ISLAMIC SOCIETIES TO THE NI.

Ira M. Lapidus' global history of Islamic societies, first published in 1988, has become a classic in the field. For more than two decades, it has enlightened students, scholars, and others with a thirst for knowledge about one of the world's great civilizations. This book, based on parts one and two of Lapidus' monumental *A History of Islamic Societies*, revised and updated, describes the transformations of Islamic societies from their beginning in the seventh century, through their diffusion across the globe, into the challenges of the nineteenth century. The story focuses on the organization of families and tribes, religious groups and states, depicts them in their varied and changing contexts, and shows how they were transformed by their interactions with other religious and political communities into a varied, global, and interconnected family of societies. The book concludes with the European commercial and imperial interventions that initiated a new set of transformations in the Islamic world, and the onset of the modern era.

Organized in narrative sections for the history of each major region, with innovative, analytic summary introductions and conclusions, this book is a unique endeavor. Its breadth, clarity, style, and thoughtful exposition will ensure its place in the classroom and beyond as a guide for the educated reader.

Ira M. Lapidus is Professor Emeritus of History at the University of California, Berkeley. His publications include *Contemporary Islamic Movements in Historical Perspective* (1983); *Muslim Cities in the Later Middle Ages* (1967, 1984); *Islam, Politics and Social Movements*, co-edited with Edmund Burke (1988); and *A History of Islamic Societies* (1988, 2002).

ISLAMIC SOCIETIES TO THE NINETEENTH CENTURY

A GLOBAL HISTORY

IRA M. LAPIDUS

University of California, Berkeley

CAMBRIDGE
UNIVERSITY PRESS

CAMBRIDGE
UNIVERSITY PRESS

University Printing House, Cambridge CB2 8BS, United Kingdom

One Liberty Plaza, 20th Floor, New York, NY 10006, USA

477 Williamstown Road, Port Melbourne, VIC 3207, Australia

4843/24, 2nd Floor, Ansari Road, Daryaganj, Delhi - 110002, India

79 Anson Road, #06-04/06, Singapore 079906

Cambridge University Press is part of the University of Cambridge.

It furthers the University's mission by disseminating knowledge in the pursuit of
education, learning and research at the highest international levels of excellence.

www.cambridge.org
Information on this title: www.cambridge.org/9780521732987

© Cambridge University Press 2012

First published 2012
Reprinted 2017

A catalogue record for this publication is available from the British Library

Library of Congress Cataloging in Publication data
Lapidus, Ira M. (Ira Marvin)
Islamic societies to the nineteenth century: a global history / Ira Lapidus.
p. cm.
Includes bibliographical references and index.
ISBN 978-0-521-51441-5 (hardback) – ISBN 978-0-521-73298-7 (paperback)
1. Islamic countries – History. 2. Islamic civilization 3. Islam – History. I. Title.
DS35.63.L36   2012
909'.09767–dc23   2011043732

ISBN 978-0-521-51441-5 Hardback
ISBN 978-0-521-73298-7 Paperback

CONTENTS

PART III THE GLOBAL EXPANSION OF ISLAM FROM THE SEVENTH TO THE NINETEENTH CENTURIES

THE WESTERN ISLAMIC SOCIETIES

LIST OF ILLUSTRATIONS

LIST OF FIGURES

LIST OF MAPS

LIST OF TABLES

PREFACE

Islam is the religion of peoples who inhabit the "middle" regions of the planet from the Atlantic shores of Africa to the South Pacific and from the steppes of Siberia to the remote islands of South Asia: Berbers, West Africans, Sudanese, Swahili-speaking East Africans, Middle Eastern Arabs, Turks, Iranians, Turkish and Persian peoples of Central Asia, Afghans, Pakistanis, many millions of Indians and Chinese, most of the peoples of Malaysia and Indonesia, and minorities in the Philippines – some 1.5 billion people adhere to Islam. In ethnic background, language, customs, social and political organization, and forms of culture and technology, they represent innumerable variations of human experience. Yet Islam unites them. Although Islam is not often the totality of their lives, it permeates their self-conception, regulates their daily existence, provides the bonds of society, and fulfills the yearning for salvation. For all its diversity, Islam forges one of the great spiritual families of mankind.

This book is the history of how these multitudes have become Muslims and what Islam means to them. In this book we ask the following questions: What is Islam? What are its values? How did so many peoples, so different and dispersed, become Muslims? What does Islam contribute to their character, to their way of living, to the ordering of their communities, and to their aspirations and identity? What are the historical conditions that have given rise to Islamic religious and cultural values? What are the manifold ways in which it is understood and practiced? To answer these questions, we shall see how religious concepts about the nature of reality and the meaning of human experience, embedded at once in holy scripture and works of commentary and as thoughts and feelings in the minds and hearts of Muslim believers, have given shape to the lifestyles and institutions of Muslim peoples, and how reciprocally the political and social experiences of Muslim peoples have been given expression in the values and symbols of Islam. Our history of Islam is the history of a dialogue between religious symbols and everyday reality.

This book covers the history of the Islamic world from its beginnings in the seventh century to the beginning of the era of European economic and political domination that began in the late eighteenth and nineteenth centuries – the "modern" era. It includes the first two parts of the original *A History of Islamic Societies*, which covered the history of the Islamic world to the present day and was first published in 1988. A second edition, revising and bringing contemporary history up to date, was published in 2002.

Reviewing this work only a few years later, it is striking not only that recent events call for a still further updating but that as a result of scholarly research the past is changing too. The changes are generated in some instances by the discovery of new sources, but more commonly by new historical methods and theories that lead to both controversy and fresh insights.

To take account of these changes, the editors of Cambridge University Press and I have decided to modify the format of this work. This new edition will be published as two books. The first will contain a very substantially revised history of Islamic societies from their beginnings in early seventh-century Arabia to the eve of the modern era. The second will contain the entire work, recounting the history of Islamic societies from their beginnings to the present. The part devoted to modern history will be updated on crucial issues, such as contemporary Islamic movements, the recent uprising in the Arab world, the place of women in Muslim societies, and Islam in Europe and North America. *Islamic Societies to the Nineteenth Century: A Global History* will serve the needs of students and others interested in the early foundation and worldwide diffusion of Islam. *A History of Islamic Societies* is directed to readers who would like the entire history in one volume.

Both books have two goals. One is to tell the history of each particular population, country, or region of the Islamic world. The second is to identify the themes that give cohesion to the concept of Islamic societies. In this book, history is understood not as a sequence of stories but as an integral process in which state, religion, community, and cultures are related in many variable but definable ways. In all periods, Islam has to be understood in the context of previous and contemporary cultures. Islamic cultures are shaped by their connections to the ancient world before it; to other contemporary Islamic societies; to non-Islamic cultures; and to economic, technological, and political conditions that are not connected to religion and culture. In the present era, it has become debatable as to whether Islamic societies will continue to develop in their historic forms.

Although there are many controversies among Muslims and others over the correct version of Islam, this book attempts to recognize, depict, and respect its enormous richness and diversity.

THE BEGINNINGS OF ISLAM IN THE MIDDLE EAST

The first part of this book deals with the beginnings and early development of Middle Eastern Islamic societies. The new edition emphasizes how early Islam was a part of and a continuation of the civilizations that preceded it. We review the basic structures of ancient empires, including a new section on women and family, tracing the precedents set by ancient norms for Islamic laws and values. The controversial historiography of the last thirty years dealing with the "origins" of Islam, the validity of the early sources, and the authenticity of the Quran is reevaluated, and new perspectives are incorporated into the text. There are important changes in the study of architecture as a display of imperial legitimacy. A revised history of early Islamic law and the veneration of the prophet give new perspectives on early Islamic religiosity. A new chapter situates the non-Muslim minorities under Muslim rule.

These new themes are integrated into an overall perspective on the interconnections of ancient, Mediterranean, and early Islamic cultures. Although bedouin elements made pre-Islamic Arabia different from many of the settled regions of the Middle East, in politics, trade, material development, and religious cultures, Arabia was already closely connected to the larger Middle Eastern region. Pre-Islamic Arabian religious and literary culture not only stemmed from bedouin practices but was modeled on the general system of culture found in the cities of the Middle East since the third century.

Cultural interactions continued and were intensified after the Arab-Islamic conquests. Arab-Muslim participation in the antique heritage continued approximately to the eleventh century. Islamic civilization developed out of a cultural matrix that included Arabian tribal culture and religious practices; Jewish beliefs, religious practices, and community institutions; Christian theology and eschatology; and Roman and Sasanian arts, literatures, legal systems, and political institutions. Pre-Islamic cultures were adapted through specific texts and translations, oral recitations, and ordinary social and business contacts among peoples with different backgrounds. Arab-Muslims shaped the linguistic and religious cultures of the region, while the emerging Islamic civilization was itself shaped by the earlier Middle Eastern and Mediterranean civilizations. I call this phase the Arab-Islamic renaissance, a period of assimilation, adaptation, and creative transformation of previous, late antique Middle Eastern cultures into an Arabic-Islamic form.

Similarly, political, economic, and social institutions were carried over from the ancient into the Islamic epoch. The modes of production in agriculture, trade, services, and taxation remained the same – indeed they were ratified in Islamic law for commerce and property. The Caliphate understood imperial rule as it was understood and proclaimed by the Roman-Byzantine and Sasanian emperors and similarly defined and legitimated its rule through architecture, art, and the patronage of literary and religious activities. Family life and the position of women in society carried on the concepts and practices of late antique societies.

The religion of Islam itself, although newly revealed, shared the theology of its predecessors and provided similar codes for ritual and social behavior and communal loyalties. The Quran presents Islam as a correction and the true version of corrupted older religions. Jews, Christians, Zoroastrians, and Muslims all believed in God, the angels and the prophets, the last judgment, and the purpose of human existence as being the fulfillment of God's commands and faith in his truth. Early Islam also shared folk traditions and popular spirituality with non-Muslims. Eastern Syriac Christians who believed in the human nature of Jesus had common ground with Muslims. Jews were, like Muslims, committed monotheists. Sufism drew inspiration from the Quran and from neo-Platonism and Hindu mysticism. To all Middle Eastern peoples, similar beliefs implied a community, and all believed that religious communities had a founding prophet. Gnosticism, messianism, magic, mysticism, science, and philosophy were also found in all the Middle Eastern religions.

The distinctive cultural achievements of the early Arab-Islamic era linked Islamic civilization to its predecessors. Philosophy was translated from Greek and Syriac into Arabic, and Muslim theology (*kalam*) was built on the same dialectics and concepts as Christian theology. Islamic law (*fiqh*) was a continuation of Roman provincial law, canon law, Talmudic law, and Persian law, progressively integrated with the teachings of the Quran and hadith to form what we now know as Islamic law. The Arabian poetic forms (*qasida*) became the basis of classical Arabic poetry. Persian literature (*adab*) was translated into Arabic. Poetry and *adab* became the basis of the literary "formation" of the cultivated gentleman. In architecture, the basics of the design and decoration of mosques and even their placement in the urban environment created a distinctive Arab-Muslim presence, although based on an older visual vocabulary. A substantially new chapter deals with the interactions of Muslims, Jews, and Christians in Spain.

In all these respects, a new civilization had come into being, one that was creative and distinctive and yet a continuation of the basic institutional structures and cultural forms of previous Middle Eastern and Mediterranean civilizations – an innovative expression of the historic Middle Eastern cultures. Over centuries, however, the process of assimilating, Arabizing, and Islamizing historic cultures led to the consolidation of a distinctively new civilization whose ancient sources were forgotten, concealed, and perhaps obliterated, and whose roots can now only be uncovered by scholarly investigation.

Thus, Islam is part of a common Eurasian civilization. It continues directly from Roman, Byzantine, and Persian late antiquity. Islam integrated the existing political forms, modes of economic production, religious values, and family structures. It shares the conceptual world of Judaism and Christianity, although there are major differences due to the accidents of language and vocabulary and of historical and cultural references. Islam did not change the fundamental institutions of civilization so much as it changed languages, ideologies, and identities.

This distinctively Middle Eastern Islamic civilization achieved dominance in the period from the eleventh to the fifteenth centuries. In the midst of repeated nomadic invasions from the east and Crusades from the west, a new quasi-imperial, quasi-feudal system of political institutions was consolidated. Nomadic forces and military slavery supported by the assignment of benefices and fiefs became the regional norm. Muslim communities were organized into Sunni schools of law, Sufi fraternities or brotherhoods, and Shi'i sects. This was the era of the cultural consolidation of "normative Islam" based on the integration of law and Sufism and of alternative forms of Muslim belief based on philosophy, theosophy, and the popular veneration of saints. In this era, a political ethic was defined. Most important, there grew up alongside Arabic literatures a new Persian literary and poetic culture that became the dominant language and culture for the eastern regions of the Muslim world. Henceforth, Islamic culture would be expressed in both Arabic and Persian media (and later in Turkish media and that of other languages). This new edition contains newly written or extensively reworked chapters on the Timurid Empire and its political and cultural importance, the development of Persianate Islam, the social structure of Middle Eastern communities, and women and family.

THE GLOBAL DIFFUSION OF ISLAM TO THE NINETEENTH CENTURY

The third part of the book describes how Arab–Middle Eastern Islam was the paradigm for the re-creation of Islamic societies in other languages, cultures, and regions of the world. Everywhere Islam took shape as a hybrid of local cultures and Middle Eastern Islam. From the seventh to the tenth centuries, Arab conquerors brought Islam and the Arabic language and culture to North Africa and Spain, Iran and Transoxania. Persians, Turks, and Soghdians in the east and Berbers and Goths in the west were incorporated into the Arab-Muslim empire. Merchants and missionaries, often Sufis, brought Islam to the steppes of Inner Asia. From Egypt, the Sudan, and North Africa, Islam and Arab culture reached Saharan and Sudanic Africa.

After these direct contacts, Islam was carried further by newly Islamized Persian, Turkish, and African peoples. Arab-Islamic culture followed later conquests, colonization, missionary proselytization, and commerce. On the mainland of Eurasia, migrating, conquering, and empire-building Turkish peoples brought Islam westward into Anatolia, the Balkans, and southeastern Europe; eastward into Inner Asia and China; and southward into Afghanistan and the Indian subcontinent. Here, they established the Mongol, Timurid, Shaybanid, Mughal, Safavid, and Ottoman empires. The new empires patronized Muslim schools, courts, Sufi hospices, and other religious and communal institutions. The empires are newly described in terms of recent scholarship. The Ottoman chapters have been expanded to discuss women, family, and religious minorities. The three great early modern Muslim empires – the Safavid, Ottoman, and Mughal empires – are discussed in terms of processes of decentralization and networking among central and local elites. The Muslim empires are presented in the context of the worldwide development of early modern empires and are compared with one another.

In the Indian Ocean region, merchants and Sufi missionaries carried Islam from Arabia to India and East Africa (tenth to twelfth centuries). From Arabia and India,

Islam reached the Malay Peninsula and the Indonesian archipelago (thirteenth to fifteenth centuries). From the coastal zones, it spread to the interior of the islands and continents.

In Africa, Arab and Berber traders and settlers in the Saharan and Sudanic regions, Arab and Persian settlers on the East African coasts, and Dyula communities in West Africa were the nuclei of Muslim influences. Often, colonies of Muslim traders allied with local political elites and induced the rulers of the states of Ghana, Mali, Kanem, Songhay, Hausaland, and Dogomba to accept Islam. African history chapters have been expanded and updated to deal with not only Islam but also slavery and European colonialism.

The global diffusion of Islam is discussed in the context of the rising power of Europe and in terms of the regional interconnectedness of Muslim societies – in the Mediterranean, the Indian Ocean and the great inner "seas," the Taklamakan desert in Inner Asia, and the Sahara in Africa.

As I explain later in this volume,

> By the nineteenth century, Islamic societies the world over had acquired similar types of Muslim elites, beliefs, religious practices, and social organizations. In each Muslim region, we find not one but several variant types of Islam. There were the scholars who represented formal learning, organized education, and judicial administration, affiliated through schools of law. There were also the scholars-cum-Sufis, who combined legal learning with mystical discipline and contemplation, in an effort to live their lives in imitation of the Prophet. Such religious teachers perpetuated a tradition of learning that combined law, theology, and Sufi wisdom representing Sunni–Shariʿa (orthoprax)–Sufi Islam. There were ecstatic visionary Sufis in the tradition of Ibn al-ʿArabi and the gnostic forms of Islamic mysticism, as well as the popular forms of Sufi Islam expressed in veneration of saints, faith in their charismatic powers, and belief in the magic of their shrines. Throughout the Muslim world, Sufism in all its forms became the most widespread and popular expression of Islam.

THE BEGINNING OF THE MODERN ERA

By the eighteenth century, Islamic societies had begun to decline in political power. The Safavid state had been defeated by Afghan invaders and, deserted by its tribal vassals, disintegrated completely. The Ottoman Empire went through a period of decentralization that impaired the imperial state. The Mughal Empire disintegrated into numerous competing provincial and feudal regimes. In Southeast Asia, a centralized regime had never been established over the Indonesian archipelago or the Malay Peninsula. In North Africa, Muslim states were being subverted by their declining commercial position in the Mediterranean while provincial, tribal, and Sufi resistance was on the increase. The Sudanic states had long passed the peak of their commercial prosperity, although Muslim communities were growing in influence.

A critical, but hardly the only, factor in the political decline of many Muslim regimes was the rising power of Europe. European societies were generating technological inventions, economic wealth, and military power that would profoundly change the conditions of life not only for Muslims, but for all the world's peoples. On the northern flanks of majority-Muslim areas, the steppes of Inner Asia came under Russian control. The Russian conquests culminated in the colonizing of Transoxania and the Transcaspian regions in the late nineteenth century. At the same time, China established its suzerainty in eastern Turkestan in the eighteenth century and made it a province of China in the late nineteenth. Russia and China took control of most of the Muslim populations of Inner Asia.

On the southern flanks of majority-Muslim areas, European expansion began with Portuguese, Dutch, and British merchant adventurers, who won naval and trading empires in the southern seas and ended by establishing colonial regimes. The Portuguese established a series of bases in the Indian Ocean and at Malacca in the early sixteenth century, but they were displaced by the Dutch, who took control of the Southeast Asian trade in the seventeenth century, made themselves suzerains of Java by the middle of the eighteenth century, and conquered the rest of the Indies in the course of the nineteenth. The British also began by establishing trading bases and ended by conquering an empire in India. In 1858, in the wake of the Indian mutiny, the British removed the last of the Mughal emperors and brought India under their direct control. They took control of the Indian Ocean – with bases in Malaya, the Persian Gulf, the Red Sea, and East Africa – and Egypt. The French took territorial control of North Africa. Africa was the last region with a large Muslim population to be subjected to colonial domination. At the Congress of Berlin in 1884–85, Britain, France, Belgium, Italy, and Germany agreed on the partition of Africa and seized pieces of the continent for themselves. All of Africa except Liberia and Ethiopia came under European rule by World War I. Only the Ottoman Empire and Iran maintained their political identities without experiencing direct colonial rule.

By the nineteenth century, Europe was not only seizing the trade and the territory of Muslim states; it was beginning to seize the imagination of Muslim peoples. European military and technological efficiency and artistic styles, as well as political (especially nationalist) concepts and moral values, began to influence Muslim populations. These influences opened a new era in the history of Muslim peoples. This book, then, concludes with the Muslim world on the eve of its modern transformations.

The scope of the book itself implies that it is not a narrative history, a telling of stories, but history seen as a holistic process in which the relations among and the variations in state, economic, religious, communal, and cultural forms help us to analyze both the organization and the evolution of societies. It is not a history of events, but a history of civilizations.

As a historian, however, my primary interest is not in theory but in the adaptation of theory to the needs of a coherent and meaningful exposition. The central problem of this book is how to present a history of enormous diversity – the history of societies that to sight and sound are utterly different – and yet preserve some sense of their historical and institutional relatedness. For the reader, this book is intended to provide a coherent overview of Islamic history. As a teacher, I think that the endless everyday flow of events and news confuses rather than enlightens us and that a large "map" of the subject as a whole is essential to the understanding of particular occurrences. Only from an overall point of view can we acquire the poise, distance, and perspective that make it possible to identify basic contextual factors and long-term historical trends, and to distinguish them from accidental and short-term considerations.

The reader should be cautioned, however, that the factual narrative approach of this book conceals great uncertainties of historical judgment, incomplete knowledge, conflicts of opinion and interpretation among experts, and constantly changing research that brings new knowledge and new points of view to the fore. Little has been said about the degree of reliability or the margin of error in the presentation of information, but the book is based on the most reliable research and interpretation. The reader should be aware that parts of the work are provisional and exploratory in nature and represent the author's best judgment about particular subjects.

A few comments about the organization of the book may help readers find their way through this large volume. The book is divided into three parts, each of which has an introduction and conclusion that deals with the organizing concepts on which the book is based and summarizes the important themes implied in the narrative chapters. For an overview of the transformation of Islamic societies, these introductory and concluding chapters may be read separately or in conjunction with selected period or regional histories. The table of contents and the index are of course the reader's guide, but the reader or teacher using this book as text could also create an alternative table of contents, following particular regional or state histories – Middle Eastern, South Asian, African – through successive periods, or following subjects such as women and family, scholars and law, Sufism, art, and philosophy.

The definition of geographic regions requires some arbitrary simplifications. Muslim world areas are by and large defined in regional terms such as Middle East, North Africa, Indian subcontinent, Southeast Asia, and West and East Africa. For convenience of reference, and despite the obvious anachronism, these areas or parts of them are commonly identified by the names of present national states such as India, Indonesia, or Nigeria. This is to simplify identification for readers unfamiliar with the geography of these vast regions and to avoid such cumbersome locutions as "areas now part of the state of ___," but it should be clear that the use of these terms does not necessarily imply any similarity of state and social organization or of cultural style between pre-modern and contemporary times.

Transliterations from the numerous native languages of Muslim peoples have been simplified for the convenience of English readers. In general, I have tried to follow standard scholarly usage for each world area, modified by the elimination of diacritical marks and sometimes adapted to give a fair sense of pronunciation. Certain standard Arabic terms and names are given in their original, usually Arabic, literary form despite actual variations in spelling and pronunciation the world over. Dates are given in the Common Era.

Ira M. Lapidus
University of California at Berkeley

ACKNOWLEDGMENTS

The preparation of this new book has provided me with two great joys for nearly five years. One is the joy of learning, catching up and coming to terms with recent scholarship. The other, even more important, is the collaboration of young scholars who contributed their erudition, their methodological sophistication, and their friendship and encouragement. I value them for the opportunity to know and work with them as much as for the work itself.

For the long duration of this project, Lena Salaymeh has contributed her great knowledge of the early Islamic sources and the late antique, early Islamic history; her understanding of Islamic law; her methodological sophistication; and her exacting standards for historical rhetoric. She has reviewed, commented on, and edited the entire book, with a view to each of these considerations. She has done wide-ranging research on women, family, and law in the pre-modern Islamic era, and she is the co-author of new and revised chapters on these subjects. Her practical know-how has been invaluable with computer-connected matters and with the preparation of the text for publication. Our conversations have informed me, sharpened my judgment, and stimulated my interest. I am very grateful for her colleagueship. She is writing an innovative and deeply researched book on Islamic legal history.

David Moshfegh has briefed me on the history of Jews in Muslim lands with a sensitive ear for historiographical controversies and the influence of political positions on historical writing. His own dissertation concerns early European orientalism and shows a keen sensitivity to the conjunction of personal needs, cultural controversies, and political engagements in the shaping of late nineteenth- and early twentieth-century orientalist scholarship. He is the co-author of the sections on Jews in the early Islamic era and in Spain and has contributed to the history of Jews in the Ottoman Empire.

Kevin Schwartz was my informant about new writing on Persian and Indian history, and the construction and diffusion of Persianate culture throughout western,

Central, and southern Asia and in the Indian Ocean region. He was an alert and forthright critic of the previous versions of these topics and helped bring me up to date with current scholarship.

Heather Ferguson provided a fresh orientation to the new historiography on Ottoman history and helped me interpret it and integrate it into the revised account in this volume. She alerted me to the new historiography on empire formation in the early modern period. Her dissertation on the circle of justice gave me a fresh conceptual approach to understanding Ottoman government.

Murat Dagli provided me with important insights from his rich knowledge of Ottoman history, brought me up to date in the new historiography, and read my draft chapter with an informed and critical eye.

Nadia Nader did research on the position of women, especially in Egypt in the nineteenth and twentieth centuries, and provided me with materials from her reading of the Egyptian press, TV, and her personal experiences.

The important contribution of Lisa Pollard to the study of women and family in the second edition carries over to this volume.

My professorial colleagues have been inspiring and helpful. I am indebted to Huricihan Islamoghlu for many conversations enriched by her sophisticated knowledge of comparative economic and world history. Yuen Gen-Liang read a draft of Part I and made many helpful suggestions for its improvement. Jeffrey Handler introduced me to the latest work in Southeast Asian history, including his own contributions to the history of Minangkabau. Munis Faroqui was supportive of my studies of Islamic history in the Indian subcontinent. Max Lecar helped correct the chapter on Islamic Spain. Jed Harris read portions of the manuscript and gave me helpful suggestions from the point of view of the lay reader.

Briana Flin was my library and secretarial assistant. Her careful attention to detail is a welcome and important contribution to the project.

I am especially grateful to the Andrew W. Mellon Foundation and to its administrative officers and staff. The Mellon Foundation has generously supported this project with an Emeritus Fellowship, and its officers and staff have been throughout responsive and supportive of the special needs of this project.

I am deeply grateful to my wife, Brenda Webster, for her constant love and support.

Finally, but not least, I want to thank Marigold Acland and the staff of Cambridge University Press for their encouragement and unfailing enthusiasm for this book. They sustained me through the work and motivated me to finish at last.

ACKNOWLEDGMENTS TO THE FIRST EDITION OF
A HISTORY OF ISLAMIC SOCIETIES

With continuing gratitude and respect for the many people who helped with the previous editions and versions of this subject, I reproduce the acknowledgments from the first and second editions of *A History of Islamic Societies*.

In the preparation of the book I have been greatly aided by my students, research assistants, and colleagues. They have helped me, depending on their skills and my background in a given world area, in the following ways: by the preparation of bibliographies; reading, review, and preparation of digests on relevant literatures; research into particular themes and topics in both secondary and source materials; summaries or translations of materials in languages I do not read; and discussion of historiographical or methodological problems in their particular fields or disciplines. They have made an important contribution to my understanding of the role of Islam in several world areas and have enormously facilitated the completion of the book.

I would like to thank David Goodwin, Margaret Malamud, Ann Taboroff, and Sahar von Schlegell (Islamic history and Sufism); James Reid (Iran); Corrine Blake (Arab Middle East); Elaine Combs-Schilling (North Africa); Sandria Freitag and David Gilmartin (India); Mary Judd and Allan Samson (Indonesia); William McFarren and Leslie Sharp (Africa); Rose Glickman and Mark Saroyan (Russian Inner Asia); and John Foran and Michael Hughes (modernization and political economy). I am also grateful for the bibliographical help of Melissa MacCauly and Susan Mattern.

For the selection of illustrations, I benefited from the advice and assistance of Guitty Azarpay, Jere Bacharach, Sheila Blair, Jonathan Bloom, Herbert Bodman, Gordon Holler, Thomas Lentz, Kim Lyon, Amy Newhall, and Labelle Prussin. I warmly thank the individuals and institutions by whose kind permission they are reproduced here. I am grateful to Cherie A. Semans of the Department of Geography, University of California, Berkeley, for the preparation of the designs and sketch maps on which the maps in this volume are based.

Many friends and colleagues have read portions or even the whole of the manuscript and have given me invaluable corrections, suggestions, and reflective thoughts. Each of them has enriched this volume, although none of them is responsible for the remaining faults. It gives me great pleasure to thank Jere Bacharach, Thomas Bisson, William Brinner, Edmund Burke III, Elaine Combs-Schilling, Shmuel Eisenstadt, Sandria Freitag, David Gilmartin, Albert Hourani, Suad Joseph, Barbara Metcalf, Thomas Metcalf, Martha Olcott, James Reid, Richard Roberts, William Roff, Allan Samson, Stanford Shaw, David Skinner, Ilkay Sunar, Ilter Turan, Abraham Udovitch, Lucette Valensi, and Reginald Zelnik. As much as the writing, the friendship and generosity of these people have blessed many years of work.

Several colleagues have had a particularly strong effect on the development of my understanding and have generously shared with me their views and unpublished work on various aspects of this book. In particular I would like to thank Barbara Metcalf (India), Elaine Combs-Schilling (North Africa), Suad Joseph (women's studies), Martha Olcott (Soviet Inner Asia), James Reid (Iran and Inner Asia), Allan Samson (Indonesia), Warren Fusfeld (for his dissertation on the Naqshbandiyya in India), and Sandria Freitag and David Gilmartin (India). Morris Rossabi has graciously allowed me to see a copy of an unpublished article by Joseph Fletcher on the Naqshbandiyya in China.

I am equally indebted to the many people who have helped prepare the manuscript and the published book. The staff of the Center for Advanced Studies in the Behavioral Sciences, Stanford, California, prepared an early draft of the manuscript. Muriel Bell edited several of the chapters. Lynn Gale helped to arrange the transmission of this material to the word processor of the Institute of International Studies at Berkeley, where Nadine Zelinski and Christine Peterson worked with great skill on the preparation of the manuscript and have given me endless friendly support; they are among the close collaborators to whom I owe this book. The staff of Cambridge University Press, Elizabeth Wetton, editor, Susan Moore, subeditor, and Jane Williams, designer, have been especially helpful. Finally, but not least, I am grateful to my wife, Brenda Webster, for her amazed, and amazing, patience as this book grew larger and larger, for her suggestions and criticism, and, above all, for her faith in the work.

The research for this project has been generously supported by the Institute of International Studies of the University of California, Berkeley. I would like to express my thanks to Professor Carl Rosberg, Director of the Institute; to Mrs. Karin Beros, Management Services Officer of the Institute; and to the Institute staff, who have been generous and gracious in their support. The preparation of this volume has also been made possible by a year in residence at the Center for Advanced Studies in the Behavioral Sciences, Stanford, California, with the support of the National Endowment for the Humanities, and by a research grant from the Hoover Institution, Stanford University. The completion of this work has been made possible by a grant from the Division of Research of the National Endowment for the Humanities, an independent federal agency. To these institutions I express my deep appreciation for affording me the opportunity to concentrate on research and writing.

Information and ideas for the maps in this book are derived from R. Roolvink, *Historical Atlas of the Muslim Peoples*, Cambridge, Mass., 1957; J. L. Bacharach, *A Middle East Studies Handbook*, Seattle, Wash., 1984; W. C. Bryce, *An Historical Atlas of Islam*, Leiden, 1981; F. Robinson, *Atlas of the Islamic World*, Oxford, 1982; and J. D. Fage, *An Atlas of African History*, New York, 1978.

With the permission of the publishers extensive passages have been quoted or adapted from my previous publications:

"Adulthood in Islam: Religious Maturity in the Islamic Tradition," *Daedalus*, Spring 1976, pp. 93–108.

"Islam and the Historical Experience of Muslim Peoples," *Islamic Studies: A Tradition and Its Problems*, ed. Malcolm H. Kerr, Malibu, Calif.: Undena Publications, 1980, pp. 89–102.

"Arab Settlement and Economic Development of Iraq and Iran in the Age of the Umayyad and Early Abbasid Caliphs," *The Islamic Middle East, 700–1900: Studies in Economic and Social History*, ed. A. L. Udovitch, Princeton, N.J.: Darwin Press, 1981, pp. 177–208.

"The Arab Conquests and the Formation of Islamic Society," *Studies on the First Century of Islamic Society*, ed. G. H. A. Juynboll, Carbondale: Southern Illinois University Press, 1982, pp. 49–72.

"Knowledge, Virtue and Action: The Classical Muslim Conception of Adab and the Nature of Religious Fulfillment in Islam," *Moral Conduct and Authority in South Asian Islam*, ed. Barbara Metcalf, Berkeley: University of California Press, 1984, pp. 38–61. © 1984, The Regents of the University of California.

Contemporary Islamic Movements in Historical Perspective, Policy Papers No. 18, Institute of International Studies, University of California, Berkeley, 83.

"Mamluk Patronage and the Arts in Egypt," *Muqarnas*, 11, 1984, New Haven, Conn.: Yale University Press, pp. 173–81.

Ira M. Lapidus
Berkeley, California, 1985

ACKNOWLEDGMENTS TO THE SECOND EDITION OF A HISTORY OF ISLAMIC SOCIETIES

In preparing the new edition I have again been blessed with the help of many friends and colleagues. To Marigold Acland, my Cambridge editor, I owe the inspiration for a new edition, the determination to awaken me to my duty, and helpful interventions throughout the process of revision. Murat Dagli tracked down data, maps, photos, and bibliography. Scott Strauss helped with the research on Africa. Nancy Reynolds prepared a first draft of the new parts of the revised chapter on Islam in South Asia. Renate Holub and Laurence Michalak gave me good insights and helped correct the text for the chapter on Muslims in Europe and America. David Yaghoubian read through the whole of revised Part III and gave me innumerable suggestions for improvements. Saba Mahmood thoughtfully reviewed the conclusion. The chapter on women and gender has been revised with the help of and co-authored with Lisa Pollard. She has provided good counsel, insights, corrections, and new textual material. Nadine Ghammache skillfully prepared the manuscript. Mary Starkey did very thoughtful and tasteful work in her copyediting, and Bennett Katrina Brown carefully checked part of the proofs. The Cambridge University Press editorial staff, Paul Watt and Karen Hildebrandt, have generously given their indispensable help in the preparation of the text. I am deeply grateful to each of them for their work, their collegiality, and their support. To my wife, Brenda Webster, I owe the happiness and peace of mind that allowed me to undertake this venture.

Maps 36 and 37 are based on maps printed in *Le Monde diplomatique*, November 2001. I would also like to thank the publishers of my previous work for their permission to print extracts and adaptations from the following articles:

"A Sober Survey of the Islamic World," *Orbis*, 40, 1996, pp. 391–404.

"The Middle East's Discomforting Continuities," *Orbis*, 42, 1998, pp. 619–30.

"Between Universalism and Particularism: The Historical Bases of Muslim Communal, National, and Global Identities," *Global Networks*, 1, 2001, pp. 19–36.

Ira M. Lapidus
Berkeley, California, 2002

PUBLISHER'S PREFACE

The Press Syndicate originally commissioned Ira Lapidus to write *A History of Islamic Societies* as a supplement to *The Cambridge History of Islam*, which was published in 1970 in two volumes. His would be a unique enterprise, a monumental work with the status of a Cambridge History, but by one hand and integrated by one coherent vision. Since its publication in 1988, it has surpassed all expectations. The book has become a classic work of history. This new volume, focusing on the early history of Islamic societies, brings a revised version of this definitive and best-selling book to a new generation of readers.

INTRODUCTION TO ISLAMIC SOCIETIES

The history of Islamic societies to the nineteenth century will be presented in two dimensions: one historical, an effort to account for the formation of Islamic societies and their change over time; the other analytic and comparative, which attempts to understand the variations among them. Three methodological and historical assumptions underlie these approaches. The first is that the history of whole societies may be presented in terms of their institutional systems. An institution, whether an empire, a mode of economic exchange, a family, or a religious practice, is an activity carried out in a patterned relationship with other persons as defined and legitimized in the mental world of the participants. An institution encompasses at once an activity, a pattern of social relations, and a set of mental constructs.

The second assumption is that the history of Islamic societies may be told in terms of four basic types of institutions: familial, including tribal, ethnic, and other small-scale community groups; economic, the organization of production and distribution of material goods; cultural or religious, the concepts of ultimate values and human goals and the collectivities built on such commitments; and political, the organization of conflict resolution, defense, and domination.

The third assumption is that the institutional patterns characteristic of Islamic societies had their origin in ancient Mesopotamia in the third millennium BCE. The constellation of lineage and tribal, religious, and political structures created by the Mesopotamian city-states and empires set the foundations for the later development of Middle Eastern societies before and during the Islamic era. Later Middle Eastern Islamic societies were built on the infusion of ancient institutions with an Islamic cultural style and identity. These Middle Eastern Islamic institutions and cultures in turn interacted with the institutions and cultures of other world regions to create a number of variant Islamic societies. In the modern era these variant societies were again transformed, this time by interaction with Europe. Modern Islamic countries are each the product of the interaction of a particular regional form of Islamic society with different European political, economic, and cultural influences. Thus, the variation among modern Islamic societies may be traced to older patterns.

Parts I and II of this book examine the formative era of Islamic civilization from the revelation of the Quran to the fifteenth century. Part I begins with the Prophet Muhammad and continues through the classical Islamic era. This era gave rise to Arabic literature, Islamic religious teaching, and cosmopolitan artistic achievements – a complex of tribal-ethnic, religious, and courtly-aristocratic cultures from which all later versions of Islamic civilization derive. Here I attempt to explain the development of Islamic civilization in terms of its relationships to past patterns of Middle Eastern societies, and in terms of the cultural effects of urbanization, social change, and the formation of new empires. Part II discusses the history of Iran, Iraq, Syria, and Egypt from the tenth to the fifteenth centuries and attempts to explain the transformation of Islam from a complex of doctrines and cultural systems into the operative principles of Middle Eastern societies. In this period, Islam became the religion of the masses of Middle Eastern peoples, who formed new state and communal institutions (Shi'i "sects," Sunni schools of law, and Sufi brotherhoods) and redefined the relations of political regimes to religious bodies.

The emergence of Islamic civilization is striking for its basic continuity with late Roman and Persian antiquity. In political forms, modes of economic production, religious values, and family structures, it is basically similar to its predecessors. It shares the conceptual world of Judaism and Christianity. The major differences are the accidents of language and vocabulary, and historical and cultural references. Thus, Islamic civilization is not a different civilization from our own, but part of a shared European–West Asian heritage.

In its turn Middle Eastern Islam became a paradigm for the creation of similar societies in other parts of the world. Part III traces the diffusion of the Middle Eastern Islamic paradigm. From the seventh to the nineteenth centuries, Islam became the religion of peoples in the Middle East, North Africa and Spain, Anatolia and the Balkans, the Indian subcontinent, Inner Asia and China, Southeast Asia, and sub-Saharan Africa. In Part III we consider the forces behind the diffusion of Islam, and the interaction between Islamic religious values and existing cultures and societies. We see how Islamic cultural and political norms were subject to change and transformation as they interacted with already-established non-Islamic societies. We also examine the consolidation of Islamic regimes, including the Ottoman, Safavid, and Mughal empires, and Islamic states in Southeast Asia, Africa, and elsewhere, and their varied ways of integrating political regimes, Islamic religious institutions, and non-Islamic values and forms of community.

By the eighteenth century the Middle Eastern paradigm for an Islamic society had been replicated, multiplied, and modified into a worldwide family of societies. Each was a recognizable variant on an underlying structure of familial-communal, religious, and state institutions. Each also represented a version of the various ways in which Islamic belief, culture, and social institutions interacted with the still-broader complex of human organization – including the non-Islamic institutions of political regimes; systems of economic production and exchange; non-Islamic forms of kinship, tribal, and ethnic communities; and pre-Islamic or non-Islamic modes of culture. We explore the relation of Islamic to pre-Islamic institutions in these regions. What were the similarities and differences among these numerous Islamic societies?

Part III concludes in the late eighteenth and early nineteenth centuries, when Islamic societies were profoundly disrupted by the breakup of Muslim empires, economic decline, internal religious conflict, and the establishment of European economic, political, and cultural domination. These forces would lead to the creation of national states, to the modernization of agriculture, to industrialization, to major changes in class structure, and to the acceptance of secular nationalist and other modern ideologies. The further history of nineteenth- and twentieth-century Islamic societies will be considered in a forthcoming edition of *A History of Islamic Societies*.

This is not, it should be clear, an effort to define an essential Islam, but rather an attempt to develop a comparative method for assessing the role of Islamic beliefs, institutions, and identities in particular historical contexts. The mechanism I have adopted to do this – the expository framework – is based on the assumptions that Islamic societies are built on institutions and that these institutions are subject to internal variation, to variations in the relationships among them, and to variations over time. The limited number of institutional factors imposes a constraint that allows us to conceive this large subject in some ordered way, but also allows for the depiction of individual societies as concrete and different entities. By exploring the variation of institutions in differing contexts, we may be able to comprehend why Islamic societies are similar in general form and yet differ so much in specific qualities.

In this volume primary emphasis is placed on the communal, religious, and political institutions of Islamic societies rather than on technologies and economies. I subordinate economic to noneconomic institutions because the distinctive historical developments in Islamic societies in the last millennium have been cultural and political, and because differences of culture and institutions differentiate Islamic societies from one another and from other human civilizations. In Muslim societies the basic forms of economic production and exchange were set down in the pre-Islamic era. The forms of agricultural and pastoral production, handicrafts, manufacturing, prevailing systems of exchange, and technological capacities are all older than, and continue through, the Islamic era in their inherited forms. This is not to deny that there has been considerable variation in economic activity in and among Muslim societies – such as in the relative role of pastoral, agricultural, commercial, and manufacturing activities; or in degrees of poverty and prosperity; or in the distribution of wealth – or that these differences have important cultural and political implications, or that economic considerations are an essential aspect of all human values and social action. Still, the fundamental modes of economic production and exchange were basically unaltered until the modern era, and economic and technological changes were not the primary sources of political and cultural variation or of changes in class structure and social organization. Until the modern era economic activity remained embedded in communal and political structures, and class divisions in society did not determine, but were inherent in, state and religious organizations. Although cultures, sociopolitical institutions, and economic and technological forces can be autonomous causal factors in historical change, in the history of Islamic societies, cultural and sociopolitical forces have been the significant loci of historical individuation. Whether twentieth-century technological and economic change now calls into question the existence of an Islamic group of societies is an open question.

PART I

THE BEGINNINGS OF ISLAMIC CIVILIZATIONS

THE MIDDLE EAST FROM c. 600
TO c. 1000

CHAPTER 1

MIDDLE EASTERN SOCIETIES BEFORE ISLAM

Islamic societies were built on the framework of already established and ancient Middle Eastern civilizations. From the pre-Islamic Middle East, Islamic societies inherited a pattern of institutions that would shape daily life until the modern age. These institutions included small communities based on family, lineage, clientage, and ethnic ties; agricultural and urban societies, market economies, monotheistic religions, and bureaucratic empires. Along with their political and social characteristics, Islamic societies also inherited many of the religious, literary, and artistic practices of the pre-Islamic past. The civilization of Islam, although initiated in Mecca, also had its precursors in Palestine, Babylon, and Persepolis.

Islamic societies developed in an environment that since the earliest history of mankind had exhibited two fundamental and enduring qualities. The first was the organization of human societies into small, often familial groups. The earliest hunting and gathering communities lived and moved in small bands. Since the advent of agriculture and the domestication of animals, the vast majority of Middle Eastern peoples have lived in agricultural villages or in the tent camps of nomadic pastoralists. Even town peoples were bound into small groups by ties of kinship and neighborhood, with all that implies of strong affections and hatreds. These groups raised the young, arranged marriages, arbitrated disputes, and formed a common front vis-à-vis the outside world.

The second was the creation of unities of culture, religion, and empire on an ever-larger scale. In pre-modern times, this tendency was manifested in the expansion of trade and the acceptance of common decorative styles and religious ideas, but its most important early manifestation was the emergence of the city-state in ancient Mesopotamia (3500 BCE–2400 BCE). The formation of cities in lower Iraq was a revolution in the history of humankind: it brought about the integration of diverse clans, villages, and other small groups into a single community. It led to

7

new cultural and artistic achievements such as the invention of writing, the creation of great works of myth and religion, the construction of architectural masterpieces, and the fashioning of sensuous sculpture.

The first cities developed from the integration of small village communities into temple communities built on shared commitment to the service of the gods. The Sumerians, the people of southern Iraq, believed that the lands they inhabited were the property of the gods and that their primary duty was the construction of a great temple to worship the forces of the universe. The priests who presided over the worship were also judges and "political" chiefs. Moreover, the temple-cities were necessarily communities of economic as well as religious interests. The construction of the great temples required masses of organized workers; their rituals required specialists in administrative, professional, and artisanal activities. The earliest cities were communities in which religious leaders and religious ideas governed the economic and political affairs of the temples' adherents.

ANCIENT, ROMAN, AND PERSIAN EMPIRES

Beginning about 2400 BCE, the temple-cities of Mesopotamia were superseded by new unifying institutions – kingship and empires. Kingship in ancient Mesopotamia emanated from two sources: the warrior or warlord houses of the ancient Sumerian cities and the tribal peoples of northern Mesopotamia. Between 2700 and 2500 BCE, city kings established ephemeral states among their neighbors. About 2400 BCE, Sargon of Akkad, the chief of pastoral peoples in northern Mesopotamia, founded the first of the world's empires. Sargon's empire soon failed, and the temple-cities temporarily regained their independence. From Sargon to Hammurapi, the great lawgiver (d. 1750 BCE), Mesopotamian empires rose and fell, but each one, although relatively short lived, reinforced the institutions of kingship and of multicity regimes.

Kingship as it developed from Sargon to Hammurapi increasingly assumed a sacred aura. Kings usurped the authority of priests and became the chief servants of the gods. They took over the priestly functions of mediating between the gods and the people. Kingship was justified as the divine plan for the ordering of human societies. Sacralized political power, as well as religion, became a vehicle for the unification of disparate peoples.

The successive empires of this ancient period also established the institutions that would henceforth be the medium for imperial rule. At the center was the ruler's household; the king was surrounded by his family, retainers, soldiers, servants, and palace administrators. Standing armies were founded; feudal grants of land were awarded to loyal retainers. Governors, administrators, and spies were assigned to control cities and provinces.

The superimposition of empires on smaller communities transformed local life and fostered the emergence of social individuality by providing the linguistic, religious, and legal conditions that freed individuals from absorption into clans, temples, and royal households. Temples were reduced to cogs in the imperial machine, and priests lost their judicial and political authority. The empires also intervened in small communities by freeing individuals from their commitments to clans and temples. To defend, administer, and maintain communications across wide territories required some decentralization of authority and greater mobility and autonomy for individuals. Warriors and administrators were assigned land and became independent proprietors. Merchants became entrepreneurs working with their own capital. Craftsmen began to work for the market rather than for the temple or royal household. A market economy emerged to facilitate exchanges among independent producers and consumers and progressively supplanted the older forms of household redistributive economy. The spread of markets and the introduction, by the seventh or sixth century BCE, of money as the medium of exchange transformed the economic structures of the ancient world. For increasing numbers of people, the cash nexus replaced patrimonial authority as the mechanism that regulated the way they earned a living.

Furthermore, the language of the dominant elites became the language of the cosmopolitan elements of the society; the remote and powerful gods of the king and the empire – the gods of the cosmos, organized into a pantheon – superseded the intimate gods of individual localities. Imperial law regulated the distribution of property, economic exchange, and relations between the strong and the weak. Ancient empires, then, not only were political agencies but provided the cultural, religious, and legal bases of society.

For ancient peoples, the empires symbolized the realm of civilization. The function of empires was to defend the civilized world against outsiders, often called barbarians, and to assimilate them into the sphere of higher culture. For their part, the so-called barbarians, mostly nomadic peoples, wanted to conquer empires, share in their wealth and sophistication, and join the ranks of civilized peoples. Empires commanded allegiance because they were thought to represent civilized peoples. They commanded allegiance because kingship was perceived as a divine institution and the king a divinely selected agent, who – if not himself a god – shared in the aura, magnificence, sacredness, and mystery of the divine. The ruler was God's agent, his priest, the channel between this world and the heavens, designated by the divine being to bring justice and right order to men so that they might in turn serve God. The king thus assured the prosperity and well being of his subjects. Magically, he upheld the order of the universe against chaos.

From these earliest empires to the eve of the Islamic era, the history of the Middle East may be summarized as the elaboration and expansion of the institutions formed in this early period. While parochial communities and local cultures were a continuing force in Middle Eastern society, empires grew progressively larger, each wave of expansion and contraction bringing new peoples into the sphere of imperial civilization. Empires came and went, but the legacy of interchange of populations – the movement of soldiers, administrators, merchants, priests, scholars, and workers – left a permanent imprint of cosmopolitan culture and a heritage of shared laws, languages, scripts, and social identity.

From Sargon to Hammurapi, Middle Eastern empires were restricted to Mesopotamia, but later Hittite, Kassite, and other "barbarian" empires brought Mesopotamia, Anatolia, and Iran into a common network. The empire of Assyria (911–612 BCE) brought Iraq, western Iran, and, for a time, Egypt into a single state. The Achaemenid Empire (550–331 BCE) incorporated eastern Iran and formed the first universal Middle Eastern empire – the first to include all settled peoples from the Oxus River to the Nile and the Dardanelles.

The Roman empire

With the destruction of the Achaemenid Empire by Alexander the Great, the Middle East was divided into two empires. In the west, the successor states to the empire of Alexander became part of the Roman Empire. In the east, Iraq and Iran as far as the Oxus River became part of Persian empires – the Parthian Empire (226 BCE–234 CE) and its successor, the Sasanian Empire (234–634 CE).

The Roman Empire encompassed the whole of the Mediterranean basin from Spain in the west to Anatolia, Syria, and Egypt in the east. Rome was its capital, but in the fourth century a second capital was founded at Constantinople. With the fall of Rome to "barbarian" invaders, the remaining provinces, governed from Constantinople, constituted the late Roman or Byzantine Empire and continued to rule the Balkans, Anatolia, Syria, and some of Mesopotamia, Egypt, and North Africa. Its official language until the reign of Heraclius (610–41 CE) was Latin, although the ordinary language of Constantinople was Greek.

The emperor stood at the apex of government, in theory an absolute authority in all matters of state, law, and religion. Considered divine in the pre-Christian era, emperors after Constantine (306–37 CE) were thought to be representatives of God on earth. The ruler maintained the cosmic order and suppressed the evils that come from men.

In practice, emperors were not omnipotent. They were dependent on subordinates to carry out their decisions and were strongly influenced by their families and other aristocrats, advisers, and courtiers. The bureaucracies might not implement their wishes; their subjects might circumvent them. To help make their authority effective, emperors tried to rotate appointments and cultivate patronage networks and popular factions. To enhance their prestige, they sponsored court ceremonies and public festivals and placed their portraits on coins.

The Roman Empire ruled its diverse ethnic, linguistic, and religious populations through a political machine centered on the emperor, supported by his armies and bureaucratic connections to the cities. Local notables, wealthy and educated landowners, administrators, and lawyers governed the cities. Cities controlled the land and the taxation of the countryside and supplied a portion of its revenues to the center. A shared Greco-Roman culture linked the elites and provided the rationale for the legitimacy and authority of the empire.

In the sixth and seventh centuries, however, this system was transformed. Professional bureaucrats were replaced by imperial favorites who undermined the civic notables by acquiring large rural estates. Great landed estates and large rural villas were established in Egypt, Syria, Lebanon, Cilicia, Cyprus, and Asia Minor. The church and its bishops took on ever-larger administrative roles. The new social regime was linked by a Hellenistic Christian – rather than by a Hellenistic pagan – culture.

In Egypt, aristocratic landowning families directly managed some of their estates using peasant labor, leased some to tenants under contract, and used sharecroppers on still other portions of their holdings. As the power of the aristocratic landowners grew, the regional economies declined. Still, a rural bourgeoisie encompassing lower landed gentry, entrepreneurial farmers leasing land, peasant village collectives, and merchants and artisans continued to exist in Egypt and Syria. The peasants and the poor, however, were alienated from the empire and ever more closely attached to their churches. The center was losing power in the periphery.

The consequences of these political and social transformations were marked in the economies and even in the physical appearance of the cities. As town councils lost control over taxes and land, cities lost their classical form. The agoras were turned into churches; the street grid pattern was cluttered with shops; theaters and baths gave way to houses built with enclosed courtyards walled off from the outside world. Churches remained the only public facilities.

The Sasanian empire

The Sasanian dynasty was founded in 224 CE. The Sasanians grounded their authority in the symbols of ancient Iranian monarchy. Early emperors were considered divine, an echo of Hellenistic and Old Persian ideas of kingship. The themes of Assyrian palace reliefs – the ruler enthroned by the gods, the protector of the fertility of the realm, the heroic warrior – were repeated in Sasanian palaces. Everything from cylinder seals to gardens proclaimed the grandeur of the emperor.

The Sasanian Empire has been described either as a centralized state or as a feudal confederation. In fact, it was a hybrid regime. The power of the Sasanian dynasty was grounded in Iraq and southern Iran, where the state drew its revenues from cities, the taxation of agriculture, land reclamation, and the international Indian Ocean trade. Extraordinary Sasanian development projects – the Nahrawan canal and Diyala basin development, the canalizations of southern Iraq and Khuzistan, the development of Isfahan and the Helmand basin, the fortifications of Ctesiphon, the Darband and the Gurgan walls defending against nomadic invaders – are evidence of a strongly centralized state. Similarly, a hierarchical tax and civil administration, a justice system, an organized Zoroastrian priesthood, and a rigid class hierarchy imply a state with monetary revenues and centralized direction. The power of this regime was manifest in great military victories over the Romans that indicate a large standing army as well as feudal levies.

In Iraq, the state drew its power from the *dihqans* (landowners), soldiers, and courtiers, who manned the Sasanian army and tax administration. They were united by a shared eclectic culture, combining Greek philosophy and medicine, Byzantine architecture, Indian tales, and sports and games such as chess, polo, and hunting. This hybrid culture would flourish again in the 'Abbasid age.

At the same time, the Sasanian Empire was a confederacy in which the Sasanians, as the Kings of Kings, ruled in conjunction with an aristocracy of Parthian clans. The great Parthian families were subordinate kings or feudal lords, rulers of vast provinces to the north and east of the Iranian plateau – from Azarbayjan to Gilan and Tabaristan to Khurasan – with royal and noble powers based on landownership. Whereas the Sasanians were Parsi speaking and Zoroastrian in religion, these families spoke Parthian languages and worshiped the god Mithra. The Sasanians relied on the military contributions of the Parthians and maintained their supremacy largely because of the rivalries among the Parthian dynasts. Conversely, Parthian revolts and collaboration with the Byzantines led in 628 to the defeat of the Sasanians in the great Roman-Persian wars and soon after to the extinction of the dynasty by the Arab conquests.

In sum, the Byzantine Empire was built on urban elites, bureaucracy, and a standing army. The Persian Empire was built on an alliance of a warrior, landed, horse-borne fighting aristocracy, with lower-ranking landowners (*dihqans*) as the base of the Sasanian army and tax administration.

RELIGION AND SOCIETY BEFORE ISLAM

The development of more encompassing empires and empire-wide civilizations paralleled the transformation of religions. The earliest religions were based on nature and associated with small communities. The gods of Middle Eastern peoples were the gods of families, tribes, villages, and towns; but with the growing connections among peoples through empire and trade, universal gods came to be recognized. Polytheism evolved toward monotheism. The gods of empires, the gods of dominant peoples, and the gods of conquerors, travelers, merchants, and priests whose activities were not circumscribed by a single locality came to be worshiped over large areas. Mithraism, for example, was a pagan religion uniting soldiers and officials of all races across the Roman Empire, providing uniform places for the worship of a supreme god. Sacred places, such as Rome and Alexandria, allowed the worshiper to be in contact with all the gods at once. The tendency toward unification was expressed by the idea of a pantheon and hierarchy of gods, which allowed different peoples to share in the same universe while preserving local cults and forms of worship. Local gods came to be seen as the manifestations of a universal god.

The concept of the universality of the great gods evolved into a belief in one god, who was the god of the whole universe and of all mankind. The oneness of God was preached by the prophets of ancient Israel and, in the seventh century BCE, by the Iranian prophet Zoroaster. Christianity, and later Islam, would also teach the unity of God, the universality of his sway, and the obligation of all of mankind to acknowledge his glory.

Between the third and seventh centuries, the missionary force of the new ideas and doctrines, the widening net of contacts among Middle Eastern peoples, and especially the support of the great empires made Christianity and Zoroastrianism the dominant religions in the Roman-Byzantine and Sasanian empires. Empires promoted religious conformity to help overcome ethnic and provincial differences. The boundaries between paganism and monotheism disappeared as pagans adopted monotheistic ideas about God and as the confessional religions incorporated pagan practices. Each of these confessional religions was defined by faith in an absolute truth, the possession of a holy scripture, a learned or priestly authority, and communal organizations in the form of congregations, churches, and sects.

Although different in orientation, Judaism, Zoroastrianism, and Christianity shared a common vision. All were transcendental. They held that beyond the world of this life there is a higher world, the realm of the divine, to be attained either through ethical action or through faith in God. Through sacrifice, prayer, and sacrament, they sought salvation from sin and death, and entrance for men into the eternal reality beyond the ephemeral appearances of this world. Furthermore, they were universal religions, believing that God created and governed the whole universe and all people. Believers are thus brothers in a common religious way of life and a common quest for salvation.

Jews believed that there was a single god of the universe who commanded his people (Israel) to fulfill his holy law and who would judge them in this world and the next. Judaism, however, was not a universal religion but was the religion of an ethnic group or nation. After the Romans destroyed the Jewish state in Palestine in the second century, Jewish communities were scattered throughout both the Roman and the Sasanian empires. Judaism had no political structure but was organized in numerous small communities that shared faith in the Torah (the holy scripture), a national history and law, and similar legal, educational, and charitable institutions. Jews did not have a hierarchical ecclesiastical organization but were linked by informal ties to and respect for the great academies of learning.

Under the Sasanians, Jews had their own law courts, schools, and synagogues. The exilarch was the civic chieftain officer of the Jewish community. He collected taxes and represented the Jews at the imperial court. Rabbis interpreted Jewish law and were employed by the exilarch as judges, market inspectors, and tax collectors.

Jews emphasized the observance of religious law and fulfillment of God's commands in everyday life. There were also mystical, spiritual, and eschatological elements to Judaism. In the seventh century, perhaps in response to the

Sasanian-Roman wars, messianic and apocalyptic Jewish sects, including Rabbinites, Karaites, Samaritans, ʿIsawiyya, and gnostics, proliferated. There were "hybrid" Jewish-Christian sects that accepted Jesus as a human prophet but maintained Jewish practices. In Iran and Inner Asia, a region with a long tradition as a refuge for deviant groups, there were numerous Jewish communities.

Christianity was in principle not the religion of a particular people but was universal, a religion for all mankind. The central Christian doctrine is faith in a triune God – God the Father, the Son, and the Holy Spirit. The Son is the Logos, the word of God, Christ incarnate, who was crucified so that believers might be saved. Christians developed a strong ethical strand, but their central aspiration was salvation through faith in Christ from the evil and suffering that is inherent in the material world and in man's nature.

By the sixth century, however, Christians differed profoundly among themselves about the nature of Christ's being. Was Christ human or divine, man or God, and how were the two aspects of his being related? Most Christians believed that Christ was both fully divine and fully human, but they disagreed over how to express this. The church Council of Nicaea ruled in 325 CE that Christ was not only human but also unbegotten and consubstantial with God, divine in his being. In 451 CE, the Council of Chalcedon explained that Christ had two natures, divine and human, expressed in one concrete instance (hypostasis) and in one person (prosopon); this was the position of the Orthodox Church. The Miaphysites held that Christ has one nature, one hypostasis, and one prosopon. The Nestorians held that he had two natures, two hypostases, and one prosopon. These arcane distinctions spelled out rivalries among clerics and jurisdictional and regional conflicts, as well as differences in spiritual vision.

These different religious beliefs were the foundation of the various Christian churches. Modeling themselves on the empires, the churches were territorially organized hierarchies in which the highest authority in both doctrinal and organizational matters belonged to popes and patriarchs who appointed the bishops, the heads of provinces called dioceses, who in turn appointed the local parish priests.

Parishes implemented church teachings at the local level in what we would now consider secular as well as religious matters. Bishops were sometimes the governors and administrators of the cities in which their dioceses were located. Formal ecclesiastical courts came into being in the fourth century and had jurisdiction in family, property, and commercial matters, and even in some matters of criminal law. They were also important educational institutions.

Furthermore, Christian affiliations were closely tied to political identifications. The Byzantine Empire enforced the Chalcedonian creed as its official doctrine. Miaphysitism was the religion of the Aramaic-speaking village populations of Syria and of the Coptic-speaking (the Egyptian language written in modified Greek script) peasants of Egypt. Minorities loyal to Chalcedon, known as Melkites or Eastern Orthodox Christians, however, were also found in Egypt and Syria.

Miaphysitism was also the religion of Georgia and Armenia. In the sixth century, Axum (Ethiopia) and Himyar in southern Arabia became Miaphysite. Miaphysites evangelized Nubia in the sixth century. Arabs on the edge of the Syrian desert patronized Miaphysite holy men and clerics. The Ghassanid princes on the Arabian borders of the Byzantine Empire were Miaphysites. (The Lakhmids, on the Arabian borders of Sasanian Iraq, were Nestorians.) Miaphysitism was an expression of provincial autonomy and resistance to Roman-Byzantine suzerainty.

Despite these doctrinal and organizational differences, Christianity created a common culture in multiple languages: Greek or Aramaic in Syria, Persian or Aramaic in Iraq, Greek or Coptic in Egypt. Christian Greek literature influenced and was influenced by Syriac, Armenian, Coptic, Georgian, and Arabic literature, thereby generating a shared cultural heritage.

The spread of Christian culture, however, marginalized Greco-Roman culture. Notables and the people came to share a common Christian culture. In the fifth and sixth centuries, the clergy took over many of the functions of the declining town councils. This introduced a period of lavish church constructions and decoration in the village societies of Egypt and Syria.

While urban and rural clergy were implicated in the world of power, holy men, shrines, and monasteries became the popularly accepted intermediaries between humans and God. Holy men and ascetics popularized the spiritual purity of the desert. Pilgrimage to the column of St. Simeon Stylites became a form of mass worship. In the seventh century, veneration of icons and the cults of saints and the Virgin became alternatives to the authority of the emperor and the church. In Egypt, wealthier peasants and townspeople introduced the veneration of icons. Syrian merchants developed fine stone carvings; bands of Syrian monks were noted for their musical litanies. Music, holy relics, and Christian ceremonies became the means of cultural transmission. Personal access to God displaced imperial and church-defined religious ceremony. Throughout the old Roman Empire, east and west, culture and identity were recast in Christian terms.

In the Sasanian Empire, Zoroastrianism was the religion of the political and social elites. Zoroastrians believed in a supreme god, Ahura Mazda, the creator of the world, a god of light and truth. At the creation, however, there were two independent powers: Ohrmazd, the god of goodness and light, and Ahreman, the god of evil and darkness. There was also a third principle, a mediating figure, Mihr, and other gods of the pantheon.

In Zoroastrian eschatology, the destiny of the world was to be decided by God's struggle with the forces of evil and darkness. Zoroastrian teachings included a cosmic struggle for redemption culminating in the coming of the messiah, the resurrection of the dead, and the last judgment. Human beings are part of this cosmic struggle. Both gods and demons reside in the human soul: the goal of human existence is to make the divine prevail over the demonic. Human beings must contribute to the victory of the Good and Light by their actions and beliefs and will be judged at the day of judgment. The fate of the wicked is either to be damned for eternity or to be purified by punishment and accepted into universal salvation at the end of the world. In the end, Ahura Mazda will prevail, evil will be eliminated, and human beings will be transformed into spiritualized bodies and souls. Zoroastrianism, like Judaism, emphasizes individual ethical responsibility.

Zoroastrian worship turned around the mobads (magi) or fire priests, who at some time in the third century acquired a chief mobad, and thus a hierarchy of clergy. The fire temples, tended by the magi, kept alive the flame of purity. In the fourth century, Zoroastrians collected their scriptures into the Avesta. The magian legal system helped diffuse a magian way of life, parallel to Judaism and Christianity.

Zoroastrianism, however, had no unified tradition and no identifiable orthodoxy, but many varieties of belief and practice. Elite religion involved spiritual programs of self-transcendence. Popular religion included demon worship and magical practices to propitiate the demons. Ritual religious practices included astrology and divination. Mazdakism was a reform movement within Zoroastrianism advocating communal property and marriages.

The Parthian nobility, however, were devotees of Mithra. Mithra was the god of contracts, alliances, pacts, and justice, fighting on the side of goodness and light. Mithraism was the religious heritage of northern and eastern Iran – Khurasan, Tabaristan, Gilan, and Azarbayjan – and of popular opposition to the Sasanians and the mobads.

The Sasanian Empire was also home to numerous other religions and cults, including Judaism, Christianity, Manichaeanism, Buddhism, and gnostic sects. In Mesopotamia there was no congruence of language or religion between government and the town populations. Parsi-speaking Zoroastrians ruled Iraq, but the local populations were Aramaic-speaking Nestorians and Jews. Jewish communities were also found in Armenia, Azarbayjan, and Isfahan. Christians were settled in Marw and Soghdia, where they spread their religion among the Turkic nomads. Transoxania also harbored a great diversity of religions, including Nestorianism, local Zoroastrianism, Buddhism, and colonies of Jews and Hindus.

Under the Sasanian Empire, from the fourth century, religious communities were organized as legal corporations owning property; maintaining courts; regulating marriages, divorces, and inheritances; and through their chiefs, holding responsibility to the state for taxes and discipline. In 410 CE, Shah Yazadgard recognized the administrative autonomy of the Christians and the bishop of Seleucia-Ctesiphon as the head of the church. Bishops began to preside over legal cases. The Sasanians appointed a catholicos or patriarch and a metropolitan to preside over the bishops in parallel with the Sasanian administrative hierarchy. Magians had a hierarchy parallel to that of the state, a hierarchical judicial administration specifically for Zoroastrians, a cult, scriptures, religious laws, and distinctive customs. It was the religion of the elite and rulers.

In the fifth century, the Nestorian Church was reinforced by the migration of persecuted Christians from the Roman Empire. The emperors allowed the transfer of the theological school of Edessa to Nisibis, bringing Christian theology into the Sasanian domains, fortifying the Nestorian Church, and preparing the later amalgamation of Christian theology and philosophy with Arab-Islamic thought. Scholars from Edessa also established a medical school at Gundeshapur.

In the sixth century, Nestorians extended church government and canon law to deal with marriage, inheritance, and property. Unlike the Syriac Church, which referred to Roman codes for civil issues, the Nestorian Church did not distinguish between civil and religious law. Competing clerical and lay factions invoked royal support and brought the government into church decisions. Royal permission was required for the election of the head of the church, construction of buildings, burials, and even the establishment of monastic rules.

Alongside the monotheistic religions, numerous sects and cults continued to flourish. Manichaeanism, a universal dualist religion asserting separate cosmic forces for good and evil, was a heresy to both Christianity and Zoroastrianism and flourished in Iraq and Iran. Its founder, Mani (216–76 CE), preached the division of the universe between spirit and matter. Manichaeans believed that spirit was good, but that matter was derived from Satan and was evil. Manichaeanism was never attached to a particular ethnicity nor organized as a church. It spread to Iran, India, Central Asia, and North Africa; its texts were translated from Aramaic into Greek and Pahlavi.

In this religious environment, paganism also remained important. Pagans adopted monotheistic ideas about God, and monotheistic religions incorporated pagan practices. In Iraq, there were Marcionites who believed in three principles – good, evil, and the demiurge of justice. Pagan Hellenistic cults – Hermetics, Elkasaites, Mandeens, gnostics, Chaldeans, astrologers, occult scientists, and others – flourished. In Syria, Hellenism was a powerful influence: many towns still had cults of Apollo, Hermes, Ares, and other gods. Even Christians used Greek mythology to decorate homes and churches.

RELIGIONS AND EMPIRES

The relations between religious elites and imperial administrators were ambivalent. Each laid claim to an absolute truth and a universal authority. In principle, they were competitors in representing the highest values, but simultaneously they could be uneasy allies. Empires gained legitimacy and administrative help from cooperative religious elites; religions gained protection, material assistance, power, and glory from the support of empires. Each could either deliver or withhold popular support from the other.

The Roman Empire made Christianity a state religion. Constantine, the first Roman emperor to convert to Christianity, enforced orthodoxy and attempted to punish heretics. He thereby joined the emperor and the empire to Christianity, merging a universal religion with missionary goals and a strong scriptural authority to the political and military apparatus of the state. Empire and Christianity under the theme of one God and one empire were united in opposition to heresy and to provincial independence.

After Constantine, the Roman state considered itself the domain of the chosen people, and the emperor considered himself representative of God and defender of orthodoxy. Royal decrees regulated the organization of the church. Roman emperors called convocations of bishops, supplied them authority, and enforced their decisions. False belief was defiance of imperial authority. Emperor Justinian (r. 527–65 CE) persecuted pagans, heretics, homosexuals, and Jews. Emperor Heraclius (r. 610–41 CE) tried to force Chalcedonian doctrine on all Christians.

The Byzantine Empire, however, never succeeded in consolidating its religious domination. Local power holders, including archbishops and bishops, used doctrinal differences to contest the authority of the emperor. Miaphysitism articulated both a doctrinal opposition to the Chalcedonian doctrine and provincial resistance to imperial power. The struggle between competing doctrines and competing political powers resulted in the establishment of several forms of regional Christianity.

The Sasanian Empire sometimes promoted a centralized state collaborating with Zoroastrian clergy in imitation of Byzantine Caesaropapism. There were periods of religious repression – against Manichaeanism in the fourth century, Christianity in the fourth and fifth centuries, Mazdakism in the late fifth century, and Judaism in the third and fifth centuries. In general, however, unlike the late Roman Empire, the Sasanian Empire accepted its diverse Zoroastrian, Nestorian, and Jewish communities as legitimate social bodies. The Sasanians surrounded themselves with the Nestorian catholicos and the Jewish exilarchs as well as Zoroastrian mobads. Nestorian and Zoroastrian communities had a bureaucracy and system of titles parallel to that of the state. Royal permission was required for the election of the heads of churches, for construction of buildings, for burials, and even for the issuing of monastic rules. Competing clerical and lay factions invoked royal support and brought the government into church decisions. The Sasanian state used the churches as intermediaries to regulate and tax the population. The long-term Sasanian policy was to accept and to utilize all religious communities as instruments of rule.

Thus, Byzantine and Sasanian religious policies differed. The late Roman Empire strove for religious uniformity as a basis for imperial rule. It was prepared to punish and persecute religious deviants. But the rising power of religion as the principle organizing forces in the lives of masses of peoples gave power to bishops, saints, holy men, and icons. The growing importance of religion limited the effective authority of the emperors. By contrast, the Sasanian Empire maintained a preferred cult and, despite episodes of persecution of Jews and Christians, tolerated and utilized all the major religious communities as vehicles of state control. Churches and religious communities saw themselves as both potential collaborators and potential opponents of the empires.

WOMEN, FAMILY, AND SOCIETY (CO-AUTHOR, LENA SALAYMEH)

Empires and religions were the great overarching institutions, but the fundamental units of society were families living in small communities. Unfortunately, we know very little about the legal and social institutions or the patterns of daily life that regulated family behavior and the relations of men and women in late antiquity. Most of what we know comes from the records of royalty and aristocracy and from legal texts; little is known about the populace as a whole. Thus any account of families in antiquity is tentative and must be taken with great reserve.

Still, it appears that all the pre-Islamic Middle Eastern and Mediterranean societies had, with variations, similar family institutions and norms for the relations of men and women. In ideology – and to a large degree in behavior – late antique societies made a sharp distinction between men's and women's roles. The middle- and upper-class ideal was the isolation of women from the marketplace, politics, and social life with men. Generally, in the upper classes, war, politics, and worship were men's work, although the wives of kings, public officials, and warriors occasionally rose to unofficial prominence and substituted for men in moments of crisis. In the ancient Persian empires, women of royal and noble rank owned and administered landed estates. In the lower classes, men did craft work and trading, hard labor and heavy agricultural work, including plowing and irrigation. Women of the lower classes were engaged in household and domestic craft work, care of children, light agriculture, and stock herding.

In extended families and lineages, women were subject to the authority of fathers, brothers, husbands, and husbands' male kin. It is probably fair to say that in the pre-Islamic Mediterranean and Middle East men looked on women as inferior in rational, moral, and physical capacities, and as requiring the support, supervision, and control of men. In ancient Greece, women were wards of their fathers and then of their husbands. In early Roman law, only men were considered citizens empowered to act in the political arena and as the heads of families. According to the Jewish scholar Flavius Josephus, "Woman, the Law says, is inferior to man in all things. Hence she must obey not force but authority, because God has given power to man." Although women were subordinated to men, their social, economic, and marital functions were highly valued. Women were socially weak, but men were obliged to be considerate, protective, and solicitous of their women. In all the regional pre-Islamic societies, the authority of men and their social and economic advantages were institutionalized in the arrangements of marriage and divorce, sexual morality, property, and engagement in public life.

Marriage, divorce, and sexual morality

The authority of men was clearly expressed in the institutions of marriage. Ancient Iranian, Greek and Roman, and Jewish and Christian communities had similar concepts of marriage. Marriage was a mechanism for producing children who would carry on the family name and family fortunes. Betrothal and marriage agreements were entered into by families. Marriages were regulated in the interests of families and their property and were not an expression of the sentiments of the couple. Normally, a father negotiated a betrothal for a female child, possibly before the child had reached puberty. Ancient Roman women, for example, could not marry without the consent or representation of a guardian. According to Sasanian law, a woman had to give her consent before marriage, but her father had to represent her in drawing a marriage contract. However, she had the legal right to keep her wages after marriage. For a Jewish marriage, consent was required, but a woman's consent could be tacit. In general, a very young woman was expected to accept her parents' wishes – silence was considered consent. Women were expected to be faithful and loyal, to bear children, prepare food, and keep house. A bride would ordinarily move to the house of her husband and reside with his kin, but her male guardians were ultimately responsible for her welfare.

In later centuries, a more egalitarian ideal based on mutual affection emerged. By the early Roman Empire period, people above the age of puberty could declare a marriage by mutual consent without parental permission. Upper-class women owned property, were entitled to the return of their dowries if divorced, and attended social and public events without restriction. Women's funeral steles were inscribed with loving sentiments by their husbands. This was the beginning of the ideal of marriage as a monogamous loving union. However, divorce was common, especially in the upper classes.

Throughout the Mediterranean and the Middle East, men had privileges and powers regarding divorce that women did not. Mesopotamian, Sumerian, biblical-era, and pre-Islamic Arab practices indicate that men generally had unrestricted rights to divorce, although they had to announce it publicly. According to Sasanian law, divorce occurred either through mutual consent or the husband's repudiation of a wife for committing a sin (adultery, ignoring purity rules, etc.). Sasanian women of the lower classes could not divorce their husbands, whereas upper-class women could.

In early Roman law, only a husband could make a declaration of divorce, but by the time of Constantine (fourth century), either spouse could unilaterally end a marriage. Emperor Constantine at first tried to forbid divorce, but he was unsuccessful. He then ruled that wives or husbands could divorce in cases of grave misconduct. If the wife were responsible for the breakup of the marriage, the husband could retain money from her dowry and take custody of any children. If the husband were at fault, he would have to repay the dowry. In actuality, there was considerable leeway for individual cases.

In rabbinic law, a husband, but not a wife, could end a marriage at will, but he was required to return the dowry – unless the wife was judicially found to be at fault. The rabbis, however, differed on the legal rights of women to initiate divorce. The majority of Babylonian Talmudists gave a woman the right to divorce in the case of a major flaw in the husband, such as impotence or a serious disease. The Palestinian Talmud suggests that Jewish women had the right to sue for divorce. Rabbis acknowledged divorce by mutual consent. A widow or divorcee could remarry after a waiting period to ascertain that she was not pregnant by her previous husband.

The spread of Christianity modified perceptions of divorce. Christian values prohibited divorce except in cases of adultery and prohibited remarriage after divorce. By the eighth century, marriage was widely accepted as an indissoluble sacrament, although this did not enter canon law until 1563.

Late antique sexual morality was governed by a double standard. All late antique societies denounced adultery by women but in practice condoned nonmarried sexual opportunities for men. Roman law recognized concubinage as a long-term relationship between people whose social status precluded the legal arrangements of a marriage; the law permitted concubines in addition to a wife. Although adultery and premarital sex were condemned, the relations of married men with slaves, prostitutes, or other less than respectable women were not considered adultery. Roman society expected unmarried women to be chaste. The distinctions between wife, concubine, and mistress were ambiguous.

Zoroastrian, Jewish, and Christian traditions all required virginity in a bride. The Avesta (Zoroastrian scripture) encouraged chastity and forbade sex outside marriage. The Bible (Leviticus) orders that women who have had premarital sex should be stoned to death, and a Jewish bride found not to be a virgin was subject to punishment. In practice, however, Palestinian rabbis developed a process by which a woman could prove that she was still a virgin despite having a "damaged" hymen. Until the tenth century CE, if not later, Jews also practiced polygyny. Rabbinic law permitted multiple marriages if a man could fulfill his commitments to each of his wives. Still, there were hesitations among Palestinian rabbis who recommended that a man divorce his first wife before remarrying. Also some rabbis granted a first wife the right to divorce or to put a provision in the marriage contract to prevent her husband from marrying a second wife.

Early Christians also condemned premarital sex but pardoned the offense if the couple married. Although opposed in principle to extramarital relations, Christians in late antiquity did not in fact penalize a married man's extramarital relations with women of low status. It was most severely reproved if a man tried to bequeath property to illegitimate children.

Property and inheritance

In late antique societies, women could own property and acquire it by gift, dowry, inheritance, or work. Commonly, however, fathers, husbands, and other guardians were empowered to control their assets. In ancient Greek law, a woman retained legal ownership of her property, but her husband was the manager of his wife's dowry and received its income as long as the marriage lasted. He had to represent her in court cases and in drawing of contracts in much the same way as he was the guardian of his children. Roman law did not recognize women as legally independent. Their property came under the control of their *patras familias* – father, husband, or other guardian. A woman could own and bequeath property, but her choices had to be approved by her guardian and her heirs. Many Roman jurists believed that these restrictions were justified by women's weakness of mind. Despite such limitations, women in the Roman Empire often managed their own properties and entered into legal arrangements. Sasanian women had the right to own property, but – because they were not considered full legal persons – a male relative or spouse would administer the property. Jewish husbands acquired control over their wives' property, because the rabbis reasoned that a husband was entitled to the profits of some kinds of property because he was obligated to ransom her if she were taken captive.

In late antique law, with the possible exception of Roman law, women did not inherit equally with men. However, families commonly arranged to transfer property to wives and daughters by gifts or wills. Under Sasanian rules wives of full legal status could inherit the same portion as sons, but lower-status wives and their children could not inherit. Unmarried daughters received half of a son's share in an estate; married daughters could not inherit, because, presumably, they had received a dowry equivalent to their share. Under Sasanian law, however, wills and dowries were often used to alter inheritance shares. Biblical laws prevented widows (unless childless) from inheriting and allowed a daughter to inherit only if there was no male heir or if she married within the same clan. By late antiquity, however, it was common for Jewish fathers to give daughters bridal dowries to compensate for their omission from inheritance.

The limitations on women's control of property extended to their participation in the judicial system. The dominant pre-Islamic norm was to limit women's testimony or involvement in court proceedings. The Emperor Constantine disapproved of women being present in court. The Zoroastrian clergy did not allow women's testimony in a court of law. Rabbis considered women incompetent to testify in court, but they appear to have accepted women's testimony in matters considered under their purview (such as purity).

Seclusion and veiling
Although it is not possible to assess the extent of gender segregation across classes and communities in pre-Islamic Middle Eastern and Mediterranean societies, the lives of women in the ruling classes were generally marked by seclusion and veiling. Textual evidence from the mid-Assyrian period (1132–1115 BCE) indicates that women lived in separate areas and were guarded by eunuchs. Elite Greek women were absent from public life. Jewish women in the time of Jesus were admonished

to stay within the household. Seclusion may have been related to ritual and social restrictions placed on women during menstruation. In the Zoroastrian tradition, menstruating women were considered polluted and could not perform temple rituals. Rabbinic law also restricted women from social activities during menstruation or after childbirth, even though marriage and sexuality were seen as positive.

The seclusion of women, however, was by no means absolute. Women appeared in public to work. Some Jewish women were educated. Christian and pagan women in Byzantium appear to have studied the classics, but they studied different texts than men and were expected to speak in a distinctive manner. Christian women also played an important role in the church, as patrons, as teachers for women who could not read the gospels, as assistants in the baptism of women, and as caregivers of the sick and the needy. Through their contacts with other women, Christian women could help promote conversions to Christianity or adherence to Christian social and moral norms.

Veiling was widely practiced throughout the pre-Islamic Mediterranean and Middle East. It is known that a style of clothing that covered women from head to toe existed in ancient Mesopotamia around 3000 BCE. The oldest statute regarding the veiling of women known today is in middle Assyrian law (c. 1300 BCE). The pre-Islamic inhabitants of the Iranian plateau practiced veiling of women. Elite Sasanian women (and Sasanian kings) were veiled. Jewish women were required to cover their heads and faces when in public. Some passages in the Talmud indicate that the rabbis associated a woman's hair covering with piety and chastity.

Women in ancient Roman society wore a long cloth called a *palla*, which may have changed into veils of different sizes around the second century BCE. Later, early Christian churches requested women to cover their heads in the chapel, and Tertullian (a second-\third-century Christian writer), in his essay "On the Veiling of Virgins," declared that unmarried women must wear the veil.

There are many different interpretations of veiling. In late antiquity the veil, generally, represented high status. The veil distinguished respectable women from slaves and prostitutes. Numismatic and other evidence from the sixth century BCE to the seventh century CE suggest that veiling may also have been decorative or fashionable. In some contexts, it may have signified that a woman was the ward of her husband or father. Still, how widely veiling was practiced, in what circumstances, or how the veil was actually worn is not known.

The fragmentary evidence suggests that women in third-century Sasanian communities, or fourth-century Jewish societies, or sixth-century Byzantium lived in worlds of similar values and similar social and legal practices. These values and practices would be perpetuated in the Muslim era.

CONCLUSION

On the eve of the Islamic era, the Middle East was divided into two great realms of polity and culture (Byzantine and Sasanian) and two main spheres of religious

Table 1. *Islam in world history*

Early village farming communities	c. 7000 BCE
Cities	c. 3000 BCE
Empires	c. 2400 BCE
Axial-age and monotheistic religions	c. 800 BCE
Muhammad	c. 570–632
Middle Eastern Islamic societies	622–c. 1200
Worldwide diffusion of Islam	c. 650 to present
Rise of European world empires	1200–1900
Modern transformation of Islamic societies	1800 to present

belief (Christian and Zoroastrian, with Jewish minorities). Religion and empire were intertwined. The empires sustained, patronized, endowed, and enforced organized worship. In turn, the religious communities legitimized the emperors' reigns and helped govern the subjects in their name. Alternatively, Miaphysite churches embodied political as well as religious resistance to the state. Within each society, a myriad of small communities retained their social and cultural distinctiveness. Their headmen, chiefs, and elders mediated their integration into the overarching realms of common religion and empire.

These two political and religious regions – with their common institutional forms and overlapping popular cultures –would become part of a single Middle Eastern civilization. (See Table 1.) In the late sixth and early seventh centuries, the two empires fought exhausting wars for the control of Syria and Egypt, which paved the way for the Arab-Muslim conquests and the formation of an Arab-Islamic empire in the former domains of both. The new empire preserved the continuity of Middle Eastern institutions. The basic forms of state organization – including the emperorship, the bureaucratic administration and large-scale landownership, and the predominant style of religious life focusing on universal and transcendental beliefs and a parish-like community organization – were maintained.

Early Islamic societies adapted both the Roman model uniting imperial authority and religious identity and the Sasanian model of religious pluralism. As in the late Roman and Sasanian empires, culture and identity came to be defined in religious terms – Muslim identity would also be defined by religious affiliation. Both the hierarchical Christian churches and the decentralized Jewish communities would be precedents for the later organization of Muslim religious associations. Just as Christianity had created a translinguistic religious culture, Islam would be expressed in Arabic, Persian, Turkish, and many other languages. The basic structures of empire, economy, religion, society, and family continued, but they were gradually redefined in terms of a new religion, new cultures, and new social identities.

Similarly, the regional ecology continued to be based on agrarian and urban communities, and the economy functioned on the basis of marketing and money exchanges. Ancient cultures – philosophy, literature, law, and art – continued to flourish and would be carried on in the Arab-Islamic era.

Family, lineage, clientele, and ethnic communities also continued to be the building blocks of society. Just as the institutions of empire and state and of religious-communal organization descended from the pre-Islamic era and continued to be the governing template for the Muslim era, so too were ancient patterns of family and gender relations – revised, modified, freshly detailed, and given a new religious and cultural context – carried over from the ancient to the Islamic era.

The progressive transformation of late antique societies into Islamic societies took place in three main phases: first, the creation of a new Islamic community in Arabia; second, the conquest of the Middle East by this new Arabian-Muslim community; and third, the generation in the period of the early caliphate (to 945 CE) of an Islamic empire and culture. In the post-imperial or sultanate period (945–c. 1200) the institutional and cultural prototypes of the caliphal era were transformed into new types of Islamic states and religious communities. In the first phase, we see the emergence of Islam in Arabian society. In the second, we consider Islam as it became the religion of an imperial state and urban elite. In the third phase, we see how Islamic values and elites transformed the lives of Middle Eastern peoples.

THE PREACHING OF ISLAM

CHAPTER 2

HISTORIANS AND THE SOURCES

For more than a century, Western scholarship on the "origins" of Islam – Arabia, the life of Muhammad, the Quran, and the Arab conquests – was based on the traditional Arabic sources. Western scholars added commentaries on themes important in Anglo-European historiography such as the psychology of the Prophet Muhammad, the social and economic environment, and the relationships of early Islam to Judeo-Christian and Arabian cultures. The theme of political and religious leadership was particularly prominent.

In recent decades an intensive reexamination of the Arabic sources has challenged the traditional narratives. A number of scholars have argued that we do not and cannot know much about the early Islamic era. Every aspect of the "origins" of Islam – the paganism of Arabian society, the advent of the Prophet Muhammad, the provenance of the Quran, and the story of prophecy, community, and state formation in early seventh-century Arabia, and many aspects of the Arab conquests – has become the subject of scholarly controversy. The skeptics point out that the sources did not begin to be transcribed from oral to written form until a century or so after Muhammad's death. Texts in hadith, law, theology, and history were not compiled in written form until the late seventh century, when oral reminiscences began to be written down, scraps of documents collected, stories assembled, biographies remembered, exploits celebrated, and chronologies worked out, decades and even a century after the events in question. These materials were not organized into books until the middle decades of the eighth century and often as late as the ninth century. The historical record could not but be shaped by later political, social, and religious commitments; factional, tribal, sectarian, and ethnic rivalries; the interests of caliphs and scholars; and the competition among elites for political and religious authority.

Because the Arabic-Muslim accounts of the Prophet and early Islamic history are based on later materials, some scholars reasoned that the only way to know the true history is to use non-Muslim sources. One result was an account of the origin of Islam as a messianic Jewish sect in Palestine and North Arabia that much later was redefined as a new religion. In general, however, this effort has failed, because the non-Muslim sources are themselves fragmentary, poorly informed, and prejudiced.

Other scholars argued that the traditional story of the origins and the early history of Islam was a later invention intended to demonstrate, via historical narrative, the mythical, doctrinal, and other beliefs of Muslims and their superiority to religious rivals, including pagan Arabians, Jews, and Christians. Thus, they see the materials in the biography of the Prophet not as a factual history but as part of later inter-confessional polemics, and as designed to explicate the Quran, validate Muhammad's historical role, establish legal precedents, and reinforce the Muslim religious beliefs and community identity of a later era. The biography of Muhammad is an expression of the superiority of Muslims to Jews and Christians. For this reason we have traditions about his perfect character, his appearance, his miracles, and his triumphs over infidel Arabs and Jews. In the revisionist view, the story of Muhammad is a creation of literary history rather than the documentation of a life. It embodies the construction of a religion rather than a biography.

These interpretations – modeled after biblical criticism and other forms of literary analysis – make a valid point. Given the compositional history of the biography of Muhammad (*sira*), the traditions of his sayings (hadith), his campaigns (*al-maghazi*), and Quranic exegesis (*tafsir*), the intrusion of a later mentality and later religious, political, and social concerns was unavoidable – as it is for any literary tradition in any time period.

This skepticism was part of a larger cultural and political tendency. A far-reaching critique of "orientalist" scholarship rejected the attitudes and the findings of earlier generations of Anglo-European scholars as prejudiced and distorted. This critique merged with a "post-modernist" phase in academic scholarship in which scholars in literature, history, and anthropology began to examine the hidden political and cultural motivations for the production of academic scholarship. Feminism and third world studies were the leaders in this movement. Texts could no longer be taken as objective accounts of reality. We know what people said and we try to decipher what they thought, but we do not know what "actually happened." In early Islamic studies, radical skepticism has sharpened our minds to the importance of careful questioning of the sources, but it goes too far in its root and branch criticism of the traditional story. From a healthy skepticism the radical view eventuates in the outright rejection of the only historical material we actually possess. It excludes epoch-transforming events from history and makes the origins of a worldwide civilization incomprehensible.

The radical skeptical approach underestimates the abundance and variety of historical materials, culled and transmitted from the very earliest years of Islam and embedded in later texts. We know a great deal about the ancient history of Arabia from inscriptions and archeological findings and from Greco-Roman historical and ecclesiastical sources. Arabian tribal genealogies, poetry, and other lore were passed on in oral form at first and later in writing. Early written documents include contracts, treaties, and diplomatic correspondence such as the Constitution of Medina, the Treaty of Hudaybiya, and Muhammad's epistles to the tribes. The early written compilation of the Quran suggests that writing was a common method of transmission in the Prophet's lifetime.

Later in the first Islamic century, Arab scholars collected tribal lore, Judeo-Christian exegetical stories, Yemeni genealogies and battle tales, and the sayings and stories about the Prophet Muhammad and his battles. Materials embedded in later texts show that stories related to the Quran were compiled in the 650s and 660s, within a generation of the death of Muhammad. Tax and pay documents, records of public works, papyri, coins, inscriptions, monuments and archeological remains, and lists of caliphs add to the data. The abundance of data and the variety of sources make it possible to critically reconstruct many aspects of the early period.

Furthermore, the radical skeptical view neglects recent studies of late antiquity. Scholars of the late Roman period, especially versed in Syriac sources, are reexamining the cultural, social, economic, and political conditions of the eastern Mediterranean in the centuries before and after the Arab conquests. The new scholarship emphasizes cultural, social, and political continuities between late antiquity and the early Islamic era. This scholarship has had an important impact on the conception of early Islamic civilization presented in this book.

Finally, the radical skeptical approach is based on a misunderstanding of the transmission of knowledge in late antiquity and the early Islamic era, and on a misleading, anachronistic application of our own culture of book learning and book production to a different culture. In the seventh and later centuries, books – fixed texts transmitted in unchanging detail – were not the only or even the predominant mode of learning. Late antique and early Islamic cultures were neither book nor oral cultures, but rather a hybrid based on recitations, lectures, and note taking. In this system of learning, poets and scholars presented their work orally, either from memory or from written notes – likely with variations in each repetition. Students made notes during the recitation and/or reproduced the presentation from memory. To control the learning process, teachers might dictate, prepare scripts of their own lectures, or correct and authorize students' notebooks.

At a later stage, the material in notebooks would be compiled and edited into a text, which was still subject to new variations. The ninth century was rich in the production of compilations based on either one authority or an assemblage of earlier authorities. By the tenth century, definitive texts – books – became the norm. Thus, there was a sequence of narrator, note takers, successive compilers, and eventually the editors or authors of books. There was no single act of authoring. This process cannot be described by the dichotomy of oral and written and defies the notion of tracing all books back to an original source.

This system of lecturing and note taking had precedents in both Hellenistic and Jewish learning. The Greek language distinguishes between a mnemonic aid for a lecture (*hypomnema*) and a literary work (*syngramma*). The classical method of instruction was oral lectures and note taking. Galen's medical works were taught in this way into the Muslim era. There were also Jewish, Syrian, and Persian traditions for this type of knowledge transmission. In Jewish learning, Haggadoth (oral traditions) and Talmudic studies were *hypomnemata* (at least until and probably even after the codification of the Talmud in the late antiquity). The Bible, however, was probably both read from the text and recited from memory.

In early Muslim culture this quasi-oral, quasi-written method of transmission was often preferred to fixed texts. Verified auditory transmission was regarded as more reliable than writing, which was easily manipulated. Before the era of mechanical reproduction of books, when texts had to be copied by hand, there was too much leeway for errors, distortions, and forgeries. The uncertainties of early Arabic orthography also led many scholars and poets to prefer recitation to texts. Poets were also suspicious of writing because it could distort the sensory impact of speech. To be accepted in court, legal documents required oral confirmation. Indeed, early Muslim scholars did not necessarily value ownership, originality, or fixity. The goal was not the literal preservation of the text, but continuity, correction, and improvement. Not the fixed text but the living, ongoing adaptation of tradition was the key to truth.

Withal, books did have an important and growing place in this system of transmission. The Quran was the earliest Muslim book. The early caliphs sponsored literary, theological, and historical writing. For example, Ibn Ishaq's biography of Muhammad was commissioned by the 'Abbasid Caliph al-Mansur (754–75). Sibawayhi's (d. 796) grammar – perhaps too complex and theoretical for oral transmission – was composed as a book, and other books followed in the ninth century. The need for tax records, correspondence, and legal administration made writing ever more important.

Thus, the rich, vivid, and extensive materials in the early Arab-Muslim histories were not invented in a later period. Although the Arabic literary tradition was indeed shaped by the later eras in which it was compiled and edited, it embodies an historical recollection of the Arabian milieu and of Muhammad that preserves a core of genuine collective memory. The history of Arabia and the life of the Prophet were passed on by a variety of oral, quasi-oral, quasi-written, and written methods. These methods allowed for the preservation of a multiplicity of voices within the literary tradition and give the rich possibilities that diversity affords for historical reconstruction. A gradual, incremental process seems more realistic than to imagine the creation of a belated and elaborate myth out of whole cloth.

This is not to say that these sources – or any historical sources – can be taken at face value. In later eras historians wanted to explain the conquests as the outcome of Muhammad's teaching and career, and to depict them as both tribal heroism and pious commitment to Islam. The process of historical transmission allowed, indeed inevitably included, variations, selection, and reinterpretations influenced by the mentality, cultural and political contexts, and personal, factional, and sectarian interests of the transmitters and their patrons and students. Moreover, in the transmission of all historical narratives, variation is inevitable. Any history requires selection; combination; a chronological and causal framework; a narrative, dramatic, or thematic strategy; and fitting the data into a coherent narrative that alters and reshapes the story. History is not only a record of past events; it is a story about those events.

CHAPTER 3

ARABIA

On the eve of the Islamic era, Arabia stood on the periphery of the Middle Eastern imperial societies. (See Map 1.) In Arabia, the primary communities remained especially powerful, and urban, religious, and royal institutions were less developed. Whereas the imperial world was predominantly agricultural, Arabia was primarily pastoral. Whereas the imperial world was citied, Arabia was the home of camps and oases. Whereas the imperial peoples were committed to the monotheistic religions, Arabia was largely pagan. The imperial world was politically organized; Arabia was politically fragmented.

At the same time, pre-Islamic Arabia was in many ways an integral part, a provincial variant, of the larger Middle Eastern civilization. There were no physical or political boundaries between Arabia and the larger region; no great walls, nor rigid ethnic or demographic frontiers. Migrating Arabian peoples made up much of the population of the desert margins of Syria and Iraq. Arabs in the Fertile Crescent region shared political forms, religious beliefs, economic connections, and physical space with the societies around them.

Arabia was also connected to the larger region by the interventions of the imperial powers. The Byzantines and the Sasanians disputed control of Yemen, and both were active in creating spheres of influence in North Arabia. They intervened diplomatically and politically to extend their trading privileges, protect sympathetic religious populations, and advance their strategic interests. The Ghassanid kingdom (in southern Syria, Jordan, and northwestern Arabia) and the Lakhmid kingdom (in southern Iraq and northeastern Arabia) were vassals of the Byzantine and Sasanian empires, respectively. The client kingdoms, like the empires, had systems for rapid communications by couriers. From the Romans and the Persians, the Arabs obtained new arms and armor and learned new tactics, often through the enrollment of Arabs as auxiliaries in the Roman or Persian armies. As a result, Arabia was probably more politically sophisticated and institutionally developed

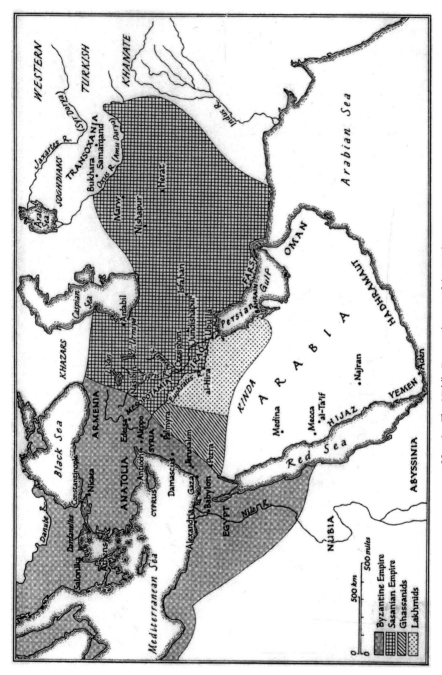

Map 1. The Middle East on the eve of the Muslim era.

Western Turkish Khanate

Soghdiana

Transoxania

Jaxartes R. (Syr Darya)

Bukhara Samarqand Oxus R. (Amu Darya)

Marv

Nishapur

Herat

Aral Sea

Khazars

Caspian Sea

Ardabil

Isfahan

FARS

OMAN

Persian Gulf

Arabian Sea

HADHRAMAUT

Armenia

L. Urmiya

Nasibin

Mesopotamia

Tigris

Euphrates

Cteshipon

Junishapur

IRAQ

Ubulla

al-Hira

KINDA

ARABIA

Aden

YEMEN

Najran

Black Sea

Anatolia

Edessa

Aleppo

Syria

Antioch

Palmyra

Damascus

Jerusalem

Gaza

Petra

HIJAZ

Mecca

al-Ta'if

Medina

Red Sea

Constantinople

Nicaea

Dardanelles

Cyprus

Alexandria

Babylon

Egypt

Nile R.

Mediterranean Sea

Salonika

Athens

Danube R.

NUBIA

ABYSSINIA

500 km

500 miles

Byzantine Empire

Sasanian Empire

Ghassanids

Lakhmids

32

than scholars have recognized. The later Arab-Muslim conquests were organized as armies and not as migrating tribes.

Furthermore, the diffusion of Judaism, Christianity, and gnosticism in southern, west-central, and northern Arabia made these regions parts of the Hellenistic world. In southern Arabia, Judaism was established in the fourth and fifth centuries. Monotheistic, probably Jewish, inscriptions in Yemen date to the fifth century, and there were many Jews in the Arabian tribes of Himyar and Kinda. In northern Arabia, there were Jews at Khaybar and Medina. Jewish Arab tribes in Medina were rich in land, fortresses, and weapons.

In the north, Christianity was established in the fifth century. Christian churches were active in eastern Arabia in the Sasanian sphere of influence, especially at Al-Hira (the Lakhmid capital). Christianity was also represented by merchants who traveled in Arabian caravans from Najran (in southern Arabia) to Busra (in Syria). The market fair at 'Ukaz attracted Christian preachers. Extensive networks of monasteries, police posts, and markets carried Miaphysite literary and religious ideas from Edessa, Coptic culture from Egypt, and Ethiopian Christianity to Arabia. Many names, religious terms, and historical references also indicate Iraqi Aramaic influences in pre-Islamic Arabia. In the border regions of northern Arabia, Syrian and Iraqi holy personages, saints, and ascetics were venerated by pagan Arabs and Christians alike.

In the south, Christianity was established in the sixth century by intensive Byzantine missionary activity on both the Ethiopian and the Yemeni sides of the Red Sea. Abyssinians invaded southern Arabia in 525 and left Christian settlements in the small oases of Yemen. Nestorians returned to Najran with the Persian conquest of 570. Najran was also the home of Arians, Miaphysites, and Julianites who believed that not Jesus but a substitute died on the cross. This religious environment tended to emphasize the humanity of Christ.

Arabia included many economically developed, productive areas. Sasanians helped develop silver and copper mining in Yemen; copper and silver were also mined in eastern Arabia. Leather and cloth was produced in Yemen. 'Uman and Bahrayn were agriculture producers; Bahrayn exported grain to Mecca. At least one small town in north-central Arabia – al-Rabadha, on the Kufa-Medina road – produced metal, glass, ceramics, and soapstone wares. Internal Arabian trade linked all the regions together. Trade also linked Arabia with the wider region. Merchants brought textiles, jewelry, weapons, grain, and wine into Arabia. Arabia exported hides, leather, and animals. Arabian markets intersected with Indian Ocean commerce on the east and south coasts.

Thus, by the end of the sixth century, Arabia had experience in trade, stratified elites, royal institutions, and the capacity for large-scale political coalitions. Many Arabians shared the religious identities and cultures of the settled peoples. These political, economic, and religio-cultural contacts allowed for the eventual amalgamation of the empires and the outside areas into a single society. From one point of view, Islam was a foreign force bursting in from a peripheral region; from another, it originated within the framework of the existing Middle Eastern civilization.

CLANS AND KINGDOMS

In many ways, Arabian societies were defined by geography. The interior of Arabia is largely desert with scattered oases, and from the beginning of camel domestication (in the thirteenth and twelfth centuries BCE) the desert was inhabited by peoples who migrated seasonally in search of pasturage. They passed the winter in desert reserves, moving to spring pasturage at the first signs of rain. In the summer they camped near villages or oases, where they exchanged animal products for grain, dates, utensils, weapons, and cloth. They provided caravans with animals, guides, and guards.

We know from ancient poetry, from later histories, and from anthropological observation that the migratory peoples lived in tight-knit kinship groups – patriarchal families formed of a father, his sons, and their families. These families were further grouped into clans of several hundred tents, which migrated together, owned pasturage in common, and fought as one. Each clan was fundamentally an independent unit. All loyalties were absorbed by the group, which acted collectively to defend its individual members and to meet their responsibilities. If a member was harmed, the clan would avenge him. If he did harm, it would stand responsible with him.

As a consequence of this group solidarity (*'asabiyya*), bedouin clans recognized no external authority. Each clan was led by a chief (*shaykh*), who was usually selected by the clan elders from one of the prominent families and who always acted in accordance with their counsel. He settled internal disputes according to the group's traditions, but he could not legislate or command. The chief had to be wealthy and show generosity to the needy and to his supporters; he had to be a man of tact and prudence – forbearing, resolute, and practical.

Bedouin poetry expressed absolute devotion to the prestige and security of the clan. Bedouins were probably animists and polytheists, believing that all natural objects and events were living spirits who could be either helpful or harmful to man. Demons (jinn) had to be propitiated or controlled and defeated by magic. Bedouins also worshiped their ancestors, moon and star gods, and gods in the form of stones or trees placed in protective sanctuaries. The sacred was vested mysteriously in the plethora of forces that dominated the natural world and the being of man.

In contrast with the desert regions, the southwest, the northwest, and the northeast are agricultural regions. Although they were outside of the Roman and Sasanian empires, the oases of Yemen, the borders of greater Syria, and the borders of the

Euphrates-Tigris water systems had a long history of agriculture, peasant societies, and monarchical governments. At the points of contact between the fertile parts of Arabia and the desert, the bedouins could be integrated into more inclusive, often stratified, bodies. In these areas, clan confederations organized caravans and trade. The formation of a haram, a common sanctuary, also allowed for worship of the same gods, economic exchange, sociability, and political bargaining. Monarchies were also established on the Arabian peripheries. In South Arabia, royal authority was first founded about 1000 BCE and lasted until the Muslim era. By the fifth century BCE, Yemen was organized into kingdoms encompassing agricultural, trading, and pastoral peoples, with monarchs, landed elites, a religious pantheon, and organized temple worship of the gods. The political elite was drawn from aristocratic tribes and controlled extensive landed estates. Temples also had substantial holdings, whereas the commoners were organized into clans that were obliged to provide agricultural and military services to the elites. South Arabian sedentary communities had a more elaborate institutional framework than tribal groups, including a council with a king and delegates from the principal tribes. Tributary and vassal tribes extended the power of the Yemeni kingdoms well into the interior of Arabia.

However, in the first century BCE, the opening of sea routes for international trade and the collapse of the overland trade routes from Yemen to the north brought financial and political disaster. The Yemeni kingdoms were weakened, and bedouins pushed in against agricultural areas and cut off Yemeni influence in the Hijaz and central Arabia. In 328 CE, Imru' al-Qays b. 'Amr seized control of Najran. An inscription, in Arabic language and Nabatean script, refers to him as King of the Arabs; it is the oldest surviving indication of an Arab identity.

In the north, kingdoms were less fully institutionalized. The Nabatean kingdom (sixth century BCE–106 CE) was ruled by a king but really depended on a supporting coalition of clan and tribal chiefs. From 85 BCE, the Nabateans – their capital at Petra, in modern-day Jordan – controlled much of Jordan and Syria and traded with Yemen, Egypt, Damascus, and the coastal cities of Palestine.

The Nabatean kingdom was destroyed by the Romans in 106 CE. Palmyra, in the desert to the east of Damascus, succeeded Petra, extending monarchical control over the deserts and surrounding border areas. An urban capital, elaborate temples, a strong agricultural base, wide commercial networks, and Hellenistic culture marked Palmyran supremacy. Palmyra was destroyed in 271 CE – a victim, as were the Nabateans, of Roman efforts to incorporate northern Arabia directly into the empire.

Thus, from about 1000 BCE until about 300 CE, Yemen and the northern kingdoms organized the interior of the peninsula and kept the bedouins under the control of the agricultural and commercial economies of the settled kingdoms. By the end of the third century, however, the peripheral kingdoms had lost control of the center of the peninsula. Violent conflicts between clans and tribes became more frequent. In the fourth, fifth, and sixth centuries, bedouin marauders harassed the caravan trade, and bedouin migrations converted marginal regions in Yemen and on the borders of Iraq and Syria to pasturage. The bedouinization of Arabia was a gradual and cumulative process, shifting the balance between organized polities and clan societies in favor of the latter.

From the early fourth century to the end of the sixth century, there were several efforts to reestablish the dominance of the peripheral kingdoms and protect trade and oasis cultivation. In Yemen, the Himyarite kingdom was reestablished, and its influence – mediated by the tribal confederation of Kinda – extended over the bedouins of the Hijaz and central Arabia. But in the sixth century, after the Abyssinians invaded Yemen in 525 CE and a civil war between Jews and Christians, South Arabian agriculture was again in ruins, and Arabian tribes were shifting from sedentary to nomadic life.

In the north, after the destruction of Petra and Palmyra, both the Roman and the Sasanian empires attempted to restore their spheres of influence. By the end of the fifth century, the Romans had come to depend on the Ghassanids, an Arab-Christian clan, to defend Syria and Palestine against the bedouins and the Persians. The Sasanian Empire also maintained a buffer state: a coalition of Aramean and Christian tribes along the border between Iraq and the desert, organized under the leadership of the Lakhmids, whose capital was al-Hira on the lower reaches of the Euphrates.

For a time, the empires promoted sedentarization, trade, and the diffusion of cultural influences (especially Christianity), but the Arabian kingdoms of this later era were less powerful than the caravan city-kingdoms of earlier times. The early kingdoms were based on sedentary populations that were assimilated to Greco-Roman culture, earned a living in agriculture and trade, and sponsored art and architecture. The later kingdoms were tribal confederations, nomadic rather than agricultural. Then, in the late sixth century, the Romans and Persians removed their vassals altogether and attempted to partition northern Arabia and absorb it into their respective empires. By the early seventh century, the empires were at war with each other; the result was a breakdown of the Arabian economy and of political order on the Arabian frontiers of both empires.

MECCA

In the sixth century, only Mecca stood against the trend toward political and social fragmentation. Mecca remained the center of a tribal- and trade-oriented confederation and the most important place for Arabian cultural and religious life. A religious sanctuary whose shrine, the Ka'ba, attracted pilgrims from all over Arabia, Mecca became the repository of the various idols and tribal gods of the peninsula, and the destination of an annual pilgrimage. The pilgrimage also entailed a period of truce, which served not only for religious worship, but also for trade, the arbitration of disputes, and the settlement of claims and debts. The annual trade fair at ʿUkaz and the pilgrimage to Mina and ʿArafat (near Mecca) were important commercial occasions.

In the fifth century, the Quraysh, an alliance of tribal groups, took control of Mecca. The Quraysh were united in a religious cult and defensive coalition, called the Hums, centered on the sanctuary (*haram*) and shrine of the Kaʿba. They governed Mecca through a council of clans (*malaʾ*). The Quraysh further defined their identity by codes of diet, dress, domestic taboos, and endogamous marriages within the Quraysh confederation. United by religion as well as by kinship, the Quraysh had a social structure similar to that of Jews and Christians, albeit based on polytheistic rather than monotheistic religious beliefs.

The Quraysh were active in local fairs and regional trade. In the mid-sixth century, Mecca participated in the trade linking northeastern Arabia with Yemen or with Abyssinia by sea. The Quraysh were also engaged in trade with bedouin tribes on the borders of Syria and Iraq, exchanging textiles and oil for bedouin products. They ferried goods to the Byzantine frontier and were especially important in selling hides when demand for leather in the empires rose due to its military uses (such as saddles, bridles, body and horse armor, shields, belts, and straps). It is presumed that Mecca had also been engaged in the international spice trade from Yemen to Syria; however, by the sixth century, these routes had been severed.

Trade gave Mecca a sphere of political as well as commercial influence. Trade required treaties with Byzantine officials and with bedouins to assure safe passage of the caravans, protection of water and pasture rights, and guides and scouts. In association with the Tamim tribes, such arrangements gave Mecca a loose diplomatic hegemony in northern Arabia. With the decline of Abyssinia, Ghassanids, and Lakhmids, Meccan influence was the main integrative force in late sixth-century Arabia.

LANGUAGE, POETRY, AND THE GODS

The political, social, religious, and economic complexity of the several Arabian societies implied a rich and sophisticated cultural environment. Arabia was multilingual. Although Aramaic was probably the most widely spoken language in pre-Islamic Arabia, by the sixth century Arabic was both written and spoken in the region. Arabic script appeared about a century before the Islamic era; it was derived from earlier writing in Aramean, influenced by Nabatean script, and then reshaped in al-Hira by Syriac-writing Christians or Aramean Jews. Arabic writing may have been stimulated by the patronage of the Arab client kings. There was also an Arabic poetic *koine* (a common dialect used by reciters of poems throughout Arabia) that fostered a collective identity transcending the individual clans.

Pre-Islamic poetry cultivated an Arab identity manifest in the virtues of *muruwwa* –
bravery, loyalty to kin, and generosity.

Arabic was also a language of religion. Iraqi and Himyarite Christians had Arabic
translations of the Old and New Testaments as early as the fourth century. There
were Christian liturgies and prayer books in Arabic. Arabs in Medina may also have
studied Arabic, Aramaic, and Hebrew in Jewish schools.

The Meccan Kaʿba expressed this diversity in religious form. It was the sanctuary
of numerous gods. Al-Ilah was the highest deity in the Meccan pantheon. Sacrifices
of livestock and produce were made; individuals "called" on their god for help.
The gods, then, were not simply identified with nature but were defined as distinct
persons separate from the natural forces that, as willful beings, they controlled.
Such gods had to be propitiated by sacrifices; one could communicate with them
as persons. The formation of a *haram*, a shared sanctuary, allowed for worship
of the same gods. The very concept of the worship of numerous gods at festivals
or fairs indicates a Hellenistic connection and a parallel with religious practices
in Syria.

In the shared sanctuaries, new conceptions of collective identity could emerge.
The *haram* focused the worship of tribal peoples on common cults, allowed them
to observe one another's mores, and helped standardize their language and customs. Furthermore, Mecca was also one of the few places in Arabia to have a
floating, nontribal population of individual exiles, refugees, outlaws, and foreign
merchants. Arabian-wide commercial contacts and the very presence of different
peoples and clans – people belonging to no clan, foreigners, people with diverse
religious convictions – set some individuals free from the traditions of their clans,
fostering new conceptions of personal worth and status and new social relationships. In Medina, the beginnings of a new society were based on geographical
proximity rather than tribal ties. Individuals or groups from tribes living adjacent
to one another began to coalesce into political groups, the "people of a locality."

Commerce, however, also brought economic competition, social conflict, and
moral confusion. Commercial activities intensified social stratification on the basis
of wealth and morally inassimilable discrepancies between individual interests
and clan loyalty. The Quran would condemn the displacement of tribal virtues
by the ambition, greed, arrogance, and hedonism of the new rich. Mecca, which
had begun to give Arabia some measure of political and commercial order, was
changing its moral and social identity.

Thus, Arabia was in ferment: a society touched by imperial influences but
without a central government; marked by the monotheistic religions but with competing polytheistic and henotheistic beliefs; a prospering society caught in social
and moral conflicts. Here Muhammad was born, was entrusted with the Quran,
and here he became the Prophet of Islam.

CHAPTER 4

MUHAMMAD: PREACHING, COMMUNITY, AND STATE FORMATION

THE LIFE OF THE PROPHET

Prophecy is a rare phenomenon, and all the more extraordinary is the prophet whose influence permanently transforms the lives of his people and leaves as a legacy one of the world's great religions. Thus the life of Muhammad and the rise of Islam have to be understood in terms of both religious vision and worldly impact. In this chapter, I outline the Prophet's biography as reported in the earliest Muslim sources and review critical themes in the scholarly interpretation of Muhammad's life.

Compared with those of the founders of other great religions, the sources of our knowledge of the Prophet's life are abundant. The life of Muhammad is reported in *sira* (biographical narratives of the Prophet), *maghazi* (campaign and battle narratives of the early Muslim community), and hadith (narratives of the Prophet's words and deeds). They were first transmitted as quasi-oral, quasi-written materials, some of which can be traced back to the students of Muhammad's companions or the companions themselves. 'Abdallah ibn Abi Bakr (d. 747–48 or 752–53) was the first to put them in chronological order. The earliest surviving biography, the *sira* of Ibn Ishaq (d. 768–69) dates to the middle of the eighth century. Ibn Ishaq located Muhammad in Near Eastern prophetic history and emphasized the religious and miraculous aspects of his life. Al-Waqidi (d. 822) highlighted the political and military dimensions of the early Muslim community. Ibn Hisham (d. 833–34) edited the work of Ibn Ishaq, leaving out biblical history from Adam to Abraham and poetry and stories in which the Prophet was not involved. Much of the material rejected by Ibn Hisham is found in the later work of al-Tabari and others.

From these works, we know that Muhammad was born in Mecca around 570 CE into the clan of Banu Hashim. (See Figure 1.) His ancestors had been guardians of the sacred well of Zamzam. Muhammad's father died before he was born. He was

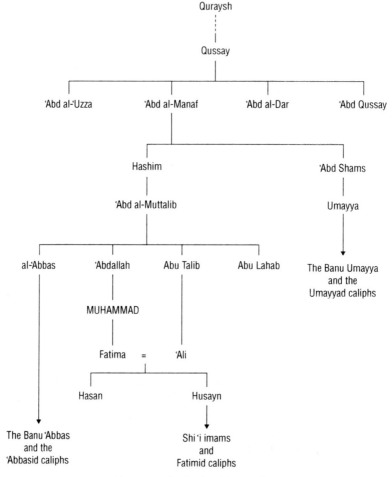

Figure 1. The family of the Prophet.

raised by his grandfather and then by his uncle, Abu Talib. Muhammad worked
as a caravaner and at twenty-five married his employer, Khadija, a wealthy, older
widow. They had four daughters and several sons; all the boys died in infancy. In
the years before the revelations, Muhammad was wont to retreat to the mountains
outside Mecca to pray in solitude. A tradition reported by Ibn Ishaq (but not found
in Ibn Hisham's recension) indicates that Muhammad received advice and support
from a *hanif* – an Arabian monotheist, a believer in one God, although not a Jew
or a Christian – who taught him about the futility of worshiping idols.

About the year 610, this seeker of religious truth received his first revelations.
They came upon him like the breaking of dawn. The first words revealed to
him were the opening five lines of chapter (sura) 96: "Recite! In the name of

thy Lord who created, created man of a blood-clot. Recite! And thy Lord is the Most Generous, who taught by the pen, taught man that he knew not."[1] In the early years, the content of these revelations was the vision of a great, just God (Allah), who would on the day of judgment weigh every man's deeds and consign him to bliss or damnation. The early revelations emphasized the immanence and fear of the last judgment, piety, and good works and warned against neglect of duties and heedlessness of the final day of reckoning. Opposed to the worship of God and fear of the last judgment were presumption, pride in human powers, and attachment to the things of this world. Such was the false pride of the pagan Meccans that led them to neglect almsgiving and the care of widows, orphans, the weak, and the poor. Eschatological piety and ethical nobility were the bases of Muhammad's revelatory message.

For three years after the first revelations, Muhammad remained a private person, coming to terms with God's message. He related his experiences to his family and friends. A small group of people accepted his ideas and gathered around him to hear and recite the Quran. These were the first converts, and they included Khadija (his wife), as well as Abu Bakr and ʿAli, who later became caliphs, the Prophet's successors as leaders of the Muslims.

About 613 CE, Muhammad received the revelation that begins, "O thou shrouded in thy mantle, arise, and warn!" (sura LXXIV, verse 1). He began to preach publicly. Apart from a small following, Muhammad's preaching met with almost universal opposition. From the Quran and later historical sources, we know that the Quraysh – the traders who dominated Meccan life – belittled Muhammad's revelations. They scoffed at the bizarre notion of a last judgment and resurrection and asked for miracles as proof of his message. Muhammad's only response – still the Muslim response – was that the Quran itself, with its unique beauty of language, is a miracle and a sign of revelation. Nonetheless, the Quraysh denounced Muhammad as a soothsayer (*kahin*), a disreputable magician or madman. Then came insults, harassment of Muhammad and his followers, and an economic boycott that extended to keeping his followers from purchasing food in the markets.

Quranic revelations provided Muhammad with a response to this opposition. He was justified in his preaching because he was sent by God to rescue his people from ignorance and guide them on the path to righteousness. He was a prophet in the long succession of Old and New Testament and Arabian prophets; he was a prophet sent to declare God's will in Arabic.

Nonetheless, his situation in Mecca began to deteriorate. In 615, a group of his followers departed for Abyssinia. Few Meccans were converting. By 619, his wife Khadija and his uncle Abu Talib were dead, and Muhammad's situation became precarious. He began to look for support away from home. He was rejected in

---

[1] A. S. Arberry, *The Koran Interpreted*, London: Allen & Unwin, 1955, II, p. 345. Hereafter all quotations from the Quran are taken from the Arberry translation.

al-Ta'if and by bedouins but finally found converts in Medina. In 620, six men of the Khazraj tribe accepted him as a prophet. In 621, a dozen men representing both Khazraj and Aws pledged to obey Muhammad and to avoid sin; in 622, a delegation of seventy-five Medinans paved the way for his coming to Medina by taking the pledge of al-ʿAqaba – the pledge to defend Muhammad.

With the guarantees provided by the pledge, Muhammad and his followers made the journey to Medina – the most dramatic event in early Islamic history. The Muslim calendar dates the Christian year 622 as the year 1. The journey is called the *hijra* (meaning the migration) and signifies a change of place and entry into the community of Muslims. The *hijra* is the transition from the pagan to the Muslim world – from kinship to religious belief.

In Medina, Muhammad and his Medinan hosts came to a formal political agreement. The charter specified that all disputes would be brought before Muhammad, and he and his Meccan followers were to form one political group with the clans of Medina, called an *umma* (community).

From Medina, small parties of the exiled Meccans (*muhajirun*) raided Meccan trade caravans for booty. At first, only Meccans were involved in the raids, but in 624, Muhammad assembled a large force of Meccan exiles and Medinan supporters to attack an important Meccan caravan. At the Battle of Badr, he defeated a larger Meccan force and decimated Mecca's leadership. The battle led to the defection of some of the bedouin tribes that protected Mecca's caravan lines, thus disrupting the major trade routes between Mecca and the north. In the following years, the initiative passed to the Meccans, who twice attacked Muhammad and Medina – first at the Battle of Uhud (625) and then at the Battle of the Ditch (627). The former was a defeat for Muhammad and the latter was a stalemate.

Within Medina, pagans and possibly some Jews accepted the politico-religious leadership of the Prophet. A critical issue, however, was the place of the Jewish clans. The early Meccan verses of the Quran presented Muhammad as a prophet sent by God to restore the purity of a faith already revealed, preach a renewal, and end the corruption that had crept into daily life. This implied a message to all Arabians – Jews and Christians, as well as pagans. In Medina, Muhammad instituted religious practices similar to the Jewish Day of Atonement and designated Jerusalem as the direction of prayer. Some of the Jewish clans, however, rejected Muhammad's claim to being a prophet in the Hebrew tradition; they disputed his accounts of sacred history. New revelations denounced the Jews for having broken their covenant and emphasized that Muhammad was sent to restore the pure monotheism of Abraham. These verses claimed that Abraham, already well known and considered the ancestor of the Arabs, was the prophet par excellence. He was depicted as the first nonsectarian monotheist (*hanif*) and the founder of the Kaʿba. The direction of prayer (*qibla*) was changed from Jerusalem to the Kaʿba. A new form of prayer was introduced that defined a Muslim community different from the others. The religious differences were amplified by political conflict. Allegedly, as punishment for desertion and betrayal in the war with Mecca, two of the larger

Jewish clans were exiled, and the male members of a third were executed and their property confiscated.

In 628, Muhammad and a large group of followers made a pilgrimage to the Ka'ba and proposed adopting it as part of Islam. The Meccans intercepted him at a place called al-Hudaybiya, where he concluded a truce in which the Meccans agreed to admit the Muslims for the pilgrimage and Muhammad dropped his demand that the Quraysh recognize him as the Prophet of God.

This proved to be a temporary agreement. Two years later, in 630, a dispute between client tribes of Mecca and Medina broke the truce, and Meccan leaders surrendered the city. Muhammad gave amnesty to almost everyone and generous gifts to the leading Quraysh. The idols of the Ka'ba were destroyed, and it was declared the holiest shrine of Islam. With Mecca finally subdued, many more Arabian tribes accepted Islam.

Muhammad died in 632. His life was at once a story of religious revelation, community building, and political expansion.

THE QURAN

The Quran (Muslim scripture) is believed by Muslims to have been revealed by God through the angel Gabriel and is the ultimate source of belief, the final revelation, which supersedes the previous Jewish and Christian versions.

Muslims believe in the Quran as a book of guidance. It begins:

> In the Name of God, the Merciful, the Compassionate,
> Praise belongs to God, the Lord of all Being,
> the All-merciful, the All-compassionate,
> the Master of the Day of Doom.
> Thee only we serve; to Thee alone we pray for succor.
> Guide us in the straight path,
> the path of those whom Thou hast blessed,
> not of those against whom Thou art wrathful,
> nor of those who are astray. (sura 1, verses 1–7)

At the center of the Quranic guidance is a vision of the reality of God's being. God is transcendent, eternal, utterly other, unfettered in will or action, and the almighty creator of the world and its creatures. The Quran demands belief in God and submission to his will and carries strong exhortations to believe, as well as warnings, proofs, threats of judgment, and appeals to gratitude to God. God will judge human beings at the end of days and mete out eternal reward or eternal punishment. The reality of the world to come is presented with potent eschatological symbols whose influence continues to be a living force in Muslim faith.

As guidance, the Quran teaches what people should believe about God, nature, and history. It gives rules about what people should and should not do in religious rituals and in relation to their fellow men. It prescribes the basic beliefs of Islam and the five pillars: profession of faith, prayer, fasting, the giving of alms, and pilgrimage. It sets out some basic laws of marriage, divorce, inheritance, and business matters. It also presents the spiritual qualities that should infuse ritual, social, and legal obligations. These qualities include gratitude to God for one's existence, repentance, moral earnestness, fear of the last judgment, loyalty to the faith, sincerity, and truthfulness. It condemns arrogance, thanklessness, and pride.

Beyond precise specifications, the Quran leaves each individual to judge what constitutes proper fulfillment of God's command. For example, the law defining the supererogatory night prayers is given not as a rule but as permission to adapt the injunction to pray to individual circumstances:

> Therefore recite of the Koran so much as is feasible.
> He knows that some of you are sick, and others
> journeying in the land, seeking the bounty of God,
> and others fighting in the way of God.
> So recite of it so much as is feasible. (sura LXXIII, verse 20)

Because the guidance is open, the boundaries of human responsibility are problematic, and the prospects of achieving eternal reward are uncertain. Some passages in the Quran stress the full measure of human responsibility. God is just and he will weigh every deed and thought on the day of judgment. Other passages, however, stress God's power, his predetermination of all events, and man's helpless insufficiency before his majesty.

Recent, conflicting, and controversial scholarship has raised questions about the composition and compilation of the Quran. There are several theories about the origins of the Quran. One is the traditional theory that Muhammad was the sole author, or the sole recipient of the Quranic revelations. A second is that the Quran is a compilation – including Christian hymns and prayers – composed a century before Muhammad and then rendered in Arabic. A third is that the Quran was the product of a much later Muslim community in dialogue with non-Muslims – perhaps as late as the ninth and tenth centuries – intended to validate Muhammad's credentials as a prophet and establish a direct line from Adam to Muhammad, bypassing Moses and Jesus. The definitive edition of the Quran is variously dated to the ninth and early tenth centuries.

The latter two theories are not widely accepted among scholars of the language and history of the Quran. The skeptics all have different theories, and all of them select only the passages that seem favorable to their case. The most persuasive view in my judgment is that of Neuwirth, who holds that the new scholarship has failed to discredit the authenticity of the Quran. The rhyme and literary structure of verses and suras indicate that the Quran has an inner intentional design and is the product of one voice. The Quran is also a dramatic text that bears the marks of direct communication with an audience. The audience responds as it is exhorted, encouraged, commanded, or rebuked. Moreover, reports or comments on contemporary events appear in the Medinan suras, thereby challenging the dating of the two aforementioned theories.

The style of Quranic verses and chapters differs from the Meccan to the Medinan period. The early Meccan suras, powerful short poems, were most likely recited; later Medinan suras, which are long and have multiple topics, were most likely written down or even composed in writing. The Meccan rhymes have the resounding voice patterns of the *saj* type of oral recitation; the late Meccan and Medinan verses are marked by a cadenza – a moral reflection on the significance of a narrative that marks the conclusion of a passage.

Nonetheless the text is unified. The Quran reads like a running commentary on the events of the time. Later suras sometimes presuppose the existence of earlier ones and imply an ongoing discourse. Nothing about it suggests a deliberate literary work. If it were composed in later centuries, the Quran would presumably have had a more ordered narrative or more formal legal instructions.

The history of the text confirms its early origin. The Quran was probably presented as both recitation and text. Muhammad and the *qurra'* (Quran reciters, similar to the public poetry reciters) recited the Quran. The Prophet himself probably began compiling a written scripture by dictating to scribes and instructing them on how to order the verses of the revelation. In the Medinan period, passages in the Quran imply that it was beginning to be considered as scripture, a proper book (*kitab*), perhaps like the Old Testament. Later suras refer to a heavenly book from which the Quran is taken.

Muhammad did not himself leave a fixed text or book, but after his death a collection was made from oral witnesses and scattered records on slips of papyrus or parchment, chips of stone, bone, leather, palm stalks, or slates. Some traditions say that the first compilation was in the reign of Abu Bakr; other traditions claim that 'Umar and his daughter Hafsa made the first codex. Historical sources indicate that Caliph 'Uthman (r. 644–54) ordered a definitive codex in order to prevent the proliferation of variant versions. The existing materials were arranged in order of the longest suras first and the shortest last. 'Uthman's codex was supposed to be definitive, but many verses defended by their recipients as genuinely Quranic were not included. As many as fifteen major codices were collected by other companions of Muhammad and Quran reciters and were cherished in the garrison towns after the Arab conquests.

Moreover, the 'Uthmanic text was written in a still-incomplete Arabic orthography (related to Nabatean Syriac script), which left uncertainties in the readings of vowels and some consonants. Thus, the early Quran had the qualities both of a fixed text and of a variable recitation and left open a debate as to whether the text or the recited versions were more authentic. In 714, the Caliph al-Walid ordered the governor of Iraq, Al-Hajjaj, to improve the orthography.

Material evidence indicates that the Quran was in existence at the end of the seventh century. Surviving manuscripts are dated to the end of the seventh century by the calligraphy of Arab coins and inscriptions. Inscriptions from the reign of the Caliph 'Abd al-Malik (685–705), including the inscriptions on the Dome of the Rock in Jerusalem (692), quote or paraphrase the Quran.

In the 'Abbasid period, a developing literature of exegesis, history, and law made a fixed text more important, and, in the late eighth and ninth centuries, a consensus was reached to unify the presentation to conform with the emerging standardized Arabic grammar. Finally, Ibn al-Mujahid (d. 935/6) established the seven canonical readings of the Quran on the basis of literary, lexicographical, and grammatical studies – although alternative readings remained in circulation.

THE JUDEO-CHRISTIAN AND ARABIAN HERITAGE

The Quran was produced in a religiously and culturally rich environment; in language and in concepts, it bears the marks of the milieu in which it was delivered. Aramaic dialects were spoken in Arabia, and it is no surprise that the Quran contains many names, religious terms, and historical references derived from Aramaic.

Quranic teachings also resemble Judaism and Christianity, because the revelations came from the same God. Biblical tales were retold. Ideas similar to Judaism – such as uncompromising monotheism, belief in written revelations and divine guidance, the conception of a prophet sent to a chosen people, and religious practices such as regular daily prayer – are found in the Quran. Indeed, the idea of the Apostle is rooted in Jewish-Christian sects.

Christian beliefs and concepts are equally important. The Quran reflects Muhammad's encounter with Arabic-speaking Christian preachers from Najran. Parallels to the preaching of itinerant Christian monks are evident in the Quranic vision of the last judgment – the prediction that it would come with thunder, trumpets, and earthquakes; that the world would be destroyed and the dead resurrected; and that it would be a terrifying moment when, one by one, all men passed before God, the angels interceding only for the good. The Quranic emphasis on the humanity of Christ suggests the influence of Arab-Christians, such as those in Najran – the home of Arabic-speaking Arians, Nestorians, and Julianites.

The Islamic way of praying may be an adaptation of Syrian monastic prayer – with its sequence of recitations, prostrations, and hand raising – simplified and limited in duration. Also, the month-long fast of Ramadan may be an adaptation of the practice of Syriac monks.

Ethiopian Christian influence was also strong in Mecca. There is a tradition that some Ethiopians read the Torah and Gospels aloud in Mecca. Muhammad must have had information about Ethiopia and contacts with Ethiopians in order to send some of his early followers there. The words "Jesus" and "Bible" appear in the Quran in Ethiopic form: 'Isa and Injil.

There are also striking parallels to Manichaean beliefs. As in the tradition of Mani, Muhammad insisted on the historical unity of the prophetic messages. The concept of a chain of apostles appears in Manichaean writings. Mani was considered by his followers to be the apostle of his generation. The idea that earlier revelations had been corrupted is also found in Manichaean and Mandaean teachings.

There has been much scholarly debate about the sources of the Quranic versions of biblical stories. Some scholars point to textual sources: parallels to Quranic passages can be found in the Bible, in the Dead Sea Scrolls, and in Zoroastrian texts. Yet the Quranic telling of biblical tales does not match the textual sources in detail, for the Bible was not just a written book but an endless flow of stories told by Jews, Christians, Jewish-Christians, and Manichaeans. Scripture was understood not only as text but also as oral tradition. Muhammad had probably heard haggadic stories from Jews and learned about Jesus from Christians. Quranic stories show that there must also have been an Arabian culture of legends and stories about the origins of peoples and the histories of prophets.

Whatever the sources, biblical stories are retold with original variations and with new literary panache. In fact, even within the Quran, stories are amplified and retold from earlier to later verses. The originality of the treatment is more compelling than the derivation of the materials.

The closeness of the Quran to Jewish and Christian beliefs and cultures is not surprising; it was intended. Islam is avowedly a continuation and renewal of the older monotheistic traditions. The Quran teaches the existence of a single God who requires human beings to live righteously and who will reward them with everlasting bliss or punish them with eternal misery. God has sent previous prophets to warn and to instruct his people, give moral guidance, and lay down laws and rules. The Quran tells the stories of the prophets who have preceded Muhammad, but now the divine mission is vouchsafed to him. The biblical elements in the Quran are part of a shared Jewish, Christian, and Muslim heritage. Islam is not "borrowed" from other cultural traditions but inhabits the same cultural world.

These connections are so close that many scholars see early Islam as a reborn version of the previous religions. Ruthven sees early Islam as a hybrid Hebrew monotheism with Christian, gnostic, and Arabian elements. Donner sees early Islam as a pan-religious movement. Muhammad's early followers were the believers (*mu'minun*), who share belief in one God, the soon-to-be last day, and the need for righteousness on earth. A Muslim, then, is someone who submits to God's will and his law – or to the law of the Torah or Gospels or earlier versions of revelation – and in particular those who submit to Quranic law.

Many verses in the Quran can be construed as including Christians and Jews in the Muslim community, because Muhammad saw himself at first as a missionary to all peoples but later narrowed his intended audience to pagan Arabs. Muhammad became disillusioned with the People of the Book and condemned them as "unbelievers." Conflict with the Jews led to the redefinition of Islam as a new confessional religion and led to new laws and rituals to provide Muslims with a separate identity.

Although identified with the monotheistic religions, the Quran also embodied a summation and transformation of traditional Arabian values. The Muslim *umma* redefined the meaning of the tribe as a group that defended its brothers to include religious as well as blood brothers. The biblical and tribal law of blood revenge was accepted, but now the *umma* as a whole was substituted for the clan. In family life, the patriarchal clan was reaffirmed as the ideal Muslim family but redefined to include a new concern for women and children and the stability of marriages. In the Prophet's lifetime, acceptance of Islam was probably a gesture at once of political obeisance and of religious allegiance.

In the realm of individual morality, a similar reshaping of values took place. The traditional Arabian virtues were vested with new Islamic meanings. Bedouin courage in battle and reckless bravery in defense of one's tribe became persistent dedication to the new faith of Islam and the capacity for disciplined sacrifice in the name of the new community. Patience in the face of adversity (*sabr*) became unshakable faith in God in the face of trials and temptations. Generosity – shorn of its impulsive and ostentatious aspects – was transmuted into the virtue of almsgiving and care for the weak and the poor as part of a pious and restrained, but regular, commitment. The Quranic teachings and Muhammad's leadership extracted the virtues of the bedouin culture from the context of *jahl* (passion, ignorance, and thoughtlessness), to reestablish them on the basis of *hilm* (self-control) and *'aql* (rational judgment), based on *islam* (submission to Allah).

Thus, the new religion reaffirmed Arabian moral traditions by joining them to new concepts of brotherhood and authority. By giving old concepts new meaning, it made possible a new religious sensibility and the integration of disparate peoples into a new community.

COMMUNITY AND POLITICS

Finally, Muhammad is seen as a warrior, a political leader defending a community's interests, expanding its domains, and propagating its truths. In the histories of Christianity and Buddhism, the founding teacher is portrayed as a spiritual person divorced from the concerns not only of politics but of everyday life. Muhammad, by contrast, was immersed in both. His teachings and the norms he transmitted bear on the ethics of everyday behavior, marriage, family, commercial practices, tribal relations, politics, and war. Western scholars tend to emphasize the political over the moral and social aspects of Muhammad's teaching. For Muslims, he encompasses both the holy man engaged in the world and the ideal warrior-saint.

The worldly dimension of his life was implied at the very outset. When Muhammad began to recite his revelations in public, he had launched a worldly mission. Significantly, the first converts were rootless migrants, poor men, members of weak clans, and younger sons of strong clans – those people most dissatisfied with the hierarchical moral, social, and economic climate of Mecca.

Muhammad provoked fierce opposition because preaching was an implicit challenge to the existing institutions of the society: the worship of gods, the economic life attached to pagan shrines, the values of tribal tradition, the authority of chiefs, and the solidarity of clans. Religion, moral belief, social structure, and economic life formed a system of ideas and institutions inextricably bound up with one another. To attack them at any major point was to attack the whole society – root and branch.

As Muhammad's mission unfolded, it became clear that it involved not only the presentation of the Quranic revelation but also the leadership of a community. Prophecy implied eschatological vision and knowledge of God's will, which in turn entailed right guidance and social leadership. As early as 615, Muhammad had become the leader of a community. A group of his followers departed for Abyssinia. For the sake of their faith, they were willing to leave their families and clans and take up life together in a foreign land. For them, the bonds of common belief were stronger than the bonds of blood.

Opposition to Muhammad revealed yet another dimension of the relations between religion and society. It exposed the extent to which Muhammad's very survival in Mecca, to say nothing of his preaching, depended on his uncle Abu Talib and his clansmen, the Banu Hashim, who protected him because he was their kinsman. With their support, Muhammad could, despite harassment, continue preaching – although in the later Meccan years, the flow of converts dried up. To protect himself and his followers, to overcome the resistance of the Quraysh, and to gain a hearing from Arabians beyond the small circles spontaneously attracted to him, some kind of political base was necessary.

Muhammad tried to win support at al-Ta'if and from some bedouins but was rebuffed. Then he turned to Medina, which, like Mecca, was inhabited by various clans; however, unlike Mecca, it was a settlement racked by bitter and even anarchic feuding between the leading tribal groups – the Aws and the Khazraj. Prolonged strife threatened the safety of men in the fields and called into question Medina's very existence. Unlike the bedouins, Medinans had to live as neighbors and could not move from place to place. Like Mecca, Medina was undergoing social changes that rendered obsolete the underlying bedouin form of kinship society. Agricultural, rather than pastoral, needs governed its economy. Its social life came increasingly to be dictated by spatial proximity rather than by kinship. Also, Medina had a large Jewish population, which may have made the populace as a whole more sympathetic to monotheism.

A coterie of Medinans invited Muhammad to Medina. This was based on a well-established precedent. Feuding clans often selected someone reputed to have religious vision and to be just, politic, and disinterested to be their arbitrator (*hakam*). It was common practice for a potential arbitrator to interview the disputants and assure himself that they would accept his decisions.

In Medina, Muhammad defined his powers as an arbitrator in the so-called Constitution of Medina. This was an agreement to fight together and to accept

Muhammad's authority to resolve internal disputes. The treaty was drawn between the émigré Meccans and Medinans, the latter representing Jewish tribes in alliance with them. There are numerous Jewish tribes mentioned in the treaty, but the three largest Jewish clans (the Banu Nadir, Banu Qaynuqa, and Banu Qurayza) appear not to have been party to this agreement. The Jews who became allies were not expected to embrace Islam. Meccans and Medinans, including several of the Jewish clans, would act as one in the defense of Muhammad and of Medina against outsiders. No clan would make a separate peace. No one would aid the Quraysh of Mecca, the presumptive enemy.

In the next few years, Muhammad consolidated his powers. His political work in Medina was to build the confederation that would extend his teachings and authority to Mecca and to the rest of Arabia. This was part of Muhammad's religious ambition, but it was also a matter of political necessity. If Mecca remained antagonistic, it might eventually defeat him. However, to bring Mecca under his influence required controlling the bedouin tribes whose cooperation was essential to Meccan trade. Both religious ambition and the political logic of Muhammad's removal to Medina required an Arabian confederation. Thus, Muhammad raided the Meccan caravans. In 624, he won a great victory at the Battle of Badr. In the Battle of Uhud (625) and the Battle of the Ditch (627), he successfully resisted Meccan counterattacks.

Within Medina, the pagan clans converted to Islam. Muhammad wanted to include the Jews in his nascent community, for he saw himself as sent by God to all Arabians – Jews and Christians as well as pagans – to restore the purity of the faith already revealed, preach a renewal, and end the corruption that had crept into daily life. Relations with some of the Jewish tribes, however, broke down because of disputes over the authenticity of Muhammad's teachings and competition over resources. Some of the Jewish clans rejected Muhammad's claim to be a prophet in the Hebrew tradition and disputed his accounts of sacred history. In the course of this struggle, new revelations denounced the Jews for having broken their covenant. These verses revealed that Abraham was the prophet par excellence (the first *hanif*), the builder of the Ka'ba, and the father of the Arabs. The Quran now stressed that Muhammad was sent to restore the pure monotheism of Abraham. In effect, Muhammad's mission and his community would no longer include Jews and Christians but would be a distinct religion alongside them.

Muhammad's disputes with three of the Jewish clans also involved long-simmering political and economic grievances. In the sixth century, the Banu Nadir and the Banu Qurayza had collected taxes on behalf of Persian overlords. The growing hostility may have been related to land and the location of the Muslim community's newly established market. After a quarrel, the Banu Qaynuqa were expelled. The Banu Nadir were accused of trying to assassinate Muhammad and were expelled. The Banu Qurayza were accused of aiding the enemy; the males were executed. The elimination of these powerful Jewish clans enhanced the political and material power of the Muslims. Muhammad seized the lands of the Banu Nadir and the Banu Qurayza, confiscating their weapons and horses. Women and children were sold as slaves. After the Battle of the Ditch and the decimation of the Banu Qurayza, Muhammad's power was clearly established, and there seems to have been a more widespread acceptance of Islam.

At this point, however, Muhammad relaxed, rather than intensified, the pressure on Mecca. In 628, in a seeming turnaround, Muhammad proposed to make a peaceful pilgrimage to the Ka'ba. The Meccans, however, intercepted him at a place called al-Hudaybiya. There, he concluded a truce in which the Meccans agreed to admit the Muslims for the pilgrimage and Muhammad agreed to drop his demand that he be recognized as the Prophet of God. He agreed to an unequal arrangement whereby children who left Mecca to become Muslims would have to be returned if they did not have parental consent, whereas Muslim apostates would not be returned. The treaty may seem like an embarrassment to Muhammad, but he made important political gains. Meccan hostility was allayed, and the treaty confirmed what Meccan failures at the Battle of Uhud and the Battle of the Ditch had shown: that Meccans could not defeat him.

Throughout this struggle, Muhammad tried to gain control of the tribes. Missionaries and embassies were sent throughout Arabia, factions loyal to Muhammad were supported, and tribes were raided to compel them to pay allegiance and the alms tax (*zakat*). Many of the recalcitrant tribes accepted his leadership. Muhammad expanded his sphere of influence to the settled regions in the north. He subdued the oasis of Khaybar, made a foray into Syria in 629, and defeated a bedouin alliance in 630.

As Muhammad's position grew stronger, his attitude toward other Arab tribes became more defined. Early in the Medinan years, Muhammad made alliances with peoples who were not Muslims. He did not require his allies to believe in God and accept him as the Prophet of God. Non-Muslims could choose between accepting Islam or paying an annual tribute. Without one or the other, they would be attacked and, if defeated, killed or enslaved. Typically, Christians and Jews agreed to pay the tribute (*jizya*). In 630/1, he granted the Christians of Najran protection in return for payment of taxes. This was a critical precedent for the later Muslim policies toward conquered peoples.

Muhammad's occupation of Mecca, however, showed that his policy toward non-Muslims would be adapted to circumstances. On his entry into Mecca, Muhammad proclaimed a general amnesty, and it seems that Meccans freely accepted Islam. In 632, the pilgrimage was modified and transformed into a Muslim ritual. (See Illustration 1.)

By the end of his life, Muhammad had created a large-scale Arabian federation of oases and tribes, based in Mecca and Medina, appointing officials and collecting taxes and tributes from the member groups.

Illustration 1. The Pilgrimage to the Kaʿba. *Source:* Newspix.com.au.

Perhaps the most contested aspect of Muhammad's career is warfare and the presumed legacy of jihad (holy struggle). In fact, Quranic statements about war are quite different from later Muslim interpretations and from contemporary Western concepts. Jihad in the Quran does not mean holy war. In the Quran, the words for war are "*qital*" – generally used for religiously authorized war – and "*harb*" – generally used for profane war. "Jihad" means striving to one's utmost, including striving to be pious, showing religious loyalty through the observance of rituals, and supporting one's fellow believers.

The Quran does not present a consistent doctrinal position on warfare. The earliest statements from the Meccan period counsel patient endurance (*sabr*), rather than fighting. In Medina, the Quran specifies that Muslims may fight enemies who attack them and may defend the oppressed. There are verses placing restrictions on fighting, presumably in the sacred month, except in cases of self-defense. Gradually, over time, the tone of Quranic statements changed. Some verses exhort apparently reluctant followers to fight. At Badr, Muhammad first promised paradise to his warriors. Later verses advocate war in the path of God and call on Muslims to subdue their enemies. Thus, in Medina, there was a progression from a time when the early Muslims could not imagine a war against their own kin, to booty raids even against kin, and to war against all opponents of Islam. The changing tone of the Quran may reflect divisions in the community among people less and more willing to fight. It may also reflect changing economic and political realities, and a transition from a more conciliatory to a more militant stance, as the power of the Muslims grew greater.

The Quran set diverse precedents, but later Muslim jurists linked jihad to offensive war. Mid-eighth-century jurists did not consider warfare obligatory, and Hanafi jurists held that war was legitimate only in self-defense, but under the 'Abbasid dynasty the term jihad became increasingly linked to imperial policy. Al-Shafi'i (d. 802) appears to be one of the first jurists to permit offensive war. By the mid-ninth century, collections of hadith generally advocated war on behalf of Islam, although hadith that counseled against war and martyrdom were not eliminated from the tradition. An important concept in the later doctrine of warfare – the concept of *dar al-Islam* (Islamic territory) and *dar al-harb* (non-Islamic territory) and of a constant cold war between the two – has no basis in the Quran. Whatever sanction jihad has in later Muslim thinking, the Quran supports a variety of positions.

CONCLUSION: THE *UMMA* OF ISLAM

By the time of his death in 632, Muhammad had provided his followers with the design for a political community based on religious affiliation. Acceptance of Islam was a gesture at once of political obeisance and of religious allegiance. The word "Islam" could mean submission to the Prophet in both a worldly and a spiritual sense Religiously, the new community was grounded in the vision of the oneness of God. In the revelations of the Quran, Muhammad synthesized Arabian religious concepts, Judaism, and Christianity into a new monotheism. Eschatological piety and fear of hellfire resemble Syriac monastic preaching. The role of a prophet, the significance of written revelations, obedience to God's commands, and stress on communal life as the context of religious fulfillment all parallel Jewish ideas. Although resembling Jewish and Christian beliefs, emphasis on God's utter transcendence, majesty, omnipotence, and untrammeled will; the submission of one's own will to God's; surrender to God's commands; and acceptance of God's judgment all gave Quranic teachings a special originality within the framework of the monotheistic religions.

The translation of monotheistic values into the principles of a reformed Arabian society and the formation of a new community with its own congregational life, rituals, and legal norms made Islam a new religion. This was the *umma*, the brotherhood that integrated individuals, clans, cities, and even ethnic groups into a larger community in which religious loyalties encompassed all other loyalties without abolishing them and in which a new common law and political authority regulated the affairs of the populace as a whole. In a fragmented society, Muhammad had integrated otherwise anarchic small clans into a larger confederacy and built a churchlike religious community and an incipient imperial organization.

What made Muhammad so rare a figure in history, what made him a prophet, was his ability to convey his vision to people around him so that concepts long known to everyone took on the power to transform other people's lives as they had transformed his. This was accomplished by direct preaching about God, by changing family life and institutions, and by introducing new ritual practices, social mores, and political loyalties. Muhammad was a prophet who caused a religious vision to operate in the body of a whole society.

In the Quran and Muhammad's teachings and example, Muslims have ever after found a revelation of the spiritual reality of God's transcendence and man's humble place in the universe. They find a revelation of the laws by which people should live in a community of believers, dedicated to the care of the weak and the poor, to education, and to social reform. Equally, they are dedicated to a political community organized to administer justice, to defend itself, and to wage war in the name of the true faith. Islam proved particularly effective in unifying tribal societies and in motivating militant struggle in the interests of the community as a whole. To this day, to be a Muslim implies a combination of personal religious belief and membership in the community of fellow believers.

THE ARAB-MUSLIM IMPERIUM
(632–945)

CHAPTER 5

INTRODUCTION TO THE ARAB-MUSLIM EMPIRES

The death of Muhammad and the Arab-Muslim conquests opened a new era in Middle Eastern civilizations. The Arab-Muslim conquests initiated the long historical process that culminated in the amalgamation of Arabia, the Sasanian Empire, and the eastern regions of the Byzantine Empire within an Islamic empire; in the eventual conversion of the majority of Jewish, Christian, and Zoroastrian peoples to Islam; and in the formation of an Islamic society and culture.

On Muhammad's death, many of his followers decided on the appointment of a caliph or executor of the Prophet's legacy. The first four caliphs – Abu Bakr (632–34), 'Umar (634–44), 'Uthman (644–56), and 'Ali (656–61) – ruled by virtue of their personal connections with Muhammad and Arabian ideas of authority. They were later called the Rashidun, the Rightly Guided Caliphs. These caliphs, in part following the precedents set by Muhammad, launched a great wave of military campaigns and a migration of Arabian peoples leading to the conquest of all the lands of the former Sasanian Empire and the Near Eastern and North African provinces of the Byzantine Empire. Iraq, Syria, and Egypt were conquered by 641; Iran by 654. North Africa was conquered between 643 and 711; Spain between 711 and 759. In the east, the region of Inner Asia between the Oxus and the Jaxartes rivers, Transoxania, was fully conquered by 751. Thus, the "Middle East," North Africa, Spain, and Transoxania were incorporated into a single empire. The Islamic religion and related cultures and an Islamic sociopolitical identity would be formed in this region.

The conquests made the caliphs the military and administrative chiefs of the newly conquered lands. The Rightly Guided Caliphs (632–61) represented the religio-political leadership of a coalition of town-dwelling and nomadic tribes. The Umayyad dynasty (661–750) reconstructed the governing apparatuses of the Byzantine and Sasanian empires and began the work of molding them into an

Table 2. *Outline chronology of early Islamic history*

Muhammad	c. 570–632
Rashidun caliphs	632–61
First civil war	656–61
Umayyad caliphs	661–750
Reign of Mu'awiya	661–80
Second civil war	680–92
Reign of 'Abd al-Malik	685–705
Marwanid caliphs	685–744
Third civil war	744–50
'Abbasid caliphs	750–1258
Consolidation of empire	750–c. 850
Reign of al-Ma'mun	813–33
Breakup of empire	c. 835–945
Independent succession states	945–c. 1220
Mongol invasions	c. 1220–c. 1260

Arab-Muslim regime. After several periods of civil wars, the Umayyad were over-thrown by the 'Abbasid dynasty, which would reign from 750 to 1258. The 'Abbasids brought the Arab-Muslim empire to the height of its political organization, the furthest boundaries of its conquests, and the peak of its political powers and cultural creativity. The 'Abbasid Empire, however, disintegrated in the course of the ninth and tenth centuries. Although the 'Abbasid caliphs continued as the nominal rulers from 945 to 1258, the territories of the former empire were ruled by new conquerors and new regimes. (See Table 2.)

The historical character of the Arab-Muslim empires was grounded in the economic and social changes generated by the Arab conquests. Economic development and urbanization generated the resources for the organization of a new and powerful empire. The unification of former Sasanian and Byzantine territories and the integration of the trans-Oxus region created a vast new trading zone. Basra and later Baghdad became two of the most important trading cities in the world. Samarqand, Bukhara, Nishapur, and many other Iranian cities prospered. New agricultural zones were developed in Iraq and Mesopotamia.

The conquests also had profound demographic, social, and cultural implications. With the defeat of the Byzantine and Sasanian empires, a frontier between populations broke down. Families and whole tribes followed the conquering men. Arab-Muslim migrants created new cities and also settled in older towns, villages, citadels, and country estates, mingling with other ethnic and language groups, races, religions, sects, and cults. They interacted as rulers and ruled, patrons and clients, and in marketplaces as merchants and customers, as employers and employees, and as landlords and tenants. The settlements stimulated intermarriages, conversions, and exchanges of religious ideas and languages. A new society came into being integrating Arab-Muslim conquerors and conquered peoples on the basis of Islam and widespread Arabic and/or Persian linguistic identities.

In turn, the elites of cities and empire gave birth to new imperial and religious cultures. Imperial Islam was the Islam of the caliphate, the court, political elites, and the literati and artists patronized by the government. The court milieus contributed especially to Islamic art, architecture, philosophy, science, and Iranian and Hellenistic forms of literature in Arabic. Urban Islam embodied the religious beliefs and moral and social values of Muslim communities as expressed by the companions of the Prophet and their successors, the learned and holy men of Islam. The city milieus contributed to the literatures of Quranic exegesis, law, mysticism, and theology in conjunction with an Arabic belles lettres. Some subjects – such as poetry, theology, and history – were cultivated in both milieus. Both the imperial and the city versions of Islam were the cultural product of the new communities created by the economic and social upheavals of the Arab-Muslim conquests.

In the following chapters, we will explore first the conquests and the economic and social changes that formed the bases for the new empires. In successive chapters, we will discuss the history and politics of the caliphate and then the courtly imperial and the urban religious forms of early Islamic cultures.

CHAPTER 6

THE ARAB-MUSLIM CONQUESTS AND THE
SOCIOECONOMIC BASES OF EMPIRE

THE CONQUESTS

With the death of the Prophet Muhammad, a new era began, an era of vast
conquests and the formation of a Middle Eastern–wide Arab-Islamic empire. The
Arab-Muslim conquests began the processes that culminated in the formation of a
new empire, which included all of the former Sasanian Empire and much of the
Byzantine Empire, and in the emergence in that geographic and political framework of Islamic cultures and societies.

When Muhammad died in 632, he left no instructions concerning succession,
and, in the absence of an agreement with regard to a successor, the Muslim
community – a conglomeration of diverse elements – was on the verge of disintegrating. To prevent this, some of the tribes and factions elected Abu Bakr –
one of Muhammad's closest associates and his father-in-law – as caliph or successor. Abu Bakr was the first of those who were later identified as the Rashidun, the
Rightly Guided Caliphs: Abu Bakr (632–34), 'Umar (634–44), 'Uthman (644–56),
and 'Ali (656–61), who ruled by virtue of their personal connections with Muhammad and Arabian ideas of authority. The conquests made the caliphs the rulers of
the newly conquered lands as well.

There are two principal interpretations of what motivated the Arab-Islamic conquests. One finds the origin of the conquest movement in the dynamics of tribal
conflict. At Muhammad's death, many of the allied Arabians sought to regain their
independence. Tribes in the Najd and Hijaz – but not tribes living in the region
between Mecca and Medina – refused to pay the alms tax or tribute. Some considered their tribute payments personal to Muhammad; other tribes refused tributes
and taxes, although they did not renounce Islam. Some put forth prophets and
religions of their own. In some tribes, pro-Muslim factions had taken control, and,
at Muhammad's death, other factions tried to subvert their dominance.

Abu Bakr, however, refused any concessions to demands for relief from taxes, waged war on recalcitrant tribes, forced them into subjection, and even expanded the sphere of Muslim power beyond what it had been in Muhammad's time. At the Battle of al-Aqraba (633), Muslims defeated a rival tribal confederation and extended their power over eastern Arabia. These wars (known as *ridda*) were waged on a scale unprecedented in Arabia; in effect, Medina had become a state capable of marshaling large armies.

The immediate outcome of the Muslim victories was turmoil. Medina's victories led allied tribes to attack the nonaligned to compensate for their own losses. The pressure drove tribes to Hadramawt and Yemen in the far south, to Bahrain and Oman in the east, and then across the imperial frontiers into Iraq and Syria. The Bakr tribe, which had defeated a Persian detachment in 606, joined forces with the Muslims and led them on a raid in southern Iraq to Ubulla and al-Hira, the former Lakhmid capital. A similar spilling over of tribal raiding occurred on the Syrian frontiers.

Abu Bakr encouraged these movements. At first, small tribal groups were searching for booty, but, when Arab-Muslim raids forced the Byzantines to send a major expedition into southern Palestine, the raiding parties had to concentrate their forces east of Gaza. There, under the leadership of Khalid b. al-Walid (sent by Abu Bakr from Iraq to take the generalship of the Arab clans), they defeated a Byzantine army at the Battle of Ajnadayn (634). What began as intertribal skirmishing to consolidate a political confederation in Arabia ended in a full-scale war against the two empires.

A second view is that the Arab-Muslim conquests were not spontaneous raids but a planned military venture already under way in the lifetime of the Prophet. New but still controversial research in Persian sources argues that the Muslim campaigns in Iraq had already begun in 628 and that Muhammad's raiding parties had already entered Syria in 629.

In either case, in the wake of the Battle of Ajnadayn, the Arab-Muslims moved against the Byzantine province of Syria. They took Damascus in 636. Baalbek, Homs, and Hama soon surrendered. The rest of the province, however, continued to resist. Only in 638 was Jerusalem taken. Caesarea fell in 640. Finally, in 641, the Arabs took the northern Syrian and Mesopotamian towns of Harran, Edessa, and Nasibin. The conquest of Syria took so long because victories over Byzantine armies did not necessarily bring about the surrender of fortified towns, which had to be conquered individually.

The next Byzantine province to fall to the Arab-Muslims was Egypt. Egypt's attractions were its position as the granary of Constantinople, its proximity to the Hijaz, important naval yards, and a strategic location for further conquests in Africa. General 'Amr b. al-'As, on his own initiative, began the conquest of the province in 641. Within the year, he had taken Heliopolis, Babylon, and the whole of the country except Alexandria, which capitulated in 643. Because Egypt was politically centralized and scarcely urbanized, the conquest was virtually instantaneous. The next Arab-Muslim objective was North Africa. Tripoli was taken in 643, but the subjugation of the rest of North Africa took another seventy-five years. Instead of sudden, dramatic victories, painfully prolonged wars were waged to establish Arab-Muslim suzerainty.

Within a decade, Arab-Muslims had captured Syria and Egypt, but the Byzantine Empire retained its richest and most populous provinces (Anatolia and the Balkans) and would engage in almost continuous border warfare on land and on sea, always threatening to retake territories that had for hundreds of years been part of the Greco-Roman, Christian world. The survival of Byzantium left the Arabs with a contested and dangerous frontier and a permanent barrier to their expansion.

The Sasanian Empire, by contrast, was utterly destroyed. The Arab-Muslims defeated the Persians at the Battle of Qadisiyya (637), seized the capital of the empire (Ctesiphon), and forced the last emperor (Yazdagird) to flee to the protection of Turkish princes in Inner Asia. All of Iraq fell into Arab-Muslim hands. With the collapse of the empire, the Arab-Muslims were faced in Iran with a number of small and weak but inaccessible principalities, protected by mountains and deserts. The problem in conquering Iran was not a strong resisting state but the large number of remote areas that had to be invaded and occupied. It took decades to subdue all the quasi-independent principalities that had comprised the Sasanian Empire.

From the garrison base of Kufa, the Arab-Muslims moved north, occupying Mosul in 641. Nihawand, Hamadhan, Rayy, Isfahan, and all the main cities of western Iran fell by 644. Azarbayjan, to the west of the Caspian Sea, was captured about the same time. Other forces operating from Basra captured Ahwaz (Khuzistan) in 640 but took until 649 to complete the conquest of Fars. Only then did the conquest of more outlying regions begin. Marw was occupied as a military base in 650–51 and Khurasan was conquered by 654.

This first wave of conquests was followed several decades later by new campaigns on a grand scale. To the west, North Africa was conquered between 643 and 711; Spain was absorbed by the Arabs between 711 and 759. In the east, the Transoxus region was fully conquered only after a century of effort. The capitals of Transoxania, Bukhara, and Samarqand fell in 712 and 713. Inner Asian Turkish peoples recognized Arab-Muslim suzerainty after more decades of warfare. In 751, the Battle of Talas secured Arab-Muslim-dominated Transoxania against Chinese expansion. In the north, Arab-Muslims attacked Anatolia and launched in 660, 668, and 717 three great but failed expeditions to capture Constantinople. They fought against the Khazars in the Caucasus and established small principalities in Sind, the lower Indus Valley.

For the first time in history, the region we now call the Middle East, as well as North Africa, Spain, and Transoxania were incorporated into a single empire. Thus the Arab-Muslims established the geographical arena for the eventual diffusion of a common culture and a common sociopolitical identity in the name of Islam. (See Map 2.)

The reasons for the relatively rapid success of the Arab-Muslim conquests are not hard to find. Arabians had long experience of military conflict with the bordering empires and, therefore, acquired military sophistication. The Byzantine and Sasanian empires were both militarily exhausted by decades of warfare prior to the Arab-Muslim invasions. The Christian populations – the Copts in Egypt, the Miaphysites in Syria, and the Nestorians in Iraq – all had long histories of troubled relations with their Byzantine and Sasanian rulers. Their disaffection was important in the cases where Christian-Arab border tribes and military auxiliaries joined the conquerors and where fortified cities capitulated. The conquests, then, were due to victories over militarily weakened powers and were consolidated because, by and large, local populations accepted the new regime.

The conquests were further secured by a large migration of Arabian peoples. With the defeat of the Byzantine and Sasanian empires, a frontier between populations broke down. Families and whole tribes soon followed the conquering men, leading to a massive movement of peoples from Arabia into the lands of the Middle East. Arab-Muslim migrants created new cities and settled in a great variety of milieus – older towns, villages, citadels, and country estates – mingling with a great variety of ethnic and language groups, races, religions, sects, and cults. They interacted in marketplaces as merchants and customers, as employers and employees, as patrons and clients, and as landlords and peasants. The settlements stimulated intermarriages, conversions, and exchanges of religious ideas and languages.

In effect, Arab-Muslim settlements promoted the partial integration of Arab and non-Arab populations into new cosmopolitan communities. In turn, urbanization, economic change, and the formation of new communities generated resources for the organization of a new and powerful empire; the elites of city and empire gave birth to new expressions of imperial and religious cultures. What we identify as Islamic civilization was the cultural expression of the integrated elites thrown up by the forces of economic and social change generated by the Arab-Muslim conquests.

THE ADMINISTRATION OF THE NEW EMPIRE

The conquerors represented an already complex and sophisticated society. The soldiers came from both nomadic and sedentary tribes, but the leaders were primarily Hijazi merchants. They brought with them exposure to the agricultural, urban, and monarchical culture of Yemen; to the Ghassanid and Lakhmid experiences of tribal confederation and intermediation with the empires; and to the court cultures of palaces, poetry, and hunting, as well as the merchant skills of Mecca. They would

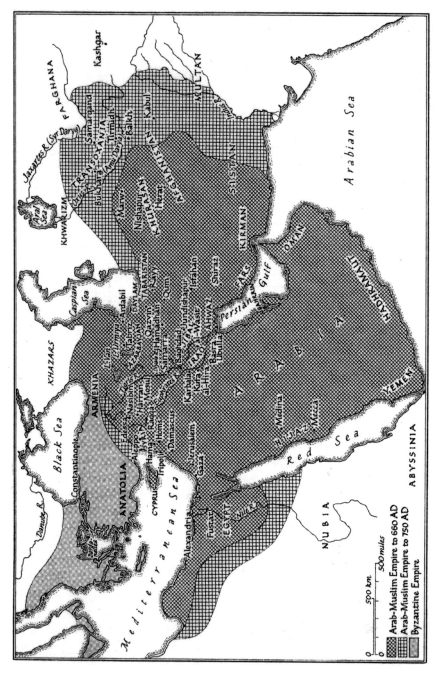

Map 2. The Arab-Muslim empire to 750 CE.

Kashgar

FARGHANA

Jaxartes R. (Syr Darya)

Aral Sea

KHWARIZM

Samarqand

TRANSOXANIA

Bukhara (Amu Darya)

Tirmidh

Balkh

Kabul

MULTAN

AFGHANISTAN

Marv

Nishapur

KHURASAN

Herat

Indus R.

Arabian Sea

SIJISTAN

KIRMAN

FARS

Shiraz

Isfahan

Rayy

Qum

TABARISTAN

DAILAM

Qazvin

Hamadhan

Jundishapur

Ardabil

Caspian Sea

KHAZARS

ARMENIA

Tabriz

Maragha

Zanjan

KHUZISTAN

AHWAZ

Basra

Ubulla

OMAN

Persian Gulf

HADRAMAWT

ARABIA

YEMEN

Edessa

Nisibin

Harran

Mosul

al-Mada'in

Samarra

al-Qadisiyya

Kufa

al-Hira

Wasit

Karbala

al-Anbar

Baghdad

Aleppo

Hama

Raqqa

Homs

Damascus

Jerusalem

Gaza

Tripoli

CYPRUS

Black Sea

Constantinople

Danube R.

ANATOLIA

Mediterranean Sea

Alexandria

Fustat

EGYPT

Nile R.

Red Sea

HIJAZ

Medina

Mecca

NUBIA

ABYSSINIA

500 km.

500 miles

Arab-Muslim Empire to 660 AD

Arab-Muslim Empire to 750 AD

Byzantine Empire

62

quickly add Byzantine and Persian landowning and administrative experience and adopt the imperial tax systems.

From the outset, the chiefs of the Muslim community in Medina sought to channel the bedouin migrations for both their individual and the common advantage. Meccans and Medinans decided on the two basic principles of the postconquest government: the bedouins would be prevented from damaging the agricultural society and the new elite would cooperate with the chiefs and notables of the conquered population. The necessary arrangements between conqueror and conquered were implemented in the reign of the second caliph, 'Umar (634–44).

The first principle of 'Umar's settlement entailed the transformation of the Arab conquerors into a military caste that garrisoned the subdued areas and carried out further conquests. To prevent the bedouins from raiding indiscriminately, to forestall the destruction of the productive agricultural lands, and to segregate the Arabs from the conquered peoples, the Arab-Muslim armies were settled in garrison cities (*amsar* [plural], or *misr* [singular]). The three most important were new cities founded in Iraq and Egypt. Basra, at the head of the Persian Gulf, was strategically located for easy communication with Medina and for expeditions into southern Iran. Kufa, on the Euphrates River to the north of the marshes near al-Hira, became the administrative capital of northern Iraq, Mesopotamia, and northern and eastern Iran. Fustat, the new capital of Egypt, was located just below the delta of the Nile and served as the base for Arab-Muslim expansion into North Africa until Qayrawan (Tunisia) was founded in 670.

In other provinces, the Arabs did not usually create new cities but settled in towns, and in suburbs and villages on the outskirts of existing towns. In Syria, the important Arab-Muslim bases were Damascus, Jerusalem, and a number of desert palaces. In Iran, they included Hamadhan, Isfahan, Rayy, and Marw.

The garrisons served not only to house the bedouin migrants and organize the armies but to distribute the spoils of victory. Soldiers were entitled to a stipend paid out of the taxes collected from peasants and the tributes paid by townspeople. In principle, soldiers and clans were not permitted to seize landed property as their own. Conquered property (*fay'*) was considered the permanent possession of the community; the revenues, but not the land, could be given to the conquerors. These arrangements both protected the cultivated areas from pillaging and distributed the spoils of victory more equitably.

The second principle of 'Umar's settlement was that the conquered populations should be disturbed as little as possible. This meant that the Arab-Muslims did not – contrary to reputation – attempt to convert conquered peoples to Islam. Muhammad had set the precedent of permitting Jews and Christians in Arabia to keep their religions if they paid a tribute tax; the caliphate extended the same privilege to Jews, Christians, and Zoroastrians in the conquered lands, whom they considered protected peoples (*ahl al-dhimma*) or Peoples of the Book, the adherents of earlier written revelations. At the time of the conquests, Islam was primarily understood as a religion of the Arabs, a mark of unity and superiority. When conversions did occur, they could cause embarrassment, because they created status problems and led to claims for financial privileges.

Just as Arab-Muslims had no interest in changing the religious demographics of conquered lands, they had no desire to disturb the social and administrative order. Caliphs sent governors to oversee the collection of tributes and taxes, supervise the distribution of tax revenues as salary to the troops, and lead the soldiers in war and in prayer – but, otherwise, local situations were left in local hands. The old elites and the administrative machinery of the Byzantine and Sasanian empires were incorporated into the new regime. Iranian, Aramean, Coptic, and Greek scribes and accountants worked for their new masters as they had for the old. The old landowners, chiefs, and headmen kept their authority in the villages and assisted in collecting taxes. The former social and religious order was left intact.

In practice, the relationship established between the Arab-Muslims and local elites varied from region to region, depending on the circumstances of the conquests and on the available social and administrative machinery. Some provinces came under direct bureaucratic administration, but many others retained their autonomy. Places that had stubbornly resisted Arab-Muslim incursions forced the invaders to concede favorable terms in return for local compliance. Numerous formal treaties were made with town notables or the chiefs and princes of small provinces, promising to leave the old elites in power and respecting their property and their religion in return for the payment of a tribute, usually a fixed sum, which the notables could collect from their subjects. In these cases, the conquerors simply collected taxes from sub-rulers who were their vassals. In the citied areas of upper Mesopotamia and Syria, in Khurasan and elsewhere, the Arab-Muslims were at first remote suzerains.

The arrangements made in the wake of the conquests, however, were not permanent. As the conquerors consolidated their power, they sought to increase their control over local affairs, to set the bureaucratic machinery of the old regimes to work for the new, and to adapt the preexisting tax system. Taxation was important not only for the incomes of the elites but also for the very viability of the tax-paying societies. Taxes on peasants often reached 50 percent of the value of their produce, and at such levels the incidence of taxation determined whether life for the mass of the people would be tolerable. Taxation affected the care given to soil nutrition, the level of investment in maintaining productivity, and the choice of crops. It determined whether or not the peasants would stay in the villages and work the land or flee, leaving their homes and lands to decay. Furthermore, taxation defined social structure. Taxes were duties levied on some classes of the population for the support of others. Peasants, workers, and merchants paid taxes. Landowners, administrators, clergymen, soldiers, and emperors collected them. To pay taxes was not only an economic burden; it was a sign of social inferiority.

The Arab-Muslim conquests thus followed a pattern familiar from past nomadic conquests of settled regions. The conquering peoples became the military elite, and the settled societies were exploited to support them. The governing arrangements were a compromise between the elites of the conquering peoples and the elites of the conquered or settled peoples: the interests of the former in military power and adequate revenues were assured in exchange for permitting the latter to retain their local political, religious, and financial autonomy. Both leaned on the tax-paying peasantry.

CHAPTER 7

REGIONAL DEVELOPMENTS: ECONOMIC AND SOCIAL CHANGE

Despite conservative intentions, the conquests, the settlement of large Arab-Muslim populations in numerous garrisons, and the consolidation of a new imperial regime set in motion vast changes in the patterns of international trade, local commerce, and agriculture. The unification of former Sasanian and Byzantine territories removed political and strategic barriers to trade and laid the foundations for a major economic revival. The Euphrates frontier between the Persian and the Roman worlds disappeared, and Transoxania, for the first time in history, was incorporated into a Middle Eastern empire. Commercial considerations inspired Arab-Muslim expansion in Inner Asia and India. Cities prospered in Iraq, Iran, and Transoxania. Basra and later Baghdad became two of the leading trading cities in the world. Samarqand, Bukhara, and Nishapur prospered. However, a new frontier was drawn between Syria and Anatolia, which had formerly been part of a single Byzantine state, and trade between these regions declined.

Each region of the new empire fared differently under Arab-Muslim rule. Some prospered, some declined. Agricultural production shifted from one area to another. Arab-Muslim landowners often replaced the previous elites. Soldiers settled on the land, and non-Arabs moved to Arab settlements. These changes created a high degree of mobility and interaction between different peoples and set the basis for the ultimate integration of populations into a shared culture.

IRAQ

The Sasanians had developed Iraq to a level of productivity never to be reached again. Iraq was watered by two great rivers – the Tigris to the east and the Euphrates to the west. In central Iraq, parallel west-to-east canals carried water from the Euphrates to the Tigris. The extensive irrigation system made possible the production of crops such as rice, sugarcane, and cotton. Other common crops were wheat, barley, dates, olives, wine grapes, and alfalfa. In late antiquity, the countryside was organized in village-scale estates, owned by absentee landlords called *dihqans* and worked by servile renters.

On the eve of the conquests, Iraq suffered from neglect of irrigation, exploitative taxation, and wars with the Roman Empire. In southern Iraq, the irrigation works had been allowed to degenerate; in 627–28, a major agricultural disaster took place. In a year of high water flow, the dikes in the Tigris River system of canals burst, and there was a major shift in the riverbed. The Tigris flowed westward through the canals into the Euphrates at a point to the north and west of its previous channel, creating a desert in the east but flooding the lower course of the Euphrates, which remains a marsh to the present day. Repeated floods and plagues devastated southern Iraq, destroying capital facilities and decimating the population. Agricultural production also declined in the Diyala region, which depended on state-maintained irrigation.

Arab Muslim rule provided a stable government and encouraged recovery. The conquerors immediately took charge of fiscal and land policy in Iraq. The caliph 'Umar confiscated the land that once had belonged to the Sasanian crown, along with the estates of notables who had fled with the defeated Sasanian emperor, and made them part of the caliphal domains. However, village-scale estates survived into the Islamic period, and their owners (*dihqans*) paid taxes to the conquerors. 'Umar adopted the Sasanian system of collecting both a land tax (*kharaj*) and a poll tax (*jizya*). Land was measured, and a tax was fixed for every *jarib* (2,400 square meters); the actual rate of taxation per *jarib* varied with the quality of land, the crop, the expected productivity, and the estimated value of the produce. The rates also varied with distance from market, availability of water, type of irrigation, transportation, and so on. In addition, everyone was expected to pay a poll tax in gold coins. A per-capita tax was levied on the towns based on estimated population.

The caliphate also created a Muslim landowning class. 'Uthman awarded confiscated Sasanian crown estates around Kufa to Meccan and tribal aristocrats, and Mu'awiya (661–80) made similar grants from reclaimed lands around Basra. These lands were tithed rather than taxed at *kharaj* rates, the difference given as patronage for members of the ruling family and other loyalists. These richly productive lands were devoted to market-oriented production of high-value specialized crops such as cotton, sugar, and rice. The composition of the Muslim landlord elite then rotated as new caliphs and governors promoted their favorites.

More drastic changes in landownership followed. Al-Hajjaj, governor under the caliphs 'Abd al-Malik (r. 685–705) and al-Walid (r. 705–15), broke the power of the old elites in lower Iraq by refusing investments in irrigation; he reduced the *dihqans* to the status of tenants. In 718–19, the Umayyads stopped the sale of *kharaj* taxable lands, extending the concept of *fay'* (Muslim communally owned property) to the whole of Iraq. In effect, this eliminated both the remaining *dihqans* and earlier Muslim landowners, giving control of the land to the caliphate. The 'Abbasids in turn took over Umayyad properties, sometimes by confiscation.

Wherever the Arab-Muslims established garrison and administrative capitals – as at Basra, Kufa, and al-Wasit – efforts were made to stimulate agricultural output and develop fresh sources of food for the new cities. The swamps around Kufa were drained and brought under cultivation. Basra was planted with date-palm forests. To the east of Basra, the salt marshes were reclaimed by caliphs, governors, and rich tribal *shaykhs*, encouraged by the policy of land and tax concessions. Slaves were imported from East Africa to work the newly reclaimed lands. Thus, the Arab-Muslim regime created the only plantation-type economy in the region. This would lead to Zanj revolts in 690 and 760 and to sporadic Zutt rebellions in the early eighth century.

Imperial investments, however, were highly selective and favored new areas to the detriment of old areas of production, probably because the revenues of the latter were already assigned to peasants, local landowners, and the garrison armies. By the end of the eighth century, however, soil exhaustion, salinization, the high cost of irrigation, absentee landlordism, and the use of imported, rebellious slave labor rendered further development uneconomical. Thus the net effect of the government's efforts was to restore regions in Iraq that had Arab settlements and to allow others to decay. All in all, the total output of Iraq was less than the best levels in Sasanian times.

SYRIA AND MESOPOTAMIA

In late antiquity, Syria was prosperous. The first half of the sixth century was a period of agricultural expansion and population growth. There were many prosperous, large villages in northern Syria, the Hawran, and the Negev (where they were supported by sophisticated water-conserving irrigation). Wine production centered in Gaza. Towns and villages invested heavily in walls, gates, paved and colonnaded streets, and lavishly decorated churches. Churches replaced theaters and bathhouses as the dominant civic institution.

Landownership differed from place to place. Small-scale farming was the dominant form of agriculture in northern Syria, the Hawran, and Palestine – although some monasteries and lords owned villages and extensive tracts of land worked by village-dwelling farmers. In Palestine, Christian landowners dominated a Samaritan peasantry. Arabian tribes had settled in Jordan and in Palestine from the Dead Sea to Gaza. Meccan merchants owned land in Jordan, where the Umayyads would later have their palace-estates.

Urban transformations probably began in the late sixth century. In many towns, the regular classical street plans were converted to the bazaar configuration even before the Arab-Muslim conquests. The Persian invasion of 611–19 caused enormous damage to urban life. The Christian population of Jerusalem and the monasteries of the wilderness of Judaea suffered particularly badly.

The Arab-Muslim conquests, which followed almost immediately after, seem to have allowed for consolidation and rehabilitation. The conquest battles were fought in open country and did little damage to the towns. The invading Arab tribesmen were billeted in the towns and forbidden to engage in agriculture, thus protecting the countryside from some of the risks of nomadic incursions.

Towns, churches, and monasteries continued to flourish; many new churches were built even in the conquest years. Hama remained prosperous into the Islamic era. The dead cities region (a region of deserted stone towns and villages) of northern Syria, the Hawran, and parts of Palestine and Jordan continued to flourish in the seventh and into the eighth century. Production and commerce in olives and wine continued. For a time, the location of the caliphate at Damascus and the creation of "desert palaces" – sometimes the center of agricultural estates – promoted development in selected places. Coastal towns, the locus of Arab-Muslim defenses against Byzantine attack, were fortified and repopulated.

Papyri from the village of Nessana in the Negev give us an intimate glimpse into the social and political structure of the region. They show a village society independent of the larger towns. The village had an informal leadership of local headmen and landowners. There is no evidence of social hierarchy, or of collective leadership or councils, or of tenancy and dependency. Families were constituted by sibling groups.

In Syria and Mesopotamia, the conquerors made innumerable treaties with the local populations, but after a time the Arab-Muslims refused to renegotiate tributes and insisted on payment of taxes in direct proportion to population and resources. Arab-Muslim rule was more closely engaged in village communities than Byzantine rule had been. Mu'awiya made the first census and levied land taxes on the basis of the *iugum,* or the amount of land that could be worked by one man and a team of animals in a day. A special poll tax was levied on urban, nonfarming populations. In 691–92, the caliphate ordered a census and land survey to record individuals, households, land, crops, and animals and assigned a four-dinar poll tax and a rate for every land unit that varied with distance from the market. In the early eighth century, the Umayyad caliphs took over old crown lands and granted estates to favorites or allowed the Quraysh and tribal notables to buy them. Thus, the countryside was transformed from peasant-owned to large-scale landed estates. The 'Abbasids eventually took over the Umayyad holdings.

The Arab-Muslim regime also separated town and rural administration. Since classical antiquity, the Mediterranean region had been divided into self-governing city-states. Although the municipalities eventually became cogs in the machine of the Roman bureaucracy, the city-state with its surrounding rural area continued as a basic element in Roman administration. The new conquerors abolished the city-state as a political form and placed Syria and Mesopotamia under a territorial bureaucracy.

By the eighth century, the prosperity of Syria and Palestine was fading. Palestinian exports of wine and olives seem to have declined after 700. Syria ceased to import grain, oil, and pottery from the west. Gaza and Antioch withered. By the mid-eighth and early ninth centuries, many monasteries in Syria and Mesopotamia had been abandoned, and many monks went to Byzantium and some even to Rome. Although coastal trade declined, the interior continued to prosper into the ninth century, producing textiles and ceramics on a small scale. The Iraq trade, built around Aleppo and Aqaba, increased in the ninth century. Ultimately, the loss of Mediterranean markets, the decline of Christian pilgrimage, the rise of the ʿAbbasids, and the shift of imperial regime from Damascus to Baghdad rendered Syria a backwater.

In contrast with Syria, the caliphs did not intervene in the administration of Mesopotamia until the reign of ʿAbd al-Malik (685–705). Mosul was first ruled from Kufa by a conquest garrison that levied taxes through the local Christian landowning notables. The revenue surpluses probably went to Kufa. The later Umayyads created the first imperial-type administration in Mosul by appointing governors. ʿAbd al-Malik ordered a census and land survey for Mesopotamia to record individuals, households, land, crops, and animals; he assigned a four-dinar poll tax and a rate for every land unit.

In northern Mesopotamia, there were areas of economic growth and others of economic decline. Production in the Edessa region was high in the sixth century but was then abandoned in the late sixth and seventh centuries. At al-Raqqa, Marwanid and ʿAbbasid investments in irrigation helped increase settlement density and production. At Mosul, the Marwanid caliphs distributed estates and developed urban facilities – including a mosque, a palace, canals, and mills. Lavish construction was both an economic measure and a symbol of legitimacy. In the countryside, Christian landed gentry kept their power well into the tenth century. Progressively, Mosuli families took on a provincial identity. For many of them, scholarship and administration were the keys to preservation of family status.

Apart from these zones of development, the migration of Arab bedouins seeking pasture, Khariji opposition to the caliphate, and banditry damaged the agricultural productivity of northern Syria and Mesopotamia.

EGYPT

In Egypt, Byzantine administration had deteriorated before the conquests, but the Arab-Muslims immediately restored effective government. Arab officials were installed at the highest levels of tax administration and supervised the countryside. The division of taxes among villages and individuals and the collection of taxes were left to local Egyptian lay and church notables. There were both land and poll taxes. The poll tax was assessed on entire village populations and then divided up internally by the villagers. Greek and Coptic continued to be used in administration, but Arabic documents and bilingual Greek-Arabic documents were in use from the beginning.

The conquerors simplified the administrative system by breaking the power of large estates, subjecting them to taxation, and abolishing the fiscally independent estates (*autopragia*) and municipalities. Two essential concerns of the new Arab-Muslim government were to organize the transport of grain from Egypt to the Hijaz and to construct the fleets that would be used to attack Constantinople.

Under the Marwanids, administrative regulation was intensified. The tax registers were translated into Arabic, with a new formulary and fiscal procedures. This began the process of replacing Coptic village headmen with Arab-Muslims and assessing taxes on individuals rather than communities. In 693–94, poll taxes were imposed on monks and a proportional tax was levied on crops. In 705, registers show records of landholdings by lists of individual taxpayers, minors, fugitives, and even deceased former taxpayers. Between 715 and 718, all travelers were required to have an internal passport identifying name, date, place of origin, and work permit. A comprehensive land survey was undertaken in 724–25. In the next year there was a great Coptic revolt. With the defeat of these rebellions, the influence of the church and of Coptic notables was further diminished.

By the middle of the eighth century, Muslims were living in the countryside. Some Arab-Muslims or converts may have been officials of the postal service, whereas others were landholders. In later Umayyad and early 'Abbasid times, there was no longer a distinction in taxes paid by Muslims and non-Muslims; they were equally subjects of the state. By the time of the Caliph al-Mansur (754–75), Egyptian and Khurasanian documents were using the same formulas, suggesting a highly centralized empire-wide administration.

In general, the Egyptian economy flourished from Byzantine times to the Middle Ages. Wines, woolens, linen, papyrus, textiles, and grain continued to be exported – although they declined somewhat between 800 and 1000. Although the productivity of agriculture probably declined, grain surpluses continued to be exported to the Hijaz rather than to Constantinople.

IRAN

In Iran, the Arab-Muslim conquest and migrations also favored urban and agricultural development. Security, trade, a new population, and new policies regarding settlement, city building, and irrigation stimulated economic growth. In Iran, the conquerors did not found new cities (except Shiraz) but settled in already-established ones. Important places such as Hamadhan, Isfahan, Qazvin, Rayy, Nishapur, and Marw received Arab-Muslim garrisons. These were usually housed in newly constructed quarters and in villages surrounding the town centers.

Moreover, in Iran, construction and settlement continued beyond the initial conquest. Throughout the seventh and eighth centuries, each important governor imported his own clientele of guards, soldiers, and administrators and built new quarters, palaces, mosques, barracks, gardens, and canals. Surrounding agricultural lands were brought into cultivation. Later caliphs also constructed walls and redefined administrative jurisdictions, thus converting groups of quarters and villages into cities. By this process, Isfahan, Rayy, and Qazvin became large cities. Qum grew from a simple complex of agricultural villages into a major town. Whole regions – such as the districts around Samarqand and Bukhara, favored with new quarters and villages, irrigation works, and walls to defend them against Turkish nomads – prospered. Khwarizm, the delta of the Oxus River, which before the conquests had contained small hamlets and farmsteads interspersed with feudal castles, became highly urbanized and densely settled.

In Khurasan and other parts of Iran, however, only the loosest suzerainty and tributes were imposed, and virtually complete autonomy was conceded to local notables. By the 'Abbasid period, however, Iranian lordly families (often continuing from Sasanian times) had been incorporated into the bureaucracy, and taxes were being collected by the central government.

Thus, the net effect of the Arab-Muslim conquests and empire formation was prosperity in Iran, a redistribution of the pattern of development in Iraq, and the partial economic decline of Mesopotamia, Syria, and Egypt.

THE INTEGRATION OF CONQUERING AND CONQUERED PEOPLES

Under pressures of war, migration, and intensive economic changes, the fundamental assumption of the conquest empire – that Arab and non-Arab populations would be segregated, with the former serving as a military elite and the latter as producers and taxpayers – proved untenable. Instead, conquered and conquering peoples assimilated to each other on the basis of new communities and new Arab and Islamic identities.

Sedentarization itself created pressures for the assimilation of Arabs into the surrounding societies. Under the pressures of town life, Arabian kinship and lineage societies became socially stratified, occupationally differentiated, and communally organized. In the garrison cities, each major clan or tribal group originally had its own quarter, mosque, cemetery, and meeting place. Over time, however, the tent dwellings were replaced by reed huts; the huts were reinforced with earthen walls and then replaced with mud-brick houses. The bedouins, once accustomed to migration, found themselves immured in brick.

The military and administrative systems also generated profound changes by requiring that the preexisting units of Arabian society be rearranged into artificial groups. To make uniform regiments and to pay units of about a thousand men, large clans were subdivided and smaller ones combined. In 670, tens of thousands of families were moved from Basra and Kufa to garrison Marw in Khurasan, and all the remaining groups were reorganized. Also, newcomers who came in continuous streams to partake in the Arab-Muslim wars had to be integrated into the basic units. Even though the military units kept their clan and tribal names – perhaps also their kinship core – they no longer represented the pre-Islamic Arabian social structure.

Furthermore, class distinctions separated the chiefs and ordinary tribesmen. Military and administrative functions widened the gap between the chiefs and their followers. The existence of privately owned palaces and agricultural estates suggests that the chiefs were enjoying wealth, privileges, and a style of life far removed from that of the mass of their clansmen. The military elites began to form a new class stratum, fortified by marriage ties. Tribal society was being transformed into a society stratified into classes based on wealth and power.

Settlement also entailed the transformation of bedouins and soldiers into an economically differentiated working population. As Basra developed into an important administrative capital, a center of cloth manufacturing, and a trading city connected with Iran, India, China, and Arabia, Arab settlers became merchants, traders, artisans, and workers – supplementing their meager military allotments with new incomes. Similarly, the new religion of Islam offered opportunities for social mobility through careers in teaching, scholarship, and legal administration.

Simultaneously, settlements obfuscated the distinctions between Arabs and non-Arabs. As a capital and commercial center, Basra attracted non-Arab settlers. The soldiers and administrators of the old regime came to seek their fortunes. Iranian regiments were enlisted en masse as Arab governors brought back troops from the east. Sasanian soldiers were important as private retainers, bodyguards, and police in the service of Arab elites. The Asawira – Persian archers taken on as clients of the Tamim tribe in Basra – maintained their own language and resided in their own quarter. Bukharan archers were added in 673. Shakiriyya – the personal guards of Persian princes and landowners – became clients of Arab generals, setting a precedent for the Persian and Turkish military units that would later constitute the 'Abbasid armies. Numerous other ethnic groups – Armenians, Azarbayjanis, Ethiopians, Sudanese, Berbers, Qiqaniyya from India, and Saqaliba (freed Slavs from the Antakya region) – were recruited in the course of the Arab-Muslim campaigns to provide loyal, reliable troops for the caliphs, governors, and Arab generals. Progressively, these new forces replaced Arabian forces. As the tribesmen of Basra and Kufa were demobilized and became civilian town dwellers, other ethnicities became the mainstay of the caliphal armies. These diverse ethnic groups were assimilated into Arab-Muslim society.

Furthermore, clerks, tax collectors, estate managers, village chiefs, and landowners flocked to the centers of government. Merchants in lucrative, long-distance trade and humble workers (including bath attendants, weavers, and spinners) migrated to the new towns. Slaves (captured and purchased), itinerant construction workers, fugitive peasants, and migrant laborers – seeking employment and relief from the harshness of the countryside – also flooded the new cities. The most numerous elements of these diverse, non-Arab groups were Iranians and Arameans (the people of Iraq). Most of them were originally Nestorian Christians, but many were Jews. Indians, Malays, Gypsies, Africans, and Turks also came in small numbers from remote areas. As intermarriage and assimilation occurred, the meaning of "Arab" was less and less definable.

The assimilation of these non-Arabs had important repercussions for Arab society and identity. Arabs tried to absorb the newcomers into the old clan structure as clients (*mawali* [plural], or *mawla* [singular]). The concept of clientage was inherited from pre-Islamic Arabia, where a client was an inferior associate of an Arab clan. Very often, he was a former slave who was freed and then raised to the level of client, although many people were adopted or contracted directly into the status. The client was almost a member of the clan; his heirs were also clients. Clients could expect support and protection and would be helped in arranging marriages. The protection of the powerful was exchanged for the loyalty of the subordinates.

However, as they absorbed clients, Arab clans ceased to be kin units and became stratified political and economic groups built around a kinship core. The gap between aristocratic and plebeian clans widened. For example, in the Tamim tribe, the noble clans acquired former Persian cavalry units as their clients, whereas others had slave laborers and weavers as theirs.

Clientage also generated conflicts between clients and patrons. Even clients with skills in war, administration, commerce, medicine, and religious life were viewed as social inferiors. They were exploited economically and could not intermarry with Arabs or inherit equally. The active soldiers resented exclusion from the military payrolls (*diwans*), because enrollment was not only a financial benefit but a symbol of social privilege. Clients wanted to be recognized as part of the elite, but to the upper class (mostly, but not exclusively, Arabs) this was unthinkable. They clung to their status and privileges and resented the importance of the clients in the army and administration, their religious precocity, their commercial skill, and the shadow they cast over Arab primacy.

In Iran, different circumstances led to similar outcomes. At Isfahan, Marw, Nishapur, and Balkh, the Arab-Muslim garrisons were settled in villages (rather than in cities) and conquerors rapidly became landowners or peasants. Of the 50,000 families initially settled in Marw in 670, only 15,000 were still in active military service by 730. Most of the Arab-Muslim army had by then left active service for civilian occupations. In Azarbayjan, parties of Arabs from Basra and Kufa seized lands and villages and established themselves as a local landowning aristocracy. In Kirman, Arab migrants reclaimed abandoned lands, founded new villages, and settled as a peasant population. In all these provinces, Arab landowning elites came into being. These Arabs refused to take up military duties and found themselves – although in principle an elite caste – in fact absorbed into the occupations of the subject population. Furthermore, in Iran, occupational assimilation was accompanied by social assimilation. Although some Persians became Muslim or Arabized, Arabs by and large assimilated to the Persian milieu. Arabs spoke Persian, dressed like Persians, celebrated Persian holidays, and married Persian women.

Thus, within fifty years, the founding of new cities and the transfer of economic opportunities and political power to new peoples and new places stimulated the interpenetration of Arab and non-Arab peoples. Non-Arabs permeated the Arab-Muslim military caste as converts and associates, and Arabs became landowners, merchants, and settlers. The pressures generated by sedentarization and urbanization and by contact with other Middle Eastern peoples dissolved the lineage structure of the old tribal society, fostered new group and communal structures, intensified the stratification of society and the division of labor, and led to the formation of new mixed Arab and non-Arab communities.

CONVERSIONS TO ISLAM

Conversion was a very gradual process. Although earlier Muslim and Western writers assumed that the region was forcibly, quickly, and massively converted to Islam, nowhere in the sources is there mention of the conversion of large numbers of people, or of whole villages, towns, and regions. The only known exception may be on the Byzantine frontier. The available evidence points, rather, to a slow and uneven process of social and religious transformations. Moreover, the modern notion of conversion does not correspond to the historical process by which individuals came to identify themselves as Muslim for a variety of political, economic, and social reasons. Conversion did not necessarily imply a profound inner spiritual change.

There are a number of reasons for the slow pace of conversions. The Arab-Muslim elite assumed that they would form a dual society in which the conquerors would constitute an aristocracy and the conquered peoples a subject population: the former Muslim, the latter not. Arab elites were resistant to the conversion of masses of people partly to defend their exclusive privileges and partly to preserve the full revenue base of the regime.

The early Muslim regime was also religiously tolerant of the non-Muslim populations. In the highly fluid social world of the seventh century, peoples of all ethnicities and religions blended into public life. Muslims and non-Muslims were not segregated in public spaces such as markets, baths, and festivals. In Syria, they even shared churches before the conquerors were ready to build mosques for themselves. The Muslims recognized or accepted these churches as holy places and may not have fully distinguished Islam from Christianity.

Furthermore, in the seventh century, the Arab-Muslim regime helped reorganize the Christian churches. The Nestorian Church in Iraq resumed its roles in the educational, judicial, and even political administration of the Christian population. In Egypt, the Muslim authorities cooperated with Coptic lay and clerical notables. Christian scribes served in the administration of Syria, Iraq, and Egypt. In Iraq, Azarbayjan, Khuzistan, and Sistan, relations with local notables were generally cooperative and allowed for the survival of the fire temples. For the sake of political inclusiveness and effective administration, the empire collaborated with non-Muslim elites, permitted them partial access to power, and protected them against disruptive social and economic changes.

Nonetheless, in the postconquest mingling of peoples, conversions began to take place. The earliest converts to Islam were those Christian-bedouin tribes living on the margin of the Fertile Crescent who were swept up in the great migrations. Later, in the first century of Arab rule, other Mesopotamian Arab tribes also accepted Islam – although many remained Christian. The Taghlib living on the Byzantine frontier, for example, remained Christian well into the 'Abbasid era but were considered loyal forces and were exempt from the poll tax levied on non-Muslim subjects.

Once the Arab conquests were secure, conversions began among the elites of the former Sasanian Empire. Soldiers, officials, and landowners made common cause with the conquerors and accepted Islam. Client soldiers and scribes serving the Arab elite converted. Conversions implied the ratification of old privileges and paved the way for entry into the dominant elite. Other strata of the population attracted to the Arab garrisons, including merchants, workers, and peasants fleeing the land, also converted. Prisoners were likely converts. In these cases, conversions involved mobile individuals and not classes or whole communities.

Islam was not imposed on the population but attracted people who wanted to escape from social and fiscal constraints and join the ruling elite. Converts might gain tax and political advantages, protection of landed property, employment, or perhaps manumission from slavery. The weakening of the older clerical and political elites facilitated the breakdown of communities and social mobility.

By the beginning of the eighth century, conversions became a policy issue for the caliphate and the Arab elite. Elite elements resisted the dilution of their status and revenues. Religious activists favored conversions. Widespread Arab assimilation into the general population and numerous conversions led many Arabs to accept the equality of Arabs and non-Arabs and to value Muslim as well as Arab identities.

Transoxania reflects both attitudes. In Khurasan and Transoxania, converts began to demand exemptions from the poll tax (*jizya*). The political response was inconsistent. Some governors favored exemption in the interest of mobilizing local support for the struggle against Soghdian and Turkish peoples in the east;

others resisted or revoked the changes in order to maintain the revenues and the support of Arab military cadres.

Caliphs also were divided. 'Umar II (r. 717–21) favored the equality of all Muslims regardless of social origin. He sought to put the empire on a Muslim, rather than a strictly Arab, basis; he accepted the fundamental equality of all Muslims, Arab and non-Arab, and promulgated new laws giving fiscal equality to Muslims regardless of origin. Although later caliphs abandoned this policy, the sporadic attempts at encouraging conversion to Islam marked a turning point in the ongoing integration of Arabs and conquered peoples as Arab religious intellectuals undertook missionary activity in Khurasan and Transoxania.

Moreover, the religious and cultural barriers to conversion were low, because Islam was similar to Judaism and Christianity and because conversion may not have been understood in this period as a radical change. Converts may have signified their conversion by praying, by going to a mosque, by changing their names, or by dressing like an Arab; intellectual study or a change in moral or spiritual beliefs may not have been required. Some Muslim theological and legal schools – such as the Murji'a and Hanafis – held that a simple declaration of Muslim allegiance, rather than performance of works, made a true Muslim – a position favorable to new converts. Thus, in the first Muslim century, as myriad converts entered Islam – bringing the cultural, ritual, and legal practices of their old religions and societies – the religious beliefs and practices of new Muslims must have been exceedingly varied.

Reciprocally, Arab-Muslims were open to the incorporation of past religious beliefs, symbols, practices, and holy places into their own culture. This openness would persist for centuries until Islam became fully consolidated in its own cultural identity.

The potential religious position of converts in the seventh and eighth centuries may parallel that of converts in Central and southern Asia during later Muslim conquests. People who worked for the new governments or who had business with them were the first to convert. These converts had many different stances toward Islam. Many were nominal converts who pronounced the testimonial (*shahada*) but who otherwise continued to live in their non-Muslim families and communities, taking part in the worship and festival life of the old religions. They were Muslims without Islamic orthodox teachings and practices. Still others would have been won over by the preaching, piety, and miracles of Muslim holy men. Others would have assimilated more deeply, perhaps taking positions that led to the acquisition of new languages and religious knowledge, perhaps becoming scholars of Islam (*'ulama'*). They may or may not have remained connected to nonconverted families and communities. In time, with education and incessant pressure from Muslim scholars, their practice would increasingly conform to the Islamic orthodoxy of that period.

Several scholarly efforts have been made to assess the amount and the historical rhythm of conversions. One method is to study family names in later biographical dictionaries and identify the earliest Muslim members. Based on this methodology, Bulliet concluded that conversions before 695 were minimal. The numbers of converts significantly rose between 695 and 762; by then, perhaps 10 percent of the town populations had converted. Conversions rapidly increased in the 'Abbasid period until perhaps half of the town populations were Muslim by 850.

A second approach is to mine the chronicles for specific cases. By the late seventh century, Christian writers in Syria were concerned with apostasy. By the middle of the eighth century, there seems to have been a steady progress of conversions in Iraq, Egypt, and Syria. Significant numbers of converts were located in and around the Muslim garrison centers.

In Iran, the chronicles indicate a very irregular pattern. As early as 666, Zoroastrians in Sistan were converting. In the 720s, masses of Samarqandis converted – probably in response to pledges of equality and tax relief. Between 723 and 738, there were 30,000 converts in Marw. By the end of the eighth century, sources report that Hanafi missionaries had converted 100,000 people in Farghana, Shash, and Balkh. The chronicles do not support Bulliet's hypothesis about the rate of conversion and instead indicate that conversions were episodic and driven by local circumstances. Despite this rising tide of converts to Islam, outside the garrison towns, the mass of Middle Eastern peoples remained non-Muslims.

ARABIC AND OTHER MIDDLE EASTERN LANGUAGES

Along with conversion to Islam, common languages emerged. In general, Arabic became the language of written communication in administration, literature, and religion. It also became the predominant spoken dialect in the western parts of the Middle East – North Africa, Egypt, Syria, Mesopotamia, and Iraq – where languages close to Arabic (such as Aramaic and Syriac) were already spoken. The adoption of Arabic as a language of literature, learning, politics, and everyday life was a critical milestone in the transformation of Middle Eastern cultures.

The spread of Arabic was faster than the diffusion of Islam, but this is not to say that the process was rapid or complete. In Syria, Greek was the language of the elites, intellectuals, and clergy, but Aramaic and Armenian were the ordinary spoken languages. Arabic became more prominent than Greek during the eighth century, but Greek continued to exist as both a literary and a spoken language. Arabic became the lingua franca of Melkites, but until the end of the eighth century, inscriptions in churches and ecclesiastical literature were written in Greek, and Greek continued to be used in monastic contexts until the Crusades. Theodore of Abu Qurra (d. c. 825) was the first important Christian theologian to write in Arabic. Coptic was still spoken in Fustat in the eighth century. In Syria and Iraq, there continued to be Aramaic-speaking populations.

In western Iran, however, Arabic did not predominate. Arab settlers were absorbed into the local populations and became bilingual. Not only did Arabs learn Persian, but the Arab-Muslim conquests became the vehicle for the introduction of Persian as the lingua franca of the peoples east of the Oxus. In Transoxania, Persian – the spoken language of Arabs in eastern Iran – replaced Soghdian as the common language for Arabs, Persians, and Soghdians.

Thus, within a century of the Arab-Muslim conquests, the basic principles on which the empire was organized were no longer valid. In the nomadic kingdom organized by Caliph 'Umar, Arabian peoples were to constitute a "nation in arms," settled in garrison centers, segregated from the subject peoples, restricted to military activities, and barred from commerce and agriculture. Membership in Islam was their prerogative. Non-Arab peoples were to keep their communal ties and religions and continue to work in the productive occupations that enabled them to support the ruling elite.

In the course of the first Muslim century, the Arabs changed from primarily (although not exclusively) a clan or tribal people into a primarily urban people; they assimilated with non-Arab peoples, abandoned military affairs, took on civilian occupations, and lost their monopoly on Islam. Correspondingly, non-Arab peoples entered the military and government services, converted to Islam, adopted the Arabic language, and claimed a place in the government of the empire in which they were initially subjects. Economic and social changes in the garrison centers, conversions, and shared languages paved the way for the society of the future: no longer divided between Arab conqueror and conquered peoples but united on the basis of their commitment to Islam, sharing an Arabic and/or Persian linguistic identity.

The mutual assimilation of peoples and the emergence of Islamic Middle Eastern communities took place, however, only in a restricted number of garrison centers. Most of the Middle Eastern population remained outside the influence of the new societies, still bound to their more ancient heritage. Nonetheless, the cosmopolitan communities would set the tone of Middle Eastern politics and culture for centuries to come. The integration of Arab-Muslims and others in the garrison settlements was the social foundation for the integration of old and new religions and cultures.

CHAPTER 8

THE CALIPHATE TO 750

The caliphate was established as the succession to Muhammad and became a defining institution of Muslim societies. It was, however, an evolving institution with a different political and religious meaning in successive eras. The first phase, the period of the Rightly Guided Caliphs (632–61; known as Rashidun), was the religious chieftainship of a community and the political leadership of a coalition of nomadic conquerors. In the succeeding early Umayyad period (661–85), the caliphate was refashioned as a Syrian-Arab monarchy. In the later Umayyad (685–750), the caliphate was transformed into a new form of Middle Eastern empire defined and legitimized both in older imperial and in Islamic terms.

THE RIGHTLY GUIDED CALIPHS

The bare outlines of the historical record suggest a very uncertain and contested beginning. At the death of the Prophet, there was no instruction from him and no agreement among his followers that there should be a succession at all. 'Umar and other Muslims persuaded a partial gathering of the community to accept Abu Bakr as caliph. Abu Bakr (632–34), the first of the Rashidun caliphs, was named *amir al-mu'minin* (commander of the believers), a *shaykh* or chief who led the collectivity, arbitrated disputes, and followed the precedents set by Muhammad. His authority derived from tribal tradition, his personal connection to the Prophet, and the community's election of him. According to tradition, on assuming his office, Abu Bakr said simply that he would obey the precedent (sunna) of the Prophet and that people should obey him as long as he obeyed it.

Nonetheless, Abu Bakr made a number of decisions that defined the political direction of the new regime. He decided that all tribes formerly allied to Muhammad would have to continue to pay taxes (*zakat*), and he waged war on those who refused, a period known as the apostasy (*ridda*) wars. He installed the governors who administered the conquered territories. He made legal decisions about the property of Muhammad, ruling that it belonged to the community and could not be inherited by Muhammad's family. The traditions say both that Abu Bakr named his colleague 'Umar to succeed him and that 'Umar was elected by the community.

'Umar's reign (634–44) continued the roles of the caliph as head of a religious community and ruler of a growing empire. 'Umar promulgated laws abolishing temporary marriage, increasing punishment for adultery, and regulating parentage by concubines. He established the *hijra* calendar and promoted religious identity by building mosques and appointing religious officials such as judges, preachers, and Quran reciters. From the beginning, however, there were deep divisions within the Muslim community. The succession of caliphs was disputed. 'Ali was regarded by his supporters as the intended heir of the Prophet because of his personal piety and the great importance placed in Arabian society on blood kinship. Madelung makes a strong case that 'Ali was the intended heir of the Prophet, but that there was in effect a coup in which a minority brought Abu Bakr to power. The bitterness was heightened by Abu Bakr's denial of Muhammad's property as inheritances for the family of 'Ali.

In addition, a political rivalry developed between the Quraysh (the Meccan tribal leaders) and the early Meccan and Medinan followers of the Prophet. The Caliph 'Umar adopted a Muslim-centric policy, favoring the Meccan companions of the Prophet (the *muhajirun*), his Medinan helpers (the *ansar*), and the clans who had supported Medina in the Arabian wars and had been early participants in the conquest of Iraq. 'Umar appointed them to governorships, generalships, and administrative posts; he gave them the highest stipends and allowed them to administer the abandoned Sasanian crown lands (*sawafi*). The Quraysh aristocracy resented 'Umar's policies. In the provinces, powerful Arabian clans and the chiefs of the earlier tribal opposition also claimed a share of power.

'Uthman (644–56) succeeded 'Umar by the vote of a council of notables appointed by 'Umar. He was a Meccan aristocrat of the Umayyad clan, and he reversed 'Umar's policies and favored Umayyads, other Meccans, and large clans at the expense of the emigrants and Medinans. To accomplish this redistribution of power, 'Uthman increased central control over provincial revenues. He also took initiatives in religious matters, including the promulgation of a standard edition of the Quran. This expressly laid claim to religious authority and was resented by other companions of the Prophet, who viewed themselves as custodians of the holy book. 'Uthman thus reasserted the pre-Islamic coalition of Meccan and Arabian tribal aristocrats against the new Islamized elements and claimed an enlarged authority for the caliph to effect social, economic, and religious changes.

In implementing these policies, 'Uthman provoked bitter opposition, conspiracies, and, eventually, civil war. In 656, he was murdered by a party of about 500 soldiers from Fustat. In the wake of this murder, 'Ali was elected caliph. As the cousin and son-in-law of Muhammad, as well as one of the earliest converts to Islam, 'Ali had claimed the caliphate on the basis of his devotion to Muhammad and Islam, but he was compromised because he had come to power with the support of 'Uthman's assassins and without the legitimacy conferred by a council (*shura*) of companions (*sahaba*). He opposed the centralization of caliphal control over provincial revenues and favored an equal distribution of taxes and booty among Arab-Muslims.

'Ali's accession led to factional fighting. First, he was opposed by a faction led by the Meccan aristocrats Talha and Zubayr and 'A'isha (the Prophet's favorite wife), whom he defeated at the Battle of the Camel in 656. He was then challenged by Mu'awiya ('Uthman's cousin and the governor of Syria), who refused 'Ali's demands for allegiance and demanded revenge for 'Uthman's assassination and punishment for his killers. The opponents and their armies met at the Battle of Siffin (657), where after months of desultory confrontation and negotiations, the moderates forced an agreement to arbitrate the question of whether 'Uthman's murder was justified. Some of 'Ali's supporters, called the secessionists (Kharijis), held that they were loyal to the ruler only so long as he upheld the Quran and the sunna; they saw 'Ali's willingness to submit to arbitration as a violation of religious principles. They turned against him and were defeated in battle, but this new round of bloodshed further fragmented the Muslim community.

The results of the two arbitration meetings are not clearly known, but it seems that the arbitrators agreed that 'Uthman's murder was not justified (a boost for Umayyad claims) and did not agree on the continuation of 'Ali's caliphate. In the course of the next two years, 'Ali's support disintegrated. The protracted struggle had begun to threaten the security of the empire and the flow of revenues. As rebellions in eastern Iran cut off the payment of taxes to the tribesmen of Basra and Kufa, Arab opinion turned in favor of Mu'awiya. He was backed by disciplined forces; he seemed able to maintain order within the Arab-Muslim elite and to sustain control over the empire. After 'Ali's assassination by a Khariji, Mu'awiya declared himself caliph and was accepted as such by the political elites. He was the founder of the Umayyad dynasty (661–750).

This protracted civil war initiated a lasting division within Muslim society: henceforth, Muslims were divided over who had the legitimate right to occupy the caliphate. Muslims who accepted the succession of Mu'awiya and the historical sequence of caliphs after him are called the Sunnis. Those who held that 'Ali was the only rightful caliph and that only his descendants should succeed him are called the Shi'is. For the Shi'is, 'Ali gradually became not only a family claimant but the repository of high religious authority – the living embodiment of God's continuing guidance. Shi'is tended to stress the religious functions of the caliphate and to deplore its political compromises; Sunnis were inclined to circumscribe its religious role and to be more tolerant of its political involvements. Kharijis held that the caliph should be elected by the community of Muslims at large and hold his position only so long as he was sinless in the conduct of his office. As these early differences were vested with ever-widening religious importance, Sunnis, Shi'is, and Kharijis developed separate versions of Islam and formed distinct religious bodies within the community as a whole.

The precise nature and the boundaries of the caliph's authority have always been in dispute. The caliphs were cited in administrative documents and inscriptions as successors to the Prophet, and they claimed to be heirs of the Prophet's mantle and staff. In Medina, the caliphs were dignified as the companions of the Prophet, tribal chiefs, jurists, arbitrators, exemplars, and holy men. In Muslim historiography, the Rightly Guided Caliphs (Rashidun) – or some of them – are seen as the saintly perpetuators of the teachings of Muhammad. The conquests emphasized the military and political dimensions of the succession to Muhammad. Non-Muslim scholars have long perceived the caliphate as representing both Muhammad's political and religious leadership.

This authority, however, was by no means absolute. Apart from the caliphate, the companions of the Prophet – repositories of Prophetic memories and scholars of hadith and religious knowledge – exerted an important local, communal, and religious authority. From an early time, the collective authority of the companions was an implied alternative to the disputed authority of the caliphs.

The titles taken by the early caliphs also imply modest claims. The one official title attested from early times was "commander of the believers" (*amir al-mu'minin*). Crone and Hinds insisted that the title "deputy of God" (*khalifat allah*) was used by both Abu Bakr and 'Umar as a sign of transcending authority, but Sunni sources – which they mistakenly dismiss as propaganda – indicate that Abu Bakr and 'Umar used the more modest title "deputy of the prophet of God" (*khalifat rasul allah*) as well as "commander of the believers." Similarly, the term "imam" – adopted by the Shi'is to mean divinely gifted spiritual leader and source of law – was, in later Umayyad times, applied to all persons and texts deemed authoritative. It was applied to the Quran, to the early caliphs, to companions, and to later jurists. It also referred to military leaders. Thus, the titles "*khalifat allah*" and "imam" were adopted in later literature and perhaps by later caliphs but did not originate with a defined meaning in the early period.

THE UMAYYAD MONARCHY (661–685)

(See Figure 2.) The first civil war created permanent sectarian divisions within the Muslim community. Driven by changing historical circumstances and by political and religious conflicts among Arab-Muslim elites, the caliphate had to rebuild its institutions, validate its authority, and mobilize the political, economic, and ideological resources it needed to rule. Its response was to strengthen its institutional bases among Arab tribes and to give new voice to its Muslim credentials. On seizing power, Mu'awiya (661–80) expanded the military and administrative powers of the state. He appointed regional governors atop the network of tribal forces but did not yet establish a centralized government apparatus. His dynasty, the

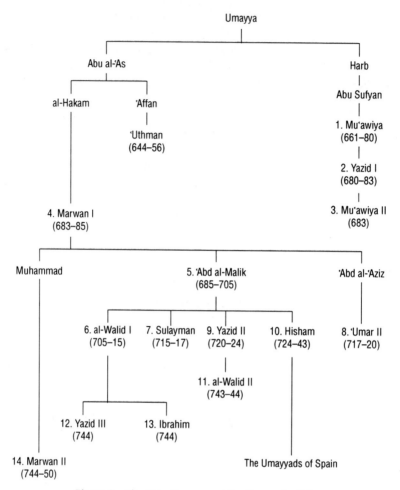

Figure 2. The Banu Umayya and the Umayyad caliphs.

Sufyanid, ruled as a family regime through tributaries with a minimal bureaucracy; they were the directors of a tribal coalition. To satisfy the interests of the tribal chiefs, the conquests were resumed in North Africa and eastern Iran. On the Syrian front, Mu'awiya kept peace with the Byzantine Empire so that he could hold Syrian forces in reserve for purposes of internal policing. Further, he sought to build up revenues from private royal incomes, from confiscated Byzantine and Sasanian crown lands, and from investments in reclamation and irrigation.

Mu'awiya also devised new moral and political grounds for loyalty to the caliphate. He tried to cloak his growing police and financial powers under religious gestures. He minted Sasanian-type coins "in the name of God" and called himself commander of the believers. Notably, there is no surviving mention of the Prophet.

The regime patronized Arabic poetry, genealogy, and history. Tribal lore, genealogies, and histories of Yemen were among the first matters to be set down in writing. Arabic poetry was adopted as sponsored court poetry. It derived from the *qasida* form of poetry, featuring praise of oneself and one's tribe and praise of the Lakhmid and Ghassanid kings. The presentation of praise poems was a ceremonial and ritual function in which lauding of the ruler was exchanged for gifts and honors to the poet; the recognition of royal power exchanged for royal beneficence. The *qasida* form attached the past to the present by making both patron and poet heirs of the Arabic cultural heritage. For the ruling elite in this period, however, Arab identity and Muslim identity were likely indistinguishable.

Mu'awiya's personal qualities were more important than any institutions. He embodied the traditional Arab virtues of conciliation, consultation, generosity, and respect for tribal tradition. He is legendary for his *hilm* – clemency, patience, and the power to do harm restrained by forbearance – his talent for dealing with his followers so that they cooperated without feeling that their dignity had been offended. If the caliphate of 'Umar fundamentally rested on his closeness to Muhammad and religious integrity, Mu'awiya's reign was based on state power, his networks of clientele ties, and his ability to exemplify the Arab tribal patriarch.

Despite these efforts, the decades of Mu'awiya's rule did not do away with the causes of the first civil war. Arab aristocrats continued to vie for control of the caliphate. Shi'is aspired to bring Husayn ('Ali's son) to power; Kharijis resisted any impious candidate. Arab factional conflict simmered beneath the surface. When Mu'awiya died, civil war broke out again; this time, it lasted from 680 to 692.

At Mu'awiya's death, his son and successor, Yazid (680–83), fought against Meccan rivals led by 'Abdallah b. al-Zubayr. 'Ali's son Husayn attempted to move from Medina to Kufa to lead his followers, but his small party was intercepted at Karbala (Iraq) and destroyed. At the time, the episode had few repercussions, but Husayn's death gradually assumed the significance of martyrdom. Today, Husayn's shrine at Karbala is one of the great pilgrimage sites of the Muslim world. Along with the defeat of his father, Husayn's death at the hands of the Umayyads deeply divided Muslims. 'Ali is the ancestor of Shi'ism; Husayn is its martyr.

Apart from these direct challenges to the Umayyad caliphate, the civil war period was marked by widespread factional fighting. Whereas the factions of the first civil war were based on Islamic versus tribal loyalties, the new factions were based on ad hoc alliances between clans that had come together in the insecure and changing societies of the garrison towns. Although defined in tribal terms, the warring coalitions were probably composed of older- and younger-generation migrants. The Syrian tribal coalitions – which had for decades been the mainstay of Mu'awiya's reign – divided into two warring coalitions called Yemen (or Kalb) and Qays; they were mainly located in Syria and northern Mesopotamia. The fighting spread to Iraq, where the factions were called Mudar and Tamim, and to Khurasan, where they were called Rabi'a and Qays.

The Kharijis who had repudiated 'Ali after the battle of Siffin formed small bands, usually of between thirty and a hundred men. Each group was at once an outlaw gang and a fanatical religious sect. They were held together by the conviction that they were the only true Muslims and that their rebellions had profound religious justification. A group of Kharijis (called Najda) controlled a good part of Arabia – including Bahrain, Oman, Hadhramaut, and Yemen – before they were finally crushed. These Khariji bands were most likely formed by uprooted individuals looking for communal affiliation through sectarian movements. The second civil war, then, was a crisis for the cohesion of the Arab-Muslim elite, for its political authority, and for its concepts of true belief and communal leadership.

THE IMPERIAL CALIPHATE: THE MARWANIDS (685–750)

The Caliph 'Abd al-Malik (685–705), backed by Syrian Yemeni armies, eventually crushed his numerous opponents. The new caliph and his successor, al-Walid (705–15), faced with endemic religious opposition – both Shi'i and Khariji – and tribal factionalism, set in motion a new phase in the process of defining the beliefs, symbols, and institutions of Arab-Muslim society. The caliphate was transformed from a coalition of nomadic conquerors into a new form of Middle Eastern empire, defined and legitimized in both historic imperial and Islamic terms. The reigns of 'Abd al-Malik, his son al-Walid, and their successors generated reinventions of the caliphate with profound implications for Islamic societies.

The new caliphate was built on the further centralization of state power. In domestic policy, 'Abd al-Malik demilitarized the Arabs in the garrison cities of Iraq. A Syrian army policed Iraq from a new garrison town built at al-Wasit. Syrian forces replaced Iraqi soldiers in all the eastern campaigns. The Arabs of Kufa and Basra were now treated as pensioned subjects of the empire they had founded.

In foreign policy, the caliphate resumed conquests on a massive scale. The early conquests, which made use of tribal migrations and the annual campaigns of Arab forces based in the garrison cities, were superseded by planned attacks on remote places, carried out with the aid of non-Arab forces. These new wars were not fought for tribal expansion but were imperial wars waged for world domination. They brought North Africa, Spain, Transoxania, and Sind into the Muslim empire. Three failed attempts to conquer Constantinople indicate the ambition to inherit the Roman Empire.

The caliphal court was also reorganized. In Mu'awiya's time, the caliph was surrounded by Arab chiefs. Now a chamberlain kept visitors in order and regulated daily business. The officials of the chancery, the officer of the royal seal, guards, and scribes, as well as Arab favorites, surrounded the ruler. Important governorships were still assigned to Arab leaders, but the business of government was conducted by professional administrators (both Arab and non-Arab) rather than by councils of Arab chiefs. The caliphate had transformed itself from tribal-based rule into an imperial government.

In administration, 'Abd al-Malik and al-Walid rebuilt roads, put in milestones, and reorganized the postal service. Large numbers of uniform tax seals were issued, suggesting a standardized procedure for producing them. Passports were issued with formulaic language invoking the name of God (the *basmala*) and stating that the document was "ordered by [name of caliph] commander of the believers" on a particular *hijra* date. Passports named the hierarchy of issuing authorities from caliph to scribe.

The Marwanids also arranged for the translation of the tax registers from Greek and Persian into Arabic. Résumés, copies, and reports appeared in Arabic. The changeover was made in 697 in Iraq, in 700 in Syria and Egypt, and shortly afterward in Khurasan. Umayyad administration also began to delineate a unique organizational identity. In the first decades of the Arab empire, administration had been carried out by Greek- and Persian-speaking officials inherited from the older empires. By 700, however, a new generation of Arabic-speaking clients came to power – an indication of a broad process of Arabization in the region. They and their descendants formed the secretarial backbone of the Arab-Muslim empire until the tenth century. With new personnel, the Marwanids carried out extensive censuses and land surveys and introduced empire-wide systematic record keeping and taxation. The caliphs then proceeded to reorganize the finances of various regions.

THE CRISIS OF THE DYNASTY AND THE RISE OF THE 'ABBASIDS

The assertion of a new form of Arab-Muslim imperium, however, did not allay political and social unrest. Tribal-factional struggles within the military elite continued. In the Sufyanid period, the Arab-Muslim forces were still identified along tribal lines (Qays or Yemen), but by the Marwanid period, they had become military factions. As generals took over governorships and appointed their kin and clients to office, the factionalism intensified. Syria had previously been governed by the caliph's kin. By the time of the third civil war, it was ruled by the generals. Syria was largely in the control of the Yemeni faction and the Jazira was largely controlled by the Qays.

Furthermore, the clients who served as soldiers in the armies and as administrators in the government bureaucracy demanded equality of status and privilege with the Arabs. Peasant converts claimed the right to exemption from the taxes levied on non-Muslims. In the face of these demands, caliphs did not implement a consistent policy. 'Abd al-Malik did not discriminate against clients, but he was opposed to the conversion of peasants. 'Umar II reversed this policy, accepted converts, and enrolled them in the army

The struggle among these competing interests came to a head in the reign of 'Umar II (717–20). 'Umar believed that the domination of one ethnic caste over other peoples was un-Islamic. The peoples who filled the armies and staffed the administration, the merchants and artisans who took a leading part in the propagation of Islam, would all have to be accepted as participants in the empire. The antagonisms between Arabs and non-Arabs would have to be dissolved into a universal Muslim unity. He felt that the empire could no longer be an Arab empire but had to be the imperium of all Muslims. He thus promoted the conversion of all of the peoples of West Asia to Islam and their acceptance as equals to Arabs.

In his actual policies, 'Umar demonstrated a pragmatic approach. He accepted the claim of the clients that all active Muslim soldiers (Arabs or not) were entitled to equal pay, and he also accepted the tax equality of all Muslims, but he implemented his decisions in ways that protected the interests of the state. Although converts claimed exemption from land and poll taxes as a form of equality with Arabs, 'Umar ruled that land taxes applied to all landowners regardless of social status and that both Arab-Muslim landlords and converts would have to pay them. The poll tax was to be paid only by non-Muslims, but Arab-Muslim settlers and converts were expected to pay the alms tax, which partially compensated the state for the loss of poll tax revenues.

Later caliphs attempted to implement these principles, but with very limited success. Throughout the late Umayyad period, the interest in reconciliation and justice conflicted with maintenance of the status quo; caliphal policy oscillated between tax concessions and cancellation of concessions.

These circumstances provoked opposition, and the stage was set for a third Muslim civil war. In Sunni religious circles, there was deep suspicion of and hostility toward the caliphate. Although supporting the caliphate in principle as the expression of the Muslim community, many Sunni religious leaders were alienated by the military and administrative policies of the regime and by its evident assumption of an imperial authority. Some Sunni thinkers wished to dissociate themselves from the regime, but not from the concept of the caliphate and its religious significance as the succession to the Prophet.

The Shi'is claimed that the caliphate rightly belonged to the family of 'Ali, chosen by God to teach Islam and to rule the Islamic community. They raised the hopes of many disgruntled Arabs and converts that out of this family would come a savior (Mahdi). If Banu Hashim had borne Muhammad and 'Ali, might they not produce the messiah to come? Since the second civil war, however, the 'Alids had scarcely been manifest in public, although various members were organizing underground conspiracies against the Umayyads. Between 736 and 740, Shi'i agitation finally broke out in Kufa, and a number of Kufans were seized by the police and executed. In 740, Zayd b. 'Ali, a grandson of Husayn, rebelled and was defeated.

Meanwhile, another branch of the Banu Hashim (the 'Abbasids) was biding its time. The 'Abbasids, like the 'Alids, were descended from an uncle of Muhammad, named 'Abbas, but their immediate claim to the caliphate rested on the allegation that a great-grandson of 'Ali, Abu Hashim, had bequeathed them leadership of the family and of the opposition movement. While the 'Alid branch of the family concentrated on Kufa with no success, the 'Abbasid branch proselytized in Khurasan, sending a succession of missionaries to mobilize all the opponents of the Umayyads. 'Abbasid agents agitated for revenge for 'Ali, for the overthrow of the Umayyads, and for a new era of peace and justice. From 744, the leading 'Abbasid agent, Abu Muslim, built up an underground movement and organized military support in Khurasan. The 'Abbasids attempted to exploit factional fighting among Arabs, messianic movements, and provincial rebellions. The Hashimite propaganda was an effort to find a common denominator for all the political hopes of a return to a just caliphate.

With the death of the Caliph Hisham in 743, the Umayyad regime collapsed. The later Umayyad caliphs had increasingly used the military power of Syria to control other Arab-Muslims and to stiffen the armies fighting on the frontiers of the empire with professional, battle-hardened troops. Garrison duties exposed Syrian troops in these areas to the brunt of warfare precisely at a time when the empire was suffering temporary setbacks. The Turks had driven the Muslim army from Transoxania. The Khazars (a nomadic people living beyond the Caucasus) had broken through Muslim defenses, defeated them at Ardabil, invaded Armenia, and penetrated as far as Mosul in 730. In 740, the Byzantines won a decisive victory over Umayyad invaders at Acrazas in Anatolia and destroyed a major Syrian army. Arab and Berber invaders were defeated in central France in 732. Berber rebellions under the banner of Kharijism broke out in North Africa and destroyed a Syrian army of 27,000 men. What remained of this army made its way to Spain, where parts of it helped establish the Spanish Umayyad dynasty. It took yet another Syrian army to quell these rebellions in 742. These defeats brought an end to the imperial phase of Arab-Muslim empire building and left Syria militarily depleted. Having based a century of rule on the ever-increasing power of the state, the Umayyad dynasty now found itself without the military basis for effective central government. From 744 to 750, not only the 'Abbasids but Shi'is, Kharijis, tribal factions, and ambitious provincial governors struggled to seize the throne.

In 747, the 'Abbasids were ready to move. In the villages of Khurasan – especially around Marw – Abu Muslim (the 'Abbasid agent) found the support he needed. Khurasan was in a fever of political agitation and eschatological expectation. Popular apocryphal writings called *Jafr* and *al-Malahim* foretold fateful battles, the imminent end of the world, the coming of the messiah (Mahdi), and the beginning of a new era of universal justice. In this atmosphere, Abu Muslim rallied peoples aggrieved by loss of status and by unjust taxes and, with only about 3,000 fighting men, defeated rival factions and seized the caliphate.

On the basis of support in Khurasan, the 'Abbasids prevailed. Yet after centuries of scholarly research, it is still not entirely clear who these supporters were. There are two principal theories. One is that the 'Abbasid organization was founded by Yamani Arabs and their clients in Kufa, whose agents in Khurasan mobilized the support of disaffected Persians. These Persians were Umayyad clients angry with the Umayyads because of the failure to reward them with a place on the military payrolls, and Persian converts to Islam who had been subjected to unjust taxation. Arabs were generally, but not exclusively, on the Umayyad side.

The alternative theory is that the 'Abbasids were supported primarily by Arabs from the villages around Marw, belonging to the Yamani faction. They had been part of the armies sent to conquer the eastern region but had in the intervening years settled in villages, become peasants, acculturated to Iran, and were then subject to taxation by the Persian *dihqans*.

A hybrid theory is the most persuasive. The 'Abbasid revolution was a revolt against the dominant alliance of the Arab military chieftains, mainly of the Qays faction, and high-ranking Iranian nobles. The 'Abbasids were supported by a coalition of middling landowners (both Arab and Persian). The Persian landowners and tax collectors were alienated by Umayyad policies excusing converts from the poll taxes. The Arab settlers and their clients were opposed to the Umayyads because they were subject to the tax-raising authority of the Persian *dihqans*. They were backed by masses of oppressed Arab and Iranian peasants. The 'Abbasid movement included Arabized Persians and Persianized Arabs who were ideologically united by their commitment to the family of the Prophet as the only legitimate caliphs and to the idea that Islamic identity should replace ethnicity and nobility as the basic principle of society.

Thus, the 'Abbasid movement was based on interest groups in an integrated society in which Arabs and Persians were assimilating to each other. On their victory, representing just one of a number of factions that had been competing for power, the 'Abbasids would face the Umayyad problem of translating the title of caliph into institutions of effective and legitimate dynastic rule.

CHAPTER 9

THE 'ABBASID EMPIRE

BAGHDAD

The first venture of the new regime was the creation of a new capital. From ancient times, Middle Eastern rulers had built new cities as headquarters for their armies and administrative staffs and as symbols of the advent of a new order. The rulers of the Assyrian Empire created the famous cities of Nineveh and Nimrud; the Sasanians founded Ctesiphon. In a strategic location on the main routes between Iraq, Iran, and Syria – in one of the most fertile parts of Iraq with ready access to the Tigris-Euphrates water system – the 'Abbasids built Baghdad to be their palace and administrative base. (See Map 3.)

Like its predecessors, Baghdad rapidly transcended the intentions of its founders and grew from a military and administrative center into a major city. The very decision to build the administrative center – called the City of Peace (Madinat al-Salam) – generated two large settlements in the vicinity. One was the extensive camp of the 'Abbasid army in the districts to the north of the palace complex (al-Harbiya), and the other, to the south (al-Karkh), was inhabited by thousands of construction workers brought from Iraq, Syria, Egypt, and Iran. Here were markets to provision the workers and their families and workshops to produce their clothes, as well as utensils, tools, and factories to supply the building materials for the construction project. The original Baghdad, then, was a three-part complex – the troop settlement in al-Harbiya, the working populations in al-Karkh, and the administrative city itself, Madinat al-Salam. No sooner was the City of Peace completed than the decisions of the caliphs to build additional palace residences and administrative complexes in the immediate vicinity stimulated the growth of additional quarters. Across the Tigris, the new palace district of al-Rusafa also promoted urban development.

Baghdad was the largest city in the history of the region; it was not a single city but a metropolitan center, made up of a conglomeration of districts on both sides

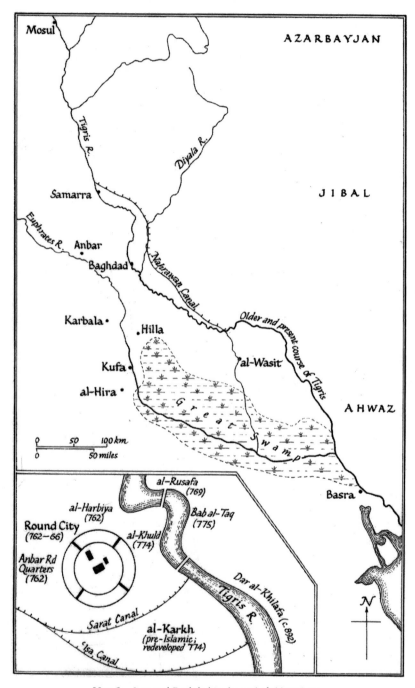

Map 3. Iraq and Baghdad in the early ʿAbbasid era.

of the Tigris River. In the ninth century, it measured about 25 square miles and had a population of between 300,000 and 500,000. It was ten times the size of Sasanian Ctesiphon, and it was larger than all of the settled places – cities, towns, villages, and hamlets combined – in the Diyala region. It was larger than Constantinople (which is estimated to have had a population of 200,000) or any other Middle Eastern city until Istanbul in the sixteenth century. In its time, Baghdad was the largest city in the world outside China.

Its vast size is an index of its importance in the formation of the 'Abbasid Empire, society, and culture. A capital city, Baghdad became a great commercial city for international trade and textile, leather, paper, and other industries. Its cosmopolitan population included people of different religions (Jews, Christians, Muslims, and secret pagans) and ethnicities (Persians, Iraqis, Arabians, Syrians, and Central Asians). Soldiers and officials, the workers who built the new city, the people who lived in the surrounding villages, and merchants from Khurasan and the East who engaged in the India traffic through the Persian Gulf also settled in Baghdad. Basrans seeking intellectual contacts and business fortunes; notables and landowners from Ahwaz; cloth workers from Khuzistan; prisoners of war from Anatolia; scholars from Alexandria, Harran, and Jundishapur; and Nestorian Christians from villages all over Iraq made Baghdad their home. Baghdad, then, was the product of the upheavals, population movements, economic changes, and conversions of the preceding century; it was the home of a new Middle Eastern society, heterogeneous and cosmopolitan, embracing numerous Arab and non-Arab elements, integrated into a single society under the auspices of an Arab-Islamic empire and religion. It provided the wealth and manpower to govern a vast empire; it crystallized the culture that came to be identified as Islamic civilization.

'ABBASID ADMINISTRATION: THE CENTRAL GOVERNMENT

The creation of Baghdad was part of the 'Abbasid strategy to cope with the problems that had destroyed the Umayyad dynasty. They had to build effective governing institutions and mobilize political support from Arab-Muslims, converts, and the non-Muslim communities that paid the empire's taxes. The new dynasty had to secure the loyalty and obedience of its subjects and to justify itself in imperial and Islamic terms. (See Figure 3.)

To deal with these problems, the 'Abbasids returned to the principles of 'Umar II. The 'Abbasids swept away Arab caste supremacy and accepted the universal equality of Muslims. Arab caste supremacy had lost its political meaning, and only a coalition regime – uniting Arab and non-Arab elements – could govern a Middle Eastern empire. The propagation of Arabic as a lingua franca, the spread of Islam, the conversion of at least some proportion of the population, the tremendous expansion of commercial activities, and the economic and demographic upheavals that set people free from their old lives and launched them on new careers in new

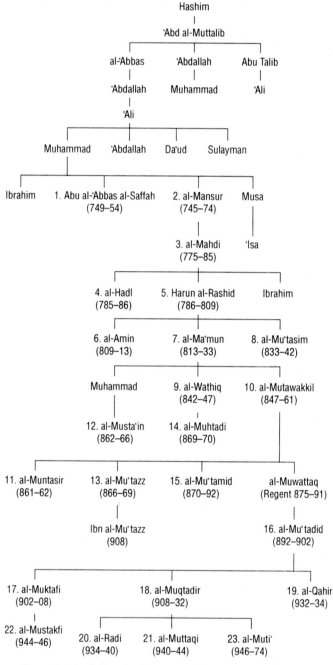

Figure 3. The ʿAbbasid caliphs to the disintegration of the empire.

cities such as Baghdad made possible an empire-wide recruitment of personnel and of political support for the new regime. Under the ʿAbbasids, the empire no longer belonged entirely to the Arabs – although they had conquered its territories – but belonged to all those peoples who would share in Islam and in the emerging networks of political and cultural loyalties that defined a new cosmopolitan Middle Eastern society.

Arabs continued to play important roles in the new regime. Until the reign of Harun al-Rashid (785–809), the regime was supported by the extensive ʿAbbasid family, whose members were appointed to top military and governmental posts in Baghdad, Kufa, Basra, and Syria. The early elites were further drawn from Arab notables, tribal leaders, and Khurasanian-Arab officers. The ʿAbbasids continued to use Arab troops as the central army (known as the *ahl-khurasan* units, which probably included non-Arab officers and soldiers too) and employed Arab forces in Syria, Mesopotamia, Yemen, India, Armenia, and the Byzantine frontiers.

The end of the conquests, however, meant that Arabs in Iraq, Khurasan, Syria, and Egypt could be retired from military service. The ʿAbbasids no longer needed vast reserves of manpower. Rather, they required only limited frontier forces and a central army to make occasional expeditions against the Byzantines and to suppress internal opposition. The ʿAbbasids established new forces, which – although partly Arab – were recruited and organized so that they would be loyal to the dynasty alone and not to tribal or caste interests. In this regard, they followed the practice of the late Umayyads, who had also tried to concentrate military and political power in the hands of selected Syrian regiments and had begun to replace provincial Arab forces with Syrians, non-Arab converts to Islam, clients, and local non-Arab, non-Muslim forces.

The inclusiveness of the ʿAbbasid regime was particularly evident in administration. The ʿAbbasid dynasty was Arab in the paternal line, because every ʿAbbasid caliph had a non-Arab mother; the judicial and legal life of Baghdad and other important cities was in Arab hands. The prominence of Arabs, however, was no longer a prescriptive right but was dependent on loyalty to the dynasty. Many of the scribes in the expanding ʿAbbasid bureaucracy were former Umayyad administrative personnel. Persians from Khurasan and Nestorian Christians (who made up a large proportion of the population of Iraq) were heavily represented. Jews were active in administrative and commercial activities. Shiʿi families were also prominent. Arab theologians, jurists, and literati were patronized and welcomed at court.

At the same time, the ʿAbbasids perpetuated Umayyad administrative and governmental precedents. Just as the Umayyads had inherited Roman and Sasanian bureaucratic practices and remnants of their old organizations, the ʿAbbasids inherited the traditions and the personnel of Umayyad administration. Clientele ties to the caliphs were the essence of government organization. At first, the ministries were just the clerical staffs of the leading officials, and the caliphs were consulted about everything. In time, however, the ad hoc, household character of the caliphate was substantially (although by no means entirely) superseded by a more rationalized form of administration. The business of the government became more routinized, and three types of services or bureaus (*diwans*) developed. The first was the chancery (*diwan al-rasa'il*), the records and correspondence office. The second was the bureaus for tax collection (such as *diwan al-kharaj*). Third, there were bureaus to pay the expenses of the caliphs' armies, court, and pensioners; the army bureau (*diwan al-jaysh*) was the most important of these. Gradually, the conduct of government grew more elaborate and more specialized. Each function – revenue, chancery, disbursement – was subdivided into a host of offices, and each office was subdivided to carry on auxiliary activities.

Alongside the bureaucratic staffs, the caliphs also appointed judges (*qadis*). Caliphal appointment of judges began in 642. They were at first multicompetent state officials dealing with justice, police, tax, and finance issues. Judges in the Umayyad period had a variety of administrative and political duties in addition to their judicial duties, including policing, tax collecting, making payments to soldiers, and preaching and leading the community in prayer. They adjudicated on the basis of Islamic law and local, customary law. Their status depended not only on government appointment but also on acceptance in legal circles and ties to local elites.

By the time of Caliph Harun al-Rashid, judges were usually selected from among the community leaders and scholars of Islamic law, and their duty was to apply this law to the civil affairs of the Muslim population, administer charitable endowments, perhaps collect the Muslim charity tax, and serve as a check on the activities of other officials. Other judicial officials dealt with state-related issues; customary law continued to be used in small communities. Harun was the first caliph to appoint a chief judge and adopt the Sasanian model of hierarchical judicial administration – a chief judge to oversee provincial judges, who in turn appointed delegates. The state also had a separate court (*mazalim*) – similar to courts of equity – to which subjects could appeal.

With this elaboration of functions and offices, the caliphs found themselves less and less able to directly supervise the business of the state. To keep the organization responsive to the will of the ruler, they instituted internal bureaucratic checks. Financial affairs were supervised by the controller's office (*diwan al-azimma*), which was originally attached to each bureau but later evolved into an independent bureau of the budget. Correspondence went through the drafting agency (the *diwan al-tawqi'*) for countersignature and then to the keeper of the seal (*khatam*). In a special administrative court (*mazalim*), the caliphs – advised by leading jurists – adjudicated fiscal and administrative problems. The official messenger and information service (*barid*) spied on the rest of the government.

Finally, the office of the chief minister (*wazir*) was developed to coordinate, supervise, and check on the operations of the bureaucracy. *Wazir* was the title originally applied to the secretaries or administrators who were close assistants of the caliphs and whose powers varied according to the wishes of their patrons. Under the Caliphs al-Mahdi (775–85) and Harun al-Rashid (786–809), the Barmakid family rose to particular prominence. Originally a Buddhist priestly family from Balkh, they were appointed as generals, provincial governors, and the tutors of young princes. Still, however powerful, the Barmakids were not chiefs of the whole administration but depended on the changing impulses of the caliphs for their positions. In 803, Harun al-Rashid executed the leading members of the family. Not until the middle of the ninth century did the minister become the chief of administration, with the combined duties of controlling the bureaucracy, nominating provincial officials, and sitting on the *mazalim* or administrative court.

This elaborate central government was the nerve center of the empire. From Baghdad, the caliphs maintained communications with the provinces. But despite the propensities of the central administration, the provinces were not all governed in a bureaucratic manner. The degree of control ran from highly centralized administration to loosely held suzerainty. The empire was tolerant and inclusive rather than monolithic.

PROVINCIAL GOVERNMENT

The centrally governed provinces were Iraq, Mesopotamia, Egypt, Syria, western Iran, and Khuzistan – the provinces physically closest to the capital. Khurasan was sometimes, but not always, included in this group. These provinces were organized to maximize the obedience of officials to the will of the central government and to assure the remittance of tax revenues from the provinces to the center. Governors' appointments were limited to a short term so that their careers would be entirely at the mercy of the caliphs. They were rotated to prevent them from developing local support. In addition, the powers of provincial governments were often divided among several officials. The governor was usually the military commander, and a different man was appointed by the central treasury to be in charge of taxation and financial affairs; yet another official headed the judiciary. These officials checked one another's powers, and all officials were subject to the supervision of the information service (*barid*).

The ideal of frequent rotation of governors, separation of civil and military powers, and inspection by the information service was difficult to implement. Governorships were often awarded in payment of political debts to warlords, generals, and members of the royal family who had acquiesced to the accession of a caliph or to his succession plans. Caliphs had to give these appointees wide latitude. In such cases, frequent rotation and the separation of civil and military functions might be waived.

Iraq remained the crucial agricultural, commercial, and financial base of the empire; the land and tax policies begun by the Umayyads were perpetuated. However, over the course of the first hundred years of 'Abbasid rule, the agricultural economy of Iraq was progressively undermined by underinvestment in irrigation and by the usurpation of tax revenues by high-ranking military officers, local notable families (sometimes dating back to pre-Islamic times), and tribal elites. Later efforts at reform failed to restore Iraqi revenues to earlier levels.

Syria was governed by 'Abbasid governors. These were initially family members, but, later, 'Abbasid clients and military officers were appointed. The 'Abbasids retained Umayyad military and administrative personnel. Syrian and Arabian military forces were active in the Byzantine wars. Umayyad nobles were welcome in the 'Abbasid court, and Umayyad clerks and some judges were employed. 'Abbasid governors worked to win the support of the local notables (*ashraf*), often Umayyads, who felt entitled to rule. They also dealt with Qays and Yamani tribal competition for benefits and influence. Tribal factionalism and apocalyptic hopes led to occasional Umayyad-led rebellions, but generally the Syrian notables reached an accommodation with the new rulers.

In Egypt, the Umayyads had begun and the 'Abbasids continued the process of centralizing administrative control. At the beginning of the eighth century, Syrian Arabs began to replace Coptic functionaries and to substitute taxation of individuals for communal levies. The 'Abbasids appointed Persian administrators and assigned assessment and collection of taxes at the local level to government officials. This made peasants directly responsible to the state and not to an intermediary notable. Although this arrangement had advantages in terms of central control, it also allowed local officials to embezzle revenues by falsely reporting that tax payments were in arrears or that there had been crop failures. Starting in the late eighth century, assessment and collection were separated. Government officials assessed but did not collect the taxes. Instead, the caliphate appointed a guarantor (*damin*), who was responsible for collection and payments to the state officers.

The guarantor could also collect rents. In effect, the state had created a new landlord elite that was responsible for taxes but was also given concessions for bringing land into cultivation. Ownership created incentives for the production of high-value crops and for using the peasants as laborers rather than as tenants.

Under the 'Abbasids, Khurasan also became a centrally administered province. In the Umayyad period, taxes were collected by Iranian lords, but by the 'Abbasid period, Iranian lordly families had been incorporated into the bureaucracy, and taxes were collected by the central government. As early as the reign of al-Mansur, Egyptian and Khurasanian documents were using the same formulas, suggesting a highly centralized, empire-wide administration.

Outside the directly administered provinces were affiliated regions that were scarcely, if at all, controlled by the central government. Geographically, these were the provinces of the Caspian highlands (Jilan, Tabaristan, Daylam, and Jurjan), the Inner Asian provinces (Transoxania, Farghana, Ushrusana, and Kabul), and most of North Africa. In some peripheral provinces, the caliphs appointed a supervising military governor and assigned a garrison to collect taxes and tribute payments. For example, until the middle of the ninth century, Armenia and Tabaristan had Arab governors who overawed the local rulers and collected tribute. These governors had no direct administrative contact with the subject people; the actual collection of taxes was in local hands.

In other cases, the caliphate merely confirmed local dynasties as "governors of the caliphs." Khurasan, which until 820 was directly ruled by caliphal appointees, came under the control of the Tahirid family (820–73). Officially, the Tahirids were selected by the caliphs, but the caliphs always confirmed the family heirs. The Tahirids paid very substantial tributes, but no one from the central government intervened to assure the payments or to inspect their administration. Transoxania under the Samanids was governed in the same way. The Samanids had been a local ruling family since Sasanian times, but in the wake of the incorporation of Transoxania into the Islamic empire, they converted to Islam. During the caliphate of al-Ma'mun (813–33), the ruling members of the family were named hereditary governors of Samarqand, Farghana, and Herat – without further supervision.

LOCAL GOVERNMENT

Local government similarly varied. Iraq was divided into a hierarchy of districts (called *kura, tassuj,* and *rustaq*). The *rustaq* was the bottom unit in the hierarchy and consisted of a market and administrative town surrounded by a number of villages. The same hierarchy and even the same names were used in parts of Khurasan and western Iran. In Egypt, the administrative structure was similar.

Local government was organized for taxation. Surveys were taken in the villages to determine the amount of land under cultivation, the crops grown, and their expected yield. The information was passed up to the central administration. The taxes for whole regions would be estimated, the sums divided up for each district, and demand notices sent out describing the responsibilities of each subdivision. Each subunit received its bill and divided it among the smaller units. At the next stage, taxes were collected, local expenses deducted, and the balance passed upward until the surplus eventually reached Baghdad.

This hierarchical administration did not encompass all cultivated lands. The crown lands – which included the estates of the former empires, church properties, reclaimed wastelands, and lands purchased or confiscated by the caliphate – were not part of the usual provincial tax administration. Such lands were very extensive in Iraq and western Iran.

Other lands (*iqta's*) were also cut off from regular provincial administration. Specifically, the *iqta' tamlik* was frequently (although not always) ceded out of wastelands, for the sake of stimulating agricultural investment. The concessionaire was expected to reclaim the land and assure its cultivation in return for a three-year grace period and a long-term reduction of taxes. Ultimately, such lands became private property, because a concession holder could pass it on to his heirs.

A second type, *iqta' istighlal*, resembled a tax farm. In this case, lands already in cultivation and part of the general revenue administration were assigned to individuals who agreed to pay the treasury a fixed sum of money in return for the right to tax the peasantry. The assignee's payment was assessed at a rate of ten percent (*'ushr*), but he was permitted to exact from the peasants full taxes at the land tax (*kharaj*) rates, which usually amounted to a third or a half of the value of the crop. The benefit given the assignee was the difference between what the peasants paid him and what he paid the government.

There were several reasons for making these kinds of grants. They were a way of paying off political debts to the 'Abbasid family, important courtiers, officials, and military officers who had claims on the state for rewards, pensions, or bribes for their support and cooperation. Such grants simplified administration by obviating the need for collecting revenues in the provinces, bringing the specie to Baghdad, and redistributing the income through yet other bureaus. Instead of keeping surveys and records for large areas, all that was necessary was the description of the assignment and the amount due. Nevertheless, before the middle of the ninth century, taxable lands were assigned with relative restraint, for they represented an important concession of state revenues and state powers. Never in this period were they assigned in lieu of payment of military salaries.

Regardless of the organizational forms of local government, local administration and tax collection posed delicate political problems. Despite the immense power of the bureaucratic organization, it was extremely difficult to make that power effective in the villages. The bureaucracy was admirably suited to the communication of orders and to clerical and financial tasks, but in the villages, the power of the state was limited by ignorance. How could the government tax the peasantry without knowing who owned the land, how much was produced, who had money, and who did not? How was the state to work its way through the millennia-old complications of landownership, water rights, and other legal matters? How was the state to know if crops were concealed? The state came to the villages with staffs of technical specialists, including surveyors to make land measurements, weighers and measurers to estimate the size of crops, and bankers and money changers to convert currencies or to give credits. It came with legal specialists – judges to adjudicate disputes, witnesses to transactions, registrars of deeds, and the like. Alongside the technicians came the specialists in violence – collectors, soldiers, police, extortionists, stool pigeons, and thugs. Fear was no small part of the business of tax collection.

Yet, even with all this, the potential for passive resistance and the problem of inadequate information could not be solved without the cooperation of local people. These included family patriarchs, village headmen (such as the *ra'is* in Iran or the *shaykh al-balad* in Egypt), and village landowners; they controlled a large part of the village land and were much richer than the average peasant, but not so wealthy as the great estate or *iqta'* holders. In Iraq and Iran, the *dihqans* included native elites and Arabs who had acquired land, village-dwelling and town-dwelling absentee landlords, grain merchants, and money changers who bought the peasants' crops or lent them money to pay their taxes.

These notables played an important intermediary role in the taxation process. As the most powerful people connected with the villages, they handled negotiations, made a deal on behalf of the peasants, and paid the taxes. The arrangement suited everyone. The bureaucratic agents were never absolutely sure how much money they could raise and wished to avoid the nuisance of dealing with individuals. The peasants did not have to confront the exorbitant demands of the tax collectors directly. The notables underestimated the taxes to the state, overestimated them to the peasants, and pocketed the difference. 'Abbasid officials understood perfectly well the importance of these people, whom they called their helpers (*'awan*). They understood that – for the ultimate tasks of assessment, division, and collection of taxes – the bureaucracy had to depend on people who were not subordinates, but whose cooperation had to be enlisted nonetheless.

Thus, the 'Abbasid imperial organization was a complex bureaucracy – highly elaborate at the center and connected with provincial and local forces throughout the empire. Yet, the arrangements between the central government and the provincial and local levels were not simply hierarchical. At each level, the business of administration was carried on by independent people. In some cases, these were princes or independent governors who controlled whole provinces, whereas in others, they were the local village chiefs and landowners without whom the central and provincial governments were helpless. Because the ties of government were not strictly hierarchical, a complex system of constraints and opportunities, obligations and loyalties, bound the central, provincial, and local notables to the regime.

These ties depended first of all on the fact that the army, the police, and the inspectors of the information system could compel obedience. Also, self-interest dictated the collaboration of village chiefs and landowners, because participation in the tax-collecting apparatus consolidated their local position. It increased their political importance; conferred on them the prestige, authority, and respect of the state; and provided financial opportunities. Apart from force and interest, class and clientele loyalties drew together central administrators and local elites. The officials of the central government were drawn from the provincial notable families. Provincial landowning and notable families sent their sons to careers in the central government. Merchant families maintained branches in Baghdad and facilitated financial contacts between the administrative center and the provinces.

Patronage and clienteles were crucial to this system. Central administrators appointed their provincial representatives, and patronage – fortified by ethnic, religious, regional, and family affiliations – helped to smooth the operations of the ʿAbbasid state. For example, a governor of Khurasan, Tahir (820–22), explained that only he could govern the province because all the notable families were allied to him by marriage and clientage. Clientele ties also crossed religious lines. Muslim converts at the center dealt with provincial cousins who remained Christians or Zoroastrians. Conversion to the new religion did not necessarily disrupt family, clientele, and regional ties. Thus, the ʿAbbasid policy of recruiting notables regardless of ethnic background not only soothed the conflicts that racked the Umayyad dynasty but was essential if a centralized government was to be built at all. Because effective administration was based on sympathetic communication between central officials and local notables, the wider the recruitment, the greater the possibility for effective rule. The ʿAbbasid Empire, then, was formed by a coalition of provincial and capital city elites. Sharing a common concept of the dynasty and the purposes of political power, they were organized through bureaucratic and other political institutions to impose their rule.

RESISTANCE AND REBELLION

This regime imposed itself not in a single moment but only after decades of political struggle. The process of empire building was not smooth and uninterrupted but depended on the forcible subjection of many dissident and unwilling populations. Mountainous provinces remote from Baghdad resisted subordination. The Caspian region (the rulers of Tabaristan and Daylam) and parts of Inner Asia (the semi-independent provinces of Kabul, Ushrusana, and Farghana) refused tribute or allegiance, obliging the caliphs to send military expeditions to recover their suzerainty. By the reign of al-Maʾmun (813–33), however, most of these places were incorporated into the empire and their rulers and officials converted to Islam. In North Africa, the tendency after 800 was toward independence, although local ruling houses recognized the suzerainty of the caliphate.

Arab opposition was also important. The old military caste – displaced by a single professional army and deprived of employment, salaries, and prestige – sporadically resisted the ʿAbbasid settlement. Syrian Arabs rebelled in 760 and were defeated. In Egypt, the ʿAbbasids established their own garrisons at al-Askar near Fustat, provoking Arab tribal fighting (785) and rebellions (793–94). Bedouins in Syria, Arabia, Sistan, Kirman, Fars, Khurasan, and particularly in upper Mesopotamia (where Arab and Kurdish outbreaks were virtually incessant) rebelled against the consolidation of any government that might restrict their autonomy. Until the beginning of the ninth century, bedouin rebels adopted Kharijism to articulate their opposition to the empire. From then on, Shiʿism became the main expression of tribal opposition to centralized government.

In Iran, local lords, *dihqans*, peasant villagers, and mountaineers maintained their own staccato opposition to the ʿAbbasid regime, sometimes led by former elites. Resistance to the caliphate took the form of syncretistic sects, blending Shiʿism and Mazdakism – perceived by the mainstream as heresies in both Islam and Zoroastrianism, respectively. The first of these Iranian rebellions was the rebellion of Bihafarid (a peasant leader near Nishapur), which spread widely in Khurasan in 747–50; he advocated a combination of Muslim ideas and the ancient worship of Ahura Mazda. The rebellion was put down by the ʿAbbasid governor Abu Muslim – significantly, at the request of the Zoroastrian priests (*mobads*), for it was a threat to the notables and to both Islamic and Zoroastrian beliefs.

This same Abu Muslim later became the symbol of religious and social opposition. His role in the ʿAbbasid revolution made him – in the popular imagination – a precursor of the messiah and inspired Shiʿi-Mazdakite syncretic heresies and rebellions in his name. The first of these broke out in the region of Nishapur under the leadership of a man named Sunpadh. Supported by the mountain peoples of Khurasan, it spread as far west as Rayy and Qum. Sunpadh preached that Abu Muslim was not dead but lived on in the company of Mazdak and the savior until he would return again.

Similar outbreaks followed in Rayy, Herat, and Sistan. The most important of these was the movement led by a self-styled prophet called al-Muqannaʿ (the Veiled One). Al-Muqannaʿ preached that he was God incarnate and that the spirit of God had passed from Muhammad to ʿAli to Abu Muslim to him. He would, he said, die and return to rule the world. His emphasis on the passage of the spirit and his return as imam was parallel to extremist Shiʿi views, and he was accused of advocating Mazdakite social doctrines – communism of money and community of women. Most of his support came from peasant villages.

Insofar as the ʿAbbasid regime in Iran depended on the collaboration of local notables who were both Muslims and Zoroastrians, the empire presented itself as a dual orthodoxy based on a joint Muslim-Zoroastrian elite. Thus, resistance to the consolidation of the empire cast itself in the form of syncretic religious heterodoxy. The unusual degree of religious ferment may have resulted from the disorganization of both the older religions (Zoroastrianism and Christianity) and the newer religion (Islam) in the wake of the Arab-Muslim invasions and decades of warfare in Transoxania. The eighth century was a time of unique freedom for religious invention as part of social and political conflict.

Throughout the ʿAbbasid Empire, the most profound opposition to the caliphate took the form of Shiʿism. The Shiʿis had supported the ʿAbbasid movement before it came to power, expecting that one of the heirs of ʿAli would succeed the Umayyads, but the ʿAbbasids disappointed these expectations by seizing the caliphate for themselves. Once in power, the ʿAbbasids were resisted by Muhammad al-Nafs al-Zakiyya – a Shiʿi claimant to the caliphate who seems to have had support among the families of Muhammad's Medinan companions. There were a number of other minor Shi'i rebellions in Basra, Kufa, Mecca, and Medina. A major Shi'i rebellion, backed by the bedouin tribes of upper Mesopotamia, took place between 813 and 816. In the early tenth century, the Isma'ili movement (an offshoot of Shi'ism) would provoke a new wave of anti-'Abbasid provincial resistance.

The 'Abbasid Empire, as a political system, has to be understood in terms of its organization, its social dynamics, its political concepts, and its opponents. As an empire, it was a regime governing a vast territory composed of small communities. Each community was headed by its notables: headmen, landowners, and other men of wealth and standing, who characteristically were allied to superiors and patrons with positions in the provincial or central governments. Government organization, communication, and tax collection was bureaucratic in form, but the social mechanisms that facilitated the organization work were the contacts between central officials and provincial elites. The bureaucracy mobilized the skills and social influence of prominent persons throughout the empire and put these assets at the disposal of Baghdad. This system of alliances was justified as an expression of God's will. By God's will – expressed both in Muslim and in pre-Islamic cultural terms – the exalted person of the caliph reigned in expectation of passive obedience from all his subjects.

However, not all peoples and provinces of the empire submitted to the imperial order. Mountain peoples, semisedentarized villagers, peasants, nomads, and segments of the town populations (including strata of the upper as well as the lower classes) refused to accept the system. They denied its legitimacy and rebelled against it, although they could not overthrow it. Nor could they be altogether repressed. The 'Abbasid regime was locked into constant struggle with its opponents.

CHAPTER 10

DECLINE AND FALL OF THE ʿABBASID EMPIRE

THE DECLINE OF THE CENTRAL GOVERNMENT

The very processes that led to the rise of the early Islamic empire, its elites, and its cultural forms resulted in its collapse and transformation. The decline of the ʿAbbasid Empire began even in the midst of consolidation. While the regime was strengthening its military and administrative institutions and encouraging a flourishing economy and culture, other forces were set in motion that would eventually unravel the ʿAbbasid Empire.

As early as Harun al-Rashid's reign (786–809), the problems of succession had become critical. Harun bequeathed the caliphate to his elder son, al-Amin, and the governorship of Khurasan and the right to succeed his brother to his younger son, al-Maʾmun. The independence of Khurasan under al-Maʾmun was probably set up by Harun to satisfy the demands of the eastern Iranian warlords. With the death of Harun, al-Amin attempted to displace his brother in favor of his own son. Civil war resulted. Al-Amin was backed by the Baghdadi population (the *abna'*). These forces may have included the descendants of the original ʿAbbasid forces from Khurasan but most likely were forces rallied for the civil war on the basis of royal patronage and not on any abiding ethnic or historical loyalty. Al-Maʾmun turned to Arab forces in Khurasan and to the independent Khurasanian warlords. In a bitter civil war, al-Maʾmun defeated his brother and in 813 assumed the caliphate. With Maʾmun's conquest of Baghdad, the empire was dominated by Khurasanians.

Once in office, al-Maʾmun attempted to deal with his unreconciled opponents by means of a double policy. One goal was to restore the legitimacy of the caliphate by manipulating Shiʿi loyalties and Muʿtazili theological doctrines to give the caliphate control over religious affairs. (See Chapter 13.) This policy failed and thereby deprived the caliphate of an important measure of popular support.

Al-Maʾmun also adopted a new military policy. To win control of the caliphate, he had depended on the support of a Khurasanian lord, Tahir, who in return was made governor of Khurasan (820–22) and general of ʿAbbasid forces throughout the empire, with the promise that the offices would be inherited by his heirs. Tahir's forces included Khurasanian warlords and their followers, as well as Turks, Bukharis, and Khwarizmis from the Transoxus region. From this point, the Arab component in the military disappeared. Furthermore, despite the momentary usefulness of the arrangement, the concession of a hereditary governorship defeated the caliphal objective of integrating provincial notables into the central government. Now the empire was to be governed by an alliance of the caliph with the most important provincial lord.

To offset the power of the Tahirids and regain direct control of the provinces, the caliphs were eager to create new military forces. Thus, al-Maʾmun and al-Muʿtasim (833–42) raised forces of two types. The first were intact units (*shakiriyya*) under the leadership of their local chiefs from Transoxania, Armenia, and North Africa. Although the soldiers were not directly beholden to the caliphs, they served as a counterweight to the Tahirids. The second type of forces was Turkish slaves (*ghilman* [plural]), who were purchased or captured individually in the frontier regions. They were then grouped into regiments. For the sake of efficiency, morale, and a balance of power between the regiments, each lived in its own neighborhood, had its own mosque and markets, and was trained, supplied, and paid by its commander. Thus, slave regiments also became self-contained units that gave their primary loyalty to their officers rather than to the caliphs.

The system of recruiting, training, and employing slave soldiers was a major innovation in Middle Eastern history and the beginning of an institution that would characterize many later Muslim regimes. The pressing military and political need for loyal troops directed the attention of the caliphs to long-established precedents for the employment of military forces from peripheral regions and marginal populations. The Romans had recruited Illyrians and Germans. Since Umayyad times, the caliphs and governors of the Arab-Muslim empire had raised supplementary troops in eastern Iran and had depended on servile, client, and even slave troops for their personal bodyguards. The new system of slave regiments was a rationalization of earlier practices that became the centerpiece of ʿAbbasid military organization.

These new regiments strengthened the hand of the caliphs, but the Transoxanian and Turkish soldiers soon ran afoul of the Baghdadi populace and of the former Arab soldiers in the Baghdadi army. Bloody clashes ensued. Eventually, Caliph al-Muʿtasim built a new capital (Samarraʿ) about 70 miles north of Baghdad to isolate the troops from the masses. Although Baghdad remained the cultural and commercial capital of the region, from 836 to 870, Samarraʿ was the military and administrative headquarters of the caliphate.

The new city only created further difficulties. The caliphs, who had hoped to avoid clashes between the populace and the troops, instead became embroiled in rivalries among the various guard regiments. The officers took civilian bureaucrats into their patronage, won control of provincial governorships, and eventually attempted to control succession to the caliphate itself. Regimental rivalries led to anarchy. Between 861 and 870, all the leading officers were killed and the troops turned to banditry. The employment of slave armies further alienated the caliphate from the populace it ruled. Whereas the early 'Abbasid Empire had depended on the military support of its own subjects, the late empire tried to dominate its peoples with foreign troops.

In the same period, changes in administrative organization also reduced the capacity of the central government to control the empire. These changes in administration were due partly to the interference of the army and partly to the rise of independent provincial powers, but they were also due to overwhelming internal stresses inherent in the normal operation of the bureaucracy. In 'Abbasid government, all high-ranking officers employed their personal followers to do their staff work. To learn the art of being an accountant or scribe, a young man had to enter the service of a master, live in his household, and become a dedicated personal servant. He owed his master respect and obedience for life, and the patron was obliged not only to train him but to protect him and advance his career. In time, the bureaucracy came to be dominated by cliques and factions formed among the functionaries, whose main interest was to exploit bureaucratic office for private gain. The bureaucracy ceased to serve the interests of the ruler and the empire and began to act on behalf of the personal and factional interests of the scribes.

By the late ninth century, the numerous small cliques attached to many leading officials had become polarized into two great factions: the Banu Furat and the Banu Jarrah. Each of these factions was built around a *wazir* and his relatives and clients. The families also had a larger following based on social and ideological affiliations. The Banu Jarrah faction was composed mainly – although not exclusively – of Nestorian Christians or Christian converts, often educated in the monastery of Dayr Qunna in southern Iraq. By the middle of the ninth century, this faction had already grown powerful enough to influence state policy. In 852, Caliph al-Mutawakkil (847–61) was persuaded to assure Christians freedom of religion, freedom from military service, and the right to construct churches; he also gave the Nestorian catholicos full jurisdiction over all Christians. The caliph conceded the right of converts to inherit the property of parents who were still Christians, although Muslim law did not permit such transfers. These concessions, however, were soon revoked. The other major faction, the Banu Furat, was mainly composed of Baghdadi Shi'is.

The chiefs of these factions eventually gained control of the entire government service. In the reign of al-Mutawakkil (847–61), the *wazirs* were put in charge of all the administrative bureaus. Although they could be appointed and removed by the caliph at will, in practice the caliphs rarely intervened in the routine operations of the bureaucracy. A minister and his faction would come to power by intrigues and by bribing the caliph and other influential courtiers. Their main concern then would be to exploit their offices, earn back their bribes, and prepare for future hard times by various frauds, such as padded payrolls, false bookkeeping, illegal speculations, and taking bribes. The officials regarded their positions as property rights that they bought, sold, and exploited for private gain.

When a faction had been in power and was known to have become rich, the caliph and the opposing faction would be eager to seize the fortunes accumulated by the incumbents. The caliph would then appoint a new minister; a rival group would come to power, which would then confiscate the assets of the defeated party. Some of the money would go to the caliph and back to the treasury, but some of it went into the pockets of the victorious faction. Special bureaus were set up to handle the reclaimed monies: the *diwan al-musadarat* for confiscated estates and the *diwan al-marafiq* for confiscated bribes. The caliphate could maintain only a modicum of influence by rotating the leading factions in office and using each change of government as an occasion to extort the resources stolen by the faction last in power.

The cost, however, was extremely high, for the central government was forced to look to new administrative devices to counterbalance the political and financial losses occasioned by a corrupt bureaucracy. One method was to distribute or sell tax-collecting rights (*iqta's*) to soldiers, courtiers, and officials, who collected the taxes ordinarily due from the peasants and paid a portion to the central government. Although it brought in a short-term income, selling *iqta's* reduced long-term revenues and subverted the normal operation of provincial and local administration. In addition, *iqta's* acted as crystals to collect and aggregate small holdings. Peasants, under pressure from the tax bureaus, would appeal for protection to the powerful property holders and sign over their lands. The practice was called commendation (*talji'a*) or protection (*himaya*). The growth of large landed estates further diminished the areas under routine administration. Instead of taxing peasants in a relatively direct way, the government found itself dealing more and more often with powerful local landowning notables, who reduced the task of the administration to the collection of negotiated fees. In addition to the sale of *iqta's*, the central government introduced tax farming in Iraq and western Iran. To obtain revenues in advance, the government sold the right to collect taxes to tax farmers. Tax farming, however, was not merely a financial arrangement; it was a substitute form of administration. The tax farmer not only paid a sum to collect taxes but also agreed to maintain local administration, meet all the government's local expenses, invest in irrigation, and support the local police. Although government inspectors tried to protect the peasants from abuse, the basic apparatus of local administration was being displaced by private governments. Through the distribution of *iqta's* and the sale of tax farms, the government forfeited its control over the revenue-bearing countryside.

PROVINCIAL AUTONOMY AND THE RISE OF INDEPENDENT STATES

With the decline of the military and financial capacities of the central government, the provinces became increasingly independent. The peripheral provinces – governed by tributary rulers – freed themselves altogether from their subordination to the empire, and many of the core provinces – once directly administered by Baghdad – became peripheral provinces under the control of semi-independent governors. (See Table 3.)

The devolution of provincial powers occurred in two main ways. In some cases, Turkish guard officers usurped provincial governorships and made themselves independent of the central government. Egypt, between 868 and 905, came under the control of the Tulunid dynasty. The founder of the dynasty, Ahmad b. Tulun (r. 868–84), originally a subgovernor of Egypt, built up a private slave army, seized control of Egypt's finances, and established his own dynasty – all while being protected by patrons at the caliphal court. In other areas, governors chipped away at the prerogatives of the central government; some ceased to remit tax revenues; others negotiated a fixed payment in return for their assignments.

Elsewhere, the decline of central authority triggered popular resistance to central control. Rebellions in Armenia, Azarbayjan, and Arran were led by local princes. In the middle of the ninth century, there was a mass uprising of frontier soldiers (*ghazis*) in Sijistan (southeastern Iran) under the leadership of the Saffarids. The Saffarids took control of Sijistan, Kirman, and northern India; seized Khurasan from the Tahirids; and then conquered western Iran and invaded Iraq. Although they were defeated in Iraq, the caliphate recognized Saffarid control of Khurasan and most of western Iran. The Saffarid victory displaced the older landowning and administrative elites with military leadership. Iraq was the scene of a prolonged revolt of the Zanj slave laborers led by dissident 'Abbasid notables, by agricultural capitalists, and by an alliance of Bahrayni and Basran merchants involved in long-distance trade.

Despite the loss of control of Egypt and Iran, the caliphate was able to reassert itself. In 900, the Samanid rulers of Transoxania defeated the Saffarids. The Samanid victory was a great gain for the 'Abbasids, because the Samanids represented the same landowning and administrative notables as those who governed the 'Abbasid Empire and because they restored cooperation between a major independent provincial dynasty and the 'Abbasid central government. In 905, the caliphs also managed to defeat the Tulunid dynasty in Egypt and Syria. The restoration of central authority, however, was short lived. With the bureaucracy in disarray, the caliphate could not use its temporary military victories to reorganize the empire. These victories were but a pause in a downward course that became headlong between 905 and 945.

In the early decades of the tenth century, Shi'ism again became the leading form of popular resistance to the 'Abbasid Empire. Isma'ilism was preached in

Table 3. *Middle Eastern provincial regimes: the 'Abbasid Empire and the post-imperial era*

	Iraq	Western Iran	Khurasan	Mesopotamia (Mosul)	Egypt	Syria
700	'Abbasids, 750–945	'Abbasids, 750–934	'Abbasids, 750–821	'Abbasids, 750–905	'Abbasids, 750–868	'Abbasids, 750–945
800			Tahirids, 821–73 Saffarids, 873–900		Tulunids, 868–905	
900		Buwayhids, 934–c. 1040	Samanids, 900–99	Hamdanids, 905–91	'Abbasids, 905–35 Ikhshidids, 935–69	
	Buwayhids, 945–1055				Fatimids, 969–1171	Partitioned between Hamdanids in Aleppo, 945–1004, and Fatimids in Damascus, 978–1076
				'Uqaylids, 992–1096		
			Ghaznavids, 999–1040 (in Afghanistan, 961–1186)			
1000						Mirdasids, 1023–79, in Aleppo
	Saljuqs, 1055–1194	Saljuqs, 1055–1194	Saljuqs, 1038–1157			
						Saljuq conquest, 1078; Saljuqid states, 1078–1183; crusader states, 1099–1291
1100				Zangids, 1127–1222	Conquest by Saladin, 1169	
					Ayyubids, 1169–1250	Ayyubids, 1183–1260
1200	Mongols, 1258	Nomadic invasions culminating in Mongols, 1256–1353	Mongols, Il-Khans, 1256–1353		Mamluks, 1250–1517	Mamluks, 1260–1517
					Ottomans, 1517–1805	Ottomans, 1517–1918

southern Iraq, Bahrain, Syria, Mesopotamia, Yemen, Daylam, eastern Iran, and North Africa. The Isma'ilis seem to have had a central directorate, but the Isma'ili missions tended to adapt to the prior religious convictions and understandings of the persons being proselytized. The movement addressed itself to all classes of the population, whether peasants in Iraq and Syria, bedouins in Arabia, villagers in Iran, Berbers in North Africa, or the upper classes of eastern Iran.

Isma'ili religio-political agitation led to a series of rebellions called the Qarmatian movement. Around 900, there were peasant jacqueries in Iraq and bedouin revolts in Syria and northeastern Arabia; these led to the formation of a Qarmatian state in Bahrain. In the 920s, the Qarmatians attacked Basra and Kufa, threatened Baghdad, cut the pilgrimage routes, pillaged Mecca, and took the black stone of the Ka'ba. Shi'ism also inspired resistance to the 'Abbasids in Mesopotamia, where Arab bedouins under the leadership of the Hamdanid family extended their influence southward from Mosul to Baghdad, westward into northern Syria, and northward into Armenia.

In North Africa, another offshoot of the Isma'ili movement founded the Fatimid dynasty (909), which conquered all of North Africa and Egypt by 969. Fatimids claimed to be the rightful successors to the Prophet, not only for their own provinces but for the whole of the Muslim world. They adopted the title of caliph, thus breaking the symbolic unity of the Muslim community. They were followed by the Umayyad dynasty in Spain and by other North African states (see Part III) that thus debased the title, prestige, and legitimacy of the 'Abbasid dynasty.

In the Caspian province of Daylam, Shi'i refugees fleeing 'Abbasid persecution converted the local people to Islam. In 864, the Daylam Shi'is declared their independence from the caliphate, forced out the 'Abbasid governor, and established an independent state. In the early tenth century, a local Daylamite ruler named Mardawij b. Ziyar conquered most of western Iran. When he was killed in 937, his empire was inherited by the Daylamite mercenaries in his service, led by the Buwayhid brothers, who established their dominion in the region.

Other governors and warlords also seized extensive territories. By 935, the caliphate had lost control of virtually all of its provinces except the region around Baghdad. Administratively and militarily helpless, the caliphs could only appeal for protection to one or another of the provincial forces or play them off against one another. In 936, to stave off the enemies pressing in on Baghdad, the caliphs created the post of general-in-chief (*amir al-umara'*) and divested themselves of all actual power – except the formal right to select the most powerful of their subjects as chief of state. After a complex, many-sided struggle, the Buwayhids took control of Baghdad in 945. The caliphs were allowed to continue in nominal authority – indeed, the 'Abbasid dynasty lasted until 1258 – but they no longer ruled; the 'Abbasid Empire had ceased to exist.

The disintegration of the 'Abbasid Empire into a number of independent provincial regimes implied vast changes in the organization of society. The emergence of a slave military elite and the new property-based form of administration assured not only the breakup of the empire but also the transfer of power from old to new elites. Early ʿAbbasid government had been built on a coalition of the central government staffs with provincial landowning and other notable families. The empire attracted into central government service the scions of provincial families whose contacts and goodwill served to unify the empire and make the central government effective in the provinces. Over time, however, the staffs of the central administration tended increasingly to be composed of the descendants of former scribes, rather than being drawn from provincial families. As generations of scribes succeeded each other, the bureaucracy became a city-based organization, scarcely connected to the provinces. It ceased to represent the diverse populations of the empire. Moreover, the introduction of tax farming, which required large investments, favored the interests of merchants wealthy from involvement in slave, grain, and international trade. Bankers who could raise the necessary sums and channel them into state investments became politically ever more important. Thus, a merchant elite – the product of the empire's fiscal centralization, tax-collecting methods, and the opportunities it offered for worldwide trade – began to displace the scribal class, with its provincial contacts, as the political mainstay of the central government.

The decline of the central government brought in its wake the ultimate destruction of the provincial landowning notables who had originally supported the ʿAbbasid Empire. The rise of military warlords and of a new capital-city-based financial and administrative elite, as well as the development of new forms of land tenure (including *iqtaʿ* assignments and tax farms) brought to the countryside a new elite, backed by the waning but still significant powers of the central government, to compete with the old provincial notables. In many regions a new class of large land controllers and landowners foisted on the countryside by central government policies displaced the small-scale landholding notables of the villages.

These extensive political and social changes were accompanied by widespread economic regression. In the course of the late ninth and early tenth centuries, the economy of Iraq was ruined. For more than a century, the caliphate had neglected investment in irrigation and reclamation projects. Irrigation in the Tigris region was severely damaged by almost incessant warfare, and large districts became depopulated. The distribution of *iqtaʿs* and the creation of tax farms removed the incentives for maintaining rural productivity. In southern Iraq, the slave rebellions also led to agricultural losses. Although the early Buwayhid rulers attempted to restore canals and to reclaim abandoned lands, political instability and fiscal exploitation ruined the countryside. Iraq, once the most prosperous area in the region, became one of the poorest and would not recover its agricultural prosperity until the twentieth century.

Iraq also suffered from declining international trade. The Qarmatian rebellions hurt the trade of the Persian Gulf and the trade between Arabia and Iraq. The disruption of the caliphate interfered with the international routes that brought goods from the Far East and South Asia to Baghdad for transshipment to the Mediterranean. In the late tenth century, the Fatimid regime helped to promote an alternative international route through the Red Sea and Cairo, which also damaged the commercial prosperity of Iraq.

Other provinces were similarly in decline. Mesopotamia – which had been settled in the seventh century by large numbers of bedouins – suffered economically from the encroachment of pastoralism on agriculture. In the late eighth century, peasants suffering from bedouin raids and excessive taxation began to abandon the land. In the course of the ninth century, there was a regression of sedentary life under nomadic pressure. The emergence of the Hamdanid dynasty ratified the dominance of pastoral over sedentary peoples.

Egypt, however, continued to prosper. The landowning elites formed in the ninth century continued in power through the Tulunid phase and into the Fatimid period. These elites invested in the growing of flax and the manufacture of linens. There was a government factory to produce embroidered fabrics for official use (*tiraz*), some private factories, and some cottage production. This opened up employment for weavers, dyers, tailors, and merchants. Egypt also produced wines, woolens, and papyrus and continued to export grain to the Hijaz. Iran also maintained its high levels of urban and agricultural development well into the eleventh century.

Thus, the breakup of the 'Abbasid Empire was at once a political, a social, and an economic transformation. It led to the substitution of small states for a single, unified empire. The bureaucratic and small landowning elites who favored centralized government were replaced by large-scale landowners and military lords who opposed it. The overall decline of the economy further contributed to the weakening of the empire. Finally, the military, administrative, and cultural policies of the empire themselves led to its collapse and the eventual formation of a new type of state and society.

COSMOPOLITAN ISLAM: THE ISLAM OF THE IMPERIAL ELITE

CHAPTER 11

INTRODUCTION: RELIGION AND IDENTITY

The delineation of Arabic-Islamic religion and culture and Muslim identities was a centuries-long process. Its social basis was the integration of Arab-Muslim, convert, and non-Muslim populations in the cities founded or settled by the Arab-Muslims. Mecca, Medina, Damascus, Kufa, Basra, Baghdad, and other cities were the homes of new Islamic societies that integrated the cultures of Arabia and the conquered peoples. The new civilization amalgamated Arabian language, poetry, and religion and late antique imperial symbols and literary and artistic cultures, as well as Jewish, Christian, and Zoroastrian religious values and family and communal institutions.

Islamic identities developed only slowly, and some scholars have questioned if there was a "Muslim" identity at all in the years after the death of Muhammad. If not, when did a Muslim identity come into being? One theory is that the conquerors first identified themselves not as Muslims but as a community of believers, a coalition of peoples of faith fighting the enemies of God. They were an assembly of monotheists, and the people of each faith had their own book and their own laws. Only after a century did they accept Muhammad as their prophet and the Quran as their holy book. The idea of a multireligious community was indeed implied in Muhammad's early teaching, but with the struggles for power in Medina and the exile or execution of the most powerful Jewish clans, it is not likely that this concept lasted even to the end of Muhammad's life. In Medina, the revelation of new ritual and family laws and of a sacred Arabian history for Muslims already implied the beginnings of a separate communal identity.

Moreover, there is no Middle Eastern precedent for a collectivity of religious groups. Each religious group regarded itself as the possessor of the true religion and the others as false – even though they held similar beliefs. As later polemics show, their clerics vigorously defended each religious group's monopoly on the truth. Also, the later incorporation of Christian tribes (such as the Taghlib) and

Persian regiments into the conquering Arab armies indicates not a multireligious army but Arab-Muslim tribal forces reinforced by the inclusion of captured or defeated soldiers as clients (*mawali*).

Another theory is that the initial movement was not Muslim but rather a movement of sectarian Jews. Only later did Islam become a distinct religion based on a new version of monotheistic concepts. From this perspective, the story of Arabia and Muhammad was invented later to demonstrate by historical narrative the mythical, doctrinal, and other beliefs of Muslims and their superiority to religious rivals.

This theory too does not stand up to the evidence. The Arab conquerors were from the beginning identified as Muslims, followers and heirs of the Arabian Prophet Muhammad with a distinctive religion of their own. Non-Muslim sources of the seventh century indicate a distinctive cult – one God, a sacred place in Arabia, a teacher named Muhammad, a holy book, the name *muhajirun*, and a calendar based on the Christian year 622 as the year one. Non-Muslims knew Muhammad as the teacher whose laws forbade the consumption of wine and carrion and who condemned fornication. They knew that the conquerors had their own places of worship and prayed in the direction of the Ka'ba in Mecca. They depicted the new rulers as monotheists, but deniers of the divinity of Christ and hostile to images.

Studies of papyri, inscriptions, coins, and archeological excavations indicate the early existence of an Islamic identity. A papyrus of 642 included the phrase, "In the name of Allah," and a document of 643 shows that the Arab-Muslims were dating by an era beginning in 622. Sasanian-type Arab coins from 651–52 were inscribed, "In the name of God," and later coins of 676–78 bore the inscription, "Allah is the lord of judgment." Early inscriptions in rock were permeated by expressions of Quranic piety, declarations of faith, and requests for forgiveness and compassion.

Furthermore, there is Arabic literary evidence for the existence of mosques in Muhammad's lifetime and soon after. The architectural elements of the mosque date to the era of the Prophet and the Umayyads. Mosques are attested for Medina in the time of the Caliph 'Umar (634–44), rebuilt in 665; Fustat (Cairo) in 641–42; Basra in 665; Jerusalem in the 660s; Kufa in 675; and Qayrawan in 670. An elevated platform for the preacher (*minbar*) goes back to Muhammad; a *minbar* in Damascus is attested for 657, and 'Ali had one in Kufa. Caliph Mu'awiya (661–80) in 665 put it on a six-step base. A royal enclosure (*maqsura*) is described for Damascus and Basra by 665 and was probably introduced by the Umayyad caliphs. The arrangements for mosques descended from Greco-Roman temples, churches, and synagogues. Like earlier places of worship, mosques had a distinctive orientation (*qibla*), a niche to mark a sacred place (*mihrab*), a seat of honor (*minbar*), and a place for ablutions in an exterior courtyard. Early Muslim religious buildings were distinctive because they were not decorated with images. However, archeological evidence only confirms the building of mosques from the construction of the Dome of the Rock in Jerusalem in 692 and thereafter.

Thus, in the seventh century Islamic identity was based on the Quran, the memory of the Prophet, and the collective experience of Arab-Muslim peoples as conquerors. The Islamic presence was asserted in documents, inscriptions, and the construction of places of worship, but there was little development of the political, ideological, religious, or cultural dimensions of this identity. Neither the caliphate nor the holy men and scholars had yet generated the public symbols and the literary content of Islam. Until the reign of 'Abd al-Malik (685–705), the caliphate scarcely defined itself publicly in Muslim terms. Hadith, law, theology, and history were circulated orally but were not compiled in written form until late in the seventh century; they were organized into books in the middle decades of the eighth century.

Islamic civilization, then, dates to the time of the Prophet Muhammad, the revelation of the Quran, and the first Muslim community in Medina and Mecca, and it was perpetuated throughout the first century after Muhammad's death and ever after. The Islam we recognize, however, is the elaboration of these teachings, carried out in later centuries – not only in the original home of Islam in Arabia but throughout the whole of the vast region from Spain to Inner Asia conquered by the Arab-Muslims. Islamic religion came to encompass not only the Quran and the example of Muhammad but a vastly expanded range of religious study and practices – including law, theology, and mysticism – developed in numerous schools and subcommunities. Furthermore, religion was part of a larger civilization encompassing poetry and belles lettres, arts, philosophy, and sciences, which would be the cultural expressions of the new Islamic empire and societies.

There were two principal foci of Islamic religious and cultural development in the postconquest era. One was Islam as expressed by the caliphate, the court, political elites, and the literati and artists patronized by the government. The court milieus contributed especially to Islamic art, architecture, philosophy, science, and Iranian and Hellenistic forms of literature in Arabic. The other was Islam as the religious beliefs and moral and social values of the Muslim urban populations – as expressed by the companions of the Prophet and their successors, the learned and holy men of Islam. The city milieus contributed to the literatures of Quranic exegesis, law, mysticism, and theology in conjunction with an Arabic belles lettres. Some subjects – such as poetry, theology, and history – were cultivated in both milieus. In the chapters that follow, we will consider first the cultural production and Islamic identities of the caliphal elites and then the Islam of the literati, the scholars, and the holy men. Their different understandings and experiences of Islamic identity coexisted and sometimes overlapped.

CHAPTER 12

THE IDEOLOGY OF IMPERIAL ISLAM

With the centralization of state power came a new rhetoric of legitimacy. The early caliphate had been a series of individual reigns deeply dependent on the religious qualities of the caliphs, and their personal connection to the Prophet. After the first four caliphs, the various contenders for the position adopted different claims. 'Ali and his descendants claimed the right to the caliphate as a matter of family relation to the Prophet, the Kharijis on the basis of religious purity, and others on the basis of their Meccan tribal heritage. The Caliph Mu'awiya asserted the legitimacy of his reign in terms of Arabian tribal culture, but after the second civil war 'Abd al-Malik based his claim to rule on his services to Islam.

At the same time, the caliphs adopted the ancient symbols of divinely granted rule expressed in poetry and literature, philosophy and science, and art and architecture. To define the authority of the regime and the legitimacy of the ruling classes, they propagated a cosmopolitan culture implicitly wider in scope than Islam. A literary and philosophical culture presented a vision of the universe as a whole, of the role of the state and the ruler in the divine plan, of the functioning of human society, and of the nature of human beings and their destiny in this world and the next. In Umayyad and 'Abbasid times, this vision was expressed partly in Islamic religious terms and partly in literary and artistic terms inherited from Greco-Roman, Persian, and Indian cultures.

In the Umayyad period, this imperial culture included Arabic poetry and oral traditions concerning Arab history, the life of the Prophet, the beginnings of Islam, and the deeds of the early caliphs. It also incorporated Byzantine and Sasanian artistic and literary materials. Thus, Umayyad mosques and palaces fused Christian and Byzantine decorative and iconographic motifs with Muslim uses and concepts to create new modes of Islamic architecture. The Umayyads also sponsored formal debates among Muslims and Christians, which contributed to the absorption of Hellenistic concepts into Muslim theology. Byzantium was both a source to emulate and a foil against which to define the distinctiveness of the Muslim regime.

An early expression of imperial Islam was the issuance of uniquely Islamic gold and silver coinage in place of Byzantine and Sasanian money – coinage being the historic prerogative of emperors and the principle vehicle of their propaganda. The new coinage replaced Christian and Zoroastrian symbolism with Arabic script to signify the sovereignty of the caliphs, their commitment to Islam, and their triumph over the previous empires. A coin dated 694–95 reads on one side: "There is no god but God and Muhammad is the messenger of God"; the reverse side lists the titles, "commander of the believers, caliph of God" (*amir al-mu'minin, khalifat allah*).

UMAYYAD ARCHITECTURE

The state also symbolized its sovereignty by undertaking monumental constructions. 'Abd al-Malik elaborated the status of Jerusalem (the most sacred city of Judaism and Christianity) as a holy place for Islam. The Dome of the Rock, the first great Muslim shrine, was built between 692 and 702 on the site of the ancient Hebrew temple and near the place of Christ's crucifixion and resurrection. This was also the legendary site of Abraham's intended sacrifice of Ishmael (the favored son in Muslim tradition), thus establishing a direct connection to the common ancestor of monotheism. (See Illustration 2.)

In Muslim tradition, this site is also the location of the Prophet's ascent to heaven. Muslims believe that Muhammad's miraculous night journey from Mecca to Jerusalem (*isra'*) and his ascension to heaven (*mi'raj*) took place from the rock and that Jerusalem will be the site of the last judgment and entry to paradise. Traditions defining the religious merit to be gained by visiting Jerusalem were already in circulation in the early eighth century; some urged a visit to Jerusalem in conjunction with the pilgrimage (*hajj*).

Apart from its religious prestige, there may have been practical reasons for the construction of a great Muslim shrine in Jerusalem. Jerusalem was an important town for the subject populations. Christians maintained a lively presence at least until the end of the seventh century. Jews – possibly from Arabia and Babylonia – were returning. By the 670s and 680s, there was a mosque, and laborers were moving into the city for construction work. The construction of the first great shrine of the Islamic era may also have been part of an attempt to make Jerusalem – in the heart of Umayyad domains – a rival to Mecca – then in the hands of the counter-caliph, Ibn al-Zubayr. The Dome has the shape of a reliquary built over a sacred place or object, suggesting a pilgrimage destination at a time when the pilgrimage to Mecca appears not yet to have been established as a Muslim worldwide ritual.

The building – a dome resting on an octagon – resembles the Greco-Roman churches of Rome, Ravenna, and Jerusalem and other smaller churches in the surrounding region. The construction of a Muslim shrine on the site of the ancient

Illustration 2. The Dome of the Rock.

Hebrew temple and the adoption of the design of local Syrian churches implied that Muslims were the heirs of the ancient religious traditions and rivals of the nearby churches that marked the ascension and resurrection of Christ.

Muslim triumph was further celebrated in the decoration of the building. Its ornamental motifs, expressing holiness and power, were adapted from Byzantine and Persian forms to illustrate the sovereignty of Islam. The Dome appears as a kind of royal pavilion covering God's throne on the Rock. Its mosaic decorations – crowns, jewels and hanging pearls, acanthus scrolls, grapes, and pomegranates – evoke pre-Islamic church decoration, trophies of rulers and gifts to the temple. Eggs, pearls, lamps, stars, and gardens are symbols of the luminosity and radiance of paradise. Jewels and pearls also appear in Islamic texts as part of the decoration of paradise.

Inscriptions in the Dome of the Rock proclaimed the mission of Islam, the truth of the new faith, and the surpassing of the old faith. These passages name Muhammad as the envoy of God, but they bless Jesus and acknowledge him as a prophet and messiah. They acknowledge blessings for the day when Jesus is

Illustration 3. The central portico of the Umayyad Mosque of Damascus. Courtesy of Isabelle Chiosso.

raised up again but deny that he is the son of God. Is the mention of Jesus meant to include him in the Muslim pantheon and thus appeal to Christians? Or is the intention to refute the Christian doctrines of Jesus's divinity and to convert them to Islam?

The Dome of the Rock was the first of a series of great mosques built in the late Umayyad period. In the Umayyad Mosque of Damascus, ʿAbd al-Malik's successor, al-Walid (705–15), combined the aesthetics of a pagan sanctuary (with its classical, Roman, and Hellenistic motifs) and a Christian church to create a new and distinctly Muslim architecture. (See Illustration 3.) Before al-Walid, Christians and Muslims had both worshiped on the platform of the church (*temonos*). The church was then demolished and replaced by a triple-aisled hall placed against the south side of the

Illustration 4. Mosaics of the Damascus mosque (detail). Courtesy of Isabelle Chiosso.

temonos and decorated with colored marbles, glass mosaics, gilding, and lamps. The mosque is decorated with scenes of idyllic buildings and landscapes that may represent heaven or may imply the subjection of the world to the new caliphs and the new faith. (See Illustration 4.) In 706, the Umayyad Mosque of Damascus was inscribed, "Our lord is one God, our religion is Islam and our prophet is Muhammad." The old church was preserved by the incorporation of materials and by its location.

Moreover, the location of the clock gates, the caliph's box (*maqsura*), the nearby royal palace, and the colonnades that link palace and mosque correspond to the topography of the imperial complex in Constantinople. This suggests that Damascus was displacing both Jerusalem as a holy place and Constantinople as the center of imperial power. It was a message to both Muslims and non-Muslims about the replacement of the old imperium by the new.

Then, in 707–09, al-Walid rebuilt the Mosque of the Prophet in Medina. The very structure of the mosque evoked the caliph's glory. It was built in the manner of Hellenistic royal architecture and contained a longitudinal hall, absidal niche, and pulpit (*minbar*) from which the official Friday sermon recognizing the sovereignty of the caliph and important political announcements were made. This was the first known mosque to have the decorated, semicircular niche that marks the direction of prayer (*mihrab*). The mosque also contained a box (*maqsura*) to seclude the caliph from his subjects, much as he was secluded at court. Umayyad caliphs sent necklaces, ruby-encrusted crescents, cups, and thrones to emphasize the submission of non-Muslim peoples to Islam and the triumphs and primacy of the caliph.

Al-Walid carried the decorative scheme of the Damascus mosque to other places in his empire, perhaps to create a uniform imperial-religious iconography in all Islamic lands. He rebuilt the Aqsa mosque adjacent to the Dome of the Rock and, in 710–12, he rebuilt the Mosque of 'Amr and the governor's palace in Fustat. The Mosque of San'a was remodeled by his governors. The Haram of Mecca and the Haram al-Sharif in Jerusalem were also completed. As a consequence of these constructions, a characteristic Arab-Islamic mosque emerged, defined by a longitudinal courtyard, a concave niche to mark the direction of prayer, a dome, a minaret, a wide axial nave, elevated transepts, and a decorative scheme of vines, marbles, mosaics, gilded epigraphy, and jewels.

In these works, the caliph as conqueror and endower treated religion as an intrinsic aspect of his own identity and the mosque as a symbol of the compact union of the political and religious aspects of his rule. Before entering the mosque, the Caliph al-Walid would change from perfumed and multicolored clothes to pure white garments. On returning to the palace, he would again put on the worldly and splendid garb of the court. Although the caliphate took Islam into its political majesty, Islam absorbed the caliph into the service of religion. The same motifs served both imperial and religious purposes. They testified to the glory and power of kings and sacred presences.

THE DESERT PALACES

Alongside the religious program of the caliph, there was a secular-imperial program manifested in court ceremony, art, and architecture. Like its predecessor courts, the court of the Umayyad caliphs became a theater enacting the drama of royalty. The caliph's residence was approached by ceremonial gates; its central feature was a longitudinal hall culminating in an absidal or domed room – a pattern found at Damascus, al-Wasit, Mushatta, and later Baghdad – adapted from Hellenistic, Roman, Byzantine, and Sasanian patterns for the emperor's court. The court, with its domed room, was the center of the universe; its decorations signified the gathering of the living cosmos to glorify the caliph.

Court symbols conveyed the august majesty and unique rank of the caliph among men. He was entitled to dress and furnishings, to ceremonies and amusements, and to gestures of respect that no other humans enjoyed. Court poetry glorified the ruler and surrounded him with a divine aura. The Umayyad court poets addressed the caliph as the deputy of God (*khalifat allah*). Poetry of the late seventh and early eighth centuries also identified the caliph as the axis of the universe (*qutb*), as the light of guidance, and as the direction of Muslim prayer (*qibla*). The panegyrics sometimes imputed supernatural powers to him; his intercession brought rain. The oath of allegiance (*bay'a*) became a gesture of the humble servitude of the courtier and subject before his overlord.

In 742, al-Walid II was the first caliph to claim that the title "*khalifa*" meant "*khalifat allah*," that is, "deputy of God" instead of "deputy of the Prophet." A letter ascribed to al-Walid presented the caliph as God's agent on par with the Prophet and as a source of guidance (imam). The titles "*khalifat allah*" and "imam," however, were used only in poetry and rhetoric; they were not official titles and not recognized by Muslim scholars. The recognized titles of caliphs were *khalifat rasul allah* (deputy of the prophet of God) and *amir al-mu'minin* (commander of the believers).

The caliph held audience seated on a throne, dressed in a crown and royal robes, and veiled from his audience by a curtain. His courtiers stood or sat on each side of the long hall. His day included consultations, receptions, prayer, and private entertainments – hunting, music, dancing girls, wine drinking, and poetry reading. A chamberlain controlled access to the royal person; everyone addressed him in submissive tones and with panegyrical greetings. Obedience and fidelity to an adored majestic personage was a leading theme in later Umayyad court life.

Love of the steppe, its climate, its healthfulness, its seclusion, and its hunting brought Umayyad princes to their desert palaces. There, decorations depicted the caliph's majesty and power. In a fresco at Qasr al-Khayr, the caliph appears in a formal, frontal pose; at Khirbat al-Mafjar, he assumes a martial figure. Paintings at Qusayr 'Amr portray the Caliph al-Walid as Adam, in an hieratic manner adopted from Byzantine depictions of the Christ as Pantocrator. At Qusayr 'Amr, his majesty appears in full triumph in a painting depicting the shah of Iran, the emperor of Byzantium, Roderic of Spain, the negus of Abyssinia, the emperor of China, and the emperor of the Turks greeting the caliph as their master. The caliph is shown at the head of the family of kings, preeminent among rulers who are shown as deriving their authority from their new suzerain, the Muslim caliph, whose power embraces not only Islam but the whole world. At Qusayr 'Amr, a villa set in gardens or a small-scale agricultural estate, the paintings depict the luxury and extravagance of hunting, gardens, birds, animals, banquets, and dancing girls. All this defined the prerogatives of royalty. It was a statement of royal transcendence of religious identities.

In these ways, the Umayyads not only gave cultural legitimacy to the Arab-Muslim imperium but also welded the disparate elements of the governing class – the caliph, his family and boon companions, Arab tribal chiefs and generals, Inner Asian soldiers, Iranian administrators, Christian ecclesiastics, and Muslim religious scholars – into a cohesive imperial elite.

THE UMAYYADS AND THE ANCIENT EMPIRES

These policies and monuments were continuations of Byzantine and Sasanian practices. The sublimity of the emperor-caliph, the official support of the state for religion, and the construction of monumental churches – or, in this case, mosques – all had Byzantine precedents. In Syria and Egypt, the whole administrative apparatus – including the revenue administration and even the form of chancery documents – maintained Byzantine systems. Syrian military organization also followed Byzantine models. In Iraq, the Sasanian pattern of administrative organization – the fourfold division of finance, military, correspondence, and chancellery services – was adopted by Arab administrators.

In adopting the practices of the previous empires, the Umayyads transformed the traditional motifs. Although the Umayyads employed Byzantine designs and even builders, artists, and workers (from Damascus, Jerusalem, the Biqa Valley, Syria, Egypt, and Byzantium) to decorate their mosques and palaces, the artistic inspiration was not entirely Byzantine. Umayyad art was a fusion of Byzantine, ancient Roman, and Sasanian art, creating a uniquely Islamic aesthetic. The Umayyad Mosque of Damascus was built on the Roman *temonos*; the desert palaces resembled Roman villas in their fortification, isolation, and close connection to the land. In their palaces, the Umayyads integrated Sasanian motifs – images of hunting, drinking, music, dancing, and beautiful women. The portraits of princes were presented in Byzantine style, but with Sasanian overtones. Conversely, the six kings painting was a Sasanian motif presented frontally in Byzantine style. Thus, Greek, Roman, and Persian themes and techniques were used to create a decorative scheme that was distinctly Umayyad. In utilizing the art of their predecessors, the Umayyads chose, rejected, combined, and juxtaposed ancient themes in a new art.

The artistic symbolism communicated a double meaning. Early Islamic art suggested both that the new empire was an integral continuation of the existing civilizations and that it had superseded them. It called for the cooperation of non-Muslim notables and local power holders and for the acquiescence of its non-Muslim subjects, while also proclaiming a new Muslim empire replacing the Byzantine Empire and a new religion taking over from Christianity and Judaism.

ISLAM AND ICONOCLASM

From an early period, Muslim religious and public art was characterized by vegetal and calligraphic decoration covering large surfaces and by the use of Arabic script as both a decorative motif and an emblem of identity. Muslim coins were embossed with script, but not portraits. However, royal and private Umayyad decorations did portray human and animal figures. Later Muslim practice was also mixed. Mosques, schools, and other places of religious significance were never decorated with human or animal figures, but representational images were found in ʿAbbasid, Fatimid, Persian, Indian, and Ottoman art produced under royal patronage and for court consumption, although this was much less common in the Arab world.

What does this tell us about Muslim religious attitudes toward the representation of people and animals in art? There is nothing in the Quran or early Muslim religious literature to suggest an iconoclastic attitude. Grabar has argued that Muslim calligraphy and vegetal arts were most likely a pragmatic adaptation to the need for a new imperial-Islamic emblem distinct from the Byzantine and Sasanian portraits of emperors. The use of vegetal designs and writing was prior to any religious theory about them. Once adopted, they became the norm for Islamic public art. Theories about Islamic iconoclasm were developed later.

However, the absence of human images in Muslim public art may not be accidental. It may have been an implied choice of a fundamental religious orientation. The inscription in the Dome of the Rock demotes the status of Christ from son of God to a human prophet and instead extolls the Quran (the text of the revelation) as the only contact with God. It implicitly denies any human or material intermediary between man and God and thus rejects the veneration of icons and images. Early Islam favored the communal rather than the salvific forms of religion that look to human intermediaries as the medium of salvation. Because God alone is reality and cannot be represented, nothing material can substitute for him. Abstraction signifies transcendence.

CHAPTER 13

THE 'ABBASIDS: CALIPHS AND EMPERORS

THE CALIPHATE AND ISLAM

Like the Umayyads, the 'Abbasids pursued two kinds of legitimation, Islamic and imperial. From the beginning, the caliphs were involved in religious matters, but their engagement was limited. The Rashidun caliphs – as companions of the Prophet – left authoritative precedents in many matters of law. 'Uthman promulgated an official edition of the Quran. Mu'awiya tried to exert influence over communal-religious leaders by appointing Quran readers and judges. Caliphs built mosques, protected the pilgrimage, proffered justice to the people, and waged war on behalf of the Islamic empire. In the reigns of 'Abd al-Malik and his successors, the construction of great mosques defined the caliphs as patrons of Islam who glorified their religion and made it prevail over Byzantine Christianity. The Caliph 'Umar II came to the throne from an earlier career in Medina engaged in legal and religious activity and brought to the caliphate a renewed concern for communal-religious issues. The later Umayyads assumed the right to intervene in theological matters; they executed Qadari theologians who proclaimed God's power absolute and, by implication, subordinated the authority of the caliphs. Their court poets bestowed on them the grandiose title of God's deputy (*khalifat Allah*).

The 'Abbasids reaffirmed the Islamic basis of their legitimacy. In the course of their anti-Umayyad revolution, the early 'Abbasids tried to promote their claim to rule as Hashimites; being the family of the Prophet, this revered lineage stood above all ethnic, tribal, regional, and local interests. They also maintained that the right to rule was assigned to the founder of their lineage, Ibn al-'Abbas, by the Prophet himself. As caliphs, they inherited the attributes of religious authority: the Prophet's cloak, stave, and ring. The royal name was inscribed on coins and the borders of ceremonial garments (*tiraz*) and was invoked in the Friday sermon (*khutba*). They themselves claimed to be appointed by God to follow in the ways of the Prophet and to lead the Muslim community along the path of

Islam. The idea of God's caliph was invoked in 'Abbasid as well as in Umayyad poetry.

The 'Abbasids had come to power on a current of messianic hopes, and their titles stressed their imagined role as saviors. 'Abbasid caliphs – including Al-Mansur (the Victorious), al-Mahdi (the Savior), al-Hadi (the Guide), and al-Rashid (the Rightly Guided) – claimed to bring enlightenment and to return Muslims to the true path. They patronized scholars and promoted the pilgrimage to Mecca by organizing way stations, by providing military security in the desert, and by making gifts to the holy places. They performed the pilgrimage. The 'Abbasid caliphs also tried to draw Muslim religious leaders into public service as judges and administrators. They expanded the judicial hierarchy and tried to use the judges as intermediaries to organize scholars, teachers, and legists under the jurisdiction and patronage of the state.

Furthermore, the 'Abbasids intervened directly in religious matters. In 777, the Caliph al-Mahdi began persecuting freethinkers and heretics (*zanadiqa*) in order to set the boundaries of acceptable doctrine and to unify his cadres on common religious grounds. The term "*zanadiqa*" was applied to people who held a variety of religious beliefs and social practices. In the narrow sense, it referred to Manichaeans or dualists who believed in the existence of two divine powers – one for good and one for evil – as opposed to the unitary conception of monotheism. However, the term was used more generally to refer to atheists who denied the existence of God, creation ex nihilo, prophecy, or the next world. It referred to people who denied that the Quran was a miraculous revelation from God. It referred to libertines or antinomians who did not believe in reward or punishment after death. The *zanadiqa* were those who believed in freedom from law and were therefore political subversives. Included in the denunciations were poets, theologians, scribes, and many Shi'is. By the reign of Harun al-Rashid, however, the campaign had petered out.

The effort to bring Muslim religious life under state supervision was similar to both Byzantine and Sasanian imperial practices. Byzantine emperors did not have the right to define doctrine – only the church itself as represented by the collectivity of the bishops could do that – but they saw to it that the decisions taken suited imperial political interests as well as the convictions of the bishops. They presided over church councils and suggested formulas for the creed. The emperors also appointed the leading patriarchs, archbishops, and bishops.

The Sasanian system is less well known. However, the early 'Abbasid scribe and translator of Sasanian literature into Arabic, Ibn al-Muqaffa', may represent the Sasanian situation. He wrote that religious matters were of utmost importance to the state and that uniformity in doctrine and control over religious organization were indispensable bases of power. He argued that the caliphs could not afford doctrinal disputes in the administration and the army and could not permit religious scholars and judges to be outside state control. Ibn al-Muqaffa' urged the caliphs to promulgate doctrine, organize a hierarchical judiciary, and appoint the leading judges.

The early 'Abbasid caliphs did appoint judges and tried to define the boundaries of acceptable belief, but their influence in the formation of religious laws and doctrines was limited. The caliphate was constrained by widespread resistance to its religious claims (even among its Sunni supporters) and vigorously opposed by sectarian movements.

Still, the authority of the caliphs was not recognized as absolute or even compre-hensive. Among Sunnis who supported both the Umayyad and 'Abbasid dynasties, the ever-growing importance of the religious intellectuals and the independent development of Quranic studies, hadith, law, and theology limited the author-ity of the ruler. Many Sunnis held that the Prophet's guidance had been passed on to the companions collectively, not solely to any one of them, and to their students, followers, and successors. The consensus, or collective agreement, of scholars defined law and belief. At best, the caliphs were considered equivalent to the scholars and could decide questions not otherwise decided by the religious authorities. Primarily, the caliph was the guardian of Islam. By the time of Harun, the caliphate also seems to have accepted its role as the guardian but not the source of Islamic teaching. The caliphs distanced themselves from claims to be imams in the Shi'i sense of divinely inspired teachers.

Shi'is opposed the established caliphs in principle. They claimed that only the family of 'Ali, a holy lineage related to the Prophet, was entitled to hold the office. Then, with the anti-Umayyad rebellion of al-Mukhtar in 687, gnosticism – the belief that human beings embodied a divine spark trapped in this world and that they must return to their true divine realm – entered Shi'i intellectual circles. The gnostics were eschatological dreamers who believed in incarnation, transmigration of souls, and continuous, living prophethood. They thought of the imam as the savior (Mahdi). By the eighth century the Shi'is had evolved into a movement claiming not only the rights of the family of 'Ali but also that this family was divinely blessed with supernatural powers and moral perfection.

However, although they all agreed that leadership (imamate) was inherited in the family of 'Ali, they differed over which descendant was the true heir. Zaydis believed that the true heir had to prove himself in active struggle for the office. Imami Shi'is defined the leader as the person who inherited the position or was designated by the previous imam, but he did not have to be a political activist. They introduced the idea of an imam who is not a political ruler, but a teacher and savior. Eventually the leadership of Imami Shi'ism passed to scholars. Quietism, accommodation, dissimulation, and martyrdom became the dominant sociopolitical motifs.

The Inquisition
The Caliph al-Ma'mun (813–33), however, attempted to expand the religious func-tions of the caliphate. Al-Ma'mun came to power as the result of a civil war in

which – supported by a new military force from Khurasan – he overthrew a legitimate caliph and brought a new governing entourage to Baghdad. To legitimate his
regime, al-Ma'mun assumed an austere lifestyle, emphasized his Hashimite descent,
and adopted the slogan of "command good and forbid evil." This was intended to
co-opt vigilante religious activity in Baghdad. He declared himself Imam al-Huda,
the guide inspired by God, and the caliph of God (*khalifat Allah*). Al-Ma'mun then
nominated 'Ali al-Rida – the Shi'i eighth imam – as his successor. This has variously
been interpreted as an effort to co-opt the Shi'is or to implicitly adopt Shi'i ideas
of the authority of imams for himself.

These measures to bolster his religious prestige and authority were preliminary
to the decisive measure of his regime: the declaration of a theological policy and an
inquisition (*mihna*) to enforce his views. Al-Ma'mun declared the Quran "created."
This was the position of the rationalist Mu'tazilite theologians (see Chapter 15)
and implied that the Quran was a worldly object, not itself part of the divine
being. This stood in contrast to the idea that the Quran was "uncreated" – like
the Logos in Christian theology – an emanation of and part of the divine being.
The practical import of the doctrine of the created Quran was that reason and/or
caliphal authority could define religious belief and practice, whereas the contrary
position placed revelation (including Quran and hadith) above all human authority.

The inquisition supported the rationalist theological schools that valued reason
(Mu'tazilis, Zaydis, Murji'is) and the quasi-rationalist Shafi'i and Hanafi law groups,
which accepted the use of analogical reasoning – against the traditionalists or
hadith scholars who stressed revelation as the source of religious knowledge. The
inquisition required the religious scholars to accept both the doctrine and the
caliph's right to promulgate it.

The inquisition was prosecuted by judges of the Hanafi school. It was aimed
in particular at the followers of Ahmad ibn Hanbal, the leading hadith scholar in
Baghdad. Scholars who refused to accept the caliph's doctrine were beaten, denied
court positions, disqualified as judges and legal witnesses, denied the legal right
to pass on property to relatives, and forbidden from teaching or praying in the
mosques, from narrating hadith, or from giving binding legal opinions (*fatawa*).

The motives for the inquisition were probably as much political as theological.
Although the Hanbalis accepted the authority of the caliphate, they were opposed
to the arbitrary or abusive exercise of power. They were temperamentally hostile to
the luxury and self-indulgence of the elites. In addition, they had strong support not
only among religious scholars but also among shopkeepers, craftsmen, and skilled
workers, who made up their following. The "street" was allied with the Hanbalis.
Baghdadi Khurasanians, descended, as was Ibn Hanbal, from the original 'Abbasid
conquering army, were their principal supporters. Thus al-Ma'mun's intervention
was also an effort to restore the authority of *al-khass* (intellectuals and theologians)
over *al-'amma* (the common people).

The inquisition continued into the reigns of al-Ma'mun's successors until the
Caliph al-Mutawakkil (r. 847–61) abandoned the inquisition after years of tumult

and popular opposition. His goal seems to have been to quiet the controversy, rather than to accept the uncreatedness of the Quran or to promote traditionalism. Judges who professed createdness were not removed; traditionalists were not appointed. Successive caliphs supported moderate rationalism but did not press the doctrine of created Quran. After this cultural and political ordeal, the caliphate limited its religious claims.

The defeat of the caliphal position marked a victory not only for the Hanbalis but for the independence of all the legal and theological schools. The outcome of the inquisition showed that the religious scholars had achieved both social authority and permanent political power vis-à-vis the caliphate. Specialists in Islamic law and theology were an autonomous pious and scholarly community operating as a private enterprise, distinct from the political sector. Once this was established, the caliphate was due obedience in all matters of state and politics. Scholars accepted the caliph as a symbolic religious leader and protector of religious law – having the authority to decide some questions of religious law not otherwise decided by the scholars. Only then did the caliphate become the symbol of the unity of Islam and empire, of a golden age in Islamic history.

The confrontation with religious scholars, however, by no means fully defined the concept of the caliphate and its authority. The caliphate was not only a Muslim regime; it was an imperial regime, the successor of ancient empires. Although they appealed to Muslim sentiment so that Muslims would recognize them as the legitimate successors to the Prophet and as the protectors and organizers of Islam, the caliphs simultaneously appealed to non-Muslims and converts as divinely selected rulers or exalted princes sent by God for the right ordering of worldly affairs. In ceremony, art, and architecture they expressed an imperial ideal. They sponsored a cosmopolitan literary and artistic Islamic culture and viewed themselves as heirs to the ancient cultures, which they incorporated into the amalgam of Islamic identities. The ʿAbbasid dynasty patronized Arabic poetry in both old bedouin and new courtly genres; they commissioned the translation into Arabic of Iranian literary classics, including works of history, polite literature, fables, political precepts, and manuals of protocol and behavior for scribes, as well as the mythic and scientific lore of Persia and India. Similarly, classical logical, scientific, and philosophical works were translated from Greek and Syriac into Arabic.

Architecture and court ceremony
The caliphal conception of the majesty of the ruler was expressed in Arabic, Persian, Hellenistic, and other Middle Eastern terms. The caliph was the vice-regent of God on earth. Court poets and court protocol elevated the caliphs above angels and prophets, calling them the chosen of God, God's shadow on earth, a refuge for all of his lesser creatures. By his magical powers, the caliph upheld the order of the cosmos, providing for the rain and the harvests, keeping all persons in their places, and seeing to it that they fulfilled their functions in society. He was the symbol

of civilization: agriculture, cities, arts, and learning depended on his blessings. In the middle of the tenth century, a court chronicler reports that an unsophisticated provincial soldier, overcome by the splendor of the caliph's appearance, thought he was in the presence of God.

Palaces and palace-cities manifested the majesty of the caliphate. Baghdad incorporated materials taken from the ruins of Sasanian palaces. Its design had symbolic implications. The city of peace was a round city divided into quadrants by axial streets running from east to west and north to south, with the palace in the very center. The structure of the city reproduced the symmetry and hierarchy of society and the central position of the caliph within it. The central placement of the caliph symbolized his sovereignty over the four quarters of the world. It also symbolized the cosmic and heavenly world. Since ancient times, the founding of a city had signified the creation of order out of chaos in the geographic, social, and cosmic levels of the universe. With the construction of a new city, the caliph became the creator of order in the otherwise formless, boundless, and threatening experience of mankind.

The inner life of the court was marked by an elaborate protocol. The Umayyads had inscribed themselves in a universal history of power: processions, formal audiences, presentation of gifts, the screen shielding the ruler from view, and the privilege of wearing textiles embroidered with sacred words that were reserved for the ruler alone. These practices were continued by the ʿAbbasids. The caliph was presented as capricious, inscrutable, and terrifying. One of the prerogatives of the ruler was ceremonial and deferential behavior in his presence, marked by silence and kissing the ground. The court was governed by elaborate regulations for eating, drinking, and dressing. The protocol was also designed to signify the order of courtly ranks as determined by the caliph, who conferred on his servitors the symbols of rank and honor, such as weapons, banners, food, and royal robes. Court etiquette, manners, gaze, and speech were all fashioned to enunciate royalty. Carnal pleasures – wine, women, and song – were part of a Dionysian atmosphere featuring bacchic and homoerotic love poetry. Court protocol and the pleasures the caliphs promoted a vision of the ruler as transcending ordinary limits.

THE ARABIC HUMANITIES

Literature also served the imperial program. Arabic literature was cultivated in both court and urban circles, but the caliphate patronized poetry and history in particular as an expression of its legitimacy and of its affinity with the conquering armies, as well as an adornment of imperial rule. The caliphs were strongly influenced by the heritage of pre-Islamic bedouin Arabia and by Arab interest in glorifying of the conquests.

The classical poetry of the desert became a part of courtly entertainment. The pre-Islamic ideas of sacred kingship became an Arabic-Islamic ideology of royal legitimacy. Panegyrics recited at the Umayyad and 'Abbasid courts celebrated ruler-ship in terms of victory and enshrined the idea of Arabs as masculine, dominant, aggressive, and active rather than feminine and submissive. Furthermore, pane-gyrics deified the patron. The poet praised him and prayed to him for blessings and gifts. The generosity of the ruler was compared to the divine overflowing of grace, except that the caliph's benefits were present and real, whereas God was distant and unresponsive. Court poetry implied that the benefits conferred by rulers elevated them above the powers of God.

Love poetry was particularly important. Pre-Islamic love poetry was nostalgic for lost loves but also unsentimental and intensely physical. In the caliphal era, there were two kinds of love poetry. One was a brazenly physical celebration of fulfillment in love. The other was *'udhri* poetry, yearning for an impossible and unrealizable love. 'Abbasid court poetry made unfulfilled love fashionable. Yearning showed a refined sensibility and thus marked a man as part of the court elite. Esteemed poets, moreover, wrote about homoerotic desires and celebrated the blessings of wine.

Court poetry contradicted orthodox Muslim religious values. The scholars believed that Islam required mindfulness, concentration, clarity, attention to God, and resistance to the seductions of the body (including music, dance, secular songs, poetry, drinking, hashish, and gambling). They viewed Islam as regulating erotic relations and all attachments other than those to God. Yet, the puritanism of ortho-dox Islam did not erase the seduction of poetry about love and war, intoxication, ecstasy, and freedom. When the power of the caliphate declined, later courts in Egypt, Syria, Mesopotamia, and North Africa continued this literary tradition and made it a universal Muslim world expression of royalty.

Historical studies were also a product of both court and urban milieus. Historical literature embodied the desire to celebrate and validate the conquests as an Arab tribal and Muslim achievement. Muslim histories served to legitimate Muslim hege-mony over non-Muslims and to assert the superiority of Islam to the older religions and of Arab kingship to the Byzantine and Sasanian empires. History was also writ-ten to advance the claims of contenders in Arab and intra-Muslim rivalries. In the seventh and eighth centuries, Arab scholars collected tribal lore, pre-Islamic Jewish lore (*isra'iliyyat*), information on Yemeni antiquity, genealogies, battle tales, tales of ancient kings and prophets, and the Prophet's biographical information. Papyri, coins, inscriptions, name lists, and lists of caliphs provided basic information.

Biographies of Muhammad, books about the conquests, and stories of the early civil wars were written down in the early decades of the eighth century. In these early works, Arab-Muslims defined their communities and the bases of their polit-ical community and imperial power. They told stories about the conquests and the battles they had fought, developing a narrative about the piety and religious virtues of the conquerors. Martial valor was equated with piety. The Arab-Muslim community was memorialized through the deeds of its heroes, defenders, and holy martyrs.

From the middle of the eighth century, these early accounts were reworked – in accordance with theological, political, and social needs – into narrative histories. Persian historiography provided the model of histories focused on the reigns of kings; historians (*akhbaris*) provided lists of caliphs, governors, judges, and officials. "Authored" texts replaced students' and scholars' notebooks circulated among colleagues. There was a boom in learning at the end of the eighth century as the production of paper made the reproduction and dissemination of knowledge easier.

One of the primary concerns in early historiography was to establish the distinctness of Islam from both paganism and other monotheistic religions. Pre-Muhammad prophetic history was narrated to elaborate Quranic stories and to give Muslims a history validating Muhammad as a true prophet. Muslim historians portrayed the emergence of a religious people out of a tribal wilderness, they pointed to the Islamic calendar, the direction of prayer, and a sacred language and script to validate the divine inspiration of the Arab-Muslim community. Some scholars condemned pagan, tribal, sectarian, and other monotheistic cultures as the enemies of the true community. Middle Eastern ideas of the cyclical history of prophecy and God's selection of Muslims for virtue and victory shaped the way early Muslim history was narrated. This was salvation history, the history of how God has ordered mankind and its destiny, told from the creation to the present, from former prophets to the final prophet, from the pagan era in Arabia (*jahiliyya*) to Islam.

Other cultural and social forces shaped the way in which history was conceived. History was often written by non-Arabs. Assimilated converts brought with them the literary concepts of their own traditions. Ancient Greek topoi – familiar to both Arabs and non-Arabs – appear in Arab-Muslim histories: the dual between two warriors, the small incident that triggers a momentous event, the eye witness confirming the truth, love of lists and famous "firsts," and speeches to exhort to battle or belief in Islam.

The study of hadith was both a component of and an influence on Muslim historiography. Whereas cultivated courtiers were interested in the entertainment and instructional value of a story more than its literal truth, traditionalists believed that the wisdom of the ancestors was the highest knowledge and had to be conserved. Knowledge was not created – it was passed on. The past was a source of models for behavior, and so accuracy of transmission became critical. For some hadith scholars, historical tales and hadith both had to be valid; invention and any use of reasoning that made the teller anything other than the medium of transmission was frowned upon. In a multiethnic, multilingual society, these attitudes helped maintain the ties of ʿAbbasid-era Arab-Islam to the Quran and to the Arabian past.

In the tenth and eleventh centuries, historiography began to feature a variety of rhetorical styles. Two main subgenres emerged. First, history became important because of its connection to politics, because it was produced for rulers, courts, secretaries, and officials as a repository of prescriptions for, examples of, and knowledge about how to live. Scribes and secretaries replaced traditionalists as the sources for this kind of history. Second, local histories and biographical dictionaries were written to glorify the scholars – especially the collectivity of scholars of particular towns – and to ennoble the merchant and landowning strata from which they derived.

Thus, Arabic culture of this period was partly of the court and caliphal patronage, partly of Arab tribal milieus, and partly the product of the urban middle-class and scholarly communities. This culture had a crucial role to play in defining the political elite. Although Arabic culture was subtly merged with Islamic culture, the development of Arabic literature preserved an ethnic and linguistic distinctness from and within Islam. Arabism would later stand apart from Islam as the foundation of political and cultural identity.

PERSIAN LITERATURE

Arabic poetry and history were not the only elements of cultural identity in this period. The incorporation of new peoples into the Arab-Muslim empire and the empire-wide recruitment of late Umayyad and 'Abbasid political elites from all parts of the empire brought Persian officials and cultural influences into the caliphate. Persian court procedures were adopted and the first translations of Persian political documents were undertaken in the reign of the Umayyad Caliph Hisham (724–43). Under the 'Abbasids, Persian and Nestorian officials, scribes, physicians, merchants, and soldiers oversaw the translation of Persian texts into Arabic. Persian courtiers translated manuals on how to conduct affairs of state, carry out the duties of various offices, behave in the presence of rulers, and fulfill the duties required for different positions. This advice was embedded in tales and anecdotes about the great Persian rulers of the past. This was done partly as a partisan measure to enhance the prestige and authority of their own ethnic or factional groups, and partly to signify the supremacy of the caliphs and the political class to ordinary Muslims.

With political advice came technical and scientific knowledge. Iran was an important transmitter of Indian and Hellenistic medical, mathematical, astronomical, and astrological ideas. Works on horsemanship and the care and use of weapons and practical knowledge about government, agricultural management, and irrigation were all translated into Arabic. So too were literary masterworks such as the fables of Kalila and Dimna and some of the tales of the Arabian Nights. The literature of Persian courtly etiquette (*adab*) integrated Persian, Indian, and Hellenistic cultures. Valuing originality, wit, and style, this literature emphasized experiential knowledge, scientific understandings of nature and society, and historical knowledge discovered by research and reason.

The flourishing of Persian translations led to rivalry between Persian courtiers and their Arab counterparts. A literary movement, the Shuʿubiya, asserted the cultural superiority of the Persians to the Arabs and influenced the official culture of the ʿAbbasid caliphate. Persians emphasized the absolute and unlimited authority of the monarch, his divine selection, and his superiority in matters of religion as well as state. Persian literature also espoused a hierarchical view of society in which each person – ruler, noble, warrior, scribe, priest, merchant, worker, or peasant – had a fixed place. The duty of government was to preserve everyone in his place, giving each class its due.

These ideas differed profoundly from the prevailing sentiment in Arab-Muslim circles. Arab-Muslim sentiment was more egalitarian and less hierarchical. Urban Arab-Muslims tended to deny the ruler authority in religious matters and refused to accept that the ruler was a law unto himself. Arabs generally believed that the ruler was chosen by and was responsible to the community and its religion. Also embedded in Persian literature was a religious challenge to Islam. Although Iranian administrators were Muslims, many were still sympathetic to Zoroastrianism; others may have been Manichaeans, gnostics, or even agnostics and atheists.

Arab scholars resisted Persian ideas and attempted to meet the temptations of Persian literary sophistication on its own grounds. In response to Persian literature, Arabic literary culture explored new directions for the sake of defending its old essence: the result, occurring primarily in the ninth century, was an Arab-Persian synthesis. Ibn Qutayba (828–89) compiled treatises on such themes as government, war, nobility, scholarship, asceticism, love, friendship, and women. His selections were organized in the manner of Arabic literature and included quotations from the Quran, hadith, and Arabic histories of the early caliphs and the Arab empire; he also incorporated Persian *adab* works, Indian tales, and Aristotle's philosophy to attract the Persian elites.

Another ninth-century writer, al-Jahiz (d. 869) – who is regarded as the finest prose stylist in the history of Arabic letters – also synthesized the literary interests of Arab- and Persian-minded elites. Out of the encyclopedic works of his predecessors, he selected, adapted, edited, and made attractive a body of literature that would serve as a common culture for both Arabs and Arabic-speaking Persians. Arabic writers thus offered some of the fruits of Persian thought to Muslims but obscured the elements that were in conflict with Islam and Arab values. The flood of translations from Persian was diverted and rechanneled into a stream of literature bearing a Persian imprint in manner, style, and subject but firmly wedded to Arabic and Islamic ideas.

Thus, elements of the Persian heritage became an integral part of Islamic imperial administrative and aesthetic culture. Still, the Persian language and Iranian political and religious ideas survived outside the Islamic synthesis. The Persian language would be the basis of a later Persian literary and artistic revival. Persian political ideas continued to influence the practice of Middle Eastern governments; Persian gnosticism would return to inspire later Islamic religious developments. In a later era, Persian would be the foundation of a variant Perso-Islamic culture in the Middle East, and in Central and southern Asia.

HELLENISTIC LITERATURE AND PHILOSOPHY

Hellenistic thought also had a complex role in Islamic civilization. Greek culture as it became known in the Islamic era was not the thought of ancient Greece but rather Greek thought as preserved and interpreted in the late Roman Empire. Plato's ideas were represented by his political works and some of his dialogues. Aristotle's logical and scientific works, ethics, and metaphysics were also known. However, most of the materials attributed to Aristotle and Plato had actually been written in the centuries following the deaths of the two master philosophers, when they were reinterpreted in neo-Platonic terms as teachings of a path to spiritual salvation. The Greek heritage also included the science and medicine and the semimystical, semiscientific ideas of the alchemists, neo-Pythagoreans, and Hermetics.

The transmission of Hellenistic culture to Islamic societies depended on the survival of the ancient academies. The most important ancient academies were originally located in Athens and Alexandria, but with the Christianization of the Roman Empire in the fourth and fifth centuries, pagan schools were dispersed. They found a haven in the Christian but non-Roman parts of the Middle East. The school of Athens was rescued by the Nestorian Church, which sponsored the translation of Greek works into Syriac. From the fifth to the eighth centuries, the school of Edessa translated the works of Aristotle and Porphyry, as well as many philosophical, historical, geographical, and astronomical works from Greek into Syriac. In the sixth century, the school of Nasibin, staffed mainly by Nestorian Christians, was transferred to Jundishapur, a Sasanian royal city in Fars. Here, Hellenistic philosophical and scientific studies flourished under the influence of Persian and Indian religious and occult conceptions. This school was eventually transferred to Baghdad.

Hellenistic schools were also active in Harran, Qinnesrin, Mosul, the Dayr Qunna monastery, al-Hira, and Marw. Secular topics – including Greek rhetoric, dialectics, mathematics, music, geometry, astronomy, and philosophy – were taught privately in Damascus, but as private secular education waned in the seventh and eighth centuries, Syrian monasteries became the centers of Greek studies and translation into Syriac. A Syriac literature of hagiography, homilies, miracles, and disputations also blossomed. Syriac translations of Greek work continued to be made in the Umayyad period, but in the late Umayyad and ʿAbbasid era, Arabic replaced Syriac as the new common language. Arab princes commissioned the translation of works on alchemy from Greek and Coptic into Arabic.

Alexandrian Hellenistic thought also became a part of Islamic intellectual culture. Philosophical studies based on the canon of Porphyry (d. 305), including Aristotelian and neo-Platonic works, were taught in Alexandria, Beirut, and Gaza. The Alexandrian school was moved to Antioch (in Syria) under Jacobite auspices, then to Harran in Mesopotamia and Marw in Khurasan. Some of the scholars were Nestorian Christians, but others (at Harran) were pagans. From Mesopotamia, this school also moved to Baghdad at the end of the ninth and the beginning of the tenth centuries. Iraqi-Persian Hellenism and Pahlavi culture, with its Indian connections, were other sources of late antique thought. In the Sasanian Empire, Greek works were translated into Pahlavi and were considered part of the Sasanian cultural heritage. Some works of logic and medicine came into Arabic from Persian translations.

Muslims interested in theological questions were drawn to the Hellenistic heritage. Debates between Muslims and Christians in the courts of the Umayyad caliphs conveyed Christian or Hellenistic vocabularies, forms of rational argument, and literary methods. In Baghdad, translations were undertaken by professional translators instead of clerics and often by scholars oriented to the culture of Iran rather than Syria. Translations in the reign of al-Mahdi (775–85) reinforced theological and cosmological arguments against heretics. In the eighth century, even before the great Arab grammarian Sibawayhi (d. 796), there was a Kufan grammatical school strongly influenced by Greek logic and philosophy. In the early ninth century, there was increased interest in theological texts and practical works of alchemy and medicine.

In the reigns of al-Ma'mun (813–33) and al-Mu'tasim (833–42), under the guidance of Hunayn b. Ishaq (d. 873), works in medicine, optics, mechanics, geography, occult sciences, mathematics, and philosophy – including Aristotle's logic and the works of Galen and Hippocrates – were translated. The output of Hunayn's school was prodigious. This school of philologically competent editors created a body of translations and a spirit of critical inquiry that made philosophical studies in the Islamic era rigorous and exacting. Muslim and Christian scholars commented and glossed the translated works and prepared lectures, compendiums, and texts to disseminate their ideas. Al-Ma'mun and later caliphs also sent scholars to Byzantium to gather works on philosophy, geometry, music, arithmetic, and medicine for translation. The greater part of the translations was completed by the end of the tenth century. After that, philosophers and scientists worked with the corpus of earlier translations.

Translations were sponsored by caliphs, the royal family, ministers, officials, physicians, and scholars – whether Arabs, Persians, or Nestorians. In general, scholarly life was focused in patron households. Institutions – such as colleges or research centers – were few. Harun al-Rashid established a library and center for translations and scholarship (*khizanat al-hikma*). The Caliph al-Ma'mun is said to have established an academy and observatory (*bayt al-hikma*) to stimulate the translation of logical, scientific, and philosophical works into Arabic, but this may have been a center for Zoroastrian studies rather than philosophical translations.

Hellenistic philosophy played a profound intellectual role in the Islamic era. Philosophy – including logic, natural science, and metaphysics – was an intellectual movement with a great variety of positions united by a shared vocabulary and by a commitment to a rational program of investigations. Philosophers in the Islamic era also dealt with theological issues, such as the nature of God and his attributes, the theory of prophecy, ethics, and the relationship of philosophy to scriptural revelation.

Philosophy, however, was not a neutral form of analysis but was itself a kind of religious ideology. Its ultimate goal was not merely intellectual knowledge but the reabsorption of the human soul into the spiritual universe from which it had come. Philosophical teachings differed from Islamic teachings on such questions as the resurrection of the body, whether the universe was eternal or created, and whether God had knowledge of particulars as well as universals. Hellenistic philosophy – as a heritage of rational reflection – could be understood as posing a challenge to the Quranic revelation as a source of complete and infallible truth.

There were several responses to this challenge. One of the earliest Muslim philosophers, al-Kindi (d. ninth century), believed that philosophy and Muslim theology could be combined as an expression of wisdom (*hikma*) and could jointly refute heresy, gnosticism, and dualism. Still, al-Kindi believed in the primacy of the Quran and the superiority of faith over reason as the way to the discovery of religious truths. He believed that the teachings of the Quran required no philosophical justification. He advocated the superiority of the Prophet to the philosophers in providing knowledge of the divine world. He did not accept Platonic and Aristotelian opinions about the creation of the world, which he believed was created ex nihilo. He held that the role of reason was to clarify and to extend faith into areas left vague by Quranic pronouncements

Later Muslim philosophers (*falasifa*), however, gave primacy to philosophy as a means of finding truth and regarded Islam as no more than an acceptable approximation. Al-Farabi (d. 950) established the broad outlines of philosophy and defined its relation to Muslim scripture. He believed in a supreme and eternal being who was the first cause of all existing things. He also believed that the supreme being was connected to the world by a hierarchical series of emanations, intelligences, which constituted the structure of the spiritual world and gave form to the material world. The successive levels of intellect mediated between God and the material world. Human beings, like all created beings, were formed by the intelligences of the spiritual world but at the same time were objects in the material world. Implanted in the human being was the faculty of reason, which is a counterpart of the spiritual intelligences. Human beings, therefore, must cultivate rational intelligence to the utmost and use intellect and reason to control behavior and feeling so that the soul may be purified and returned to its ultimate destiny: knowledge of, vision of, and reintegration into spiritual reality.

Religion for al-Farabi was only an inferior and indirect way of symbolizing the truth, suitable for the masses. The imagination of the prophet, he believed, was inferior to the intelligence of the sage. To reconcile philosophy with Islam, al-Farabi held that Islam was indeed a true religion and that Muhammad was the perfect sage and philosopher, as well as a prophet who could express the truth in a fashion persuasive to ordinary people. Insofar as al-Farabi valued Muhammad, it was not as prophet but as philosopher. Still, philosophers saw themselves not as opposed to Islam but as Muslims vested in one of many dimensions of the ancient culture that they regarded as part of their heritage.

Other aspects of Greek heritage remained the pursuits of a cosmopolitan aristocracy remote from the mainstream of Islamic religious and cultural trends. Islamic-era scientists showed a great talent for direct observation and experiment, and their contributions to astronomy, mathematics, medicine, chemistry, zoology, mineralogy, and meteorology often surpassed the received heritage of Greek, Persian, and Indian ideas. Alchemy, occult physics, and occult neo-Pythagorean mathematics, however, were motivated by the quest for esoteric revelations rather than by scientific understanding. Neo-Pythagorean numbers, for example, were not mathematical entities but symbols of a higher and unseen reality that the occult scientist tried to conjure forth. In alchemy, the object was not only to transform materials but to discover the hidden relation of the material to the immaterial world. Hellenistic thought in this mode introduced not an experimental endeavor or practical technology but a nontheistic spiritual and religious program.

CULTURE, LEGITIMACY, AND THE STATE

There were important cultural and political reasons for the translation of Persian and Hellenistic literatures. Translations were in part a continuation of a traditional form of culture, in part an appropriation of past culture by a new political elite, and in part a partisan project to enhance the prestige and authority of specific ethnic groups or factions. Translations were made to gain access to scientific, medical, mathematical, astronomical, and astrological skills and data. The caliphate, as sponsor and patron of philosophical literature, likely perceived it as an assertion of the superiority of rationality to revelation and of philosophers to prophets; by implication, an assertion of the superiority of caliphs as philosopher-kings over the scholars of religion. Philosophy was a literature appropriate to the transcendental claims of the ruler. Translations were also intended to symbolize the superiority of the Islamic empire to the Byzantine Empire, and the supremacy of the caliphs and the political elites to ordinary Muslims.

Furthermore, the 'Abbasids created a universal, transethnic, and pan-religious empire by promoting both conversions to Islam and translations of all cultures into Arabic as the shared imperial language. The incorporation of old elites into the new empire and the need to legitimate the caliphate in all the cultural languages of the conquered societies were important motives for the translation movement.

Translations acknowledged the growing importance of converts and clients, the founding of Baghdad as a multicultural society, and the need for the education of an ever more cosmopolitan elite.

Persian and Greek thought were also important in court circles, because they introduced the ideal of aristocratic self-cultivation. Courtiers, administrators, and the servants of caliphs were to be refined, learned, and worldly gentlemen. The aristocrat had to be knowledgeable in all the sciences, literature, history, philosophy, and religion. He was to be gentlemanly in manners, gracious, and sensitive to the nuances of rank and honor. He should also be competent in finance, in letter writing, in horsemanship, and in technical matters of administration. The aristocrat's cultivation included Islamic virtues, but its essential quality was a worldly refinement that set him apart from the lowly and justified his claim to power. Indirectly, the cultivation of Persian and Greek letters implied a common culture for a heterogeneous elite based on the presumption of inherent aristocratic superiority.

Furthermore, all the court literatures served to propagate a pre-Islamic concept of the ruler and the empire. Interest in the secular aspects of Arabic literature, Persian *adab*, and Hellenistic philosophies and sciences signified the adaptation of a cultural heritage that could be used to legitimize caliphal rule. They provided, in the Arabic case, an ethnic concept of political leadership; in the Persian case, a continuation of the heritage of ancient Middle Eastern kings; and in the Hellenistic case, a concept of the structure of the universe itself, in philosophic and scientific form, as the ultimate justification for imperial rule. The patronage of these several literatures implied that the caliph, although a Muslim ruler, was legitimized by the non-Islamic heritage of the ancient Middle East.

In sum, the 'Abbasids fostered ideological or religious loyalty to the caliphate using both Islamic and pre-Islamic motifs. They appealed to Muslim sentiment to recognize them as the legitimate successors to the Prophet and as the protectors and organizers of Islam. At the same time, they presented themselves to their subjects – Muslims and non-Muslims – as divinely selected rulers sent by God for the right ordering of worldly affairs. The caliphs expressed their claims in universalistic themes prevalent in ancient Near Eastern, Persian, Indian, Roman, and Hellenistic thought; they based their legitimacy not only on religious doctrine but on architectural symbols, literature, science, and philosophy, and on a style of court life marked by extraordinary possessions, pleasures, and powers. Their worldly power was construed as divine power, a power to be worshiped.

URBAN ISLAM: THE ISLAM OF SCHOLARS AND HOLY MEN

CHAPTER 14

INTRODUCTION

Two principal forms of state and society stemmed from the Prophet Muhammad. One was the caliphate, his successors who were deemed competent to give both political and religious leadership. The other was that of a community (*umma*), a religious body headed by those learned in law and theology who provided schools and courts, teachers and judges. Whereas the caliphate sponsored a version of Islam as a culture of imperial power and courtly accomplishments, in the oases of Arabia and garrison cities of the Middle East, the learned and the holy men cultivated Islam as a religion of law and piety, theology and devotion.

The formal teaching of Islam as a religion embedded in a community began with the Prophet. Later hadith reported that the Prophet used to sit in the mosque surrounded by students, whom he instructed in passages of the Quran. Other hadith recount how he sent teachers of the Quran (*qurra'*) to the Arabian tribes.

After Muhammad's death, his companions became the bearers of his religious legacy and authority. They preserved the Quran and were the repositories of memories, stories, and the sayings of the Prophet. They were committed to the precedents he had set for ritual, family, social, and legal behavior and were venerated because of their contact with him. For a long period, the memory of the Prophet was oral and personal. Only gradually were the first written records, themselves embedded in later texts, set down.

The companions also formed study circles for Quran and hadith, as well as for theological, historical, and legal studies that were not yet considered distinct or specialized subjects. These study groups probably resembled ancient classical academies and Jewish schools of religious study. In the postconquest period, mosques, private homes, and shops were all used as schools.

Although concentrated in Medina and Mecca, the companions carried the story of the Prophet throughout the empire. Wherever Arab conquerors settled, men who had known the Prophet, or the disciples of these men, accompanied the migration. In the garrison cities, these students of religion, who were without office, institutional means of support, or priestly status – including the *qurra'*, the *'ulama'* (religious scholars), and the Sufis (the ascetics) – became the teachers of Islam and the leaders of their communities.

The relationship between the scholars and teachers and the caliphate varied. Some considered the caliphs to be the heirs of the Prophet's religious as well as political leadership, and they supported the regime. Many scholars accepted their authority and took official positions as teachers, judges, and preachers. Others were opponents of the imperial vision of Islam. They held that not only the caliphs but all the companions of the Prophet who had direct experience of Muhammad's teaching, and through them their followers, were the custodians of his legacy and heirs to his religious authority.

The politics of the caliphate intensified this opposition. The Umayyad dynasty provoked Shi'i, Khariji, and Yemeni Arab opposition in the name of religious principles. 'Abbasid efforts to build up a strong state apparatus and to give the ruler a ceremonial grandeur that bordered on divinity also provoked rebellions. Even Sunnis, who supported the caliphate in principle, often withdrew from public commitments and concentrated on small-scale community life and personal piety.

Under the leadership of the scholars and holy men, the Muslim community was extremely diverse. At Muhammad's death, the earliest Meccan recruits who migrated with him to Medina (the *muhajirun*) and the earliest Medinan converts (the *ansar*) were the most closely identified as Muslims – those who accepted the Quran as revelation, Muhammad as the messenger of God, and the *umma* as the community of the true believers. His following also included converts from some of the Medinan Jewish tribes. Also included in the *umma* were "converts," allies, and factional chiefs from the tribes surrounding Mecca and Medina. The Quraysh of Mecca accepted Islam when, defeated by Muhammad, they recognized him as Prophet and leader in 630. These new Muslims, scarcely exposed to his teachings and influence, were less likely to be imbued with the moral sense of his teaching. Still, they were part of the Muslim community.

Postconquest settlements added further to this diversity as non-Arab clients and converts to Islam were assimilated into the tribal, religious, and literary traditions of the conquering elite. New Muslims – from pagan, Jewish, and Christian communities – brought with them a great variety of cultural understandings, ritual practices, and political sentiments. To some, Islam was a commitment to a way of life; to others it may have been little more than a political affiliation.

Under the pressure of this diversity, the community fragmented into a plethora of religio-political movements. The conflict between the Sunnis (the supporters of the established caliphate) and the Shi'is (those who campaigned for the succession of an imam descended in the family of 'Ali) led to a division within the Muslim *umma*. The political divisions, justified and sustained by religious concepts, led to separate versions of Islamic religion and identity. Kharijism had similar consequences, although on a smaller scale.

By the end of the first century, a new generation of scholars, disciples, and students (much augmented in number) succeeded the companions of the Prophet. The study circles became more specialized. Some circles focused on the legacy of the Prophet, the stories told about his person, his actions, and his sayings. Others focused on the text of the Quran itself, and the explications of its meanings (*tafsir*). Still others were engaged in legal analysis. Always present were the ascetics and holy men seeking a more direct experience of God rather than mere knowledge of his commands. These groups promoted alternative conceptions of political authority and religious merit and created diverse political and communal loyalties buttressed by theological speculation, historical narratives, mystical practices, and legal codes. Among Sunnis, the complex social and political situations of the first Muslim century led to a variety of theological sects and social movements, such as the Mu'tazili, Murji'i, and Qadari.

Among the Shi'is, the same tendencies toward diversity prevailed. The Shi'is divided over the proper line of succession to 'Ali and over the question of whether the succession (the imamate) was a political or a purely religious office. The Shi'i movement fragmented into numerous sects.

The diversity of beliefs and practices was further intensified by the close relationships of Muslims and non-Muslims. In the first century after Muhammad, there was no clear boundary between Muslims and non-Muslims. Islam began in a complex religious milieu in which paganism and monotheism had already begun to converge. Muslims shared religious beliefs and practices, folk traditions, and popular spirituality with non-Muslims. Jews, Christians, and Muslims all believed in God, angels and prophets, the last judgment, and the purpose of human existence as being the fulfillment of God's commands and faith in his revealed truth. Eastern Syriac Christians who believed in the humanity of Christ had common ground with Muslims. Jews were committed monotheists. Christians and Muslims believed in the sanctity of holy men, equating the warrior and the ascetic as militant defenders of religion. All Middle Eastern peoples thought of communities as religious bodies and believed that religious communities had a founding prophet. Gnosticism, messianism, magic, apocalypticism, mysticism, science, and philosophy were found in all the Middle Eastern religions.

Moreover, in the highly fluid social world of the seventh century, peoples of all religions interacted on a regular basis in commerce, social life, and festivals. Many Muslims were married to non-Muslims. In some cases, Muslims and Christians worshiped in the same spaces and venerated the same holy men. There were also political pressures for common views. The early caliphs were the rulers of Christians, Jews, and Zoroastrians as well as the leaders of Muslims; they sought to win the cooperation of non-Muslim elites and the acceptance of the majority of their subjects.

In these circumstances, the new empire did not at first separate adherents of Islam from other religions, nor from past social, cultural, ethnic, and literary identities. Converts to Islam brought with them the cultural, ritual, and legal practices of their old religions and societies – Arabian tribal culture, Jewish ideas and practices, Christian eschatology, and late Roman and Sasanian political and legal institutions. Muslim family life and the relations of men and women followed earlier West Asian patterns. Jewish community organization – the authority of the rabbis or scholars of Jewish law, as well as the organization of schools, courts, and charities – was a model for Muslim institutions.

Furthermore, Muslims and non-Muslims participated in a dynamic, living culture. There was much integration and mutual influence among Muslims, Christians, and Jews. This is exemplified in the many shared religious narratives. Muslims, for example, absorbed stories from Jewish tradition (*isra'iliyyat*). The educational system – based on oral recitation followed by transmission of texts – was similar in Roman, Jewish, and Muslim study circles. Theological debates fostered a shared discourse. Arabic literary culture stemmed not only from Arabian traditions but also from the traditions of the cities of the Middle East. In addition, Hellenistic and Persian literatures flourished, partly sponsored by the caliphate, partly the expression of the urban elites. The past provided models for the new religious community and made Islam one of a family of religions.

In many ways, the first century was probably similar to the later diffusions of Islam in other parts of the world. People who served the new elite, court, and government were often the first to convert. Others were won over by the preaching, piety, and miracles of Muslim holy men. Many may have been nominal converts who pronounced the Muslim profession of faith – "There is no God but God, and Muhammad is the Prophet of God" (*shahada*) – but otherwise continued to live among their non-Muslim families and communities, taking part in the worship and festivals of the old religions. Others would be more deeply transformed, adopting new languages, beliefs, and customs.

In this fluid cultural situation, the multiplication of divergences in the teaching of the scholars, the intensification of sectarian competition, and the strong influences of other religions led to fears of losing the true legacy of Muhammad. Caliphs, scholars, and holy men strove to articulate their Islamic credentials, to define beliefs and behaviors that were properly Muslim, and to distinguish Muslims from other peoples.

The policies of the Umayyad caliphate lent further urgency to the question of who had the authority to define Muslim beliefs, practices, and symbols. With the minting of Muslim slogans on coinage and the construction of the Dome of the Rock and other mosques, the caliphs (beginning with ʿAbd al-Malik) dramatically declared their patronage of Islam and laid claim to a more exalted status for themselves as divinely selected rulers.

In response, Sunni scholars, literati, and holy men gradually shifted their intellectual activities from oral transmission to written literature in order to consolidate and to propagate their teachings. Some were concerned primarily with scripture, the study and explication of the Quran, the recollection of the sayings of the Prophet, and the elaboration of law. They considered laws, rituals, and norms of behavior the critical aspect of Islam. They wanted to know how to live their daily lives in the image of the Prophet – how to pray, how much to give in alms, how to dress, how to greet each other, what pious formulas to apply on everyday occasions, and what laws should regulate marriage, divorce, inheritance, contracts, and other social and familial issues.

Others were committed to theology and were primarily concerned with understanding the meaning of faith and true belief, the nature of God's being, and what will be rewarded and what will be punished in the afterlife. Still others identified with the presence of the sacred (in the person or memory of the Prophet and the holy men) or in mystic realization of God. The never-ending process of delineating a Muslim identity invoked not only law, theology, and asceticism, but also the writing of history.

At the same time, the Shi'is maintained that the true leadership of Muslims was vested in the person of 'Ali and his descendants; they developed their own communities, conceptions, and practice of daily living under the authority of the imams. For most Muslims, however, Islam probably meant commitment to everyday life in everyday communities, with one's valor marked by restraint in thought and behavior, and a sense of humility before God.

Thus, between the seventh and the tenth centuries, the religion of Muslims was elaborated in Quranic exegesis, hadith, law, theology, mystical discourses, and the Shi'i concept of the imamate – incorporating into Islam the heritage of Greece and Iran as well as of Arabia and Muhammad. The historical religions of the Middle East were recast into a new high cultural monotheistic vision. Urban Islamic religious culture was ultimately the amalgamation of all of these orientations, of the struggles among them, and of those between them and the courtly practices of Islam. In the following chapters, we will explore in greater depth the varieties of religious experience in early Islam.

CHAPTER 15

SUNNI ISLAM

In the century following the founding of Basra, Kufa, and other Arab-Muslim cities, Arabic literary interests were pursued in conjunction with Quranic, legal, theological, and other religious subjects. An Arabic lingua franca emerged for the diverse tribes. Persian and Aramaic speakers contributed to rapid changes in Arabic's vocabulary, grammar, style, and syntax. As the Arabic language changed, religious scholars feared that they would lose touch with the Arabic of the Quran and thus lose the meaning of God's revelations. In eighth-century Basra, philosophical, lexicographical, and grammatical studies were undertaken to recapture the pure Arabic of Mecca and of the desert tribes and to clarify the usage of Arabic in the Quran and hadith. The roots of words had to be specified, vocabulary selected and explained, and proper speech given rules of grammar and syntax. These linguistic efforts persisted for more than a century and produced what we now know as classical Arabic. The grammar of Sibawayhi (d. 796) and the early dictionaries of Arabic were the products of this period.

The cultural ramifications of these studies went beyond linguistic analysis. The basis of linguistic studies was the collection of examples of old Arabic. Much in the manner of contemporary linguists or anthropologists, the scholars of Basra and Kufa sought out the bedouins and recorded their poems and sayings. Gradually, a large body of lore was accumulated and transcribed from oral into written form. This lore included bedouin poetry, as well as information about the life of the Prophet, Quranic revelations, the early conquests, and the behavior of the early leaders of the Muslim community. From the eighth to the tenth centuries, the totality of this literary and religious culture was gathered into several encyclopedic collections. Arabic literary culture was not purely the heritage of the desert but was shaped in the early Islamic era out of the religious and historical concerns of the Umayyad and early 'Abbasid periods.

History was an important part of this literature. Partly the product of caliphal patronage, it was also compiled and transmitted by the Muslim urban literati. In addition to the stories of the Arab conquests and empire, history was written to enshrine Muhammad as a prophet, to establish the credentials of the Muslims as a monotheistic people, and to explain their origins out of Arabian paganism. History portrayed the emergence of a religious people out of a tribal wilderness; it pointed to the Islamic calendar, the direction of prayer (*qibla*), and a sacred language and script to validate the origins of the Arab-Muslim community. Pre-Muhammadan prophetic history was elaborated to explain Quranic stories and to give Muslims their own prophetic history validating Muhammad as a true prophet.

The early caliphs promoted Muslim beliefs and practices by building mosques; they also appointed storytellers, teachers, and preachers who interpreted the Quran to ordinary people, related the sayings of Muhammad (hadith), and recounted stories of his life and of the ancient prophets. As moral preachers – much like the holy men of late antiquity – they admonished against sin and inculcated religious beliefs and norms of behavior. In the garrison cities, reciters of the Quran, preachers, and storytellers told of Muhammad and his exploits, his sayings, and his behavior. Historical materials embedded in later texts show that stories related to the Quran were compiled in the 650s and 660s. In the early decades of the eighth century, Medina was a center for the compilation and transmission of Prophetic reports (hadith), biography (*sira*), and campaigns (*maghazi*). The earliest extant biographies of the Prophet are attributed to authors who died in the second decade of the eighth century.

THE VENERATION OF THE PROPHET

A profound aspect of early Muslim religious feeling was the veneration of the Prophet. Next to the Quran, the veneration of the Prophet was – and arguably remains – the defining feature of Islam. In early biographical materials Muhammad is presented as having an immaculate character and providing ideal leadership. Traditions about his perfect character, his appearance, his miracles, his triumphs over infidels, and his superiority to all past prophets abound.

There were two main themes in the accounts of Muhammad as prophet. One was that he was an ordinary man selected by God for this task. He was a lawgiver and chief of a community. Hadith dating to the end of the seventh and early eighth centuries made the practice of the Prophet a model for ritual and social behavior. Muslims wanted to know about the Prophet in intimate detail: how he cared for his body, his personality, his kindness, his love of children, and his moral example.

The second theme was that Muhammad was a miraculous being, to be venerated as were Moses and Jesus. In the Quran, Muhammad is presented as the beloved of God; angels invoke blessings on him; he is a model human being, a mercy to the world. Hadith and biographies cultivated an image of the Prophet as the bearer of divine qualities and earthly perfection. Some hadith incorporated materials about ancient Israel or those derived from Jewish sources, as well as folkloric themes passed on by Jewish converts (*isra'iliyyat*), placing Muhammad in the lineage of ancient prophets. Muhammad as prophet was put on par with earlier holy men, saints, and apostles – all of whom are wise, trusted exemplars; teachers and healers; and just and holy friends of God.

The earliest biographies are replete with stories of miraculous deeds and events. Stories from Jewish, Christian, Zoroastrian, and Buddhist legends were applied to Muhammad. At his birth, his mother saw a miraculous light; signs were seen by holy men. Extraordinary events occurred in his lifetime: he won easy victories in battle, fed many from little, and died by his own choice.

The greatest miracle was the Prophet's ascent to heaven. A Quranic verse states that God transported Muhammad from the Masjid al-Haram to the Masjid al-Aqsa. The location of al-Aqsa is not specified, but early hadith place it in Jerusalem. In the Umayyad period – possibly in the reign of al-Walid – al-Aqsa became particularly sanctified because of its associations with Jesus and with the ascension, and/or to bolster the prestige of the caliphs in nearby Damascus. The story narrates that Gabriel awakened Muhammad and provided him with a winged beast (*buraq*) to carry him on a night journey (*isra'*) from Medina to Jerusalem. There, Muhammad ascended to heaven (*mi'raj*). He met Abraham, Moses, and Jesus and led them in prayer; he spoke with God, face to face, and learned about obligatory prayers. He visited paradise and hell. Muhammad acquired a heavenly book, echoing the lore of Jewish, Samaritan, and Judeo-Christian sects. In later centuries, the story was vastly elaborated and was told in resurrection (*qiyama*) literature, which describes the heavenly world. It was used as a symbol of mystical ascension to vision of God and was depicted in later Persian and Indian painting.

Superior to earlier prophets and on par with Jesus, Muhammad was also imagined as a kind of angel. Early narratives claim that Muhammad embodied the primordial light. He preceded all existence, and his birth was the manifestation of that light in human form. In Sufi theosophy, the light of Muhammad is the first expression of God's being – it is an emanation of the perfect man, the prototype of existence (i.e., the Logos). In the eighteenth century, Sufis defined their spiritual goal as the remaking of the person in the image of the Prophet.

Many Muslims believe that Muhammad can intercede for individuals with God and that his intercession may be won by prayer to implore God to bless him and his family, by repetition of the name of God (*dhikr*), and by the recitation of poetry. The appearance of the Prophet in a dream is considered a great blessing.

The adoration of the Prophet was expressed in poetry, prose, and festivals. The birth of the Prophet (*mawlid*) came to be celebrated almost everywhere with prayers, stories, sweets, festivals of lights, recitations, and ceremonies giving thanks to God, as well as expressing love of the Prophet and hope for salvation. The *mawlid* is marked by giving gifts that reciprocate the blessings of God and Muhammad. These may include money for charity, the sharing of food, and the reading of sacred texts or stories about the Prophet's life. Reverence for the Prophet is expressed by standing or praying in ceremonies to express deference and awe (*qiyam*).

Mawlid celebrations probably originated within Shi'i circles in the tenth century, but the narratives recited during them date to the first century of Islam. Al-Khayzuran (d. 789), the mother of Harun al-Rashid, transformed Muhammad's birthplace (as well as his tomb in Medina) into a place for prayers. The Fatimids (969–1171) celebrated the *mawlid* in Egypt with a ceremony that included a mosque recitation from the Quran, prayers, processions, and a sermon, mainly for the ruling elite. *Mawlid* practices then spread to Sunnis and became popular in Syria, Mesopotamia, and Egypt in the twelfth century. In thirteenth-century Cairo, it was celebrated by Sufis and the common people. *Mawlids* came to include Sufi exercises (*dhikr*), as well as recitations of mystical verses, the canonical collections of hadith (*sahih*), and panegyrical poems and blessings of Muhammad. The *mawlid* is an auspicious time of year because in that season God's responsiveness and generosity is believed to be greater. A prayer at this time is vastly more efficacious than at other times.

The *mawlids* of the Prophet set a precedent for the celebration of the birthday (here meaning the death day and the beginning of the afterlife) of saints. Prayers, recitations of poems, processions, *dhikr*, and readings from the Quran were and are conducted at the shrines of saints throughout the Muslim world.

Some scholars were opposed to these celebrations. They saw the *mawlids* as religion made easy for poor, uneducated, and "undisciplined" people. But they were unable to suppress these beliefs and ceremonies. In modern times, Wahhabis vigorously oppose *mawlid* celebrations because, for them, obedience is more important than love, and observance of tradition (*sunna*) is more important than an emotional attachment or spiritual relationship. Under Wahhabi influence, the *mawlid* is being redefined as a historical commemoration whose didactic aspect matters more than the experienced presence of the Prophet.

This changing attitude reflects a still deeper transformation in Muslim religiosity. The traditional *mawlid* is premised on the idea that a person is constituted by ties to a community and by shared emotions that have to be publicly dramatized. The modern view emphasizes individuality, so that religious obligations are defined by adherence to precepts; emotions are purely private and personal. The modern idea rejects the transactional bargain through which Muslims sought blessings from God.

EARLY MUSLIM THEOLOGY

Theology (*kalam*) – the investigation of the nature of God's being and his relation to human beings – was as much the product of Islamic urban milieus as of the caliphal court. Theological questions were prompted by political disputes. The Kharijis opposed 'Ali's agreement to arbitrate the murder of 'Uthman and opposed attempts to define the imamate in terms of lineage or ethnicity, arguing instead that individual piety and ability should be the criterion. They held that 'Ali's failure to decide by the Quran disqualified him as caliph. The supporters of Mu'awiya, however, did not want to scrutinize the personal religious qualifications of a caliph and held that all persons who professed Islam were ipso facto true Muslims. Later Kharijis extended the implications of their position to argue that anyone who failed to follow God's command was not a true Muslim and would be condemned to hell.

Kharijis also broached the problem of free will and predestination. Kharijis claimed that children of Muslims are not by definition Muslims, because individuals must elect to be Muslim; it was consistent with their view that only a blameless person was a true Muslim and, by implication, that every person had a choice and was responsible for his choices. They believed in freedom of will.

Other opponents of the Umayyads adopted a similar position. The Qadaris, a theological sect active between the end of the seventh and the beginning of the ninth centuries, held that a ruler is responsible for his actions. He has freedom of choice and should abdicate or be deposed if unrighteous. (The name Qadaris, however, was used to define the advocates both of free will and of the opposite, predestination – human power of choice or God's power of determination.)

Emerging from the Qadaris in Basra, the Mu'tazilis took a politically neutral position. They agreed with the Qadaris that every individual is the author of his actions and is responsible for them, but they refused to draw the same political implication. The Mu'tazilis held that a sinful Muslim is an intermediate between a believer and a nonbeliever, neither true Muslim nor infidel, and continues to belong to the Muslim community. Mu'tazilism began as a political position but went on to become a proselytizing movement and a theological defense of Islam. Mu'tazilis were in political favor during the inquisition era until 849. After the loss of political support in the reign of al-Mutawakkil, Mu'tazilis were no longer accepted in Sunni law schools but were still engaged in Shi'i Imami and Zaydi schools and continued to be an influential theological movement until the eleventh century.

Another politically neutral theological position was that of the Murji'a. Murji'a argued that anyone who professed to be a Muslim was a true Muslim, regardless of whether he practiced Muslim rituals. In the Murji'a view, faith and intention – not behavior – defined a true Muslim. Murji'a were active supporters of the equality of non-Arab converts with Arab-Muslims and defended the genuineness of their conversions whether or not they performed Muslim rituals.

The Murji'a and the Mu'tazilis prompted a host of theological issues. The debate about free will and predestination raised the question of God's powers and attributes. Do humans have free will, and, if so, does this compromise God's powers? If God determines human behavior, is he responsible for evil? What is to be understood by such Quranic phrases as "God's power" and "God's knowledge"? The question of attributes raised the further question of God's unity. Do his attributes imply that he is a composite being? Theologians thus debated the importance of faith versus works, of free will and predestination, and of the nature of God's being and how his seemingly contradictory qualities should be understood.

In the course of these discussions, Muslims engaged the works of Greek philosophers and Christian theologians who had already devised a tradition of theological argumentation. Converts brought earlier traditions into Muslim circles. Debates between Muslims and Christians at the court of the Umayyad caliphs, other polemical confrontations with Christians, and the translation of Greek and Syriac literature into Arabic integrated Hellenistic vocabulary and Greco-Christian practices of rational argument into early Muslim theology. The translation of Aristotle into Syriac and then into Arabic provided common methods and materials for intra-Muslim and Muslim-Christian disputations.

In Muslim theological circles, the people most interested in Greek dialectics were Mu'tazilis. At the forefront of debates – competing with Christian Trinitarianism, Manichaean dualism, pagan materialism, and even anthropomorphic conceptions widespread among Muslims – the Mu'tazilis upheld God's unity and transcendence. They affirmed that there was but one God, who is pure, ultimate being. As pure being, God is not like any created matter, nor like a human person, nor divided in any way. They denied that the attributes of God mentioned in the Quran are physical and literal.

Other Mu'tazili doctrines were a corollary of their conception of God's transcendence and unity. For example, they held that the Quran was a created message inspired by God in Muhammad and not part of God's essence or divine itself – as opposed to the Christian view that Christ, the Logos, the word of God, proceeds from God as part of his essence and is co-eternal with him. Other Muslims held that the Quran was "uncreated." The issue became a cause célèbre in Muslim theology and the most important issue in the religious politics of the 'Abbasid caliphate.

A further corollary of the Mu'tazili conception of God's transcendence and unity was the doctrine of God's justice and man's moral freedom and responsibility: men choose their own acts; they are not created by nor determined by God. God rightly rewards and punishes men for their deeds. They also upheld God's goodness: men, not God, are the authors of evil. If men were not morally free, they argued, God would by implication be the cause of evil.

From this followed the Mu'tazili principle of the promise and the threat: a Muslim who obeyed God's revealed law would be rewarded in heaven; a Muslim who ignored the law would be punished in hell. For the Mu'tazilis (as opposed to the Murji'a), faith included works.

The main tenets of the Mu'tazilis were profoundly Islamic in inspiration. Although other Muslims might disagree, their stress on God's unity and man's responsibility seemed to be the essence of the Quranic message. Yet, the Mu'tazilis raised issues that were not found in the discourses of the people of hadith and the jurists. They developed a metaphysics of being, a theory of the origin of the universe, a physics of created things, and a psychology of man – building on the teachings of Aristotle, Democritus, Empedocles, and other Greek philosophers.

A crucial tenet in their philosophy was that God's being, the universe, and human nature are all rationally ordered and knowable to human reason. God is defined by his essence, which is reason. The created world functions according to rational laws and, once created, is independent of God and not changeable by him. Similarly, in moral matters, good and evil have an intrinsic value. They are not dependent on, or changed by, divine will. God's justice is constrained by the laws of good and evil. Revelation can complete, confirm, or complement reason, but there are no truths unknown, unknowable, or inconsistent with the dictates of reason. Revelation can do no more than amplify or make the teachings of reason more specific. A possible corollary of the Mu'tazili position is that revelation is only supplementary guidance and of secondary importance.

These positions are summed up as the five theses of the Mu'tazili school: (1) *Tawhid*, the unity of God's being (with the implication that the Quran is created). (2) *'Adl*, God is just and does not do or make humans do evil. (3) Reward and punishment are in the hereafter without intercession for grave sinners. Repentance may win God's grace, but it is not assured. (4) A sinner is neither a true Muslim nor an apostate (the intermediate position). (5) Muslims are responsible for promoting good and suppressing evil.

Although the Mu'tazilis served Islam in their defense of the unity of God and in their clarification of man's free will and responsibility, their larger philosophy was at odds with the majority sentiment of the Arab-Muslim milieu about the nature of God and his creation. For other Muslims, the Quran and Muhammad – not reason – were the central experiences of Islam. They believed that the Quran contained God's will for men and the duties he had assigned them and that Muhammad was the messenger of God who delivered the last revelation. For most Muslims, man must submit to God, not presume to know better than God. The people of hadith – who severely criticized the legalists for the application of personal judgment to legal problems – were especially incensed that Muslim theologians were relying on reason for the discussion of religious matters. Some hadith scholars rejected Greek methods of discussion; they believed that reason had no place in religion at all because hadith were God's will and not to be questioned. They rejected the siren song of Greek ideas as incompatible with complete and unassuming devotion to God and his revelations.

Hadith scholars opposed the Mu'tazili conception of *tawhid* by insisting that the attributes of God – the independent existence of which was denied by the Mu'tazilis – must exist because they are mentioned in the Quran. To deny or explain them away would be to derogate from God's own revelation of his being. They rejected the Mu'tazili notion of the createdness of the Quran; they affirmed the contrary (uncreatedness) and made this a fundamental tenet of faith, as a way of asserting the superiority of the Quran to all human reasoning and knowledge.

Finally, they held that man's acts are predetermined by God alone. For hadith scholars, God's omnipotent power and his untrammeled, inscrutable will – not his rationality or his justice – were the heartfelt attributes.

Thus, by the ninth century, two basic positions had emerged in Muslim theology. One was a rationalist-oriented position that emphasized the centrality of reason as an ordering principle in the understanding of God's being, of the structure of the universe, and of the governance of human behavior. The rationalist position included, as its corollary, belief in free will and individual responsibility for moral choices. A contrary position stressed the absolute omnipotence and inscrutability of the divine being, who can be known only insofar as he has chosen to reveal himself through the Quran. This view denied the utility of reason in religious or moral choices. All human action is ultimately an expression of the power of the creator, rather than an autonomous exercise of free judgment and will. Embedded in the debate over God's determination and human freedom was a conflict of worldviews. The rationalists had confidence in the world as knowable and in the human mind as attuned to reality. The traditionalists believed in the limitations of human capacities and had a pessimistic view of human life as fated and controlled by the unfathomable power of God.

Ash'arism

Dissatisfied with both the excesses of Mu'tazili rationalism and the constricting literalism of the hadith scholars, ninth- and tenth-century Muslim theologians tried to find a middle ground consistent with emphasis on the importance of hadith, while preserving some role for reason in the discussion of theological issues. The most important middle position in the history of Muslim theology was the work of al-Ash'ari (d. 935). On doctrinal matters, al-Ash'ari adopted the views of the hadith scholars but refined them to meet the standards of Mu'tazili reasoning. For example, he held that the words of the Quran subsist in the divine essence, but their expression in letters and sounds is created. Thus, the Quran is uncreated, but any particular copy of it is created. On the question of free will, al-Ash'ari held that God is the ultimate author of man's actions, but man is an instrument of and participant in these actions and has responsibility for them by acquisition (*kasb*).

On the role of reason, al-Ash'ari stressed the overwhelming importance of the divine revelation and the humble quality of man's own will and rational faculties. Al-Ash'ari claimed that revelation is the only source of knowledge of good and evil. He rejected rational metaphysics as the key to the nature of God and the universe, but nonetheless he used Greek concepts to defend his position. Reason, he allowed, can spell out the meanings embodied in the Quran and hadith, defend the truth against its adversaries, and be used to persuade others of its validity. Theology does not of itself discover truths but reinforces belief in God and obedience to God's will by rational comprehension. Thus, Muslim theologians may use rational arguments to support theological tenets derived from tradition.

Maturidism, based on the work of al-Maturidi (d. c. 944), a Hanafi theologian and jurist, became the main rival to Ash'arism. His views were integrated into Transoxanian Hanafism in the tenth and eleventh centuries and moved westward to Iraq, Anatolia, Syria, and Egypt in the eleventh and twelfth centuries. Contrary to the Ash'aris, al-Maturidi agreed with the Mu'tazilis that man knows God through reason independently of revelation. He believed that there is a rational and universal basis for good and evil, that man has free choice, and that faith does not require works. Still, he believed that God has foreknowledge of who will be a believer and who a sinner. Unlike the Mu'tazili, he considered divine attributes – such as power and knowledge – to be real and eternal. Maturidis considered the word (*kalam*) of God to be uncreated but acknowledged that the ink, paper, and writing of Quranic texts are created.

In its modified Ash'ari and Maturidi forms, theology became an integral part of the intellectual life of the law schools. Great scholars of the eleventh century, such as al-Juwayni and al-Ghazali, held that reason cannot be the ultimate source of true knowledge but is rather a tool for prudential, useful, and worldly evaluations.

The turn to a more limited concept of the role of reason coincided with important sociopolitical changes in early Muslim societies. The emphasis on reason seems to have been correlated with Muslim minority hegemony in a mixed society and the need for Muslim elites to maintain ties with the non-Muslim population and broader cultural and religious traditions. The insistence on the priority of revelation belongs to a later period in which Muslims had become the dominant majority, although they were beset by intense intra-Muslim sectarian conflicts. The result was an Islam both dominant and threatened – concerned primarily with consolidating Muslim identities and defining boundaries between Muslims and the minority non-Muslim populations and between truly Islamic beliefs and heresy. With these historical changes came a transformation of cultural mood from an open and optimistic to a guarded and pessimistic view of human nature; from revelation as parallel to reason to revelation as absolute and transcendent.

SCRIPTURALISM: QURAN, HADITH, AND LAW
(CO-AUTHOR, LENA SALAYMEH)

However, for the great majority of Muslims (both Sunnis and Shi'is, not theology but adherence to scripture is the first principle of Islam. Islam is defined as living in accordance with the law of God. The law is contained in the texts of the Quran and in the precedents of the Prophet (hadith). For early readers and commentators, the Quran was more than a text. Scholars were eager to mold their own lives by it and to infuse the lives of their contemporaries with the spirit and teachings of the holy book. They wanted the Quran to be the basis of a Muslim style of personal behavior and of ritual, family, and business matters, and also of political questions

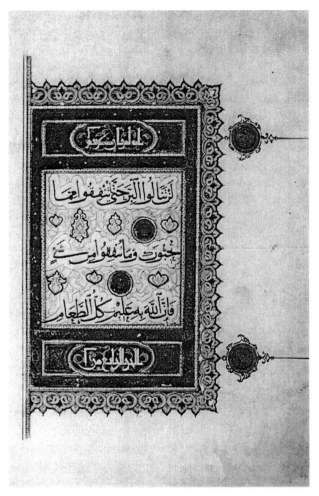

Illustration 5. A page of an illuminated Quran. Reproduced by permission of the Trustees of the Chester Beatty Library, Dublin.

such as the selection of rulers, justice, and taxation. They aspired to cast the whole of life in the mold of the Quranic message. (See Illustration 5.)

This interest in the application of the Quran led to works of interpretation, commentary, and explanation (i.e., exegesis, or *tafsir*). Two of the most important and extant early works were by al-Tabari (d. 923) and al-Tha'labi (d. 1035). Exegetical works are often encyclopedic, including earlier interpretations and embracing many aspects of the Sunni tradition – including poetry, hadith, *adab*, theology, law, and Sufi hermeneutics. Exegesis is not only philological but also doctrinal and devotional.

The centrality of the Quran also led to the study of the sayings and deeds of the Prophet, which were considered authoritative examples of how a proper Muslim life should be led. Hadith, which had been primarily transmitted in oral tradition, began to be collected in written form from the beginning of the eighth century. In the ninth century, several canons were compiled that stand second only to the Quran as authoritative Muslim scripture. The impulse to fashion a divinely guided way of life further inspired the elaboration of Islamic law. Law (*fiqh*, which is misidentified as Shari'a in contemporary usage) is not strictly speaking the revealed word of God, but it was widely understood to be a divinely inspired extension of the teachings of the Quran and hadith. The development of Islamic law was driven both by pragmatic considerations and by the impulse to actualize the teachings of the Quran and the Prophet.

Law in the seventh and eighth centuries

Islamic law, like all legal systems, first developed out of practical everyday concerns and the need to set out norms for behavior and to adjudicate disputes. Muslim legal thought and practice had deep roots in the ongoing functioning of Middle Eastern societies. Islamic law continued and modified pre-Islamic practices in familial, commercial, criminal, and administrative matters. Arabian customary law in commerce, marriage, and criminal matters was an important precedent. So too were deep traditions of Roman law and provincial variations on Roman, Persian, canon, and Jewish law. In the early Islamic era, Jewish and Christian legal systems were also evolving, and there likely were interchanges between these legal systems. Customary social and business practices, the experiences of converts, discussions among experts, and the reading of texts brought ancient laws into early Muslim juridical reflection and practice.

Quranic teaching added to the ongoing practice of law. It set out religious rituals such as prayer, fasting, and pilgrimage; it regulated social behavior in such matters as almsgiving, feuds, marriage, and inheritance. After the death of Muhammad, law was amplified by the decisions and policies of the early caliphs and the Prophet's companions (who acted as judges and arbitrators). Caliph 'Umar is said to have promulgated laws on temporary marriage, adultery, parentage by concubines, and other issues.

Furthermore, caliphs appointed governors who in turn appointed judges (*qadis*). Judges were initially multicompetent state officials dealing with justice, police, tax, and finance issues. Many, but not all, were religious scholars and teachers who in addition to their judicial duties led the community in prayer. Between 700 and 740 courts became more professional due to formal record keeping, the appointment of functionaries such as scribes, official witnesses, and the consultation of outside legal authorities (muftis). After 740 or 750, caliphs – rather than governors – appointed judges, whose nonjudicial functions ceased as a bureaucratic court apparatus emerged. By the reign of Harun al-Rashid, only religious scholars (*'ulama'*) were appointed as professional judges. Generally, the considered personal judgments (*ra'y*) of the judges, or of the judges and their legal advisers, set the precedents for what would be Islamic law.

Simultaneously, Islamic legal traditions were formed by discussions within communities. This was not the work of any single person or group but was carried out in geographically distinct centers of religious and legal scholarship. Mecca, Medina, Kufa, Basra, Baghdad, and Fustat were the most important. Independent scholars reflected on legal issues, cultivated students and disciples, and created study circles for discussion and instruction. Students participated in several study circles and studied with their master or masters, either at once or successively. These early study circles were not confined to law but included students of theology, history, and hadith who were being trained not only as lawyers but as religious intellectuals. Students in the same legal circles might hold different views about both legal and nonlegal religious subjects. Thus, Islamic legal systems were formed and implemented by both state appointed officials and independent scholars, surrounded by their students, patrons, clients, and communities.

As legal, theological, and other study groups multiplied under the leadership of prominent local scholars in important cities, students disseminated their teachings, expanding local legal study groups into empire-wide networks of shared legal studies and practice. The Hanafis were the first of the legal study circles to become an empire-wide legal network. They had their origins in Kufa and Basra. They traced their origins back to Abu Hanifa (d. 767) and his prolific students, Abu Yusuf (d. 798) and al-Shaybani (d. c. 805). By the second half of the eighth century, the earlier legal circles were absorbed or displaced by the Hanafis. In Iraq, Hanafi legal activity had a politically and socially pragmatic orientation. The Hanafis based their judgments on established (even pre-Islamic) precedents, individual judgment of the scholars (*ra'y*), and Islamic norms.

Hanafism spread, in part because it had the support of the 'Abbasid regime and was propagated by appointments to judgeships. Baghdad, being a newly created city, had no prior history of legal studies, and the legal cadres there were generated entirely by 'Abbasid appointments. Hanafi traditions soon reached beyond Iraq. They circulated in Isfahan and spread throughout Khurasan before the middle of the eighth century, to Transoxania in the late eighth and early ninth centuries, and to Egypt and Qayrawan in the early decades of the ninth century. In the first half of the ninth century, Hanafi opinions are attested in Mosul and Qazwin. In the late eighth and ninth centuries, a Hanafi-Murji'a orientation was strong in Isfahan, Rayy, and Khurasan, while in Baghdad some Hanafis were Mu'tazilis and others were Sunnis. However, the Hanafi network was not a monolith. Students of Hanafi scholars studied with a variety of masters and could hold different legal and theological opinions.

The legal tradition of Medina was the basis of a second legal network and of the later Maliki school of law. The *Muwatta'* of Malik (d. 767) is one of the earliest surviving and comprehensive legal works. It contains the results of a continuous tradition of legally defined social and ritual practices going back to the Prophet. In the *Muwatta'*, law is understood as deriving from the teaching of the Quran, the example of the Prophet (*sunna*), the judgment (*ijtihad*) of the companions, and the practice of the people of Medina. Thus, law was based on the practice of the Prophet, but as transmitted, agreed on, and modified by successive generations of Medinan scholars. Religious authority lay in Medinan custom, the recollected, vetted, and practiced norms and rules of law, a continuous living tradition (*'amal*).

Malikis also developed widespread networks, although at first they were without political support. The disciples (*ashab*) of Malik appeared in Egypt at the end of the eighth century. Then in the late ninth century, Malikis were appointed as judges in Egypt, Wasit, Basra, and Baghdad. These appointees were not locals but officials of the central government. The Maliki school would become the most prominent school in Egypt, North Africa, and West Africa.

Little is known about the early Shafi'is. The Shafi'is spread from Egypt to Iraq and Iran around the middle of the ninth century and from Baghdad to western Iran and Khurasan in the tenth century. The expansion of the Shafi'is and the Malikis was probably favored because both had a balanced way of integrating hadith and legal practice in comparison with the Hanbalis, who emphasized hadith, and the Hanafis, who leaned toward practice. They attracted independents and new jurists to their ranks.

Some places – such as Syria and the Jazira, where pro-Umayyad sentiment was strong and 'Abbasid influence weak – remained outside of the predominant law networks. The judges of Mosul were local scholars from dominant Yemeni tribal families. Syrian scholars were often Awza'is (members of a school that did not survive) or Malikis related to the Umayyads or to local tribes.

A key factor in the development of legal networks was the ever-growing recourse to written texts. The production of texts and consolidation of study circles led to the coalescence of jurists around a limited number of authorities and traditions. The underlying stratum of legal texts was oral material. Oral transmissions were collected by students in the form of notes that – with successive interpolations – became books. Teachers would either check the materials in students' notebooks or produce their own texts. By about 750, important legal texts had been compiled. From then on, more formal, codified learning, driven by authoritative compilations, generated a school tradition defined by the transmission of and commentary on authoritative texts.

Most texts were independently produced by private scholars, but some texts were sponsored by the government. Abu Yusuf's *Kitab al-Kharaj*, for example, originated in order to gather documents to unify the tax system of Iraq and to validate the caliphal claim that Iraq was conquered by force and was therefore subject to taxation at the discretion of the caliphs. This was disputed by jurists who claimed exemptions for lands set aside for taxation at reduced rates.

Tradition and law: Hadith

Before these legal networks and their traditions would be consolidated into the final schools of law, there was a crucial and defining struggle among the lawyers and the scholars of hadith. Although the Quran was an important source of law, it was not exclusive and not necessarily the primary source of law. The living practice of the Prophet (sunna), the practice of local communities (such as Medina) transmitted by personal example, and customary Arab law were also authoritative sources of ritual, social, and legal norms. The Quran was often interpreted in the light of living practices. Many Muslims believed that their practices were consistent with the Quran, or were justified by the visually perceived behavior of the Prophet, by the authority of the companions, or by the authority of the caliphs or claimants to the caliphate. The views of prominent *shaykhs* and teachers and the judgment of courts, scholars, and lawyers were also taken to be authoritative. In specific instances – such as stoning as punishment for adultery – actual practice could take precedence over Quranic texts. There was a lively debate among texts, practices, and political authorities. Only much later would legal discourse come to emphasize the Quran and hadith as the overriding legal sources, as part of a general process in which Islamic culture came to be dominated by traditionalism.

In the late Umayyad period, for example, Marwanid court circles debated whether purity laws and ablutions should be based on living practice, on the personal example of the Prophet, on visual memory, or on Quranic texts. In the reign of 'Umar II (717–21), almost a century after the death of Muhammad, the Quranic text finally prevailed. The Quranic ritual laws then came to be seen as God's gift, which marked the covenant with his people that was first given to Abraham and then to Moses and then to the Christians, but finally given to the Muslims. The application of Quranic and Prophetic norms to ritual matters thus separated Muslims from non-Muslims and defined a confessional community.

Similarly, rules about the charity tax (*zakat*) were elaborated in the first half of the eighth century. Quranic texts barring interest on loans (*riba*) were applied to challenge Umayyad coinage practices, in which the state took a commission or minted new coins lighter than the old ones, because these practices entailed a fee or tax on the exchange of coins. The prohibition of taking interest was then applied to various kinds of sharecropping transactions.

Alongsidey of the Quran, hadith – the sayings of the Prophet – became the most important source of law. According to the orthodox Muslim view, these sayings are Muhammad's own inspired utterances dealing with ritual, moral, and social matters, but they are not revelations (as is the Quran). Hadith probably originated as stories told by Muhammad's companions and their pupils in Mecca and Medina and then in the postconquest garrison cities of Kufa, Basra, and other cities. As veneration of the Prophet increasingly became central to Muslim identity, interest in emulating his every behavior intensified. Everything Muhammad said and did came to be of prime religious importance.

Initially, the transmission was primarily oral. Many hadith were recalled from the actual sayings of the Prophet; others carried the remembered sense of what he said, or intended, and not necessarily his exact words. Still others were thought to be consistent with the Prophet's intentions, but some were ascribed to the Prophet based on ideas that were considered good, right, and true in the time of their formulation. Others may have attributed words and ideas to Muhammad for ulterior motives. In late Umayyad and early ʿAbbasid times, scholars who were devoted to a companion of Muhammad or perhaps interested in particular subjects gathered circles of students and began to make written compilations. Although hadith were supposed to be transmitted by personal contact, many were probably transmitted through written collections. They could therefore be transmitted in parallel but varying versions. There was, however, resistance to written copies, because of the desire not to rival the Quran and because scholars wanted to maintain flexibility and a living tradition. Scholars in Basra, Kufa, and Medina continued to favor hadith transmission from memory, but this was abandoned in Baghdad and elsewhere outside of Iraq. Even scholars who permitted writing did not like copying from texts but preferred note taking from oral presentation. In the eighth century, chains of transmission (*isnads*) became necessary (because of the generational changes) to validate the genealogy of the reported sayings. At first, many transmission chains were incomplete or traced back to one of the companions rather than directly to the Prophet himself. Gradually, the use of transmission chains with continuous links back to the Prophet became the standard.

The progressive enlargement of the appeal to hadith can be traced in the history of Meccan law. Ibn al-ʿAbbas (d. 687–88) gave legal opinions explicitly supported by the Quran and by *raʾy* (individual judgment), but not by traditions from the Prophet. Ibn ʿAbbas's students expanded the authoritative role of hadith. In the work of Ibn Jurayj (d. 767), hadith from the Prophet were more numerous, but transmission chains – although more common – were not fully developed. By the late eighth century, there were systematically organized books of hadith and hadith transmitter criticism. In the early ninth century, hadith books organized by legal topics or as Quranic commentaries were produced.

Collectors of hadith determined authenticity based on the reliability of the men who transmitted the stories and the verifiability of the chains of transmitters. One had to demonstrate that Muhammad's sayings were reported by a person of known probity, who in turn had heard them from earlier holy men. Then, and later, hadith were accepted based on their probability and plausibility, on the authority of the *shaykhs* who transmitted them, and on collective agreement. Hadith compilers were strongly opposed to individual judgment and any use of reasoning that made the teller anything other than the medium of transmission. In the culture of early Islam, what mattered were oral transmissions and the authority of the *shaykhs* who transmitted them. Regardless of theory, in practice it was the authority and reputation of the scholars and their acceptance by students and by the larger community that defined religious beliefs and practices.

In the ninth century, six Sunni canons of hadith – including the collections of al-Bukhari and Muslim – were compiled. The classical compilations were organized by topic to serve as reference works on ritual and legal issues. The Sahih of Bukhari uses such headings as faith, purification, prayer, alms, fasting, pilgrimage, commerce, inheritance, wills, vows and oaths, crimes, murders, judicial procedure, war, hunting, and wine. In each chapter, there are anecdotal descriptions of how the Prophet dealt with these matters. Muslims read hadith in close relationship with the Quran to clarify and supplement the Quran's specific guidance. However, the hadith are so varied that no matter what a Muslim believes and does there are infinite aspects that elude him. There is an endless tension among precepts fulfilled, precepts neglected, and precepts not understood.

Hadith literature also flourished in later centuries. In the tenth century, Baghdad, Iran, and Cordoba were the main centers of hadith scholarship. In the eleventh century, Spain, Iran, and Baghdad were centers for more specialized biographical and technical works bearing on hadith. By then, the process of hadith compilation and criticism was extensive, and later generations would edit, synthesize, and transmit them. Abridgements, commentaries, and reference works became the norm.

Almost a century of Western scholarship has called the validity of hadith into question. Many studies have alleged that some hadith were first put into circulation long after the death of the Prophet. Many others were provided at a later date with *isnads* that were expanded backwards to make contact with the Prophet as the original source. Because hadith are the basis of so much of Muslim religious and social practice, Muslim scholars have defended their authenticity. Scholars caught between root-and-branch criticism of hadith and Muslim acceptance of them as valid transmissions from the Prophet often take the middle ground and argue that transmission chains are a late invention attached to material that genuinely goes back to a time when it might plausibly be remembered by the Prophet's companions.

Other scholars – both Muslim and non-Muslim – have recently argued that the issue of the fabrication of hadith is misconceived. Hadith, they argue, were always understood to represent Muslim acceptance of certain views as authoritative expressions of Islam, rather than a mechanical connection to the Prophet. Early hadith scholars made no claim to absolute certainty that a hadith derived expressly from the Prophet. They were interested in probability, plausibility, and soundness (*sahih*). The consensus of scholars on the acceptability of a hadith added validation. The addition of transmission chains, then, was not a conspiracy to mislead Muslim believers, but an expression of the consensus of scholars at a given time about the acceptable range of opinions and the authority of those opinions. The key objective was to capture the charisma of the Prophet.

Reasoned opinion versus traditionalism

Toward the end of the eighth century, the work of some legal scholars came under attack from scholars of hadith. The "people of hadith" – often minority members of the various law schools – differed with the majority on specific doctrines and about the proper sources of legal judgment. Whereas most legal scholars believed in the traditions of their school and in a certain amount of personal discretion, the hadith-minded (*ahl al-hadith*) opposed any source of law or morals other than the Quran and the sayings of the Prophet. They objected to the arbitrary personal opinions of their opponents (*ra'y*) and questioned the validity of the Madinan concept of normative practice (*'amal*).

Although hadith scholars were found in all the law circles, in the early decades of the ninth century, hadith advocacy was organized into a separate movement under the leadership of Ahmad ibn Hanbal (d. 855). Ahmad ibn Hanbal and his followers became the leading spokesmen for hadith due to their resistance to the inquisition (*mihna*) of the Caliph al-Ma'mun (r. 813–33). Al-Ma'mun tried to define a religious orthodoxy in terms of the created Quran – a theological position that held that the Quran itself was an object in the material world. This doctrine defended the unity of God's being – nothing other was akin to God – but implicitly diminished the sanctity of the Quran and made it subject to interpretation by caliphs and scholars. The jurists held that human reasoning was essential to extend and to apply the law in areas not covered by revelation.

Ahmad ibn Hanbal defended instead the principle of the uncreated Quran, which implied that the revelation was on par with the divine being. Traditionalists believed that only the revealed word – including the authenticated words of Muhammad – could be the source of law. They opposed the use of reason in legal matters in any form – whether analogy (*qiyas*), consideration of the public interest (*istislah*), or casuistic manipulation of the letter of the law (*hiyal*). Whereas theological positions were integral to the worldview of the people of *ra'y*, traditionalists objected to reasoning itself.

These jurisprudential differences were reinforced by political differences. The people of *ra'y* tended to cooperate with the state and serve in the administration of justice; the traditionalists, inclined to asceticism and puritanism, tended to refuse state service and state patronage. The Hanbalis were also an activist public movement. They enforced Muslim values, "commanding the good, and forbidding evil," by preaching an ascetic and puritanical version of Islam, and they launched vigilante attacks, breaking wine bottles, musical instruments, and chessboards.

Nonetheless, the theological and juristic debates prompted the formulation of a middle position that combined hadith and rational legal judgment, reason and revelation. In the late ninth and tenth centuries, Hanafi, Maliki, and Shafi'i jurists in principle accepted Quran and hadith as the fundamental bases of law, but in practice continued to base legal judgments on analogical reasoning and the consensus of the learned.

Although the people of hadith in principle relied on whatever was dependably reported as a Prophetic hadith – without appeal to external sources of appraisal or criticism – in practice Hanbalis and hadith scholars accepted the utility of rational arguments for defending their positions, for making consistent judgments, and for validating their views vis-à-vis other jurists. Also, jurists and traditionalists united to resist the more extreme position that only the Quran was a valid source of Muslim law – a position that would have undermined both the people of *ra'y* and the people of hadith – and to oppose the Shi'is and Mu'tazilis.

These compromises are manifest in the literature of legal methodology (*usul al-fiqh*). One of the best-known early works on methodology is the Risala, which is attributed to al-Shafi'i (767–820). The theory of the Risala was further developed by Ibn Surayj (d. 918) and his students and became a textbook in the tenth century. The methodology espoused in the Risala and similar jurisprudential texts accepted that the Quran and Prophetic traditions are the ultimate sources of law; indeed only hadith going back to the Prophet himself are considered valid. Still, legal rulings based on individual judgment, analogy (*qiyas*), and consensus are valid insofar as they keep within strict logical boundaries and are extensions of revealed texts. Although this methodology curbed the use of *ra'y*, it also controlled the use of hadith by holding that only the consensus of qualified scholars could determine the authenticity of hadith.

As in all legal systems, jurisprudential texts identified the sources of law and the procedures that allowed for extrapolation or application of the law to different circumstances. In the Islamic context, these methodologies replaced free reasoning based on experiential considerations with hermeneutic reasoning based on specific texts. They provided standards and methods to discover the will of God from the revealed texts and thus legitimated the positions of the law schools by showing them to be based on proper methods – even if the results varied by school.

The proliferation of legal methodology also had important implications for the relations of theology and law. In their early history, the law study circles were at once schools of law, theology, and historiography. Hanafis gave primacy to revelation but held a variety of theological views that accepted some role for human reason, choice, and responsibility. The Hanafi school harbored a variety of theological sects, including the Maturidi, the Murji'a, the Najjari, and the Ash'ari. Shafi'is were primarily Ash'aris in theology, although up to the eleventh century many were Mu'tazilis. Hanbalism, however, rejected theological speculation and took a deterministic view of God's absolute omnipotence, calling for submission, obedience, humility, and strict respect for the literal words of the Quran and sunna.

Despite the importance of Aristotelian logic in theology and philosophy, Islamic jurisprudence does not appear to have explicitly incorporated Aristotelian logic until the works of al-Ghazali (d. 1111), the Hanbali jurist Ibn Qudama (d. 1223), the Shafi'i jurist al-Amidi (d. 1233), and the Maliki jurist Ibn al-Hajib (d. 1248). The use of logic as known through the organon of Aristotle helped give legal thought a greater consistency and logical coherence and grounded legal theory in a still wider field of knowledge. However, in practice, it does not seem to have had much effect on legal argument.

Thus, the outcome of the long struggle between the people of hadith and the people of *ra'y* was to reconcile two vaguely defined religious orientations. Law came to be defined as a code of religious teaching based on revelation in Quran and hadith, as interpreted and amplified by the consensus of the legal scholars and by the use of analogical reasoning. The long debate refined the shape of law and hadith and persuaded most Muslims that both Quran and hadith were the scriptures of Islam.

Concealed within this consensus was a profound disagreement over the meaning of a truly religious life. The proponents of hadith thought of Islam as a completely revealed faith, a religion of submission to the revealed word of God and acceptance of the words of Muhammad. The proponents of community consensus and of individual judgment held that Islam was a religion based on scripture, but one that must be adapted and applied to changing circumstances based on individual judgment and the agreement of the community. Thus, there was profound disagreement about the boundaries between revealed truth and human interpretation, the requirements of faith and the use of reason, the degree of man's submission to God, or his autonomy in living a Muslim life. The same outer life implied radically different forms of spirituality.

The schools of law

The struggle between *ashab al-hadith* and *ashab al-ra'y* also had important institutional effects on the study of law. It prompted the further development of legal study circles and networks of study groups into what we now identify as the classical legal schools (*madhhab* [singular], or *madhahib* [plural]). The social organization of Muslim legal activity evolved from broadly defined religious study circles, to more focused legal study circles, to networked legal study circles, and finally to the schools of law. As both hadith scholars and jurists defined their methodological and theological positions, the study circles and networks were provided with a more formal doctrinal identity. Their doctrines were then presented in authoritative compilations and a school tradition emerged from the transmission of and commentary on authoritative texts. The culmination of this process was the production of an authored summary of school teachings (known as *mukhtasar*).

School identity was fostered by naming the school after a past great figure and by compiling biographical dictionaries of past and present members. Teaching was organized under a single head (*ra'is*). The transition from study circles to schools of law with a defined identity, programs of study, and historical tradition established institutions that functioned as guilds insofar as they regulated entry, training, and certification in law. The schools also gave some consistency and predictability to

Table 4. *Early schools of law*

Founding "father"	Region	School
al-Awza'i (d. 744)	Syria	Awza'i
Abu Hanifa (d. 767)	Iraq	Hanafi
Malik b. Anas (d. 795)	Medina	Maliki
al-Shafi'i (d. 820)	Egypt	Shafi'i
Ibn Hanbal (d. 855)	Iraq	Hanbali
Dawud b. Khalaf (d. 883)	Iraq	Zahiri

Note: Of the hundreds of legal schools that once existed, primarily four Sunni schools of law survive and they are Hanafi, Maliki, Shafi'i, and Hanbali.

Islamic law, although they continued to reflect geographical diversity and did not eliminate the individual judgment of prominent jurists (*ijtihad*). (See Table 4.)

In the late ninth and early tenth centuries, Baghdad was the center of these transformations in legal education. A Shafi'i jurist, Ibn Surayj (d. 918), started the practice of a regular course of study, a defined student body under a single teacher, a defined succession of teachers, and a written dissertation. He was a leader in the synthesis of hadith texts and rational jurisprudential procedures. Theology was often, but not necessarily, studied by the law students. Many Shafi'is were Ash'aris in theology and Sufis in devotional practices.

Al-Karkhi (d. 952) played a similar role for the Hanafis. As late as the first half of the tenth century, the Hanafis were defined as followers not of Abu Hanifa but of several of his disciples. The Hanafi school solidified in the tenth century with the writing of commentaries, the transmission of an authoritative doctrine, and the training of students – but there was still considerable variation and free choice of opinions. The Hanafi school perpetuated its identity not by teaching students to imitate but by introducing them to controversies within the school and by inculcating a sense of the boundaries of controversies and of respect for competing authorities. For example, Hanafi texts from the thirteenth century took the form of commentaries on the Muhtasar of al-Qudari. These commentaries focused heavily on differences (*ikhtilafat*), which gave students a sense of the history of the school, the positions of earlier scholars, and the connections of later authorities to earlier authorities. This became the basis of legal reasoning according to Hanafi methodologies.

Abu Bakr al-Khallal (d. 923) was the effective founder of the Hanbali school. The basic text of this school, Ibn Hanbal's Musnad, was – strictly speaking – a work of hadith and not of law. It was arranged by transmitter and not by legal subject and gave no opinions from later jurisprudents. Hanbalism, however, became a law school, as Hanbal's followers collected his opinions and began to order and classify collections of hadith by subject matter. Al-Khallal (d. 923) gathered Ibn Hanbal's opinions, elaborated them, taught them to his disciples, and wrote a biographical dictionary of earlier Hanbalis. The institutional aspects of the Maliki school are less known.

By the end of the tenth century, most jurists were adherents of one or another of the schools. They disagreed over details, but they recognized one another's legitimacy, and they had fairly similar jurisprudential systems based on the integration of hadith and rationalism. Many differing opinions attributed to the companions and earlier jurists allowed for flexibility and diversity. Change came from commentaries, and from judicial opinions on specific matters raised by petitioners. Every scholar was entitled to independent reasoning (*ijtihad*), and only discussion and debate could resolve differences of opinion. Contrary to a common opinion, the gates of *ijtihad* were never closed.

Legal schools divided law into three substantive categories: *'ibadat* (ritual regulations), *mu'amalat* (rules of social relations), and *imama* (theory of collective organization). Under these categories, the law dealt with prayer, almsgiving, and fasting; matters of marriage, divorce, slavery, partnerships, debts, wills, and other legal and social concerns; and a concept of the selection and authority of rulers. Many aspects of law were derived from the world of everyday affairs. The system of taxation employed by the caliphate was a continuation of Sasanian practices – rather than the legal outcome of a specific Quranic verse or hadith. Similarly, many aspects of contracts, property law, criminal law, and family law found in the region's pre-Islamic legal systems persisted in Islamic legal practice through the acceptance of customary social norms. Islamic law was not a theoretical construct but was developed in discourse with the real world of Muslims.

The legal opinions and methods of each school were applied in daily practice. Jurist-consultants (muftis) adopted the schools' opinions. Judges applied the schools' teachings in courts. Courts rendered decisions in family and commercial matters and maintained communal records for marriages, divorces, and commercial and property transactions. There were also informal means of adjudication outside of the courts based on customary law and the mediation of community notables.

The tenth-century shift in the character of legal discourse and practice also indicates important changes in the social and political meaning of law. In the ninth century, jurists were still the informal elders of their communities – merchants, officials, and perhaps artisans, meeting in the marketplace or mosque. By the eleventh century, they were professionals. Authority had shifted from a diffuse community to a specialized elite. Within that elite, authority was vested in the legal scholars (*shaykhs* and *mujtahids*) who were the qualified interpreters of the law. Shi'is are well known for having a hierarchy of jurists, but Sunnis in effect had an informal but similar respect for hierarchical authority. The authority of the legal scholar, however, was not spoken of as a present phenomenon but was held to inhere in past great teachers whose charisma was manifest in the present. Sunni jurists also accepted the overriding authority of the consensus of jurists (*ijma'*), but this consensus was said to exist as long as there was no dissenting opinion on a particular issue.

Politically, the emergence of consolidated legal schools represented the triumph of the pious and scholarly community as a private socioreligious rather than a governmental enterprise; law was the product of discussion within communities and competition among schools rather than state legislation. After the inquisition of the early ninth century (*mihna*), caliphs did not usually interfere in either legal education or adjudication. Law developed in an autonomous domain not shaped by the state.

The consolidation of the schools of law was an important moment in the history of Middle Eastern societies. In the early conquest era, Islamic law was the continuation of a living tradition of legal study and adjudication enhanced by Quranic and prophetic teachings, and the judgments of caliphs and companions. Progressively, however, legal practice and doctrine were overtaken by traditionalist demands that the Quran and hadith be the supreme – if not the only sources of law. Although traditional methods of legal reasoning remained in play, in the course of three centuries, ancient law was traditionalized. Pre-Islamic legal traditions were assimilated and transformed into the distinctive system of Islamic law that functions, albeit with modifications, to the present.

ASCETICISM AND MYSTICISM (SUFISM)

An ascetic life, renouncement of the world, and a mystical vision of an integral connection to God are additional experiences of Islamic belief. Whereas legists concentrated on the laws of daily life and theologians focused on rationalizing their beliefs, mystics attempted to acquire an immediate and personal experience of God's reality. They sought to order their lives, channel their thoughts and feelings, and hone a language that would make possible a direct experience of the presence of a God who was otherwise acknowledged to be transcendent and inaccessible. In this quest, language was particularly important, because only right language could unify the soul of the individual, break down the barriers between human and divine discourse, and enable the mystic to symbolize the reality he experienced. In religious terms, this is a quest for unity with the divine being; in humanistic terms, it is an effort to overcome the divided self, to realize the truths by which life must be lived, and to attain wholeness of being.

Islamic asceticism and mysticism originated in the spiritual aspirations and religious practices of the Prophet Muhammad, his companions, and their successors. Arab-Muslim spiritual seekers questioned the value of a worldly life. Some withdrew from the world; militant ascetics devoted themselves to holy war. They chose a piety that emphasized memorization of the Quran, devotion to hadith and law, and the fulfillment of God's teachings in their daily lives. They sought a deeper spiritual meaning through contemplation of the Quran, imitation of the Prophet, poverty, renunciation, and bodily mortification. Ascetics stressed abstinence and opposed injustice, luxury, and hypocrisy.

They questioned the value of marriage versus celibacy, wealth versus poverty, and active engagement versus retreat. Some chose utmost poverty and isolation; constant watchfulness to avoid any sin, great or small; and yearning for the paradise promised for true believers. Their lives were marked by fear of heedlessness, of temptation or sin, and of the last judgment. They wept for their sins and the punishment to come; they wept for the misery of the world. They taught that the only proper life for a good Muslim was one of humility and poverty; that the only proper expression was tears, rather than laughter; and that silence was best of all. In silence, one could concentrate on the recollection of God and on waiting for the last judgment.

For others, however, the purgative way implied a more moderate asceticism and discipline of bodily desires. For still others, asceticism implied an attitude of emotional disinterest, of detachment, without requiring physical renunciation. Goodness in following the teachings of the Quran, avoidance of sin, and a humble, yearning attitude toward God were summed up in the word "*zuhd*" (renunciation).

Although the inspiration of early Muslim ascetics was Quranic, their beliefs and practices were profoundly shaped by their own pre-Islamic traditions and contact with other religions and cultures. Syrian and Iraqi Christian holy men, monks, and hermits provided examples of deep spirituality. The combined militancy and piety of Christian monks became a model for the ascetic, self-denying Muslim warrior and, by extension, a model for ethical and pious renunciation in daily life. Muslim missionaries in India came into contact with Hindu thought. Contacts with teachers of philosophy, medicine, alchemy, mathematics, and astrology were important influences.

Hasan al-Basri (d. 728) is said to have wept for his unworthiness and feared death, the last judgment, and the hellfire to come. He also taught obedience to the commands of the Quran and the strict practice of the rules of religion reinforced by ascetic devotions, patient acceptance of the trials of this world, submission to God's will, and constant anticipation of the last judgment. For Hasan, the cultivation of proper acts and attitudes was an individual responsibility. While accepting God's determination and guidance in all matters, he sought to reconcile the power of God with the responsibility of individuals through the mystical concept of contentment (*rida*), an attitude that brought the soul into harmony with God's will and thus reconciled freedom of choice with God's power to determine all things.

The story of Hasan became a model for renunciation and self-restraint as the bases of responsibility and moral conduct in communal and political affairs. He lived an active life devoted to holy war (jihad), teaching, preaching, and administration. He fought in the frontier wars to expand Islam and held public office in Basra. He held it a responsibility of good Muslims to counsel ordinary believers on their obligations to God and to give moral advice to rulers. Even when rulers were unjust, the proper response was moral counsel and not violent rebellion. Paradoxically, renunciation of the world led back to the actual fulfillment of the divine law for both the individual and the community.

Recent scholarship has cast doubt on the factuality of some of the legends associated with Hasan, which now appear to be mythical inventions projected backward into an earlier time. Still, his life story gives a vivid image of a Muslim conception of holy life as it was narrated over the generations.

In the late eighth and ninth centuries, the mystical dimension embedded in early Islamic asceticism became more distinct. As ascetics cultivated psychological, emotional, and spiritual awareness, Islamic mysticism emerged in full flower. Recitation of the Quran, the remembrance of God and repetition of his name (*dhikr*), litanies, and meditation – along with the struggle to suppress inner vices – liberated the deepest capacities of the soul and prepared it for the vision of God. The overriding goal of closeness to and vision of God set the Muslim ascetic and mystic against the ordinary demands of familial and communal life.

The name "Sufi" came into use in the late eighth and early ninth centuries as applied to ascetics and recluses in Iraq, Syria, and Egypt. The earliest person we can identify as a Sufi was a Kufan, Abu Hashim (d. 767–68). Many Sufis, especially in Basra and Kufa, wore a rough wool robe, from which their name may be derived. In Khursan and Transoxania, they were called *hukama* – wise men or gnostics. Abu Hafs al-Naysaburi (d. 883–84) may have been the first in Khurasan to use the term "Sufi."

Nishapur was also the home of the mystical-ethical movements of the Malamatiya and the Karramiya. The Malamatiya believed in a normal working daily life inspired by inward mystical devotions, and they organized young men's clubs devoted to good deeds. The Karramiya were world-renouncing ascetics who built hospices and carried out missionary work. Nishapur was also a center of Shi'ism, and this may be the basis of a shared Shi'i-Sufi tradition in ethics, exegesis, and devotions. In the tenth and eleventh centuries, the Malamatiya and the Karramiya merged with Baghdadi Sufism.

Sufis maintained ties to other religious movements. Both Hanbalis and Mu'tazilis shared Sufi ascetic values and a commitment to "commanding the good." Some early Mu'tazilis were called Sufis. There were overlaps in the religious views of different groups that did not belong to the same party.

The Quran provided Sufis with inspiration, guidance, and a vocabulary for this quest. Muqatil b. Sulayman (d. 767) developed a form of commentary that allowed the interpreter of the Quran to transcend its literal meaning and arrive at its spiritual meaning. Ja'far al-Sadiq (d. 765), the sixth imam of the Shi'is, taught that every passage of the Quran spoke on four levels of meaning, which could be appreciated by people having the requisite spiritual experience. These levels were the physical words of the Quran (*'ibara*); allusion to an outside object (*ishara*);

the mysterious fruit within the Quran (*latifa*); and, finally, the truth or reality of the Quran (*haqiqa*).

Mystics did not rely entirely on the vocabulary of the Quran but developed their own language to express the stages of ascent toward God. Shaqiq al-Balkhi (d. 810) was one of the first known Sufi writers to discuss four stages. The first was renunciation of the appetites of the body (*zuhd*); the second was fear of God and constant humility; the third was yearning for paradise; and the fourth was love of God. Dhu'l Nun al-Misri (d. 860–61) developed the concepts of states of being (*ahwal*) and stages of ascent (*maqamat*) in his discussions of love of God – the transition from asceticism to real mysticism. Dhu'l-Nun is considered the first theosophical mystic. Later writers – such as Abu Sa'id Kharraz (d. 890 or 899) – described seven stages on the way to God in which the term "*qurb*" (nearness) was the central metaphor. Each stage was partly a product of the Sufi's own disciplined efforts (*maqam*) and partly a gift of God's grace (*hal*). Al-Kharraz (d. 890–91) is the first known mystic to use the terms "*fana*'" (annihilation of self) and "*baqa*'" (persistence in the self).

As the stages of ascent became more elaborate, Sufis emphasized patience in accepting God's will and in renunciation of the world (*sabr*); gratitude (*shukr*); trust in God (*tawakkul*), which implied utter reliance on God and acceptance of his will without recourse or hope in worldly things; and acceptance of the vicissitudes of life and the reality of the divine decree with equanimity and even with joy and love (*rida*). Love implied yearning for God, obedience to God's will, complete surrender, and dying to one's self in the hope of closeness to God. Rabi'a (d. 801), a female mystic, put into passionate poems her desire to be joined to God. Some Sufis saw love as yearning; others understood it as union. Still others thought of love of God in terms of God's mercy and forgiveness, on which sinful man was always dependent. Love of God opened the way to a still higher stage, unity (*tawhid*), the loss of self, and absorption in the divine being.

By the ninth century, two broad tendencies had emerged within the Sufi movement. The Khurasanian tendency was characterized by emphasis on resignation to God's will (*tawakkul*) expressed through voluntary poverty. Abu Yazid al-Bistami (d. 873) epitomized the quest for an intoxicated, rapturous union with God. In al-Bistami's view, the mystic seeks annihilation of self and union with the divine names or attributes. The mystic's identification with God is expressed in theopathic utterances (*shath*), which are the voice of God speaking through his person. Al-Bistami represents a change from world-renouncing piety to true mystical self-annihilation and union with God. This mysticism ruptured the ordinary pattern of Muslim religious activities and ignored obedience to Quranic law in search of a transcending religious self-realization.

Al-Hallaj (d. 923), who lived as a preacher and missionary in Khurasan and Afghanistan, also sought loss of self and unity in God. As a manifestation of this union, al-Hallaj proclaimed, "I am the Truth," performed miracles, and claimed a religious authority greater than that of caliphs and scholars because it was the authority of the divine presence. His claims to miracles and the doctrine of divine love and union led to prosecution for heresy and his execution in 923.

Other mystics held back from the radical implications of ecstatic Sufism and the concept of annihilation of the self in God. The Baghdadi tendency placed heavy stress on asceticism and renunciation of worldly things, combined with the cultivation of practical virtues such as patience, trust, gratitude, and love of God. The daily life of Sufis was marked by kindness, charity, and good deeds. The Baghdadis, however, as opposed to the Khurasanians, believed in observance of the Quran and conformity with Muslim law. Practically and intellectually, the Baghdadi Sufis were more closely integrated with mainstream Muslim religious practice and belief.

Al-Harith al-Muhasabi (d. 857) was the leading ninth-century proponent of this position, but al-Junayd (d. 910) was the great master of the effort to integrate Sufism with other aspects of Islamic religious life. Al-Junayd laid stress on renunciation, purification, and mental struggle in order to return to the preexistent state, in which the human being is a concept in the mind of God. Al-Junayd professed a two-stage concept of Sufi union. Beyond annihilation of the self (*fana'*) he found *baqa'* or persistence in his own identity. He held that the mystic's goal was not the loss of self as the final end but, through a loss of self, a return to daily life transformed by the vision of God and ever after conducted in the presence of God. As opposed to the Khurasanians, al-Junayd taught that beyond the ecstasy of loss of self there was a sober persistence of the self in never-failing worldly devotion to God's will as expressed in the teachings of the Quran and the Prophet. For the Baghdadis, visionary insight into the reality of God's being was not an escape from but an intensification of the Sufi's commitment to the fulfillment of God's will in daily life. In opposition to Khurasanian intoxication, al-Junayd advocated Baghdadi sobriety. Thus, al-Junayd made mysticism acceptable in other pious circles. His emphasis on austerity, outward behavior in conformity with law, and inward trust in God integrated the ascetic and the mystical camps.

Although mystics differed on the stages of the ascent toward God, they had – by the end of the ninth century – collectively articulated a theory of spiritual progress that combined Quranic inspiration with the lived experience of generations of seekers. Later Sufis, such as Niffari (d. 985), further elaborated the language of Sufism. He employed symbols that came into being in the moment of mystic experience and cultivated a language that condensed human experience with its transcendent reference. Through symbols, the mystic became familiar with the God who reveals himself in the language of men without compromising his transcendence. Symbolic language became a symbol of the mystic's absorption into the divine reality.

In addition to their pragmatic program, Sufis also cultivated a metaphysical, theosophical, and philosophical concept of the divine reality. By the early tenth century, several metaphysical theories of the creation of the material world and the relation of human beings to God had been put forth. All of them in one form or another posited a transcendent God, but one whose spiritual radiance or emanation was implanted in human beings. A human being must overcome the bodily and animal forces within him, restore purity of will and intellect, and thus realize his inherently divine nature. Through this realization he returns to his origins in God.

Sahl al-Tustari (d. 896) elaborated that God's essence is light, which is a single and transcendent illumination that radiates from him to create the spiritual pro-totypes of the material world. Enshrined in this light are the prototypes of the prophets and of ordinary people, who exist before their worldly birth as particles of the divine light. In this preexistent state, human beings recognize and testify to the oneness and the lordship of God, a primordial covenant. In the life of this world, man attempts to reactualize this preexistent covenant. In prayer, he contem-plates God's existence; in *dhikr* or Sufi ceremony, he attempts to recollect God's primordial self-revelation. To do this, he must purify the heart and make it triumph over the forces of the bodily self, following Quran and hadith with sincerity and repentance, living according to God's commands and prohibitions. Penitence and inner struggle free him from his bodily self (*nafs*) and allow him to realize his spiritual self, heart (*qalb*), reason (*'aql*), or spirit (*ruh*). By the resurrection of this preexisting reality, the mystic prepares himself for the vision of God and life eternal in the presence of the divine being.

With the translation of the Syriac and Greek classics into Arabic, the intellectual mysticism that stemmed from the thought of Plotinus (d. 270) provided a similar theosophical concept of the mystic way. Neo-Platonism introduced the idea that the universe radiated from the divine being in successive stages of spiritual and then material manifestation. Man – who stood at the juncture of the spiritual and material worlds – was capable by inner knowledge or illumination of rising up in the hierarchy of being to the ultimate vision of God. By discovery of the inward truths of the heart, which correspond to the cosmological structure of the universe, the mystic ascends from his material state toward ever-higher levels of spiritual being and the ultimate illuminative knowledge of God.

Thus, in several forms, early Sufi metaphysics combined a transcendentalist with an immanentist view of God's existence. God is utterly different from any created reality; yet he is also the source of spiritual illuminations that make it possible for human beings – in whom there dwells some aspect of the reality of God – to return from their material exile to their spiritual home.

Finally, there was a miraculous and magical aspect to Sufism. The individual who had achieved knowledge of God's being through his daily behavior and visionary insight was considered more than human. In his person, he was an epiphany, a manifestation, of the divine being, and the vehicle of communication between man and God. The mystic was considered a healer, a magician, a worker of miracles, and a pillar of the universe. For many Muslim believers, the Sufi was not only a person of great moral and spiritual quality but a living expression of God's power in the world. Al-Tirmidhi (d. 932) advanced the theory that the Sufi adept was a saint who by his spiritual achievements upheld the order of the universe. Standing in the hierarchy of God's emanation, he was capable of miraculous deeds. Al-Tirmidhi's doctrine of sainthood became the basis of an almost universal Muslim belief in saints as intercessors with God and of a veneration of saints and their descendants, disciples, and tombs as repositories of the divine presence. In metaphysical doctrine and in magical practice, the Sufis represented the possibility of salvation by entry into the presence of God.

Sufism, which began as the quest for individual spiritual redemption, became by the late eighth century a collective religious movement. By this period, Sufis had developed a concept of themselves – the people of the coarse white wool garment – as initiates in a form of Muslim religious life that was distinct from the piety enshrined in scholarship and legal practice. Sufis gathered to recite the Quran and to sit in the presence of great masters. In the houses of rich merchant patrons, in collective retreats such as the *khanaqa* at Abadan, and in castles and towns on the Byzantine frontier, Sufis were provided with a living and sometimes even with stipends. The beginnings of a collective life helped give coherence to Sufism as a movement.

Combining ascetic renunciation with spiritual growth leading toward union with God, and grounded in philosophical and metaphysical conceptions of God's being and a doctrine of the venerable and miraculous nature of saints, Sufism began to manifest both a social organization and a public mission. All of these trends would be consolidated and further developed in the centuries following the collapse of the ʿAbbasid Empire.

CHAPTER 16

SHI'I ISLAM

Alongside Sunni communities, the Shi'is developed their own expressions of Islam. In one Shi'i view, the source of true belief in each generation was ultimately not the text of tradition, nor the consensus of jurists, nor the piety of holy men, but loyalty to the Caliph 'Ali and his descendants. The true imamate or caliphate belonged in the family of the Prophet, the Hashimite clan. In the seventh and eighth centuries, this led to a number of political movements opposing the Umayyad and 'Abbasid dynasties. Family loyalists tried again and again to seize the caliphate. (See Figure 4.)

Defeat channeled many Shi'is from political activity into religious reflection. The defeat of the Kufan uprising led by al-Mukhtar in 687 prompted a turn to gnosticism – the belief that human beings embody a divine spark and that they must return from this world to their true divine realm. Gnosticism generated a large number of Shi'i sects that denied the resurrection and believed in incarnation, transmigration of souls, and continuous living prophethood. Collectively these were called extremist sects (*ghulat*).

By the mid-eighth century, there were two principle branches of Shi'ism – the Zaydis and the Imamis. They differed over which descendant of 'Ali was the true imam. Zaydis held that the true imam proved himself by active struggle for the office and by being both a political and a religious leader. A Zaydi-sponsored revolt occurred in Kufa in 740, and Zaydis were active in a number of later anti-'Abbasid rebellions. Eventually, they established local regimes in Yemen and the Caspian Sea region.

The Imamis held that the imamate descended directly in the family of 'Ali and Fatima, but they did not have a unified position on whether political activism was required for a claimant to the imamate. At least one faction in the Baghdadi community called for an immediate restoration of the true imamate as political ruler and in 762 backed the anti-'Abbasid revolt of Muhammad al-Nafs al-Zakiyya. After the defeat of this revolt, the Baghdadi Shi'is became a pacific religious congregation. Shi'is were important in merchant and scribal circles and had access to the 'Abbasid court. By the ninth century, the Baghdadi Shi'is had renounced political aspirations in favor of local community affairs and pious personal lives and lived in an atmosphere of mourning for lost hopes and messianic dreams. Instead of trying to transform the world, they withdrew to a pious existence within it. Thus, the early political movement developed into a sectarian religious community.

The earliest Imami community was resident in Kufa and Baghdad, but in the ninth century, Qum replaced Kufa as the chief center of Imami Shi'ism. In the tenth century, Baghdad became the most important center. In the eleventh century, the community moved to Najaf and Hilla. From Qum, it was widely dispersed in Iran.

For the Baghdadi Shi'is, the critical issue was the authority of the imam and the succession to the imamate. Ja'far al-Sadiq (d. 765), the sixth imam in the line of 'Ali, taught that the true caliph and ruler of the Muslim community descended in the family of 'Ali by virtue of *nass* – each incumbent imam's designation of his successor. Through designation, the imam inherited a secret knowledge and exclusive authority to interpret the Quran and hadith and to elaborate the legal system of Islam. Many Shi'is, however, yearned instead for a savior. Although the movement to ascribe supernatural powers to the imam began in the imamate of Ja'far, he both refused an active political role and denied that he was the expected redeemer (*qa'im*). Until 874, the living imams gave guidance to their community and left a legacy of precedents that would shape later Imami Shi'ism.

A central issue for the Baghdadi Shi'is was whether the imam possessed supernatural inspiration or was an ordinary – although learned and pious – human being. The historical succession after Ja'far reinforced the tendencies toward belief in the supernatural qualities of the imam. A succession of child imams who could not qualify for their office by virtue of learning led to the idea that imams became imams through divine grace or an indwelling divine light. In the extremist (*ghulat*) view, which would become integral to some later Shi'i ideas, the imam was vested with an indwelling spirit of God and was the messiah (Mahdi) chosen by God to restore the true faith of Islam and to establish justice and the kingdom of God in the world. By the ninth century, Shi'i concepts of the imam came to include the notion that he was *ma'sum*, a sinless and infallible guide to religious truth. The ordinary believer was obliged to obey and give unquestioning loyalty to the imam. These views provoked an intense intellectual struggle between the Baghdadi believers in the quasi-divinity of the Imam and the Shi'i scholars of Qum who held that the imam was merely a person with true knowledge of the Quran and the law.

In the tenth century, the concept of the imam was reformulated in neo-Platonic and gnostic terms that provided a new metaphysical context. The imam came to be understood as an emanation of the divine being and the universal intelligence (*'aql al-kull*) and thus a bearer of direct knowledge of the secret truths

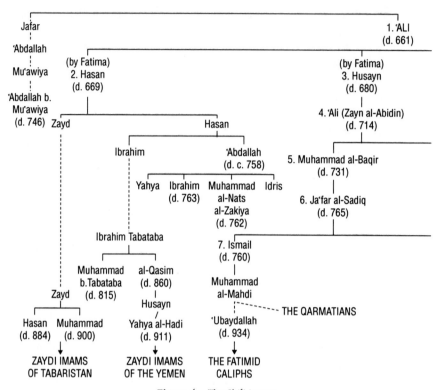

Figure 4. The Shiʿi imams.

and states of spirituality that lead to the reunion of the soul of man with God. From this vantage point, Shiʿism moved toward Sufi ideas in that the divinely graced imam became the exemplar and teacher of a mystical reunion with God.

In a divided community, the succession to the imamate was often problematic. After Jaʿfar's death, the Shiʿi community split into two groups – the followers of his sons Musa and Ismaʿil. The followers of Musa and the ninth-century imams who were his descendants maintained the religious and social policies we know as Imami. But the followers of Ismaʿil created a new messianic and politically active movement.

In 874, after the death of the eleventh imam, Hasan al-Askari, who left no heirs, the line of succession from Jaʿfar came to an end. The Shiʿis then elaborated their concept of the hidden twelfth imam, who is not dead but is in retreat until he shall return as the messiah at the end of days. In the absence of a living imam, the

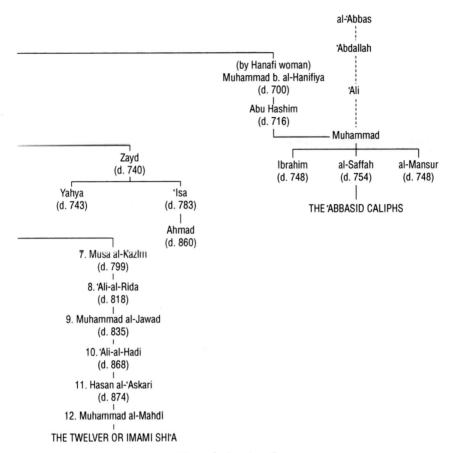

Figure 4 (*continued*).

Banu Nawbakht, an important Shi'i family of Baghdad, took up the leadership of the community, and from 874 until 941 acted as agents of the hidden imam. This first period, in which the twelfth imam was hidden but still in direct contact with his agents, was called the lesser occultation. The period that followed, in which all direct contact was lost, is called the greater occultation. The *ithna 'ashari* (Twelver), or Imami, Shi'i community has come to be defined by its eschatological conception of the imamate and doctrine of the historical succession of twelve imams culminating in the occultation of the twelfth imam, who will return as the messiah.

With the loss of direct divine guidance, Baghdadi Shi'is began to codify their religious and cultural heritage to compensate for the missing imam. In the late decades of the tenth century, they began the public ritual cursing of Mu'awiya ('Ali's political rival) and marked the holiday of mourning for the death of Husayn at Karbala (*'ashura'*) as well as the day of celebration for Muhammad's adoption of 'Ali as his successor (*ghadir khumm*). Pilgrimages to the tombs of 'Ali at Najaf, of Husayn at Karbala, and of 'Ali al-Rida at Mashhad became important rituals. The passionate mourning for Husayn, identification with the suffering of the martyr, and the messianic hopes implicit in the commemoration of Karbala gave emotional and religious depth to Twelver Shi'ism.

Politically, this meant that the Twelvers – although opposed to the 'Abbasid regime in principle – were willing to postpone their expectations of a Shi'i imam until the indefinite future. Some Imamis recognized that the occultation (*ghayba*) was permanent and that scholars would take over the leadership roles of the hidden imam. By the twelfth century, Imamis generally believed that a layperson must consult a learned scholar on all matters of belief and practice. Quietism, accommodation, dissimulation of true beliefs, and martyrdom became the dominant sociopolitical motifs.

In the same period, Twelver teaching in hadith, law, and theology also became more established. In the eighth and ninth centuries, hadith were central to the Imami Shi'i practice of Islam. Because the Shi'is denied the legitimacy of Sunni succession of caliphs, Abu Bakr and 'Umar could not be accepted as authoritative sources of Muslim religious teaching; nor could the other companions or the Umayyads and 'Abbasids. Therefore, an independent hadith and law in which 'Ali was the prime authority was elaborated.

An Imami legal and theological school came into being in the imamate of Muhammad b. 'Ali al-Baqir (d. 732). Legal traditions became common in the imamate of Ja'far al-Sadiq (d. 765). Because in Imami tradition all truth derives from the teaching of the imams, hadith was primary and law and theology were secondary pursuits. However, the Shi'is were also in close touch with political sympathizers such as Mu'tazili theologians, and, by the end of the ninth century, they were also debating the questions of free will and God's attributes.

The first extant compilation of Shi'i hadith on ritual and law was made by al-Kulayni (d. 940). His hadith collections were organized under legal subject headings. In time, the emphasis shifted from hadith to more general rules of law. Sunni legal development preceded Shi'i law, and Shi'is studied and taught in Sunni schools.

Shi'is were divided, like Sunnis, between a traditionalist position and a modified rationalist position. Scholars debated the teachings of the imams as the sole source of beliefs and the permissibility of exercising individual legal judgment (*ijtihad*). Shi'i traditionalists (*akhbaris*) rejected rational methods and insisted on strict reliance on hadith. Traditionalists were dominant until the middle of the tenth century when rationalism was revived in law. Usulis (rationalists) favored a reasoned judgment in legal matters. Some Twelvers also adopted consensus (*ijma'*) and claimed that the Twelvers constituted a fifth school of law (*madhhab*) on par with the Sunni schools. Shi'is thus left a legacy of religious teachings basically similar to the Sunni types, but differing mainly in matters of detail and in chains of transmission.

By the mid-eleventh century, Imami Shi'is had created a worldly life lived in perpetual expectation of the world to come. In permanent opposition to the established political regimes, Imamism had become a religion of salvation. This salvation might be attained by living in accordance with the hadith of the Prophet and the imams, by emotional absorption into their martyrdom, or by gnostic vision and mystical identification with the emanations of the divine being. With the consolidation of their doctrinal beliefs in written form, the development of a public ritual life, and political recognition by the reigning authorities, the Baghdadi Shi'is emerged as a sectarian community within the body of Islam.

ISMA'ILI SHI'ISM

The second branch of Shi'ism is composed of followers of Ja'far's son, Isma'il. Early Isma'ilis differed from the Imami Shi'is in recognizing Isma'il rather than Musa as the true imam. Moreover, their strong messianic orientation led to doctrinal changes and to political activism. In Isma'ili doctrine, the Quran revealed two truths – the external, literal (*zahir*) truth of the divine message and the inner, esoteric (*batin*) truth of the Quran – which could only be known by proper exegesis of the Quranic text and by comprehension of the external meanings as the symbols of an inner spiritual principle. For Isma'ilis of the ninth century, the doctrine implied a conception of the imam as teacher and guide to the inner meanings of the Quranic revelation.

Isma'ilis generated a historical and eschatological concept of the imam. According to their doctrine, prophetic revelation was always complemented by the appearance of a *wasi*, who was the executor and interpreter of the inner meaning of the revelation. In history, there were to be seven prophets, each followed by a cycle of seven imams. Muhammad was the sixth prophet. His *wasi* was 'Ali, who was to be followed by a cycle of imams culminating in Muhammad the son of Isma'il (the Mahdi), who would return as the seventh and final prophet to reveal the truth in its fullness and establish everlasting justice. Isma'ilism combined a historical, cyclical concept of prophetology with eschatological messianism.

Furthermore, Isma'ilis held that the imams were figures in a universal hierarchy as well as participants in prophetic cycles. The prophet (*natiq*) was superior to the imams, who in turn were superior to the proofs (*hujjas*), who represented the imams in their absence and were in turn represented by missionaries (*da'is*). This structure of communal authority was at once a hierarchy of leadership and the mark of successive stages of spiritual initiation. Isma'ilism, Sufi messianism, and philosophical ideas about governance made the ruler a cosmological figure, a semieternal, semidivine emanation on whom a just political order depends. In this worldview, the ruler was also the redeemer and savior.

Isma'ilis of the ninth century were active missionaries and political organizers. Whereas the Shi'is of Baghdad maintained their position in 'Abbasid society and government, Isma'ilis set out to proselytize tribal and peasant peoples in Arabia, Syria, Iraq, North Africa, and the towns of Iran. They preached equality and justice, the need for reform, and the coming of the savior. Isma'ili missionaries converted new peoples to their version of Islam and led extensive rebellions against the 'Abbasid caliphate. Isma'ili dynasties were founded in North Africa, the Caspian region, Bahrain, Multan, and other places. Whereas Imami Shi'ism was politically quietist, Isma'ili Shi'ism carried the banner of Islamic revolution.

In either form, Shi'ism was characterized by a religious mood that stressed messianic hopes and chiliastic expectations. Shi'is believed in the return of the imam as a messiah and that the historical world would come to an end with the fulfillment of successive cycles of prophets and imams in a cataclysmic era, out of which would come a reborn mankind and the establishment of a kingdom of God on earth. Although Sunni and Shi'i Muslims did not vary much in the practice of their daily lives, they differed profoundly in the emotional mood through which they saw worldly reality.

WOMEN, FAMILIES, AND COMMUNITIES

CHAPTER 17

MUSLIM URBAN SOCIETIES TO THE TENTH CENTURY

WOMEN AND FAMILY (CO-AUTHOR, LENA SALAYMEH)

Of the topics that we have discussed thus far, the position of women in Muslim societies is the most controversial. It requires a digression to discuss the political, cultural, and methodological considerations that shape our views. Contemporary European and American public discourses are driven by religious rivalry, geopolitical issues such as the Israeli-Palestinian conflict, and ongoing wars in the Middle East. This situation promotes an atmosphere of suspicion, prejudice, and hostility toward Islam and Muslims. These same considerations also motivate widespread Muslim hostility against the West.

A key theme in this atmosphere of conflict is the position of women in Muslim families, communities, and countries. Westerners often allege that in Muslim societies women are oppressed and subordinated to men, without opportunities for independence, education and careers, or the cultivation of their talents and full potentials. Islamic law is perceived as discriminating against women, and Islamist demands for a return to Shari'a are understood as being a campaign against the emancipation of women. The wearing of the veil or the burqa is viewed as the foremost sign of this subordination.

Conversely, conservative Muslims (and indeed some Christians and Jews) see women in Western societies as economically exploited for their labor, sexually abused, and commercially commodified by Western media's fixation on the female body. Most Muslims experience their faith as liberating or fair to women. Some find it offensive that Westerners do not fully understand the rich historical and contemporary realities of women's lives.

Some perspective on these issues may be helpful. Such strongly held convictions and prejudices make it difficult to fairly and realistically discuss the experiences of women in numerous Islamic societies. Western discourses about Muslim women ignore the problems and challenges Western women experience in their own societies. We tend to compare Western societies as we perceive them to be in the present moment without taking into account their recent histories or contemporary realities. A little more than a hundred years ago in America, women could not vote, nor, if married, manage their own property. Today, there is widespread resistance in the West to modern women's roles and widespread conservative convictions that the place of women is in the home and family. We fail to recognize that there are many different varieties of feminism and feminist movements throughout the world.

Rather, we have to come to terms with realities that are more varied, complex, and ambiguous than we generally imagine. There are myriad historical, geographical, socioeconomic, religious-doctrinal, and legal differences within the category of women and Islam. Much of the variation in the situations of women in the Muslim world is governed by class as well as religious, ethnic, and social considerations. Women of the same social class have similar life experiences across ethnic, national, or religious lines. Wealthy women and working-class women in different societies may have more in common with one another than with women of other classes in their own communities. In addition, women who are Muslims are affected by non-Muslim practices, beliefs, and cultures.

Finally, we do not usually think of women in the Muslim world in the context of global variations in the roles and identities of women. How are the contemporary or historical experiences of women in Muslim-majority societies different from those of women in non-Muslim-majority societies? Here and in the chapters that follow we will attempt to relate "Muslim women" to the historical, political, and socioeconomic realities of their times and places and in terms that are not unique to Islam.

In the period from the seventh to the tenth century, we have little evidence about the lives of women. Most of what we know comes from later legal and historical texts. The extant literature generally articulates the perspectives of upper-class men with religious and social influence. Our sources may not represent the daily reality of women's lives. In later chapters (Chapters 21 and 31) dealing with the period from the tenth to the eighteenth centuries, as the source material becomes more abundant, we can better describe the functions, status, and relationships of women.

In the early Islamic era, the overall status of women remained much the same as it was in pre-Islamic late antiquity. Middle Eastern societies continued to make a relatively sharp division between men's and women's roles. The family, the household, light agricultural labor, and domestic craftwork were the domain of women. The middle- and upper-class ideal was isolation from the marketplace, politics, and social life with men. In the early Islamic era, in extended families and lineages, women were subject to the authority of fathers, brothers, husbands, and husbands' male kin. This basic attitude was reinforced by the belief that the honor of a man and his family, lineage, or tribe depended on the honorable conduct of all its members, including women. Common attitudes about the roles of men and women, however, did not preclude wide variation in institutional and social arrangements.

Women and family in the lifetime of the Prophet

In late antique Arabia, the basic family unit was the patriarchal agnatic clan, a group of people descended directly in the male line from a common ancestor and under the authority of the eldest male or chief member of the family. This was an extended family of several generations – several groups of married couples and their offspring, with collaterals and clients – and they were all considered part of one household. Status, duties, and rights stemmed entirely from the clan. The group was responsible for defending individual members and making restitution in case of any crime committed by a member. Property was regulated by the customs of the group. Marriages were arranged by the heads of the families with a view to the interests of the families. A good marriage brought honor to the clan; if any of its members, especially the women, were violated or breached social norms, the clan was dishonored.

However, alongside the agnatic clan, various forms of polyandrous marriage of one woman to several men with varying degrees of permanence and responsibility for paternity, including temporary marriages, were also known in Arabia. Polygynous arrangements varied from multiple wives in one residence to several wives living with their own tribes, where they were visited by the husband on a rotating basis. It is unclear if women were secluded in pre-Islamic Arabia, and it seems improbable considering nomadic ways of life. However, it is conceivable that men's and women's economic activities and socializing patterns kept them apart. No single norm was universally accepted.

With the advent of Islam, the Prophet presented a value system and regulations that in many ways reflected and consolidated, but also significantly modified, the pre-Islamic Arabian context. Quranic verses seem to strengthen the agnatic clan. Quranic rules against incest were crucial for the viability of group life, for biological heredity, and for the creation of marriage bonds between families. Divorce, although still relatively easy, was discouraged. Because lineage was traced through its male heirs, the Quran provided rules to assure knowledge of paternity. (For example, in the event of divorce, a woman could only remarry after three menstrual cycles.) Polyandrous marriages were condemned because they undermined identification of lineage.

The agnatic family ideal was buttressed by a clear definition of its collective duties in the all-important matter of responsibility for crimes. As in pre-Islamic times, all the male kin were held responsible for the protection of family members, but Quranic teachings tried to reduce the devastating effects of the blood feuds that often resulted from this obligation. They urged the aggrieved party to accept compensation in money rather than blood and ruled that, if blood retaliation were insisted on, only the culprit himself could be slain – instead of any male relative. This modification did not end the law of blood revenge or the strong common responsibilities of family members to one another, but it restricted feuds, to give security to families, who no longer had to fear that the indiscretion of one member would in the end destroy them all.

The moral and spiritual reform advocated in Quranic verses enhanced the status of women. The Quran addresses women directly and charges them to uphold morality in the community. It recommends respect for their modesty and privacy. Marriage was recognized as having important spiritual and religious values because it was a relationship sanctioned by the will of God. Furthermore, the Quran and Prophetic teachings recognized women's property rights. A woman was given the right to inherit up to a quarter of her husband's estate and, in case of divorce, to retain the agreed-upon bridal gift. In addition, the Quran tried to prevent hasty and willful divorces by urging delay, reconciliation, and mediation by families. A waiting period following a divorce also served to assure a woman of interim support and of support for a future child if she were pregnant. Finally, Prophetic practice indicates that women also had the right to initiate divorce.

Because the Prophet's practices set precedents for Muslim jurisprudence and social values, it is important to explore concrete examples of how the Prophet treated women. The Prophet's first wife was his employer, Khadija. This was a monogamous relationship with a widowed woman significantly older and wealthier than him. She is reported to have been forty and he twenty-five when she proposed marriage and he accepted. Historical sources describe her as the Prophet's confidante and note that he did not oppose her wishes. She appears to have provided him with both financial and emotional support. Khadija died after some twenty-five years of marriage to the Prophet, during which time she was his only wife.

The Prophet's monogamous marital life with Khadija in Mecca was followed by more than a decade of multiple marriages in Medina, mainly with widowed and divorced women, with the exception of his young bride, 'A'isha. His first marriage after Khadija's death was to Sawdah bint Zam'ah, a middle-aged widow; ostensibly, he needed her to care for his daughters. His second wife was 'A'isha, the daughter of Abu Bakr (the first caliph). 'A'isha was the youngest of the Prophet's wives – probably just entering puberty – and the only one not to have been previously married. The Prophet chose to remain in her quarters during his last illness, and he died there. 'A'isha became an important transmitter of hadith, a jurist, and a political activist. Muhammad's other wives were widows and divorcees, and one was a captive. Many of these relationships appear to have had political motivations because they established alliances with various clans.

Hadith report him as regularly conversing with his wives and generally treating them with respect, patience, and gentleness.

Little research systematically examines the Prophet's interactions with women who were not related to him as wives, daughters, or other relatives. From what we now know, he appears not to have imposed seclusion or avoided contact with women. When he first began preaching in Mecca, the sources report him teaching men and women together. They specifically depict the Prophet as making social visits to various female companions; many women other than his wives transmitted hadith from him. Women were present as political representatives at the ʿAqaba meeting between the Prophet and members of the Medinan community; later, women fought in raids and battles. Women are also reported to have provided food and nursed the wounded during battles.

There is no evidence for seclusion of women in the lifetime of the Prophet. In the Quran, women are enjoined, when in public, for the sake of modesty and chastity, to draw their scarves around them and not to display adornments. Later hadith interpreted this to mean a head covering and to be the basis of exclusion from public life, but the historical evidence of these practices in the Prophet's lifetime is scant. Narrative sources from the Medinan period depict female companions as marrying, divorcing, and remarrying with relative ease. Women in this period were instrumental in the transmission of knowledge – whether Prophetic traditions, folk remedies, or dream interpretations.

Women and family in the Caliphal era

We do not have sufficient biographical and historically detailed narratives to recon-struct women's lives immediately after the Prophet died. Unfortunately, this period was especially influential for later constructions of the status of women, because this was the era when Quranic exegesis and hadith – two sources of Islamic legal doctrines – began to flourish.

The Arab-Muslim conquests and the organization of the empire affected the position of women connected to the political and military elites. It seems likely that the taking of captives and slavery enforced a turn toward polygyny, harems, and the subordination of women. Slavery had profound effects on family and identities, because it created complex families with multiple relationships and loyalties and a fluid distribution of power. Slave women had minimal rights unless they bore acknowledged children. Yet slave women, as is known from ʿAbbasid court history, could become politically and economically powerful, and this may have been true for families at all levels of society. As is shown in early Arabic literature, slave women might also become love objects and thus an outlet for male imagination and individuality. Slave men could bring wealth into a family by virtue of their work and the accumulation of property and thus enhance the power of the extended family unit. In these circumstances, reinforced by laws that made divorce easy for men, the nuclear family would be a weak element.

The caliphal family was a special case. Under the early ʿAbbasids, royal women had their own households; but after the death of Harun, caliphs did not marry, and their mothers were the chief women at court. By the tenth century, women were housed in a special structure within the royal palace – much like the Byzantine equivalent, the *gynaikonitis*.

Family behavior and the role of women in society were shaped by the settlement of Arab-Muslim conquerors in the garrison cities. The new cities were first settled by tribal units, but after a century of sedentarization they were thoroughly urbanized. Tribal structures evolved into groups defined by family, geographical proximity in town quarters and markets, and religious associations. In Basra, by the eighth century, nontribal names and identifications became dramatically more important. Mixed Arab and non-Arab Muslim populations included merchants, artisans, workers, teachers, and scholars. Independently of the caliphate, town populations developed sociocommunal and even political organizations of their own, under the leadership of both nonreligious and religious leaders. In these new conditions, from the seventh to the tenth centuries, Muslim jurists worked out a legal system to regulate family and property relations. With some variations, this system carried on the fundamentals of late antique legal practice.

Late antique marriage practices and sexual morality did not significantly change in early Muslim communities. Generally, an Islamic marriage is a contract between the bride (who makes a marriage offer) and a groom (who accepts the offer and pays the dower) in the presence of two witnesses – with or without particular contractual stipulations. Consanguinity, foster relationships, and marriage to mother and daughter or two sisters at the same time were forbidden. A marriage contract required the payment of a dower. Usually, two witnesses were required; some public celebration or notice was considered desirable, and most jurists disapproved of secret marriages. A marriage contract and consummation could be separated by a long interval. Marriage did not result in the creation of community property; men were solely responsible for family maintenance.

Most Muslim jurists required women to be represented by a male guardian, who accepted an offer for the woman from a suitor of appropriate class and status, but the bride had to give her consent for the marriage contract to be valid. Before puberty, a father's authority was virtually unlimited; minors, both girls and boys, could be forcibly married by a father. With a mature virgin, some gesture of assent was needed; a previously married woman had to give express verbal consent. Different rules applied if the guardian was not the father. Judges did intervene in cases in which there was no guardian or in which a guardian refused to let a woman marry an appropriate person.

Islamic legal traditions from the first several generations do not indicate any clear ruling on non-virgin brides – that is, women who were not previously married but were not virgins. However, later Muslim juristic practice corresponded to rabbinic practice in minimizing the significance of prior sexual activity. Likewise, polygyny and female concubinage were accepted practices. The Shi'is permitted temporary marriages, whereas Sunnis prohibited it. There are reports of the Prophet punishing a Muslim man for adultery, and succeeding generations appear to have continued to do so.

Quranic verses and Prophetic practice indicate an interest in both preventing divorce and limiting its potential for harm. A man had the right to dissolve a marriage by declaring his wife divorced, but the Prophet's companions narrated hadith that encouraged arbitration and dissuaded couples from divorce. A husband could reconcile with his wife after two divorce declarations, but a third declaration of divorce was irrevocable. The divorced wife would have to be married to and divorced by another man before remarriage to her first husband. Unlike Sunni jurists, Shi'i jurists require two witnesses for the divorce declaration to be valid. Although there are reports that the Prophet granted women's requests for divorce with little questioning, this was limited by later juristic practice. Women could petition for divorce in a variety of situations: if a husband was unable or unwilling to provide an appropriate standard of living, if a husband was unable or unwilling to engage in sexual intercourse, or if a husband was abusive.

Once a divorce declaration was made, a waiting period (*'idda*) of three menstrual cycles would begin. This waiting period provided an opportunity for reconciliation and reflection, as well as, in cases of pregnancy, determination of paternity. Men were required to provide lodging and support during this waiting period and child support during the duration of an ex-wife's custody.

Property and inheritance

The Islamic juristic tradition guaranteed women certain property rights. In contrast to some late antique precedents, there were no legal restrictions on a Muslim woman's right to own or to manage property. Women appear as property owners in pre-Islamic Arabian practice, in historical sources from the early Islamic period, and in Egyptian papyri of the ninth and tenth centuries. Muslim women had the right to hold property in their own names and were not expected to contribute to the support of the household. Muslim women were given the right to inherit up to a quarter of a husband's estate, to receive gifts of property, and, in case of divorce, to retain the agreed-upon bridal gift. Also, in contrast to prevailing pre-Islamic late antique practices, Muslim women could inherit from a number of relatives. Women could use their wealth to negotiate favorable marriage contract stipulations or to arrange divorces on their own initiative. Although adult women were not legally required to have guardians, Muslim jurists generally restricted women from testifying in commercial transactions.

Inheritance is a particularly complicated area of Islamic law, with a complex history, differences among the legal schools, and a variety of special cases. The Quran favors direct descent of property from father to sons but allows for testamentary disposal of property and emphasizes the rights of women to own property. Similarly, very early Islamic law allowed a person to designate heirs and dispose of property as he wished. The testator could designate parents, or wife, or daughter-in-law. The testator could leave a will that favored particular heirs, such that certain relatives who would have inherited if the testator died without a will would get a smaller share. To meet their political and economic interests, some early caliphs manipulated Quranic exegesis to eliminate unrestricted designation of an heir. In the conquest period – probably for the sake of social cohesion at a time when great wealth was being accumulated – a system of fixed shares was made compulsory. Then, Islamic trusts (*waqf*) evolved to provide testators with the ability to evade the system of fixed shares.

Muslim jurists followed Quranic inheritance stipulations and upheld gender-based differences in apportionment that were common in late antiquity. Generally, Sunni jurists ruled that women receive half the share of men who are related to the deceased in the same degree. A mother or a father inherits one-sixth of a child's estate; a grandmother receives one-sixth. A full sister receives half of her brother's estate (if he does not have children). A widow receives one-quarter of her husband's estate if there are children. However, there are significant differences between Sunni and Shi'i jurists in matters of inheritance; the latter generally provide larger shares for daughters without brothers.

In many respects, these legal norms favored men over women. Marriages were commonly arranged by families; a bride's male guardians were ultimately responsible for her welfare. A bride would ordinarily move to the house of her husband and reside with his kin. The Quran also gives a husband authority over his family because he is responsible for the family's economic well-being. Muslim jurists afforded men easier terms on which to initiate divorce, whereas women were given fewer opportunities. In the case of divorce, children beyond a certain age were under the guardianship of the husband and his family. In Islamic law, however, women had important economic rights and could come to court to enforce their economic and marital rights. In the ninth century, this was easy for a lower-class woman, but it was considered shameful for higher-class women to leave their homes and be seen in public. Eventually, arrangements were made for such women to send a representative. Although in law women could own property, in many instances non-Islamic social practices restricted their opportunities to accumulate or inherit property. Contrary to Islamic law, customary norms prevailed when families refused women their Islamic inheritance shares from the properties of husbands or other relatives.

Although legal and cultural norms advantaged men, this was tempered by economic and social realities. From later historical materials and theoretical considerations, we know that the relations between the sexes were more complicated than is implied in the simple concepts of male dominance and gender segregation. Although women had a lesser role in the "public" sphere, the public domain was much smaller in pre-modern than in modern societies; families played a much larger role in economic life and politics. Women were commonly the custodians of the family's social status, and they had influence in arranging marriages and maintaining reciprocal relations with other families. Educated upper-class women taught the Quran and the sayings of the Prophet to the girls in their family networks. The nominal domain of women was thus more consequential than it would seem today.

Other factors could also give women considerable autonomy – and even dominance – in domestic affairs. In the direct relations between husband and wife, a wife's personal influence, manipulation of her husband, conspiracies and intrigues, threats to humiliate her husband by denouncing him for neglect or impotence, and setting sons against fathers all worked to subvert the domestic power of men. The dependence of men on domestic life and the opinion of their neighbors and kin also helped to equalize the relationship between husbands and wives. Furthermore, women had their own bases of social and personal autonomy in their networks of friendships and social gatherings.

Moreover, the relationships between men and women and women's standing in the public world were not fixed by culture or by law but varied by context. Wealthy upper-class women were more likely to be limited to the household, but they also had the resources and opportunities to take control of their lives and advance their interests. They became property owners through inheritance, dower, and gifts. Educated women were likely valued for their opinions on religious, family, and political matters.

Lower-class women had a measure of independence because of their work and relative mobility. Women played a significant economic role in animal husbandry, agriculture, home crafts, and cottage industries. Rural women produced tents, bedding, clothing, mats, rugs, sacks, pottery, and baskets – both for the household and the market. They acted as healers, midwives, cooks, prostitutes, musicians, savants, and traders. In towns, women did embroidery and washed, carded, and spun wool. Women's lending and marketing networks were a source of income. Although there were important variations by region and class, the economic contributions of women's incomes and assets and their control over the distribution of family food and other resources gave them considerable familial and social power.

Nonetheless, women's options were more limited than those of men. Jurists granted men rights that women did not have – to polygyny, to marrying non-Muslims, and to advantages in divorce and in inheritance. Women – in both Islamic and other late antique societies – had to operate within a patriarchal framework of unequal power and unequal legal rights, finding or creating whatever amelioration they could.

Thus, the personal relations and attitudes of men and women toward each other have several dimensions, corresponding to the complexity of their social and economic roles. Women were perceived by some men as erotic objects, but to others they were partners in earning a living and in family relations. Although, from a contemporary point of view, men were dominant, women cannot be thought of as an oppressed class. They most likely did not see themselves as forming a collectivity with interests opposed to those of men, because women themselves had varying experiences depending on their social class and local community. Most women probably saw themselves as playing a valued, legitimate, and important role in family and social life, one that differed from but was complementary to that of men.

URBAN COMMUNITIES

Beyond the family, Muslim populations belonged to larger-scale communities, but we have little information about the organization of communal and social life for the period from the seventh to the tenth centuries. Extended families and tribal connections seem to have mattered less in towns than in the countryside. Nor were ethnicity or national identifications the basis of community and political organization.

Scattered throughout the sources, and bearing mainly on Baghdad, there are indications that the settlers of the Arab-Muslim cities and garrison towns were organized by quarter, by market, and by religious associations. From the chronicles, we learn that in the middle of the ninth century *shaykhs* of the quarters represented their people to the military. In 919, the chief of police designated legal scholars in the quarters to give judgments to guide the officers. We find references to the headmen of artisans, which suggests some kind of market organization, and the headmen of soldiers, functionaries, merchants, and scholars. These were most likely titles for prominent notables, but they may imply a spokesman for an informal group. There is no evidence for communes or guilds.

Yet the chronicles show that the populace was well enough organized to intervene in political crises. In 812, the common people joined in the fight against the Khurasanian forces of al-Ma'mun on behalf of the Caliph al-Amin. Gangs of young men (*'ayyarun*) were organized in military fashion with a leader for each street and for each quarter. The groups were also active in battles with slave soldiers and in antitax or bread riots, which took place sporadically throughout the late ninth, tenth, and eleventh centuries. While resisting the state, they also preyed on rich property owners and merchants.

Apart from the residential quarters and the markets, religious congregations or associations were a critical aspect of city communal organization. In the Muslim garrison cities, the imams of the Shi'is, Khariji chieftains, charismatic preachers, Quran readers, jurists, theologians, ascetics, and mystics won over students, followers, and disciples. The learned and holy men became the leaders of sects, teaching circles, and prayer groups. Local legal scholars, teachers, storytellers, and preachers in the mosques assumed an independent authority as Islamic law, theology, and ritual developed largely without state interference.

Religious teachers were the social elites, notables in their communities, and assumed authority in all sorts of local matters. As in ancient times, scholarship and education were aligned with social and communal prestige and were connected to tribal chiefs, landowners, merchants, and government officials. Social prestige was attached to roles of mediating and adjudicating disputes and therefore to the study of law. Conversely, learning provided opportunities for upward mobility. Judges were particularly important. Often selected from among the heads of prominent families or clans, judges had important social and administrative as well as religious roles. In the Umayyad and early 'Abbasid periods, judges were often appointed in consultation with local scholars (*'ulama'*) and study circles. At first, many (but not all) judges were legal scholars, but after the reign of Harun they were drawn from the legal study circles. Law courts and their personnel became a focus of local consultation on legal issues, of mediation, and of adjudication of disputes.

Study groups and informal congregations were commonly attached to prominent families and tribes. They sometimes constituted a clientele or a faction, consisting of students, client workers, and/or residents of a neighbourhood or market supporting prominent local leaders. Judges, in particular, had the support of a faction consisting of students, functionaries, official witnesses, notaries, and other clients. Some circles were engaged in social or political activism, in their words, "commanding the good and forbidding evil," by vigilante campaigns against vice, or defending the people against governmental injustice. Others had close political ties to the caliphate. Thus, in this early period, a legal study group was also likely to be a political faction, a school of theological dogma, and sometimes a religious movement. Political support, whether caliphal, tribal, or familial, was everywhere crucial to the influence of jurists.

Kharijis set early precedents for community formation on a religious basis among Muslims. Through their insistence on the equality of all Muslims regardless of tribe and through their conception of the true imam or caliph as a person without blemish or sin, they pioneered the notion of a Muslim community based on faith rather than politics or tribe. Kharijis appointed different leaders for war and for prayer, thus separating the functions of head of state from head of community. Shi'i opposition to the Umayyads and the formation of dissident communities in Iran and Iraq early defined the Shi'is as a sectarian community.

Theological positions also had important sociopolitical implications. Some of them became the basis of communal movements. Murji'a, Hanbalis, Mu'tazilis, Qadaris, and others had their own preachers, who reached out for popular support. The Murji'a, who held that profession of Islam rather than performance of works made a true Muslim, were political and social activists. Their position on faith and works made them active missionaries in eastern Iran. Some of them fought on behalf of abused clients and converts in Transoxania. Other Murji'a made "command the good and forbid evil" the highest ideal and opposed Umayyad injustices. A moderate Murji'a position was adopted by Hanafi lawyers and spread in the eastern Iranian areas of Balkh and Turkharistan.

The Karramiya were also connected to the Murji'a-Hanafi tradition. The Karramiya were an ascetic missionary movement whose members preached poverty and set up residences (*khanaqa*) for their missionaries and adherents throughout Iran. Their theological opponents, the Hanbalis, also constituted a political-activist movement. They enforced Muslim values by vigilante action, breaking wine bottles, musical instruments, and chessboards, and preached an ascetic and puritanical version of Islam. In Baghdad, Hanbalis were typically drawn from the milieu of former Khurasanian fighters for the 'Abbasids. They were opposed to Shi'ism, to Mu'tazili theology, and to the Murji'a view that all professed Muslims were equal. They gave priority to the Prophet, his companions, and his Arab followers. Especially in the tenth century, under the leadership of al-Barbahari, they repeatedly engaged in demonstrations and street battles against the Shi'is and other religious factions.

Many of these religious "congregations" were small, even esoteric, cults, but some of them acquired a mass following. Muslim masses turned to them rather than to the caliphs for moral instruction and religious guidance. Learned and pious people who held no official position but who had acquired a reputation for knowledge of and devotion to the faith were accepted by ordinary Muslims as the true authorities on Islam.

CHAPTER 18

THE NON-MUSLIM MINORITIES

The situation of religious minorities – Jews, Christians, Zoroastrians, and others – under Muslim rule or in Muslim-majority societies is highly controversial. Some contemporary scholars see them as an assimilated and integral part of the Middle Eastern (or Muslim) world. Others see them as ethnic enclaves. Still others see them as persecuted minorities.

In Muslim domains, non-Muslims had a legally and culturally legitimate standing. Non-Muslims were entitled to the practice of their religion, to autonomy in internal communal matters, to commercial activity, and to political safety or protection in return for the payment of a special tax and acceptance of Muslim rule and social supremacy. Although non-Muslims bore significant legal and social disabilities and often suffered the disdain of Muslims, in general, the security and prosperity of the religious minorities was assured in 'Abbasid Iraq, Fatimid Egypt, Umayyad Spain, and the Ottoman Empire. In politically and economically troubled times, there were periods of exploitation, harassment, and persecution.

Although Jews, Christians, and others had a separate religio-communal identity, they were integrated into Middle Eastern societies in language, trade, and scholarship, and sometimes in government. Non-Muslims were participants in a shared nonreligious high culture of science and philosophy, theology and poetry, and many aspects of folk culture, such as norms of daily living in eating, dressing, social behavior, and commerce that were much the same regardless of religious affiliation. Even religious beliefs were similar. Whatever their religion, most peoples believed in the existence of God, the creation of the world ex nihilo, the last judgment, eternal life, prophecy, and the efficacy of the veneration of saint's tombs and other holy places. The cultural, religious, and social customs of non-Muslims were shaped by their interactions with the dominant societies, but they also contributed to forming Muslim beliefs and lifestyles.

THE EARLY ISLAMIC ERA

The practices pertaining to the place of non-Muslims in Muslim-dominated societies developed slowly over time. The Arab conquests established Muslim predominance. At the outset, some monasteries were sacked, and magian fire temples were confiscated in Syria and Iraq. A period of tolerance followed the depredations of war. For the Arab-Muslim conquerors, the perpetuation of the ruling class was necessary for the efficient administration of the new empire. The old military, administrative, and landowning elites continued in power and transferred their allegiances to the new regime. Christian landowners and monasteries survived in Upper Egypt, Syria, and northern Iraq for centuries, as did lower-level village headmen and landlords. Bishops, rabbis, mobads, and their academies and places of worship continued to function.

The historic relationship of state and religious communities was slowly restored, often at the initiative of the subjects. In the period of Roman and Sasanian domination, Christians, Jews, and Zoroastrians had been organized as self-governing, socio-legal corporations. Nestorians and Jews pressed for and were granted a restoration of Sasanian policies that gave religious bodies political and social roles. Arab-Muslim conquerors accepted that personal law was attached to religious status and acknowledged separate legal systems for different religions. The old religious communities were consolidated as the Arab rulers sought to pacify and to integrate their new subjects into the empire.

Indeed, in the wake of the Arab conquests, the old communities not only survived but experienced religious revivals. The Arab conquests inspired apocalyptic literatures among Muslims, Zoroastrians, Christians, and Jews. Populations were roiled by predictions of the coming of the anti-Christ and the end of the world. Zoroastrian literature envisioned a period of defeat and decline as a prelude to eventual resurrection and triumph.

The defeat of the Byzantine Empire allowed Christian heresies to flourish. The destruction of the Zoroastrian aristocracy allowed many sects and cults to flourish. In the eighth century, the population of Iraq included Melkites, Jacobites, Nestorians, Messaliens, Jewish Christians, Jews, Hermetics, Marcionites, Daysanites, Elkasaites, Mandaeans, Chaldeans, and others. The Khurasanian population included Christians, Manichaeans, Marcionites, and Buddhists. In the late Umayyad period, syncretistic religious movements, combining Muslim and Iranian beliefs and symbols, rose in opposition to Arab rule. Bihafrid, Sunbad, Ustadis, and Muqanna launched anti-Arab messianic movements. Mazdakite opposition – a conglomerate of movements based on cosmic dualism, gnostic syncretism, allegiance to Mazdak, and Muslim ideas – flourished in Khurasan under the name Khurramiyya and in Azarbayjan under the leadership of Babak. Under Muslim rule, Christianity expanded in the Caspian region and in Inner Asia. Some of these churches and heresies were intensely engaged in missionary activity. A non-Islamic religious revival was competing with nascent Islam.

MUSLIM LEGISLATION FOR NON-MUSLIMS

Muslim legal views on the status of non-Muslims had their beginnings in the precedents set by Muhammad. Although Muhammad had battles with the Jews of Medina and killed and expropriated many of them, he made agreements with the Jews of Khaybar and the Christians of Najran to pay taxes in exchange for protection and permission to function under their own laws and leadership. These precedents were applied in the early years of the conquest, when the Arab-Muslim invaders made treaties for the surrender of numerous cities and towns.

Islam treated Judaism and Christianity as precursor religions, ordained by God but superseded by the new revelations. Islam had its own direct linkage and descent from Abraham and Ishmael and a comparable authenticity and venerable antiquity. There were no important theological differences between Jews and Muslims. Each considered the other an imperfect but related monotheism. However, there were significant theological differences between Jews and Muslims, on the one hand, and Christians, on the other, over the doctrines of the Trinity, the divinity of Christ, and the virgin birth.

Despite these beginnings, Muslim policy evolved toward more strict regulation of non-Muslims. Early caliphs began to tighten controls on non-Muslims to affirm the separateness and higher status of Muslims, precisely because Arabic-speaking peoples of different religions were not easy to distinguish from one another. Muslims and non-Muslims shared beliefs, cultures, and market and social connections, and devout Muslims became concerned with the identification of non-Muslims, perhaps for security reasons, and concerned about their own possible assimilation into the non-Muslim populations. 'Umar II (r. 717–20) forbade Christians from holding powerful government positions and promulgated restrictive sumptuary codes. After his reign, Muslims increasingly treated Jews and Christians as subordinate minorities, forbidding non-Muslims to ride horses, bear weapons, ring church bells, stage processions, or display religious symbols in public. Christians and Jews were forbidden to change their dress and hairstyles to look like Muslims, and some sources report that Muslims were forbidden to dress like Christians. Business transactions with Muslims had to be conducted in terms of Islamic (or state) law. These rules also made it easier to identify the people subject to the poll tax (*jizya*).

Later caliphs sporadically harassed and persecuted non-Muslims. Yazid II (r. 721–24) promulgated an iconoclastic measure – perhaps in response to an internal Christian controversy – calling for destruction of human and animal figures in churches. In many Christian churches, human figures were dug out of marble mosaics. Harun al-Rashid (r. 786–809) – possibly in response to Muslim opposition to the important positions of non-Muslims in the government bureaucracy, banking, and trade – is reported to have issued restrictions on non-Muslims. Caliph al-Mutawakkil (in 850) promulgated regulations to require distinctive garments for non-Muslims. He ruled that houses of worship built after the Muslim conquests were to be destroyed, barred non-Muslims from government offices and positions of authority, and prohibited displays of crosses or chanting in public. There is no evidence of physical persecution or any indication of whether these rules were enforced or for how long.

Muslim historians and jurists also promoted a Muslim identity. Their deliberations took place in the context of ongoing warfare with the Byzantine (Christian) Empire. The threat of espionage and collaboration on the part of non-Muslim subjects was likely a concern. In juristic treatises, restrictions on non-Muslims were first applied to predominantly Muslim cities and then extended to all cities. Jurists debated whether old prayer houses should be destroyed or only new ones prohibited. There was even discussion over whether non-Muslims should be allowed to live in Muslim cities.

Nevertheless, the jurists differed among themselves. The Hanafi jurist Abu Yusuf (d. 798) favored a relatively tolerant approach to win non-Muslim acquiescence and support. He held that treaty-based rights of non-Muslims should be respected. As long as Christians paid the poll tax, their churches should not be destroyed – although no new ones could be built. In fact, archaeological evidence indicates that new churches were built. Public displays of religion should be restricted, though Abu Yusuf would have allowed the parade of the cross on Palm Sunday. Pigs were forbidden in public.

Al-Shafi'i (d. 820) accepted former treaties but sought to ensure the submission of non-Muslims and to protect Muslims from insult, injury, or undue influence. He prohibited defaming Muhammad, apostatizing, and selling wine and pork to Muslims. Dress and saddles should distinguish Christians from Muslims. Ahmad ibn Hanbal (d. 855) took a more subtle approach. To maintain Muslim identity in daily interactions, he recommended that Muslims remain conscious of and assert their identity – their differences, their separateness from other people.

Although early Islamic law on the whole protected non-Muslims (*dhimmi*), by the turn of the tenth century, regulations for non-Muslims came to include many restrictions not considered by earlier jurists. Later regulations required personal deference and respect to be shown by non-Muslims to Muslims – an emphatic demand for the subordination of the ruled to the rulers. Non-Muslims suffered other practical disadvantages. A non-Muslim man could not marry a Muslim woman, although a Muslim man was allowed to marry non-Muslim women. The blood wit for non-Muslims was two-thirds or one-half that for Muslims. Non-Muslim merchants, in theory, had to pay twice as much in customs taxes at the frontiers, although this was not always enforced.

Nonetheless, legal and political regulation and the degree of enforcement varied in different political and socioeconomic conditions. Payment of the poll tax (*jizya*) seems to have been regular, but other obligations were inconsistently enforced and did not prevent many non-Muslims from being important political, business, and scholarly figures. In the late ninth and early tenth centuries, Jewish bankers and financiers were important at the ʿAbbasid court.

CHRISTIANS AND CHRISTIANITY

Early Islamic era to the ninth century

At the time of the Arab conquests, large Christian populations were found in Syria and Palestine, Iraq, Egypt, and North Africa. The Christian population maintained from Hellenistic and Roman times a rich religious, literary, and intellectual culture, but they were deeply divided by theological principles and church loyalties. In Syria and Palestine, most Christians were Jacobites or Miaphysites who spoke Aramaic. A small percentage were ethnically Greek, although Greek was widely spoken as a diplomatic and administrative language. The Melkite or Syrian Orthodox Church was prominent in Jerusalem and Antioch. In Iraq, most Christians were Nestorians; in Egypt, they were Copts (Egyptian Miaphysites).

Although the Arab-Muslim conquests brought destruction, pillaging, and killing, the overall impact of the invasions was limited. The battles were fought in open country and probably did limited damage to the towns. Caliph ʿUmar visited Palestine in 638 and established political order. Christians were at first divided as to whether to accommodate passively or to resist Muslim rule. Greek Orthodox Christians saw the Arab conquests as a disaster. Other Christians were ambivalent, because they were relieved of Byzantine persecution and found support in the new Arab-Muslim regime.

Later caliphs and the Umayyad dynasty brought administrative organization and partial agricultural and economic development. While Egypt and Iraq remained relatively prosperous, the economy of Syria and Palestine went into decline in the eighth and ninth centuries due to the transfer of the capital to Baghdad and the decline of Mediterranean trade and Christian pilgrimage to Jerusalem.

For the sake of political inclusiveness and effective administration, the ecclesiastical hierarchies remained intact. In the Umayyad period, numerous churches were repaired and new ones built. Monasteries continued to function. The Nestorian Church in Iraq resumed its roles in the educational, judicial, tax, and political administration of the Christian population. Christian scribes and landowners assisted in the administration of Syria, Mesopotamia, and Iraq. In Egypt, the Muslim authorities cooperated with Coptic lay and clerical notables.

Muslims and non-Muslims circulated together in town markets and other public spaces, but Muslims came to insist ever more on their hegemony in public spaces.

The inscriptions of the Dome of the Rock challenged the idea of the Trinity, and Muslims derided the veneration of icons. There was a wave of persecution during the reign of the Umayyad Caliph ʿUmar II (r. 717–20). According to Christian authors, Harun al-Rashid is said to have destroyed innumerable churches in Syria and Palestine; many priests, monks, and nuns were killed or fled to Constantinople. By the ʿAbbasid period, the numbers of churches in Syria and Palestine were also reduced by general economic decline and lack of resources for repairs. Under the ʿAbbasid Caliph al-Mutawakkil (r. 847–61), non-Muslims were dismissed from government jobs and required to wear clothing that distinguished them from Muslims. Restrictions on church building, displays of the cross, and other manifestations of Christian religious life were imposed.

From the seventh to the end of the eleventh century, around half of the world's Christians lived under Muslim governments, but the Arab-Muslim rulers did not attempt to convert the populations to Islam. Under Muslim government, as a protected community, Christians were entitled to laws and courts of their own, but in many instances the Christians had no clear-cut legal tradition and adopted Islamic law for both administrative and communal affairs. Many individuals converted out of belief, desire to avoid the poll tax, fear of discrimination, and social, economic, and political ambitions. By the late seventh century, Christian writers in Syria were already concerned with apostasy. Christian communities prohibited intermarriage and forbade apostates to Islam from inheriting from their Christian families. Christian clerics, however, could not prevent appeals to Muslim courts and the mingling of people in ordinary commerce, social life, and festivals. By the middle of the eighth century, there seems to have been a steady progress of conversions in Iraq, Egypt, and Syria. Perhaps half of the town populations were Muslims by 850, and by the tenth and eleventh centuries Muslims were probably a small majority in Syria, Mesopotamia, Egypt, and Iraq.

In the decades before and during the Arab invasions, the Christian churches were only beginning to form their distinct ecclesial identities and hierarchies, a process that continued in the Islamic era. The churches, however, fared differently under Muslim rule. After the Arab conquest, the Greek Orthodox Church lost the privileged status it had enjoyed under the Byzantines but also benefited from its independence from Constantinople. It came to be known as the Syrian Orthodox Church. The caliphate delayed the appointment of Orthodox patriarchs and left their sees vacant in the cases of Jerusalem from 638 to 705 and Antioch from 702 to 742, but new patriarchs were elected to Jerusalem in 706, Alexandria in 727, and Antioch in 744. The Orthodox Church, however, remained an important landowner and was able to shelter Christian peasants especially around Bethlehem, Nazareth, and Mount Tabor, perhaps prolonging their attachment to Christianity.

In Syria and Palestine, the Syriac (or Jacobite, Miaphysite) Church had the largest following, especially among the peasant populations. The Coptic Church in Egypt was also Miaphysite by doctrine. The senior ecclesiastical offices were open only to monks, and the bishops were selected from monasteries in Syria, Mesopotamia, Asia Minor, and Egypt. The Jacobite Church, however, developed its own civil law and court system, incorporating both Roman and Muslim civil regulations, so that it would have a legal system to compete with the Muslim courts.

In Iraq, Nestorians consolidated their own legal and ecclesiastical administrative systems and in general benefited from close associations with the Muslim authorities. Bishops sometimes designated judges; sometimes a layperson usurped power; sometimes the judges were appointed by the state. In general, the church was independent, but internal disputes often led to the engagement of the Arab-Muslim government in church affairs. Eventually, the Umayyad government required that any newly elected catholicos have governmental ratification. Other Christian churches included the Armenians and the Maronites.

Before the Islamic era, Christians spoke different dialects of Aramaic. Orthodox Christians around the patriarchate of Jerusalem spoke "Christian Palestinian Aramaic," but Greek was the language of the clergy and the liturgy. The Jacobite Christians of Syria and Mesopotamia used the Syriac dialect of Aramaic as their ecclesiastical and liturgical language. Arabic, however, became the vernacular of everyday life in late eighth-century Palestine, late eighth- and ninth-century Syria and Mesopotamia, tenth-century Egypt, and Iraq and North Africa. Arabic also displaced Aramaic and Syriac as the predominant written language of administration, literature, and religion. The linguistic changes helped reinforce a transition from the greater Christian orthodox world to more local Christian identities. Greek continued to exist, however, as both a literary and a spoken language in Syria. Inscriptions in churches and ecclesiastical literature were written in Greek, and Greek continued to be used in monasteries until the Crusades. Also, Christians did not pray in Arabic until the tenth century.

Christian literature in Arabic
The new religio-political situation of the early Islamic era motivated Christian theologians to restate and defend the teachings of their churches against both Muslims and other churches. The Melkite author John of Damascus (d. 749/764) thus composed the first *summa theologiae* in Christian intellectual history, *The Fount of Knowledge*, refuting Islam and Christian heresies. Similar systematic statements, such as Theodore bar Koni's *Scholion* (c. 792), were written by Nestorian theologians. From the middle of the eighth century until late in the tenth century, the bishopric of Jerusalem and the surrounding monastic communities, cut off from Constantinople, also began to translate Greek texts in history, philosophy, prose, and poetry into Syriac. A Syriac literature of hagiography, homilies, miracles, and disputations flourished.

Translations into Syriac were followed by translations into Arabic. The Melkites were in the forefront of the transition from Greek into Arabic and the composition of polemical works in Arabic. The Melkite monasteries in the Judean desert, particularly Mar Sabas and Mar Chariton, produced the first sustained translations of the Gospels and the Christian patristic literature and also the first original theological compositions in Arabic. Theodore of Abu Qurra (d. c. 825) was the first important Christian theologian to write in Arabic. A primary reason for the adoption of Arabic for ecclesiastical texts was the need to reach Arabic-speaking and Arabic-reading Christians and defend the tenets of orthodoxy from their ever-growing familiarity with an Arabic-Muslim vocabulary and Muslim religious ideas. Christian beliefs and practices concerning the Trinity, incarnation, baptism, the Eucharist, and the veneration of the cross and of icons were vigorously defended against the Muslim insistence on the unity and oneness of God. The Christian concept of the divinity of Christ was defended against the Muslim view of Christ as a human prophet. Nestorian and Jacobite theologians and philosophers soon developed their own theologies, a Christian *kalam*, to defend their Christological positions in Arabic.

The leading theologians were Theodore Abu Qurra (d. 830), the Jacobite Habib ibn Khidmah Abu Raitah (d. c. 851), and the Nestorian Ammar al-Basri (fl. c. 850). In later generations, there were the Jacobite philosopher and theologian Yahya ibn 'Adi (d. 974), the Nestorian Elias of Nisibis (d. 1046), and the Melkite Paul of Antioch (d. c. 1180). Thus, only in the early Islamic period and in the Arabic language did the Melkites, the Jacobites, and the Nestorians come to a full statement of their theological identities. After the thirteenth century, Coptic Egypt became the primary center of Arab-Christian thought.

Hellenistic philosophy, science, and literature also flourished in Christian circles, and Christian scholars and theologians were the principle intermediaries in the translation of Greek and Hellenistic learning into Arabic. Theodore Abu Qurra translated a pseudo-Aristotelian work, *De virtutibus animae*, for one of the Caliph al-Ma'mun's generals. The Nestorian philosopher Hunayn ibn Ishaq (d. 873) coordinated a vast translation enterprise. By their appropriation (initially into Syriac) of the sixth-century Alexandrian school of Aristotelianism (a form of rationalism committed to the philosophical defense of religious truths), Christian thinkers provided the basis for the eventual development of Islamic theology (*kalam*) and philosophy. They stood for the ideal of a philosophical way of life in which universal truths transcended religious particularisms.

Crusades and reaction

Despite the conversions of many Syrian and Palestinian Christians in the Umayyad and 'Abbasid periods, Christians remained a very large proportion of the total population, possibly even a majority in some areas until after the Crusades. Byzantine and crusader invasions of Syria, however, undermined the Syrian and Palestinian Christians, and the Mamluk era (1250–1517) brought economic and political pressures and persecution, leading to the conversion of the great majority of regional Christians.

In the tenth century, the Byzantine Empire reconquered the northern part of Syria and ruled for almost 120 years (969–1084), sheltering the Greek Orthodox from Muslim temptations and pressures. At the same time, there were large-scale conversions in southern Syria and Palestine. The Crusades and Latin dominance deeply alienated native Christians. The Latins took control of the Christian holy places, including the Church of the Nativity in Bethlehem and the Church of the Holy Sepulcher in Jerusalem, and made many Syrian and Palestinian Christians look to Muslims for relief from coercion by the Latins. Indeed, in 1187 the churches were returned to native Christians by Saladin.

The rise of the Mamluks in Egypt and Syria and the Mongol invasions permanently changed the place of Christians. Many Christians in Syria sided with the Mongol invaders; the Mamluks, fighting both the Mongols and the crusader occupants of coastal Syria and Palestine, embraced Islam as an ideology of resistance to the invaders. Muslim jurists called for the strict enforcement of regulations for non-Muslims and the punishment of Christians who collaborated with the enemy. There were repeated efforts to drive Christians from government jobs and to rigorously enforce the collection of the poll tax. Moreover, in the fourteenth and fifteenth centuries, nomadic Arab migrations into Palestine added to the forces of Arabization and Islamization. In the Mamluk period, the Christian population was reduced to the small proportions that endure to the present. One major exception was the Maronite population of the Lebanon, protected by their mountainous country, who paid tribute and were free from direct Mamluk administrative interventions.

The Egyptian copts

After the Arab conquest of Egypt, the patriarch was returned to his office; the Cathedral church of Alexandria, St. Marks, was rebuilt; and the patriarch played a diplomatic role in the Arab relations with Nubia and Ethiopia. The church also established a network of shrines commemorating the itinerary of the flight of the holy family into Egypt that would serve as a foundation for Coptic devotions and identity. A network of churches, monasteries, and shrines was the foundation of the Coptic community. At first, new churches were built, but in time the Muslim attitude hardened and required government authorization or at least tacit consent. By the tenth century, Muslim jurists had ruled that churches existing before the conquest might be repaired, but new ones should not be constructed.

Arabic diffused rapidly among the Christian population; by the ninth century, it was in use by the clergy as well. Conversion to Islam progressed more slowly and painfully, associated over the centuries with social, fiscal, and political pressure from the dominant Muslims. Fiscal administration played a large part in the pressure or incentives for conversion. Under the Umayyads, administrative regulation was progressively intensified. The tax registers were translated into Arabic. Many Coptic village headmen were replaced with Arab-Muslims, and taxes were assessed on individuals rather than communities. Converts were promised exemption from the poll tax. There were repeated popular revolts. A comprehensive land survey was undertaken in 724–25, and in the next year there was a great Coptic revolt. There were thirteen more between 767 and 832. With the defeat of these rebellions, the influence of the church and of Coptic notables was further diminished, and the conversion of Egyptians to Islam increased. The limited evidence indicates a steady flow of converts in the ninth and tenth centuries.

In the early Fatimid era (909–1171), Christians and Jews were well treated. Christians – mostly Coptic Orthodox, although there were also Greek Orthodox and Armenian Orthodox churches – are estimated to have composed at least a third of the population of Egypt. Christians and Jews were employed in the financial administration and frequently at the highest levels. Bureaucratic skills were passed on from generation to generation. Copts prospered as farmers, ceramicists, papyrus makers, textile producers, and in many other trades. The state generally tolerated non-Muslim places of worship and even provided financial support and gifts of land for the endowment of churches and Jewish courts and schools. Coptic festivals and ceremonies such as the feasts of Nairouz, Christmas, Epiphany, Maundy Thursday, and Martyr's Day were celebrated by both Copts and Muslims. Copts and Muslims venerated the same saints and holy men. The patriarchs promoted the interests of the state in their relations with the Nubian and Ethiopian churches and in diplomatic relations with the Byzantine Empire. The one major exception was a period of persecution in the reign of the Caliph al-Hakim (996–1021). In his reign, Christian officials were pushed out of office, the sale of alcoholic drinks forbidden, sumptuary regulations enforced, and many churches closed or torn down.

In the twelfth century, the crusader invasions of Palestine increased religious tensions. Copts were again subjected to heavy taxation. Many converted to Islam. At the same time, Arabic was consolidated as the vernacular language of Copts. Books on canon law, theology, and church history were now written in Arabic. By the thirteenth century Arabic Christian texts from Syria and Iraq reinforced Coptic Arabic scholarship.

In the Mamluk era (1250–1517), the pressures for conversion and the numbers of conversions grew ever greater. In this period, the Coptic population of Egypt was reduced to the small percentages of today (variously estimated at 5 to 15 percent). The wars against the crusaders and the Mongols generated high tension among Muslims and Christians, a more assertive Muslim militancy, resentment of the favored position of Copts in the government financial bureaucracy, and demands by Muslim clerics for conformity to the more restrictive *dhimmi* laws. The Mamluks found it convenient to vent these pressures by repeated requirements that non-Muslim functionaries either convert to Islam or be removed from office, and reenactment of the Covenant of 'Umar sumptuary laws (1293, 1301, 1321, and 1354). In 1321, major anti-Christian rioting led to the destruction of some sixty churches. In 1354, there were riots and destruction of churches in Cairo and other parts of Egypt. Christian bureaucrats were dismissed or compelled to convert to Islam. The government confiscated church properties. The result was a sharp decline in church revenues and increased conversions to Islam. The restrictive regulations for non-Muslims were renewed in 1417, 1419, 1422, 1437–39, and 1463, which indicates both that they were not enforced and that the harassment of Copts was endemic.

The Coptic secretarial class, which had in effect displaced the clergy as the leaders of the community, was the key player in this ongoing drama. Its members provided patronage to the clergy and the resources to rebuild the churches. Lay notables played significant roles in negotiating and managing the church's relations with the Muslim authorities. Coptic officials were also indispensable to the state. Even after centuries, the state continued to depend on Christians to staff the financial administration. In consequence, they were resented and hated by the Egyptian-Muslim population. Conversion did not necessarily resolve this tension, because many Copts were reluctant converts, perhaps with continuing family and church connections, and in any case Muslims were suspicious of their genuineness and loyalty.

The Coptic Church and communities nonetheless survive to the present. The church maintains its theological Miaphysite position. Its deep historical continuity, its shrines and sermons, and above all its identity as a church of martyrs sustain it to the present.

Christians in North Africa

The Muslim conquests of North Africa dealt a lasting blow to the Christian communities. The fall of Carthage in 698 led to a mass exodus of Christians. The church nonetheless survived, and in time Christians became socially and commercially engaged with Muslims as they were in the Levant and the Middle East. The Christian trading communities involved in the Mediterranean trade and connected to the Italian city-states and the Saharan trading community of Tahert maintained their prominence into the eleventh century. The eleventh century, however, was a turning point and the beginning of the effective extinction of ancient Christianity in North Africa. The Hilali invasions and succeeding Almoravid and Almohad conquests drove the remaining Christians into exile. The loss of the intelligentsia is marked by the absence of a Christian North African culture in Arabic. In the thirteenth century, under Spanish-Muslim auspices, there was a countermovement of Christian soldiers, mercenaries, and merchants returning to North Africa, but indigenous Berber Christianity continued to fade away. A church-based community survived in Tunis, but without an intellectual class, strong church leadership, or external support, Berber Christians were absorbed into the Muslim populace.

JEWS AND JUDAISM (CO-AUTHOR, DAVID MOSHFEGH)

The place of Jews in Muslim societies is best seen against the background of their place in medieval European Christian societies. In Europe, there was an endemic conflict between Judaism and Christianity. Jews were held responsible for the murder of Christ. Early Christians, a persecuted sect, aspired to converts all Jews and gentiles and to replace Judaism rather than coexist with it.

The Christian treatment of Jews in Europe goes back to the Theodosian Code. In late Roman law, Jewish life, property, and religious observance was considered legitimate, but intermarriage with Christians, the construction of new synagogues, holding public office, and ownership of Christian slaves were forbidden. The Fourth Lateran Council in 1215 added new restrictions. Jews were required to wear identifying clothing so as to inhibit mingling with Christians; excessive usury by which Jews oppressed Christians was prohibited. From 1239, the popes began to interfere in Jewish worship by banning and burning the Talmud.

At the same time, European princes, eager to promote commerce, assured Jews of privileges – including protection under municipal laws, judicial autonomy, and freedom of movement. Over centuries, however, Jews were excluded from participation in (Christian) artisan and merchant guilds and from representation in the "estates" and were confined to money lending and usury to earn a living. Excluded from all social groupings, they were vulnerable to taxes and extortion and eventually to expropriation and expulsion. Jews were expelled from England in 1290; from France in 1306, 1322, and 1394; from Spain in 1492; from Portugal in 1497; and from numerous German towns and princedoms.

The long-term situation of Jews in Muslim societies was very different. Before the Arab conquests, Jews were economically and culturally well integrated into pre-Islamic Arabian society. Under Sasanian rule, Jews were generally secure, although there were three episodes of persecution in the late fifth and sixth centuries. However, oppressed Jews in Byzantine Syria and Palestine supported the Persian invasions in 614 and attacked Christians. The advent of Islam and the revelations of the Quran inspired messianic expectations. Jews in Arabia, Palestine, and Syria were swept by a wave of hopes for immediate redemption. Some accepted Muhammad. Others recognized him only as a prophet to pagan Arabs. Indeed, Jews had an endemic history of sectarianism. There were various Jewish sects – Samaritans, ʿIsawiyya, and gnostics – in Persia and Central Asia, where there was a long tradition of frontier refuge for deviant sects. Hybrid Jewish-Christian sects accepted Jesus as a human prophet but practiced Jewish traditions. Jewish messianists also joined the early Shiʿi movement. In the ninth century, Jews were primarily divided among Karaites and Rabbinites.

The largest Jewish communities were found in Iraq. They were Aramaic speaking and well integrated into Iraqi society; they called themselves Babylonians. The great majority of Jews, however, were agriculturalists and workers, often in menial and despised trades such as viniculture and tavern keeping, weaving, dying, tanning, and butchering. An elite cadre of merchants (the Radhanites) was engaged in very long distance international trade, bringing goods to and from Western Europe through the Middle East and on to India and China. By the late ninth century the Jewish population was increasingly urban, as is indicated by rabbinic responsa that increasingly deal with movable property. There were high-ranking Jewish courtiers, physicians, astrologers, bankers, merchants, and some functionaries in the 'Abbasid financial administration. Some Jews belonged to the rich middle class – including landowners, physicians and pharmacists, merchants, and gold- and silversmiths. The majority was engaged in commerce and craft work.

Under Sasanian and later Muslim rule, Jewish communities were governed by the exilarchs, or leaders of the civil community who claimed descent from King David, collected taxes, and represented the Jews at court. Over time, however, the most important Jewish institutions became the rabbinic academies (yeshivas) in Iraq and Palestine. The heads of the academies were the most respected scholars and the highest authorities of Jewish law. The academies served as appellate courts; trained the rabbis who were at once religious teachers, judges, and community administrators; and sometimes appointed them to their local posts. The heads of the Babylonian and Palestinian academies were seen as spiritual leaders whose views were passed on throughout the Jewish world to local teachers and judges. It is hard to determine how much of a formal hierarchy there was, how much client loyalty, and how much independence for local rabbis. There was probably a constant power struggle between the rival academies and between the central academies and local communities. Expert laymen could also take on judicial functions.

At the time of the Arab conquests, the gap in state control allowed the heads of the yeshivas, known as *gaonim*, to contest the authority of the exilarchs, and by the 'Abbasid era to become the stronger power. Although the exilarch maintained some administrative functions, the rabbis chose the exilarch, though only from within the exilarch's family. In the 'Abbasid era, the Babylonian academy moved from Sura and Pumbedita to Baghdad and gained primacy throughout the Jewish world.

In the early Muslim era, the foundations of Rabbinic Judaism evolved into the form we recognize today. Some rabbinic texts appear to have been recorded or redacted in their extant forms during the early Islamic era. The text of the Bible, the Babylonian Talmud, Jewish law and ritual, the synagogue and the prayer book, much of the Hebrew language, and Jewish philosophy and theology all date to this epoch. Jewish thought was influenced by both Christian and Muslim contemporaries, often through interconfessional discussions and debates. Jewish apologetics were influenced by Muslim and Christian writings. Comparative research into Quranic exegesis, Islamic law, and rabbinic texts suggests direct contact between Muslim and Jewish scholars. Not all Jews, however, accepted the authority of the rabbis. Karaite Jews rejected rabbinic law and believed the Bible was the sole and complete religious authority.

Although Jews in Iraq seem to have been generally safe and prosperous, as under the Sasanians, there were periods of persecution. In all periods, the non-Muslim communities, including Jews, were vulnerable to changes of political mood. There were persecutions of Jews in ninth- and twelfth-century Baghdad.

Jews were at least temporarily removed from government offices, and synagogues were attacked for violating the rules against new constructions. In eleventh- and twelfth-century Baghdad, the Saljuq era, rioting commoners and mobs repeatedly demanded the enforcement of the non-Muslim dress code, and the Saljuqs frequently expropriated Jewish merchants.

In an era of upheavals, conversions, and the mingling of people of different religions, the leaders of all confessional communities tried to maintain the allegiance of their followers. Clerical leaders in all communities strove to corral people within communal boundaries and insistently claimed judicial exclusiveness. In debates, religious leaders used much the same arsenal of scriptures, authenticated traditions, and dialectical arguments. Nonetheless, Muslims and non-Muslims mingled in public life. Muslim jurists permitted non-Muslims to appeal to Muslim (i.e., state) courts, and, by the ninth century, Jews and Christians were going to Muslim courts for commercial issues, wills, inheritances, and even marriages. They likely sought to reverse the decisions of ecclesiastical courts, or to find better terms, or to have access to more enforceable legal decisions.

Egyptian and North African Jews: the Geniza era

With the breakdown of the ʿAbbasid Empire in the tenth century, the Jewish communities of Iraq declined in international importance. Large numbers of Jews migrated from Iraq to Egypt and later from North Africa to Egypt. Jewish communities in Egypt, North Africa, and Spain became the leading centers of Jewish community life, commerce, and Judeo-Arabic and rabbinic culture. From the tenth to the thirteenth century, Jews were heavily engaged in international trade, especially in the Muslim-dominated, Arabic-speaking parts of the Mediterranean. Political stability in Egypt and the weakness of medieval European states allowed for an era of commercial freedom and opportunity for Jews.

In the first half of the eleventh century, Qayrawan was the ecumenical financial center of the Babylonian yeshivas. Qayrawan had an active scholarly academy that created its own synthesis of Palestinian and Babylonian Talmudic commentaries. Its scholars were responsible for gathering and relaying both religious queries and contributions of funds from the Maghreb, through Fustat, and to the Babylonian and Palestinian yeshivas.

This was not accidental but was based on the deep history of Jewish communities in North Africa. The Jews of North Africa date back to the Phoenician period, although many of the Jews at the time of the Arab conquests were likely to have been Berber converts and their descendants. Jews lived in the commercial cities of Tripoli, Qayrawan, Tahert, Tlemcen, Sijilmassa, and Fez. In the tenth and eleventh centuries, the merchants of Qayrawan were the hub of the Mediterranean trade with Sicily, Spain, Morocco, and Egypt.

The Jewish merchant elites, based in Fustat-Cairo, Qayrawan, Tunis, and Spain, were the leaders of their local communities. While engaged in commerce, this elite also cultivated learning and piety. They supported the yeshivas, synagogues, and Jewish education. They supported extensive charities, especially for the ransom of Jewish captives, whomever and wherever they might be; for Jewish foreigners in their communities; for education; and for the relief of the poor. A "proper" person was defined by a combination of business success, family, scholarship, etiquette, personal probity, and communal responsibility. Through commercial and scholarly networks, family alliances, and marriages, the Jewish elite linked together the Jewish communities of the Mediterranean. They supported both local identities and a coherent international community able to represent and defend the community before the political authorities and to enforce cohesion and discipline within it.

Most Jews were craftsmen and workers. Most business was conducted on the basis of informal partnerships, friendships, and mutual trust. Most craftspeople were independent partners rather than employees. Jewish-Muslim partnerships were common. Formal contracts were important because they were enforceable in Muslim courts. The Jewish communities themselves generated a great number of positions for officials, functionaries, and servants connected to the synagogues, courts, and schools – notably, judges, teachers, cantors, ritual slaughterers, scribes, and court clerks. Jewish charities supported resident foreign Jews and other Jewish communities. Collections were regularly taken for bread for the poor, wheat, clothing, educational expenses, burials, traveling scholars, ransom of captives, and payment of officials.

The Yeshivas and Rabbinic Judaism
The breakdown of the 'Abbasid Empire and the migration of Jews westward also promoted the rise of *gaonim* and the yeshivas as worldwide Jewish authorities. The Babylonian yeshivas at Pumbedita and Sura formed close bonds with new "Babylonian" congregations in Fustat (Cairo), Qayrawan, Fez, and Sijilmassa and eventually gained primacy throughout the Jewish world.

The yeshivas functioned as the highest courts of the Jewish community and conceived of themselves as substituting for the Sanhedrin of the Second Temple. The Palestinian yeshiva in fact literally designated itself a Sanhedrin. The yeshivas fulfilled the functions both of the jurisconsults in giving responsa to legal questions and of the judges in adjudicating disputes. Each local Jewish congregation was under the religio-legal direction of one of the yeshivas and its *gaon*. The *gaonim* sent letters of instructions to be read to the congregations, and the congregations made regular financial contributions. Local congregations accepted legal and administrative oversight, and the chief judges and leaders in the important Jewish communities were generally members of the academies; as such, they were also scholars and students who were expected to continue their studies and maintain a scholarly relationship and correspondence with the yeshivas. The *gaonic* yeshiva was a much more hierarchal institution than the Talmudic one. The Talmud was created by discussion among scholars, but the *gaon* was a single, final authority. The members of the yeshiva were organized in an elaborate hierarchy. In discussion, the senior members participated while the others listened. Ranking members expected to pass on their position to their heirs.

The *gaonim* of the Babylonian yeshivas depended on a local personage, usually a court physician, with prominent ties to the Muslim authorities who could serve as the secular head of the community, supervise its affairs, and guarantee the financial support of the yeshiva. The yeshivas also depended on the great mercantile families to act as trustees and treasurers who handled the international aspects of yeshiva finances. Although the *gaonim* had great authority, their power was also limited by the autonomy of Jewish congregations. Local congregations were in many respects independent communities. Although the *gaonim* appointed judges and communal leaders, they generally confirmed a congregation's own choices. In general, Jewish communities tried to minimize outside intervention by arbitrating disputes among themselves. Their critical goal was to maintain communal confidence, trust, and solidarity.

The authority of the yeshivas, the universality of *gaonic* authority, and the hierarchies of appointed functionaries resembles in many ways the organization of the Christian churches, but the religio-communal order of the Jews in Muslim lands lay somewhere between the defined hierarchy of the churches and the more informal networking arrangements of the Islamic legal schools. The attitude of the three yeshivas to one another can be compared to that of the Islamic schools of law toward one another. Notwithstanding many differences, each viewed the others as equally orthodox. There were some serious differences between the two Babylonian yeshivas; for example, Sura obligated levirate marriage, whereas Pumbedita forbade it and obliged the parties to grant each other a release. In Palestinian family law, half the dowry of a woman who died without children reverted to her own family, but not in Babylonian law. The most protracted struggle between the Babylonian yeshivas and the Palestinian yeshivas revolved around the Jewish calendar. The Babylonians celebrated the six yearly holidays for two days, the Palestinians for one.

Pumbedita was the dominant yeshiva in the last decades of the tenth century and the first half of the eleventh. Between the tenth and the thirteenth century, the authority of the yeshivas and the *gaonim* rose to their apogee and faded away. In the early twelfth century, the two Iraqi academies moved to Baghdad, where they may have coalesced into one. Around 1200, the ʿAbbasid caliphs made financial support of the Baghdad yeshiva a legal obligation of the Jewish population. Yet the *gaonim* disappeared by the end of the thirteenth century, and the remaining authority of the exilarch gradually disappeared after the fourteenth century.

The Palestinian yeshiva, having moved from Tiberius to Jerusalem, was at its peak in the tenth and eleventh centuries. The Fatimids, who held Jerusalem for around a century, recognized the claims of the Palestinian yeshiva to jurisdiction over all rabbinic Jewry. The Palestinian *gaon* was responsible not only for expounding the law but for administering it in all matters of personal status, such as marriage and divorce. He had the right of appointment over all communal officials (cantors, preachers, ritual slaughterers, etc.), especially judges. For decades, except for the crisis under Caliph al-Hakim, the Palestinian yeshiva received funding from the Fatimid state. However, after the Seljuk conquest of Jerusalem in 1071, it moved to Tyre, then to Damascus, and ultimately to Fustat in 1127. The school that formed around Moses Maimonides (d. 1204) replaced it.

The *Nagid*

From the eleventh century, a countertendency emerged in the organization of the Jewish communities – a tendency toward a local leader who combined religio-legal and civil authority; in effect, this was a return to the exilarchate of a previous era, but in a local context. The *nagid* was the highest religio-legal Jewish authority, with a competence comparable to the *gaonim*, and also the secular head of the Jewish community, responsible for its affairs and for representing its interests before the Muslim authorities. The new authority reemerged in Egypt, where Fatimid and later Mamluk governments favored the concentration of power in the hands of one supreme authority. From c. 1200 to c. 1370, the position was passed on in the Maimonides family. In Mamluk times (1250–1517), it was described as the office of the *ra'is al-yahud*, headman of the Jews.

The Jews of Egypt and Syria under the Fatimids were, despite their general security and prosperity, subject to waves of persecution. In the reign of the Fatimid Caliph al-Hakim, there was a wave of anxiety about the free mingling and perhaps sexual connections of Muslim women and non-Muslim men. Laws to inhibit the social interaction of Jews and Muslims were promulgated. Non-Muslims were excluded from the baths on certain days; Jews and Christians were required to wear special colors or identifying clothing.

Under the Mamluk regime of Egypt and Syria (1250–1517), social tension turned into political persecution. Political instability, rivalries among Mamluk warlords, and the incessant demand for new revenues led to hardship and insecurity for all their subjects – especially for minorities. A slave, military elite, embroiled in war with the crusaders and dependent on Muslim support for its legitimacy, waged harsh campaigns against Christian minorities in the Lebanon and Syria and Jews in Cairo. Similarly, in Iran, the rise to power of the Safavids (a Shi'i regime) led to the persecution of Sunni Muslims, Jews, and other non-Muslim religious minorities in the sixteenth and seventeenth centuries.

Jewish culture in the Islamic context

Just as Jews participated socially and economically in Arabic-Islamic societies while maintaining a separate communal identity, Jews participated in the Middle Eastern Arab/Islamic culture while cultivating a parallel and separate Judaic culture.

Generally, Jewish communities employed two languages: a vernacular (Aramaic in Babylonia and Palestine, Persian in Iran, Aramaic and Greek in Egypt, Berber and Latin in North Africa, and Romance in Spain) for general communication and a sacred language, Hebrew, for religious and ceremonial purposes. Aramaic, however, was also used for Talmud and other sacred purposes. After the Muslim conquests, Arabic replaced Aramaic as the colloquial language, although scholars continued for some time to use Aramaic in writing.

In the tenth century, Saadya Gaon (d. 942) is the first known rabbinic leader to use Arabic, written in Hebrew script. Saadya translated the Hebrew Bible into Arabic and wrote short, focused treatises on specific topics in Talmudic law. The reception of Arabic extended to grammatical studies, theology, and poetry. The great works of Judeo-Arabic culture, from Saadya's *The Book of Beliefs and Opinions* to Maimonides's *Guide for the Perplexed*, were written in Middle Arabic. Responsa literature was written in Arabic, Hebrew, or Aramaic, depending on the language used by the questioner. Aramaic was the language of the Talmuds, but after Saadya, most of the scholarship on the Talmud was conducted in Judeo-Arabic.

At the same time that Saadya pioneered the dissemination of Judeo-Arabic, he originated a Hebrew-language revival. In reaction to multireligious discussion in ninth- and tenth-century Iraq and speculation about ethical rationalism and universal religious values, he championed the concept that universal truths were found within one's own religion. He became a leader in defending Rabbinic Judaism against Christian and Muslim polemics, Jewish gnostic skepticism, and Karaite sectarianism. He compiled the first Hebrew dictionary.

Jews shared not only the literary culture of the Arab world but also religious practices (such as pilgrimage to sacred shrines). The veneration of saints became a mass practice among both Jews and Muslims. In northern Palestine, Jews visited the alleged tombs of the great rabbis of the ancient world; in Egypt, Jewish pilgrims flocked to ancient synagogues that became associated with biblical figures and sometimes invited Muslim friends. In Iraq, both Muslims and Jews attended the presumed tombs of the prophet Ezekiel and Ezra the Scribe. Jews in Egypt later debated whether to wash before prayer or to pray in rows, as did Muslims. The relation of Jews to Muslims (and of Christians to Muslims) might be defined as separate but similar.

CHAPTER 19

CONTINUITY AND CHANGE IN THE HISTORIC CULTURES OF THE MIDDLE EAST

In the first part of this book we reviewed the beginnings and early development of Islam and attempted to show how early Islam was a part and continuation of late antique Greco-Roman and Persian civilizations. Islam goes back to the Prophet Muhammad, the revelation of the Quran, and the first Muslim communities in Mecca and Medina, but the Islamic religion was the amplification of these teachings, carried out in later centuries, not only in the original home of Islam in Arabia but throughout the whole of the vast region from Spain to Inner Asia conquered by the Arab-Muslims. The Islamic religion came to encompass not only the Quran and the example of Muhammad but a vastly expanded range of religious literatures and practices, including law, theology, and mysticism, developed in numerous schools and subcommunities. Islam in this sense refers to the whole panoply of religious concepts and practices through which the original inspiration was later expressed. Similarly, Islamic-era philosophy, poetry and belles lettres, arts, and sciences were also continuations of both the Arabian and the broader regional cultures of late antiquity. In this larger body of literature, arts, and sciences, religious and nonreligious influences intermingled. Islamic political, economic, and social institutions were also built on the same template as those of past empires, economies, and societies.

The appropriation of the past was in part unconscious and in part deliberate. The vast reach of the Islamic empires, the broad recruitment of the imperial elite, and the cosmopolitan quality of Baghdad brought the whole of the ancient Middle Eastern heritage into the purview of Islam. The new elites were impelled to generate a unified culture to provide a coherent way of life in their melting-pot cities, to integrate the disparate elements of the new elite, and to articulate the triumph, the legitimacy, and the permanence of the new order. These needs could only be fulfilled by the assimilation of the crucial elements of the ancient heritage.

In the new era, the past was a living presence. Prior cultures were transmitted through ongoing institutions; political, social, and business contacts among peoples with different backgrounds; texts; translations; and oral recitations. Family, village, neighborhood, tribal, and other forms of small-scale community organization were generally not affected by the Arab conquests and the Muslim empires. Despite geographical changes in the distribution of economic activity, the basic institutions of agricultural production and urban commerce remained unchanged. Byzantine and Sasanian imperial institutions, including the concept of the ruler and his responsibility for religion, were directly taken over by the Arab-Muslim caliphate. Monotheistic religious beliefs and congregational forms of religious organization became the template for the newly forming Muslim religious communities. Converts brought their previous education, cultural style, and political identifications into the new faith. Christian eschatology and theology and neo-Platonic and Hellenistic philosophy became part of Islamic theology and mysticism. Jewish scriptural, prophetic, ritual, and legal precedents were absorbed into Islamic law. Hellenistic science and Sasanian and Byzantine court ceremony, art and architecture, administrative precedents, and political concepts were assimilated by the Umayyad and ʿAbbasid empires.

Arab-Muslim participation in and transformations of antique heritage began in the seventh century and continued approximately to the eleventh century. The process of cultural creation occurred in several periods. The first was the beginning of Islam in a complex Arabian cultural environment. Bedouin elements made pre-Islamic Arabian culture different in many respects from the settled regions of the Middle East, but in politics, trade, material development, and religion, Arabia was already closely connected to the larger region. Pre-Islamic Arabian religious and literary cultures not only stemmed from bedouin origins but were modeled on the general system of culture found in the cities of the Middle East since the third century. Thus, Islam had its beginnings in a religious milieu in which paganism and monotheism had already begun to converge, and Arabian Islam absorbed religious beliefs and practices, poetry, folk traditions, and popular spirituality from its environment.

The second period included the Arab conquests and the consequent political, social, economic, and demographic upheavals. In the seventh century, there was an Islamic identity, but there was little development of the political, ideological, religious, or cultural dimensions of this identity. The Quran was preserved. The memory of the Prophet was kept alive, and an Islamic presence was asserted in documents, inscriptions, and the construction of places of worship, but neither the caliphate nor the holy men and scholars had yet generated the public symbols or the literary content of what later became Islam.

The third period began in the late seventh century and continued approximately to the early eleventh century. This was the Arab-Islamic renaissance phase, a period of the assimilation, adaptation, and creative transformation of late antique Middle Eastern cultures. In this phase, Arab-Islam absorbed Roman and Sasanian arts and literatures, legal systems, political institutions, and economic practices. It absorbed

Arabian tribal culture, Middle Eastern family practices, Jewish religious concepts and community institutions, and Christian theology and eschatology. Under the auspices of both the caliphate and the urban religious literati, Persian literature (*adab*), Hellenistic philosophy and science, and Greco-Roman law were translated, summarized, paraphrased, adapted, and integrated into new Arabic literatures. In each case, Islamic identities were a continuation of, a variation on, and at the same time, a discernibly innovative expression of the historic Middle Eastern cultural background. Each institutional and cultural type, however, had a different mode of reconfiguration and reconstruction in Arab-Islamic culture. These differences must be considered to grasp the variety and subtlety of the transmission and transformational process.

Islam infused inherited institutions with a new vocabulary, concepts, and value preferences, as well as a new definition of personal, social, and political identity. It redefined pre-Islamic institutions in Muslim cultural terms. The appropriation of Christian, Byzantine, and Sasanian artistic motifs resulted in a configuration original and unmistakably Islamic. In literature, law, theology, mysticism, and philosophy, the materials of the past were reshaped. Islamic civilization had to find a balance between the tendency to incorporate the past and the need to assert a new identity, between the ancient religions of the book and the new dispensation, and between the continuity of Middle Eastern imperial regimes and the novelty of the Muslim caliphate.

In economy and society, the fundamental institutions of the ancient world were carried over into the new era. The modes of production in agriculture, trade, services, and taxation remained the same – indeed they were ratified in Islamic law for commerce and property. Muslim family life and the position of women in society continued the concepts and practices of late antique societies with some changes in details, now legitimated as part of Islamic law. The caliphate constructed an imperial regime as it was understood and proclaimed by the Roman-Byzantine and Sasanian emperors, similarly expressing its political identity and legitimating its rule partly on the basis of historic Middle Eastern imperial symbols expressed in art and architecture, poetry, philosophy, and science, and partly on the basis of Muslim concepts.

Architectural styles were assimilated not as a finished text but as a malleable vocabulary to allow for different results. Many aspects of art and architecture were developed on the basis of an earlier repertoire of images, motifs, and styles but yet were subtly rearranged and set into new contexts so as to create art forms that were based on ancient motifs but were recognizably original. The design and decoration of mosques, and even their placement in the urban environment, created a distinctive Arab-Muslim presence. At the same time, there emerged in Islamic art certain characteristic preferences, none of them by themselves wholly novel – the preference for complete decoration of surfaces; the ubiquity of geometric, vegetal, and calligraphic decoration; and the opposition to human or animal images in religious buildings – that, in combination, expressed a distinctive Arab-Muslim sensibility.

In the realm of literature, the Arabian *qasida*, the classical panegyrical ode, became the basis of later Arabic poetry and was adapted as a form of court poetry. Philosophy was translated from Greek and Syriac into Arabic, and ancient philosophy was carried into the Arab-Muslim era with little change apart from translation. Persian *adab*, however, although translated into Arabic, was very selectively incorporated into anthologies along with Arab, Indian, and other materials. *Adab* in this vetted form became the basis of the literary education of the cultivated gentleman. Philosophy, *adab*, and other Persian literatures and tales also maintained a position as distinct subcultures within early Islamic civilization.

In the third period, Muslim scholars and holy men launched a more determined effort to define Islamic orthodoxy. A new generation of scholars, disciples, and students, much augmented in number, succeeded the first generation of companions of the Prophet. Small groups of masters and disciplines took shape. Out of these study circles came a variety of specialized religious activities. Some circles focused on the legacy of the Prophet, the stories told about his person, his actions, and his sayings, all of which would constitute hadith and biography. Others focused on the text of the Quran itself and its exegesis. Still others were engaged in legal analysis and theology. Always, there were ascetics and holy men seeking a more direct experience of God. Allied to these interests were historical and linguistic studies that would be the basis of the Arabic humanities.

In the postconquest era, Islam became a parallel religion, different in the details of its expression but similar in its basic orientations to the previous monotheistic religions. Islam was a newly revealed religion, but it shared the mentality of its predecessors. Already in the Quran, Islam is avowedly a continuation and renewal of the older monotheistic traditions. Jews, Christians, Zoroastrians, and Muslims all believed in God, the angels and the prophets, the last judgment, and the purpose of human existence being the fulfillment of God's commands and faith in his truth. Islamic teaching and practice overlapped with that of the other religions. Eastern Syriac Christians who believed in the human nature of Jesus had common ground with Muslims. Jews were committed monotheists. All Middle Eastern peoples believed that religion implied community, and all believed that religious communities had a founding prophet.

Each religion provided for communal loyalties and made regulations for ritual and social behavior. As in Judaism and Christianity, Islam is expressed through participation in a community and adherence to its laws. It is expressed through acts of ritual and worship such as prayer, fasting, almsgiving, and pilgrimage. Sayings of the Prophet and stories about his deeds, faith in the miraculous events surrounding his life, veneration of his goodness, imitation of his example, and adherence to the laws he transmitted became the hallmarks of a Muslim life, just as stories of the ancient patriarchs and prophets in Judaism or the gospels of Jesus in

Christianity defined the earlier monotheisms. Belief in the visions, healing powers, and miraculous deeds of holy men became a part of Muslim religious life, just as they had been a part of Christian and Jewish religious life. Muslim ascetics and mystics resembled Christian monks and Hindu holy men.

Greco-Roman provincial law, canon law, rabbinic law, and Sasanian law formed the customary legal background that was integrated with the teachings of the Quran and hadith to form what we now know as Islamic law. Family law was redefined in terms of Quran and hadith but differed mainly in detail from pre-Islamic law. Commercial, property, and contract law were essentially the same.

Muslim theology (*kalam*), reasoned argument on the basis of religious belief, was partly adapted from and partly developed in parallel with Christian theology. It shared the same dialectical form of discussion but drew distinctive conclusions for issues central to Muslim concerns, such as determination and free will and the createdness of the Quran. Sufism drew inspiration from the Quran and from neo-Platonism and Hindu mysticism. Early Islam shared folk traditions and popular spirituality with non-Muslims. Belief in revealed scripture, prophecy, mysticism, gnosticism, messianism, magical and apocalyptic thinking, science, philosophy, and law were interconfessional, that is, found in all the Middle Eastern religions.

By mutual influences, Islam, Judaism, and Christianity were all reshaped in the Islamic period. As Arabic became the common language of peoples of all religions, despite communal differences and loyalties to different authorities, texts, and traditions, the religious discourses became similar. Islamic religion, culture, and literature was neither derived from a bedouin past nor directly borrowed from other religions but developed in parallel with others as part of a shared Middle Eastern heritage.

The process of forming Islamic civilization, however, was not a passive assimilation but an active struggle among the proponents of different views. Within court circles, representatives of Arabic, Persian, and Hellenistic literatures struggled to shape the identity of the caliphate. The proponents of Arabic and Persian identities fought for a century, until Arabic triumphed as the primary language of the empire, and Persian and Hellenistic literatures were absorbed into Arabic literary forms.

Similarly, the Muslim urban communities embodied not one but a number of conflicting orientations. Some Muslims emphasized the authority of the scholarly tradition, others the teaching of the imams or the charismatic presence of the saints. The Sunnis tended to stress the revealed text itself, the chain of commentary and interpretation going back through the generations directly to the Prophet, and the collective authority of learned men as the basis of Islamic belief and practice, but they were divided among those who emphasized good works and correct practice and those who were concerned with doctrine and true belief. Still others urged the importance of direct experience of the being of God. The Shi'is emphasized personal loyalty to the imams and their teachings. Urban Islam embodied fundamentalist, conservative, puritanical, accommodationist, realist, and millenarian religious attitudes.

Each of these positions was formed by debate. We have seen how the scripturalists held different views about the authority of the Quran, hadith, and law and differed over the boundaries of revelation and human judgment. The theologians disputed the nature of God's being and his attributes, free will, and predestination. The relative weight of revelation and reason, although defined in terms of a limited use of reason, was yet to be resolved. The mystics were divided by world-renouncing and world-accepting attitudes, and by ecstatic and sober practices. Just as there were intense debates within each orientation over the proper values of the religious life, there were intense conflicts among them. Scholars of law questioned the validity of mysticism. Theologians wrestled with the hadith-minded commitment to revelation rather than reason. The relations of scripture, theology, mysticism, and philosophy would have to be reconsidered in a later era.

The most fateful confrontations, however, were between the courtly cosmopolitan and the urban religious versions of Islamic civilization. Each represented a selection and synthesis of the heritage of Middle Eastern Jewish, Christian, Hellenistic, Byzantine, and Sasanian cultures. Islamic court culture was visual, literary, philosophic, and scientific. As opposed to the courtly concern for symbols to articulate a vision of the universe that justified the authority of the caliph and the supremacy of the dominant elite, the urban version of Islam emphasized individual piety. The pious set their concept of humbleness and devotion against aristocratic elegance and refinement. For the courtly milieu, Islam was but an aspect of a cosmopolitan identity and worldview. For the urban milieus, Islam defined the good life.

These differences led to conflict on several levels. The Shu'ubiya controversy over the supremacy of Arabic or Persian literary values was partly a court-centered dispute, but it also spilled over into a confrontation between court and urban milieus. Whereas the proponents of Persian literature espoused political domination, social hierarchy, and aristocratic refinement, the urban *'ulama'*, the legal scholars, affirmed religious equality, political accountability, and personal values based on the Quranic revelation and the Arabic identity of the town populations.

An equally important struggle was waged over the legitimacy of Hellenistic thought. Hellenism represented both a reinforcement of and a challenge to the worldview of the urban *'ulama'*. Court and urban theologians welcomed logical methods of argument to clarify Muslim perspectives and to defend them against philosophic attack, but insofar as philosophy was conceived as an alternative source of divine truths, they rejected the primacy of reason in religious matters. Similarly, neo-Platonism was in one sense intrinsic to the philosophic vision and was therefore a court-sponsored alternative to urban Islam, but in another sense it reinforced an already-existing strand of Muslim mysticism and gave Sufi asceticism a rationale and a method for the mystical quest. Other aspects of Hellenistic teaching such as science, philosophy, and occult metaphysics, which were acceptable in court milieus, were rejected in urban *'ulama'* Islam. Like Persian *adab*, Hellenistic culture was screened, adapted, and utilized to reinforce the basic moral and religious positions of the urban *'ulama'*. Nonetheless, it continued to be sponsored in court circles as a part of cosmopolitan and aristocratic cultivation. In this guise Hellenistic philosophy and science would be preserved for future confrontations and interactions with Islamic religious thought and for eventual transmission to Christian Europe.

RELIGION AND EMPIRE

The conflict of worldviews also led to a struggle between the caliphate and the urban *'ulama'* over the content of Islamic belief and the role of the caliphate in the governance of the Muslim community. As we have seen in the history of both Roman and Sasanian societies, empires and religious communities both laid claim to absolute truth and absolute authority. They were at times collaborators in maintaining control of society and at other times rivals for political, social, and cultural power. The critical issue was the boundaries between imperial and religious – church, congregational, or communal – authority. The Roman Empire supported one official religion, Christianity, in one orthodox form, but the Roman orthodox world was but one part of a more extensive grouping of politically independent and religiously diverse Christian societies. The Sasanian Empire made Zoroastrianism an official religion but accepted a plurality of religions.

The caliphate went through several phases of competing concepts of the office and its powers. In the Rightly Guided period, caliphs were both religious-community leaders and military and political rulers, continuing Muhammad's integral connection of political and religious-communal authority. The Rightly Guided Caliphs not only directed armies and governments but also gave authoritative legal judgments and set precedents for later Muslim practice. 'Uthman promulgated an authorized edition of the Quran. Mu'awiya appointed judges and tried to regulate preachers, Quran readers, and judges. 'Abd al-Malik's issuance of coinage and construction of the Dome of the Rock defined the caliphate as the supreme patron and protector of Islam. 'Umar II came to the throne from an earlier career in Medina engaged in legal and religious activity and brought a new concern for communal-religious matters to the caliphate. Later Umayyads expanded on the religious significance of the caliphate: they executed Qadari theologians as heretics and justified their reigns by claiming to be God's caliphs, *khalifat allah*, rather than *khalifat rasul allah* (successors to the Prophet of God).

Despite the lofty titles, 'Abbasid caliphs also took limited positions in religious affairs. They persecuted and executed so-called heretics. Generally, they supervised the judicial administration and appointed judges from favored factions. They condemned certain religious positions. The ʿAbbasid Caliph al-Mahdi (r. 775–85) claimed to be the protector of Islam against heresy and arrogated the right to proscribe unacceptable beliefs. But caliphs did not define theological or legal positions nor legislate personal, familial, or commercial law.

Moreover, from the beginning of the Islamic era, there were alternative and competing conceptions of the caliphate. The caliphate was vigorously opposed by several sectarian movements and constrained by widespread resistance to its religious claims, even among its Sunni supporters. In the first civil war, a number of factions contested the succession. Kharijis called for the election by the community of a person without sin. In their view, the imam was simply the most righteous person in the community. Kharijis fused Islam with tribal equalitarianism and a communal idea of consensus, solidarity, and unity.

Shiʿis also opposed the historic succession of the caliphs. They claimed that only the family of ʿAli, a holy lineage related to the Prophet, was entitled to the caliphate. Shiʿis evolved into a movement claiming not only the rights of the family of ʿAli but also that this family was divinely blessed with supernatural powers and moral perfection. Whereas Zaydis believed that the true heir to the authority of ʿAli had to be both a political and a religious leader, Imami Shiʿis did not require political activism. They introduced the idea of an imam who is not a caliph or political ruler but a teacher and savior.

Many Sunnis, who accepted the legitimacy of the historical succession and supported both the Umayyad and ʿAbbasid dynasties, sought to limit the authority of the ruler. They held that the Prophet's guidance was not confined to a single leader but had been passed on to the companions collectively, and to their students and successors. By the late Umayyad period, many Sunnis held that the caliphs were simply *mujtahids*, scholars entitled to express an authoritative opinion on legal matters, on par with other jurists. Hadith and law, not the caliph, were the real rulers of the community; the collective agreement of the learned was the key to guidance.

By the time of ʿAbbasid Caliph Harun, the caliphate too accepted its role as the guardian but not the source of Islamic teaching. Caliphs distanced themselves from claims to be imams in the Shiʿi sense of divinely inspired teachers. Later, however, al-Maʾmun (r. 813–33) tried to remake the religious foundations of the caliphate in the wake of the disruptive civil war that brought him to power. He tried to win over his opponents by making a Shiʿi imam, ʿAli al-Rida, the eighth descendant of ʿAli, heir to the caliphate. The rapprochement with Shiʿism implied that al-Maʾmun accepted the Shiʿi view of the caliph as divinely chosen by God with the authority to define religious belief and law. ʿAli al-Rida, however, died within a year. Al-Maʾmun then tried to accomplish the same objective by adopting the Muʿtazili thesis that the Quran was created and not of the divine essence. This doctrine served to emphasize the religious importance of the caliph by implying that the Quran, as a created thing, was, like all created things, subject to authoritative caliphal interpretation. These were not idle claims. Al-Ma'mun initiated an inquisition to force Muslim scholars to accept this doctrine and his right to proclaim it.

The inquisition was the most radical assertion of 'Abbasid religious authority and has been interpreted in various ways. Some view it as an effort to claim supreme authority for the caliph in matters of religious belief; the doctrine of the created Quran implies that reason and/or caliphal authority can define law. Others view the inquisition as a political tactic; in the religious struggles of the time, al-Ma'mun's intervention supported the rationalists against the opposing hadith scholars.

Among religious leaders, only Ahmad b. Hanbal refused to accept the caliph's contentions. He denied that the Quran was created and affirmed the transcendent authority of the written word over its human interpreters. Islamic religious obligations, he argued, were derived not from caliphal pronouncements but from the fundamental texts known to the leading scholars. The caliph was merely the executor of the Islamic community, and not the source of its beliefs. A protracted struggle between the caliphate and the *'ulama'* eventually ended with the victory of the latter. In 848–49, Caliph al-Mutawakkil reversed the policy of his predecessors, abandoned the Mu'tazili thesis, and accepted the contention that the Quran was not the created word of God. The caliph in effect conceded both the point of doctrine and his claims to be the ultimate source of religious beliefs. Al-Ma'mun had tried to overcome an entrenched communal structure but did not succeed. The caliphate had to abandon its claims, because they provoked widespread popular opposition. After this cultural and political ordeal, the caliphate limited its religious claims. Only later would it become the symbol of the unity of Islam and empire, of a golden age in Islamic history.

The claims of the caliphate brought out a long-smoldering resentment. It had become suspect to the *'ulama'* and other pious Muslims, who saw it as falling away from true religious principles. Although the caliphate remained head of the Muslim community (*umma*) and a symbol of Muslim unity, a gulf had opened between the state and some of the religious communities. Henceforth, the caliph would represent the administrative and executive interests of Islam, while the scholars and Sufis defined Islamic religious belief. Islam began to evolve independently under the aegis of the religious teachers. The struggle over the createdness of the Quran widened the differences of the two forms of early Islamic culture and community – the division of state and religious communities, of court and urban *'ulama'*, and of cosmopolitan and religious forms of Islamic civilization.

Because its religious authority was always contested, the caliphate attempted to provide itself with an imperial, indeed cosmic, authority apart from Islam. The caliphate constructed an imperial regime as it was understood and proclaimed by the Roman-Byzantine and Sasanian emperors. Early Umayyad caliphs reverted to Arabian conceptions of monarchy as the basis of their legitimacy. Later Umayyad caliphs defined themselves as successors to the Byzantine emperors as well as the guardians and promoters of Islam; they also claimed to be God-sent rulers.

They expressed this royal, nonreligious authority in architecture and decoration, court protocol, poetry, and philosophy. In court life and in the decorations of the desert palaces, they assumed the prerogatives of all kings and royal families. In the ʿAbbasid period, the assertion of a quasi-divine authority – integrating Persian cultures as well – grew more explicit and more elaborate. Court protocol, poetry, architectural design, and bacchic pleasures promoted a henotheistic ideal.

In theory, early Islamic institutions resembled the Roman model of unified imperial authority and religious identity. The early caliphate had a double identity and legitimation: one explicitly Muslim derived from the Prophet; the other universal or cosmic derived from the pre-Islamic, imperial cultures of the region. Like the Roman emperor, the caliph as head of state was also in a generalized sense head of religion. The administrative authority of both was widely accepted, but in both cases their religious authority was contested by congregations that drew their authority directly from scripture or charismatic succession to the founder of the religion (Jesus or Muhammad). In the Islamic case, by contrast with Roman practice, matters of ritual, civil, and family laws were regulated by the scholars (rather than the state) and were the nonpolitical function of an independent religious elite. Yet the power of the caliphate always made some government intervention possible, especially in matters that concerned the state (such as taxation), and undoubtedly allowed for a great deal of variation in the administration of law and justice.

Islamic governance, however, differed from the Roman and resembled the Sasanian model in its acceptance of the legitimacy of other religions. The Roman Empire recognized only one orthodox form of Christianity, whereas the Sasanian Empire accepted Zoroastrianism, Christianity, and Judaism as approved religions organized to govern the internal affairs of their communities and to act as administrative conduits for the state.

Furthermore, Muslim communities under the caliphate were organized in a way closer to Jewish communities than to Christian churches. Unlike the Christian churches, there was no centralization or hierarchy of religious authority. Islamic society was a network of local communities under the leadership of scholars and judges who were linked by travels, by teaching, and eventually by schools and brotherhoods. Unlike the Jewish communities, most of the Muslim communities were linked under the authority of the caliphate. The regime accepted many or most, but not all, of the Muslim theological sects, law circles and schools, socioreligious movements, congregations, and communities. The state accepted a variety of Islamic positions, always maneuvering to draw support and legitimacy from them. The Islamic structure of state, society, and religion may be described, then, as a religious commonwealth of independent and religiously diverse groups, under the general leadership and partial authority of the caliphate. The collapse of the caliphal empire in the tenth century resulted in a religious commonwealth of both politically independent and religiously diverse Muslim regions.

CONCLUSION

Thus, there was an historical rhythm to the emergence of a distinctive Islamic civilization. In the first instances, the emerging Islamic civilization was closely modeled on its predecessors, but older cultural materials took on new qualities as they were not merely translated but freshly expressed in Arabic, and attuned to the religious sensibilities of Muslims. In architecture, in some forms of literature (such as courtly *adab*), and in law and theology, ancient materials were Islamized. Intense debates, cultural wars, and political struggles occurred over which elements of the overall culture should and would be considered legitimate and essential to Islam. Thus, ancient precedents outgrew their pasts and became distinctive expressions of an Islamic civilization.

By the late tenth and eleventh centuries, a new cultural world had come into being, superseding its ancient heritage – a period in which an Islamic "orthodoxy" had been consolidated, the alternative visions of Islam articulated, and boundaries with non-Islamic Middle Eastern cultures defined. Over centuries the process of assimilating, Arabizing, and Islamizing historic cultures led to the consolidation of a new civilization whose ancient sources were then forgotten and concealed and whose roots and history can now only be uncovered by scholarly investigation.

Nonetheless, in the new civilization, the past lived on. The deep historical past embodied meanings and concepts that defined what life is about and how it is lived, and it could not easily be reinvented. In perpetuating earlier civilizations, Islamic civilization is based on a newly revealed religion, but it shared the mentality of its predecessors and grew from the same Greco-Roman and Persian roots as did what we now call Western civilization.

PART II

FROM ISLAMIC COMMUNITY TO ISLAMIC SOCIETY

EGYPT, IRAQ, AND IRAN, 945–c. 1500

CHAPTER 20

THE POST-'ABBASID MIDDLE EASTERN STATE SYSTEM

The "medieval" era in the Middle East is the period after the breakup of the 'Abbasid Empire and before the consolidation of the Ottoman and Safavid empires. Numerous and often ephemeral regional states replaced a unified empire. (See Map 4.) With the weakening of central governments and the rise of semiautonomous military, civic-religious, and land-controlling elites, it is no longer possible to recount Middle Eastern history from a central point of view. Its history is best understood by distinguishing the eastern parts of the Middle East – including Transoxania, Iran, and Iraq – from the western parts – consisting primarily of Syria and Egypt.

In the east, the first generation of regimes that succeeded to the domains of the 'Abbasid Empire included the Buwayhids, mercenary soldier-conquerors from the Caspian Sea region, in Iraq and western Iran (945–1055); the Samanids, a provincial noble family already in power in the late 'Abbasid era, in eastern Iran and Transoxania (to 999); and the Ghaznavids, a dynasty founded by slave soldiers in Afghanistan and Khurasan (to 1040). These regimes gave way to a succession of nomadic empires as the collapse of the 'Abbasid Empire broke down the frontiers between the settled parts of the Middle East and Inner Asia and allowed Turkish nomadic peoples to infiltrate the region. In the tenth century, the Qarakhanids took control of Transoxania. In the eleventh century, the Saljuqs seized Iran, Iraq, and Anatolia. Ghuzz and Nayman followed in the twelfth century; the Mongols conquered most of the region in the thirteenth.

In the west, the Fatimids (an offshoot of the Isma'ili movement) conquered the former 'Abbasid province of Egypt and parts of Syria. However, the collapse of political order in Syria permitted a succession of further foreign invasions. In the tenth century, the Byzantine Empire reoccupied northern Syria and even attempted to conquer Jerusalem. Byzantine armies were followed by Latin crusaders and

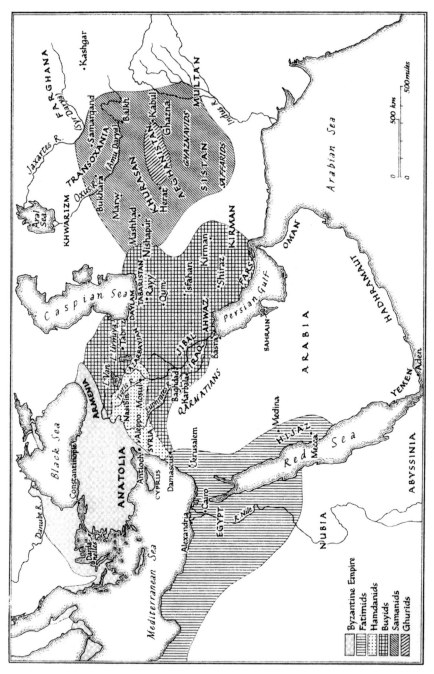

Map 4. The post-imperial succession regimes, late tenth century.

Byzantine Empire
Fatimids
Hamdanids
Buyids
Samanids
Ghurids

ARMENIA

Black Sea

Constantinople

ANATOLIA

Dardanelles

CYPRUS

Antioch

Aleppo · Mosul · Nasibin

SYRIA

Damascus

Jerusalem

Mediterranean Sea

Alexandria

Cairo

EGYPT

R. Nile

NUBIA

ABYSSINIA

Red Sea

Medina

Mecca

HIJAZ

ARABIA

YEMEN

Aden

HADRAMAUT

OMAN

BAHRAIN

QARMATIANS

Basra

IRAQ

Baghdad · Karbala

Euphrates

Tigris

JIBAL

AHWAZ

Qum · Rayy

Isfahan

TABARISTAN

AZARBAYJAN

Tabriz · Urmiya · Van

DAYLAM

Caspian Sea

Aral Sea

KHWARIZM

Oxus R. (Amu Darya)

TRANSOXANIA

Bukhara · Samarqand

Marv

FARGHANA

Jaxartes R. (Syr Darya)

· Kashgar

KHURASAN

Mashhad · Nishapur

Herat

AFGHANISTAN

Balkh

Kabul · Ghazna

GHAZNAVIDS

SISTAN

SAFFARIDS

MULTAN

Indus R.

KIRMAN

Kirman

FARS

Shiraz

Persian Gulf

Arabian Sea

500 km
500 miles

226

finally by the Saljuqs. With the establishment of Saljuq-derived regimes, the western parts of the Middle East rejoined the stream of eastern developments.

IRAQ, IRAN, AND THE EASTERN PROVINCES

After the disintegration of the ʿAbbasid Empire, Iraq and Iran became the crucial centers for the formation of new state, communal, and religious institutions. Middle Eastern states came to be built around similar elites and institutions. The old landowning and bureaucratic elites lost their power and were replaced by nomadic chieftains and slave soldiers. These several new states came to depend on slave armies and a semifeudal form of administration. Each state became the patron of a regional culture. In the Arab provinces, poetry, manuscript illumination, architecture, and minor arts developed. In Iran, new Islamic cultural expressions based on the Persian language and arts emerged. At the same time, scholars and mystics – who in the imperial age had been the informal spokesmen of Islam – became the heads of communal organizations. They encouraged the conversion of Middle Eastern peoples, standardized Islamic religious teachings, articulated an Islamic social and political ethic, and organized schools of law, Sufi orders, and Shiʿi sects. Despite political fragmentation, a new form of Islamic state, community, and religious orthodoxy came into being.

The Buwayhids, who ruled western Iran, Iraq, and Mesopotamia, pioneered this new type of regime. They left the caliphs in position as titular heads of state, recognized them as the chiefs of all Sunni Muslims, conceded their right to make appointments to religious offices, and accepted the idea that their own right to govern was based on caliphal recognition. The sermon at Friday prayers, government coinage, and (in Iraq) even grants of land and appointments to offices referenced the names of the caliphs. Although it was deprived of actual administrative and military power, this allowed the caliphate to mobilize the support of the Sunni population of Baghdad and to retain an important role in Baghdadi politics.

In practice, the Buwayhid regime was based on a family coalition in which each of the conquering brothers was assigned a province of Iran or Iraq as his appanage. The armies, composed partly of Daylamite infantry and partly of slave Turkish cavalry, were, like the forces of the latter-day caliphate, organized into regiments loyal more to their own leaders and to their own ambitions for wealth and power than to the state itself. These regiments fought one another and encouraged conflicts among various Buwayhid princes, which further reduced the powers of the central government. The established bureaucratic families were replaced with Christians, Jews, and Zoroastrians. The Buwayhids sold landed estates to the soldiers, assigned them revenues from designated lands (*tashib*), or allowed them to collect taxes in lieu of salaries. To these new military grants, the old name *iqtaʿ* was often applied. In Kirman, Fars, and Khuzistan, foreign Turkish and Daylamite soldiers neglected investments in agriculture and exploited the peasants for short-term gain. Arab and Kurdish tribes dominated northern Iraq, leading to a further regression of the agricultural economy of Iraq and western Iran.

In eastern Iran and Transoxania, the Samanid dynasty maintained the ʿAbbasid system for another half century. The regime was administered by a bureaucratic elite that depended on the local notables and landlord families, whereas the attached provinces of Sijistan, Khwarizm, and Afghanistan were governed by tributary lords or slave governors. Like the ʿAbbasids, the Samanids were the patrons of a fabulously creative Islamic culture. In the tenth century, Bukhara emerged as the center of new Persian-Islamic literatures and arts – as Arabic religious, legal, philosophic, and literary ideas were recast into Persian. For the first time, Islam became available in a language other than Arabic.

However, the Samanid regime disintegrated in the tenth century, and its domains in Khurasan and Afghanistan fell to Alptigin, a slave governor whose capital was Ghazna (Afghanistan). Alptigin founded a regime of slave soldiers who conquered and ruled Khurasan from 999 to 1040 and Afghanistan until 1186. They attacked Transoxania and western Iran, plundered Lahore in 1030, and occupied parts of northern India until 1187. Everywhere they destroyed established elites and replaced them with slave soldiers; the rulers were themselves former slaves. Like the Buwayhids, they gave land tax allotments to their soldiers, but they also maintained the vestiges of Samanid bureaucratic administration to keep central control over the distribution of landed estates and to collect tributes, booty, and the revenues of crown estates. The Ghaznavids also started the policy of cultivating the support of Muslim religious leaders by declaring allegiance to the caliphate and supporting Islamic education and a Persian literary revival. A slave army, decentralized administration, and patronage of Persian-Islamic culture were henceforth the defining features of Iranian and Inner Asian regimes.

By the middle of the eleventh century, Ghaznavid rule gave way to new forces that had their origin in Inner Asia (i.e., between the borders of the Iranian and the Chinese empires).(See Map 5.) This region was inhabited by pastoral peoples who raised horses and sheep for their livelihood. These people generally lived in small bands, but they could form confederations to contest control of pasture lands and to attack settled areas. In the course of the seventh and eighth centuries, nomadic peoples on the eastern frontiers of China, prevented from entering China by the Tang dynasty, began to push westward in search of pasturage. This started a wave of migrations pushing Inner Asian peoples into the region of the Aral Sea, Transoxania, Khwarizm, and Afghanistan.

These peoples were organized under the leadership of royal families and other chiefs. They entered regular commercial and cultural relations with the settled areas. From the settled peoples, the nomads purchased grain, spices, textiles, and weapons. In return, they sold livestock, hides, wool, and slaves. This lively exchange induced settled peoples to extend trading posts and towns out onto the steppes and involved Inner Asian nomads in the caravan traffic between Transoxania, the Volga and Siberian regions to the north, and China to the east.

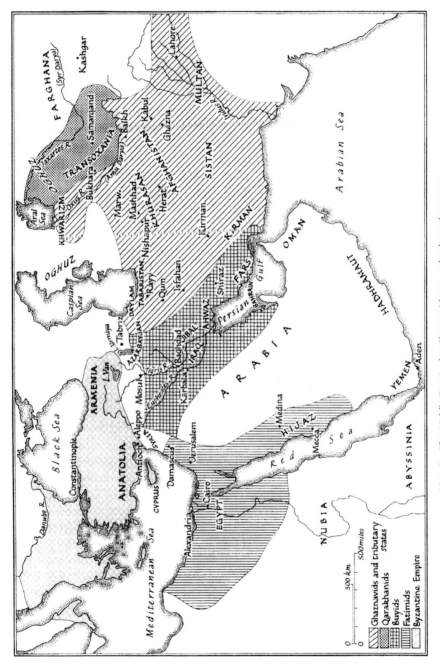

Map 5. The Middle East in the Ghaznavid era, early eleventh century.

Ghaznavids and tributary states
Qarakhanids
Buyids
Fatimids
Byzantine Empire

500 km

500 miles

Through contacts with Muslim merchants, scholars, and Sufis, nomadic peoples were introduced to Islam. Originally they were pagans (who believed that the world, animate and inanimate, was peopled by living and vital spirits) and shamanists (who believed that some of their members had the capacity to separate body and soul and, in ecstatic moments, rise up to heaven or descend to the underworld). Knowledge of the realms and powers beyond made the shamans healers and interpreters of dreams. Inner Asian peoples, however, were familiar with Nestorian Christianity, which had been preached on the steppes. Many were Buddhists; some were Manichaeans. In the middle of the tenth century, the Qarluq peoples – who would later establish the Qarakhanid Empire – converted to Islam. Shortly before the end of the century, Oghuz peoples associated with the Saljuq family also converted to Islam. Thus, by the end of the tenth century, Turkish–Inner Asian peoples had developed the capacity for large-scale coalitions, possessed stratified elites and royal institutions, had gained experience in trade, and had adopted the religious identity of the settled peoples. They would enter the Middle East with the political and cultural capacities to become a new imperial elite.

This leveling of political and cultural capacities opened the way for the breakdown of the frontier between steppes and settled areas. With the conversion of Inner Asian peoples, the settled frontier warriors (*ghazis*), who had hitherto resisted Turkish incursions on the grounds that they were defending their Muslim civilization against barbarians, gave up the holy war. With the conversion of the Turks, the whole rationale of the frontier life was subverted, and these warriors abandoned the eastern frontiers. Many made their way with the Ghaznavids into India; others moved to the Byzantine frontier. With the frontier defenses in disarray, Qarluq peoples, led by the Qarakhanid dynasty, took Bukhara in 992 and Samarqand in 999.

The Qarakhanid elites were quickly assimilated to the traditions of eastern Iranian-Islamic states. In Inner Asian fashion, the new rulers divided their domains into a western khanate that ruled Transoxania until 1211 and an eastern khanate for Farghana and Kashgaria. The new rulers of Transoxania accepted the nominal authority of the ʿAbbasid caliphs and directly or indirectly promoted the spread of Islam among the populace of Transoxania, Kashgar, and the Tarim basin. The Qarakhanids also patronized the formation of a new Turkish literature, based on Arabic and Persian models, which made it possible to re-create the religious and literary content of Islamic Middle Eastern civilization in Turkish dress. Just as the Samanids had presided over the formation of a Persian-Islamic culture, the Qarakhanids were the patrons of a new Turkish-Islamic civilization.

THE SALJUQ EMPIRE, THE MONGOLS, AND THE TIMURIDS

The Saljuq empire
While the Qarluq peoples occupied Transoxania, Oghuz peoples, under the leadership of the Saljuq family, crossed the Oxus River in 1025. In 1037, they took

Nishapur; in 1040, they defeated the Ghaznavids and became the new rulers of Khurasan. This was the beginning of a Saljuq empire. (See Map 6.) The Saljuq chiefs, Tughril Beg and his brother Chagri Beg, led their followers into western Iran, defeated the Buwayhids, seized control of Baghdad and the caliphate in 1055, and were named sultans and rulers of a new Middle Eastern empire from Khurasan to Iraq. Nomadic bands pushed into Armenia, Azarbayjan, and Byzantine Anatolia, where, in 1071, at the Battle of Manzikert, they defeated the Byzantine army, captured the emperor, and opened the whole of Asia Minor to Turkish penetration. The advancing Turkish peoples also entered Iraq and Mesopotamia and extended Saljuq domination as far as the Mediterranean. (See Figure 5.)

Thus the Saljuqs reunited most of the former 'Abbasid Empire and rekindled the dream of Muslim unity and universal empire. They sought to rebuild bureaucratic forms of administration, and they sponsored Muslim religious activity as the basis of their legitimacy. But although the Saljuqs aspired to a unified Middle Eastern empire, the organizational and institutional capacities needed to sustain a large empire were not available. The economy of Iraq could no longer support a centralized government; bureaucratic administration could not be effectively restored in a society dominated by the military landowners who had replaced the smallholding notables of the late Sasanian and 'Abbasid periods.

Moreover, the Saljuq nomadic heritage proved detrimental to their imperial ambitions. Although nominally unified under the authority of a single sultan, the Saljuqs had no fixed idea about legitimate succession and considered the right to rule to be vested in the leading family as a whole. Thus, members of the ruling house were entitled to share the family domains on behalf of the tribal subgroups whom they led. Furthermore, tribal tradition cherished the institution of the *atabeg*, who was a tutor or regent assigned to raise a minor prince and govern in his name. The *atabeg* was entitled to marry the mother of a ward who died and to become a governor in his own right. This was the start of many independent Saljuq-related principalities. Finally, tribal groups were entitled to regions for habitation and grazing. All these aspects of the nomadic heritage worked against imperial unity under the leadership of a single ruler.

To overcome these inherent liabilities, the Saljuq sultans adopted Buwayhid and Ghaznavid institutions. They tried to reduce their dependence on the Turkish peoples who had conquered the empire by creating slave armies of Turks, Greeks, Khurasanians, Kurds, Georgians, and others. They adopted the Buwayhid practice of granting lands as payment of the salaries of soldiers. Nonetheless, the unified empire lasted only from 1055 until the death of Malik Shah in 1092. His sons then divided the provinces among themselves, establishing independent dynasties in Iraq, Anatolia, Azarbayjan, Mesopotamia, Syria, Khuzistan, Fars, Kirman, and Khurasan. These proved to be ephemeral regimes, unable to consolidate power or defend their frontiers.

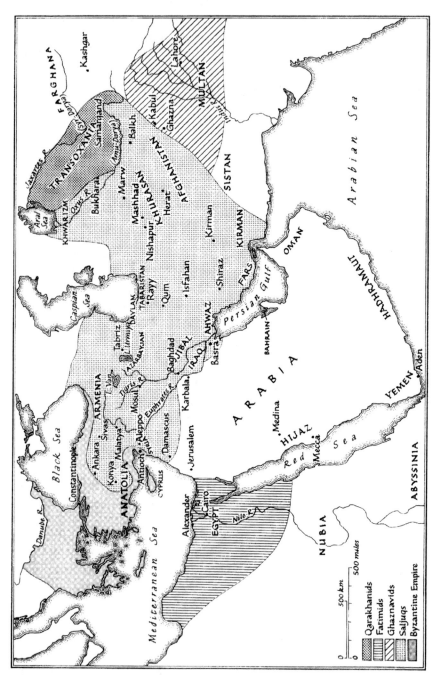

Map 6. The Saljuq Empire in the late eleventh century.

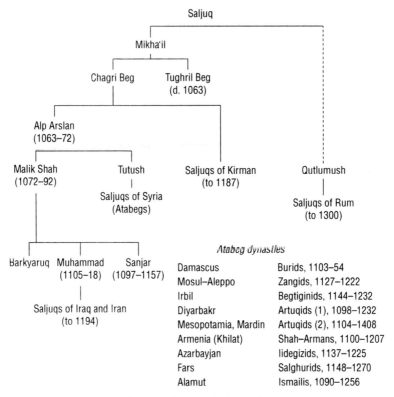

Figure 5. Saljuq period dynasties.

The result was renewed nomadic invasions. In the late twelfth century, the Qarakhitay, a Mongol people who had ruled northern China in the eleventh century, took control of Transoxania from the Qarakhanids. Ghuzz peoples, displaced by the Qarakhitay, invaded Khurasan and, in 1153, destroyed the last Saljuq resistance to further nomadic incursion from Inner Asia. They were followed by the Naymans and the Mongols.

These invasions had long-term demographic consequences. In the eleventh century, Armenia, Azarbayjan, and parts of Mesopotamia, which had been Iranian or Kurdish, became Turkish. The Greeks of Anatolia were in the process of converting. Iran experienced an almost complete breakdown of state authority, unremitting nomadic invasions, and unprecedented destruction. The ultimate symbol of this chaotic era was the execution of the last 'Abbasid caliph in 1258.

The Mongols

The Mongol invasions dealt a devastating blow to Iranian-Muslim civilization. The Mongols originated with the formation of a confederation of Inner Asian peoples under the leadership of Chinggis Khan. Believing in a God-given destiny, the Mongols set out to conquer the whole of the known world and brought East Asia, the Middle East, and the Eastern European steppes under their rule. Within a few decades, they ruled all of Eurasia from central Europe to the Pacific. This vast empire was divided among the four sons of Chinggis, partly for administrative convenience and partly because the conquered territories were considered the joint possession of the ruling family. Because there was neither a defined succession nor any way to assure unity, the descendants of Chinggis fought among themselves. Out of these disputes came several independent and even hostile Mongol states. These included Mongol regimes in Mongolia and China, the Golden Horde on the northern steppes, the Chaghatay khanate in Transoxania and eastern Turkestan, and the Ilkhan regime in Iran and Anatolia. (See Map 7.)

The first impact of the Mongol invasions in Iran was disastrous and amounted to a holocaust. The populations of many cities and towns were systematically exterminated. Whole regions were depopulated by invading armies and by the influx of Mongol nomads who drove the peasants from the land. The conquerors plundered their subjects, made them serfs, and taxed them ruinously. The result was a catastrophic fall in population, income, and state revenue. For more than a century, fine pottery and metalwares ceased to be produced. A period of urban autonomy and cultural vitality was brought to an end.

Whereas the first century of Mongol rule wreaked havoc, beginning with the reign of Ghazan (1295–1304), the Ilkhans rebuilt cities, redeveloped irrigation works, and sponsored agriculture and trade in the familiar way of Middle Eastern empires. Despite their self-conscious superiority, however, the Ilkhans did not bring a new linguistic or religious identity to the Middle East. Unlike the Arabs, who changed both the language and the religion of the region, the Mongols were absorbed by Islam and Persian culture. In the reign of Ghazan, the Mongol and Turkish military elite converted to Islam and began a new phase of creativity in Persian-Islamic culture. Later Mongol empires opened a new era of economic and cultural exchange across Asia. In an earlier era, the Arab conquests reached well into Inner Asia, making possible the exchange of Persian fruits, medicinal plants, and drugs to China and the importation of Chinese paper silks, porcelains, and other products. From about 1250 to 1350, exchanges between the Mongolian courts of China and Iran included not only regional products but also the travels of diplomats, scholars, merchants, and artisans, bringing important cultural and technological contacts.

The Ilkhans also resumed historical patterns of governance. The Mongol regime in Iran was made up of a single large army composed of a tribal aristocracy allied to the ruling dynasty. This aristocracy conceived of itself as a privileged people whose right to dominate and tax its subjects was enshrined in its supreme law, the *yasa*. The Mongols ruled Iran by distributing the land to military chiefs for pasturage or for tax revenues. The chiefs, in turn, divided it among their followers. Pasture and plow

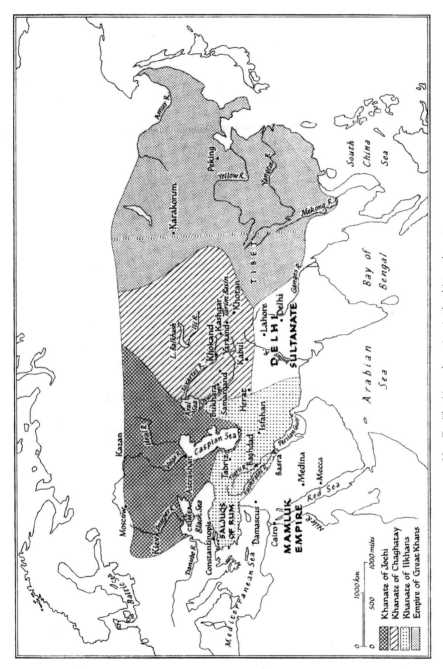

Map 7. The Mongol empires in the thirteenth century.

Khanate of Jochi
Khanate of Chaghatay
Khanate of Ilkhans
Empire of Great Khans

1000 km.
0   500   1000 miles

lands were combined in estates called *tuyul*, a concept that combined Mongolian ideas about the distribution of pasturage and Iranian administrative concepts about the distribution of the right to collect taxes. Mongol rule, moreover, depended – as did the preceding Saljuq regimes – on the support of local notable families. The Ilkhans allied themselves with Iranian urban bureaucrats, merchants, and scholars. Scholars continued or resumed their positions as local elites, filling the offices of judge, preacher, market inspector, and other posts. Urban elites – whose prestige was based on Islamic learning; whose social power was built on ownership of urban quarters, gardens, and village land and control of trusts (*awqaf*); and whose functions included financial and judicial administration – provided continuity in local government and buffered the impact of changing military regimes. They also provided the administrative personnel for the construction of successive Mongol and Timurid governments.

The Timurids

The Ilkhan regime lasted until 1336, when, like the Saljuq Empire, it dissolved into competing provincial states. The small successor states were in turn absorbed into a new empire established by Timur (d. 1405; famous in the West as Tamerlane) and his heirs, who introduced a new phase in the development of Iranian monarchical culture. Timur was a military adventurer who came to power by building up loyal bands of followers and defeating other chieftains. In 1370, he made Samarqand his capital and claimed to revive the house of Chinggis Khan and thus to be an heir to the Chaghatay branch of Mongol rulers in Transoxania. Timur and his successors considered themselves at once warrior conquerors, administrators in the Persian-Islamic tradition, and cultivated patrons of literature and the arts.

The Timurid military was composed of Turko-Mongolian, Chaghatay warriors in a standing (not tribal) army headed by clients of Timur. The amirs were also governors of provinces and advisers of the ruler.. Timur appointed his sons and grandsons as provincial governors, but he was careful to restrict their power by frequently rotating the gubernatorial assignments, appointing generals and tax collectors who were directly responsible to him, and assigning his personal representatives to oversee their rule At the same time, Timur continued the ongoing Persian-Islamic bureaucratic administration. Timur was supported by the local Muslim elites, including the chief jurisconsult of Samarqand and the Sufis who became his spiritual advisors. Muslim religious leaders served Timur as judges, diplomats, and tutors for young princes. They helped rally support from both nomadic and town populations to legitimize his new regime. The regime thus combined a Mongol patrimonial household guard and military elite with Persian bureaucratic administrative practices, thereby transforming a booty-seeking conquest into a routinized regime.

Once in power, Timur began his extraordinary conquests. From 1379 to 1402, zigzagging between east and west, he conquered Iran, northern India, Anatolia,

Table 5. *Iran: outline chronology*

Mongol conquests begin	1219
Ilkhan dynasty	1256–1336
Iran partitioned among several local regimes	1336–70
Conquest by Timur (Tamerlane)	1370–1405
Succession states	
Qara Qoyunlu, Azarbayjan	1380–1468
Aq Qoyunlu	1378–1508
Timurids of Samarqand	1370–1500
Timurids of Herat	1407–1506

and northern Syria. These conquests were made in the name of Islam. Timur's death in 1405 led to civil war among his heirs. Like the Saljuqs, the Timurids considered the ruling family in its entirety as sovereign and all able warriors in the ruling family as eligible for succession. Indeed, the sons of Timur had already been allotted individual domains.

The successors of Timur carried on this rich tradition of patronage for Perso-Islamic culture. (See Table 5.) Under Ulugh-beg (r. 1404–49), Samarqand became a center of Muslim architectural, philosophic, and scientific achievement, generating a new variant of Mongol-Iranian-Islamic royal civilization. Muslim religious culture was represented in Samarqand by the Naqshbandi Sufis and their merchant and artisan followers. In Bukhara, Sufi leaders led revolts against political authorities, and Ulugh-beg sought to pacify them by endowing schools (*madrasas*) in both Bukhara and Samarqand. He also built a retreat (*khanaqa*) for Sufis and a great new mosque. The veneration of Muslim saints and Sufi *shaykhs* (masters or teachers) became one of the most important indications of the Timurid integration of Islamic principles. The accommodation of Timurid princes to the Sufi *shaykhs*, both Sunni and Shi'i, provided the former with temporal legitimacy and religious prestige and the latter with state support and grants of landed income. The Kubrawi, Naqshbandi, Khalwati, Hurufi, and other Sufi movements prospered; the Khalwati appealed to the lower classes, and the Hurufis were considered heretical. After the death of Ulugh-beg, although Timurid princes remained nominally in power, effective local control was assumed by Khwaja Ahrar (d. 1490), a Naqshbandi holy man who denounced the lifestyle of the upper classes and had a strong influence on the army and the common people.

Herat was the second principle center of Timurid Persian-Islamic culture. Shah Rukh (r. 1405–47) lived in an observant Muslim style, attending prayers, fasting during Ramadan, and listening to Quran recitations. Shah Rukh adopted the title of sultan, instead of adopting specifically Mongol honors, and publicly proclaimed his adherence to Islamic law, patronized Muslim learning, and enforced Muslim morals in the streets and markets. Shah Rukh built and embellished Muslim shrines – such as the shrine of Imam Riza at Mashhad, the tomb of 'Abdullah Ansari at Gazargah near Herat, and the shrine at Mazar-i Sharif. His successor, Sultan Husayn

Bayqara (r. 1469–1506) also endowed numerous shrines of saints as expressions of piety, and as mechanisms for economic development. He purchased private properties to donate in trust (*waqf*) and turned over state lands to the shrine of the eleventh-century Sufi saint ʿAbdullah Ansari at Herat, the shrine of the eighth Shiʿi imam ʿAli Riza at Mashhad, and the shrine of ʿAli b. Abi Talib at Mazar-i Sharif near Balkh, all strategically located in rich agrarian oases. Through careful investment and agricultural and financial management, these shrines served as vehicles for economic development and for the enrichment of the military and bureaucratic elites and the Sufi brotherhoods.

Whereas Khurasan, Transoxania, Fars, Azarbayjan, and Central Asia were governed by a Chaghatay military elite, the central political fact of the Timurid era was that the regime did not have a monopoly of force. All strata of the population were politically organized and capable of military action. Local rulers maintained a measure of power and autonomy. Tribes were a military force. Princes who were given land tax allotments and government positions to offset the power of the governors became independent lords. Artisans were organized under the leadership of town notables; regional armies were made up of peasants and artisans. Local as well as central military elites were contenders for power. The fate of would-be conquerors and reigning dynasties turned on whether tribes and townspeople would accept their authority. Thus, the cooperation of local elites was essential for the central government.

The state ruled through the mediation of local power holders. The administration was not so much a bureaucracy as an assemblage of notables drawn from financial and administrative officials, notable or scholarly families, and the landed and merchant elites. In their localities, notables exercised influence as a consequence of individual and family prominence rather than official or representative positions. The elites were expected but not required to contribute irrigation, mosques, bazaars, baths, and other public facilities. Timurid society functioned not through structured institutions but through a culture of personal loyalties and political entrepreneurship.

THE WESTERN REGIONS

Fatimid Egypt

Egypt and Syria were among the first Middle Eastern provinces to be absorbed into the Arab-Muslim caliphate. They were both conquered in 641, and their populations rapidly adopted the Arabic language, although they were slow to accept Islam. Under the Umayyad and early ʿAbbasid caliphates, Egypt was a subsidiary province, but from the middle of the ninth century, slave soldiers appointed by the ʿAbbasids established short-lived dynasties. The Tulunids ruled Egypt from 868 to 905 and the Ikhshidids from 935 to 969. In 969, the Fatimids conquered the country and established a new caliphate that lasted until 1171.

The Fatimid dynasty was not merely an independent governorship but a revolutionary regime that claimed universal authority. It had its origin in the Ismaʿili movement. The Qarmatians in the Fertile Crescent and Arabia had roused peasant and bedouin opposition around 900. Similarly, the Fatimids incited Kitama Berbers to overthrow the Aghlabid regime of Tunisia in 909 and established a new government based on the claim of ʿUbaydallah to be the living imam. Under the leadership of the Fatimid imams, the Berbers conquered North Africa, Egypt, and parts of Syria. Based on Berber tribal forces and Turkish and Sudanese slave regiments, they controlled Egypt by means of an efficient administration inherited from the ʿAbbasids, staffed by Jewish and Christian officials. The agricultural riches of Egypt were augmented by the redirection of international trade. With the collapse of the ʿAbbasid Empire, the exchange of goods between the Indian Ocean and the Mediterranean Sea was rerouted through the Red Sea and Egypt. The revived trade route favored the Egyptian economy and the Fatimid coffers. The Italian city-states brought metals, wood, and protein-rich cheese to Egypt. Silk came from Spain and Sicily. North Africa sent gold and silver and other metals, olive oil, hides, and leather. Egypt exported flax and sugarcane.

The Fatimid dynasty (969–1171), like the ʿAbbasids, claimed to be the true Islamic regime. This claim was advanced in the multiple vocabularies of Mediterranean civilization. The Fatimids presented an Ismaʿili, a philosophical, a Byzantine, and an ʿAbbasid symbolism of political authority. They proclaimed that they were the true imams, the descendants of ʿAli. (See Figure 6.) This declaration required a redefinition of the historical succession of imams and of the eschatological cycles of history. The Fatimids asserted that they were the continuation of the sixth cycle of imams and that the coming of the messiah and the closure of the historical cycles were postponed to the indefinite future. Under the auspices of the new theory, neo-Platonic and gnostic concepts were incorporated into Ismaʿili thinking. At the beginning of the tenth century, al-Nasafi, an Ismaʿili missionary in eastern Iran, taught that the universe was brought into being by divine emanations in the form of intellectual essences. The imams corresponded to these emanations. Through them, the believers would be initiated into spiritual truth; by gnostic illumination, they would become the Truth. The imam, then, was the center of faith – to believe in him was to obey God. The palace was a spiritual as well as an administrative center.

Fatimid concepts of ruler and imperium were also expressed in court ceremony, art, and architecture. Emulating the rival ʿAbbasid and Byzantine empires, the palace of the ruler was decorated with extraordinary splendor. Court decorations – some the gifts of foreign ambassadors, some of Byzantine manufacture, and some ʿAbbasid relics – depicted his glory. A huge silk hanging with a map of all the lands of the world and their rulers expressed the Fatimid claim to belong to the family of kings. Fatimid paintings and illuminated manuscripts reflected the influence of the ʿAbbasid court at Samarra. Fatimid ceramics were decorated with vegetal and

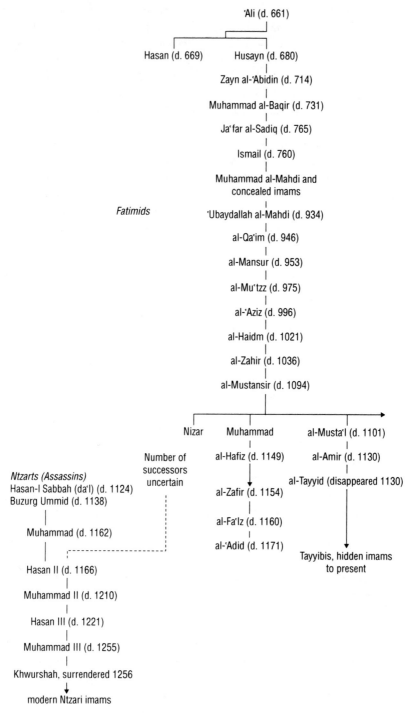

Figure 6. The Isma'ili imams.

animal themes (symbolizing good luck) and with hunters, musicians, dancers, and human figures (depicting court life). Their intent was to magically re-create the splendor of Fatimid rule.

Gold rafters supported the ceiling; rare birds and animals decorated the walls and the furniture; fountains of cascading water cooled the air. The ruler himself sat on a gold throne protected by a curtain in a fashion inspired by the ʿAbbasids and resembling Byzantine enthronement. He was entitled to a special crown, sword, scepter, parasol, weapons, and other implements that were signs of his sovereignty. An elaborate protocol regulated eating, drinking, and dressing. One of the prerogatives of the ruler was deferential behavior in his presence – silence, dismounting, and kissing the ground. The protocol was also designed to signify the ranks of courtiers. The court was highly stratified, and the caliph could confer on his servitors symbols of rank and honor, such as weapons, banners, food, clothes, and robes of honor.

Court decorations and utensils were housed in royal treasuries, for they were not only useful ornamentations but rare and exotic objects reserved for the sole use of the sovereign and the court. In 1067, however, in the course of a civil war, the Fatimid treasury was looted and royal objects became accessible for imitation. Fatimid ceramics, metalworks, and woodcraft inspired an Egyptian craft culture based on international imperial motifs.

Equally important were palace and public celebrations. Audiences with the caliph, formal processions, reviews of the soldiers, and receptions of ambassadors signified the sublime importance of the monarchy. The Fatimids gave an Ismaʿili turn to Egyptian festivals that had no necessary connection to Shiʿism. Ramadan and New Year processions, the Shiʿi festivals of *ʿashura* and *ghadir khumm*, and the opening of the Nile canals brought the caliph and his entourage, arranged in order of rank, to the mosques of the city, where he delivered the sermon, celebrated the festivals, and displayed the magnificent and sacred objects of the Fatimid treasury. The holidays marking the end of Ramadan and of Hajj were celebrated with great banquets. Thus the caliph brought home to the populace the importance of the ruler both in the spheres of war and politics and in those of religion, nature, and magic.

The public architecture of the Fatimids was an extension of the ceremonial aspect of the royal court. The new Fatimid capital city, al-Qahira (Cairo), founded in 969, with its magnificent palaces and grand mosques, was an imperial city designed for imperial pageants. The principal mosques – al-Azhar and al-Hakim – were constructed with minarets and cupolas, which symbolized the preeminence of the imam and recalled the holy places of Mecca and Medina as a way of glorifying the ruler in the service of God and Islam.

The Fatimids further cultivated religious glory by sponsoring the cult of the family of ʿAli. The cult of saints had its roots in pre-Fatimid popular beliefs and practices, especially in the visitation of the cemeteries. The Fatimids initiated the celebration of the birth of Muhammad and constructed numerous mausoleums over the supposed graves of the family of 'Ali in order to encourage pilgrimage and to inculcate a popular enthusiasm for shrines and relics. Quranic inscriptions encouraged obedience to the imam and called on people to accept his authority as an expression of God's will. In 1153, the head of the martyr Husayn was moved from Ascalon, and a new mausoleum, Sayyidna al-Husayn, was constructed to house it. Pilgrims circumambulated the tomb, kissed his final resting place, wept, and begged for the imam's favor. The graves of caliphs were considered holy, but they were buried in the palace precincts and could be venerated only by court personnel. From the eleventh century, wealthy officials and private persons also built mausoleums over their tombs. These constructions introduced artistic motifs, such as the stalactite decoration (*muqarnas*), facades with decorated gates and minarets, and the use of figural representation, which would become staple features of later royal Islamic art.

The new regime made Isma'ilism the state religion, and the Fatimids created an elaborate missionary and educational structure. The palace contained halls for the teaching of Isma'ili beliefs. Judges, missionaries, reciters of the Quran, and prayer leaders were regularly present for court ceremonies. Ministers patronized intellectuals and organized palace debates among Muslims, Jews, and Christians. The Fatimids sponsored palace and mosque lectures, research institutes, libraries, and an astronomical observatory. Their teachings, however, were directed at the regime elite, and they made no effort to change the allegiances of the Egyptian population. The Muslim population of Egypt remained predominantly Sunni, and Sunni schools of law flourished, especially in Alexandria.

The international missionary movement (*da'wa*) was in principle directed by the Fatimid imam in Egypt, but the provincial leaders had virtually complete autonomy. The Isma'ili missions reached North Africa, Sicily, Lebanon, northern Iran, and India. The decline of the Fatimid caliphate, however, accentuated the contradiction between its revolutionary pretensions and the actualities of its Egyptian political base. The decline of caliphal authority led to schisms as the messianic and politically radical branches of the Isma'ili movement split off. In Lebanon, the sectarians who believed that the Caliph al-Hakim (d. 1021) was the last imam and was indeed God himself established the Druze religion and community. Then, at the death of the Caliph al-Mustansir in 1094, his son al-Musta'li succeeded him, but the missionary movement in Syria, Mesopotamia, and Iran cut itself off from the Fatimids in Egypt, broke with the parent regime, recognized al-Mustansir's son Nizar as the true imam, and founded a new branch of Isma'ilism. The Nizari Isma'ilis, later known as the Assassins, would carry on the Isma'ili challenge to Sunni Islam.

With the shattering of the 'Abbasid Empire, Egypt emerged as a principal center of Arabic-Islamic civilization, but the rhythm of Fatimid history was similar to that of 'Abbasid history. The period from 969 to 1021 was one of political and religious consolidation. The second phase, from 1021 to 1073, saw a breakdown of political order, warfare between military factions, and the division of the country into land tax allotments controlled by the leading military officers. This decline was partially arrested by the administration of Badr al-Jamali and his son, al-Afdal, from 1073 to 1121, in which the military chiefs replaced the caliphs as the effective heads of government. In 1171, Saladin conquered Egypt, removed the Fatimid caliphs, and established a Sunni-oriented regime.

Syria and the Crusades

While the Fatimids ruled Egypt, Syria – a province characterized by numerous ecological and political zones (coastal, mountain, town, and desert) and exposed to multiple influences from Anatolia, the Mediterranean, Egypt, and Iraq – was divided into several small states. The Fatimids established their authority in southern Syria and took control of Damascus from 978 to 1076. Northern Syria, after a brief interlude of Hamdanid, Buwayhid, and Byzantine warfare, came under Byzantine control from 968 to 1086. The balance of power between the Byzantine and Fatimid empires allowed for a proliferation of bedouin principalities in Mesopotamia and northern Syria under the aegis of the 'Uqaylid (990–1096), Marwanid (983–1085), and Mirdasid (1023–79) dynasties. Southern Syria was in the hands of Kalb tribes. Towns such as Tripoli became independent city-states. Mountain populations in Lebanon preserved their autonomy. In this fragmented condition, Syria was overrun by the Saljuqs. They conquered Damascus in 1079 and took Antioch and Aleppo in 1085. Syria was then divided between two Saljuq succession regimes, one based in Aleppo and one in Damascus.

Syria was subsequently exposed to yet another wave of invasions, this time by Latin crusaders. The Crusades had their origin, in part, in already long-standing struggles between Western European Christians and their Byzantine and Muslim adversaries in the Mediterranean; Italian towns pushed back Muslim pirates. The Reconquista had begun in Spain and by 1085 Toledo was in Christian hands. In 1087, Pisa and Genoa destroyed Mahdiyya, the political and commercial capital of Muslim North Africa. The Normans conquered Sicily between 1061 and 1091 and moved on to attack the Byzantine Empire. The papacy encouraged the Crusades, because it was eager to reconcile the Greek and Western churches and to support the Byzantine Empire against the Saljuq Turks. It wanted to establish new states under its auspices in the eastern Mediterranean in order to spread the influence of the Latin church among Eastern Christians. Alongside these political currents ran a strong passion for pilgrimage to Jerusalem, the heavenly city, which symbolized salvation, penance, and the remission of sins. The Saljuq conquests raised European anxieties about access to Jerusalem and generated a passionate desire to secure the holy city in Christian hands.

These trends came together in 1096. Pope Urban II, speaking to an audience of restive warriors at Clermont in France, conscious of papal policy needs, and influenced by the pilgrimage sensibility, broached the idea of an armed pilgrimage to capture the holy places from the infidels. To those who would undertake this mission, Urban offered protection of property at home, new lands in the East, plenary indulgences, and the total remission of all temporal punishments that might be imposed by the church for the commission of past sins. His audience probably heard this as a promise of absolution from sin and of salvation.

By sea and by land, European warriors set out for the East. Between 1099 and 1109, they captured Edessa, Antioch, and Tripoli, and also established the Latin Kingdom of Jerusalem. Baldwin was elected king, ruling as a feudal lord with the support of the Knights Templar and Hospitalers. Latin clergy took control of Christian administration in Palestine, but the Eastern Christian sects were not eliminated.

The Muslim response to the Crusades was slow to develop; when it did, it led eventually to the unification of Syria and Egypt into a single Muslim state. The initial Muslim reaction was, by and large, indifference. Syria was so fragmented as to preclude any unified opposition to the intruders; several more little states among many did not much disturb existing interests. The fact that these new states were Christian was not exceptional – the Byzantines had also ruled northern Syria and, there was a substantial, if not a majority, local Christian population.

Gradually, however, a Muslim counterattack emerged in three phases. (See Map 8.) From 1099 to 1146 was the phase of Mesopotamian leadership. The Saljuq Atabegs of Mosul, who had nominal authority over Syria, attempted to create their own small empire in Mesopotamia and northern Syria. In 1128, a new governor of Mosul, Zengi (c. 1127–46), seized Aleppo; in 1144, he managed by chance to capture Edessa. When Zengi died in 1146, however, Mosul and Aleppo were severed from each other to make independent principalities for his surviving sons. Throughout this period, the Mosul campaigns were not primarily directed against the crusaders but were aimed at winning territory from either Muslim or Christian rulers whenever possible. There was little consciousness of Muslim-Christian antagonism per se. In fact, Christian and Muslim princelings often allied to resist Zengi's encroachments. A second phase began with the succession of Nur al-Din (c. 1146–74), the son of Zengi, who inherited Aleppo. Nur al-Din made the capture of Damascus his main goal. In 1147, he helped relieve the siege of Damascus by the Second Crusade. In 1154, a local rebellion expelled the ruling Saljuqid governors, and the populace of the city turned it over to Nur al-Din.

The Crusades revealed the underground growth of a new Muslim communal and religious spirit, which was frankly anti-Christian and opposed to the crusader presence. Jerusalem was the focus of a new Muslim self-awareness. The Dome of the Rock had been built in Jerusalem by the Umayyad caliphs to symbolize the Muslim continuation of the sacred past of Judaism and Christianity. In the course of the eighth, ninth, and tenth centuries, Jewish and Christian ideas about Jerusalem were assimilated into Islamic teachings. Jerusalem was an axis of communication

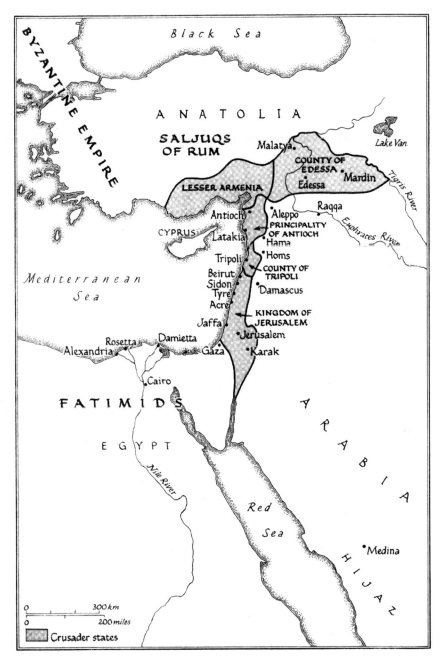

Map 8. Egypt and Syria, showing the crusader states in the twelfth century.

between this world and the next. It became venerable to Muslims as part of their own prophetic history, because Muhammad was believed to have ascended to heaven from Jerusalem. Refugees waged a literary and religious campaign about the merits of Jerusalem and the importance of jihad. By the middle of the twelfth century, this sentiment had become a popular force, and this helps to account for the surrender of Damascus to Nur al-Din, who was at the time seen as the Muslim prince who would redeem Jerusalem.

In fact, the reign of Nur al-Din in Damascus from 1154 to 1174 was concentrated not on the redemption of Jerusalem but on the consolidation of his little kingdom in Syria. He made treaties with the Byzantines and the Latins and concentrated on the conquest of Mosul, which he took in 1170, thus fulfilling a family ambition to reunite Syria and Mesopotamia. He also entered into the struggle for control of Egypt. With the Fatimid regime in total disarray and Amalric (the Latin King of Jerusalem) maneuvering to seize the country, in 1169 Nur al-Din sent his general Shirkuh and Shirkuh's nephew Salah al-Din (Saladin) with Muslim forces to take control of Egypt. In 1171, they removed the last of the Fatimid caliphs and established a Sunni regime. The histories of Egypt and Syria would be joined until the nineteenth century.

The advent of Saladin to the sultanate of Egypt opened a third phase of the Muslim response to the Crusades. From Egypt, Saladin brought Syria and Mesopotamia into a single Muslim state. In 1174, he took Damascus; in 1183, Aleppo; in 1186, Mosul. He then defeated the crusaders at the Battle of Hattin (1187) and brought an end to the Latin occupation of Jerusalem. At the siege of Acre (1192), however, Saladin made a truce with Richard the Lion-Heart, which allowed the crusading principalities to maintain their foothold on the coasts of Palestine and Syria.

On Saladin's death in 1193, his family, the Ayyubids, succeeded to the rule of Egypt (to 1250) and Syria (to 1260). The family divided his empire into the smaller kingdoms of Egypt, Damascus, Aleppo, and Mosul in accordance with the Saljuq idea that the state was the patrimony of the royal family. Nonetheless, the Ayyubids did not revert to the fragmentation of earlier regimes. The sultan of Egypt usually managed to assert his suzerainty over the rest of the family and to make use of family loyalties to integrate the regime. The Ayyubids ruled Egypt and Syria through a military aristocracy composed of Kurdish and Turkish troops and some slave forces. In Syria they adopted the Saljuq land tax allotment (*iqta'*) system, took over the feudal estates of the Latin crusaders, and converted Latin church properties into endowments for Muslim institutions. They administered Egypt by the age-old bureaucratic system that prevailed in that country and by the distribution of feudal lands (*iqta's*) to leading military officers.

The Ayyubids were notably reluctant to continue the struggle against the remaining crusader principalities. Having achieved a tenuous unity and a prosperous Mediterranean trade between Syria and Egypt and the ports of Italy and Europe, the Ayyubids drew back from the struggle for Palestine and gave priority to the protection of Egypt. Realizing that Egypt was the key to the recovery of the holy land, the Christians attacked it in 1197, 1217, 1229, and 1249. In 1217, to divert the crusaders from Egypt, al-Kamil (1218–38) offered concessions in Palestine. In 1229, the Ayyubids negotiated a treaty with Frederick II, agreeing to return Jerusalem to Christian hands on the condition that the city would not be fortified and that the temple area would remain open to Muslim pilgrims. Thus, the Ayyubids gave preference to political and economic over religious and symbolic considerations. However deep Muslim anti-Christian sentiment might be, its effective expression still required that religious feeling correspond to the interests of the political elite.

The Mamluk Empire

In 1250, the Ayyubid house was overthrown by a rebellion of one of its Mamluk or slave regiments, which killed the last Ayyubid ruler of Egypt and named one of its own officers, Aybeg, as the new sultan. The Mamluks defended Syria against the Mongols at the Battle of 'Ayn Jalut in 1260, crushed the last of the independent Syrian principalities, expelled the remaining crusader states by 1291, and expanded the boundaries of their empire into the upper Euphrates Valley and Armenia. Thus, they were able to unify Egypt and Syria until the Ottoman conquest in 1517. This was the longest-lived Muslim state in the Middle East between the 'Abbasid and the Ottoman empires.

The Mamluk era was noted for the perfection of the post-'Abbasid slave military system. Before the Mamluk period, slave regiments had been employed in all Middle Eastern armies, but the Mamluks, like the Ghaznavids, were based entirely on the slave military machine. The elite personnel of the regime, including the sultan, were slaves or former slaves. In principle, although there were important exceptions, no one could be a member of the military elite unless he was of foreign origin (usually Turkish or Circassian), purchased and raised as a slave, and trained to be a soldier and administrator. No native of Egypt or Syria could ever belong to this elite, nor, in principle, could the sons of slaves. The raison d'être of this arrangement was that every man who served the regime belonged entirely to the state and was without any family or local ties to compromise his total dedication to his master and to the service of the military caste.

Mamluks were purchased from abroad at the age of ten or twelve, converted to Islam, and raised in barracks, where they not only learned military technique but were imbued with loyalty to their masters and to their comrades-in-arms. On graduating from the barrack schools, the fully trained Mamluks served either in the sultan's Mamluk regiment or as soldiers in the service of other leading officers. The officers possessed their own personal slaves apart from the regiments of the sultan. A Mamluk army, then, may be imagined as a grouping of slave regiments, made up of the sultan's troops and of the regiments loyal to individual officers, who were in turn personally loyal to the sultan. This army was not organized so much by hierarchy of rank as by personal allegiance.

In Mamluk Egypt, the bureaucratic tradition of Egypt and the land tax allotments of Syria were combined. The tax revenues of Egypt and Syria were assigned to pay the salaries of the sultan and the Mamluk officers, but the central bureaucracy kept close control over taxation. The bureaucracy made surveys to determine the available resources and to prevent the Mamluks from acquiring excessive revenues or other rights in the countryside. With the decline of the Mamluk state in the late fourteenth century, central controls became less effective, and the amirs usurped the revenues of the land tax allotments.

The need to legitimize the regime led to a program of imperial and court ceremony and of cultural patronage designed to glorify the rulers. The presence at court of the caliph and the chief judges, the guardianship of the annual pilgrimage caravan to the holy places of Mecca and Medina, the formal presence of the sultan in the Hall of Justice, and the celebration of Islamic religious feasts emphasized the religious importance of the regime. The magical as well as religious aspects of royal power were also celebrated. The ruler was revered as someone who had in his control the powers of the cosmos. A good ruler could bring rain and abundant harvests; a bad ruler could bring ruin. The tomb of al-Mansur Qalawun (r. 1279–90) copied features of the Dome of the Rock in Jerusalem to signify the Mamluk pretension to be heirs to the glory of the first Islamic dynasty. In a similar spirit, royal libraries were provided with copies of Persian illuminated manuscripts telling of the conquests of Alexander the Great and the histories of Persian kings. Late Mamluk-era culture was rich in Persian and Ottoman influences. The cosmopolitan heritage of Mamluk Egypt was also reinforced by the migration of Iranian, Turkish, Spanish, and Mesopotamian craftsmen and scholars, who brought with them metalwork, textile, ceramic, and building crafts, which were adopted by the Mamluks to adorn the life of the court and the military aristocracy. The religious and cosmopolitan aspects of Mamluk court culture were tempered by a parochial ethnic and military emphasis. The Mamluk court listened to Turkish and Circassian poetry; they reveled in military reviews, tournaments, and displays of martial arts. In the course of this effort to legitimize themselves, the Mamluks left a distinctive Egyptian-Islamic artistic legacy.

The Ayyubids and the Mamluks also continued the Saljuq policy of strong state support for and control of Islam. The decisive force behind Ayyubid- and Mamluk-era Egyptian culture was the commitment of the state to Sunni rather than Shiʿi Islam. The early Mamluk period was dominated by intense Muslim religious feeling expressed in warfare against the crusaders, the Mongols, and the Ismaʿilis, and hostility to Christians and Jews, coupled with pressures for the conversion of non-Muslims to Islam. In addition, both the Ayyubids and the Mamluks sponsored a revival of Sunni Islamic religious activity. In the Ayyubid period (1193–1260) there were no fewer than 255 religious structures built in Damascus. This was followed by an equally intense period of construction in the first century of Mamluk rule, at the instance of governors, generals, judges, and rich merchants. The Ayyubids and

Mamluks also followed Fatimid precedents by constructing tombs for venerated Muslim ancestors and for deceased rulers. One of the first Ayyubid projects was the construction of a madrasa near the grave of al-Shafi'i, the founder of the principal Egyptian school of law. Colleges and *khanaqas* came to be provided with mausoleums for the remains of their founders. A tomb advertised the sanctity of the ruler, and his devotion to Islam.

A characteristic architectural design emerged for the religious architecture of this period. Mosques, madrasas, and *khanaqas* were often built with an open central courtyard surrounded by four galleries or *liwans* on the principal sides of the courtyard, with the intervening spaces filled in with rooms for students. The mausoleum itself was often topped by a dome, and the whole structure provided with tall, slender minarets. Such buildings, clustered along main streets or in the cemeteries, created a vast visual display, shaped the physical fabric of the city, and symbolized the integral relation of the state, Islam, and the urban society. With strong state support, the schools of law became the foci for the spread of Islamic teaching among the common people. In Damascus, lawyers issued legal advice, preachers exhorted the general populace, and religious manuals instructed the people.

In Syria and Egypt, the Saljuq succession states converted the routine patronage of the *'ulama'* (legal scholars and teachers) and Sufis into a system of state control. Nur al-Din selected the appointees to judicial and teaching offices and created a supervisory post for the administration of Sufi *khanaqas*. He pioneered a policy of making the *'ulama'* and Sufis directly dependent on state patronage and appointments. Saladin appointed a chief judge (*qadi*) and a chief *shaykh* for the Sufis. In 1263, Sultan Baybars (1260–77) appointed a chief *qadi* for each of the four major schools of law, a chief *shaykh* (master, teacher) for the Sufis, and a syndic for the corporation of descendants of the Prophet (*naqib al-ashraf*). Under the Mamluks the state appointed judges, legal administrators, professors, Sufi *shaykhs*, prayer leaders, and other Muslim officials. They paid the salaries of religious personnel, endowed their schools, and thus brought the religious establishment into a state bureaucracy. Never did the state attempt to define the content of religious teaching. Thus, the Mamluks extended the Saljuq-Iranian pattern of organized religious life to Syria and Egypt. Owing to this strong support for Islam, Mamluk royal culture emphasized its Islamic rather than its cosmopolitan bases. It was thus typical of the tendency in the Arab provinces to legitimize states in Muslim rather than universalist terms.

MILITARY SLAVERY

New institutional arrangements characterized the post-imperial era. All post-'Abbasid regimes included an alien military elite. The Buwayhid, Ghaznavid, Qarakhanid, and Saljuq regimes were built by ethnic minorities, including mercenaries from the Caspian Sea and nomadic Turkish peoples from Inner Asia. These elites had no ethnic, cultural, linguistic, or historical connection with the peoples they ruled. Nomadic forces were supplemented by a praetorian guard of slave soldiers organized to offset the influence of the nomadic elites. These slaves were commonly purchased in Inner Asia while still young and then raised at the courts of their masters. Every regime followed a policy of pitting slave regiments against one another to maintain the authority of the ruler. Occasionally, as in the Ghaznavid case, the slaves seized control of the state, and the leading generals became sultans. They were not hereditary, landed, or aristocratic and depended on the continuous recruitment of new cadres.

The slave elites were organized as households, held together by interests, surrogate kinship, and patronage. The patronage of an amir or a sultan who raised, trained, and empowered his men created a lifelong obligation and affection like the relation of parent and child. Such ties might last for generations. Loyalties were created by the giving and taking of benefits. Oaths of allegiance, such as the oath of allegiance to a caliph or to a prominent official, were even used to consolidate conspiracies to seize power.

Military slavery and slave states were peculiar institutions. However, the translation of the word "*ghulam*" or "*mamluk*" into English as "slave" carries inappropriate connotations. The concept of *ghulam* or *mamluk* designated a binding personal obedience but not necessarily a humble situation in society. In its Arab-Muslim sense, the slave soldier was the personal property of a master and could be bought and sold. He was a servile retainer, depending on the master for security and support. The social position of the slave, however, did not reflect his personal servitude but rather reflected the status of his master. The slave of the sultan could be a general or minister of state, and the slave of a general could be an officer in the army or administration. Furthermore, military slaves were eventually manumitted and became freedmen, clients of their former masters, which gave them limited legal rights to property, marriage, and personal security. In this institution, the exclusive personal loyalty of the slave or client soldier to his master was crucial.

THE *IQTA'* SYSTEM AND MIDDLE EASTERN FEUDALISM

The system of state fiscal administration was closely related to military organization. 'Abbasid government had been based on bureaucratic methods of taxation and disbursements to the court and the army. The central government staffs collected revenues from the countryside and made payments in cash and kind to the officials and soldiers who served the state. With the decline of 'Abbasid administration, the central bureaucracy progressively lost control of the countryside; with the advent of the Buwayhid dynasty in 945, soldiers were for the first time assigned *iqta's* (land tax allotments) in payment for military service. The Ghaznavids adopted a similar system, and the Saljuqs extended this means of paying the army from Iraq and western Iran to Khurasan. They also introduced the system into Syria and eventually, under the Ayyubid dynasty, into Egypt.

The terms of assignments varied considerably. In the Ghaznavid and early Saljuq cases, a strong central government maintained control over the assigned lands. Assignees were held to their military responsibilities and rotated at the will of the ruler; hereditary succession was not permitted. Central government officials kept registers indicating the value of the tax assignment, the number of troops to be provided, and the terms of service.

Later in the Saljuq period, the central government was unable to maintain control. Land tax allotments became hereditary, and the assignees usurped the land and turned their tax-collecting rights into private property. The assignees became landlords over peasants. Hereditary control of rural districts in the hands of military assignees gave rise to virtually independent principalities in Mesopotamia and Syria. The Saljuq practice of giving appanages to the members of the ruling family, the encouragement to independence inherent in the institution of the *ulubeg*, the decline of central checks on the authority of provincial governors, the widespread assignment of salary *iqta's*, and the usurpation of *iqta's* dispersed political power. Saljuq administrative practices led to a drastic fragmentation of political power and to the substitution of small principalities for large-scale states.

Many scholars have referred to these changes as a period of Middle Eastern feudalism. The decline of the 'Abbasid Empire may be seen as parallel to the breakup of the Roman Empire and the widespread distribution of *iqta's* in the Middle East as analogous to the widespread distribution of fiefs in Europe. European feudalism also had its origin in the breakup of a centralized state (the Carolingian Empire) and the distribution of land to a multitude of small lords in France in the late tenth and eleventh centuries. In fact, however, the Middle Eastern development is different from the European. The essence of feudalism did not lie simply in the decentralization of power and in the multiplication of numerous and relatively small principalities; rather, it lay in certain characteristic institutions governing the relationships between the peasant populations and their lords and the relationships among the lords themselves.

In European feudalism, the relationship of peasant and lord was defined by the manor, an agricultural estate made up of the residence of the lord and his private properties surrounded by the small plots of the peasants. The manor, when assigned to a lord by his overlord as a benefice, was a grant of the services of peasants, who became tenants of the lord and owed him economic dues for the use of the land. Benefices, moreover, were also conceded with immunity from central inspection. Then the lord was made judge, and his tenants became his political subjects. Finally, and perhaps most important, they became his personal servitors as well. They could not leave the land, and their heirs were automatically serfs. They had to work his lands; they were conveyable by him; they had to ransom the right to marry and to pass on their property. The economic powers of the landlord and the fiscal and jurisdictional rights of the state were united with the power of the patriarch over his household. The combination of powers defined the manor as a fief.

In the twelfth century, some hierarchical order was brought into the distribution of fiefs, and they came to be considered as the concession of a higher lord to one of his vassals in return for military service. All lords of fiefs were in principle the vassals of higher-ranking lords. The king, highest lord of all, was the source of everyone's tenures and jurisdictions. In the feudal system, the relationships among lords were not governmental relations of superior to subordinate but were relations of personal dependence. A vassal was the sworn client of his lord, exchanging service and devotion for protection and support. The relation between vassal and lord, moreover, was a contractual one, in which violation of the agreement on either side resulted in the termination of the contract, the dismissal or withdrawal of the vassal from service, and the return of the fief to the lord. One crucial aspect of this relationship was that disputes were judged in a court composed of other vassals. Every vassal, as part of his obligations and rights, had to attend his lord's court for the settlement of disputes between the vassals and the lord and the judgment of other matters.

Time and the weakness of lords in France favored the entrenchment of vassals in their fiefs. The fief ceased to be granted solely on condition of service but became a hereditary right. Eventually all connections with military service and clientage were dissociated from the possession of a fief, which became simply a hereditary governmental jurisdiction and personal property.

As inheritable property, the possession of a fief also defined the social status of the warrior class. A fief not only meant economic rights, personal servants, and governmental jurisdiction but also conferred the privileges of nobility. Feudalism thus became not only a system that confounded public and private powers but also a kind of society in which function or occupation, social status, political power, styles of life and culture, and economic wealth were all tied to the possession of land.

The Middle Eastern system was not feudal in this European sense. Indeed, the collapse of the 'Abbasid Empire led to a decentralization of political authority, to the emergence of many petty rulers, and to the distribution of land in *iqta's*, but the situation differed in several ways. In the Middle East, the idea of public authority and the distinctions between governmental powers and personal possessions and rights were never abandoned. However decentralized the powers of government became, a subordinate was never considered a vassal but was always a delegate of the ruler. The ruler assigned a post to an official, and he could unilaterally, at his pleasure, remove his agent from office. He made no contracts with his appointees and gave them no rights to be consulted. It was common in the Middle East for the governor to be a personal dependent of the sultan, just as the vassal in Europe was a personal dependent, but still the relations were different. The vassal was a free man who contracted his dependency, whereas dependents in the Muslim world were slaves or freedmen. Also in the Middle East, the personal relationship did not entirely substitute for the political relationship. It was not the personal relationship as such but the designation of the ruler that conferred authority on a governor.

A second difference was the distinction between an *iqta'* and a fief. In principle, an *iqta'* was a grant of the right to collect taxes and to keep them in lieu of salary, a mechanism to decentralize the collection and disbursement of revenues due to the state. In principle, *iqta's* were conceded only on condition of military service being rendered and were valid only for the lifetime of the incumbent. They could be increased or decreased, revoked, or reassigned by the ruler. An *iqta'* was not a personal property; it could not be sold, leased, or willed. Nor was it a government jurisdiction; it brought no political, judicial, or personal powers over the peasants, who were considered subjects of the state, and not serfs or slaves of the *iqta'* holder. Nor did the possession of an *iqta'* confer status privileges or legal rights. The status of the holder had nothing to do with the land but was determined by his rank and duties as a soldier or administrator and his closeness to the ruler. Finally, *iqta's* could not be reassigned to subordinates. Officers were responsible for bringing men to service in proportion to the size of their *iqta's*, but in principle they did not pay their men by granting them land tax allotments in turn.

In practice, certain powers not originally envisaged in the grants of an *iqta'* were usurped. Often an *iqta'* gave the holder enough local wealth to accumulate other properties and, eventually, by merging his *iqta'* with other lands, to make it hereditary private property as well. Furthermore, *iqta'* holders might force the peasants to surrender their land and to become personal dependents. In some cases, *iqta'* holders even acquired governmental powers by usurpation or immunities. When coupled with private power over land and peasants, this created a fief-like or "feudal" condition. Such aberrations, even though widespread in the Saljuq period, never became a recognized system of governmental relations. Muslim rulers always maintained substantial slave bodyguards and the scribal staffs and records essential to the enforcement of obligations and the utilization of *iqta's* as a component of state power. Although some *iqta's* became fiefs, a feudal system did not materialize. In the Middle East, then, decentralization entailed no fundamental institutional changes and could, in changed circumstances, be reversed. Imperial governments could and would be reconstructed by the later Mamluk, Ottoman, and Safavid empires.

Thus, from 950 to 1200, the unity of the 'Abbasid age was lost. Still, despite the numerous different regimes, certain uniformities in the political concepts and institutions of the period emerged. The supremacy of the caliphate and of the Islamic identity it represented was universally accepted, whereas effective political power was conceded to nomadic conquerors and slave warlords. Similar institutions of nomadic family practice, military slavery, and *iqta'* administration were developed, with variations, throughout the region. Everywhere the political concepts and military and administrative institutions adumbrated in the 'Abbasid age were integrated with the institutions and concepts of the nomadic conquerors and worked into a new system of government. In an era of unprecedented fragmentation of power and instability, these institutions were similar throughout the region. They constituted, via numerous small experiments, an enduring legacy in the experience of Middle Eastern Islamic government.

ROYAL COURTS AND REGIONAL CULTURES: ISLAM IN PERSIAN GARB

The new system of Middle Eastern states also opened a new era in the development of aristocratic and cosmopolitan Islamic culture. The post-imperial era reveals two dominant trends. One was the continuation of 'Abbasid tendencies toward the bifurcation of Islamic cosmopolitan and Islamic religious culture, although, in many respects, an intimate relationship was maintained between the two. Art and architecture, poetry, science, and certain forms of prose literature were usually expressions of court, regime, and governing elites, but court patronage also extended to Islamic religious studies. Some genres, such as history, political studies, and some forms of philosophy and theology, were cultivated in both court and private urban milieus.

The second trend was toward regional diversity. As Baghdad dwindled, Samarqand and Bukhara, Nishapur and Isfahan, Cairo, Fez, and Cordova became the new capitals of Islamic civilization. In place of the single cosmopolitan court culture, each capital generated its own blend of Islamic motifs and local heritage. Islamic architecture differed from region to region. Samanid brickwork, Ghaznavid minarets, Isfahan domes, and Fatimid shrines were emblematic of a new cultural diversity.

Within this diversity, there was a tendency to divide the former regions of the 'Abbasid Empire into two linguistic and cultural zones. In the western regions – including Iraq, Syria, and Egypt, and the lands of the far Islamic west, including North Africa and Spain – Arabic became the predominant language of both high literary culture and spoken discourse. In the eastern lands – including Iran and Transoxania – Persian became the predominant literary language. During this period the poems and epics of the east would be composed in Persian, whereas the odes and quatrains of Baghdad and Cordova would be written in Arabic. The two cultural regions, however, continued to share a common system of religious values and institutions.

In the post-'Abbasid era, Baghdad maintained its position as a capital of Islamic religious and Arabic literary studies. Baghdadi poetry continued to follow ninth-century forms; the *qasida* or panegyric and the *ghazal* or lyric were still the most important forms of poetic expression. Al-Mutanabbi (d. 965) and Abu al-'Ala' al-Ma'rri (d. 1057) were the most important poets. Sufi poetry celebrated ecstatic experiences in the imagery of the intoxication of wine and love. In the tenth and eleventh centuries, under the influence of Ibn Qutayba's compilations, anthologies of poetry, history, and other subjects were composed. Arabic letter writing and secretarial correspondence became an art of elaborate rhymed prose displaying great technical skill. The *Maqamat* of al-Hariri (d. 1122), done in virtuoso prose and with philological subtlety, was perhaps the greatest achievement of this type. Historical writing also flourished. Histories of the caliphate were superseded by new world histories, city histories, collections of biographies, and historical anecdotes written to entertain and enlighten. Arabic prose literature was profoundly influenced by a new literary criticism that insisted on formal qualities in writing and deemphasized novelty or significance in content.

In the eastern provinces of the 'Abbasid Empire, a Persian literary and artistic revival generated a parallel Muslim civilization. Persian culture developed in a multitude of places over a period of many centuries but was nonetheless strikingly unified. Persian culture drew on deep and wide-ranging roots. Ancient Mesopotamian law, Zoroastrian mythology, Buddhist mysticism, Indian mathematics and literature, and Hellenistic philosophy all flourished in the early Islamic era. In the ninth century, Sijistan, Khurasan, and Transoxania; the courts of the Tahirids of Nishapur and Marw; the Samanids of Bukhara; and the Ghaznavids were the primary centers for the patronage of a new phase in Persian linguistic, literary, and artistic development pursued by Iranian courtiers, administrators, scholars, painters, and poets. In the late tenth and eleventh centuries, the new Persian language and literature written in Arabic script and created in eastern Iran became the literature of western Iran. In later generations, Saljuqs, Ghurids, Ilkhans, and Timurids produced their own contributions to the common culture. Persian culture not only became the characteristic style of Iran but also had an important influence on the development of Muslim culture in Inner Asia, India, and Indonesia. Persian literary and artistic styles superseded Arabic as the predominant cultural influence in the formation of the eastern Islamic world.

The development of new Persian was conditioned by two factors. One was the linguistic situation in eastern Iran just prior to the Arab conquests. In late Sasanian times, Parsi (Pahlavi) or Middle Persian was the official religious and literary language of the empire. Dari was the dialect version of this language spoken throughout much of Iran. Alongside formal Parsi and spoken Dari, poets and entertainers cultivated a popular oral literature for the amusement of the common people and the local lords, also expressed in a version of Dari. All three levels of Persian would contribute to the formation of the new Persian language.

The second factor was the Arab-Muslim conquests. Under Arab rule, Arabic became the principal language for administration and religion. The substitution of Arabic for Middle Persian was facilitated by the translation of Persian classics into Arabic. Arabic became the main vehicle of Persian high culture and remained as such well into the eleventh century. Parsi declined and was kept alive mainly by the Zoroastrian priesthood in western Iran. The Arab conquests, however, helped make

Dari rather than Arabic the common spoken language in Khurasan, Afghanistan, and the lands beyond the Oxus River. Paradoxically, Arab-Islamic domination created a Persian cultural region in areas never before unified by Persian speech.

The new Persian language evolved out of this complex linguistic situation. In the ninth century, the Tahirid governors of Khurasan (820–73) began to have the old Persian language written in Arabic script rather than in Pahlavi characters. At the same time, eastern Iranian lords in the small principalities began to patronize local court poetry in an elevated form of Dari. The new poetry was inspired by Arabic verse forms, so that Iranian patrons who did not understand Arabic could comprehend and enjoy the presentation of an elevated and dignified poetry in the manner of Baghdad. This new poetry flourished in regions where the influence of ʿAbbasid Arabic culture was attenuated and where it had no competition from the surviving tradition of Middle Persian literary classics cultivated for religious purposes – as in western Iran.

The new poetry borrowed both from Arabic literary forms and oral Iranian literature. The *qasida* became its chief expression. Based on Arabic rhyming schemes, it was used mainly for panegyrics praising Iranian princes. Oral Persian poetry contributed a distinctive rhythmic pattern. The most important early poets in the new vein were the Samanid court poets Rudaki (d. 940–41), who was considered the father of the new Persian poetry, and Daqiqi (d. c. 980), who was especially successful in conveying daily life in his poems. Bilingual poets translated Arabic poems into Persian and began to compose poems of their own in both Arabic and Persian.

The Persian literary heritage of stories, romances, fables, and dynastic histories also formed the basis of a new type of epic poetry. The Samanids revived Iranian interest in the ancient history of kings and in the literary collections of the Sasanian period. From the pen of Firdawsi (d. 1020–21 or 1025–26) emerged an immense historical epic. His *Shah-name* or *Book of Kings* contains not only the court histories collected by the Sasanians but also a cycle concerning the life of the great hero Rustam. For patrons who were attempting to legitimize their rule by virtue of their historical descent from ancient Iranian rulers and their emulation of ancient Iranian virtues, Firdawsi composed a new epic preoccupied with sovereignty, feudalism, and the war of good and evil. Poems written in the new Persian language with a moderate influence of Arabic vocabulary became the literary standard of the new era.

Prose was equally important in the new Persian language. The historical works of al-Tabari were translated, and a small number of geographical, philosophic, and scientific works were written in Persian. Commentaries on the Quran, mystical treatises, and legal and other religious texts were translated from Arabic. Such works were generally written in a utilitarian style without the elaborate literary pretensions of lyric and epic poetry. Under the influence of these translations and new compositions, Dari became more and more highly Arabized, and Persian evolved into "new Persian," which was heavily influenced by Arabic vocabulary and syntax.

This new language and literature flourished at other regional courts. Mahmud of Ghazna (d. 1030) sought the help of poets to legitimize his regime. Mahmud patronized Unsuri (d. 1039/40), whose *qasida* celebrated court festivals, the changing of the seasons, royal entertainments, and the pleasures of music and wine. Mahmud was also the patron of Firdawsi, the scientist and geographer Biruni, and a host of historians who chronicled the events of the era. Poetry also flourished brilliantly in the Saljuq courts of the eleventh and twelfth centuries. The poets moved from court to court looking for patrons, giving continuity and unity to a literary activity carried on in numerous places throughout Iran.

Under Samanid and Ghaznavid patronage, the new Persian literature favored several poetic and prose genres. Poetry was commonly composed in one of four metric forms. The *ghazal* is a lyric poem of some seven to fifteen lines on the theme of love that expresses private sentiments but in standard images and symbols – such as the nightingale in love with the rose. The *ruba'i*, or quatrain, was a lyric that usually expressed mystical or profane love. The *masnavi*, or rhyming couplet, was a loose form used for narratives such as tales, romances, legends, and histories. Persian literature was rich in such materials, including the tales of Sindbad, the heroic accounts of the life of Alexander the Great, the fables of *Kalila wa-Dimna*, and the lives of saints. A characteristic product of court poets was panegyrical poems produced for money in *qasida* and sometimes in *masnavi* form. Characteristically, the poems contained images of the king as ruler over cities, generous in gifts, noble in ancestry. The most important representative of this type of poetry was Anvari (d. 1189), who lived at times in Marw, Nishapur, and Balkh. Persian poets did not aim at self-expression, originality, creativity, or personal insight. Poetry was a public recitation, an adornment for court life, and the main value was virtuosity in handling familiar forms and content. This was a poetry of masks that wandered from theme to theme, so as to be a vehicle of sensuous appreciations or philosophical thoughts.

In Azarbayjan, romantic poetry was favored. Courtly romances based not on personal experience but on literary convention told the stories of heroes consumed by physical passion and heroes who sublimated their love into an idealization of a perfect but inaccessible woman. Court poetry dwelt on the theme of the lover who suffers just for a glance, while his only comfort is wine. Perhaps the most important writer in this genre was Nizami (d. 1209), who wrote the stories of Alexander's quest for the water of life; the love story of Shirin and the emperor Khusraw Parviz; and the story of Majnun, who became mad with longing for Layla, whom he could never attain. Nizami's poetry brought a vernacular vocabulary into the high Persian poetic tradition.

In Sufi poetry, images of wine, drinking, and love were adopted to express yearning for and love of God. The most important writer of this genre was Farid al-Din ʿAttar (d. 1221), who was famous for his histories of the Sufis and his books of wisdom, the *Language of the Birds* and the *Book of God*, whose principal themes were renunciation of worldly desires and the soul's journey toward metaphysical vision. His works describe the forty stations of the visionary and cosmic passage by which the traveler progressively leaves behind this world in his quest for the world to come. Rumi (d. 1273) was perhaps the greatest of the Persian mystical poets seeking the identification of the human self with the divine being. His *Mathnavi* combined impassioned lyrics with gentle storytelling, merging profane and mystical themes. Persian poetry would continue to inspire brilliant composition throughout Iran, Inner Asia, and the Indian subcontinent. Saʿdi (c. 1213–91) and Hafiz (c. 1320/25–88/89) in Iran, Rumi (1207–73) in Anatolia, Amir Khusrau Dihlavi (1253–1325) in Delhi, and Jami (1414–92) in Herat are among the great names of succeeding centuries.

With the blossoming of Persian literature, Islamic culture was no longer wholly identified with Arabic. Then, under the auspices of the Qarakhanids, who succeeded the Samanids as the rulers of Transoxania, Islamic culture was re-created in Turkish. A new Turkish language, developed first by translation and then by scholarly and literary recreation of Persian literature, became the bearer of Islamic civilization throughout Inner Asia. Islam was becoming a universal religion and civilization in several linguistic media.

The visual arts became as important as the literary. In the ninth century, under the influence of Chinese wares, Nishapur and Samarqand produced white pottery decorated with Kufic writing. Pottery decorated with animals, birds, and vegetal elements was made to please an urban middle-class taste; silver and gold objects were produced in imitation of Sasanian models. Kashan and Rayy produced new types of ceramics. One type was a blue-black or turquoise floral with calligraphic design under glaze; another was a polychrome painting over glaze in which court scenes or historic legends were depicted. The court scenes included hunting, polo, music, and dancing. The objects were illustrated with astronomical signs. Ceramics were often decorated with texts on the theme of love. Another type of ceramic depicted one or two persons sitting together, sometimes playing a musical instrument, perhaps an illustration of love or meditation. Ceramic manufacture of this sort continued until the middle of the fourteenth century.

In architecture, the most important buildings were the tombs of holy men and rulers. These were covered by a dome and surrounded by a complex of buildings dedicated to worship and study. The most famous of these was the Samanid mausoleum at Bukhara built before 943 and the Gumbad-i Qabus dated 1006–07. Mosques with cupolas, round minarets, and monumental arcades derived from Iranian precedents were also built. By the middle of the eleventh century, the characteristic features of Iranian architecture included brick construction, arcades, stalactite projections, and stucco decorated with geometric and vegetal designs to cover the surfaces of large buildings.

By the twelfth century, in the Saljuq era, a new standard form of mosque architecture spread throughout Iran and replaced the earlier Arab-inspired mosque built around a colonnaded courtyard. The new design consisted of a large central courtyard surrounded by arcades, the largest being on the *qibla* (toward Mecca) side of the mosque and surmounted by a large dome.

The mosques were built mainly of brick and with pointed barreled vaults. They also had *muqarnas* (stalactite-like projections) at the junctions between the domes and the substructures. In addition to mosques, numerous tower tombs and mausoleums with cupolas were built in the twelfth and thirteenth centuries, especially in Azarbayjan and Transoxania.

The patronage of the Mongols and their successors the Timurids brought Persian-Islamic literature and arts to new levels of brilliance. Under Mongol sponsorship, history writing flourished, reflecting the Mongol sense of universal destiny. Al-Juvayni's (d. 1283) *History of the World Conquerors* told the story of Chinggis Khan and the conquest of Iran. His near-contemporary Rashid al-Din (d. 1318), a physician and vizier, wrote the *Compendium of Histories*, integrating Chinese, Indian, European, Muslim, and Mongol histories into a new cosmopolitan perspective on the fate of mankind. The Ilkhans, like previous (Turkish) conquerors, were devoted to the construction of monumental tombs and adapted older Iranian architectural forms for the monuments of Tabriz, Sultaniyya, and Varamin. The most important Ilkhan construction was the mausoleum of Oljeytu (1304–17) at Sultaniyya, whose large central dome was a major technical achievement. Stucco, terracotta, and colored bricks or tiles were used to decorate the exterior surfaces.

The Mongol contribution to the revival of the glory of Iranian monarchy was most brilliantly expressed in painting and manuscript illustration. Tabriz became the center of a flourishing school. The historical works of Rashid al-Din were frequently copied and illustrated. So were the epic poems of the *Shahname*, the *Life of Alexander*, and the fables of *Kalila wa-Dimna*. Chinese influences were introduced by the travels of Mongol administrators, soldiers, and merchants across Inner Asia and by the importation of Chinese silks and pottery. Chinese artistic techniques are evident in the treatment of landscapes, birds, flowers, and clouds; in the composition of scenes that appear to be drawn on receding planes; and in new ways of grouping human figures. One type of human figure was aristocratic, elongated, and motionless, with facial features precisely drawn, perhaps gesturing slightly with a movement of the head or finger; a second type was a caricature with highly exaggerated expressions of comedy or pain. Thus, the Ilkhan regime continued the cosmopolitan aspect of Iranian monarchy, reinforced by Mongol concepts of authority and political destiny.

The succeeding Timurid regimes both adopted and re-created Iranian Islamic culture. Tent pavilions and garden residences, palaces, mosques, and tombs defined the ruler's glory in terms of both nomadic and sedentary traditions. The labors of craftsmen from Syria, Iran, and India conveyed the boundless reach of

Timur's rule. Persian, which had a much greater literary reach than Chaghatay, was patronized as the language of court poetry, epic, history, and science. Great monuments were built at Samarqand, including the square of the Registan, the tomb complex of the Shah-i Zindah, and the mausoleum of Timur, the Gur-i amir, which is famous for its blue and turquoise tile decorations and gorgeous dome. Timur's successor in Samarqand, Ulugh-beg, presided over a court of musicians, poets, and singers. He was himself an astronomer and had a large observatory built for his studies. In Herat, Sultan Husayn (r. 1469–1506) reaffirmed his ties to Timurid and Mongol traditions by sponsoring Turkish and Persian histories. The great figures of his time were the classical poets Jami (d. 1492) and Mir 'Ali Shir Nava'i (d. 1501). Born in Herat of a bureaucratic family, Nava'i was a leading poet and patron of the arts and sciences. As a courtier, he was an intermediary between state and town religious elites; he was initiated into the Naqshbandi order. He was most famous as a translator of Persian literature into Chaghatay and as the poet who made Chaghatay Turkish, alongside Persian, an important language of Islamic high culture.

Perhaps the most dramatic and lasting achievement of Timurid rule was the production of illustrated manuscripts. Royal workshops produced the books and other fine art and craft work, whose distinction legitimated the Timurid regimes. Herat and Bukhara became the principal centers of manuscript illustration. Under the patronage of the Timurid Shah Rukh's son, Baisunghur (d. 1434), the reign of Shah Rukh witnessed the creation of a standard repertoire of scenes, which repeated, modified, embellished, and established a visual record of the descent and continuity of the Timurid dynasty; this would shape later Ottoman, Safavid, and Mughal painting and royal imagery. Later, the school of Bihzad (d. c. 1530s) at Herat, and then Tabriz, further developed the Persian style of painting. Persian manuscript illustrations are among the most celebrated of Persian art forms. These miniature paintings are rich with colorful figures and depict victorious armies and royal hunting, trysts and garden feasts, and figures in conference and worship. The paintings are decorated with architectural motifs, flowers, and shrubs. In the fifteenth century, the images became illustrations that accompany a story, but they were not illustrations of specific passages or depictions of the narrative. They were a surprising, exciting enhancement of the book that called on readers to immerse themselves in a parallel world, apart from the text but related through the sequences of images. The most popular work was the classic Persian epic history the *Shahnama* of Firdawsi.

Yet these are not realistic paintings. Timurid period paintings were composed in a way that broke up the surface of the painting into several scenes, each of which seemed to be independent of the others. Each wall, floor, or garden had its own self-contained pattern. Yet all the beautifully decorated objects within a painting – houses, gardens, tiles, carpets, animals, and human figures – were expected to form part of a larger ensemble. Landscapes were transformed in fantastic ways with exotic vegetation, animals, and rocks depicted in surging rhythms, suggesting Chinese sources. The result was an idealized, abstracted ordering of space. In late Timurid paintings, everything was subordinated to design. Even human figures were presented in a way that stressed graceful lines rather than conveying the feeling of a human presence. Faces were expressionless. There were no shadows and no expressions of emotion – a mood of abstract detachment prevailed.

The Timurid painter, like the court poet, wanted to adorn, delight the spectator, and perhaps convey the glory of a patron, but not reveal emotional depths. This was not a tradition of naturalism or illusionist realism but one of detachment, formality, and the transcendence of everyday life. The stylized realm suggested the transcending domain of the ruler. Since ʿAbbasid times, the princely realm had been portrayed as private, separate, luxurious, and otherworldly. Based on the Persian royal artistic tradition carried to exquisite refinement, painting conveyed the ruler's claim to the obedience of the Persian elites. Luxury, refinement, and high culture were joined to political power.

Sufi influences also had a powerful effect on late fifteenth-century Persian painting. Classic Persian love stories, such as the story of Layla and Majnun, were depicted to suggest a spiritual ideal. The final meeting of the two lovers, which causes them to lose consciousness before they can consummate their love, was a symbol of the belief that the Sufi can only attain the object of his devotion after death. Physical features took on a spiritual meaning. For example, doorways and gates implied the movement from outer to inner worlds, the passage from the physical to the spiritual plane. Themes such as love and union inspired the dynasty's literature as well as its art. Given the allegorical character of Persian poetry, a love poem might evoke either (or both) profane love or spiritual devotion, the intoxication of wine or imagination, or the beloved as lover, Sufi master, or royal patron, who all had the power to bestow or withhold their gifts.

Royal patronage for poetry, literature, architecture, and art indicates a profound integration of the political and religious meanings of artistic composition. Kingship was justified by the construction and decoration of mosques, schools, tombs, minarets, and other religious buildings. The blending of profane and spiritual themes in Persian love poetry also bespeaks the inseparability of art and literature from religion.

Whereas in the early ʿAbbasid era aristocratic culture maintained a certain distance from Islam, in the Saljuq era and later the education of an aristocrat combined literary or secular studies (such as poetry, belles lettres, history, mathematics, and philosophy) with religious studies. The secular aspects of the training were designed to develop the courtier as an elegant stylist, technician, and engineer who was competent in finance and public works, as well as a refined and graceful adornment to the court of his king; the religious aspects were a moral and spiritual initiation intended to provide the deeper qualities of soul essential for the successful pursuit of both a worldly career and otherworldly blessings. Whereas the arts served both religious and political purposes, the images and motifs employed in Islamic art avoided cosmological or mythical meanings. Sculpture was almost unknown; religious arts avoided the reproduction of human and animal figures. Islamic arts concentrated on purely visual or verbal demonstrations of richness, quality of craftsmanship, elaboration of invention, and compositional effects. The unifying element in Islamic art was the repetition of calligraphic motifs, arabesques, or geometric designs.

By avoiding cosmic myths and minimizing visual forms, Muslim artists created an art form that conformed to dominant Muslim theological and philosophical views of the universe as being without an overall pattern or causal interconnectedness. This world, created ex nihilo and maintained by continuous creation and recreation, is governed by God's will; its apparent regularity is not intrinsic in nature but is his bounty. This aspect accords with a human ideal. Moral and spiritual qualities do not correspond to the ontological order of the world but derive from the fulfillment of God's will as expressed in the teachings of the Quran and the tradition. A human life is a sequence of actions correctly performed according to the divine command. Islamic art and literature, then, cultivated for the glory of the court, the ruler, and the elite, were expressive of the universal aspects of Islamic religious culture. Whereas they intruded the claims of the ruler on Islamic religious sensibility, they were close enough to expressing that sensibility to be acceptable as an expression of the genius not only of regimes but of the whole civilization.

This flourishing Timurid society, carrying on earlier Turkic and Iranian institutions, would be the political, administrative, and cultural model for the later Ottoman, Safavid, Uzbek, and Mughal empires.

THE POST-'ABBASID CONCEPT OF THE STATE

Despite the numerous and short-lived provincial regimes, between 950 and 1500, a region-wide pattern of governmental institutions took shape. These institutions began with the late 'Abbasid practice of the caliphate, the use of slave military forces and *iqta'* forms of tax administration, and nomadic concepts of family and state authority. This new order first took shape in the eastern provinces of the former 'Abbasid Empire under the aegis of the Buwayhids, the Ghaznavids, and the early Saljuqs.

With the demise of the 'Abbasid Empire, a new concept of governmental authority was devised to accommodate changing political realities. Although the 'Abbasid dynasty continued in office until 1258, the caliphs no longer possessed exclusive political authority. Other rulers in Egypt, North Africa, and Spain claimed the caliphate's once-privileged title, and the caliphs lost effective military and administrative power. They retained, however, a role in judicial and religious affairs in that the caliph was considered the head of the religious establishment and could suspend the administration of justice and worship. The caliphs also retained an important moral authority and were able to intervene to temper the policies of the secular lords. Above all, they retained their symbolic standing as heads of the Muslim community; all provincial authorities were considered delegates of the caliphs.

At the same time, the conquerors and reigning warlords sought to establish an independent basis for their authority. The Buwayhids – whose power was based on the lifelong patronage of slaves in exchange for their loyal service and sworn oaths exchanged among warriors and officials – still sought to generate a public aura of legitimacy. They revived an ancient Iranian nomenclature including the title *Shah-en-shah* (King of Kings), adopted sonorous-sounding Muslim names, practiced ceremonies to display royal insignias such as the crown and the throne, and cultivated a mystique of kingship suggesting divine selection revealed in dreams, miracles, and prophecies. The Buwayhids fabricated genealogies that connected them to ancient Iranian kings and patronized public works, literature, and the arts as symbols of kingship. Similarly, the Ghaznavids sought recognition by the caliphs and implicitly assumed responsibility for the protection of Islam; they also glorified their reigns by the creation of splendid palace architecture and court ceremony and by the erection of magnificent mosques and minarets as a sign of their service to the faith, to society, and to civilization. Like their predecessors, the Saljuqs professed to be the appointees of the caliph, to serve Islam, and to support the institutions of religion. The first Saljuq ruler, Tughril Beg, adopted the title "sultan" to assert supreme and exclusive power, although the title eventually became the ordinary name for Middle Eastern rulers.

The division of authority and power between caliphs and sultans was uncertain. As long as Saljuq sultans were effective rulers, the caliphs had a limited political position. Whenever the reigning sultans were weak, however, the caliphs were tempted to assert their political authority in Baghdad and the surrounding regions. Sultans, although dependent on caliphs for recognition of their legitimate rule, sought religious prestige through the patronage of Islamic religious life and through claims, in the Iranian fashion, to hold their authority and responsibility for the protection of their subjects directly from God. Thus, in the course of the post-'Abbasid era, the Islamic aspect of political authority increasingly came to the fore. Appointment by the caliph was considered essential to legitimacy. Responsibility for Islamic institutions became the main justification of political authority, although ancient Iranian and Turkish concepts of rulership did not disappear.

CHAPTER 21

MUSLIM COMMUNITIES AND MIDDLE EASTERN SOCIETIES: 1000–1500 CE

In this period we have more abundant source materials on the community life not only of Baghdad but of many Middle Eastern cities. In this era, the town populations included four main strata: the military elites and their administrative adjuncts, as well as the notability defined by religious learning connected through family ties to the landowning, bureaucratic, and merchant elites; the common people – tradesmen, peddlers, craftsmen in both luxury and ordinary trades; and the lumpen proletariat, an underworld of illicit entertainers such as prostitutes, dancers, wine sellers, and cock fighters; and finally menial workers (especially in despised trades such as tanning, scavenging, and waste removal) and beggars, vagabonds, drifters, migrants, and refugees. These, however, were not amorphous masses. They were organized into a variety of communities, including families, quarters, markets, and religious associations.

WOMEN AND FAMILY: IDEOLOGY VERSUS REALITY
(CO-AUTHOR, LENA SALAYMEH)

In the early Islamic era (roughly from the seventh to the tenth centuries), our sources for women in society are meager. Chronicles and poetry primarily depict women in the caliphal court, but not in everyday life; legal sources communicate the expectations of jurists, rather than daily behavior. In the "medieval" era (roughly from the eleventh through the fifteenth centuries), although our sources are still limited, we can broadly reconstruct the lives of women as they function in the politics, economics, and social life of their communities. However, most of our sources come from Egypt and Syria and therefore do not represent the full geographic scope of medieval Islamic societies.

Our understanding, moreover, remains obstructed by two ideological positions: one is that of medieval, orthodox Muslim scholarly and moralist opinions; the other is that of contemporary Western stereotypes. These ideological views share the assumption that Muslim women are or should be secluded, passive persons (veiled or otherwise), restricted in their access to public life, and under the authority and control of men. Muslim scholars writing in the medieval period unwittingly reveal the counterreality; in their jeremiads about the decline of morality and their objections to the liveliness, assertiveness, and independence of women, they reveal women's normal activities and behaviors. The reality of women's lives in medieval Islamic societies was more varied and complex than the representations of either ideology.

The norms for and the behavior of women in the medieval period differ in time and place, according to religious affiliation, popular culture, and – above all – socioeconomic class. Contrary to popular assumptions, polygyny and seclusion of women were elite practices that do not reflect the daily lives of the vast majority of women in medieval Islamic societies. Whereas veiling was part of the public image of elite women in the medieval period, there is not much evidence of veiling by other socioeconomic classes. In all classes, financial independence – wealth acquired through inheritance, gifts, dowries, and investments, as well as salaries and wages for trading and working activities – allowed women to exercise political and social power, mobility, and independence. Many women divorced and remarried with relative ease and enjoyed a public social life interacting with men in mosques, markets, Sufi celebrations, cemeteries, and other public places.

Royal women

Royal women were housed in special quarters (*haram*). The occupants of the women's quarters included the caliph's or sultan's mother, wives, concubines, children (both sons and daughters), unmarried sisters, aunts, cousins, and their female slaves and servants. The widows of former rulers, the queen mother, and the wives (or concubines) of rulers had the highest status. Concubines served as musicians, singers, poetesses, and entertainers and often became romantic love objects. Based on their relationships to men and through palace conspiracies, royal women exercised political and economic power in matters of succession, appointments, and finances. Mothers, wives, and concubines sometimes received diplomatic and other official correspondence. In the Fatimid state, one particularly prominent woman, Sitt al-Mulk (d. 1023), had her own military guard, engaged in diplomatic negotiations with the Byzantine Empire, issued laws on tax matters, redistributed confiscated properties, and helped reform the state's finances. Strictly speaking, however, women needed the authorization of a male family member or high-ranking official for their political dealings.

Apart from the Fatimids in Egypt, there were many cases of royal women exercising political influence. Women attached to ʿAbbasid, Saljuq, and Mongol rule were similarly powerful. A woman reigned on behalf of the Fatimid caliphs in Yemen during the eleventh and twelfth centuries. Shajar ad-Durr, the Turkish widow of the Ayyubid ruler of Egypt, reigned briefly in her own name in 1250.

Royal women commanded great wealth. Mothers, wives, daughters, and concubines of caliphs and sultans received incomes from agricultural and commercial taxes. They acquired property by inheritance, dowries, gifts, and allowances. They accumulated rents from land and urban real estate, incomes from investments in trade, and material possessions such as jewelry and textiles. Rarely leaving the palace, women conducted their political and business affairs through proxies, whether husbands, male or female servants, or eunuchs. Their deputies and agents managed properties outside the palace walls. In both the Fatimid and Mamluk eras, unmarried daughters of the ruling family were particularly favored as depositaries for family wealth, perhaps because of their greater life expectancy and safety from political violence or as an inducement to remain unmarried and celibate so as to forestall disputes over succession to the throne. Astute personal servants of royal women could also become wealthy.

Royal women spent their money to establish political loyalties, to finance their administrative staffs, and to fund charitable institutions, usually through trusts (*awqaf*). They built and endowed palaces, mosques, schools/colleges, mausoleums, fountains, and baths. Women of scholarly and upper-middle-class families also endowed and managed charitable trusts. The same factors that favored their accumulation of wealth – youth and security – also favored their selection as the supervisors and administrators of endowed properties. In these positions, they were able to secure the futures of their children and the continuity of their families. They counteracted the inherent instability in military and political households. A woman who outlived the men of her generation became a dowager and de facto head of her family.

Women of urban notable families

Among urban notable families, polygyny and seclusion of women were expensive and rare. Notable women who appeared in public and at prayers most likely wore a covering over their heads and shoulders, but precisely what was covered or how is unclear. Nonroyal elite women were also able to accumulate and manage property, including revenues from lands, orchards, residential rents, and other investments. They acquired wealth in jewelry, textiles, gold and silver, and other movable property. They often endowed charitable institutions, some of whose administrators and beneficiaries could be family members. Trusts (*awqaf*) were an effective way to transfer incomes to children and unmarried daughters in particular. In urban notable families – especially the families of judges, scholars, and scribes – wives and daughters were commonly educated. Male relatives, informal women's study circles, and private lessons in the mosques all taught women to read and write and to memorize Quran, hadith, and important legal texts. Many women are included in the biographical dictionaries as transmitters of hadith, reciters of poetry, or calligraphers. Few were jurisconsults or theologians and virtually none were judges, teachers, or students in the formal colleges where they might exert authority over men. Still, women did teach and learn in informal settings.

Women also had an independent religious life in women's Sufi orders. Women conducted female-only Sufi sessions and participated in Sufi festivals. The Muslim equivalent of convents (*ribats*) housed Sufi women and were found throughout Syria and Iraq in the twelfth and thirteenth centuries. It is unclear if Sufi women were primarily from the notable or working classes. Women's participation in scholarly activities and Sufi orders appears to have decreased after the sixteenth century, as reflected in their absence from late medieval biographical dictionaries.

Working women and popular culture

Unlike royal and notable women, working-class women were generally not secluded, and it is not clear when or if they were veiled. Women patronized markets regularly as both consumers and suppliers. Working-class women often facilitated the seclusion of upper-class women, who relied on delivery women to transport goods between the women's quarters and the markets. Women traders visited women in their homes to sell various household goods, beauty products, and fabrics. Middle- and lower-class women worked in agriculture and food preparation and sales. Perhaps the most common profession of working women was spinning and weaving. Women served as doctors, midwives, and nurses. Undertakers, washers of female corpses, official mourners, bath attendants, and hairdressers were exclusively women. Women entertainers performed in both private and public spaces. Prostitutes operated in market areas. As a result of their economic activities and inheritance rights, women often functioned as moneylenders to husbands, other family members, and business associates.

Working women primarily educated one another – in apprenticeships (for nursing, embroidery, funeral rites, hairdressing, etc.) and religious learning (recitation of Quran and hadith). Working women also learned in the company of men in mosques or private homes, where they jointly listened to recitations of books or sermons.

Studies of marriage and divorce in Cairo, Damascus, and Jerusalem in the Mamluk era (1250–1517) indicate that women were often financially independent because they earned their own livelihoods and received dowries and other gifts of parental property. These gifts were effectively a premortem distribution of jewelry, household furnishings, and clothing to daughters that remained a woman's personal property throughout marriage and after. Women's wages and property were the key to a high degree of independence and mobility. In Mamluk-era society, repeated divorces and remarriages were the norm, with an estimated 30 percent of marriages ending in divorce. Thus, instead of patriarchal families, we find a highly individualized society in which marital relations were independent of clan relations; a highly monetary society in which women could earn a living and own property; a mobile society in which divorce, migration, and remarriage were common; and even an equalitarian society in terms of marital bargaining.

The material and social situation of women points to a popular culture – although frequently denounced by juristic and moralistic writers – in which women were lively, expressive, emotional, and fun loving, and sometimes defiant of male attempts to curtail their independence. Women used a variety of economically based strategies to stake out their independence; if husbands attempted to restrain them, they could resort to threats of costly divorce or deny them sex.

Women had frequent occasions to socialize with other women (and men) when visiting, celebrating weddings and childbirths, mourning at funerals, and participating in Sufi festivals. Some quasi-public spaces were frequented or dominated by women. In bathhouses, women socialized and competed – in terms of beauty, clothing, and jewelry – with one another. In medieval Cairo, plump women were highly regarded, and some women even refrained from fasting to avoid becoming thin and thereby losing potential suitors; sometimes they showed off their figures in form-fitting clothing.

Women celebrated religious events and other occasions with merriment and music. Weddings were loud, boisterous celebrations that could include music, dancing, singing, and wine drinking in gatherings of men and women – at least some of whom were likely unveiled. At weddings, women trilled cries of joy, clapped, danced, and sang to the accompaniment of tambourines. The birth of a baby was celebrated with music, dancing, and sweets – distributed among family and neighbors. Women mourned the dead in public expressions that had been normative in the region for centuries (as evidenced in Jewish texts): disheveling their hair, blackening their faces and bodies, and wailing. To commemorate the martyrdom of Husayn (on the day of *'ashura'*), they purchased and burned incense. Sufi *mawlids* were the occasion of lively festivities in which men and women mingled in the streets and cemeteries. Women, unveiled, greeted the Sufi celebrants with ululations and gifts of food. Men and women danced to the Sufi chants and songs. Thus, women interacted with men in markets and shops, in mosques and shrines, in visits to the cemeteries, and in Sufi ceremonies.

Muslim and non-Muslim women interacted freely and regularly throughout the medieval period and shared similar norms for social behavior. Elite Christian and Jewish women were secluded in the manner of their elite Muslim counterparts. Geniza documents suggest that elite Jewish women went veiled and accepted the same ideas of modesty as elite Muslim women. (Jews adopted Islamic dress wherever possible and permitted.) But non-elite Jewish women, like Muslim women of their social class, worked as spinners and embroiderers, traders, midwives and nurses, and body washers. They frequented markets, bathhouses, synagogues, shrines, and courts.

This behavior of women was criticized by religious scholars as too "free." A surviving text from one particular scholar is replete with criticisms of women's activities. Ibn al-Hajj, a Maliki jurist who lived in Cairo in the fourteenth century, objected to the weekly routines of visiting shrines and going to markets without compelling reasons. He opposed women's visits to cemeteries and participation in Christian festivals, another occasion for purchasing jewelry and perfumes. He was appalled by women who wore tight and short chemises and trousers below the navel instead of form-concealing clothing. This scholar frowned on the emotional commemoration of marriage, of the birth of a child, or of the death of a family member, as well as funerals and festivals that brought women and men together. In his view, men were as much to blame as women, because they were responsible for controlling the behavior of women and appeared indifferent to intermingling. The real mores of both men and women did not correspond to orthodox or moralist expectations. (Yet, the very same scholars who advocated for women's seclusion did not question or neglect to use hadith transmitted or reported by women; nor did they deny the validity of a woman's testimony in court.)

Restrictions on women's daily lives came not only from jurists but from rulers. In the early eleventh century, the Fatimid Caliph al-Hakim promulgated a variety of restrictions on women's movement and behavior; these regulations may have been motivated by contemporaneous crises of plague, famine, and drought. Al-Hakim's decrees prohibited women from unveiling, going out in the evening, going to cemeteries, gathering at the Nile's shores, or boating with men. Caliph al-Hakim's regulations attempted to curtail women's visits to cemeteries, bathhouses, and markets. These restrictions most likely affected middle-class women, because upper-class women rarely went out, due to their status and the availability of servants and agents, and because lower-class, working women could obtain exemptions from the restrictions. When al-Hakim's half-sister, Sitt al-Mulk, became regent, she overruled her half-brother's legislation and permitted wine drinking, musical entertainment, and the unrestricted mobility of women.

Jurisprudence and courts

Contrary to the stereotype that the law was resolutely biased in favor of men, Islamic legal systems provided a variety of norms that could be manipulated to the advantage of either men or women. For example, both Sunni and Shi'i schools of law differed considerably in their norms for family relations. Although Malikis insisted on a guardian for a first marriage, Hanafis and Imami Shi'is allowed women to marry independently. In contrast to the other Sunni legal schools, Hanafis gave women broad discretion in marriage contract stipulations (including preventing spouses from contracting multiple marriages). Although most schools provided little leeway for annulment, Malikis allowed it for desertion, nonmaintenance, bodily harm, or impotence. Medieval jurists affirmed a man's obligation to satisfy a wife's sexual desires. Fatimid-era legal practice, based on Isma'ili jurisprudence, allowed daughters (without brothers) to fully inherit, including inheriting land; unlike Imami (Ja'fari) law, Isma'ili jurists outlawed temporary marriages and invalidated a contractual clause giving the wife the right to demand a divorce. Most Hanafi jurists did not permit women to frequent mosques, but Hanbalis generally did, and Malikis and Shafiʿis fell in between. There were few legal restrictions to abortions in this period. (These few examples only offer a glimpse of a complex and diverse legal situation for women living in various medieval Islamic societies.)

In economic terms, medieval Muslim jurists gave great advantages to women, more so than other Mediterranean and Middle Eastern legal systems. The contractual nature of marriage defined a spousal relationship in monetary terms that were favorable to women. A husband was obliged to feed, clothe, and house his wife; pay for domestic expenses; and also make a marriage gift that could be paid in yearly installments. Furthermore, medieval Muslim jurists maintained earlier Islamic legal traditions in respecting a woman's right to own and manage her property without male guardianship. A married woman kept both title and control of her property; she could gift or bequeath it to whom she wished. It did not become the property of her husband or community property. Women also had the resources of family and women's networks to support them.

Furthermore, although jurists granted men greater rights to divorce, they were limited by legal ramifications. Divorce was generally expensive, because it entailed payment of any uncompensated expenses, delayed dower, three months of alimony for the wife, child support, nursing fees, and any debts owed to the wife (which were not uncommon). In many medieval Islamic areas, the unpaid balance of the dower was considered a debt due on demand. In the fifteenth century, for example, a husband might well owe his wife a daily cash allowance, an annual installment of the marriage gift, and even rent – if he were living in her house. As a result, men often chose not to exercise their right to unilateral divorce, and women (despite limited legal rights to demand a divorce) commonly had the financial assets to buy out their husbands or to compel them to agree to a divorce. (This is known as *khulʿ*.) Still, most divorces were consensual and were informally negotiated or mediated by in-laws, kin, or neighbors.

Women had just as much access to courts as men, because the law recognized women as full legal persons and because women had economic power that translated into legal autonomy. Women were both plaintiffs and defendants in an array of cases related to contractual disputes, marriage, divorce, and alimony. Women used courts to procure a variety of marital advantages: opportunities for divorces and annulments, control of dowers, custody of children, and restriction of a husband's right to take another wife. Women also frequented courts to challenge any attempted limitations on their inheritances or to manage their property or other economic interests. Courts often appointed a woman as trustee for an orphan's inheritance. Women owned substantial amounts of urban property and were important contributors to educational and charitable trusts. Trusts (*awqaf*) were in effect an alternative to the patrilineal inheritance rules outlined in Islamic legal texts and thereby promoted matrilineal inheritance. In some medieval cities, more endowments were established or managed by women than by men.

Thus, married couples possessed separate economic assets, and both men and women had access to divorce and to multiple marriages. In medieval Muslim societies, all individuals engaged their extended family networks to assist them in protecting their economic or legal interests, as well as to mediate domestic disputes. Customary practices or social norms, however, could act as limitations on women even in the absence of any Islamic legal basis. For example, social norms that dictated the seclusion of elite women limited their access to the courts. Also, women's inheritance or control of property could be curtailed if they were forced to relinquish their legal rights because of social pressure or non-Islamic customary practices.

Thus, the status of women and their real-life situations in the medieval era differed greatly from the expectations embedded in Islamic legal texts, from pious moral literature, and from common contemporary Western expectations about the place of women in Islamic societies. Women in royal households, women in wealthy and educated middle-class households, and working women lived by different norms. Whether they were Muslim, Christian, or Jewish, women lived similar lives depending on their socioeconomic class. Muslim women enjoyed economic rights and powers that gave them a measure of independence and mobility and opportunities to engage in the social and economic world. Working-class women in particular lived by cultural norms and practices that gave them opportunities to socialize with men as well as other women. Scholarly Muslim cultural and religious attitudes about the relations of men and women were incongruent with the complex socioeconomic and political forces that generated alternative cultural values.

URBAN SOCIETIES: THE QUARTERS AND THE MARKETS

Towns and cities were divided into neighborhoods typically defined by religious or ethnic minorities, actual or presumed common ancestry, or village origins. The clienteles of notable families (business or professional staff members, servants, and workers) and certain crafts (especially in peripheral quarters, where tanning or other noxious industries were concentrated) were also the bases of quarter communities.

Quarters not only had a recognizable social base but were also administrative, tax, and police units. A *shaykh* or headman, appointed by the town governor, was responsible for maintaining discipline, representing the quarters to the military regimes, and conveying their orders to the people. Quarters were often political units in that they could be engaged in feuds or hostilities with other groups. In Syria, for example, these rivalries went under the names of the seventh-century tribal moieties, Qays and Yemen. In Iran, they were typically organized in the name of the schools of law, Shafi'is and Hanafis. Thus, a quarter was a small, fairly integrated community based on family, religious, or ethnic solidarity and economic and political functions. Quarters were village-scale communities, typically physically distinct but not necessarily walled, gated, or barred to the rest of the city.

Although the quarters had local markets, there were also extensive central markets, bazaars, or *suqs*; these were physically organized by trade or craft, but they were not socially or politically highly organized. The markets were under the supervision of the governor's police (*shurta*) and the market and morals inspector (*muhtasib*). Market inspectors were appointed by military governors to keep discipline and enforce regulations in the markets. They supervised the coinage and the standardization of weights and measures. They were responsible for maintaining the streets, supplying water, and providing a night watch. Gradually, religious and moral duties were added to their portfolio; market inspectors became responsible for preventing illicit meetings of men and women and for investigating extremism, heresy, and political sedition. Their authority over the market populations was mediated by the leaders of the crafts and trades, but there is little evidence to suggest that there were guilds, unions, mutual benefit associations, or religious confraternities based on trade or craft.

Another important locus of community organization (besides the quarters and markets) was young men's fraternities and gangs, variously called *ahdath*, *'ayyarun*, or *zu'ar*. The term "*ahdath*" was sometimes applied to the gangs allied with a quarter or faction, whereas the term "*'ayyarun*" seems to have applied more generally to gangs under their own leadership. Some of these gangs were devoted to an ideology of chivalry, bravery, and honor (*futuwwa*). Some were gymnastic or sporting associations. Some were constituted by the young men of the quarters recruited from the working population. There were also organized gangs of beggars, vagabonds, and menial workers – sometimes in the guise of Sufi orders.

These clubs and gangs were largely autonomous and played a complicated and ambivalent role in city life. They would from time to time defend their quarters against abusive taxation, fight the gangs of other quarters, and resist military regime control. But they also served as strong-arm men for local notables, quarters, or religious sects and acted as "mafias," running protection rackets and other criminal activities. Sometimes they served as military auxiliaries for as well as against the government. The gangs were particularly powerful in interregnums between military regimes. In Baghdad just before the consolidations of the Buwayhid and later of the Saljuq regimes, lower-class elements took over policing and some taxation and collected tolls and protection money from merchants. Standing between the regimes and the urban populations, they had an important political and military role.

The learned and scholarly elites (*'ulama'*) were a particularly important stratum of the populations. They were important in worship and education – as prayer leaders, scholars, and mosque functionaries. They were managers of educational, religious, philanthropic, and legal institutions. They were judges, lawyers, legal witnesses, and registrars central to family, commerce, and property. They organized clienteles of students and lesser functionaries; judges were surrounded by a clientele of deputies, witnesses, orderlies, clerks, and agents. They represented the people of the quarters and the markets. Especially in times of trouble, the people turned to the judges, the scholars, and the merchants and landowners for leadership.

The notables, however, were unable to govern the cities by themselves. They did not have military power, they did not control rural resources, and they did not have the capital to sustain their own cadres and to provide for big urban infrastructure investments – such as walls, canals, mosques and colleges, caravanserais, and shops; for these, they depended on the military elites. Reciprocally, the military did not have the local knowledge, administrative cadres, and legitimacy to govern directly.

Although the local units of society remained the same in the centuries following the collapse of the ʿAbbasid Empire, a new political elite of nomadic and slave warlords – and the ruin of local landowners and other notables – paved the way for far-reaching changes in the organization of town and village communities. The crucial change in this period was the widespread diffusion of Muslim identities, the assumption of social leadership by Muslim teachers and holy men, and the crystallization of Muslim sectarian communities, including Shiʿi sects, Sunni schools of law and theology, and Sufi orders.

The creation of an Islamic communal and religious identity (distinct from the caliphate) had already begun in the seventh century. In his ideal and early form, the caliph was the sole ruler of a single community and custodian of both its religious principles and its political interests. From the outset, however, pious believers were disenchanted with the worldliness of the early caliphate. This disenchantment first expressed itself in the form of the Khariji, Shiʿi, and ʿAbbasid movements, which aimed to return the caliphate to its ideal incumbents.

With the victory of the ʿAbbasids, and the defeat of both Khariji and Shiʿi aspirations, the political opponents of the caliphate evolved into religious sects. Bitter rivalries among them and strong state support for both Shiʿi and Sunni movements hastened their diffusion. Popular religious organizations that had their origin in an earlier period became normative and universal throughout the region. In the same period, masses of Middle Eastern peoples converted to Islam and were absorbed into Muslim social bodies. Islam, originally the religion of a political and urban elite, became the religion and social identity of most Middle Eastern peoples.

RELIGIOUS COMMUNITIES

Shiʿis

Shiʿis are the earliest example of a new form of sectarian community. Early Shiʿis were divided into different groups, depending on their theory of the true succession of imams. One of these was the Baghdadi Twelver community, which believed in the imamate of Ja'far's son Musa al-Kazim and his descendants; another was the believers in the imamate of Ja'far's son Isma'il and his descendants. From the time of Ja'far, the Baghdadi community denied in theory, but accepted in practice, the reign of the 'Abbasid caliphs and concentrated more and more on religious teaching. In 873, however, the last of its living imams, the twelfth in line of succession, "disappeared," and in 941 direct communication with the imam was lost altogether.

In place of the presence of a divinely guided leader, Twelver teaching in hadith, law, and theology was consolidated. Al-Kulayni (d. 940) compiled the earliest surviving compilation of Shi'i hadith, ritual, and law. Later scholars debated whether their beliefs were based solely on the teachings of the imams or whether *ijtihad*, the exercise of individual judgment in matters of law, was permissible. The concept of the imam was reformulated in neo-Platonic and gnostic terms, and he came to be understood as an emanation of the divine being, the universal intelligence (*'aql al-kull*), and thus a bearer of direct knowledge of the secret truths and states of spirituality that lead to the reunion of the soul of man with God.

At the same time, Baghdadi Shi'is organized a new communal life. In the late tenth century, they began a day of celebration for Muhammad's adoption of 'Ali as his successor (*ghadir khumm*), the public ritual cursing of Mu'awiya (the enemy of 'Ali), a public holiday of mourning for the death of Husayn at Karbala (*'ashura'*), and pilgrimages to the tombs of 'Ali at Najaf, Husayn at Karbala, and 'Ali al-Rida at Mashhad. The passionate mourning for Husayn, identification with the suffering of the martyr, and the messianic hopes implicit in the commemoration of Karbala gave emotional and religious depth to Twelver Shi'ism.

By the mid-eleventh century, Imami Shi'is had created a worldly life lived in perpetual expectation of the world to come. In permanent opposition to the established political regimes, Imamism had become a religion of salvation. This salvation might be attained by living in accordance with the hadith of the Prophet and the imams, by emotional absorption into their martyrdom, or by gnostic vision and mystical identification with the emanations of the divine being. With the consolidation of their doctrinal beliefs in written form, the development of a public ritual life, and political recognition by the reigning authorities, the Baghdadi Shi'is emerged as a sectarian community within the body of Islam.

Schools of law

The consolidation of the Baghdadi Shi'i community and the success of the Isma'ili missions stimulated Sunni scholars to further institutionalize their practice of Islam and to make their schools of law, theology, and Sufism the focus of community affairs. Legal circles began to organize in the late seventh century as groups of scholars committed to a common legal doctrine and method of legal analysis. There were innumerable legal circles and networks in the early centuries of Islam, but by the eleventh century most of them had disappeared, and most jurists became identified with one of the four now-surviving legal schools: Hanafi, Shafi'i, Hanbali, and Maliki. The consolidation of the jurisprudential schools was favored both by the appeal of their teaching and doctrines and by the support of the caliphate and other governments that oversaw the appointment of judges and the distribution of patronage to favored schools. Eventually, the Mamluks of Egypt appointed a chief judge for each of the four main Sunni legal schools.

From their beginnings in Medina, Basra, Baghdad, and Fustat, the four surviving schools spread throughout the 'Abbasid realm. The travels of scholars and students in search of hadith and the appointment of judges with law school affiliations introduced the schools into new provinces. The Hanafi school began in Iraq and was soon established in western Iran and Transoxania. The Hanbali school, Baghdadi in origin, spread to northern Iraq and Syria. Hanbali judges (*qadis*) were appointed in Damascus and Homs; Hanbalism also had followers in the important cities of Iran. The Shafi'i school first developed in Egypt but, by the tenth century, was established in Syria, Baghdad, and in all of the important towns of western Iran, Khurasan, and Transoxania. The Maliki school was concentrated primarily in Egypt and North Africa. In twelfth-century Baghdad, Hanafis dominated as judges, Shafi'is as "professors" in the colleges, and Hanbalis as preachers and teachers in the larger mosques of the city. There were also jurists who identified with the Maliki and Zahiri legal schools in medieval Baghdad, but they were marginal.

The schools were united by the travels of students, who came to study with great masters and to obtain certificates certifying their achievements. Having acquired a wide range of learning from different teachers, a successful student would sometimes settle down with a single professor and, in time, perhaps succeed him. This international system of connections was informal but was sufficient to generate a jurisprudential identity for each of the major schools. Identification with a particular legal school, however, was not necessarily exclusive. Law students studied with scholars outside their own legal school – particularly on the topic of hadith transmission – and freely switched legal school affiliation. Some jurists shifted their legal school affiliation in order to procure administrative or judicial appointments.

Muslim theological schools also acquired a coherent social identity. Although they did not have judicial and administrative functions, the Mu'tazilis and Ash'aris became important religious movements. The Karrami movement, which combined theological tenets and Sufi practices, appealing mainly to the lower classes, was influential in Khurasan, Transoxania, and Afghanistan.

In the course of the tenth and eleventh centuries, professional law schools were increasingly established. Islamic law was initially taught in mosques and private homes, which were then converted into hostels for traveling scholars and students. In Khurasan, this was the prototype for the madrasa, or college of legal studies. In Baghdad, the college was organized by combining the mosque in which the teaching was carried out, the *khan* or boarding house for students, private libraries, and the practice of community financial support. A madrasa then was a building used for study and a residence for teachers and students, commonly provided with a library. As buildings, madrasas were used for teaching, prayer, public fountains, tombs, libraries, and dormitories for teachers and students.

Furthermore, the colleges were also endowed with permanent sources of income, such as land or rent-bearing urban property, set aside in perpetuity. These trusts (*awqaf*) paid the salaries of the faculty and stipends for students. Endowments usually paid for a staff of religious functionaries, a maintenance staff (gatekeepers, carpet sweepers, candle maintainers, etc.), and an administrative staff. By giving such gifts, donors could preserve their property intact against fragmentation due to inheritance laws. Trusts also protected the wealth of mamluks, officials, or merchants from confiscation, allowing them to appoint their heirs, associates, or clients to an income and garnering social prestige. A trust could even be used to circumvent Islamic inheritance laws by providing an income for daughters. It also provided a tomb for the grantor.

The curriculum of colleges was determined by the professor and was therefore variable. Most were academies of law, teaching the particular version of the professor's own legal school. Although law was the master science, the schools taught what the teacher wanted to teach. All subjects – law, medicine, philosophy, and hadith – were transmitted from a single teacher to a single student (or to many students simultaneously). Colleges also commonly taught the related subjects of Quran, hadith, and Arabic grammar; some professors taught theology or Sufism. A broad education garnered from many teachers rather than specialized learning was the ideal. The madrasa was not a college in the modern sense, because it lacked a graded curriculum or a uniform system for certification. Islamic education was basically informal, flexible, and built on the individual teacher and student, rather than institutional ties. A student "heard" his subjects from a variety of teachers on a variety of topics in a variety of places and study circles.

Thus, the transmission of religious learning went on both in endowed colleges, madrasas, and in informal study circles. In both cases, learning revolved around the reputation of a respected scholar, who in his individual capacity could give students who "graduated" a specific license to teach, to transmit hadith, to judge, or to participate in scholarly debates, depending on the course of study.

The relationship of teacher and student was intensely personal, for the master communicated not only specialized learning but religious insight and a stylized mode of behavior that signified the rank of scholar. In that relationship, the teacher's authority was absolute, like that of a parent over a child or a Sufi master over a disciple. Through this scholarly devotion, a student acquired knowledge (*'ilm*), literary cultivation (*adab*), blessing (*baraka*), a set of ritual and performative practices, and a style and presence that signified honor, dignity, and blessing. The true object of education was not merely knowledge but the whole style of personal behavior and deportment. The personal relationship between master and disciple, which could be traced generation by generation back to the Prophet himself, was the primary vehicle for the communication of Islamic traditions.

Teaching was not separate from other religious activities, because study was considered an act of piety. What mattered was the creation of a spiritual environment for Islamic faith, teaching, and practice. Thus, we even find colleges whose endowments provided for prayer leaders, muezzins, Sufis, and Quran and hadith readers, but not for teachers and students. In all cases, there was an intense consciousness of the importance of training Sunni Muslim scholars to combat Shi'ism and Isma'ilism. Madrasas were not only colleges but centers for religious propaganda and political action.

Education extended far beyond colleges. Teaching went on in public mosques and in private homes, without endowments; students could come to a madrasa without being a resident or receiving a stipend. Women studied with relatives but also received certification from outside scholars, including women scholars. Women most commonly transmitted hadith. Teachers, hadith and Quran reciters, book readers, and storytellers reached out to the common people.

In sum, medieval colleges consolidated informal legal instruction into an institution with a physical center and permanently endowed funds, thereby facilitating professional full-time study of Islamic law and the expanded training of cadres of Islamic legal teachers and administrators. It became the standard Sunni Muslim organization of religious and legal instruction, spreading from Iran throughout Samanid and Ghaznavid domains and then westward with the Saljuq conquests. Nizam al-Mulk, the leading minister of the early Saljuq period (1063–92), endowed Hanafi and Shafi'i schools in all the major cities of the empire and made it the state's policy to support organized Muslim religious scholarship. The Hanbalis adopted the madrasa form of instruction early in the twelfth century. In earlier centuries, jurists typically had earned their living through trade or craft work, but with the institutionalization of education in the form of endowed colleges, religious scholars became professionals, officials, and salaried employees. Through state patronage, salaries, and the administration of endowments, scholars rose to the position of a rentier class.

Coinciding with the rise of official colleges and the consolidation of the schools of law was an increase in the importance of the jurisconsult (mufti). The earliest surviving collections of a jurisconsult's opinions (*fatawa*) date to the tenth century. The general public consulted a jurisconsult in much the same manner that we now consult attorneys for legal advice; indeed, some even "shopped" for a legal decree (*fatwa*), asking several jurisconsults until they found a desired outcome. A legal decree consisted of both the question sent in writing to the jurisconsult and his answer. In addition, judges often consulted with jurisconsults for their expertise in complicated cases, as evidenced by the inclusion of a jurisconsult's legal decree within the court register. Although generally jurisconsults were not affiliated with

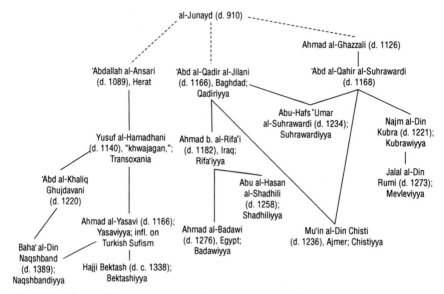

Illustration 6. An old woman petitions Sultan Sanjar. Source: The Metropolitan Museum of Art, Gift of Alexander Smith Cochran, 1913. 13.228.7 fol.17.

or regulated by the state, the Mamluks did appoint some jurisconsults to courts of equity. In the eleventh century, jurists defined a jurisconsult as being a *mujtahid* (i.e., one who has the ability to independently reason; the highest rank of a jurist). By the middle of the thirteenth century, however, it appears that the prerequisites were lowered, and jurisconsults were expected – by most, but not all scholars – to be *muqallids* (i.e., able to articulate a legal opinion based on the precedents and methodology of a particular legal school; a lower rank than *mujtahid*). Under the Mamluks, jurisconsults were appointed to special courts of equity.

A judge (*qadi*) was responsible for the administration of the courts and therefore selected both his own court recorders and witness certifiers (responsible for evaluating the reliability of witnesses). Judges were also involved in managing charitable endowments and, sometimes, managing the assets of orphans. There was no equivalent to attorney representation, because plaintiffs and defendants interacted directly with the judge. Although court recorders wrote down case proceedings, these documents were not effectively preserved, and Islamic court records are largely lost for periods before the sixteenth century. One exception is a significant repository of fourteenth-century Mamluk court documents that were found in Jerusalem's Islamic museum.

In addition to the formal court system, there were other judicial or quasi-judicial authorities. As early as the ʿAbbasid Caliph al-Mahdi, if not earlier, caliphs and sultans heard complaints or petitions in courts of equity (*mazalim*). (See Illustration 6.) Market inspectors enforced commercial regulations and morally proper behavior in the marketplace. A genre of legal literature (*hisba*) emerged that reflected juristic attempts to delineate the duties and limitations of a market inspector. It is likely that market inspectors gained more discretion to regulate public behavior as a result of the growing social influence of legal schools.

Thus, the medieval period was a time of bureaucratization and centralization that shaped the legal profession. All aspects of legal activity became confined to fewer legal schools that gained in power and prominence. Professionalization of jurists and institutionalization of learning contributed to the growing dominance of a religious orthodoxy. The diversity of opinions on a variety of legal and theological matters gradually became narrower and, after the tenth century, came to form a religious canon. As legal education became more systematized and salaries of judges increased, the legal profession most likely attracted students drawn to the pragmatic – rather than spiritual – aspects of the vocation of law.

As law schools (*madhahib*) consolidated, they also became popular religious movements. Initially, each legal school was built around a core of scholars, judges, students, court functionaries, wealthy patrons, and local followers. Progressively, the leadership of the law schools was extended to the masses, beginning with charitable, educational, and judicial services and carrying on to informal social and political leadership.

Hanbalis were the first to convert informal, popular influence and sympathy into a sectarian movement. They resisted the efforts of the ʿAbbasid caliphate to promulgate religious doctrine. They opposed al-Maʾmun's claims to authority and held that while obedience was due to the caliph in matters of state, authority in religion rested with the scholars of Quran and hadith. Preaching to their followers among former ʿAbbasid soldiers and residents of the Harbiyya quarter of Baghdad, the scholars mobilized popular support. Throughout the ninth and tenth centuries, Hanbali preachers raised popular demonstrations for or against caliphal policy; they led anti-Shiʿi riots and opposed the Muʿtazili and Ashʿari theological schools. They organized groups of vigilantes, who attacked their opponents and suppressed such immoral activities as wine drinking and prostitution.

Under the Buwayhids, Shiʿis – perhaps in response to Hanbali activism – introduced the festivals of *ghadir khumm* and *ʿashura*, and Sunnis responded by celebrating the nomination of Abu Bakr to the caliphate, the reigns of the Rashidun caliphs and Muʿawiya, and other symbols of Sunni identity. Preachers and religious storytellers provided incitements. Festivals, processions, and demonstrations led in the tenth and eleventh centuries to riots and street battles between Sunnis and Shiʿis. Baghdad was frequently in turmoil because of battles between religious factions.

In eastern Iran, the schools of law also turned into popular factions. In the tenth and eleventh centuries, Hanafis, Shafiʿis, Karramis, and Ismaʿilis struggled for local political power. The schools had become exclusive and mutually hostile small communities. In this guise, they resembled the neighborhood, lineage, or other parochial bodies into which Middle Eastern towns had always been divided. Religious creed now superseded tribal or quarter identifications.

The history of Nishapur in the eleventh and twelfth centuries is the best-known example of the law schools as factions. Here, the Hanafi school was built around leading merchant, official, and scholarly families who controlled the judiciary of the city, important *waqf* revenues, colleges, and mosques. Their main opponents were the Shafi'is, who controlled most of the teaching positions in the colleges and the revenues of important endowments. The Shafi'i following, however, was broader than the Hanafi, because the Shafi'is were united with Ash'aris and Sufis and seemed to enjoy mass support. The antagonism of the two schools of law spread from disputes over control of teaching and judicial positions, to competition for governmental support, and to pitched battles in which large segments of the town and the surrounding rural populace were mobilized to fight for their group. As a result, Nishapur was physically and socially destroyed by the middle of the twelfth century. These conflicts were not simply disputes about legal reasoning but rather conflicts over theological and political issues. After this crisis, intraurban conflicts seem to have abated.

In many of these cases, however, the label "schools of law" obscures the fact that the common people gave their allegiance not to the abstract school but to local pious, charismatic teachers and *shaykhs*. From studies of Palestine in the twelfth and thirteenth centuries, we see how Hanbali *shaykhs* became leaders of small communities and watched over the well-being of their villages. They protected them from enemies, gave aid to the sick and the poor, and mediated between their villages, other communities, and the military authorities. They taught orthodox practice of Islam, including adherence to the five pillars and the norms of ritual and social behavior. They were avatars of altruism and generosity and embodied the practical spirituality of Sufi attitudes, if not of Sufi doctrine. The schools of law came to the people in the guise of pious teachers and leaders.

Sufis

The development of the Sufi movement paralleled the development of the schools of law. From the tenth to the fourteenth centuries, Sufis worked out their mystical practice and metaphysics, integrated their thought and practice with other forms of Islamic belief and worship, and became a social movement. (See Figure 7.)

Sufism was highly individual. Sufis met in private houses, initially, and then later in Sufi meeting houses. On the model of *ribats* – which were originally residences for Muslim warriors scattered along the frontiers of the Byzantine Empire in North Africa and the frontiers of eastern Iran – meetinghouses were founded at Abadan, Damascus, and Ramla in the course of the eighth century. In imitation of Christian monks, there were grottoes in Khurasan.

The term *"khanaqa"* appeared in the late ninth century and came to be widely used for Sufi residences in Khurasan and Transoxania. The word was applied

Figure 7. The early Sufi orders and their founders.

to residences for migrant individuals without a shared affiliation to a particular master. The *khanaqa* was adapted to more sectarian purposes by the mystic and theologian Muhammad b. Karram (d. 869), a student of hadith and an ascetic preacher in southern and eastern Iran. He taught a God-fearing way of life based on mortification of the flesh and pious devotion to God's will and a theological doctrine emphasizing an anthropomorphic view of God – interpreting literally the Quranic usages that suggest that God has substance and a body. Ibn Karram won a large lower-class following in Transoxania, Afghanistan, and eastern Iran, where he built *khanaqas* as centers of missionary activity.

Other Sufi masters followed his example. Shaykh Abu Ishaq Ibrahim al-Kazaruni (d. 1033) cultivated a large following in his home district in western Iran and converted numerous Zoroastrians and Jews to Islam. His warriors also fought on the Byzantine frontier. They built some sixty-five *khanaqas* in southwestern Iran as centers for teaching and missionary activity and as places to distribute charity to the poor. His near contemporary Abu Saʿid b. Abi Khayr (d. 1049), who was born and died in the region of Nishapur, was the first Sufi master to set up rules for worship and a code of behavior to regulate the communal life of the *khanaqa*. By the end of the eleventh century, in addition to their devotional, instructional, and missionary functions, the *khanaqas* came to be used as tombs for venerated Sufi masters and sites of pilgrimage for ordinary believers.

From the tenth to the thirteenth centuries, important changes in Sufi concepts reinforced the trend toward organized groups. A developing concept of the relations between masters and disciples paved the way for a more formal type of organization. In the ninth and tenth centuries, a Sufi novice was understood to be a student who took lessons from his master. By the eleventh century, he was a disciple who owed total obedience to his master, just as any man owes obedience to God. By then, the master was considered not only a teacher but a healer of souls and a repository of God's blessing. These new and deeper bonds were the basis of a more lasting loyalty of disciple to master and of the perpetuation of the authority of miraculous teachers over the generations.

New forms of Sufi ceremony emerged to symbolize the new relationships. In the earlier era, a student received an *ijaza*, or license to teach the subject he had learned from his master. In the new era, the *khirqa*, or cloak of the master, was conferred on him, and ceremonies of initiation were instituted to induct disciples of the same master into shared vigils, litanies, devotions, and other forms of worship. With the elaboration of the master's authority, the spiritual genealogy of masters and disciples also became important. In the course of the twelfth and thirteenth centuries, chains of authority (*silsila*) reaching from the present masters across the generations to ʿAli and to the Prophet were formulated. The authority of Sufi teaching in any given generation was guaranteed by a chain of contacts that connected the present to the Prophet. Initiation into Sufism bore with it a spiritual power derived directly from the original revelation of Islam.

The beginnings of Sufi orders are shadowy, but we may surmise that they coalesced in the thirteenth and fourteenth centuries among disciples of the great twelfth- and thirteenth-century masters. These Sufis attributed their practices and doctrine to famous earlier *shaykhs* or originating masters, who were recognized as the transmitters of Sufi teaching and the founders of later Sufi orders. They were thought to have appointed the delegates (*khalifas*) who established new chapters of the order (*tariqa*) and who would in turn appoint their lieutenants and successors.

The known historical facts about the founding of these orders are few. The Suhrawardi order attributed to Abu Najib al-Suhrawardi was actually founded by his nephew ʿUmar al-Suhrawardi (d. 1234). ʿUmar was appointed by the Caliph al-Nasir (d. 1225) to be the head of a group of *ribats* founded in Baghdad. ʿUmar wrote a treatise on the behavior of Sufi novices and thus established a monastic rule. The Shadhili order, which was introduced into Egypt in the late thirteenth century, began in Morocco with the teachings of Abu Madyan (d. 1197). His student al-Shadhili (d. 1258) moved to Alexandria in 1244, gathered followers and disciples, and created the particular pattern of devotional activities, social life, and avoidance of close relations with government authorities that would later characterize the order. The Qadiriyya was at first a local chapter centered around the tomb of 'Abd al-Qadir al-Jilani in Baghdad, but a hospice for Qadiris was founded in Damascus at the end of the fourteenth century. Later, the order spread throughout the Arab world and sub-Saharan Africa. The order named after Najm al-Din Kubra was in fact organized in Iran by al-Simnani (d. 1336) and spread widely in Khurasan, Khwarizm, and Transoxania. Al-Simnani was the founder of a movement that emphasized the unity of the Islamic community. His following embraced both Sunnis and Shi'is; venerated the family of the Prophet, including 'Ali, along with the great Sunni masters; and appealed to Buddhists and pagans to convert to Islam. Sufism, in the view of this order, was an all-embracing form of Islam that transcended sectarian divisions.

By the end of the fourteenth century, the Sufi orders were well established throughout the Middle East. In eastern Iran and Transoxania, the Kubrawiyya was most important. In Iraq, the Suhrawardiyya was dominant. In Syria, the Qadiriyya and the Rifa'iyya were well established. In Egypt, the Rifa'iyya, the Qadiriyya, the Shadhiliyya, and the Badawiyya were widespread. Sufi orders in Egypt enjoyed government patronage, the attendance of sultans at Sufi devotions, and a considerable popular following.

The influence of Sufism was considerable. In each community, Sufis represented, in competition with the schools of law and theological sects, an alternative form of social affiliation. The alliance of Sufism with the *ghazi* commitment to holy war and its tradition of missionary activity made the peripheral rather than the historical regions of Islam – such as North Africa, Inner Asia, and India – centers of Sufi expansion. Still, Sufis were received at the courts of rulers, called on to give their blessings and counsel, and allowed to intercede on behalf of their constituents. They also became integrated into the Shafi'i and the Hanbali schools of law. Most important, they exerted a vast influence on the common people. The Sufi *khanaqa* was a center of public preaching, of religious instruction, and of shared worship for lay followers. Insofar as the *khanaqa* was also the tomb of a venerated saint, Muslims made pilgrimages to worship, to be cured, and to receive spiritual blessing and material aid. Worship at the tombs of saints, increasingly widespread in the thirteenth and fourteenth centuries, would become the main vehicle of the Sufi expression of Islam.

Individual Sufis – with their followings of disciples and lay believers – remained the heart of the Sufi movement, despite the formation of small discipleships, the establishment of the *khanaqa* as a focus of collective life, and the institutionalization of the concept of *tariqa*. Although the orders served to bring some uniformity

into the teachings of the myriad of local Sufi masters and saints, Sufism was fundamentally the shared culture of individual teachers. Sufi insight was ultimately the
product not of institutions but of otherworldly inspiration.

Thus, the schools of law and the Sufi orders were the backbone of larger-scale
but diffuse communities that gave people a common law, common authorities,
and common facilities, such as mosques, schools, and charities. They gave large
numbers of people a common identity that transcended parochial and local membership in quarters and gangs. Religious communities diffusely organized under
the leadership of scholars and Sufis were the most inclusive groups and linked the
quarters within cities as well as the cities to one another.

Within the context of these communities, religious affiliations, identities, and
authority were fluid and diffuse. The law schools and Sufi orders were not rigidly
institutional but decentralized and focused on individuals. Even though offices,
endowments, and family connections gave power to religious leaders, they had
to attract followers by their personal qualities and performances, competing for
recognition and influence. Rivalries, jealousies, and competition for patronage and
followers embroiled leaders in disputes.

Moreover, competition for religious authority came from diverse sources. Apart
from the legal schools and the Sufi orders, spiritual authority was widely distributed.
Given the prevailing beliefs in the intercession of saints, visitation of graves to ask
for divine favors, magic, charms, amulets, and exorcism, as well as Quran, law,
theology, and mysticism, many people had access to the spiritual realm. Thus,
rulers, scholars, *sayyids* (descendants of the Prophet), Sufis, poets, madmen, and
ordinary worshipers might hold an independent religious authority.

ISLAMIC INSTITUTIONS AND A MASS ISLAMIC SOCIETY

The institutionalization of Shi'i sects, Sunni schools of law, and Sufi orders was but
one aspect of a larger process by which Middle Eastern communities transformed
into an Islamic civilization. The translation of Islamic institutions into an Islamic
society also depended on the mass conversion of Middle Eastern peoples to Islam.
Curiously, mass conversion was not achieved in the age of the Umayyad and
'Abbasid empires. The early empires that nurtured Islamic literary, religious, and
court cultures never attempted or succeeded in making Islam the religion of the
majority of Middle Eastern peoples. Despite numerous conversions, substantial
Christian populations remained in Iraq, Mesopotamia, Syria, and Egypt; substantial
Zoroastrian populations survived in Iran. Although there were conversions among
individuals who migrated to the Arab capitals and became Muslims, as late as
two centuries after the conquests, Muslims remained an elite minority among non-
Muslim peoples.

The first known mass conversion of a Middle Eastern population took place in
Egypt in the middle of the ninth century. A massive Coptic peasant rebellion was

crushed in 832. In the wake of the rebellion, bedouins attacked Christian villages; money was extorted from the church. Under pressure of communal defeat, bedouin attack, and the impotence of the church, Christian loyalties were subverted. In regions that had been partially settled by an Arab population, such as the eastern delta and parts of Upper Egypt, mass conversions to Islam took place. Other parts of Egypt, however, especially the western delta, remained Christian.

Only with the breakup of the 'Abbasid Empire and the vast upheavals attendant on the destruction of the established elites did the masses of Middle Eastern people convert. Extensive warfare, rural insecurity, and the decline of the old elites and village communities resulted in large numbers of Persians converting to Islam. Sufi missionaries seem to have played a crucial role. In western Iran, Shaykh al-Kazaruni and his followers converted numerous villages. Islamic missionary activity also had substantial success in eastern Iran, where Mu'tazili and Karrami missions made converts. The Caspian regions were converted by Shi'is fleeing from Baghdad. In Daylam, Tabaristan, Gurgan, and Transoxania, most urbanites had converted by the year 1000. Between 1000 and 1200, missionary Sufis and preachers brought Islam to the villages; rural mosques proliferated. By 1250 or 1300, an estimated 80 percent of the population was Muslim. Sufis pushed out into Inner Asia, where they converted Turkish peoples. In northern Mesopotamia, Egypt, and Syria, however, the bulk of the population remained Christian until the late thirteenth century and probably later. By the thirteenth century, as far as we can tell from exceedingly fragmentary evidence, Islam was no longer the faith of a dominant minority but was the majority faith of Middle Eastern peoples.

Whereas in the imperial era Islam was the identity of the political aristocracy and the dominant Arab-Muslim urban society, in the new era it progressively adapted to express the communal identity of the masses of Middle Eastern peoples. In the course of the tenth to the thirteenth centuries, Islamic communal groups and religious leaders were able to take charge of Middle Eastern communities and infuse them with their interpretations of Islamic identifications. This was possible because old landowning and officeholding notables lost their power to new military regimes dominated by slave soldiers or migratory nomadic chiefs. As foreigners with no historical ties to the societies they had conquered, warlords could restore provincial government, but they could not take the place of the old official and landowning classes and offer, on a local level, the protection, advice, and assistance that the powerful traditionally offered the poor. Faced with military elites unfamiliar with local traditions, scholars emerged as a new communal notability. Religious scholars married into established merchant, administrative, and landowning families and merged with the older local elites to form a new upper class defined by religious qualifications. They took charge of local taxation, irrigation, and judicial and police affairs and often became scribes and officials in the Saljuq states. The elites, both local and central, were not required but were expected to contribute irrigation, mosques, bazaars, baths, and other public facilities. The scholars thus developed from a purely academic and religious elite with judicial functions into a broad social and political elite. In many instances, given the instability of military regimes, they became the effective representatives and even governors of their towns and territories. Like tribal chiefs, local landowners, princes, and military governors, leading scholarly families sometimes ruled their towns in de facto independence from the military regimes. The families descended from Abu Burda governed Shiraz for centuries; the Mikalis family served as leaders of Nishapur, and the Burhan family of Bukhara provided local governors who collaborated with the nomadic regimes that successively conquered eastern Iran and Transoxania. The acceptance of this new responsibility was a reversal of the earlier scholarly resistance to involvement in politics and is explained by the dramatic breakdown of the caliphate.

Scholarly authority was derived from achieved learning and a reputation for sanctity, because there was no central or churchlike agency to ordain, license, or validate religious leadership. Authority was personal, grounded in the relationship of individual religious teachers to their disciples and followers. In the case of a Shi'i imam, the head of a school of law, or a Sufi *shaykh*, the personal relationship of layman to scholar, of worshiper to preacher, of sectarian to religious guide, and of disciple to master was crucial. Religious authority was validated by the recognition of other scholars and ordinary people. The influence of the scholars with the general populace was further reinforced by the exercise of patronage, which bound ordinary people to the educated elite. The binding force in society was not a structure of offices and institutions but the networks of personal ties that enabled the scholars to uphold family and religious community as the essential expressions of an Islamic social order.

Shi'i sects, Sunni schools of law, and Sufi orders also served as cadres for local political organization. The legal schools – made up of study groups, teachers and students, interested members of the community and patrons, and legal functionaries such as deputies, witnesses, orderlies, and clerks grouped around the important judges – formed organized parties or factions. Scholars had close ties to merchant families, bureaucrats, and officials. Their popular following was often found in the quarters where their mosques and schools were organized, among the people who sought their advice and protection. By the thirteenth century, everyone was considered to be a member of one of the four schools of law or one of the Shi'i sects, on the basis of birth or the traditional membership of his quarter, city, or region. The common people belonged in that they looked to one or another of the schools for authoritative opinions on what they saw as the divinely commanded rules of behavior. They went to the scholars of the law for judgments in uncertain cases and to the witnesses and judges for commercial and legal matters.

Although Muslim religious bodies became the usual organizing cadres for local communities, they were by no means the only ones. Primary groups – including families, villages, and town quarters defined by family, ethnic, or sectarian homogeneity, or by shared employment in some craft or trade – remained active forces. Young men's gangs (*fityan, 'ayyarun, zu'ar,* or *ghazis*) – made up of unmarried men of working-class backgrounds, separate from family, tribal, or craft organizations – played a complex role in the social life of towns and villages. An already venerable culture of masculine honor and social sanction for revenge helped reinforce the tendency to factionalism and feuds in Middle Eastern town and village communities. These factions made Middle Eastern towns quarrelsome places but also gave them a limited capacity for organized resistance to nomadic and slave regimes.

The Islamic schools of law and Sufi orders played a double role. They were often parochial and factional bodies struggling for control of judicial offices and teaching positions and often involved in pitched battles with rival schools over doctrine, prestige, and control of the streets. In other cases, the schools of law and the Sufi orders served to integrate disparate town populations and bring factional groups into a more embracing Muslim community. Transcending loyalties to any particular place, membership in a law school or a Sufi order created a feeling of participation in the worldwide Muslim community (*umma*) and was an important aspect of social consciousness. United by the travels of scholars, Sufis, merchants, and students, the schools of law and Sufi orders were crucial both in the formation of local community life and in linking each small locality to the worldwide community of Islam.

Towns and villages were thus segmentary societies made up of numerous groups, defined by neighborhood or by religious sect, and sometimes by occupation, but never by economic class. This is not to deny that the notables formed an elite stratum or that lower-class groups could be independently organized. In Iranian towns, the patriarchates, consisting of officials, professionals, landowners, and merchants, tended to dominate lower-class groups but, by and large, social and political groups were organized in communal rather than in class terms.

This pattern of social affiliations and identifications excluded one alternative pattern of communal organization – the corporation of citizens resident in a particular locality. The town or village from which a person hailed, however important in his consciousness, did not constitute a corporate body, had no territorial administration, and conveyed no political citizenship. No institutions corresponded to the social or psychological facts of town or village life. In this type of society – with its combination of parochial and cosmopolitan identifications and its weak geographic solidarity – people depended on the informal authority and mediation of the scholarly notables to cope with shared concerns. Informal consultation of respected notables and their networks of patronage ties allowed for mediation of local disputes, for mobilization across parochial group lines, and for the expression of shared religious and political interests.

Town and village societies of this type were not ordinarily self-governing. Scholarly notables were neither a military nor a territorial elite. They did not have the skills for warfare; nor did they control land and revenues. Middle Eastern localities lacked the technical, organizational, and economic bases for political independence. They lacked the internal cohesion necessary for political autonomy, and they feared the breakdown of internal order more than the heavy hand of alien regimes.

Conquest by nomadic peoples and slave warlords who militarily and economically dominated both town and country precluded the possibility of communal independence. Only in interregnum periods, in the absence of strong military regimes, could mediation by scholars and parochial clienteles give local forces temporary independence. When the ruling empires were weak, urban resistance to exploitation, revolts against unpopular governors, and protests against taxation were common. Town resistance based on religious leadership and local armed forces could even settle the fate of empires. In 992, when the Samanids were faced with the advancing Qarakhanids, their last hope lay with the masses of Bukhara, whose religious spokesmen counseled neutrality. Similarly, the notables and the scholars of Nishapur determined the success of the Saljuq invasion. Deciding that the Ghaznavids could no longer defend Khurasan, they surrendered to the Saljuqs and offered the services of a socially and administratively skilled elite to the new regime. Otherwise, empires reigned.

Thus, in the period between 950 and 1200, local elites and communities in Iran and Iraq became Muslim and transformed Islamic identities. By 1400, the same was substantially true for Syria and Egypt. Through the schools of law, Sufi orders, and Shi'i sects, Islamic religious leaders provided the cadres of communal organization not only for a small sectarian following but, in an age of conversions, for the masses of Middle Eastern peoples. Islam thus gave the post-imperial Middle East a new identity. While conquerors and regimes came and went, Islam became ever more firmly and widely entrenched as the basis of the social and political order.

MUSLIM RELIGIOUS MOVEMENTS AND THE STATE

The religious and social roles of the Sunni schools of law, theological sects, Shi'i communities, and Sufi orders made them of the utmost importance to Middle Eastern military regimes. In the ninth and tenth centuries, the Buwayhids, the Hamdanids, and the Qarmatians were officially Shi'i. The Buwayhids authorized, patronized, and guided the organization of the Imami community in Baghdad. They introduced the festivals of *ghadir khumm* and *'ashura'*. The Fatimids were the sponsors of Isma'ili missions that reached from North Africa to Khurasan, Afghanistan, and Transoxania. The triumph of the Shi'i dynasties also prompted a literary and cultural renaissance in which Hellenistic, philosophical, and secular views flourished.

Caliph al-Qadir (d. 1031) took the lead in the Sunni response to Shi'ism by trying to organize a Sunni religious mission to restore the true practice of the faith. He helped Sunnis set up their own festivals, commemorating the nomination of Abu Bakr and the death of Mus'ab ibn al-Zubayr, to rival the Shi'i celebrations; by proclamation, he made Hanbalism the state's official Islamic legal school. In 1019, the caliph condemned allegorical explanations of the Quran and the thesis of the created Quran and proclaimed the excellence of the first four caliphs in order of their access to office. His successor, al-Qa'im (d. 1075), renewed the effort to define Islamic orthodoxy in Hanbali terms and to mobilize popular support for caliphal supremacy. In reaction to Shi'ism, the Sunni revival of the eleventh century aspired not only to define Islamic orthodoxy but also to restore the caliphs as the heads of the Islamic community.

The advent of the Saljuqs in 1055 profoundly changed the relations between religious communities and the state. From the very beginning of their conquests in Khurasan, the Saljuqs became embroiled in religious controversy and soon devised a policy of alliance with selected Islamic movements. They espoused an uncompromising anti-Shi'i policy and helped suppress Shi'i activities throughout their domains. Their hostility was motivated partly by rivalry with the Fatimids and partly by Sunni anxiety over subversion by Shi'i movements. Saljuq opposition to Shi'ism was vigorously pursued in order to create Sunni solidarity and to promote the legitimacy of Saljuq states in the name of the "true" Islam.

The Saljuqs also took positions vis-à-vis the competing Sunni schools. First, they intervened in the Hanafi-Shafi'i and Hanbali-Ash'ari struggles, favoring the Hanafi school of law and forcibly suppressing Shafi'i and Ash'ari activity. In 1063, however, Nizam al-Mulk, newly appointed as minister (*wazir*), proposed to calm Sunni religious quarrels by patronizing both the Hanafis and the Shafi'is. The major instrument of this policy was the construction and endowment of religious schools (madrasas) in every major city of the Saljuq domains. Saljuq support created a broad base for the education of Sunni teachers, for Sunni missions to the general populace, and for opposition to the Fatimids and the Isma'ilis. Nizam al-Mulk probably aimed at state control over the Sunni movements and used the major legal and theological schools as a vehicle for political influence over the masses.

After the death of Nizam al-Mulk, Saljuq policy oscillated between patronizing the Hanafis and patronizing the Shafi'is. The late twelfth century, however, brought a shift from sponsorship of individual schools to equal recognition of the four major schools of law. Alongside the colleges, which taught the legal doctrine of each of the four main schools, a new type of college, called *dar al-hadith*, was created to teach the sayings and deeds of Muhammad. The *dar al-hadith*, however, was not assigned to a particular school of law but represented the common Muslim interest in the legacy of the Prophet. In 1234, as a further expression of a pan-Sunni policy, a new madrasa, al-Mustansiriyya, was founded in Baghdad to house all four of the law schools. In the course of a century and a half, government policy had moved from identifying itself with particular sectarian movements to delineating Islamic orthodoxy to include all the major schools of law and the most prominent theological groups.

The Saljuqs endowed *khanaqas* as well as colleges. They brought the institution to Baghdad, where these centers were known as *ribats*. *Ribats* housed scholars of hadith, legists, and theologians and were, in particular, residences for preachers engaged in religious and political propaganda on behalf of the Saljuq sultans.

Thus, by sponsorship of colleges, schools of law, theological groups, and *khanaqas*, Nizam al-Mulk initiated a state policy of seeking legitimacy and political stability by patronage and sponsorship of Sunni religious institutions. State support and sponsorship of religious schools helped overcome factional antagonisms. The madrasas and *khanaqas* served as an organizational base for legal teaching, as a vehicle for providing financial support for religious scholarship, as centers for the training of religious and administrative cadres, and as bases for missionary activity with the goal of achieving the universal acceptance of Sunnism. In return for Sunni support and legitimization of state policy, the Saljuqs helped to realize the Sunni ambition for a universal Muslim society.

The conquest of Syria and then of Egypt by Turkish (and Kurdish) warriors and the establishment of Saljuqid regimes introduced the system of state and religious organization that was being worked out in the eastern provinces into the former western provinces of the 'Abbasid Empire. The Ayyubids in Syria and the Mamluks in Syria and Egypt continued the Saljuq policy of strong state support for and control of Sunni Islam. Under the patronage of Nur al-Din, new colleges of law were founded in Damascus and were endowed with permanent funds. In the Ayyubid period (1193–1260), there were no fewer than 255 religious structures built in Damascus.

Stimulated by Hanafi and Shafi'i scholars from Iran and Spain, the Syrian provinces were integrated into what was becoming the prevalent system of education in the Middle East.

The conquest of Egypt by Saladin in 1171 opened the way for the installation of the Sunni schools in Egypt. The Shafi'i school had survived under Fatimid rule, but Saladin introduced the Hanafi school, endowed colleges of law, and recruited prominent teachers and judges from abroad. In the early thirteenth century, the Ayyubid government in Egypt adopted a pan-Sunni policy of equal recognition and equal sponsorship of all schools of law. The al-Kamiliyya, a school of hadith, was founded in 1222 to teach the points of law that were held in common among the schools. The madrasa, al-Salihiyya, was founded in 1239 to house all four schools of law in the same building.

Similarly, Saljuq sponsorship of *khanaqas* and *ribats* spread these institutions from eastern Iran to Baghdad and to the western Arab provinces. The first Syrian *khanaqa* was built in Aleppo in 1115. Nur al-Din established one in Damascus after 1154. Saladin founded a *khanaqa* in Egypt in 1173 as a hostel for foreign Sufis and one in Jerusalem in 1189.

The Ayyubids also followed Fatimid precedents by constructing tombs for venerated Muslim ancestors and for deceased rulers. One of the first Ayyubid projects was the construction of a college near the grave of al-Shafi'i, the founder of the principal Egyptian school of law. Colleges and Sufi retreats were provided with mausoleums for the remains of their founders. A tomb advertised the sanctity of the ruler and his devotion to Islam.

This Ayyubid sponsorship of Sunni institutions was followed by another equally intense period of construction and endowment under the Mamluks. The early Mamluk period was dominated by intense Muslim religious feeling expressed in warfare against the crusaders, the Mongols, and the Isma'ilis and by hostility to Christians and Jews, coupled with pressures for the conversion of non-Muslims to Islam. At the instance of governors, generals, judges, and rich merchants, Cairo and other towns were provided with ever-enhanced facilities for worship, education, and charity. Thus, the Mamluks extended the Saljuq-Iranian pattern of organized religious life to Syria and Egypt. Owing to this strong support for Sunnism, Mamluk royal culture emphasized its Islamic rather than its cosmopolitan bases. It was thus typical of the tendency in the Arab provinces to legitimize states in Muslim rather than universalistic terms.

By the thirteenth century, from Iran to Egypt, a new system of government based on the collaboration of military elites and local religious notables was consolidated. As culturally and linguistically alien conquerors, the military elites did not have the legitimacy or bureaucratic personnel to control and tax the city populations, suppress urban factions and gangs, and forestall the emergence of independent civic associations. For this, they depended on the support of local notables – scholars, teachers, judges, market inspectors, and local officials. To win this needed assistance, rulers and high-ranking officers (amirs) supported the notables with endowed incomes, gifts, and stipends and thereby built up factional political support.

The endowment of colleges and other religious and urban facilities also served the personal interests of the rulers and officers. They could be used to perpetuate their private and household fortunes. The gift of a trust (*waqf*) allowed the donors to keep control of their properties until death and pass control to their heirs. They provided the donors with tombs. Trusts were often endowed by the women of warrior households, helping to safeguard their fortunes.

Although their power was sometimes based on local groups of young men (with chivalric ideals and gangster behavior), notables and scholars were limited, because they were divided by faction, school, and other interests. Thus, they depended on stipends, gifts, and endowments for their influence and for the continuity of family power. Moreover, they had no title to such stipends – rulers could change the beneficiaries at will – and had to compete for favors and depend on the success of the military factions to which they were allied. The notables competed by prestige in learning and reputation for *hurma* (honor and cultivated personality) and by the transmission to their heirs of the knowledge, deportment, and behaviors that defined high status.

In Timurid Iran, we find a variant version of the relationship between political-military and religious-notable elites. The ruler showed respect for learning, Sufism, and shrines. Herat was the premier city of religion, with important scholarly lineages, Sufi masters, descendants of the Prophet, and tombs. The ruler did not try to promote his own religious program but appointed a chief judge to oversee the religious personnel. He showed respect for the existing local authorities by distributing the highest posts to students of religious leaders promoted by Timur, but other posts went to local Khurasanian families. However, given the diversity of religious beliefs and authorities and the intense competition among them, influence and power were largely individual achievements.

In sum, government was based on a dynasty, the ruler, and his men, who were supposed to protect the religion and the community. The ruler was supposed to balance the varied interests in the society and to prevent any one of them from becoming disproportionately powerful and therefore oppressive. He achieved this by an elaborate and ever-changing network of patronage ties to the men of power, influence, and status in the larger society.

CHAPTER 22

THE COLLECTIVE IDEAL

The new realities of state and religious institutions were reflected in an abundant literature of political theory. This theory had three principal branches: a Sunni theory of the caliphate that was the work of the scholars, a Persian-inspired genre of mirrors for princes, and a philosophical theory of the ideal state composed by commentators on Plato and Aristotle. Each of them responded in part to the changing social universe and in part to their own literary canons, but they also embodied a common perception of the ultimate significance of politics and community. The shared values and assumptions bring us to the core of the post-imperial conception of an Islamic society.

SUNNI THEORY

The Sunni theory of the caliphate was set forth in theological and juridical treatises. Sunni writers tried to explain why there should be a caliphate at all, what purposes the office served, what qualifications were required of its incumbents, how they were to be selected, and what were the obligations of subjects. The underlying assumption of the Sunni literature was that rulers held office to implement Islamic law and maintain the existence of the Muslim community. Before the middle of the tenth century, Muslim political debates turned on the question of who was qualified to hold this office. Sunnis proposed certain personal qualifications combined with an electoral process to guarantee the legitimacy of a ruler. Whereas Sunni authors discussed the formalities of assuming the office, including the formal act of designation, consultation with the religious scholars, the oath of investiture, and the contract with the community, legal thinking in effect justified the actual pattern of succession and especially the designation by the incumbent of his heir.

By the tenth and eleventh centuries, it was clear that the caliphs could no longer fulfill their political and religious roles. The sultanates had stripped the caliphate of its actual powers; sectarian quarrels diminished its religious authority. Sunni theorists accommodated to these realities. Al-Mawardi (d. 1058), a Shafi'i jurist, wrote *al-Ahkam al-Sultaniyya* (Principles of Government) to show that the primary duties of the caliph are to maintain religion according to early precedents, enforce judicial decisions, and protect the people of Islam. For al-Mawardi, the caliphate was both a religious commitment and a political actuality. Thus, his theoretical views were supplemented with a discussion of the delegation of authority, the conditions of appointments and tenure for all classes of government officials, and the personal and moral qualities required of each officeholder. He described the organization of judicial administration, tax collection, government measures to stimulate agricultural production, and the application of legal penalties for criminal offenses. In effect, he set out a comprehensive blueprint for the exercise of an Islamic government. Embedded in this elaborate literary exercise is a poignant mixture of scholarly devotion, religious idealism, and political ambition.

Al-Ghazali (d. 1111) similarly combined allegiance to religious tradition with a pragmatic awareness of political realities. He too wanted to restore the caliphate to its "true" function as the protector of the tradition of the Prophet and of Islamic law, to recapture the unity of Muslim peoples, and to restore their military and worldly might. To do this, he realized, it was necessary to assimilate the Turkish military aristocracy, subordinate them to the caliphate, reform political administration, and above all use the combined powers of caliphs and reigning sultans to suppress dissidents, especially the Shi'is. Most important for al-Ghazali was the need to inculcate in every individual Muslim true belief, true piety, and true practice of Islamic law. Despite his continuing commitment to the caliphate, al-Ghazali was realistic enough to recognize that military commanders often appointed the caliphs, who in turn legitimized their power. His theory conceived of Islamic government as a condominium of the authority of the caliphs and the effective powers of the sultans.

More important was the ever-increasing emphasis on obedience. Obedience is counseled in the Quran and in hadiths. The Hanbali theologian Ibn Batta (d. 997) condemned armed revolt against an established government. He held that obedience was required of all subjects, but that this obedience was limited, in that the individual should refuse to disobey a command of God. Al-Ghazali held that rulers should be obeyed because resistance, even to tyranny, was a worse alternative. He believed that in the absence of a strong government, factional hostilities could lead to anarchy. These fears were not unrealistic. Under the pressure of political necessity, Muslim jurists were led to accept any established government as legitimate and to put aside their insistence on the supremacy of the caliphate.

With the demise of the caliphate in 1258, Sunni political thinkers could finally articulate a concept of Islamic government based on the collaboration of secular rulers and religious teachers. Just as the authority of caliphs was based on succession to the Prophet and on the presumption that they had the knowledge, understanding, and moral qualities essential to implement the revealed law, so the authority of the scholars and Sufis was based on a combination of personal achievements and of *silsila* (chain of initiations going back to the Prophet). Thus, the followers of the caliphate, the students of the scholars, and the devotees of the Sufis respected the same essential principle: the transmitted teachings of the Prophet. Political theorists then assigned the scholars an ever-larger role in the government of Muslim communities as advisors and counselors to reigning princes. As early as the ninth century, the Hanbalis had emphasized the Quranic injunction to "command the good and forbid the evil" as the basis of the responsibility of every scholar and of every Muslim to apply God's law in community affairs. With the rise to power of slave and nomadic chieftains, Hanbalis and other Muslim theologians also stressed the requirement of advising and admonishing (*nasiha*) the ruling elites to induce them to observe and implement Islam.

In both practice and theory, Ahmad b. Taymiyya (d. 1328) represented the epitome of the trend to focus Muslim religio-communal interests on scholars. Ibn Taymiyya was an outstanding Hanbali scholar of Quran and hadith and a prolific writer on a great variety of religious questions. Born in Harran in Mesopotamia, he fled from the Mongol invasions to Damascus. He first achieved notoriety in 1293 when he led a campaign to execute a Christian who was accused of insulting the Prophet. In sermons and speeches, legal responsa, and published creeds, he violently denounced his religious enemies. He opposed the Ash'aris and speculative theology in all its forms; he opposed all forms of metaphysical Sufism; he denounced esoteric and antinomian religious views and the veneration of saints' tombs; he involved himself in violent controversies on legal matters such as the law of divorce. He took part in demonstrations to destroy cultic forms of worship and expeditions against the Isma'ilis in the mountains of the Lebanon and led Muslim resistance to the Mongol invasions of Damascus. He insistently demanded that Islamic law be a continuing and vital force in the everyday life of every Muslim.

In accordance with his own political role, Ibn Taymiyya held that scholars were responsible for upholding the law by giving religious advice to rulers, teaching true principles to the community of Muslims, and "commanding the good and forbidding the evil." He set aside the traditional question of the caliphate – arguing that true caliphs had not ruled since the early days of Islam – and defined Muslim governments in terms of the actual ruling authorities and their attention to the advice of the scholars. His political activism thus embodied a new concept of state and society in which the scholars rather than the caliphs became the principal actors. Sunni political theory had shifted slowly to deemphasize the caliphate and to accept the reality of sultan and scholar as the key figures in the Muslim political order.

MIRRORS FOR PRINCES

While Sunni theory developed in Islamic religious circles, mirror literature arose out of a Persian tradition of manuals of statecraft. The first works of this kind were translated into Arabic in the course of the eighth and ninth centuries to counsel

Illustration 7. A youth prostrating himself before a ruler. Source: Los Angeles County Museum of Art, the Edward Binney, 3rd, Collection of Turkish Art. Photograph © 2002 Museum Associates LACMA.

the 'Abbasid caliphs. The upheavals of the tenth and eleventh centuries led to a new wave of mirrors for princes, written by government officials and religious scholars, to define the rules of good government for their new Turkish overlords. (See Illustration 7.)

The most important treatise of this kind was *The Book of Government* by Nizam al-Mulk (d. 1092). This text urges the sultan to do justice and gives him specific advice on the techniques of rule. The work is devoted to explicating the proper role of soldiers, police, spies, and finance officials; it tells anecdotes about the great ancient rulers to illustrate its lessons. Another important work, the "Qabus-nameh" of Kay Ka'us (d. c. 1082), was a compendium of the wisdom of an old king written for his favorite son, containing advice on the proper conduct of a household, agriculture, the professions, and government. The "Qabus-nameh" tries to teach a youth how to be a statesman, a gentleman, and a good Muslim. The *Book of Counsel for Kings* by al-Ghazali is an altogether different kind of mirror. Whereas Nizam al-Mulk concentrated on pragmatic political questions and Kay Ka'us was concerned with the education of an aristocrat, al-Ghazali's *Book of Counsel* sets out the beliefs of Islam, the moral qualities and attitudes expected of a ruler, and his duty to uphold the true religion. The example of ancient Persian kings and the sayings of sages are quoted to illustrate these teachings and to give a work with Muslim religious content a Persian literary flavor.

These works are strikingly diverse in tone and content, but they are all concerned with the ultimate ends of government and with the cultivation of rulers who have the vision, the character, and the technique to realize these ends. The purpose of government is to uphold justice and to preserve the Islamic tradition. In the work of Nizam al-Mulk, justice means that each class of the population – soldiers, administrators, merchants, and peasants – shall have its due; the weak shall be protected, and the productivity of the population assured. In concrete circumstances, justice is defined by custom and by Islamic law. For these obligations, a ruler is considered a shepherd responsible to God for his flock.

Al-Ghazali's *Book of Counsel for Kings* also stresses the importance of justice. The ruler should understand that God loves a just sultan and that God will judge him on the final day. The ruler should also see that his officers, servants, and slaves are disciplined. His most important responsibility is to shun heresy and evil actions, to keep to the tradition of the Prophet, and to reward virtuous people and condemn evil ones. For al-Ghazali as well as for the secular writers, the principal function of kingship is to uphold order in society and the teachings of the true faith.

According to the implicit theory of the mirrors for princes, the principal means for realizing justice is that the ruler himself be a just person. Although there are numerous pragmatic or political matters that must be managed, societies depend ultimately on the intellectual and moral qualities of their rulers. The good ruler must be a man of intelligence, knowledge, and experience, deliberate and circumspect, patient and self-restrained. This nobility must be expressed in a grave, dignified, and stern manner, for the ruler must inspire awe, loyalty, and good behavior in his subordinates. He must therefore avoid lying, avarice, anger, envy, and cowardice. If the ruler is a liar, men will have no fear; if he is avaricious, they will have no hope; if he is angry, they will not confide in him. The most desirable trait is generosity: he must reward his servants and spend his treasure on those who help him. His good character not only wins the support of his subordinates but serves as an example and induces them to be good to the people. Thus the moral qualities of the ruler are at the heart of his capacity to make justice reign. For al-Ghazali, this essential goodness is based on religious humility. The virtues of princes come from fear of God, for we are temporary sojourners in this world and our ultimate destiny is in the world to come.

To achieve goodness, the ruler must consult with the sages and the scholars. They will teach him what God requires; they will divert him from heresy and innovation; they will help make his soul into the image of a just ruler. The scholars thus define the goodness incumbent on the ruler and help instill it in him. The literature of the mirror for princes, then, trusts to personal virtue as the basis of social justice.

THE PHILOSOPHER-KING

A third genre of literature stems from the Greek heritage: Muslim commentators on Plato and Aristotle – including al-Farabi (d. 950), Ibn Sina (Avicenna, d. 1037), Ibn Rushd (Averroes, d. 1198), and others – who examine the ideal state and the ideal ruler. The highest goal in philosophic political theory is the perfection of the human speculative intelligence and the attainment of happiness through the rational contemplation of the divine reality. For the realization of this blessed state, the cooperation of human beings is essential.

Al-Farabi was the premier political theorist in the philosophic tradition. His *al-Madina al-Fadila* (The Virtuous State) begins with a résumé of the principles covering the divine being, the emanation of the celestial intelligences, and the relation of human intelligence and imagination to the spiritual universe. His objective is to understand the nature of being and intellect and to attain a spiritual vision of reality; his principal concern is the person of the philosopher, who must know the truth and be responsible for actualizing it in human society. The philosopher who has attained a theoretical vision of the truth is the only person qualified to rule, instruct his people, form their character in accordance with moral principles, teach them practical arts, and rouse them to do good acts so that they in turn reach their highest possible perfection.

In *Aphorisms of the Statesman*, al-Farabi explains that there are two levels of ideal state. One is the state ruled by the philosopher-prophet-prince, whose personal guiding presence is the inspiration for a virtuous society. The second type is the state ruled in accordance with the law set down by the original philosopher-prophet. In this state, the ruler must have knowledge of ancient laws, good judgment about how to apply them, initiative in coping with new situations, and practical wisdom to handle matters in which tradition does not suffice. The second type of ideal state corresponds to the Islamic society governed by the revealed law under the guidance of a ruler who implements the law – it is akin to the ideal caliphate of Sunni legal theory.

Later political philosophers held much the same position. Ibn Rushd offered a comprehensive vision of the spiritual universe and the place of human society within it. This is presented in his commentary on Plato's *Republic*. The perfection of speculative intelligence is the highest goal of human existence; human society exists for the sake of this perfection. The ideal society requires a philosopher-king and lawgiver who will create an order in which each person fulfills the tasks appropriate to his nature. When the virtues of the soul – intellect, temperament, and appetite – receive proper expression, there is justice in the society and in each person. The ruler establishes this perfect order by teaching philosophy to the elect and theology and poetry to the others. He trains the people by providing laws that guide them toward proper actions. Ibn Rushd, like al-Farabi, posits two levels of ideal society. One is established by the philosopher-prophet, who combines wisdom, intelligence, and the imaginative capacity to communicate the truth directly to the masses. The other is based on law, which is a way of implementing the speculative truth known to philosophers and is conducive to the perfection of the soul. In either case, a good ruler is essential to the realization of a good society.

All three forms of Muslim political theory are ultimately grounded in the premise that the goal of the social order is the formation of individuals who live rightly in this world in accordance with the truth and are so prepared to achieve salvation in the world to come. Politics is but part of a larger quest for religious salvation. Nonetheless, in each theory, the definition of that truth is somewhat different. In the Sunni theory, the fulfillment of the law is the fulfillment of God's revealed will. In the mirror theory, the substance of religious fulfillment is not discussed, but it is assumed that justice corresponds to the realization of religious principles. In the philosophical theory, knowledge of the intelligences and purification of the soul free the human intellect to regain its visionary attachment to the spiritual world.

The three genres of Muslim political theory also agree that political society is essential to the realization of this perfection. In the philosophical theory, a properly ordered society is necessary for the cultivation of souls who may comprehend the ultimate reality. In both philosophical and Sunni theory, law is the essential device for instructing, educating, and forming the morals of human beings. In turn, the state is essential for the enforcement of laws and the protection of individuals from being harmed or doing harm. In all three theories, society is necessary to enforce justice and order, sustain basic human needs, teach and instruct individuals in their moral duties, and support their spiritual quests.

All three genres insist that the proper social order requires a good ruler, whether he is a philosopher, caliph, or sultan. In all three forms of Muslim political literature, the ruler symbolizes the integration or the orderly relation of human beings to the cosmos and to God. In the philosophical literature, the ruler stands not only for personal religious fulfillment but for the harmony of the individual and society with the spiritual cosmos. The ruler who actualizes his rational potential brings his own soul into contact with the active intellect and the spiritual intelligences. He symbolizes in mythic terms the integration of man and God. In Sunni and mirror theory, the ruler does not have a mythic function: the caliph is not divine, or semidivine, or an incarnate savior, or a perfect man. He is, however, God's vice-regent, God's shadow, his vehicle for the maintenance of order in society and for fulfilling the conditions essential to the implementation of Islamic law. The caliph is seen as the upholder of order and justice in the image of God. He is mighty, capricious, inscrutable, and deserving of loyalty regardless of his actual deeds. An ordered society is unimaginable without a ruler, just as an ordered universe is unimaginable without God.

The ideal ruler is presented as ethical, just, and God-fearing, but the unspoken motive for the composition of these literatures is that actual rulers are capricious, willful, self-serving, and tyrannical. The unspoken contrast symbolizes the deep conflict that is experienced in the soul of every individual and in the body of society – the conflict between the forces of unbridled passion and unrestrained exercise of power and the discipline of moderation and self-control. It also symbolizes the ever-present conflict in society generated by family antagonisms, tribal wars, factional struggles, conquests, and the rise and fall of regimes, as opposed to the hope for peace. The ruler signifies not merely order but the quest for order in a society composed of self-seeking human beings and groups. These genres are indicative of a broader concern among intellectuals that Muslim leaders of the medieval period were significantly less qualified or worthy of leadership than their early Islamic predecessors. Similarly, Sunni-Shi'i disputes over legitimate Muslim leadership provoked an intellectual interest in analyzing and delineating the characteristics and functions of a successful leader.

The person of the ruler is so important that all of these works, with the partial exception of those of Nizam al-Mulk, neglect actual political institutions. In the Sunni theory, the emphasis is on the person of the caliph and not on the mechanisms that could bring religious principles into practice. The mirror literatures are similarly vague about the meaning of justice and hierarchy. The philosophical writers give no concrete description of the ideal government. Society is described as organized into classes, but the classes are only metaphors for the virtues of the well-ordered soul. In none of these literatures do economic issues have an important place.

There are several reasons for this emphasis on the person of the ruler. One is that these literatures reflect the realities of their time. Whereas modern political theory may focus on institutions because of the highly bureaucratic and legalistic structure of modern societies, Muslim writers of that era turned their attention to the ruler because authority was vested in patriarchal figures who depended on the personal loyalty of their soldiers and officials to maintain their regimes. In a society that depended on men rather than institutions, the only conceivable check on the powers of rulers was their character as human beings.

Furthermore, the emphasis on the ruler also reflects the weakness of organized institutions. Although ubiquitous in influence, scholars and Sufis had no central organization. Urban communities were divided into factions. Landowners and other economic elites were divided by region and faction and had no formal ways of generating solidarity. Apart from the small urban family or rural clans, lineages, and tribes, there was no organized political society. Even the state was often the household of the prince.

Finally, the person of the ruler was emphasized because the ruler symbolized not only the aspiration for political justice but the hope for individual religious perfection. In the philosophic literature, the ultimate concern of political theory is the education of the philosopher. Analogously, the ultimate concern of Sunni writers was not politics but religious and moral perfection to be attained by adherence to the law. The caliph was a symbol of that perfection. Similarly, the mirror literature describes the ruler as a person in control of his own evil impulses and those of others. He is not an administrator but a model for how men should live. While addressing the question of the state, the underlying premise of Islamic "political literatures" is that a good state is the product of good human beings.

CHAPTER 23

THE PERSONAL ETHIC

The consolidation of a post-imperial Islamic society was accompanied by the consolidation of Islamic religious literatures, beliefs, and values and by the canonization of an Islamic ortho doxy. Although the basic literatures of exegesis, hadith, law, theology, and mysticism had originated in an earlier era, during the tenth to the thirteenth centuries these literatures were merged into the forms that we now identify as "classical Islam." A Sunni-scripturalist-Sufi orientation became the most commonly accepted version of Islam. Shi'ism, philosophy, theosophy, and popular religion were the alternatives to the Sunni consensus. The post-imperial era constructed both the normative forms of Islamic religious belief and practice and the alternatives, thus defining the issues that would ever after constitute the *problématique* of Muslim religious discourse.

NORMATIVE ISLAM: SCRIPTURE, SUFISM, AND THEOLOGY

Sunni consensus became grounded in scripture during the medieval period. In the post-imperial era, the Quran was understood to require each person to do the good deeds commanded by God; to be moderate, humble, kind, and just; and to be steadfast and tranquil in the face of his own passions. The true Muslim is the slave of God. He accepts his humble place in the world and takes no pride or consolation in human prowess but recognizes the limited worth of all worldly things and the greater importance of pleasing God.

By the ninth century, hadith had achieved a central place in Muslim religious life. Once the basic canons had been codified, hadith studies tended to concentrate on the criticism of chains of transmission (*isnad*) and on the compilation of anthologies garnered from the earlier canons. Sunni works of law, theology, and mysticism continued to quote proof-texts from the Quran and hadith. Also, by the middle of the tenth century, the schools of law had developed their basic jurisprudential procedures and had elaborated a considerable body of legal materials. By

Table 6. *Central concepts in law*

fatwa	Advisory opinion on a matter of law given by a *mufti* (jurisconsult)
fiqh	Understanding, law
ijtihad	Independent judgment of qualified legal scholar (*mujtahid*)
'ilm	Knowledge, especially of law; the learning of the *'alim* (pl. *'ulama'*)
qada'	Court judgment made by a judge (*qadi*) on the basis of *fiqh*
Shari'a	The way, the total corpus of law
taqlid	Imitation, following the established teachings
usul al-fiqh	Jurisprudence; sources of law: Quran, hadith (sayings of the Prophet), *ijma'* (consensus of schools and community), *qiyas* (reasoning by analogy)

then, it was evident that there were four principle schools of Sunni jurisprudence with large followings, although there were also numerous independent scholars and small personal schools, in addition to the Shi'i schools. In time, only the four major Sunni schools – the Hanafi, Shafi'i, Maliki, and Hanbali – survived.

Despite the consolidation of schools of law, there was considerable legal development after 950. (See Table 6.) The formalization and professionalization of legal schools is reflected in changing genres of legal literature. Whereas previously legal texts tended to compile the opinions of a single jurist, in later periods, the legal opinions of groups of jurists who belonged to the same school were combined. In the tenth century, legal schools began codifying their doctrines in compendia (*mukhtasar*) based on each school's most authoritative or widely accepted legal opinions. The law took the form of a vast reservoir of case materials and precedents that could be used as the basis of judicial decisions. This genre became increasingly more prevalent in subsequent centuries. The *Hidaya* (Guide) by the Hanafi jurist al-Marghinani (d. 1196) is representative of compilation, repetition, and formalism in Islamic legal scholarship. By selectively choosing which legal opinions would be considered authoritative, these compendia created a resource for later jurists to perpetuate and disseminate the rulings and the methodology of their school. Another genre of legal literature that intensified in the medieval period is the etiquette of judging (*adab al-qadi*). These texts outlined the duties and proper behavior of a judge, further formalizing the legal profession.

Whereas the Hanafi, Maliki, and Shafi'i schools agreed that the "gate of *ijtihad*" or independent reasoning was closed and that scholars of later generations were not free to give personal or independent interpretations of the law, the Hanbalis and a minority of Shafi'i writers never accepted the principle of *taqlid*, or obedience to the traditional canon, and upheld the authority of every qualified legal scholar to use rational judgment in legal questions. Even the more conservative schools allowed for flexible accommodation of legal principles to custom and tradition. Surviving court records suggest that jurists applied legal doctrines of schools other than their own. The application of the law to practical situations and the procedure of consulting scholars for legal opinions also resulted in legal changes.

The possibilities for individual interpretation and selection out of the repertoire of numerous jurists gave Islamic law almost boundless flexibility in practice.

Legal rules were mixed with moral injunctions. Some actions were required, others were recommended; some were forbidden, others discouraged. In some matters, the law was neutral. In many categories, it did not provide sanctions, and its application was left to conscience. The universal tension between ethical ideals and legal rules, between fulfillment in spirit and in letter, and between law as a symbol of truth and as a system of rules manifested itself in Islamic societies. Furthermore, custom or socioeconomic circumstances often decided whether or not aspects of the law were applied. As in all legal systems, legalistic devices (*hiyal*) allowed for exceptions to the principles of the law while keeping to its letter. Actual legal practice was infinitely varied, according to locality, legal school, and many other circumstantial factors.

Embedded in the problem of adherence to the law was the question of its sources. Was law based on divine authority, the rational judgment of experts, or allegiance to the tradition and consensus of the community? Revelation, reason, consensus, and tradition all played a role in the formulation of religious judgments. Acceptance of scripture, then, implied faith in revelation, commitment to a specific way of life, and a search for personal realization of the moral and spiritual as well as the behavioral qualities implied in the Muslim revelation. In Quran, hadith, and law, we find not only prescriptive rules but the vocabulary of an open religious quest.

SUFISM IN THE POST-ʿABBASID ERA

Sufism was another way of pursuing this quest. It devalued worldly things in the search for an ecstatic experience of God's being. It also carried with it a theosophical view of the universe that explained the structure of the cosmos and the possibility of religious ascent toward union with God. Finally, it encompassed belief in the miraculous powers of saints as channels for God's action in the world. Sufism thus encompassed piety and ethical behavior, ascetic and ecstatic practices, theosophical metaphysics, and magical beliefs. It embraced at once a scripturalist, an agnostic, and a miraculous concept of Islam. Some forms of Sufism would be integrated with law, whereas others tended to gnosticism and the veneration of saints. Its ascetic and theosophical aspects were consistent with devoted practice of Islamic law, but the veneration of the magical powers of Sufi saints led rather to religious practices that were expected to produce miracles or to induce ecstatic visions. Sufism was thus not one but several forms of religious inspiration united under the same name.

By the end of the tenth century, Sufis had defined their movement as a science, parallel to that of law, capable of leading to true knowledge of God by virtue of correct doctrine, religious practices, and methods of mystical contemplation. Leading Sufis developed wide and complex religious views including legal and theological interests. Sufi writers worked out a technical vocabulary to define, defend, and standardize Sufi practice; integrate it with law and theology; and thus legitimize it within the framework of Islam.

In the eleventh and twelfth centuries, a postclassical period began. God was seen as the only reality; meditation techniques, music, and love poetry were introduced, and emphasis was placed on the moral and ethical aspect of Sufism consistent with legal Islam.

Sufi positions were expressed in a growing body of literature. Biographies linked Sufi initiates with a chain of teachers leading back through al-Junayd to Hasan al-Basri and the companions of the Prophet Muhammad. Other Sufi treatises set forth the main ideas derived from Sufi experience and tried to communicate the actual experiences of the masters through anecdotes and sayings. They illustrated the great piety and scrupulousness of Sufis, their trust in God, their detachment from the material world, and their qualities of heart and soul. Such works included the *Qut al-Qulub* (The Food of Hearts) of al-Makki (d. 998), which set out Sufi prayers and recitations. The *Kashf al-Mahjub* (Unveiling of the Hidden) of al-Hujwiri (d. 1071) and the *Risala* (Epistle) of al-Qushayri (d. 1074), head of the Shafi'i-Ash'ari party in Nishapur, explained the meaning of key Sufi terms, discussed metaphysical and theological issues, and gave the biographies of famous masters.

The central motif of this literature is renunciation of individual will, of worldly concerns, and of everything except God. This renunciation, however, refers to an attitude of mind rather than a literal state of emptiness or vacuum. The Sufi lives with material things but does not care about them. He owns things but does not derive his esteem from them.

Further, the Sufis taught that true Islam is the submission of man's will to God's will. Al-Hujwiri says, "Divine grace is this – that God through His will should restrain a man from his own will and should overpower him with will-lessness, so that if he were thirsty and plunged into a river, the river would become dry." And further: "What we choose for ourselves is noxious to us. I desire only that God should desire for me and therein preserve me from the evil thereof and save me from the wickedness of my soul. . . . I have no choice beyond His choice."[1] The Sufi does not wish his own wishes but makes his wish whatever God has commanded; he is satisfied with whatever God decrees for his life; indeed, he embraces God's choices, doing God's will joyfully.

This does not mean that the Sufi does not have a "will" in the ordinary sense; it means he has fused the chaotic wishes of every person into his authentic will,

---

[1] Al-Hujwiri, *The Kashf al-Mahjub*, trans. R. A. Nicolson, London: Luzac, 1970, pp. 378–79.

his willing acceptance of God's command. In this, Sufism is consistent with the Quran, which sees that the unbeliever is one who gives free reign to unchecked passions and who only serves his apparent needs for wealth, honor, fame, and power. Controlling this false willfulness, obeying God's command, restraint, and modesty are the "true Islam."

Sufism further teaches that the will is tamed by the love of God. The politicians would curb men by force; the moralists, by public opinion; the philosophers, by reason; the theologians, by faith. Sufis teach that the true love of God is to love his will as one's own. They yearn to do God's will as a lover yearns to fulfill the wishes of his beloved. "God's choice for His servant with His knowledge of His servant is better than His servant's choice for himself with his ignorance of his Lord, because love, as all agree, is the negation of the lover's choice by affirmation of the Beloved's choice."[2] Love of God makes his every command the Sufi's own heartfelt wish.

The love of God was wedded to a profound Sufi determination to fuse personal religious experience with the practice of Islam according to law and tradition. Sufis of the tenth and eleventh centuries grappled with the tension between scripturalist Islam – an orthopraxy of external laws, rituals, and moral and social norms required of all Muslims – and Sufism – a mystical experience of the subjective being of man inculcating purity of heart, visionary knowledge, and love of God. Despite the efforts of generations of Sufis, including al-Junayd and al-Qushayri, and the growing rapprochement of law and Sufism in the tenth and eleventh centuries, these two understandings of Islam continued to be taken as alternative paths to religious fulfillment. Scripturalism or orthopraxy meant the conformity of outer behavior to legal requirements, whereas Sufism meant the purification of the heart for the sake of the vision of God. Finally, al-Ghazali was able to combine the authority of scripture and historical tradition with the personal experience of the Sufi master. Seizing on currents in philosophy, theology, law, and Sufi practice, he integrated Sufism and law in a way that has become authoritative in Islamic civilization. (See Table 7.)

AL-GHAZALI: HIS LIFE AND VISION

Al-Ghazali still stands as the master of this era. He came to his vocation in a crisis, described in his memoir, whose immediacy and poignancy is vivid to the present day. He studied law and theology in Tus and Nishapur. At the age of thirty-three he was appointed professor at the Nizamiyya school in Baghdad, one of the most prestigious positions of the time. He wrote treatises on law and theology, mastered philosophy and esoteric subjects, gave authoritative legal decisions, and lectured

---

[2] Ibid, p. 379.

Table 7. *The vocabulary of Sufism*

The anthropology of the soul

'aql	Reasoning faculty, often equivalent of *qalb*
al-fitra	Pure state of being, before investment of soul in the body
nafs	The passions and appetites to be subdued and ordered by reason
qalb	Heart, soul, seat of knowledge and conscience

The spiritual path

baqa'	Remaining in God
dhawq	Tasting of divine reality
fana'	Annihilation of the self
hal	State of rapture by grace of God
'ibadat and mu'amalat	Ritual and social obligations
'ishq	Love, yearning for God
islam	Submission to God's will
kashf	Unveiling, revelation
maqam	Achieved status on the way to God
ma'rifa	Immediate experience of truth
rida	Contentment; acceptance of the divine will
sabr	Patience in accepting God's will
shukr	Gratitude
tawakkul	Trust in God
tawba	Repentance
tawhid	Unity of God and union in God
zuhd	Piety, asceticism, renunciation

to hundreds of students. He was widely regarded as living an exemplary Muslim life. Yet he was beset by doubts: at the time of his greatest success, his doubts flowed into a deep sense of unworthiness.

> Next I considered the circumstances of my life, and realized that I was caught in a veritable thicket of attachments. I also considered my activities, of which the best was my teaching and lecturing, and realized that in them I was dealing with sciences that were unimportant and contributed nothing to the attainment of eternal life.

> After that I examined my motive in my work of teaching, and realized that it was not a pure desire for the things of God, but that the impulse moving me . . . was the desire for an influential position and public recognition.

> One day I would form the resolution to quit Baghdad and get rid of these adverse circumstances; . . . the next day I would abandon my resolution. I put one foot forward and drew the other back. If in the morning I had a genuine longing to seek eternal life, by the evening the attack of a whole host of desires had reduced it to impotence. . . . The voice of faith was calling, "To the road. To the road!" . . . Soon, however, Satan would return. "This is a passing mood, . . . do not yield to it, for it will quickly disappear. . . ."

It did not.

> For nearly six months beginning with Rajab 488 AH [July 1095 CE], I was continuously
> tossed about between the attractions of worldly desires and the impulses towards eternal
> life. In that month the matter ceased to be one of choice and became one of compul-
> sion. God caused my tongue to dry up so that I was prevented from lecturing. One
> particular day I would make an effort to lecture in order to gratify the hearts of my
> following, but my tongue would not utter a single word nor could I accomplish anything
> at all.

> This impediment in my speech produced grief in my heart, and at the same time my
> power to digest and assimilate food and drink was impaired; I could hardly swallow or
> digest a single mouthful of food.[3]

Al-Ghazali had come to an emotional crisis. His doctors said wisely but helplessly:
"This trouble arises from the heart... and from there it has spread through the
constitution; the only method of treatment is that the anxiety which has come over
the heart should be allayed."[4]

His decision was made. He took up the life of a wandering Sufi. For ten years,
he pursued the mysteries of Sufism. His retreat, however, was neither total nor
permanent. After ten years, he took up his public career again, returned to a
professorship at Nishapur, and wrote his major treatises. He had resolved the doubt
in his heart; he had come to certain knowledge of the truth of God's existence and
of the nature of his obligations to him. He saw his return as a return to his old
work in a new way.

> In myself I know that, even if I went back to the work of disseminating knowledge, yet
> I did not go back. To go back is to return to the previous state of things. Previously,
> however, I had been disseminating the knowledge by which worldly success is attained;
> by word and deed I had called men to it; and that had been my aim and intention. But
> now I am calling men to the knowledge whereby worldly success is given up and its low
> position in the scale of real worth is recognized.[5]

Al-Ghazali did not renounce the world; he abandoned false goals in worldly
activity.

Sufism brought al-Ghazali to certain knowledge of God, and certain knowledge
brought him back to Muslim beliefs, prayer, and teaching, to the given way of
scripture and tradition. His master of theology, al-Juwayni, had already said:

> I had read thousands of books; then I left the people of Islam with their religion and
> their manifest sciences in these books, and I embarked on the open sea, plunging into

[3] W. M. Watt, *The Faith and Practice of al-Ghazali*, London: Allen & Unwin, 1953, pp. 56–57.
[4] Ibid, pp. 57–58.
[5] Ibid, p. 76.

the literature the people of Islam rejected. All this was in quest of the truth. At an early age, I fled from the acceptance of others' opinions [*taqlid*]. But now I have returned from everything to the word of truth. "Hold to the religion of the old women."[6]

In the *Ihya' 'Ulum al-Din* (Revivification of the Religious Sciences), al-Ghazali gives his mature conception of the relationship between the outer and inner life, between law and spirituality. His position was rooted in a philosophic concept of the nature of the human being. In his view, the essence of the human being is the soul, which is a spiritual substance variously called *qalb, ruh, nafs,* or *'aql*. In its original state, *al-fitra,* before it is joined to the body, it is a pure, angelic, eternal substance. In this state, the soul possesses reason – the capacity to know the essence of things and the capacity for the knowledge of God. The highest good is the actualization of this inherent potential.

For this to be achieved, the soul must be joined to the body, for the body is the vehicle that carries the soul on its journey to God. The body, however, necessarily corrupts the pure state of the soul. In the combined constitution of man, desire, anger, and the inclination to do evil (*shaytaniyya*) are joined to the purely spiritual elements. The human being thus comes to possess both an animal soul made up of the faculties of desire and anger (*nafs*) and a divine soul (*rabbaniyya*) possessing the faculties of reason and justice. To perfect the soul, every person must subordinate the animal faculties to the higher faculties and perfect the virtues – temperance, courage, wisdom, and justice – appropriate to each faculty. *'Aql* (reason) has to prevail over *nafs*. The proper channeling of the animal parts and the achievement of some harmony of faculties is called justice in the soul. This does not mean, however, the destruction or abandonment of the lesser parts of the soul, but rather the dominance of reason over the other faculties. The goal is not to destroy but to make use of *nafs* in the interest of *'aql*.

The Sufi quest is aimed at such purification. Sufis seek to empty the mind of all distracting passions by retreat to the *khanaqa* (where the Sufi can concentrate on renunciation of worldly attachments), and by repetition and remembrance of the name of God (*dhikr*). As al-Ghazali explains, the Sufi path to knowledge is to shut the gate on sense perception, sexual passion, and worldly ties; to shut the gate on the material side of the mind. To do this, one does not need education or book learning – and here is the quarrel of Sufism with the scholars. The certain knowledge of God comes not from learning but from piety.

Sufi detachment, however, is but an extreme tactic in a more broadly conceived reform of the heart. This reform has both an outer and an inner aspect. It involves the triad of good actions, virtues, and knowledge. According to the *Ihya',* actions come first. The first book of the *Ihya',* after the introduction on knowledge, is entirely devoted to ritual actions (*'ibadat*). These include ablutions, prayer, alms,

---

[6] W. M. Watt, *A Muslim Intellectual: A Study of al-Ghazali,* Edinburgh: University Press, 1963, pp. 23–24.

fasting, pilgrimage, reading the Quran, *dhikr*, and *wird* (the continual remembering of God). Book II of the *Ihya'* is devoted to social actions – to table manners, marriage, earning a living, friendship, and journeys. These actions, ritual and social, are important precisely because they are God's revealed ways to cleanse the soul of passions and invoke the remembrance that is inherent in the original soul (*al-fitra*). The prescribed acts are themselves purifying.

The second aspect of purification is a direct assault on inner vices. The vices include the sins of speech (cursing, false promises, lying, slander, and backbiting), anger, envy, greed, jealousy, gluttony, miserliness, ostentation, pride, love of wealth and power, and love of this world. These vices sully the heart and stand in the way of ultimate happiness, not to speak of ordinary well-being.

The elimination of these vices is a lifelong process. Children must be raised properly with praise and blame, reward and punishment, to discipline their desires and habituate them to good acts. As children become adults, the discipline of society, the admonition of friends, the counsel of elders, and the imitation of good people is also helpful. In adulthood, however, the process of rooting out the vices becomes an individual responsibility. The individual must himself become aware that he is beset by vice, and self-awareness must be followed by inner struggle (*mujahada*), self-training (*riyada*), and habituation, by sturdy resistance to any external expression of bad impulses in speech or action. Indeed, not only must the individual control his impulses, he must oppose his vices by deliberately acting contrary to them. He has to create in the soul a struggle between vices and their opposites so that the faculties are driven from extremes toward the virtuous mean.

The elimination of vices paves the way for a new level of inward achievement, the acquisition of the mystical virtues. Book IV is devoted to these virtues – the states and stations on the way to God. They include repentance, fear, asceticism, and patience, which are preliminary to gratitude, trust, love, and intimacy. In one sense, these virtues develop spontaneously. They flourish like flowers in a garden, when the garden is weeded. In another sense, they can only be won through God's guidance and grace (*rahma*). A good Muslim strives for ethical self-control, but the mystical virtues flourish only by passive acceptance of God's will.

Passive fulfillment is at the heart of al-Ghazali's discussion of abandonment of self or trust in God (*tawakkul*). In the *Revivification of the Religious Sciences*, al-Ghazali explains that trust in God means to leave everything to God and to have no will, initiative, or activity of one's own. There are three levels of this extraordinary state. One is akin to the trust of a man in the attorney who represents his interests. The man turns over his affairs to the management of another, in whose honesty, energy, and ability he has confidence. This delegation, however, is limited to a particular case, and the subject does not surrender his awareness of what is going on, his judgment, or his ultimate right to make choices. This modest degree of trust may continue indefinitely.

The second degree of trust is akin to the dependence and confidence of a very small child in his mother. The infant cannot take care of himself; he knows only his mother, seeks refuge with her, and depends on her support. He has no capacity for initiative of his own, but he can cry, call for his mother, run after her, and tug her dress. At any distress, his first thought is of his mother; he has complete confidence that she will meet his needs. This is like the man who trusts entirely to God and has complete confidence that he will be nourished by the Almighty, to whom he addresses his prayers and petitions. This state of passivity may last a day or two, like a fever, before it passes and the mystic is returned to an everyday condition.

The third state is to be in the hands of God as a corpse in the hands of the washer. The mystic sees himself as dead, moved by God, and certain that he does not move, or will, or know, save by God's decree. In this state, the mystic trusts completely that he will be sustained. He does not call out like a child or pray like an adult. This third state, al-Ghazali says, lasts no longer than the pallor produced by fear.

These images convey the state of being that al-Ghazali has in mind. The trust of the child in his mother is a man's trust in his basic security, his confidence that his being will be sustained. The trust of the corpse in the washer, that passivity that can only be communicated by images of death, whose interval is the moment of fear, lies beyond the infant's trust. To know it, one passes through the helplessness of infancy, through the fear of death, through the terror of nonexistence. This trust is known by the abandonment of one's own efforts and resources, by the testing of one's capacity to endure a total surrender of one's own life to the very ground of all life. To know this trust is to know that one's existence is assured without striving, effort, or will of one's own. It is assured as such.

Renunciation of the will, of the self, abandonment to God, and trust in God represent not detachment in a physical sense from the ongoing life of the world, but rather moments that come to pass and return as part of the flow of man's psychic reality. These moments of passive grounding in trust become the basis of an active Muslim life and of the active virtues that pervade the scriptural and traditional imagery.

The third aspect of purification is knowledge. Knowledge has the most complex implications. It is at once a means and a goal to be attained. It is also a metaphor for the whole of the process by which religious vision is achieved. First, knowledge is basic. Knowledge of the principles of the faith; belief in God and his attributes, the angelic world, paradise, and the last judgment; knowledge of the character and actions of the Prophet; knowledge of which actions are commanded and which are prohibited; and knowledge of the heart and how to cure evil impulses – all of this is essential. The scholar's knowledge – indeed, the knowledge contained in the volumes of the *Ihya'* – is important information.

In another sense, knowledge for al-Ghazali is not what is learned but what is experienced. It is precisely the insights impressed on the heart by the actions and the inner traits of the person. Every action of the heart or the limbs, or inner movement of the soul, impresses itself as an image (*athar*) on the heart. Or, he sometimes says, the heart is like a mirror that reflects the form or the essence of the actions (*sura*). Sometimes al-Ghazali speaks of the heart as acquiring a *hal* (condition) or a *sifa* (attribute). In effect, every action implants a thought, an idea on the soul, for the essence of the soul is intellect. This knowledge of the heart is more than just information. It so impregnates the mind that all thinking runs by allusion from one passage of the Quran or Sunna to another, totally controlling the will and the actions of the believer. Deeply rooted in the soul, this knowledge generates actions without the mediation of reflection or judgment. Such knowledge is not only what we know but what we feel. It is knowledge that is not only known but meant. The fusion of knowing, feeling, and doing integrates the outer and the inner man.

Finally, this maturation of the soul through good deeds and virtues leads to knowledge in yet another sense, to mystical vision and love of God. Purification brings *kashf,* the lifting of veils and a vision of God as real beyond doubt. How is this to be interpreted? In one sense, it seems to mean that the soul once purified is set free from the trammels of the body and rises up to a transcending vision of God, but in fact al-Ghazali does not allow any direct contact, vision, or unity between man and God. The vision, *ma'rifa*, means knowledge of the truths of religion known with utmost clarity without any intervening screen. In this sense, the vision of God is not another reality but a way of understanding reality and a way of living life as a whole that results from the good deeds and virtues that impress themselves on the heart as truth. *Ma'rifa* is not an extra experience but insight into the meaning of reality that rises from intellect and conviction, from behavior in the world and conformity to the principles of one's culture.

Actions, virtues, and knowledge are provisions for the eternal happiness of the soul. The three factors, however, are not cultivated successively or independently. They are altogether interrelated. In al-Ghazali's view, doing good deeds establishes inner virtues. In turn, the virtues of the heart govern the actions of the limbs. As each act, each thought, each deed presses itself as an image on the heart or becomes an attribute of the heart, the acquired attributes become all the more continuous, deeply rooted, and seemingly natural. Moreover, because the heart is the seat of knowledge, this maturation of the soul through good deeds and virtues leads to mystical vision and love of God. Reciprocally, mystical vision is the source of virtue and channels all action according to God's will. What al-Ghazali tells us about the relations of inward and outward deeds, of acts and knowledge, and of the struggle for virtue and the vision of God is that they are aspects of a single progressive achievement in the course of which the believer becomes more wise, more just, and more obedient at each step, until he achieves a totality of being that entails at once mystical vision and ordinary piety. This kind of Sufism reinforces the everyday fulfillment of Islamic law by providing the believer with a still-deeper insight into the reality of God's existence. Thus, al-Ghazali gives expression to a cultural ideal, the integration of orthopraxy and Sufism, the outer and the inner ways – an ideal that is manifest in his return from Sufi retreat to his work as teacher, advisor, and reformer. In these terms, al-Ghazali unified orthopraxy based on scripture and Sufism and made them the normative form of Sunni Islam.

THEOLOGY

Theology offered another option for the deepening of scriptural Islam. It arose out of the need to give rational expression to religious concerns. After the early debates over the proper understanding of the divine revelation, three basic positions had been accepted by the middle of the tenth century. The Mu'tazilis and the philosophers emphasized the centrality of reason as an ordering principle in God's being, in the human understanding of the universe, and in the governing of human behavior. The rationalist position had as its corollary belief in free will and individual responsibility for moral choice. A contrary position stressed the absolute omnipotence and inscrutability of the divine being, who could be known only insofar as he had chosen to reveal himself through the Quran. Religious insight could only be attained by accepting the teachings of the Quran and hadith. By extension, all human action was ultimately an expression of the power of the creator – rather than an autonomous exercise of free judgment – and will and reason was of no use for religious knowledge or moral choice. The Hanbalis, who held this position, rejected allegorical interpretation or rational speculation on the text of the Quran or hadith.

The Ash'aris and the Maturidis steered a middle course between Mu'tazili rationalism and Hanbali literalism. Religious truths, according to the Ash'ari position, can only be known through revelation, although reason may play a subordinate role in defending the truth and persuading others. In moral matters, all human action is governed by God's power, but human beings acquire responsibility for or participate in their own actions. From the tenth to the twelfth centuries, the Ash'aris continued to hold the intermediate position, but they evolved away from the thought of the master in the direction of a more philosophical form of theology. In the work of al-Ash'ari, theological argumentation (*kalam*) was not methodical, like philosophical proofs, but indicative, in the sense of persuading or demonstrating the validity of a proposition. The main point of *kalam* was to attack and denounce all false religious views, but as the foremost opponent of philosophy, Ash'arism absorbed the strategies of the opposition. Philosophic methods and reasoning became an integral part of a new type of philosophical *kalam*.

Al-Juwayni (d. 1085) and al-Ghazali were key figures in the development of a new form of Ash'ari theology. In the prevailing mode of dialectical argumentation, the theologians reasoned by analogy to draw conclusions about new subjects. Al-Juwayni supplemented this form of argumentation by using the Aristotelian syllogism to deduce conclusions from universal principles or logical premises. Al-Juwayni shifted the contours of *kalam* from rationalistic argumentation toward systematic philosophical discussion of the principles of religion. Al-Ghazali further advanced the use of Aristotelian logic, and Fakhr al-Din Razi (d. 1209) completed the integration of theology and philosophy. In later manuals of theology, virtually two-thirds of the text was devoted to logic, natural philosophy, and ontology.

The absorption of a philosophic format did not imply a reconciliation of theology with the principal teachings of philosophy. On the contrary, Ash'ari *kalam*, revitalized by a more sophisticated method of argument, was all the more vigorous in its condemnation of philosophic teachings that were contrary to the scriptural revelation. Al-Ghazali's *Incoherence of the Philosophers* exposed the contradictions among philosophical writers and affirmed that a transcendent God could not be known by rational insight. From this vantage, al-Ghazali denied the philosophic concept of the eternity of the world in favor of the Quranic idea of its creation in time, defended the doctrine of the resurrection of the body against the philosophic belief in the eternity of the soul, and affirmed God's knowledge of particulars against the philosophic belief that limited God's knowledge to universals. Al-Ghazali employed Aristotelian logic and acknowledged the importance of philosophy in the study of nature and mathematics, but in religious matters he insisted on the primacy of God's revelation, the divine will, and God's command over human acts. For al-Ghazali, theology was useful for the defense of religious truth against certain kinds of intellectual confusion, but it was not itself a way of confirming the reality of God's existence. Insight into religious truth could be found neither in philosophy nor in theology, but only in the direct religious experience of mysticism.

Through the synthesis of philosophy and theology, rational inquiry found an integral place in Islamic religious culture, but philosophy and theology continued to diverge, despite the close alliance between them. Whereas philosophy operated with the conviction that reason alone would reveal reality, most theologians held that reason alone without support of revelation could not address ultimate realities. What was believed could not be changed by rational speculation, nor could reason discover God's will in matters of good and evil, or control moral behavior. At best, the knowledge that comes from divine revelation could be enlarged by rational insight and transformed from faith based on tradition to reasoned faith.

For Muslim theologians, faith (*iman*) was the key to religious fulfillment, and they defined it as knowing the truth and believing in it. Faith begins in the intellect: knowing that God exists; knowing his attributes, his prophets, and his will; and accepting this knowledge as the truth (*tasdiq*).*Tasdiq* is a conviction about what has been preached and recorded, which becomes the basis of a commitment to live one's life in accordance with that reality. It is an emotion of the heart as well as a thought in the mind. It is a state of devotion; it entails trust in and submission to God, fear and love of God, and above all love of what God wants men to do and hatred for what he has forbidden. Faith issues in devoted worship; every deed of everyday life is carried out as an expression of God's will.

Ibn Khaldun, a North African scribe and historian (d. 1406), explained that there were several degrees of faith. First, faith is simply genuine belief in the teachings of Islam as traditionally defined: "The affirmation by the heart of what the tongue says."[7] Beyond simple faith, there is a higher degree of faith, perfect faith. Calling on Sufi thought, Ibn Khaldun defined perfect faith as knowledge of the oneness of God. This knowledge, however, is not merely a knowledge known, but knowledge that has become a built-in attribute (*sifa*), modifying the very nature of a man's being. The difference, Ibn Khaldun explained, between "'state' and knowledge in questions of dogma is the same as that between talking [about attributes] and having them."[8] It is the difference between knowing that mercy for orphans is recommended and gladly giving alms. This quality of faith can only be acquired by repeated affirmation of belief and by acts of worship and good deeds. Faith, like any habit, arises from actions, is perfected by actions, and then governs all actions.

> The highest degree is the acquisition, from the belief of the heart and the resulting actions, of a quality that has complete control over the heart. It commands the actions of the limbs. Every activity takes place in submissiveness to it. Thus all actions, eventually, become subservient to this affirmation of faith, and this is the highest degree of faith. It is perfect faith. The believer who has it will commit neither a great nor a small sin.[9]

In the theological tradition, the capacity for faith rather than reason sums up the human potential for religious salvation. Yet faith includes intellect and implies acceptance of a rational dimension in human religiosity. Thus, theology transcended its purely apologetic functions and allowed an essential role for rational speculation in the elucidation of Islamic beliefs.

ALTERNATIVE ISLAM: PHILOSOPHY AND GNOSTIC AND POPULAR SUFISM

The integration of scripturalism, theology, and Sufism constitutes the normative, orthodox forms of Islamic belief and practices. The supreme authority of scripture as revealed truth was integrated with rational judgment. Commitment to the fulfillment of God's command in everyday life was allied to the quest for spiritual insight. Within the purview of Islamic culture, however, there were alternative visions of human nature and religious salvation. They were embodied in intellectual form in

---

[7] F. Rosenthal, *Ibn Khaldun, The Muqaddimah*, New York: Pantheon, 1958, III, p. 41.

[8] Ibid, p. 39.

[9] Ibid, pp. 41–42.

philosophy and gnosticism; they were expressed in popular rituals and worship. These other forms of Islam overlapped with theology and Sufism, but they were at the same time profound challenges to Sunni-scriptural-Sufi Islam.

Islamic philosophy and theosophy

Islamic philosophy was the work of a small group of scholars committed to rational inquiry and to the Hellenistic philosophical tradition. Al-Farabi defined philosophy as a comprehensive vision of the divine reality and the human condition. His successor, Ibn Sina (Avicenna), the great physician and metaphysician, was the son of a Persian official serving the Samanid regime near Bukhara, who by the age of eighteen was a master of logic, natural science, and medicine. He became a Samanid minister but as a result of court intrigues was forced to flee from place to place. He lived for fourteen years in Isfahan and died at Hamadhan in 1037. A man of action, he produced numerous scholarly works. He contributed to all the natural sciences (including physics, chemistry, astronomy, mathematics, and natural history) and composed the monumental *Qanun fi al-Tibb* (Canon of Medicine). The *Canon* includes an introduction to the general study of medicine and volumes on the pharmacology of herbs, pathology of organs, fevers, surgery, and other books. His most important philosophical work was the *Kitab al-Shifa'* (Book of Remedy). Like his philosophic predecessors, Ibn Sina wrote on neo-Platonic metaphysics, natural science, and mysticism.

The core of Ibn Sina's teaching was his ontology, or doctrine of being. God is conceived as transcendent and prior to the universe. He stands utterly beyond all being. However, Ibn Sina allowed for a continuity between the necessary being and the contingent universe. Although distinct from him in essence, the universe is brought forth from God. As he conceived it, God is the necessary being whose essence is by definition inseparable from existence. All other beings are contingent, for their existence does not follow from their essence. They come into being, following the neo-Platonic tradition, by the self-contemplation of the necessary being. The first being brings forth the first intellect, which, contemplating the essence of the necessary being and its own being, brings forth the second intellect. The process of contemplation proceeds until it brings forth the tenth intellect, which completes the celestial and spiritual universe. Thus, there are successive levels of heavenly being, each of which is an intellect emanating from the divine being, comprising a substance generated by the next higher level of being; each level includes an angel, a soul, and a heavenly sphere. The tenth or active intellect apprehends itself and forms ideas that bring into existence the concrete beings of the terrestrial realm. The tenth intellect also illuminates the minds of human beings and enables them to contemplate the universals existing in the angelic sphere.

This theory of creation also defines the ultimate relation of human beings to God. In Ibn Sina's view, the human soul is composed of several faculties. The rational faculty includes the theoretical or speculative faculty. This may be perfected through several stages until it reaches the level of intellect, in which the human soul becomes an image of the spiritual world, receiving illumination from the active intellect. This religious vision is essentially an intellectual one, for there is no suggestion of direct union between the human being and the necessary being. In Ibn Sina's view, the highest level of interaction belongs to prophets, who come to know all things perfectly and directly from the active intellect and who communicate their knowledge in imaginative images to ordinary human beings. Prophets teach the existence of God and the practical and ritual aspects of religion. Religion, then, is an imaginative presentation of truths that are known in a pure form to the purely rational soul.

The *Recital of Hayy*, the *Recital of the Bird*, and the *Recital of Salmon and Absal*, three allegorized texts believed to have been written by Ibn Sina, develop the mystical aspects of his philosophical concepts. They recount how a beautiful stranger, an angel of initiation, leads the soul to the orient, to the source of light and the vision of God. This journey of the soul is at once an inward exploration of its own being and a progress through the cosmos. The consciousness that attains knowledge of itself attains knowledge of the successive levels of the divine emanation in the form of angels' souls and celestial spheres. This journey is motivated by love of the divine being and by the realization that the soul is a stranger in the world seeking to return to its origin. The method of this journey is *ta'wil*, interpretation of all existing things in a symbolic way so as to arrive at a new insight into reality. The study of the visionary recitals is then a psychic event leading the soul back to the experience that these texts symbolize.

This journey requires that the soul be detached from every worldly and corrupting influence. Like a steel mirror, it must be polished to perfection to see the divine radiance reflected in itself. In this vision, the soul loses consciousness of itself as the medium of vision and retains consciousness only of the divine presence. This mode of union, however, is not a substantial union of the soul with God, but an intellectual vision of God as the necessary being who is the cause of the contingent world. By purifying imagination and by concentrating the intellect, the soul, driven by love of God, may lose itself in contemplation of the divine truth, but it has no prospect of merger with a transcendent God.

Ibn Sina's philosophy is thus a form of intellectual mysticism, which attempted to reconcile Greek philosophical and theosophical views with scriptural traditions. The doctrine of the necessary being attempts to be consistent with the scripturalist view of the transcendence of God and the separation of the created world from him. The concept of human salvation, although allowing for human intellectual and philosophic comprehension of divine reality, is presented in a way that maintains the ultimate distance between man and God.

Whereas Ibn Sina tried to reconcile the scriptural vision of the transcending oneness and otherness of God with the philosophical and mystical conviction that God and humanity share the same spiritual essence, his efforts were in tension with scriptural traditions. His images and vocabulary come from Greek philosophy, rather than the Quran. Some of his specific doctrines are perceived as heretical. His doctrine of the eternity of the world and its creation as a form of emanation from the divine being contradicts the dominant interpretation of revelation that the world was created ex nihilo. His emphasis on the inherent rationality of human beings contradicts the scripturalist conviction that all that exists is the product of God's inscrutable will. His view that the soul survives by union with the spiritual world contradicts the orthodox view that man, constituted of both body and soul, will at the day of judgment be resurrected as an entity and rewarded or punished as such. His philosophy attempted to define positions in accordance with scripture, but its inspiration and religious vision remained profoundly distinct from orthodox, scripturalist concepts. Moreover, Ibn Sina's metaphysical universe corresponded to gnostic Sufi visions of the quest for salvation. Whereas the orthoprax forms of Sufism stressed the fulfillment of God's commands, gnostics did not think it was necessary to follow ritual laws. The former was an active fulfillment of God's commands; the latter a contemplative state of being.

Ibn Sina stands therefore not only as a central figure in philosophy but as a precursor to Suhrawardi, Ibn al-ʿArabi, and later philosophers and mystics of the sixteenth- and seventeenth-century Iranian school of *hikma* (wisdom). His concepts stand at the center of a long tradition of philosophic speculation and gnostic experimentation – a tradition that continues to appeal to intellectual and religious minorities in Muslim countries to the present day.

In the post-imperial era, two figures stood out as the spokesmen of a theosophical and gnostic form of Sufism oriented toward metaphysical comprehension and ecstatic contemplation. Shihab al-Din Suhrawardi was born in 1153 and was executed for heresy in 1191. He combined the philosophical and theosophical aspects of Sufism with Ibn Sina's philosophy of emanations and with ancient Zoroastrian, Platonic, and Hermetic symbols, thereby synthesizing them into a new form of Islamic mysticism. In Suhrawardi's view, he was reviving an ancient esoteric wisdom, revealed to Hermes Trismegistus and then communicated via Greece, Persia, and Egypt to Islam. He believed himself to be the spokesman of a universal wisdom known to the ancient sages of Iran, Greece, and India and revealed once again in the Quran. Thus, Sufi gnosticism was fed by strong currents in Islamic philosophy, neo-Platonism, Ismaʿili metaphysics, ancient Greek or Hermetic occult sciences, and other Middle Eastern religious ideas.

In his *Hikmat al-Ishraq* (Theosophy of the Orient of Lights) and other symbolic and mystical narratives, Suhrawardi taught that the divine essence was pure light, the source of all existence, and that the reality of all other things was derived from the supreme light. Degrees of light were associated with degrees of knowledge and self-awareness. For Suhrawardi, as for Ibn Sina, the emanation of light from the primary being established a hierarchy of angelic substances standing between God and this world. The angels were limitless in number. In Suhrawardi's vision, there were two orders of angels: a vertical order in which each higher angel generated and dominated the lower ones and each lower angel loved the higher. The vertical order of angels gave rise to the celestial spheres, whereas the horizontal order of angels constituted the world of Platonic forms and archetypes and gave rise to the angels who governed human souls.

In this spiritual universe, the human soul stood in a privileged position. The soul was a heavenly body imprisoned in an earthly body. The imprisoned part sought to reunite with its angelic half and to escape its material and pitiful state. The souls who succeeded in freeing themselves would enjoy the proximity of the supreme light. In Suhrawardi's theosophy, the hierarchy of being was a ladder of illumination along which the purified soul could return from the material world to the world of archetypes. In its own symbols, this vision resembles neo-Platonic, Sufi, and Avicennan ideas.

Ibn al-ʿArabi

Another great theosophist, Ibn al-ʿArabi (d. 1240), born in Murcia in Spain and educated in Seville, made the pilgrimage to Mecca, where he had a vision of the spiritual universe. He saw the divine throne upheld by pillars of light. In the vision, he was told that he was the seal of sainthood, the supreme figure in the hierarchy of saints who upheld the universe. As a result of these visions, he wrote the *Meccan Revelations*. From Mecca, he moved to Konya (in Turkey) and then Damascus. In Damascus, he wrote *The Bezels of Wisdom*, dictated to him by God through the angel Gabriel. This book was the masterpiece of esoteric sciences, for it synthesized Hermetic, neo-Platonic, Ismaʿili, and Sufi influences into a religious vision for which Ibn al-ʿArabi claimed an authority equivalent to that of the Prophet.

In Ibn al-ʿArabi's thought, all reality is one. This is the doctrine of *wahdat al-wujud*, the unity of being. Everything that exists is God. The divine reality transcends all manifestations, but the manifested world is identical with him in essence. A hadith says: "I was a hidden treasure and I wanted to be known so I created the world."[10] The reality of the universe is manifested on several planes, the lower planes being symbols of the higher. The highest is the absolute essence of God; following in the hierarchy of being are the attributes and names of God, the actions and the presence of lordship, the world of spiritual existences, archetypes and forms, and, finally, the world of senses and sensible experience.

The hierarchy of being is understood in terms of theophanies (*tajalliyat*). Each level of reality is a theophany of the divine names, which is brought into being by the self-consciousness of a higher level, which, becoming conscious, generates another state of spiritual being. The process of creation is further imagined as the result of the divine breath, just as words are formed by human breath. The creation

---

[10] A. M. Schimmel, *Mystical Dimensions of Islam*, Chapel Hill, NC, 1975, pp. 189, 268.

is renewed at every breath of the Lord. Existence gushes out from the absolute being, whose mercy and love of his own fulfillment bestows existence.

Ibn al-ʿArabi's vision of the unfolding of the divine being and the creation of the material world follows in broad outline philosophic and neo-Platonic theory. To these theories he adds a rich and original vocabulary and corollary symbols. For example, in his vision, the first intellect of the philosophers, the primary manifestation of the divine being, is variously symbolized as the attributes and names of God, the Logos, the prototypes of creation, the *insan al-kamil* (perfect man), and the *haqiqa muhammadiya* (Muhammadan reality). The divine names symbolize at once the creation of the world, the revelation and the appearance of prophets, and the spiritual capacities of human beings. The symbols of the perfect man and the Muhammadan reality compress the universe into a personified image. The prophets and the saints symbolize the fact that man himself is a manifestation of and ultimately an aspect of the absolute. The person who understands the nature of reality and the unity of existence is a perfect saint. Having discovered the truth, he in turn becomes a guide for the rest of mankind. This condensation of symbols also links the gnostic concept of spiritual reality to the Muslim concept of the historical actuality of the revelation and of Muhammad as Prophet.

In the continuous hierarchy of existence extending from God to the spiritual world to the lowliest beings, man stands in a central position linked to both the world of spirit and the world of matter. By understanding the symbolism of this reality, human beings may pass from this world to the world beyond. Because the spiritual world is a hierarchy of intelligences, through the human capacity for knowledge we may participate in the divine reality. By contemplating the cosmos, we become one with the universe. Thus the intellectual and spiritual task of Muslim gnostics was to understand the nature of symbolic discourse and its relation to concrete reality and to integrate the two by making speech and thought correspond to the physical and social actuality of the world. In gnostic thought, the intangible reality of meaning carried in language and conveyed between persons is a realm of reality separate from the physical world; yet it is the model of the physical world, the image of it, and the guide of our actions in it. Thought and language in the theosophy of Ibn al-ʿArabi are ever the same and ever different from the actualities they define.

Ultimately, the return to God is motivated by love; it is driven by prayer and worship. In the vision of Ibn al-ʿArabi, God is the mirror in which man contemplates his own reality, and man is the mirror in which God knows his essence. Man needs God to exist, and God needs the world to know him.

The doctrine of Ibn al-ʿArabi was the culmination of centuries of Sufi gnostic and philosophical contemplation. His theoretical vision and his personal authority shaped for centuries to come the further development of Sufi theosophy and practice. However, his thought had profound, although unintended, implications for later Sufi practice and for the daily life of Muslim believers. By implication, theosophical metaphysics diminished the importance of observance of law and ritual. For Sufis, cosmic harmony became a justification for abandoning Islamic laws and for seeking states of intoxicated ecstasy. It justified an antinomian morality. Such doctrines were also used to minimize the importance of communal loyalties, for truth is universal. Theosophical views increased the importance of dreams, visions, and ecstasy rather than ordinary Muslim devotions. In some cases, it was allied to the use of drugs and physical techniques to gain ecstatic vision. The doctrines of the perfect man and the invisible hierarchy of saints, the doctrine of the *qutb*, or pole of the universe around which the cosmos revolves, reinforced popular belief in miracles. Although consistent in principle with the orthoprax Sufi orientation, the theosophical doctrines of Ibn al-ʿArabi allowed for religious practices and popular belief by which Muslims sought to short-circuit the trying discipline of the orthoprax way of life and to directly achieve spiritual redemption by contemplative, miraculous, and magical means. For the Sufi masters, Sufism was a devotional practice or gnostic illumination. For ordinary believers, it came to mean the veneration of saints and the tombs of saints. (See Illustration 8.)

Popular Sufism: the veneration of saints
The veneration of saints has its Islamic beginning in the Quran and the hadith, which mention the Prophet, the angels, the scholars, and holy men as potential intercessors between ordinary Muslim believers and God. The earliest form of Muslim veneration of human intermediaries was the cult of the Prophet. By the end of the eighth century, his burial place had become an important place for prayer. ʿAbbasid queen mother Khayzuran (d. 789) built a mosque over the Prophet's grave in Medina. The story of his ascension to heaven from Jerusalem (*miʿraj*) became a focus of popular piety and Sufi inspiration. Al-Bistami (d. 873) used the ascension as a model for his mystical journey, in which the stages of the Prophet's ascent became equivalent to the stations of the Sufis' progress toward God. Other Sufis wrote their own stories of heavenly visits, modeled on that of the Prophet. They organized the levels of heaven into stages corresponding to the emotional levels of the journey toward unity. In the tenth and eleventh centuries, the site of the Prophet's ascension in Jerusalem became a popular place for Muslim worship. Already theologians were explaining that Muhammad was not of ordinary flesh and that he was immune from ordinary sins.

Shiʿis were probably the first to revere the family of the Prophet. In the early tenth century, Shiʿi holy places were provided with elaborate tombs and became centers of pilgrimage. Najaf, the burial place of ʿAli, became a hallowed cemetery; Mashhad, Karbala, and Qum became Shiʿi shrines. The Fatimid caliphs (969–1171) marked the Prophet's birthday (*mawlid*) with recitations from the Quran, prayers, sermons, and a procession of court dignitaries. The Fatimids also built a number of monumental shrines on the graves of descendants of the Prophet, which became

Illustration 8. A Sufi preaching. Source: The Bodleian Library, University of Oxford.

the object of popular pilgrimage in the course of the twelfth century. In 1154 and 1155, the head of Husayn, the martyred son of ʿAli, was transferred to Cairo, where it became the focus of a popular Sunni cult lasting to the present day.

Sunni veneration of the Prophet, the family of the Prophet, and later Muslim martyrs and saints developed either in parallel with or in reaction to Shiʿi pilgrimage and worship at the tombs of the family of ʿAli. By the end of the eleventh century, the *mawlid* (the celebration of the birth of the Prophet) had also become a popular custom among Sunnis in Mesopotamia and Syria; Saladin is credited with bringing it to Egypt as a popular festival. In thirteenth-century Cairo, it was celebrated by Sufis and the common people.

The birth of the Prophet is celebrated in popular narratives, ceremonies, and festivals that express love and closeness to the Prophet and bear the hope of salvation. *Mawlid*s came to include Sufi exercises (*dhikr*) and recitations of mystical verses, hadith, and poems and blessings of Muhammad. Celebrants give thanks to God, express love of the Prophet, and give charity to the poor. These activities are considered an exchange of gifts with the Prophet, a transaction that wins blessings for the donor. The *mawlid* is an auspicious time of year because in that season God's responsiveness and generosity is believed to be greater. A prayer at this time is vastly more efficacious than at other times.

Some scholars were opposed to these celebrations. They saw the *mawlid*s as religion made easy for poor, uneducated, and "undisciplined" people. But they were unable to suppress these beliefs and ceremonies. In modern times, Wahhabis vigorously oppose *mawlid* celebrations, because for them obedience is more important than love, and observance of tradition (sunna) is more important than an emotional attachment or spiritual relationship. Under contemporary Wahhabi influence, the *mawlid* is being redefined as a historical commemoration whose didactic aspect matters more than the experienced presence of the Prophet.

This changing attitude reflects a still deeper transformation in Muslim religiosity. The traditional *mawlid* is premised on the idea that a person is constituted by ties to a community and by shared emotions that have to be publicly dramatized. The modern view emphasizes individuality, so that religious obligations are defined by adherence to precepts; emotions are purely private and personal. The modern idea rejects the transactional bargain through which Muslims sought blessings from God.

In the medieval period, the *mawlid*s of the Prophet set a precedent for the celebration of the birthday (here meaning the death day and the beginning of the afterlife) of saints. Prayers, recitations of poems, processions, *dhikr*, and readings from the Quran were and are conducted at the shrines of saints throughout the Muslim world. In the eleventh century, a mausoleum and school in the memory of Abu Hanifa, the founder of the Hanafi school of law, was reconstructed in Baghdad. In 1176, the Ayyubid dynasty rebuilt the college and tomb of al-Shafi'i in Cairo. It became customary for pilgrims to visit the tombs of companions of the Prophet and to pray at the graves of holy men who martyred themselves for Islam or through whom miracles had been performed. By the beginning of the thirteenth century, there were hundreds of sanctuaries all over the Muslim world. Guides and manuals were written to tell the miracles of the saints and to prescribe the rituals and prayers that would bring blessings on the pilgrim. Early thirteenth-century guidebooks show shrines dispersed throughout Syria, Egypt, Turkey, Iraq, and Iran.

Formal theology and mystical writing gave support to popular belief. As early as the tenth century, al-Tirmidhi (d. 932) developed a theory of sainthood as an explanation of the mysterious power of Sufis. Al-Baqillani (d. 1013) wrote that Sufi masters were friends of God who were capable of performing miracles and of interceding on behalf of ordinary Muslims. He elaborated a theological doctrine to distinguish saints from the Prophet and to define the nature of their miraculous powers. Al-Qushayri and al-Ghazali accepted this doctrine and made it part of formal Muslim belief. Ibn al-ʿArabi elaborated it into a cosmological doctrine of the hierarchy of saints who upheld the order of the universe.

These teachings gave support to popular faith in Sufi ceremonies, belief in the efficacy of prayers performed at the tombs of saints, and the quest for ecstatic experiences. Many Muslims believe that saints do miracles of telepathy and healing, feed the poor, and intervene with the government on their behalf. Funerals and visitations of graves continue the faith in miracles. Thus, the equation of holy men and martyrs with the spiritual universe became an integral aspect of Islamic religious culture. Whatever the legal, intellectual, or doctrinal basis of Sufism, its power and appeal to the masses of everyday Muslim believers came from faith in the miraculous power of saints.

In Mamluk-era Egypt, popular festivals echoed the *mawlid* of the Prophet and the visitation of saints' tombs. ʿId al-Adha (the day of sacrifice for pilgrims on the *hajj* to Mecca) was commemorated by the sacrifice of an animal. On ʿId al-Fitr (the breaking of the fast of Ramadan) Muslims dressed up, gave presents, and went to the cemeteries, often sleeping out in tents. Nawruz, the first day of the Persian solar year (usually midsummer solstice, coinciding with harvest), came to be celebrated in Iraq, Syria, and Egypt in Muslim times. In Egypt, it corresponded with the peak rise of the Nile and was a day to don new clothes, eat good food, and give gifts to friends, and also for carnival-like celebrations. The pilgrimage (*mahmal*) was an occasion for carnival.

DIALOGUES WITHIN ISLAM

By the ninth century, Sunnis accepted the Quran, hadith, and law as the core of Islamic practice; schools of law and colleges had become the central institutions. Each legal school had its own, although similar, jurisprudential methods. They varied in matters of detail, but there was widespread agreement on basic religious issues. With the consolidation of scripturalism as the central expression of Islamic identity, the great debates of the tenth to the thirteenth centuries turned on the relation of hadith and law to theology and Sufism. The debate over law and theology was especially complex, for it involved a debate over the role of rationalism that was carried out at several levels. At one level, there was a debate between philosophy and theology over reason and revelation. At another, there was a general debate between theology and scripturalism over the role theology itself would have in Islamic belief.

The result of these debates was the integration of theological rationalism into the legal mentality. Theology (*kalam*) became an acceptable adjunct of Islamic belief. Some scholars held that rational understanding of the truth was essential to being a good Muslim. For many others, however, theology was but a secondary concern limited to the defense of revealed truth, a kind of medicine for doubters.

It was necessary that at least some members of the community pursue it, but it was not essential for all believers.

The schools of theology became closely linked to the schools of law. The Hanafi school of law harbored the Maturidi school of theology. The Shafi'i law school was the home of Ash'arism. However, not all legists in each school were committed to a theological position; nor was a theological position necessarily part of the teaching of the law schools. Hanbalis, however, rejected rational speculation in any form. Thus, in general, jurists treated theology as an enrichment of their intellectual and religious life rather than as the center of their scriptural position. By a broad, but not quite complete, consensus, theology in various forms was accepted as an important adjunct to Islamic religious faith and activity.

Sufism was similarly integrated with scripturalism. Sufis began with a religious community and forms of worship separate from those of the schools of law. Progressively, however, there was a rapprochement between the legal and the Sufi approaches to Islam. Sufis accepted hadith and law as the basis of Muslim belief and practice. Legists recognized the importance of the inner life to the full realization of the law. In this period, the term "Shari'a" was applied both to the legal and moral norms for behavior specified in the Quran, hadith, and law and also to a rich intellectual, spiritual, and mystical life. (See Table 8.)

Law, theology, and Sufism shaped Muslim consensus around belief in a transcendent God who had created the world and revealed his will to human beings through the agency of his prophets. Muslims believed in the authority of Muhammad and his prophethood and in the tradition of the community. They accepted the goodness of the companions, the genius of the leaders of the law schools, and the piety of Sufi masters as the sources of right guidance. They accepted the literatures of law, theology, and mysticism as setting forth the beliefs, practices, and ethical and moral attitudes required of a good Muslim. The integrated concept of Islam thus combined the scriptural revelation of required actions with philosophical, theosophical, and mystical views of the nature of the universe and the meaning of human action within it.

The Sunni consensus presented a Muslim ideal of an individual who lives in society according to the rules he has been brought up to respect; according to the norms and laws of the Quran, hadith, law, and social custom; yet in harmony with his own inner knowledge, dispositions, choices, and feelings. This cultural ideal combined legal practice and the cultivation of mystical knowledge. The scripturalist-Sufi form of Islam sought salvation in this-worldly conduct of the ritual and social prescriptions of Islam. For Sunni Muslims, a religious life was an active life, consisting of everyday occupations in politics and business, of marriage and family, intermixed with the practice of ritual and other religious obligations. For the Muslim merchant or artisan in the marketplace, the scholar at school, the scribe at court, or the mystic at worship, worldly action and fulfillment of religious commands were the soil in which intellectual and moral skills could grow.

Table 8. *Muslim religious movements and sects*

Kharijism

Azariqa (684–c. 700)	Southwestern Iran: sinners must be excluded from the Muslim community; call for election of caliph; declaration of war on all other Muslims
Ibadis	States founded in Oman, North Africa: sinners may remain Muslims with limited rights; permit political compromise

Philosophers (falasifa)

al-Farabi (d. 950)	Tradition of Alexandrian Hellenistic thought, superiority of reason to revelation
Hunayn b. Ishaq (d. 873)	Translator of Greek texts
Ibn Rushd (Averroes, d. 1198)	Aristotelian, reconciliation with Shari'a
Ibn Sina (Avicenna, d. 1037)	Neo-Platonic philosophy and medicine
al-Kindi (d. c. 866)	Accepts Mu'tazili *kalam*

Shi'ism

'Alid imams	Claim to be sole rightful leaders of Muslim community
Isma'ilis	Militant, established Fatimid and Qarmatian movements
Ithna'ashari	Twelvers, Imamis, pacifist, primarily in Iraq
Zaydis	Followers of Zayd; established dynasties in the Caspian region and Yemen

Sufism

School of Baghdad	al-Junayd (d. 910), sober
School of Khurasan	al-Hallaj (d. 923), ecstatic

Sunni schools of law

Hanafi
Hanbali (*ahl al-hadith*)
Maliki
Shafi'i

Theological schools

Ash'aris	al-Ash'ari (d. 935); compromise between Mu'tazili and Hanbali theological positions
Murji'a	Define good Muslims by faith rather than works; refuse to judge between 'Uthman and 'Ali
Mu'tazilis	Neutral in the disputes over the proper succession to the caliphate; affirm human free will and createdness of the Quran
Qadaris	Hasan al-Basri (d. 728); discuss God's determination and human autonomy

Religious knowledge and virtue could only be achieved by engaging in worldly affairs, although worldly activity has no ultimate value unless it is infused by religious purpose. The orthoprax-Sufi tradition rejected worldly values pursued for their own sake; the enjoyment of family, economic well-being, and power is of secondary importance. This tradition did not incorporate the *areté* of the warrior, the civic responsibility of the Greek citizen, the intellectualism of professionals, and the aestheticism of aristocrats. Still, it did not embrace otherworldly detachment, such as the spirituality of the monk, the creativity of the romantic, or the abstract knowledge of the scientist. It was neither a surrender to the world nor an escape from it. It was a way of living in the world without being absorbed by it or fleeing from it. The goal of the scripturalist-orthoprax-Sufi view of life was devotion to God as the basis of an active worldly personality.

The complex of views contained in orthoprax-Sufi Islam never became a formal system. Islam has no master science as Christianity has in theology. Within the Sunni complex, there were numerous collections of hadith, several equally valid versions of the law, several acceptable theological positions, and different schools of mysticism. Within the Sunni consensus, the range of theological viewpoints could vary from sophisticated philosophical reasoning in theology and law to complete exclusion of the use of reasoning and literal reliance on scripture. Muslim mystics varied from strict adherence to the law to complete antinomian lack of interest in convention, ritual, and morality.

Whereas the orthoprax-Sufi consensus allowed considerable flexibility within itself, the Sunni community also permitted major religious positions to develop outside its framework. Although devotional, rational Sufi positions were partly merged into the general position, philosophy, gnosticism, and popular religion maintained an independent stance, challenging Islamic orthodoxy. The availability of religious alternatives and the debates concerning their validity made up a more comprehensive program of Islamic religious discussions.

The most important religious alternative came from within Sufism. The gnostic and theosophical tradition influenced by philosophy, although partly accepted into the Sunni consensus, represented an altogether different view of human religious goals. Whereas the scripturalist view insisted on the fulfillment of God's commands in worldly action, the gnostic goal, embodied in Sufism, Isma'ilism, and philosophical literatures, was insight and contemplative union with the divine reality, to be achieved by purification of the soul and its detachment from bodily and material concerns.

The various forms of gnosticism, however, differed in their comprehension of the mechanism of this purification, vision, and union with God. The peripatetic philosophers stressed reason as the basis of knowledge of God and as the key to a total transformation of the soul that enabled the gnostic not only to comprehend but to enter into the divine presence. Some gnostics stressed reason as the essential aspect of the human soul and the metaphysical structure of the universe. Others stressed emotional forms of illumination; still others stressed the authority of imams and spiritual guides. In all its variations, gnosticism was a quest for a direct contemplative realization of the divine for which scripturalist symbols, rational dialectics, ritual practices, and ethical behavior were all secondary considerations. It was a religion of the visionary soul rather than the active person.

Another religious alternative within the Sunni tradition was popular Islam. Faith in direct divine intervention in human affairs put aside the whole of the Sunni effort to build a morally disciplined worldly life on the teachings of the scriptural tradition. Popular faith held that the saints could intercede on behalf of human

Table 9. *Muslim worship*

Five pillars of Islam	
hajj	Pilgrimage to Mecca
salah	Prayer performed five times daily: before dawn, midday, mid-afternoon, before sunset, mid-evening
shahada	Statement of faith: There is no God but God, and Muhammad is the Prophet of God
zakat	Almsgiving
Prayer rituals	
Friday midday prayer	Performed in *jami'* (mosque for the whole community), sermon
imam	Leader of prayer
khutba	Preached by *khatib* from the *minbar*, in which the authority of the ruler is acknowledged
masjid	Mosque; place of prayer furnished with a *mihrab* (niche to mark direction of Mecca), *minbar* (pulpit), *maqsura* (box for caliph)
muezzin	Stands in the minaret to summon worshipers to prayer
qibla	Facing in the direction of Mecca, which is necessary for performing prayer
wudu'	Ablutions prior to prayer
Festivals	
'id al-adha	Greater *'id*: celebration and animal sacrifices to mark end of the pilgrimage
'id al-fitr	Lesser *'id*: festival celebrating the end of Ramadan
laylat al qadr	27th of Ramadan: Night of Majesty commemorating first revelation of the Quran
Ramadan	Ninth lunar month, dedicated to daytime fasting
Optional festivals	
'ashura'	10th of Muharram: Shi'i festival commemorating martyrdom of Husayn
laylat al-mi'raj	Night of Muhammad's ascent to heaven from Jerusalem
mawlid al-nabi	Birthday of the Prophet

beings and could transmit God's miraculous powers into the world through the person of his saints and the physical things with which they had come into contact. The tombs of saints were considered especially potent.

Outside the Sunni fold, there were also communal alternatives. For the Shi'is, the critical issue was loyalty to the family of 'Ali. They believed that the divine spirit passed from imam to imam in each successive generation. This divine grace both entitled the 'Alids to the caliphate and made them an infallible source of knowledge of the divine will. Whereas Muhammad had revealed the Quran, its interpretation was vested in the infallible imams. In their view, the true source of belief in each generation was ultimately not the text of tradition, the consensus of the jurists, or the piety of other Muslims, but an imam descended from 'Ali. From this vantage point, Shi'ism left a legacy of religious teachings similar to the Sunni types, but it also moved toward a merger with Sufism, in that the divinely graced imam became the example of a mystical reunion with God. Shi'ism is characterized by a religious mood that stresses hope in the return of the imam as a messiah who will redeem Muslims from the burdens of the world. Shiʿism is also chiliastic in believing that history will come to an end. The cycles of prophets and imams will culminate in a cataclysm, out of which will emerge a reborn mankind and the kingdom of God on earth.

The partitions of Shiʿi Islam are different from those of Sunni Islam. Instead of schools of law, there are sects founded by the followers of the various imams. The Twelver branch followed one line of succession; the Ismaʿilis followed another. In time, there would be more disagreements, each leading to the development of a new sect with different religious principles. Shiʿi communities, often at war with their Sunni neighbors, were established throughout the Middle East. (See Table 9.)

With all these variations, what did it mean to be a Muslim? It meant that one believed in the truth of God's existence and in the revelation of the Quran, and that one adhered to at least some of the positions in a wide range of religious expression. Muslim believers clustered around one of several Sunni schools of law or one of several Shiʿi sects. Islam, then, included a variety of religious positions sharing the same historical tradition. To be a Muslim meant to ponder these positions in the terms set down in the medieval era of Islamic civilization.

CHAPTER 24

CONCLUSION: MIDDLE EASTERN ISLAMIC PATTERNS

What we now classify as a Middle Eastern Islamic civilization is actually the by-product of a process that occupied six hundred years, from the beginning of the seventh to the beginning of the thirteenth centuries. However innovative, Islamic civilization was constructed on a framework of institutions and cultures inherited from the ancient Middle East. On the eve of the Islamic era, Middle Eastern societies were organized on several levels. At the base, there were numerous local, parochial communities built around factional, lineage, tribal, and village groups. These communities were integrated by market exchanges and by great religious associations – Jewish, Christian, or Zoroastrian. The larger-scale economic networks and religious associations were in turn under the rule of the Byzantine and Sasanian empires. On the cultural level, the ancient heritage included the monotheistic religions, imperial arts and literatures, and philosophy and science. This complex institutional and cultural heritage was carried over into the Islamic era. Despite the rise and fall of empires and shifts in economic activity, the fundamental aspects of technology, modes of production, and the relation of human communities to the natural environment continued unaltered. Also, the basic modes of state organization and family and religious association remained the same. The characteristic changes of the Islamic era were the formation of new political and social identities, the organization of new religious communities, and the generation, out of the elements of the past, of a new cultural style.

New political and religious identities for Middle Eastern societies began in Arabia. While under the influence of Byzantine and Sasanian civilizations, Arabia was not fully integrated into the rest of the region. It was basically a lineage society in which the conflicts of lineage and commercial communities and the religious and cultural influences emanating from the rest of the Middle East made possible the emergence of a new prophet, Muhammad, and the revelation of a new religion, Islam. To Muhammad, God revealed a new monotheism, which differed in its specific teachings, eschatological consciousness, and literary qualities from Judaism and Christianity. The Prophet also organized a new community parallel in form to Jewish and Christian religious associations.

The Muslim community in Mecca and Medina acted as an integrating force in a lineage society. The Prophet and his disciples mediated among lineage groups, regulated the economy, created a state, and inspired moral reform while maintaining basic lineage structures. In Arabia, the existence of the two levels of segmentary and religious organization resulted in a complex system of values. In principle, the Quran introduced a concept of transcendent reality, as opposed to the aggrandizement of tribal groups and the *areté* of the tyrannical, boastful, and hedonistic warrior, and a community based on religious brotherhood and personal humility, modesty, and self-restraint. In practice, however, the family and lineage structures of Arabian peoples became part of Islamic society. Pagan virtues were preserved by being vested with new meaning as Islamic ethics, and bedouin identities persisted alongside Islamic loyalties. In its first guise, the Islamic mission became a model for the way in which radical religious values and sectarian impulses would later function in lineage and tribal societies.

IMPERIAL ISLAMIC SOCIETY

The next phase in the transformation of Middle Eastern Islamic societies was the Arab-Muslim conquests and migrations. They led to the creation of a new regime (the caliphate), the settlement of new cities and towns, the formation of new urban communities, the rise of trade, and the growth of agriculture. In the garrison cities of the Middle East, warrior-bedouin migrants were assimilated to non-Arab populations to form new mixed communities. Migrant Arabs were transformed into an urban-dwelling, occupationally differentiated population that included workers, artisans, merchants, and a new religious elite of Quran readers, scholars of law and Arabic letters, and ascetic and charismatic preachers. The town populations were also stratified on the basis of political officeholding, landownership, and tribal chieftainship and organized into new religious sects and political movements.

The new urban societies generated both the resources and the conflicts that would shape the caliphate and the imperial regime. From the towns, the caliphate could draw skilled manpower and economic resources. The ʿAbbasids in particular based their regime on the diverse populations that flocked to Baghdad as well as other Arab cities. The pressures of urban social change also generated conflict over political interests and over the caliphate. The first Muslim century witnessed a series of civil wars. Initially, the problem was factional divisions in the Arab elite, the balance of central and local power, and the role of religious versus political factors in the concept and identity of the regime. The major struggle was between factions united by commitment to Islam and Arab tribal coalitions. The second civil war was motivated by sectarian Khariji and Shiʿi opposition and by continuing factionalism within the Arab elite. The third civil war, which brought the ʿAbbasids to power, was the product of the division between Arabs assimilated into the general society and those active in the military, a struggle marked by strong ideological conflict over "Arab" versus "Muslim" identity.

Each of the civil wars forced the caliphate to develop the institutional mechanisms to keep political power and to legitimize dynastic rule. To consolidate its position, the caliphate adopted Byzantine and Sasanian institutions and concepts of imperial rule while giving them a new Islamic definition. The Umayyads adopted the bureaucratic administration of the older empires and patronized architectural works that integrated Byzantine, Sasanian, and Christian symbols into Islamic designs. The ʿAbbasids continued the Umayyad trend toward consolidation of an imperial regime and its definition in transmuted Middle Eastern terms. Their regime was centered on a royal court; they governed the provinces through clients and servants of the rulers, using a combination of bureaucratic tax-collecting methods and quasi-feudal forms of administration in which local princes and chieftains were confirmed in power and given status as servants of the caliph. ʿAbbasid administration depended on a coalition of elites throughout the Middle East. The regime brought together Arab soldiers; Iraqi, Egyptian, and Iranian landlords; Nestorian scribes; Jewish merchants; Inner Asian warlords; and others to serve the central regime. These elites were united by loyalty to the caliphate, by clientele and family ties linking the center and the provinces, and by common interests in the exploitation of the empire. These were the people made available by the extended period of economic change, social mobility, and urbanization that followed the Arab conquests. They transformed the Arab conquest kingdom into a universal Middle Eastern empire.

To legitimize their domination, the ʿAbbasids patronized cultural activities that made clear the historical roots of the regime and its cosmopolitan inclusiveness. The court culture signified the superiority of the Arab-Muslim imperium by adapting the artistic and ceremonial themes of its ancestors and incorporating them into a new ritual of state. It signified its universality by patronizing the various Middle Eastern cultures: the poetic and historical traditions of the Arabs, the *adab* literature of Iran, and the Hellenistic philosophy and sciences of the Mediterranean. Imperial culture justified the exercise of power as a divine necessity and stressed the hierarchy of society, the responsibility of masters, and the subordination of the masses. The new culture gave the new elite a shared language, literary expression, and personal values based on the validation of worldly power and wealth. In the ancient debate over whether it was legitimate to enjoy the goods of this world, the ʿAbbasid imperial culture was resoundingly positive. As in the past, out of the formation of an empire came a new civilization. Empire was a moral and cultural entity as well as a system of political exploitation.

However, the very social processes that had made it possible to construct an empire extending over all the Middle East – the new urban centers, economic growth, and the formation of cosmopolitan communities – also created an independent urban population, led by religious chiefs and organized into sectarian communities, who would oppose the imperial vision with one of their own. The family or companions of the Prophet and their descendants, reciters of the Quran, scholars of Islamic law and history, and Sufi ascetics won over groups of disciples, students, and followers and thus generated numerous Shi'i and Khariji associations, Sunni schools of law, and, later, Sufi discipleships. Most of these groups were small, even esoteric, cults. Some of them acquired a mass following. In opposition to the caliphs, all of these groups claimed to embody the tradition of the Prophet and the true teachings of Islam. Shi'is and the Kharijis at first violently opposed the caliphate, but by the ninth century the Twelver Shi'is and many Kharijis had renounced world-transforming political aspirations in favor of local community affairs and pious personal lives, living in an atmosphere of mourning for lost hopes and of messianic dreams. Instead of trying to transform the world, they withdrew to a pious existence within it. Even Sunnis, who supported the caliphate in principle, withdrew from public commitments and concentrated on small-scale community life and personal piety. In the urban milieu, the crucial question was the following: what is the proper way to live the life of this world in view of the eternity to come? Was a good Muslim a person of good deeds or of inner faith, one who fulfilled his obligations to the law or who cultivated a spiritual contact with God? Between the seventh and the tenth centuries, the Muslim urban response to these questions was elaborated in Quran commentary, hadith, law, theology, and mystical discourses that incorporated into Islam the heritage of Greece and Iran as well as of Arabia and Muhammad, and recast the historical religions of the Middle East into a new high cultural monotheistic vision.

Imperial and urban versions of Islamic culture were closely related. The court accepted the religious supremacy of the Quran, the validity of hadith, and the Islamic historical tradition. Law had important political, regulatory, and moral functions; many legists and jurists were employed by the state. Mu'tazili theology was as much a court as an urban science. Similarly, urban scholars and Sufis accepted many aspects of court culture. The symbols of palace and mosque, the legitimacy of the caliph's authority, the cultural primacy of the Arabic language, poetry and history, and aspects of philosophy, neo-Platonism, and theology were all accepted in urban circles. Still, despite the interpenetration of cultural interests, the two milieus were in conflict over basic values. The Hanbalis, in particular, resisted the religious authority of the caliphs. As a result of ninth-century struggles between caliph and scholars, it became clear that two elites – caliphate and court versus scholars and Sufis – would elaborate two distinct concepts of Islam – one imperial and one urban, one political and one communal, one worldly and one pietistic. Ever after, Islamic societies have been characterized, in fact if not in culturally recognized principle, by separate state and religious institutions.

At the end of the ninth century, Muslim elites and their cultural vision still represented only a limited population, including the state elites and the populace of the Arab-Muslim towns and converted rural districts. The translation of these elite influences and cultural paradigms into a mass Islamic society accelerated with the disintegration of the ʿAbbasid Empire in the ninth and tenth centuries. The empire disintegrated not as the result of external shocks but as the outcome of the inherent evolution of its basic institutions. The caliphate, caught in the dilemma of representing both worldly power and religious values, compromised its political authority and was forced to depend more and more on military force. Both army and administration broke up into independent and self-serving factions; factional competition made it impossible for the caliphate to maintain control over the central government and the provinces. The result was the rise to power of independent warlords and the outbreak of popular rebellions. By 945, the empire was no more. The process of disintegration, moreover, destroyed the bureaucratic and landowning classes that had controlled the empire and opened the way to power for nomadic elites, slave soldiers, local warlords, and others who had no interest in collaboration with a central government.

STATES AND COMMUNITIES IN A FRAGMENTED MIDDLE EAST

With the breakdown of the ʿAbbasid Empire, the separation of state and religious elites and institutions became more marked. The Middle East was conquered by Turkish nomadic warriors and by slave warlords. In the post-imperial era, the ʿAbbasid caliphs kept only nominal authority, whereas Buwayhid, Ghaznavid, and Saljuq sultans organized the military-political regimes. Muslim religious associations took on the task of organizing the populace.

Under the Saljuqs, a standard pattern of institutions developed, in which the power of the ruler was based on a praetorian slave guard and the manipulation of nomadic tribal levies. Court bureaucrats and scholars helped maintain administrative services; in the provinces, the sultans were represented by governors, garrisons, and fiscal inspectors. *Iqtaʿs* (quasi-feudal grants of tax income to soldiers) were distributed widely, decentralizing control over rural revenues. These institutions did not suffice to provide a lasting political order. Disputes among competing members of aristocratic lineages, tribal lords, and slave generals prevented the centralization of power. The *iqtaʿ* system of administration, in which tax-collecting privileges were parceled out among the military elite, also contributed to the fragmentation of power. Nevertheless, the institution of the sultanate, slave military forces, and *iqtaʿ* administration formed a pattern of government that would become the norm.

The consolidation of these institutions was accompanied by the articulation of concepts to define, rationalize, and legitimize the exercise of power. Muslims viewed the caliphate as the institution mandated by the Prophet to uphold Islamic law, protect the security of Muslim peoples, and wage jihads. All legitimate power was delegated from the caliph to sultans and from sultans to their subordinates. Sultans were expected to uphold Islamic justice and education, patronize the scholars, and suppress heresy. If he upheld Islamic law, a ruler was considered legitimate regardless of how he had come to power. Government was also legitimized in personal terms. All regimes were built on the loyalties of slaves, clients, and retainers to their masters and patrons. A subordinate officer conceived of himself not as a functionary of the state but as an elevated servant of the ruler. Slavery was but the most forceful expression of the personal bonds that complemented concepts of delegated authority. Furthermore, the state was identified with the person of the ruler. In all the political literatures of the time – Muslim, Persian, and Greek – the ruler was portrayed as the prototype of the perfected human being. He embodied wisdom and virtue, restrained the evil inclinations of his subordinates, and inspired goodness in his subjects. Government functioned as a consequence of personal ties and was considered legitimate because it was conducive to the fulfillment of religious ideals.

Finally, government was legitimized in terms of historical descent from ancient empires and of the fulfillment of cosmic and divine purposes. Architecture, art, and poetry, in Arabic or Persian regional variants, symbolized the attachment of the political regimes to the divinely given order of the universe, the inherent glory of the ruler, the rightness of the pursuit and exercise of power, and the legitimacy of aesthetic refinement and luxury. The sultanal regimes patronized historical writing to trace the genealogical descent and mythic connection of present rulers to ancient Persian and Turkish kings. As God's own servant, the ruler was entrusted with the care of the world and given authority over men whose fate was confided to him. The ruler ordered society, promoted the construction of civilization, and even had magical powers, which could affect the course of nature. Despite the arbitrary exercise of powers, states were an image of the cosmos. They were vital not only to daily life but to the mythic wholeness of the social order. However damaged the great empires, however many military lords became independent, however much control of the land was distributed in *iqta's*, however much authority was conceded to local notables and local militias, the state continued to represent a commitment to a transcending order. Thus, whereas the sultanates had Islamic functions and identities, their Islamic aspect was paralleled by non-Islamic Persian and Turkish concepts of the nature of government. An "Islamic" state was also an expression of a non-Islamic territorial and cultural identity.

As states became militarized and disconnected from religious institutions, Muslim associations became the almost universal basis of Middle Eastern communal organization. Until the ninth century, Islam was the religion of the Arab populations and assimilated urban groups, but from the tenth to the thirteenth centuries the mass of Middle Eastern peoples converted to Islam. This was due to the dissolution of the 'Abbasid Empire, its replacement by foreign military elites, the ruin of the landowning and administrative classes, and their replacement by Muslim religious leaders – who converted the uprooted masses and provided them with leadership and religious organization through the Sunni schools of law, Sufi orders, Shi'i sects, and other Muslim groups.

The schools of law were not colleges and institutions but were schools in the sense that the adherents shared a common legal tradition. They were associations of scholars, teachers, and students adhering to the law codes developed by discussion among legal scholars in the eighth and ninth centuries. Through the law schools, scholars organized higher education and trained teachers and judicial administrators; from the schools came consultants, notaries, and judges. The schools also gathered a popular following. The students considered themselves personal disciples of their masters; the communities in which the schools were located provided patrons and supporters, especially from the merchant and artisan classes. Sufi orders were based on the disciples of each master and on the groups of Sufis who lived in common residences called *khanaqas*. Orders were formed when Sufi masters in the twelfth and thirteenth centuries began to reckon themselves the descendants of earlier teachers. Those who descended from the same teacher regarded themselves as perpetuating a common spiritual discipline and as units of a much larger religious movement accepting the same higher authority. Such formations grew beyond their local origins and became regional and even worldwide brotherhoods.

In an urban context, the legal communities and Sufi orders served as confessional collectivities that could recruit individuals across the lines of existing community structures and unify smaller-scale family, clan, or residential collectivities into larger units. But Muslim religious associations could also operate wholly within the framework of existing collective units. Sunni legal schools, Sufi orders, or Shi'i sects were often identified with particular neighborhoods, or occupational and ethnic minorities, and gave previously existing collectivities an Islamic identity.

COPING WITH THE LIMITS OF WORLDLY LIFE

The ethos of these associations varied on a spectrum ranging from otherworldly ecstatic, contemplative forms of Sufism to very worldly family and business orientations. There was a broad middle ground – the orthoprax-Sufi position. This was represented by the Hanafi and Shafi'i schools of law, the Ash'ari and Maturidi schools of theology, and the "sober" Sufi tradition of al-Junayd, al-Qushayri, and al-Ghazali. This middle ground attempted to integrate commitment to the principle of the caliphate as the basis of the ideal Muslim community, devotion to the fulfillment of Islamic law, belief in the limited use of reason for understanding religious truths, and the practice of Sufi ethical and meditational exercises. It was an attempt to combine the correct external forms of social and ritual behavior with inner emotional and spiritual awareness.

Sunnis with this orientation had a nuanced attitude toward worldly actualities. They accepted existing regimes as legitimate by virtue of the inherent need for order in society, and they worked out routine ways of collaborating with states. Political obedience was highly emphasized. Scholars reserved for themselves a consultative role and the right to admonish, to educate, and to give moral advice to rulers; they expected rulers to give them control over legal administration and to patronize Muslim educational and charitable activities. Within this framework, however, Sunnis were involved not so much in politics as in community affairs. Their concern was to uphold public morality, to apply Islamic law to family and commercial affairs, to educate, to heal, and to mediate local conflicts.

Sunni Muslims accepted the given clan, lineage, tribal, or clientele substructures of Middle Eastern societies and with them inequalities of wealth and property. They regarded social and economic justice as matters of individual behavior. Sunni values were thus neutral with regard to different economic systems; there was no Muslim teaching on the proper structure of the economy and no obvious correlation between Islamic beliefs and any particular economic organization. Furthermore, if we compare the dominant Sunni attitude toward economic activity with later Protestant attitudes, we find that, although Muslims were highly motivated in economic matters, they did not see such activity as a vehicle for the transformation of the world or of the individual. Sunni Muslim leaders did not try to mobilize people for economic ends but called on them to lead a pious life in the context of economic and other worldly activities.

Acceptance of the world was modified, however, by an attitude of detachment and a rejection of commitment. Although many scholars and Sufis accepted the responsibilities of political power, held office, accumulated land and property, and served as spokesmen for the needs of their people, there was a deep strand of feeling opposed to such engagements. The companions of princes were regarded as morally corrupt. Scholars and Sufis characteristically refused official positions and turned down royal gifts. Disengagement was taken as a mark of piety and of the highest moral virtue. The refusal to give moral assent to the world as it is was accompanied by a nostalgia for the restoration of the true caliphate and a yearning for the coming of the savior. Nostalgia expressed withdrawal from the actual world, but it also served to ratify things as they were.

The Hanbalis cultivated a more active stance. They undertook vigilante action to enforce morality, suppress alcohol consumption and prostitution, and attack rival sects. They rallied Muslim volunteers for holy war and on occasion attempted to restore the political power of the caliphate. This activism, however, was channeled mainly into pressuring existing political regimes to uphold Muslim morality, rather than being aimed at changing the political order. Thus, the majority of Sunnis accepted the world as it was, yet withheld their full assent by refusing to be directly involved in politics, by actively campaigning to improve public morals, and by nostalgic reflection and eschatological yearning.

The reasons for this complex orientation can be understood when we consider that Muslim religious associations were partially but never fully differentiated from other sociopolitical institutions. The Sunni positions reflected a transcendent religious vision embedded in sectarian associations, but these associations existed within the overall political framework of the sultanal regimes, and they were inter-locked with parochial lineage, residential, and other solidarities. Therefore, the tension between religious and other commitments could not be absolute, and the complex relationships among them had to be expressed in subtle modes of acceptance, detachment, and rejection.

Islamic organizations and identities were also institutionalized in rural societies, although on different terms. Throughout the Middle East, clans, lineages, and vil-lage communities led by independent chieftains – legitimized in terms of tribal tradition and by the acceptance of an age-old pattern of culture – continued to be the backbone of the social order. The basic lineage and factional structures were reinforced by Arab and Turkish migrations. In these societies, Muslim religious leadership and Islamic symbols were used to unite factionalized peoples into more unified religious-political movements. The Arab-Muslim conquests were prototyp-ical. In addition, Berbers in North Africa were united under Kharijism, Shi'ism, Sunni reformism, and later Sufism, into conquering religious movements such as the Fatimids, the Almoravids, and the Almohads. Kharijis in eastern Arabia, Qarma-tis in the Fertile Crescent, and later the Safavids in western Iran are other examples of Muslim religious leaders and symbols becoming the basis of rural unification in the quest for the ever-elusive just Islamic society.

There is also evidence for the beginnings of widespread acceptance of Islamic identity by rural collectivities in the form of the veneration of Sufis and worship at shrines. By the thirteenth century, the doctrinal basis for the veneration of Sufis as intercessors between man and God had been established, and pre-Islamic magi-cal practices and superstitions were accepted as part of popular Islam. Sufis were commonly believed to be saints and were venerated as intermediaries between the material and the spiritual worlds, as miracle workers and as dispensers of blessings. On this basis, they served to mediate disputes; facilitate the selection of chiefs; organize long-distance trade; teach the young; heal the sick; provide amulets; officiate at circumcisions, marriages, and funerals; celebrate festivals; do white magic; and otherwise uphold the tenuous connection of human beings with the world of the spirits and the divine. This type of Sufism also led to venera-tion of the tomb, and the disciples and descendants, of the holy man, and to a religious life of sacrifices and festivals around the tombs. Belief in Islam did not necessarily lead to the formation of an organized association capable of collec-tive action but served as a shared identity among diverse peoples who preserved their own kinship, territorial, linguistic, ethnic, and other bases of non-Islamic culture.

STATE AND RELIGION IN THE MEDIEVAL ISLAMIC PARADIGM

The crucial feature of this system of states and religious communities was the tacit collaboration of state military, local scholars, and Sufi elites. The foreign origin and the militarization of the ruling elites emphasized the distinction between the state and the religious elites and required their political cooperation. The nomadic and slave military elites needed the collaboration of the scholars in order to govern. The Saljuqs were leaders of tribal groups with no experience in ruling an agriculturally based empire. Scribes, finance officials, estate managers, and other technicians were vital. Furthermore, the nomadic and slave elites needed scholars, for both political and psychological reasons, to recognize the rightfulness of their regimes. Scholars were the guardians of tradition and to the Saljuqs – who were at first lacking in technical skills and literary and social knowledge – represented the epitome of a desired way of life. They looked to the scholars to be tutored, educated, and guided in acceptable courses of action. Thus, the conquerors were conquered by their subjects.

In return, the scholars accepted the need for a military regime because it alone could protect the trade routes and the agricultural villages from bedouins and bandits. The scholars favored a strong state to repress factional strife and gang warfare and to act as an arbiter of disputes that the communities themselves could not regulate. Moreover, they were interested in an accommodation with military regimes because they could, by serving in the state administration, transform themselves from local elites into an imperial governing class. The state accorded them positions that could consolidate their local power. Finally, military elites could give valuable support to Sunni social and educational missions.

To work out this tacit bargain, the Ghaznavids and the Saljuqs restored mosques, built colleges and Sufi retreats, endowed trusts, and appointed members of the law schools to official positions. The Saljuqs suppressed Shi'ism and gave vigorous support to Sunni Islam. In return, Sunni scholars preached the legitimacy of established regimes, supported favored princes against their rivals, supplied cadres for the state administration, facilitated taxation, and accepted the nomadic and slave conquest states as part of the legitimate and necessary order of Islamic societies. Although the religious notables could mediate between military regimes and city populations, they lacked the ideological and economic bases to be fully independent. Their inevitable collaboration with the state elites brought the rest of society under control.

In the post-imperial period, new forms of state organization, community life, and culture were integrated into a new order. The post-imperial system of government and society was profoundly different from that of the earlier era. The earlier 'Abbasid era had been characterized by a universal empire built on the support of Middle Eastern landowning, bureaucratic, and merchant elites who forged a common religious and cultural identity. In the post-imperial period, the unity of the Middle East was no longer to be found in empire but was found in the almost universal diffusion of certain forms of social and political organization and of allegiance to common values and symbols. For the first time in Middle Eastern history, the peoples of western Asia belonged, if not to the same empire, to the

same culture, religion, and type of political society. Islam had become a universal
society without a universal empire.

The institutions and traditions of Middle Eastern Islamic societies held a crucial
place in the development of later Islamic societies. They bequeathed a repertoire
of cultural and religious ideas that remain operative in Islamic lands to the present
day. From this era came the forms of Islamic orthopraxis contained in hadith and
law, Sufi forms of ethical and spiritual self-cultivation, Shiʿi concepts of religious
leadership, ideals of mystical and gnostic transcendence, popular saint worship
and magical practices, and a socially active and reformist Islamic ideal.

This period also gave rise to the basic elements of Islamic social organization:
states, schools of law, and Sufi orders. Finally, this era set the precedents for a
distinction between state institutions and Muslim religious communities. All the
while, the persistence of non-Islamic modes of social and economic organization
and non-Islamic cultures generated an endlessly rich variety of social and communal possibilities and an abiding ambiguity as to what constitutes an Islamic society.
Wherever Islam was established, these institutions and cultural concepts would be
combined and recombined and merged with local traditions to form new types of
Islamic societies. Each of them would bear profoundly the imprint of the Middle
Eastern beginnings of Islamic societies.

PART III

THE GLOBAL EXPANSION OF ISLAM FROM THE SEVENTH TO THE NINETEENTH CENTURIES

CHAPTER 25

INTRODUCTION: ISLAMIC INSTITUTIONS

Between the seventh and the thirteenth centuries, the historical institutions of pre-Islamic Middle Eastern societies were recast in Islamic forms. New empires and states were organized under Islamic practices of authority and symbols of legitimacy. Muslim religious elites, including scholars (*'ulama'*) and Sufi holy men, generated Islamic forms of worship, education, and legal administration. The majority of Middle Eastern peoples became Muslim, although what that meant in practice varied by region; pastoral tribes, peasants, urban artisans, merchants, and state elites elaborated diverse Islamic identities. A new civilization, in part royal and artistic, in part urban and pietistic, came into being.

In subsequent eras, an Islamic system of institutions and its various cultures would continue to evolve in the already Islamized regions of the Middle East – including Iran, Transoxania, and the Arab provinces. These societies would also serve as a paradigm for the establishment of Islamic societies in other parts of the world. From the seventh to the nineteenth centuries, Islamic societies – based on the interaction of local institutions and cultures and Middle Eastern influences – were established in Anatolia and the Balkans, Inner Asia, South and Southeast Asia, and sub-Saharan Africa. The development of a global system of Islamic societies, however, was blocked in the eighteenth and nineteenth centuries by the growing political and economic power of Europe. The consolidation of European colonial rule in most of the Muslim world marks the end of the pre-modern era and the beginning of the modern transformation of Muslim societies. (See Map 9.)

CONVERSION TO ISLAM

North Africa and the Middle East
From the seventh to the tenth centuries, Islam was carried by Arab-Muslim conquests to North Africa, Spain, Sicily, and the Mediterranean coasts of Europe. Muslim warriors, merchants, and scholars spread the religion to Saharan and Sudanic

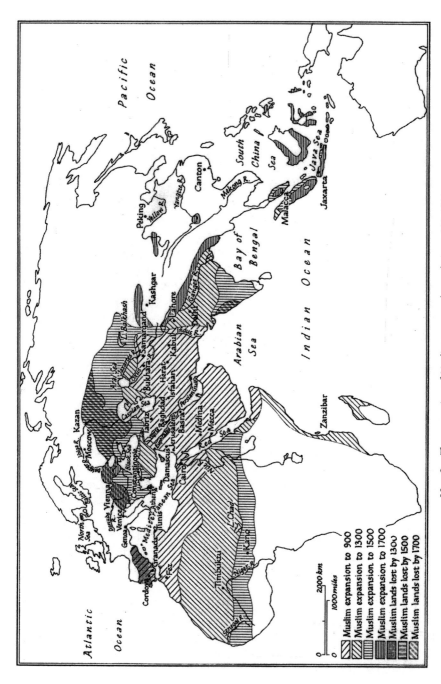

Map 9. The expansion of Muslim states and populations, 900–1700

Muslim expansion to 900
Muslim expansion to 1300
Muslim expansion to 1500
Muslim expansion to 1700
Muslim lands lost by 1300
Muslim lands lost by 1500
Muslim lands lost by 1700

2000 km
1000 miles

Atlantic Ocean
Pacific Ocean
Indian Ocean
Arabian Sea
Bay of Bengal
South China Sea
Java Sea
Red Sea
Caspian Sea
Black Sea
North Sea
L. Balkhash

Cordoba
Toledo
Granada
Fez
Tunis
Venice
Rome
Vienna
Constantinople
Moscow
Kazan
Volga R.
Samarkand
Bukhara
Kashgar
Peking
Canton
Yellow R.
Yangtze R.
Mekong R.
Malacca
Jaxarta
Zanzibar
Kano
Timbuktu
Niger R.
Senegal R.
Cairo
Medina
Mecca
Baghdad
Basra
Jerusalem
Damascus
Isfahan
Herat
Kabul
Lahore
Delhi
Ganges R.
Indus R.
Oman
Persian Gulf

344

Africa. Other Islamic societies originated from the conversion of Inner Asian Turkish peoples to Islam and their migrations, conquests, and empire building. From the tenth to the fourteenth centuries, Turkish peoples took Islam westward into Anatolia, the Balkans, and southeastern Europe; eastward into Inner Asia and China; and southward into Afghanistan and the Indian subcontinent. They thus played a crucial historical role in the diffusion of Islam and in the founding of the Saljuq, Mongol, Timurid, Safavid, Ottoman, Uzbek, and Mughal empires. Finally, another cluster of Islamic societies originated from the expansion of Muslim merchants in the Indian Ocean. From Arabia, Islam reached India and East Africa (tenth to twelfth centuries); from Arabia and India, it reached the Malay Peninsula and the Indonesian archipelago (thirteenth to fifteenth centuries); from the coastal zones, it spread to the interior of the islands and continents.

The expansion of Islam involved different factors in different regions. In North Africa, Anatolia, the Balkans, and India, it was carried by nomadic Arab or Turkish conquerors. In the Indian Ocean and West Africa, it spread by peaceful contacts among merchants or through the preaching of missionaries. In some cases, the diffusion of Islam depended on its adoption by local ruling families; in others, it appealed to urban classes of the population or tribal communities. Its appeal was couched in interwoven terms of political and economic benefits and of a sophisticated culture and religion.

The question of why people convert to Islam has always generated intense feeling. Earlier generations of Western scholars believed that conversions to Islam were made at the point of the sword and that conquered peoples were given the choice of conversion or death. It is now apparent that conversion by force, although not unknown in Muslim countries, was, in fact, rare. Muslim conquerors ordinarily wished to dominate, rather than convert, and most conversions to Islam were voluntary.

Even voluntary conversions are suspect to Western observers. Were they made out of true belief, or for opportunistic political or social reasons? Surely there are innumerable cases of conversion to Islam by the illumination of faith or by virtue of the perceived sanctity of Muslim scholars and holy men, as well as by calculation of political and economic advantage. In most cases, worldly and spiritual motives for conversion blended together. Moreover, conversion to Islam did not necessarily imply a complete turning from an old to a totally new life. Although it entailed the acceptance of new religious beliefs and membership in a new religious community, most converts retained a deep attachment to the cultures and communities in which they were raised and continued to live. In the sections that follow, I stress the historical circumstances that have induced large numbers of people to adhere to Islam, rather than analyzing the spiritual or material motives of individuals for becoming Muslims. This is not to diminish the centrality of belief and commitment in the subjective experience of individual converts, but to account on a historical basis for the responses of great numbers of human beings.

Initial conversions to Islam occurred in the Middle East between the seventh and the thirteenth centuries. These took place in two phases: the first was the conversion of animists and polytheists belonging to the tribal societies of the Arabian desert and the periphery of the Fertile Crescent; the second was the conversion of the monotheistic populations of the Middle Eastern agrarian, urbanized, and imperial societies.

The conversion of Arabian populations was part of a process in which the civilization of the sedentarized imperial societies spread to the nomadic periphery. Arabian peoples, living on the borders of the wealthier agricultural and commercial zones of the Middle East, strongly influenced by Middle Eastern commerce and religious thought, found in Muhammad's teaching a way to formulate a kind of Middle Eastern monotheistic religion parallel to, but distinct from, the established Jewish, Christian, and Zoroastrian religions. Indeed there were prior efforts to define an Arabian monotheism. The conversion of pagan – as well as Jewish and Christian – Arabian peoples to Islam represented the response of a tribal, pastoral population (and of the sedentary oasis and town populations) to the need for a larger framework for political and economic integration, a more stable state, and a more imaginative and encompassing moral vision to cope with the problems of a tumultuous society. Conversion intensified the ongoing process of Arabians integrating into a new cultural and political order defined in monotheistic religious terms.

The conversion of non-Arabian peoples to Islam was a different process. In this case, Islam substituted for Byzantine or Sasanian political identity and for Jewish, Christian, or Zoroastrian religious affiliation. The transformation of identities among Middle Eastern peoples took place in two stages. In the first century of the Islamic imperium, Arab-Muslim conquerors attempted to maintain themselves as an exclusive Muslim elite. They did not demand the conversion as much as the subordination of non-Muslim peoples. At the outset, they were hostile to conversions, because new Muslims diluted the economic and social status advantages of Arab-Muslims. Nonetheless, Muslim rule offered substantial incentives for conversion. It formed a protective umbrella over and conferred the prestige of the state on Muslim communities. Political patronage allowed for the establishment of mosques, the organization of the pilgrimage, and the creation of Muslim judicial institutions. The establishment of an Arab-Muslim empire made Islam attractive to elements of the former Byzantine and Sasanian aristocracies, including soldiers, officials, landlords, and others. Arab garrison cities attracted non-Arab migrants who found careers in the army and administration open to converts. Merchants, artisans, workers, and fugitive peasants seeking the patronage of the new elite were also tempted to accept Islam.

Despite these attractions, the mass of Middle Eastern peoples did not quickly or easily convert. Only with the breakdown of the social and religious structures of non-Muslim communities in the tenth to the twelfth centuries did the weakening of churches, the awakening of Muslim hostility to non-Muslims, sporadic and localized persecution, and the destruction of the landed gentry of Iraq and Iran weaken the communal organization of non-Muslim peoples. Muslim teachers were then able to take the lead in the reconstruction of local communities on the basis of Islamic beliefs and identities. Large parts of Egypt and Iran were probably converted in the tenth and eleventh centuries. In northern Syria, however, Christian majorities survived through the twelfth century, until – compromised by their sympathies with and assistance to the crusaders – they were put under severe pressure. Most converted in the thirteenth and fourteenth centuries, but substantial Christian minorities remained. Similarly, most of the remaining Christian population of Egypt adopted Islam in the fourteenth century. To adherents of the monotheistic and communalist faiths, Islam offered the same variety of intellectual, legal, theological, and mystical appeals. Although Islam had a specific religious orientation toward the inscrutable and untrammeled will of God and the necessity for submission of spirit and actions to the will of God, its basic religious positions were fundamentally similar to those of the other monotheistic religions.

The conversion of North Africa also began with the Arab-Muslim conquests but unfolded in a different process because it primarily involved the adoption of Islam, notably in sectarian form, by the chiefs of Berber societies as the basis of tribal coalitions and state formation. Khariji states in Algeria and Morocco adopted Islam to help regulate tribal relations and long-distance trade. The process of Islamization of the masses of Christians and Jews is not known, but it may be related to the spread of *ribat*s (forts manned by warriors for the faith), trade, and Sufis. In any case, it seems to have been rapid when compared to conversion in the Middle East.

Turkish conquests and conversions in Anatolia, the Balkans, the Middle East, Inner Asia, and India

The diffusion of Islam to regions beyond the Middle East involved analogous processes. The spread of Islam in Inner Asia, Anatolia, the Balkans, and India was closely tied to the conversion of pastoral Turkish (rather than Arab) peoples, which began in the tenth century. Inner Asian peoples came into contact with Muslims through caravan trade and commerce with merchants who operated on the steppes as brokers between nomadic and settled populations. Muslim missionaries and Sufis also moved out to proselytize among the Turks. Political ambition prompted the Qarakhanid and Saljuq elites to take up the new religion. Later Inner Asian regimes – including the Mongols of the Golden Horde and the Chaghatay Khanates – also adopted Islam and brought it to the northern steppes and eastern Turkestan. In Inner Asia, Islamization was important for the establishment of nomadic regimes over sedentary populations, for the organization of long-distance trade, and for the creation of politically cohesive ethnic identities among Tatars, Uzbeks, Kazakhs, and others.

The spread of Islam into Anatolia and the Balkans paralleled the historical process of the spread of Islam in the Middle East. (See Illustration 9.) The Saljuq and Ottoman conquests of the eleventh to the fourteenth centuries established Muslim regimes that patronized Sunni law schools, Islamic judicial administration, the construction of schools and colleges, and other religious and communal facilities. They gave protection to scholars and Sufis who founded centers for teaching and social services in the conquered territories. The migration of a substantial Turkish population under the leadership of Muslim holy men uprooted Anatolian agricultural communities and replaced them with Turkish Muslim peoples. Nomadic conquests and the hostility of the Saljuq government to the Byzantine Empire and the Greek Orthodox Church also led in Anatolia to the progressive reduction of church lands, administrative capacities, and authority. The weakening of the church deprived the Christian population of leadership and organization. In Anatolia, as in Inner Asia, India, and Africa, Sufi warriors and activist missionaries helped to establish Islam among a newly conquered peasant population. The assimilation of Anatolian peoples was facilitated on the cultural as well as the social level by the familiarity to Christians of Islamic religious concepts. In Anatolia, as in the rest of the Middle East, the conjunction of Muslim state power, the decline of organized Christian societies, and the social and cultural relevance of Islam facilitated mass conversions to the new religion.

In the Balkans, the factors favoring Islamization and conversion of local peoples were similar to those in Anatolia: the establishment of a regime that favored Islam and the migration and settlement of a substantial Turkish population. Islamization under these pressures was especially pronounced in the towns. In the Balkans, however, the spread of Islam was limited by the vitality of the Christian churches. It came at a later stage of Turkish conquests, at a time when Ottoman policy favored Christian nobles and churches as vehicles of Ottoman administration and so maintained – and, indeed, reinforced – the social structure of Balkan communities. Most Balkan peoples, buttressed by the continuity of organized Christian community life, maintained their confessional affiliation.

The history of Islam in India most closely resembles that of the Balkans. Islam was brought into India by a conquering Afghan and Turkish military elite that established the Delhi sultanate in the thirteenth century. Conversions occurred as a result of the political attraction of the dominant regime to both non-Muslim elites and dependent peasants and workers. Also, as in the Middle East, the construction of new cities favored the conversion of mobile peoples attracted to the centers of Muslim administration and trade. In most of India, however, as in the Balkans, the appeal of Islam was relatively restricted. Only in the Northwest Frontier, the Punjab, Sind, and Bengal were the populations converted en masse. In these regions the transition from hunter-gatherer and pastoral activities to settled agriculture was the occasion for a total reconstruction of society under Muslim leadership and for the

Illustration 9. The Battle of the Twelve Heroes. Source: Los Angeles County Museum of Art, the Nasli M. Heeramaneck Collection, Gift of Joan Palevsky, by Exchange Photograph © 2002 Museum Associates / LACMA / Art Resource / Art Resource, NY.

development of new Islamic identifications. Conversion to Islam on a mass scale was most likely among populations lacking prior organized institutions.

In general, however, the assimilative capacity of Islam in the subcontinent was limited by the relative thinness of the Muslim elite. Although Muslim rule in India attracted numerous warriors, administrators, and religious teachers, the Muslim conquest was not accompanied by massive migrations, as in the cases of the Arab conquest of the Middle East or the Turkish conquest of Anatolia. Furthermore, the social structure of conquered peoples remained intact. Hindu Rajputs, for example, maintained their authority under Muslim suzerainty; Brahmanic Hinduism and the caste system were not challenged by Muslim rule. Indeed, Hindu philosophy and popular religions were invigorated by Muslim competition. In the face of an ordered social and religious structure, conversions to Islam were inhibited.

When conversions did occur, Sufism played a considerable part. Following the scent of battle, Sufis streamed into India from Afghanistan, Iran, and Inner Asia. Many came as warriors to establish Muslim supremacy and convert the infidels. Some tied their fortunes to the state. Others fanned out in North India, establishing their influence by personal merit. Here too, the adaptability of Sufis to traditional religious cultures was important in the transition from Hindu and Buddhist identities to Islam. In India, the boundary between Hindu and Muslim beliefs, ritual practices, and social loyalties was thin. As in the Middle East and the Ottoman Empire, Islam was established under the auspices both of a political elite and of independent religious teachers.

Conversions in Southeast Asia and Sub-Saharan Africa

The conversion of Malaya, Indonesia, and sub-Saharan Africa to Islam followed a different pattern. In these regions, Islam was not established by conquest, by the imposition of a single centralized state, or by the settlement of a substantial foreign Muslim population; nor was it associated with massive social change. It was, rather, due to the diffusion of Muslim merchants and missionaries who founded small communities and sometimes induced (or forced) local elites interested in state formation, trade, and political legitimization to accept their religion. Islam spread as the result of commercial contacts and political and business rivalries, and by the progressive acceptance of new symbols of identity by ongoing societies.

Islam was first introduced into Indonesia at the end of the thirteenth century by merchants and Sufis from India, Arabia, and perhaps China. It appealed to the rulers of small coastal and riverine principalities who had close trading contacts with the Muslims and intense rivalries with other Indonesian and Chinese traders. Acceptance of Islam by local merchant princes won them social and administrative support and an entrée into extensive trading networks. Portuguese (sixteenth century) and later Dutch (seventeenth century) intervention in the Indies further stimulated the acceptance of Islam, because the struggle against the Portuguese and the Dutch made Islam a bond of solidarity in resistance to the efforts of Christian powers to establish trading monopolies. Local competition facilitated the further spread of Islam. The struggle of the coastal principalities with the interior states of Java eventually led to the establishment of Islam as the official religion of the whole of Java. As a result, Indonesian state and elite culture was shaped not by an aristocracy coming from the Middle East but by a local elite that preserved its political and cultural continuity and adopted Islam as an additional expression – or reinforcement – of its earlier legitimacy. Throughout Indonesia and Malaya, Islam was also integrated into popular culture. Sufi missionaries and village teachers settled widely and made Islam part of folk culture and folk identity. In Southeast Asia, as opposed to India and the Balkans, where it reached only a minority, Islam became the religion of great majorities of the population.

In most of Africa, Islam was established by processes more closely resembling those of Southeast Asia than those of the Middle East and India. Muslim merchants and missionary colonies, rather than conquest and empire, were central to Islamization. Arab and Berber traders and settlers in the Saharan and Sudanic regions, Arab and Persian settlers on the East African coasts, and Dyula communities in West Africa were the nuclei of Muslim influences. In Sudanic Africa, colonies of Muslim traders allied with local political elites and induced the rulers of the states of Ghana, Mali, Kanem, Songhay, Hausaland, and Dogomba to accept Islam. It is possible that Muslims themselves seized kingships and created small states. Islam was adopted to consolidate political power, reinforce commercial contacts, recruit skilled personnel, and mobilize spiritual and magical powers in the interests of state elites. As in North Africa, acceptance of Islam provided an additional basis for legitimization of state regimes, coalition formation among disparate peoples, organization of trading networks, and the employment of skilled personnel. Under the auspices of Muslim states, a small scholarly elite of judges, scholars, and imams was established, but no evidence for conversion of the lower classes is available. Islam was primarily the religion of the political and economic elites.

In other parts of West Africa, the Islamic presence was established by Dyula traders, landowners, missionaries, and teachers scattered throughout the region, all of whom created an Islamic presence without necessarily generating Islamic states and without attendant Islamization of the population. These family communities seem to have fitted into a highly stratified and subdivided society, whose internal divisions made it acceptable to have unassimilated communities but were a barrier to the further diffusion of Islam.

Whereas in West Africa Arab merchants inspired warrior elites to convert to Islam, in East Africa Arab traders themselves took over the leadership of small states. In Somalia and Ethiopia, Arab merchants married into local lineages and assumed leadership of tribal coalitions, which then adopted an Arab and Islamic identity. In East African city-states, Arab settlers intermarried with local peoples and became the elites of the coastal Swahili society, based on a new language and cultural style that symbolized the merger of populations. Muslim communities were consolidated by the integration of peoples and the formation of new cultural idioms. As the religion of the state and trading classes, Islam in Africa appeared in highly syncretic forms. Because African elites were not conquered and replaced but converted and maintained power, they brought with them a strong component of traditional, non-Islamic African practices.

In some cases, the formation of African-Muslim states was followed by the conversion of the masses. In Somalia, Mauritania, and other Saharan regions, the large numbers of Arab migrants, the close identification of pastoral peoples with Arab nomads, and the utility of holy leadership for the regulation of relations among tribal communities explain why Islam was so widely accepted. In the Funj and Darfur sultanates, state elites adopted Islam as a result of trading contacts and opened the way for a large influx of Sufi missionaries. Muslim holy men, supported by state grants of land, introduced Islam to the common people. In the Sudan, the spread of Arabic and contacts with Egypt and the Middle East helped establish Islam among the common people.

By the eighteenth and nineteenth centuries, throughout West Africa, the spread of Muslim trading communities linked by lineage, trade, teaching, and Sufi affiliations had reached a critical mass that enabled Muslims to fight larger-scale political regimes. Motivated by a tradition of hostility to rulers among both trading and pastoral peoples, African-Muslim communities attempted to seize political power and to Islamize both state regimes and the masses of the African population. In Sudanic, savannah, and forest West Africa, Muslim jihads were equivalent to Islamic conquests in other parts of the world and led to the Islamization of northern Nigeria, Senegambia, and parts of the upper Guinea coast. However, even when colonial conquest put an end to Muslim jihad, Islam – without state support – served to express anticolonialism and to unite uprooted peoples into new communal structures. In Africa, the process of conversion was tied to a double mechanism of peaceful expansion of traders, settlers, and teachers and to militant conquest. As in other parts of the world, the two could work either separately or in tandem.

Throughout the Old World, the diffusion of Islam led to the formation of new communities and states or to the redefinition of existing communities and empires in Islamic terms. In many parts of Africa and Inner Asia, the introduction of Islam was the basis for conversions from animistic to monotheistic religions and for the construction of states in hitherto stateless societies. In most places, however, the advent of Islam inspired the reconstruction of societies that already had monotheistic religions and state institutions. If there is an underlying common factor in the global diffusion of Islam, it seems to be its capacity to generate religious fellowship, larger-order communities, and states among peoples otherwise living in factionalized or fragmented societies. Islam became the religion of tribal peoples and merchant groups seeking economic integration and state elites seeking consolidated political power. In general, it seems to have been most effective when it gave a new social identity to peoples severed from traditional social structures.

In all these cases, the Middle Eastern experience anticipated the formation of later Islamic societies. Middle Eastern Islamic societies were built around three different types of collectivities: parochial groups, religious associations, and states. Parochial groups were based on family, clan, lineage, tribal, clientele, and neighborhood ties. At the level of religious associations, scholars and Sufi elites were organized around schools of law, Sufi fraternities, and shrines. States were characterized by such institutions as nomadic or ethnic elite armies, slave or mercenary military forces, a combination of bureaucratic and quasi-feudal forms of administration, and an Islamic legal terminology for taxation. These components of the Middle Eastern societies involved a combination of Islamic and non-Islamic institutions and concepts. Although religious associations and certain aspects of states were specifically Islamic, state bureaucratic, administrative, and feudal-like systems of taxation were not. Furthermore, the prevailing concepts of legitimacy were formulated in patrimonial, ethnic, historical, or cosmopolitan cultural terms as well as in Islamic symbols. Similarly, the social systems and cultural expressions of parochial communities were not unique to Muslims. Thus what we classify as "Islamic societies" by definition includes non-Islamic institutions and cultures. It is impossible to disassociate Islam from its regional (i.e., Middle Eastern) context.

In the diffusion of Islamic institutions and identities, Middle Eastern precedents were transmitted sometimes as a whole system and sometimes in parts, depending on who were the bearers of Islam and what were the conditions of its diffusion and reception in different societies. For example, conquest by nomadic peoples as opposed to contact among small groups of merchants made a significant difference in the way in which Middle Eastern Islamic influences were transmitted and received. In all instances, however, the diffusion of Islam released tremendous artistic and cultural forces as each new Islamic state and society created its own synthesis of Middle Eastern Islamic institutions and local traditions. The history of Islamic societies illustrates the originality of Muslim regimes the world over and yet reveals them to be variations on an underlying pattern shaped by indigenous conditions in each part of the Muslim world.

MUSLIM ELITES AND ISLAMIC COMMUNITIES

In every Islamic society, scholars (*'ulama'*) and Sufis were the teachers, exemplars, and leaders of Muslim communities. The scholars were knowledgeable about Muslim history, law, and theology. Their primary function was instruction and judicial administration. In West Africa, we find scholars under the local names of *mallam* or *karamoko* teaching in villages and town quarters. In Indonesia, they were called *kiyayi*, the teachers in boarding schools (*pesantren*). In Iran, Inner Asia, and the Ottoman Empire, they were the mullahs, who taught in Quran and higher-level schools. Despite important differences of knowledge, lineage, and wealth among higher- and lower-ranking scholars, there were rarely formal distinctions among them. Only in Bukhara and West Africa were scholars graded by rank.

Scholars were commonly organized into schools of law, which were associations of scholars, teachers, and students adhering to the codes of law developed by discussion and debate among legal scholars in the eighth and ninth centuries. By the late medieval period, the principal Sunni schools were the Hanafi, Shafi'i, Maliki, and Hanbali schools. Shi'i scholars were organized in two main schools. Through the law schools, scholars organized higher education and trained teachers and judicial administrators. The law schools trained legal consultants (muftis), notaries, and judges. (See Map 10.)

These activities generated a popular following for the scholars and their schools. The students usually considered themselves the personal disciples and loyal clients of their masters. In Africa and Indonesia, they worked in their masters' employ to pay their tuition. They commonly married into their masters' families. As an organized following, they could have considerable local political importance. The students of Istanbul and Bukhara were ready to take to the streets to defend their collective interests. Patrons and supporters came from the merchant and artisan classes. In eastern Iran and Transoxania, under Mongol and Timurid suzerainty, and in West African Dyula settlements, scholars were political leaders as well.

The religious authority of scholars, their expertise in law, and their social leadership made it important for states to control them. The Ottoman, the Safavid, and the Mughal empires, as well as the states of Tunisia and Bukhara, provide – in differing degrees – examples of the bureaucratic organization of scholars. In other North and Sudanic African states, scholars were not bureaucratically organized but were still courtiers and clients of the political elites. By contrast, Hanbalis in Egypt and Syria, Malikis in North and West Africa, and Naqshbandis in India not only maintained their autonomy but were active opponents of state elites in the name of Islamic principles.

Scholars performed different political roles depending on their status and the type of political system in which they were embedded. Higher-ranking scholars were commonly state functionaries, whereas lower-level teachers were often spiritual counselors for the common people. In the Ottoman Empire, scholar-bureaucrats belonged to the state elites and lower-ranking students and teachers to the opposition. In Iran, the Shi'i scholars evolved from a position of subordination to the state to autonomy and leadership of the common people.

The most striking socioreligious development of post-thirteenth-century Islamic societies was the emergence of Sufism in innumerable variations as the principal expression of Islamic beliefs and communal identities. Personified in scholar-mystics, ardent reformers, ecstatic preachers, and miracle-working holy men, Sufism became the almost universal sign of the Muslim presence. It is difficult to characterize Sufism briefly, because the word was used to apply to extremely varied religious and social practices. In general, Sufism is Islamic mysticism, or

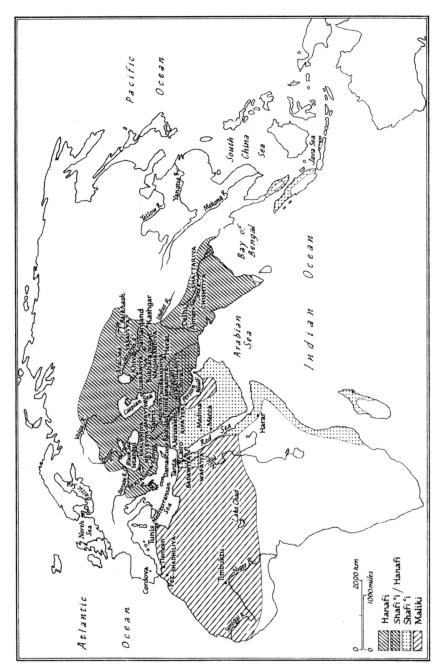

Map 10. Muslim schools of law and Sufi brotherhoods, c. 1500

the spiritual quest that leads to direct experience of the reality of God's being. With variations, the term covers two basic, sometimes overlapping, constellations of religious ideas. One kind of Sufism is a religious and ethical discipline built on adherence to the teachings of the Quran, the hadith, and the law, supplemented by spiritual practices designed to cultivate an outward conformity to Islamic norms and an inner insight into the ultimate spiritual realities. Muslim holy men of this type are commonly integrated with the scholars and cultivate religious knowledge, ethical discipline, and spiritual insight. The ordinary Sufi of this type is at once a scholar and a spiritual master.

A second kind of Sufism emphasizes faith in Sufi saints and relates to preexisting beliefs in the world of spirits and the magical powers of holy men. To many ordinary Muslims, a Sufi is a person who has attained a quality of inner consciousness that makes him close to God. The saint is directly connected to the cosmos because he participates in the essential forces of rational or spiritual power. The Sufi is considered by his followers to be a spiritual teacher, a miracle worker, a dispenser of blessings, and a mediator between men and God. This type of Sufism led to veneration of the person of the holy man and the heirs of his *baraka* (power of blessing) in the form of his tomb or shrine, or his disciples and descendants. It led to a religious life of offerings, sacrifices, and communal festivals around the shrines of saints. Shrine-Sufism, then, is a religion of magical acquisition of divine powers rather than of ethical or emotional self-cultivation. Although both types of Sufism are Islamic, they represent profoundly contrasting concepts of religious life.

In either case, the social organization of Sufism followed from the authority of Sufi masters. The ultimate social unit was the individual Sufi, surrounded by his disciples. The individual holy man (and his disciples) could also win lay followers among the people of his village, quarter, or camp. Such small communities might in turn be linked together in lineages or brotherhoods, sharing a common religious identity.

An individual Sufi's authority was built on a combination of knowledge of the Quran, mystical achievements, and inherited powers transmitted by spiritual and/or genealogical descent from an earlier saint or from the Prophet himself. Just as the chain of transmission (*silsila*) went back to the companions of the Prophet, the genealogies of Sufis were commonly traced back to the caliphs and the Prophet. Such was the case for the *mirs, khwajas,* and *sayyids* of Transoxania and the *shurafaʾ* of Morocco. The fusion of spiritual and genealogical descent was easy to make, for the Sufi was indeed a child of the Prophet; one who imitated his ways, recreated his life, and concentrated within himself the noble qualities or the image of the Prophet (*sura*). Given the widespread Muslim veneration of the holiness of ancestors, it was natural to identify present holiness with descent from superior beings. In many respects, this is parallel to the descent of the Shiʿi imams.

In turn, the personal authority and spiritual power of the master was transmitted to his descendants, to his disciples, and to his tomb. The descendants of a famous saint constituted a holy community based on inheritance of his spiritual qualities and lineage ties. Descent from the Prophet became particularly important in many regions in the fourteenth century and later. Certain lineages in Egypt, the *khwajas* of Bukhara and Kashgar, the *shurafa'* of Morocco, Jakhanke lineages in West Africa, *evliadi* groups among Turkmens, and Berber *zawaya* lineages in Mauritania were identified as holy communities – every male member of which was a descendant of a saint and heir to his spiritual qualities.

More common was the organization of a Sufi order (*tariqa*). A Sufi order was formed when several Sufi masters considered themselves the disciples of an earlier teacher, perpetuating a common spiritual discipline. Although Sufi cells were independent of one another, they recognized the same higher authority and became units of a larger-order association. Some of these associations were regional in scale. In India, the introduction of the Sufi order was the basis of a region-wide Islamic society. In West Africa, the consolidation of such brotherhoods in the eighteenth and nineteenth centuries was in part the basis of the effort to create Muslim states. Some of these brotherhoods – such as the Naqshbandi, the Qadiri, and others – became worldwide.

Veneration of shrines also led to special forms of communal or political organization. As the tombs of saints became centers for worship, administered by their descendants, tomb complexes became the focus of communities composed of people who believed that the saints could perform miracles. Shrines were endowed with agricultural estates to provide funds for their upkeep and for charitable activities. In such cases, a Sufi order included not only the descendants of the saint and the active disciples but all of the people who believed in the saint and worshiped at his tomb. This fellowship of believers, however, remained highly diffuse, segmented, and unorganized. Still, from the thirteenth to the end of the eighteenth centuries, the veneration of shrines and holy places became the most widespread form of popular Islamic practice. Sufis and their shrines provided ritual and spiritual counsel, medical cures, and mediation among different groups and strata of the population. Sufis helped to integrate corporate bodies (such as guilds) and to form political organizations among diverse lineage groups.

Sufism embodied myriad religious and social practices. The individual Sufi may have subscribed to any of a wide variety of religious or theosophical beliefs, may have come from any walk of life, may have had multiple affiliations (including simultaneous membership in different schools of law and Sufi brotherhoods), and may have coupled his mystical insights and practices with any of a number of worldly vocations, combining the roles of Sufi and scholar, merchant, artisan, or political chieftain. Similarly, the disciples and followers, although united by their adherence to the master and to the religious practices of their order, represented

Table 10. *The social organization of Sufism*

The Sufi master	
'arif	Gnostic
khalifa	Deputy, head of branch of Sufi order with authority to initiate new members
murshid, pir, ishan	Guide
shaykh	Teacher
wali	Friend of God, saint
Sufi lineages	
ashraf, shurafa', zawaya, insilimen, evliad	Descendants of the Prophet, of companions of the Prophet and of saints
Sufi brotherhoods	
dargah, khanaqa, tekke, zawiya	Residences and facilities of an order
khirqa	Patched cloak of the master transmitted to the disciple as a sign of initiation
murshid, khalifa, murid	Hierarchy of members
silsila	Chain of transmission of blessing from the Prophet to a present master
waqf	Endowed financial support
Tombs and shrines	
baraka	Blessing, God's power communicated through the saints
karamat	Miracles of saints
'urs	Celebration of the anniversary of the death of a saint, his marriage to God
ziyara	Visit to venerate a saint's tomb and seek his intercession before God

every conceivable social milieu. Given all this variation, Sufism cannot generally be defined but may only be described case by case. The underlying common factor is the exercise of religious insight, discipline, or authority in worldly affairs and a reputation for sanctity.

By the nineteenth century, Islamic societies the world over had acquired similar types of Muslim elites, beliefs, religious practices, and social organizations. In each Muslim region, we find not one but several variant types of Islam. There were the scholars who represented formal scholastic learning, organized education, and judicial administration, affiliated through schools of law. There were also the scholars-cum-Sufis, who combined legal learning with mystical discipline and contemplation, in an effort to live their lives in imitation of the Prophet. Such religious teachers perpetuated a tradition of learning that combined law, theology, and Sufi wisdom representing Sunni–Shari'a (orthoprax)–Sufi Islam. There were ecstatic visionary Sufis in the tradition of Ibn al-'Arabi and the gnostic forms of Islamic mysticism, as well as the popular forms of Sufi Islam expressed in veneration of saints, faith in their charismatic powers, and belief in the magic of their shrines. Throughout the Muslim world, Sufism in all its forms became the most widespread and popular form of Islam. (See Table 10.)

THE REFORM MOVEMENT

The seventeenth and eighteenth centuries witnessed the rise of a reformist (*tajdid*) movement opposed to both the rigidities of the schools of law and the cultic aspects of shrine-Sufism. The reformist mentality theoretically traces back to the early Hanbali movement, which emphasized commitment to the hadith of the Prophet (rather than law or cultic worship) and to social activism to improve the quality of Muslim political and communal life. The imitation of the Prophet Muhammad became the ideal of a Muslim life. These reformers, aided by the conviction that God was punishing Muslims for failure to heed his will, opposed the tolerant attitude of Muslim states toward non-Muslim peoples and cultures, sought to abolish the veneration of saints and the more florid cults and ceremonies, and worked to dispel superstitious or magical beliefs and practices. The reformers espoused, instead, a religion of personal discipline, moral responsibility, and commitment to a universal Muslim society. They were committed, if need be, to militant action to destroy corrupt versions of Islam and to create a just and truly Islamic community.

These various protoreformist tendencies came together in seventeenth- and eighteenth-century Mecca, Medina, and Cairo, where scholars representing the new trends in Morocco, Iraq, India, and elsewhere met in informal '*ulama*' and Sufi study groups. They advocated a purified version of Islamic belief and practice based on the study of the Quran, hadith, and law combined with Sufi asceticism. They worked on the earliest possible texts of hadith, rather than the later standard collections, and sought to eliminate religious practices that were not found in the Quran and in the teachings of the Prophet. They celebrated al-Ghazali as the premier teacher of Sufism and set the foundation for religious orders that would propagate the new devotional seriousness.

From Arabia and Cairo, traveling scholars, students and Sufis, and merchants and craftsmen carried the reformist doctrine to India, Indonesia, and North and West Africa. In Cairo, al-Azhar emerged as an important center of the new tendency, marked by hadith scholarship, the teachings of al-Ghazali, and repudiating the traditions of Ibn al-ʿArabi; visiting North African scholars taught their doctrine of imitation of and union with the spirit of the Prophet rather than pantheistic union with God. Muslim scholars in the Ottoman Empire again emphasized the primacy of hadith. The Naqshbandi and Khalwati orders combined hadith and law with Sufi asceticism and meditation in opposition to shrine worship and festivals. Naqshbandi teachers brought the order from Yemen to Egypt and from India to Syria. Social reformers were active in India, where they stressed a combination of hadith and Sufism because their religious goal was not union with God but identification with the spirit and active life of the Prophet.

Reformism also inspired political action. The reformist discourse appealed to two milieus. First, it appealed to fragmented lineage and village societies, to whom it offered Islamic authority and leadership for the unification of diverse groups in the struggle against local rivals and states. Reformism could be used as an ideology of mobilization for conquests, the formation of new states, and for anticolonial resistance.

The earliest example of a reformist movement in a pastoral and tribal society was the Wahhabi movement in Arabia. Born out of an alliance between a reform preacher and the Sa'udi family, the Wahhabis united diverse tribal groups into a movement that conquered most of Arabia. The religious goal of Wahhabi teaching was the purification of the heart from vices and sin and acknowledgment of the unity and transcendence of God. Wahhabis rejected Sufism, the veneration of any human being, and any authority except the Prophet himself.

Wahhabism set an example of militant moral and social reform. In India – which was in continuous interaction with Arabia through the travels of merchants, the movements of scholars, and the journeys of pilgrims – reform movements took root in Delhi, the Northwest Frontier, and Bengal. In the Indian Northwest Frontier, Sayyid Ahmad Barelwi tried to organize the Pashtuns against the British and the Sikhs on the basis of reformist teaching. Reformism inspired the Padri movement in Minangkabau in Sumatra. Reformism also became the basis of the local struggle against colonialism in the Caucasus and Inner Asia, where the Naqshbandi order became the bearer of new religious inspiration and, ultimately, of political resistance to both Russian and Chinese expansion.

In West Africa, Islamic reform had both indigenous roots and international Muslim connections. Eighteenth- and nineteenth-century reformist movements in the Senegambian region represented a local tradition of Muslim resistance to non-Muslim political elites, but the Fulani conquests, led by 'Uthman don Fodio (1754–1817), who established the caliphate of Sokoto (1809–1903) in the region between the Niger and Lake Chad, had mixed local and Arabian inspiration. Reformism inspired the Sanusiya, the Tijaniyya, the jihad of al-Hajj 'Umar, and Sufi orders in the Sudan. International reformist influences, introduced by the Tijani order, spread in Algeria, Morocco, and West Africa and interacted with local forces to inspire the formation of the regime of al-Hajj 'Umar (1794?–1864) in the regions from the Niger to Senegal. In Libya, the Sanusiya unified tribal peoples and created a loose confederation of tribes and oases that served to mediate disputes and to organize trade.

Second, reformism took root in agricultural and urban merchant milieus, in direct response to European political intervention and economic changes. In Bengal the reformist Fara'idi movement was associated with the introduction of British rule and the rise of Hindu and British landlords. In northern India, British rule and the collapse of the Mughal Empire led to reform movements in urban and small-town, middle-class milieus. Based at Deoband, reformist *'ulama'* created a network of colleges that trained cadres to proselytize, educate, and make true Muslims out of Indian believers. Deoband and subsequent reformist movements in India contributed heavily to the creation of a sense of Muslim identity throughout the subcontinent.

In Southeast Asia there were successive waves of reformism. The early nineteenth-century Padri movement in Sumatra was associated with the commercialization of coffee production. Coffee farmers were receptive to the influence of the reformist pilgrims and scholars returning to Sumatra from Mecca and Medina, who launched a movement to Islamize Muslim villages. At the end of the nineteenth century, reformism became the creed of the Indo-Malay merchant communities of Singapore and other Southeast Asian ports. Enlarged world trade; pilgrimage; the creation of a capitalist plantation economy in Sumatra and Malaya producing rubber, coffee, tobacco, pepper, sugar, pineapples, and palm oil for export; the formation of a plantation and mining proletariat; commercialization; urbanization; and other forces of socioeconomic change broke down traditional family and social structures, favored the growth of a Muslim merchant class in Singapore and other inland ports and of commercial planters in Sumatra and Malaya, and led to the adoption of Muslim reformism as the doctrine of new communities. These and similar milieus were the basis of the early twentieth-century Muhammadiya movement in Indonesia and the Kaum Muda (Young Group) in Malaya. In Inner Asia, merchants and intelligentsia adopted *usul-i jadid* (the New Method) in response to Russian domination and the need to revitalize a threatened Muslim community.

In sum, Islamic reformism was the political and moral response of '*ulama*', tribal, and urban communities to the transformation of the traditional structures of Muslim societies and to the threat of European political, economic, and cultural domination. It had its origin in the seventeenth and eighteenth centuries in response not to European pressures but to purely internal conditions, and it was later adapted to anticolonial resistance. Reformism appealed to tribal societies seeking political unification and to merchant and farmer milieus undergoing commercialization and urbanization, where reformist doctrine provided a cultural basis for larger-scale communities. Although often politically passive, reformism contributed to the psychological mobilization of colonized peoples and became the vehicle for the reconstruction of Muslim political identities among subnational populations in the Caucasus, Inner Asia, India, and Indonesia and the basis for national movements in Algeria and Morocco. The political breakdown of Muslim countries and the rise of European imperialism would give reformed Sufism a new role in the mobilization of Muslim peoples for defense against European colonial domination.

SOCIAL STRUCTURES OF ISLAMIC SOCIETIES

These various types of Muslim elites, beliefs, and associations gave Muslim societies complex structures. On one level, Islam may be considered an international religion in which all Muslims are linked by a shared tradition of learning and belief, by travel and pilgrimage to common centers of learning and worship, and by membership in international schools of law and religious brotherhoods. For example, Istanbul was the religious capital not only of the Ottoman Empire and of many of the Arab provinces but also of Inner Asia. Cairo drew students to al-Azhar from as far away as Indonesia and West Africa. Schools of law found their affiliates over broad regions. The Malikis were predominant in North and West Africa; the Hanafis in the Ottoman Empire, Inner Asia, and India; and the Shafi'is in India, Southeast Asia, and East Africa. Similarly, the Sufi brotherhoods generated regional and international loyalties. The Naqshbandis spread throughout India, Inner Asia, China, the Caucasus, and the Middle East. The Tijaniyya in the eighteenth and nineteenth centuries became a North and West Africa–wide brotherhood with important branches in the Arab Middle East. The reform movement was centered on Mecca and Medina but radiated its influence to India, West Africa, Inner Asia, and China. This international Muslim community enables us to speak of "the Muslim world." Still, on another level, Muslim identities remained intensely local, in that scholars and Sufis were embedded in particular communities and represented concepts and practices that were a fusion of the mainstream interpretations of Islam with local customs, beliefs, and lifestyles. Islam, then, has to be understood both as a universal religion and in its numerous particular contexts.

Islamic religious leadership and beliefs had a profound effect on the social organization of Muslim peoples. In urban societies, which were commonly divided into strong family, clan, clientele, and residential groups, Islam could be the basis for the organization of neighborhood communities around a mosque, Sufi retreat, or college. Within the urban fabric, there were schools of law, Sufi brotherhoods, or Shi'i sects identified with particular neighborhoods, occupations, or ethnic minorities. For example, in eleventh- and twelfth-century Iranian cities, neighborhood communities were closely identified with schools of law. In India and East Africa, merchant groups sometimes had a sectarian Isma'ili identity. Isma'ilis formed *jamathandis*, or collective associations, which provided political leadership and organized worship and instruction for a self-contained small community. Similarly, Dyula or Hausa merchant groups formed close-knit communities in West Africa. In these cases, the special trust and cohesion required for commercial activities came from religiously reinforced familial and ethnic loyalties.

Towns and cities, however, also provided a setting for social and political integration. This took place through markets, direct political negotiations among town notables, and the activities of scholars and Sufis. Schools of law and Sufi orders drew diverse elements of the population into common religious bodies. Islamic collectivities formed a superordinate community. Their integrative function was expressed in terms of allegiance to Islamic law. Through urban communities, Islam also played an important role in creating regional and international trading networks, administrative organizations, and states.

In many village societies, Muslim identity was often superimposed on preexisting village identity. In Minangkabau Sumatra, peasant villages had a double social structure, in which family and property were treated on matriarchal lines, whereas trade and politics were symbolized in patriarchal terms. In other cases, the merger of Islamic and non-Islamic cultural identity was expressed through shrine worship, festivals, belief in spirits, and shamanistic or magical curing practices that blended faith in the miraculous powers of Islamic holy men with pre-Islamic beliefs. Religious conviction was expressed through worship at shrines and holy places in an annual cycle of religious festivals, magical activities, and other rituals that incorporated non- or pre-Islamic concepts and ceremonies. Islamic belief, then, did not necessarily lead to the formation of an organized body of believers but could serve as a shared identity among diverse peoples who preserved their own kinship, territorial, linguistic, ethnic, and other bases of non-Islamic culture in group organization and social relations.

After the thirteenth century, Sufism became central to lineage societies, wherein Muslim holy men appeared as individual charismatic teachers – sometimes the custodians of local shrines, sometimes affiliated with brotherhoods. Sufis also appeared as members of their own holy lineages. Sufi lineages in Algeria, Morocco, southern Somalia, Mauritania, and Turkmenistan are among the many examples of groups tracing their descent to the Prophet or the early caliphs, who were organized as separate communities within the framework of the surrounding tribal societies. Similarly, African Dyula communities were made up of lineages or specialized occupational castes operating as components of complex, usually non-Muslim segmented societies. The authority of these lineages was based in part on descent and in part on Sufi qualities. Whether as individuals or lineages, Sufis served to facilitate the selection of chiefs, mediate disputes, and organize long-distance trade or other economic ventures.

Sufi leadership could also unite clans, lineages, and tribes into larger movements and tribal conquests and assist in the formation of states. In such cases, religious leadership and loyalties created a double structure of society in which religious elites represented the larger movement and secular tribal or group chieftains represented the smaller units. In these cases, the larger religious identity did not efface other aspects of ethnic, tribal, or clan loyalties but rather was superimposed on them. Movements created in this way were likely to fragment into their component parts.

The unification of pastoral or tribal peoples under Islamic religious leadership was a recurring phenomenon. The prime example is the initial integration of Arabian bedouins into a conquering movement by the preaching of Islam. Later, in Oman, Arab tribesmen were united and governed by the 'Ibadi (Khariji) imams. In North Africa from the seventh to the thirteenth centuries, Berber peoples were united under Kharijism, Shi'ism, Sunni reformism, and Sufism to form

Table 11. *Muslim religious leaders*

caliph	Head of Sunni Muslim *umma*
Mosques	
imam	Leader of prayer
khatib	Preacher of official sermon
muezzin	Crier of calls to prayer
Schools	
faqih or *ʿalim* (*pl. ʿulama'*)	Scholar of law
mudarris	Professor of madrasa
Legal administrators	
mufti	Jurisconsult
muhtasib	Market inspector and enforcer of morals
shaykh al-Islam	Chief mufti and head of judicial establishment
qadi	Judge
Sufi brotherhoods	
khalifa	Deputy
muqqadam	Local headman in brotherhood
sajjada nishin	Successor, chief of shrine
shaykh (*murshid, etc.*)	Master and guide
shaykh al-shuyukh	Chief of Sufi *shaykhs* (Egypt)
Descendants of Prophet	
sayyid, sharif (*pl. ashraf,* *shurafa'*), *naqib al-ashraf*	Syndic of the descendants of the Prophet
Ithna ʿashari Shiʿis	
ayatollah	Sign of God: highest-ranking *mujtahid*
hujjatollah	Proof of God: higher-ranking *mujtahid*
marjaʿ-i taqlid	Religious teacher to whom obedience is due
mujtahid	Scholar of law qualified to give independent legal judgment
Ismaʿilis	
daʿi	Missionary
hujja	Proof, the representative of imam
imams	Successors to the Prophet and leaders of the Muslims

the Fatimid, Almoravid, Almohad, and other movements. After the twelfth century, Sufism played a particularly important role in tribal unification. Rural populations throughout North Africa came to be organized in Sufi-led communities. In Morocco, the Saʿdian and the ʿAlawi dynasties were based on Sufi-led coalitions of pastoral and mountain peasant peoples. The Safavids united individuals, clienteles, and clans to conquer and govern Iran. The Saljuq and Ottoman conquerors of Anatolia and the Balkans, although under overall dynastic direction, were at the local level led by Sufis. In Inner Asia, the *khwajas* created coalitions of pastoral peoples. The tribes that occupied Somalia were united by allegiance to Sufis. The West African Fulani jihads of the eighteenth and nineteenth centuries were built on reform preaching. (See Table 11.)

Thus many of the great "tribal" movements that led to the formation of Islamic states were built on Muslim religious leadership or the integration of Muslim religious and secular chieftainship. In tribal societies, Muslim leadership inspired millenarian revolts and radical opposition to established regimes. Before the modern era, these were the principal expressions of Islamic societies.

ISLAMIC STATES

Most early modern Muslim societies were ruled by states often based on similar concepts, institutions, and vocabularies. Generally, a Muslim ruler was the symbol of a legitimate regime, the guarantor that Muslim laws would be enforced, and the representative of the historical continuity of Muslim communities. Islamic states and empires were expected to maintain worship, education, and law. In times of war, they were to defend against infidel enemies; in times of peace, they patronized scholars and saints,

Islamic states differed greatly in their religious legitimization. In many cases, this legitimization was attached to the person of the ruler. The Umayyads of Damascus, 'Abbasids, Fatimids, Almoravids, Almohads, Umayyads in Spain, and the leaders of West African jihads in the nineteenth century all considered themselves hierocratic rulers. They were the heirs to the authority of the Prophet; they were at once teachers and rulers. Similarly, the *khwajas* of Kashgar, the Sufi masters of small Moroccan states, and the Safavids of Iran regarded themselves as the repositories of religious as well as temporal authority. In Morocco, the legitimacy of the ruler depended on his prophetic descent and Sufi qualities. The reform movements of the nineteenth century would bring a resurgence of the aspiration to unite religious and political leadership.

In other Muslim societies, legitimacy was attached directly to the state institutions. The Ottoman Empire was legitimized by its reputation as a warrior regime that expanded the frontiers of Islam and defended Muslim peoples against the infidels. Even in the nineteenth century, when the Ottoman state was in decline and overwhelmed by European powers, its importance to Muslim security remained unquestioned.

Legitimization, more generally, depended on a combination of Islamic and non-Islamic patrimonial, cosmopolitan, or cosmological symbols. The 'Abbasid regime and its Mamluk, Ottoman, Safavid, and Mughal successors appealed to genealogical descent from earlier Arab, Persian, or Turkish nobility to justify their rule. Each regime also patronized a cosmopolitan culture to define its political identity. A continuing tradition of Persian language and literature linked the Samanids, Saljuqs, Timurids, Ottomans, Safavids, and Mughals. Architecture, painting, and music received royal patronage. Through their patronage of philosophy and science, Islamic regimes appealed to universal symbols as the basis of political order.

Islamic statecraft was also conceived of as being regulated by rules derived from secular monarchical traditions. The state elites distanced themselves from Islamic commitments by cultivating artistic, literary, and scientific achievements that had little to do with Islam but were part of the historical political culture of the various Muslim regions. The multiple levels of legitimization responded to the need to win political support or acquiescence from the multiethnic, multireligious populations who were commonly subjected to Muslim rule.

Furthermore, each regime showed originality in the selection of cultural and artistic styles and in the fusion of Islamic, cosmopolitan, cosmological, and patrimonial symbols. Thus, Arab regimes tended to be strongly Arab-Islamic, without noteworthy cosmopolitan symbols; the Indian Mughal Empire was highly syncretic. Indonesian and Malayan regimes perpetuated a non-Islamic culture of imperium with little more than Islamic titles. By contrast, the nineteenth-century African jihads were dedicated to an Islamic utopia.

Islamic states tended to adopt similar political practices and to redefine local political precedents in Islamic terms. The militias of tribal-founded Islamic empires were commonly transformed into slave or client forces. This was especially important in the Middle East, where slave troops were recruited to supplement or to displace tribal levies, as in the cases of the 'Abbasid, Ghaznavid, Saljuq, Mamluk, Ottoman, and Safavid empires. Slaves were also used in North and West Africa. Slaves were generally recruited in Inner Asia and the Caucasus but were also taken from non-Muslim populations in the Balkans, Georgia, and sub-Saharan Africa. Slaves commonly retained an ethnic and cultural identity based on their non-Muslim past.

In administration, Islamic states also shared practices based on regional precedents. The 'Abbasids inherited Byzantine and Sasanian practices in granting tax revenues for military services, and the Saljuqs molded the *iqta'* of late 'Abbasid times into a system of financial administration that, under various names, was later adapted by the Mongol, Timurid, Ottoman, Safavid, Uzbek, and Mughal empires. The *iqta'*, *timar*, *tuyul*, and *jagir* (all names for grants of tax revenues) represent a similar principle of decentralized financial support for the state military elite. Other examples of administrative uniformities among Muslim states are taxation on a land- (*kharaj*) and poll- (*jizya*) tax basis and the endowment of trusts (*awqaf*) for religious purposes. In many cases, as in Inner Asia and North Africa, these uniformities were due to the direct transfer of Middle Eastern institutions, but in many others, they were due to the inheritance of similar institutions from earlier non-Islamic regimes and to the adoption of a common Islamic terminology for separate precedents.

Alongside Islamic practices and symbols, Islamic states were defined by their relationship to the scholars and the Sufis. The Ottoman, Safavid, and Bukhara monarchies were strongly supported by an organized scholarly bureaucracy, which viewed the state as indispensable to Islam. These states suppressed antagonistic

Sufi brotherhoods and appropriated the political functions of Sufis by endowing government officials with extensive powers to dispense justice, regulate economic matters, protect trade, and sponsor education. Sunni scholars commonly held the view that even a corrupt and evil state had to be accepted and obeyed, for any regime was better than none. In their view, the alternative to state control was anarchy and factional violence. In some African kingdoms, the scholars, although not highly organized by the state, were still the source of political legitimization – even from non-Muslim subjects, who accepted the superior magic of literate Muslim courtiers. In India, the Mughals drew limited support and much criticism from the scholars. In Indonesia, by contrast, Muslim elites had little or no role in the legitimization of regimes and were, if anything, the leaders of peasant resistance.

Whereas the relations between states and scholars tended toward interdependence, those between states and Sufis tended toward opposition. Some Sufi orders cooperated with central governments and transmitted governmental authority to the common people, as did the Suhrawardis of India and the Mevlevis of the Ottoman Empire, but Sufism was usually apolitical, as in the case of the Chistis in India. Many Sufi orders opposed governments, as in eighteenth-century Algeria and Morocco. In general, highly organized states regarded the scholars as politically compatible but considered the Sufis as political competitors to be suppressed or co-opted.

Even in cases in which Sufis were independent, there was an intimate connection between Sufis and state authorities. Rulers patronized Sufi masters in order to acquire some of the blessings attributed to the saints and to transfer Sufi legitimacy to the princes. In India, the same rituals and ceremonies were observed in both the courts of the Sufis and the court of the ruler. Both courts were called by the same name – *dargah*. Conversely, the authority of Sufi masters was built around worldly success, power, and efficacy in daily affairs.

These states fused Islamic and non-Islamic practices. The state's "Muslim" elites were often warriors for whom tribal identity was more salient than Muslim identity. Moreover, such tribal military forces were frequently supplemented or replaced by non-Muslim levies. The Mughal regime, for example, absorbed Hindu lords; North African regimes depended on Catalan or Aragonese forces. The subordinate vassal principalities of large Muslim empires included non-Muslim tribal chiefs, feudal lords, and other local notables. These subordinate regimes were ordinarily legitimized in patriarchal or patrimonial terms and not by recourse to Islamic symbols or ideology.

Thus, Muslim regimes and empires were usually composite formations that embodied Islamic institutions in the matrix of a broader political culture. On one level, they were Muslim; on another, they were cosmopolitan patrons of a style of monarchical culture that, despite variations, gave a similar gestalt to Ottoman, Safavid, Mughal, and other Muslim state cultures. The production of illuminated manuscripts, the diffusion of Persian literary forms into Turkish and Urdu, the construction of domed architectural monuments, and many other features identify an imperial expression of Islamic civilization. On another level, the culture of Muslim regimes was also regional and derived from the pre-Islamic and non-Islamic substrates of the societies they ruled. Local languages, poetic traditions, literary forms, architectural motifs, musical motifs, and cultic practices made each Muslim regime an expression of a particular locality. The several interacting levels of universal Islamic, cosmopolitan, imperial, and local cultural styles afforded each regime a distinctive identity.

THE WESTERN ISLAMIC SOCIETIES

CHAPTER 26

ISLAMIC NORTH AFRICA TO
THE THIRTEENTH CENTURY

From the origins of the Islamic era to the nineteenth century, the history of North African society turned on two essential motifs: state formation and Islamization. Historically the basic units of society – families, hamlets, or groups of hamlets – were embedded in factional and tribal groups. The economy was based on small-scale grain, fruit, and olive production; stock raising by pastoral peoples; and limited urban-based textile and other small-scale manufacturing. Although trade was important, the merchant middle class was not highly developed. Unlike the Middle East, North Africa did not have a long experience of imperial organization, monotheistic religious communities, sedentarized agriculture, and urban commerce. It had a veneer of imperial and urban Christian civilization set down by the Phoenicians and Romans, and confined to relatively limited coastal territories.

Islamic civilization was brought to North Africa and Spain by the Arab conquests in the seventh and eighth centuries. The Arab conquests led to the formation of not one but several political centers, and an ever-changing political geography. North African forces conquered Spain in the eighth century. From the seventh to the eleventh centuries, North Africa and Spain were divided among governments formed by the Arab conquerors, by Berber tribes, or by Arab-Berber coalitions. The smaller Berber kingdoms defined themselves in varying forms of Khariji Islam, while the Umayyad dynasty in Spain and the Fatimids in North Africa claimed to be the caliphs of the whole Islamic world.

A period of political consolidation began in the eleventh century. In the eleventh and twelfth centuries the Almoravids and the Almohads brought large regions of Saharan, North African, and Spanish territory under their control. In the twelfth and thirteenth centuries the Muslim states of North Africa took on an institutional configuration resembling that of the Saljuq Empire in Iraq and Iran and the Mamluk Empire of Egypt and Syria. By the end of the fifteenth century Muslim states in Spain had been defeated by Spanish Christians, and North Africa assumed the political configuration we know today – the region encompassing the separate states of

Libya, Tunisia, Algeria, and Morocco. (For convenience, however, I will refer to the various subregions of North Africa in the early period by these names.) In the sixteenth century most of North Africa (with the exception of Morocco) came under Ottoman suzerainty. Finally, in the eighteenth and nineteenth centuries, these societies were undermined by European economic competition and brought under colonial rule.

MUSLIM STATES TO THE ELEVENTH CENTURY

(See Map 11.) The Arab conquest of both Berber peoples and Byzantine towns began with scattered raids from Egypt. Around 670 Tunisia was occupied, and Arab garrisons were established in Qayrawan, Tripoli, Tunis, and Tobna, and in numerous Byzantine forts or frontier *ribats*. The people who manned these *ribats* were committed to Muslim holy war and cultivated an ideology of piety and longing for martyrdom. From North Africa, Arab and Berber forces reached Spain in 711.

Arab-Islamic civilization in North Africa was based on the integration of Arab conquerors, Berbers, and the populations of the Mediterranean cities. Berber speakers who made up the great majority of the indigenous population were known under the names of Masmuda, Sanhaja, and Zenata. Some lived in farms, villages, and towns in the coastal regions of what are now Tunisia and Algeria. The majority were camel-herding nomads in the Sahara, and pastoralists in the mountain regions. They shared a common culture, but they had rarely, if ever, formed states. With the Arab conquests, sedentarized Berbers remained Christians, but nomadic Berbers enlisted in the Arab armies and helped spread Islam westward into Algeria, Morocco, and Spain. They also became merchants engaged in the trans-Sahara trade. Arabic replaced Latin as the language of administration. Berbers became Muslims long before they became speakers of Arabic. (See Table 12.)

The Arab conquests lead not to a single state but to numerous small Arab and Berber states, often with sectarian identities. The earliest Muslim kingdoms in North Africa were founded not by Arabs but by Berbers, often in the name of Kharijism. Thus they expressed both acceptance of Islam and affiliation with the conquerors, but also their cultural and religious autonomy. In the middle of the eighth century Berber-Khariji principalities were established at Tlemsen, Tahert, and Sijilmassa. Another kingdom was founded by Kharijis of the Sufri sect around Tangier.

The Ibadi-Khariji kingdom of Tahert (761–909) founded by 'Abd al-Rahman b. Rustam may be taken as typical. The Ibadi imamate of Tahart was a kind of theocracy. The imam was elected by the notables and lived an ascetic life interpreting laws, rendering justice, and leading his warriors in battle. Life at Tahert was conducted in a perpetual state of religious fervor. The theocratic community enforced a high standard of social behavior by physical punishment and imprisonment.

In Tunis, the Arab governors founded the Aghlabid dynasty, which ruled Tunisia, Tripolitania, and eastern Algeria from 800 to 909. The region of what is now Tunisia

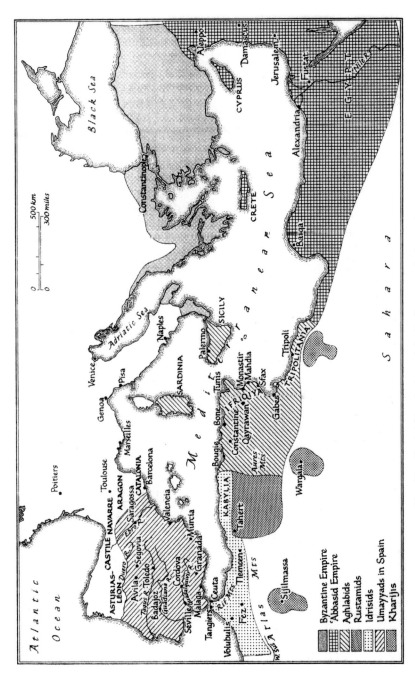

Map 11. North Africa, Spain, and the Mediterranean in the ninth century.

Byzantine Empire
'Abbasid Empire
Aghlabids
Rustamids
Idrisids
Umayyads in Spain
Kharijis

Atlantic Ocean

ASTURIAS–CASTILE NAVARRE
LEÓN
Poitiers
Toulouse
ARAGON
CATALONIA
Saragossa
Barcelona
Marseilles
Genoa
Pisa
Venice
Ebro R.
Duero R.
Avila
Segovia
Valencia
SARDINIA
Adriatic Sea
Naples
Toledo
Murcia
Tagus R.
Guadiana R.
Cordova
Guadalquivir R.
Badajoz
Granada
Malaga
Seville
Ceuta
Tangiers
KABYLIA
Bougie
Bone
Tunis
Palermo
SICILY
Fez
Volubulis
Tlemcen
Atlas Mts.
Ksur Mts.
Sijilmassa
Tahert
Wargala
Constantine
Qayrawan
Monastir
Mahdia
Sfax
Gabes
Aures Mts.
TRIPOLITANIA
Tripoli
Mediterranean Sea
CRETE
CYPRUS
Aleppo
Damascus
Jerusalem
Fustat
Alexandria
Barqa
EGYPT
Sahara

Black Sea

Constantinople

500 km
300 miles
0
0

Table 12. *North Africa: outline chronology*

	Libya	Tunisia (Ifrīqiya)	Algeria	Morocco	Spain
700	Arab conquests begin, 643				Arab conquests begin, 711; the Umayyad dynasty, 756–1031
800		Aghlabids (Tunisia and eastern Algeria) (Qayrawan), 800–909	Rustamids (Tahert), 761–909	Idrisids (Fez), 789–926	
900		Fatimids, 909–72; Zirids, 972–1148	Fatimids	Fatimids, 921–72	First Caliph 'Abd al-Rahman III, 912–61
1000			Hammadids, 1015–1152		Muluk al-Tawā'if, c. 1030–c. 1090; the party kings in Malaga, Seville, Cordoba, Toledo, Valencia, Saragossa, etc.
1100	Hilali migrations and conquests begin, 1052	Almohads, 1160–1228	Almohads, 1147–1236	Almoravids (Marrakesh), 1056–1147	Christian conquest of Toledo, 1085; Almoravid conquest, 1086–1106
1200		Hafsids (Tunisia and eastern Algeria), 1228–1574	'Abd al-Wadids (Tlemsen), 1236–1550	Almohads, 1130–1269 Marinids, 1196–1549 (take Marrakesh in 1269)	Almohad conquest, 1145 Defeat of the Almohads, Las Navas de Tolosa, 1212; Christian conquest of Cordoba, 1236, and Seville, 1248

Year	Spain	Morocco	Algeria	Tunisia	Libya
1300	Nasrids of Granada, 1230–1492				
1400		Portuguese take Ceuta, 1415; Wattasid regency and sultanate, 1428–1549			
1500		Sa'dians, 1511–1659	Ottomans capture Algiers, 1529, Tlemsen, 155.	Ottomans capture Tunis, 1574; deys of Tunisia, 1591–1705	Ottoman conquests / Ottomans, 1551–1711
1600		'Alawis, 1631–present	Deys, 1689–1830		
1700				Beys 1705–1957	Qaramanlis, 1711–1835
1800			French occupation begins, 1830	French protectorate, 1881	Ottomans, 1835–1912; Sanusiya, 1837–1902 (Cyrenaica)
1900		French protectorate, 1912–56; Independence, 1956	Independence 1962	Independence, 1956	Italian conquest, 1911; Independence, 1951

was a natural center for an Arab-Islamic regime and society. In North Africa, only Tunisia had the urban, agricultural, and commercial infrastructures essential for a centralized state on the model of the eastern Islamic state. The Aghlabid military elites were drawn from the descendants of Arab invaders, Islamized and Arabized Berbers, and black slave soldiers. The administrative staffs comprised dependent client Arab and Persian immigrants, bilingual natives, and some Christians and Jews.

Tunisia flourished under Arab rule. Extensive irrigation works were installed to supply royal gardens and towns with water, and to promote olive production. In the Qayrawan region hundreds of basins were built to store water to support horse breeding. Important trade routes linked Tunisia with the Sahara, the Sudan, and the Mediterranean. A flourishing economy permitted a refined and luxurious court life and the construction of the new palace cities of al-ʿAbbasiya (809) and Raqqada (877).

The region we now know as northern Morocco was the center of another cluster of Arab-Berber principalities, and eventually of a territorially defined Islamic state, this time in the name of Shiʿism. The Idrisid regime was founded in 786 at the former Roman capital of Volubilis by a descendant of ʿAli and Fatima, Idris I. His son Idris II was the founder of Fez, built in 808. Despite its small size, the Idrisid kingdom was the first Moroccan-Islamic state and a center of active proselytization among Berbers on behalf of Islam.

The rest of Morocco was divided among a number of localized states, including that of the Barghwata peoples on the coastal plains of north-central Morocco. Derived from Sufri Kharijism, their leader, Salih b. Tarif, declared himself a prophet, composed a "revealed book" in Berber, gave rules for fasting and prayer, and otherwise established a Berber version of Islam. These regimes were islands of kingly rule in a sea of independent Berber peoples living in pre-state communities.

For a time, these North African states maintained a flourishing economy. The countryside produced olives, grapes, and cereals; the towns had lively textile and ceramic industries. The towns produced carpets and textiles, ceramics, pottery, and glasswares. Trade with Europe, Egypt, and sub-Saharan Africa enriched the economy. North African commerce with Saharan and sub-Saharan Africa went from Tripoli to the Fezzan and from Qayrawan to Walata. Tahert and Tlemcen were linked to the Sudan through Sijilmassa. Sijilmassa was a critical nodule in the trade among the Morocco Khariji states and the Sudan and an important base for the southward diffusion of Islam. On the Sudanic routes the principal products were slaves and gold, which allowed the North African regimes and the Umayyads in Spain to mint gold coins. From Qayrawan, cereals, oils, and slaves were sent to Alexandria. From Morocco, sugar, hides, horses, and sheep were sent to Spain.

THE FATIMID AND ZIRID EMPIRES AND THE BANU HILAL

The era of small states was brought to an end by the Fatimid movement. At the end of the ninth century, an Ismaʿili missionary converted Kutama Berber villagers in the mountains of Kabylia in eastern Algeria to the Fatimid cause. The leader of the movement, Ubaydallah, proclaimed himself caliph in 910. The Fatimids conquered Sijilmassa, Tahert, Qayrawan, and much of the rest of North Africa. They destroyed the Khariji principalities. Warfare also destroyed the trade routes and led to the rise of nomadism. The Fatimids conquered Egypt in 969. Moving their capital to Cairo, they abandoned North Africa to local Zirid (972–1148) and Hammadid (1015–1152) vassals.

In the eleventh century, the invasions of nomadic peoples, the Banu Hilal Arabs from the east and the Almoravids from southern Morocco, transformed the political and religio-cultural geography of North Africa and Spain. The Banu Hilal and the Banu Sulaym, coming from Arabia and Egypt, defeated the Zirid and Hammadid states and sacked Qayrawan (1057). Qayrawan and other cities, created by the first wave of Arab conquests, were ruined by the second. The Banu Hilal collected tributes in kind: wheat, dates, and olives from the farmers and taxes and tributes from the cities. As the invaders took control of the plains, sedentary peoples were forced to take refuge in the mountains. In central and northern Tunisia, and later in Algeria and Morocco, farming gave way to pastoralism. Tunisian trade and agriculture declined as the result of the Arab invasions, the internal weakness of local regimes, and the shift of the Sahara trading economy to other routes.

A politically weakened North Africa was also subject to attacks from Europe. The Genoese and Pisans attacked Bone in 1034. The Normans conquered Sicily between 1061 and 1092, devastated Mahdiya in 1087, and between 1135 and 1153 conquered the coastal strip from Tripoli to Cape Bon.

The destruction, however, was not total. The coastal regions survived. Tripoli retained its palm, olive, fig, and other fruit plantations, and Tunis remained an important city for textiles, ceramics, glass, oil, soap, leather, and other urban manufactures. Moreover, some of the factors that led to decline of the Tunisian and Algerian regions of North Africa favored economic development in Egypt and Morocco. The transfer of the Fatimid regime to Egypt favored eastern Egyptian trade routes to sub-Saharan Africa. Spanish-patronized western routes to the Sahara favored Morocco and the exchange of salt and luxury products from the north for gold, slaves, hides, ivory, and wood from the south.

The most important cultural consequence of the Banu Hilal migrations was the blending of Arab and Berber cultures and the diffusion of an Arabic dialect as a common spoken as well as official language of North Africa. (See Map 12.)

THE ALMORAVIDS AND THE ALMOHADS

In the eleventh century, a second nomadic invasion came from southern Morocco. This one, however, led to the political unification of Morocco and Spain under the Almoravid movement. Like the Fatimids, the Almoravids were a coalition of Berber peoples united by religious leadership and doctrine. The movement rose among Sanhaja Berbers in the western Sahara who were being pushed out of their trading

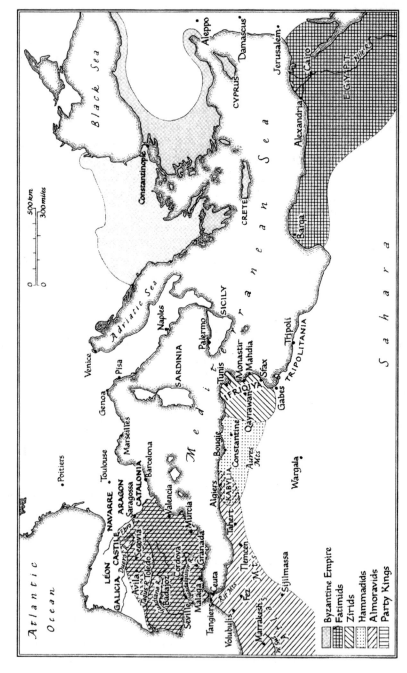

Map 12. North Africa, Spain, and the Mediterranean in the late eleventh century and the Almoravid conquests.

livelihood by Zanata Berbers at the northern ends of the trans-Saharan trade routes, and by the Sudanic state of Ghana, which was taking over the southern outlets of the trans-Saharan trade. Islam played an important role in the Sanhaja adaptation to these pressures. An Islamic reformist movement provided the religious cement for a Sanhaja counterattack, under the leadership of the Lamtuna tribe, against pagan Sudanese kingdoms to the south and impious Zanata domination in the north.

Returning from his pilgrimage to Mecca, a Sanhaja chieftain brought back a Moroccan student, ʿAbdallah b. Yasin, who taught Quran, hadith, and law. Ibn Yasin called for repentance and warned that the last day was coming. He imposed a strict moral and religious discipline on his followers. He closed taverns, destroyed musical instruments, abolished illegal taxes, and implemented Muslim laws for the distribution of booty. The inner jihad – the purification of body and soul – had to precede the warriors' outer jihad. The name of the movement he founded, al-Murabitun, was derived from the Quranic root *r-b-t*, referring to the technique of fighting in closed ranks, with infantry in front and camels and horsemen in the rear, rather than in the long, loose lines common to Berber battles. "Almoravid," then, refers to those who wage holy war in the quranically prescribed fashion.

The Almoravids defeated the kingdom of Ghana and took control of the trading cities of Sigilmassa in 1055 and Awdaghost in 1056. This gave them control of the trans-Saharan trade routes. They went on to conquer Morocco. They founded Marrakesh as their capital around 1070 and conquered the central Maghrib between 1070 and 1080. In 1082 a delegation of *ʿulama*ʾ urged the Almoravids to intervene on behalf of the Spanish-Muslims. Thus, in 1086 a Moroccan army crossed the straits and defeated Alfonso VI. From 1090 to 1145, the North Africans conquered the Spanish-Muslim cities and governed Spain as a province of Marrakesh. The Almoravids thus linked the Sahara, Morocco, and Spain into a single political regime and trading zone with Marrakesh and Seville as their two capitals. Morocco, benefiting from trade and empire, became in the course of the eleventh to the thirteenth centuries a commercial and urbanized society.

The Almoravid regime was built around the Lamtuna tribal aristocracy, but the Almoravids also employed Spanish scribes, Christian mercenaries, and black slaves to form a cavalry bodyguard for the ruler. This gave him predominance over camel-riding Berber troops. The legitimacy of the regime was based on claims to religious purity. Almoravid rulers were titled *amir al-muslimin*. Scholars of Maliki law sat in executive council with the ruler and gave legal advice. The legalists condemned Muslim theology and opposed Sufism. Despite their narrow religious position, the Almoravids promoted the final triumph of Sunni Islam and the Maliki school of law over Shiʿi and Khariji rivals. With their victories in Spain, the North African rulers became patrons of Spanish scribes, philosophers, poets, and architects and engineers and brought many of them to North Africa. The great Mosque of Tlemcen, built in 1136, and the rebuilt Qarawiyin Mosque of Fez were designed in the Andalusian manner. As a result of the conquests, Spanish and Moroccan cultures were integrated.

By the middle of the twelfth century the Almoravid state began to unravel. In southern Morocco a new religious movement challenged its legitimacy. The Almohad movement (al-Muwahhidun) was founded by Muhammad b.'Abdallah b. Tumart, who had made the pilgrimage to Mecca and studied in Baghdad and Damascus. He regarded himself as the heir of the Prophet, his career as a duplication of the Prophet's career, and his teaching an effort to restore the Islamic community as it had existed in the Prophet's lifetime. On his return he preached the transcendence and oneness of God, the supremacy of Quran and hadith over the law schools, and the need for moral reform. Grounding himself in the theology of al-Ash'ari, he rejected anthropomorphism and a physical interpretation of the attributes of God mentioned in the Quran. Ibn Tumart also denounced pagan Berber customs taken into Islamic practice and proscribed wine drinking, music, and the enjoyment of luxurious clothing.

At Tinmal in southern Morocco he received the support of a local chieftain, Abu Hafs 'Umar. He then declared himself Mahdi (messiah), imam, and *ma'sum* (sinless) or infallible leader sent by God. His regime depended on a military aristocracy made up of the tribes that supported the movement. Under his authority a new government was organized under a council of ten disciples, who in turn were advised by an assembly of fifty tribal delegates. A religious hierarchy was thus superimposed on a tribal society.

After the death of Ibn Tumart, his successor, 'Abd al-Mu'min (1130–63), took the title "caliph of Ibn Tumart." 'Abd al-Mu'min governed his empire through his family but attached an Almohad *shaykh* as a teacher to each of its youthful members. The Almohad government was much more Berber than that of the Almoravids; Berbers played an important role as court counselors, secretaries, poets, physicians, and ministers of finance. The military was augmented by slaves, Arab tribes, and contingents of Turkish, Kurdish, and black soldiers, as well as urban auxiliaries. An elaborate religious administration including a keeper of morals (*mizwar*), muezzins, and instructors in the Quran was also established. Among the duties of the *mizwar* were the destruction of musical instruments and the prohibition of alcohol. A civil bureaucracy of the Andalusian type was mobilized to support the government. Thus the Almohad regime was based on a combination of a royal household, an hierarchical religious organization, a tribal military elite with Berber and Arab tribal allies, and a Spanish-type administration.

Despite the power of the regime, the Almohad doctrine was never successfully implemented. Alternative expressions of Islam, including that of the Maliki jurists, the popular cult of saints and Sufis, and the philosophy of Averroes, were always tolerated. Later rulers abandoned Almohad doctrine, and conflict within the ruling elite led in 1229 to the formal renunciation of the teachings of Ibn Tumart and a return to Maliki law.

Under al-Mu'min's leadership, the Almohad movement defeated the Almoravid dynasty and captured Tlemcen in 1144, Fez in 1145, and Marrakech in 1146. In 1151–52 the Almohads conquered the central Maghrib and ended the Hammadid emirate. The coastal zones, however, remained in the control of the Normans and the Genoese. The Almohads also accepted the Almoravid precedent of a Moroccan empire reaching from the Sahara to Spain. They took Seville and Cordoba in 1149, and the rest of Muslim Spain by 1172. The Almohads, however, were defeated in 1212 by the combined Christian forces of Leon, Castile, Navarre, and Aragon at the Battle of Las Navas de Tolosa. Southern Morocco was invaded by Arab tribes of Banu Ma'qil, who ruined the villages and undermined the authority of the central government. In turn they would construct a new state. By the middle of the thirteenth century, however, through a succession of invaders and state builders, Morocco had evolved from a region divided among Arab and Berber principalities into a society with a lasting territorial identity.

The collapse of the Almohad Empire marked the conclusion of the first phase of state formation and Islamization in North Africa. In this era a succession of regimes – Rustamid, Idrisid, Fatimid, Almoravid, and Almohad – had used Islamic religious beliefs to legitimize new political elites and to unify Berber tribal peoples. Islam had become the basis of political solidarity among factious populations, but the role of religion in the formation of these states varied. The Idrisid, Fatimid, Almoravid, and Almohad rulers all claimed an unmediated, divine authority based on their personal qualifications and their descent in the family of the Prophet. In some respects these regimes were the ideological equivalents of the caliphate. The Khariji states of southern Tunisia and Algeria, however, stressed ideology rather than the person of the rulers. They were built on an ascetic, egalitarian concept of the social order in which the imam was a representative of collective values rather than an embodiment of the divine mystery.

To build these states, religious authority was joined to revenues from commerce and the support of tribes. Yet the North African states were short lived and subject to changing patterns of trade, the rise of new tribal movements, and the breakdown of coalitions. Moreover, they did not fully control the territories under their nominal domain but were suzerainties over independent peoples. Sometimes the states were no more than islands in a sea of autonomous and unorganized Berber populations.

SCHOLARS AND SUFIS: ISLAMIC RELIGIOUS COMMUNITIES

Although Islamization was associated with state formation, as early as the eighth century, religious elites, separate from the state and committed to Islamic values above state interests, had also come into being.Under Aghlabid patronage Qayrawan became the leading North African center of the Maliki school of law. Despite criticism that the Maliki school was rigid and literal minded, it was not monolithic.

Theological issues were hotly debated. Such topics as the creation of the Quran, free will and predestination, and the meaning of the caliphate were debated as much in Qayrawan as in Baghdad. In the course of the tenth century Ash'arism was assimilated into the Maliki school and was later transmitted to the Almohads. Maliki scholars were also students of grammar, philology, mathematics, astronomy, and medicine. Ibn al-Tabban (d. 981) was a student of law, philology, grammar, mathematics, astronomy, medicine, and the interpretation of dreams. Al-Qabisi (d. 1012) was a theologian who stressed hadith and mysticism, and an intensely pious religious practice. These men exemplified divergent orientations within the Maliki school parallel to those in the eastern Shafi'i school.

The schools of law were the vehicles for the mobilization of public opinion in the struggles among political regimes. In Qayrawan, the Hanafis, representing an upper-class milieu, were favored by the Aghlabids. They later collaborated with the Fatimids. The Malikis, by contrast, eschewed appointments to office and won popular support. Under Fatimid rule, the Malikis denounced Shi'ism, provoked anti-Shi'i riots and massacres in Qayrawan, and in 1049 forced the Zirids to accept Sunni allegiance and to recognize the 'Abbasid caliphs. Although Qayrawan and Tunis were the main centers of Maliki teaching, the Maliki position was also strongly supported in the coastal *ribats* and spread to southern Morocco, across the Sahara, and into Sudanic West Africa.

Along with the Maliki school of law, Sufi asceticism – stressing sadness, silence, suffering, fear of God, attention to the coming of the last judgment, and the virtues of humility and charity – was cultivated in Qayrawan. The *ribats* combined holy war with pious devotions. The common people believed in saints who had the power to heal, bring rain, perform miracles, communicate with spiritual forces, interpret dreams, and otherwise act as intermediaries between men and God. Sufism in North Africa, as in the Middle East, was not so much an organized religious movement as a religious sensibility.

In the eleventh and twelfth centuries, a new form of Sufism, based on both Spanish and Eastern teachings, was introduced to North Africa and spread in reaction to the Almoravid and Almohad conquests. Abu Madyan al-Andalusi (d. 1197) brought the Spanish form of Sufism that integrated ascetic mysticism with the study of law. His tomb became a venerated place of pilgrimage, and his successors continued the tradition of combining the study of hadith and law with mystical practices. Sufi scholars were established in Tunisia at Tunis, Bone, and Qayrawan and were represented in Morocco at Aghmat, Marrakesh, and other places. Abu al Hasan al-Shadhili (d.1258) introduced a new brotherhood to the Islamic West. The Maliki school, the early *ribats*, Khariji teachers, and Sufis helped to diffuse Islam from its Tunisian base into southern Morocco. Traders and scholars also brought it to the Saharan region.

Alongside the formal and legal Islam of the Sunni *'ulama'* and the scholarly mysticism of the Sufi leaders, a popular form of Sufism, here called Maraboutism, developed among the common people. As in the case of parallel developments in the eastern Islamic world, popular Sufism derived from the tradition of the popular storyteller-teacher-missionary and from the warrior traditions of the *ribat* or frontier fortress dedicated to the expansion of Islam. The holy warrior or popular saint was believed to possess magical powers of divination and healing and ultimately the power to convey God's grace (*baraka*) into worldly affairs and to intercede with him at the last judgment. The holy man gathered his disciples into a community and ultimately a brotherhood with many branches that carried on his teaching and conveyed his blessing. His tomb came to possess the magical powers he embodied in his lifetime. The Almohads helped to popularize this form of Sufism.

Our knowledge of this early period is too scattered to give an assured account of the rhythm of the development and diffusion of the several varieties of Islam. Libya appears to have been relatively quickly converted in the wake of the early conquests. Large numbers of Berbers accepted Khariji Islam, but Qayrawan, Tunis, Tripoli, Sfax, Mahdiya, Bougie, Bone, and other cities still had Christian communities in the eleventh and twelfth centuries. Nonetheless, the 200 bishoprics known in the seventh century had been reduced to 5 by 1053 and to 3 by 1076. The Almohads effectively put an end to Christianity in North Africa; Christians survived only in isolated villages. Jews were reduced in number.

Thus, by the middle of the thirteenth century, the Arab invasions and the introduction of Islam had inspired a centuries-long wave of state construction culminating in the integration of Tunisia and Morocco into territorial states. At the same time, Islam had been established as the dominant religion. Informal schools of legal instruction, theology, and mysticism emerged, and Islamic religious teachers acquired a large popular following. Religious leadership and communal ties were differentiated from state institutions. Only in the thirteenth century, after numerous experiments – Kharijism, Zaydism, Shi'ism, Malikism, Almohadism – was the full panoply of Sunni scriptural, mystical, and popular Islam established. As a result of state formation, the defeat of the great tribal and religious movements that sought to unify North Africa, and the formation of an autonomous Islamic religious elite, the way was prepared for a new historic phase of the relationships between state and Islam in North African societies.

CHAPTER 27

SPANISH-ISLAMIC CIVILIZATION

Muslim Spain from the Arab conquest to the liquidation of the last Muslim possessions in Granada in 1492 represents yet another expression of the caliphal type
of early Islamic civilization. This civilization assimilated the Spanish, Jewish, and
Berber populations to Arab-Islamic culture, fostering extraordinary economic prosperity. Muslim Spain bears an aura of glory. The great Mosque of Cordoba; the
gardens, fountains, and courtyards of the Alhambra; the *muwashshah* and *zajal*
poetry, with their Arabic verses and Romance language refrains; the irrigated gardens of Seville and Valencia; the wisdom of philosophy and science – these are
the monuments of Spanish Islam. Spain was the focal point for the transmission
of Greek philosophy from the Arab world to Europe. No less important was the
drama of the defeat of this brilliant Muslim civilization by its European enemies,
the expulsion of the Jews and Muslims, and the reabsorption of Spain into Christian
Europe.

For all its brilliance, Muslim Spain was a province of the Arab caliphate. Already
overrun by successive waves of Alaric and Vandal invasions from the north, Spain
was conquered by Arab and Berber forces from North Africa led by Tariq, who
defeated the Visigothic King Roderic at the River Barbate in 711. The Arab advance
into France was checked by Charles Martel at the Battle of Poitiers in 732. Whereas
in the East Arab conquerors were generally forced to settle in garrison towns and
villages – leaving the land in the direct control of its preconquest landlord elite and
a tax-collecting bureaucracy – in Spain large territories were parceled out among
Arab and Berber clans. This was both the basis of the complex integration of ethnic
groups, religions, and cultures and the tumultuous political competition that would
characterize Hispano-Arabic civilization.

Arabs and Berbers alike were organized as patrilineal clans and tribes that
facilitated factional quarrels. The Arabs in Spain (like those in the East) were
divided into quarreling tribal factions called Qays and Yemen, representing the
first-generation settlers and later immigrants. In the very first decades of Muslim

rule, Berbers, allocated poor mountain lands in Galicia and Cantabria, rebelled against Arab governors. The rebellions were put down by Syrian Arabs and the new forces were in turn given fiefs. As in the Middle East, by the eleventh century long-term processes (such as sedentarization, urbanization, and the centralization of political power in the caliphate) had greatly reduced the importance of tribal segmentation.

Cultural development was abetted by extraordinary economic prosperity in the ninth and tenth centuries. The introduction of irrigation agriculture based on Eastern models led to the cultivation of valuable new crops, including cherries, apples, pears, almonds, pomegranates, figs, dates, sugarcane, bananas, cotton, flax, and silk. A Damascus type of irrigation assigned water to each cultivator in proportion to the size of his land. In the irrigated, oasis-like gardens (*huertas*) of Valencia, a Yemeni type of irrigation distributed water by a fixed time flow. Irrigation was administered either by a town authority under the control of the *sahib al-saqiya*, who policed the distribution of water and assured equity, or by local communities who selected their own irrigation managers. Luxury manufactures abounded, including perfumes and incenses, silk textiles and clothing, ceramics, ivories, jewelry, and metal objects. At the same time, Spain prospered due to the breakdown of Byzantine naval control over the western Mediterranean. Cities such as Seville and Cordoba prospered from both agricultural production and international trade.

Economic development led to political consolidation. After a succession of weak governors appointed from North Africa, three great rulers built up the Spanish-Muslim state. ʿAbd al-Rahman I (r. 756–88), a grandson of the Umayyad Caliph Hisham, supported by Berbers from North Africa and by Syrian clients of the Umayyads, founded the Umayyad dynasty in Spain. The new regime followed the ʿAbbasid pattern. It suppressed local revolts and built up a client army of soldiers coming from north of the Pyrenees. ʿAbd al-Rahman II (r. 822–52) further centralized administration, brought into being a new secretarial class made up of merchants and clients, and created state monopolies and controls over urban markets. ʿAbd al-Rahman III (r. 912–61) built his army with captives from northern Spain, Germany, and the Slavic countries. These troops, known as *saqaliba*, were later reinforced with detribalized professional Berber soldiers and local levies. A *hajib*, equal in rank to a vizier, was in charge of administration and taxation. Provincial tax collectors were appointed to raise revenues and to send the surplus to Cordoba. While twenty-one provinces were governed by appointees of the central government, frontier districts were managed by local officials (*qaʾid*) and hereditary petty lords. A chief judge supervised the judicial administration and managed the properties endowed for religious and charitable purposes.

ʿAbd al-Rahman III also sought a new basis for the legitimization of his regime by adopting Baghdadi ʿAbbasid cultural forms. Although Islamic culture in Spain assimilated some aspects of local culture, it was primarily an outpost of Middle Eastern Arab-Islamic civilization. As in the East, court culture tried to integrate

Muslim and cosmopolitan symbols. 'Abd al-Rahman adopted the title caliph, or *amir al-mu'minin*, in reaction to the claims of the Fatimids in North Africa. Thus, the precious title signifying the unity of the Muslim community was claimed by no fewer than three rulers in the tenth century. 'Abd al-Rahman expanded the Cordoba mosque, installed irrigation works, and waged war to check Christian attacks in northern Spain.

HISPANO-ARABIC SOCIETY (CO-AUTHOR, DAVID MOSHFEGH)

Dispersed settlement contributed enormously to the Arabization and Islamization of Spain. In the period of the caliphate and the succeeding factional (*taifa*) states, Muslims constituted the political elite, but "Muslim" identities were complex. Some considered themselves Arabs by lineage; others Berber by family heritage. For others the Arabic language defined their status. Then rulers took on clients, captured slaves, hired mercenaries, and married into local families. By the ninth century, Arabic was widely used by the indigenous population, and there were many converts (*muwalladun*). As converts multiplied, the distinction between the original Arab elite and assimilated Arabs blurred, and a more homogeneous Hispano-Arab society came into being.

The Spanish caliphate defined itself by its heritage of high culture in poetry, courtly literatures, entertainments, architecture, philosophy, and science. It was also Islamic and adopted much of the religious culture of the eastern Arab world. As in the cases of the Umayyad and 'Abbasid empires, the Spanish caliphate considered its non-Muslim subjects to be protected minorities (*dhimmi*), permitted to exercise their own religion. Native Christians and Jews were given communal autonomy and continued to administer themselves in terms of their Visigothic Christian rite or Jewish law. As in the East, the way was often open for a blending or merger of populations in language and everyday culture and indeed in some religious matters as well.

In Spain, the complex identities of the Muslim populations were matched by an equally complex situation among the Christian and Jewish populations. Jews considered themselves notables, if not nobles. They may have assisted in the Arab-Berber-Muslim conquest and served in administration and financial affairs. Sephardic Jews identified with the ruling elite and acted as intermediaries between the Muslim rulers and the Christian powers. Leading Jewish administrators carried on an international correspondence and assumed an implied spokesmanship for Jewish communities in Europe.

The language of the non-Muslim population of Cordoba during the ninth and tenth centuries was principally a Romance dialect, but there were many variations of religious, linguistic, and ethnic identities. Many Muslims came to speak Romance. Some Christians retained both their Romance language and Visigothic Christian culture. Others Christians converted to Islam but spoke only Romance and knew no Arabic. Still others took on Arabic language and cultural traits without becoming Muslims. Mozarab was the name applied to Christians acculturated to Arabic but not converted to Islam. These Christians may have included Visigothic nobles who were allied with the Muslim conquerors, or others who served in the Umayyad and *taifa* periods as government officials and soldiers. People in all three categories married each other, creating new layers of hybrid family, religion, and culture. Their progeny were raised as Muslims but born into a non-Arab-Muslim family and were called *muwalladun*, which means "those born of two races." In sum, there were Romance-speaking Christians and Romance-speaking Muslims, as well as Arabic-speaking Muslims and Christians. Both a Romance vernacular and spoken Arabic were used across confessional lines. With the Arabization of the Christian population and the reciprocal transmission of the Romance and Roman-Visigothic heritage to the Muslim elite, a new cultural blend came into being.

This cultural blending was strongly resisted by elements of the Christian church hierarchy who feared not only the ever-growing numbers of Christian conversions but also cultural assimilation, Arabization, as a religio-communal defeat. Indeed, Christian Visigothic texts were being translated into Arabic. Between 850 and 859, some forty-eight monks, nuns, priests, and other fervent Christians committed to the Latin Christian Visigothic heritage, promoted by a priest named Eulogius, martyred themselves to protest Arab-Muslim rule. This was an effort to draw a clear boundary between Muslims and Christians. Some of these activists deliberately courted execution by denouncing Muhammad. Some were the children, especially daughters, of mixed families who were Muslim according to Islamic law but who considered themselves Christians and renounced their putative religion. In reaction to these protests, the Umayyad regime dismissed Christians from court service, levied new taxes, and had some churches destroyed. Christian extremism was also repudiated by many Christians who maintained good relations with Muslims.

This complex society in many ways resembled the eastern Islamic societies. In the eastern case, too, Muslims held the highest political status, but in everyday life there was a great deal of interaction between Muslims, Christians, Jews, Zoroastrians, and others, depending on the locale. Non-Muslims converted and adopted Arabic (or Persian) as a common language; others adopted the common culture without converting. Muslims often adopted the cultural and material styles of the older Middle Eastern populations. Especially in marketing and business affairs, the caliphal-era societies were fairly well integrated. Jews and Christians were prominent in Baghdad and in Cairo, as well as in many other places, in trade, banking, and government administration. Among the educated elites, there were shared religious, philosophical, scientific and legal, and literary interests and a shared pursuit of these interests. Despite these shared lives, there were still episodes of religious-political tension, competition, and persecution.

Thus, the societies of Spain under the caliphate and the *taifa* principalities were based on the eastern Arab-Muslim imperial models. This was the Mediterranean and

Middle Eastern–wide mode of Muslim rule and the prevailing mode of acculturation and quasi-integration of populations.

HISPANO-ARABIC CULTURE

Poetry became the primary expression of Spanish cosmopolitan culture. Spanish poetry was originally based on Arabic models, which carried with them the warrior sentiments and factional interests of the Arab conquerors. The urbane Baghdadi style was introduced when the poet, musician, and singer Ziryab (d. 857) came to Cordoba. In early Hispano-Arabic poetry, the *qasida*, which praised the virtues of the ruler and served official purposes, was the dominant form. A new poetic form, the *muwashshah*, combined Arabic strophes with a responding refrain (*kharja*) in the Romance dialect. The Arabic part, usually a love poem, was courtly in theme, masculine in tone; the *kharja* was usually the voice of the lower classes, or of a Christian slave girl, and feminine in inspiration. The metrical system, the syllabic prosody, and the rhyme scheme of the Arabic verses indicate Romance traditions.

Other literary activities flourished under caliphal patronage. Eastern scholars emigrated to Spain, and the royal libraries were enlarged. Grammar and philology came from Iraq. *Adab*, or belles lettres in Eastern style, was first composed in Spain by Ibn 'Abd al-Rabbih (d. 940). Caliphal patronage broadened scientific learning. Aristotle's philosophy was introduced by the reception of the *Organon*; the *Republic*, the *Laws*, and the *Timaeus* of Plato were known. Galen became the standard medical author. A new translation of a classic work – Dioscorides' *Materia Medica* – was made in Spain. The earliest translations of astronomical and geometric works from Arabic into Latin were made in the tenth century.

The architecture of the caliphate, including mosques, palaces, and baths, was also Eastern in inspiration. The Mosque of Cordoba was expanded and rebuilt by successive rulers. It was a vast hall divided by columns surmounted by horseshoe arches, a hallmark of Hispano-Roman architecture of the Visigothic period. A niche with a fluted shell-like vault and a horseshoe arch indicated the direction of prayer. Red and white banded arches evoked the grand Umayyad monuments of Damascus and Jerusalem. Visigothic and Roman elements were built into the Muslim design, including horseshoe arches and classical orders. The mosque was redecorated between 961 and 966 by mosaic workers, who gave it a vivid and brilliant interior. The Mosque of Cordoba, like the Mosque of Damascus, was a symbol of the incorporation of ancient values and their supersession by Islamic civilization. In the tenth century, the caliphs also built the royal city of Madinat al-Zahra, a city of splendid palaces, fountains, and gardens that echoed the palace complexes of Baghdad.

Under the auspices of the Spanish Umayyad regime, Islamic legal and religious studies were promoted. The Syrian school of law, founded by al-Awza'i, favored by Syrian-Arab military lords, was imported into Spain, but the town populations favored the Maliki school from North Africa. From the East came Shafi'i concepts. Hadith studies were introduced in the ninth century, and Muslim scholars were divided between those who emphasized law and those who favored hadith and theology. This distinction may have represented a division between Arab elites and later converts. Shafi'i scholars, however, had to accept Maliki law, and Malikism remained the primary legal school of Muslim Spain. Mu'tazilism was also introduced from Baghdad in the ninth century. Muhammad b. Masarra (d. 931), whose father had studied in Basra, amalgamated neo-Platonic, Shi'i, and Sufi thought. The legal scholars, however, restricted the public expression of mystical tendencies.

Arab-Islamic culture in Spain was thus associated with different social milieus and sociopolitical movements. Monumental architecture, formal poetry, and philosophic interests characterized the royal style of culture in Spain as in Baghdad. The scribal class was identified with Arabic belles lettres. As in the East, the secretarial class, composed of Spanish converts, generated an Arabic literature that was intended to prove their equality with the Arab warrior elites. The *Risala* of Abu 'Amir b. Garcia provoked an avalanche of contemptuous Arabic poetry in response.

Important lower-class social movements were also connected with religious trends. In circumstances that still remain obscure, the scholars (*'ulama'*) of the Rabad quarter of Cordoba led local rebellions in 805 and 818. They denounced the regime for corruption, fiscal exploitation, use of foreign military forces, and chronic insecurity. As in North Africa, Baghdad, and other parts of the Muslim world, the scholars assumed political responsibilities and a voice in the direction of society. Sufis also led a lower-class movement opposed to the exploitative accumulation of wealth by the upper classes and espoused an ascetic, mystical, and communalist doctrine. The revolts, however, were put down, and 'Abd al-Rahman II created a religious council to demonstrate that he ruled in accordance with Islam. Thus, the Umayyad princes sought to legitimize their rule by co-opting the scholars of law.

Like its 'Abbasid model, the Spanish-Muslim state was subverted by internal conflicts. The hostilities between provincial and urban mercantile elites, between townsmen and Berber troops, and between converts and Arabs made it impossible to stabilize the regime. In the early eleventh century, the caliphs lost control of the central government, provincial governors became independent, and Arab clans revolted. The caliphate was abolished, and Spain was divided into petty warring principalities, the *taifa* states. Arab, Slav, and Berber soldiers and local elites took power, and each province became an independent state with an army, court, and administration of its own. The Amirids – descendants of former caliphal administrators – ruled the eastern coast of Andalus. Regimes based on local Arab families were founded at Cordoba, Seville, and Saragossa. Berber-dominated states were founded at Toledo, Badajoz, and Granada. The Christian states of the north joined in the free-for-all. Small states made opportunistic alliances with one another and employed mercenary soldiers regardless of religion. In Granada, the Berber ruling elite governed with the help of the Jewish Banu Naghrila family. This provoked intense Muslim hostility and a pogrom against Jews in 1066.

Although the emergence of provincial regimes was a defeat for centralized government, Spanish society was not as fragmented as the political divisions of power would imply. Islamic law and a Muslim-Arab identity were widely accepted; scholars continued to represent the urban populations. Spanish-Muslim society was also integrated by a flourishing regional and international commerce. Andalusia traded with Morocco, importing wood, alum, antimony, and cloth, and exporting cloth and copper. It traded with Tunisia and through Tunisia with Egypt, importing the wool, flax, and dyes that came to Egypt from Iran, Arabia, India, and China. Spanish-Muslims also traded with the Christian north, where growing wealth and the rising power of new states created ever larger markets.

The disintegration of the caliphate did not disrupt Spanish-Muslim cultural life. With the decline of the caliphate, the patronage of art and culture shifted to the courts of the provincial rulers and merchants. In place of grand mosques, private palaces became the characteristic symbols of Hispano-Arabic civilization. In the late tenth century, the *muwashshahat* poetry flourished, as city dwellers rediscovered the beauties of nature. Poems in *qasida* form devoted to descriptions of nature and gardens, wine and war, and love and passion were composed. Ibn Quzman (d. 1160) cultivated the *zajal*, a form of poetry in colloquial Arabic, whose themes were the life of towns and markets, the common people, and the underworld. This was a deliberately irreligious form of art. After a long period in which the Baghdadi style had dominated Arabic-Spanish literature, poetic interests were transferred from the political to the personal. Love and art for art's sake became the dominant themes.

Love was the central theme in the philosophy of Ibn Hazm (d. 1093). He taught that the attraction of two people was based on an eternal affinity, a timeless connection of souls. Ibn al-ʿArabi later explained that a man loves a woman because she is the mirror that reveals his innermost true being – the spiritual being that transcends his animal reality. The love of a woman is the love of the original nature of the soul and therefore a reminder of God. Love stems from the creation of man in the image of God, and sexual love is a symbol of the extinction of the separate natures in the divine reality.

With the breakdown of the caliphate, Sufism also became important. From Almeria came Abu al-ʿAbbas b. al-ʾArif (d. 1141), whose writings described the stages of mystical ascent to the realization that only God exists. Ibn al-ʿArabi, also from Spain, was probably the greatest Muslim mystical metaphysician. Theological and philosophic debates took place under Almohad rule (1149–1212). Al-Ghazali had taught that direct apprehension was the basis for the knowledge of the divine being, and that the Quran was a direct expression of God's being. Ibn Rushd (Averroes, d. 1198) held that reason was the basis of human knowledge of the divine being, and that the Quran was an allegory requiring rational interpretation.

THE RECONQUISTA

Despite its great prosperity and cultivated urban life, the extreme degree of political fragmentation eventually undermined Islamic Spain. The initial Muslim advance had left a small belt of northern territories along the Pyrenees in Christian hands. In the course of the eighth and ninth centuries, skirmishes among the small kingdoms in this region led to the beginnings of an ideological movement to reconquer and recolonize the Muslim areas of Spain. Christian sentiment was also expressed in the founding of Benedictine monasteries and the pilgrimage of Santiago de Compostela. Pope Gregory VII made the reconquest a religious duty of Christians as well as a territorial ambition of Spanish kings.

The disintegration of the Muslim states in the eleventh century allowed for the rapid expansion of various Christian kingdoms. In 1085 Alfonso VI, on the strength of the unified kingdoms of Castile, Leon, and Galicia, conquered Toledo. This was a signal event in the struggle between Muslims and Christians, for a brilliant center of Muslim civilization, once the capital of Visigothic Spain, again fell into Christian hands. Christian migrants flocked to Toledo, but the Muslim, Jewish, and Mozarab populations were allowed to remain. In the meantime, the kingdom of Aragon captured Huesca (1096), Saragossa (1118), Tortosa (1148), and Lerida (1149). In the second half of the twelfth century, the reconquest became institutionalized in the founding of monastic-military fraternities, such as the orders of Calatrava and Santiago, financed by landed estates, and conquered and colonized Muslim territories.

The Christian advance was countered by the Muslims. The Muslim sense of retreat and decline prompted, in 1082, a delegation of scholars to urge the Almoravids to intervene on behalf of the Spanish-Muslims. Thus, in 1086, a Moroccan army crossed the straits and defeated Alfonso VI. From 1090 to 1145, the North Africans conquered the Spanish-Muslim cities and governed Spain as a province of Marrakesh. The Almoravids polarized religio-communal relationships. Although they grudgingly accepted the *dhimmi* status of Christians and Jews, Christians began to emigrate from Almoravid domains. There were Sufi-led revolts in Silves and Niebla and scholar-led revolts in Cordoba and Valencia that eventually overthrew Almoravid rule. The Almohads, who took Marrakesh in 1147, accepted the concept of a Moroccan empire reaching from the Sahara to Spain. They took Seville and Cordoba in 1149 and the rest of Muslim Spain by 1172. A new Moroccan suzerainty was imposed on Spain, but the Almohads did not honor the *dhimmi* pact, and much of the Andalusian Jewish and Christian population moved to other regions.

Nonetheless, the Muslim position continued to weaken under the combination of Christian pressures and regional anarchy. The Almohads were defeated in 1212 by the combined Christian forces of Leon, Castile, Navarre, and Aragon at the Battle of Las Navas de Tolosa. With the defeat of the Almohads, the Spanish-Muslim states again found themselves independent but helpless before the resumption of the Christian reconquest. The union of Castile and Leon in 1230 opened the way for the conquest of Cordoba in 1236 and Seville in 1248. The Aragonese advanced along the coast to take Valencia in 1238 and Murcia in 1243. By 1249–50 the Portuguese had taken all of the lands west of the Guadiana River.

By the middle of the thirteenth century, only Granada remained in Muslim hands. It was protected by a large populace, a mountainous territory, and a productive economy that paid a heavy tribute to the princes of Castile. Castilian attacks on Granadan farmers weakened the Muslim state, as did internal factional disputes, but divisions in Castile long protected it from defeat. The union of Castile and Aragon opened the way for the final conquest of the last Muslim possession in Spain in 1492. (See Map 13.)

MUSLIMS UNDER CHRISTIAN RULE

The attitudes of the Spanish Christians toward their Muslim subjects were deeply ambivalent. In all the conquered places, the monarchies and especially the local Christian nobility wanted to retain the productive working and agricultural populations. Yet they feared Muslims and Jews, and especially converts to Christianity, as a subversive and dangerous presence.

There was substantial continuity in the social and political organization of the Muslim population. Treaties guaranteed Muslims religious, judicial, and communal autonomy. Some Muslims were pushed out of urban neighborhoods, but Muslims generally kept their residences; merchants and artisans continued to flourish. Small farmers, property owners, and tenants kept their tenures. The kings of Aragon at first maintained the authority of the Muslim elites by treating them as vassals of the crown. They required oaths of loyalty and military service. The old rural social structure, consisting of small village or castle-scale communities governed by a *qa'id*, was maintained. In the cities, Muslims and Jews were allowed to govern themselves in local affairs. They became – as the Christians had been – a protected population. Muslims retained control of civil courts and of internal matters. The judge (*qadi*) was the chief Muslim official, the *amin* was the main administrator and tax collector, and the *sahib al-madina* was in charge of the police. The organized Muslim communities could thus both cooperate with and ward off state interference. Apart from the small crusading principalities in Palestine, Lebanon, and Sicily, this was the first experience of Muslims under non-Muslim rule.

In Spain, the living together of Muslims, Christians, and Jews is called *convivencia*. The Muslim conquest, Muslim governments, and its substantial Muslim and Jewish populations made Spain, perhaps apart from Sicily, a unique part of Western Europe. In Europe Spain has a distinctive history because of the synthesis of Christian, Muslim, and Jewish cultures. *Convivencia* signifies the acceptance of Jews and Muslims in royal courts and administration, in economic life and daily

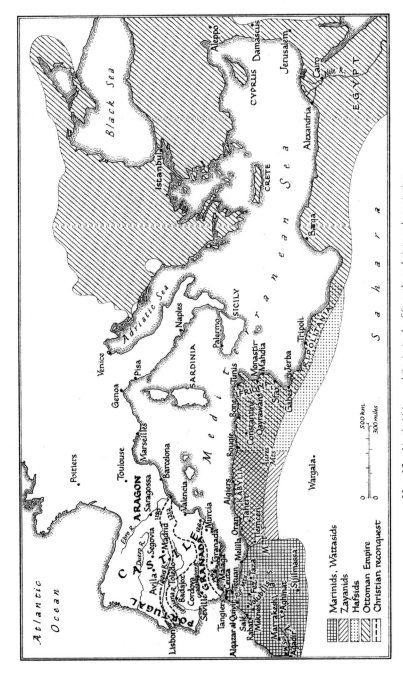

Map 13. North Africa and Spain in the fifteenth and sixteen h centuries

social relations, and in intellectual collaboration among Jews, Christians, and Muslims. Recently, it has come to be celebrated as an epoch when Muslims, Christians, and Jews lived in harmony and in economic and cultural collaboration. Now it is often presented as a model for pluralistic societies in the Mediterranean and the Middle East.

The historical story, however, is more complex. Historians who celebrate the *convivencia* overlook the parallel history of the breakdown of the security and prosperity of the Muslim and Jewish communities, economic exploitation, violent assaults, religious persecution, and indeed their eventual expulsion from Spain. In fact, the history of Jews and Muslims under Christian rule falls into two phases. The first phase was a period of autonomy and relative security for the governed populations and cultural collaboration among the elites; the second phase was a period of increasing harassment, persecution, and eventually expulsion from Spain.

The conditions of Muslim and Jewish community life under Christian rule differed from kingdom to kingdom and from province to province. In Castile, Alfonso adopted the previous Muslim policy of respecting the religious, communal, and economic interests of the subordinate populations. The Castilian treatment of its Mozarab population – meaning Christians of Visigothic rite who spoke Arabic – is emblematic of the treatment accorded the Muslims and Jews. In the early postconquest era, the Mozarabs were treated as a favored minority. Alfonso granted a special dispensation to six parish churches to use the Visigothic or Hispano-Gothic rite rather than the Catholic liturgy. They were granted their own communal legal jurisdiction and many fiscal advantages. This allowed Arabized Christians and Muslim converts to Christianity to occupy a favored position in the expanding Christian states. In 1371, Enrique II confirmed the privileges of the Mozarabs of Toledo, but by the end of the fifteenth century the Mozarabic tradition had virtually disappeared.

Muslims and Jews were at first given similar treatment. Within two years, however, the central Mosque of Toledo was confiscated and converted into a cathedral. In Andalusia, the Muslims of the Guadalquivir Valley were forced to leave their town quarters and to settle in outlying suburbs or hamlets. In general, however, Muslims could keep their properties and govern their internal affairs and were assured freedom of worship. In Aragon, Muslims, perhaps 20 percent of the population, were bilingual in Romance and Arabic and were highly integrated into Christian society. They served Christian lords and in the market had Christian employers and customers. Navarrese Muslims often held high office under the crown and served in the army.

Of the reconquered territories, Valencia had the largest Muslim population. At first, the Muslims of Valencia province, called Mudejars, some of whom lived in towns but most of whom lived in country villages, constituted about 80 percent of the population. They were Arabic speaking. The Mudejars made up most of the work force. They were free farmers, small landowners, and artisans. They dominated the ceramics and paper industries. They were important as merchants, shopkeepers, entertainers, household servants, and slaves.

They were ruled by Christian lords assisted by Christian and Jewish administrators. The conqueror, James I of Aragon, attempted to consolidate Christian hegemony by bringing in Christian and Jewish settlers from Catalonia and Aragon, by establishing religious orders, by giving lands to Christian landlords, and by organizing a tax-collecting administration. However, Christian power was not consolidated until the fourteenth century when, as a result of Christian and Jewish immigration and Muslim emigration, Mudejars constituted only one-half of the population. By the fifteenth century, they were probably less than one-third of the total. Relations between Muslims and Christians were not always peaceful. The Mudejars did not passively accept Christian rule. From the 1240s through the 1270s, they repeatedly rose in revolt, often aided by Moroccan and Granadan allies. There were anti-Muslim riots in 1275–76.

Muslims continued to live in self-governing communities. By royal decree, Muslims were permitted to live under their own laws, to offer public prayers, and to educate their children. The chief Muslim official under the crown of Aragon was the *qadi* general, or royal *qadi*. In each Muslim community (*al-jama‘a*) there was a local judge and an *amin* or fiscal officer responsible for the collection of taxes. The local jurists advised the Muslim and Christian judges and officials called in to arbitrate disputes among Muslims. In this role, the jurists sought to preserve Islamic ethics, mediate the needs of a subjugated population, and maintain Muslim communal identity.

Communal identity was reinforced by commercial, family, clan, and linguistic ties. The religious scholars, preachers, and teachers traveled widely, maintaining extensive networks that linked the communities together. Valencian Mudejars spoke a dialect of Arabic and created their own vernacular written version (Aljamiado). At the same time, standard literary Arabic was used in Quranic, legal, and other religious studies and for drawing contracts for marriages, commercial obligations, and tax records. Because Valencian Muslims were not versed in Romance dialects, their linguistic knowledge created both an inner solidarity and a barrier to the Christian world.

The Reconquista did not extinguish the cultural vitality of Muslim Spain. On the contrary, in Castile and Aragon, a new Islamic devotional literature written in Arabic script and in Arabized Spanish, Aljamiado, emerged as the literary language of the Mudejars. Granada, the surviving Muslim enclave, maintained a sophisticated style of life. The city was adorned with patios, fountains, and pavements; Granada copied Eastern styles in bronzes, ivories, ceramics, and furniture. In order to meet its huge burden of tribute, Granada developed an export trade in ceramics, porcelains, silks, and weapons. (See Illustration 10.)

The Alhambra was one of the great achievements of Islamic urban art. It was first constructed as a fortress and royal residence in the eleventh century. By

Illustration 10.   Patio de los Leones, Alhambra (Granada, Spain). Source: Ray Lifchez Collection, Architecture Visual Resources Library, University of California at Berkeley.

the thirteenth century, it had been enlarged into a princely city. Like Baghdad and Cairo, it was a symbol of the power and aloofness of royalty. The Nasrid dynasty of Granada (1230–1492) built the famous Court of the Myrtles, the Court of the Lions, and innumerable gardens and pavilions. The palace complex was decorated with Islamic symbols and water motifs. It was embellished with Quranic inscriptions and provided with a large mosque, an open prayer field, and the "Gate of the Law." Pools and fountains symbolized refuge, repose, and paradise. Inscriptions bore allusions to the legend of the glass floor built by King Solomon to resemble a pool of water – the Solomonic story linked Granada with the royal art of the ancient Near East and its later Islamic versions. It was a last echo of the courtly cosmopolitan civilization of the Arab East in the western Mediterranean.

In the Christian kingdoms as well, Hispano-Islamic culture was a powerful influence. Nobles and churchmen built their houses in the Moorish manner and borrowed Hispanic-Islamic motifs for their heraldry. They dressed in Arab fabrics. Even before the conquest of Toledo, buildings in northern Spain were built or remodeled with some of the characteristic features of the Umayyad and *taifa* period. Mozarab churches blended Visigothic plans and elevation with Cordoban arches and decoration. In Toledo after 1085, the construction of the apses of churches joined semicircular Roman arches characteristic of Castilian construction with horseshoe and scalloped niches for the portraits of saints characteristic of Mudejar art. In the fifteenth and sixteenth centuries, Castilian monuments – such as the Alcazar of Seville, the palace of Tordesillas, and other buildings – shared Mudejar architectural features with the buildings of Granada. Indeed, Granadan and North African craftsmen may have worked on these Castilian projects. As in eastern Umayyad and 'Abbasid art or Spanish Umayyad art, the appropriation of the artistic styles of past regimes was used to express victory, dominance, and authority. It signified the appropriation of the wealth, refinement, sophistication, and mythic power of Islamic culture. Islamic motifs also distinguished Castilian architecture from European art represented by Romanesque and Gothic styles.

THE JEWS IN SPAIN (CO-AUTHOR, DAVID MOSHFEGH)

The Jews of Spain probably date back to the destruction of the Second Temple (70 CE), when Jews were dispersed throughout the Roman Empire. After the conversion of Visigothic kings from Arianism to Catholicism, in 613 Jews were given the choice of conversion or exile. Later, Jews cooperated with the Arab/Berber invasions of 711. They made up a substantial part of the population of cities such as Lucena and Granada and soon came to speak Arabic and dress in the Muslim fashion.

The golden age of Jewish culture in Spain opened under the reign of the Umayyad Caliph 'Abd al-Rahman III (912–61). The leaders of the Jewish community, such as Hasdai ben Shaprut (c. 915–70) and Samuel ibn Naghrela (993–1055), were at once courtiers, physicians, diplomats, and scholars of Hebrew, Arabic, Latin, and Romance. Hasdai ben Shaprut was the impresario behind the invitation of scholars of Bible and Talmud, philosophers, scientists, poets, and linguists to the court. Aware of the importance of poetry in Arab social and political life, Hasdai encouraged the development of Hebrew "court poetry" on Arabic models.From North Africa came Issac al-Fasi, a Jew from Algiers and later Fez, who established at Lucena the first Spanish school of Talmudic studies. Another Fasi scholar, Judah b. David Hayyuj (c. 945–c. 1000), the founder of comparative grammatical studies of Hebrew and Arabic, recognized the common word structure built on three-letter roots.

The renaissance of Hebrew poetry (and philosophy) defined the golden age of Spanish-Jewish culture. Following Arab examples, a worldly Hebrew poetry celebrated the pleasures of earthly life. Jewish secular poetry included poetry about the ecstasies of sensual pleasure and homoerotic love, but with the language and narrative background of the Bible. The poetic genres included the *qasida*, and later the *maqama*, with its mix of narrative and rhetorical text, as well as the Spanish-Arabic *muwashshah* (ending in a colloquial Arabic or Romance couplet resetting the scene of the poem). Samuel bin Naghrela (c. 993–1056), the vizier of Granada, was the first true master of secular Hebrew poetry. Solomon bin Gabirol (1021 to 1058 or 1070), a Jewish neo-Platonist and the foremost Hebrew poet of his time, turned poetry into a means of cultivating an intimate and personal religious sensibility. Judah Halevi (1085–1141) was a distinguished philosopher as well as poet. The eleventh century marked the high point of both Arabic- and Romance-inspired Jewish poetry.

With the breakdown of the caliphate, the succession of the numerous Muslim *taifa* kingdoms, and the Almoravid and the Almohad invasions, the security of the Jewish communities in Spain eventually broke down. The *taifa* kingdoms protected a small Jewish elite who served at *taifa* courts and who perpetuated Hebrew culture. However, under the Almoravids and Almohads, the non-Muslim populations suffered. The Christians of North Africa had already disappeared, and the Jews of Granada were massacred. Many Jews converted to Islam, but they remained suspect to the Almohad ruler al-Mansur (1184–99), who imposed the *dhimmi* regulations, which included distinctive clothing meant to distinguish Jews from Muslims. Many Jews migrated to the Christian states of Portugal, Castile, Navarre, and Aragon, where they were valued for their financial, administrative, and diplomatic skills. Toleration and assimilation led many to voluntarily convert to Christianity. From the late twelfth to the fourteenth centuries, Jewish culture and Jewish communities flourished in the Christian kingdoms. Highly educated Jews, fluent in classical Arabic as well as Hebrew and Romance, served as royal secretaries and translators and participated in the interconfessional cultural life of the reconquest kingdoms.

In this period, biblical and Talmudic commentary resumed. Writing in Hebrew became the hallmark of Jewish scholarship. In the mid-twelfth century Abraham ibn Ezra wrote his Bible commentaries in Hebrew, and from then on a good part of the vast corpus of Judeo-Arabic literature was translated into Hebrew for Jews in Europe and Spain. Maimonides's (1135–1204) epochal work, *Mishneh Torah*, written in Hebrew, was completed in 1180. His "codification" of the Talmud replaced its wide-ranging discussions with a logically ordered treatise and short historical accounts of legal problems. By the mid-thirteenth century, Hebrew had become the exclusive language of Jewish scholarship in Spain; in the Arab

East, Arabic held out as the normative language of scholarship until the sixteenth century.

Philosophical reasoning on religious issues also became an integral part of Hebrew culture. Much of medieval Jewish philosophy and theology followed Philo's attempt to reconcile divine revelation and Hellenistic thought. Saadya Gaon brought medieval Jewish theology, the Jewish *kalam*, into being. He adopted the positions of Muslim Mu'tazili theology to demonstrate the oneness and unity of God, his justice, and the Hebrew Bible as the true revelation of God.

Neo-Platonism became characteristic of Jewish thinking in the eleventh and early twelfth centuries, especially in Spain in the work of thinkers like Solomon bin Gabirol and Bahya bin Paquda. Neo-Platonism was a metaphysical system that held that the world emanated out of the singular divine origin toward increasing multiplicity, ending in the material world. The philosopher sought reunion with the divine by ecstatic or meditative consciousness of the source of all being. Jewish neo-Platonists often sought to retain some vestige of the personal God of Judaism, and to reconcile the idea of the creation of the world out of nothingness with the schema of creation by spiritual emanations.

Jewish neo-Platonists also relied on the example of Sufism. Jewish mysticism was shaped by Isma'ili ideas. Avicenna's philosophical mysticism (Illuminationism or Ishraq) and its successors, such as the mysticism of Suhrawardi, were taught to Jews, Jewish converts, and Muslims identifying with Judaism. Hermetic mysticism influenced such Jewish thinkers as Moses ibn Ezra, Judah Halevi, and Abraham ibn Ezra. Ibn al-'Arabi was also an important influence. Mysticism may have appealed to Jewish scholars because it represented a universal religious truth, transcending confessional loyalties and traditions. The study of esoteric mysticisms implied a transcendence of ordinary religious cultures. In any case, the aim of Jewish mystics was a spiritualization of the Jewish heritage and a new emphasis on inward devotion to God. The focus on the Hebrew language and the spiritualization of the Jewish tradition effected by Jewish neo-Platonism led to a new genre of meditative poetry (*piyyut*). This form of Hebrew poetry imported ideas from Arabic poetry, while drawing on the new spiritual philosophy, to bring a new profundity to the Hebrew liturgical canon.

In the twelfth and thirteenth centuries, Aristotelianism became the dominant philosophical outlook. Maimonides established a middle position between the Jewish tradition and Aristotelianism. He demonstrated the existence of God by arguing that his being was necessary for the always-contingent world to subsist, but he drew a strict line between the necessity of the divine and the contingent, although regular and rational, effects of his will on the world. In this way, he was able philosophically to demarcate the personal God of Judaism from the rationally ordered but contingent cosmos that was his creation.

Jewish and Muslim scholars shared in the philosophical enterprise. Alongside of biblical and Talmudic commentary, the entire corpus of Arabic Aristotelian philosophy was translated into Hebrew. Aristotelianism opened the way, as it had done in Arabic and would do in Latin, for the interpretation of the Bible or Talmud and for theological speculation. It also opened scientific studies to Jewish scholars. The integration of Muslim and Jewish philosophical scholarship set the foundations for Muslim, Jewish, and Christian interactions at the court of Alfonso X and for the translation of the Aristotelian and Greek philosophical and scientific corpus into Latin.

In poetry and architecture, as well as in philosophy, science, and mysticism, Jewish and Muslim cultures were blended. Arabized Jews continued the tradition of Hebrew poetry based on Arabic models, including the *muwashshah* poetry that combined Hebrew verses with a Romance refrain. The congregational synagogue in Toledo (today the Church of Santa Maria la Blanca), the Synagogue of Samuel Halevi in Toledo (El Tránsito), the Synagogue of Isaac Mehab in Cordoba, and a Mudejar-style synagogue in Segovia, now destroyed, show the close integration of Almohad, Spanish Mudejar, and Jewish impulses in design.

THE SYNTHESIS OF ARABIC, HEBREW, AND LATIN CULTURES

In philosophy and science as well as in art, Islamic, Jewish, and Christian cultures were brought together in one of the great achievements of European culture: the translation of classical Greek, Arabic, and Hebrew science and philosophy into Latin. Churchmen eager to persuade Muslims of the truth of their beliefs and to convert them to Christianity first sponsored the translation of the Quran. The first translation of the Quran into Latin, indeed into any non-Muslim language, was completed around 1141 under the guidance of Peter the Venerable. Later translations were made into Castilian and Catalan.

Toledo was the center of these translations, because of its church patronage and great libraries. By the 1140s, the translation of Arabic philosophy was being promoted by Toledo's French archbishop, Francis Raymond (r. 1125–52), who established the Toledo school of translators. The presence of scholars of Romance languages, Arabic, Hebrew, and Latin in the same milieu was critical. Teams of translators – including Mozarab Christians, Muslim and Jewish scholars, and Cluniac monks – who were often bilingual or multilingual, worked together to translate books from Arabic into Castilian or Latin, and from Castilian to Latin. A Mozarab, a Christian native speaker of Arabic, might first render an Arabic text word for word into the vernacular; then a Latin expert would redo the vernacular into formal Latin.

Key texts of the Aristotelian tradition were translated in Toledo shortly after being written in Cordoba or Seville. Aristotle and Muslim philosophers – such as al-Kindi, al-Farabi, and Avicenna – were translated into Latin. Between 1160 and 1187, Gerard of Cremona translated some eighty-seven works, including the

Quran, Aristotle's *Posterior Analytics* and *Physics*, and many works on mathematics, astronomy, medicine, and philosophy. He translated the *Qanun* of Avicenna. Between 1220 and 1250, Averroes's commentaries on Aristotle and the works of Maimonides were also rendered into Latin and were later quoted by St. Thomas Aquinas. Thus Greek philosophic thought came through the Arab world to Europe.

The translation project was of immense historical cultural importance. It brought together the scholarly worlds of the three Mediterranean religions. It brought the teachings of Aristotle into the European worldview and introduced a new metaphysical mentality and empirical orientation to Western European Christianity. By the end of the twelfth century, Latin Europe had been reconnected with the classical Greek, Arabic, and Hebrew philosophy and science that would shape its religious and intellectual outlook to the present day.

In the thirteenth century, the movement of translation was given royal patronage. Jewish and Muslim literatures were translated into Castilian and Latin. Alfonso X (d. 1284) arranged for the translation of the Bible, the Talmud, and the Quran into Castilian. He commissioned lavishly illustrated books of chess; monumental histories of civilization from biblical times to the Castilian era; illustrated treatises on astronomy, astrology, geology, and codes of law; and handbooks of philosophy. The use of the astrolabe was learned from treatises written in Arabic and Hebrew and then in Latin. In frank emulation of the ʿAbbasid caliphs of Baghdad, Alfonso had translated *Kitab al-Jawarih*, a Baghdadi treatise on falconry and other hunting practices, and *Kalila wa-Dimna*, the centerpiece of the Baghdadi adoption of ancient Iranian imperial culture. Scholars from northern Europe worked with Spanish scholars to translate medical, religious, scientific, philosophical, and literary texts into Castilian and Latin.

From ancient Iran to ʿAbbasid Baghdad to Castilian Toledo and from Zoroastrian to Islamic to Christian monarchies, a single trail of literary legitimization for monarchical authority was blazed. In the interests of empire, in the ambition to rival and replace both the Umayyad Empire and the Holy Roman Empire, Alfonso sought to create a Castilian imperial literature that would supersede both Latin and Arabic. These appropriations gave Islamic culture an afterlife in Christian Spain. Some of these translations were carried into old French and Latin. The works of Ptolemy were translated. The story of the ascent of the Prophet into heaven (*miʿraj*) was translated into Castilian and then into old French and Latin, where it may have become available to Dante.

Integration of Muslim, Jewish, and Christian experts also took place in fourteenth- and fifteenth-century medical studies. By the fourteenth century, Spanish Jews were studying Latin scholastic medicine and philosophy with Christian scholars. The medieval system of separate examinations for each ethno-religious group was replaced by an examination system under Christian authority. All medical students were examined by Christian overseers.

THE BREAKDOWN OF *CONVIVENCIA* (CO-AUTHOR, DAVID MOSHFEGH)

Convivencia under Christian rule reached its apogee in the twelfth and thirteenth centuries. Although there were incidents of harassment – such as the confiscation of the Mosque of Toledo and its conversion into a church – and there were frequent riots and pogroms against the Muslims of Valencia between 1276 and 1291, Muslim and Jewish communities remained relatively secure, and cooperation among scholars and intellectuals continued to be productive. The first major Muslim experience of Christian rule showed how in the multiethnic and multireligious societies of the Mediterranean, Middle Eastern and Muslim concepts of autonomous religious community could serve for a time to accommodate Muslims in a Christian society, just as they had accommodated Christians in a Muslim society.

In the long run, however, several factors worked against this outcome. The rulers of Castile and Aragon had no abiding or principled commitment to the autonomy of their Muslim and Jewish populations. They saw them as economically important, but also as a political threat. Jews were both assets and a danger, because of their economic importance and administrative positions at court. Jews were the recalcitrant stiff-necked people who had refused Christ, but also potential converts. Muslims were important as workers and taxpayers, especially in Valencia, but were a political danger because of their large numbers. As the economic importance of Muslims and Jews diminished, their vulnerability to Christian religious hostility and Christian demands for religious purity, conformity, and homogeneity increased. This led in the end to forced conversion, forced assimilation, and finally the expulsion of the Jewish and Muslim populations.

By the middle of the fourteenth century, the position of the Muslims of Valencia, the largest Mudejar population, had sharply deteriorated. The Mudejars were burdened with growing financial obligations. Free Muslim peasants were pushed into servitude. They were pushed out of the irrigated *huertas* of Valencia into nonirrigated, less productive dry farming areas. Christian political control also led to a progressive restriction of Muslim religious liberties. By the middle of the fourteenth century, some 80 percent of judicial cases were heard in Christian rather than Muslim courts and were tried under Christian rather than Muslim law. Muslim communities were losing their internal autonomy.

In the critical reign of Fernando II (1479–1516), the situation of Valencian Muslims was stabilized. Economic interests for a time prevailed. Fernando tried to increase the population of royal *morerías* (Muslim communities) by attracting the vassals of Christian lords and by bringing in new settlers from the Granada region. Many Mudejars thus obtained better working and living conditions; purchased, leased, or reclaimed additional land; launched new commercial ventures; and shared in the relative prosperity of late fifteenth-century Valencia. Popular antagonism was curtailed by Muslim-Christian cooperation in workplaces and marketplaces. For a time, neither kings nor subjects showed marked hostility toward the Mudejars.

The Dominicans wanted to convert the Muslims and sponsored schools of Arabic to prepare cadres for rationalistic debate with elite Muslims. By contrast, the Franciscans adopted a confrontational approach, preaching the evil of Islam and the triumph of the cross in mosques and to Muslim crowds. Sporadic riots and pogroms underlined the rise of Christian anger and hatred. Still, the monarchy kept these forces in control. In this uncertain situation, Valencian Muslims maintained their identity. They continued to speak Arabic and to identify with Granada and North Africa. Language differences were a powerful factor in the alienation of Muslims and Christians.

THE EXPULSION OF THE JEWS FROM SPAIN AND PORTUGAL (CO-AUTHOR, DAVID MOSHFEGH)

Despite their cultural brilliance, the economic and political position of the Jewish communities began to deteriorate in the fourteenth century. The Jews of Valencia are the best known of these communities. In Valencia, Jews lived in their own self-governing community, with their own court of law, schools, charities, synagogues, ritual baths, and slaughterhouses, as had been the pattern under Muslim rule. They were the tax farmers of Castile and served the kings of Aragon as government officials, translators, physicians, and diplomats, but most of all as tax collectors, helping to govern a majority Muslim population. They were moneylenders to Christians and Muslims who collected debts with interests to pay off their obligations to the king. In the kingdom of Aragon they were allowed to buy and own land.

The powerful position of Jews was a double affront to Christians, and especially to Christian nobles, who felt themselves subordinate both to Jews and through Jewish intermediaries to the power of the sovereign. As early as the twelfth century the municipality of Toledo attempted to limit Jewish prerogatives. The Cortes, the assembly of the estates of the Spanish realms, expressed its hostility to Jews. In the thirteenth century even the crown of Aragon, although in practice depending on Jewish tax collectors and moneylenders, declared itself opposed to usury and to Jewish officeholding and by the end of the century did indeed remove Jews from positions at court, obliged them to sell their landholdings, and imposed heavy taxes on the Jewish communities. A critical factor in Aragon was the rise of a Christian merchant and professional class that could take over the moneylending, tax collecting, and administrative positions of the Jews. Jews were relegated to small-scale lending to Muslims and to an increasing diversity of occupations. Less and less important as tax collectors for the monarchy, Jews were left ever more vulnerable to a rising Christian socioeconomic and religio-ideological antagonism.

In Castile, however, in a semifeudal military society, Jews remained important for their bureaucratic and economic roles until the end of the fourteenth century.

The increasing political and economic pressure opened a class and cultural divide within the Jewish communities. Because the royal demands were laid collectively on the communities, elite families competed for control of the Aljamas and disputed the division of taxes with the common people. These socioeconomic splits may have been related to a cultural divide as well. The elites favored rationalism, an expression of religion transcending specific community laws. The common people favored pietism and mysticism.

More important for the survival of the Jews was the hostility of the church. To many Christians, the failure of the Jews to recognize the mission and the divinity of Christ – the very existence of Jews – was a repudiation and an outrage. Furthermore, Christians were unnerved by the conversion of Jews and Muslims, because converts often maintained good relations with their natal families and communities. Christians were doubtful about the loyalty, commitment, and religious practices of these converts. They saw a grave danger in the mixing of peoples and feared the subversion of Christian purity and solidarity. Some of the most rabid anti-Jewish agitators were apostates from Judaism.

These fears have a deep history. As a result of the Fourth Lateran Council in 1215, Jews and Muslims were required to dress differently than Christians, because it was difficult to separate Christian, Jewish, and Muslim men by physical appearance, and this could lead to sexual intercourse between Christians and non-Christians. A cape and badge of colored cloth for Jews and a special haircut and dress for Muslims were prescribed to define a sexual boundary.

Increasing pressure on both Muslims and Jews, however, came from the church. Franciscans and Dominicans, and notably apostates from Judaism, denounced the Jews in public sermons. An ever-increasing Eucharistic devotion and brooding over the torment of Christ led to harassment, persecution, and mob violence. The period from 1391 to 1416 brought massacres and massive forced conversions in the kingdoms of both Castile and Aragon. Jews were attacked in Seville, Cordoba, Jaén, Ubeda, Baeza, Carmona, and many other cities. The Jewish population of Valencia was destroyed in 1391 and was relocated in Morvedre. The largest surviving Jewish community in Valencia province was unmolested until the expulsion in 1492. There the Jews were protected in part by their lack of political importance. Also, the king of Aragon protected the Jewish populations in Catalonia and Palma de Mallorca.

Throughout Spain, however, masses of Jews were forced to convert to Christianity, enlarging the class of conversos, converted Jews who retained their family contacts and many Jewish religious practices. This ambiguous situation made converts suspect and seemingly ever more subversive and threatening to the Christian population. Thus in 1478 Isabel I of Castile and Fernando II of Aragon established the Spanish Inquisition in both Castile and Aragon to suppress the Judaizing conversos. In 1483 the inquisitors persuaded the monarchy that the only way to eliminate the continued Judaic practices of the conversos was to expel the Jews – not necessarily the converts themselves – from Spain. In 1483, the Jews were expelled from Andalusia, and, in 1492, Ferdinand and Isabella ordered the Jews to either convert or be banished from the kingdoms of Castile and Aragon. Perhaps one half of the Jewish population converted; many of the others went to Navarre and Portugal.

The Catholic monarchs then imposed this policy on Portugal. In 1497, in negotiations for the marriage of Infanta Isabella of Aragon and the Portuguese monarch, Manuel, the Spanish insisted on the conversion or expulsion of Portuguese Jews as a condition of the marriage. In 1497 the Portuguese also required Jews to convert or go onto exile. Jews were banished from the Iberian Peninsula. The Jewish population, once a flourishing commercial and cultural community, estimated at its height to have numbered hundreds of thousands, was expelled to other parts of Europe, North Africa, and the Ottoman Empire.

The converted Jews who remained were cut off from Hebrew literature, synagogues, and the other facilities of Jewish ritual life, but secret observance of Jewish rituals and beliefs continued. In the absence of formal institutions, women played an ever-greater role in maintaining a Jewish family life. Converts also maintained a kind of ethnic solidarity in the Christian framework by living in the same parish, selecting convents for their daughters, and burying their dead in the same chapels.

Jews in North Africa

With the expulsion of the Jews from the Iberian Peninsula, many Spanish and Portuguese Jews took refuge in North Africa and in the Ottoman Empire. As early as the thirteenth century the defeat of the Almohads allowed for the revival of Jewish communities in North Africa under the succeeding Hafsid, Ziyanid, and Marinid regimes. Jews began to repopulate North African cities and to act as diplomatic and commercial links between European and North African polities.

The Marinids and the Hafsids employed Jews to conduct diplomatic missions with Europeans. The Marinids of Morocco employed Christian captives, merchants, Iberian Jews, and conversos. At the same time, Morocco experienced an influx of new and diverse populations – Atlas villagers; Christian artisans from Europe; merchants from Holland and Britain, including Franciscans; and Iberian Catholics. To reconcile the Muslim identity of the sultanate with the actualities of its social base, the Moroccan sultans created a special quarter for the Jews and other foreign servants of the regime adjacent to the Kasba or fortress quarter where the government was housed. The first walled and gated Jewish quarter (mellah) was organized in Fez (1438). The mellah of Marrakesh was founded around 1557, followed by the mellah in Meknes (1679). The mellahs did not isolate Jews but facilitated their interactions with the sultan and the reception of Europeans, both Jewish and non-Jewish, and helped mediate between Europe and Morocco.

The mellah, long misconceived as a Jewish ghetto, was also the quarter for foreigners and for the dealings of Muslims with foreigners, thus sheltering Muslims from foreign influences. Despite the intentions of their royal founders, however, Muslims had a large presence in the mellahs. Muslims owned about 10 percent of the property in the mellahs, and landlords came to collect rents. Muslim shoppers came to the mellah, especially on Friday mornings. Muslim pilgrims came to saints' tombs. Mostly, the mellah was the illicit entertainment quarter, where Muslims could find alcohol, gambling, contacts with Europeans, and Jewish prostitutes. Reciprocally, Jews were not allowed to own property in Medina, the Muslim city, but they rented storage and selling space. When they went to Medina, however, they risked insults and relegation to the inferior status of *dhimmi*. Sumptuary rules required Jews in Medina to remove their shoes.

THE EXPULSION OF THE MUSLIMS (CO-AUTHOR, DAVID MOSHFEGH)

In the kingdom of Castile and Aragon, the conquest of Granada in 1492 marked the beginning of the end of the Muslim population in Spain. Although the treaty of surrender guaranteed Muslim religious liberty and property, in practice these rights were ignored. On the arrival of Christian immigrants in 1498, the city was divided into two halves, with the Muslims confined to the Albaicin district. All the mosques of Granada were converted to churches. The Muslims of Albaicin and other areas revolted and, in 1502, were given an ultimatum requiring the conversion or emigration of all the Mudejars of Castile. Some Granadan notables who collaborated with the crown were permitted to practice their religion in the confines of their own estates. Many Granadans became crypto-Muslims who practiced Islam in secret while outwardly professing Christianity. Many fled to North Africa.

In 1511, measures were taken to suppress even the everyday culture of Muslims. Tailors were forbidden to make Muslim-style garments. Then, in 1526, the Arabic language, local dress, jewelry, and baths were outlawed. Only Christian midwives could assist in deliveries, and the Inquisition, rather than the parish clergy, was charged with supervision. Not only religion but Mudejar culture was banned.

Forcible conversions were extended to other parts of Spain. In 1515–16 Navarre was incorporated into Castile, and its anti-Mudejar laws were extended to Navarre and later to Valencia. The Inquisition was empowered to enforce conversions. In 1525, King Carlos received a papal brief allowing him to retract earlier promises to the Muslims. By early 1526, Mudejars living in the crown of Aragon had to convert to Christianity or face expulsion from the peninsula. Mosques were shut down; Arabic books and documents were banned.

The converted Mudejars defined themselves as Muslims, but the names "moriscos" and "moros" were given to them by outsiders. They were by definition crypto-Muslims living their religion secretly because the law considered them Christians. Their nominal conversion implied important changes in lifestyle. Important legal changes ensued. Endogamous marriages, accepted in Islamic law and Arab and Berber social practice, were now forbidden. Property would no longer be distributed to heirs by the terms of Islamic law.

Still Muslim jurists helped keep alive an underground Muslim culture. Books in Arabic and Aljamiado, including the Quran, continued to circulate. Notaries drew up contracts in Arabic, and marriages, circumcisions, and burials were still performed in traditional Islamic ways. Teachers continued to instruct the young about Islam.

In 1556, Arab and Muslim dress was again forbidden, and in 1566 Philip II decreed that the Arabic language could no longer be used. In 1570, there were Muslim rebellions in Granada that led to the crown deciding that the only solution to the morisco problem was the removal of the formerly Muslim population of Granada. Thousands of moriscos were sent to Seville, Cordoba, Toledo, and other towns. Finally, in 1609, Philip III decreed the expulsion of the Muslims from all of Spain. They took refuge in North Africa, where Andalusian communities once again contributed to a flourishing Islamic civilization. The religion of Islam introduced in Spain in 711 was driven out in 1614, 903 years later.

CHAPTER 28

LIBYA, TUNISIA, ALGERIA, AND MOROCCO FROM THE THIRTEENTH TO THE NINETEENTH CENTURIES

While the Muslim presence in Spain was being liquidated, Islamic societies in North Africa were entering a new stage of development. With the collapse of the Almohads, North Africa began to take on a new configuration of state and society. Although older claims to a "caliphal" type of religious authority were carried into the new era, with the exception of Libya, North African states increasingly moved toward the Saljuq (and Egyptian Ayyubid-Mamluk) type of Middle Eastern Islamic institutional structure. The new states would be based on client, slave, or mercenary armies and a small household bureaucracy but would depend on a governing coalition of tribal forces. The larger society would be organized into Sufi-led communities. Inspired by developments in the eastern Muslim world and Spain, Sufism took root throughout North Africa in the twelfth and later centuries. The states of the post-Almohad era would have to develop a new relationship with the religious notables. Some of them would surrender their claims to direct religious authority; all would accept the 'ulama' and Sufis as the bearers of Islamic legitimacy and as intermediaries in the government of their societies. In different forms, they implemented the Eastern patronage concept of a Muslim state.

LIBYA

Libya is an exception to this pattern. Until the Ottoman occupation, Libya was a territory without a history. The invasions of the seventh century helped to Arabize and Islamize the population but did not establish a central regime. Almohad authority was nominal. The Mamluks of Egypt had alliances with tribes in Cyrenaica, which allowed them to claim that they were suzerains of the country. This claim was inherited by the Ottomans. They had conquered Egypt in 1517 and Tripoli in 1551. From 1551 until 1711 Tripoli was governed by Ottoman pashas and janissary soldiers. Ottoman rule established the first state in the territories of Tripolitania, Cyrenaica, and the Fezzan, which make up modern Libya.

In 1711 Ahmad Qaramanli, a local janissary officer, seized power and founded a dynasty, nominally under Ottoman suzerainty, which lasted until 1835. Qaramanli power waned in the early nineteenth century as a result of the suppression of piracy and of growing British and French influence, and the Ottomans again intervened in Libya and brought the dynasty to an end. Ottoman governors ruled Tripolitania and were suzerains of Cyrenaica until the Italian occupation of 1911 and Ottoman withdrawal in 1912.

From 1835 to 1911 the Ottomans made extensive changes in Tripolitania. By 1858 they had defeated local resistance, established their government throughout the region, and introduced Tanzimat reforms. The Ottoman governors strengthened the central authority, encouraged the sedentarization of the bedouins, developed towns and agriculture, and helped revive the trans-Saharan trade, which flourished in Libya as the abolition of the slave traffic closed down Saharan routes going through Tunisia and Algeria. Ottoman rule encouraged local education and the formation of an intelligentsia inspired by the political and cultural life of Istanbul. In this phase of Ottoman administration, Tripolitanian officials, intellectuals, and tribal and village *shaykhs* acquired a sense of common identity as part of a larger provincial, Ottoman, Arab, and Muslim universe.

Cyrenaica remained a separate province under Ottoman suzerainty but went through a similar phase of development, owing to Ottoman cooperation with the Sanusiya order. The Sanusiya was founded in 1837 by Muhammad b. ʿAli al-Sanusi (1787–1859), who was born in Algeria and educated in Fez and Mecca. Al-Sanusi, under the influence of reformist Sufi currents, declared that his purpose was to return to the basic precepts of the Quran and hadith and affirmed the right of believers to use independent rational judgment to deduce the principles by which a Muslim life should be conducted. The Sanusiya wished to unite all of the Muslim brotherhoods, and to contribute to the spread and revitalization of Islam.

His mission led al-Sanusi to Cyrenaica, where he established a number of *zawiyas*. The Sanusi *zawiyas* became centers of religious mission and teaching, but also of agricultural settlement and trade. The *zawiyas*, strung out along the trade routes linking Cyrenaica with Kufra and Wadai, helped organize caravans. The brotherhood progressively acquired a quasi-political authority among the bedouins of the region by negotiating cooperation in trade, mediating disputes, and providing urban services such as religious instruction, exchange of products, charity, and political representation. By the end of the century the Sanusi network of *zawiyas* had built up a large tribal coalition in the regions west of Egypt and the Sudan. Under Sanusi leadership this coalition resisted both French expansion in the region of Lake Chad and the Italian invasion of Libya.

After the Congress of Berlin in 1878, the Italians considered Tripolitania part of their imperial sphere of influence and attempted to establish an economic presence in the province. Ottoman resistance to Italian economic penetration provided a pretext for an Italian invasion in 1911. The Italians occupied the towns and forced the Ottomans to concede their suzerainty over Tripolitania and Cyrenaica, but the Sanusiya also claimed to be the heirs of Ottoman authority in Libya. Only after World War I was Italy able to defeat local opposition in Tripolitania, and not until a protracted and destructive war that lasted from 1923 to 1932 were the Italians able to defeat the bedouins of Cyrenaica, seize the majority of their lands, and colonize the country. The Sanusi leaders were forced into exile. In 1934 the Italians completed the conquest of Cyrenaica and Tripolitania and united the two into modern Libya.

TUNISIA

Tunisia by contrast had a deep history of centralized states. The Tunisian state from the thirteenth to the nineteenth centuries was essentially a reconstruction of a past form of centralized state based on an urbanized economy and relatively close political control over rural and pastoral populations. Although the regime of the eighth and ninth centuries had lapsed under the pressure of the Hilali invasions and economic decline, it was rebuilt with significant innovations by the Hafsid dynasty (1228–1574). Despite repeated phases of consolidation and disintegration, the Hafsids defined the institutional framework of Tunisian society until the modern era.

The Hafsid regime grew directly out of the Almohad Empire. The dynasty descended from an aristocratic Almohad family and was supported by the former Almohad elites. The Hafsid armies included Almohad tribes, Arab nomads, Berbers from the Constantine and Bougie regions, Turks and Kurds, black slaves, and a Christian militia sent from Aragon. In the fifteenth century, the descendants of earlier generations of mercenaries, by then Arabized, continued to form a bodyguard for the rulers. The Hafsids also maintained a weak navy supplemented by privateers.

The civil administration was dominated by Andalusian scribes who provided the ministers for the army, finance, and chancery services. They were the principal officers for court affairs, governors of the royal palace, secretaries, chamberlains, and treasurers. The elites were supported by the distribution of *iqta's* to government officials, Almohad *shaykhs*, and tribal chiefs. The Hafsids tried to control nomadic tribes by influencing the choice of the chiefs, by putting them under military pressure, by winning favor through fiscal or territorial concessions, or by integrating tribal factions into the royal armies. Still, southern tribes were likely to be independent.

The strength of the state was related to the revenues of international trade. A series of thirteenth-century treaties with Sicily, Venice, Marseille, Genoa, and Florence helped revive Tunisian prosperity. At the end of the fourteenth century Tunis was exporting cereals, dried fruits, dates, olive oil, fish, salt, spices, sugar, wool, leather, cotton goods, coral, weapons, and slaves, and it was importing cereals, spices, wine, cloth goods, dyes, wood, metal, weapons, and jewelry. At the end of the fifteenth century the Portuguese discovery of a route to India and the aggressive expansion of Portugal and Spain along the coasts of North Africa undermined Tunisian trade.

Out of the broad possibilities afforded by the historic repertoire of Muslim, cosmopolitan, and patrimonial concepts of rule, the Hafsids chose to portray themselves as Muslim rulers. They took the titles of caliph and *amir al-mu'minin*; the head of state was later called *malik al-sultan* in imitation of Mamluk Egyptian rulers. Succession was legitimized by the oath of allegiance and the recognition of the ruler in the Friday prayer. Solemn public processions accompanied by flags and drums were also prerogatives of the sovereign.

The rulers conducted state business in a formal court attended by tribal chiefs, soldiers, men of religion, intellectuals, and other courtiers. Mornings were reserved for military business, afternoons for civil administration, and evenings for entertainment. The households of the rulers were centers not only of political administration but also of mosques and academies of learning. Scholars from all over North Africa and Spain gathered to instruct the rulers, minister to religious needs, and symbolize the religious credentials of the sultans. The Hafsid court produced studies of the Quran, hadith, law, and Arabic grammar; biographies of the Prophet and of saints; dictionaries of famous scholars; histories; and works of theology. The architectural style of the Hafsid period was derived from Morocco and Egypt. Science and medicine, however, languished.

Like the Mamluks in Egypt, the Hafsids sponsored Muslim law and a Maliki restoration. They maintained an Islamic religious administration under the authority of the *qadi al-jama'a*, a title that goes back to Umayyad Spain. Tunis had a second *qadi* who specialized in marriage law. A weekly council of *qadis* and muftis met to review important cases in the presence of the rulers. In 1257 the Hafsids endowed the al-Mustansiriya madrasa. The feast of the end of Ramadan and the feast of the conclusion of the pilgrimage were celebrated by massive public prayers led by the sovereign. The birthday of the Prophet, marked first in Egypt in the thirteenth century and declared an official festival in Morocco in 1292, was accepted as an official feast in Tunisia at the end of the fourteenth century. The sultans also sponsored the daily reading of hadith and of the biography of the Prophet in the great Mosque of Tunis.

Gradually, however, Sufism began to displace law as the most important expression of Tunisian Islam. Between the eleventh and the thirteenth centuries, Sufism spread from the towns into rural areas. Al-Shadhili, who was born in Morocco, educated in Egypt, and died in Tunis in 1258, left numerous disciples who combined formal scholarship with mystical exercises. As friends of God, they were believed to perform miracles, know what would happen at a distance, see or dream the future, transport themselves magically over time and space, cure the sick, and intercede before God on behalf of ordinary believers. They gathered groups of disciples, sworn to absolute obedience, to whom they taught the special techniques that had given them their mystical powers, and whom they initiated by transmitting the *khirqa*, or cloak of the Sufi. The more puritanical Sufis deplored the common practices of visits to tombs and the use of music to achieve ecstasy.

From the late thirteenth century, Sufi *zawiyas* (hospices) began to assume social and political functions. Sufis organized tribal coalitions to safeguard the trade routes, suppress brigandage, promote religious piety, and oppose illegal taxation. In the course of the fourteenth century Sufism was sufficiently consolidated for the political authorities to seek the favor of the Sufis. Territorial or fiscal concessions were given to the *zawiyas*. In Tunis a combination *zawiya*-madrasa, founded in 1399, marked the integration of urban Sufism and Maliki Islam. The breakup of the Hafsid state in the fourteenth century, its subsequent reconstruction in the fifteenth century, and its final decline in the sixteenth century allowed organized Sufi Islam to become the most powerful force in Tunisian society. The breakdown of the regime shifted the balance of power in North Africa to Sufi-led tribal communities that united rural peoples to meet the needs of political order, defense, economic organization, mediation of disputes, and other essential functions.

With the decline of the Hafsid dynasty, the Tunisian state was rebuilt by the Ottomans. The Ottomans made Tunisia a province of their empire in 1574 and garrisoned Tunis with 4,000 janissaries recruited in Anatolia, reinforced by renegade Christians from Italy, Spain, and Provence. In 1591, however, the local janissary officers replaced the sultan's governor with one of their own men, called the deys. The deys ruled over Tunis, but a Corsican-born Tunisian tax collector (bey) named Murad (d. 1640), and his descendants, dominated the rest of the country. The struggle for power made allies of the deys, the janissaries, and bedouin tribes against the beys, the towns, and the fertile regions of the countryside. The beys eventually triumphed and ruled until 1705, when Husayn b. ʿAli came to power and established a dynasty that would reign until 1957. In theory Tunisia continued to be a vassal of the Ottoman Empire – the Friday prayer was pronounced in the name of the Ottoman sultan, money was coined in his honor, and an annual ambassador brought gifts to Istanbul – but the Ottomans never again exacted obedience.

Under Ottoman suzerainty Tunisia resumed the system of political control over the religious elites developed under the Hafsids. Under the Husaynids both Hanafi and Maliki *qadis* were appointed to high offices. The leading *qadis* and muftis participated in the bey's council. The bey could appoint and dismiss the judges, jurisconsults, teachers in madrasas, and Sufi *shaykhs* of *zawiyas*. The central government also controlled the rural tribes. It broke the power of the great tribal chiefs and left only lesser chieftainships and smaller units intact. Tunisia was ruled by some sixty *qaʾids* (district governors) and some two thousand local *shaykhs*. Much of the rural population, however, was partly independent on the basis of organized lineages, Sufi brotherhoods, and political alliances.

The migration of Spanish-Muslims to North Africa reinforced the sedentary and commercial sectors of Tunisian society. After the fall of Granada in 1492, increasing Christian pressure on the Muslim population in Spain led to a steady emigration to North Africa, which reached its peak with the expulsion of the *moriscos* at the beginning of the seventeenth century. Andalusian poets, scribes, scholars, and soldiers took refuge with the Hafsids. Many newcomers settled in the Zuqaq al-Andalus and other suburbs of Tunis. Numerous Andalusian villages were founded. As cultivators, the Andalusians introduced new irrigation systems, mills, gardens, and vineyards in the Spanish fashion. The migrants were accorded autonomy in tax collections; an official spokesman, the *shaykh al-Andalus*, represented them to the government. A cultured community, they continued to speak their own languages and founded mosques and colleges.

Until the late eighteenth and early nineteenth centuries, the Tunisian economy functioned in the traditional way. It was divided into a sector of self-sufficient nomads and cultivators, and a sector attached to international trade. Tunisia exported meat, wool, olive oil, hides, beeswax, dates, and sponges and imported European cloth and paper. The beys entered the trade, gathering taxes of wheat and wool in kind, which they sold to European merchants. In the eighteenth century ʿAli (1759–82) and Hammuda Pasha (1782–1813) seized the opportunities provided by European wars to enlarge Tunisian trade, improve ports, and encourage cloth production.

The felt cap industry, introduced by Andalusians, was one of the most important. The *shashiya* was the standard cap worn throughout the Mediterranean by Christians, Jews, Armenians, and Muslims and was widely sold throughout the Ottoman Empire, the Balkans, and Iran. Hundreds of workshops were organized by merchant investors, and Tunisian production often reached 100,000 dozen hats per year. There were between 15,000 and 50,000 people engaged in the trade. The production of these caps also depended on international trade. Wool came from Spain, vermilion from Portugal, and alum from Rome. The imports, however, were generally in the control of French merchants from Marseille and Jewish merchants from Livorno. Although Tunisians suffered from regulations imposed by the bey of Tunis, European control of raw materials, a rigid corporate organization, and high costs of production, they had the advantage of understanding the market and producing an appropriate commodity.

In the late eighteenth century, however, the Tunisian economy went into decline. From 1784 to 1820 there were repeated crop failures and outbreaks of plague. Olive oil replaced wheat as the major export, and the *shashiya* was forced off the market by French competition. The industrial revolution and the tremendous increase of European production undermined the industry. By the middle decades of the nineteenth century, the most profitable and highly capitalized Tunisian industry was in decline. At the same time the price of olive oil declined drastically, and

Tunisia was left importing manufactured and luxury products with an unfavorable balance of payments.

In spite of economic decline, the government attempted to build up the army and the state apparatus. Rapid increases in taxes provoked a great peasant uprising in 1864. Even though the regime put down the revolt, it still did not have adequate revenues to maintain the army. Borrowing from European banks led to bankruptcy in 1867. In 1869 Tunisia had to submit to a French, British, and Italian commission to collect tax revenues and repay the bondholders. At the Congress of Berlin in 1878, the European powers encouraged France to establish a protectorate over Tunisia to divert it from the loss of Alsace-Lorraine and to compensate it for Russian gains in the Balkans and the British occupation of Cyprus. The protectorate was declared in 1881.

ALGERIA

Whereas Tunisia had a long history of centralized states in addition to Khariji principalities and tribal dynasties, Algeria had no history of central states and no territorial identity. From the thirteenth to the fifteenth centuries it was generally under Hafsid suzerainty, but in the course of the fifteenth century Sufi teachers gathered followers, acquired large territories as gifts from local rulers or from their devotees, and became landowners, patrons, and spiritual counselors for multitudes of small cultivators. Henceforth the political structure of Algeria would be based on lineage or tribal groups and Sufi-led communities.

An Algerian state first came into being as a result of the Ottoman conquest. With the help of Ottoman guns and janissaries, Khayr al-Din Barbarossa captured Algiers in 1529. From 1529 to 1587 Algiers was ruled by a beylerbey (provincial governor), supported by janissaries. In the period of its ascendancy, the Turkish regime managed to define the territorial identity of Algeria and to create a central-ized state in the region between Tunisia and Morocco. The state apparatus was highly institutionalized in the Ottoman manner, but its control over the country was limited by independent rural communities. In the sixteenth and seventeenth centuries a small professional army could deal with dispersed tribal coalitions.

Eventually, the agha of Algiers, the chief officer of the janissaries, made himself independent with the title of dey. Although tribute was sent to Istanbul in exchange for the sultan's political and ideological support and the right to recruit janissaries in Anatolia, from 1659 to 1830 Algeria was ruled by the deys and the local Turkish janissaries. The sons of Turkish soldiers and local women, called *kulughlis*, were in principle excluded from the janissary corps but served as subordinate militias. The dey was elected by the officers to administer the city of Algiers and its agricultural environs. The rest of the country was divided into three regions – Constantine, Mascara, and Titteri – governed by representatives of the dey, who were called beys. To subdistricts within their jurisdiction the beys named *qa'ids*, who controlled the local tribal leaders, levied taxes, settled judicial disputes, and presided over the markets. Apart from the judicial administration, there is little evidence for a large *'ulama'* establishment or for state sponsorship of a Muslim education system. There was no institution in Algeria comparable to the Qarawiyin college of Fez or the Zaytuna Mosque of Tunis.

Apart from zones of direct administration, the people were organized under the authority of religious and tribal chieftains. Many of the local chiefs were Sufis. Because the state could not control the tribal populations, it allowed *zawiya shaykhs* to assume political functions, such as arbitration in tribal disputes and collection of taxes, and to maintain their own soldiers. To win their support, the Algerian regime endowed mosques and tombs, appointed them to judicial positions, and gave them land and tax revenues. The Sufi-organized tribal communities were particularly important on the Moroccan frontier. The Turkish-Algerian regime also required all persons wishing to trade or work in the marketplace to have a permit issued by the agha of the janissaries. The Kabyle region, in particular, was dependent on these permits because it was overpopulated and relied on the export of olive oil, figs, craft products, and surplus labor for survival. In southern Algeria the government controlled the movements of pastoralists by manipulating the price of grain and levying a tax on each camel load. To collect taxes the government also had recourse to military expeditions to coerce the local population. Some districts, such as the Kabyle, Aurès, and the Sahara, remained fully autonomous.

In the course of the sixteenth century privateering was a flourishing enterprise. Algerian corsairs, often manned by Turkish and Greek seamen, seized European ships at sea, confiscated their goods, and sold their crews into slavery. Portions of the booty went to support the government and repay merchants who helped finance the ventures, but there was also a great increase in the number of mosques and pious foundations endowed by the earnings of the corsairs.

By the eighteenth century, the dominance of the state was greatly diminished. Algerian naval power and sea revenues declined, fewer recruits came from Anatolia, and modern weapons were more widely dispersed. As the state depended increasingly on Jewish, French, and English merchants, its legitimacy was compromised. In the decades between 1800 and 1830 there were Sufi-led rebellions by the Darqawa, the Qadiriyya, and the Tijaniyya brotherhoods. The Tijaniyya represented a kind of Islam with deep roots in North African popular culture. Founded by Ahmad al-Tijani (1737–1815) and carried by numerous deputies, the central Tijani teaching was the concept of the *hadrat*, the stages of the metaphysical cosmos and of the ascent to the divine essence, which is suffused by the light of Muhammad, the divine light that can only be approached through the mediation of the Prophet. The devotees must believe that the *shaykhs* of the brotherhood, their litanies, or their tombs open the way to heaven. Such beliefs and the organized brotherhoods that espoused them were a powerful political force. In the early nineteenth century the balance of power between a limited central government and the Sufi brotherhoods was turned against the Turkish state. This was the moment for the French invasion of 1830.

MOROCCO: THE MARINID AND SAʿDIAN STATES

The Almoravids and Almohads created the basis for a Moroccan territorial state. Morocco would go through successive cycles of political consolidation and decline as the Marinid, Saʿdian, and ʿAlawi dynasties in turn captured the state and lost control to other forces.

The Marinids were the dominant group in a coalition of Zenata Berbers who overthrew the Almohads and conquered Morocco between 1244 and 1274. The Marinids built Fez Jadid in 1275 as a military and administrative residence for the ruler and his family, officials, and troops. Here were quartered Castilian or Catalonian militias. The dynasty was supported by a coalition of Moroccan tribes that included the Banu Marin; the Banu Maʾqil, who controlled the territory south of the Atlas; and various Zenata Berber chieftains in the Atlas region. Government control was effective on the plains of central and northern Morocco, but not in the mountain regions. To legitimize the regime, the Friday prayers were first said in the name of the Hafsid caliphs; the Marinid princes claimed the title of *amir al-muslimin*. Gradually, however, they abandoned Almohad doctrine and simply claimed to be the protectors of Sunni Islam. They favored *ʿulamaʾ* and madrasa forms of religious instruction. In 1437 they attempted to co-opt the legitimacy attached to descendants of the Prophet by their discovery of the tomb of Idris II and the creation of a Marinid-sponsored cult around his tomb.

The Marinid regime, however, was undermined by a variety of economic problems. In the course of the fourteenth century there were profound changes in the pattern of international trade that were detrimental to Moroccan prosperity. The kingdom of Mali entered into competition for the southern sectors of the Sahara-Sudan routes and helped revitalize competing trade routes via Tlemcen, Bougie, Tunis, and Egypt, which substantially cut into Morocco's share of the profitable traffic. Throughout the fourteenth and fifteenth centuries, ships from Venice, Genoa, Pisa, Marseille, Catalonia, and Aragon regularly traded in Moroccan ports. Morocco imported metals, hardware, textiles, woolens, spices, and wine and exported leather, hides, carpets, wool, coral, grain, slaves, and sugar, but from the beginning of the fifteenth century it was damaged by Portuguese efforts to establish their political and commercial supremacy in the western Mediterranean. In 1415 the Portuguese seized Ceuta and in 1471 Tangiers. Between 1486 and 1550 they established themselves on the Atlantic coast of Morocco. The Portuguese did not use their forts for further inland conquests. Rather, they moved along the African coast, opening the way for direct trade with Sudanic Africa.

Even in the short term, the Portuguese threat brought about both a crisis of economy and one of political legitimacy. Within Morocco the precarious balance between the state and tribal forces shifted in favor of the latter. Already Hilali Arabs had pushed their way into the Sus and Saharan regions of Morocco and had done severe damage to agriculture. The Banu Ma'qil took control of Sijilmassa and created their own small empire south of the Atlas. Marrakesh fell into the control of tribal chiefs. The Wattasids, originally tribal allies of the Marinids, became regents for the dynasty in 1428 and then assumed the sultanate from 1472 to 1549. Under the Wattasids the weakness of the central state allowed nomadic peoples to make further gains at the expense of peasant cultivation and permitted the Portuguese to seize and fortify numerous coastal ports.

The economic and political regression of Morocco in the Marinid and Wattasid periods led to the rise of Sufism. Moroccan Sufis were generally religious scholars living in village communities. A typical Moroccan Sufi of the fourteenth century combined knowledge of mysticism and law, literate scholarship, and esoteric practices. In the Moroccan ideal of the time the perfected Sufi was a symbol of the religious qualities of the Prophet, who was in turn a symbol of the reality of God. The Sufi was venerated not in his person but as a symbol of the *surat al-muhammadiya* – the laudable qualities that belong to the spiritual universe and are concentrated in the person of the Prophet. Sufis were affiliated with *zawiyas* as centers of worship and teaching, but in this period they did not have political functions.

In the fifteenth century, however, Sufism became crucial for organizing local self-defense and mobilizing popular resistance to the Portuguese. Sufis became the leaders of local tribal coalitions, and the scale of Sufi organization was greatly enlarged by the introduction of the Sufi orders. Under the inspiration of Abu 'Abdallah Muhammad al-Jazuli (d. 1465), master *zawiyas* created satellite communities, or combined into single brotherhoods based on shared spiritual lineages. Loyalty to the *shaykhs*, shared *dhikrs* (chanting of the name of God), and ceremonies of initiation bound together the members of the brotherhoods.

Sufi authority was also buttressed by the acceptance of a new concept of religious authority. In addition to authority based on the imitation of the Prophet, descent was taken to assure religious sanctity. The descendants of the Prophet (*shurafa'*) were already a privileged caste in local society, supported by religious endowments and organized under the leadership of a *naqib*, who acted as judge, maintained records, and represented the interests of the group. With the decline of the Marinid state, the *shurafa'* claimed the right to oversee political affairs. Ever after, Moroccan Sufis and princes would claim *sharifian* descent.

The authority of the Sufis and the *shurafa'* challenged both tribal and state concepts of the political order and allowed for the creation of local coalitions on the basis of tribal allegiances to the Sufi orders. Henceforth, no Moroccan regime could come to power or maintain itself without integrating this new concept of authority and the organizational form in which it was embedded into its own political practice.

By the fifteenth century, then, Morocco, like Tunisia and Algeria, was a society with a central state and a Sufi-led rural population. In the course of the fifteenth and sixteenth centuries, the central regime temporarily broke down, and Sufi-led communities became the dominant force, but in the late sixteenth century the Moroccan state was seized by the Sa'dians and restored to a precarious sovereignty. The Sa'dians had their origins in a local jihad led by Muhammad al-Mahdi against the Portuguese fortress of Agadir. The holy war gathered the support of Sufi and tribal chiefs, and Muhammad was elected amir of the Sus. From the Sus the Sa'dians conquered and ruled all of Morocco from 1554 to 1659.

Whereas Algeria and Tunisia were shaped by Ottoman institutions, the Sa'dians provided Morocco with another type of Islamic regime. Like that of the Ottomans, the authority of the new regime rested on its service to Islam in the holy war, but the Sa'dians claimed descent from the Prophet Muhammad and thus identified themselves with a concept that had, in the course of the fifteenth century, become central to Moroccan notions of political authority. This descent was conceived partly in genealogical terms, partly in terms of devotion to the teachings of the Prophet, and partly in terms of the symbolic embodiment of divine virtues.

The Sa'dians linked themselves to the Sufis by the discovery of the tomb of Mawlay Idris II in Fez in 1437 and by encouragement of a popular cult. They also moved the body of al-Jazuli, who had popularized the teaching of Abu al-Hasan al-Shadhili, to Marrakesh to symbolize the formation of a coalition of Sufi brotherhoods around the venerated tomb. The Sa'dians appealed to the Sufi brotherhoods, because they too claimed physical and spiritual closeness to Muhammad and gave the common people a worshipful closeness to the principal figure in their religion. The celebration of the Prophet's birthday gave added import to the political claims of the dynasty.

Sultan al-Mansur (1578–1603) also tried to embellish the ritual paraphernalia of his office by introducing a more elaborate court ceremonial. In the absence of Ottoman institutions, the sultans ruled not only by administrative means but also by the *baraka* (power of blessing) derived from *sharifian* descent, by dynastic inheritance, and by elective authority conferred by tribe, city, and the army. Thus the Sa'dian sultanate embodied Islamic religious unity and authority in a territory dominated by tribal and Sufi concepts of society. In this regard Moroccan authority resembled that of the Safavids rather than the Ottomans.

Al-Mansur emerged as the great organizer of the regime. He conquered Timbuktu and thus gained direct access to the gold of the western Sudan. He expanded the army from its Berber tribal base to include mercenaries from Spain, Turkey, and Africa who were competent in the use of firearms. In 1603 there were 4,000 European renegades, 4,000 Andalusians, and 1,500 Turks in an army of some 40,000. Modern artillery units were incorporated. Fortifications capable of mounting artillery were built at Taza, Fez, and Marrakesh. England and the Netherlands, in their shared enmity to Habsburg Spain, provided Morocco with ships, cannons, and powder. Al-Mansur also built up a civil administration, called the Makhzan. Loyal tribes enabled the regime to control the plains of northern Morocco and the Atlantic coastal regions.

Despite the favorable economic conditions, the Moroccan state broke down on the death of al-Mansur. Sa'dian princes established separate regimes at Fez and Marrakesh; Sufi chiefs created independent principalities. In the ensuing struggles for power, the brothers Maulay Muhammad and Maulay Rashid, leaders of a *sharifian* faction in Tafilalt, triumphed over other factions and established the dynasty that governs Morocco to the present day.

THE 'ALAWI DYNASTY TO THE FRENCH PROTECTORATE

Like the Sa'dians, the 'Alawis came to power on the basis of the religious legitimacy provided by descent from the Prophet and war against the infidels. Maulay Isma'il (1672–1727) was the first great ruler of the dynasty. He reconstructed the centralized state by building up a professional army of some 30,000 to 50,000 slaves. These slaves were probably recruited from the existing Moroccan slave population and from the subordinate, client tribes called *haratin*. The slave army was supplemented by the tribes who furnished troops in return for tax exemptions and rights to land. High government functionaries were recruited from the dominant tribes and from the town bourgeoisies, including the leading families of Fez and families of Andalusian descent. *'Ulama'* filled the offices of judge, market inspector, administrator of intestate properties, and other posts. In the provinces the government was represented by *qa'ids*, who varied in power from subordinate functionaries to independent local lords.

Despite the ostensible strength of the central government, it had limited power in the provinces. Although rural peoples did not question the sultan's authority, in practice defiance of his power was the norm. In principle the Sufi leaders were also subordinate to the authority of the central government, but in fact they remained independent. Sufi chiefs played an important role in trade, and their headquarters were commonly located along trade routes or along the boundaries between tribal groups, where they could facilitate traffic and negotiate disputes. The *zawiyas* were also centers of agriculture and provided educational and judicial services. A *zawiya* was at once a hotel, a hospital, a school, a market, a mosque, a court of law, and a refuge. Nonetheless, the 'Alawis tried to overcome Sufi influence by using the authority of the sultan over religious activities. They took over the right to ratify succession to the chieftainships of the *zawiyas* and the control of their properties, and they conferred on the Sufis both spiritual titles and land and revenues. The relation of the Sufi orders to governments was a complicated combination of antagonism and cooperation. In some cases the Sufi orders helped the state consolidate its authority; in others they resisted.

Sufi influence continued to expand as new brotherhoods were founded throughout the seventeenth, eighteenth, and nineteenth centuries. These included the Nasiriya, which claimed to represent the purest Islamic orthodoxy. Its rituals consisted of supplementary prayers and the recitation of the profession of faith, "There is no God but God," a thousand times a day. Its chiefs refused to use the name of the ʿAlawi sultan in the Friday prayers on the grounds that it was blasphemous to mention a human being in the course of divine supplication. The Darqawa, founded in the late eighteenth century, denounced the pointless repetition of prayers and sought to restore direct communication with the divine being through a prayer and dance designed to induce religious ecstasy.

The ʿAlawis were able to consolidate their power with the help of economic resources gained from trade with Europe and the Sudan. They first captured the Portuguese forts along the Atlantic coast and then, in 1591, seized Timbuktu and took control of the trans-Saharan region. Moroccan sugar was an important source of royal revenues. The industry was owned by the sultans, managed by Jews and European Christians, and operated by slave labor. As early as the late thirteenth century, Moroccan sugar was being exported to Flanders, Venice, and later to Spain, but in the seventeenth century new plantations in Madeira, the Canary Islands, and the Americas squeezed Morocco out of the international market.

In the eighteenth century Morocco was exporting large numbers of slaves in return for cloth, leather, silk, jewelry, iron, lead, and weapons, and European-derived tea, coffee, sugar, paper, tin, copper utensils, and Indian spices. Britain and France were Morocco's principal trading partners, but dyes came from Spain, and woolen goods, other textiles, spices, and metals came from Holland. Italy supplied alum and artisanal products. From the eastern Mediterranean came silk, cotton, and opium. Salé was the most frequented port, but Agadir and then Mogador were important for the contacts between Europe, the Sus, and the Sudan. Trade, however, did not necessarily benefit the central government, because it could be organized by tribal confederations under religious protection. Local *shurafaʾ* played an important part in providing the liaisons and guarantees of security for caravans. For example, descendants of Maulay Ismaʿil, residing in the fortresses of Tafilalt, had a monopoly on guiding caravan traffic to Touat.

In the nineteenth century European trade led to the economic penetration of the country. In 1856 Morocco was forced by British pressure to conclude a treaty, which opened the country to free trade on the basis of a 10 percent customs duty. After the middle of the century the Europeans were no longer content to maintain a strictly commercial relationship and tried to directly control the means of production. They began to purchase land, extend loans at high rates of interest, and take Moroccans under extraterritorial protection. Also, Moroccan exports declined after the opening of the Suez Canal (1869) and the introduction of steamships and railroads that made it possible for American, Russian, and Australian producers to provide wheat and wool to European markets in competition with Moroccan products. The Moroccan Saharan trade also dwindled, owing to French expansion in West Africa that drew Sudanic and Saharan goods to Atlantic ports.

As a result, elements of the Moroccan population prospered while others suffered. A new Moroccan bourgeoisie, including the merchant intermediaries between the European and the local markets and a host of petty traders and retailers, prospered. Customs officials and other functionaries also profited from trade. The merchants of Fez maintained their dominant position, and Fassi families established colonies in Manchester, Marseille, Genoa, and French West Africa. The Fez textile industry survived European competition by cultivating new Middle Eastern, African, and domestic markets. The production of straw mats, rugs, carpets, and wool blankets, as well as the building trades, also continued to prosper. Other Moroccan crafts suffered from European competition. Imported products destroyed cotton farming and manufacturing and the Moroccan shoe industry. The Moroccan state was among the economic losers.

Faced with declining revenues, power, and territory, Sultan Hasan (1873–95) attempted to reform the army by means of military instructors and weapons obtained from Europe, and to reform the state bureaucracy by a reorganization of provincial administration. He also proposed to improve the economic infrastructure of the country by building bridges and railroads and by establishing cotton and sugar plantations. These reforms had only a limited success. Most of the religious and political elite opposed them as infringements of tradition and law; the European powers were hostile to changes that might reduce their economic privileges.

Furthermore, in the course of the nineteenth century, Berbers pushed government forces out of the Middle and Central Atlas. The High Atlas fell into the hands of the quasi-independent great *qa'ids*. By the end of the century the central government controlled scarcely a third of the land and about half of the population, concentrated in the plains of eastern Morocco, the Rif, Fez, and the Atlantic zones from Tangiers to the Atlas. Even in these regions local chieftains were often paramount. To maintain his influence, the ruler commonly had to move a small army into noncomplying or rebellious territory, camp, live off the resources of the country, and compel payment of taxes in arrears. The local people were thus put under pressure to save their crops; the sultan, however, was also under pressure to conclude an agreement so that he could move on to another rebellious district. Religious chieftains would mediate between the tribes and the ruler until some kind of deal was made.

This kind of polity was scarcely able to resist European colonization. Between 1899 and 1912 the French occupied Morocco, abetted by diplomatic agreements with Italy, Spain, Britain, and eventually Germany. To consolidate their gains, the French manipulated the various players in the Moroccan political system. Thus in the region of Touat, faced with French intervention, local chiefs demanded that the sultan wage jihad, but at the same time they resisted his efforts to collect taxes.

The shortage of revenues made the sultan dependent on French financial support, and in turn he lost legitimacy in the eyes of local people, who then felt justified in yielding to French military superiority. The autonomy of local officials, religious leaders, and chiefs made it impossible for Morocco to put up a unified resistance to French aggression.

The sultan's efforts to increase the power of the state only played into the hands of the French. From 1901 to 1903 Sultan 'Abd-'Aziz tried to strengthen the central government by implementing a new tax on agriculture and livestock, and by the appointment of new officials to assure the collection of taxes. He proposed to tax tribes, religious leaders, government officials, and others hitherto exempt. The opposition of the rural notables and the *'ulama'* however, was resolute, and 'Abd-'Aziz was forced instead to mortgage the customs revenues and borrow heavily from the French. For this he was greeted with widespread revolt and a revolution that deposed him in favor of his brother 'Abd al-Hafiz.

The intervention of the *'ulama'* was a novelty in Moroccan history. Traditionally the Moroccan *'ulama'* were a group of officials but not an organized corporate body. The chief *qadi* of Fez named the professors of the major mosques and colleges and controlled their endowed properties. For more than half a century, however, the government had been increasing its control over the appointment of judges and professors and of madrasa graduates who entered the state bureaucracy. Nonetheless, after 1900 many *'ulama'* joined the opposition because they could not accept the collaboration of the sultan with the French, his failure to protect Moroccan territory, and his tax reforms, loans, and European advisors. The result of *'ulama'* and rural tribal opposition was the loss of independence and the declaration of French and Spanish protectorates in 1912.

CHAPTER 29

STATES AND ISLAM: NORTH AFRICAN VARIATIONS

From the origins of the Islamic era to the nineteenth century, the history of North African society turned on two essential motifs: state formation and Islamization. The Arab conquests gave new impetus to state formation and to the organization of North African society into Muslim communities. Tunisia in the eighth century, Morocco in the eleventh, and Algeria in the sixteenth acquired territorial identity and state regimes. The conquests also led to the institutionalization of Islam for the masses of the population. From the eighth century, the Maliki school of law became rooted throughout North Africa and remained the mainstay of legal administration, education, and state legitimization until the nineteenth century. From about the twelfth century, Sufis became the chieftains of rural communities in Tunisia, Algeria, and Morocco and the leaders of tribal coalitions, in parallel with and in opposition to states. Much of the history of North Africa from the thirteenth to the nineteenth centuries may be defined in terms of the relations between state and Sufi forces. Finally, the Arab conquests also gave North Africa an Arab identity due to successive waves of Arab migration, and Arab dominance of states. Large parts of southern Tunisia, Algeria, and Morocco, however, were primarily Berber. Only in the twentieth century would Arabic become the universal language of societies that had been Muslim since the Almohad era.

Each society, however, exhibited its own variations on state, religious, and tribal institutions. At the time of the Arab conquests, Tunisia was already the center of a developed civilization and remained throughout its history a society marked by a highly developed agricultural and commercial economy governed by an aristocracy of landowners, merchants, and urban intellectuals. Tunisia in the early Muslim era, like the Middle East, maintained its inherited institutional base but accepted an Islamic version of ancient civilization. Under the early Arab and Aghlabid governors a caliphal type of administration and the Maliki school of law flourished. The Hafsid regime adopted the sultanal type of administration and *'ulama'* and Sufi forms of Islam. With the Ottoman conquest at the end of

421

the sixteenth century, Ottoman janissary and administrative institutions and the Ottoman type of *'ulama'* bureaucracy modified the structure of the Tunisian state. Throughout this era Tunisia maintained its state institutions, despite a large pastoral and tribal population in the southern parts of the country, and despite constant fluctuations in the balance of power between the state and the tribal parts of the society. Until the nineteenth century Tunisia was in all respects a provincial variant of the Middle Eastern Islamic world.

Algeria has a different history. As a whole it remained without state organization well into the Islamic era, although it supported a number of local dynasties, such as the Hammadids, on the basis of a share of Saharan and European trade. These regimes, however, never controlled the whole of the territory and gave way readily to tribal opposition. A stable state was finally introduced by the Ottomans, who provided a ready-made military elite, administrative cadres who were supervised from Istanbul, and the rudiments of a religious bureaucracy. The concepts of jihad against Christians and of sultanal authority served to legitimize this regime.

At first the Algerian regime was confined to the city-state of Algiers and was based on privateering and on direct support from Istanbul, but progressively Algiers established its own administrative, tax-collecting, and judicial authority over a large territory. Ottoman-Turkish authority came to be recognized throughout Algeria, although it was not uniformly effective. Provincial, tribal, and Sufi resistance, however, grew in the eighteenth and nineteenth centuries. Thus Algeria resembled Ottoman Syria and Iraq, where a centralized state governed a segmented society. The Ottoman-Algerian regime succeeded in creating an Algerian territorial and administrative identity, while the spread of Sufism among rural populations gave it Islamic identity.

The history of Morocco shows a third variation on the theme of Islam and state formation in a highly fragmented society. Although Volubilis was the capital of a Roman province, Morocco on the eve of the Arab conquests had neither territorial identity nor a history of centralized regimes. A number of local principalities emerged in the wake of the Arab conquests, based on the personal religious authority of the rulers, but from the eighth to the eleventh centuries the process of state formation was inhibited by internal fragmentation and external Fatimid and Umayyad interventions. The Almoravid conquests began the process of creating the territorial base for a Moroccan state. The Almoravids, the first of a series of conquest regimes set up by coalitions of tribal peoples from the south united on the basis of religious principles, were succeeded by the Almohads, the Marinids, the Sa'dians, and the 'Alawis, each of whom was legitimized by an appeal to the charismatic authority of the ruler, although this authority was articulated in different ways. In the Almoravid and Almohad cases, the leaders were heads of reform movements. Later Sa'dian and 'Alawi rulers possessed the *baraka* of descent from the Prophet and were believed to have the charismatic powers of Sufi saints. They were also regarded as caliphs, successors to the Prophet in the defense and administration of an Islamic society. The sultan was at once caliph, imam, *sharif*, *wali*, and *mujtahid*. He had important ritual roles at the Muslim holidays and shared in the national veneration for religious leaders.

Moroccan sultans, however, did not have a monopoly of religious legitimacy but shared *sharifian* descent and Sufi *baraka* with other religious leaders. This sharing of authority was both supportive and competitive. It was supportive in that the Sufis provided the sultans with a cultural basis for their claims to worldly authority. It was competitive in that the sources of moral judgment and political authority were independent of the state and dispersed among many individuals in the society. This dispersion meant that Morocco could not easily create a unified national regime.

The highly personal nature of the Moroccan monarchy assured its legitimacy and historical continuity but was also a source of weakness. Power was effected by means of personal contacts between the ruler and his clients. The highly personal nature of the state implied weak institutions. The central regime was supported by household administration and by mercenary and slave soldiers, but the *makhzan*, or coalition of independent, tribal, or Sufi power holders supplying military forces to the regime, was crucial to its effectiveness. With the help of the *makhzan* the government could control the towns and the central plains, but not the mountains and the deserts. Morocco thus preserved a distinctive territorial and monarchical identity, based on the personal religious authority of the sultans. This differed from Tunisia, which combined a Muslim statist concept of political legitimacy with centralized political administration, and from Algeria, which had a highly developed central government but a weak sense of political identity.

There are several reasons for the failure to consolidate a central Moroccan state. Although Morocco was a relatively wealthy region, its agricultural and commercial sectors were small in comparison to its pastoral populations. Successive bedouin invasions destroyed peasant village life. Furthermore, the weakness of the state made it difficult to collect regular taxes. To supplement poor tax revenues the sultans attempted to exploit long-distance trade, but rival Moroccan chiefs, and Sudanese, Algerian, and European competitors, appropriated important shares. Although Moroccan dynasties often came to power on the basis of control of trade, it proved impossible to monopolize trade revenues for extended periods.

A related factor was the weakness of the urban bureaucratic, commercial, and intellectual elites. Andalusian minorities provided the cadres of administration. Without links to either the rural or urban masses, however, they could serve only as secretaries. The *'ulama'*, also, were merely a slim stratum of the population, dependent on the sultans, restricted to the urban areas, and without politically potent ties to the common people. They also had to compete for religious prestige with the sultans, the saintly lineages, and the Sufi brotherhoods.

The corollary of the weakness of the sedentary society was the strength of autonomous tribal and Sufi groups. Their independence was enhanced in the seventeenth and eighteenth centuries by their access to European weapons. The effort to control the tribes and Sufi coalitions was continually subverted by intra-elite struggles for power and by the need to make fiscal, territorial, and other concessions to pacify communities that could not be defeated. In any case, Moroccan tribes were themselves unstable constellations. They used the patrilineal idiom, but they did not have a firm hierarchy or permanent constituencies. Tribal chieftainships were temporary positions subject to a constant competition for power. Sufi lineages and coalitions were similarly unstable, for the power of Sufis was personal rather than organizational and depended on the voluntary adherence of the tribes to the saints.

The late eighteenth and nineteenth centuries were a period of protracted crisis for North African–Muslim societies. Their Ottoman suzerain could no longer protect them. Their states were no longer capable of exerting close political control or of generating large revenues and strong armies. Their economies were increasingly in bondage to Europe. The decline of economic power made them prey to French conquest and French protectorates.

ISLAM IN ASIA

CHAPTER 30

INTRODUCTION: EMPIRES AND SOCIETIES

Within the global framework of Muslim regimes and societies, the great Muslim empires of the Middle East and South Asia – the Ottoman, the Safavid, and the Mughal – were linked by shared historical, ethnic, and cultural traditions. Western scholarship has been preoccupied by their similarities and differences from the states of Western Europe. Karl Wittfogal's *Oriental Despotism* characterized Asian empires as centralized, authoritarian, monolithic, and despotic regimes that governed subordinate and supine societies; as opposed to Western societies, which were seen as ruled by law (rather than tyrants). The West was the domain of autonomous classes (nobility, clergy, and bourgeoisies), of autonomous collective institutions (communes, councils, parliaments, courts, guilds, and other corporations), and of free men.

This extreme dichotomy is challenged by revisionist scholars. In recent work, East and West are no longer seen as having separate histories. They develop in the same global context. As early as the eleventh or thirteenth centuries, depending on different authors, there was already a global system of political and economic interaction. War and trade brought empires and states into close interaction and awareness of technological, military and administrative, intellectual, scientific, and artistic developments. In both Asian and European societies, there was a trend toward the consolidation of centralized states that dominated local nobles, warlords, tribes, and other potentially autonomous forces. This was partly due to new military tactics (the use of gunpowder weapons), international trade, and new financial and administrative methods. Competition among these states and empires led to intensified warfare and new military technologies, mobilization of resources from the population (or simple exploitation), and sometimes the promotion of economic development. International trade was also a powerful factor in the interrelated growth of early modern empires. From the fourteenth century onward, throughout Eurasia, political regimes were becoming larger, more powerful, and more centralized.

Furthermore, although centralized to different degrees, both Asian and European states were engaged in fluid political interactions with other forces in their societies – military officers, administrators, landowners, merchants, and religious spokesmen – who were at least partially independent and on whose cooperation imperial regimes depended. More recent studies understand state formation as a negotiated process involving subordinate or subaltern elites. Empires are understood, as they are in this book, as built on networks of political relationships with regional and local forces. Islamic-Asian and Islamic-African states, as much as European states, governed by means of ever-shifting negotiated relationships with their political constituencies. All Eurasian empires depended on the collaboration of independent or quasi-independent elites, and on legitimacy, consensus, and the support of their populations. In some revisionist studies, however, royal authority and military and administrative powers are dissolved into an infinitely flexible system of negotiations, which may underestimate the power of the central states and the long-term historical importance of the institutional distinctions between South and West Asian empires and Europe. In some European states the legal rights of nobles, the autonomy of the churches, bourgeois corporations, and popular communes were the basis for the emergence of parliamentary governments and for exceptional economic development.

In the succeeding chapters, we will first examine the institutions and operations of the early-modern-era Islamic empires of South and West Asia: the Ottoman Empire in Anatolia and the Balkans (1281–1924), the Safavid Empire in Iran (1501–1732), and the Mughal Empire in India (1526–1858). All three were built on the legacy of the Timurid Empire (1370–1526), and on both Iranian and Inner Asian governmental practices. The Ottoman, the Safavid, and the Mughal empires had similar institutions for succession, military recruitment, patrimonial or bureaucratic administration, and relations of central government and local elites. In conclusion, we will compare the similarities and differences among them.

CHAPTER 31

THE TURKISH MIGRATIONS AND
THE OTTOMAN EMPIRE

TURKISH-ISLAMIC STATES IN ANATOLIA (1071–1243)

The Turkish migrations that gave rise to the Saljuq, Mongol, and Timurid empires in Iran also gave birth to a succession of Western Muslim empires. Oghuz peoples pushed their way into Georgia, Armenia, and Byzantine Anatolia, bringing Islam into territories not hitherto reached by the Arab conquests or Muslim expansion. At the Battle of Manzikert in 1071, the Turks captured the Byzantine emperor, Romanos I. In the next century, they spread across Asia Minor.

The migrating peoples were organized into small bands of warriors (*ghazis*) under the leadership of chieftains (beys) or Sufi holy men (*babas*). Veneration of the chiefs and the desire to find rich pasturage, gather booty, and win victories against the infidels in the name of Islam held them together. The migrants did extensive damage to the countryside and cut off cities from their hinterlands and trading connections, but Turkish expansion was soon counterbalanced by the formation of states that attempted to stabilize and reconstruct the region.

Anatolia came under the Saljuq sultanate of Rum (c. 1077–c. 1308), whose rulers were remote relatives of the Saljuqs of Baghdad, with its capital at Konya. The Saljuqs of Rum, like earlier Middle Eastern Muslim states, employed Turkish nomadic forces but built up a large standing army of Turkish and Christian slaves and mercenaries. The administration was composed of Iranian scribes. In the early thirteenth century, a fiscal survey was taken, and tax revenue grants (*iqta‘*) were distributed in return for military service. The Saljuqs appointed provincial governors. Energetic efforts were made to sedentarize and extract taxes from the pastoral population. The Saljuqs built caravansaries and encouraged maritime commerce on the Black Sea, the Aegean, and the Mediterranean. Still, there were many regions in tribal hands and a number of minor principalities outside of Saljuq control.

The Saljuqs built up the infrastructure of Sunni Islam by inviting scholars from Iran to settle in Anatolia. Judges were appointed, colleges were endowed, and funds were provided for the education of converts. The money came primarily from levies on Christian villages and expropriated ecclesiastical properties. The Saljuqs also attempted to bring independent Sufi fraternities under government influence by providing them with schools, hospices, and endowments. Sufis were particularly important in Anatolia. Members of the Qalandariyya, Rifaʿiyya, and other Sufi brotherhoods came into Anatolia from Inner Asia and eastern Iran; some were driven westward by the Mongol invasions. The Sufi *babas* helped bring new territories into cultivation. They built hospices, schools, and mills; planted orchards; provided for the safety of travelers; and mediated disputes among tribes. Thus, they brought order into a fragmented warrior society.

Rural Sufis also adopted a tolerant attitude toward Christians and facilitated the conversion of Greeks and Armenians to Islam. Hajji Bektash (d. c. 1297), who was widely revered in Anatolia, synthesized Sunni and Shiʿi beliefs and Muslim and Christian religious practices. Urban religious fraternities – groups of unmarried young men devoted to the youth (*futuwwa*) ethic of bravery and hospitality (known as *akhis*) – recruited from the artisan and merchant strata of the population, organized commerce among towns and between towns and rural areas, protected people from abuse, and gave charity to strangers and the poor. These fraternities were closely allied to the Mevlevi order, whose Friday prayers and common meals were a focus of town life.

In 1242–43, the Mongol invasions destroyed the existing urbanization and sedentarization. The Mongols defeated the Saljuqs, made them vassals, and tipped the balance of power in Anatolia from the central state back to the pastoral warrior populations. Large numbers of new migrants entered Anatolia in the 1230s and settled on the frontiers of the Byzantine Empire. Small groups of warriors, nomads, refugees, adventurers, and bandits, eager for booty and glory in the holy war, resumed the struggle against the Byzantine Empire and founded new principalities. The most important of these new states were the Karaman beylik in Cilicia, which in 1335 made Konya its capital and claimed to inherit Saljuq authority; the dynasty of Dulgadir in the northern reaches of the Euphrates River; and Menteshe and Germiyan in the region of Kutahya.

The absorption of the former Byzantine territories by Turkish-Muslim conquerors led to the Islamization of Anatolia. Before the Turkish migrations, the vast majority of the Greek, Armenian, Georgian, and Syrian populations of Anatolia were Christians. By the end of the fifteenth century, the great majority was Muslim. Some of this change was due to the immigration of a large Muslim population and the ravages of war, but in great part it was due to the conversion of Christians to Islam. These conversions reflected the weakening of the Byzantine state and the Greek Orthodox Church. In the late thirteenth and fourteenth centuries, the Turks excluded bishops and metropolitans from their sees. Church revenues and properties were confiscated. Hospitals, schools, orphanages, and monasteries were destroyed or abandoned, and the Anatolian Christian population was left without leadership and social services. Muslim holy men appealed to a demoralized Christian population by presenting Islam as a syncretism of Muslim and Christian religious beliefs. Jesus and Christian holy places were venerated by Muslims. Byzantine princes, lords, and administrators were tempted to convert to Islam in order to join the Turkish elite. At the same time, the Saljuq state and the Turkish emirates built palaces, mosques, colleges, caravansaries, and hospitals, supported by endowments and staffed with Persian and Arab scholars.

THE RISE OF THE OTTOMANS (c. 1280–1453): FROM *GHAZI* STATE TO EMPIRE

The Ottoman state arose as one of the Turkish principalities on the Byzantine frontier. Its ruling dynasty would hold power from 1300 to 1924. In its early period, the Ottomans were bands of frontier raiders (*ghazi*) under the leadership of the Ottoman family. The frontier warriors, however, were not ideological, and the Ottomans developed a network of alliances with local tribes, farmers, and townspeople; Muslim dervishes; and Christian lords. This was superseded in the fifteenth and sixteenth centuries by a centralized patrimonial state based on slave elites and *timar* (quasi-feudal grants of tax revenue equivalent to *iqta'*s) holding soldiers, and on an imperial ideology. In the seventeenth and eighteenth centuries, the centralized empire evolved into a network regime in which provincial notables played an ever-growing role in the empire's military, landholding, mercantile, and tax-collecting arrangements. The nineteenth century was marked by a renewed concentration of power at the center. Through all these changes in the political apparatus, the dynasty survived and maintained its authority. (See Table 13.)

The Ottoman dynasty was initiated by frontier warriors under the leadership of Ertugrul (d. c. 1280) and his son Osman, who gave his name to the dynasty. Struggling for control of pasturage, they expanded their domains from hills to plains, and in 1326 Orhan, son of Osman, seized the important towns of Bursa and Iznik. In 1345 he crossed the straits from Anatolia to the Balkans. Having established a foothold in Europe, the Ottomans occupied northern Greece, Macedonia, and Bulgaria. Ottoman control of the western Balkans was decisively established by their victory at the Battle of Kosovo in 1389. The papacy and a coalition of European powers tried in 1396 and again in 1444 to push back the Ottomans but were defeated both times.

Then, on the basis of their European empire, the Ottomans began to annex rival Turkish principalities in western Anatolia. Ottoman expansion was temporarily set back in 1402 by the invasion of Timur, who defeated Bayazid I (r. 1389–1402) and reduced the Ottoman state to vassalage. The Ottomans, however, survived this defeat and continued to enlarge their domains in both Anatolia and Serbia.

Table 13. *The Ottoman dynasty*

Accession date	Sultan
1281	Osman
1324	Orhan
1360	Murad I
1389	Bayazid I
1402	Interregnum
1413	Mehmed I
1421	Murad II (first reign)
1444	Mehmed II the Conqueror (first reign)
1446	Murad II (second reign)
1451	Mehmed II the Conqueror (second reign)
1481	Bayazid II
1512	Selim I
1520	Suleyman I ("the Law-Giver" or "the Magnificent")
1566	Selim II
1574	Murad III
1594	Mehmed III
1603	Ahmed I
1617	Mustafa I (first reign)
1618	Osman II
1622	Mustafa I (second reign)
1623	Murad IV
1640	Ibrahim
1648	Mehmed IV
1678	Suleyman II
1691	Ahmad II
1695	Mustafa II
1703	Ahmed III
1730	Mahmud I
1754	Osman III
1757	Mustafa III
1774	'Abdul-Hamid I
1789	Selim III
1807	Mustafa IV
1808	Mahmud II
1839	'Abdul-Majid I
1861	'Abdul-Aziz
1876	Murad V
1876	'Abdul-Hamid II
1909	Mehmed V Rashid
1918	Mehmed VI Wahid al-Din
1922–24	'Abdul-Majid II (as caliph only)

By 1449, the Ottomans had reached the Danube and in the next half century would absorb Greece, Bosnia, Herzegovina, and Albania. In 1453, they conquered Constantinople, a triumph that fulfilled an age-old Muslim ambition to inherit the domains of the Roman Empire. (See Map 14.)

Ottoman institutions were based on the Saljuq state in Anatolia and the Byzantine Empire. The regime was built on Turkish chiefs, religious leaders (such as

Turkish *babas* and dervishes), Greek warlords and castle chieftains, and former Byzantine civil servants and Christian nobles who were integrated into the Ottoman armies and administration. Ottoman elites intermarried with Christian nobles. The courts of the Ottoman sultans brought together Muslim scholars, Sufi teachers, and Christian and Jewish theologians. The Ottomans inherited Middle Eastern practices such as the slave military corps and *iqta'* form of administration. Reflecting its conquests, some administrative practices, some architectural styles, patronage of Christian churches, the guild system, and controls over the provincial economy were integrated from Byzantine precedents.

The Ottoman conquests in the Balkans also established Muslim hegemony over large Christian populations but did not lead, as in Anatolia, to substantial conversion of the populations to Islam. In the Balkans, the Turkish-Muslim presence was first established by Turkish migrants who entered Thrace, the Maritsa Valley, northern Bulgaria, and Albania in the course of the fourteenth and fifteenth centuries. Hundreds of new villages were founded, often around Sufi hospices (*tekkes*). The major towns were settled by Muslims. Still, in the Balkans the pressure to convert to Islam was much less than in Anatolia. There was no large-scale Turkish immigration comparable to that in Anatolia. After the conquest of Constantinople, the Orthodox Church in the Balkans was reorganized, confirmed in its jurisdictions and properties, and allowed to protect Christian communities. Although there were some cases of forced conversion in Serbia, Albania, and Bulgaria, there was no systematic persecution.

In the Balkans, as in Anatolia, some conversions were facilitated by the preaching of the Sufi orders, such as the Bektashis and the Mevlevis. Converts to Islam often maintained their Christian beliefs and practices. Baptism, worship of saints, the celebration of Easter, and belief in the healing efficacy of churches were continued from Christian into Muslim practices. In the Balkans, Islam was also influenced by pagan practices, which had remained a strong aspect of Balkan folk Christianity.

A census of 1520–30 indicates that about 19 percent of the Balkan population was Muslim, and 81 percent was Christian, with a small Jewish minority. The Bosnian Muslim population, one of the most numerous, made up 45 percent of the total population. In general, Muslims were concentrated in towns. Much later, in the seventeenth century, Islam came to the Rhodope, northern Albania, and Montenegro. Greeks in southwestern Macedonia and Crete converted in the course of the seventeenth and eighteenth centuries.

THE OTTOMAN WORLD EMPIRE

The conquest of Constantinople and the Balkans was a turning point in Ottoman history. Rather than satisfying Turkish, Ottoman, and Muslim ambitions, it made them boundless. Mehmed II the Conqueror (r. 1444–46, 1451–81) combined Turkish interest in victories over the infidels with the imperial ambitions of the Muslim

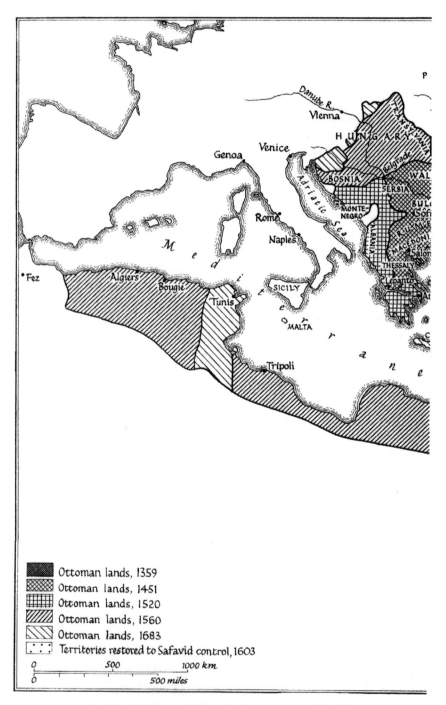

Map 14. The expansion of the Ottoman Empire, c. 1280–1683.

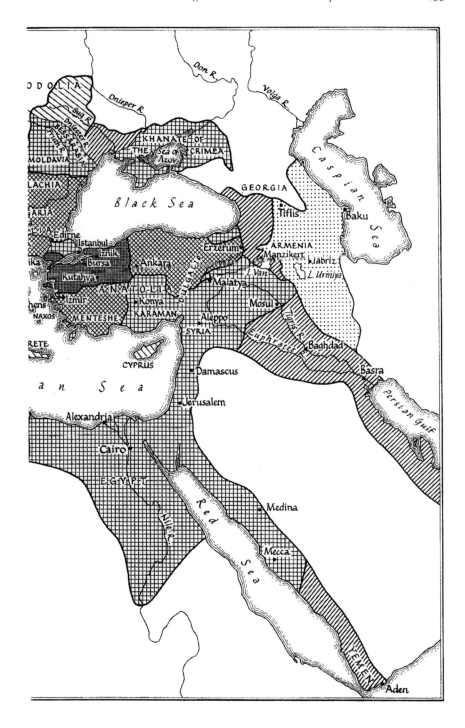

Don R.

Volga R.

ODOLIA

Dnieper R.

Bug R.

Dniester

BESSARABIA

KHANATE OF

THE CRIMEA

Sea of Azov

MOLDAVIA

GEORGIA

LACHIA

Black Sea

ARIA

Tiflis

Baku

Caspian Sea

L IA

Edirne

Istanbul

Iznik

Erzerum

ARMENIA

Manzikert

Bursa

Ankara

Tabriz

ika

Kutahya

BULGAR

L. Van

L. Urmiya

A N A T O L I A

Malatya

Izmir

Konya

Mosul

hens

MENTESHE

KARAMAN

Aleppo

Euphrates

Baghdad

NAXOS

SYRIA

Tigris R.

Basra

RETE

CYPRUS

Damascus

Persian Gulf

a n   S e a

Jerusalem

Alexandria

Cairo

EGYPT

Nile R.

Medina

Red

Sea

Mecca

YEMEN

Aden

caliphate and the Roman Empire. This empire would sweep eastward to the borders of Iran, subsume the Arab provinces of the Middle East and North Africa and the holy places of Arabia, and defend Muslim interests in the Indian Ocean region. Westward it would expand into the Russian steppes, Eastern Europe, and across the Mediterranean Sea.

Ottoman expansion, exacerbated by Sunni-Shiʿi religious antagonism, brought the Ottomans into rivalry with the Safavids for control of eastern Anatolia and western Iran. The decisive Battle of Chaldiran (1514) enabled the Ottomans to annex eastern Anatolia and northern Mesopotamia and to take control of the important trade routes leading from Tabriz to Aleppo and Bursa. The Ottoman struggle with Iran continued sporadically for more than a century until the treaty of Qasr Shirin (1639) gave Baghdad and Iraq to the Ottomans and the Caucasus to Iran. This treaty delineated the modern boundaries between Iraq and Iran.

In 1516 and 1517, the Ottomans took over the Mamluk Empire of Syria and Egypt and the Islamic holy places of Arabia. (See Illustration 11.) From this vantage, the Ottomans maintained their participation in the Red Sea and Indian Ocean international trade. With the conquest of the former lands of the ʿAbbasid caliphate, the Ottomans inherited Muslim world leadership. The absorption of Damascus, Cairo, Mecca, and Medina brought a great influx of Muslim scholars to Istanbul. In addition to the title of "Warrior for the Faith," Ottoman rulers took the titles of "Servitor of the Two Holy Sanctuaries" and "Defender of the Shariʿa." Muslims the world over appealed to them for military and political support. Muslims in Spain appealed for Ottoman help against the Christian Reconquista. Sunnis in Inner Asia called to their Ottoman brothers to protect them against the Safavids and the Russians.

The Muslims of Gujarat and Aceh invoked their aid in the Indian Ocean struggle against the Portuguese efforts to divert the international spice trade from the Mediterranean to Atlantic routes. By 1507, the Portuguese had established a series of bases in the Indian Ocean, cutting off commerce to the Red Sea and the Mediterranean, but after 1517, the Ottomans established their own bases in Arabia and East Africa, including Sawakin, Aden, and Yemen. From these bases, the Red Sea fleets under the leadership of Piri Reʾis (d. 1554) reopened the routes to Alexandria and Aleppo. In the Persian Gulf region, the Ottomans occupied Baghdad in 1534, Basra in 1538, and Bahrain in 1554. In this epic struggle, the Portuguese relied on maritime commerce and the control of trade. The Ottomans depended on the revenues of their vast territorial empire.

From their dominant position in the Muslim East, the Ottomans also swept northward and westward over Eastern Europe and the Mediterranean. The conquest of the Balkans opened the way for a two-century-long struggle against the powers of Europe. In these wars, the Ottomans were primarily allied to France against their principal enemies: the Habsburg Empire in Spain, the Netherlands, Austria, Hungary, and Tsarist Russia.

Illustration 11. Sultan Selim the First. *Source:* Sonia Halliday Photographs.

A world war unfolded in three principal theaters. In central Europe, the Ottomans pushed beyond the Danube and absorbed the Romanian principalities by 1504. They confirmed local princes in power but maintained forts and garrisons and received a tribute of cereals, honey, hides, and cloth. The Hungarian monarchy, crippled by aristocratic factional quarrels and by unrest among the peasants, lost Belgrade in 1521 and was forced to accept Ottoman suzerainty in 1526. In 1529, the Ottomans besieged Vienna, and although the siege failed, it assured the Ottomans control of Hungary. Still expanding, the Ottomans made Transylvania a vassal in 1559. Finally, the long war of 1593–1606 brought an end to Ottoman expansion. By the treaty of Zsitva Torok (1606), Ottoman rule over Romania, Hungary, and Transylvania was confirmed, but the Ottoman sultans had to recognize the Habsburg emperors as their equals. The struggle to break the stalemate went on and culminated in the last, and fruitless, Ottoman siege of Vienna in 1683.

These wars in central Europe were accompanied by an equally vast Ottoman-Habsburg struggle for control of the Mediterranean. In the early days of Ottoman expansion, the dominant naval powers were Venice and Genoa, each of which had established a series of fortified trading posts along the Mediterranean and Aegean coasts in order to sustain their commerce. After the conquest of Constantinople, Mehmed II built a new navy based on Italian designs and Greek seamanship. Ottoman naval policy was directed to the control of trade routes and the acquisition of productive resources. In wars that lasted from 1463 to 1479 and from 1499 to 1503, Venetian possessions in Greece and the Aegean were conquered. Muslim privateers led by Hayreddin Barbarossa carried Ottoman power into the western Mediterranean. Barbarossa took Algiers in 1529 and was made grand admiral of the Ottoman fleets in 1533.

The Spanish Habsburgs counterattacked by building a series of fortified posts along the coast of North Africa, reaching as far as Tripoli in 1510 and La Goletta in 1535, but eventually the Ottomans seized Tripoli (1551), Bougie (1555), Jerba (1560), Malta (1565), and Cyprus (1570 or 1571). This provoked the formation of a coalition among the papacy, Venice, and the Habsburgs, who defeated the Ottomans at the Battle of Lepanto in 1571. Lepanto was celebrated as a triumph of Christian Europe over the Muslim Turks. The Europeans regained their confidence, but the Ottomans restored their fleets and, in a resounding victory, seized Tunis in 1574. By 1580, both protagonists recognized that they could no longer change Mediterranean boundaries. An Ottoman-Habsburg truce of 1580 confirmed the porous frontier between Christian Europe and Muslim North Africa that lasts to the present day.

The regions north of the Black Sea and between the Black and the Caspian seas were disputed by the Ottomans and the Russians. After 1484, the Ottomans excluded foreigners from the Black Sea, with the exception of ships bringing wine from Crete or Chios. The Black Sea trade, in general, passed from the Genoese to Armenians, Jews, Greeks, Turks, and Romanians in the course of the fifteenth century. In the late fifteenth century, the Ottomans established their suzerainty over Romania and the Crimea, but the Russians seized Kazan (1552) and Astrakhan (1556) and thus won control of the lower Volga. In response, the Ottomans determined on the bold strategy of building a channel between the Don and the Volga rivers, which would enable them to transfer ships from the Black to the Caspian seas, block Russian expansion into the Caucasus, and keep open the trade and pilgrimage routes from Inner Asia. An Ottoman expedition of 1569–70, however, was defeated. Russian expansion led eventually to a three-way Polish, Russian, and Ottoman struggle for control of the Ukraine that culminated (in 1676) with Ottoman control of the Black Sea and part of the Ukraine. Here, the Ottomans reached the apogee of their expansion in northern Europe.

Thus, the sixteenth century was the period of the most aggressive expansion, and the seventeenth century was a period of maintenance. By the end of the seventeenth century, the Ottomans had created a world-scale empire, reaching from the western Mediterranean to Iran and from the Ukraine to Yemen. The dynamism of the worldwide expansion of Ottoman rule came from the inner motivations of Turkish and Ottoman society. The spearhead of the early Ottoman conquests was *ghazi* warrior adventurers under the leadership of popular military chieftains or venerated holy men united under Ottoman authority. The later conquests were backed by an imperial state of exceptional organizational capacities, employing an advanced military technology (based on cannons and massed infantry musket fire), tolerating and assimilating non-Muslim populations and reconciling them to Ottoman rule. By the seventeenth century, however, the logistical problems of further expansion and increasingly organized resistance in central Europe brought an end to Ottoman advances.

THE PATRIMONIAL REGIME: FIFTEENTH AND SIXTEENTH CENTURIES

From the middle of the fourteenth to the end of the sixteenth century, the early Ottoman state was slowly transformed into a centralized empire in parallel with similar processes throughout the Middle East, the Indian subcontinent, and Europe. Kings and emperors were consolidating their authority over feudal, tribal, and local elites. In the Ottoman case, the critical transformations were the institutionalization of succession to the sultanate, the creation of a standing army exclusively loyal to the sultan, the regularization of the *timar* system and provincial administration, and the construction of a central bureaucratic administration to replace reliance on Turkish and Christian vassals. Yet the degree of centralization should not be overestimated. The Ottoman Empire operated within the limits of pre-modern communications and transportation; extensive territories remained in the control of nomadic tribes and local rulers. The quasi-feudal *timar* system used in the directly governed regions was by definition a decentralized system. Crucial to the empire in this early period, as in later ones, were the arrangements for shared power with provincial elites and the clientele networks that bound together center and periphery.

The Ottoman Empire was not only governed but "owned" by the sultan. All the revenues of the empire were his property – although he assigned a portion to his military and administrative servants and a portion to charitable endowments. All the officers of the state were his "slaves" and servants. By the seventeenth century, the imperial household, including the armies and the administration, numbered about 100,000 people.

At the center of the centralizing Ottoman state was an elaborate court, palace, and household government. The Istanbul palace, the Topkapi Saray, which was built in 1470, itself a symbol of patrimonial power, was divided into an inner and an outer section. The inner section was the very heart of the empire. It included the residence of the sultan and his harem, secluded from public view; the privy chambers and treasury of the ruler; the royal kitchens; and the schools for the training of pages and slaves for the inner service. The outer section housed the state offices for military, civil, and religious administration; kitchen staffs; artisans; and gardeners, who maintained the palace grounds and performed military service. Whereas the inner courtiers enjoyed a direct relationship with the sultan, the outer household was in effect the government of the empire.

At the very heart of the palace was the royal family. The rules and customs governing the royal family were designed to serve the political interests of the regime, yet dynastic marriage policy and succession policy led to profound political uncertainties. The authority of the sultan was absolute, but there was an ambiguity about the transmission of authority. According to Turkish practice, the authority of the sultan was passed on to his sons (females and descendants in the female line had no right to the throne), but the line of succession was not specified. The sultan's sons were given provincial commands, and the death of a reigning sultan led to a struggle for power among them. The sultanate was inherited by whichever son defeated and killed his brothers. This practice favored politically and militarily competent sons but undermined the stability of the realm.

Multiple children compounded the problems of succession. Because a child's legal status was defined by his father, and because it made no difference in law if the mother was a legal wife or a concubine, to reduce the number of potential claimants to the sultanate, Ottoman rulers began to make celibate marriages for political purposes and to restrict sexual relations and childbearing to concubines. Furthermore, they limited each concubine to one child. This was the system of reproduction until the reign of Suleyman (1520–66). Suleyman, however, fell in love with his slave, Hurrem; married her; and allowed her to have several children, thereby assuming the role of queen mother on his death. After Suleyman, seniority rather than civil war became the normal route to succession. Still, until the end of the sixteenth century, the successor sultan executed brothers and half brothers. When this practice was abolished, the brothers were instead imprisoned in the royal harem.

The Janissaries and civil and religious administration

The driving force in the centralization of the Ottoman state was the conflict between the Turkish warrior or *ghazi* party, which was powerful in the provincial armies and the religious administration, and the slave or *devshirme* party, which was powerful in the imperial service and in the janissary corps. The warriors were concerned about the excessive power of the sultan and wanted a decentralized government with a Muslim and Turkish – as opposed to a cosmopolitan and impe-rial – cultural style. Successive sultans favored the policies of one party or another, or manipulated them against each other. Bayazid I (r. 1389–1402) consolidated the slave party by introducing the slave soldiers into administrative positions and by bringing the provinces under central control, but Mehmed I (r. 1413–21), in the wake of defeat by Timur, gave full support to the Turkish and *ghazi* elements. He removed Byzantine advisors from the court and made Turkish and Persian, rather than Greek, the official languages of administration.

Mehmed II (r. 1444–46, 1451–81) returned power to the slave soldiers. He removed the Turkish nobility and all competing members of the Ottoman family from power and reserved the most important positions in the central government for his own slaves. To maintain some balance of power, a functional division was made between the offices of the grand vizier, the religious notables, the treasury administration, and the chancery services. Some Turkish families were restored to favor and allowed to keep their properties. Mehmed II also sought the support of the Greek Orthodox clergy by recognizing their civil as well as religious authority over the laity. He centralized government controls by taking tax surveys and absorbing independent vassal territories into the *timar* system, and he promulgated the first systematic legal codes dealing with the organization of the state and the obligations of subjects. Bayazid II (r. 1481–1512) reversed his policies by sponsoring an Islamo-Turkic policy, but by the reign of Suleyman I (r. 1520–66), the dominance of the janissaries was uncontested. The centralizing program triumphed by defeating rival Ottoman claimants to the sultanate, subduing the independent Turkish states in Anatolia, co-opting noble Turkish families, and building an administrative apparatus based on slaves.

The slave military forces were critical to the Ottoman system. Murad I (r. 1360–89) was the first sultan to use slave military units (*kapikullari*) organized either as infantry (the famous janissaries) or as cavalry. The new troops were at first taken from prisoners and volunteers, but in 1395 the *devshirme* was instituted as a kind of tax in manpower taken on the Christian population of the Balkans. Whereas the slave soldiers of previous Middle Eastern regimes had been recruited from outside the territories of the empires they served, the Ottoman janissaries were taken from the subject population. This afforded a regular supply of soldiers and perhaps a cheaper source of slaves, but it permitted the complication that the system had originally been designed to avoid: slaves recruited in the Balkans could resume family and social contacts in their home region. Murad II (r. 1421–44) expanded the janissary corps and also built a navy to combat the Venetians in the Aegean and Black seas. In his reign, the Ottomans first armed their infantry with muskets and cannons. Gunpowder weapons were a critical factor in decreasing the power of noblemen fighting from horseback.

The most promising of the slave recruits were educated in the palace schools to be pages in the royal household or officers in the army or administration. They were given a Turkish, Arabic, and Islamic education and were cultivated as gentlemen in the Ottoman style. Other recruits were apprenticed to Turkish officers in Anatolia and were trained to operate as infantry in organized formations using firearms.

These "slaves" – as in the Mamluk case – were not an oppressed class but were the highest-ranking officers of Ottoman society and were "slaves" only in the sense that they were the servants of the sultan.

The janissary corps was complemented by provincial cavalry, most of whom continued to be recruited from the free Turkish population and supported by assignments of tax revenues in return for military service. In 1527, there were about 28,000 slave infantrymen and some 70–80,000 cavalrymen, of whom 37,500 were *timar* holders. In addition, there were auxiliary garrison and frontier raiders who were financed by tax exemptions.

Civilian institutional changes followed from military developments. A bureaucracy was essential to the financing of the slave armies. Orhan (r. 1324–60) appointed a minister for the central administration and military and civil governors for the conquered provinces. From the reign of Mehmed II to the accession of Suleyman, ministers were drawn from among the Christian noblemen of the Balkans and thereafter from among the *devshirme* recruits. Chancery officials came from the Muslim colleges.

Muslim religious administration was another pillar of the empire. Ottoman political policy promoted Muslim identities. The postconquest reconstruction of Istanbul society reaffirmed and strengthened the state's connections to the religious elites and to Muslim communities. Abu Ayyub al-Ansari, a Muslim hero of the Umayyad assault on Constantinople, was made "patron saint" of the city. Some churches were converted into mosques and colleges. Ottoman wars with the Shiʻi Safavids for control of eastern Anatolia, conquest of the Mamluk Empire of Egypt and Syria, and the establishment of Ottoman suzerainty over the holy places of Arabia reinforced Ottoman Sunni identity.

The Ottomans were keen to bring scholars (*ʻulama*ʼ) and Sufis under state control. From the earliest days of the regime, the Ottomans patronized both groups by endowing schools (*madrasas*) and Sufi retreats. The first Ottoman college was established in Iznik in 1331, when scholars were invited from Iran and Egypt to augment Muslim instruction in the new territories. Later sultans founded colleges in Bursa, Edirne, and Istanbul. In the late fifteenth century, these were arranged in a hierarchy that defined the career path for the promotion of leading scholars. The college built by Suleyman between 1550 and 1559 as part of his great mosque complex was made the highest ranking. Beneath it were ranked the colleges founded by previous sultans and beneath these the colleges founded by state officials and religious scholars. The colleges were not only organized by rank but also distinguished by their educational functions. The lowest-level colleges taught Arabic grammar and syntax, logic, theology, astronomy, geometry, and rhetoric. The second-level kind stressed literature and rhetoric. The higher-level colleges taught law and theology. The Ottoman state appointed all important judges, jurisconsults, and professors of law.

Suleyman consolidated the bureaucratic system of control over the scholars. The head of Ottoman legal administration was the *şeyhü'lislām* (*shaykh al-Islam*), the leader of an organization of jurisconsults (muftis) that paralleled the organization of judges. The *shaykh al-Islam*, the chief jurisconsult of Istanbul, had direct access to the sultan. He issued legal decrees (*fatawa*) and intervened in political matters by issuing legal opinions related to the state's foreign policies. Ebu's-su'ud (d. 1574), a sixteenth-century Ottoman *shaykh al-Islam*, is one of the best-known Ottoman jurists to hold the position. Ebu's-su'ud gave the Ottoman sultan the title of caliph, justified interest-bearing loans, and modified tax practices.

A similar elaboration took place in judicial administration. The judicial appointments of Istanbul, Bursa, and Edirne were originally the most important, but the hierarchy came to include judgeships in Damascus, Aleppo, Cairo, Baghdad, Medina, Izmir, and Konya. The educational and judicial hierarchies were interlocked. Appointments to judgeships required the attainment of appropriate levels in the educational system. The judicial service was headed by two military judges (*qadi-askers*), one for the Balkans and one for Anatolia. Ordinary judges were graded into several ranks. Ottoman court records show that judges followed well-known procedural and substantive rules. Indeed, they were bureaucrats, and their methods of adjudication were systematized, as was administration in general.

Judges had important administrative as well as judicial responsibilities. The judges and their deputies served as notaries public, registrars of deeds, and administrators of the properties of orphans and minors. Judges supervised the administration of colleges and had an important role in certification of taxes, overseeing harvests, inspection of military forces, and supervision of the urban economy, including government regulations for artisan guilds and markets. The state courts also took control of religious endowments and charities. Trusts represented approximately 16 percent of the economy in the seventeenth century and 27 percent in the eighteenth century. Trusts funded educational institutions, charities, transportation, and inns and meals for students and teachers, pilgrims or travelers, and indigents.

Ottoman law (co-author, Lena Salaymeh)

In earlier Islamic societies, legal training, the formulation of law, and judicial decisions had been the preserve of jurists with minimal state intervention. The Ottoman state, however, became intimately involved in every aspect of judicial activity – from training jurists and court personnel, to selecting judges, and to applying legal codes. Ottoman courts became the primary venue for litigation throughout the empire.

The Ottomans made Hanafi *fiqh* (laws derived from the jurisprudential methodology of jurists) the official legal school. The Ottoman courts applied Islamic legal precedents, which, however, did not cover all aspects of Ottoman political and social life. On a broad range of issues, the sultans issued *firmans*, decrees that were later gathered in codes called *kanun*. These administrative laws were considered to be a valid extension of religious law. Medieval Muslim jurists' law, state (*kanun*) law, and customary law were all integrated in the Ottoman codes. Suleyman compiled the judgments of predecessor sultans in his legal code, the *kanuni Osmani*, which became the law of the Ottoman Empire for several centuries. The law codes dealt with administrative and criminal justice, property and tax, the discipline of officials, military affairs, the relations of *timar* holders and peasants, and the organization of the religious hierarchy. This systematic codification of law was an extension of the centralizing and bureaucratizing tendencies of the Ottoman Empire.

In matters of government administration, Ottoman law was applied to all subjects, but in matters of family and business law, it applied only to Muslims. Non-Muslims had their own communal law and courts. In practice, however, Jews and Christians commonly had recourse to Ottoman courts in order to assure enforcement, or to have state guarantees for commercial and property transactions, or to win an advantage in marital and inheritance disputes. Rabbinic courts were aware of the Jewish community's venue shopping and would sometimes decide cases according to Ottoman law, rather than rabbinic precedents. For example, Jews often established trusts according to Ottoman law rather than Jewish law in order to avoid Jewish laws of inheritance. In general, Jewish and Ottoman courts appear to have regularly communicated – even collaborated – in the fifteenth and sixteenth centuries.

Ottoman law was contested. Some Ottoman subjects objected to Ottoman laws that they perceived as not being based on Islamic law. This was often an expression of opposition to the authority of the state and to the usurpation of the prerogatives of Muslim jurists. The Ottoman criminal code differed from Muslim law in that it changed a variety of penalties into fixed fines and permitted some circumstantial evidence in determining adultery. Ottoman law accepted payment of interest on loans, although this was proscribed by the earlier Islamic schools of law.

There was also local resistance to Ottoman legal hegemony. Local customs competed with jurisprudential texts, and Ottoman judges sometimes deferred to customary law. Ottoman courts honored guild law and customs in adjudicating disputes between guild members. Islamic law had always been an amalgam of *fiqh* and *kanun*. What makes the Ottoman period distinctive in Islamic legal history is the leading role of the state in law making and adjudication.

Provincial government
In matters of provincial government, the empire was never truly centralized. In the fourteenth and fifteenth centuries, it was still common for newly conquered regions to remain vassal provinces under the control of their former lords, often Christians, in return for tribute and military manpower. Former Byzantine, Serbian, and Greek cavalry were incorporated into Ottoman armies as *timar* holders. As the empire

expanded, provinces that had initially been tributaries were annexed and brought under routine administration. In the Balkans, direct controls were implemented as early as 1400, but many Anatolian regimes held out for another century. By 1500, the four central provinces of the empire – Rumelia, Anatolia, Rum, and Karaman – were under direct rule, and by 1550 most provinces were administered by salaried officials who collected taxes and sent the surplus to Istanbul. The largest provincial units, called *beylerbeyliks*, were subdivided into *sanjak beyliks* and further divided into *timarliks*, which were the districts assigned to military officers in lieu of salary.

A *timar* typically consisted of the right to collect taxes from a village or group of villages and their lands in return for military services. For tax purposes, cadastral surveys (*tahrirs*) listed the villages, the households, the adult males who were responsible for the payment of taxes, and their crops and other resources. In addition, a *timar* holder was the chief law enforcement officer on his lands. Although the assignment of *timars* indicated a greater degree of central control than the earlier contracts with vassal lords, this was a quasi-feudal dispersal of authority. Furthermore, *timar* holders themselves used intermediaries to oversee their domains. Local landowners, merchants, and village notables or headmen were important in tax collection and the administration of local affairs.

Although all provinces were in principle subordinate to the central authority and subject to taxation, in each region there was tension between Ottoman control and local autonomy. Anatolia was the home of a bellicose pastoral population whose chieftains were important local political figures and Sufi-led resistance was almost endemic. In the Balkans, Ottoman rule perpetuated the historic social structure and thus a considerable measure of local autonomy. Tribal groups, the Serbian *zadruga* or joint family, and independent churches such as the Serbian patriarchate at Pech (between 1557 and 1766) were all partially independent. The Orthodox Church helped to preserve the ethnic and linguistic character of Greek and other Balkan peoples.

In peripheral areas, the state had to make further compromises with local princes, chieftains, and tribes. The Crimean khanate, Albania and Montenegro, and principalities north of the Danube including Transylvania, Wallachia, and Moldavia remained under the rule of native tribute-paying dynasties. The Greek aristocracy of Istanbul (Phanariot) controlled church properties, tax farms, and the commerce of much of the Balkans. In the eighteenth century, leading Phanariot merchants were appointed as rulers of Romania. Control over the Arab provinces – Egypt, Yemen, Abyssinia, Basra, Baghdad, Libya, Tunis, and Algeria – was never fully established. The Arab provinces were virtually subsidiary regions organized around their own capitals, such as Cairo, Damascus, Aleppo, and Baghdad. The Ottoman regime was in continual negotiation with Arab tribes, *shaykhs*, and notables.

Despite these zones of autonomy, the Ottoman regime was striking among pre-modern empires for the degree of state control over the subject societies. The state inhibited organized elite resistance by manipulating factions and individuals and by rotating officials rapidly. The Ottomans extracted from each village and locality the surplus wealth that supported the central government and sustained the wars of expansion. Among Muslims, the state resisted the formation of independent loci of authority such as scholarly schools, Sufi brotherhoods, *akhi* fraternities, or independent merchant and artisan associations. The empire assured its dominance not only through force but also through its hold on the minds of men. It stood for Islam and the arts of civilization. It won the cooperation of local chiefs, landlords, village headmen, and religious leaders, all of whom had to respect the power of the central regime and all of whom benefited from being its accomplices.

Nonetheless, the power of the central government was always limited, because the people who served the state had ambivalent purposes. The men who made up the armies, the *timar* holders, and the central administration always looked for ways to advance their private, familial, and factional interests. The local notables who supported the regime also resisted an excessive encroachment on their pre-rogatives. Nevertheless, the Ottoman regime was vastly more powerful than the Safavid, and, until the end of the sixteenth century, autonomous chiefs played a much smaller role in its history.

ROYAL AUTHORITY, CULTURAL LEGITIMIZATION, AND OTTOMAN IDENTITY

Like the rulers of the ʿAbbasid and Saljuq empires, the authority of the Ottoman sultans combined patrimonial, Islamic, and imperial dimensions. The Ottoman regime, in both concept and practice, integrated caliphal, Saljuq, Timurid, and Mamluk Middle Eastern precedents. Christian European influences were relatively limited. The patrimonial authority of the Ottoman sultan was foremost. The state was his household; the subjects his personal retainers. The soldiers were his slaves. The territory of the empire was his personal property.

The sultan was glorified as a warrior prince, as a Muslim caliph, and as a conquering emperor. At the core of this absolute authority was the Ottoman descent from the original khan of the Oghuz peoples, with echoes of pre-Islamic Iranian, Roman imperial, Byzantine, and Timurid authority. After the defeat of the Ottomans by Timur in 1402, they adopted the concept of *ghazi*-warrior to reinforce their damaged authority. Murad II and later Ottoman rulers presented themselves as the embodiment of the *ghazi*-warrior-king. Mehmed II, the conqueror of Constantinople, declared himself Caesar and traced his lineage to both the Byzantine and Saljuk royal houses. Bayazid claimed to be successor to the caliphate. In 1547, after Suleyman received tribute for Habsburg lands in Hungary, he added "Caesar of Caesars" to Ottoman nomenclature. Suleyman also styled himself "sultan of the Arabs, Persians, and Romans," as well as caliph and imam of the Muslims. The titles of holy warrior, successor to the Saljuks, and caliph would survive into the twentieth century. The Muslim character of the sultanate, expressed in its control of the religious establishment, was at the core of Ottoman legitimacy.

Timurid precedents enhanced the Ottoman self-conception. The garden kiosks in the Topkapi Palace, court poetry, histories, manuscript illustration, and astronomical observation all followed Timurid patterns. From their wars with the Safavids, the Ottomans brought back important Persian art and craft collections to signify their inheritance of Timurid authority.

Poetry was the principal expression of royal style. Court poetry was based on the *aruz* (a prosodic meter derived from Arabic meters) and was heavily infused with Arabic and Persian words. The basic poetic forms were those already pioneered in Persian court poetry – the *qasida*, the *ghazal*, the *masnavi*, and the *ruba'i*. The greatest Ottoman poet of the classical period was Baki (d. 1600). Nef'i (d. 1636), a panegyrist and satirist, composed poetry celebrating power and struggle. Yahya Efendi (d. 1644) developed an original subject matter based on direct observation of life and nature and the expression of personal emotion.

Ottoman prose literature was strongly influenced by imperial ambitions. Early Ottoman historical writing was composed in both Turkish and Arabic to legitimize the origin of the dynasty, its rise to power, and its everyday court and military events. In the course of the sixteenth century, Ottoman world ambitions were given expression in the composition of universal histories. Mustafa 'Ali's (d. 1599) *Kunh al-Akhbar* (which was strongly influenced by Persian histories) contained a history of the world from Adam to Jesus, of early Islam, of Turkish peoples up to the rise of the Ottomans, and of the Ottoman Empire. In the seventeenth century, historians were employed to compile daily court chronicles. Geographical writing was stimulated by the expansion of Ottoman naval power. Piri Re'is, the Ottoman commander in the Indian Ocean, was the author of an important atlas. Evliya Chelebi's (d. 1682) *Seyahat-name* (Book of Travels) contains a comprehensive description of journeys throughout the Ottoman Empire and his observations of Ottoman society and economy.

Manuscript illustration also expressed the Ottoman sense of an imperial destiny. From the time of Mehmed II, the Ottoman regime maintained a court studio (*nakkashhane*) that employed calligraphers, painters, illuminators, and bookbinders to produce manuscripts and to design Ottoman ceramics, woodwork, metalwork, textiles, and carpets. Between 1451 and 1520, Persian precedents formed the basis of Ottoman manuscript art. Artists from Shiraz, Tabriz, and Herat were brought to Istanbul. The earliest works were illustrated copies of Persian classics such as 'Attar's *Language of the Birds*, the *Love Story of Khosraw and Shirin*, the *Khamsa* of Amir Khosraw, and the fables of *Kalila wa-Dimna*. The history of Alexander's conquests and illustrated contemporary histories became staple products of the Ottoman workshop.

Sixteenth-century manuscripts turned from the illustration of classic literature to contemporary events, such as the ceremonial reception of ambassadors, the collection of taxes, and the conquests of famous fortresses in the Balkans. Victories, festivals, accessions, royal processions, battles, sieges, banquets, and celebrations were the subject of manuscript illustrations. The *Shahinshah-name* of 1581 depicts the circumcision festivals held in Istanbul, athletic performances, guild parades, and other court events. Viziers, janissaries, cavalrymen, scholars, guildsmen, merchants, and sultans appear in profusion. The *Shah-Name-i Al-i Osman* (Book of Kings of the House of Osman) by Arifi (d. 1561/2) is one of the most famous productions of this period. By the end of the sixteenth century, illustrated history, celebrating the splendor of the Ottoman state and its conquests, had become a special Turkish contribution to the tradition of Middle Eastern and Islamic manuscript illumination. Ottoman manuscript art celebrated the self-consciousness of the Ottoman elite as a world historical force. Ottoman miniature painting gave up the warmth, the whimsy, the theatricality, and the multiple meanings of Iranian art in favor of realism, which was also expressed in Ottoman maps, fortress plans, and geographies. Ottoman painting – unlike Safavid and Mughal art in the sixteenth and seventeenth centuries – was not much influenced by European painting, despite Ottoman proximity and exposure to the West.

The Ottoman imperial sensibility was similarly reflected in architecture. Koja Sinan (d. 1578) was the master of the Ottoman style of architecture. Sinan designed buildings for mosques, schools, hospitals, libraries, kitchens, and mausoleums that were donated by the rich and powerful. Ottoman design features, such as single large domes, tall minarets, and colonnaded courtyards, showed the strong influence of Aya Sophia, the greatest of Byzantine churches. The dome, independently supported apart from the rest of the building, and the echoing half domes, expressed (as did the Dome of the Rock in Jerusalem) the triumph of Muslims over Christian rivals. (See Illustrations 12 and 13.) By 1600, Ottoman architecture, miniature painting, poetry, historical writing, and numerous crafts had created a new style, a new aesthetic, and a distinctive Ottoman identity.

THE OTTOMAN ECONOMY

In many respects, the Ottoman economy was fostered and directed by the Ottoman state. Ottoman expansion was directed toward securing a powerful position in the international luxury trade in spices, drugs, dyes, and silk. In the fifteenth century, the Ottomans took control of Mediterranean and Black Sea trade away from Venice and Genoa. The naval war against the Portuguese in the Red Sea and the Indian Ocean and Ottoman conquests in Iran, Iraq, Egypt, and Arabia gave the Ottomans access to the Indian Ocean trade. Baghdad and Basra traded with Iran and India. By the beginning of the sixteenth century, the Ottoman Empire was the principal intermediary between Europe and southern and eastern Asia. It maintained a trade surplus with Europe, receiving payment in silver, and in turn used the silver to cover its purchases of Iranian silk and Indian spices and cotton cloth. Precious Eastern

Illustration 12. The Sultan Ahmed (Blue) Mosque, Istanbul. *Source:* Photodisc/Getty Images.

goods came on various routes: overland from Jidda to Mecca, Damascus, and Aleppo and from the Persian Gulf to Basra and Aleppo. At the end of the sixteenth century, Aleppo was the most important silk market in the Ottoman Empire. From Aleppo and Tabriz, silk came to Bursa, the terminus for the Asian silk trade and an important producing center, where it was exchanged for Florentine and other European woolens and metalwares.

Added to the luxury trades was a growing trade in bulk goods for mass consumption, such as grain, cotton, wool, hides, fish, wine, olive oil, and ordinary textiles. Bursa was also a principal market for the Black Sea trade. From Bursa, silks, spices, cotton, and other products were shipped across the Black Sea to the Crimea, whence they were carried into the Ukraine, Poland, and Russia in

Illustration 13. The Sultan Ahmed (Blue) Mosque, Istanbul (interior). *Source:* Photodisc/Getty Images.

exchange for Eastern European cattle, fish, wheat, and hides. Bursa's rich merchant elites included Muslims, Greeks, Jews, and Armenians who invested in specie, real estate, slaves, and cloth.

The Ottoman conquests brought prosperity to other parts of Anatolia and the Balkans. Silk industries flourished in Amasya, Bursa, Istanbul, Mardin, and Diyarbekir. The European market stimulated Ottoman exports from the Balkans. Salonika woolens were exported north of the Danube. Edirne had a "capitalist" population, including money changers, jewelers, long-distance traders, local landowners growing wheat or raising cattle, and moneylenders who invested in textiles or milling. Soldiers and government officials were prominent among the wealthy.

Interregional trade was lively. Egypt traded with Anatolia, Syria, and the Sudan and with North and West Africa. Syrian pistachios, dates, spices, and slaves were sent to Anatolia. The pilgrimage routes brought people from all over the empire to Mecca and Medina. Mecca was an emporium for spices, pearls, pepper, and coffee, and almost every pilgrim financed his journey by bringing goods to sell in Mecca and returning with goods to sell at home. The provisioning of the pilgrimage caravans in Damascus, Cairo, and Baghdad was an important business.

Internally, the Ottomans stimulated land traffic by building bridges and caravansaries, digging wells, and garrisoning major road junctions. They also endowed towns and villages with religious and social facilities, including *imarets* and Sufi hospices (*tekke*). An *imaret* was a complex of buildings, including a mosque, a college, a hospital, and a hospice for travelers and students. Endowment funds for mosques, colleges, hospitals, bridges, convents, soup kitchens, libraries, and other institutions were invested in baths, bazaars, shops, tenements, workshops, mills, presses, slaughterhouses, tanneries, and tile factories; they were an important source of capital for commerce and agriculture. Sufi *tekkes* became centers of cultivation, trade, and local administration, as well as of educational and charitable activities. Numerous villages founded by Sufis in Anatolia and the Balkans were backed by the state.

The single greatest state project was the reconstruction of Istanbul for the glory of the sultan and the needs of administration and trade. At the time of the conquest, Constantinople probably had a population of between 50,000 and 60,000 people. To repopulate it, the Ottoman government obliged Muslim merchants from Bursa, Konya, and other Anatolian and Balkan places to move to Istanbul. The government gave land, houses, and tax concessions to the new migrants. Numerous villages in the vicinity were settled with slaves, prisoners, and deportees from the Balkans. According to the census of 1478, there were about 9,000 Muslim, 3,100 Greek Christian, 1,650 Jewish, and about 1,000 Armenian and gypsy dwellings in Istanbul. Thus the population was about 60 percent Muslim, 20 percent Christian, and 10 percent Jewish, and it totaled less than 100,000. Within a century, it would rise to more than 700,000, more than twice the population of the largest European cities of the time.

The city was rebuilt by constructing public institutions such as mosques, schools, hospitals, baths, and caravansaries with attached bazaars, bakeries, mills, or factories in several districts. Each neighborhood was centered around an important religious and public institution and its attendant facilities. Between 1453 and 1481 alone, 209 mosques, 24 schools or seminaries, 32 public baths, and 12 inns or bazaars were built in Istanbul. Many thousands of houses and shops were constructed by trust administrators in order to generate revenue.

A critical Ottoman concern was the provisioning of Istanbul. This was accomplished not by reliance on market forces but by close government regulation of production and trade. The produce of Bulgaria, Thessaly, the Ukraine, western Anatolia, and Egypt was mobilized to feed the capital. Ottoman regulations applied to ports and caravans and specified roads and customs houses to assure the collection, transit, and delivery of supplies. The state required traders to guarantee delivery of wheat, rice, salt, meat, oil, fish, honey, and wax directly to the palace and the capital city at fixed prices. Merchants were thus made agents of the state to meet the fiscal and provisioning needs of the capital.

Guilds were the basic units for the organization of the urban economy. Merchants, craftsmen, transport workers, and even entertainers and prostitutes were organized into corporate bodies to enforce economic discipline. The administrative apparatus that supervised the activity of professional corporations was elaborate. The grand vizier, the chief (*agha*) of the janissaries, judges, and market inspectors enforced guild regulations. Guild officials were appointed by the government in consultation with guild members in order to implement state rules and collect taxes. The chiefs of guilds acted through an informal body of guild elders, who were collectively responsible to the state. Guild regulation, however, was flexible. Outside of Istanbul, guilds had more leeway in the selection of officials, and disputes were typically settled by negotiations among state officials, guild spokesmen, and local notables.

In conjunction with the guilds, the authorities regulated entry into trades, opening of new shops, and the types and quality of merchandise produced. Maximum prices designed to protect consumer interests were set by the state. Weights and measures were regulated by government inspection. Guilds were expected to supply workers to accompany military campaigns, to provide labor services, and to take part in royal processions.

Ottoman guilds served not only the state but also the economic, social, and religious interests of the members. They operated under an internally generated guild law and took on certain social and religious functions. Guilds arbitrated disputes among their members and collected funds for mutual aid, religious ceremonies, and charities. They staged picnics and celebrations. The guilds were also religious confraternities with a patron saint and initiation ceremonies modeled on Sufi lines, which sponsored prayers and pilgrimages, and heard lectures on the value of sobriety and honesty. Guilds were usually confined to people of the same religious community. Only a minority had a mixed Muslim and Christian, or Muslim and Jewish, membership.

Some sectors of the Ottoman economy escaped direct administrative control. Merchants engaged in money changing and international trade were usually able to operate without close governmental supervision. Some merchants organized a putting-out system of manufacture in rural areas to compete with the monopolies of town guilds. Also, as janissaries penetrated into commerce and craft production in the seventeenth and eighteenth centuries, it became increasingly difficult for the government to regulate the artisan population.

RULERS AND SUBJECTS: JEWS AND CHRISTIANS IN THE OTTOMAN EMPIRE

The Ottomans reigned over an extraordinarily diverse population in terms of language, ethnicity, culture, religion, occupation, and social class. They classified this society in two dimensions. One was the distinction between *askeri* and *reʿaya*, which corresponds to the distinction between rulers and ruled, elites and subjects, warriors and producers, and tax collectors and taxpayers. The chief attributes of the ruling elite (the military, civil, and religious administrators) were the right to exploit the wealth of the subjects, exemption from taxes, and trial only by military court. In addition, to be a member of the ruling class, one had to be cultivated in the distinctive language and manners known as "the Ottoman way." One could become an Ottoman either by birth or by education in the imperial, military, or Islamic schools. By contrast, commoners paid taxes and were subject to the laws of their religious communities.

The distinction between rulers and ruled was not the same as that between Muslims and non-Muslims. Although non-Muslim populations were considered subordinate to Muslims, elite non-Muslims held positions of power and influence in the government, the royal court, tax administration, banking, and commerce. They shared the same style of consumption as the Ottoman elites. Some prominent Jews were excused payment of the poll tax paid by non-Muslims. Alongside Turkish soldiers and Arab and Persian scribes and scholars, the ruling elite also included Balkan Christian lords and scribes. The patrician Greek families of the Phanar district of Istanbul (who were prominent merchants, bankers, and government functionaries) and the higher clergy of the Orthodox Church (who collected the poll tax and administered communal affairs) were part of the Ottoman elite. Armenian bankers (*sarraf*) directed the flow of capital to the purchase of shares in tax farms, linked provincial merchants to the ruling class, and provided the elites with credit. Greeks and Jews were active in tax farming and international trade. Galata had large populations of Greek, Armenian, Jewish, and European as well as Muslim merchants.

Jewish refugees from Spain also became important in Ottoman trade and banking in the fifteenth and sixteenth centuries. Joseph Nasi (d. 1579), for example, was a refugee descended from a Portuguese Jewish family that had moved to Antwerp and then to Italy after the expulsion of the Jews from Spain. In 1554, he arrived in Istanbul, where he had European business and diplomatic connections; he became a close adviser to Sultan Suleyman, played an influential role in French-Ottoman diplomatic relations, and in 1566 was made Duke of Naxos, entitling him to a monopoly of customs revenues and the export of wine. Nasi was also a patron of Jewish community life and of Jewish settlement in Palestine. Thus, the Ottoman system was in a sense a condominium of elites, some Muslim, some non-Muslim, who had partitioned the various dimensions of the political economy among ethnically or religiously defined subelites.

In practice, the subjects (*re'aya*) included both Muslims and non-Muslims organized into small communities, which were primarily religious but also territorial and economic. Non-Muslims were known by the generic term "*dhimmi*" (protected peoples). In return for the payment of taxes and their acceptance of Muslim supremacy, they could retain their religious practices, communal associations, and identities. The religious communities administered the educational, judicial, and charitable affairs of the subject population, provided worship services and burials, and collected taxes. Like previous Muslim regimes, the Ottomans considered their non-Muslim subjects autonomous but subordinate peoples whose internal social, religious, and communal life was regulated by their own religious organizations, but whose leaders were appointed by and were responsible to a Muslim state.

Religious communities, however, were not the only form of non-Muslim social organization. Many communities were organized as ethnic, language, or family groups, including, for example, the Serbian joint family organization (*zadruga*) and self-governing community (*knezina*), the Balkan pastoral community (*katun*), and the Greek free communities (*eleuthe-rochoria*). These communities maintained a separate identity, because many Greek, Serbian, Albanian, or other Slavic communities were not fully integrated into religious bodies.

At the conquest of Constantinople, Mehmed II reaffirmed the Ottoman history of collaboration with Christians and permitted the religious, legal, and commercial autonomy of both indigenous and foreign non-Muslim merchants. Ottoman non-Muslims belonged to three recognized communities: Greek Orthodox, Armenian, and Jewish. The non-Muslim communal administration (the millet system) was not a uniform or centralized system, but a great number of ad hoc local arrangements with great variations over time and place. Internal authority could be held by either clerics or laymen, but the leadership and the communal regulations had to be registered with the Muslim authorities, who could be called on to enforce communal rules and/or to resolve internal disputes.

In public life, such as in the markets, Jews, Christians, and Muslims mingled freely. Although there were some exclusively Christian or Jewish crafts, Muslims and non-Muslims together belonged to many of the same craft and trade associations. Muslims and non-Muslims bought and sold, contracted, and employed each other. Some specialization was evident in commerce. Muslims dominated the caravan commerce linking Aleppo, Damascus, Baghdad, and Cairo and the cities to their hinterlands. Non-Muslims were prominent on the Anatolian and Balkan trade routes and in trade with Western Europe. Relatively homogeneous residential neighborhoods clustered around places of worship, but exclusively Muslim, Jewish, or Christian neighborhoods were rare. Music, cuisine, and material culture were generally indistinguishable.

Jews, Christians, and Muslims also shared religious beliefs and festivals. Sufi and popular practices integrated Jewish and Christian beliefs and practices. Regardless of religion, people exchanged food on religious holidays, often celebrated the same saints' days, and venerated the same shrines, such as the tomb of Abel in Damascus and the tombs of the patriarchs in Hebron. In Homs, a popular Sufi festival coincided with the Christian Holy Week. In Egypt, the Monday after Easter spring holiday was celebrated by both Muslims and Copts.

Non-Muslims, however, were not fully accepted as equals. Just as noncitizens have limited rights in contemporary states, so too did non-Muslims have specific legal disabilities as compared to Muslims. Although a Muslim man might marry a non-Muslim woman, non-Muslim men could not marry Muslim women. The testimony of non-Muslims against Muslims was not accepted in court. Non-Muslims were required to keep their place. Public manifestations of certain non-Islamic religious practices, such as processions or ringing of church bells, were forbidden. Riding horses was proscribed. Muslim officials often insisted on a clear separation of the communities. Non-Muslims were supposed to wear distinctive clothing in public or at least not wear the Muslim color green or white turbans. In the bath houses of Syria and Egypt, non-Muslim men had to wear an identifying amulet or towel. Judges sometimes ruled that Muslim and non-Muslim women must visit the baths on different days. Such regulations, however, were enforced only intermittently and usually in times of high sociopolitical tension.

Persecution was rare, but despite the general harmony, there were episodes of intense pressure on non-Muslims to convert. Sultan Beyazid II (r. 1481–1512) pressured Jews to convert and Selim I (r. 1512–20) pressured Bulgarians. The most serious episode of this sort was a wave of religious zealotry under Mehmed IV (r. 1648–87). The Kadizadeli "fundamentalist" preachers insisted on clear boundaries between Muslims and non-Muslims (especially the separation of Muslim women from non-Muslim men). Due to their influence, Jews were made the scapegoats for a great Istanbul fire in 1660, were banned from living in the city, and were required to sell their properties to Muslims. In the following year, the sumptuary codes regulating dress were reapplied, Jewish and Christian property was confiscated, and some churches and synagogues were destroyed. Assaults on Jews and Christians included the destruction of taverns and the prohibition of the wine and spirits trade. These actions were supported by imperial decrees and encouraged by contemporary Muslim jurists. Between 1666 and 1670, the population of the Rhodope and Pirin mountains of Bulgaria converted under pressure. Between 1663 and 1687, Jewish palace physicians and others converted, or were made to convert, to Islam. The sultans stopped appointing Jewish physicians, translators, and diplomats to court positions and replaced them with Greek Orthodox personnel.

Jews

The Jews in the Ottoman Empire stemmed from diverse populations. Romaniot (Greek) and Karaite Jews were part of the Anatolian and Balkan populations at the time of the Ottoman conquests. They spoke either Turkish or Greek. Mehmed the Conqueror resettled many Anatolian and Balkan Jews in Istanbul. Emigrants from northern Europe and then refugees from the Inquisition and from the expulsion of Jews from Spain followed. Sephardic or Spanish Jews also settled in Istanbul, Salonica, Edirne, Bursa and other towns. In general, Istanbuli Jews spoke Turkish, and Jews everywhere tended to amalgamate their dialect with the ambient language – Turkish, Slavic, Greek, or Arabic.

Jewish communities were found throughout the empire. At the time of the Ottoman conquests of Egypt and the Fertile Crescent, there were numerous Jews in the Arab cities of Cairo, Aleppo, Damascus, and Baghdad. In the Levant, some Jews were peasant farmers in predominantly Muslim villages. Jews were found as craftsmen, especially goldsmiths and jewelers, in the major Kurdish towns of northern Iraq. Jews in the Arab provinces generally spoke Arabic, but Jewish communities in Palestine had diverse ethnic origins and spoke many languages. Sephardic immigrants settled in Aleppo, Damascus, Jerusalem, Cairo, and Safed. In Aleppo and Jerusalem, the Sephardim kept their dialects, but elsewhere they assimilated the local languages. Sephardic Jews established the first Ottoman printing presses.

The wealthiest Jewish communities were those of Istanbul, Salonica, Izmir, Damascus, and Cairo, due to the importance of Mediterranean international commerce, in which Jews acted as middlemen between Europe and the Ottoman domains. The Jewish communities of Izmir and Aleppo flourished in the second half of the seventeenth century. The commercial cities also attracted small numbers of European Jews – Portuguese Marranos and Italian and French Jews – all of whom were known as Francos.

Toward the end of the sixteenth and the beginning of the seventeenth century, Jewish prosperity diminished. Jewish immigration to the Ottoman Empire ceased. The textile industry was in decline due to competition from the quality products of England, France, Italy, and Holland. Salonica, the largest Jewish textile-producing town, never recovered. In Bursa and other towns, the Jewish upper class was pushed out of tax farming by Ottoman officials and soldiers and reduced to secondary positions as agents or managers of tax farms. Worsening economic conditions also reduced the number of Jewish physicians and advisors at the Ottoman court. During the eighteenth and nineteenth centuries, the middle classes remained strong, but more and more Jews turned to craft work. In Iraq, however, Jewish merchants enjoyed renewed prosperity in the nineteenth century under British patronage; they dominated the trade of Baghdad and Basra with India.

A major factor in the decline of Jewish economic activities was competition from Greeks, Armenians, and Syrian Christians of both Eastern and Roman Catholic denominations. In the eighteenth century, these communities entered the international trade as the preferred middlemen of the Europeans and sent their children to be educated in Western Europe. They took over prominent positions as merchants, financiers, translators, and court physicians. In Cairo, Jews had served since the Ottoman conquest as moneylenders, customs officers, and masters of Cairo's mint;

but in 1768 a new ruler, Bulut Kapan ʿAli Pasha, removed Jews from their positions in the customs office, confiscated their wealth, and executed several leading figures. Syrian Catholics replaced Jews in the customs house and as translators for the European merchants. Armenians took the post of customs inspector in Aleppo in 1831, and by the mid-nineteenth century, Christian Arabs replaced Jews in the customs house of Damascus.

Within the empire, Jews were organized into local congregations (*kahal* or *jamaʿat*) under the authority of both lay and religious leaders who managed communal educational, legal, and tax concerns. Small congregations were sometimes united in citywide communities. In the seventeenth century, the independent rabbinic courts of Istanbul were consolidated into three district courts united under a single supreme court. Similarly, in Salonica, the Jewish communities built a central school, hospital, and charitable complex. Jews, unlike Christians, had no formal representative to the Ottoman government but were represented by court favorites and special envoys. In the eighteenth century, the title of chief rabbi emerged, but it was often held by more than one person. In 1835, the Ottomans finally designated a *haham basi*, a chief rabbi.

In accord with Ottoman recognition of the civil law of non-Muslims, Jewish courts were permitted to function in all matters except criminal cases that involved a death penalty. From the Ottoman point of view, cases involving Jews brought to Jewish courts were matters of arbitration. Jews turned to Jewish courts for not only religious but also family and commercial issues. Jewish courts were effective as long as Jewish litigants themselves did not refuse their judgments, for they always had the option of appealing to Ottoman courts. Jews went to Muslim courts for marriage, divorce, inheritance, and commercial cases.

The persecutions of the late seventeenth century led to a profound upheaval in Jewish identity. Great numbers of Jews became followers of the self-declared messiah Shabbatai Zvi and converted to Islam when he did so in 1665. The converts, known as Donme, formed a separate community that observed Muslim customs (such as praying in mosques and fasting during Ramadan), but held private beliefs in Shabbatai Zvi as the messiah, performed rituals from the kabala, and prayed in Hebrew and Ladino (the Judeo-Spanish dialect). They married only within their community and buried the dead in their own cemeteries. Nonetheless, in the nineteenth century, while Christian communities in the Balkans and the Arab provinces turned to nationalism, Jews remained attached to their religio-communal and Ottoman identities.

Greek Orthodox and Armenian Christians

The Christian populations of the empire were extremely diverse. In Istanbul, Christians spoke the languages of their ancestral roots. Orthodox Christians spoke Greek or Slavic languages, and Armenians spoke Armenian. In the Balkans, Orthodox and Armenian Christians spoke Turkish, and in the Arab provinces the Christians

generally spoke Arabic. Most Christians were considered part of the Eastern Orthodox Church, which included Greek, Romanian, Slavic, and Arab believers. In
Ottoman parlance, the Orthodox speakers of Slavic, Romance, Semitic, and other
languages – whether in Europe, Asia, or Africa – were all described as "Rum"
(literally Roman), designating them as Greek Orthodox.

Mehmed, the conqueror of Constantinople, appointed Gennadius as patriarch
and, in principle, subordinated the Slavic churches to the patriarchate of Constantinople. In addition to collecting taxes for the Ottomans, the Orthodox Church
had authority over and managed church lands, education, and the legal institutions
of the Orthodox community. Church courts dealt with births, deaths, marriages,
and other civil issues. By the end of the seventeenth century, the Greek merchant
elite of Istanbul, the Phanariots, chose patriarchs and administered the church's
internal affairs. The authority of the patriarch of Constantinople outside of the capital, however, was never clearly defined but rather evolved gradually over time.
In the eighteenth century, the church attempted to convert the local authority of
the patriarch of Constantinople into an empire-wide authority. The independent
patriarchates of Ohrid (Bulgaria) and Pech (Serbia) were abolished in 1766 and
1767.

The Armenian Church in the Ottoman Empire was a separate administrative
body founded in 1461. In 1441, the catholicos of the Armenian Church moved to
Persia, and, in response, the Ottomans established two new centers in Istanbul and
Jerusalem, appointing a patriarch for each. With the growth of the Istanbul Armenian population, the patriarch of Istanbul was able to dominate the entire church.
The Armenian patriarch was responsible for tax collection and civil administration
and, in principle, was the administrative authority for the non-Orthodox Christians
of the Ottoman Empire – Miaphysites in Syria and Egypt, Assyrians, the Bogomils
of Bosnia, and Copts.

Although in Anatolia most Armenians were peasants, in Istanbul, Izmir, Aleppo,
and Basra they prospered in international trade. By the nineteenth century, they
had become supervisors of customs houses, bankers to local pashas, purveyors of
luxury goods, and minters of coins, as well as long-distance merchants. An Armenian lay elite (*amiras*) came to dominate the church and influence the Ottoman
selection of patriarchs.

Coptic Christians

Egyptian non-Muslims included Melkites, Armenians, Jews, and later a growing
community of Syrian Catholics, but the majority were Copts. Over the centuries
since the Arab conquests and especially in the Mamluk period, the Coptic population had been drastically reduced by conversion and waves of persecution to a
small minority of the total population. According to one visitor, in the years 1530–
40, there were only seven Orthodox churches in Egypt – four in Cairo and one

each in Alexandria, Damietta, and Raithou. In the Ottoman period, conversions to Islam seem to have been rare.

The majority of Copts were farmers and village craftsmen. In the towns, Copts worked as goldsmiths and jewelers, shoemakers, masons, engravers, carpenters, weavers, tailors, furriers, construction workers, laborers, candlemakers, and purveyors of wines and distilled alcoholic drinks (especially *'araq*). Copts were employed as bureaucrats, financial and tax administrators, secretaries, and stewards to the political elite. In the eighteenth century, they staffed the households of the leading military officers and tax farmers.

The Coptic Church was hierarchical. The patriarch appointed the metropolitans of Ethiopia, Damietta, and Jerusalem, and the bishops below them. Bishops commonly purchased their positions. They ordained the priests, consecrated churches and altars, administered the finances of their dioceses, and helped care for the poor. A Coptic priest could be married so long as his marriage took place before ordination. Coptic monks were laymen and, apart from those who were appointed bishops and patriarchs, were not considered clergy.

As in the Orthodox and Armenian churches, the lay elite (archons) came to rival the clergy and often to dominate church affairs. They made large contributions to charity and religious affairs, and they had political connections to the Mamluk military elite.

Despite these internal conflicts, the Coptic Church preserved the identity of Coptic Egyptian Christians. The Coptic Church perceived two main challenges: Muslim influences and the competition of Catholic missionaries. Copts began to adopt Muslim practices. They circumcised their sons around the age of ten and would eat only properly slaughtered meat. They participated in religious festivals with Muslims and Jews. In the sixteenth century, Copts turned to Sufis for blessings and miracles. At the same time, Catholic missionaries – backed by the riches and prestige of European states and merchants – sought to proselytize the Coptic population and converted the wealthy and the intelligentsia. In the eighteenth century, Syrian Catholics came as traders to Damietta and Rosetta, and by the end of the century they controlled the coastal trade between Syria and Egypt and along the Red Sea coast. By the mid-nineteenth century, they were eclipsed by Greek merchants.

In response to these pressures, the Coptic clergy promoted the beliefs and ceremonies that kept Coptic commitments alive. The church promoted a cult of martyrs, the veneration of saints, and pilgrimage to and religious festivals at Coptic shrines and sanctuaries. The clergy preached homilies and sermons to discourage conversion to Islam or Catholicism and to promote uniformity in Coptic beliefs and practices. The archons patronized Coptic scholarship and sponsored a renaissance of architectural, literary, and artistic projects. Manuscripts were copied and restored; icons were produced for churches and homes.

Christians in the Ottoman Near East

The Christian population of geographical Syria at the time of the Ottoman conquest is variously estimated at between 20 percent and 35 percent of the total population. Christians centered around Aleppo, Damascus, Tripoli, and Tyre with concentrations on Mount Lebanon and the villages surrounding Jerusalem, Bethlehem, and Nazareth. The populations of the major cities grew substantially in the seventeenth century. Palestinian Christian villagers moved to Jerusalem, and, by the nineteenth century, villages that had been Christian in the sixteenth century were Muslim. Most of these Christians were Arabic-speaking Greek Orthodox, known as Melkites. The Ottoman conquests made the patriarchs of Alexandria, Antioch, and Jerusalem administratively subordinate to the patriarch of Constantinople. The Orthodox patriarchate of Jerusalem supervised the holy places in constant struggle with other Christian churches. The Jacobites – Aramaic speaking and much depleted in number by earlier conversions – were concentrated in the Jazira of northern Iraq and southeastern Turkey, with large numbers in Aleppo, Damascus, and Urfa. Aramaic-speaking Nestorians inhabited Kurdistan and Mosul.

The most important religious development among Christians was the spread of Catholicism. The Maronites of the Lebanon were the first Christian communities to accept the authority of Rome, although they retained their rites and dogma. In 1584, a Maronite college was established in Rome under Jesuit auspices.

The spread of Catholicism was fostered by treaties between the Ottomans and the European countries. The French-Ottoman treaty of 1604 gave Catholic pilgrims and priests the right to visit the holy places in Palestine and permission for French clerics to reside in Jerusalem. A treaty of 1673 accorded diplomatic status to priests serving the French consuls in Galata, Izmir, Sidon, and Alexandria, and other cities. In 1690, with the help of the French ambassador in Istanbul, Catholic missionaries were permitted to preach in Ottoman territories. These and later treaties allowed the Europeans to designate local translators and agents who would enjoy the same favorable customs rates as the Europeans themselves. France was named guardian of the holy places, and other European powers then claimed to be the protectors of Ottoman non-Muslims. The Russians claimed the Orthodox; the French adopted the Catholics. Britain and Prussia competed for the small Protestant communities and the Jews.

In the seventeenth century, Catholics began to proselytize openly in the Ottoman Empire. Colleges were founded in Rome to educate Eastern students. Schools and hospitals were founded in Ottoman domains. The missionary effort included the adoption of the vernacular languages of the Christian populations (Greek, Arabic, Coptic, Syriac, and Armenian) for teaching and preaching, and the composition or translation of Catholic religious works into these languages. To spread the new dogma, in 1706 the Metropolitan Athanasios Dabbas established in Aleppo the first Arabic printing press in the Ottoman Empire. New monastic orders were founded in the Lebanon. Catholic missionaries were much appreciated for the practical education they provided and for involving women in parish activities. Many women converted to Catholicism apart from their husbands or other male relatives. Economically upwardly mobile Christians, disillusioned with the traditional churches, found encouragement in the Catholic Church.

Catholicism appealed particularly to the Orthodox merchants of Aleppo. To prosper in the Mediterranean trade, they needed strong European patrons. French consuls – working in parallel with missionaries – helped promote conversions by protecting Syrian Christian merchants and issuing berats that gave them legal and diplomatic status and reduced tariffs. Catholic Arabs would hold the post of dragoman in Aleppo throughout the eighteenth century. In Aleppo, missionaries succeeded in converting the majority of native Orthodox and Jacobite Christians.

The unsettled political conditions of the eighteenth century gave rise to both intense competition among religious-commercial communities and political alliances across the sectarian divides. In Egypt, Syrian Catholics replaced Jews working for the European merchants and displaced Muslims in the Cairo and coastal trade. The improved position of the Catholic merchants in the Arab Levant also came at the expense of Jewish bankers and merchants. Rivalry between Catholic and Jewish merchants flared in Palestine in the eighteenth century. In the nineteenth century, Aleppo Armenians regained control of the custom revenues from Jews.

There was financial and political collaboration between Muslims and Christians. Muslims realized that non-Muslims could provide financial assistance; non-Muslims understood that politically powerful Muslims could assure their safety, access to opportunity, and continued economic prosperity. By the end of the eighteenth century, the leading Muslim families in Aleppo were allied with equally prominent Catholic families. The Catholics supplied the bankers, business partners, and even political agents in Istanbul for their Muslim associates. The Muslims brought Catholics into the tax farming business. In Mosul, Christian businessmen sought the patronage of Muslim warlords.

The rise of Syrian Catholicism led to profound changes in the organization and relations of the several Christian churches. Pope Benedict XIII (r. 1724–30) was the first pope to recognize the communion of the Melkite Catholics with Rome. Henceforth, the Melkite Church was divided between the Orthodox patriarchs appointed by the patriarch of Istanbul and the Catholic pope. Only the Catholics continued to use the title Melkite. In current usage, the term refers to Arabic-speaking Catholics. In the course of the eighteenth century, similar splits occurred among the Armenians and other churches that accepted the authority of Rome. The Uniate churches included the Melkite Catholic Church of Antioch, the Maronite Church, the Chaldean Catholic Church (which grew out of the Nestorians), and the Armenian Catholic Church and Catholics in Hungary, Croatia, and Albania. The Uniate churches kept their liturgies, calendars, and holidays. Their clergy retained the right to marry. However, in the Uniate churches, Arabic began to replace Greek, Syriac, and Armenian.

The rupture in the churches was ratified by the Ottoman authorities, who recognized the Catholics as constituting a separate millet in Aleppo, although not in the empire at large. The Armenian Catholic Church was recognized as an autonomous millet in 1831. Throughout the Ottoman provinces, the strong authority of the Roman pontiff subverted the influence of the patriarch of Constantinople and greatly reduced the autonomy of the Eastern patriarchs.

A still more profound and lasting impact on the Christian communities was the transformation from millet to secular and national identities. The identification with Western Europe, Catholicism, and "modernity" led to new political identities. For example, the long struggle of Syrian Christians with the Greek authorities in their millet led them to think of themselves first as Syrians and then as Arabs. The millets functioned as both administrative entities and social communities, joining people who shared both religion and language and making it possible to imagine a national identity.

The millets also empowered new classes of the population – rural notables, commercial entrepreneurs, and secular intellectuals and professionals – for whom a national identity could be a route to political and economic power. Lay elites defined in ethnic and secular terms displaced clerical elites and increasingly defined a secular political identity for their co-religionists. At first, in alignment with the program of the Ottoman Tanzimat, this was an Ottoman citizen identity, but progressively Ottomanism was displaced by an Arab nationalism. The emergence of new elites made it possible to redefine the cultural union of religion and language as the basis of ethnic and national identity. These changes corresponded to broader, global changes as nationalism replaced religion and localism as the most important expression of social and political identity.

MUSLIM COMMUNITIES

The Muslim masses, as a subject (*re'aya*) population, were organized in a parallel way. They were grouped in families, residential units (such as villages or town quarters), merchant and craft associations, and religious communities. Each group was represented by its elders and headman, who were responsible for order and for the payment of taxes. The schools of law and the Sufi brotherhoods were the framework for popular religious associations. Ordinary people looked to – and sometimes loyally followed – the scholars, teachers, and judges for leadership in ritual, law, and communal matters. Even more potent were their allegiances to Sufi *shaykhs*.

From the earliest Ottoman times, the Bektashis, the Central Asian-Indian Naqshbandis, and the Anatolian Halvetis had widespread popular support. Sufi *babas* mobilized bands of Turkish warriors and led them to holy war, protected travelers, and mediated in disputes. Wandering dervishes, called Malamatiyya or Qalandariyya, who openly disregarded Islamic law and opposed contact with government authorities, were nonetheless venerated by rural people as bearers of God's blessings and of magical powers. Sufis attracted landless and dispossessed peasants in the countryside and artisans, traders, and merchants in the towns.

The Bektashis were among the most influential of these Sufis. Hajji Bektash, the founder of the order, probably lived toward the end of the thirteenth century. According to legend, he and some forty followers set up hospices (*tekkes*) throughout eastern Anatolia and among Turkomans in Macedonia, Thessaly, and the Rhodope. Bektashis spread throughout Anatolia and the Balkans in the course of the fifteenth century. Around 1500, Balim Sultan organized the rituals of the order and perfected its system of hospices. The Bektashis were strongly influenced by both Shi'ism and Christianity. They took the sixth imam, Ja'far, as their patron saint; venerated the trinity of God, Muhammad, and 'Ali; offered bread and wine in initiation ceremonies; and required celibacy of their teachers. They taught that there were four levels of religious belief: *shari'a*, adherence to the law; *tariqa*, initiation in special ceremonies to the Sufi order; *ma'rifa*, understanding of the truth; and *haqiqa*, the direct experience of the divine reality. Initiates were introduced progressively to the secret knowledge and ceremonies of the group.

The Bektashis, although unorthodox, were taken under the wing of the Ottomans as chaplains to the janissaries. They lived and marched with the soldiers, providing them with magical protection in battle. This resulted in the order's spread throughout eastern Anatolia and among Turkish migrants in Macedonia and Albania.

Many rural Sufis were politically important because they could inspire resistance to the state. Eastern Anatolia, like northwestern Iran, was a breeding ground for Sufi messianic beliefs and Sufi-led revolts against state domination. For example, in central Anatolia and the Balkans, Bedreddin (d. 1416) denied the literal truth of heaven and hell, the day of judgment, the resurrection of the body, the creation of the world, and other basic tenets of Muslim belief. The Hurufiyya (whose doctrine spread among both Muslims and Christians in Anatolia and Bulgaria at the end of the fourteenth century) preached that the only rightful income was that earned by manual work. Sufi-led rebellions also occurred in the late fifteenth century. In 1519, a preacher named Jelal took the name of Shah Isma'il, claimed to be the messiah (Mahdi), and attracted Turkish cultivator and pastoralist opposition to the imposition of taxes. An early sixteenth-century wave of revolts was closely related to Safavid agitation and the opposition of eastern Anatolian peoples to the Ottoman-Sunni regime. The Ottoman-Safavid conflict exaggerated the differences between Sunnis and Shi'is, and the persecution of the Shi'is in the Ottoman Empire became routine in the fifteenth and sixteenth centuries.

Anatolian resistance was fostered by Turkish folk culture. Itinerant minstrel poets (*saz shairi*) toured villages, singing of the struggles of the Turks against

the Georgians, Circassians, and Byzantines and celebrating the virtues of Turkish peoples. Epic poetry was translated into shadow-play theater (*karagoz*). Sufi
poets, such as the influential Yunus Emre (d. 1329), gave expression to popular
literary and religious culture. Poets traveled with soldiers, sang in camps, enter-
tained people at fairs, and conducted contests that were the basis of an Anatolian folk consciousness. The heritage of nomadic populations, independent states,
and Sufi brotherhoods separated the Anatolian provinces from the capital city
elites.

Alongside the rural Sufis, urban religious orders also flourished in Anatolia and
the Balkans. The Mevlevis were spiritually descended from Mawlana Jalal al-Din
Rumi (d. 1273) and have become universally known for their ceremonial dancing
as the whirling dervishes. Apart from their ceremonial function, Mevlevi *tekkes*
were also important for the study of Persian literature and Sufi thought, and for
the education of the Ottoman bureaucratic elite. They attracted many intellectuals,
poets, scholars, bureaucrats, and rich merchants in Istanbul. The Mevlevis were
similarly tied to the Ottoman state; they acquired the right to gird a sultan with a
holy sword on his accession. Naqshbandis and Khalwatis were also influential and
active Sufi orders.

In the course of the fifteenth and sixteenth centuries, the Ottomans succeeded in
domesticating the major Sufi brotherhoods without entirely eliminating the independent influence of Sufi teachers. The state co-opted Sufi *tekkes* by providing
them with permanent endowments and gifts for charitable purposes, but many
Sufis remained skeptical and even hostile to the bureaucratization of the religious
elites.

WOMEN AND FAMILY IN THE OTTOMAN ERA (1400–1800)
(CO-AUTHOR, LENA SALAYMEH)

Ottoman-era literatures reveal a continuity with the mores of earlier Middle Eastern societies ('Abbasid, Fatimid, and Mamluk) but provide more abundant source
materials and reveal new dimensions of family, male-female relations, and sexuality. In previous sections, we discussed the divergences between the cultural and
legal systems espoused by religious elites and the actualities of women's lives. In
the Ottoman era too, women were expected to obey and defer to men, to be veiled
and unobtrusive in public, and to attend to the needs of husbands and households.
Yet we find the same gap between religious and social norms and the real world of
family, sexuality, and property. Although the dominant social norms did not favor
women, women nonetheless had considerable leeway to maneuver in society; their
situations varied greatly by historical context and social class. Upper-class women
were more likely to be secluded, but they also had greater access to financial,
educational, and political resources. Lower-class women had comparatively more
mobility, but more difficult daily lives.

The royal family and harem were defined by very special circumstances. The Ottoman harem was a part of the Topkapi Palace, kept exclusively as a residence for the sultan's wives, concubines, female relatives, and servants. The harem was based on a widespread and long-standing Middle Eastern and Mediterranean practice of keeping aristocratic and elite women within the household, a practice then extended to all female relatives. The harem was open only to the sultan and his eunuchs and was invisible to the outside world. However, seclusion did not imply that the royal women were cut off from the world of power, money, or culture. It was considered not a confinement but a protection from the profane world and a sign of prestige and honor.

The royal household was further marked by an intricate nexus of freedom and slavery. The wives of sultans were legally married free women, but many of the sultans' consorts were concubines. Until the late fifteenth century, Ottoman sultans typically married both Muslim and non-Muslim royal and noble women from the dominant Anatolian and Balkan dynasties and in turn gave the men from these dynasties royal daughters in marriage. These marriages fostered close political ties, but they also generated rivalry among the sons of different mothers and warfare among the sons fighting to succeed to the sultanate. To increase family and political stability, the Ottomans determined first that only the eldest son was entitled to succession and then that Ottoman sultans would restrict sexual relations to concubines – wives were henceforth celibate – and limit each concubine to a single male child. This gave great political power to concubines, who accompanied their sons when they were appointed as provincial governors. This practice was changed by Suleyman, whose concubine, Hurrem, had more than one son with Suleyman and remained in Istanbul with the sultan when her sons were appointed as provincial governors. She assumed the role of queen mother on Suleyman's death, initiating a practice that became prevalent in the late sixteenth and seventeenth centuries.

Women in the royal household enjoyed great political power and economic privileges. They maintained family and political connections with Ottoman allies and Ottoman nobles and officials and sometimes played an active role in diplomatic and political negotiations. This may have been a specifically Ottoman phenomenon, because there is no parallel in the Safavid and Mughal empires. Moreover, royal women were richly provided with properties and, as did royal women in an earlier era, generously funded endowments for educational and charitable purposes – endowments that gave them a network of social and political contacts in the wider society. Still, there were limits to these powers, because women did not have access to official positions from which they could rival high-ranking men in the accumulation of property and power.

The lives of middle-class and working women continued some of the patterns of earlier times. Women in these classes commonly possessed property and earned their own living. In the seventeenth and eighteenth centuries, the expansion and commercialization of the Ottoman economy and the engagement of the Ottoman

Empire in the world trading economy resulted in increased jobs in coastal cities and factories, which in turn gave many women increased mobility, earning power, and independence. Ordinary women inherited and received dowers and other gifts of property and land. They acted as landlords and moneylenders, had businesses and jobs, and earned and lent money. There was also a female economy in things valued by women.

Family inheritance and property practices differed in different parts of the empire. In Anatolian towns, women generally inherited cash, cloth, or jewelry. Family real estate was typically sold for the proceeds to be divided among the heirs. In Cairo and Aleppo, however, women created and administered educational, charitable, and familial trusts (*awqaf*). In eighteenth-century Cairo, women endowed 25 percent of trusts; in eighteenth-century Aleppo, women endowed between 30 and 40 percent of trusts. Women were sometimes the executors (*mutawali*) of trusts, if they stood in the line of appointed successors to a dead husband, son, or brother.

Furthermore, wealth and earnings gave women social and familial advantages. Divorces at the initiative of women (known as *khul'*) were more prevalent, as women sought to end unhappy marriages by relinquishing some of their financial rights. Women could exchange property for protection and support. Still, wherever property was considered a collective resource and household and kinship ties were strong, women were vulnerable to family pressures and could be deprived of property by male relatives.

The Ottoman legal system and the family

The Ottoman legal system continued the Islamic legal tradition, which allowed for great variability in practice. Courts responded to the realities of peoples' lives rather than strictly applying legal or cultural norms. Court records indicate that judges were flexible in their adjudication of family issues, implementing a variety of custody practices and often providing financial support for women in cases of divorce. Some examples from specific places and times reflect a great variety of practices that favored women and were prevalent throughout the Ottoman Empire. In seventeenth-century Cairo, a woman could stipulate in her marriage contract that her husband could not take a second wife. In eighteenth-century Aleppo, mothers and matrilineal female relatives were awarded custody of children in more than 50 percent of the known cases – despite the availability of patrilineal guardians. Support for pregnant or divorced women was greater in practice than legal texts suggest. The prescribed waiting period (*'idda*) helped assure paternal responsibility. Widows were often granted guardianship of children's inheritances or the right to use a child's inheritance, rather than the mother's own money, for support of the child. The courts commonly helped women keep their inheritances and gave them and maternal relatives guardianship of children. Children born of widows long periods after the deaths of husbands were assigned the paternity of the deceased spouse. Courts recognized a woman's claims to debts owed to her by a deceased husband. Parents of children conceived or born out of wedlock were allowed to marry without punishment. Court records also suggest that judges did not require or enforce seclusion of women. Seventeenth- and eighteenth-century legal opinions from Syria and Palestine indicate that even though judges believed in the gender superiority of men, they helped women by enforcing their rights and widening the grounds for divorce or annulment at the woman's initiative.

Local judges sometimes ignored Ottoman state law and looked to the several legal school traditions to find interpretations that seemed best suited to the cases they were adjudicating. The law schools differed considerably in their norms for family relations and could be manipulated to gain advantages in given situations. For example, although Malikis insisted on a guardian for a first marriage, Hanafis allowed women to marry by themselves. Whereas Hanafis gave little leeway for annulment, Malikis allowed it for desertion, nonmaintenance, or bodily harm.

The courts served a broad spectrum of the population. Upper-class women were less likely to go to court, but if they or their representative did so, they had advantages due to family and social networks, economic assets, and education. Eighteenth-century Ottoman court records include female petitioners from the countryside, which suggests a degree of state centralization that allowed appeals to the center against provincial officials and a favorable attitude toward women's needs.

Non-Muslim women frequented Ottoman courts for marital, divorce, and property issues when the Ottoman courts were more likely to favor their interests than Christian or Jewish courts. Ottoman court decisions were also more likely to be enforced. Jewish women benefited from the advantages of Islamic law in matters of inheritance. Also, a non-Muslim woman who wanted a divorce not granted by a husband or wanted to remarry, escape from a husband's decision to marry a second wife, or avoid punishment for adultery had the option of converting to Islam. By converting, a woman would automatically be divorced from a non-Muslim husband.

Freedom and slavery

As in earlier eras, women's mobility varied according to class, age, and other circumstances. In addition to employment, events such as religious festivals and other celebrations provided opportunities for women to leave domestic spaces. In eighteenth-century Cairo and Mosul, for example, women visited tombs and took part in Sufi ceremonies. Eighteenth-century miniatures depict women in public situations, including ceremonies, processions, visits to tombs, and pilgrimage. Female poets participated in the general culture. Although many women wore veils in public spaces, veiling provided a certain anonymity that could be liberating.

Slavery was a significant aspect of both the Ottoman economy and Ottoman society. Slave women differed in social status and mobility depending on their specific socio-legal category, whether concubines, mothers of free children, or manumitted slaves. Generally, slaves who had children with their owners were equivalent in status to wives. If the father acknowledged paternity, his children were legally recognized and given full inheritance rights. Jews and Christians also owned slaves, sometimes including Muslim slaves – although by law a non-Muslim would have to sell a slave who converted to Islam to a Muslim.

Family and sexuality

Economic developments and the decentralization and redistribution of political power in the eighteenth century had important ramifications for family life, socio-sexual mores, and even sexual identities. In traditional patriarchal and patrilineal households, elder males were the dominant authority, and older women – especially mothers – exerted strong influence over their sons. A young bride was commonly subject to the authority of, and perhaps abuse by, her mother-in-law but could become a dominant mother-in-law in turn. Ottoman and Egyptian women who married into extended families often stipulated protective conditions in their marriage contracts, such as assurances against domestic violence or the husband taking a second wife without their consent.

Moreover, contrary to common assumptions about Ottoman or Islamic patriarchy, there is much evidence that matrilineal relationships were as important as patrilineal ones, suggesting a relatively bilateral kinship system. Bilateral kinship appears to have been informally recognized in previous eras, as demonstrated in biographical literature, but became more prominent in the eighteenth century. Women were often married to maternal kin and maintained close emotional, financial, and property ties to their natal families. Natal families continued to support their daughters and sisters – brothers and sisters were typically closely bonded – after their marriages and, if need be, after divorces. Divorced women tended to remarry quickly. Family instability and frequent divorces and remarriages were compensated by bilateral family ties that remained important throughout the life cycle. In addition, scholars of eighteenth-century families have found that men were increasingly identified with their wives' families, especially if the wife came from a family of high status. Tombstones show a new fluidity in the way people identified their ancestors. Wives' names appear; men sometimes link themselves to women's patriline. Ottomans were creating their own lineages.

Eighteenth-century Ottoman households varied considerably according to region and class. We find both extended families and natal units, sometimes living in a house of their own within a compound and sometimes living in nuclear units. Divorced or widowed women often remarried, and women raised children from previous marriages in their new households. In the early modern period, there was a growing tendency toward the formation of nuclear families marked by affection and concern for the security of women. Earning opportunities and mobility favored the small family unit. The early modern trend toward couple autonomy and single-family homes would become more pronounced in the nineteenth century.

There were a variety of discourses shaping the Ottoman-era practices of sexuality. Although we do not have sufficient historical evidence to compare the Ottoman with the pre-Ottoman period, it seems likely that Ottoman sexual norms continued earlier practices and beliefs. Although religious scholars defined adultery and fornication by unmarried men and women as serious crimes and condemned homoerotic sexual relations, in practice Ottoman norms attached no shame to sex, viewed men and women as having the same sexual nature, and accepted both hetero- and homoerotic relations as normal. Ottoman state law (*kanun*) tended to equalize the treatment of men and women and of hetero- and homosexuals. Medical discourse, based on Galen and the humoral theory of the body, held that men and women have the same nature, blurring the distinction between hetero- and homosexual behaviors. Dream interpretation literature accepted both homo- and heterosexuality as natural. In the puppet theater, both men and women are portrayed as avidly sexual, and women as independent and assertive. The principle character (*karagoz*) is married and has children, but he chases women, has both active and passive homosexual sex, and cross-dresses. Furthermore, Sufi mystics sought spiritual inspiration by gazing on youthful male beauty. Homoerotic relations between an older man and a beardless youth – especially between a Sufi master and his disciples – were widely considered desirable, although the growing eighteenth-century Islamic reform movement rejected Sufi practices.

An important change would occur in the nineteenth century, as European ideas about sexual differences of men and women and a more judgmental tone – distinguishing natural and unnatural, normal and abnormal, and Christian and heathen forms of sexuality – led to attacks on the Ottomans for the seclusion and the promiscuity of women, sodomy, homoerotic relations, and lurid theater. This discourse connected the weakness and corruption of Ottoman government to Ottoman sexual corruption. By the 1850s, European ideas were driving Ottoman discourses into self-censorship. There was a Victorian-like regression in the autonomy of women. An embarrassed silence descended on Ottoman sexual discourses. Homoerotic love became shameful. Dream books virtually disappeared. The puppet theater was toned down. The hetero-normalization of sexuality was reinforced by massive sociopolitical changes, such as the centralization of state power, the breakdown of small communities, and the emergence of the nuclear family.

CHAPTER 32

THE POSTCLASSICAL OTTOMAN EMPIRE:
DECENTRALIZATION, COMMERCIALIZATION,
AND INCORPORATION

In the late sixteenth, seventeenth, and eighteenth centuries, foreign wars interacted with domestic political and economic problems to bring about profound changes in the Ottoman system. The pressures of war, internal social and demographic crises, and the commercialization and monetization of the economy led to new political institutions.

After centuries of conquests, the Ottomans reached a stalemate with the Portuguese in the Indian Ocean and the Habsburgs in the Mediterranean. The Austrian war of 1593–1606 showed that further Ottoman expansion was blocked. As the Ottomans reached further into central and northern Europe, logistical difficulties hampered their campaigns. A new premium was being placed on infantry armed with gunpowder weapons, muskets, and cannons, fighting from entrenched positions. As firearms and organized infantry became ever more important, the Ottoman cavalry (*sipahis*) could no longer resist German riflemen. Western economies could better afford the costs of war. Moreover, from the 1680s to the 1730s, the Ottomans became dependent on Albanian, Bosnian, Kurdish, Cossack, Tatar, Georgian, and Circassian auxiliaries who were not as well disciplined, trained, and armed as the traditional Ottoman forces.

In the late seventeenth century, both the Habsburg and the Russian empires expanded at Ottoman expense. For the first time, the European powers pushed back the frontiers of the Ottoman Empire. An Ottoman siege of Vienna failed in 1683, and the Habsburgs seized most of Hungary north of the Danube, Serbia, Transylvania, Croatia, and Slovenia. The Venetians took Dalmatia and the Morea. Poland invaded Podolia and the Ukraine. Russia, under Peter the Great, with its armies newly modernized, took Azov in the Crimea in 1696. The Ottomans, however, were able to restore their territorial positions with gains in Eastern Europe and the Black Sea.

In the late eighteenth century, however, Russian expansion resumed. Between 1768 and 1774, the Russians occupied Romania and the Crimea and by the treaty of Kuchuk Kaynarca (1774) achieved access to the Black Sea. A new series of wars, culminating in the Peace of Jassy (1792), allowed the Russians to advance to the Dniester River, to establish a protectorate over Georgia, and to consolidate its position in the Crimea. In 1798, Napoleon invaded Egypt.

The losses in foreign wars were partly due to domestic problems. In the late sixteenth century the Ottoman military system was breaking down. As early as the 1530s, there was evidence that *timars* (the grants of tax revenues from land to support soldiers) were becoming hereditary – contrary to the original intention of reserving control in the hands of the sultan. By the end of the century, further corruption in the system of grants of land income was evident in evasion of duties, assignments of *timars* to the protégés of high-ranking officials, and banditry by displaced *sipahis*. The discipline and loyalty of the janissaries were also compromised, in part due to falling incomes. As it ceased to expand, the empire ceased to acquire booty. After 1580, inflation, possibly due to the influx of American silver and certainly due to the debasement of Ottoman coinage, also reduced the value of Ottoman incomes. Inadequately paid soldiers and officials seized provincial lands and diverted the revenues for their private benefit.

Moreover, in response to political unrest, janissaries were stationed in towns and fortresses to suppress rebellion and criminality. They soon became enmeshed in local communities, took control of artisan associations, engaged in trade and crafts to supplement their incomes, married and established families, and then promoted their own children into the military corps. They became resistant to military service and used their political and military clout to extract gifts and privileges from the sultans. Janissaries soon formed an exploitative class living off illegal tax revenues. Close ties among janissaries, artisans, and scholars made it politically impossible to control the soldiers. Discipline in the army was reduced to such an extent that there were pay riots in 1622 and 1631, accompanied by the looting of Istanbul. In the following century and a half, janissary rebellions supported by artisans and scholars became almost an ordinary political event. Rebellious janissaries brought down ministers and sultans. The abandonment of the *devshirme*, the draft of Christian youths for military and court service, in 1637 made it impossible to redress these trends.

The political and military crises coincided with long-term social and economic crises. Late fifteenth- and sixteenth-century inflation raised prices and reduced the real incomes of peasants, *timar* holders, salaried soldiers, and the state. The sixteenth century also saw the beginnings of a long period of population growth, landlessness, and rural unrest. The end of Ottoman conquests in Hungary and Iran forced displaced cavalrymen and demobilized irregular infantry to return to their villages and towns. They were joined by peasants fleeing excessive taxation, footloose students, unemployed drifters, and bandits, who provided the manpower for a series of revolts between 1595 and 1610, known as the Jelali rebellions. The Jelali rebellions were led by lower-ranking military and administrative officers and were supported by commoners, fighting to gain a share of the privileges allotted to the slave forces. Jelali rebels aimed at being bought off, and the Ottoman authorities managed them by alternately paying and suppressing them. By the end of the sixteenth century, the Ottoman state had begun to adapt to the weakening of its janissary and cavalry forces by recruiting bandit gangs, peasant militias, ethnic auxiliaries, and the retainers of provincial notables for its armies.

These developments weakened the state but increased the power of the common people. Peasants moved into villages clustered around fortified manor houses and were often permitted to arm themselves for defense against bandits. This strengthened local community ties and encouraged the emergence of a stronger peasant leadership. In many parts of the Balkans, the weakening of Ottoman central authority led to a three-way struggle for power among provincial officeholding and landowning notables, janissaries and artisans, and peasant bandits.

COMMERCIALIZATION

At the same time, there were important changes in the trading and commercial economy. After centuries of increasing Ottoman power and economic advantages in the Black Sea, the Mediterranean, and the Indian Ocean, Western European powers were gaining the upper hand. Whereas in the sixteenth century the Ottomans had fended off the Portuguese intrusion into the Indian Ocean, in the seventeenth and eighteenth centuries the Dutch and the British took control of the spice trade in Asia and diverted most of it to Atlantic routes. The silk trade further declined as the demand for cotton textiles rose. The Atlantic countries also profited from the production and sale of woolen cloths and metals, the enormous expansion of trade with the Americas, and the substitution of Western for Eastern sources of colonial sugar, tobacco, and cotton. The Ottomans, however, remained active in the trade of Indian cotton goods and dyes and in control of the growing coffee trade from Yemen through Egypt to Istanbul and from Istanbul to Europe.

Control of the Asian trade helped Europeans build up a strong position in the Mediterranean as well. The Ottoman-French alliance against the Habsburg Empire disposed the Ottomans to give France a monopoly on Ottoman trade. For a time, all European ships had to sail under the French flag. In 1583, however, the British ambassador Harbourne succeeded in negotiating a trade treaty with the Ottoman Empire. The English formed the Levant Company to export cloth and tin, which was essential to make brass for cannon founding, in return for silk, mohair, cotton, wool, carpets, drugs, spices, and indigo. In the seventeenth and eighteenth centuries, competition in the Mediterranean among the French, English, and Dutch was fierce. In the late eighteenth century, France again became the dominant trading partner, but the overall volume of Mediterranean trade was probably declining due to the competition of direct shipments of spices, Indian cloth, and Persian silk to Europe over Atlantic routes. The British East India Company, buying Far Eastern goods at their source and bringing them into the Mediterranean via London, actually became a competitor of the British Levant Company, which depended on the Persian Gulf and Red Sea routes.

Moreover, European merchants penetrated Ottoman markets, especially as the decline of the Eastern trade shifted European interest from Turkey and the Arab provinces to the Balkans. European traders, with the participation of Jewish and Greek intermediaries, brought their imported products to the interior and gathered goods for export. From Salonika, European trade reached Bosnia, Albania, Serbia, and Bulgaria. The English imported luxury cloth; the French, middle-quality cloth. Venice sold silk, satin, and taffeta. The Germans brought paper, tin, iron, copper, sugar, and indigo. European merchants exported wood, cotton, silk, leather, tobacco, beeswax, and hides by sea; cattle went overland from Romania and Hungary into central Europe. Ordinarily the Ottomans prohibited the export of iron, lead, copper, and grain, but there was an active trade in contraband. In the eighteenth century, the French became dominant over other Europeans in the Istanbul market and set up their own corporate structure to strengthen their collective position. They used their influence with the Ottoman state to break the grip of Ottoman merchants and guilds over the local economy.

Changes in trade caused profound changes in the internal Ottoman economy. Some regions suffered while others prospered. Coastal areas expanded production of cotton and rice and introduced maize and tobacco. Parts of western Anatolia and the Adana region went over to cash-crop farming of grain, cotton, silk, and other raw materials for export. In general, silk, printed cottons, and carpet production expanded, but the production of Bursa silk cloth and Ankara mohair woolens fell when Europeans began to replace Turkish textiles with their own manufactures. In the seventeenth and eighteenth centuries, Ottoman consumption was reinforced by the importation of Indian textiles, Far Eastern porcelains, coffee, tobacco, and European luxury cloth goods. The Ottoman Empire was entering into a cosmopolitan consumer culture.

As Baghdad, Cairo, and Aleppo declined, Izmir emerged in the seventeenth century as the principal market for the exchange of Iranian silk for Dutch and English woolens and Italian silks and as a rendezvous for Europeans and local Armenian, Jewish, and Greek merchants. Portuguese Jews dominated tax farming; Ottoman Muslims controlled regional exchange; Greeks handled interregional trade; and Armenians predominated in the silk trade. In the eighteenth century, with European patronage, the Greeks emerged as the most important merchant community.

The Balkan economy flourished. Macedonia became a major exporter of grain and other commodities – such as cotton, livestock, tobacco, and maize. Cotton production increased enormously. Thessaly and Macedonia exported roughly half of their grain, cotton, and tobacco crops. Bulgaria produced cheap woolen cloth for the internal market. As cities grew and craft industries developed, textile production from Greek and Turkish (Muslim and Jewish) manufacturers in Izmir, Salonica, Bursa, Edirne, and Istanbul prospered.

Until the mid-eighteenth century, Ottoman manufactures seemed to have prospered in international trade, but by the last decades of the century Ottoman trade relied on the export of raw materials such as wool, cotton, furs, hides, tobacco, and olive oil. The balance of trade was shifting. As became clearer in the nineteenth century, the Ottoman Empire was increasingly importing manufactured goods and exporting raw materials.

European commercial penetration also subverted Ottoman control of trade and its revenues, helping to transfer political and economic power from the Ottoman state to foreign commercial powers, provincial elites, and non-Muslim merchants. Ethnic factors became crucial to market positions. Away from the coastal areas, Ottoman Muslim merchants controlled local markets, but English, Dutch, and French merchants allied with Greek Orthodox and Armenian merchants and bankers to push aside Jewish and Muslim merchants. The French attacked local monopolies by allying with Jews against Greeks and by mediating their relations with Muslims through the Armenian money changers. Greeks, Albanians, and Serbs gained in commercial prominence. The Phanar Greek financial aristocracy held administrative and economic power in Romania. Non-Muslim traders in Istanbul, Salonica, Izmir, Aleppo, and other important cities strengthened their commercial and cultural ties with counterparts in Livorno, Ancona, Trieste, Leipzig, Vienna, and Lwow.

Thus, economic change contributed to the development of a pluralistic, multicentered economy with substantial foreign involvement. In an earlier era, the empire was able to closely control and tax international trade and to channel the surplus produce of Anatolia to the benefit of the political elite and the populace of Istanbul. Increasing European demand for Ottoman products gave local notables, merchants, and estate owners an incentive to convert tax farms into private estates (*chiftliks*), and to bypass state regulations so as to export surplus produce to Europe. Newly independent tax farmers and local officials redirected the agricultural surpluses from the capital to provincial towns and markets. Furthermore, in the Balkans, a new landlord class made up of Muslim officials, army officers, and rich non-Muslim merchants and other notables raised new crops such as maize, rice, and animals for export, despite the fact that this was illegal under Ottoman regulations. Commercialization also stimulated the growth of towns. Absentee landlords, tax farmers, rich notables, and import-export merchants formed a new urban aristocracy. A provincial economic elite rose to power.

NEW POLITICAL INSTITUTIONS

In the decades from the late sixteenth through the eighteenth centuries, the end of the Ottoman conquests, the breakdown of the old military system, the rise of popular forces, and an increasingly commercialized economy led to profound changes in the Ottoman political system.

The key to political change was the financial system. The stabilization of frontiers meant that the incomes from booty, tributes, and taxes from new regions were lost. New and enlarged infantry forces, however, required increased cash revenue. Whereas European governments typically borrowed from moneylenders or banking houses or sold bonds to meet their revenue needs, the Ottomans attempted to maximize taxation. In the early seventeenth century, they replaced assignment of tax revenues to *timar* holders with direct collection. *Timars* were sold to wealthy investors as tax farms. The empire also levied new taxes on the growing commercial sector (*avariz*) and on the non-Muslim population (*jizya*). With the transformation of the *timar* grants into money tax revenues and the increasing trade with Europe, economic development led to the need for a more monetized economy and eventually for a single Ottoman currency. In tandem with the monetary unification of the economy came the need for a single and centralized system of law. Islamic law became ever more essential for the regulation of property and commercial transactions. The empire was evolving from a feudal to a capitalist type of economy.

Consequently, in the seventeenth century, financiers and merchants rose in political importance, joining the high-ranking military as the elites of the empire. The viziers and the pashas of the finance and scribal bureaucracies fortified their positions by building powerful households on large cadres of subordinate personnel and extensive kinship and clientele networks that rivaled the sultan, the palace hierarchy, and the religious bureaucracy. This development was abetted by the sultan's practice of marrying his daughters and sisters to leading officials. Mehmed Koprulu, a *devshirme* recruit of an Albanian Christian father, who was grand vizier from 1656 to 1661, further consolidated the power of the bureaucrats over the slave elites, undermined the influence of the religious elites by confiscating the properties of the chief judges, and suppressed the Sufi orders. As a result, the households of the leading officers of the state came to be more powerful than the imperial household. The sultans became ever more ceremonial figures. Of the nine sultans who reigned between 1617 and 1730, seven were dethroned. In effect, the Ottoman state had become distinct from the Ottoman dynasty.

The key to the enhanced power of the financial elites was the expansion of tax farming. Tax farming was an arrangement in which anticipated tax revenues were sold to private persons in return for payment in advance. This assured the government of a fixed return but deprived it of incomes exceeding the price of the farms. In 1597, the state converted the *timars* into tax farms. In 1695, tax farms were sold as life tenures (*malikane*). By 1703, lifetime tax farms were in wide use in the Balkans, Anatolia, and the Arab provinces. The state also sold tax farms for the collection of commercial and poll taxes. Eventually, shares in tax farms were sold to the public.

Due to tax farming, the tax bureaucracy dominated the central government. At first, the high-ranking central officials occupied provincial positions as well, but increasingly they appointed deputies (*mutesellim*), many of whom were local notables (*a'yan*) and employed local officials, religious leaders, notables, merchants, and landlords as subcontractors. In Egypt and the Arab provinces, these local elites were Mamluks. In Romania, they were Greek Orthodox merchants from Istanbul. Everywhere, local tax farmers increased their wealth as regional production and trade grew in response to international commerce. They invested in land, urban real estate, and money lending, thus retaining an increasing part of the provincial surplus for local use. As power and wealth shifted to the provinces, the central government depended ever more heavily on them.

In turn, the provincial elites developed their own extended political households, military forces, administrative staffs, and local patronage networks. With bands of peasants, demobilized soldiers, and idle students roaming the country, provincial officials and notables created bodyguards and even small armies. In the Arab provinces, janissary regiments took power. The tax farmers also took over local government by assisting judges and organizing troops for the Ottoman armies. From one point of view, the central government was losing power to its own officials, but at the same time it was extending and deepening its reach in the provinces. Although increasingly powerful, local officials depended on the grants of tax farms and authority from Istanbul; they collected taxes and sent military forces when required.

The balance of power between central and provincial elites was always changing. Over a period of two centuries, waves of provincial autonomy alternated with periods of state centralization. The first half of the eighteenth century was a period of consolidation. The ministerial and chancery services maintained discipline within the scribal corporation. In many provinces, the Ottomans reorganized administration and appointed effective governors. Still, the forces of decentralization and the privatization of official positions and incomes continued apace. In the latter part of the eighteenth century, a period of wars and disruption, provincial notables further built up households of servants and retainers, soldiers, and scribes, in imitation of the sultan and the great lords of the regime. The position of notable became a formal, locally elected office, and councils of notables won control over the appointment of deputy governors and judges, enforced guild regulations, prevented food shortages, and maintained public buildings. In 1809, the notables extracted formal recognition of their rights and prerogatives from the sultan.

Local dynasties entrenched themselves in power. The Karaosmanoglu dominated central and western Anatolia; the Chapanoglu, the north-central plateau; and the Caniklizadeler, the northeast. In the Balkans, 'Ali Pasha of Janina (r. 1788–1822) founded a small regional state in northern Albania and Greece. Osman Pasvanoglu (r. 1799–1807) ruled western Bulgaria and parts of Serbia and Romania. Other

Balkan lords occupied eastern Bulgaria and Thrace. In the Arab provinces, the governors of Damascus, Mosul, Baghdad, and Basra were substantially independent. Egypt was governed by the Mamluks, and North Africa was autonomous. By the end of the eighteenth century, almost all of the Ottoman Empire was in the control of independent officials. This was the high point of notables' influence and political decentralization and would be followed in the nineteenth century by strong efforts to reestablish central control.

NETWORKING

Decentralization, commercialization, and the consolidation of strong provincial elites was accompanied by the formation of new social and political networks among individuals and interest groups interacting directly with one another, rather than under the aegis of the state. In 1703, Istanbul guilds led by janissaries and supported by lower-ranking officials, merchants, and craftsmen rebelled against the burdens of war and taxes. The rebellion deposed the sultan, but a provincial lord marched on the capital and convened an assembly of powerful notables from the Balkans and Anatolia to restore him. This gave the first historically visible indication that viziers and pashas, based in Istanbul, Anatolia, and the Balkans, had created extensive patronage networks among family members, lesser notables, administrators, soldiers, merchants, religious functionaries, students, and others and had used these networks to manipulate political power. The great *a'yan* were creating what were, in effect, political parties.

A further development of the networking tendency was manifest in the Patrona Halil revolt of 1730. Led by an Albanian janissary, this revolt was joined by masses of commoners – shopkeepers, craftsmen, religious students, and ordinary soldiers – who rebelled in protest of economic hardship, taxes, and wars. As janissaries merged into the working population and merchants and craftsmen were incorporated into the military and paramilitary forces, the common people were drawn into political action.

In May 1807, a coup d'état led to another coalescence of Ottoman notables who joined to shape the policies of the central government. Sultan Selim III proposed a radical program of reforms to strengthen the army and the state and was deposed by rebellious janissaries and scholars. In response, a coalition of the notables of Anatolia and Rumelia, an ad hoc parliament, was formed to support the reform program. A "deed of agreement" between the sultan and the provincial lords exchanged the loyalty and military support of the provincial notables for the acceptance of their local authority. The Ottoman Empire was moving from state control to a multicentered participation of different interests in the governance of society. As a result of decentralization, commercialization, and the privatization of property, the Ottoman state was moving toward a post-imperial "modern" form of society.

POWER, IDEOLOGY, AND IDENTITY

These political, social, and economic changes had complex implications for the ideologies and identities of Ottoman elites and their subjects. Within the Ottoman elite, the seventeenth-century military setbacks caused consternation. Ottoman historians and court officials gave thoughtful attention to the problems of the regime and wrote volumes of advice to rulers. They recommended a restoration of traditional Ottoman institutions. The *Risale* of Mustafa Kochu Bey, written in 1631, advised the sultan to return to the direct management of the government, restore the authority of the grand vizier, reconstruct the *timars*, and suppress factions. He warned against the oppression of the peasantry. Katip Chelebi (d. 1657) analyzed the weakening of the empire in terms of the abuse of peasants, the loss of production and revenues, and the flight to the cities and called for the restoration of just taxation and lawful order. He attributed a Venetian military victory in 1656 to their superior geographical and scientific knowledge. Mustafa Naima (d. 1716), an official historian of the Ottoman court, understood the problem in terms of government financial policies and advised that the army be purged of incompetent soldiers.

By the beginning of the eighteenth century, however, there was a reorientation of Ottoman perceptions. The treaty of Karlowitz (1699), the first time that the Ottomans lost territory to a European power, showed that European innovations in military technology, economic organization, and cultural style were a direct threat to the empire. The Ottomans cautiously began to import European advisors to implement military reforms. Between 1734 and 1738, de Bonneval taught mathematics and artillery techniques to Ottoman soldiers. In 1773, Baron de Tott provided up-to-date instruction in artillery and naval warfare. An Ottoman press was established to print European technical works dealing with military subjects, engineering, geography, and history.

This new political consciousness of the balance of power was expressed in the emulation of European fashions. Ottomans became enamored of European architectural decoration and furniture. Ottoman mosques were decorated in baroque fashion. Summer palaces and water fountains, built on traditional Ottoman architectural lines, were decorated in a French-inspired rococo manner. Ottoman writers reported on French theater and opera, dress and decorations, garden design, and the freer style of social relations.

The craze for tulips in the reign of Ahmed III (r. 1703–30) became an emblem for this new sensibility. Among the Istanbul elites, the taste for European textiles, glass, clocks, flowers, architectural adornments, and home furnishings was accompanied by a mania for prize tulips. The sultans sought to enhance their standing by taking a leading role in setting standards and taste in consumption. They promulgated sumptuary laws to define the required dress and identifying marks for persons of different religions, occupations, and ranks and presented themselves as the guardians of order and morality and the arbitrators of social status. No longer in direct command of the armies or the administration, they were the leaders of high society.

Turkish poetry turned to themes of everyday life and adopted a more vernacular language. Turkish proverbs, puns, and jokes became part of the poetry of such writers as Ahmed Nedim (d. 1730). Mehmed Emin Belig (d. 1758) described bazaars, baths, and the lives of artisans. Ottoman art lost its hieratic quality; the taste for naturalistic and floral design replaced the formality of traditional geometric and Arabesque decoration. These changes indicate a shift from a self-conscious imperial style to a more personal sensibility, much in parallel with the evolution of Safavid taste in an era of imperial weakness.

Despite the administrative decentralization of the empire, however, the identity of local Turkish and Arab elites remained bound up with the empire and with Islam. The sultans continued to be recognized as legitimate suzerains, and local officials continued to be Ottomans. Indeed, the extension of elite networks and the increased reliance of the regime on the support of provincial notables and even of peasant riflemen implied the need for greater ideological and cultural ties between the ruler and the populace.

The traditional ideological expression of this bond was "the circle of justice" – the commitment of the regime to the protection and well-being of the people that was the basis of prosperity, order, and power. This was overtaken in the eighteenth century by a new statist ideology that reflected the growing power of the vizier households and the wealthy financiers of the empire – the tax-farming and merchant strata. Their identity was expressed in the historical writings of official chroniclers and in compilations of biographical dictionaries. Earlier histories were organized by the reigns of sultans; new histories were more impersonal chronicles of the Ottoman state. Earlier biographies focused on the judicial and religious notables; new biographies discussed the viziers and administrators.

A competing cultural response was framed in terms of Islam. In the sixteenth and seventeenth centuries, a strong populist movement promoted more restrictive and puritanical expressions of Islam in opposition to Sufism and the diversity of Muslim beliefs and practices. As early as the 1540s, theology and mathematics were losing popularity. In 1580, an observatory attached to the Sulaymaniya College in Istanbul was destroyed. Puritanical legalists, supported by students and tradesmen, won strong support for a more narrow definition of Islam. Nonetheless, neither the rational sciences (such as mathematics and philosophy) nor Sufism were eliminated. The college curriculum of the eighteenth century continued to include these subjects. Sufism, reoriented toward reform and social activism, also flourished.

From 1630 to 1680, the supporters of Qadizade Mehmed Efendi (d. 1635) formed a party, the Kadizadeli, to persuade the authorities to enforce a legally oriented form of Islamic practice. Many of the leaders were preachers (rather than scholars) who must have felt themselves to be in direct competition with Sufi masters for popular support. The Kadizadeli movement seems to have been a reaction against the formation of a *classe dangereuse* in Istanbul, including migrants from the countryside, gangsters, and street peddlers living in bachelor inns. The Kadizadeli opposed coffee houses and the consumption of opium, coffee, and tobacco; puppet theater shows (*karagoz*); and the relaxed behavior of women in public. Reform-minded religious scholars denounced Sufi practices, including the popular ceremonies for the dead, pilgrimages to saints' tombs, and Sufi dancing and singing. Under their influence, Sufi hospices (*tekkes*) were closed and ceremonies banned. Some Sufis were imprisoned; others executed.

The rise of a "fundamentalist" orientation was also connected with a profound change in Ottoman policy toward non-Muslims. The Kadizadeli insisted on clarifying boundaries between Muslims and non-Muslims and especially on the separation of Muslim women from non-Muslim men. In the late seventeenth century, there was intense state and public pressure on at least some of the empire's non-Muslim populations to convert to Islam. Eventually, the Ottoman authorities suppressed the Kadizadeli movement, probably out of concern at once for the authority of the state, the threat to public order, and sympathies with Sufi piety and Sufi influence with the common people.

Still, the effects of the movement were felt long after. Late eighteenth-century sultans set out their own claims to be "caliphs" and leaders of Muslims worldwide. The Ottoman scholarly families became entrenched as a religious aristocracy. Important posts were filled by a limited number of families. The scholars were a powerful interest group. Through the trust system of charitable grants, they were the only segment of the Ottoman elite that could securely pass on their property after death and appoint their heirs as administrators. The influence of scholarly families enabled them to promote their children into the higher grades of the educational and judicial hierarchies without having reached the proper preliminary levels, whereas theological students who could not find patronage were excluded. Their integration into the Ottoman regime made them the spokesmen of Ottoman legitimacy. They were less and less perceived as representing a transcendent Islamic ideal opposed to worldly corruption.

Whereas Ottoman-Muslim identities remained focused on the sultan and the empire, in the Balkans local autonomy was a harbinger of revolutionary change. In the late eighteenth and especially in the nineteenth century, Balkan peoples, predominantly Christians, never completely Ottomanized, began to conceive of national independence. Although the Orthodox Church continued to ally itself with the Ottoman regime as a bulwark against European, Latin, and Catholic influences, the centralization of power in the hands of the Greek clergy provoked ethnic resistance. Bulgarians, especially in the merchant class, cultivated a national history and a literary Bulgarian language. Local clergy fostered an interest in history and vernacular language among Rumanians. Orthodox Slavs were dissatisfied with Greek leadership. Rural lords, peasant bandits, and urban merchants began to look westward not only for economic exchange but for intellectual stimulation. Elements of the Christian urban middle classes in Greece sponsored secular schools to replace church schools and patronized secular and nationalist literary, intellectual, and political movements. Religious identity was being replaced by national identity. Progressively, segments of the Balkan mercantile and landowning elites, prospering as exporters and middlemen in the trade with Europe, developed a new political consciousness. Increasing contacts with Europe and the decentralization of the Ottoman Empire opened the way for national independence.

CENTER AND PERIPHERY

The Ottoman Empire originated in the conquests of Turkish warrior bands under the leadership of the family of Osman. As they expanded throughout western Anatolia and the Balkans, the Ottomans devised institutions to concentrate power in the hands of the sultan and his entourage. From the fourteenth through the sixteenth centuries, these institutions – the palace household, the janissary corps, the *timar*-supported cavalry, provincial governorships, and the patronage of Muslim religious elites (both scholars and Sufis) – constituted the classical Ottoman imperial configuration. These were the institutions that sustained Ottoman conquests, administered their domains, and legitimized their rule.

In the late sixteenth and early seventeenth century, changes in the military and financial systems and in the economic and social conditions of the provinces undermined the earlier institutional configuration. The succession of poorly trained sultans, the corruption of the janissaries, the breakdown of the *timar* system, and the need to recruit infantry from lower-class bandit gangs, displaced soldiers, students, and peasants all weakened the sultanate. The sultans became dependent on provincial magnates, warlords, officials, and chieftains for military manpower. Taxes were diverted from the sultans to provincial lords.

In the seventeenth and eighteenth centuries, two factors further transformed the relations of the state to its elites. One was the increasing power of local notables culminating in the privatization of politically acquired assets – the conversion of tax farms into private estates. The second was the growth of both local and international commerce that enhanced the wealth and influence of merchants, officials engaged in commerce, local notables, and non-Muslims. These officials and merchants benefited from rising rural productivity, local manufactures, and a more vibrant market economy. While the Ottoman state became increasingly decentralized, the enrichment of provincial elites and commoners was leading to a more variegated society.

These changes have been described as the "decline" of the Ottoman Empire. In terms of military power and wars with Europe, the Ottomans were stalemated and in retreat from the beginning of the seventeenth century. But from an internal perspective, these changes represented a realignment of power among the Ottoman elites. High government officials were transforming the regime in their own interests. Military leaders, tax collectors, administrators, scholars, and other wealthy and powerful persons became the beneficiaries of a more decentralized system. The Ottoman center was losing power because it was losing control over taxes and markets and no longer had the resources to be a redistributive state. From the point of view of the sultanate, the devolution of power was a corruption of Ottoman institutions. From the point of view of provincial chieftains, officials, and merchants, it was a reduction of the exploitative capacities of the center and a gain in local autonomy.

Yet, as central power was becoming less concentrated, its influence was becoming more widespread. The center was reaching out to the real holders of local power and allying them with the sultanate. Starting in the seventeenth century, in place of slave military forces and *timar* holders, it could mobilize provincial officials, landowners, merchants, financiers, and even peasant recruits for the army. With these connections, the Ottoman state succeeded in recruiting new infantry and reining in otherwise unemployed soldiers. It raised revenues and reorganized financial administration. Through tax farming, it could tap the wealth of the military and provincial elites. Thus, the era of "decline" vis-à-vis Europe also appears as a broadening of the base of regime recruitment and a co-optation of military and financial elites on the basis of negotiated relationships.

Despite decentralization, the concept of a legitimate state, its importance as the representative of Islam, and its authority as the overlord of local notables in Anatolia and the Arab provinces were unimpaired. The state maintained its dominance over the scholars and the religious establishment. In the Balkans, however, European influence enhanced the autonomy of the Christian populations and gave them new advantages in international trade that paved the way for their ultimate independence.

The change from a centralized state to a network state was probably not as radical as it has appeared to historians. Royal power was always mediated through provincial lords – warrior chieftains (*ghazis*), *timar* holders, and local satraps elevated to the rank of imperial functionaries. The Ottoman state always functioned by consultation and mediation. Not only were regional warlords and local landholding and administrative notables consulted, but the heads of religious communities (scholars and Sufi leaders, patriarchs, and rabbis), merchant leaders, and village headmen were all intermediaries – not in a chain of command, but in a web of negotiated understandings. Accommodation and incorporation were the means by which the Ottoman state maintained its authority and longevity.

At the end of the pre-modern era, Ottoman-Islamic society was still built on a strong state, which was legitimate in military, patrimonial, and cosmopolitan as well as Islamic terms; a well-organized and subordinate Islamic religious establishment; extensive patronage networks linking provincial notables to the center; and an abiding acceptance of the concept of the authority of the empire over parochial communities. These institutions would powerfully affect the modern development of Islamic societies in Turkey and other parts of the Middle East.

CHAPTER 33

THE ARAB PROVINCES UNDER OTTOMAN RULE

EGYPT

The Ottoman conquest of Egypt in 1517 perpetuated, with some modifications, the ongoing system of society. The Ottomans garrisoned Egypt with several corps of janissaries and appointed military governors, inspectors, and finance officers to assure the collection of taxes and the remittance of surpluses to Istanbul. The main functions of Ottoman administration were to pacify the country; control the bedouins; protect agriculture, irrigation, and trade; and thus assure the flow of tax revenues. In the course of the first century and a half of Ottoman rule, the irrigation system of Egypt was rebuilt, cultivation increased, and trade restored by reopening the routes between India and Egypt. Egypt was also important to Ottoman control of the Red Sea, Yemen, Nubia, and Abyssinia, and the holy places in Arabia.

In many respects, Egypt remained a separate political society. Beneath the top level of Ottoman administration, the old institutional structure remained intact. The local Mamluk households continued to be militarily important and were assigned taxable estates. Although the Ottomans appointed a chief judge and a chief syndic for the corporation of descendants of the Prophet from Istanbul, the rest of the scholarly establishment was of local origin. The muftis of the law schools, the chiefs of the holy lineages, and the rector of al-Azhar were the principal leaders of the religious establishment. They were responsible for disciplining their followers and managing the trust revenues and, in the eighteenth century, the tax farms assigned for their personal upkeep, as well as being responsible for the maintenance of the religious function of their schools and fraternities.

From the fifteenth century, there were important changes in the character of Egyptian religious life. Whereas in the early Mamluk period the schools of law and the colleges had been the most important expression of Sunni Islam, Sufism became increasingly important. The Khalwatiyya, Shadhiliyya, Ahmadiyya, and other brotherhoods were organized under centralized leadership and endowed with substantial properties. They were held in reverence by the military elites and the common people alike. The birthdays of the Prophet and of famous Sufi saints were occasions for immense celebrations in which many thousands of people participated. Visits to the tombs or shrines of saints became a routine part of Egyptian religious life.

In Egypt, as in many other parts of the Muslim world, Sufism and shrine worship precipitated a religious reaction. Reformers in Mecca, Medina, Istanbul, and Syria – including Naqshbandis and others – opposed the shrine forms of Sufism. In Egypt, reform influences made themselves felt at al-Azhar, where hadith studies were revived. The Naqshbandis and the Khalwatis reinforced the trend. Reformism was especially appealing to, or indeed the expression of, the more scholarly, ethical, and puritanical spirit of merchant-scholar milieus, with their wider range of commercial and intellectual contacts and their need for a more universal form of Islam (as opposed to the parochial and localized forms of saint worship). In the late eighteenth century, Egypt seems to have maintained a variety of religious styles, including orthoprax, Sufi-orthoprax, shrine-Sufi, and reformist types of Islam.

Throughout this period, scholars and Sufi leaders played important political and social roles. They were the intermediaries between the Mamluk elites and the common people. On the one hand, higher-ranking scholars were often the clients of Mamluk regiments, from whom they received trusts, gifts, salaries, and fees for teaching and religious services. In the eighteenth century, these ties enabled the leading scholars to become extremely prosperous from the management of trusts, control of tax farms (*iltizams*), and other incomes. They served the Mamluks as negotiators and mediators in disputes among the factions, acted as bankers and tax collectors, and communicated the demands of the regime to the common people. On the other hand, they were also closely connected to the commoners. They married into merchant families; frequently invested in trade and real estate; managed schools, hospitals, and charities; and served as patrons for their neighborhoods. A leading scholar or Sufi would arbitrate in local disputes, feed the poor, and protect his people from abuse by soldiers and tax collectors. He could either organize or calm local resistance. Thus, in Egypt, the scholars and Sufis played a critical role as intermediaries in the functioning of their society.

The late eighteenth century in Egypt was a period of violent warfare, exploitative taxation, a decline in irrigation, and rising bedouin power. As in many other parts of the empire, Ottoman governors lost authority as the Mamluks seized control of trusts and divided into factions. The Qasimiyyah and the Faqariyyah fought for political power until the Ottomans defeated the Mamluk factions in 1786–87 and restored central government control.

This was also a period of economic hardship due to inflation and a decline in commerce. In the sixteenth and seventeenth centuries, Egypt lost some of its trade to Portuguese and then Dutch competition but gained partial compensation from the coffee trade with Yemen. The eighteenth century, however, brought more severe European competition. European textiles, ceramics, and glass beat down Egyptian industries. Even coffee was imported into the Ottoman Empire from the Antilles.

THE FERTILE CRESCENT

In the Fertile Crescent, the Ottomans also perpetuated the regional political society. Unlike Egypt, which was a single province, the Ottomans ruled this region through the major towns (Damascus, Aleppo, Mosul, and Baghdad) that formed the territorial base for several Ottoman governorships. Ottoman administration had very limited means for centralizing political power. The Ottomans aimed at the minimum of governmental power needed to prevent officials from becoming independent and still allow them to maintain order, collect taxes, and remit the surplus to Istanbul. The primary concern in Istanbul was to make it difficult for its own appointees to defy central authority. Political authority was divided among military governors and independent civil and judicial officials. The army was divided into numerous units, including regiments of janissaries and cavalry sent from Istanbul, the governor's private retainers, and local janissaries. Bedouin tribes served as auxiliary military units. The weakness of the state apparatus made it necessary to depend on local notables. Their power was based on control of taxation and of trusts and on the support they could rally from town quarters, artisan guilds, and local soldiers. In any case, control of the towns did not necessarily mean control of the countryside. Bedouins, especially in southern Iraq and along the Syrian margins of the north Arabian desert, and mountain peoples in Kurdistan, northern Syria, and the Lebanon, maintained freedom from central control.

Notables differed in composition from city to city. In Damascus, the scholars were particularly important. Throughout the period of Ottoman rule, a relatively small group of notable families controlled the posts of judge, preacher, mufti, and teacher in the colleges and constituted a religious patriarchate. Although Sufism was well established in Syria, it does not seem to have played as large a role as in Egypt. The scholarly-Sufi synthesis was less manifest, and Syrian scholars tended to be hostile to less "orthoprax" forms of Sufism. Sufi brotherhoods, Sufi hospices (*khanaqas*), shrines, and celebrations of the death day of the Sufi saints (*mawlids*) seem to have had a smaller place in Syrian religious life. The major exception to this was the veneration of the shrine of Ibn al-'Arabi in Damascus.

Aleppo is an example of both a provincial capital and a cosmopolitan caravan city. In the seventeenth century, the Persian silk trade was Aleppo's primary industry. Armenians, Christian Arabs, Sephardic Jews, and merchants from Iran, India, and Europe were the principal actors in this trade. In the eighteenth century, the French surpassed the English as the predominant European merchant community, and many local Christians converted to Catholicism. Nonetheless, foreigners and minorities did not control or define the lifestyle of Aleppo as much as they did that of Izmir. Aleppo's hinterlands were as important in the political economy as trade.

Throughout the sixteenth century, the Ottomans maintained a dominant position, but by the end of the century their position had deteriorated. Janissary units, aggrieved by the declining value of their salaries, rebelled against the central government, seized tax farms, and turned them into life-tenure farms or private estates. Ottoman governors were reduced to manipulating the competing military factions. In the eighteenth century, the weakening of the central state allowed local notable families to control the rural hinterlands. Then, in the first half of the eighteenth century, the Ottomans regained control of Damascus and Syria. In 1708, the newly appointed governor of Damascus was given direct authority over other administrative subdistricts of Syria and was charged with responsibility for the pilgrimage. His job was to maintain the goodwill of the urban notables and to curb the bedouins by offering them bribes and offices. After 1758, however, the central government was defeated by local forces. In the latter part of the eighteenth century, the Ottomans could no longer control the notables or protect the pilgrimage.

With Ottoman decline, governors established local dynasties. The 'Azm family ruled Damascus from 1724 to 1780; the heirs of Hasan Pasha governed Baghdad and Basra from 1704 until the early 1830s; the Jalili family governed Mosul from 1726 to 1834. In Palestine and Lebanon, there were several small-scale regimes. Zahir al-'Umar took control of Acre in 1750 and established a local despotism based on efficient economic management. He encouraged the production of cash crops, established monopolies over production and foreign trade, and wooed European advisors. This short-lived regime ended in 1775, when the territory reverted to the governorship of Damascus. After 1780, Ahmad al-Jazzar succeeded to the control of Acre and Sidon, building up a personal domain based on a strong army, economic monopolies, and lively European trade. This new type of despotism foreshadowed the nineteenth-century reform movement in Turkey and Egypt, which led to a recentralization of power and to efficient government controls over the local economy.

The Lebanon posed special problems for Ottoman authority. In the north and in the Kisrawan region lived the Maronites. They had been Monothelite Christians until the period of the Crusades, when they accepted Catholic doctrine and papal supremacy. Turkish Muslims also inhabited the north, but in the Gharb and the Shuf the population was largely Druze. Although the Lebanese peasants were affiliated with the religious communities, the local political order was based not on religion but on allegiance to village and valley chiefs, who were subordinate to feudal suzerains, who were in turn subordinate to the governor of Damascus and the sultan in Istanbul. This hierarchy of authority was at best unstable. Between 1544 and 1697, the Ma'n family was the most powerful. The great ruler of this era, Fakhr al-Din (r. 1603–35), governed by means of a Maronite and Druze peasant coalition. In 1697, the Ma'n were succeeded by the Shihabi, who ruled from 1697 to 1840.

In other parts of the Fertile Crescent, Ottoman power was subverted by bedouin opposition. Parts of Syria east of Hama and Homs were occupied by Arab bedouins, who threatened agricultural settlement and the security of the pilgrimage route. Turkmen and Kurdish tribes occupied the regions north of Damascus. The northern Euphrates region was taken over by the ʿAnaza confederation, and the southern reaches of the river were occupied by the Shamar.

In sum, the Arab Middle East was governed by an Ottoman elite with the cooperation of local intermediaries. In Egypt, these were Mamluk households and scholars. In the Fertile Crescent, they were local janissaries, scholars, and mountain and bedouin chieftains. In the late eighteenth century, the balance of power between the central state and the provinces and even between provincial capitals and their hinterlands shifted in favor of the latter. Almost every local political power – Mamluk or janissary households, scholars, officeholders, tax farmers, guildsmen, town quarters, bedouin tribes, and mountain communities – managed to increase its autonomy. Still, the basic institutional structures of these societies and the historical system of ever-changing balances of power among state, military, religious, and parochial elites continued to function.

On the horizon, however, the clouds of new forms of highly centralized states and of European commercial and political penetration were already visible. Ottoman supremacy in the Arab provinces was being threatened by European trade and by the rising influence of Greek, Armenian, Maronite, and other Christian merchants who prospered under the protection of foreign powers while Muslim communities were in disarray. The decentralization of the late eighteenth century made it impossible to crystallize a regional political identity or to protect Ottoman Muslims against the competition of local and foreign Christians. This political disarray would also make it extremely difficult to form stable nation-states in the twentieth century.

THE ARABIAN PENINSULA

For almost a millennium, the Arabian Peninsula stood outside the mainstream of Middle Eastern developments. Although the Arab conquests began a new era in Middle Eastern civilization, they left Arabia drained of much of its population and relegated the peninsula to a marginal role in Middle Eastern history. In the Ottoman era, Egypt and the Arab Fertile Crescent became provinces of the empire, but with the exception of peripheral areas, Arabia did not. Unlike Egypt and the Fertile Crescent states, the peninsula was governed by family and tribal elites. Islam was a crucial factor in the unification of disparate clan and tribal groups into regional confederations and kingdoms. In the imamate of Yemen and the sultanates of Oman and Saudi Arabia, religion and state were closely identified. Although the *shaykhs* of the Persian Gulf region did not formally claim charismatic religious authority, the rulers were considered the heads of the religion, responsible for the implementation of Islamic values. Throughout the peninsula, the *'ulama'*, whether Zaydi, Shafi'i, Ibadi, or Wahhabi, also played an important role as political advisors to rulers, administrators of judicial and educational institutions, and a source of moral advice and political authority.

Yemen

Yemen has an exceptional position in the history of the Arabian peninsula. Throughout their history, northern and southern Yemen have had different regimes and different religious orientations based on tribal and pastoral population in the north and an agricultural and state-organized society in the south.

After Yemen was absorbed into the early Umayyad and 'Abbasid empires, it was partitioned among a number of local dynasties. In the late ninth century, like other regions far removed from Baghdad, northern Yemen became a center of Shi'ism. A Zaydi Shi'i dynasty was established in 893 and ruled the north until 1962. Southern Yemen came under the influence of Egypt. First the Fatimids and then the Ayyubids established satellite states. The Rasulid dynasty (1229–1454) organized a strong central government and won the south over to Sunni Islam. The Ottomans occupied southern Yemen from 1539 to 1636. The Qasimi branch of the Zaydi dynasty eventually expelled them, but the country was never unified. Zaydi imams, claimants to the imamate and tribal forces competed for power. In 1872 the Ottomans re-established their suzerainty, but not effective power, in the north. A treaty of 1911 confirmed Ottoman suzerainty, but divided administrative control between the Imam in the highlands and the Ottomans on the coast. This corresponded to the division into Zaydi and Sunni spheres of influence.

With the defeat of the Ottomans in World War I, Imam Yahya (r. 1904–48) won control over much of Yemen. He governed in conjunction with the Zaydi elite who were the 'ulama', governors, judges, teachers, and also merchants and military officers. They were divided into two groups: the *sada'* (sayyids), a landed aristocracy of descendants of the Prophet, and the *quda'* the descendants of early judges. In the Sunni parts of the country, the Shafi'i 'ulama' held a similar position. Yemen in this period was thoroughly isolated from the outside world; there were few secular schools and few contacts with the rest of the Middle East. Every effort was made to preserve the traditional society.

In most of the nineteenth and twentieth centuries South Yemen had a separate history. Aden came under British rule in 1839; in 1937 it was made a crown colony. Under British control, the traditional Arabian clan and religious communities remained intact. The Sultans dominated the towns; the sayyids owned the land and served as mediators among the clans. Plebeian clans were organized into specialized agricultural, craft, and servant groups. The British protectorate included some twenty-three Sultanates, Emirates, and tribal regimes.

Saudi Arabia

Central Arabia has become the domain of the Saudi kingdom and the Wahhabi movement. In 1745 'Abd al-'Aziz b. Sa'ud (Ibn Sa'ud), the chief of a small tribal principality in north-central Arabia, took up the cause of a Hanbali preacher, Muhammad b. 'Abd al-Wahhab (1703–87). Ibn 'Abd al-Wahhab had studied in Mecca, Medina, Damascus, and Basra and returned to preach the reform principles. He insisted that the Quran and the Prophet were the only valid Muslim authorities and proposed to return to the fundamental principles embodied in Muslim scripture. Wahhabi reformism took the extreme position of totally rejecting belief in and veneration of saints or of any human being as a form of *shirk*, or polytheism. It also rejected the common pantheistic types of Sufi theology and magical rituals. Ibn 'Abd al-Wahhab's preaching was the first political expression of a reform tendency that had developed in Mecca and would soon manifest itself throughout Islamic India, Indonesia, and North Africa.

With the conversion of Ibn Sa'ud to the Wahhabi cause, Wahhabism became the religious ideology of tribal unification. Ibn Sa'ud and his successors waged war against the surrounding tribes and converted them to the reformed version of Islam. As imams of the Wahhabi movement, they became the spiritual as well as the temporal chiefs of central Arabia. In 1773 they took Riyadh and made it their capital; in 1803 they captured Mecca, but they were defeated by Muhammad 'Ali, who took control of Mecca and Medina in 1812 and destroyed the Saudi state in 1818. During much of the nineteenth century, the Sa'udi house survived as a small tribal principality in the interior of Arabia, but in 1902, 'Abd al-'Aziz b. Sa'ud took control of Riyadh, proclaimed himself imam of the Wahhabis, and restored the Saudi kingdom. The principal instrument of his power was the Ikhwan – a nontribal military corps, settled in agricultural villages, which fought and proselytized for the Wahhabi movement. Ibn Sa'ud succeeded in unifying the tribes of central and eastern Arabia, declared himself sultan of the Najd (1921), and proceeded to round out the boundaries of modern Sa'udi Arabia by treaties with Iraq (1922), Jordan (1925), and Yemen (1934). In 1925 he took control of the Hijaz and the holy places.

The Saudi regime was based on a subtle combination of political and religious powers. The Saudi kings were tribal chiefs who ruled by maintaining alliances and marriage ties with the families of other chiefs. The army was made up of loyal tribes. At the same time they were religious rulers, committed to upholding the laws of Islam and protecting the pilgrimage and the holy places. The *'ulama'* of the country, largely the descendants of Ibn 'Abd al-Wahhab, married into the royal family, were financially supported by the state, and had considerable influence in government circles.

The Gulf

The history of the Persian Gulf region, like that of Yemen and central Arabia, is based on the persisting identification of political and religious authority as the basis of tribal unification. In pre-Islamic times Oman was part of a Sasanian commercial network that reached from the Persian Gulf to India. Commercial profits were invested in an Iranian type of *qanat* irrigation, and Oman became a highly agricultural society. The Arab conquests, however, introduced a large pastoral population. In 796 Oman came under the rule of Ibadi imams, who managed to contain tribal rivalries, defend agriculture, and integrate the nomadic and settled populations. Under Ibadi leadership, Omanis founded commercial colonies in Basra, Siraf, Aden, and India and traded on the east coast of Africa. At the end of the ninth century the Ibadi state and Omani commerce collapsed, and Egyptian-sponsored Red Sea routes took over the bulk of the Indian Ocean traffic. Oman, however, revived in the middle of the eleventh century, when a second imamate was founded, and a social system was created that lasts to the present day. Cultivators accepted a tribal concept of social organization and thus were integrated with pastoralists into a single society. Ibadism became a full-fledged Muslim school of law, regulating personal and family behavior and political institutions. In the Ibadi system, the imam is nominated by the elders of the community and holds power insofar as he upholds the divine law and maintains the confidence of his electors. The imamate was thus a tribal state integrated by religious authority.

Oman's prosperity was revived in the seventeenth and eighteenth centuries, when Omanis drove the Portuguese out of East Africa and the sultans of the Bu Sa'id dynasty established their own trading network. Oman renewed its control over Zanzibar and other East African towns. Although Zanzibar became a separate regime in 1856, the dynasty continues to rule Oman (and Muscat) to the present day.

In other parts of the Persian Gulf a new political system took shape at the beginning of the eighteenth century. In 1752 Sabah b. Jabr of the Banu 'Utub became the first ruler of Kuwait and established the dynasty that rules Kuwait today. Kuwait was and is a tribal state, a commercial entrepôt at the head of the Persian Gulf, and an important rival of Basra and other Persian Gulf ports. The al-Sabah family also assisted in the establishment of another branch of the 'Utub, the al-Khalifa, in Bahrain . By the end of the eighteenth century Britain had become the dominant power in the Gulf region and was paramount over the small tribal regimes. In 1798 the British made the first of a series of treaties to protect British shipping in the Gulf and to install British political agents. British treaties with Kuwait, Bahrain, Oman, and the smaller "Trucial" states helped to strengthen the tribal rulers. British influence remained predominant until 1961, when Kuwait became fully independent. In 1970 and 1971, when Britain left the Gulf region, the Trucial states were reconstituted as members of the United Arab Emirates. The modern transformation of the Persian Gulf region began with the discovery of oil in Bahrain in 1932.

CHAPTER 34

THE SAFAVID EMPIRE

THE ORIGINS OF THE SAFAVIDS

Iran had a profound historical tradition of imperial regimes and cultures. The Saljuq
governments of the eleventh and twelfth centuries were built on prior 'Abbasid
and Sasanian and more ancient institutions. The Mongol and Timurid invasions
continued many of the political and cultural achievements of the past but brought
lasting demographic, economic, and political changes to Iranian societies. In the
twelfth and thirteenth centuries, large numbers of Turkish and Mongol peoples
settled in northwestern Iran and eastern Anatolia, and, by the fourteenth century,
a large Turkish population was also established in eastern Iran and in the Oxus
region. Ever since, Turkish peoples have constituted about one-fourth of the total
population of Iran.

The Turkish presence radically changed the economy of Iran. Substantial territories were turned from agriculture into pasturage. Villagers were induced to take
up a migratory existence, farming in valley bottoms and pasturing sheep in adjacent mountain highlands. Only in the reign of Ghazan (d. 1304) did the Ilkhans
attempt to develop a more balanced relationship between agricultural and pastoral
activities and a system of property organization that maintained the position of
both agricultural and pastoral peoples. The Ilkhans began to stabilize the division
of Iran into two economic and cultural worlds – one, the world of the sedentary
village; the other, that of the pastoral camp.

From Inner Asia also came new political institutions. To the Iranian legacy of
monarchical and hierarchical institutions and Islamic communities were added
Turkish and Mongolian political traditions. Rulership in Turkish society was
achieved by victory in battle and was maintained by active struggle against rivals.
The crucial expression of chieftainship in the Turko-Mongolian societies was the
household state (*uymaq*). An *uymaq* was an elite military formation organized as a
great household under the leadership of its chief. The chief was supported by his

family and by other lesser chiefs and their followers, whose support was won by delicate negotiations and/or by success in war. The *uymaq* chief used his military support to collect taxes from townsmen and peasants and to establish, in effect, a local territorial government commonly based in a citadel or fortress. The powers of an *uymaq* chieftain could be reinforced by royal appointment to a position that gave him the right to tax and to supervise the local bureaucracy. The *uymaq*, however, was generally unstable, owing to the fact that it was based on the personal prowess of chiefs and on semi-independent warriors, clans, and vassal groups who constantly calculated their relative advantage, bitterly competed for leadership, and regularly rebelled against the dominance of the great chiefs. The authority of an *uymaq* lord was always challenged by lesser chieftains. Competition among all these groups made the *uymaq* extremely volatile and led to rapid rises and falls of fortune.

Thus, all post-Saljuq Iranian states acquired the dual heritage of an Iranian monarchical tradition and of Turkish *uymaq* polities. The Mongols, the Timurids, and the Safavids in succession had to struggle with the problems of maintaining a centralized monarchy and of coping with the tribal and military chiefs. Indeed, the later dynamic of Iranian history would turn on the relationship between state and *uymaqs*.

The shattering impact of the Mongol invasions, the succession of unstable and ruinous regimes, and the intrusion of Turkish pastoralists also provoked new forms of socioreligious organization among the common people of Iran. Islamic leadership in western Anatolia, northeastern Iran, and northern Mesopotamia passed into the hands of Sufi preachers, shamans, and sorcerers. These preachers performed miraculous cures, manipulated occult forces, and claimed a religious authority based on esoteric knowledge vouchsafed through direct revelation or the interpretation of magical texts. They taught their followers that a savior would come to redeem ordinary people and that the pillar (*qutb*) of the saintly world would provide a haven for oppressed peoples.

Responding to the need for political protection and spiritual reassurance, Sufis organized a number of local movements to unite rural populations and resist political oppression. In the thirteenth century, the Kubrawi order in western Iran, named after Najm al-Din Kubra (d. 1221) but actually founded by al-Simnani (d. 1336), stood closest to high-culture Islam. Al-Simnani preached a doctrine that attempted to transcend sectarian divisions. The order appealed to both Sunnis and Shi'is by venerating the family of the Prophet, including 'Ali, along with great Sunni masters. Kubrawi mysticism was also intended to win Buddhists and pagan converts to Islam.

The Hurufiyya, founded by Fadlallah Astarabadi (d. 1394), represented a more populist version of Islam. Astarabadi claimed to be a hidden imam, the beneficiary of a direct revelation of God's will. He taught that it was possible to gain knowledge of secret and spiritual matters through the interpretation of the alphabet and the understanding of its implicit numerical values, for the letters of the alphabet are the microcosm of the divine reality. This secret knowledge would bring his followers salvation. Nurbaksh (d. 1465), like many other militant Sufi preachers, held that the true messiah must carry out jihad in the name of Islam. He led a rebellion in Kurdistan against the local Timurid rulers. Other millenarian movements looked forward to the ultimate confrontation between good and evil, the coming of a messiah, and the redemption of mankind.

Another such movement, the Safavid, would conquer Iran and establish a dynasty that would reign from 1501 to 1722. The Safavid movement – founded by Shaykh Safi al-Din (d. 1334), a Sunni/Sufi religious teacher descended from a Kurdish family in northwestern Iran – also represented a resurgence of popular Islam in opposition to chaotic and exploitative military domination. The founder began by preaching a purified and restored Islam. His son, Sadr al-Din (r. 1334–91), transformed the movement into a hierarchical, politically sensitive, and propertied organization. He was the first head of the order to claim descent from the Prophet. He expanded the family compound in Ardabil, providing it with schools and residences, and broadened the movement's missionary activities. He organized the hierarchy of the *murshid*, who was the head of the order, and the *khalifas*, who were his direct agents, and supervised the missionaries, assistants, students, and novices.

In the fifteenth century, the Safavid movement became a powerful political force in northwestern Iran and eastern Anatolia. The Safavids took advantage of the breakup of the Timurid regime and of the bitter Turkish tribal conflicts to turn from preaching to militant action. Shaykh Junayd (d. 1460) was the first leader to fight Christian populations in Georgia and Trebizond. His wars against the Christians were soon turned against established Muslim states, which he denounced as infidel regimes.

The more militant Safavid policy depended on active recruitment of individuals and of *uymaq* and tribal groups. Anatolian followers were individual soldiers and adventurers given political organization by the Safavid order. Iranian supporters were Turkish-, Kurdish-, and Luri-speaking pastoralists, peasants, artisans, and middle-level lineage chiefs who joined the Safavids to oppose the more powerful tribal lords. In addition, Shaykh Junayd married into the families of local princes to form military alliances and to recruit whole tribes to his cause. His recruits were called Qizilbash, after their distinctive red headgear, which showed that they were the disciples and warriors of the Safavid house. As exploited peasants flocked to the Sufi brotherhoods to find leadership in their struggle for existence and to give expression to their hope for redemption, the Safavids combined the forces of religious devotees and *uymaq* clients to establish a dynasty and an empire representing a new constellation of imperial, religious, and tribal forces.

The reorientation toward militant political action was accompanied by doctrinal elaboration. The Safavids declared their Shi'i allegiances, and Shah Isma'il (d. 1524) proclaimed himself the hidden imam, the reincarnation of 'Ali, and an epiphany of the divine being. Isma'il claimed to be descended from the seventh imam, and to be the seventh descendant in the Safavid line; each successive imam was the bearer of the divine fire passed down from generation to generation to its embodiment in Isma'il. Leaning on the religious syncretism of almost two centuries of Sufi movements in northwestern Iran and Anatolia and combining diverse religious influences (including Shi'ism, Sunni messianism, Buddhism, and Zoroastrianism), Isma'il also proclaimed himself the incarnation of Khidr, the bearer of ancient wisdom, and the spirit of Jesus. He titled himself the Shadow of God on Earth in the manner of Persian emperors. This absolute authority was communicated to his followers through his role as perfect master (*murshid-i kamil*), reinforced by the cult of the Safavid ancestors at Ardabil. His claims to power were thus based on pre-Islamic Iranian and early Islamic cosmologies, Sufi mysticism, and 'Alid loyalties. He was therefore messiah and shah, possessor of both mystical rulership and temporal power.

On the basis of these religious claims, Safavid leaders called for absolute and unquestioning obedience from their Sufi and Qizilbash followers. To question the authority of the perfect master was tantamount to apostasy. The followers of Isma'il were supposed to adhere strictly to a code of conduct called *sufigare*; disobedience was punished by expulsion from the order and possibly by execution.

IRAN UNDER THE EARLY SAFAVIDS

By means of fierce and violent campaigns driven by millenarian and apocalyptic expectations, Isma'il occupied Tabriz in 1501 and proclaimed himself shah. Within a decade he had conquered the rest of Iran. While the rival Ottoman Empire to the west seized eastern Anatolia and the Shaybanid Empire to the east took control of Transoxania as far as the Oxus River, Isma'il established the borders that have defined Iran until the present day. These borders would eventually divide the region into separate realms of Turkish Ottoman, Iranian, and Inner Asian Muslim cultures.

The problems of rebuilding the Iranian state and society were formidable. Centuries of political upheaval had worn away the infrastructure of centralized imperial government. Agricultural and urban production had been undermined by nomadic invasions. Economic regression and a declining peasant population reduced the resources essential for a centralized state. Moreover, political power was widely dispersed. Qizilbash and other *uymaq* chieftains ruled over subject clans, tribal affiliates, and towns and villages. For example, the Mausillus controlled vast territories in western Iran. The chiefs held official positions in the Safavid government and received subsidies, allotments of infantry, soldiers, tax revenues, and economic rights that made them all the more powerful.

The fluid *uymaq* and tribal groups were not the only contenders for political power. The *uymaqs* were opposed by urban bourgeoisie and by peasants organized in secret religious societies. Tribal-led, merchant-led, and Sufi-led peasant groups waged a multisided struggle for political and social power. In 1537 and 1538, there was a rebellion in Astarabad of local Persians against the Turkish elites, led by Muhammad Salih Bitikchi, who preached an egalitarian doctrine and promised the deliverance of oppressed peoples from the hands of evil masters. There were similar peasant rebellions in Mazandaran, Jilan, Azarbayjan, Fars, and Afghanistan.

To fight this dispersion of power, the Safavids struggled to consolidate the religious authority of the shah and the military and administrative power of the central government. Shah Isma'il (r. 1501–24) and his successor, Shah Tahmasp (r. 1524–76), tried to control the army by appointing as generals men of lesser *uymaq* standing in order to limit the power of the great Qizilbash lords. Shah Tahmasp began to incorporate non-Qizilbash Persian tribal volunteers and captured Georgian, Circassian, and Armenian slaves into his forces. The military officers (amirs) were given land grants from which each had to pay a sum of money to the central government and support a contingent of troops.

They also built up a civil administration inherited from the governing apparatus of previous regimes. The Persian officials, and many scholars, poets, and literati, who had served the Timurid courts and local dynasties in Iran, Central Asia, and eastern Anatolia were recruited by the Safavids. Local and regional lords on the borders of the Safavid domains were brought into the regime by negotiation. Local administration was left in the hands of Persian tax collectors and landlords. Persian administration embodied Persian culture. The scholar-bureaucrats not only kept the records of the regime and carried on its correspondence; they also transmitted the literary, scientific, philosophic, and religious heritage of Persian Islam. They embodied the heritage of literary learning, rhetorical excellence, elegant manners, ethical behavior, and philosophical wisdom (collectively known as *adab*). Persian painting and crafts – including textile and carpet weaving, ceramics, and metalwork – flourished under the Safavids.

Equally important to the new regime was the consolidation of its religious authority. Parallel to the program of state formation, the Safavids created a religious establishment that would lend its authority and administrative services to the regime. Safavid religious appeals had first been addressed to their Qizilbash and tribal supporters, to whom they promised messianic fulfillment. The devotion of the Qizilbash, however, was a double-edged sword, for the millenarian impulses that had brought the Safavids to power could also be turned against them. In fact, the Ottoman victory at the Battle of Chaldiran in 1514 shattered the Qizilbash belief in the invincibility of their leader.

To cope with the complications of Qizilbash enthusiasm and the tepid response of the Iranian population, Isma'il set aside his messianic claims in favor of Twelver Shi'ism, which was proclaimed the official religion of Iran. His son Shah Tahmasp also abandoned claims to quasi-divinity and claimed only to communicate with God indirectly through dreams. Although there were Shi'is in northern Iran, the shahs imported Twelver Shiʿi scholars from Syria, Bahrain, northeastern Arabia, and Iraq. These scholars promoted a legalistic form of Shiʿism based on Jaʿfari law and rational derivation of legal principles (*ijtihad*). ʿAli al-Karaki (d. 1534) founded the first Shiʿi school in Iran, where Shiʿi texts were abridged and translated from Arabic into Persian. Arab Shiʿis defined a new orthopraxis based on Shiʿi law and spearheaded a policy of imposing a new doctrinal uniformity throughout the towns and villages of Iran.

In the early period of Iranian Shiʿism, the administrative and moral authority of the shahs over the religious establishment was virtually complete. The Safavids organized the scholars into a state-controlled bureaucracy. A chief religious bureaucrat (*sadr*) supervised judicial and teaching appointments and charitable endowments. He was initially responsible for the ritual cursing of the first three caliphs. The office of *divan bagi* was created as a high court of appeal. Grants of land called *soyurghal* were made to eminent religious families and were allowed to pass from generation to generation immune from taxation. With the influx of Arab scholars, there emerged a network of intermarried families co-opted by the Safavids through appointments to offices, grants of estates, tax immunities, and charities and endowments. The religious elite became part of the Iranian landowning aristocracy. In time, the Arab Shiʿi elite gave way to new cadres of Persian scholars (*ʿulamaʾ*) and to a much enlarged religious community of lower-ranking scholars, merchants, and artisans. These developments disposed the Shiʿi scholars to accept state authority and to stress those elements of the Shiʿi tradition that affirmed the state as an historical necessity.

To sustain the official religion, the Safavids embarked on a bold program to eliminate all rival forms of Islam in what had been a highly pluralistic society. Twelver Shiʿism was imposed by a wave of persecutions that had little or no parallel in other Muslim regions. The Safavids suppressed their messianic and extremist followers, who seemed likely to turn their religious passion against them. The millenarian Nuqtavis and Hurufis were eliminated. Popular Sufi movements and the *futuwwa* artisan cults, especially the cult of Abu Muslim, were suppressed. Shah Tahmasp forbade wine drinking, dancing, singing, and other Sufi behaviors at court. The dominance of Twelver Shiʿism was further assured by the violent suppression of Sunnism. The Safavids ritually insulted the memory of the first three caliphs and violated the tombs of Sunni scholars. Sufi shrines were destroyed. Ismaʿil desecrated Naqshbandi tombs and suppressed the Khalwatiyya and other Sunni-Sufi orders.

Despite repeated repression, however, merchants, craftsmen, and the working population of the towns maintained a religious and communal subculture built around Sufi leadership, *futuwwa* ideals, guilds, and youth associations. In these milieus, Sufi teaching and the veneration of Abu Muslim were kept alive by storytellers and poets in coffee houses. In the same population, women had a separate religious subculture centered on the visitation of shrines, especially to pray for fertility and good health. Female religiosity linked women of all communities – Jewish, Zoroastrian, and Armenian – in shared beliefs and practices. Although the Safavids repeatedly attempted to suppress these tendencies, their policy was not to completely eliminate them but to play them against one another and to maintain the supremacy of the shahs as the balancing, arbitrating, and manipulating leaders of society.

THE REIGN OF SHAH ʿABBAS

The move to centralize political power was set back by several ineffectual reigns in the late sixteenth century, but the state-building program was resumed by Shah ʿAbbas I (d. 1629). ʿAbbas reorganized the army. He rallied loyal Qizilbash supporters, known as lovers of the shah (*shah-seven*). In the tradition of earlier Islamic regimes, he supplemented these troops with Kurdish, Georgian, Circassian, and Armenian slave forces to offset the power of Turkish warlords. The financial basis of the slave armies was secured by seizing Qizilbash lands and turning them into crown lands. The ministers were made responsible for putting these lands into cultivation. They were expected to invest in irrigation works, protect the peasants from oppression, and assure the collection of rents and taxes. Bureaucratic administration, however, was not completely centralized. In order to pay the salaries of the soldiers, ʿAbbas reverted to the basic Islamic and Iranian practice of assigning *iqtaʿs* or *tuyul*, grants of land tax revenue, which often became the property of the assignees.

The new slave military elites played an important political role. On behalf of the shah, they collected revenues from the crown lands and constructed roads, bridges, and urban projects. Still, their power was limited. By the death of Shah ʿAbbas, the slave officers held eight of fourteen provincial governorships and made up about a quarter of the generals. The Qizilbash and other *uymaq* confederations held the balance of important military and provincial positions. Generally royal influence was used to tip the local balance of power against the great magnates in favor of lesser chieftains who would ally with the shah. ʿAbbas succeeded in reducing the power of the great magnates without changing the basic structure of the Turkish *uymaq* political system. On his death, the Iranian state continued to function by virtue of the shifting balance of power between the Safavid regime and the *uymaq* elites.

The military reorganization, however, had important foreign policy consequences. New musket and artillery units gave the shah's armies modern firepower and made them the equivalent of the Ottoman janissaries. Territories earlier lost to the Ottomans and the Uzbeks, including eastern Khurasan and parts of Kurdistan and Diyr Bakr, were retaken by the Safavids.

The centerpiece of Shah ʿAbbas's administrative and economic program was the creation of a great new capital city, Isfahan. (See Illustration 14.) It was essential

Illustration 14. The Maydan of Isfahan. Source: © Roger Wood/CORBIS.

both to a centralized state and to the legitimization of the Safavid dynasty. The Safavids built the new city around the Maydan-i Shah, a huge square that measures about 160 by 500 meters. The square served as market, carnival place, and polo ground. It was surrounded by two-storied rows of shops and by principal buildings or arches on each of the cardinal sides. To the east, the Masjid-i Shaykh Lutfallah, begun in 1603 and completed in 1618, was an oratory designed for the shah's private worship. To the south stood the royal mosque, begun in 1611 and completed in 1629. On the west stood the 'Ali Qapu Palace or Sublime Porte, which was the headquarters of the government. On the north side of the Maydan was the monumental arch that marked the entrance to the royal bazaar and its innumerable shops, baths, caravansaries, mosques, and colleges. From the Maydan, the Chahar Bagh Avenue ran two and a half miles to the summer palace in which the ruler gave audiences to ambassadors and held state ceremonies. On either side of the avenue were elaborate gardens, the shah's harem, and residences for courtiers and foreign ambassadors. The whole ensemble was a masterpiece of Middle Eastern city planning.

Isfahan's bazaars were essential to the state economy, for they concentrated production and marketing and brought them under the taxing authority of the state. The new capital was a reservoir for recruits to the imperial armies and administration. It was equally important to the vitality of Iranian Islam. In 1666, Isfahan, according to a European visitor, had 162 mosques, 48 colleges, 182 caravansaries, and 273 public baths – almost all of them erected by 'Abbas I and

'Abbas II (r. 1642–66). Isfahan's vast plazas and bazaars symbolized the legitimacy of the dynasty through its ordering of the world by royal decree; its religious monuments signified royal sustenance for the faith; its gorgeous decoration was the universal sign of royal splendor. Safavid claims to legitimacy were broadened from their initial religious basis to include the traditional motifs of Iranian monarchical grandeur.

The patronage of manuscript illuminations was one such motif. In 1510, the Timurid School of Painting was transferred from Herat to Tabriz. Bihzad, the greatest painter of the time, was appointed director of the royal library and supervisor of a workshop that produced illuminated manuscripts. Shah Tahmasp was also a great patron of the production of robes, silk hangings, and works in metal and ceramics. He kept these treasures as private and courtly adornments and devoted little attention to mosques, shrines, colleges, or other public expressions of imperial authority. The Timurid School produced an illuminated edition of the *Shah-name* (Book of Kings) that contains more than 250 paintings and is one of the great masterpieces of Iranian-Islamic illuminated manuscript art. 'Abbas I patronized paintings of battles, hunting scenes, and royal ceremonies. After his death, artistic effort turned to emotional expression and themes of private daily life; the great themes of the royal tradition were put aside in favor of more realistic and secular scenes, such as couples embracing, which may have appealed to an aristocracy of bureaucrats, landlords, and soldiers. Single-page drawings and paintings were made for inclusion in albums. The later seventeenth-century style combined sensuality and realism.

Shah 'Abbas's military and administrative reforms were partly financed by an elaborate mercantilist venture. The silk trade was critical to the Iranian economy. Since the fourteenth century, Iranian silk from beyond the Oxus and the Caspian littoral was shipped from Tabriz to Bursa in the Ottoman Empire, where it was used by Ottoman elites and sold to European merchants. To control this trade and its essential revenues, Shah 'Abbas turned northern Iranian silk-producing lands into crown estates. He also forced Armenian merchants to reside in Isfahan and to serve as intermediaries between the shah and foreign customers. Thus, the royal court gained a strong position in the trade between Iran, the Ottoman Empire, and Europe and indeed in the international trade from East, Southeast, and South Asia to Europe. In 1619, Shah 'Abbas declared silk production and sale a royal monopoly, managed exclusively by royal merchants, and forbade the export of specie.

Iran's entry into international commerce was facilitated by the British. Ever since the Portuguese seized control of the Indian Ocean trade in the early sixteenth century, the British had been looking for opportunities to bypass Lisbon and find direct access to eastern spices and luxury goods. The first Englishmen to make their way to Iran were Anthony and Robert Sherley, merchant adventurers who arrived in 1598. In 1616, the English East India Company acquired the right to trade freely in Iran. In return, the English helped ʿAbbas expel the Portuguese from the Persian Gulf port of Hormuz in 1622 and create Bandar ʿAbbas as a new port for the Persian–Indian Ocean trade. The British and Iranian victory encouraged the Dutch to enter the Iranian trade market, and the Dutch East India Company signed a treaty with Iran in 1627. Armenian merchants, in alliance with the British, the French, and the Dutch – and supported by the shah – competed with the Ottomans and Portuguese in the silk, wool carpet, shawl, and porcelain trades. By 1645, the English had been overrun by Dutch competition. The French East India Company entered the scene in 1664, although the first treaty between France and Iran was signed only in 1708, granting trading privileges and protection to Christian religious orders in Iran. By the late seventeenth century, however, European merchants were substantially in control of Iranian trade, and the economic benefits of international trade were probably lost to Iran. In the eighteenth and nineteenth centuries, the English reestablished their supremacy in the Indian Ocean and Persian Gulf.

ʿAbbas also established royal factories to produce luxury products for royal use and for international sale. Carpet making, which began as a cottage industry, was centralized in great factories in Isfahan. Silk making also became a royal industry, producing velvets, damasks, satins, and taffetas to be sold in Europe. Apart from the royal factories, there was a vibrant market economy. Metalwork, ceramics, painting, and carpet making flourished with middle class as well as royal patronage. Safavid ceramicists, with the help of imported Chinese workmen, produced their own china based on Chinese porcelains. Throughout Iran, trade was stimulated by the construction of roads and caravansaries.

The general economy was highly organized and highly regulated. Iranian merchants were organized by craft or trade, religion, and ethnicity under the supervision of headmen appointed by the shah. The heads of the royal workshops supervised the corresponding guilds. Déclassé workers – such as jugglers, acrobats, dancers, singers, and puppet show artists – were supervised by a government official. Brothels, gambling dens, cannabis and wine shops, and coffee houses were similarly regulated.

Under ʿAbbas I, the Safavid monarchy reached the height of its political power. His reign was a glorified household state, with the ruler surrounded by his personal servitors, soldiers, and administrators. He closely controlled the bureaucracy and tax collection, monopolized the manufacture and sale of important cloth goods and other products, built great cities, and maintained shrines and roads as an expression of his fatherly concern for the welfare of his people. Although his reign marked the apogee of the Iranian state, he never succeeded in establishing a fully centralized regime. The military and administrative policies that reduced the power of Turkish lords did not succeed in replacing them. His commercial policies had only short-lived success; his religious and artistic efforts were eventually appropriated by others. Ultimately, the tribal forces proved too strong, and urban merchant and rural landlord support too weak, to sustain a centralized state.

THE CONVERSION OF IRAN TO SHI'ISM

Shah 'Abbas I and his successors continued to promote Twelver Shi'ism as the official and only tolerated religion of Iran. By the reign of 'Abbas I, the translation and abridgement of Shi'i texts carried Shi'i legalism to an extensive community of Persian scholars, lawyers, theologians, merchants, and artisans. Shi'i law and worship spread through all classes of the population. Although the position of the legal scholars was generally dominant, Shah 'Abbas and his successors sponsored gnostic and philosophic ideas to counterbalance the influence of Shi'i legalism. A new school of philosophy, under the leadership of Mir Damad (d. 1631) and his disciple, Mulla Sadra (d. 1640), combined Shi'i scripture, theology, and mystical reflection to create a Shi'i version of Sufism and give a philosophic basis to individual religious consciousness and to Shi'i loyalty to the imams. The new philosophy was in the main an extension of the neo-Platonic (rather than Aristotelian) tradition of Greek and Muslim philosophy. It combined the Illuminationism of Suhrawardi and the gnosticism of Ibn al-'Arabi (see Chapter 23) with the sayings of 'Ali and the imams.

The central problem for Mir Damad was the creation of the universe and the place of the human being within it. He approached the classic issue of scholastic theology – whether the world is eternal or is created in time – by introducing an intermediary state. He divided temporal reality into three categories – *dahr*, *sarmad*, and *zaman*. *Dahr* means eternity and defines the divine essence, which is unitary and has no internal distinctions but is the source of the names and attributes that are integral to it and yet separate from it. The relationship between essence and attributes is characterized as *sarmad*. In turn, the names and attributes are the archetypes that generate the material and changeable world. The latter is characterized as *zaman*, or temporality. Although existing in time, the created world is not purely temporal in its origin, for it is brought into being by archetypes that exist before the creation of the world and are themselves eternal. Like the neo-Platonists, Mir Damad tried to close the gulf between God and the creation and to reconcile the transcendence of God with his immanence in the created world.

For Mir Damad, as for the neo-Platonist and Illuminationist philosophers, the human being stands in an intermediate position, a bridge between the world of eternity and the world of time. Man possesses qualities of perception, imagination, and intellect that link the visible and the invisible worlds. The soul both receives sensible perceptions from the material world and is illuminated by intelligible concepts from the spiritual world. The realm of archetypes (*'alam al-mithal*), intermediate between material sense perception and intellectual abstraction, is the ontological basis for symbolic imagination, dream experience, and religious commitment. The emphasis on this intermediary reality gave Shi'ism a rationalistic explanation of revealed truth and defined the metaphysical meaning of the individual's quest for spiritual salvation. Politically, it denied the claim of the Shi'i legal scholars to absolute authority in the absence of the true imam.

Although the shahs promoted gnosticism and theosophy, the spiritual and intellectual core of Sufism, they nonetheless suppressed Sufi movements. 'Abbas I massacred his Sufi disciples, who were accused of collaborating with the Ottomans and of failing to place the will of the master before all other concerns. Other chiliastic movements in northwestern Iran were also suppressed. At the same time, the shahs promoted popular veneration for the imams similar to the veneration of Sufi holy men and shrines. The great shrines of Mashhad and Qum were rebuilt in the reign of 'Abbas I and were endowed with extensive properties. Shah 'Abbas personally visited the shrines. Shrines built in memory of people born or related to imams (*imamzadas*) and shrines devoted to Hasan and Husayn (*imambaras*) replaced popular village shrines. The pilgrimage to Karbala became an alternative for pilgrimage to Mecca. The festivals of the month of Muharram became the ceremonial center of the Shi'i religious calendar. Recitations of the heart-rending story of Husayn and processions that included public flagellation, passion plays, sermons, and recitations of elegies marked a period of mourning and atonement for his death. Neighborhood groups, youth gangs, and religious factions competed in their veneration of Husayn and often ended up in bloody struggles. Thus, Shi'ism seized hold of popular emotions in order to attach the Iranian populace to the religious establishment. By the late Safavid period, Shi'ism had duplicated the whole complex of religious sensibility already found within Sunnism. It thus became a comprehensive alternative version of Islam.

In pursuit of a Shi'i polity, the shahs were also hostile to non-Muslim communities. After the capture of Hormuz, 'Abbas required the local Christians to convert to Islam. Decrees of 'Abbas I made it possible for a convert to Islam from Judaism or Christianity to claim the property of his relatives. In 1656, Shah 'Abbas II granted extensive powers to his ministers to force Jews to become Muslims. Shah Husayn (d. 1726) decreed the forcible conversion of Zoroastrians. Shi'i scholars, however, were less harsh in their treatment of Armenians, who maintained good relations with the Iranian regime because of their shared hostility to the Greek Orthodox Church. Also, Armenians and Georgians provided important recruits for the shah's military and commercial establishments.

STATE AND RELIGION IN LATE SAFAVID IRAN

The Safavid pattern of state, tribal, and religious institutions created by Shah 'Abbas I was profoundly altered in the late seventeenth and early eighteenth centuries. In this period, the Safavid regime was weakened and eventually destroyed by tribal forces, and Shiʿi Islam was liberated from state control. (See Map 15.)

The decine of the central government was manifest after the death of ʿAbbas I. In order to prevent violent struggle among potential successors to the throne, succeeding generations of Safavid princes were confined to the harem and palace precincts and were raised with a narrow education lacking any experience of public life. No ruler after ʿAbbas I duplicated his vision or authority. After the peace of 1639 with the Ottoman Empire, the army was neglected and declined into a number of small and ill-disciplined regiments. By the end of the seventeenth century, the Safavid army was no longer a competent military machine. With the decline of the military, the grand viziers and other high-ranking officials took control of rural estates and converted them into centrally administered crown lands, but the central administration ceased to function in the interests of the shah and the state.

The weakening of the Iranian state in the seventeenth century and its eventual destruction in the eighteenth century also had profound implications for the relations between state and religious elites. Land grants and tax immunities, the administration of endowments, and large clienteles of family, students, and administrative staffs transformed religious teachers into a clerical nobility. The centralized religious administration gave high-ranking clerical officials the power to appoint religious functionaries such as the chief judge (*shaykh al-Islam*), judges, and college professors, and to fill lower-ranking posts, such as teachers, prayer leaders, shrine attendants, and notaries. Religiously trained officials crossed over to the financial and chancery administration.

The declining power of the shahs allowed the latent claims to autonomy of Shiʿi scholars to come to the fore. The first steps were taken with the reaffirmation of the Shiʿi millenarian concept that the hidden imam would establish his personal rule only at the end of time, rather than in the era of Safavid authority. Many scholars withdrew from engagement in public affairs, and, by the seventeenth century, the religious motivation for involvement in worldly action was being replaced by a pious disdain for worldly affairs.

A parallel tendency was the growing claim to clerical supremacy. By the late seventeenth century, Shiʿi scholars cast doubt on the inherited authority of the shah as the primary bearer of Shiʿi Islam. This authority depended on descent from the seventh imam, but in Shiʿi theory biological inheritance was not sufficient. Testamentary designation (*nass*) was necessary to determine which of the descendants of a given imam had inherited his authority. The Safavid position was weak because they could not demonstrate designation by testament.

Moreover, according to Twelver Shiʿi belief, since the greater occultation of 941, religious scholars rather than rulers represented the hidden imam. Scholars capable of independent religious judgments (*mujtahids*) bore the highest religious authority. Their authority was based on knowledge of the Quran, the tradition

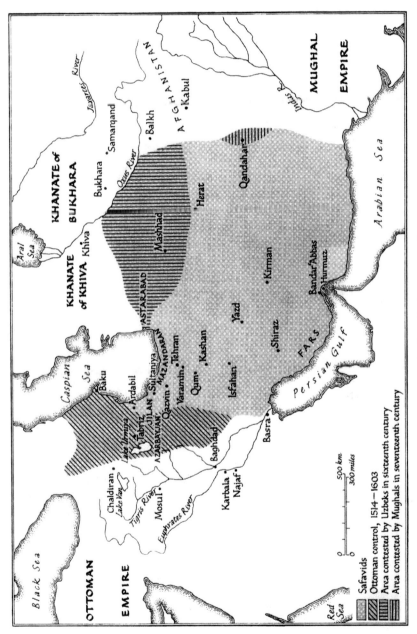

Map 15. Iran under the Safavids, seventeenth century.

Black Sea

OTTOMAN

EMPIRE

Red Sea

Chaldiran
Lake Van
Mosul
Tigris River
Euphrates River

Karbala
Najaf

Baghdad

Basra

Caspian Sea

Baku
Ardabil
Tabriz
Lake Urmiya
AZARBAYJAN
Qazvin
GILAN
Sultaniya
MAZANDARAN
Varamin
Tehran
ASTARABAD

Qum
Kashan

Isfahan

Persian Gulf

Yazd

Shiraz

FARS

Kirman

Bandar Abbas
Hurmuz

Arabian Sea

500 km
300 miles

Safavids
Ottoman control, 1514–1603
Area contested by Uzbeks in sixteenth century
Area contested by Mughals in seventeenth century

KHANATE of BUKHARA

KHANATE of KHIVA

Khiva

Aral Sea

Jaxartes River

Samarqand

Bukhara

Balkh

Oxus River

AFGHANISTAN

Kabul

Indus

MUGHAL EMPIRE

Mashhad

Herat

Qandahar

503

of 'Ali, the use of reasoned judgment in legal matters, and the consensus of the community. The people who espoused this position and gave *mujtahids* broad latitude were called the *usulis*. Their opponents, called *akhbaris*, restricted the authority of individual scholars by stressing the importance of literal adherence to the letter of the tradition passed down by the Prophet and the imams. The *usuli* rationalists harbored a claim to be the true rulers in the absence of the imams. The *akhbari* traditionalists implicitly accepted the authority of the shahs. A modus vivendi between the opposing schools was reached under the leadership of Muhammad Baqir al-Majlisi (d. 1699), the head of the Shi'i scholars, who advocated a middle way between rationalism and traditionalism. He considered traditions the crucial source of religious guidance but accepted reason and consensus as authoritative sources of judgment.

At the same time, both the shahs and the clerical elite faced a challenge from popular forms of Muslim communal organization, worship, and social customs. Sufis and gnostics found support among the common people. Despite persecution, individual Qalandaris – committed to a wandering life and rejecting all worldly connections – remained an important spiritual influence. Deviant religious practices were linked to brigandage and political revolts. To cope with these pressures, the shahs sometimes, but not consistently, adopted policies of tolerance and support for the gnostic or philosophic, Sufi, and popular versions of Shi'i Islam. Shah Sulayman (r. 1666–94), for example, patronized the popular *imamzadas*, Sufis, and philosophers as well as the legal scholars. By contrast, Shah Sultan Husayn (r. 1694–1722) and his clerics tried to suppress popular religious and social practices – ranging from music and dancing to gambling, wine drinking, cannabis consumption, and prostitution – in the name of religion and of social order. (See Illustration 15.)

THE DISSOLUTION OF THE SAFAVID EMPIRE

From the Mongol invasions to the collapse of the Safavid Empire, the history of Iran was marked by both continuity and transformation of the basic patterns of state, religion, and society inherited from the Saljuq era. From the Saljuq era, the Mongols, Timurids, and Safavids inherited a tradition of centralized monarchy and sought to strengthen the power of the central state by subordinating the tribal or *uymaq* conquerors to slave military forces and a quasi-centralized administration. Nonetheless, the Turkish and Mongol invasions had permanently consolidated the parochial *uymaq* or tribal forces in Iranian society, and all Iranian monarchs were obliged to rely on the political cooperation of *uymaq* and tribal chiefs and on *iqta'* (or *tuyul*) forms of tax administration. Iranian states remained at best household or court regimes with limited powers in the countryside. Even when the state overcame the power of the *uymaq* lords and tribal chiefs, as in the reign of Shah 'Abbas I, it could not change the underlying distribution of political power. The

Illustration 15. Persian court dress in the Safavid period. (a) Male Persian court dress in the Safavid period. (b) Female court dress. Source: Cornelius de Bruyn, *Travels in Muscovy, Persia and Part of the East Indies*, 1737.

weakening of the central state permitted the revival of *uymaq* chieftainships and provincial revolts against Safavid authority. In the eighteenth century, Iran fell into anarchy. The most important of the new competitors for political power were the Afghans, Afshars, Zands, and Qajars. Ghalzai Afghans took control of Isfahan, the Safavid capital, in 1722. Iran was then attacked by both its Ottoman and its Russian neighbors, who in 1724 agreed on a partition of Transcaucasia in which the Ottomans gained Armenia and parts of Azarbayjan and the Russians obtained the Caspian Sea provinces of Jilan, Mazandaran, and Astarabad.

With the Afghans in control of the south and the Russians and the Ottomans in control of the north, Nadir, an Afshar chieftain of Chaghatay descent, seized power. Nadir deposed the last of the Safavids and in 1736 named himself shah of Iran. His actions were not merely a Bonapartist-like adventure but harked back to an eastern Iranian frontier tradition of Turkish resistance to an Iranian central government and to ethnic Persian rule. For centuries, a frontier population, closely resembling the Cossacks of the Russian steppes, had maneuvered between the larger powers and kept alive its aspirations to establish a new khanate on the basis of a Chaghatay and Sunni identity.

In his short reign, Nadir restored the territory of the Iranian state, attempted to promote a reconciliation of Sunni and Shiʻi Islam, and integrated Afghan and eastern Iranian tribal peoples into the regime. He proposed to make Shiʻism a fifth school of law, called the Jaʻfari school, equal in status to the four Sunni legal schools. He also weakened Shiʻi scholars by confiscating properties, abolishing clerical positions in the government, and canceling the jurisdiction of religious courts. Nadir was succeeded by Karim Khan, the leader of a coalition of Zand tribal groups in western Iran, whose effective regime lasted from 1750 to 1779. In its turn, it gave way to the Qajars, who were originally Turkish lords in Safavid service and local governors in Mazandaran and Astarabad. In 1779, the Qajars defeated the Zand and established a dynasty that was to last until 1924.

Iran also went through extraordinary changes in the relationship between state and religion. In the Mongol and Timurid periods, rural Sufi movements organized popular opposition to brutal foreign regimes. The Safavids originated in a movement to unite disparate peoples, but on coming to power suppressed millenarian forms of Sufi Islam in favor of a state-constructed scholarly establishment. The Safavids made Twelver Shiʻism the official religion of Iran and eliminated their own Sufi followers as well as Sunni scholars. Safavid-period Shiʻism absorbed philosophic and gnostic ideas and popular saint worship. Iran was virtually unique among Muslim societies in the degree to which the state controlled the religious establishment and in the extent to which it absorbed all religious tendencies found within the Muslim spectrum. But with the termination of the Safavid dynasty, the all-absorbing religious establishment created by the shahs was no longer tied to the state. In the nineteenth century, it would become the leading opponent of the new regimes.

The eighteenth-century crisis brought to an end the pre-modern history of Iran. Whereas in most Muslim regions the pre-modern period ended with European intervention, conquest, and the establishment of colonial regimes, in this case the consolidation of European economic and political influence was preceded by the breakup of the Safavid Empire and the liberation of the scholars. Thus, the Safavid regime left as its legacy to modern Iran a Persian tradition of glorified monarchy, a regime based on powerful *uymaq* or tribal principalities, and a cohesive, monolithic, and partially autonomous Shiʻi religious establishment.

CHAPTER 35

THE INDIAN SUBCONTINENT: THE DELHI SULTANATES AND THE MUGHAL EMPIRE

In the Indian subcontinent, Islam was introduced into an already developed civilization defined by agriculture, urbanization, higher religions, and complex political regimes. India was defined by the caste system, by Brahmanic Hinduism and Buddhist religions, and by Rajput and other Hindu political elites. In the past, there had been great empires, but on the eve of the Muslim invasions India was divided into numerous small states. The Muslim conquests brought a new elite and a new level of political integration, beginning the process of generating a new culture blending universal Muslim concepts and symbols of statecraft, cosmopolitan artistic pursuits such as architecture and painting, and regional motifs. In India, Muslim religio-communal orientations encompassed all of the principal varieties of scholasticism, Sufi orthopraxy, shrine worship, and reformism. In India, as opposed to Iran or the Ottoman Empire, a pluralistic religious society escaped bureaucratization and state control. The special cultural qualities of Indian-Islamic civilization and the autonomy and plurality of religious tendencies made it a distinctive variant of Islamic societies.

AFGHANISTAN

The history of Islamic societies in the subcontinent began with the Arab invasions of 711–13, when Muslim rule was established in Sind, but the definitive Muslim conquest came from the post-'Abbasid military regimes in Afghanistan.

Throughout history Afghanistan has been located in the interstices between the great empires of West, Central, and South Asia. A poor, mountainous, and inaccessible country, it was never conquered as a whole by any of the surrounding empires. The population is extremely varied, divided among ethnic Turks in the north, Pashtuns in the east, Baluchis in the south, and Turkomans in the west. Tajiks are the second-biggest ethnic group, followed by Uzbeks and Hazaras. Most

(85 percent) of the population was involved in raising wheat, cotton, fruit, sheep, goats, and cattle. Half the population speaks Pashto, and Farsi is the common language of the non-Pashtun population. Farsi and Islam are the only common cultural elements, and the population is intensely parochial, tribal, and sectarian.

Historically, the country was ruled by the tribal khans, whose power varied greatly. In some cases they were the landowners as well as chiefs, and the rest of the tribesmen were serfs or tenants; in some cases power was more equally distributed. Some tribes dominated subordinate ethnic groups, who supplied labor. Within the tribes the dominant value was consensus and cooperation. The jirga existed as a larger-scale convocation of tribal elders, but in general Afghan society was highly conflicted due to blood feuds, intra- and intertribal rivalries, and the antagonisms of tribes of different ethnic, language, and religious orientations.

The most important conflicts were those between tribes and would-be central states. To survive, central rulers had to mobilize tribal support, manipulate tribes against one another, and motivate them to attack external enemies. As a central government consolidated, it put out new military outposts; built roads; established communications, such as the telegraph; and followed up with tax collectors and schoolteachers. As a central government weakened, the tribes refused payment of taxes, raided outposts, attacked small towns for arms and loot, and disseminated religious propaganda against the central government. Islam played a great social role. Mullahs had great influence in community matters such as property and honor, and many were worldly, wealthy, and prestigious. They were men of knowledge and property and power brokers in political affairs. Sufi *pirs* (holy men) formed extensive networks including prominent political and social leaders; these networks were the basis of their fund-raising and political influence.

Ghaznavids, Ghurids, Mongols, and Timurids in succession have all been rulers of Afghanistan. Mughals, Uzbeks, and Safavids partitioned it in the sixteenth to the eighteenth centuries. In the eighteenth century, rising Pashtun tribes pushed out the Safavids and fought the Mughals. Then began a long and often-repeated effort to create a centralized state. In this effort the most important Pashtun tribes, the Durranis and the Ghilzais, played the leading roles. A Durrani chieftain, Ahmed Shah Sadozai, created a small suzerainty over the tribes of Afghanistan and northern India, including the Punjab, Multan, and Kashmir (1747–73). After the death of his son Timur, Sadozai's rivals partitioned his domains. Dost Muhammad (1835–63), founder of the Muhammadzai dynasty, reestablished a central government. After his victory over the Sikhs in 1837 he called himself *amir al-mu'minin*, commander of the believers, the historical title of Muslim rulers.

In the middle of the nineteenth century, the bordering empires – British and Russian – became rivals for control of Afghanistan. The British saw it as the key to the defense of their Indian empire and invaded in 1839–42. They found this strategy too costly and then attempted to force the amirs to pacify the Pashtuns and prevent raids into India. Russian conquests in Central Asia led the British to a more "forward" policy, and another invasion in 1878–80. The British wanted an Afghanistan strong enough to be a barrier to Russia but not so strong as to threaten India. Again they had to resort to supporting the Afghan amirs as the best vehicle for controlling the tribes. In the 1880s Britain and Russia came to terms over boundaries. In 1885 the Lumsden Commission negotiated a northern border with Russia, and in 1893 the Durand Agreement defined the borders with British India. In 1907 a British-Russian treaty ratified Afghanistan's position as a buffer state.

THE MUSLIM CONQUESTS AND THE DELHI SULTANATES

The conquests of India began in earnest with the Ghaznavids. Their regime in Afghanistan was based on Turkish military slaves. They captured Lahore in 1030 and plundered North India. In the late twelfth century, free Afghan mountain war-lords, under the leadership of the Ghurid dynasty, began the systematic conquest of India. Between 1175 and 1192, the Ghurids occupied Uch, Multan, Peshawar, Lahore, and Delhi. In 1206, one of the Ghurid generals, Qutb al-Din Aybeg, the conqueror of Delhi (r. 1206–10) and his successor, Iltutmish (r. 1211–36), founded the first of a series of dynasties collectively known as the Delhi sultanates (1206–1526). (See Map 16.) Each dynasty represented a different segment of the Afghan-Turkish Inner Asian military lords and their clients, the victors of the moment in the constant jockeying for power. The successive dynasties made repeated efforts to centralize state power, but each was merely senior in a political society composed of numerous local Muslim and Hindu lords. Each dealt with the problem of establishing an Islamic state in a region of profound Hindu and Buddhist culture. In succession, they made Delhi a refuge for Persian bureaucrats, Muslim scholars, and Sufis fleeing the Mongol invasions of the Turkic, Persian, and Afghan regions to the north. Out of their collective achievement emerged a distinct kind of Indian-Muslim civilization. (See Table 14.)

The short-lived Khalji dynasty (1290–1320) succeeded the first Delhi sultanate (the dynasty of Aybeg) and extended the rule of Delhi to Gujarat, Rajasthan, the Deccan, and some parts of South India. They systematized agrarian administration. Before the Muslim conquest, agrarian taxation was based on the principle that peasants cultivated the land and paid the ruler a share of the produce. The ruler generally dealt with the villages as a unit and collected taxes with the assistance of local headmen, who would assess the individual peasants. The ruler commonly assigned his tax rights to pay the salaries of his soldiers or administrative employees. In 1300, however, 'Ala' al-Din Khalji set a new standard of revenue demand at one-half the produce, abolished the perquisites of local chiefs, and confiscated all existing land grants in an effort to deprive local lords of their military and financial power. He also controlled the grain market in Delhi, where grain was distributed at regulated prices to the soldiers and the urban population.

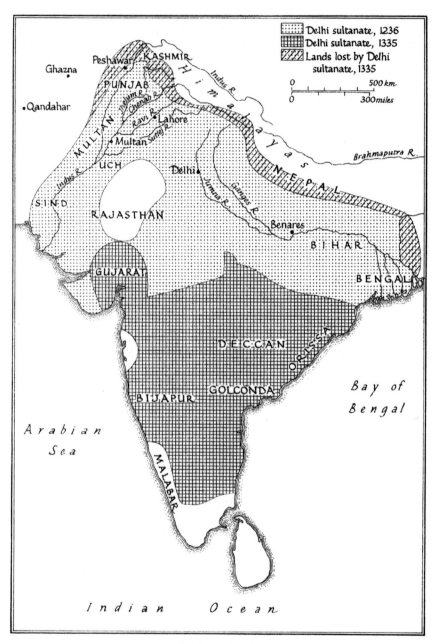

⬚	Delhi sultanate, 1236
▦	Delhi sultanate, 1335
▨	Lands lost by Delhi sultanate, 1335

Ghazna

Qandahar

Peshawar

KASHMIR

PUNJAB

Indus R.

Jhelum R.

Chenab R.

Ravi R.

Lahore

Multan

Sutlej R.

MULTAN

Indus R.

UCH

Delhi

SIND

RAJASTHAN

Jumna R.

Ganges R.

Benares

Himalayas

NEPAL

Brahmaputra R.

BIHAR

GUJARAT

BENGAL

DECCAN

ORISSA

BIJAPUR

GOLCONDA

Bay of Bengal

Arabian Sea

MALABAR

Indian   Ocean

0   500 km

0   300 miles

Map 16. The Delhi sultanates.

Table 14. *Muslim India: outline chronology*

Ghaznavids (began the Muslim conquest of India)	
Afghanistan	977–1186
Khurasan	999–1040
Ghurids	
Afghanistan and India	1173–1206
Delhi sultanates	
Dynasty of Aybeg	1206–90
Khaljis	1290–1320
Tughluqs	1320–1413
Sayyids	1414–51
Lodis	1451–1526
Suris	1540–55
Mughal empire	*1526–1858*
Akbar I	1556–1605
Aurangzeb	1658–1707
British victory at Plassey	1757
Britain becomes paramount power	1818
Independent Muslim regimes	
Kashmir	1346–1589
Deccan (Bahmanids)	1347–1527
Bengal	1356–1576
Deccan (Faruqis)	1370–1601
Jawnpur	1394–1479
Malwa	1401–1531
Gujarat	1407–1572
British Raj	*1858–1947*

For the Delhi sultanate – an offshoot of Muslim expansion sustained by a small and factious military aristocracy that ruled over the vast Indian subcontinent – cultural and ideological cohesion was essential. To soothe the factional quarrels, maintain solidarity among the Muslims, and integrate the Hindu lords into the governing elite, the Delhi sultanate elaborated its own cultural and political identity. This was at once Muslim and cosmopolitan, built on both Persian and Indic languages, literature, and arts, brought together into a new Indian-Islamic civilization.

This cultural policy, however, took time to develop. The first gesture of the Muslim conquest was to destroy major Hindu temples. They were destroyed in order to loot their riches or to signify the defeat of both Hindu rulers and their gods. Sometimes former temples were replaced with mosques that announced the victories of Muslim warlords to both Hindu and rival Muslim warriors. The Mosque of Quwwat al-Islam in Delhi, which incorporated stones and iron pillars from Hindu monuments, and the Qutb Minar, a towering brick structure, signaled the presence of a Muslim community. The Delhi regimes stressed allegiance to the caliphate and supported the judicial establishment of the scholars ('*ulama*'). Some rulers, such as 'Ala' al-Din, sought Sufi (rather than scholarly) support. Just as the Sufi saints stood at the apex of the universal spiritual order, the sultans stood at the head of secular society.

The Khalji regime was succeeded by the Tughluq dynasty (1320–1413). Muhammad b. Tughluq (r. 1325–51) was supported by newly immigrant Turkish warriors. He was the first sultan to appoint non-Muslims to military and government offices, participate in local festivals, and permit the construction of Hindu temples. To maintain the Muslim credentials, Muhammad b. Tughluq stressed his identity as a Muslim warrior by defending India against the Mongols. He gave formal adherence to Islamic law, accepted the ʿAbbasid caliph in Cairo as head of the Muslim community (*umma*), appointed a chief judge, and imposed the tax on non-Muslims. He was generally favorable to the scholars. His was the first Muslim regime to integrate Turkish warlords, Hindu feudatories, and Muslim scholars into the political elite. The Tughluq Empire, however, disintegrated rapidly under the pressure of revolts by governors, local resistance in the Deccan, and the formation of independent Hindu kingdoms.

The Indian-Islamic practice of kingship was derived from the Iranian-Muslim tradition as expressed in a treatise on kingship by Barani, a Tughluq administrator (d. c. 1360). The ruler must follow the teachings of the Prophet, enforce Islamic law, suppress rebellions, punish heretics, subordinate unbelievers, and protect the weak against the strong. The ruler and his servants must set an example of good behavior for all subjects and create the conditions that make it possible for them to fulfill their religious duties. Barani's moral principles were followed by practical advice on the management of the army, the treasury, and subordinate officials. His political theory aimed at the creation of a social order that brought men into accord with God's command by cultivating moral virtues in the governing authorities.

The Delhi regime also inherited pre-Islamic Persian traditions of kingship that promoted the exaltation of rulers and prompted them to demonstrate their authority in lavish public works. Sher Shah (r. 1540–45), for example, constructed forts, mosques, and caravansaries that provided food and fodder for travelers, troops, and merchants. He also built splendid monumental tombs for his grandfather, his father, and himself, placed in strategic locations as an assertion of legitimacy and near the tombs of saints to give himself religious respectability.

Despite its Muslim emphasis, the Delhi regime also had substantial appeal to Hindu lords. The Muslim emphasis on loyalty to the ruler, patron-client relations, and the virtues of service and honor were consistent with Hindu political ideals. Indian-Muslim recognition of the hierarchy of ranks validated the organization of Hindu society. Both subcultures accepted the dominance of kings, although the meaning of kingship was different. For Hindus, the ruler upholds the order of the world by virtue of who he is – the axis mundi; for Muslims, he fulfills his role by virtue of what he does – implementing Islamic law. In the fourteenth century, the Tughluq dynasty began to absorb Hindu motifs into Islamic architecture – both as a symbol of Muslim appropriation and as a fusion of Muslim and Hindu political authority. Tughluqid architecture borrowed such design features as the Hindu kiosk (*chatri*), heavy stone balustrades, eaves, block pillars, and capitals.

The historic task of forming a shared cosmopolitan culture was furthered by the various provincial Muslim regimes. In Bengal, Sufi writers and Muslim rulers adopted the local languages. The Hindu classic *Mahabharata* and Arabic and Persian classics, including stories from the *Arabian Nights*, were translated into Bengali at the order of Muslim rulers. Muslim poets also wrote in Bengali about Hindu deities and myths, using Arabic and Persian loan words. This synthesis of languages and literatures was the basis for the emergence of a new literary Bengali language. Similarly, the independent sultans of Gujarat (1407–1572) patronized regional languages, instead of Sanskrit or Persian.

The Deccan, Bijapur, and Golconda were important centers for the synthesis of Islam and local cultures. The Bahmanid regime in Bijapur (1347–1527) ruled a land that lay between Marathi-speaking peoples to the north and Kannada speakers to the south. In each of these regions there were local devotional movements and strong attachments to local saints. In neither was the Hindu Sanskritic tradition strong. Here, a Muslim regime encouraged the integration of elements of Marathi and Kannada culture and the formation of a new regional language, Dakhni, strongly influenced by Persian. The local Muslim elites developed a shared culture for the diverse linguistic and religious elements of the Bijapur state, defined in opposition to the northern regimes.

In Golconda, the synthesis of Muslim and Hindu aristocracies and cultures developed under the Qutb Shah dynasty (1491–1688). This regime helped to integrate the Muslim and Telugu-speaking elites by patronizing the local warrior aristocracy, providing tax-free lands for Saivite Hindu temples, and sponsoring a regional culture based on the bilingual use of Telugu and Persian. Thus, while the Delhi sultanate leaned to Muslim supremacy, the provincial Muslim regimes fostered the integration of Muslim and Hindu cultures and the formation of an Indian version of Islamic civilization.

CONVERSION AND MUSLIM COMMUNITIES

Under the cover of the conquests, Sufi warriors seeking religious merit in the holy war, Muslim scholars, scribes, poets, and intellectuals flocked to India, seeking the patronage of the new regimes, organizing colleges and Sufi retreats, and opening the way for the conversion of Indian peoples to Islam. Conversion was relatively limited; it seems doubtful that more than 20 or 25 percent of the populace of the subcontinent ever became Muslim. Muslims were concentrated in the Indus Valley, northwest India, and Bengal. In the fourteenth century, Islam spread across the Brahmaputra River into Assam and in the Deccan.

Whereas the aristocracy was composed of Muslims who came from Afghanistan, Iran, and Inner Asia, Indian converts were mostly from the lower classes. Conversions commonly occurred when Muslim lords endowed a mosque or Sufi retreat (*khanaqa*) and invited scholars or Sufis to take up residence. Around the lord and his sponsored religious teachers gathered peasants and service people who adopted the religion of their masters. However, the Turkish and Afghan warrior elite was probably hostile to conversions of nobles lest they compete for political power. Their position was similar to that of the early Arab regimes in the Middle East, for whom Islam signified the suzerainty and solidarity of an otherwise factious ruling caste.

Furthermore, the growth of cities broke down caste and geographical barriers to social interaction. People who had given up their social and political status and who were ambitious to make careers under a new regime – such as itinerant merchants, workers and peddlers, fugitive peasants, and vagabonds – found in Islam a unifying ideology. Sufi retreats were often established on the outskirts of towns and villages, where they might appeal to lower-caste elements. In North India, they were the centers for the birth of Urdu as the common language among Muslims and between Muslims and non-Muslims.

In some cases, conversions to Islam were correlated with important socio-economic changes. In the northwest provinces, where the Jats (a hunter-gatherer and pastoral population) were coming into contact with a state-based agricultural society and a literate population, Islam became the religion of people who were becoming peasants. In Bengal, conversion also represented the change of hunter-gatherer and pastoral peoples to a sedentary way of life. Before the advent of Islam, Hinduism was well established in West Bengal, where rice culture supported a Brahmin religious aristocracy and Hindu temples. In East Bengal, Brahmin and caste influences were weaker, and Buddhism was the dominant religion. Muslim rule put East and West Bengal under a single regime permeated by Islamic symbols. Under the leadership of Muslim landlords, warriors, and Sufis, agricultural expansion into East Bengal made converts out of newly sedentarized peoples.

The influence of Sufis was crucial in the spread of Islam. The story of Farid al-Din Ganj-i Shakr (d. 1245), one of the early heads of the Chisti order, is illuminating. Baba Farid settled in a place now called Pak-pattan, a village in the North Indian plain. A small dusty place of mud houses and a few shops, peopled by men reputed to be illiterate, superstitious, and quarrelsome, it had a reputation for robbing travelers. Baba Farid came to this village seeking escape from the distractions and temptations of the court in Delhi. He had for years practiced a rigorous asceticism, denying himself worldly satisfactions and concentrating his attention on devotion to God. At Pak-pattan he stopped at the edge of the village under a clump of trees, unfolded his prayer rug, and lived for days, weeks, and perhaps months in solitude, subsisting on small gifts of food that he did not acknowledge. He spent all his time in prayer.

After a time people recognized him as a holy man. The poor came for cures, amulets, and advice on family matters. They asked him to intercede with landlords and tax collectors. Officials, landowners, scholars, and the rich, weary of the emptiness of the world, went to consult him. Tribal chiefs visited to ask his help in negotiating feuds. Merchants sought his protection to pass through the town unmolested. Other holy men, both Muslim and non-Muslim, sat in his presence. As his reputation grew, Baba Farid acquired enough gifts to build a hospice. Disciples came to live with him. Stories circulated about his wisdom; he came to be venerated. People converted to Islam in his name. Thus an otherworldly man acquired worldly power. Renunciation was the basis of his worldly success. Because he no longer cared for the ordinary things of life, he was able to see matters in context and measure their relative importance. Because he did not care for himself, he was a good judge of other people's motives and interests; he was, therefore, successful as a teacher, healer, and mediator.

His followers did not see this as ordinary wisdom. They saw his powers as a sign of God's blessings being channeled into this world. They believed that he possessed *baraka*, the capacity to know things unknown and to dispense blessings that are ultimately gifts from God. When he died, his grave became the repository of his *baraka*. People visited his tomb, touched and kissed the holy place, made gifts and sacrifices, and celebrated seasonal festivals and his birth and death days.

Behind the mystical and magical powers of individual saints such as Baba Farid lay deep cultural sympathies that made the person of the Sufi and his teachings attractive to non-Muslims. The Sufi who renounced worldly gain, devoted himself to prayer, and expressed himself through poetry corresponded in the popular imagination to the Bhakti devotional preacher who had given up his past life and had access to higher wisdom. Sufism stood for detachment within the world rather than renunciation of the world. Sufis married and raised children, cared for the community, and sought to bring justice and ethical values into human affairs. Similarly, Indic philosophies valued a detached style of life that permitted the believer to outwardly fulfill the complex requirements of the social and moral code and yet inwardly be free for spiritual progress. The masses saw in the Sufis the kind of spiritual achievement they had come to expect from yogis.

Sufi teachings and practices also corresponded to the Hindu metaphysical concept of the universe. The monotheism of the Sufis was not a surprise to Hindus, because the Saivite and Vaisnavite traditions had monotheistic trends. At the same time, the claims of the Sufi masters to be the concrete manifestation of the powers of God were compatible with Hindu polytheism. Moreover, the Sufis did not wholly exclude the worship of local gods within and alongside Islam. Indeed, the veneration of Sufi graves and their annual festivals corresponded in some cases with the Hindu calendar. In Bengal and the Punjab, Muslims celebrated Hindu festivals, worshiped at Hindu shrines, offered gifts to Hindu gods and goddesses, and celebrated marriages in Hindu fashion. Hindus who converted to Islam retained many of their past beliefs and practices; many Hindus venerated Muslim saints without a change of religious identity.

Thus, in popular culture, the boundaries between Islam and Hinduism were more flexible than in formal doctrine. Islam entered into the Indian environment sometimes by assimilating converts into a new communal identity and religious beliefs and sometimes by being assimilated into the indigenous culture. Conversion to Islam was a subtle matter in which Islamic elements might be added to an existing complex of Hindu religious beliefs, without change of worldview or social identity. Alternatively, the convert could make a revolutionary change in both beliefs and allegiances.

Yet, despite considerable success in the conversion of Hindus to Islam, the great majority of the subcontinent's peoples remained Hindus. Whereas the Middle East and Indonesia were almost totally converted, India, like the Balkans, remained substantially non-Muslim. There are several reasons for this. First was the thin veneer of the Muslim conquest in India. The Muslims were small bands of warriors who were not, as in the case of the Arab or Turkish conquests of the Middle East, backed by large numbers of settlers. The Muslims established a political elite, but they could not colonize the country. Second, the pre-Islamic political structure of India remained intact. The previous regime was highly decentralized, composed of local lords and a Brahmin religious elite who retained local political power under Muslim suzerainty. The caste social structure under Brahmin leadership was also resistant to change. As in the Balkans, the thinness of the governing elite, the confirmation of local lords, and the protection of non-Muslim populations served to maintain the continuity of non-Muslim identities.

THE VARIETIES OF INDIAN ISLAM

The combination of migrations from the Middle East and Inner Asia and local conversions created many varieties of Islam in the subcontinent. Scholars often became part of the state establishment. Iltutmish patronized both Hanafi and Shafi'i scholars, who were respected as learned men, esteemed for their moral conduct, and admired for their demeanor. The sultans appointed a chief administrator (*sadr*), a chief judge, and a chief mufti; the post of *sadr-i jahan* was created in 1248 to supervise most religious activities, including justice, prayer, markets, and endowed funds. The chief justice administered the court system, and judges were appointed at provincial and district levels. Subordinate officials (*sadrs*) dealt with local land and registration matters, and judges dealt with civil and criminal cases. Preachers and prayer leaders were also state-appointed and state-paid officials. The Delhi regimes also established colleges (*madrasas*) whose teachers were salaried by the government. The curriculums of the Mu'izzi and Nasiriyya colleges included Arabic, hadith, law, logic, theology, literature, and mysticism.

However, despite the formal Muslim establishment, the influence of the scholars on the general society was limited. Rather, Sufi brotherhoods played the critical role in the creation of a Muslim community in India. The brotherhoods were built around the total devotion and obedience of the disciples to the master. The disciple was initiated into the discipline and spiritual technique taught by the master. Once the novice had been initiated, there was a ceremonial passing on of the cloak (*khirqa*) of the master to his disciple. The Sufis believed in the miraculous powers of their saints and that the very order of the universe was upheld by a hierarchy of masters, the leading one of whom was called the *qutb*. Rural mystics spread the Sufi notion of the universal hierarchy of saints and the practices of tomb veneration.

The Kazaruniyya order helped establish Islam in Kashmir; the Suhrawardiyya created an extensive network of Sufi retreats throughout North India. Multan was their main base, but the order was also important in Uch and Gujarat. The Shattari order was introduced into India by Shaykh ʿAbdallah Shattar (d. 1485), who toured the Ganges Valley dressed like a king, with followers in military uniforms, carrying banners and beating drums, in order to propagate his beliefs. His followers regarded him as being in direct contact with the saints, the Prophet, and God himself, a man possessed of both earthly and spiritual power and absolved by his detachment from the world from all ordinary legal and social norms. The Shattari order appealed to the rich and was closely identified with the state elites. It withered away when it lost the favor of the Mughal emperor Akbar.

The Chisti order was introduced into India by Muʿin al-Din Hasan Chist (d. 1236). His order spread throughout Rajasthan, Bengal, and the Deccan and was especially important in the northern Gangetic plain and the Punjab. The Chisti order accepted the doctrine of Ibn al-ʿArabi concerning the unity of being and preached a nonpolitical and nonviolent philosophy. The Chistis were committed to poverty and avoidance of the temptations of the world.

Shaykh Nizam al-Din Auliya (d. 1325), one of the founding fathers of the Chisti order, was perceived by his followers to be the head of a spiritual hierarchy who ruled a kingdom parallel to that of temporal rulers. The great Sufi leaders presided over courts that rivaled those of temporal sultans; the patched cloak, the prayer carpet, the wooden sandals, and the rosary were the mystics' insignias of chieftainship. The head of the order dispatched his lieutenants to various provinces, and they, in turn, appointed subordinates to bring the mission to towns and cities. The chief of the whole network of Sufis was often called the shah or sultan to symbolize the combination of a territorial and a spiritual sphere of influence.

The focus of Chisti devotion was the tombs of saints. The shrine festivals were held on the death day of the saint according to the Muslim lunar calendar. In these commemorations, the believers, often belonging to the same locality, clan, or professional group, brought a gift to the shrine to pray for God's assistance through the mediation of the saint and the help of the *pirs* (caretakers of the shrine, often the descendants of the saint). The caretakers provided exorcisms, incantations, amulets, and spiritual medicine to cure the ills of their followers. The donations made the *pirs* important landowners and the centers of networks of religious and political alliances.

The Sufi retreat (*khanaqa*) was the collective home of the Sufi community. A Chisti *khanaqa* consisted of a big hall called a *jamaʿat khana* in which the followers lived communally. The hall was usually a large room supported by pillars, which marked the places where the Sufis prayed, studied, and slept. Some retreats had rooms attached for the private use of the *shaykh* and senior members. Often there was a garden, a veranda, and a kitchen. Life inside a retreat was organized like that of a royal court. The Sufi master took a central place; his disciples hung about, waiting to be invited to sit near him. Similarly, the shah received the general public, listened to petitioners, gave amulets to heal the sick, mediated disputes, and dispensed spiritual counsel.

People attached to the *khanaqa* were divided between permanent residents and visitors. The permanent residents were organized in a hierarchy depending on their spiritual standing and the duties assigned them. The disciples did personal services for the master and his family and organized the housekeeping tasks of the *khanaqa*. The visitors were numerous; they included scholars, government officials, and businessmen looking for escape from worldly burdens. Poor people came for money, advice, recommendations, or intercessions with their superiors. They came for cures, sympathy, and blessings. The mystics taught them Islamic worship. Still other Sufis – Malamatis and Qalandaris, individual wandering dervishes – exemplified rejection of the worldly way of life.

Apart from the Quran and hadith, the most important religious influence on Indian Islam was the teaching of Ibn al-ʿArabi and the doctrine of the unity of being (*wahdat al-wujud*). These views were spread by both the Chistis and the Shattaris, who believed that spiritual attitude was more important than specific religious laws or practices. The philosophy of Ibn al-ʿArabi encouraged the acceptance of alternative paths to spiritual vision and led to the mutual assimilation of Sufi and Hindu beliefs about the control of emotional life as a prerequisite to the control of external behavior. The Sufis adopted Hindu ceremonies, devotional songs, and yoga techniques, as well as many details of shrine worship and etiquette. Popular religious culture became a mixture of Muslim and Hindu practices. Thus, the Sufis were divided among monist, pantheist, and syncretistic religious tendencies; between commitment to individual spirituality and to collective law; and between universal Muslim practices and specific Indian forms of worship.

Sufism was closely connected to the vernacular languages; Sufis pioneered the absorption of Indian languages, music, and poetic forms into Islamic practice. Hindi became their spoken language and inspired the birth of Urdu (a literary version of Hindi) as a Muslim language. The earliest work in Urdu was a treatise on Sufism written in 1308. Dakhni was first used by Chistis in Golconda in the early fifteenth century and was developed further by Sufis in Bijapur and Gujarat. Mystical poetry in Sindhi and Punjabi dates back to the fifteenth century; Pashto mystical poetry dates to the late sixteenth century. Poetry in vernacular languages took up classical Persian themes of the yearning for and love of God. The love of the Prophet was told and retold in poems, folk songs, riddles, and bridal songs. Hindu poets also wrote mystical poems using Islamic images and themes, including the honor of the Prophet and the mourning for Husayn.

Other Muslim movements veered away from the spiritualist and syncretic forms of Sufism. The Mahdawi movement was founded at the end of the fifteenth century by Sayyid Muhammad of Jawnpur (d. 1505). Sayyid Muhammad claimed to be the messiah (Mahdi) and traced his descent to Musa al-Kazim, the seventh in the Twelver line of imams. He preached poverty, renunciation, and prayer and sought to restore the purity of religious belief and practice by building a community based on allegiance to Islamic law. His followers established communities (*daira*) in which they lived an ascetic life, shared their earnings, and attempted to minimize their worldly involvement so as not to be distracted from their dependence on God. The members met weekly to confess their sins. The Mahdawi movement was important in Gujarat in the sixteenth century and was widely accepted during the reign of Sultan Akbar by the administrative, military, landowning, and merchant elites. With acceptance came a loss of missionary zeal, and with the passing of the millennium, the thousandth year of the Muslim era, the followers of Sayyid Muhammad lost their conviction in the imminent coming of the messiah. The movement, however, still has followers in contemporary India.

Yet another alternative was a "reformist" type of Islamic belief that stressed hadith as the basis of Muslim learning and pious practice. Opposed to the excesses both of legal studies and of Sufi spirituality, the hadith scholars found their master in Shaykh ʿAbd al-Haqq Dihlawi (d. 1642). The Suhrawardis were committed to Islamic law, taught the doctrine of unity of witness (*wahdat al-shuhud*) in contrast to the Sufi concept of unity of being, and insisted on the superiority of prophecy to sainthood. These movements would inspire Shaykh Ahmad Sirhindi (d. 1624) and the reformers of the seventeenth and eighteenth centuries.

MUSLIM HOLY MEN AND POLITICAL AUTHORITY

The relations among scholars, Sufis, and the state were varied. In principle, the scholars were servants of the state. They benefited from state protection of Islamic religious life, enforcement of Islamic laws, and state employment as bureaucratic officials, judges, prayer leaders, and teachers. The scholars and the state had a symbiotic relationship because of the division of political and religious authority.

The Sufi relationship to state authority was more ambiguous. Sufi orders, such as the Suhrawardi and the Chisti, were themselves quasi-political societies within the Delhi sultanate. The Suhrawardis maintained a close and collaborative relationship with the Delhi regimes, facilitated by their geographical distribution. Concentrated in the border regions of Multan, Uch, and Gujarat, remote from the center of power, the Suhrawardis were able to enjoy state patronage, gifts of land, and other favors, while still maintaining their autonomy as provincial notables.

Their role was to mediate between the Delhi sultanate and provincial princes and tribes. Sufism thus played an important role in integrating tribal and frontier peoples into the Delhi regime. The ability of the Suhrawardis to fulfill these political functions was the basis of their spiritual authority. Wealthy state-supported Sufi retreats were the worldly symbol of the Suhrawardi claim to mediate in the world to come.

The Chistis lived by a different political philosophy. Their *shaykhs* rejected government service, refused endowments, and expected to earn their living by cultivating wastelands or receiving unsolicited gifts from the common people. The *shaykhs* even refused interviews with sultans. For ordinary disciples, however, earning a living in some simple, productive way was considered meritorious. As part of their responsibility for improving the worldly condition of Muslims, they were permitted to take employment. For the order as a whole, charity and responsibility for the poor were primary values. The Chistis maintained their spiritual authority by detachment from rather than by mediation among worldly powers. Although rejecting worldly concerns, the Chistis were, after all, in the midst of the world. They implicitly accepted the political structures of the sultanate and indirectly endorsed the authority of the sultans by advocating a concept of universal hierarchy that sultans could use to validate their claims to be the heads of a temporal world order. Only wandering Qalandaris and Malamatis denounced and wholly withdrew from the world.

The relations of scholars and Sufis to the state and to each other changed over time. In the course of the thirteenth century, scholarly influence was ascendant, but under the Khalji dynasty (1290–1320) Sufis were promoted as a counterweight. ʿAlaʾ al-Din Khalji used the latitude given him by Chisti ties to reduce the power of Turkish nobles and scholars and to bring Indian Muslims into the governing elite. Muhammad b. Tughluq, however, called on the scholars and the Suhrawardis to condemn Chisti religious practices, such as musically accompanied religious ceremonies (*samaʿ*). Nizam al-Din Auliya, the head of the Chisti order, had to appear in person to defend himself. The Chistis were also forced to serve in military campaigns in South India and to take up missionary activities under government sponsorship. The Tughluqs succeeded in forcing them to abandon their headquarters in Delhi and to disperse all over India. Under political pressure, the Chistis split. Some collaborated with the government, and others refused. The division within the order broke the power of its all-India organization.

The political power of the Suhrawardis was also eventually broken by the authorities. Muhammad b. Tughluq gave them lands and villages and then forbade anyone to visit their retreats without permission from the governors. Disputes over succession to the leadership of the order had to be brought to the sultans for resolution. As the Suhrawardis became more dependent on the state, their mediating powers declined. Only in Gujarat, which had an independent dynasty, did the Suhrawardis continue to be regarded as patron saints. They received gifts of landed estates and maintained their influence over public opinion. With the absorption of Gujarat into the Mughal Empire in 1572, the Suhrawardis lost their political importance. Their decline allowed for the spread of the Naqshbandi and Qadiri orders and the eventual resurgence of scholars and Islamic reformist movements that demanded that state policy be based on allegiance to Islamic law, rather than on Sufi principles.

The Delhi period thus set the basis for an Islamic society, with its characteristic ambiguities of Islamic and non-Islamic aspects of state ideology and popular culture. Islam in India was marked by a pluralism of religious communities that continued during the Mughal Empire.

THE MUGHAL EMPIRE AND INDIAN CULTURE

In the early sixteenth century, the struggles over the Delhi sultanate led to the intervention of Babur (a descendant of Timur), a warrior adventurer and local lord in Farghana, who was for a short time ruler of Samarqand and then of Kabul, Herat, and Qandahar. In 1526, Babur defeated the Lodis at the Battle of Panipat and established himself as the ruler of Delhi.

Babur considered himself the heir of the Mongol destiny to rule the world. His regime was based on Timurid and Chaghatay-Mongol warriors and administrators, whom he assigned positions at court and rural estates and whom he appointed as governors of provinces and fortresses in his newly conquered empire. The Timurid military elite was backed by Persian administrators from Transoxania and eastern Iran. Babur cultivated the cultural style of his Timurid ancestors by the creation of garden palaces and the patronage of Persian poets, artists, historians, astronomers, mathematicians, and musicians from the Timurid homeland of Herat and Samarqand. At the same time, like his Timurid ancestors, he supported the Hanafi school of law and maintained a close alliance with the Naqshbandi Sufis, to the extent of marrying Mughal princesses to Ahrari Naqshbandi *shaykhs*. In his memoir and later reign, however, Babur backed away from the Timurid identity that evoked bitter historical memories of earlier invasions and stressed his role as a warrior (*ghazi*) expanding the domains of Islam.

The key to the Mughal regime was the integration of the frontier lands that supplied the conquering warriors and the settled societies. An absolute ruler governed through the imperial household, surrounded by his officers, his ministers, scholars of religion, and the servants who waited on him and the court. Household officials who dealt with domestic or palace matters were at the same time administrative officers. The imperial household had departments to manage the mint, the arsenal, the royal seals, the imperial camp, and the treasury. The ruler took a personal role in government, and the great warrior lords reported directly to him. He regulated their marriages, their leisure, and their children's education. The system of land taxation was taken over from the Delhi sultanates.

The dynamism of the regime was generated by the absence of a defined method of succession. Mughal princes were equally entitled to succeed their father and fought one another to inherit the realm. This competition was destabilizing, but it had the advantage of forcing the competing princes to rally their clients. This led to the expansion of Mughal contacts and influences in new populations and regions. Although the monarchy was not always stable, the Mughal system was constantly expanding.

Babur's grandson Akbar (r. 1556–1605) was a distinguished builder of the Mughal Empire. Akbar expanded the empire from its original territories in Hindustan and the Punjab, Gujarat, Rajasthan, Bihar, and Bengal. In the north he took Kabul, Kashmir, Sind, and Baluchistan. In the south, the Deccan was absorbed in 1600. Not until the end of the seventeenth century did the empire expand further south and absorb Bijapur, Golconda, and other hitherto independent South Indian provinces. Nonetheless, large parts of South India – especially Tamil-, Telegu-, and Kannada-speaking peoples – remained outside the Mughal realm. Rajasthan remained in the hands of local Hindu lords, and east-central India was governed by tributary tribes.

Akbar centralized and systematized Mughal rule. In addition to the Afghan, Iranian, and Turkish war lords, Akbar made native Indian Muslim and Hindi Rajputs part of the governing elite. Although the ruling elite was officially Muslim, Hindus formed about 20 percent of the Mughal aristocracy. Hindus were important as subordinate military lords, administrative officials, financiers, merchants, and landowners. Hindu officials commonly shared the Persianate cultural style of their Muslim counterparts. (See Illustration 16.)

From the Mughal point of view, the ruling elite was held together by the loyalty and service of subordinate lineages to the dominant Mughal lineage. Indian society was a condominium of noble lineages bound to the emperor by territorial or political concessions, family ties, and ceremonial and cultural style. The aristocratic lineages were called *biradari, jati,* or *qawm.* They in turn made their clients the supporters of the Mughal state. The ruling elite was further organized according to the *mansabdar* system, a military hierarchy that defined the place of the officers in the chain of command and specified the number of troops they were expected to bring to battle. The *mansab* officers were paid either in cash or by the grant of an estate called a *jagir,* which was the equivalent of a Middle Eastern *iqta'.* The *jagirs* were awarded to the sultan's officers, local princes, Rajputs, and tribal leaders. Most *jagirs* were rotated and reassigned to prevent the officers from usurping control of the land, except for the historic estates of Rajputs, which were often exempt from supervision and reassignment.

About seven-eighths of the taxable land of the Mughal Empire was distributed to military assignees, and about one-eighth was reserved as the personal estate of the ruler. A major administrative problem was to set the assignment of territories and revenues in proportion to the military obligation of the assignees. Changes in local

Illustration 16. The marriage of Akbar. Source: © Victoria and Albert Museum, London.

conditions required constant redistribution of land in order to maintain a realistic correspondence between rated values, actual income, and military obligation.

Like the emperor, each noble maintained a military contingent, a financial and administrative staff, a household staff, a harem, and servants. The household of a noble imitated the household of the ruler. Mughal nobles also assumed responsibility for building mosques, bridges, and caravansaries and for patronizing scientific and literary activity.

Beneath the level of the *mansabdars*, there were numerous local chieftains. These included *zamindars* (local notables), who had a claim to a portion of the land revenues by virtue of local conquests or caste dominance, but did not have, in principle, proprietary rights over the land. Every notable was backed by armed retainers who helped him coerce the peasants and who protected his interests against central government intervention. The notables, however, were subject to the authority of the emperor and could be expelled from office. Mughal rulers often tried to displace Rajput and other Hindu lords in favor of Muslim notables.

Beneath the level of the notables there were several classes. Moneylenders and grain merchants, rich peasants, small peasant landowners, landless laborers and agricultural workers of various castes, and untouchables made up a structured society ranked by ritual purity. Each peasant village was headed by a local official (known as *muqaddam* or *patel*), whose position was likely to be hereditary and who was responsible to the authorities for payment of revenues and for the prevention of crimes. Peasants were guaranteed permanent and hereditary occupancy of the land, but they were also bound to it. In an age when land was abundant, people scarce, and peasants prone to flee to uninhabited regions, physical force had to be used to keep them in place. (This is just the reverse of modern conditions, in which landlords dominate an excessive number of human beings by threatening to evict them.)

The system for the collection of taxes that applied to the central provinces of the empire, including Multan, Lahore, Delhi, Agra, Oudh, and Allahabad, went back to Sher Shah, was continued by Akbar, and lasted until the end of the seventeenth century. Taxation was administered according to the *zabt* system: a fixed fee was assessed for each unit of land and paid in cash. The rate of assessment was based on the value of the crop raised and the average yield of the previous ten years. The amount actually collected was ordinarily half of the total crop. Everything that could be taxed without depriving the peasants of their subsistence and their capacity to produce another crop was taken. The actual collection of taxes was entrusted to the holders of military assignments (*jagirdar*), who were supposed to be supervised by other government officials.

In town administration, the judge not only adjudicated or arbitrated disputes but also registered contracts, regulated prices, mediated the payment of taxes, maintained mosques, and supervised charities. He played a central role in the social life of his community, officiating at births, marriages, and deaths. Another local official, the *kotwal*, policed the towns, prosecuted criminal activities, and censored immoral behaviors by suppressing brothels and taverns.

In matters of property and commerce, there were complex relationships among individuals, their communities, and the state that linked together different elements of town societies. Property was often regulated by the community. Some transactions – such as the sale and purchase of property – had to be agreed not only between seller and buyer but by the relevant corporate group, kin, or neighborhood, and by the judge representing the state. In important trading towns, a corporate body of merchants negotiated with government officials, regulated commerce, collected taxes, and sometimes advanced loans to the state.

Apart from the formal system, governance depended on personal and informal arrangements among the central and local officials and notables, and the collaboration of both local officials and local nonofficial power holders. Not only nobles, warrior chieftains, and large landowners but also small landowners, merchants, tribesmen, religious leaders, and even petty clerks had some elements of authority and influence. The sultans could not make their will prevail without the aid of local notables, and no local notable could impose his authority without appearing to be loyal to the sultan. Sovereignty was shared between the central government and local authorities.

AUTHORITY AND LEGITIMACY

Akbar also set the cultural style of the Mughal era on the basis of the combined legacy of Chaghatay Inner Asia (communicated through Babur) and the Delhi sultanate. The Chaghatay heritage stressed the role of the ruler as a warrior lord. Both the Timurid and the Delhi sultanates contributed concepts of royal authority derived from the Persian monarchical tradition that made the scholars advisors, tutors, diplomats, and administrative servants of the ruler. While appealing to Muslim scholars by the endowment of colleges and libraries, Akbar also supported the Chisti order.

This policy was radically revised in 1582 after Akbar defeated his brother Mirza in a struggle for the throne. With Mirza's defeat, Akbar went beyond the indirect appeals of the Delhi sultanate to the non-Muslim elites and proclaimed a cultural policy intended to create a hybrid cosmopolitan Indian-Islamic culture. Akbar founded a new cult, Din-i Ilahi (divine religion), to bind the members to the emperor himself. The emperor claimed to be virtually a prophet, possessed of the right both to interpret the Quran and Islamic law and to be the Sufi master of a new religious order. He adopted the Shi'i title of *"imam-i 'adil"* (just imam), suspended imperial sponsorship of the pilgrimage to Mecca, and planned to replace the Islamic calendar. The *Akbar-name* of Abu'l-Fazl 'Allami (d. 1602) captures the underlying concept. It describes a court society in which the ruler is considered a philosopher-king, a protector of all his subjects regardless of their religion, a spiritual guide who brings reconciliation and love, and a fosterer of well-being in the whole of his domain.

Cultural policy also sought to focus loyalty on the ruler as the protector of a shared Hindu-Muslim elite culture in manners, dress, art, painting, architecture, poetry, and belles lettres. Persian was the literary language of high culture and became the language of Mughal administration for Hindu as well as Muslim officials. Poets from all over the Persianate world flocked to India. Hindu works on

religion, law, mathematics, medicine, astronomy, romances, and fables were translated into Persian. In the eighteenth century and later, Persian was gradually superseded by Urdu, a dialect of Hindi enriched by Persian. This was a new common
language for regional elites, service officers, gentry, and wealthy merchants.

The architectural style patronized by Akbar and exhibited in the major palace
and forts of Ajmer, Agra, Allahabad, Lahore, and Fathepur Sikri was based on
motifs drawn from both Muslim and Hindu architecture. The combination of these
elements reflects earlier Indian structures. Post and lintel construction, serpentine
brackets to support eaves, zoomorphic forms, bell-and-chain motifs, and other
devices were all used in earlier mosques and palaces. Reciprocally, Hindu palaces
and temples used abstract geometric decorations and domed roofs stemming from
the Muslim tradition. By the Delhi sultanate period, Indian architecture had already
assimilated diverse forms in ways that no longer retained sectarian implications and
transcended religious and regional origins. Adopting this architectural style for the
tomb of his father, Humayun, Akbar fostered a hybrid culture for a diverse elite.

Similarly, Indian painting integrated Persian techniques of figure drawing, illumination, and calligraphy but took on specifically Mughal qualities that emphasized
line and form rather than color. Akbar and later Mughal emperors favored portrait
groups that illustrated their descent from Timur and a mythical Mongol ancestress,
Alanqua, impregnated by a shaft of light. Although Mughal painting depicted court
and hunting scenes, battles, animals, flowers, portraits, and other motifs of Persian
art, it also drew inspiration from Hindu subjects and landscapes. Paintings were
used to illustrate both Persian and Hindu literary works, including the *Mahabharata*
and the *Ramayana*, and were produced by artists of both religious backgrounds.
Indian painting, like Indian architecture, transcended sectarian implications.

Political theory embodied a similar nonsectarian ideal. The Nasirean ethics,
along with Sufi tradition and Persian poetry, cultivated the ideal of a ruler who
ensures the well-being of all his subjects. Through the pursuit of justice and the
application of law, harmony and cooperation could be achieved in society. Mughal
cultural policy implied a vision of a society that was both Indian and Muslim.

THE DECLINE OF THE MUGHAL EMPIRE

The successive reigns of Jahangir (r. 1605–28) and Shah Jahan (r. 1628–57) were
high points in Mughal cultural creativity. Jahangir was linked to the Timurid tradition through miniature paintings, seals and inscriptions, and the creation of gardens
such as the Shalimar Bagh in Kashmir. Shah Jahan reconstructed the royal city in
Delhi and built the Taj Mahal, considered one of the most beautiful Islamic buildings ever built. (See Illustration 17.)

Shah Jahan extended the Indic-Islamic cultural policy into politics. He proclaimed himself the "second Timur" and tried to prevent a struggle over succession
by nominating one son, Dara Shikuh, on the basis of his spiritual qualities and his

Illustration 17. The Taj Mahal. Courtesy of Thomas Metcalf.

alleged leadership of the Qadari Sufi order – rather than his military or administrative achievements. Dara Shikuh was promoted as the bearer of divine favor who accepted elements of Hindu religious thought as an expression of monotheism and universally valid religious truths. He was, however, defeated by Aurangzeb in a struggle to inherit the throne. (See Map 17.)

The reign of Aurangzeb (r. 1658–1707)

Aurangzeb was the first Mughal ruler to reverse the policy of conciliation of Hindus in favor of Islamic supremacy. In 1659, he forbade drinking, gambling, prostitution, the use of narcotics, and other vices. In 1664 he forbade *sati*, the Hindu sacrifice of widows, and abolished taxes that were not legal under Islamic law. In 1668, he banned music and astrology at court, imposed the poll tax on non-Muslims, and ordered the destruction of some Hindu temples. There is some question as to whether these edicts were enforced or whether they were just political

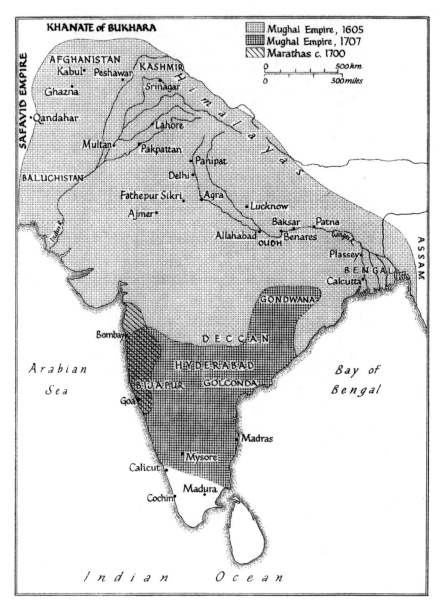

Map 17. The Mughal Empire, 1605–1707.

theater. Aurangzeb sponsored the codification of Islamic laws called the *Fatawa-i ʿAlamgiri*, intended to be the legal bases for decisions by judges and muftis. He also founded colleges to promote the study of Islamic law. Aurangzeb's reforms antagonized Hindus but still fell short of Muslim reformist demands.

The reign of Aurangzeb also saw profound changes in the structure of the Mughal nobility. He was the first ruler since Akbar to expand the frontiers of the empire. He absorbed East Bengal, pacified the Northwest Frontier, took direct control of Rajasthan, and expanded the Mughal Empire in the Deccan. The invasion of the Deccan involved the incorporation of a large number of Bijapuris, Hyderabadis, Marathas, and other Hindu lords into the imperial elite. As a result, the proportion of Hindus in the *mansabdar* system rose from approximately 20 to 30 percent; Marathas came to outnumber Rajput lords. Whereas the new lords could easily be assigned a place in the rank system, there was no way to provide estates for the enlarged military elite. The result was increased competition for scarce *jagirs*, factionalism, and the exploitation of the peasants. In the late seventeenth century, taxes began to be collected before the harvest. The poll tax on non-Muslims also increased the fiscal burden of peasants.

Moreover, by the late seventeenth and early eighteenth centuries, power was shifting from the Mughal capital and court to regional and local power holders. This was encouraged by succession struggles after the death of Aurangzeb and a series of feeble rulers that weakened the central state. Yet the redistribution of power was inherent in the political system of the empire. From the beginnings of the Mughal conquest, the power of the state depended on the acquiescence and collaboration of local notables. Higher officials took into service petty officers recruited in their jurisdictions. Networks of personal relations held together center and provinces, and capital and peripheral communities.

By the eighteenth century, however, as in the Ottoman Empire, the balance of power favored local forces. They benefited from the resources accumulated in earlier clientele relations. The arrival of new trading partners in the Indian Ocean – the Portuguese, the Dutch, the British, and the French – gave further incentives for regional, local, and commercial elites to shake off a waning imperial power. Land grantees, village headmen, and tax farmers became landlords. *Mansabdars* converted their land-tax tenures (*jagirs*) into permanent tenures, reversing the long-standing Mughal policy of rotating land revenues among the nobles to forestall the formation of independent local elites. *Zamindars* (local notables) became increasingly independent and refused payment of revenues. Village headmen became the key figures in the collection of revenues and in local negotiations with the government authorities. Rich farmers, small-town and rural shopkeepers, coin changers, moneylenders, and landlords profited from the redistribution of fiscal power.

Furthermore, the urban merchant class was growing. In the seventeenth and the first half of the eighteenth century, the Indian economy was generally prosperous. Although Delhi and parts of the Punjab were in decline, Bengal, Awadh, Rajasthan, and the Deccan were growing. India prospered from strong agricultural production, long-distance trade in cheap bulk commodities, linkages among the financial centers, exports of silk and cotton cloth, and a common monetary system supplied with European silver. The towns were lively market centers and gave employment to soldiers, servants, laborers, and artisans who worked on luxury goods. Small towns and markets throughout North India grew in commercial importance on the basis of wider market networks and rural enterprises.

Decentralization of power also favored the growth of Muslim families composed of local judges, government functionaries, landowners, urban rentiers, and religious leaders who controlled the revenues of mosques, tombs, and shrines. Muslim landlords and moneylenders acquired a corporate consciousness. In the *qasbahs* (small- and medium-sized towns) the leading Muslim families – sharing *ashraf* (noble Arab, Mughal, or Pashtun) status, united by intermarriage, and linked to the town academies and to Sufi tombs and shrines – emerged as a local elite.

In other parts of Indian society, sustained by aristocratic consumer demand in such growing cities as Lucknow and Benares, Hindu merchants, their clients, and their dependents grew wealthy. Their commercial networks overlapped with religious sects as a rising elite sought communal solidarity and corporate protection. Peasants also organized to resist exploitation. Castes, religious sects, and the clienteles of *zamindar* chiefs provided the social basis for peasant action. As in the Ottoman Empire, the widespread availability of gunpowder weapons made it all the more necessary for the empire to depend on merchant capital for resources and to negotiate with its subjects. Popular resistance and appeals to Muslim values and Islamic law constrained the exercise of authority at all levels.

With this redistribution of power in favor of local elites, the Mughal Empire came apart, and its provinces became independent. In several regions local *mansabdars* became provincial governors (*nawwabs*). The Nizam of Hyderabad became independent in 1723.

In Bengal, the change of regimes destroyed the *jagir* form of assignments, and the old Mughal aristocracy lost its position. *Zamindars* and bankers seized control of the tax system. In other parts of India, regimes based on Hindu lordships and popular uprisings came to power. Hindu-governed principalities regained control of Rajasthan. In the Punjab, religious and ethnic groups such as the Sikhs and the Jats established local regimes. The Maratha movement, based on peasant resistance to taxation, Hindu revivalism, and vernacular languages, led by Shah Shahji and his son Shivaji, defied Mughal authority. By the middle of the eighteenth century, the Marathas controlled most of South India and had replaced the Mughals as the dominant power in Gujarat.

By the middle of the century, Marathas, Sikhs, and Afghan tribesmen from the north were fighting to control the remaining territories of the moribund empire. The Marathas consolidated their grip on central and western India and formed five independent and expanding states. In 1739, Nadir Shah, the conqueror of Iran, occupied Kabul, sacked Delhi, and took control of the Mughal lands north of the Indus River. The Marathas occupied much of India south and west of Agra. The helpless Mughal regime had to call on Maratha support to resist the Afghans, but at the Battle of Panipat (1761) the Marathas were defeated by Ahmad Shah Durrani. No Indian power proved capable of resisting the foreign invaders. As a result, the Sikhs were able to expand in the Punjab between 1750 and 1799 and establish a new state with its capital at Lahore. With the empire broken into smaller political units, the way was also opened for the emergence of the British as the paramount power in India.

ISLAM UNDER THE MUGHALS

Although imperial culture tried to integrate Muslim and Hindu elites, not all Muslims were part of the ruling elite. Muslims did not constitute a single community but belonged to different ethnic groups, lineages, classes of population, and even castes. Muslims, like Hindus, were often identified with kinship and specialized occupational groups, ordered in a hierarchy that gave the highest status to warriors from Afghanistan or Inner Asia and to religious families descended from the Prophet or from Iranian and Arab scholars. Merchants, craftsmen, and service people were of lower status.

Above, all, Indian Muslims formed numerous religious bodies divided by allegiance to schools of law, Sufi orders, and the teaching of individual *shaykhs*, scholars, and saints. Some were Sunnis and some Shiʿis, although this was not an absolute distinction, owing to the strong sympathies for the family of ʿAli among Sunnis. Sunnis were themselves divided between those committed to scripturalist Islam (to the beliefs and laws set out in the Quran, the hadith of the Prophet, and the Islamic legal tradition) and those devoted to popular Sufism (in which veneration of saints, living and dead, with associated ceremonies of remembrance, mourning, and ritual marriages and funerals was the principal form of religious expression). One current in Indian Islam ran toward the disciplined, rational, and controlled practice of Islamic law; the other, toward emotional faith and identification with the miraculous powers of saints. Into the first camp fell such diverse groups as the scholars, the organized schools of law, and orthopraxy-minded Sufi orders. In the second camp, there were the Sufi saints and their descendants, who managed their tombs, shrines, and the brotherhoods founded in their names. The two orientations led to different views about the boundaries between Muslims and non-Muslims. Popular saint worship blurred the religious distinctions among Muslims and Hindus; certain Sufi theories and cosmologies blended Hindu and Muslim concepts.

In the Mughal era, the scholars were in the service of the state. The Mughals continued the Delhi sultanate system of bureaucratic religious administration. Full control over the judiciary was given to a chief judge. The provincial *sadr* was in charge of local judges, market inspectors, preachers, prayer leaders, muezzins, and trust-fund administrators. He was responsible also for the appointment of muftis and for liaisons between the government and the scholars. His office provided stipends for scholars and sometimes included the power of making grants of landed property; trusts were created to provide income for shrines, tombs, and schools. He issued the daily allowances for religious persons and made payments out of the funds of charitable endowments. The *sadr* was also responsible for charities and for feeding the poor. In the course of the seventeenth century, his power was checked by administrative arrangements that gave other officials control over land and by the creation of a more decentralized religious administration in the provinces. His judicial powers were also limited by rulers who involved themselves directly in religious affairs.

In the Mughal period, the influence of the Naqshbandis and the Qadiris replaced that of the Suhrawardis and Chistis. The Naqshbandis cultivated a spiritual discipline leading to the vision of God, but they also insisted on the necessity for active engagement in worldly affairs. The histories of two Naqshbandi *shaykhs* of the eighteenth century illustrate the religious and social principles espoused by the order. Mirza Mazhar (d. 1781), the founder of the Mujaddidiyya branch of the order, came from a family of soldiers and administrators and took up the Sufi life to avoid political conflicts and to control the violent impulses in himself. He turned to Sufism as a way of finding tranquility and security in an uncertain world. His teachings stressed the harmony of the various Sufi traditions. He minimized the differences between the theosophical and legalistic forms of Sufism. His whole life was lived in cautious efforts to protect himself from contamination by food, gifts, and other worldly things, which were all scrutinized for their legality and appropriateness. He also recommended celibacy. Mirza Mazhar never claimed the power to perform miracles, but his followers believed it of him anyway.

His successor was Shah Ghulam 'Ali (d. 1824), who stressed the social and political roles of the Naqshbandi *shaykh*, organized the *khanaqa*, sent disciples to proselytize in Iran and Afghanistan, and distributed charity and spiritual and moral advice to supplicants. He used his moral influence with political figures whenever possible.

By contrast, other Sufi orders stressed veneration of saints. The Chisti order was originally built on the personal religious insights of the founding teacher, but as time passed, the charisma of the saints was taken to reside in their tombs. Their descendants then served as the managers of their shrines and the organizers of the orders that flourished around them. The *pirzadas*, the hereditary descendants and managers of the saints' tombs, supervised the festivities commemorating the birth and death anniversaries of the saints, maintained public kitchens, led community prayers, and offered amulets along with spiritual and social advice. The growth of the shrines as centers of worship led to the accumulation of properties granted and protected by the state. The Mughals awarded landed properties to the Sufis, a practice that legitimized both donor and recipient, enabling the Mughals to intervene in succession disputes and to control the managers of the shrines. They converted the *pirzadas* into a petty gentry sensitive to the wishes of the political authorities.

In the sixteenth century, Shiʻi influence was also very strong. Golconda and Kashmir were ruled by Shiʻi princes. The Mughals had Shiʻi wives, and many Shiʻis held high offices. The Indian Shiʻi communities included the Twelvers, whose teachings we have examined in the chapter on Iran. The headquarters of these Indian Shiʻis was moved to Lucknow in 1775, and the Nawabs of Awadh later promoted a distinct set of rituals and practices.

The Nizaris had their origin in a schism among the Fatimids. They were the Assassins of twelfth-century Iran. With the collapse of the Nizari state of Alamut in 1256, the mission entered a new passive phase, concentrating on the symbolic and religious rather than political expressions of its goals. The Nizaris held that God was utterly transcendent and unknowable and that he brought into existence the world of intelligences; religious salvation was achieved by ascending the ladder of intelligences and returning to the first intelligence through which man achieved unification with God. The Nizaris believed that the cosmic order was represented in history by cycles of prophets and imams. There were seven cycles of prophets, each cycle consisting of seven imams; the final cycle ends with the resurrection. Their mission in India began in the late twelfth or early thirteenth century in Sind and Gujarat. At first, the Nizari communities in India acknowledged the supremacy of the imams in Iran, but in the sixteenth century the movement split, and only some of the Nizaris maintained this connection. Eventually, the imamate was transferred from Iran to India by Aga Khan I, Hasan ʻAli Shah, who moved to Bombay in 1845.

The Bohras had their origin in the same schism that gave rise to the Nizaris. With the disappearance of their imam, al-Tayyib, in 1133, leadership of the community was turned over to the *daʻi al-mutlaq*. The *daʻi* stands in a hierarchy that includes other missionaries, including the higher-ranking *hujja* and *natiq* and the imams. When the imams and the higher authorities are concealed, the *daʻi* becomes the highest functionary in the social world. He is empowered to teach the community, resolve internal disputes, and name his successor in accordance with divine inspiration. He operates through agents called *amils* and *shaykhs* who are the equivalent of scholars.

The Bohra branch of Ismaʻili Shiʻism was first established in Yemen, and the Bohras probably came to Gujarat in the early thirteenth century. A deputy (*wali*) ruled until 1539, when the first Indian *daʻi* was appointed. In the long history of the Bohra community, there were several major schisms. In 1846, with the death of the last *daʻi* of the Rajput line, the authority of the missionaries was compromised. The nineteenth-century Bohras tended to regard them as administrative figures rather than spiritual teachers, and their leadership was challenged by the scholars.

The diversity of Muslim religious and social groups in India inspired conflicting concepts about the social meaning of Islamic religious belief. The legally minded conceived of Muslim society as cutting across lineage and class lines. They defined Muslims not by inherited lineage, position in the state, or occupation, but by individual belief in Islam, which transcended all other social ties and made men equals and brothers in religion. Although they recognized the importance of the Mughal Empire, Islam in their view was still a universal community. Orthopraxy-minded Muslims stood for state enforcement of Islamic law and state-mandated subordination of Hindus to Muslim rule by discriminatory taxes and restrictions. By contrast, popular Sufism viewed Islam as an integral aspect of lineage, occupational, and neighborhood ties.

These differences of religious orientation were an important political issue in the seventeenth and eighteenth centuries. Whereas the state pursued a policy of conciliation among different Muslim groups and among Muslims and Hindus, scholarly critics of Akbar opposed his religious toleration, his openness to non-orthoprax religious ideas, and his assumption of the prerogatives of a Sufi. The most important opponent of imperial policies was Shaykh Ahmad Sirhindi (1564–1624). Sirhindi claimed to be the *mujaddid*, the renewer of Islam in his century, a man standing on the spiritual level of the early caliphs. Initiated into the Naqshbandi order, he became the principal Indian spokesman for Islamic law and the reformist point of view. He taught that obedience to Islamic legal norms was the key to its inner meaning and modified Ibn al-ʿArabi's doctrine of the unity of being, the metaphysical basis of religious syncretism, in favor of the doctrine of unity of witness. He opposed the insinuation into Islam of Sufi and Hindu practices, such as worship of saints, sacrifice of animals, and religious festivals. As a reformer, he waged an unrelenting crusade to persuade the Mughal authorities to adopt policies befitting an Islamic state. He regarded Hinduism and Islam as mutually exclusive. He believed it was the obligation of Muslims to subdue non-Muslims, and thus he urged rulers and nobles to impose the poll tax on non-Muslims, to permit the slaughter of cows, to remove non-Muslims from political office, and to enforce Islamic law in every way.

Sirhindi's great follower was Shah Waliallah (d. 1763), who pursued the tradition of reform in different circumstances. In the declining age of the Mughal Empire, Shah Waliallah was concerned with securing the Muslim presence in the subcontinent. After visiting Mecca, the center of reformist teaching, he stressed the importance of returning to the Prophet's teachings and the need to purge Islam of saint worship, which was subsequent to and inconsistent with the true meaning of the Prophet's life. He translated the Quran into Persian and argued for the use of independent scholarly judgment in the adaptation of the law to local conditions. While supporting the supremacy of Quran and sunna, he attempted to synthesize the different schools of law and reduce legal divergences among Muslims.

Shah Waliallah believed that reform required a Muslim state, modeled on the early caliphate, to enforce Islamic law. He defined the caliph as the religious leader who is closest to the example of the Prophet, a perfect man who strives for justice and tries to use administrative and judicial techniques to lead his people to religious virtue. In Shah Waliallah's view, the will of God radiates through the caliph into the feelings and minds of his subjects. Even in the absence of this spiritual function, a caliph provides for the political defense of Muslim peoples and the organization of Muslim law. His duty is to enforce Islamic religious practice, collect the alms tax, promote the pilgrimage, foster study and teaching, administer justice, and wage jihad. This was a program of religious consolidation in the struggle against popular Sufi Islam and in opposition to a lax Mughal regime.

As a consequence of this pluralism, there was no sense in India of a universal or unified Muslim identity. Although the state patronized the small scholarly establishment, both scholars and Sufis were generally independent. Reformist-minded scholars were critical of the Mughal state for its cosmopolitan and imperial culture, its Hindu elite, and its patrimonial loyalties. Many pious Sufis withdrew altogether from political contacts, but Sufi leaders tended to be accommodationist and to accept state support and the legitimacy of the regime. Thus, the legacy of premodern Indian-Islamic organization was not state control of doctrine, teaching, or judicial administration nor a history of well-established schools of law and scholars, but one of numerous autonomous and competitive Muslim religious movements.

Over centuries, a distinctive expression of Islamic civilization emerged in the Indian subcontinent. Like their Iranian and Middle Eastern predecessors, the Delhi sultanates and the Mughal Empire were committed to a concept of state culture that blended Islamic symbols with a royal heritage. In the Iranian case, these were the symbols of ancient Iran as transmitted through the ʿAbbasid caliphate. In India, royalty meant the heritage of Iran combined with Mongol, Timurid, and Chaghatay concepts and with Indian and Hindu motifs, which introduced new elements into Islamic imperial culture. The Mughal era bequeathed to modern India a distinctive variant of Muslim institutions and cultures.

Muslim religious life in the Indian subcontinent both resembled and departed from Middle Eastern norms. Islam in India replicated the basic forms of scholarly and Sufi Islam. Whereas in Iran Shiʿism absorbed all levels of Islam into a monolithic establishment, in India the various forms of scholarship, Sufi contemplation, worship of saints, and reformist tendencies remained in open competition with one another. In India, Islamic belief and practice on the popular level was manifestly mixed with local Hindu and Buddhist forms of belief and worship. The formation of a popular Muslim subculture in India was not, however, a departure from Muslim norms but an example of a process that was universal. In the Middle East as well, Islam had been formed as a syncretism of popular Christian and Jewish religious practices with Muslim teachings, although the passage of time has concealed the syncretic nature of Middle Eastern Islam.

THE INTERNATIONAL ECONOMY AND THE BRITISH INDIAN EMPIRE

India had long held a central position in international trade. Geographically it stood at the hub of the South China Sea, the Bay of Bengal, and the Indian Ocean. It was a bridge in the trade between the Far East and Europe and an important producer and exporter of textiles and spices. Indian trade with Europe had historically been routed through the Persian Gulf and the Red Sea, until in 1498 Portuguese mariners rounded Africa and discovered a direct sea route to South and East Asia. They established a series of bases in the Indian Ocean region (including Cochin and Goa) and sought to monopolize the spice trade. The Portuguese attacked the pepper fleets from Calicut, Kollam, and Cannanore and forced Indian Ocean traders to call at the port of Diu to pay customs duties. After 1600, the Portuguese monopoly was broken by the English and the Dutch. In the seventeenth century, the Dutch, British, and French established factories, warehouses, and residents for their merchants.

The British East India Company began trading in India in 1600. British factories were founded at Surat in 1612, Madras in 1640, Bombay in 1674, and Calcutta in 1690. They exported Indian cotton and silk cloth, cotton yarn, raw silk, saltpeter, indigo, and spices and imported silver bullion and other metals. At the outset, the East India Company depended on Indian traders and manufacturers, but it gradually set up its own networks with local producers and suppliers and undermined the older trading and manufacturing cities by concentrating commercial activity in Bombay, Calcutta, and Madras. In effect the British set up the kinds of networks that the Mughals had used to govern India, progressively extending their economic influence from one region to another and converting that power into political control. The company thus made itself into a local government and, in its struggles with competing local forces, into a colonial regime.

The critical events in the British rise to dominance were a long series of eighteenth-century wars in which the British defeated French and Indian rivals. Through the battles of Plassey (1757) and Baksar (1764), the British established themselves as the de facto rulers of Bengal. In 1772, Warren Hastings, the British governor of Bengal, took charge of the British factories of Madras and Bombay and created a unified regime.

In Bengal, the British established a new system of taxation and judicial administration. They took control of the courts and established a British-officered police and army. By means of the so-called Permanent Settlement (1793), rural taxes were set at fixed rates – a measure that ruined the old Muslim elite and opened the way for the purchase of *zamindari* tenures by wealthy Hindu merchants and investors from Calcutta. British goods came to dominate the local economy and undermined the Indian textile industry.

British power in Bengal was soon extended to other parts of India as "protection" was offered or imposed on local rulers and elites. By 1818, the remaining Rajput and Maratha rulers acknowledged the British as the paramount power. The Punjab and the Northwest Frontier were absorbed at a later date, but by the 1820s and 1830s British paramountcy was secure. In 1858, in the wake of the Indian mutiny, the British removed the last of the Mughal emperors and brought India under their direct control.

CHAPTER 36

ISLAMIC EMPIRES COMPARED

Each of the Islamic empires of West and South Asia – the Safavid, the Ottoman, and the Mughal – had a unique history, but the three had many features in common. They were all built on the combined heritage of past Middle Eastern imperial Islamic societies and the heritage of Inner Asian, Mongolian, and Turkic political institutions. In the Iranian tradition government was entrusted to hereditary rulers. The Turkish conception of society was based on military competition. Rulership in Turkish society was achieved by victory in battle and was maintained by active struggle against rivals. In the three empires, Iranian traditions of kingship, social hierarchy, and justice were combined with Turkish concepts of mythical heroes and glorious ancestors.

Whereas Mongol and Timurid precedents called for partitioning an empire among the sons of the ruler and allowed them to fight one another for power, the Safavids, Ottomans, and Mughals established, with some exceptions, a routinized dynastic succession. Each empire was built around a patrimonial or household government, elements of a centralized bureaucracy, a quasi-feudal assignment of tax revenues to support the military and to carry on local administration, and finally the extensive farming out of tax collection and other governmental functions to create patronage networks that bound soldiers, provincial officials, and local notables to the central government. All three empires had the support of royal armies (sometimes slave military forces and sometimes lower-class recruits), bureaucratic personnel, provincial feudal and tribal notables, landowners, merchants, and religious elites. There were important differences in the weight and balancing of the several bases of imperial power. The Ottomans probably had the most centralized regime; the Mughals were notably more patrimonial and less bureaucratic; the Safavid regime, the most patrimonial, was dependent on religious prestige and on the support of administrative and tribal notables. From the fourteenth century, the Ottomans relied on slave military forces; the Safavids introduced such forces in the sixteenth century, but the Mughals by and large depended on freeborn Muslims and Hindus.

The empires ruled diverse populations. The Ottoman Empire ruled over many religious (Muslim, Jewish, and Christian) and ethnic (Greek, Romanian, Hungarian, Tatar, Turkish, Kurdish, and Arabic) groups. Armenians, Georgians, Turks, and Afghans, as well as Persians and other ethnic and tribal peoples, made up the Safavid population. The Mughal Empire embraced Hindus and many ethnic and language groups.

The three great Asian-Muslim empires shared a common history and indeed many elements of a common culture. They were the heirs of central Asian, Turkish, Mongol, and, in particular, Timurid traditions of conquest and rule. Osman, Isma'il, and Babur, the founders of the Ottoman, Safavid, and Mughal empires respectively, traced at least part of their lineage to earlier Turkic commanders or rulers, spoke a Turkic dialect as their native language (Osman, Oghuz Turkish; Isma'il, Azerbaijani or Azeri Turkish, and Babur, Turki or Chaghatay Turkish), and led Turkic troops in conquests.

They all derived their historical legitimization from a mixture of pre-Islamic Iranian, Roman, and Turko-Mongol imperial traditions. The rulers depicted themselves as conquerors (*ghazis*) in the name of Islam for their victories over Christians, Hindus, or heretical Muslims. They adopted the ancient Iranian titles of shah, *padishah* or *shahanshah*. The Ottoman claim to power was enhanced by their conquest of Constantinople and later of Egypt and the holy cities of Arabia, which made them caliphs as well as Caesars. The Safavids leaned more heavily on the religious claim to be Sufi masters, representatives of the imam, and infallible guides to salvation.

All three empires perpetuated Persian as the high literary common language and cultivated Perso-Islamic architecture, painting, and poetry. In urban design, they all subscribed to the by then canonical assemblage of royal palace, Friday mosque, bazaar, and royal tombs. They all drew on the Timurid love of gardens and garden kiosks. The Topkapi Palace in Istanbul, the 'Ali Qapu and the Chihil Sutun palaces in Isfahan, and the Agra fort and Shahjahanabad complex in Delhi were at once residences for the imperial families, administrative centers, and pleasure resorts. They constructed or endowed mosques, Sufi retreats, and schools; commercial structures such as bazaars and caravanserais; and charitable institutions (such as hospitals, kitchens, and fountains). The almost-universal design motif was a square building with circular and/or semicircular domes.

The great Asian empires shared a common literary culture. Beginning in the 'Abbasid era and continuing through the Mongol and Timurid periods, Iranian scholars, poets, and administrators developed a Persian-Islamic culture. Persian language and literature became the dominant culture in the vast region from Anatolia to Central Asia and India, linking the great Asian empires through the travels of administrators, scholars, poets, and Sufis. Persian was the administrative language of the Safavid and Mughal empires and deeply influenced Ottoman court language as well. Inspired partly by ancient Iranian and Hindu literature and partly by Arabic literature, the empires created a rich corpus of religious literature, poetry and stories, history, mathematics, medicine and science, political commentary, and wisdom (*adab*) for educated gentlemen. The great figures in this tradition were Firdawsi (d. 1020), Nizami Ganjavi (d. 1209), Sa'di (d. 1291), and Hafiz (d. 1388/89) in Iran; Rumi (d. 1273) in Anatolia; Amir Khusrau Dihlavi (d. 1325) in Delhi; and Jami (d. 1492) in Herat. Only in the sixteenth and later centuries did Ottoman Turkish (literary Turkish strongly influenced by Persian) begin to displace Persian; in the eighteenth century Urdu (Persianized Hindi written in the Arabic script) displaced Persian as the dominant literary language in India.

In all three empires, poets were summoned to court to entertain and praise the ruler and to compose poetry for military victories, birthdays, and royal celebrations. Through their poetry, they expressed political, religious, and erotic concepts. From Europe to southern India, poets used similar literary conventions, meters, rhymes, images, and forms adapted to the particular linguistic, cultural, and political circumstances of each empire. The *ghazal* was the universal form to express courtly love, especially the exquisite suffering of unrequited love. Firdawsi's *Shah-nama*, a history of Iranian kings, and Nizami's *Khamsa*, five romantic epics, were universally admired.

Painting, mainly illustrations for literary works, was supported by emperors. Manuscript illustration, dating back to the Persian renaissance of the 'Abbasid era, was developed by the Mongols and Timurids and enshrined in royal workshops by the Ottomans, Safavids, and Mughals. All the regimes patronized variations on a common artistic heritage.

ASIAN EMPIRES AS ISLAMIC STATES

Each of the empires validated itself by the combined patronage and suppression of Muslim religious activities and movements. All three empires sponsored schools, mosques, Sufi retreats (*khanaqas*), and shrines. They appointed judges to apply Islamic law. The Ottomans and the Safavids organized and controlled scholars ('*ulama*') through state-organized hierarchies, but the Mughals patronized Islamic scholarship without attempting to bureaucratize the scholars.

Despite the Sunni-Shi'i divide, these regimes endorsed a similar educational curriculum. Both Sunni and Shi'i scholars agreed that knowledge was divided into religious sciences and rational sciences. The former incorporated Quranic exegesis, traditions, Arabic grammar and syntax, law, and jurisprudence. The latter included logic, philosophy, mathematics, and medicine. Theology could be placed in either category. For both the Safavids and the Ottomans, law and jurisprudence were the central subjects of study and were critical to administration. Mystical knowledge was also cultivated in all three empires. Ibn al-ʿArabi's doctrine of the unity of being (*wahdat al-wujud*) – the concept that God is the only reality and that the created world is an emanation of the divine essence into material existence – had followers in all the empires and beyond. The Persian poetry of Jami and later poetry in many regional languages (such as Sindhi, Punjabi, and Bengali) diffused his theosophy.

By the 1600s and 1700s, Ottoman scholars were emphasizing the transmitted religious subjects rather than the rational sciences. The emphasis in the Mughal and Safavid empires was changing from the rational sciences and mysticism to the transmitted religious subjects (such as hadith). In all regions, Sufism was suppressed or reoriented to stress fulfillment of worldly social obligations. In the Mughal Empire, however, the theosophy of Ibn al-ʿArabi and the pursuit of the rational sciences was not attacked and displaced until well into the nineteenth century.

International scholarly networks linked the several empires to one another and to the wider Islamic world. The Safavids brought Arab Shiʿi scholars from Syria, the Lebanon, and Bahrain to Iran; Shiʿi families and networks spread from Iraq and Iran to India, reaching from the coasts of the Mediterranean to central India. Sunni scholars and Sufis were also linked in international networks. Pilgrimage and study in the holy cities of Mecca and Medina created ties among scholars from the several regions of the Ottoman Empire, including Arabia, Cairo, Damascus, and Iraq. The reform (*tajdid*) movement was at the core of the Islamic revival and resistance to Sufism and to the theosophy of Ibn al-ʿArabi in the seventeenth and later centuries. Naqshbandi Sufis maintained connections among Inner Asian, Indian, and Arabian Muslim reformers and activists. Sufi brotherhoods were established in all the empires, and some had branches in several regions, especially the Khalwatiyya in the Ottoman Empire and the Qadiriyya and the Naqshbandiyya in the Ottoman and Mughal empires.

In the decline of all three empires, tribal forces, provincial officials, and local notables arrogated an increasing share of political power and economic resources. Everywhere central governments were thwarted and starved by their provincial clients, but they would come to very different fates. The Safavid Empire would collapse in the early eighteenth century. In 1722, the Safavid dynasty was extinguished, and Afghan warriors took control of Iran. By the late eighteenth century, the Mughal Empire was effectively reduced to a small North Indian state. The Mughal dynasty would eventually be eliminated by the British in 1858. The Ottoman dynasty was the longest lived. By the late eighteenth century, it was no longer a military threat to other European powers, but the dynasty survived until 1924, when it was replaced by the Turkish republic.

The common factor in the demise of the empires has long been thought to be economic competition and conquest by European powers. Yet the impact of commerce was mixed. Although the Ottoman and Mughal regions were exposed to competition from European manufactures, trade with Europe also stimulated demand for and exports of many local products. Nor was European military conquest the cause of their decline. The Safavids were crushed by Afghans rather than Europeans. The Mughal Empire was dismembered by both regional powers and the British. The Ottomans were most exposed to European encroachment, but the empire maintained its territorial core until World War I. In the decline and fall of these empires, internal factors played the critical role.

CHAPTER 37

INNER ASIA FROM THE MONGOL CONQUESTS
TO THE NINETEENTH CENTURY

For millennia, the central theme in the history of the vast and varied regions that lie between the settled parts of the Middle East and of China was the relationship between nomadic-pastoral and sedentary peoples. Whereas the great civilizations of the Middle East and China were primarily imperial and agricultural, the region between them was a zone of steppe lands and scattered oases. The population was predominantly pastoral and lived by raising horses and sheep. It was also organized into clans and tribes, which were sometimes assembled into great confederations. The settled peoples lived primarily in the oasis districts of Transoxania, Khwarizm, Farghana, and Kashgar, and in scattered towns along the trade routes that linked China, the Middle East, and Europe. Settled and pastoral peoples had close relationships with one another, exchanging products and participating in caravan trade. Pastoral peoples also infiltrated the settled areas and became farmers or townsmen. Sometimes they conquered the agricultural oases and became rulers and landlords. Inner Asia was also the reservoir holding a sea of peoples who, organized into great confederations, from time to time conquered the Middle East and China. From the second millennium BCE to the eighteenth century, the history of the region may be told in terms of ever-repeated nomadic conquests, the formation of empires over oasis and settled populations, and the constant tension between pastoral and agricultural peoples.

The development of an Islamic civilization in Inner Asia was closely related to that of Iran. Islam first spread in this region as a result of the Arab conquests of Iran and Transoxania and the movement of Muslim traders and Sufis from the towns to the steppes. The two regions were also linked by the Turkish migrations of the tenth to the fourteenth centuries that brought Inner Asian peoples into Iran, and Iranian monarchical culture and Islamic civilization into Inner Asia. In the tenth and eleventh centuries, Qarluq and Oghuz peoples converted and founded the Qarakhanid and Saljuq empires. Under the Qarakhanids, the Hanafi school of law and Maturidi school of theology were established in Transoxania, and a new Turkish literature inspired by Persian Islamic literature came into being. The Qarakhanids also favored the diffusion of Islam from Transoxania into the Tarim basin and the northern steppes. Sufi preachers, especially Shaykh Ahmad al-Yasavi (d. 1166), helped to spread Islam among nomadic peoples.

The connections between Iran and Inner Asia were reinforced by the Mongol invasions. In the thirteenth century, non-Muslim Mongolian peoples established their suzerainty over the whole of Inner Asia, much of the Middle East, and China. The Mongol conquests brought the steppe regions north of the Black, Caspian, and Aral seas into contact with Muslim peoples in Transoxania and Iran and linked Muslim Transoxania with eastern Inner Asia and China.

The advent of Islam in this region led to the formation of three types of Islamic societies. Among the Kazakhs, Islam became part of popular identity and belief, but not the basis of social organization. In large-scale urbanized societies such as Transoxania, state-organized Islamic societies of the Middle Eastern type were developed. Among other tribal peoples and in some oasis communities such as Kashgar, Sufi masters or Sufi lineages mediated, organized, and sometimes governed.

Eventually all of Inner Asia was brought under Russian and Chinese rule. As early as the sixteenth century, Russia absorbed the Tatar states of the Volga region. In the eighteenth and nineteenth centuries, Russia took control of the Crimea, the northern steppes, Turkestan, and the territories beyond the Caspian Sea. The Chinese occupied eastern Turkestan in the eighteenth century and divided Inner Asia into spheres of Russian and Chinese rule. The rule of settled (and non-Muslim) empires brought to an end the ancient patterns of nomadic migration and empire formation.

THE WESTERN AND NORTHERN STEPPES

The semiarid steppe region north of a line drawn across the top of the Black, Caspian, and Aral seas and Lake Balkhash was inhabited predominantly by pastoral peoples whose livelihood depended on raising cattle, horses, goats, sheep, camels, and yaks. The populace spoke Turkic-Altaic languages and was organized into families, clans, and confederations (hordes), with the clan being the basic unit of tax collection, military organization, adjudication of disputes, and other political activities. Although small communities were based on lineage, a political or territorial concept was woven into the higher levels of organization.

The Mongol conquests gave this region a semblance of political unity. In 1236, under the leadership of Batu, Mongol and Turkish nomads conquered the regions north of the Aral and Caspian seas and established their capital on the Volga River. In one of the most extraordinary campaigns in world history, the Golden Horde also conquered Russia, the Ukraine, southern Poland, Hungary, and Bulgaria, creating an empire that extended north to the forests of Russia, south to the Black Sea and the Caucasus, west to the Carpathians, and east to Khwarizm. Local princes were left in power as vassals of the Golden Horde and were used to extract tribute from the population. Moscow was the principal vassal of the Golden Horde; other Russian principalities were responsible to Moscow for the payment of tribute.

Amalgamating with the conquered peoples, the conquerors evolved over time into the Turkic-speaking Tatar population and eventually converted to Islam. Khan Berke (r. 1257–67) was the first Muslim ruler, but only from the time of Uzbek Khan (r. 1313–40) were the rulers routinely Muslims. The Islamic loyalties of the royal family were probably reinforced by contacts with the settled Muslim populations of Khwarizm and Transoxania and perhaps by the absorption of the Bulgars, who had been Muslims since the tenth century. Culturally, the Golden Horde was dependent on Egypt and Syria, which provided artists and artisans to produce wall paintings, mosaics, lamps, tombstones, and other artistic objects. In the steppes of northern Asia, the Golden Horde integrated aspects of Mediterranean-Islamic culture.

The empire of the Golden Horde maintained its suzerainty from the middle of the thirteenth to the middle of the fifteenth centuries but gradually disintegrated under the pressure of Ottoman expansion (which cut off the Golden Horde from the Mediterranean) and the rise of Moscow, Moldavia, and Lithuania. Also, in the course of the fourteenth to the sixteenth centuries, the Golden Horde broke up into smaller principalities and became differentiated into separate Crimean Tatar, Volga Tatar, Uzbek, and Kazakh ethnic and political groups. The khans of the Crimea, who claimed to be descendants of Chinggis Khan, declared themselves independent rulers in 1441. The khans of Kazan, Astrakhan, and Siberia also established their autonomy. Each of these khans had the right to conduct war and diplomacy and dispense justice, but their powers were checked by clan and tribal leaders, who had a voice in their succession. In the eastern steppes, from the Caspian-Ural region to the Tien-shan and Altai mountains, the Uzbeks probably originated as a coalition of warrior clans united under the leadership of the Shayban family. The stability and political success of the Shaybanid confederation led gradually to the development of an Uzbek language and ethnic identity.

The Kazakhs formed a second confederation in the regions north of the Caspian and Aral seas. The term "Kazakh" probably means "free" (possibly of Uzbek authority) and initially referred to a warrior stratum, then to a political confederation, and finally to an ethnic population. Kazakhs were organized into extended families called *aul* whose size was governed by the availability of pasture and ranged between three and fifteen tents. Each *aul* had its own pasturage and migrated as a unit to exploit its grazing lands. The *auls* could also be grouped into larger units (*uymaqs*), which were mixed groups of different clans. In the seventeenth century, the Kazakhs formed the Great, Middle, and Little Hordes. A fourth horde, called the Bukey (Inner Horde), was formed at the beginning of the nineteenth century. The hordes took shape only when a khan united them against a common enemy or when larger states (such as Russia) used the khans to control the nomads.

In the fifteenth and sixteenth centuries Naqshbandi and Yasavi missionaries began converting the Kazakhs. Islam, however, probably made little headway until the eighteenth century, when Tatar merchants, missionaries, secretaries, and teachers helped construct mosques and schools. Kazakh nomads accepted Muslim circumcision, marriage, burial practices, and belief in jinn as the equivalent of their spirit gods. They used Quranic amulets for protection and treated Muslim holy men as a kind of supplementary shamans. They worshiped at saints' tombs and observed Muslim holidays. Alongside Muslim festivals, however, the Kazakhs also maintained a folk culture in which wandering poets sang epic songs. Their practice of Islam, like that of nomadic and rural peoples the world over, merged ancient folk beliefs and traditions with new religious practices. Thus, the new Uzbek and Kazakh polities came into being when warrior or political elites built their power on a confederation of families and clans, who in time assumed a genealogical relatedness and ethnic identity reinforced by Muslim beliefs and by a common language.

The decline of the Golden Horde opened the way for a multisided struggle for control of the western and northern steppes. (See Table 15.) In the fifteenth century, the Ottoman Empire, Russia, Poland, Lithuania, and the Muslim states of Crimea, Kazan, and Astrakhan fought for control of the Ural-Volga region. The ultimate outcome of these wars was that Russia freed itself from Tatar and Muslim domination and itself became master of the northern steppes and the Muslim populations. By 1535, Moscow claimed the right of investiture of Kazan rulers, and Muscovy chroniclers claimed that Kazan was "Russian land" that had to be recovered to reunite Russia. Church writers stressed the perfidy of the Tatars and the bitterness of the Christian-Muslim conflict. Amid a growing sense of religious superiority and national mission, Moscow conquered Kazan in 1552 and Astrakhan in 1556. This gave it control of the Volga River and the north shore of the Caspian Sea, paving the way for the submission of the Siberian khanate in 1598.

Russian conquest of the Crimea, however, was delayed for almost two centuries. In the seventeenth century, Moscow developed adequate frontier defenses against Ottoman and Crimean attacks and began to colonize the southern steppes, which resulted ultimately in the Russian occupation of Azov in 1699. Peter the Great had to cede Azov to the Ottoman Empire in 1711, but in 1774 the Russians defeated the Ottomans and took full control of the Crimea in 1783. The Ottomans recognized the new sovereign in 1792. (See Map 18.)

From their dominant position in the Volga region, the Russians set out to conquer the Kazakh steppes. Under Peter the Great, the Russians established a string of forts across the northern steppes from the Ural to the Irtysh rivers, including Orenburg, Omsk, Barnaul, and Semipalatinsk. In 1723 the Kazakh Great Horde and in 1730 the Kazakh Little Horde were forced to accept Russian suzerainty. A century of slow consolidation was followed in 1822–24 by the abolition of the Kazakh khanates and the submission of the Kazakhs to Russian control. In 1864,

Table 15. *Inner Asia: outline chronology*

Mongol conquests	Northern and western steppes			Turkestan		
	Volga	Northern Steppes	Crimea	Khwarizm	Transoxania	Eastern Turkestan
1200 — Chinggis Khan (1206–27)						
1300	Blue Horde, Batu'ids (1227–1341), unites with White Horde to form Golden Horde (1378–1502)				Chaghatays, 1227–1370; Timurid Empire, 1370–1500	
1400	Partitioned into several khanates (fifteenth century)	Formation of Uzbek and Kazakh "nations" (fifteenth century)	Giray khans, 1426–1792			
1500 — Kazan khanate annexed by Moscow, 1552				Khans of Khiva, 1515–1920	Shaybanids, 1500–98	Chaghatays continue as nominal suzerains until 1678
1600 — Astrakhan khanate, annexed 1556; Siberian khanate, annexed 1598					Astrakhanids, 1599–1785	
1700			Annexed by Russia, 1783		Mangits, 1785–1920	Kashgar ruled by *khwajas*, 1678–1756; Khokand ruled by khanate, c. 1700–1876; Russian annexation, 1876 · Chinese conquest of Xinjiang, 1759
1800		Russian annexation of Kazakhstan completed by 1868		Russian protectorate, 1873	Russian protectorate, 1868	China annexes Xinjiang, 1884
1900						

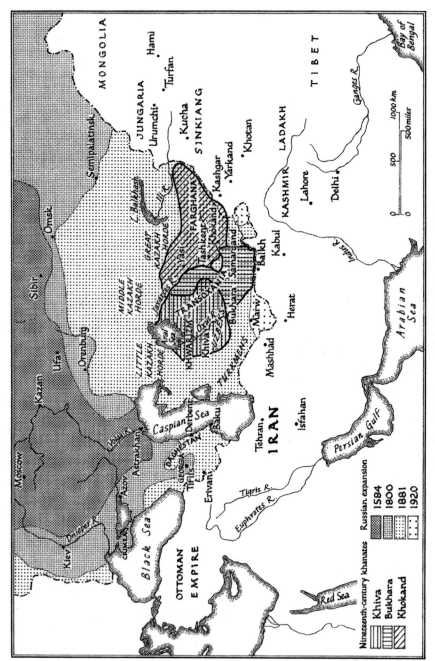

Map 18. Russian expansion in Muslim Inner Asia to 1920.

The map contains the following labels:

MONGOLIA

Hami
Turfan
JUNGARIA
Urumchi
Kucha
SINKIANG

TIBET

Bay of Bengal

Semipalatinsk

Omsk

L. Balkhash

Ili R.

Ladakh
KASHMIR

Khotan
Yarkand
Kashgar

FARGHANA
GREAT KAZAKH HORDE
Tashkent
Khokand

Lahore
Delhi

1000 km.
500 miles
500
0

Sibir.

MIDDLE KAZAKH HORDE

Bukhara Samarkand
Balkh

Kabul

Indus R.
Ganges R.

Ufa

Orenburg

LITTLE KAZAKH HORDE

TRANSOXIANA
Khiva
Oxus R.

Marw

Herat

Kazan

Moscow

Volga R.

Astrakhan

Caspian Sea

Derbent

TURKMENS

Mashhad

Arabian Sea

Dnieper R.

Sea of Azov

Baku

Tehran
Isfahan

IRAN

Persian Gulf

Kiev

Black Sea

Tiflis
GEORGIA
DAGHESTAN
Erivan

Tigris R.
Euphrates R.

Red Sea

OTTOMAN EMPIRE

Nineteenth-century khanates

Khiva
Bukhara
Khokand

Russian expansion

1584
1800
1881
1920

548

the Russians took the Syr-Darya region and completed the occupation of Kazakh territories. This victory was not easily won. Between 1783 and 1797, Batyr Srym led a series of counterattacks, followed by some sixty years of Kazakh resistance. The Bukey Horde revolted between 1836 and 1838; Khan Kenesary Kasimov led Kazakh resistance between 1837 and 1847. The last revolt, in the name of Islam, was crushed in 1868. Thus, Russia became the heir of the Golden Horde in the Ural-Volga region and on the northern and eastern steppes.

The Russian conquests were a disaster for Muslim peoples. On the conquest of Kazan and Astrakhan, the Russians expelled the Tatars from the important cities, redistributed the land to Russian nobles and monasteries, and colonized the region with Russian artisans and peasants. Mosques were destroyed, Quran schools closed, and trusts seized by the Russian treasury. The Russians aimed at no less than the complete conversion of the Tatars to Christianity. There was some success with Muslim nobles and their clients who were interested in collaboration with the Russians, but in general, Muslim resistance was fierce. From 1552 until 1610, there were repeated revolts by the Tatar nobility. Their defeat was followed by peasant uprisings from 1608 to 1615 and Tatar participation in Kazakh rebellions. In the seventeenth century, the Russians suspended their efforts at assimilation and worked mainly to prevent the apostasy of converts, but in 1710 Peter the Great began a new campaign that lasted until 1764. Converts were transferred to purely Russian villages. Muslim children were sent to Christian schools, and adults were forced to accept baptism. Churches were constructed in Muslim villages. Yet, after half a century, there were only a small number of Tatar converts. Paradoxically, Russian conquest helped to spread Islam. Driven out of the major towns and deprived of land, Tatar nobles became merchants, colonized rural areas, built mosques and schools, and propagated Islam among the nomads.

To calm her eastern provinces, Catherine the Great adopted a new policy in 1773. Aware of the importance of Tatar trading communities and eager to avoid further rebellions, Catherine ended religious persecution, gave Tatar nobles equal rights with Russian nobles, and encouraged Tatar merchants to trade between Russia and Transoxania. Decrees of 1782 and 1784 authorized the construction of mosques; in 1788, an Islamic spiritual administration was organized at Ufa under the leadership of a mufti. Under Catherine's peace, Tatar merchants flourished and invested in tanneries and in paper and woolen mills. Peasants developed cottage industries. Commercial success opened the way to European education and eventually stimulated an intellectual enlightenment.

In the Crimea, Catherine guaranteed the nobility possession of their lands and the Muslim scholars freedom of religion. A Muslim spiritual directorate for the Crimea was established in 1794; the mufti was nominated by the tsar. In time, however, the Russians began to seize Tatar estates and trusts for the benefit of the Russian aristocracy and European colonists who flocked to the country. Between

Illustration 18.   The Registan of Samarqand. Courtesy of Sheila S. Blair and Jonathan M. Bloom.

1783 and 1896, most of the Crimean Tatars were forced to migrate to the Ottoman Empire; the remnant formed a minority in their own country.

TURKESTAN (TRANSOXANIA, KHWARIZM, AND FARGHANA)

Whereas the northern steppes were the domain of the Golden Horde and later of settled Tatar and pastoral Kazakh peoples, Turkestan – the domain of the Chaghatays – was primarily agricultural and the site of numerous important oasis cities, such as Bukhara and Samarqand. The commerce of these cities reached from China to the Black Sea, linking Iran, Afghanistan, India, China, and Russia. They were also important centers of Muslim religious learning. Although nomadic peoples from the surrounding steppes time and again conquered the region, they accepted its city tradition and became patrons of its culture. (See Illustration 18.)

Throughout the period of the caliphate and the Turkish and Mongol invasions, Turkestan was tied to eastern Iran. It was ruled in succession by the Qarakhanids, the Mongols, the Chaghatays, and the Timurids. The collapse of the Timurid Empire, however, led to a permanent break between the two regions. Iran was conquered by the Safavids and Transoxania (the principal part of Turkestan) by the Uzbeks. The trade routes that linked Transoxania to Iran were disrupted by Shaybanid-Safavid hostilities. Iran converted to Shiʿism; Transoxania under Shaybanid rule remained Sunni. While Persians held sway in Iran, Turkish peoples and Chaghatay literary culture grew stronger in the east. Although it preserved a rich component of its Middle Eastern Islamic heritage, Transoxania under Uzbek rule was integrated once again into Inner Asia and became the urban and agricultural center of Inner Asian–Islamic civilization.

Uzbek domination of Transoxania began with the Shaybanid dynasty (1500–98) and endured through successive dynasties until the establishment of a Russian protectorate in 1868. The Shaybanids were in many ways typical of Turkish conquest regimes. The conquering elite was divided between the ruling dynasty and its administrative, religious, and merchant supporters, and tribal chiefs (*uymaq*) and their clients and retainers. The two segments of the elite struggled for their share of the spoils of power. The khan himself kept a portion of the territory as state lands and a portion as private revenue estates (*khasa*) that he controlled absolutely. A considerable portion of these lands was assigned as trusts to Muslim religious leaders, and the rest was assigned to the nobility. It was divided into provinces (*wilayat*), and each province was further subdivided into *iqta's* distributed to the supporters of the regional governors. The estates controlled by the members of the ruling family and the tribal chiefs (*beg*) were rated by *tumen*, probably a measure of the number of troops to be provided in return for the grant of revenues. Such grants of land tended to become hereditary, depriving the rulers of control. Strong rulers would seek to reestablish their power by seizing the *iqta's*, reducing the size of land grants, confiscating the excess properties of religious leaders, and paying their retainers in cash. In this respect, the Shaybanid khanate resembled the Safavid regime of Iran; the central rulers struggled against the *uymaq* and tribal forces that dominated the localities.

The Shaybanid khanate, like earlier Muslim regimes, legitimated itself by a combination of references to Sunni Islam and Persian literary culture. The khans took the titles of *khalifat al-rahman* (Lieutenant of the Merciful God) and *imam al-zaman* (Ruler of the Times), quoted hadith to justify their rule, and became disciples of Naqshbandi Sufi masters. Court poets wrote panegyrics, portraits were commissioned, and literary activity was patronized to depict the Shaybanids as Turkish-Persian princes. The *Shah-name* was translated into Turkish, and many Iranian scholars came to Transoxania, where they found generous Uzbek patronage. Thus, the Shaybanids maintained their own version of the Timurid heritage and created an Uzbek-dominated Irano-Islamic state.

The religious elites legitimized the regime. These elites included the judges and the scholars who taught in the colleges, but ever since the Timurid period, the leading position was held by the Naqshbandis. The Naqshbandis had their origin in the *Tariqa-yi Khwajagan* (way of the masters) founded by Yusuf Hamadhani (d. 1143). His disciple, Ahmad al-Yasavi, helped to spread Islam among Turkish peoples. Ahmad's tomb at Yasi was built by Timur as a gesture of obeisance to the Turkish Sufi tradition. His successor, 'Abd al-Khaliq Ghujdavani (d. 1220), a principal teacher of the Bukharan populace, introduced the crucial spiritual and social principle that later defined the Naqshbandi position: solitude in society – inner devotion expressed in outward social and political activity. The order received its name from Baha' al-Din Naqshband (d. 1389). 'Ubaydallah (*khavaja*) Ahrar (d. 1490), a wealthy farmer and merchant who acquired a reputation for mysticism and magical powers, was the dominant figure in the late fifteenth century. He was an advisor of princes, a teacher of famous poets, and a revered master to the common people. He and other Sufis played a large political role in protecting Muslim populations from oppression, winning over the souls of kings, and defending the Muslim way of life. Sufis who had contacts in all reaches of society united the Inner Asian communities.

While Shaybanid rule constructed a variant form of Irano-Islamic state and society, larger historical forces were profoundly altering Inner Asia. For centuries, the riches of Transoxania had been built on trade and manufactures. Merchants, rich religious leaders, and government officials had participated in the trade with China and Russia. Bukhara, Samarqand, Tashkent, Yasi, and other towns were also centers of lively silk, cotton, leather, rug, jewelry, wood carving, metal, and paper industries. Craft workers were organized into associations under the leadership of officials appointed by the rulers but maintained a social and religious solidarity of their own based on the identification of guilds with patron saints, Sufi masters, and shared religious rituals.

In the course of the sixteenth century, however, the rise of the Safavids and the closure of Iranian routes to the Indian Ocean, the Russian conquest of the Volga region, and internal disorder and insecurity undermined the Inner Asian trade. The decline of Inner Asian routes was also hastened by the discovery of new sea routes between Europe and the Indies, and later by Russian expansion across Siberia to the Pacific that opened new routes to China. Inner Asia was cut off both from economic riches and from external cultural influences, because the roads that had once brought Buddhist, Christian, and other religious and cultural influences into the region fell into disuse. Once the links to the outside Muslim world were cut, provincialism, economic stagnation, and political fragmentation set in. The decline of Inner Asian trade compromised Shaybanid efforts to maintain a centralized state. It deprived the khans of tax revenues, the merchants of profits, and the religious elites of investment opportunities. Power drifted into the hands of tribal and *uymaq* chieftains. From the end of the Shaybanid dynasty (1598) to the nineteenth century, centralized political administration was the rare and precarious achievement of exceptionally able rulers.

The nineteenth century, however, brought a revival. Bukhara (Transoxania), Khiva (Khwarizm), and Khokand (Farghana) each became the center of a newly flourishing Muslim society. In Bukhara, the Shaybanid dynasty had been succeeded by the Astrakhanid dynasty (1599–1785), which maintained only the barest continuity with Shaybanid traditions. It was in turn succeeded by the Mangit dynasty (1785–1920). Murad, the first ruler of the Mangit dynasty, ruled as amir rather than sultan but also claimed an authority based on his conquests, his services as defender and executive of the Muslim community, and his personal charisma derived from being a descendant of the Prophet.

Under the Mangit dynasty, Bukhara continued to follow the basic Shaybanid pattern. The state was ruled by the amir, who was served by a chief minister (*qush begi*) and by Persian administrative officials. The territory was subdivided into provinces and tax-collecting districts consisting of groups of villages or hamlets, each under the authority of an *aqsakal*, or elder. The territories and tax revenues were divided among the amir and the leading notables. In the nineteenth century, about 12 percent of the taxable land belonged to the ruler, 56 percent to the state, 24 percent to trusts, and 8 percent to the rest of the population. State lands could be taxed in both cash and kind, the rates being adjusted to the surface unit, water amount, and type of crop, in order to approximate the value of the produce. State lands were commonly granted to tribal notables in return for a promise to supply troops to the regime. They could also be given away as permanent rather than conditional gifts.

In the nineteenth century, the Mangit dynasty struggled successfully to reduce the power of the tribal and *uymaq* chiefs. Amir Nasrallah (r. 1826–60) removed hostile Uzbek chieftains from office and replaced them with Persian, Turkmen, and Arab functionaries. He also confiscated land, redistributed it to his supporters on a nonhereditary basis, and regulated the relations of landholders and peasants. This consolidation was aided by the sedentarization of Uzbek pastoralists, which brought both men and land under the authority of the amir. Still, the local chiefs kept their castles, their retainers, and at least part of their revenues.

As in Iran and the Ottoman Empire, Bukhara had a state-controlled religious administration under the authority of a *shaykh al-Islam* (chief jurisconsult) and a *qadi kalan*, who was in control of judicial administration, colleges, elementary schools, and mosques. The judges and subjudges were appointed to provincial districts. The muftis recorded evidence, interpreted the law, and sat in council to pass judgment on the conformity of state regulations to Islamic law. The scholars staffed more than 110 colleges and taught in the elementary schools. They were organized in a hierarchy of three ranks under the titles *auraq, sadur,* and *sadr*, which were honorific distinctions given to scholars who had a madrasa education and who served as functionaries. People who held these ranks were entitled to collect taxes and to gifts of land. A functionary (the *ra'is*) served as the equivalent of the medieval *muhtasib*, enforcing honest market practices and good public morals. The *ra'is* could require delinquent Muslims to attend mosque or school in order to improve their religious practice and knowledge. Neighborhood religious life was under the direction of imams who presided over the recitation of prayers. The term "mullah" was applied to everyone who taught in schools, presided over prayers, and officiated at marriages, funerals, and other ceremonies. The whole of this elaborate religious organization was directly controlled by the amir, who appointed the chief judges and muftis, the professors in the colleges, and other functionaries.

The social power of the scholars of Bukhara was enhanced by their corporate organization. The religious establishment included privileged groups such as the descendants of the Prophet (*sayyids*), the descendants of the first three caliphs (*mirs*), and the descendants of the early Arab conquerors (*khwajas*). These groups formed endogamous lineages that were accorded popular veneration and religious prestige. Although not formally organized, the teaching scholars also derived considerable political and social support from the mass of their students. Alongside the lineages, there were Sufi brotherhoods, including the Naqshbandiyya, the Qadiriyya, and the Kubrawiyya. Sufi masters had a considerable following of their immediate disciples and the lay brothers attached to the orders. Sufis lived in retreats and worshiped at the shrines of venerated teachers. Sufi beggars, called Qalandaris, had their own community. Sufism was also important among the rural and nomadic populations, where it was strongly oriented to saint worship, healing, and use of amulets. Together, the holy lineages, the Sufi brotherhoods, and the student clienteles made a considerable force in Bukharan society.

Religious influence was also pervasive in the mentality of the Bukharan population. This was most commonly expressed in the veneration of tombs of saints. The relics of Timur in Samarqand were the object of pilgrimage, as were the tombs of the famous Naqshbandi teachers. When a shrine began to acquire a widespread reputation, it was commonly taken over by a Sufi order, which received the gifts of the pilgrims. The cult of 'Ali was prevalent, even among Sunnis, for 'Ali was the patron saint of the canal diggers and soldiers. Bibi Seshambeh (Lady Tuesday) and "Lady Solver of Problems" were the patron saints of women. Craft guilds were organized under patron saints and had collective rituals. Guild saints included Noah, the saint of carpenters, and David, the saint of metalworkers. The Muslim populace also celebrated the *bayram* festivals (the *'ids* of the sacrifice and of the end of Ramadan) and the birthday of the Prophet. Muslim spirituality included a lively folk culture of secular entertainments by musicians, dancers, acrobats, jugglers, and gypsies. The populace also enjoyed tobacco, tea, and wine.

Despite the longevity of this state and society, important changes were taking place in the nineteenth century. First, the number of landless peasants was increasing, and the state had difficulty collecting taxes. As formerly nomadic Uzbeks were sedentarized, irrigation lagged behind the pace of settlement, partly because of the lack of skill among first-generation farmers and partly because of political struggles over the control of water. Whereas there were adequate lands for pasturage, lands suitable for cultivation were overpopulated.

The nineteenth-century consolidation of the Bukharan state also brought into being a new intermediary class between the ruling elites and the peasants and pastoralists. This class included lower-ranking functionaries, scribes, secretaries, couriers, and policemen. Promoted by an active Bukharan commerce with Afghanistan, Iran, India, and Russia, the commercial bourgeoisie also became more important. Bukhara controlled the Central Asian trade in raw silk and silk fabrics.

Its merchants organized cotton industries and financed modest banking firms. Along with the growing merchant elite, private property and private landowner-ship became more important between 1840 and 1870.

Similarly, the territories of Farghana and Khwarizm were reorganized. Before the eighteenth century, Farghana had been divided into a number of small states governed by religious chiefs, but in the early eighteenth century migrant Uzbeks assumed power and forced surrounding Kazakh and Kirgiz tribes to submit to a new state with its capital at Khokand. The consolidation of the khanate of Khokand was based on a flourishing economy in which irrigation agriculture, cotton and silk production, and trade with Kashgar, Bukhara, Khiva, and Russia were important sources of income. Khokand was the breakpoint where Russian and Chinese goods were sold and reshipped. The consolidation of state power, however, was inhibited by the struggle for control of land between the sedentary Persianized population and Qipchaq tribal peoples. Khwarizm went through a parallel phase of state consolidation and commercial development in the nineteenth century. However, the efforts of Muhammad Rahim I (r. 1806–25) to centralize the Khwarizmian state were undermined by the constant struggle with the Turkmen nomadic population supported by Sufi holy men.

Destabilized by conflicts among the ruling dynasties, *uymaq* and tribal chiefs, and pastoral and sedentary populations, Inner Asian societies became prey to Rus-sian expansion. The governing factors in Russian expansion were the ambitions of its generals and the willingness of the tsars to tolerate their initiative and benefit from their successes. Motivated by the desire to secure its borders, control trade, and exploit rich agricultural lands, Russia had already absorbed the Tatar and Kazakh steppes. Further expansion would give Russia political and trading advan-tages in relations with Iran, India, and China and enable it to forestall potential British rivalry.

From their bases on the Kazakh steppes, the Russians occupied Tashkent in 1865 and Samarqand in 1868 and forced Bukhara to pay indemnities and open up to Russian trade. Khokand was absorbed in 1876 and the Transcaspian province in 1881, and the Pamirs were taken in 1895. Great Britain also took an interest in Inner Asia as a remote extension of its Indian sphere of influence. At the Congress of Berlin (1878) and by the treaty of 1907, Central Asia, Afghanistan, and India were divided into Russian and British spheres of influence. Thus, by the late nineteenth century, the Russians had rounded out their Inner Asian empire and had become the masters of Tatar, Kazakh, Uzbek, and other Inner Asian peoples.

EASTERN TURKESTAN AND CHINA

Eastern Turkestan, the steppe and desert regions to the east of Farghana and now part of China, was also a region of nomadic peoples and important agricultural and oasis cities. From the time of the Mongol conquests, eastern Turkestan, parts of the northern steppes, and parts of Transoxania were the nominal domain of the Chaghatay khans, successors of Chinggis Khan. In the middle of the fourteenth century, the Chaghatays were restricted to eastern Turkestan. Chaghatay suzerainty was rarely more than nominal. Nomadic chieftains and the rulers of the oasis towns generally maintained their autonomy. Nonetheless, eastern Turkestan came into the domain of Turkish-Islamic culture. This was the result of a long, slow, and little-documented process in which Mongol peoples converted to Islam and began using Turkish languages. Muslim rulers tried to use Islam as legitimization for warfare against non-Muslim peoples. By the time that Komul (Hami) came under Muslim rule in 1513, Sunni Islam was widely accepted in the Tarim basin, and Chaghatay was spreading as a literary language. Mosques appeared along the trade routes between Inner Asia and China. Muslim expansion, however, was checked by Oirats (Mongols) who accepted Buddhism at the end of the sixteenth century. By then, however, much of the populace of Inner Asia outside Mongolia and Tibet was Muslim or under Muslim suzerainty.

The most striking manifestation of the influence of Islam was the role of *khwajas*, or Sufis who traced their biological as well as their spiritual lineage to the Prophet Muhammad or to the early caliphs. The earliest of these figures were probably itinerant holy men, faith healers, and miracle workers who in the fourteenth century acquired local prestige, gained a livelihood from gifts of tithes and landed estates, and married into prominent families. In many ways, they resembled the *shurafa'* of Morocco by combining Sufi qualities with descent from the Prophet. The *khwajas* gradually attained a spiritual ascendancy over secular rulers, all of whom became their disciples. The descendants of Makhdum-i ʿAzam (d. 1540), the spiritual master of Bukhara, became the principal advisors to local rulers – and eventually became the rulers themselves – in Kashgar and Yarkand. From 1678 to 1756, Kashgar was ruled by a dynasty of *khwajas* who claimed descent from Muhammad, headship of a Sufi order, and a blood relationship to Chinggis Khan. Thus, the *khwajas* united spiritual and political authority. Nonetheless, the elites of these oasis cities were divided into bitterly hostile factions. Factional wars eventually led the *khwajas* to appeal to nomadic peoples for political support – a measure that eventually cost the oases their independence.

While Chaghatay khans, *khwajas*, and tribal chiefs ruled eastern Turkestan, a new Oirat-Mongol empire called the Dzungarian Confederation, the last of the great Inner Asian nomadic empires, was being formed. The Dzungarian Confederation had its origins between 1400 and 1550, when Mongolian peoples were cut off from the markets of China and were forced to move westward and northward into eastern Turkestan, the northern steppes, and Transoxania. By the early seventeenth century, an Oirat khanate had come into existence – its power based on trade and dominance of peasants – and its leaders adopted Tibetan Lamaism as the religion of the confederation. Buddhism helped, as did Islam, to foster political unity among pastoral peoples and to unite them with sedentary populations. Expanding westward, the Oirats attacked the Kirgiz and the Uzbeks – their competitors for pasture and access to cattle markets in Transoxania – and conquered the Tarim basin. Allied with the religious factions of Kashgar and Yarkand, the Oirats took control of the oasis cities and appointed the *khwajas* as their vassals.

Oirat expansion, however, provoked Chinese intervention. China had long regarded Inner Asia as part of its inherent domain and was concerned for the protection of its frontiers against barbarian incursions. The Chinese considered Inner Asian rulers as their vassals. In the guise of tributes and exchanges of gifts, China imported horses, furs, metals, and jade in exchange for paper, textiles, drugs, tea, and porcelain. The Chinese pursued their commercial and diplomatic policy under the assumption that they possessed cultural and political supremacy and considered all exchanges as a form of tribute. By 1759, the Chinese defeated the Dzungarians, took control of the oasis cities, drove out the *khwajas*, and absorbed eastern Turkestan. In addition, the Chinese made the eastern Kazakhs and Khokand their tributaries. With these new vassals, the Chinese exchanged silk, tea, and porcelain for horses, cattle, and Russian products.

The conquest of eastern Turkestan brought a new Muslim population under Chinese control. The earliest Muslims in China were Arab troops coming from Inner Asia and Muslim merchants who settled in Canton in the eighth century. Although permanent residents, these Muslims were considered foreigners, subjects of far-off Muslim rulers, and enjoyed an extraterritorial jurisdiction under their own officials. The Mongol conquests and the formation of the Yuan dynasty (1271–1368) reinforced the Muslim population. The Mongols employed Muslim administrators and tax collectors, encouraged trade between China and Inner Asia, and sponsored the migration and settlement of Muslims not only in northwestern but also in southwestern China and Yunnan. In many cities, Muslims, living under the leadership of their own *shaykh al-Islam* and judges, occupied separate quarters provided with mosques and bazaars. Under the Ming dynasty (1368–1644), Muslims served the emperor as astronomers, diviners, translators, postal officials, and caravaners.

In the Ming period, the name Hui was applied to Chinese of Muslim faith, both to assimilated foreign Muslims and to Chinese converts to Islam. Muslims adopted the speech, names, manners, clothing, and other outward features of being Chinese. Muslim writers in this period attempted to show how Islam and Confucianism could be reconciled and how Chinese mythology and Islamic history were congruent. Still, Muslims retained an inner Muslim identity defined by their prayer rituals and communal affiliations. Under the authority of an imam, Muslims had their own mosques, schools, charities, and endowments. Chinese Muslims, however, were not an organized group. There was no unity among the numerous different congregations, and the Hui were widely dispersed. The Manchu dynasty dealt with the Hui by assurances of protection, threats of punishment, and a pragmatic policy of suppressing resistance and tolerating religious differences. As long as Muslim identity did not interfere with their outward conformity, it was acceptable to the

Chinese. This coexistence lasted until the great Muslim revolts of the nineteenth century.

The newly conquered Muslim population of eastern Turkestan was very different from the assimilated Hui. Turkestani Muslims were mainly Uighurs and Kazakhs and were not assimilated to the Chinese way of life. Under Chinese suzerainty, the Islamic identity of both the urban and the nomadic populations was fully maintained. Kashgar was the site of the much-venerated tomb of Hazrat Afaq and his family. Beggars and dervishes lived in the cemeteries; religious colonies surrounded the tomb. Pre-Islamic survivals such as fluttering flags, yak tails, and heaps of horns marked the reverence in which this place was held. Although the Muslims of China proper had become a Chinese religious minority, the Muslims of Inner Asia remained a politically subordinate non-Chinese population.

The Chinese administration of eastern Turkestan was based on a superstructure of Chinese garrisons and administrative officers in the oasis towns of Komul, Urum-chi, Kashgar, Khotan, and other places, who governed through local Muslim chieftains (*begs*). The chieftains collected taxes, controlled water supplies, administered justice, and maintained order. They were granted land and serfs to pay the costs of their offices and then tried to increase these holdings and to convert them into private properties. Chinese rule introduced a period of security and commercial prosperity. By the 1820s, the cultivated lands in the oasis district of Kashgar had doubled, and Chinese peasants were being brought in to reclaim wastelands.

Inner Asian Muslims, however, never fully accepted Chinese rule. A Muslim religious movement, the so-called New Teachings (Hsin-chiao), a variant of the Naqshbandi order, was introduced by Ma Ming-hsin, who came to China in 1761. He had studied in Yarkand and Kashgar and propagated a form of Sufism expressed in loud chanting of the Quran, prayers with dancelike head shaking and foot stamping, belief in miracles and visions, and worship of saints. New sect members believed that faith was more important than family. They were reformers who were hostile to the old practices and to the political elites. Ma attracted a following in Kansu province and, in 1781, rebelled against Chinese rule. The movement was soon repressed, but this provoked later revolts by Kirgiz warriors. The political unrest in eastern Turkestan tempted the *khwajas*, the former rulers of Kashgar who had taken refuge in Khokand, to try to regain their former possession. Between the 1820s and 1862, they led a series of attacks on Chinese territory, supported by Kirgiz and local Uighurs. The rulers of Khokand also aspired to a larger sphere of influence in eastern Turkestan. Chafing at Chinese political and trading restrictions, Khokand demanded the right to control the caravan trade and to appoint tax collectors in Kashgar. Chinese concessions only led to an expansion of Khokand's trade and influence in eastern Turkestan and to conversion of Khokandi support for the aspirations of the *khwajas*.

The weakness of the Ch'ing dynasty (1644–1911) in eastern Turkestan was only a symptom of the general breakdown of the Chinese empire. Beset by the Taiping and numerous provincial rebellions, the Ch'ing were forced to allow their subjects to organize local military forces and yet had to press them for increased taxes. Chinese hostility to Muslims and demands for their assimilation also increased with the breakdown of the Ch'ing. Ch'ing misrule provoked Muslim rebellions in Yunnan, Shensi, Kansu, and eastern Turkestan. Hanafi law, which legitimizes rebellion if non-Islamic law is enforced or if non-Muslim territory separates Muslims from one another, provided a legal basis for secret societies and revolts. Muslim religious and political consciousness was stimulated by an outpouring of Islamic literature stressing the importance of emulating the teachings of the Prophet, ritual purity, and fulfilling God's commands. This nineteenth-century literature stressed the superiority of Islam and attacked Chinese civilization rather than attempting to be reconciled to it. Chinese Muslim scholars no longer insisted on the similarities of Islam and Confucianism and urged Muslims to abide by Islamic law and to avoid Chinese customs. The nineteenth-century Muslim rebellions were also abetted by reformist Muslim influences coming from India or other parts of Inner Asia.

A series of Muslim rebellions in Yunnan culminated in the formation of an independent Muslim state from 1856 to 1873 under the leadership of Tu Wen-hsiu, who called himself commander of the faithful and sultan. The principal Muslim rebellion in Shensi province was led by Ma Hua-lung, who represented the new teaching movement. Here Muslim secession took on a peculiarly Chinese quality. Ma Hua-lung adopted the name Tsung-ta A-hung or General Grand A-hung, which is a Muslim name, but when written in Chinese characters it means "the horse became a dragon" and thus evoked Chinese as well as Muslim symbols. The new sect adopted Chinese popular symbols as the basis of a Muslim revivalism with separatist political implications. Under A-hung's leadership, Kucha and Hi rebelled, cutting off Chinese communications with Kashgar.

Taking advantage of Chinese weakness, the khan of Khokand sent the surviving *khwajas* of Kashgar with a military subordinate named Ya'qub Beg to take control of Kirgiz and Uighur peoples. Ya'qub quickly conquered most of eastern Turkestan and the oasis states. He enforced Islamic law and gave large gifts to mosques. However, he was dependent on Khokandis, Afghans, and others for his army. In a direct affront to Chinese authority, he recognized Ottoman suzerainty; the Ottomans acknowledged him as amir in 1873.

Ya'qub's fate and that of the Muslim rebellions was linked to Russian and British maneuvers. In the nineteenth century, eastern Turkestan was the object of Russian and British rivalry; both of them were interested in trading advantages and the protection of their respective territories in Russia and India. Generally, the British planned to cooperate with friendly local rulers to check Russian advances, but in the late 1860s, they backed China's efforts to suppress local rebellions, for fear that the dismemberment of China would hamper British access to Inner Asia. Russian occupation of the Hi province in 1871 led the British to see Ya'qub Beg as a potential buffer against the possibility of further Russian penetration of

Inner Asia. In 1874, they supplied him with a small number of rifles. A revival of Chinese power under the leadership of Governor Tso Tsung-t'ang (d. 1885) put an end both to Ya'qub and to British concerns. Tso reorganized Chinese forces, reconquered Shensi and Kansu, took Aksu and Kashgar by 1878, and suppressed the new teachings. In 1881, China and Russia negotiated a treaty that restored the Hi province to China and paved the way for the reorganization of eastern Turkestan as a province under civilian Chinese administration. Named Xinjiang, it became part of China in 1884. By then, all of Inner Asia had come under either Russian or Chinese rule. It remained only to define the borders between Russia and China in 1892 and between Russia and Afghanistan in 1895. The expansion of the two great imperial powers brought an end to 3,000 years of nomadic migration and empires.

Thus, Inner Asian societies, until their conquest by Russia and China, exemplified several types of Muslim society. On the northern steppes and in eastern Turkestan, Tatar, Uzbek, Kazakh, Kirgiz, Uighur, and other peoples were organized in family units and loose confederations. The *uymaq* (tribe), an alliance of family and clan units, was the effective political unit. Larger-order khanates and hordes were fragile coalitions. Nevertheless, pastoral peoples conquered the sedentary areas. In the sedentarized districts of Transoxania, Farghana, Kashgaria, and other oases, they founded centralized states, legitimized partly in Islamic and partly in cosmopolitan cultural terms. In urban areas, Islam was crucial to the viability of states. The Mangit dynasty was virtually the expression of the scholars of Bukhara, who controlled judicial administration and education and whose organized bodies of *sayyids*, *khwajas*, Sufis, students, and guilds made up the body politic. In Kashgar, dynasties of *khwajas* ruled directly. Muslim society in sedentary Inner Asia was built around the tripartite division of power and authority among tribal, state, and religious elites, but Russian and Chinese rule would – as colonial rule did everywhere in the Muslim world – profoundly change this historical configuration.

CHAPTER 38

ISLAMIC SOCIETIES IN SOUTHEAST ASIA

Just as Islam spread from the Middle East to Inner Asia and from Afghanistan to India, in the late thirteenth, fourteenth, and fifteenth centuries it spread from various parts of India and Arabia to the Malay Peninsula and the Indonesian archipelago. Whereas the history of Islamic societies in other parts of Asia can be told in terms of empires and contiguous geographical areas, maritime Southeast Asia is a region of scattered peninsulas and islands. The sea was the connection among them. The region held a central position on the trade routes that connected China to the Indian Ocean, the Persian Gulf, and the Red Sea. The population of the region included not only local peoples but Chinese, Indians from Gujarat, and Arabs from Hadramawt. Hadramawtis were especially active as teachers, traders, judges, and officials and married and sired children with local women.

Whereas in other regions Islam was established by Arab or Turkish conquests, it was introduced into Southeast Asia by traveling merchants and Sufis, often coming from Arabia and western India. Whereas in the Middle East and India, Muslim regimes were founded by new political elites, in Southeast Asia existing regimes were consolidated by conversion to Islam. The continuity of elites gave strong expression to the pre-Islamic components of Southeast Asian–Islamic civilization. The royal culture of Java seems more local and less Muslim than the corresponding royal culture of the Mughal Empire was Indian. At the same time there were Muslim merchant communities typical of international Islam and also syncretisms of Islam and village cultures. Whereas Muslims remained a minority in India, in Indonesia and Malaya they became the overwhelming majority.

PRE-ISLAMIC SOUTHEAST ASIA

Indigenous pre-Islamic maritime Southeast Asian cultures formed the basis of later Islamic civilization. By the beginning of the Christian era, the diverse populations of Southeast Asia had developed a civilization based on irrigated rice cultivation, animal husbandry, and metallurgy. The native cultures had their own religious beliefs and artistic accomplishments, such as the wayang puppet theater and the gamelan orchestra recitals of Java and Bali. The interior of Java was a region of rice agriculture and was the locus of small kingdoms. In the coastal regions of Sumatra and Java, the smaller islands, and the Malay Peninsula, the populace earned its living by trade and was strongly influenced by contacts with Hindu cultures. From earliest times, there was tension between the agrarian hierarchical society of Java and the cultures of the coastal towns.

Many of the early Southeast Asian societies were state ruled, but there was no single polity. The earliest historical known kingdoms on Java date from the fifth century CE. From the fifth to the fifteenth centuries, there were several kingdoms, each a suzerainty over petty lordships maintained by control of rice and legitimized by myth, magic, and mysticism. Each was a center for the diffusion of high culture to the surrounding countryside. Local princes borrowed Indian and Hindu political concepts to legitimize their rule. The Shailendra dynasty (c. 760–860) blended indigenous Indonesian culture with Sanskrit literature and Brahmin and Saivite versions of Hinduism. The Hindu concepts of a god king and of the terrestrial order as an analogue of the cosmic order sanctified temporal power as an expression of the spiritual universe. Great imperial palaces and Hindu and Buddhist monumental tombs were constructed by these early rulers. In the tenth century, the center of culture and power in Java shifted to Mataram, which held sway from 929 to 1222. Mataram was succeeded by a number of other regional kingdoms, notably by Majapahit (1293–1389).

The most important maritime kingdom was Srivijaya, first centered at Palembang and then at Jambi in Sumatra. This kingdom controlled both sides of the Malacca Straits, which gave it commercial hegemony over the trade between Arabia, East Africa, Iran, and India to the west and China to the east. Locally the straits area produced food, tin, gold, and pepper. Its cosmopolitan trading connections helped establish a Hinduized culture, just as it would later favor the introduction of Islam.

THE COMING OF ISLAM

The advent of Islam depended on the close trading relationships between the Indian Ocean region and Southeast Asia. (See Map 19.) The period from 1400 to 1700 saw increased commerce, the growth of cities, the monetization of the economies, and – with these fundamental socioeconomic changes – the introduction and diffusion of universalistic religions based on sacred scriptures; this included not only Islam in the island arc of what is now Indonesia and Malaysia, but Confucianism in Vietnam, Theravada Buddhism on the rest of the Southeast Asian mainland, and Christianity in the Philippines.

Seaborne commerce was crucial to the diffusion of Islam. By the thirteenth century, Southeast Asia was in contact with the Muslims of China, Bengal, Gujarat,

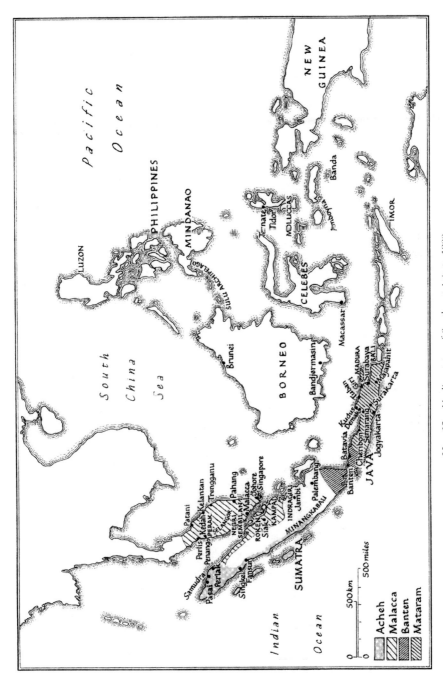

Map 19. Muslim states of Southeast Asia to 1800.

South China Sea

Pacific Ocean

Indian Ocean

LUZON

PHILIPPINES

MINDANAO

Sulu Archipelago

BORNEO

Brunei

Bandjermasin

Macassar

CELEBES

MOLUCCAS

Ternate
Tidor

Amboyna

Banda

NEW GUINEA

TIMOR

SUMATRA

MINANGKABAU

Palembang

Jambi

INDRAGIRI

Siak

KAMPAR

ROKAN

Singapore

Johore

Malacca

NEGRI SEMBILAN

PEDAS

PELANGOR

Pahang

Trengganu

Kelantan

Kedah

Perlis

Penang

Patani

Perak

Perlak

Pasai

Samudra

Singkel

Pansur

Banten

Batavia

Cheribon

Demak

Kudus

Japara

JAVA

Semarang

Surakarta

Jogyakarta

Mataram

Madjapahit

Surabaya

MADURA

GILI

BALI

500 km
500 miles

Acheh
Malacca
Banten
Mataram

Iran, Yemen, and South Arabia. Merchants, travelers, scholars, *shurafa'* (descendants of the prophet), and mystics connected by commerce, lineage, and faith flowed eastward from Yemen, Hadramawt, and Oman to Malaysia, Indonesia, and the Philippines. The fact that Malayan and Indonesian Muslims primarily adhere to Shafi'i law points to South India as a major source of Islamic influences.

The facts indicating the diffusion of Islam in the region are few. In 1282, the Hindu Malay ruler of Samudra on the island of Sumatra had Muslim advisors. A Muslim community in Pasai in North Sumatra was reported by Marco Polo in 1292. The tomb of Sultan Malik al-Salih in Perlak dated 1297 indicates the conversion of a local ruler. In 1345–46, Ibn Battuta, on his world tour of Muslim communities, found Shafi'i scholars in Samudra. In the fourteenth century, Muslims were also established in northeast Malaya, some parts of Java, Brunei, and the southern Philippines.

Malacca was one of the principal Muslim societies. At the beginning of the fifteenth century, Iskandar, the former ruler of the trading kingdom of Srivijaya, was defeated by Javanese rivals and forced to flee Palembang. He founded Malacca and converted to Islam. Iskandar based his political claims on genealogical descent from past rulers, Buddhist consecration, and Islam. By such syncretism Islam was added to the panoply of Southeast Asian cultures. Malacca built up a trading empire with extensive contacts in India, Java, and China. Ships from Malacca sailed to Gujarat, Bengal, and the smaller islands of the East Indies archipelago. Malacca also attempted to build up a Malay-Sumatran territorial empire with possessions on both sides of the straits. Malacca became a base for the spread of Islamic influence throughout the region. By 1474, the Malay rulers of Pahang, Kedah, and Patani were converted to Islam, and most of the rulers of the northeast coasts of Sumatra, from Aceh to Palembang, were Muslims.

Java's Islamization began in the fourteenth century. The first evidence suggesting that Javanese were converting to Islam is found in the gravestones of the Hindu-Buddhist court elites of Majapahit. The earliest is dated to 1368–69 CE. At Tralaya, gravestones dated from 1376–1611 CE bear Quranic quotations and pious formulas. As early as 1414, Javanese students were coming to Malacca and Pasai to study with Muslim teachers. By the middle of the fifteenth century, the coastal principalities of Java – Demak, Tuban, Madura, and Surabaya – had become Muslim. Muslim holy men established independent kingdoms centered around important sanctuaries or tombs, as at Giri, Cheribon, Kadilangu, and Semarang. Muslim scholars and preachers established mosques and schools and proselytized among Javanese. In general, however, by the fifteenth century, the coastal areas were more likely to be Islamized. Some of the coastal lords were native Javanese, but others were Chinese, Indians, Arabs, and Malays who had established trading states. Around 1500, there was constant warfare between them and the Hindu principalities of the interior.

Manuscripts of the sixteenth century show that early Javanese Islam blended Sufi teachings with Javanese cultural practices. These manuscripts use Javanese rather than Arabic terms for important mystical concepts. Muslim texts were being translated into Javanese vernacular. By the end of the century it was possible to be both Muslim and Javanese. However, as opposed to Malay texts that articulate Islamization as a conversion – the acceptance of a new identity through such rituals as the acceptance of an Arabic name and circumcision – Javanese texts envision Islamization as integrated with existing identities.

From its bases in Sumatra and Java, Islam spread further eastward. Ternate was converted in 1495. The Moluccas became Muslim in 1498 as a result of contacts with Java, and the coastal towns of Borneo were converted by Javanese contacts before the arrival of the Portuguese in 1511. Islamic influences from Sumatra, Ternate, and Borneo reached the Philippines. Conversions were made in Luzon, Sulu, and Mindanao.

Islamic influences and conversions intensified in the sixteenth and seventeenth centuries. Stimulated by commercial wealth and the availability of firearms, the established Islamic states, notably Aceh, Johor, Patani, Banten, Demak-Pajang-Mataram, and Ternate extended their control to their rural hinterlands. The concept of jihad (holy war) began to assume a major role in their legitimization. From 1580 to 1650, much of eastern Indonesia converted to Islam. Islam was adopted by the rulers of parts of Sulawesi (1603–12) and eastern Borneo. On the Southeast Asian mainland, the Cham kingdom became Muslim sometime between 1607 and 1676.

There were several interrelated factors in the diffusion and acceptance of Islam. Often, the first converts were local rulers who sought to attract Muslim commercial traffic or win allies in the struggle against Hindu traders from Java. Coastal chiefs used conversion to legitimize their resistance to the authority of Majapahit and to throw off the suzerainty of the central Javan empires. Rulers typically adopted Muslim names and dress, sponsored the construction of mosques, and made ritual gestures such as renouncing the consumption of pork. They adopted Islamic laws for commercial and family matters such as contracts, marriages, divorce, and inheritance, although the application of the law was limited. Rulers exempted themselves from the detail of the law and called on ancient gods for their spiritual authority. Rulers also created administrative hierarchies for the administration of law and prayer, including the posts of judge (*qadi*), prayer leader (imam), and preacher (*khatib*). They sponsored scholars, study circles, and debates at court and in the mosques. They set an example for and sometimes commanded their subjects to adopt Islam. At the same time, the rulers blended aspects of Islamic teaching with their historic supernatural attributes and their devotion to local spirits and gods. Court-sponsored rituals of homage to ancestral spirits and spirits of the sea, exorcisms, and artistic performances remained an important part of the regional religious cultures.

Furthermore, Islam served as the basis of shared norms and trust among Muslim traders and local rulers. Muslim merchants married into ruling families and provided important diplomatic skills, wealth, and international experience for the commercial enterprises of coastal rulers. Muslim traders were attracted to ports, where they were assured a mosque for worship and the protection of a Muslim ruler. In an era of expanding trade, conversion to Islam may have helped to create new communities to replace the village-scale communities disrupted by commerce and political change.

Missionaries from Gujarat, Bengal, and Arabia played a critical role. The Sufis came not only as teachers but also as traders and politicians who penetrated the courts of rulers, the quarters of merchants, and the villages of the countryside. They could communicate their religious vision in a form compatible with beliefs already held in Indonesia. Sufism blended indigenous spiritual and mystical beliefs and ideas of the supernatural. Pantheistic doctrines were understood because of Hindu teachings. Saint worship and faith in the saint as a healer were common to both Muslims and Indonesians. Ultimately, the success of Islam was due to its tolerance of local traditions. Rather than converting to Islam, Southeast Asians accepted Islam, adding a new body of beliefs to established local ideas.

Although there was no single process or single source for the spread of Islam in Southeast Asia, the travels of individual merchants and Sufis, the winning of apprentices and disciples, and the founding of schools seem crucial. Instruction and education in Islam developed alongside the adoption of Islamic law and Muslim identities. At the elementary level, Quran instruction and study of written Arabic was conducted in mosques, prayer houses, and the homes of learned Muslims. At a more advanced level, instruction in hadith, Quran exegesis, law, and mysticism was provided in the courts of rulers and then was taken over (in the mid-eighteenth century and later) by schools called *pondoks* in Malaya and *pesantren* in Java.

Thus, from the thirteenth to the early nineteenth century, Islam became the common religion of peoples who held different ethnic, linguistic, regional, and cultural identities. The foundations were being laid for the ultimate emergence of the modern Indonesian and Malay nations.

PORTUGUESE, DUTCH, AND MUSLIM STATES

The diffusion of Islam was paralleled by a wave of state formation lasting from the fourteenth to the eighteenth centuries. (See Map 20.) Trade led to capital accumulation and trading resources and thus to the concentration of political power. The expansion of cash crops – such as pepper in western Java, Sumatra, and Borneo and the mining of tin in the Malay Peninsula – strengthened the coastal principalities. New revenues allowed them to buy firearms and to reinforce the patronage networks that linked rulers to lesser officials and notables. Chinese, Indian, and

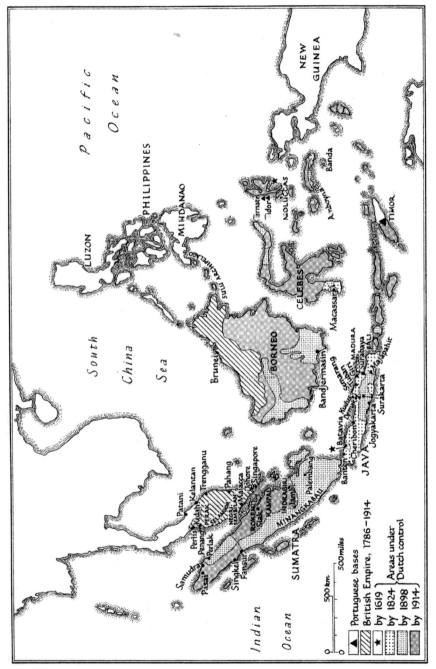

Map 20. The Portuguese, Dutch, and British empires in Southeast Asia, 1500–1914.

Portuguese bases ▲

British Empire, 1786–1914 ⧄

by 1619 ★
by 1824 } Areas under
by 1898 } Dutch control
by 1914 }

Pacific Ocean

NEW GUINEA

PHILIPPINES

LUZON

MINDANAO

Sulu Archipelago

South China Sea

Ternate
Tidore

MOLUCCAS

Amboyna

Banda

TIMOR

BORNEO

Brunei

Bandjermasin

CELEBES

Macassar

Indian Ocean

Patani

Kelantan

Trengganu

Pahang

Kedah

Penang

Perlis

PERAK

Perak

SELANGOR

Malacca

NEGRI SEMBILAN

Johore

Singapore

ROKAN

Siak

KAMPAR

Jambi

Indragiri

Palembang

MINANGKABAU

SUMATRA

Samudra

Pasai

Perlak

Singkel

Fansur

Aceh

Batavia

Bantam

Cheribon

Demak

Kudus

Semarang

GIR

MADURA

Surabaya

Mojopahit

JAVA

Jogyakarta

Surakarta

500 km.

500 miles

later Hadramawti Arab traders worked in partnership or as agents and tax farmers for local rulers.

The development of these Islamizing states and societies was profoundly affected by outside powers engaged in the pepper and spice trades. Chinese maritime activity burgeoned at the beginning of the fifteenth century, and the Portuguese established themselves as an Indian Ocean power in the early six-teenth century. In 1509, the Portuguese defeated a combined Egyptian and Indian fleet and took Goa in 1511. They conquered Malacca in 1515; they went on to take Hurmuz on the Persian Gulf and, in 1522, Ternate, in an attempt to control the trade between China, Japan, Siam, the Moluccas, the Indian Ocean, and Europe. They were expelled from Ternate in 1575, but they held on to other islands in the Moluccas. By the mid-sixteenth century, however, Portuguese interests were primarily focused on Japan and China, Brazil, and Africa.

Like the Portuguese, the Dutch came to the East Indies in quest of pepper. In 1594, Holland won its war of independence from the Habsburg monarchy and was excluded from access to pepper and spices in the Lisbon market. Instead, in 1595 Dutch fleets sailed directly to the East Indies; in 1602, the United East India Company (VOC) was chartered by the merger of competing smaller companies to control Dutch trading and to compete with the English East India Company. Holland joined the Chinese, Japanese, Spanish, Portuguese, and Indians, competing to buy pepper, cloves, nutmeg, cinnamon, sandalwood, lacquer, silk, and deer hides in return for Indian cloth and silver.

The Dutch pushed their way into the East Indies trade by naval warfare. They sought to control trade, create monopolies, and extract tributes. The spice trade required naval bases; bases needed surrounding territory. Trade required empire. By the middle of the eighteenth century, the Dutch had acquired substantial con-trol over the trade in pepper and spices by establishing forts and bases through-out the East Indies archipelago and by forcing local rulers to grant them trading monopolies, sometimes by violence and sometimes in return for political help. They defeated the Portuguese and took Amboyna in 1605. In 1619, they founded Batavia, on the island of Java, rich in rice and timber, as the new capital of their trading empire. They seized Banda in 1621, Ceylon in 1640, and Malacca in 1641. The VOC established a monopoly of nutmeg in 1621 and of cloves in the 1650s.

With these commercial advantages and fortress bases, the Dutch eliminated the Portuguese and established their supremacy over the Muslim states. Aceh came under Dutch commercial control between 1629 and 1663. Treaties of 1639, 1650, and 1659 gave the Dutch two-thirds of Aceh's tin supplies. From Aceh, Dutch economic power extended to the rest of Sumatra. They took Palembang in 1658 and in 1663 obtained a monopoly on the pepper trade of Minangkabau. The Dutch defeated resistance in the Moluccas by 1658 and established a monopoly of cloves and nutmeg. In 1669, they forced Macassar to give them a monopoly on its trade and subsequently established forts on Ternate, Macassar, and Borneo. By the 1670s, the VOC position in East Indonesia had been consolidated. With the establishment of territorial political power, Dutch interests turned from trade to a new system of economic exploitation requiring local rulers to deliver tributes. Spices declined in importance in favor of pepper, sugar, coffee, tea, and tobacco, plantation crops largely managed by Europeans and Chinese. The Dutch exchanged these products for opium rather than Indian cloth.

The British entered the regional competition in 1786, when they made an agreement with the sultan of Kedah to use Penang, an island off the coast of Malaya, to repair and equip fleets for the Indian Ocean and as a base from which they could sell British goods to raise revenues for the purchase of silk and tea in China. In 1791, they occupied Penang. The Napoleonic wars in Europe worked to the further advantage of the British. With the conquest of Holland by France in 1795, William V of Holland turned Malacca and other Dutch colonies over to the British for use in the war against France. In 1800, a strip of mainland called Province Wellesley was ceded to them. In 1810, Britain took control of Java. At the end of the Napoleonic wars, Britain agreed to return Dutch possessions in order to restore Holland as a buffer between Britain and France and to prevent the development of a French-Dutch alliance in the postwar period. However, the British retained control of the Malacca Straits and established a new base at Singapore in 1819. In a treaty of 1824, the Dutch recognized India and Malaya as being in the British sphere of influence, and the British recognized Dutch predominance in Sumatra, Java, and the rest of the Indies.

As in the steppes of Inner Asia, European economic and political intervention did not prevent but actually stimulated the spread of Islam. While the Dutch established their commercial supremacy, Islamic loyalties, Muslim regimes, and Islamic institutions were being consolidated as the indigenous expression of cultural identity, political resistance, and economic competition. In each maritime Southeast Asian region – such as Java, Aceh, Malaya, and Minangkabau – a form of Islamic society developed that was at once characteristic of the particular region, reminiscent of Indonesian-Islamic societies in other areas, and recognizably Islamic in international terms.

JAVA: THE STATE, THE '*ULAMA*', AND THE PEASANTS

On Java, the Dutch conquered already well-established Muslim states. Between 1513 and 1528, a coalition of Muslim kingdoms defeated Majapahit, and two new states emerged – Banten in central and western Java (founded in 1568) and Mataram in east-central Java. Under Sultan Agung (r. 1613–45) and Sultan Mangkurax (r. 1646–77), Mataram reduced the independent princes of the island to vassals and ministers of the Mataram state. A bitter struggle also took place between the state and the Islamic religious centers, in which Mataram progressively destroyed the political power of the Muslim lords – although not their local religious influence.

Mataram became the ruling power and the focus of Islam on Java, but the Muslim holy men retained a charisma that could be used to rally opposition to the state.

On Java the Dutch progressively established themselves as territorial overlords. They consolidated their control by founding a new capital at Batavia in 1619 and by defeating the ruler of Mataram, Sultan Agung, in 1629. In 1646, they forced Mataram to recognize their monopolies in the Spice Islands. Peace prevailed until 1675, when the rivalries of Mataram and Banten required Mataram to ask for Dutch help, for which the island was obliged to give the Dutch a monopoly over the cloth and opium trades. Dutch help was purchased again and again by tributes and concessions of land. Agrarian Java replaced the Spice Islands as the most lucrative Dutch possession. In 1723, the Dutch required an annual quota of coffee, and native princes were expected to comply with Dutch demands for timber, cotton, and indigo. At first, the local princes were autonomous intermediaries, but gradually Dutch overseers were appointed to see to the production of coffee, cloves, cinnamon, and pepper. The tributes in kind were supplemented by forced deliveries of spices at fixed prices. These goods the Dutch exported for resale in Europe.

Finally, in 1755, with the partition of Mataram into two kingdoms, Surakarta and Jogyakarta, the Dutch became suzerains of both. The rulers of the divided kingdom could no longer fight each other for supremacy and increasingly became administrative and spiritual rather than military powers. Dutch intervention brought peace to Java from 1774 to 1825.

In the early seventeenth century, the Mataram court was only partially Islamized. Despite the new Islamic titles, the Hindu cosmological conception of the state continued to be valued. Mataram maintained Hindu-Buddhist literary traditions and rituals and combined Islamic and Hindu concepts of rule. Its rulers believed that they derived their authority directly from God (the ruler was God's representative on earth, *kalipatullah*) and indirectly from the tomb of Sunan Kalijaga (the saint and holy man who represented the spiritual presence of Islam).

In the Mataram conception, the ruler was a sacred, indeed divine, figure; he was the repository of divine radiance (*wahyu*), a luminous light that suffused his person and emanated from him. *Wahyu* was seen as a concrete, tangible, creative energy that flows through the universe – a force that can be accumulated, concentrated, and preserved in individuals as a result of yogic practices and extreme self-denial. Power is concentrated by public rituals, including mass demonstrations, powerful slogans, and the presence of thousands of submissive persons. It is concentrated by the ownership of heirlooms (*pusaka*, including spears, musical instruments, and carriages) and by control over extraordinary or deformed human beings. Power is manifest in wealth and sexual energy. Fertility, political unity, prosperity, stability, and glory of the kingdom are all considered expressions of power. However, possession of power is prior to legitimacy. Power is neither good nor evil; it is just real. Thus, in the Javanese conception of kingship, the ruler was glorified by his descent from gods as well as human beings, by his possession of holy relics, and by court ceremonies in which weapons and decorations symbolized his special powers. The ruler had the deepest knowledge of reality, sense of justice, and a flawless personality acquired by ritual and by observance of taboos. The king's actions were taken to be God's will.

Royal administration was conceived in terms of maintaining order and justice in the whole of the kingdom. The ruler's subordinates were fully responsible for their districts and personally accountable to him. They formed a social class called the *priyayi*, bound to their lord by *kawula-gusti*, the bond of lord and servant. The ruler must care for his officials as a father, and the servants must give total love, submission, and gratitude to their lord. Officials were paid by benefices allotted to them by their patron. The central political problem for a ruler was to control the land granted to his supporters and not to allow it to become hereditary. When provincial notables built up an independent base of power, the ruler tried to use his household clients to offset their influence and to absorb or co-opt them. The king and the nobility lived on the labor of the peasantry. The king was entitled to part of the produce of the land. The salaries for court workers and guards were paid for by taxes from designated districts. Peasants also labored to build waterworks and bridges and provided transportation and personal services to the king and his officials.

The ideal of the Mataram aristocracy was based on individual self-cultivation. To be loyal to their lord and to fulfill their role in the cosmic order, the *priyayi* had to cultivate an inner life of refined feeling and an outer life of polite formality. For each individual, the ideal of life was to cultivate an inner tranquility that made the soul correspond to the order of society and the universe. In the pre-Islamic Javan conception, the universe was taken to be a single and unified phenomenon; the cosmos harmoniously ordered; the world of human beings grounded in cosmic principles.

The ruling elite was distinguished from the rest of the population by a quality called *halus*, which meant smoothness of spirit, beauty, elegance, politeness, and sensitivity. The opposite of *halus* was *kasar*, lack of control, coarseness, and the degradation that comes from indulging in purely selfish and personal desires. Control of emotion, equanimity, patience, acceptance of fate without protest, and detachment from the external world were the most highly regarded virtues.

This inner restraint was the basis of realistic behavior. In the outer world, the *priyayi* would express themselves by conformity to etiquette and ethics and by speaking in correct linguistic form. Language, dance, music, and art were all channeled outer expressions of a restrained inner being. The *priyayi* ethic of control over the outer world protected them against inner disturbance; a balanced inner world expressed itself in outward order. The cultivation of true feeling and of true expression, both called *rasa*, was a realization of the individual's true self and a recognition of the reality of God's existence; it was also a means to worldly power through concentration and mastery of one's spiritual capacities.

In cultural style, the *priyayi* looked to the rich Javanese tradition of *wayang* shadow theater and its spiritual imagination. They cultivated and patronized Javanese dancing, with its Hindu connotations, and the production and consumption of fine crafts such as manuscript illustration, batik dyed fabrics, symbolic ornamental daggers (*kris*), and the gamelan orchestra.

Thus, Mataram society was in name Islamic, but the actual organization of state, including its concepts of rulership and the personal ideal of the *priyayi* elite, was based on Hindu and Javanese mythical and cosmological conceptions. The strong Javanese and Hindu basis of Mataram culture was due to the continuity of political elites. Whereas Muslim regimes in India, the Ottoman Empire, and many other parts of the world were established by conquerors who brought their Muslim identity from without, the Mataram regime was converted from within. Although Islam had been introduced by the wars between the coastal principalities and the rulers of the interior, Mataram eventually destroyed the coastal powers, suppressed the sea trade, and made the aristocracy of the interior, rather than the commercial lords of the coast, the dominant elite on Java. Islamic identity then served to reinforce the legitimacy of the old order and allowed Javanese society to define its opposition to Dutch rule without disturbing the inherited structures of political order and personal values. The state continued its traditional, political, and symbolic functions in Islamic guise. As compared with Safavid Iran and even Mughal India, which also combined universal Islamic norms with local regional cultures, Mataram leaned strongly in the direction of the non-Islamic aspects of state culture.

Alongside the state, the local communal form of Islam was built around a *pesantren*, which was part school and part religious brotherhood. The pupils lived in dormitories, worked in the fields or at some craft that helped support the school, studied chanting of the Quran, and learned magical and mystical formulas. The influence of the scholars (*kiyayis*) extended from the schools to the villages, where they won a following of strict Muslim believers who looked to the teachers as their spiritual masters and who joined religious orders (particularly the Naqshbandiyya and Qadiriyya). The Shattariyya entered Java from Aceh in the late seventeenth century. The teachers, students, and village followers who adhered to this Muslim way of life were called *santris*.

The mass of villagers, however, were Muslim in a different sense. (Little is known about Javanese village life in the pre-modern era. The observations made here for the sake of completeness are based on mid-twentieth-century research.) For most Javanese villagers, Islam was not a question of political legitimacy or doctrine but was simply part of their mentality – part of their attitude toward the world seen and unseen. Islam was not a religion or a sect in the sense of being an ideology and a defined social allegiance so much as a vocabulary by which people defined the sacred forces in everyday life.

Villagers called themselves Muslims and practiced Muslim rituals. The influence of the scholars (*'ulama'* or *kiyayis*) was considerable. However, village culture was in fact compounded of animist, Hindu, and Islamic elements. The *slametan* feast was the primary village ritual; it was given to mark such important life events as birth, marriage, illness, death, personal and business occasions, village ceremonies of purification and solidarity, and Muslim holidays. The feast was meant to establish security and equanimity for the host, his family, and his guests; to dispel hostility and aggression; and to defend against evil spirits. Its symbolic purpose was to organize society, regulate behavior and feeling, and ward off the forces that threatened to bring disorder and chaos into everyday life. The ceremonial itself was marked by a short speech given by the host and a prayer or Quranic passage chanted in Arabic, followed by a meal. The Arabic recitation, the participation of the village religious teacher, and the choice of Muslim occasions, such as the birthday of the Prophet or the ending of the fast of Ramadan, made this multipurpose village ceremony an Islamic occasion. The curing of disease and the warding off of evil spirits was also the function of the village sorcerer (*dukun*), who worked his magic by spells, amulets, and herbs, sometimes giving them a Muslim orientation by chanting Quranic verses.

Islam was thus assimilated to a village religious mentality that focused on belief in a world of spirits, demons, and powers of nature. Islam in the village context was not so much a metaphysical, ethical, or legal system, or a form of social and political organization, but another metaphor for an ongoing community life based on traditional religious and social conceptions.

THE CRISIS OF IMPERIALISM AND ISLAM ON JAVA: 1795–1830

The Napoleonic wars in Europe brought a profound upheaval to Java. The Netherlands came under French domination in 1795 and in 1808 the Napoleonic regime sent Marshal Daendels to be governor-general of Java (r. 1808–11). For access to labor and economic resources, to meet its military requirements in an era of global conflict, the Dutch upset the traditional political arrangements between themselves and the Javanese princes. Daendels treated the Javanese rulers as if they were vassals, and in 1811 imposed treaties on Surakarta and Yogyakarta that involved extensive annexations to Dutch government territory. Daendels demanded a monopoly on the supply of timber, rice, and other key commodities as well as the opening of shipyards and logging enterprises to European investment. During the Napoleonic wars, however, the British took over Java in 1811–12. Thomas Stamford Raffles was appointed lieutenant-governor of Java (r. 1811–16).

In 1816, Java was returned to Dutch authority as part of the post-Napoleonic European settlement. Under renewed Dutch rule, the aristocracy continued to be alienated. The Europeans interfered in court affairs. Ever-larger tracts of sugar, coffee, indigo, and pepper plantations in Central Java were leased to Europeans and Chinese. Cultivators were ever more obliged to pay taxes in cash and thus were forced to borrow money from Chinese lenders. Chinese-run tollgates exacted a tribute from local trade. Heavy labor services were exacted by the Dutch planters on the coffee estates.

Moreover, the per-capita standard of living of the peasants was falling. The population in the rice-growing regions of Java had grown steadily from 1755 to 1825. At the same time, too much land had been converted from rice to sugar production. A cholera epidemic struck in 1821. When sugar prices collapsed in 1821–22, the price of rice remained high. In the years leading up to the crisis of 1825, harvest failures were frequent. Finally, the use of opium, promoted by the European governments and Chinese retailers, made agrarian conditions in south-central Java intolerable.

Java began to seethe with messianic expectations of a golden age of justice and plenty. In 1822, the people attacked land-tax offices, tollgates, the resident Chinese community, and the houses of European tax inspectors and estate over-seers. Then, in 1825, local resentment burst into a civil war led by Prince Dipane-gara (d. 1855), a member of the ruling family who had been passed over for succession and had devoted himself to religious studies. The corruption of the court and its subservience to the Dutch made him a spokesman for Muslim reli-gious virtues. The prince came to see himself as both temporal lord and spiritual overseer of Java; his mission was to suppress and purify Islam on the basis of a new moral order grounded in Islamic law. He also insisted on Javanese cultural norms in language, dress, and etiquette. Prince Dipanegara's supporters included the scholars, functionaries of the religious hierarchy or other courtiers, local com-munal religious officials, students of the religious schools, and masses of peasants. Their revolt lasted for five years and ended in 1830 with Dipanegara's capture and exile to Sulawesi. Although he was eventually defeated, Dipanegara became a symbol of national resistance to foreign rule. The 1825–30 revolt was the prelude to a new economy, polity, and religious culture on Java.

ACEH

Portuguese and later Dutch intervention contributed to the further spread of Islam. With the fall of Malacca, Muslim teachers and missionaries migrated to north-ern Sumatra, Java, the Moluccas, and Borneo. Aceh became the heartland of Indonesian-Islamic societies. The sixteenth and seventeenth centuries were marked by Aceh's struggle against the Portuguese and then the Dutch. Sultan ʿAli Mughayat Shah rallied the opponents of the Portuguese, defeated them at Pidie in 1521, and at Pasai, in 1524, conquered the north coast of Sumatra. Between 1529 and 1587, Aceh made continual efforts to recapture Malacca, and, finally, between 1618 and 1620, it took Pahang, Kedah, and Perak. The apogee of Acehnese power was reached under Sultan Iskandar Muda (r. 1607–36), who organized an efficient regime and established his dominance over the local lords (*uleebalang*) and village associations. Sultan Iskandar's ambition to control the whole Malay Peninsula, however, was defeated by other Malay sultans in 1629.

As an embattled Islamic land, Aceh attracted political support from the Ottoman Empire and an influx of Ottoman and Mughal scholars and Sufis. Correspondence; books; the travels of teachers, students, and pilgrims; and diplomatic missions tied Aceh directly to the international world of Islamic learning. Sufi masters formed the backbone of Acehnese Islam. The indigenous Sufi tradition goes back to Hamza Fansuri, who died around 1600. He founded the Qadari order in Indonesia, wrote mystical commentaries in Malay, and propagated the teachings of Ibn al-ʿArabi and the doctrine of the unity of being, with its emphasis on mystical unity, ecstatic experiences, and receptiveness to folk-culture versions of Islam. Hamza Fansuri was followed by a literary renaissance in both Malay and Javanese, including non-mystical texts of Quranic exegesis and law.

The integration of mysticism, Islamic ritual, and spirit worship was opposed by reformist Muslims. The reform (*tajdid*) movement was centered in Mecca and Medina, with connections in Cairo and Yemen. As early as the seventeenth century, with expanding international trade, Arab scholars, especially those from Hadramawt, came to the Indies. Southeast Asian pilgrims had more ready access to Mecca and Medina. By contrast with the Javenese and Acehnese syntheses, the reformers repudiated the theosophy of Ibn al-ʿArabi and advocated Muslim beliefs and practices derived from the Quran itself and from the most reliable hadith. They repudiated the schools of law as a deviation from the true Islam. Based on the teachings of al-Junayd, al-Qushayri, and al-Ghazali, they also opposed the excesses of Sufi devotion and spiritual practices that were not integral to orthodox Muslim views.

In Aceh, Shams al-Din Pasai (d. 1630) represented the school of Junayd, with its stress on worldly activity and the fulfillment of the religious law. The early masters were followed by ʿAbd al-Raʾuf al-Singkeli (c. 1617–90). He returned after 1661 to Aceh from Arabia, bringing with him the legal and mystical teachings of scholars in Medina and the Shattari order. Al-Singkeli taught that reason was of limited value in the understanding of God, and that union with God is achievable through the performance of ordinary religious duties and Sufi remembrance and evocation of God (*dhikr*). At the end of the eighteenth century, ʿAbd al-Samad of Palembang translated al-Ghazali's work into Malay. Acehnese Islam, then, came to encompass both the ecstatic and the reformist tendencies characteristic of Islam in the Indian subcontinent and other regions. Muslim teachings became an integral part of Acehnese identity.

Although we know little of Acehnese society before the middle of the nineteenth century, from late nineteenth- and early twentieth-century observations, we can reconstruct the role of Islam in Aceh. Acehnese village society was built around lineages (*qawm*). The lineage units, however, were not organized by territory; people of different lineages lived in the same villages. In each village there were two types of authority. One was the village headman, who ruled in the name of customary law and represented the state. The other was the *tuanku*, a combination of Muslim scholar and Sufi adept. Ordinarily, the village *tuanku* organized prayers, taught religious law, and performed feats of spirit healing. The two authorities represented two parallel cultural and social structures in village life: one based on kinship, custom, and political allegiance; the other based on Islamic belief and worship.

Outside the villages, the scholars and Sufis maintained schools that were self-supporting agricultural communities; in these, the students not only studied but worked on the land belonging to the teachers. The schools taught ritual recitation of the Quran, Sufi beliefs, and magical formulas to students who would in turn become village teachers. These schools represented a very different world from that of the village – the world of purely Islamic social and religious obligations beyond the ties of kinship and territoriality. Islam, then, was integral to the village communities and yet offered a radical alternative. In place of kinship, it offered brotherhood based on faith. In the political realm, Islam was the principle that legitimized and defined the organization of the state. The state in Aceh was represented by the sultan, originally the ruler of a small capital town and the surrounding territory. He used Islamic symbols, ideas, and rituals to legitimize his regime; waged war against the Portuguese and the Dutch; and patronized the teaching of Islam in his domains.

MALAYA

Islam in the riverine states of Malaya was also closely integrated with both village life and the state. (See Illustration 19.) As in Acehnese villages, there were two parallel authorities. The village headman, or *penghulu*, was appointed by the higher authorities to keep the local peace, arbitrate disputes, collect taxes, organize labor, and act as a healer and spirit doctor. At the same time, the imam of the mosque, supported by a muezzin and a preacher, organized local worship and taught in the local school. The holy man was often venerated for having made the pilgrimage to Mecca and for his magical powers. Islam made an important contribution to the rituals and festivals marking the solidarity of the village community and to the commemoration of important events in the life cycle of individuals (such as birth, marriage, and death).

Acehnese and Malay villagers followed both Muslim and non-Muslim religious practices and believed in holy spirits, holy places, and saints who were venerated in both Muslim and non-Muslim guise. In the villages, both Muslim and non-Muslim holy men were available to offer counsel and cures. There were both Muslim and

Illustration 19. The Ubadiah Mosque, Kuala Kangson, Malaysia. *Source:* The Photo Source.

non-Muslim festivals to mark the natural cycle of life and the agricultural year. Malay and Acehnese villagers considered themselves Muslims, but Islam did not thereby distinguish them as a group, as a community, or as a cult separate from the total fabric of the society.

Islam was also important for the Malay states. The sultans were the heads of aristocratic lineages, made up the political elite, and were the village overlords. The Malay sultans traced their descent to the sultan of Malacca. A ruler was called at once raja (sultan) and *yang di-pardon* (he who was made lord). His titles were Muslim and Hindu, and he was believed to be descended from ancient and divine Hindu lords as well as Muslim ancestors. His regalia symbolized his sacred and mystical personality. Special drums, weapons, clothing, food, and adornments were reserved for him. Whereas the ruler was believed to have supernatural powers, there was scarcely any public expression of his Islamic role. Apart from prayers at royal inaugurations and funerals, there were no Muslim public rituals. Although Islamic law was known, there is little evidence of a Muslim judicial administration. Religion, then, symbolized the legitimacy of the states but did not define political practices. Compared with other Muslim states, Islam had a minimal impact in Malaya. In a highly compartmentalized political system, it symbolized the unity of the society based on the allegiance of states and village communities to the same religious symbols.

MINANGKABAU

Minangkabau, a region on the southern side of Sumatra, and its colony, Negri Sembilan in Malaya, is another example of how Islam operated on several levels in Malay-Indonesian societies. Minangkabau was a region of rice agriculture and of trade in pepper and gold. Islam was introduced into Minangkabau in the sixteenth century by Sufi missionaries and Muslim traders. By the seventeenth century, Islamic schools were established and the Naqshbandiyya, the Qadariyya, and Shattariyya were organized. In the eighteenth century, the Shattariyya became the leading Sufi order.

Minangkabau society was built on two parallel principles – one matrilineal, the other patrilineal. On the village level, clan organization, laws of marriage, land ownership, and property were defined in matrilineal terms. The village community, called *nagari*, was a grouping of a number of clans administered by chieftains called *penghulus*. The *nagaris* were integrated into still-larger federations called *alaras*, under the authority of a prince or raja. Islam represented the masculine principle. In the villages it was institutionalized in the *surau*, young men's houses, which became schools and centers of Sufi brotherhoods.

In practice, however, there was a considerable overlap between matrilineal and patrilineal forms of organization. Marriage practices and inheritance laws were blends of Islamic and traditional Minangkabau norms. The two forms of law and social structure generated deep conflicts. Islamic inheritance, child custody, and residence laws were patrilineal and patrilocal, yet the Minangkabau were affiliated with large clan houses that were passed down from one generation of women to the next, defined by a common female ancestor.

Moreover, in the eighteenth century, both economy and society in Minangkabau were changing radically. American and European demand for coffee, pepper, and cassia created a boom in the highland economy that disrupted traditional trading systems. Marginal villages with poor soil became wealthy by planting the new cash crops, threatening the influence of the wet rice farmers. The gold and pepper trades collapsed, while coffee production expanded. In this economic upheaval, the interests of coastal trading towns locked into the Dutch trading system and upland producing communities came into conflict. Some communities disintegrated, while new entrepreneurs and peasants prospered. Rice and coffee producers came into conflict over land. Uprooted people sought their living in towns and markets. Traditional morality gave way to a new individualism.

In those troubled times, Islamic reform movements came to the fore. Through the early 1700s, scholars had been primarily concerned with states and with kingship. The reformist Islamic movements were more involved with the everyday lives of ordinary people; legal opinions addressed issues of family life, sex, and appropriate conduct. By the late eighteenth century, Islamic reformism reached the Minangkabau highlands. From West Africa through South Asia and into the Malay world, the late eighteenth and early nineteenth centuries experienced a wave of Muslim reformist and revivalist movements.

In Minangkabau, the old order was challenged by a religious revival under the leadership of Tuanku Nan Tua. He insisted that local religious and social practice be reformed to meet the demands of Islam: a more strict application of Islamic law, better attendance at Friday prayers, an end to gambling and drinking, and a cessation of the brigandage and slaving that came with increased trade. Tuanku Nan Tua (also known as Tuanku Imam Bonjol) taught that it was necessary to strictly observe Islamic law in inheritance and family matters, improve mosques and dwellings, celebrate the birthday of the Prophet, and in general make the teachings of the Prophet (rather than custom) supreme. He also taught that Islamic law and mystical vision (Shari'a and *haqiqa*) should be integrated in religious life. His reform was directed not at the village communities but at the newly mobile merchant and peasant population to whom Islamic law was offered as guidance for the regulation of economic conflict and moral problems. In Minangkabau, as in India, the reformist version of Islam challenged local usages. Minangkabau matrilineal inheritance and matrilocal residence were plainly in contradiction to majoritarian interpretations of Islamic law.

The reform movement led to bitter civil war. In 1803, the reformers were reinforced by pilgrims returning from Mecca who had imbibed the Wahhabi principles current in the holy cities of Arabia. The returned pilgrims, preaching in the coffee-producing villages, also called for the purification of Islamic life, adherence to Islamic law, and an end to gambling, cock fighting, opium consumption, drinking, smoking, robbery, and violence. They called for a Muslim way of life in strict accordance with the teachings of the Prophet and opposed the magical practices that were part of the village concept of Islam. The reformist movement soon divided. Whereas Tuanku Nan Tua advocated pacific preaching, one of his disciples, Tuanku Nan Rincheh, organized military action. This was the so-called Padri movement. His followers pledged to dress in white, wear beards, and abstain from bodily satisfactions. They were also prepared to wage war against the *nagaris*, kill the *penghulus*, confiscate their property, and establish a new regime, headed by an imam and a judge and dedicated to the enforcement of Islamic law.

Some *penghulus* accepted Islamic law peacefully and assisted in the reform movement. This was especially true in merchant communities that had extensive trading connections with other parts of Malaya and Sumatra. Most of the customary chiefs, however, refused to accept the reformist movement. To defend themselves, they invited the Dutch to intercede, and a bitter and protracted war followed (1819–39), until the Dutch finally defeated the reformers and conquered the province. By then, the internal momentum of the reform movement was spent; the collapse of the Padri in 1833 was followed by a unification of the reformist Muslims and matrilineal traditionalists in a revitalized resistance to foreign occupation. Six more years of violent warfare ensued. By 1838, the Minangkabau were defeated by the Dutch. Despite the final compromise between traditional leaders and reformist Muslims, the reform movement had a profound effect on Minang-kabau society. Whereas Aceh and Malaya maintained the traditional balance among village, school, and state forms of Islam, in Minangkabau the conflict between tra-ditional village and reformist versions of Islam strengthened orthopraxis Islamic orientations and succeeded in Islamizing the village communities.

Thus, in the early decades of the nineteenth century, both Java and Minangkabau went through profound political and religious crises. With Dutch dominance of the Indies and the attendant social and religious upheavals, the way was prepared for the radical changes of the later nineteenth and twentieth centuries.

ISLAM IN AFRICA

CHAPTER 39

THE AFRICAN CONTEXT: ISLAM, SLAVERY, AND COLONIALISM

The history of Islam in the African continent falls into three geographical and historical zones. The Mediterranean littoral was conquered by Arab-Muslims and later by the Ottoman Empire and was a region of Arab-Islamic culture. West Africa, including the Sahara desert, and the savannah, forest, and coastal country south of the Sahara constituted a second region. Coastal East Africa and its hinterlands, including inland savannah country, was the third. The history of Islam in North Africa appears in conjunction with the history of the early Arab-Islamic conquests and the Ottoman Empire. However, the history of Islam in Africa cannot be separated from the interactions between Africa and the outside Muslim world, nor from its varied connections to Europe.

ISLAM

Three themes define pan-African history. The first is Islam. The Islamic period in Africa began in the seventh century with contacts among the newly founded Arab-Islamic empire and sub-Saharan and coastal East Africa. Whereas Islamic societies in the Middle East and the Indian subcontinent were established by conquest and ordered by states, Islam in Africa, as in Indonesia, was diffused primarily by the migration of Muslim merchants, teachers, and settlers.

Islam came into East Africa through two channels. Arab Bedouins and Egyptian armies carried Islam into Nubia and the upper Nile basin. Arab- and Persian-Muslim traders settled in the towns and islands along the Red Sea and Indian Ocean coasts of East Africa. By the end of the eighth century, trade routes from the Somali coast, built around the exchange of lowland salt for highland produce, brought Islam to the Ethiopian highlands. By the thirteenth century, a chain of petty sultanates ran from Zayla to the Shoan plateau, and many of the stateless nomadic peoples, including the Afar and the Somali, had become Muslims. In the early sixteenth century, the Galla peoples also adopted Islam. The spread of Islam in Ethiopia

582   The global expansion of Islam from the seventh to the nineteenth century

again gained momentum in the nineteenth century, owing to the revival of the highland trade to the Red Sea, the pilgrimage to Mecca, and the increased demand for slaves in Arabia and elsewhere. Further south, in East and Central Africa, a thriving slave and trading economy also brought Islam to the East African interior. Nyamwezi traders came down to the coast and Arab and Swahili traders to the interior. The trade was stimulated by the commercial interests of Sultan Sa'id of Zanzibar.

In West Africa, the Arab conquests opened the way to contacts among Muslim Arabs, Berbers, and Saharan and Sudanic African peoples. North African Berbers had been converted to Khariji Islam in the seventh and eighth centuries. Mauritanian Berbers were converted to Islam in the ninth century. By the tenth century, Muslim traders from North Africa were established in Awdaghust and Tadmekka in the southern Sahara, and from there traded with the kingdom of Ghana. In addition, Sudanic Africans also accepted Islam. By the late tenth and eleventh centuries most of the Sudanese trading towns had a Muslim quarter, and Muslims were important as advisors and functionaries at the courts of local rulers. A succession of Muslim states – Takrur, Ghana, Mali, Songhay, and Bornu – governed the western and central Sudan. From the twelfth through the fourteenth century, Walata and Timbuktu were centers of Muslim trade and scholarship.

From the Sahara and the Sudan, African-Muslim merchants and scholars, known as Wangara, or Dyula (Juula), moved into the Volta River basin and the Guinean forests, trading in gold, kola nuts, and salt. Merchant communities grew up along the trade routes at the crossings of rivers, toll posts, and stopping places for caravans, where they settled down to trade with the local populace. The trading communities often developed agricultural interests, and in some cases Muslims became the custodians of specialized crafts such as weaving and dyeing. In later centuries, farming – performed mostly by slaves, clients, and students – became more important.

Scholars and holy men offered their services to local chiefs and carried on the tradition of Islamic learning, provided instruction in Islamic law and rituals, and served as prayer leaders, teachers, and healers. Many claimed that they were shurafa', descendants of the clan of Quraysh, the clan of the Prophet Muhammad, whose holiness made their charms, medicines, and prayers efficacious, and their fortune-telling and divination perspicacious. Scholars were often members of merchant families or lineages, and some individuals carried on both business and clerical activities. Linked by trading networks, family connections, teacher-student relationships, and Sufi fellowships, the Muslims were typically independent enclaves within small-scale non-Muslim regional states and in stateless societies.

Certain families provided scholars generation after generation. In the Sahara, the zawaya or insilimen clans, the religious lineages, lived by livestock rearing, agriculture, and commerce and held a high status because of their wealth, their Islamic learning and spirituality, and their claimed Arab or sharifian descent.

By the early 1800s the most important of the *zawaya* lineages was the Kunta clan, which had widespread influence throughout Mauritania, Senegambia, and other parts of the western Sudan. The Saghanughu was a Dyula lineage living in the northern and western Ivory Coast and in parts of upper Volta. The Jakhanke were prominent in Senegambia.

The Muslim communities fit readily into an African society that was in general highly segmented, built around political lineages, age-group associations, religious cults, occupational groups, and different classes of free men and slaves. Political units were based not on ideology or a history of shared culture, ethnicity, and language, but rather on sudden conquests by small minorities. Muslims were considered yet another clan or lineage with their own culture, Islam, in a society of innumerable such communities. They were treated as clients, given business patronage, and afforded safe passage and protection from bandits. In return Muslims typically became secretaries and administrators in African kingdoms and providers of religious, ritual, and magical services such as divination and the production of talismans and amulets.

Over time, however, Muslim settlements became enmeshed in the host societies. Sometimes the Muslims converted local rulers and established a joint elite of warrior rulers and Muslim merchants. Non-Muslim African rulers converted to Islam and built mosques, instituted public prayer, patronized Muslim scholars, and celebrated Muslim holidays. Nonetheless, they continued to sponsor ceremonial dances, poetry recitations, and other non-Muslim rituals. They maintained a double cultural orientation to express both the Islamic and the indigenous bases of their authority. African kings were not retrograde Muslims; they simply followed the universal tendency of Muslim regimes to blend Muslim and non-Muslim cultures. In other cases, the chiefs remained pagans but employed Muslims as officials, traders, and advisors. Sometimes they gave their daughters in marriage to Muslim clerics.

Ruling elites and merchant communities could also come into conflict. Kings might crush the Muslim merchant communities and carry on a royal household trade, often in slaves, as happened in Asante, Dahomey, and Dar Fur. Merchants could seize power and govern themselves as independent towns, as happened in Timbuktu. Even after centuries, Islam remained a class and communal religion of certain mercantile and religious groups and a royal cult and had only a limited impact on the masses of the host societies.

The cultural relations of Muslim enclaves and their hosts were ambivalent. Muslim communities wanted to maintain their special identities and wanted a superior status due to their wealth, education, religious charisma, and cosmopolitan connections. In East Africa, Arab-, Persian-, Shirazi-, Swahili-, and Asian-Muslim groups developed a racial and cultural chauvinism toward the indigenous people. Islam came to be identified with "civilization," whereas the indigenous peoples were considered "barbarians." Even converts were considered inferior Muslims. At the same time, Muslims wanted to occupy important positions in the host societies and to proselytize on behalf of Islam. Muslims and Africans both had strong cultural motives for close relationships. Muslims could express their religious worldview in local idioms. Muslim religiosity included not only a culture of scripture, law, theology, and mysticism but also a popular culture of belief in spirits, the protective and healing power of magic and divination, and the efficacy of dream interpretation, prayers, and amulets comparable to those of non-Muslim African diviners, magicians, and spiritual leaders. Quranic ideas about jinn, incorporeal beings inhabiting the physical world, were similar to African concepts of spiritual presences. Non-Muslim Africans and Muslims both constructed elaborate genealogies and venerated their ancestors.

Non-Muslim Africans could adopt Muslim beliefs and practices on a number of levels. They could be considered as isolated cultural artifacts. Elements of Islamic material culture – including ornaments and dress, religious arts, rituals, calligraphy, talismans, and amulets – were not necessarily understood as part of an integrated religious culture that had to be accepted in its entirely but could be appropriated piecemeal and without embracing the whole Islamic religious system or a Muslim identity. Africans could combine their traditional cultural and religious customs with Arab-Islamic ones. Furthermore, cultural synthesis or exchanges did not necessarily imply a profound spiritual transformation or even a break with prior African cultures but could be simply a matter of social customs expressed in dietary habits, clothing, ritual, taboos, and ethnic identity.

At yet another level, many non-Muslim Africans formally converted to Islam and recognized scholars as the representatives of God's will. The power of communal cults waned, and the worship of Allah became supreme. Converted African Muslims recognized the supremacy of Islamic law, worshiped according to the five pillars of Islam, and followed Islamic ritual practices for circumcision, marriage, and death. There may also have been legal and social changes from matrilineal to patrilineal forms of family, and from communal to private ownership of property.

Alongside peaceful Muslim colonization there was a parallel tradition of militant determination to turn small colonies into Muslim states by defeating non-Muslims and corrupt Muslim rulers who blended Islam with customary African religious and social practices, conquering the pagan populations, converting them to Islam, and ruling them according to Muslim law. With the North African Almoravid movement of the eleventh century as a shadowy precedent, the jihads of the eighteenth and nineteenth centuries rose from the *jama'at*, or rural Muslim communities, and from Fulbe pastoralists, led by Muslim scholars, teachers, and itinerant preachers. They began in Mauretania and spread to Senegambia. These were followed in the nineteenth century by the jihad of 'Uthman don Fodio, who established the Sokoto caliphate among the Hausa peoples of northern Nigeria. The jihads of al-Hajj 'Umar and Samori Ture extended the rule of Muslim states in the Voltaic regions and the Sudanic zone of West and Central Africa. Religious movements, although not jihads, were also important in North and East Africa. In Cyrenaica, part of present-day Libya, the Sanusi movement helped spread Islam. In the northern parts of present-day Sudan, an anti-British Muslim movement was led by the Mahdi.

Although great numbers of people were converted to Islam, the process of conversion was slow and the change in institutions and beliefs variable. The result was the formation not of a uniform Islamic culture but of a plethora of local variations on Islamic practice. Although we may speak about conversion and the syncretism of Islam and African practices, there was no single cultural expression of Islamic civilization in sub-Saharan Africa.

SLAVERY

A second defining theme of African history was the almost universal commerce in slaves. In West Africa slaves were carried from the central and western Sudan to Cairo, Tripoli, and Qayrawan and then to the wider Islamic world. As plantations for sugar, tobacco, cotton, and other products were developed in the Americas, Africa was exploited for slave labor to be transported across the Atlantic. In Senegambia, the Atlantic slave trade and the wars between the traditional warrior elites (*tyeddo*) and Muslim jihadists promoted slavery. The Atlantic slave trade reached its apogee in the 1780s. In the nineteenth century, slowly at first but fairly dramatically after 1850, the Atlantic slave trade was suppressed.

In West Africa, the jihads led to the enslavement of countless thousands of people who were employed in armies, administration, and trade and as concubines and domestic servants. The textile industry in cities such as Kano, Bornu, and Bundu also employed numerous slaves. The introduction of new plantation crops vastly increased the internal demand for slave labor on sugar, cotton, palm oil, groundnuts, beeswax, cloves, and – later – rubber and cotton plantations. The jihad conquests of 'Uthman don Fodio, the jihad of al-Hajj 'Umar, the reign of Samori, and the adoption of the plantation system of agriculture led to the enslavement of a substantial part of the population in the western and central Sudan.

In East Africa a vast commerce in slaves both for internal use and for export to the Mediterranean, the Middle East, and Arabia had been carried on for centuries. The slave trade flourished in Egyptian, Omani, and other Red Sea and Indian Ocean states. In the middle of the nineteenth century the island of Zanzibar, ruled by Oman, became the principal center of slave-based production of cloves. Along the East African coast, grain, coconut, and copra plantations developed between 1830 and 1884 used large numbers of slaves. Sugar plantations were established on Mauritius. In the Nilotic Sudan, slaves were widely used in Wadai, Darfur, and the Funj sultanate.

Zanzibar was also the principal center of the international slave trade. Under Omani auspices the slave trade in the Red Sea and the Indian Ocean peaked between 1830 and 1880. The Egyptian slave trade peaked at about the middle of the century. Perhaps half of the slaves for export came from the Upper Nile and the Ethiopian mountains. Slaves were sold to Arab buyers from Yemen, the Hijaz, Hadramawt, and Oman, who often resold the slaves to buyers from Iraq, Kuwait, Bahrayn, Iran, India, Malaya, and the Indonesian archipelago. In Arabia, slaves were employed as maids, sailors, soldiers, administrators, and shop assistants and in menial work. In India and the Malay archipelago, slaves worked in a plantation economy similar to that found in the Americas. In Sumatra they also did craft work as mechanics, masons, and carpenters and served as soldiers.

COLONIALISM

The third common theme in African history was the exploitation of Africa by colonial regimes. European intervention goes back to the end of the fifteenth century. The Portuguese discovery of a new route to the East Indies led to the establishment of Portuguese bases on the Atlantic, Indian Ocean, and Red Sea coasts of Africa. This was the opening phase of the incorporation of Africa into the international capitalist economy. By the seventeenth century Europeans had established bases all along the coasts of Africa from Algiers to Cape Town and had begun to move into the interior. Europeans sought palm oil, peanuts, ivory, sisal, and slaves in exchange for cotton fabric, textiles, and firearms, which in turn promoted internal warfare, enslavement, and the export of slaves to the Americas. The increase in the slave trade was especially pronounced on Atlantic routes as well as on trans-Saharan routes to North Africa.

Foreign commercial engagement in Africa was followed by the colonization and the partition of Africa. Before 1850 European "possessions" were limited. The Portuguese had claims in Angola and Mozambique. After 1815 the French revived Saint-Louis and Gorée, their trading posts in Senegambia, and conquered much of Senegal. Britain had established Freetown and agricultural villages on the neighboring peninsula. British commercial and missionary influence began to penetrate into the interior around 1850, and the British entered what is now Ghana in competition with the Danes, the Dutch, and the native Asante. Muslim colonial regimes have a more sporadic history. The Almoravids conquered Ghana in the eleventh century. The pashas of Timbuktu were vassals of Morocco in the seventeenth century. In the nineteenth century, the Mazruis of Mombasa and other East African coastal dynasties were subordinate to the Busaidi imams of Oman. Egypt conquered Sudan. The jihad states of West Africa were indigenous conquering regimes.

In the late nineteenth century, the jihad states were challenged by the French and the British. At the Congress of Berlin (1884–85) the European powers agreed on the partition of Africa among themselves. The French took possession of Senegal and of the state founded by ʿUmar in 1893, and they defeated Samori in 1898. The British defeated the Mahdi in the Sudan in 1885 and the Sokoto caliphate in 1903. Belgium, Italy, and Germany seized pieces of the continent. Only after World War II would African countries regain their independence.

CHAPTER 40

ISLAM IN SUDANIC, SAVANNAH, AND FOREST WEST AFRICA

From the seventh to the eleventh centuries, Arab and Berber Muslim traders made their way into and across the Sahara, established colonies in the Sudan, and inspired the adoption of Islam by a succession of local rulers. Then, from the thirteenth to the nineteenth centuries, African-Muslim traders, scholars, and communities settled in Mauritania, Senegambia, and the Guinean regions. From the seventeenth through the nineteenth centuries, some of these Muslim communities launched jihads and created new Muslim states. At the same time they were faced with European competition, colonization, and empire formation.

THE KINGDOMS OF THE WESTERN SUDAN

The Arab conquests opened the way to contacts among Muslim Arabs and Berbers and Saharan and Sudanic peoples. (See Map 21.) North African Berbers had been converted to Khariji Islam in the seventh century; in the eighth century Tahert, Sijilmassa, and other Moroccan towns were centers of Ibadi Kharijism. Mauritanian Berbers were converted to Islam in the ninth century. By the tenth century, Muslim traders from North Africa were established in Awdaghust and Tadmekka. By the late tenth and eleventh centuries most of the Sudanese trading towns had a Muslim quarter, and Muslims were important as advisors and functionaries at the courts of local rulers.

In the Sahara and the bordering Sudanic region, the economy was supported by pastoralism, agriculture, craft production, and above all trade. Before the coming of the Muslims the Sudanic region was already an agricultural and state-centered society. Herding was carried on in the Sahil, the grassy steppelands that border the Sahara. The Sudan, the broad savannah belt to the south, produced millet, maize, yams, groundnuts, cotton, tobacco, indigo, and other crops. The Sudan traded with other parts of Africa and the Mediterranean, often through Berber intermediaries.

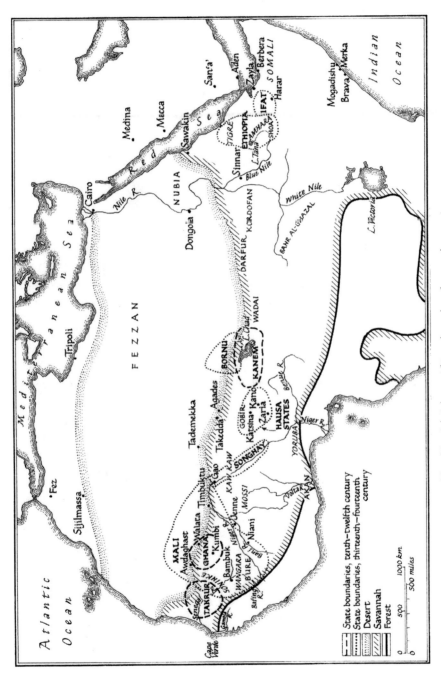

Map 21. Sub-Saharan Africa, eleventh to fourteenth centuries.

It exported gold, slaves, hides, and ivory and imported copper, silver beads, dried fruit, and cloth.

After the Arab conquests, North African cities such as Marrakesh, Fez, Tahert, Qayrawan, Sijilmassa, Tlemcen, Tunis, and Tripoli were the northern ends of the trans-Saharan trade routes that led to southern terminus cities such as Takrur, Kumbi Saleh, Kanem, Goa, Timbuktu, and Jenne. Intermediate towns such as Wargala, Ghadames, Fezzan, Tadmekka, and Awdaghust flourished on the several main routes. Sigilmassa was a key town in the nexus of trans-Saharan trade routes that linked the Sudan, sub-Sudanic Africa, the Mediterranean, and the Atlantic. The Sudan was the principal source of gold for North Africa, the Middle East, and Europe. Sudanese gold sustained the Aghlabid, Fatimid, and Spanish-Umayyad regimes and later formed the economic basis of the Almoravid Empire in Morocco and Spain.

Sudanic societies were built on small agricultural villages or herding communities, sometimes but not always integrated into larger tribal and linguistic groups. The oldest of the Sudanic kingdoms was Ghana, probably founded between the second and the fourth centuries CE. In the ninth and tenth centuries Ghana was both a partner and a rival of Berbers for the control of the trans-Saharan trade. To the west of Ghana was Takrur on the Senegal River. To the east, the kingdom of Kawkaw had its capital at Gao on the middle Niger River. To the south of Ghana there were no large kingdoms, but a number of small chieftainships and large areas that were not under state control.

Sudanic states had their origin in groups led by patriarchs, councils of elders, or village chiefs. The state came into existence when a local elder, an immigrant warrior, or perhaps a priestly ruler established his control over other communities. A Sudanic empire commonly had a core territory integrated by ethnic, linguistic, or similar ties and a larger sphere of power defined by the rule of a particular person or lineage over numerous subordinate families, castes, lineages, and village communities. The key political factor was not the control of territory but the relations that enabled the ruler to garner religious prestige, draw military support, and extract taxes or tributes. The kings were considered sacred persons and were believed to have divine powers. They did not appear in public and were not to be seen carrying out ordinary bodily functions such as eating. Around the kings were numerous officeholders who helped govern the realm and provincial and district chiefs often recruited from the junior members of the noble families.

For the sake of administrative support, legitimization, and commercial contacts, the rulers of Kawkaw, Takrur, Ghana, and Bornu adopted Islam in the late tenth and eleventh centuries. Islam became an imperial cult and the religion of state and trading elites, while the agricultural populations maintained their traditional beliefs.

From the eleventh to the sixteenth centuries, several kingdoms, in different geographical locations, succeeded one another as the principal centers of political power, trade, and Islamization. In Senegambia, south of the present-day Mauritania, the kingdom of Takrur, between the Senegal and the Gambia rivers, adopted Islam before 1040–41. The kings of Takrur introduced Islamic law and waged jihad against infidel neighbors. With the disintegration of the kingdom of Takrur, Ghana became the leading center of Islam in the western Sudan. There Muslim traders lived under the patronage of a non-Muslim ruler. The capital city of Ghana, Kumbi-Saleh, was a dual town, with one district for Muslims involved in the gold trade, and one for non-Muslims. The Muslim town was equipped with mosques and religious functionaries, including imams, muezzins, Quran reciters, and scholars. The Muslims provided the ruler with interpreters and officials. The prayers, rituals, amulets, and magical books of the Muslim traders were as important as their financial and administrative assistance.

Local Muslim influences were reinforced by Almoravid economic, diplomatic, and cultural penetration, and by the proselytizing activities of the North African Almoravid leader Abu Bakr (d. 1087) and his colleague Imam al-Hadrami (d. 1096). The Almoravid confederation had been formed in the ninth century in order to control trans-Saharan commerce from Sijilmassa to Ghana. The Almoravids conquered Morocco in the eleventh century and then took control of Ghana as well. The Almoravid invasions resulted in the adoption of Islam over wide areas and made Maliki law the dominant school in West Africa. With the decline of the Almoravids in the twelfth century, Ghana became the richest kingdom in the Sudan, but in the thirteenth century its former tributaries freed themselves from central control, and the kingdom disintegrated. The decline of Ghana gave rise to a number of small states among Soninke-speaking peoples.

Mali

From the early thirteenth to the end of the sixteenth centuries, Mali became the dominant regime in the western Sudan and the principal center of Islam. Mali had its origin among Malinke (Mande) peoples living between the Senegal and the Niger rivers. Mande-speaking peoples lived in family and village units, the head of the family being both priest and chieftain. A group of villages in turn formed a *kafs*, or *kafu*, a community of 1,000 to 15,000 people living around a mud-walled town and ruled by a hereditary chieftain called a *fama*. As in other African empires, the supreme ruler was a king of kings. He bore the military title of *mansa*, conqueror. The descendants of the *mansa* supplied the principal functionaries. Client clans, castes of dependent craftsmen, and people allied by marriage or by past service supported the ruler. Slaves and serfs worked in agricultural settlements to provide produce for the court, the army, and the administration. The *mansas* adopted the Ghanaian and Sudanic concepts of kingship to institutionalize their power. The rulers surrounded themselves with a bodyguard, servants, and elaborate ceremonies. A quasi-divine figure, the king was accepted as a symbol of the power of life and death.

The kingdom of Mali was founded by a local chieftain, Sunjata (1230–55), of the Keita dynasty. The Keita dynasty ruled, with some interruptions, from 1230 to 1390. After Islam became the royal cult, rulers built mosques and adopted Islamic law, and the king and the entire court took part in public prayers held on the great Islamic festivals. The most famous of these rulers, Mansa Musa (r. 1307–32), made a sensational pilgrimage to Cairo and Mecca in 1324 that made his kingdom legendary for its wealth in gold. Mansa Musa returned to Mali with Arab and Berber adventurers to serve in his administration. He built new mosques and palaces, appointed an imam for Friday prayers, and introduced Arabic-style poetry to his court. He encouraged Muslim scholarship in Timbuktu and sent Malian students to Fez. The rulers of Mali brought Muslim scholars from Cairo and Fez to help establish a West African tradition of Islamic learning. Arabic became important both for the diffusion of religion and for communications and trade. It was used for official correspondence in the Ghana Empire before the end of the twelfth century and in Mali in the mid-fourteenth century. The earliest known Arabic texts, though, come from Bornu at the end of the fourteenth century; fifteenth-century immigrants brought Arabic to Hausaland.

Islam as the religion of the commercial classes and portions of the political elite helped unify the kingdom and gave cultural support to the dynasty. Still, Malian rulers enforced customary law when it suited them and preserved ancient ceremonials. Muslim festivals were also occasions for the performance of pagan ceremonies and dances. This was especially important in segmented African societies in which only portions of the ruling elite and the trading classes were Muslim and the mass of the agricultural population was still pagan.

The economy of Mali was based on the gold of Bambuk and Bure on the upper Niger and on the important trading cities of Walata, Timbuktu, Gao, and Tadmakkat, where Saharan salt was traded for the cereal produce, the slave captives, and the ivory and gold of the western Sudan. In the thirteenth century, trade with North Africa increased enormously.

By the end of the fourteenth century the Malian Empire was in decline. Jenne, probably settled by Muslim traders in the thirteenth century, became the crucial link to the Akan forest region (modern Ghana and the Ivory Coast) and a source of new supplies of gold. Timbuktu, an important trade and religious center settled in the thirteenth century, replaced Walata as a terminus of the Saharan caravan traffic. As the trade routes changed, local chieftains became independent, and this reduced Mali once again to a petty chieftaincy. The people of Mali remained identifiable as having a common dialect and customs, but the empire was no more.

Songhay
With the breakup of the Malian Empire, a period of chaos ensued. Tributary states became independent. Nomadic horsemen, Mossi, Fulbe, and Tuareg raided the towns. Finally, a local warrior, Sunni ʿAli (1464/65–92), founded a new empire,

Songhay, in the region of the middle Niger and the western Sudan. He seized Timbuktu in 1468 and Jenne in 1473 and took control of the gold, kola, and trans-Saharan trade. Sunni ʿAli built his regime on the revenues of trade and the cooperation of Muslim merchants. He behaved as a Muslim in giving alms and fasting during Ramadan, but he also worshiped idols and practiced non-Muslim rites. In 1469 he made the pilgrimage to Mecca.

His successor, Askiya Muhammad Ture (r. 1493–1528), attempted to reconstruct the empire of Mali. Supported by Mande clans, he created a standing army and a central bureaucracy. Songhay acquired slave laborers by annual cavalry raids on the stateless, and therefore unprotected, peoples south of the Niger. The empire won substantial control over the salt mines of Taghaza and the copper mines of Takedda.

Askiya Muhammad made Islam the official religion, built mosques, and brought Muslim scholars, including al-Maghili (d. 1504), the founder of an important tradition of Sudanic Muslim scholarship, to Gao. Gao, the capital of his empire, was a trading city and had large communities of foreign Arabs, Berbers, and Sudanese converts to Islam, each with its own mosque. Timbuktu flourished as a center of Arabic and Islamic sciences. Askiya Muhammad appointed the first *qadi* of Jenne and extended Islamic judicial administration to other towns by establishing courts and appointing judges. War against unbelievers was considered a responsibility of the state. The legitimization of his regime also depended on his investiture by the *sharif* of Mecca as caliph of the land of Takrur. Still, Islam remained the religion of the governing elite, whereas the masses of Songhay society continued to be pagans.

The empire of Songhay was destroyed in 1591 by a Moroccan invasion that established a new ruling elite. Timbuktu became a pashalik of the Moroccan Sharifian empire. The *arma* (musketeers), the descendants of the invading army, became the ruling elite in the Niger region. The conquerors built fortresses and established permanent garrisons at the main river ports between Gao and Jenne, which enabled them to control the exchange of Saharan salt for Sudanic grain. By the mid-seventeenth century, the Moroccan regime was disintegrating. Timbuktu effectively became the capital of an independent state. By the mid-eighteenth century, the power of the *arma* was limited to the Niger River. Beyond the riverain territory, bands of freebooters lived by raiding the caravans. (See Map 22.)

A profound transformation of the position of Sudanic West Africa in the international economy took place in the seventeenth century. Although Morocco continued to be its largest market, the development of plantation agriculture in Brazil and the West Indies during the 1630s and the growth of the trans-Atlantic slave trade attracted the interest of the European commercial and naval powers. By 1642 the Dutch had expelled the Portuguese from their coastal bases in West Africa, and during the 1650s and 1660s, French, British, Danish, Swedish, and German companies were formed to develop tropical plantations and promote trade in African

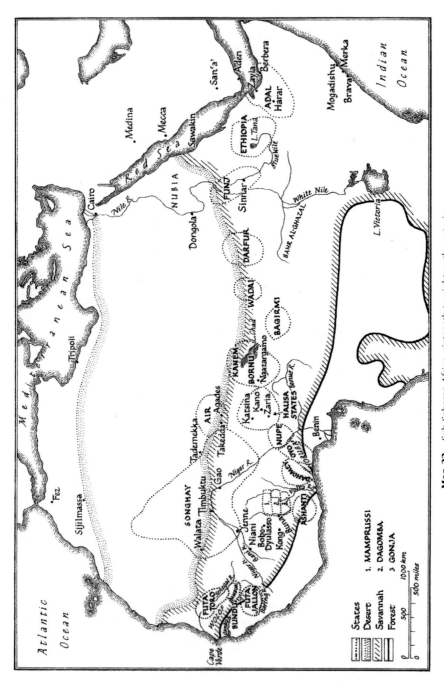

Map 22. Sub-Saharan Africa, sixteenth to eighteenth centuries.

slaves. Internal warfare and the shift of trade routes from the Sahara to the Atlantic brought an end to the history of the rise and fall of Sudanic empires. The once-great Muslim kingdoms of the western Sudan disintegrated into a plethora of small states.

THE CENTRAL SUDAN: KANEM AND BORNU

The central, like the western, Sudan was also the home of diverse ethnic and linguistic groups and was a center of state formation. The earliest state in this region was founded by Saharan nomads at some time in the ninth century, with its capital in the region of Kanem, northeast of Lake Chad. Trade routes from Tripoli through the Fezzan brought Ibadi Khariji merchants into the region. The first *mai* or king of Kanem of the Sefuwa dynasty accepted Islam in 1086 as the religion of the ruling elite. Later kings promoted Islamic scholarship, courts, and local administration. In the thirteenth century the rulers of Kanem made the pilgrimage, and in 1240 a madrasa was established in Cairo for Kanuri students, marking the integration of the central Sudan into the international network of Muslim scholarship. By about 1350 the reigning dynasty was Sunni and Maliki. By this time the state had progressively united the various peoples subject to them into the Kanuri nation.

In the fourteenth century, however, the dynasty, defeated by pagan peoples living east of Lake Chad, was forced to abandon Kanem and move to Bornu, west of Lake Chad. 'Ali b. Dunama (1476–1503) founded the new capital of Ngazargamo in Bornu. Idris b. 'Ali (1570–1602) completed the process of state formation. He developed a standing army, including a cavalry corps made up of members of the ruler's household and other chiefs, and an auxiliary infantry. The elite troops were provided with firearms.

From about the sixteenth century Bornu scholars made Ngazargamo the leading center of Quranic studies in central Sudan. Ngazargamo had four Friday mosques; the *'ulama'* engaged in learned disputations at court. Islam, however, did not have a substantial following outside court and *'ulama'* circles and was not the religion of the majority.

Bornu reached new heights of power between the middle of the sixteenth and the end of the seventeenth century. Bornu's dominant interest was the trade in gold, salt, slaves, and weapons between the central Sudan, Tripoli, and Cairo. Its major rivals were the Hausa city-states; its major ally, the Ottoman regime in Libya. Ambassadors brought rich presents of Ottoman weapons and luxury goods in exchange for slaves and gold. Bornu also maintained close trading connections with Cairo. However, by the middle of the eighteenth century Bornu's hegemony broke down, and it was transformed from a regional empire into a smaller, relatively homogeneous Kanuri state.

HAUSALAND

Hausaland, now northern Nigeria, lay between the eastern kingdoms of Kanem-Bornu and the western empires of Ghana and Mali. As a cultural and political region Hausaland took shape in the first millennium CE as a result of the westward expansion of Hausa peoples. Their expansion was marked by the conversion of woodlands into open savannah and the introduction of grain cultivation, which allowed for a denser peasant population. In large areas, there was a common language and common laws and customs.

The earliest Hausa societies were confederacies of kinship groups led by a priest-chief. The groups in the confederacy specialized in fishing, hunting, agriculture, and crafts such as blacksmithing and salt digging. The Hausa population lived in defended towns from which they went out daily to work their farms in the surrounding countryside. Hausa peoples were dominated by horse-riding military elites organized under rulers called *sarkin*. Sometimes, kings emerged through the concentration of power and wealth in the hands of one priest-chief. Such kings often turned to a universalistic religion, such as Islam, to acquire legitimization and to undermine the authority of their competitors.

The city regimes were characterized by a centralized chieftainship with a fortified capital, an elaborate court, and a substantial officialdom. By the fourteenth century, Kano had acquired a powerful military machine. The *madawaki*, or chief cavalry officer, was the commander of a professional officers' corps. The Kano armies were equipped with iron helmets and coats of mail. By conquest, Kano acquired great numbers of slaves, who were used as soldiers, officials, agricultural laborers, and porters on the trade routes. Colonies were created to produce agricultural revenues. The power of the state was also based on extensive trading networks. Kano became a base for the trans-Saharan trade in salt, cloth, leather, and grain, and for trade with the Ashanti and the Yorubas.

Islam was first introduced in Kano at the time of King Yaji (1349–85), when African Wangara or Dyula traders and clerics came from Mali, from the Volta region, and later from Songhay. He appointed a *qadi* and an imam as part of the state administration. Muhammad Rumfa (1463–99) is credited with the advancement of Islam by building mosques and schools. He commissioned al-Maghili to write a treatise on Muslim government. Other scholars from Egypt, Tunis, and Morocco turned Kano into a center of Muslim scholarship. Islamization generally facilitated the expansion of trade. It was the basis of an enlarged marketing network, for which the *'ulama'* provided legal support, guarantees, safe conducts, introductions, and other services.

Islam was introduced into Katsina by Mande immigrants. Toward the end of fifteenth century, the Wangara (Dyula) community of Muslim clerics and traders in Katsina took control of the city, and Muhammad al-Korau (d. 1541–42), a cleric, became the king of Katsina. His successors invited Muslim scholars from North

Africa and Egypt to reside in Katsina. An *'ulama'* class emerged under royal patron-age. The Hausa rulers fasted at Ramadan, built mosques, kept up the obligatory prayers, and gave alms to the poor. The reformer of Islam in Katsina, Ibrahim Maje (1549–66), ordered the implementation of Islamic marriage law. Generally, however, Islamization amounted to a nominal acceptance of Islam by the nobility, and the staffing of the courts with literate expatriate Muslims. Hausaland remained divided between a Muslim cosmopolitan urban royal society and the local kinship-based animistic rural communities. Islamic learning in Hausaland, however, was reinforced with the coming of the so-called settled Fulani, torodbe, or Tornkawa, Muslim clerics who lived in rural enclaves called *jama'at* and did not serve at the courts of the rulers.

From the time of their institutional consolidation in the fifteenth century to the end of the eighteenth century, the Hausa states were at war with one another and with neighboring peoples. In the late eighteenth century the Hausa states, like those of Bornu and the western Sudan, were economically and politically exhausted.

Thus, between the tenth and the eighteenth centuries, a succession of Sudanic kingdoms was organized under the banner of Islam. These kingdoms owed their existence to Muslim trading communities or to nomadic chieftainships that found economic support and legitimization in Islam. In some cases the traders provided the economic resources, weapons, and horses that enabled local adventurers to establish states. In other cases they were themselves the conquerors. Still, further south the savannah region remained very little influenced by Islam, and the local rulers were, in ceremonial and ritual matters, old-style divine kings.

NON-STATE MUSLIM COMMUNITIES IN WEST AFRICA: MERCHANTS AND RELIGIOUS LINEAGES

Muslim traders, scholars, and communities grew up alongside of, and indeed prior to, the adoption of Islam by Sudanic states. (See Map 23.) Lamtuna and Sanhaja Berbers became known for piety and scholarship. From the twelfth through the fourteenth century Awdaghust, Kumbi Saleh, Walata, and Timbuktu were notewor-thy for both their trading and scholarly activities. In the late fourteenth and early fifteenth centuries Timbuktu replaced Walata as the principle trading city for the trans-Saharan traffic with the Sudan.

Timbuktu is a fabled city in West African history. Timbuktu was probably the most important center of Arabic and Muslim studies. In the period of Malian rule, the imams of the Friday mosque were Sudanese, but after the Tuareg conquest of Timbuktu in 1433, they were replaced by Arab and Berber scholars from the oases of the northern Sahara. For centuries the *'ulama'* of Timbuktu maintained a rich tradition of Quranic, hadith, and legal studies, supplemented by studies in theol-ogy, linguistics, history, mathematics, and astronomy. An important biographical

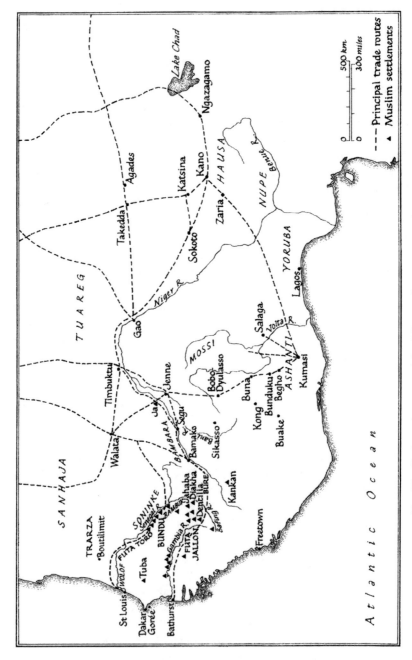

Map 23. Trade, settlements, and the diffusion of Islam in West Africa, 1500–1900.

dictionary, written by Ahmad Baba (d. 1627), indicates a high level of Arabic and Muslim learning and close contact with Mecca and Egypt.

Timbuktu's scholarly elite was drawn from a number of interrelated families representing the tribal and ethnic subgroups that made up the city populace. The *qadi* was the principal figure, speaking for the people before military regimes, and the mediator of internal commercial and religious disputes. Scholars also acted as intermediaries among the merchants and families who made up the *jama'at*, or communities of the four main (and several lesser) mosques, and the state officials.

The scholarly families were sustained by trade; by investments in cloth, camels, cattle, and urban property; by slave labor on their farms; and by the donations of their disciples, who worked as traders and tailors. The contributions of rulers and officials often took the form of slaves to work on farms. Although trade and scholarship could be specialized activities, many individuals were active in both pursuits. The commercial and the learned families were stratified by wealth. Leading scholars often came from the great merchant families; lesser scholars from the stratum of small merchants and craftsmen.

With the Moroccan conquest in 1591, Timbuktu lost its autonomy and became the seat of a military government. The authority of the *qadi* and the *'ulama'* declined as the merchants made direct contacts with the *arma* military elite. Also, the ethnic composition of the scholarly class changed as Sudanese, Soninke, Mandinge, and Dyula Muslim traders became the leading scholars. By the end of the seventeenth century, however, Timbuktu was no longer able to support a large scholarly community, and rival centers, especially at Jenne, developed in its place. Its merchant class moved into artisan work, mainly in cloth production.

Zawaya lineages: the Kunta

Instead, the leading proponents of Islam came to be not urban-based merchant families but rural clans. After the breakup of the Songhay Empire at the end of the sixteenth century, the population of the Saharan regions from Mauritania to Lake Chad was divided into dominant warrior (Hassani) clans and subordinated religious lineages called *zawaya* (or *insilimen*). The religious lineages lived by livestock rearing, agriculture, and commerce and held a high status for their wealth, their Islamic learning and spirituality, and their claimed Arab or *sharifian* descent. Each of the major caravan trading posts, such as Walata, Timbuktu, and Agades, became the center of a *zawaya* lineage and of its economic and religious networks.

By the early 1800s the most important of the *zawaya* lineages was the Kunta clan, a commercial lineage rooted in the salt trade and a scholarly lineage with widespread influence throughout Mauritania, Senegambia, and other parts of the western Sudan. The family's history goes back to Shaykh Sidi Ahmad al-Bakka'i (d. 1504), who established a Qadiri *zawiya* (Sufi residence) in Walata. In the sixteenth century the family spread across the Sahara to Timbuktu, Agades, Bornu,

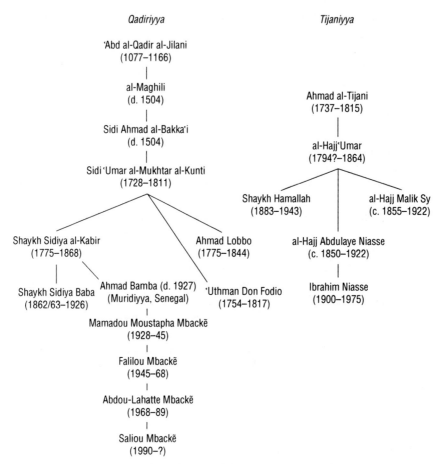

Figure 8. The Qadiriyya and the Tijaniyya in West Africa.

Hausaland, and other places, and in the eighteenth century many of the Kunta moved to the middle Niger. Sidi al-Mukhtar al-Kunti (1728–1811) united the Kunta factions and established an extensive confederation, herding livestock and trading in salt, wool, hides, dates, tobacco, and textiles between the Sahara and the Sudanic regions, linking the desert and the savannah. Students (*talamidh*), subordinate families, clients, and slaves tended the animals, especially camels, and cultivated dates and cereals. Under the leadership of Sidi al-Mukhtar, the Qadiriyya Sufi order, already established in the Sudan, was reborn in the late eighteenth century. (See Figure 8.)

A student of Sidi al-Mukhtar, Shaykh Sidiya al-Kabir (1775–1868), extended the family network to Mauritania. Sidiya began his religious education by memorizing the Quran and then went on to studies of poetry, theology, grammar, and law.

In 1809–10 he apprenticed himself to Sidi al-Mukhtar. As student, secretary, and advisor to a family that had a powerful part in the revival of the Qadiri order, extensive trading operations, and political authority in the southern Sahara, Sidiya was introduced into one of the most sophisticated of Saharan and West African communities. He studied law and mysticism, including the works of al-Ghazali and Ibn al-ʿArabi. After some thirty-five years, Sidiya returned to his home community, established his residence at Boutilimit, and, as a successful mediator, became wealthy from gifts of livestock, the revenues of gum and salt caravans, and the work of clients who cultivated his fields. The *shaykh* became the head of an association of believers who looked to him for guidance in political, economic, legal, and moral matters. As a successful social and economic organizer, Sidiya acquired a reputation as a miracle worker. After his death, his eldest son, Sidiya Baba (1862/63–1926), succeeded him. Even after France occupied Mauritania, Sidiya's family was able to maintain its political influence.

The Kunta *shaykhs* played critical religious, social, and economic roles. They served as judges and mediators. Their residences and sanctuaries (*zawiya* and *diya*) served as the equivalent of mosques and schools. Under their influence, Maliki law was reinvigorated, thus integrating Sudanic West Africa with the religious practices of North Africa. Under their auspices, the Qadiri Sufi order knit together the Muslim communities of Mauritania, Senegambia, the middle Niger, Guinea, and the Ivory Coast. In economic matters, their earnings and the taxes they collected served as a system for the redistribution of products and incomes in place of a market economy.

Islamic law and Sufism were both essential for this worldly success. In the West African context, as in many other parts of the Muslim world, Sufism and saintly qualities did not imply retreat from but rather engagement in everyday life. Sufis were valued for their learning and for their charms, amulets, talismans, and practice of divination. Their religious knowledge encompassed not only Islamic scriptures but the secret worlds of the human mind. The Sufi mission was to purify the soul as the foundation of social reform and the defense of Islam. Although both Sufism and African cultures were agreed on the veneration of ancestors and holy men, in West Africa saint veneration did not lead to cults focused on tombs. Rather, Sufi virtue was expressed in study and teaching, healing, law, and politics and war.

MERCHANTS AND MISSIONARIES IN THE FOREST AND COASTAL REGIONS

From the Sahara and the savannah, African-Muslim merchants expanded into the forest and coastal regions to the south. The opportunity for trade in gold, kola nuts, and salt attracted Muslim merchants into the Volta River basin and the Guinean forests. The empire of Mali encouraged its merchants to establish colonies close to the Akan goldfields in what is now Ghana. Muslim merchants also opened up the trade in gold from the Lobi fields in Burkina Faso. Other traders came from Kanem,

Bornu, and the Hausa city-states and moved into Gonja, Dagomba, and other parts of the Volta region. Towns like Kankan in modern Guinea, Bobo-Dyulasso in modern Ivory Coast, and Begho in modern Ghana originated in this way.

Some of these merchants were Soninke-speaking peoples linked by family ties and trading networks who became known as Wangara or Dyula (Juula). Their trading communities often developed agricultural interests and in some cases engaged in weaving and dyeing. With the Muslim merchant colonies came religious scholars and holy men, who organized festivals, offered prayers and divination at local courts, distributed talismans, and participated in anti-witchcraft rituals.

Muslims married local women and raised families, which were tied to the Muslim community through the fathers and to the local pagan communities through the mothers. The offspring of such marriages often inherited chieftainships and brought about the conversion of local peoples. As a result, Muslims in the middle Volta region were not a distinct language group but regarded themselves as part of the Dagomba, Gonja, or Mossi kingdoms.

The degree of Muslim integration into the larger African societies varied. Muslim religious influence was strongest in the kingdoms of Gonja and Dagomba. The Gonja state had been established toward the end of the sixteenth century by Mande warriors with the help of Muslim advisors and courtiers. Although the chiefs came under Muslim influence, they did not formally convert to Islam. Court ceremony and culture remained a mixture of Islamic and pagan practices. The children of chiefs were circumcised and took Muslim names, but this was done in accordance with pagan ceremonies.

Islamic influence among the political elite spread from Gonja to Dagomba. The relatively centralized political system of Dagomba favored the spread of Islam. Because the state was divided into territorial and village chieftainships – each of which, in imitation of the royal court, sought the religious and magical support of Muslim clerics – a Muslim presence was established throughout the region. Sons of Dagomba chiefs who had no prospect of obtaining ruling positions commonly converted to Islam. The chiefs also gave their daughters in marriage to Muslims in order to draw the two estates closer together. By the end of the nineteenth century, many Dagomba families had Muslim members, and Muslims were considered part of the Dagomba people.

Dagomba chiefs adopted circumcision, Muslim names, the Muslim calendar, and Muslim festivals and burial practices. Maliki law influenced customary law, and pre-Islamic pagan festivals were merged into Muslim ones. In Dagomba Muslims performed important functions, such as circumcision, washing the dead, officiating over festivals, and slaughtering animals for meat. By the early nineteenth century imams were widely appointed in Dagomba villages. The imam of Yendi, the capital city, was the leader of Friday prayers and the enforcer of Muslim law. Muslim healers gained influence by providing amulets. Non-Muslims consulted them for herbal medicines and for nightlong prayer vigils to aid the supplicants.

In other places, such as Kong in the contemporary northeastern Ivory Coast, the Dyula were the forerunners of Islamized governments. Kong was a textile-producing town; a trading junction for kola, gold, salt, and slaves; and a daily market where local villagers could sell their produce and buy salt and kola from far away or locally produced textiles, iron tools, and pottery. It was also a center for Islamic studies. Attracted by the prosperity of the Dyula, non-Muslim warrior groups settled the region in the early seventeenth century. In the early eighteenth century, Shehu Watara (d. 1745) seized power with the help of the Dyula, who provided him amulets to assure his victory and horses and guns. In return they received slaves. As a result of this alliance, the rulers brought Islamic cultural traits and Dyula teachers and traders into the villages.

In many West African areas, however, Muslims had little effect on the rest of the society. West of the Black Volta, Muslim trading communities remained isolated enclaves with their own neighborhoods, mosques, and schools and kept their own languages and a separate ethnic identity. Here Muslims were important as traders, courtiers, and religious magicians, but they had little missionary spirit and did not try to convert local peoples to Islam.

The Muslims of the Ashanti capital, Kumasi, were an example of Muslims living separate from and with little influence on other African communities. In the early nineteenth century, Kumasi had a Muslim community of about a thousand, drawn mostly from neighboring Gonja and Dagomba but also including Dyula from Senegal and Arabs from North Africa. The Muslims were headed by Muhammad al-Ghamba, who was imam and *qadi* and principal of a Quran school. The Kumasi Muslims acted as agents for the Ashanti princes in the gold, kola nut, slave, and salt trades and served Ashanti rulers as diplomats, bureaucrats, courtiers, soldiers, and religious functionaries. They provided amulets and performed rituals. In the late nineteenth century, strong reformist influences stimulated poetical and historical writing and raised Muslim exclusivist consciousness and a sense of commitment to Islam. Classical Middle Eastern and North African Arabic works and West African books produced outside the Ghana region were widely circulated. Despite the importance of Muslims, Ashanti culture was not notably influenced by Islam.

In general, the Dyula communities maintained a high standard of Muslim education. Students read Quran and commentary, hadith, and the life of the Prophet with a single teacher over a period varying from five to thirty years and earned their living as part-time farmers working on the lands of their teacher. Students and slave labor were in effect low-cost labor for their teachers. The mature students were called *karamokos*, the equivalent of *'ulama'*. The *karamokos* often started their own schools in other villages and might eventually become imams or *qadis*.

Certain families provided scholars generation after generation. The Saghanughu was a Dyula lineage living in the northern and western Ivory Coast and in parts of upper Volta. The lineage may be traced back to Timbuktu, but its principal figure was Muhammad al-Mustafa Saghanughu, the imam of Bobo-Dyulasso, who died around 1776–77. He produced a system of education based on three canonical texts of Quran commentary and hadith. His sons continued his teachings, founding Muslim schools and acting as imams and *qadis* throughout the towns of Ghana and the Ivory Coast. In the late seventeenth and the early eighteenth centuries, they sponsored a new wave of construction of mosques large enough for the whole of the Muslim population in several of the Guinean towns.

The Saghanughu continued the Suwarian tradition of accepting the existing political authorities and renouncing jihad, not even proselytizing peacefully to win converts to Islam. Muslims, they held, may accept the authority of non-Muslim rulers so long as they are allowed to pursue their own way of life in accordance with the sunna of the Prophet.

SENEGAMBIA

To the west and north of Ghana and the Ivory Coast, throughout Guinea, Sierra Leone, and Senegambia, Muslims also had a complex role to play. In Senegambia the legacy of the Takrur and Mali empires was faintly kept alive in a number of small-scale states. Kings stood at the apex of a political hierarchy, accumulating the loyalty of subordinate households and subgroups of herders, fishermen, or farmers. Vassals and slaves were the key to political and economic power.

Muslims were also organized by households and communities. By the eighteenth century there were important Muslim settlements in Kankan, the hinterlands of Sierra Leone, Gambia, Futa Jallon, and Futa Toro. These communities were typically constituted by holy lineages or were under the authority of marabouts or Sufi holy men who served as village chiefs, judges, and teachers. As early as the fifteenth and sixteenth centuries, there were numerous Mandinka marabouts spread throughout the Wolof regions. The torodbe, the Muslim scholars of Futa Toro, were the leading element of peasant society.

In Senegambia, the Jakhanke were a prominent Muslim lineage living in scattered towns and villages. The various Jakhanke villages were independent of one another and of the local chiefs. They were committed to peaceful coexistence and refused to become engaged in politics or war. Often their villages enjoyed the privileges of sanctuary, judicial independence, and freedom from military service. The Jakhanke were agriculturists supported by slave labor, but they also engaged in trade, perhaps carried on in the course of journeys as traveling teachers.

The Jakhanke had a reputation for exceptional learning. They traced their spiritual ancestry to al-Hajj Salim Suwari, who probably lived in the late fifteenth century. They adhered to Maliki law, although they were tolerant of customary practice. They stressed the importance of obedience to the *murshid*, or Sufi master. They celebrated the birthday of the Prophet and the feasts of the end of Ramadan and other Muslim holidays. They interpreted dreams and gave amulets for protection. Although saint worship was not common in West Africa, they believed that the spirits of dead saints kept guard over their followers and interceded for them before God. The graves of al-Hajj Salim and other great teachers were centers for pilgrimage. In all but name the Jakhanke extended family was a Sufi lineage.

In these Muslim communities, the signature institution was the Quran school. The Quran school was not only a center of learning; it was a center for the exercise and transmission of *baraka* or blessing. Knowledge of the Quran was taught as memorization and correct pronunciation, which were themselves considered miraculous forces that improved intelligence and combated evil spirits. The teacher who had the most intimate knowledge of the divine text had the most powerful *baraka*. The Quran school for little children was a mild discipline; for older students it might demand harsh conditions of work and submission. Wolof teachers used both student and slave labor on their farms, as was widely done throughout Muslim Africa.

Muslims fit into the Wolof system in a variety of ways. Ordinary marabouts living in their own communities could, like other households, be represented at the royal court. Muslim clerics could not be part of the hierarchy of vassals and officeholders, but they were employed by kings and nobles as personal chaplains, scribes, legal advisors, and tutors. Sometimes the royal family promoted political marriages to consolidate their ties with the Muslim clergy. Sometimes the clerics were rewarded with land, which they might distribute to followers and disciples in their home communities. Only after the jihads of the eighteenth and nineteenth centuries was the whole of Wolof society converted to Islam.

In sum, by the end of the eighteenth century, Islam in West Africa was the religion of scattered groups of Tukulors and Songhays, Dyula trading colonies, and some Hausa towns, and of the dominant classes of the central Sudanic states. Islam also had a foothold among the Wolof, the Yoruba, and the Mossi. The Kunta, the Saghanughu, the Jakhanke, and others were closely linked by trading networks, affiliation with the Qadiriyya brotherhood, and shared religious and intellectual traditions.

The Muslim settlements were centers for the diffusion of Islamic and Arabic culture. Towns such as Timbuktu made the Quran, the sayings of the Prophet, and Islamic law familiar to local peoples. The translation of religious texts into vernacular Swahili, Wolof, Hausa, Somali, and Zenaga followed. Arabic had a strong influence on Fulbe, Wolof, and other African languages, which borrowed Arab and Muslim vocabulary and came to be written in Arabic script. Arabic was used to record family histories, dowries, debts, merchants' accounts, and information about trading itineraries. It became increasingly important as an ordinary means of communication for government and merchant elites.

The Muslim communities, to a limited degree, promoted the diffusion of Islam. The political elites sometimes forged alliances with Muslim clerics and traders.

Agricultural communities might become Muslims when traditional groups broke down. Therefore, war, slave trading, and state formation favored Islam. Reciprocally, communities without extensive trading connections or political centralization found it easier to preserve a non-Muslim identity. The durability of family and village institutions, the depth of African religious culture, and the strength of traditional authorities helped to maintain a non-Islamic African majority.

CHAPTER 41

THE WEST AFRICAN JIHADS

Alongside peaceful Muslim colonization there was a parallel tradition of military campaigns to establish Muslim states and convert pagan populations to Islam. From the seventeenth through the nineteenth century, with the Almoravid movement as a shadowy precedent, jihads burst out from Mauritania to Chad. The jihads were led by Muslim scholars and teachers, the religious leaders of trading and agricultural communities, itinerant preachers, and their student followers. They were supported by the Fulbe, the Hausa, the Mande, the Wolof, and the Tuareg peoples: nomadic pastoralists, *'ulama'*, Sufi disciples, and slaves. As Muslim teachers articulated the hardships of ordinary people, they both radicalized Islamic teaching and mobilized popular support.

The jihads took their immediate inspiration from the militant reformers of the fifteenth century such as al-Maghili (d. c. 1503–06). In the fifteenth century, al-Maghili had denounced the corrupt and un-Islamic practices of West African Muslim states. He condemned illegal taxation and the seizure of private property and denounced pagan ceremonial practices and "venal" *mallams* (religious scholars) who served rulers without adequate knowledge of Arabic or Islam. Al-Maghili called for the implementation of Muslim law by a strong and committed Muslim ruler and introduced into West Africa the concept of the *mujaddid*, the renewer of Islam. The pilgrimage to Mecca and Medina also brought West African scholars into contact with reformist Sufi circles, and perhaps with the radical views of the Wahhabi movement in Arabia.

The first West African jihad took place in Mauritania and represented the resistance of Berbers to the dominance of the Arab Banu Ma'qil. Imam Nasir al-Din (d. 1674) denounced the rulers for failing to perform the prayers, consorting with musicians and jugglers, and pillaging the people. He claimed to have been sent by God to stop the oppression. He called himself *almami* (imam) and *amir al-mu'minin*, the traditional title of Muslim caliphs; proclaimed the end of time and the coming of the messiah (Mahdi); and demanded that his followers conform to the teachings of the Quran. His followers swept through southern Mauritania in 1673, but Nasir al-Din was killed in 1674, and the movement was defeated by 1677. The outcome of the war was the lasting military dominance of the Arab tribes over the Berbers. Forced to pay tribute to the Arab Hassanis, the Berbers (*zawaya*) concentrated on economic activities, engaging in the mining and marketing of salt and gum arabic, maintaining wells, organizing caravans, and raising livestock. They also took up the roles of judges and religious teachers. The *zawaya* would continue the struggle for Islamic principles and later give rise to both peaceful missionary movements and new jihads in Senegal.

THE SENEGAMBIAN JIHADS

From Mauritania the jihads spilled out into Senegambia. The jihads in Senegambia were promoted by the emissaries of Nasir al-Din, preaching among Fulbe pastoralists and the villages of Futa Toro against the tyranny of the rulers. In the Wolof and Pulaar-speaking regions of Senegal, the ruling dynasties of Cayor, Walo, Jolof, and Futa Toro were overthrown. By 1680, however, the political elites, with support from French trading interests based in Saint-Louis, regained power. Then a jihad led by the torodbe (the clerical wing of the Fulbe) in Bundu founded a Muslim regime in the 1680s or 1690s. Although they spoke Fulbe as a common language, the torodbe had no ethnic or tribal identity. Some torodbe were supported by the work of students or slaves and the contributions of artisans, but many were wandering beggars. In the early part of the eighteenth century, new jihads, led by the torodbe, were waged against the Wolof, Jalonke, and Deniake dynasties.

In Futa Jallon the jihads were due to torodbe-led Fulbe peasants and herders in conflict with the dominant landlords. Uprooted peoples, outlaws, vagrants, and runaway slaves were attracted to their ranks. In 1726 Ibrahim Musa, known as Karamoko Alfa (d. 1751), proclaimed a holy war and took the title of *almami*. He gathered the support of young men's gangs, renegades, and slaves and began a long struggle against the political elites.

The Muslims finally prevailed in 1776, when Ibrahim Sori (r. 1776–93) was named *almami*. The *almami* was selected alternately from among the descendants of Ibrahim Musa and Ibrahim Sori; the former tended to represent the more pacific tradition of Muslim learning; the latter, the more aggressive tradition of jihad. Under the authority of the *almamis* the provinces were ruled by appointed governors, and the family hamlets were ruled by local chiefs and councils of elders. The most important state activity was jihad, which was the source of slaves for export and for use on agricultural plantations. The central power, however, was gravely weakened by the emergence of a landowning aristocracy descended from the original jihad warriors and by succession disputes between the two families that provided the *almamis*. Futa Jallon eventually became a French protectorate in 1881 and recognized French suzerainty in 1896/97.

In the second part of the eighteenth century, militant Islam gave rise to a new pious literature written in Fulfulde. Poems were composed to mobilize the common people.

The jihads in Fata Jallon were followed by a new wave of jihads in Futa Toro in the valley of the Senegal River under the leadership of Sulayman Bal (d. 1776) and his successor 'Abd al-Qadir (1776–1806), a highly educated teacher, judge, and mediator, closely related to the Senegambian and Guinean network of Muslim teachers. The new jihadist state encouraged the construction of mosques and furthered settlement of the river frontiers with Mauritania. It invoked jihad to attack the Moors in 1786 and by 1790 had invaded Walo, Jolof, and Cayor. After a critical defeat in 1790, the *almamate* disintegrated. The death of Almamy Abdul in 1807 marked the end of strong central government in Futa Toro. The torodbe intermarried with the former rulers, seized land, and became an elite of local chieftains. Although *almamis* continued to be appointed throughout the nineteenth century, they no longer had any political power. However, memory of the early successes would again inspire jihads in the latter part of the nineteenth century.

The wars in Futa Toro were the inspiration for another century of jihads all across the western and central Sudan. The first of these was the jihad of 'Uthman don Fodio, which led to the formation of the Sokoto caliphate in northern Nigeria. This was followed by the caliphate of Hamdullahi on the middle Niger, which was replaced in the 1860s by the empire of Shaykh 'Umar Taal, extending from the upper Niger to the upper Senegal. From the 1870s to the 1890s, Samori Ture built a small empire in what is now upper Guinea-Conakry and Ghana. In the late nineteenth century similar religious revolutions broke out in the smaller states along the Gambia and in present-day Senegal. From Cape Verde to Lake Chad, the western and central Sahara was remade in the name of Islam.

In the central Sudan as in Senegambia, the jihads were led by Muslim clerics. Such teachers as Jibril b. 'Umar had traveled to Mecca and Medina, where they were influenced by reformist Sufi views. They returned to preach the principles of obedience to the Quran, the tradition of the Prophet, and the rule of Shari'a. Some of the leaders claimed that they had been entrusted with this mission by the Prophet himself, and/or that they were the heirs of Sufi *shaykhs* descended from him. They also taught the doctrine of the double jihad: the inner jihad, the struggle against the corruption of the body, must precede the outer jihad, the war against corrupt Muslim governments and pagan rulers. Hijra, migration to a true Muslim community, and jihad, a war in the name of the faith, were overriding obligations. For them Islam was an exclusive religion incompatible with African cults. They introduced a universalistic and theocratic concept of Islam as the supreme arbiter of social life and as the transforming force in the lives of individuals. This message was preached with messianic fervor. Throughout West and Central Africa, the thirteenth Muslim century (corresponding to the nineteenth century) was expected to mark the victory of Islam over the infidel world. This was to be the age of the *mujaddid*, or renewer of Islam, who comes once every century, and of the caliph of Takrur, the twelfth caliph, whose rule would be followed by the coming of the messiah.

'Uthman don Fodio and the Sokoto Caliphate

'Uthman don Fodio (1754–1817) was the greatest of these new leaders. 'Uthman was a descendant of a torodbe family that was well established in Hausaland, and a student of Jibril b. 'Umar, who was an uncompromising opponent of corrupt practices and a proponent of jihad. He began his African preaching in 1774–75, wandering from place to place as an itinerant *mallam*. For a time he accepted the patronage of the Hausa state of Gobir. But, publicly expressing his frustration with the failure of the rulers to put Islam into practice, 'Uthman criticized the Hausa rulers for unjust and illegal taxes, confiscations of property, compulsory military service, bribery, gift taking, and the enslavement of Muslims. He also criticized them for condoning polytheism, worshiping fetishes, and believing in the power of talismans, divination, and conjuring. Another strand in his preaching derived from the tradition of Maliki law, communicated through Timbuktu and Bornu and reinforced by reformist religious currents emanating from Mecca and Medina. He insisted on the observance of Islamic commercial, criminal, and personal law. 'Uthman denounced pagan customs, the free socializing of men and women, dancing at bridal feasts, and inheritance practices that were contrary to Muslim law. 'Uthman broke with the royal court. Disillusioned, he returned to Degel to preach to his followers. As in other Islamic societies, the autonomy of Muslim communities under *'ulama'* leadership made it possible to resist the state and the state version of Islam in the name of the Shari'a and the ideal caliphate.

'Uthman was also motivated by mystical visions. In 1789 a vision led him to believe he had the power to work miracles, and to teach his own mystical *wird*, or litany. He later had visions of 'Abd al-Qadir al-Jilani, the founder of the Qadiriyya brotherhood, and an experience of ascension to heaven, where he was initiated into the Qadiriyya and the spiritual lineage of the Prophet. His theological writings dealt with the concepts of the renewer (*mujaddid*) and the role of *'ulama'* in teaching the true faith. Out of these concerns, 'Uthman produced numerous tracts on political theory, biographies, histories, and other works in Arabic and Fulbe. Many people regarded him as the Mahdi (messiah) come in fulfillment of popular prophecies.

'Uthman's appeal to justice and morality rallied the outcasts of Hausa society. He found his followers among the Fulbe or Fulani. Primarily cattle pastoralists, they were dependent on peasants for access to riverbeds and grazing lands and were taxed accordingly. The leadership, however, came from the clerics living in rural communities who were Fulfulde speakers and closely connected to the pastoralists. The Fulani would later hold the most important offices of the new states. Hausa peasants, runaway slaves, itinerant preachers, and others also responded to 'Uthman's preaching. His jihad served to integrate a number of peoples into a single religio-political movement.

In 1804, the conflict between 'Uthman and the rulers of Gobir came into the open. The rulers forbade Muslims to wear turbans and veils, prohibited conversions, and ordered converts to return to their old religion. 'Uthman declared the hijra and moved from Degel to Gudu, where he was elected imam, *amir al-mu'minin*, and *sarkin muslim* – head of the Muslim community. There he declared the jihad. By 1808 'Uthman had defeated the rulers of Gobir, Kano, Katsina, and other Hausa states. He expanded into the territory south of Lake Chad and into Nupe and Yorubaland as far as the forest zone. By 1830 the jihad had engulfed most of what are now northern Nigeria and the northern Cameroons.

The regime founded by 'Uthman is known as the caliphate of Sokoto. 'Uthman was caliph; his brother 'Abdallah, based in Gwandu, and his son Muhammad Bello, based in Sokoto, were his viceroys. 'Uthman retired to teaching and writing, and in 1817 Muhammad Bello succeeded him. Sokoto was a combination of an Islamic state and a modified Hausa monarchy. Bello introduced an Islamic administration. Muslim judges, market inspectors, and prayer leaders were appointed, and an Islamic tax and land system was instituted with revenues on the land considered *kharaj* and the fees levied on individual subjects called *jizya*, as in classical Islamic times. The Fulani cattle-herding nomads were sedentarized and converted to sheep and goat raising as part of an effort to bring them under the rule of Muslim law.

Although the Hausa people continued to retain much of their pre-Islamic culture, including traditional medicine, folklore, music, and dancing, Islamic mores were well established by the end of the nineteenth century. Mosques and schools were built to teach the populace Islam. The state patronized large numbers of religious scholars (*mallams*). The jihad movement helped to fortify the practice of Islamic law in Hausaland. Kano became famous for law, Zaria for Arabic grammar, and Sokoto for mysticism. Sufism became widespread. The Muslim revival also generated a theological, legal, astrological, and vernacular poetic literature in the Hausa language. Most important books were written in Arabic or Hausa, although texts designed for recitation were also composed in Fulfulde. The poetry of Nana Asma'u, 'Uthman's daughter, in Fulfulde, Hausa, and Arabic, and her teacher training programs helped diffuse knowledge of Islam.

Under the authority of the caliphate, the territories were divided into emirates appointed by and responsible to the caliphs. (See Illustration 20.) The power of the amirs was based on military force, but they governed with the aid of the Fulani lineages and the advice of the *mallams*. Each emirate had a judicial officer with the title of *alkali* or *qadi*, and there were minor judges in the countryside appointed by local chiefs. Although the caliphs issued orders to the amirs, there were no Sokoto officials resident in the provincial capitals to enforce them. Many emirates corresponded to the former Hausa states and accepted Hausa methods of administration and palace organization. Officials maintained large polygynous households

Illustration 20. Hausa horsemen during tenth anniversary of independence celebration, Niamey, Niger. *Source:* Photograph by Eliot Elisofon, 1970. EEPA EENG 02671, Eliot Elisofon Photographic Archives, National Museum of African Art, Smithsonian Institution.

staffed with concubines and servants. The wives of the major officeholders were kept in purdah.

For rural administration the emirates were divided into fiefs, some of which were controlled by the rulers and some by local Fulani chiefs. Village chiefs administered their subjects through appointed ward heads and through the chiefs of organized craftsmen. The crafts were also the fiefs of officials who were responsible for the collection of taxes, observance of Muslim law, and maintenance of public property, such as mosques, roads, and walls. The fact that the greater part of the territory nominally ruled by Sokoto remained in the hands of local fief holders and chieftains meant that Islamic ideas were only occasionally applied in the provinces. Government by secular-minded Fulani chieftains led quickly away from Muslim norms, and many of the practices that had been criticized by the Muslims flourished again.

The economy of the Sokoto caliphate was based on slave villages or plantations. First developed in the Sokoto region after 1760 (and again after the jihad of 1804–08), the plantations produced cotton, indigo, grain, rice, tobacco, kola nuts, and other crops. The plantation economy flourished until the late nineteenth century, when colonial rule and the suppression of slavery allowed for a revitalization of the peasant economy. Slave labor was also used for construction of defenses, houses, and mosques. The state also promoted indigo and textile industries. Trade within West Africa and between West Africa and North Africa flourished. Hausa traders expanded their range of operations to the frontiers of the empire and exported cloth to other areas of the Sudan and ivory and oils to Europe.

The jihad inspired by 'Uthman also helped spread Islam into southern Nigeria and inspired other jihads in the western Sudan and Senegambia. With the help of the Sokoto caliphate, Muslims won control of Ilorin, and Muslim quarters were formed in Abeokuta, Lagos, and other towns. Their communities were organized under the leadership of imams, who led the prayers and festivals and mediated disputes.

The influence of the Sokoto caliphate also reached Bornu. Bornu was already a center of Muslim learning, but it had a substantial Fulani population aggrieved by landlord domination. Inspired by 'Uthman, the Fulani rose up to attack their rulers. Bornu, however, successfully resisted the jihad by revitalizing its own Muslim credentials. Al-Kanemi, a *mallam* living in Ngala, helped the rulers to defeat the Fulani and became the most powerful chieftain in Bornu. In 1814 he built his own town, Kukawa, appointed his own officials, and essentially displaced the former rulers. The new regime was built on an aristocracy consisting of the royal family, courtiers, and nobles called *kogonas*, but it also appointed *qadis* and imams. It had a double structure of administration. One system was applied to the control of territories and all the resident populations; the other was directed to clans and ethnic and craft associations. The existence of both territorial and group administrations indicates a society in transition from clan-lineage to territorial forms of organization.

Still other jihads led to the formation of Muslim states south of Lake Chad in Air, north of Sokoto among the Tuaregs, and in Masina. The Masina state, south of Timbuktu (in what is now Mali), was led by Ahmad Lobbo, had its capital at Hamdallahi, and lasted from 1816 to 1861. It was based on a highly organized army supported by a system of granaries created to provision the soldiers and spare the local population from abuse. A council of state was made up of religious teachers; the local administrative apparatus was filled with relatives and clients of the leading counselors. New morals legislation introduced controls over women and suppressed fortune-telling, tobacco smoking, and prostitution.

THE JIHAD OF AL-HAJJ 'UMAR

The jihads of the central Sudan indirectly inspired a revival of jihad in the Senegambian region. Al-Hajj 'Umar (1794?–1864) was born in Futa Toro, became one of the torodbe, and in 1826 made the pilgrimage to Mecca, where he was initiated into the Tijaniyya order. He returned as the order's *khalifa* (successor of the Prophet) for the Sudan. He stayed in Sokoto from 1831 to 1837 and married a daughter of Muhammad Bello. In 1840 he settled in Jagunku on the frontiers of Futa Jallon, where he could preach to local peoples. Growing tension with the leaders of Futa Jallon forced him to move in 1851 to Dingiray, where he began the militant phase of his mission. There he organized his followers into a professional army equipped with French weapons. In 1852 he proclaimed a jihad against pagan peoples, lapsed Muslims, European intruders, and the backsliding rulers of Futa Toro and Futa Jallon.

'Umar claimed a transcendental personal authority. He denied the importance of adherence to a school of law and favored *ijtihad* or personal religious judgment. He taught that a believer should follow the guidance of a Sufi *shaykh* who has immediate personal knowledge of the divine truth. 'Umar claimed the titles of *amir al-mu'minin*, *khalifa*, *qutb* (pole of the universe), and vizier of the Mahdi. Although 'Umar never took the title of either *mujaddid* or Mahdi, he assumed the title of *Khalifat Khatim al-Awlyya'* (successor of the Seal of Saints), a Tijani-Sufi title. He claimed to possess divine guidance in times of difficulty. His followers regarded him as their *almami* and reviver of the eighteenth-century revolutions.

'Umar appealed to the populace of Futa Toro on the basis of local grievances against the military elites. His community also appealed to rootless individuals of mixed ethnic background who found new social identity and opportunities for conquest under the aegis of Islam. He came to embody the torodbe ideal of religious revival and conquest of pagans.

His jihad began with the conquest of Futa Toro. By 1862 his empire included Timbuktu, Masina, Hamdallahi, and Segu. In Futa Toro, however, he came into conflict with the French, who were attempting to establish their commercial supremacy along the Senegal River. In 1857 they defeated 'Umar in a battle at Medina, and in 1860 'Umar made a treaty with the French that recognized their sphere of influence in Futa Toro and assigned him the Bambara states of Kaarta and Segu. In quest of new territory, 'Umar and masses of followers invaded Masina. His enemies, led by Ahmad al-Kunta al-Bakka'i (of the Qadiri order), denounced this as an illegitimate war of Muslims on Muslims and promoted a coalition of local states, including Masina and Timbuktu, to resist. 'Umar's enemies defeated and killed him in 1864, but his followers captured Hamdallahi and established a state that lasted until 1893. With the state in disarray, local chieftains took to raiding to support their troops. Muslim jihad shaded over into a purely military exploitation of the surrounding peoples. Finally, the jihad state was absorbed into the growing French West African empire.

'Umar was strongly influenced not only by West African concepts but also by the teachings of the Tijaniyya and of other reformist movements, which stressed the importance of strict obedience to Muslim practice. 'Umar's state forbade dancing and the use of tobacco, alcohol, and charms and prohibited pagan ceremonies and the worship of idols. Many un-Islamic practices were banned. The prohibition on drinking of alcohol was strictly enforced; he abolished uncanonical taxes and replaced them with the *zakat* (tithe), *kharaj* (land tax), and *jizya*. Polygamists were restricted to four wives. However, 'Umar seems to have had little interest in the practical aspects of inculcating Islam, such as building courts, schools, and mosques. The primary function of the state was predatory warfare, slaving, and the accumulation of booty. (See Map 24.)

THE LATE NINETEENTH-CENTURY JIHADS

After 'Umar's death, jihad flared again in other parts of Senegambia. In the nineteenth century Muslim influence increased further, owing to the suppression of the slave trade and the growth of the peanut, oil, and soap industries, which favored the economic and political power of the peasantry. Islam provided the idiom for peasant resistance to the military elites and for the integration of peasants and traders into a larger economy.

The great Senegambian jihad of this period was led by Ma Ba (c. 1809–67), a Quran teacher and the founder of an independent settlement. Rebelling against *tyeddo* (military) domination, his followers swept through Senegambia, burning villages, killing pagans, and enslaving their enemies. Ma Ba himself never actively participated in battle and retired whenever possible from political affairs, but the cumulative effect of the Senegambian jihads was the substantial conversion of the Wolof to Islam.

Jihad also spread into the stateless regions of the upper Volta, the Ivory Coast, and Guinea. The torodbe revolutionary tradition was kept alive by Mahmadu Lamin of Senegambia (1885–88). The most important campaigns in this region were launched in Guinea by Mori-Ule Sise, who gathered bandits, vagrants, and other rootless people; built the city of Medina; and launched a jihad in 1835 in the region of Toron and Konyan. Defeated and killed in 1845, he was succeeded by a local adventurer named Samori Ture (1879–98).

Samori was born in about 1830 of a Dyula family. He served the Medina state; engaged in various local struggles, sometimes on the pagan side; and worked relentlessly to enlarge his personal army. In 1871, he gained control over the Milo River valley, seized Kankan in 1881, and became the principal power holder on the upper Niger. By 1883 he had brought under his control the local

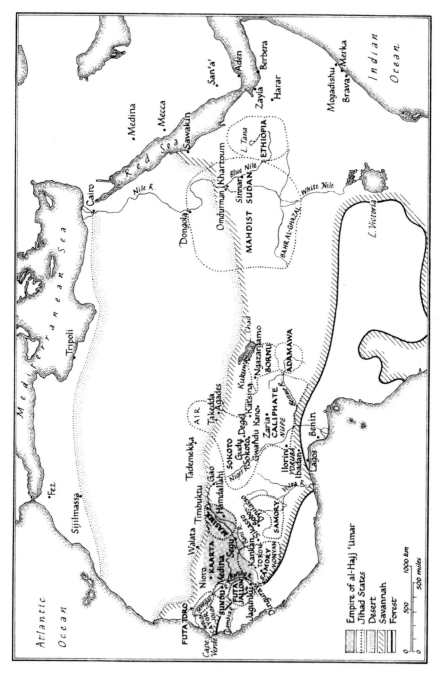

Map 24. The Jihad states of the nineteenth century.

chieftains in the territory southwest of 'Umar's state and founded the kingdom of Wasulu.

This new state was governed by Samori and a council of kinsmen and clients who took on the management of the chancery and the treasury and administered justice, religious affairs, and foreign relations. The army was the essential institution. Samori imported horses and weapons and modernized his army along European lines. Samori attempted to convert his regime into an Islamic state. In 1884 he took the title of *almami*, opened Muslim schools, forbade the use of alcohol, and required his followers to pray. He destroyed pagan sacred groves and cult symbols and forbade pagan worship. Muslim teachers and holy men were posted as officials in non-Muslim areas to enforce the Shari'a, and defeated peoples were forced to convert to Islam. Dyula traders supported Samori because of his encouragement of commerce, although they did not play a central part in the creation of the state. His Muslim policy, however, eventually led in 1888 to revolts that forced him to tolerate pagan religious associations and cults.

Samori's would-be Muslim empire was undone by the French, who pushed him eastward to upper Volta and the Ivory Coast, where he conquered new territories and set up a new state between 1892 and 1896. In this eastern zone, Samori came into conflict with both the French and the British. The French took Sikasso in 1898 and sent Samori into exile, where he died in 1900.

JIHAD AND CONVERSION

With the defeat of Samori, the era of eighteenth- and nineteenth-century jihads came to an end. Beginning in the western territories of Mauritania and Senegambia in the seventeenth and eighteenth centuries, they had spread throughout Sudanic and Guinean Africa in the nineteenth century. These movements represented an uprising of Muslim religious teachers and their followers against the military elites. The uprisings, however, took various forms. Most common were the revolts of Fulani pastoral peoples against landowning elites in Bundu, Futa Jallon, Hausaland, Bornu, Fombina, and other places. In some cases Muslim Fulanis formed coalitions with non-Muslim Fulani clans or with Muslim communities formed of uprooted peoples, former slaves, and oppressed peasants. In other cases the jihads represented peasant rebellions. Throughout Senegambia, Muslims who opposed the *tyeddo* slave military elite overthrew their masters. In some of the Wolof-inhabited parts of Senegal, the Muslim assault overthrew the old social structure and paved the way for massive conversions. In the Volta region, Ivory Coast, and Guinea, Dyula peoples established independent states.

The Muslim mission involved not only local social struggles but also wars of expansion and conquest. In certain cases, such as that of Samori in Guinea, revolts in the name of Islam were the work of military adventurers manipulating Muslim symbols. Throughout West Africa, Islam had become the almost-universal language of political ambition and moral reform.

In many cases Islam provided for the unification of heterogeneous peoples and the creation of new state-centered societies. As a result of the jihads, Muslim populations were consolidated in much of what are now northern Nigeria, Niger, Mali, Senegal, Gambia, Togo, Benin, Sierra Leone, Ivory Coast, and Burkina Faso. New states were also founded in Masina, parts of Guinea, and Senegambia. The formation of these states led to the conversion of local peoples to Islam. Parts of Senegambia and Masina became Muslim. Converts were made among the Fulani, Soninke, and Wolof peoples. Conquest was accompanied by educational and missionary activities promoting literacy and scholarship. During the spread of Islam, not only conquest but the enslavement of substantial populations led to conversions, as slaves took up the religion of their masters or sought emancipation through conversion.

The widespread conversion of Sudanic farmers marks the breakdown of the traditional order of society and the emergence of Islam as a principal organizing force in the creation of new societies. Whereas Islam had frequently been adopted as an imperial cult without being spread among the subjects, the nineteenth-century jihads created Islamic states that sought to include the whole population rather than a limited aristocracy, and to create a political people out of smaller groups of diverse racial, ethnic, and linguistic backgrounds.

Yet the successes of Islamization did not break down the profoundly rooted African culture. Traditional religions and social loyalties maintained their hold on a great part of the population. Furthermore, at the very moment when masses of Sudanese peoples were being converted to Islam, Muslim expansion was being checked by European intervention. By the late nineteenth century the French had taken possession of Senegal and of the state founded by 'Umar, and they subsequently defeated Samori in 1898. The British defeated the Sokoto caliphate in 1903. The great century of jihads came to an end with the defeat of all the Muslim states and their absorption into European colonial empires.

CHAPTER 42

ISLAM IN EAST AFRICA AND THE EUROPEAN
COLONIAL EMPIRES

East Africa, including the eastern Sudan, the East African coasts, and the hinterlands of Ethiopia, Somalia, and Kenya, formed another major zone of Muslim population. Here the sources of Islamic influences were primarily Egypt, Arabia, and the Indian Ocean region, rather than North Africa. (See Map 25.)

SUDAN

The history of the eastern Sudan (the modern state of Sudan) was separate from that of the central and western Sudan, due to the fact that Islam reached the eastern Sudan from Egypt rather than from North Africa. Over centuries Arab-Muslims moved deeper and deeper into Sudan. The Arab-Muslim conquerors occupied Egypt as far as Aswan in 641. In the ninth century, Egyptians swarmed to the newly discovered Allaqi goldfields between the Nile and the Red Sea. An early pact, renewed in 975, between Egypt and the king of Maqurra, the northern provinces of the Sudan, provided for a tribute of slaves in exchange for wheat and wine for the Christian Eucharist and for free passage of merchants. In the twelfth and thirteenth centuries Arab bedouins migrated south and married into local families, who adopted Arabic and were drawn into the Islamic cultural orbit. Through matrilineal succession, their children inherited local chieftainships. Arab penetration was followed by the Mamluk conquest of Nubia in 1276, the first of a number of campaigns lasting through the fourteenth century. In 1317 the church of Dongola was rededicated as a mosque. Most of the country, however, was in the hands of local Arab tribal chiefs who continued to push south across northern Kordofan and Darfur and into the Chad basin. In 1517 the Ottoman sultan, Selim I, occupied Nubia as far as the third cataract of the Nile. Nubia remained under Ottoman rule for some 300 years.

While Arabs were pushing south, herding peoples from the region of the Blue Nile, called Funj, were pushing north. The first historically known Funj ruler, Amara

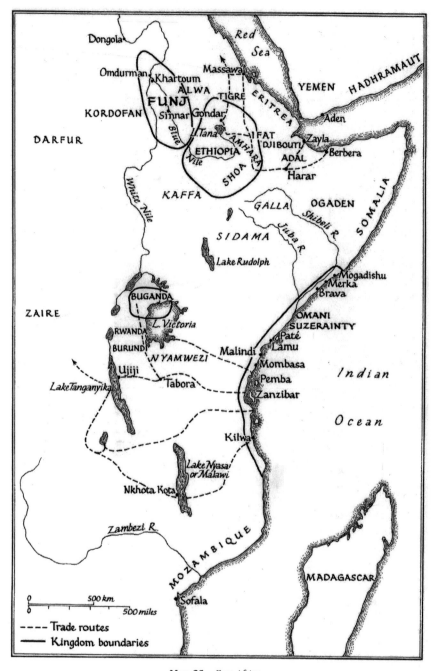

Map 25. East Africa.

Dunqas, defeated the Christian kingdom of Aiwa in 1504 and founded Sinnar as the capital of a Funj kingdom that reached north to the third cataract, south to the foothills of Ethiopia, and east to the desert of Kordofan. Its rulers were Muslims and used Arabic as the lingua franca of trade, although the court at Sinnar continued to speak Funj. Only in the eighteenth century did state documents appear in Arabic.

The Funj monarchy was a patrimonial regime built on a Sudanese concept of semidivine kingship. The public appearance of the sultans was accompanied by pomp and ceremony, but Funj rulers spent most of their reigns secluded from public view. The ruler was in principle absolute but was in practice very much under the sway of his ministers, courtiers, and family. Provincial nobles lived in castles supported by their own slave retainers. Provincial nobles, however, had to appear before the sultan each year to perform obeisance, account for their behavior, and deliver tribute. Each lesser lord was also required to take a wife from the royal family so that every vassal was related to the ruler. The ruling community formed a caste-like group that avoided intermarriage with the local population. The Funj sultanate reached its maximum power in the reign of Badi II (1644–80). In the mid-eighteenth century, the state disintegrated into regional warlord-ships, supported by rich merchants and landowners.

Islam spread in the Funj sultanate not only as the result of its acceptance by the governing elite and the trading communities but also as the result of the migration of Muslim scholars and holy men into the region. In the sixteenth century Funj patronage attracted scholars from Egypt, North Africa, and Arabia. These holy men, known locally as *faqis*, were scholars of the Quran and Muslim law and Sufi mystics and magicians. The *faqis* gained considerable influence, because they could intercede with and even rebuke the rulers, and because they were venerated by the common people for their magical powers. Many *faqis* were merchants who founded lineages, settled in villages, established schools, and won the populace over to Islam. Their *zawiyas* were residences and places of prayer in which the holy men lived surrounded by their families, servants, and disciples. Their schools (*khalwas*) taught young boys the Quran, law, and Muslim theology. In time the *zawiyas* grew into colonies and villages in which the descendants of the original holy men maintained a spiritual or temporal authority. They administered Maliki law, arbitrated local disputes, and instructed the people in Islam. They were believed to possess *baraka*, the power given by God to perform miracles. The eastern Sudanic *faqis* were also members of the Sufi brotherhoods. The Shadhiliyya was brought into the Sudan in the fifteenth century, the Qadiriyya in the middle of the sixteenth, and the Majdhubiyya in the eighteenth.

The Funj kingdom depended for its economic viability on the gold trade. All gold mined within the kingdom belonged to the sultan, who also organized long-distance commerce. Important revenues came from customs dues levied on the caravan routes leading to Egypt and the Red Sea ports and on the pilgrimage traffic from the Western Sudan. In the late seventeenth century the Funj opened trading relations with the Ottoman Empire. By 1700, with the introduction of coinage, an unregulated market system took hold, and the sultans lost control of trade to a new merchant middle class. At the same time, civil wars forced the peasants to look to the holy men for protection; the sultans lost the peasant population to the *faqis*.

The autonomy of provincial vassals, merchant communities, and *faqis* and their peasant clients subverted the power of the Funj sultanate. After a long and fitful history, the Funj kingdom disintegrated in the eighteenth century. The system of marriage alliances and princely hostages on which the power of the state depended broke down; local dynasties became autonomous. The Funj kingdom was finally brought to an end by the Egyptian conquest of 1820–21. Muhammad ʿAli, the ruler of Egypt, established a government of Egyptian and Turkish offices based in the new city of Khartoum to exact tribute in slaves for the Egyptian army. The Egyptians created a counter-religious elite to the *faqis* by setting up a hierarchy of judges (*qadis*) and muftis and a new court system, and by educating young Sudanese scholars at al-Azhar in Cairo.

DARFUR

The Arabization and Islamization of Funj was followed by the spread of Islam and the formation of kingdoms further south and west. In Darfur, the Keira lineage of the Fur peoples established a new dynasty in the late sixteenth century and inherited Sudanic concepts of divine kingship. Between 1660 and 1680 Sulayman made Islam the royal cult, built mosques, and added Shariʿa principles to his claims to legitimacy. Arabic became the language of the chancery; Fur remained the spoken language of the court.

At the end of the eighteenth century ʿAbd al-Rahman al-Rashid (1786/87–1800/01) consolidated the Darfur sultanate around a palace complex called al-Fashir. Al-Fashir was the hub of administration, a training ground for officers and courtiers, a center for the redistribution of goods, a final court of justice, and a stage for festivals, ceremonies, and parades. An important part of the economy was the trade in slaves and ivory. The Keira dynasty ruled their Fur subjects through a centralized administrative hierarchy, but their non-Fur subjects, the majority of the population, were divided into five provinces ruled by local chieftains. In the late eighteenth century the central government attempted to replace the traditional territorial leaders with the sultan's slaves and clients, including merchants and Muslim holy men. The new elite progressively took control of outlying areas. The rulers also rewarded their retainers with landed estates and slaves. The land grantees, however, made their holdings hereditary, married into the local elites, and emerged as a quasi-independent aristocracy. Islam came to be identified, as in Funj, with a middle class of merchants, jurists, and officials.

The political consolidation of Darfur was accompanied by further Islamization. Through the protection and patronage of the sultans, and under the stimulus of trade with Egypt, traders and Sufis from the northern Sudan, Egypt, Arabia, and West Africa settled in Darfur. In eastern Darfur Muslim holy men married local women and opened *khalwas* and mosques. Young boys left home to study with the *faqis* and cultivate their fields, and they then returned home to further spread the teachings of the faith. These holy men sustained the regime by creating nontribal communities, and by providing it with legitimizing genealogies and proper Arabic documents. The Muslim holy men were particularly successful in consolidating their local power. Endowed with land, subjects, and immunities, they became in effect independent local rulers. Nineteenth-century sultans attempted to bring the holy men under bureaucratic control, and after 1898 the *faqis* were organized district by district under supervisors responsible for their discipline.

THE COASTAL CITIES AND SWAHILI ISLAM

On the coasts of the Red Sea and the Indian Ocean another form of Islamic civilization came into being as a result of the contacts of Muslim merchants and teachers with indigenous African societies. As early as the seventh century, Arab and Persian seafaring merchants from the Red Sea and the Indian Ocean had established trading posts along the shores and islands of the East African coast. Muslim burials on Shanga date from 780 to 850 CE. Muslims settled Pemba and Zanzibar soon after. By the tenth century, there were Arab merchants from Aden, Yemen, Hadramawt, and Oman in Mogadishu, Brava, and Merka. Muslims reached the Comoro Islands and Madagascar by the eleventh century, but on Madagascar Arab immigrants were gradually assimilated, and Islam did not displace the local Malagasy cultures. It left only the Arabic script, vague echoes of the Quran, and some magical practices.

There were no Muslim communities on the southern coast before 1100. After 1100 the Muslim presence began to expand, stimulated by intensified trade. In the twelfth century, when the first mosques were built, Zanzibar became the most important Muslim settlement. By 1200 Persian merchants and Afro-Shirazis ruled the islands of Mafia and Pemba and the coastal town of Kilwa. The earliest mosque at Kilwa dates to the thirteenth century. By the thirteenth century, there were some three dozen towns between Mogadishu and Kilwa, the most important of which were Malindi, Mombasa, Zanzibar, and Sofala. Muslim migrants had come from the towns on the Somali coast, Oman, and Iran, but the early settlers were superseded in influence in the thirteenth century by migrants from Yemen and Hadramawt. By the fifteenth century, there were about forty Arab settlements or petty sultanates on the East African coast and islands.

The period of greatest prosperity for the East African coastal towns was roughly 1250 to 1500 CE. By 1300, Mogadishu, Malindi, Mombasa, Pemba, Mozambique, and Sofala were linked into the Indian Ocean trade. These towns traded with Arabia and the Persian Gulf and via Indonesian intermediaries with China. Kilwa exported copper; Malindi and Mombasa, iron; and Mogadishu, cloth. Tortoise shells, rhinoceros horns, amber, leopard skins, slaves, ivory, and gold were traded. There were also extensive coconut-palm, orange, sugarcane, rice, and sesame cultivations along the coast. As Kilwa prospered, stone palaces, city walls, and a Friday mosque were constructed; copper coins were minted. By the end of the century a stone mosque was built, with domes in the Indian style.

The small towns running along the 2,000 miles of the East African coast from Moghadishu in the north to Sofala in the south were essentially autonomous entities but shared many elements of common culture. Little is known about the political system of these towns, but it may be surmised that they were composed of lineages. Each town may have had a council of clan chiefs, although such councils were probably superseded by a dominant lineage or by an outside Arab or Persian chief who became ruler and mediator among the local clans. The rulers were legitimized in terms both of hereditary succession and of African symbols.

By 1400 Islam had become the religion of most of the coastal peoples. Ibn Battuta, who visited around 1332, saw the towns at the height of their prosperity and culture. He described Mogadishu as a Muslim community with a madrasa, scholars of Shafi'i law, and a community of descendants of the Prophet. It was ruled by a sultan and officials called *wazirs*, amirs, *qadis*, and *muhtasibs*, using the traditional vocabulary for administrators, military officers, judges, and market inspectors. It showed South Arabian influences in court ceremony.

Swahili was the common language of speech, and Arabic was used primarily for religious texts and correspondence. An earlier generation of scholars regarded Swahili East African coastal Islamic society as a colonial society based on the settlement of Arab or Persian migrants amid a primitive African population. The Swahili language and culture was thought to be the product of the assimilation of Africans into an Arab-Muslim or Persian-Muslim society. More recent scholarship stresses the indigenous African basis of Swahili civilization. The archeological evidence reveals a pre-Islamic urban society inhabiting mud-and-thatched-hut settlements with some stone buildings. Most of these settlements were agricultural, growing fruit, rice, millet, and cotton, and keeping livestock. A few, on the islands, were oriented to commerce. Some southern towns, such as Kilwa, ruled by African chiefs, traded in the Indian Ocean. In these already-developed societies, Arab and Persian migrants took local women as concubines, married into local families, and spawned a Muslim-African culture in language, architecture, and dress. They produced the local variations of Arab-Islamic, Persian-Islamic (Shirazi), mixed-Arab, Somali and Ethiopian (Zeilwali), and Swahili (a mixture of Arab and Bantu) cultures. The rise of an East African Islamic civilization, then, was due in part to migration, settlement, and the founding of new towns and in part to the further development of a previously established society.

This prosperous East African society was destroyed by the Portuguese. Vasco da Gama discovered the region in 1498, and he was followed by a Portuguese campaign to control the Indian Ocean and the Eastern spice trade. Admiral d'Almeida took Kilwa in 1505 and sacked Mombasa. By 1530 the Portuguese controlled the entire coast, basing themselves on the offshore islands of Zanzibar, Pemba, and other places. The Portuguese fought off the Ottomans and in 1542 helped defend Christian Ethiopia against Muslim expansion. Portuguese domination lasted until Oman expelled them from the Persian Gulf region in 1650, attacked Pemba and Zanzibar in 1652, and finally took Mombasa in 1698. The Portuguese were finally expelled from all their coastal positions by 1728.

This conquest opened the way for a new wave of migrants from Oman and Hadramawt. Between 1550 and 1800, Hadrami migrants made the Lamu archipelago the religious and cultural heartland of the coast. The Hadramis brought a scholarly tradition and a written literature, at first in Arabic, then in KiSwahili. The earliest written poetry dates from the middle of the seventeenth century. A handicraft industry produced copies of religious texts. In the nineteenth century, the Hadrami presence and the establishment of an Omani sultanate consolidated the Arabization of Swahili culture.

In the nineteenth century Omani influence in East Africa was revived by Imam Sayyid Sa'id b. Sultan (1804–56) of the Busaidi dynasty, who in 1840 replaced Muscat with Zanzibar as the capital of the Omani Empire. His authority was at first accepted in Zanzibar and Kilwa, but progressively he forced Lamu, Pate, and Mombasa to recognize his regime. The new ruler appointed his own officials but allowed for local autonomy through the appointment of officers nominated by the local lineages. The sultan also promoted Islam by appointed *qadis*. The pilgrimage became more popular. *'Ulama'* sought training at the feet of scholars in Arabia, and Sufi orders played a greater part in local religious practices. After the death of Imam Sayyid Sa'id, his sons divided Oman and Zanzibar into separate kingdoms.

The Busaidis promoted a thriving Zanzibar economy. They developed clove and coconut plantations worked by slave labor and dominated the international market for cloves. The ruler of Zanzibar monopolized the ivory and gum copal trade. Zanzibar became a center for the East African slave trade and a market for ivory, rice, tobacco, and gum copal, which were exchanged for European and American cottons, beads, ironwares, and weapons. The United States became its most important trading partner.

ETHIOPIA AND SOMALIA

The influence of Arabs and Muslims established on the coasts of the Red Sea and the Indian Ocean reached inland to the Somali and Ethiopian hinterlands. A number of small Muslim kingdoms developed in the lowlands of today's Eritrea, Djibouti, and Somalia and the eastern parts of Ethiopia. They were supported by the proximity and the trade of the Hijaz and Yemen. Arab merchants propagated Islam among their servants, trading partners, and in market villages. They also married into Somali pastoral lineages and created an Arab-Muslim-Somali identity.

By the end of the eighth century, trade routes from the island of Dahlak and the town of Zayla, built around the exchange of lowland salt for highland produce, brought Islam to the Ethiopian highlands. Merchants settled along the northern edges of the Sidama country, took wives from the local ruling families, and brought Muslim clerics to teach their children. By 896–97, an Arab state was founded on the Shoan plateau under the Mahzumite family that lasted until it was annexed by the Muslim kingdom of Ifat in 1285. By the thirteenth century, a chain of petty sultanates ran from Zayla on the Red Sea coast to the eastern corner of the Shoan plateau, encircling the Christian kingdom of Ethiopia. By the thirteenth century, many of the stateless nomadic peoples of the region, including the 'Afar and the Somali, had also become Muslims.

The Muslim principalities bordered on an ancient and powerful Christian Ethiopian civilization. The dominant population of Ethiopia spoke Amharic, a Semitic language related to South Arabian, Arabic, and Hebrew. The ancient kingdom of Axum had been converted to Christianity in the fourth century; from 451 Axum adhered to the Miaphysite doctrine. The head of the Ethiopian church was appointed by the patriarch of Alexandria (until 1948). The Ethiopians were ruled by a Christian monarch bearing the title of *nejashi*, who reigned over tributary local rules. The church identified the Ethiopian Christian nation with the Israel of the Old Testament, as a beleaguered state surrounded by hostile pagan and Muslim neighbors. By the mid-thirteenth century, a revived Ethiopian monarchy challenged Muslim merchants for control of the caravan routes to the coast. Thus began a long, bitter, and still unresolved conflict among rival kingdoms, trading peoples, and religions for control of Ethiopia. To this day, the history of this region has been shaped by the struggle between Muslims and Christians.

Victory in the first phase of this struggle went to the Christians, who by 1415 had subdued the Muslim kingdom of Ifat and the lesser principalities. Whereas some Muslims accepted Christian rule, descendants of the former rulers of Ifat founded a new Muslim kingdom called Adal along the coast of Somalia. Supported by nomadic peoples from 'Afar and Somalia, Adal resumed the war with Christian Ethiopia. Muslim forces under the leadership of Imam Ahmad b. Ibrahim (r. 1529–43), supported by Ottoman troops and firearms, conquered much of southern Ethiopia, but in a decisive battle between Muslims and Christians near Lake Tana in 1542, the Portuguese intervened to help Christian Ethiopia prevail over the Muslims.

The Christian victory shattered the Muslim regimes. Only the plains of 'Afar, Somalia, and parts of southwestern Ethiopia remained Muslim. Muslim sultanates and chieftainships disintegrated into Beja, 'Afar, and Somali tribal and village communities, although Harar and the coastal towns survived as centers of Islamic trade and religious activity. In the mid-seventeenth century 'Ali b. Daud founded a new sultanate of Harar. Prosperity in the Red Sea and on the Horn of Africa and trade with Zayla and the Funj sultanate helped maintain the Harar sultanate until the middle of the nineteenth century.

Without a strong centralized state to oppose it, Muslim expansion resumed. The Galla (Oromo) peoples, pastoralists with a common language, culture, and sociopolitical organization, had begun to move into Ethiopia in the early sixteenth century. They settled in the vicinity of Harar, slowly expanded in the Shoa and 'Afar regions, adopted Islam, and accepted the ruler of Harar as their nominal master. In practice they maintained their tribal system and an independent political hierarchy. By the early nineteenth century, the Galla tribes effectively dominated the region. Harar remained a Muslim town with numerous shrines of saints, and its peoples made the pilgrimage to Mecca.

In the early nineteenth century Muslim influence began to spread again, owing to the revival of the highland trade to the Red Sea, the pilgrimage to Mecca, and the increased demand for slaves in Arabia and elsewhere. Gondar was revived by Sudanese and Ethiopian merchants, who brought European products and Maria Theresa gold thalers in exchange for coffee, wax, musk, and slaves. Merchant caravans also penetrated the Galla country of south and southwestern Ethiopia, importing copper, brass, knives, swords, spices, and cloth in exchange for coffee, skins, wax, and slaves. By the second quarter of the nineteenth century, thousands of Ethiopian slaves, mostly pagans of Galla and Sidama origin, were being exported from Ethiopian ports. The trade benefited Muslims, and the penetration of Muslim caravans furthered the Islamization of Gallas.

In northern Ethiopia the Gallas expanded into the Sidama highlands and the Amhara provinces. Their growing influence gave Muslim merchants and scholars a foothold in these regions. In the southwest, the Innarya kingdom was founded by an adventurer named Bofo Abba Gomol, who adopted Islam soon after coming to power and employed Muslim merchants and advisors. As in Sudanic Africa, a local ruler relied on Muslim officials, scribes, and financiers to consolidate his power. The capital of Innarya, Sakka, had a population of some 10,000 to 12,000, with several hundred *'ulama'*. Sakka traded in ivory, skins, and incense from Lake Rudolph; musk, gold, ivory, and spices from Kaffa; and thousands of slaves. Gold was a royal monopoly.

Muslim holy men married into the families of local chiefs and reared children who succeeded to chieftainships and brought whole peoples over to Islam. These new Muslims venerated the shrines of local saints. At these shrines cultic practices mixed influences from the Meccan pilgrimage, Muslim saint worship, and pre-Islamic Galla and other local ceremonies. Numerous Ethiopians converted to Islam in the troubled nineteenth century. By the 1860s, Oromo commoners began to use Islamic rather than customary law in marriage and inheritance, paid the *zakat* levied by the kings, circumcised their sons, adopted the Islamic calendar, and went on pilgrimage to Mecca.

While Gallas occupied the Harar plateau, Somalis moving southward and west-ward from 'Afar took over the Ogaden. By the eighteenth century, they had pushed as far as the Juba River and controlled the coastal towns of Mogadishu, Zayla, and Berbera. In the nineteenth century they moved as far south as northern Kenya. In the course of this centuries-long migration, Somalis pushed out or assimilated the original Galla inhabitants of the region. The movement of Galla and Somali lineages thus established a Muslim bloc of peoples in southern Ethiopia and on the Horn of Africa.

Islamic reformist Sufism became more influential in the late eighteenth century and early nineteenth centuries. Agricultural production and exports prospered, and this stimulated trade with Egypt, pilgrimage to Arabia, and the settlement of Arab traders and clerics near the coast. The Qadiriyya Sufi order, which had been established in Harar by Abu Bakr ibn 'Abdullah al-'Aydarus (d. 1503), spread into Somalia and Eritrea in the nineteenth century. The Qadiri *shaykhs* were known for their humble lifestyle, their miracles, and their commitment to teaching. New brotherhoods founded by students of Ahmad ibn Idris (1785–1837) followed the reformist teaching by avoiding sensual stimulation from coffee, qat, dancing, or drumming, and rejected the belief in the intercession of saints. Other brother-hoods such as the Salihiyya, founded by Muhammad Salih of Arabia (1854–1919), appealed to Somalis, who already had a long history of religious leadership in deal-ing with interclan problems. The Salihiyya were established in Ogaden after 1850. Their agricultural settlements attracted runaway slaves and detribalized individu-als. The Ahmadiyya were established among Somalis by 'Ali Maye Durogba and founded agricultural settlements. In Eritrea, the revitalization of Islamic belief and practice was led by the Mirghaniyya, who were Arabian in origin but intermarried with African women to generate an indigenous class of Muslim *'ulama'*.

Muslim reform turned to militancy in the turn-of-the-century era of Euro-pean, Egyptian, and Ethiopian Christian conflicts. European and Omani capitalists expanded their trade and political influence in the Red Sea region. Egypt invaded Ethiopia, taking Zayla in 1870 and occupying Harar from 1875–85. Defeated by the Mahdi of the Sudan, however, Egypt retreated to the north. The Christian Ethiopian empire recovered in the reign of the Emperor Menelik II (1889). Militant Sufi movements were then directed against non-Muslims, lax Muslims, local and foreign Christian states, and rival Muslim powers.

CENTRAL AFRICA

For centuries the Muslim presence had been confined to coastal ports, whereas the hinterland remained pagan, composed of self-sufficient farming communities. Although the Swahili-Arab sultans raided for booty and slaves, they made little effort to colonize the hinterlands. From the eighteenth century, the growth of population and the formation of small states in the interior made it possible to organize caravans that brought Nyamwezi traders to the coast and Arab and Swahili traders to the interior. The trade was stimulated by the commercial interests of Sultan Sa'id of Zanzibar. By the 1820s and 1830s, a handful of Arab and Swahili merchants and adventurers, responding to the increased demand for ivory and slaves, had become active in the interior. Swahili and Omani merchants from Zanzibar were often active missionaries, and their influence permeated Mozambique, reaching the Yao of northwestern Mozambique and southern Malawi. The conversion of the Yao after a long history of contacts with the coast was probably due to closer association with Muslim trading partners, the role of Islam as a political ideology in the consolidation of chiefly authority, the importance of Swahili scribes and traders as healers, and a growing awareness and resistance to encroaching colonial rule.

Islam was carried inland along two major trade routes. A southern route connected the coastal towns of Kilwa and Malindi with the Lake Malawi region, south and southeast of Lake Victoria. On this route 'Abdallah b. Salim settled in Nkhota Kota, dominated its trade, and became a local chieftain. His successors instituted Arabic and religious instruction. Yao peoples living on the eastern side of Lake Malawi adopted the new religion. The first local chieftain converted in 1870; the arrival of Muslim missionaries in 1885 helped persuade other Yao of the cultural as well as the economic value of ties to the coast. Islam brought literacy, international commerce, social contacts, and administrative expertise into central Africa.

A second route was the trade network connecting Zanzibar and the coastal town of Dar-al-Salaam with the Manyema region and Buganda. On this route Tabora was the key town; from Tabora Arab traders reached Lake Tanganyika, where they established Ujiji, which became the center of an Arab and Muslim community, although there is little indication of the diffusion of Islamic influences in Zaire, Burundi, and Rwanda. In this region Arab and Swahili traders supplied local chieftains with firearms in exchange for slaves and ivory. Local adventurers, often supported by uprooted young men who had become warriors, took advantage of the situation to conquer small kingdoms. Tippu Tip, a Swahili trader and warrior, set up a small Muslim state. In Buganda, however, where there was a centralized state, King Mutesa I (1856–84) Islamized his regime by observing Ramadan, building mosques, and introducing the Muslim calendar.

By the late nineteenth century Islam had only a scattered representation in East Africa. It spread as the result of individual conversions rather than by the conversion of tribes or lineages. Chiefs who cooperated with Arabs in trade adopted Islam. So too did the entourages of Arab and Swahili merchants, including wives, porters, slaves, and others rooted out of their home communities to settle in Muslim towns. Still, there were cases in which non-Muslim Africans adopted Islam and continued to reside in their rural villages. Because Islam was accepted as a religion rather than a political or communal identification, Muslims, Christians, and pagans could live in the same villages and even in the same families. In this way the Swahili language, some Quranic prayers, healing rituals, and cotton clothing spread to the interior.

In South Africa the Muslim communities had very different origins. In the eighteenth century most Muslims came from South and Southeast Asia. Many were converted slaves. By the 1790s, free Muslims formed a small mercantile community in Cape Town. Exiled convict imams provided religious and social leadership.

COLONIALISM AND THE DEFEAT OF MUSLIM EXPANSION

The spread of Islamic polities in both West and East Africa was checked at the beginning of the twentieth century by the imposition of European colonial rule. (See Map 26.) Although European domination was secured in a sudden burst of conquests, European involvement in Africa goes back to the fifteenth century. The Portuguese were the first Europeans to explore the African coast, establish trading stations, and open commerce between West Africa and Europe. They were eager to find gold, break the monopoly of the Muslims over the traffic of the Sudan, and convert local peoples to Christianity. In an extraordinary century of exploration, the Portuguese discovered Madeira, the Azores, the mouth of the Senegal River, and Cape Verde; visited the Gold Coast; and finally in 1482 built the fortress of Elmina as the headquarters of a garrison that enforced the Portuguese monopoly on the Gold Coast trade.

With the discovery of the Americas and the potential for growing sugar and other crops, slaves became more important than gold, and human beings became the principal African export. By the middle of the seventeenth century, the Dutch had seized all of the major Portuguese bases on the Gold Coast, but in the eighteenth century the English won control of the Gold Coast and became the leading European commercial and slave-trading nation. In the meantime, in 1637 the French established themselves on the Senegal River at Saint-Louis and Gorée and developed a trade in gum, wax, ivory, hides, and slaves. Europeans were almost entirely involved in exporting slaves and had little impact on the technological or cultural development of African societies. The growth of the slave trade, however, stimulated local warfare, increased the power of African rulers over their subjects, and brought new states into being. Kings and officials became the principal slavers, exchanging slaves for weapons and other goods. Thus, most of southwestern Nigeria came under the control of the Oyo Empire and much of Ghana was ruled by the Ashanti.

In the nineteenth century, the British took the lead in suppressing the Atlantic slave trade. In 1807, an act of the British parliament made it illegal for Britons to engage in the slave trade, and in 1833 Parliament abolished slavery in the British Empire. The British used their navy to enforce the anti-slave-trade laws and forced other countries to join in the prohibition. Behind the British resolve to abolish the trade was a combination of humanitarian concerns and the interest of manufacturers in a growing African market. From Bathurst, Freetown, and fortresses

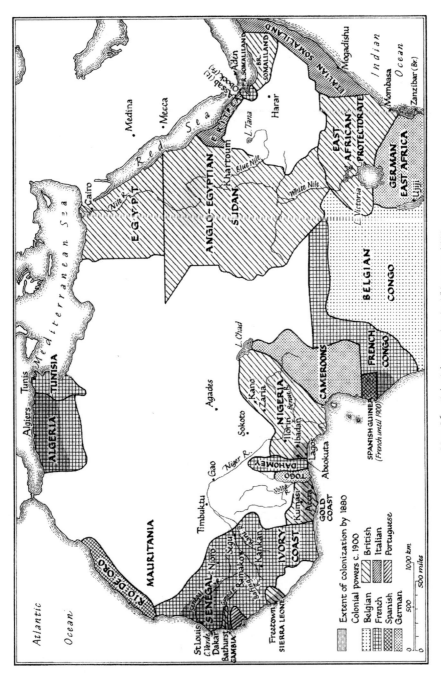

Map 26. Colonial expansion in Africa to c. 1900.

631

on the Gold Coast and the coast of Nigeria, British traders promoted traffic in palm oil, timber, ivory, and beeswax.

European explorers, missionaries, and colonists also sought to convert Africans to Christianity and to create a new class of Europeanized Africans. European trade stimulated the rise of Western-educated Africans, a proto-bourgeoisie who would later become the pioneers of African nationalism. For much of the nineteenth century, Europeans still held the notion that Africans could be equals once they had acquired a European education and had become Christians. French and British colonies were supplied with legislative and executive councils to introduce Africans to European modes of government; Africans were prepared to hold the highest offices of state. By the end of the century, however, with their rising determination to conquer Africa, Europeans came to consider them inherently inferior.

In the second part of the nineteenth century, the British began to expand from the coasts into the interior, looking for new markets and new sources of supply. Lagos, the main port for Yorubaland, was annexed in 1861. Britain's policy was to use sufficient military and political force to protect trading interests but not to seek commercial or political monopolies. As long as interior African states were well enough organized to hold up their end of the trade and as long as other European powers did not intervene, Britain was at first content with minimal political engagement. The British debated whether they should keep their settlements as small and inexpensive as possible or whether they should develop strong political controls to suppress the slave trade and to promote commerce and missionary work. British policies oscillated between the two alternatives, but after 1865, the British generally moved toward direct intervention and control. Traders, explorers, and missionaries, who cried out for increased political protection, won their cause. In 1874 the British made the Gold Coast a crown colony.

The French developed their colonial empire in Senegambia. After the defeat of Napoleon, Saint-Louis and Gorée were returned to France and became the main bases of French expansion. Suppression of the slave trade and the growth of the gum arabic and peanut trades prompted the French to establish inland fortified trading posts on territories rented from local rulers. In 1849 they obtained rights to open factories at Joal and Kaolack. After 1851 the French adopted a more aggressive expansionist policy. Under Louis Faidherbe, military governor from 1854 to 1865, they annexed Dakar (1857) and pushed French trading posts into the African interior. They blocked the western expansion of al-Hajj 'Umar and took control of the lower Senegal River. In 1859 Faidherbe forced Sine and Saloum to guarantee freedom of French commerce and to give the French a monopoly on trade and the right to buy land. A second phase of French expansion completed the absorption of the Senegambian region. After 1863 the French laid plans to establish a series of garrisons and a railroad to link the Senegal and the Niger rivers. They occupied Bamako in 1883, Cayor in 1886, and Nioro in 1887. The telegraph, the railroad, and the cannon assured French domination. Henceforth, the French would not only protect trade but try to assure their permanent authority by constructing roads, establishing formal administration, and introducing legal and educational policies.

Thus the European powers turned from trading interests to political annexation. As late as 1880, Britain's Lord Salisbury denied any British or European interest in African colonies, but by 1884 the expansion of the several powers, their mutual rivalries, and their competition for prestige stimulated a wave of chauvinistic nationalism in all the European countries. The winds of nationalism fanned the flames of trading interests and political rivalry into a scramble for African colonies. At the Congress of Berlin (1884–85) the European powers agreed on the partition of Africa among themselves. Already the French had created protectorates in Senegal; the British had seized Egypt in 1882; and the Germans had created protectorates over Togo and the Cameroons in 1884. In 1886 the Niger Company was given a royal charter to administer law and customs in its territories, and in 1897 the company took control of Nupe, Ilorin, and Bida. The British built a railroad from Lagos to Ibadan. Progressively, in 1885, 1891, and 1900 the British government took control of the Niger Company's territories and reorganized them under the colonial office as the Protectorate of Southern and Northern Nigeria. Between 1900 and 1906 Sir Frederick Lugard subordinated the northern Muslim emirates and brought the Sokoto caliphate under his control. Elsewhere, in 1891 the British assumed a protectorate over the hinterlands of Sierra Leone. Having defeated the Ashanti in 1874, they took control of Kumasi and declared a protectorate over Ghana in 1896.

While the British took Nigeria, Ghana, and Sierra Leone, the French went on to complete their West African empire. By a treaty of 1889 they delineated the boundaries between French and British possessions in Senegal, Gambia, Sierra Leone, Guinea, and the Ivory Coast. By 1893 they took Masina and eliminated the state established by al-Hajj 'Umar. They pushed back Samori and established French colonies in Guinea and the Ivory Coast. From their bases in Senegal and the Ivory Coast, the French moved on to establish a protectorate over Futa Jallon in 1897, defeated Samori in 1898, and took control of the upper Volta. By 1900 they had swept across the whole of the Sudan and conquered the Sahara as far as Lake Chad. Although fighting continued in the Ivory Coast until 1908 and in the Niger region until 1921, the French and British African empires were essentially established by 1900.

As in West Africa, European rivalries provoked a scramble for East Africa. British interests were inspired by the desire for trade, by opposition to slavery, and by Christian missionary zeal. Britain also had established interests in India, South Africa, Aden, and other Indian Ocean ports. In 1841, the British appointed a consul to Zanzibar and by 1873 had sufficiently consolidated their influence to force the sultan of Zanzibar to prohibit the slave trade. Britain began to look on Zanzibar as its proxy for the penetration of explorers, missionaries, and traders. In 1890 Zanzibar became a British protectorate.

British expansion provoked Germany to seek compensation. Between 1884 and 1888 the Germans took control of Tanganyika, including the territories that are now Rwanda and Burundi. By agreement between the Germans and the British in 1886 and 1891, East Africa was partitioned. In 1888 the British East Africa Company acquired Kenya, which was ruled from Zanzibar until 1904, when the Kenya protectorate received its first commissioner. Britain also created a protectorate in Uganda in 1893 by treaty with Mwanga II, the kabaka of Buganda, by the terms of which the slave trade was prohibited. By 1914 the British had extended their control over most of the local chiefs of the region.

The British also led the way to the partition of the Somali and Red Sea coasts, primarily because of their concern for the security of traffic to Aden and the Indian Ocean. First, they encouraged Egyptian and Italian interests as a barrier to French expansion. Then in 1887 they established a protectorate on the Harar-Somali coast and by agreement with the French defined the boundaries between their respective territories as lying between the ports of Zayla and Djibouti. In 1891 the British and Italians agreed on boundaries between British and Italian protectorates in Somaliland. Further treaties in 1897 among Ethiopia, Britain, France, and Italy regulated the Somali protectorates. Italy achieved only a nominal and disputed protectorate over Ethiopia. In the meantime, on another front, the British, who had occupied Egypt in 1882, conquered most of the Sudan in 1898 and Darfur in 1916. Thus all of Muslim Africa – indeed, all of Africa except Liberia and Ethiopia – came under European rule by World War I.

CONCLUSION

CHAPTER 43

THE VARIETIES OF ISLAMIC SOCIETIES

By the eighteenth century Muslim societies had come into being throughout Asia, Africa, and Eastern Europe. Each was built on the interaction of Middle Eastern Islamic state, religious, and communal institutions with local social institutions and cultures, and in each case the interactions generated a different type of Islamic society. Although each society was unique, they resembled one another in form and were interconnected by political and religious contacts and shared values. Thus they made up a world system of Islamic societies.

Islamic societies from the tenth to the nineteenth centuries had a complex structure. In some cases Muslim communities were isolated pastoral, village, or urban minorities living within non-Islamic societies. Examples of this type are lineage groups united by shrine veneration in the northern steppes of Inner Asia and parts of the Sahara and merchant communities in China or West Africa. In African societies the Muslim presence was centered around small communities such as lineage groups, teachers and disciples, Sufi brotherhoods, or networks of merchants. Merchant communities were established as early as the eleventh and twelfth centuries in the western Sudan. By the eighteenth century, there were Muslim merchant enclaves in the central Sudan, Berber holy lineages in the Sahara region (*zawaya* or *insilimen*), cultivator and merchant communities and scholarly lineages such as the Saghanughu (called Wangara or Dyula) in the Volta River basin and Guinean forests, and Jakhanke lineages of cultivators and scholars in the Senegambia region. In East Africa, Muslim communities were settled in the coastal towns. In Ethiopia and Somalia they were present among Galla and Somali peoples. In general the Muslim communities were scattered, had no territorial identity, and did not constitute governments.

The Muslim communities were connected to state formation in two ways. First, they often had great influence with military nobles. Muslim advisors gave an Islamic identity to the rulers of the ancient empires of Kawkaw, Takrur, Ghana, Bornu, Mali, and Songhay. Learned Muslim merchants served to legitimize the authority of the rulers and provide administrative services and economic resources, cultural identity, and guidance for festivals, rituals, and magic. Several of these regimes, such as the Mali and Songhay empires, became centers of Muslim worship, scholarship, and legal administration. These regimes were built on a condominium of military and Muslim merchant elites. In these societies, however, the mass of the population remained committed to their traditional religions and were not converted to Islam.

Second, Muslim communities repeatedly attempted to build states of their own. Torodbe or Muslim clerics and teachers were the leaders of these movements. They were a kind of free-floating intelligentsia hostile to the powers, sometimes outraged at their moral shortcomings and failure to implement Islamic policies, sometimes aggrieved over economic exploitation. They were backed by marginalized pastoralists and peasants, rootless wanderers, and gangs of youths. From the seventeenth century, jihads were launched in Mauritania, Bundu, Futa Jallon, and Futa Toro. The most famous of these was the jihad of 'Uthman don Fodio, who created the Sokoto caliphate in 1804, and the nineteenth-century jihad of al-Hajj 'Umar in Futa Toro. These jihads overthrew military elites and created states in hitherto stateless regions. They were an expression of both moral reformism and political expansionism. Their greatest consequence was to bring masses of common people into the faith of Islam. The jihad states, however, were crushed by British and French colonial intervention at the end of the nineteenth century. Apart from Hausaland and Senegal, they left little or no political legacy in the structuring of twentieth-century African states.

More commonly we find the various types of Muslim collectivities bound together in a larger system governed by a state. Islamic states were generally made up of numerous religious collectivities, village and tribal segmentary societies, urban *jama'at*, Sufi brotherhoods, schools of law, and feudal principalities. In theory, state and religion are unified and Islam is a total way of life, which defines political as well as social and familial matters. This is the Muslim view embodied in the ideal of the Prophet and the early caliphs, who were rulers and teachers, repositories of both temporal and religious authority, and whose mission was to lead the community in war and morality. This ideal inspired the efforts of reformist, revivalist, and caliphal movements to create an integrated Muslim state and society. Such movements were common in lineage communities, in which adherence to Islam led to tribal unification, conquest, and the formation of new empires, as in the case of the Fatimid, Almoravid, and Almohad movements in North Africa, the Safavid movement in Iran, and others. In the eighteenth and nineteenth centuries, reformist movements with similar intentions led to conquests and state formation in such cases as the Sokoto caliphate in what is now Nigeria and the Mahdist state in the Sudan. In different terms, the ideal is invoked by contemporary neo-Islamic movements.

Most Muslim societies did not and do not conform to this ideal and were and are built around separate state and religious institutions. By the eighth and ninth centuries, the early caliphate was already evolving into an imperial and secular political regime, while Muslim populations were being formed into a multitude of religiously defined communal groups. These included schools of law, reformist movements, Sufi lineages, brotherhoods, shrine communities, Shi'i sects, and ethnic associations. Such groups were or became independent of states; most withdrew from participation in government and were primarily concerned with solidarity, worship, education, law, personal morality, and upholding the public symbols of Islam. The separation on an institutional level of state institutions and religious associations became the norm for the late 'Abbasid caliphate; the Saljuq and Mamluk sultanates; the Ottoman, Safavid, and Mughal empires; and other Muslim regimes.

This separation, however, was neither clear-cut nor complete. Although the separation was well defined on an institutional level and in terms of organizations, personnel, and ethos, in cultural concept there was a deep ambiguity about both states and religio-communal associations. On the one hand, Muslim states were considered instruments of worldly secular power and were legitimized in terms of patrimonial claims to superior ancestry, state-patronized artistic and literary cultures, and appeals to universal cosmological or philosophical concepts. Their culture derived from the pre-Islamic and non-Islamic substrates of the societies they ruled. On the other hand, these states also had a Muslim religious value derived from historical continuity with the early caliphate, or based on their role as defenders, patrons, and supporters of Muslim worship, education, law, and jihad. They also had an inherent sacred value, for in many Muslim societies the state was conceived as the direct expression of God's will for the ordering of human affairs. Their religious worth was derived both from service to Islam and directly from divine decree.

Similarly, Muslim religious associations, although basically committed to small communal and individual religious pursuits, were involved in politics. Although Muslim religious leaders were in fact committed to an apolitical form of religiosity, in concept they could not imagine their associations as entirely independent of an all-embracing Islamic political order. In concept a Muslim state was necessary for a complete Muslim way of life.

Conceptual ambiguities were translated into a variety of institutional patterns in the relationship between states and religious associations. In the Ottoman and Safavid empires, the states themselves controlled Muslim judicial, educational, and social functions. The Ottoman and Safavid monarchies were strongly supported by an *'ulama'* bureaucracy. In these empires Muslim religious associations became virtual departments of state, although in Iran the religious elites were eventually able to assert their autonomy. In Mughal India, or Mataram Java, Muslim religious leaders, associations, and activities were largely autonomous and often critical of state policies and state-patronized culture.

Thus in the pre-modern era there were two alternative concepts of Islamic society. One was the caliphate, which integrated the state and the community, the realms of politics and religion, into an inseparable whole. The second was the sultanate, or secular state, which ruled over the quasi-independent religious associations that were the true bearers of Muslim religious life. In one image the state was the all-encompassing expression of an Islamic society; in the other, an Islamic society was divided into separate state and religious institutions. The relationship between Muslim communities and states was variable and ambiguous. The former were sometimes subordinate and committed, sometimes independent and hostile. Sometimes they accepted the inherent legitimacy of ruling regimes; sometimes they rejected them as antithetical to a truly Muslim society. Most often they regarded states with detachment. While accepting the necessity of political order, they disdained political involvement and withdrew into communal and personal religious affairs. While accepting political realities, they were nostalgic for the better days of the true caliphate and yearned for the era of justice. The legacy of pre-modern societies to the modern era, then, was not a defined structure of state and society but a spectrum of variation and an inherent ambiguity about the relations between the two.

In practice, the most common state type of Islamic society was modeled on the Saljuq-period form of Middle Eastern Islamic society. The early Islamic model, although modified, persisted in Iran, and Turkish migrations and conquests brought it directly to Inner Asia, India, and the Arab Middle East, and via Anatolia to the Ottoman Empire in the Balkans and North Africa. Although based on the same model, in each case there were differences in state organization, religious institutions, concepts of legitimacy, and religious beliefs. In the Ottoman, Mughal, Egyptian Mamluk, and Hafsid states, the government was strongly centralized. In Iran, Algeria, Morocco, and parts of the Arab world, states were weak because they were opposed by strong tribal societies, sometimes under Sufi leadership. State control of religious elites was marked in the Ottoman Empire, Safavid Iran, and the state of Bukhara, but *'ulama'* and Sufis in India, Algeria, and Morocco were relatively independent. Similarly, the bases of legitimacy varied considerably. The Ottoman and Safavid empires emphasized a combination of Islamic and cosmopolitan qualities. In the Arab provinces of the Middle East and North Africa, Islamic elements predominated. Other variations occurred in the prevailing religious orientation of Muslim societies. *'Ulama'* Islam was particularly strong in the Ottoman Empire, Inner Asia, and Iran. Shrine-Sufism was pronounced in India and North Africa. Everywhere Islamic culture was marked by strong local syncretisms. To fully understand the variations, however, each of the regional societies has to be considered not only with regard to specific features but also as a whole system in which state, religious, and parochial collectivities and cultures interacted.

The Iranian type of Islamic society may be understood in terms of the relations among state, religious, and tribal (*uymaq*) populations. The forces that gave shape to Iran go back to the Safavid conquest in 1500. The Safavids were the religious leaders of *uymaq* and tribal peoples, but their empire was gradually rebuilt on the basis of slave forces and a bureaucratic administration. The Safavid regime became a suzerainty superimposed on a society parceled out into *uymaq* kingdoms, each region actually ruled by a tribal lord and his warriors, descended often from Mongol Inner Asian families, who organized a local government and economy and taxed the local population. In Iran political power was from the outset divided between an imperial state and tribal societies.

The central government attempted to legitimize its reign in Muslim terms. Safavid authority was based on the claim that the rulers were descendants of the seventh imam and therefore were quasi-divine persons. As chiefs of the dominant Sufi movement, they claimed the absolute obedience of all their disciples. To bolster the prestige of the state, the Safavid dynasty sponsored an Iranian-Islamic style of culture concentrating on court poetry, painting, and monumental architecture that symbolized not only the Islamic credentials of the state but also the glory of the ancient Persian tradition. The symbolism of the regime was essentially Muslim, but included strong overtones of an independent Iranian cultural heritage.

In the course of Safavid rule, Iran was converted from Sunni to Shi'i Islam. After the Safavids conquered Iran, they made Shi'ism the official religion of the country, built up cadres of Shi'i *'ulama'* (mainly imported from Iraq), and ruthlessly suppressed rival religious movements. Sunni *'ulama'* and Sufi movements, even including the Safavids' own supporters, were crushed or driven from the country. By the seventeenth century the Safavids had built up a virtually monolithic religious establishment and had eliminated rival forms of Islamic belief and organization.

Still, the relationship between the state and the Shi'i *'ulama'* was ambiguous. The *'ulama'* of Iran depended on state support, deferred to state authority, and benefited from state appointments to political and religious offices and from state endowment of religious shrines. They played the role of intermediaries and mediators between the regime and the general populace. Altogether subordinate to the Safavid state, the *'ulama'* served to legitimize and support the central regime against its tribal and religious rivals and took the lead in the persecution of Sunnis and Sufis. There were some doctrinal and social indications, however, of an *'ulama'* claim to autonomy and freedom from state control and of religious doubts about the legitimacy of the Safavid regime. With the decline and eventual destruction of the Safavids, some *'ulama'* argued that the true leaders of the Islamic community were not the rulers but the scholars themselves – the *mujtahids*. They had the wisdom to give guidance on spiritual matters in the absence of the true imam, and the people were bound, according to their teaching, to follow their advice.

The Iranian Shi'i *'ulama'* differed from Sunni *'ulama'* in several respects. One was that the *'ulama'* of Iran formed a relatively cohesive body, related through the spiritual and intellectual genealogies of teachers and students, geographically defined by the boundaries of the country, and in communication with one another. Moreover, they held a large degree of authority over the common people and did not, as did the *'ulama'* of the Ottoman Empire, India, or Indonesia, have important Sufi or reformist movements as competitors. Thus, Iranian society before the eighteenth century was characterized by a legitimate but not powerfully centralized monarchy, a distribution of power among tribal principalities, and a monolithic religious establishment patronized by the regime.

The Ottoman Empire represented a different constellation of state, religious, and small community relations. The Ottoman regime was highly centralized. A slave military elite, bureaucratic financial administration, and Muslim religious administration gave the central government control over the subject population. As early as the fourteenth and fifteenth centuries, the Ottoman state had effectively subordinated the Turkish and Kurdish tribal populations of eastern Anatolia.

Within the Ottoman Empire, however, there was considerable variation in the degree of centralization of power and in the distribution of power from province to province. Whereas the central regime was powerful in the Balkans, most of Anatolia, the Nile Valley, Tunisia, and Algiers, much of Iraq, Upper Egypt, parts of Algeria, southern Tunisia, and Syria were dominated by segmentary populations. In these regions the authority of the central state was tenuous, and the local populations were organized in tribal or Sufi-led coalitions. In Tunisia, itself a subordinate state within the Ottoman Empire, the centralized state was based on a highly sedentarized and urbanized population, and tribal domains were limited to the south of the country. In Algeria, another vassal state based on a small janissary militia, the state governed some of the coastal regions, but most of the country was ruled by tribal and Sufi chiefs. The weakening of the Ottoman state in the seventeenth and eighteenth centuries allowed, in general, for a strengthening of local elites and communities.

Ottoman success in centralizing state power depended on a number of factors. The first factor was the power of the central regime and the relative weakness of the tribal populations. As opposed to Iran, which came under the control of the *uymaqs*, the Oghuz peoples who entered Anatolia in the eleventh and twelfth centuries did not bring Mongol and Chaghatay concepts of political authority and were not organized under chiefs who controlled a large central household and smaller segmentary groups. They were dispersed peoples operating in small bands, united by successful warrior lords or by charismatic Sufi leaders. The small size of these bands made it easy for the Ottoman state to suppress them, absorb the chiefs into Ottoman administration, and deprive the Sufis of their military and political authority.

Equally important was the concept of Ottoman legitimacy. Unlike the Safavids, the legitimacy of the Ottoman regime was never questioned from a Muslim point of view. Ottoman authority was based on a Turkish tradition of patrimonial leadership, the legacy of previous Muslim states in Anatolia and the Middle East, and the conquest of the Byzantine Empire. The Ottomans thus inherited the responsibilities of the historical caliphates and the imperial aura of the ancient empires. Above all, their legitimacy was based on their success as a warrior state, which fulfilled the Muslim duty of jihad, protected the holy cities of Arabia, and organized the pilgrimage. The kind of doubts about royal authority raised in the Safavid Empire by the Shi'i *'ulama'*, and those raised in the Mughal Empire by the accommodation of non-Muslim cultures, were minimal.

The organized religious life of Ottoman Muslims was also different from that of Iranian Muslims. The Ottoman Empire, like the Safavid, organized a bureaucracy of scholars, but unlike the Safavids the Ottomans kept the loyalty of the religious establishment. Government patronage and the creation of an elaborate bureaucracy absorbed the *'ulama'* into the state machine. A graded judicial and professorial hierarchy, state salaries, and state endowments effectively committed the *'ulama'* to the Ottoman regime. Even the Sufi brotherhoods, despite their large followings, were attached to the state machine and were neutralized or suppressed. The Sunni *'ulama'* were totally committed to the authority of the sultan and stressed the legacy of religious attitudes that legitimized the state. In Iran, by contrast, the *'ulama'* came to be independent of and hostile to the state.

Thus, by the eighteenth century the Ottoman Empire had an institutional pattern that emphasized the centralized state, legitimized in Muslim terms, and a centralized and unified Sunni religious establishment that served virtually as a department of state. Only in bedouin-populated regions of the Arab world and North Africa was some degree of autonomy possible.

The Mughal state, like the Ottoman and Safavid empires, was a patrimonial regime. The emperor ruled through a royal household supported by a quasi-feudal elite. The armies were composed of Muslim officers, mainly of Afghan and Inner Asian descent, who were assigned tax revenues from the land in return for supplying contingents for military service. Native Hindu vassals such as the Rajputs formed an important part of the military establishment. Muslims were the original conquering elite, but the Hindus were important as subordinate lords, administrative officials, financiers, merchants, and landowners. The regime was also supported by a bureaucratic administration that served to tax the subject populace and to register landed incomes. The bureaucracy was staffed by both Muslim and Hindu officials.

The Mughal regime wove together Muslim and Indian social and cultural considerations. The identity of the Muslim elites was based not only on Islam but on noble lineage. All members of the elite were members of extended families linked by ceremonies, gifts, and concessions of property and office. Muslim peasants and pastoralists were as much subjects of the empire as were Hindus.

The Mughal Empire was officially Muslim. It defended Islam, patronized Muslim religious life, and appointed Muslim judicial and other religious officials, but the Mughals also claimed the loyalty of Hindu lords and subjects and elaborated a court culture in which painting, music, literature, philosophy, and architecture embodied aspects of the Hindu as well as the Muslim heritage and blended them into a single stylistic form. In contrast to the Ottoman and Safavid regimes, the Mughal Empire had a strong non-Islamic expression as its cultural and political identity.

In religious organization proper, Mughal India – as opposed to Safavid Iran – recognized no single dominant concept of Islam and no single Muslim community or religious establishment. Indian Muslims formed numerous religious bodies, divided by allegiance to points of doctrine, schools of law, Sufi brotherhoods, and the teaching of individual *shaykhs*, scholars, and saints. Indian Muslims qua Muslims appeared as a congeries of religious groups rather than as a single communal body. Despite state patronage of a small *'ulama'* establishment, both *'ulama'* and Sufis were generally independent – and often critical – of the cosmopolitan and imperial culture, the Hindu elites, and the patrimonial loyalties of the Mughal regime. Thus, Indian Islamic society was organized not in terms of an Ottoman type of state control or an Iranian type of uniformity, but in terms of numerous independent and competitive Muslim religious movements.

Southeast Asia had a similar heritage of an agrarian and commercial economic base and a history of state regimes legitimized in terms of high religious culture, but there political fragmentation rather than imperial unity was the rule. Southeast Asia was never conquered by Muslim tribal peoples; nor were indigenous regimes able to achieve political unity. The coastal and regional states of Malaya and Sumatra and the principalities of Java took on an Islamic identity, but they were derived historically from pre-Islamic states. Characteristically, Indo-Malay Muslim states depended heavily on symbolic and cultural attachments to implement their rule. Although Islam was woven into the symbolism of state authority, legitimization still depended on the heritage of Hindu and Buddhist concepts. Even as compared with Mughal India, the non-Islamic cultural aspect of the political system was strongly pronounced.

The Muslim religious communities of Southeast Asia also tended to be decentralized. Religious life was built around individual teachers and holy men; the Sufi brotherhoods and the *'ulama'* schools were institutionally weak, and there were no significant tribal communities. Scholars functioned independently, teaching in schools and seminaries (*pesantren*). The village holy men were also important influences. In Indonesia, the mass of villagers considered themselves Muslims but were not strongly influenced by Islamic rituals, concepts, laws, ethics, or institutions. They followed a customary religious and social life that had existed prior to the establishment of Islam and assimilated Islam into this preexisting culture.

Islam in Indonesia was manifest as identity rather than as social organization. Some regions were exceptions to this Indo-Malay pattern. In Minangkabau the Sufi orders were strongly organized and generated intense conflict as reformers struggled to bring Minangkabau into accord with Muslim norms.

Southeast Asian Islamic societies differed from Middle Eastern societies in that there was little state participation in the organization of Muslim religious life. The village *'ulama'*, Sufis, and other popular teachers were wholly independent. Indeed, deep in the history of the *'ulama'* of Java and the outer islands there was a tradition of resistance to state authority. The common people believed that a savior or just ruler would eventually overthrow the state to create a truly Islamic society. In India and Southeast Asia the initiative passed to independent Sufi and *'ulama'* reformers and other charismatic leaders who would struggle among themselves, and with foreign and non-Islamic forces, to try to shape the Islamic destiny of the area in the modern era.

CHAPTER 44

THE GLOBAL CONTEXT

THE INNER SPACES OF THE MUSLIM WORLD

Although much of this book is about the history of Muslim states and empires, regions that lay outside of the boundaries and authority of individual states or empires are essential to understanding the political and cultural geography of the Islamic world. These regions are the Mediterranean Sea, the Indian Ocean, and the great inner deserts of Central Asia and the African Sahara. The oceans, steppes, and deserts both isolated regions from one another and allowed them to be linked together by travelers, traders, missionaries, and conquerors. Each of these regions cultivated cultural and religious practices and social networks that crossed political borders. The cross-regional connections help explain the diffusion of Islam from the seventh to the eighteenth century. They were arenas of religio-cultural transmission. From the sixteenth century, however, they also became arenas for the growing power of European states and their subsequent commercial and colonial domination of both the inner spaces and the regional territories of the Muslim world.

The Mediterranean and the Indian Ocean

The Mediterranean – from Spain in the northwest and Morocco in the southwest to Anatolia, Syria, and Egypt in the east – was first integrated under the rule of the Roman Empire and Hellenistic culture. With the creation of a second capital at Constantinople and the fall of Rome to "barbarian" invaders, the region began to fragment. The late Roman or Byzantine Empire continued to rule over the Balkans, Anatolia, Syria, and Egypt, but independent states were formed by Gothic and Celtic peoples in the former Western European provinces of the Roman Empire and in parts of North Africa. The region was further divided by religious differences among Christians.

In the seventh century, the Arab conquests partitioned the Mediterranean among Muslim- and Christian-dominated regions. The Arab-Muslim conquests made Egypt and Syria part of the Umayyad and ʿAbbasid empires. North Africa, Spain, and Sicily were governed by numerous independent Arab-Muslim rulers. In the tenth century, the Fatimids brought most of North Africa, Egypt, and Syria under their rule, but the historic political unity of the region would never be reconstituted.

From the tenth century, Muslim and Christian states were constantly at war. On many fronts Christian states pushed back the Muslims. The Byzantine Empire regained northern Syria. Italian city-states fought off Muslim pirates and attacked North Africa. In Spain, the small Christian kingdoms of the north captured Muslim Toledo in 1085. The Normans conquered Sicily by 1091. European warriors and pilgrims established the Latin Kingdom of Jerusalem and other principalities in Syria, Lebanon, and Palestine that would last from 1096 to 1291. A Muslim counterattack followed. The Moroccan Almoravids invaded Spain in 1086; the Almohads, who succeeded them in Morocco, conquered Spain in 1172 and extended their domains further east to what are now Algeria and Tunisia. The two dynasties brought the Sahara, Morocco, and Spain into a single polity and a new trading zone. Morocco, benefiting from trade and empire, became a commercial and urbanized society. Christian forces, however, defeated the Almohads at the Battle of Las Navas de Tolosa in 1212. Within half a century, all of Spain except the kingdom of Granada was under Christian rule. Granada fell to Ferdinand and Isabella in 1492. In the east, however, the Ayyubids, led by Saladin, and the Mamluk rulers of Egypt and Syria pushed out the Latin states by 1291, bringing a long period of Muslim-Christian struggle over control of the Levant coasts of the Mediterranean to a temporary end.

Despite wars, the Mediterranean was crisscrossed by commercial routes that linked its many regions and states and allowed for the transmission of cultural artifacts and ideas. Although trade between East and West diminished in the early Middle Ages due to the breakup of the Roman Empire and the Arab-Muslim conquests, it never was entirely extinguished. Jewish merchants (Radhanites) conducted trade from the western Mediterranean to China and India, bringing spices and rare woods to the West and carrying slaves, weapons, and hides to the East. In the eleventh and later centuries, a lively trade flourished among the Italian city-states, Egypt, Spain, Sicily, and North Africa. From the tenth to the thirteenth century, Venice and Genoa created extensive networks of fortified trading posts and colonies in the eastern Mediterranean and the Black Sea where they could purchase spices, drugs, dyes, silk, and other exotic products. The Italian city-states maintained an active trade with Mamluk Egypt and Syria. Thirteenth-century treaties among Sicily, Venice, Marseille, Genoa, and Florence promoted Tunisian prosperity. Jews were heavily engaged in international trade – particularly in the Muslim, Arabic-speaking parts of the Mediterranean.

The Ottoman era renewed the historic Mediterranean combination of political rivalry, warfare, trade, and cultural exchange. The Ottomans originated in Anatolia, crossed the straits of Gallipoli in 1345, and by 1389 had conquered Greece, Macedonia, and Bulgaria. In 1453, they captured Constantinople and made it their capital, Istanbul. In the late fifteenth and early sixteenth centuries, they extended their domains in the Balkans as far as the Danube in the north and the Adriatic in the west. In Hungary, they established a new frontier with the Hapsburg Empire of Austria, Spain, and Holland. Ottoman expansion forced the Genoese and then the Venetians out of their extensive trading empires in the eastern Mediterranean and the Black Sea. In 1516 and 1517, the Ottomans took over the Mamluk Empire of Syria and Egypt, Iraq, and the Islamic holy places of Arabia, giving them control of the routes from southern and eastern Asia to Europe. At the same time, they launched a nearly century-long naval struggle against the Hapsburgs for control of the Mediterranean. In time the Ottomans established their suzerainty over North Africa, except for Morocco.

Ottoman expansion gave the empire a powerful position in the international trade of the Mediterranean, the Black Sea, the Red Sea, and the Indian Ocean. By the beginning of the sixteenth century, the Ottoman Empire was at the heart of the world trading system between Europe and southern and eastern Asia. From Jeddah to Mecca, Damascus, and Aleppo; from the Persian Gulf to Basra and Aleppo; and from Aleppo to Bursa came Iranian silk, Indian spices, and cotton cloth, where it was sold in return for European woolens and metalwares. Bursa was also a principal market for the Black Sea trade to the Crimea and from there to the Ukraine, Poland, and Russia. Eastern luxuries were exchanged for European bulk goods for mass consumption, such as grain, cotton, wool, hides, fish, and ordinary textiles.

The Ottomans, however, reached their limits in the late sixteenth century. The Portuguese discoveries of new sea routes around Africa to the Indian Ocean in the end of the fifteenth and the beginning of the sixteenth century undermined the Ottoman trading position. Allied European powers checked Ottoman expansion in southeastern Europe and challenged Ottoman supremacy in the Mediterranean. Finally, an Ottoman-Hapsburg truce of 1580 confirmed each in its possessions and defined the frontier between Christian Europe and Muslim North Africa and the Levant that endures to the present.

Like the Mediterranean, the Indian Ocean both divided and united the surrounding territories. However, it has a very different history. With the partial exception of the Indian subcontinent and Iran, the history of the territories surrounding the Indian Ocean, including East Africa, Arabia, and maritime and mainland Southeast Asia, cannot be told in terms of empires and contiguous geographical areas but rather must be told in terms of scattered coastal towns, peninsulas, and islands. The population of the region included Chinese, Indians from Gujarat, Bantus and Swahili-speaking peoples of East Africa, Omanis, Hadramawtis and other Arabians, Malays, Javanese, Siamese, Thais, and the innumerable peoples of the islands. The sea was the connection among them. The Indian Ocean held a central position on the trade routes that connected China to the Persian Gulf and the Red Sea, linking Arabia to East Africa, India, and island Southeast Asia, now Indonesia. Then the

Turkish-Muslim conquests of India brought northern and western India into the zone of Muslim regimes and cultural influences.

By the thirteenth century, the nearly simultaneous rise of the Ottoman, Mughal, and Safavid empires gave an increasingly Muslim coloration to the region. The Ottomans conquered Egypt, Iraq, Arabia, and Yemen in the early decades of the sixteenth century; the Safavids and the Mughals took control of the coasts of Iran and western India. Egypt, Yemen, Hadramawt, East Africa, West India, the Malabar coast, and Malaysia/Indonesia were connected by commerce. As the coastal and island populations converted to Islam, the Indian Ocean was becoming a Muslim sea, a trans-ocean new world of Islam.

The Muslim commercial presence was reinforced by traveling scholars, *shurafa'* (descendants of the prophet), and mystics who flowed out of Yemen, Hadramawt, and Oman to East Africa from about 1250, and to Malaysia, Indonesia, and the Philippines after 1300. Hadrami networks reached Surat in India in the sixteenth and seventeenth centuries, Mecca a little later, and then Malaya from the eighteenth to the twentieth century. Hadramis and other Arabian scholars were particularly active as teachers, judges, officials, religious counselors, and holy men. They married and sired children with local women – connections favored by the matrilineal and uxorilocal marriage traditions of Swahili East Africa, the South Arabian coast, the Malabar coast of India, and West Sumatra – and created dispersed families with half siblings, offspring of the same father, often living in separate countries and speaking different languages. The dispersion of families created familial, social, and economic networks spanning the whole of the Indian Ocean region. At the same time, there was a reverse tide of migration – Muslims visiting the holy places of Arabia on pilgrimage and settling in Arabia, Yemen, and Cairo for prolonged periods of study.

The desert as ocean: Inner Asia and the Sahara
Not only seas but also deserts defined arenas for political, commercial, and cultural interaction. Historically, the great steppelands of Central Asia from the Oxus River, the border of Iran, to the frontiers of agricultural China were inhabited by pastoral peoples who spoke Turkic-Altaic languages and were organized into families, clans, and confederations (hordes). The settled peoples lived primarily in the oasis districts of Transoxania, Khwarizm, Farghana, and Kashgar and in scattered towns along the trade routes that linked China, the Middle East, and Europe. The steppes allowed the nomads to invade the peripheral settled societies of Europe, the Middle East, and China. From the second millennium BCE to the eighteenth century, the history of the region may be told in terms of ever-repeated nomadic conquests and of the formation of empires over oases and settled populations.

Islam first spread in this region as a result of the Arab conquests of Iran and Transoxania and the movement of Muslim traders and Sufis from the towns to the steppes. In the tenth and eleventh centuries, Qarluq and Oghuz peoples converted and founded the Qarakhanid and Saljuq empires. The Qarakhanids divided their domains into a western khanate that ruled Transoxania until 1211 and an eastern khanate for Farghana and Kashgaria. They promoted the spread of Islam among the populace of Transoxania, Kashgar, and the Tarim basin, patronizing a new Turkish literature based on Arabic and Persian models – the basis of Turkish-Islamic civilization. The Saljuqs moved westward to conquer Iran, Iraq, and Anatolia. Out of the Turkish peoples in Anatolia came the later Ottoman Empire.

In the thirteenth century, the Mongols followed the Qarakhanids and the Saljuqs. The Mongols originated with the formation of a confederation of Inner Asian peoples under the leadership of Chinggis Khan. They established their suzerainty over the whole of Inner Asia; much of the Middle East; parts of Eastern Europe, including Russia, the Ukraine, southern Poland, Hungary, and Bulgaria; and China. The Mongols accomplished what could never be achieved in the Mediterranean, the Indian Ocean, or the Sahara – a vast transregional empire. This vast empire was divided among the four sons of Chinggis. Out of their disputes came several independent and even hostile Mongol states. These included Mongol regimes in Mongolia and China, the Golden Horde on the northern steppes, the Chaghatay khanate in Transoxania and eastern Turkestan, and the Ilkhan regime in Iran and Anatolia. These states were the basis of several distinct Islamic societies in Inner Asia.

On the western and northern steppes, the breakup of the Golden Horde allowed for the emergence of separate Crimean Tatar, Volga Tatar, Uzbek, and Kazakh ethnic and political groups. In the fifteenth and sixteenth centuries, Naqshbandi and Yasavi missionaries began converting the Kazakhs. Islam, however, probably made little headway until the eighteenth century, when Tatar merchants, missionaries, secretaries, and teachers helped construct mosques and schools.

In western Turkestan – including Transoxania, Farghana, and Kashgaria – the Timurids and the Chaghatays were succeeded by Uzbek domination under the Shaybanid dynasty (1500–98). The Shaybanid Empire was succeeded by a number of city-states, including Khokand, Kashgar, and Bukhara. Islam became the political basis of several of these states as well as the religion of the people. Sufi masters or Sufi lineages mediated and sometimes governed. Bukhara was ruled by the Mangit dynasty and by the scholars who controlled judicial administration and education and whose organized bodies of *sayyids*, *khwajas*, *mirs*, Sufis, students, and guilds made up the body politic. Eastern Turkestan, now part of China, the domain of the Chaghatay khans, was also integrated into the domains of Turkish-Islamic culture. At the end of the sixteenth century, much of the populace of Inner Asia outside of Mongolia and Tibet was Muslim or under Muslim suzerainty.

The great Sahara desert, like the Taklamakan in Inner Asia, led both to the separation of populations and to trade and the communication of culture. On both sides of the desert the economies were based on a similar mixture of pastoralism, agriculture, craft production, and trade. From the seventh to the eleventh centuries, in west and central Saharan Africa, Arab and Berber Muslim traders made their way into and across the Sahara, settled in the trading towns, and became courtiers and secretaries for the local rulers and for a succession of regional empires – Takrur, Ghana, Mali, Songhay, and Bornu. In the eleventh and twelfth centuries the Almoravids and the Almohads brought large regions of the Sahara, North Africa, and Spain into north-south empires, including Sudanic Africa, North Africa, and the Iberian Peninsula.

From the Sudanic regions, African-Muslim merchants and scholars, known as Wangara, or Dyula (Juula), settled in Mauritania, Senegambia, the Volta River basin, and the Guinean forests, establishing their own communities and in some cases converting the local peoples to Islam. From the seventeenth through the nineteenth century, some of these communities launched jihads and created new Muslim states. In East Africa, Arab Bedouins and Egyptian armies brought Islam into Nubia. Arab- and Persian-Muslim traders settled the towns and islands along the Red Sea and Indian Ocean coasts. From there, over centuries, the traders reached into the interior, bringing Islam to Somalia, Ethiopia, Kenya, and Tanzania.

THE RISE OF EUROPE AND THE WORLD ECONOMY

By the eighteenth century, Islamic societies had begun to decline in political power. The Safavid state had been defeated by Afghan invaders and, deserted by its tribal vassals, disintegrated completely. The Ottoman Empire went through a period of decentralization that impaired the concept of an imperial state. The Mughal Empire disintegrated into numerous competing provincial and feudal regimes. In Southeast Asia, a centralized regime had never been established over the Indonesian archipelago or the Malay Peninsula. The largest Indonesian state, the Mataram Empire of Java, came under direct Dutch economic and indirect Dutch political control. In North Africa, Muslim states were being subverted by their declining commercial position in the Mediterranean, while provincial, tribal, and Sufi resistance was increasing. The Sudanic states had long passed the peak of their commercial prosperity, although Muslim communities were growing in influence in other parts of Africa. By this period, much of the northern steppes of Inner Asia had come under Russian control, and eastern Turkestan had come under Chinese rule.

An important but hardly the only factor in the political decline of many Muslim regimes was the rising power of Europe. On the far western fringe of the Eurasian land mass, Europeans were making a revolution in world history. From the late Middle Ages to modern times, European societies were generating technological inventions, economic wealth, and military power. These developments would profoundly change the conditions of life not only for Muslims but for all the world's peoples.

European world power emerged from a set of intertwined socioeconomic and cultural conditions that led to the formation of highly pluralistic societies. Unlike

Middle Eastern societies, European societies were not organized on the threefold template of kinship, religious community, and empire. Medieval European family structure, with some exceptions among the feudal nobility, was based not on closed lineage groups but rather on interlocking social networks built on bilateral ties of both husbands and wives. Moreover, with the fall of Rome and the failure of the Carolingian and Holy Roman empires, European states no longer had the all-embracing political and mythic importance still held by states in the Middle East. In place of empires, feudal governments based on personal and contractual loyalties, governments by oath association, and communes or assemblies based on Roman or Germanic notions of popular sovereignty were accepted as legitimate.

Most important was the tendency toward secularization. The potentiality for secularization was implicit in the Christian church, because it was a highly organized, corporate institution governed under laws and norms appropriate to itself but not to lay society, making it possible to define a profane realm – "the world" – outside the church, a world governed by nonchurch or noncanonical laws. Greek and Roman political and legal ideas and German communal and feudal concepts defined a realm of legal authority and secular values that, although not Christian, were viewed as legitimate.

Historical changes in the twelfth and thirteenth centuries enhanced the pluralism implicit in European family, state, and religious organization. The growth of commerce, a money economy, and towns broke up village communities, favored the mobility of individuals, and promoted occupational specialization. New urban classes of landowning and capital-investing patricians, merchants and bankers, artisans, journeymen, workers, and entrepreneurs in manufacturing, shipbuilding, and commerce grew in size. With the expansion of secular learning in literature, philosophy, law, and medicine, a nonclerical intelligentsia of poets, writers, physicians, lawyers, professors, administrators, and judges increased. Thus, European society was divided into numerous social strata and classes: nobles, knights, clergy, and a bourgeoisie, subdivided again among merchants, artisans, intellectuals, lawyers, and other groups.

The differentiation of late medieval European society stimulated the formation of corporate groups to advance the interests of their members. Some groups served the need for political security. Feudal fiefdoms, aristocratic factions, church governments, peace associations, and communes all became active centers of political power. Within the church, monastic orders and confraternities were formed to express new religious orientations. Merchant and artisan guilds and commercial companies organized economic activities. Universities were founded to carry on secular learning. Corporate structures were critical to the formation of a civil society that was a counterweight to centralized political power.

This pluralism was expressed in values as well as social organization. European societies recognized the legitimacy of several culture systems, including feudal chivalry and romance, Roman law, philosophy, and bourgeois business ethics – each of which constituted a world of independent values. Each type of government, each stratum, and each group operated in accordance with its own laws and regulations, its own moral concepts, and its own implicit idea of the nature of the human being and of human fulfillment. Muslim societies were also built on a similar multiplicity of culture and value systems, but they maintained at least a rhetorical commitment to Islamic law and community.

In this pluralistic society, the relationship between the individual and society was different from that of the Middle East. Whereas in the Middle East individual obligations were defined primarily in terms of participation in a community and secondarily in terms of specialized roles, in Europe the prioritization was reversed. The cultural heterogeneity of Europeans led to identification of individuals in terms of the specialized roles they played in occupational, corporate, and officeholding situations, and also in terms of an individual spiritual identity. Society itself came to be conceived in terms of individuals fulfilling a function, a calling, and a role in a corporate, pluralistic, and secular world.

EUROPEAN TRADE, NAVAL POWER, AND EMPIRE

These social conditions were amplified by economic and technological development. By the thirteenth and fourteenth centuries, the towns of Italy, Flanders, and the Baltic were already committed to commerce and industry, rather than agriculture, as sources of wealth. Out of these towns came novel techniques for investment, banking, and insurance, and other methods of economic organization and exchange. The pursuit of wealth and sophisticated means to generate it led to a tremendous outward expansion of European city-states in search of exotic luxury products and of new sources of food, fuel, and raw materials for their growing and ambitious populations.

The trading impulse led by stages to a revolution in world commerce and politics. Venice and Genoa had already created extensive networks of colonies and trading posts in the eastern Mediterranean and the Black Sea, where they could purchase spices, drugs, dyes, silk, and other products of the East. When the rise of the Ottoman Empire cut off the Italian city-states from their Eastern sources, Genoa was forced to turn to the western Mediterranean and the Atlantic for its supplies of wool, sugar, alum, silk, cereals, dyes, and spices. The Portuguese undertook the search for a new route to the Indies that would bypass Middle Eastern routes and enable them to bring Eastern products directly to Lisbon. By 1507 they had established bases in the Indian Ocean, reducing commerce in the Red Sea and the Mediterranean. Spanish and Italian explorers discovered new continents. Portugal and Spain conquered empires in the southern seas and the New World and brought home untold wealth.

In the sixteenth century, the great empires vied to dominate the global economy. The Ottomans fought the Habsburgs in Italy, Eastern Europe, and the

Mediterranean and the Portuguese in the Indian Ocean. By the late sixteenth century, the Ottomans had consolidated their position in the Balkans and North Africa, but the entry of northern trading and warships into the Mediterranean heralded a major change in the international capitalist economy and a shift of commercial and military power to northern Europe. Holland, England, and France emerged as the dominant forces in world trade. Each of them would create a global commercial empire based on sophisticated trading, advanced gunnery and sailing techniques, and utter ruthlessness.

Although the discovery of new routes to the Orient did not close the traditional Middle Eastern international routes, it created a revolution in the distribution of wealth. As a result, Europe would prosper on the captured gold and silver, spices, and other products of both the New World and the Old. The Baltic and the Atlantic replaced the Mediterranean and the Indian Ocean as the most important centers of world trade. The growth of Atlantic trade meant not only a change of routes but also a change in the nature of the goods being exchanged. Whereas the traditional trade was largely a trade in luxury goods, the new commerce was a trade in agricultural and industrial products (timber, grain, fish, salt, etc.) on a mass scale and represented a new level of commodity production and division of labor in the world economy. The formation of the new commercial empires made possible a system of economic exploitation in which Europe became the principal beneficiary of a division of labor between colonies producing raw materials and metropoles producing high-value industrial goods and commercial services. European commercial dominance in the seventeenth and eighteenth centuries led ultimately to the emergence of capitalist industrial economies.

In the seventeenth century the Portuguese in the Indian Ocean were displaced by the Dutch. The Dutch conquered key commercial centers such as Makassar (1669) and Banten (1682), gaining control of the vital ports and products of the Indies. By the middle of the eighteenth century, they had conquered the rest of the Indies and converted their commercial empire into a territorial empire. They made themselves suzerains of Java and conquered the rest of the Indies in the course of the nineteenth century. In the eighteenth century, new products – plantation crops largely managed by Europeans and Chinese, including sugar, coffee, and tobacco – were added to Dutch exports. Instead of cloth and silver, these exports were paid for in opium.

Malaya and India also became part of European trading and then territorial empires. In the seventeenth century, the Dutch, the British, and the French established factories, warehouses, and residences for their merchants in India. The British East India Company began trading in India in 1600, exporting cotton, silk cloth, and spices and importing silver bullion and other metals. The British progressively extended their economic influence from one region to another, converting their economic power into political control. After bitter rivalries with the French, the British took control of Bengal in the late eighteenth century and went on to dominate the rest of the Indian subcontinent in the early decades of the nineteenth. At the same time, they took control of the Indian Ocean, with bases in Malaya, the Persian Gulf, the Red Sea, and East Africa. By the late nineteenth century, the Indian Ocean region was Muslim in religion and culture and largely under colonial rule.

On the basis of their dominance of international and East Asian routes, the British, the French, and the Dutch also gained commercial supremacy in the Mediterranean and went on to take territorial control of Egypt, North Africa, and the Fertile Crescent. The French occupied Algeria from 1830 and declared a pro-tectorate over Tunisia in 1881 and over Morocco in 1912. Egypt came under British control in 1882. Libya was invaded by Italy in 1911. In the aftermath of World War I, the Ottoman Empire was partitioned, with Lebanon and Syria coming under French control and Palestine, Jordan, and Iraq placed under British suzerainty. Only parts of the Ottoman Empire remained independent and were reborn as the Turkish Republic in 1924. Even in the colonial era and the contemporary period of independent national states, the Mediterranean remains, at least in concept, despite centuries of political division, a region with an intrinsic geographical, commercial, and cultural unity.

Africa was the last region with a large Muslim population to be subjected to colonial domination. Plantation agriculture in Brazil and the West Indies created a huge demand for African slaves. During the 1650s and 1660s, French, British, Dan-ish, Swedish, and German companies were formed to develop tropical plantations and promote the slave trade. In the seventeenth and later centuries, the Europeans began to move into the interior. Europeans sought palm oil, peanuts, ivory, sisal, and slaves in exchange for cotton fabric, textiles, and firearms, which in turn pro-moted internal warfare, enslavement, and the export of slaves to the Americas as well as an increase in the slave trade on trans-Saharan routes to North Africa. French expansion in the nineteenth century further drew Sudanic and Saharan goods to Atlantic ports. Colonialism, the capitalist economy, and the technologies of industrialism vastly reduced the historic roles of the Sahara in trade and the transmission of culture.

In the late nineteenth century the European powers turned from trading interests to political annexation. At the Congress of Berlin (1884–85) the European powers agreed on the partition of Africa among themselves. Already the French had created protectorates in Senegal; the British had seized Egypt in 1882; and the Germans had created protectorates over Togo and the Cameroons in 1884 and added new territories in Tanganyika, Rwanda, and Burundi. While the British took Nigeria, Ghana, and Sierra Leone, the French went on to complete their West African empire in Senegal, Gambia, Sierra Leone, Guinea, and the Ivory Coast and conquered the Sahara as far as Lake Chad. In 1890 Zanzibar became a British protectorate, followed by Kenya and Uganda. Treaties in 1897 among Ethiopia, Britain, France, and Italy regulated the Somali protectorates. The British conquered most of the

Sudan in 1898 and Darfur in 1916. Thus all of Muslim Africa – indeed, all of Africa except Liberia and Ethiopia – came under European rule by World War I.

On the northern reaches of the Muslim world, Russia began its expansion across Inner Asia and Siberia to the Pacific, conquering and absorbing Muslim populations. In the sixteenth century, Russia absorbed the Tatar states in the Volga basin; by the nineteenth century, most of the Kazakh population of the northern steppes was under Russian control. The Russian conquests culminated in the colonization of Transoxania and the Transcaspian regions in the late nineteenth century. At the same time, China established its suzerainty in eastern Turkestan in the eighteenth century and made it a province of China in the late nineteenth. Russia and China took control of most of the Muslim populations of Inner Asia.

Only the Ottoman Empire and Iran maintained their political identity without experiencing direct colonial rule. (See Map 27.)

EUROPEAN IMPERIALISM AND THE BEGINNING OF THE MODERN ERA

By the eighteenth century, the reorganization of the global economy and the consolidation of European commercial and political dominance subverted Muslim societies, weakened Muslim states that depended on commercial revenues, and promoted factional strife and the exploitation of the peasantries. European imperial ascendancy took a cultural as well as a political and economic form. By the nineteenth century, Europe was beginning to seize the imagination of Muslim peoples. The Ottomans, for example, were impressed with European military and technological efficiency and artistic styles. European political – and especially nationalist – concepts and moral values began to influence Muslim populations. These influences opened a new era in the history of Muslim peoples.

As Muslim societies entered the modern era, they would be drastically changed by internal reorganization and by the impact of European imperialism and the world commercial economy. By the late eighteenth century, the Russians, the Dutch, and the British had established territorial suzerainty in parts of the northern steppes of Asia, Southeast Asia, and the Indian subcontinent, and European commercial and diplomatic intervention was well advanced in other regions. In the nineteenth and early twentieth centuries, European states, driven by the need of industrial economies for raw materials and markets, and by economic and political competition with one another, established worldwide territorial empires. The Dutch completed the conquest of Indonesia; the Russians (and the Chinese) absorbed Inner Asia; the British consolidated their empires in India and Malaya and took control of parts of the Middle East, East Africa, Nigeria, and other parts of West Africa. France seized North Africa and much of West Africa, parts of the Middle East, and other territories. Small German and Italian colonies were also founded in Africa. By the beginning of the twentieth century, the European powers (and China) had completed their conquest of almost all of the Muslim world.

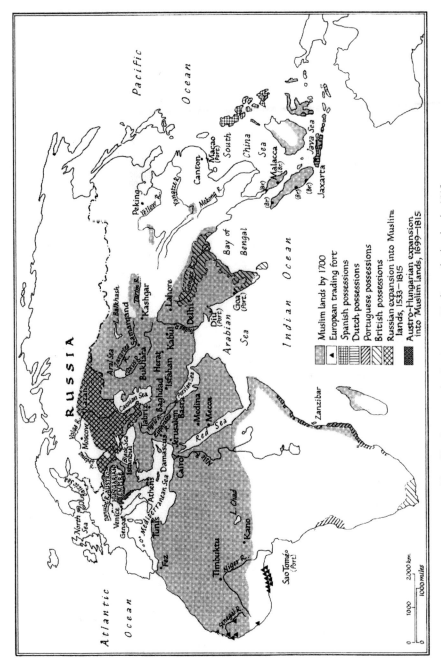

Map 27. European domination over Muslim and other lands, 1815.

Muslim lands by 1700

European trading fort

Spanish possessions

Dutch possessions

Portuguese possessions

British possessions

Russian expansion into Muslim lands, 1533–1815

Austro-Hungarian expansion into Muslim lands, 1699–1815

Atlantic Ocean

Pacific Ocean

Indian Ocean

RUSSIA

AUSTRO-HUNGARIAN EMPIRE

North Sea

Black Sea

Mediterranean Sea

Red Sea

Arabian Sea

Caspian Sea

Aral Sea

Bay of Bengal

South China Sea

Java Sea

Malacca

Macao (Port.)

Canton

Peking

Yellow R.

Yangtze R.

Mekong R.

Jaxarta

Goa (Port.)

Diu (Port.)

Delhi

Lahore

Kabul

Herat

Isfahan

Tehran

Baghdad

Basra

Tabriz

Bukhara

Samarqand

Kashgar

Tarim R.

L. Balkhash

Volga R.

Moscow

Kazan

Istanbul

Athens

Venice

Genoa

Tunis

Fez

Damascus

Jerusalem

Cairo

Mecca

Medina

Persian G.

Nile R.

L. Chad

Kano

Timbuktu

Niger R.

Senegal R.

São Tomé (Port.)

Zanzibar

0   1000   2000 km.

0   1000 miles

655

These conquests were driven by rapid changes within European societies. The Industrial Revolution in Britain in the eighteenth century – and in France, Germany, and other countries in the nineteenth – the development of bureaucratic forms of economic organization, new technologies for the production of steam and electricity, and the expansion of scientific knowledge further enhanced the economic dominance of European countries.

The American and French revolutions brought equally profound changes in the realm of politics and statecraft. They brought into being the modern nation-state built on the relative equality and participation of its citizens, close identification of populations with the state, and a merging of national, political, and cultural identities. They also pioneered the creation of parliamentary institutions that allowed for widespread political representation and state structures that diffused or moderated the exercise of power in the interests of the autonomy of the civil society and the political freedom of individual citizens.

Furthermore, the European and American Enlightenments completed the historical process of secularization. Political and economic institutions were generally differentiated from religious norms. The cultivation of scientific and of humanistic mentalities relegated religion to a narrowed sphere of worship and communal activities. The scientific mentality "disenchanted" and demystified the world of nature and of human relations. Nature, society, and even the human personality became accessible to rational understanding and to the conviction that they could be modified by conscious human intervention.

Throughout the Muslim world, European dominance led to the construction of centralized bureaucratic territorial states. European economic and capitalist penetration usually led to increased and often exploitative trade, stimulated the production of raw materials, and undermined local industries. The European powers forced or induced others to create modern schools, and to promote the values of European civilization, blended as best they could be with indigenous cultures. These changes in non-European societies involved the creation of new patterns of economic production and exchange and new technologies. In turn the new state and economic structures were the bases for the rise of new elites. Political managers, soldiers, technocrats, comprador merchants, intelligentsia, intellectuals, commercial farmers, and industrial workers became important forces in Muslim societies. European influence also stimulated the acceptance of new value systems – an appreciation for national identity and political participation, economic engagement, moral activism, and a new scientific worldview. All of these changes involved the adoption or re-creation of the basic features of European civilization in the matrix of older Islamic societies.

In each case, however, the European impact was different – and these differences, combined with the institutional and cultural variations among the Muslim societies, would generate the various contemporary Islamic societies. Just as each Islamic society was the product of the interaction of a regional society with Middle

Eastern influences, modern Islamic countries are the products of the interaction of the historical Islamic societies with Europe. Because there was no single European model of modern society, and because the impact of Europe was different in every part of the world, the result was a multiplicity of societies. Like the great empires, religions, and civilizations of the past, Europe challenged existing elites, institutions, and cultures and forced them to define their own version of modernity. Modernity engendered plurality because it resulted from the efforts of third world indigenous elites to reconstruct their own societies. Such transformations, of course, were not peculiar to the Muslim world. In the nineteenth and twentieth centuries European influence reached all civilizations, provoked profound changes, and helped shape their contemporary development.

The role of indigenous elites, institutions, and cultures in determining the pattern of development must be emphasized, because of some important differences between Muslim and European societies. In the nineteenth and twentieth centuries European societies were to a considerable extent organized in terms of economically derived social classes. In many European countries, bourgeois elites were the principal forces behind economic development, state organization, and world conquest. Industrial working classes were a principal force in production. Despite the importance of merchant elites, in Muslim societies economically defined social classes were relatively less significant. In these societies, the economy was embedded in and regulated by tribal, communal, associational, and state political structures. State elites – and tribal and religious notables – used political power to control land and trading resources and to extract the surplus product of peasants and other producers.

The impact of Europe on Muslim societies was mediated by the collaboration or resistance of these elites. The changes that took place in Muslim societies were forged in terms of the interests, perceptions, and responses of internal elites to the pressures and incentives generated by European power and by their desire to exploit European influences in the struggle for power within their own societies. Whatever the economic forces that impinged from without, in Muslim countries these elites had primarily a political or cultural orientation and tended to define the problem of European intervention in sociocultural rather than economic terms. In Muslim societies economic influences commonly led to political and cultural responses. Thus, indigenous elites, institutions, and cultural codes were as important to the shape of modernity as were European imperial and economic systems.

The history of the modern transformation of Islamic societies falls into several phases and shows certain common features throughout the Muslim world. The first phase was the period from the late eighteenth to the early twentieth century, marked by the breakup of the Muslim state system and the imposition of European commercial and territorial domination. In this phase Muslim political, religious, and tribal elites attempted to define new ideological and religious approaches to the internal development of their own societies. Out of these responses came a second phase of development, the twentieth-century formation of national states through which the elites of Muslim countries tried to win their independence, to give a modern political identity to their societies and to promote economic development and social change. The phase of national state building began after World War I and persists to the present. The consolidation of independent national states in turn led to the rise of Islamist or Islamic revival movements, struggle over the ultimate role of Islam in these societies, and new conflicts between authoritarian regimes and popular demands for democratic governments.

GLOSSARY

'abd: a slave; property rights in a person, regulated by law and Quranic ethics. In Muslim countries slaves were commonly employed as household servants and soldiers; *see also mamluk*.

adab: habit, upbringing, behavior, refinement of manners, literary cultivation, urbanity; the ideal behavior of a scribe or spiritual cultivation of a Sufi.

adat: in Indonesia and Malaysia, custom or customary law as opposed to Shari'a or Muslim law.

'adl: justice; in law, the quality required to be a legal witness; in religion, the state of personal perfection of one who fulfills God's teaching; in philosophy, the harmony among the faculties of the soul.

agha: Turkish word for elder brother, chief, or master; in Ottoman usage, the title of a high-ranking military official; in Algeria, the head of the janissary corps.

ahl: people who occupy a tent; family or community.

ahl al-bayt: people of the house, family of the Prophet.

ahl al-dhimma: the people of the covenant; Jews, Christians, and others accepted as subjects under Muslim rule and entitled to legal protection in return for payment of taxes; also called *ahl al-kitab*, or people of the book.

ahl al-hadith: partisans of hadith as a principal source of Muslim law and morals; a term for the supporters of the Hanbali school of law.

ahl i-hadith: a community in India and Pakistan that professes to follow only the Quran and hadith as sources of Muslim law and does not accept the traditional schools of law.

akhi: a member of fourteenth-century Anatolian groups of young men who held to the ideals of *futuwwa* (q.v.); generally urban, artisan, and middle class.

akhlaq: ethics; Greek ethics conveyed into Islamic thought by the translation of Aristotle and Galen and incorporated into the writings of Miskawayh, al-Ghazali, and others.

'Alids: descendants of the Prophet's cousin 'Ali; the family that claims to be the heirs of the Prophet's religious and political legacy and the rightful heads of the Muslim community.

'alim (pl. *'ulama'*): a learned man, particularly in Muslim legal and religious studies; occurs in varying forms such as *mallam, mullah*, etc.

amin: trustworthy; title for the holder of an official position such as the head of a guild.

amir: the title of a military commander, governor, or prince; commonly transliterated "emir"; equivalent of the Turkish *bey* or *beg*.

amir al-mu'minin: the commander of the faithful, the proper title of the caliph or successor to the Prophet.

amir al-umara': the supreme commander; title used for the military rulers who took over 'Abbasid government.

amsar: see *misr*.

anjuman: an assembly; refers to religious, educational, and political associations of Muslims, especially in Iran, India, Pakistan, and Turkey.

ansar: "helpers" of Muhammad at Medina; later used as designation for members of Muslim religious and political associations.

'aql: reason, reasoning, intelligence; the rational faculty as opposed to the lower faculties of body and soul.

'asabiyya: the spirit of kinship or faction; the tribal solidarity that enables a small pastoral community to conquer city dwellers and create new empires; the political solidarity of ruling elites.

ashraf: people who trace their lineage to the Prophet or his companions; in India, the noble classes; *see also sharif*.

'ashura': supererogatory fast day on the tenth of Muharram, the first month in the Muslim calendar; commemoration of the martyrdom of Husayn.

atabeg: the tutor of a Saljuq prince, his principal military advisor; later, independent governors.

awqaf: charitable foundations, endowed for religious purposes; *see also waqf*.

a'yan: local notables; in late Ottoman times, holders of officially recognized political power.

ayatollah: a miraculous sign of God, the highest-ranking scholar of law in the Twelver Shi'i religious hierarchy.

'ayyarun: vagabonds; tenth- to twelfth-century urban gangs who subscribed to *futuwwa* (q.v.) ideals and often appeared as military opponents of state regimes.

baba: Turkish for father, old man, Sufi leader.

baqa': survival in God, the divinely granted attribute of the mystic, who experiences the unity of God but returns to the world of daily activity.

baraka: blessing; the divine power emanating from a holy man.

barid: the courier, information, and spy service.

batin: the inner, esoteric meaning of a text.

bay'a: a contract; oath of allegiance recognizing the authority of a caliph.

bayram: *see 'id*.

beg: *see bey*.

bey: a Turkish title for army officer, official, or ruler of a small principality; also transliterated *beg*; *see also amir*.

Bohras: a Muslim community in India, mainly Isma'ilis. Most are merchants but many are Sunnis and peasants.

caliph: *see khalifa*.

da'i: "summoner"; propagandist or missionary for Shi'i movements; usually the lowest-ranking figure in a Shi'i hierarchy.

dar al-harb: the land of war, territory not under Islamic law and subject to conquest by Muslims; contrasts with *dar al-Islam*.

dar al-Islam: the lands in which Islamic law prevails.

dargah: the royal court or residence; shrine and tomb of a Sufi master.

da'wa: the summons to acknowledge religious truth and join a religious community; missionary movement; used in the variant form *da'wah* in Southeast Asia.

da'wah: *see da'wa*.

dawla: a dynasty; by extension, a government or state.

devshirme: an Ottoman levy of Christian youths to be trained as janissaries and court officers.

dhikr: reminding the self; continuous and rhythmic repetition of the name of God, a Sufi form of prayer that varies with the different Sufi orders.

dhimmi: the contract of hospitality and protection for peoples of the revealed religions; *see also ahl al-dhimma*.

dihqan: a landowner, village chief, the local notables of the late Sasanian and early Muslim empires.

diwan: a collection of poetry or prose; a register, the name applied to government bureaus that keep tax, military, and other records.

evliad: used in Inner Asia to refer to the Sufis descended from the Prophet and the early caliphs.

falasifa: wise men, philosophers, the Muslim proponents of Greek philosophy.

fana': in Sufi usage, annihilation of the self, the state that precedes the experience of the unity of God.

faqi: a poverty-stricken mendicant who lives only for God; in East Africa, a scholar of the Quran and Muslim law or a Sufi mystic and magician; *see also Sufi. faqih* (pl. *fuqaba'*): a scholar of Islamic law, jurist; *see also 'alim.*

fata: (pl. *fityan*): a young man, member of a group or gang devoted to the ideals of *futuwwa* (q.v.).

fatawa: *see fatwa.*

fatwa: (pl. *fatawa*): an opinion on Islamic law given by a *mufti* (q.v.); collected legal opinions form a corpus that modifies the application of the early codes of Islamic law.

fay': Muslim communally owned property.

fiqh: understanding, jurisprudence, Islamic religious law.

firman: a command, edict of a ruler.

fitra: the inherent original state of the soul before it is vested in the body.

fityan: *see fata.*

fuqaba': *see faqih.*

futuwwa: virtues or qualities of young men, including bravery and nobility; the ideology of fraternities and young men's street gangs; *see also 'ayyarun, akhi.*

ghadir khumm: a Shi'i day of celebration for Muhammad's adoption of 'Ali as his successor.

ghazal: a love song; an Arabic poetic form that passes with variations into Persian, Turkish, and Urdu poetry.

ghazi: a frontier warrior for the faith.

ghulam: a young male slave in military or palace service; *see also 'abd, mamluk.*

ghulat: Shi'is who hold "extreme" views of the spiritual qualities of the imam.

hadith: a report of the sayings or deeds of the Prophet transmitted by his companions; collections of *hadith* are second in authority to the Quran as a source of Muslim belief and practice.

hajib: a chamberlain, chief of palace administration, and sometimes head of government.

hajj: the annual pilgrimage to Mecca required of every Muslim at least once in his lifetime.

hal: a Sufi term for a spiritual state received by the grace of God; opposed to *maqam*, a station on the way toward mystical union achieved by the Sufi's own effort.

hanif: an Arabian believer in the unity of God before the revelation of Islam.

haqiqa: in Sufism, truth or reality that is experienced through union with God; ultimate reality.

haram: the portion of a house reserved for the women, from which males are excluded.

hijra: the emigration of the Prophet from Mecca to Medina in 622, the base year of the Muslim era.

hikma: the wisdom attained through philosophy, science, or occult knowledge.

hila (pl. *hiyal*): legal stratagem.

hilm: forbearance, moderation, tranquility in the face of passion.

himaya: the commendation or protection given by nomads to settlers, landlords to peasants, or the powerful to the weak, in return for payment; the protection of European consuls for local clients.

hiyal: *see hila*.

hujja: proof; the person through whom God's presence becomes accessible; a rank in the hierarchy of Shi'i missionaries; *see also da'i*.

'ibada (pl. *'ibadat*): obedience to ritual religious practices, including ablutions, prayer, fasting, pilgrimage, and so on.

'ibadat: *see 'ibada*.

'id: the Muslim festivals; *'id al-fitr*, the breaking of the fast of Ramadan, and *'id al-adha*, the sacrificial festival of the tenth of Dhu al-hijja; in Turkish called *bayram*.

ijaza: a certificate given by a teacher to a student certifying his capacity to transmit a particular text.

ijma': the consensus of legal scholars or of the community as a whole; a basis of Muslim law.

ijtihad: "exerting oneself" in Islamic law; reasoning by analogy, free from received opinions, in order to reinterpret Islamic law; *see also mujtahid*.

'ilm: knowledge, especially of religious truths; the knowledge that guides behavior.

iltizam: a form of tax farm in the Ottoman Empire and Egypt.

imam: the supreme leader of the Muslim community; the successor to the Prophet, used commonly by the Shi'is for 'Ali and his descendants.

imama: the legal theory of collective organization.

imambaras: shrines devoted to Hasan and Husayn.

imamzada: a descendant of a Shi'i imam; the shrines of sanctified descendants of 'Ali revered by pilgrims, who believe they have miraculous qualities.

iman: faith, fidelity, belief.

imaret: in Ottoman usage, an endowed complex of religious and charitable facilities, commonly including a place for prayer, a college, a library, and soup kitchens.

insilimen: a term used in the Sahara for religious scholars and venerated holy lineages; *see also zawaya*.

iqta': a grant of the rights to collect taxes from land conceded in return for development or administrative and military service; *see also jagir, timar*.

ishan: an honorific used in Inner Asia as the equivalent of a Sufi *shaykh* or spiritual leader.

islah: reform, purification, and revitalization of the Muslim community based on a return to the first principles of the Quran and hadith; *see also tajdid.*

islam, Islam: submission, unconditional surrender to God, the name of the religion of Muslims, the institutions and cultural style of states and societies formed by the Islamic religion.

Isma'ilis: a branch of the Shi'is who look to the leadership of Isma'il, a son of Ja'far, and his descendants; this branch includes the Fatimids; later divided into several branches, including the Nizariya, who spread from Syria and Iran into India; subcommunities include the Khojas, Bohras, and others.

isnad: a chain of authorities, the series of transmitters of *hadith* (q.v.) whose names guarantee their validity.

isra'iliyyat: narratives in the Quran and Arabic literature derived from Jewish sources.

ithna 'ashari: the branch of the Shi'is who believe in the twelve imams descended from 'Ali, the last of whom disappeared and went into hiding in 873 and will return as the messiah; the branch of Shi'ism to which the majority of the populace of Iran adheres.

jagir: an assignment of revenues in Mughal India in lieu of payment of salary; *see also iqta', timar.*

jama'a (pl. *jama'at*): a meeting, assembly, the community of believers, the *umma* (q.v.).

jamathandi: a collectivity or small community; used especially of the Shi'i sects.

jami': a mosque for Friday prayers.

janissary: a member of the Ottoman infantry corps, the elite regiments of the Ottoman regime.

jihad: striving; effort directed toward inner religious perfection and toward holy war of the Muslims against the infidels.

jinn: spirit beings, composed of vapors or flames, who are imperceptible but malevolent influences.

jizya: the poll tax levied on non-Muslims in a Muslim-ruled society.

Ka'ba: the central sanctuary of Islam, located in Mecca; the principal object of the *hajj.*

kafir: an unbeliever, one who is ungrateful to God for his gifts.

kalam: theology, the subject that attempts to give rational proofs for religious beliefs; deals with such problems as the divine unity, attributes, human free will, and self-determination.

kanun: state-promulgated administrative regulations or codes of law, usually dealing with financial and criminal matters; in contemporary usage, all codes of law promulgated by governments.

karamoko: a West African title for scholar and teacher; *see also 'alim.*

kash: economic gain; in theology, the technical term for acquisition of responsibility and of reward or punishment for good or bad deeds.

kashf: lifting of the veils, the realization or vision of God as ultimate reality.

khalifa: the successor of the Prophet and head of the Muslim community; the caliph; in Sufism, the disciple of the master authorized to transmit prayers, initiate new members, and act as a deputy or head of the Sufi order.

khan: a Turkish title, originally the ruler of state but then applied to subordinate chiefs and nobles; also a caravansary.

khanaqa: a building for Sufi activities where the *shaykh* may live, instruct his disciples, and carry on Sufi worship; *see also ribat, tekke, zawiya.*

kharaj: the tax on land.

Kharijism: early religio-political movements whose followers held that the caliph should be elected by the community.

kharja: *see muwashshah.*

khatam: the keeper of the seal.

khatib: the official preacher who presents the Friday sermon; in principle, the representative of the ruler.

khirqa: the patched cloak worn by Sufis and passed from master to initiate as a symbol of the communication of the blessings inherited from the Prophet.

Khojas: a sect of Nizari Isma'ilis in India.

khutba: the Friday sermon.

khwaja: a title variously used by merchants, scholars, and officials; in modern Turkish, *hoja*, a professional man of religion.

kiyayi: the Indonesian term for *'ulama'*, the scholars and teachers of Islam.

madhahib: *see madhhab. madhhab* (pl. *madhahib*): a Muslim school of law; the four principal schools are the Hanafi, Maliki, Shafi'i, and Hanbali schools.

madrasa: a college whose primary function is the teaching of law and related religious subjects.

mahalla: a town quarter.

Mahdi: the "guided" one; the person who will appear on the last day and establish Islam and the reign of justice.

mahr: in Muslim law, the gift that the bridegroom gives the bride, which becomes her personal property.

majlis: a gathering, assembly, or council.

makhzan: the Moroccan central government administration; royal court, army, and provincial officials.

maktab: an elementary school for teaching children recitation of the Quran and the basics of reading and writing.

mallam: the term used in West Africa for a religious scholar; *see also 'alim.*

mamluk: a slave or freedman in military service.

maqam: a station on the Sufi path to unity with God acquired by the Sufi's own efforts.

maqsura: the enclosed space in the mosque reserved for the ruler.

marja'-i taqlid: the source of imitation; in Iran, just and learned scholars of law qualified to give authoritative legal opinions; the common people are obliged to accept them as absolute religious authorities.

masjid: a mosque or place of prostration and prayer; a center for Muslim communal affairs.

masnavi: an epic poem in Persian and related literatures.

ma'sum: a person who possesses infallibility, freedom from committing sins.

mawali: see *mawla*. *mawla* (pl. *mawali*): a client or freedman, servant; the word also applies to the patron or master.

mawlid: the celebration of the birth of the Prophet; also applies to celebrations at saints' shrines.

mazalim: a royal administrative court for the adjudication of governmental problems, to which subjects could bring petitions or appeals.

mihna: an inquisition, in particular the inquisition of the Caliph al-Ma'mun.

mihrab: the ornamented niche in the wall of a mosque that indicates the direction of prayer.

millet: religion or religious communities; in contemporary usage, nation.

minaret: the tower of a mosque from which the call to prayer is proclaimed.

minbar: the high seat or chair in a mosque from which the preacher delivers the sermon.

mi'raj: the ascent of the Prophet to heaven in Jerusalem after the miraculous night journey from Medina.

mirs: the descendants of the Prophet.

misr (pl. *amsar*): the military camps and garrisons constructed in the early Islamic conquests; administrative capitals for the conquered provinces.

mobad: a Zoroastrian clergyman.

mu'amalat: Muslim laws pertaining to social relations.

mufti: an expert in Muslim law qualified to give authoritative legal opinions.

muhajirun: the emigrants who accompanied the Prophet on the *hijra* (q.v.) from Mecca to Medina.

muhtasib: an official who supervises fair market practices and public morals.

mujaddid: "the renewer"; the scholar or holy man who comes once every century to restore the true knowledge and practice of Islam.

mujtahid: a person qualified to exercise *ijtihad* (q.v.) and give authoritative opinions on Islamic law.

mullah: a learned man; often used in the Indian subcontinent; the equivalent of *'alim* (q.v.).

muqarnas: the stalactite decoration of ceilings.

murshid: a guide; a Sufi master and teacher; *see also Sufi*.

muwashshah: a love poem; a form of Arabic verse popular in Spain, commonly ending in a *kharja*, or refrain of Romance origin.

nafs: the soul; the animal faculties as opposed to the rational or angelic faculties.

naqib: a syndic or headman.

naqib al-ashraf: the syndic or headman of the groups of descendants of the Prophet found in many Muslim countries.

nasiha: faithful advice to a ruler; exhortation to do good.

nass: in Shi'i usage, the explicit designation of a successor to the imamate, which confers on him knowledge and power appropriate to the office.

niya: intention, the necessary state of mind for the validity of religious actions.

padishah: a nineteenth-century title for the Ottoman sultans.

pançasila: the five principles of Indonesian independence.

penghulu: a headman, used in Indonesia as a title of a village administrator.

pesantren: in Indonesia, a school or seminary for Muslim students.

pir: a title for a Sufi *shaykh*.

pirzada: the descendant of a *pir* or saint, or the manager of his tomb.

priyayi: the governing and scribal class; the elite of pre-modern Indonesian society.

qadi: a judge; the caliph's designated representative to adjudicate disputes on the basis of Islamic law.

qa'id: a tribal, district, or military chief; a term widely used in North Africa.

qalb: in Sufism, the heart, the soul, the seat of conscience and knowledge.

qanat: an underground irrigation canal, commonly used in Iran.

qasaba: a fortified castle, residence of government officials; a chief town; in India, *qashah*.

qashah: see *qasaba*.

qasida: the classical Arabic ode that often eulogizes the tribe of the poet or a great man; the Persian *qasida* is a lyric poem.

qawm: lineage, tribe, religious community, nation.

qibla: the direction of the *Ka'ba* (q.v.) in Mecca, which Muslims face during prayers.

Quran: Muslim scripture, the book containing the revelations of God to Muhammad.

qurra': Quran reciters, similar to the public poetry reciters.

quth: the pivot around which something revolves; the head of the invisible hierarchy of saints on whom the order of the universe depends.

ra'is (pl. *ru'asa'*): a person of high rank, a headman or chief.

Ramadan: the ninth month of the Muslim calendar, the month of annual fasting.

Rashidun: the rightly guided; a title applied to the first four caliphs.

ra'y: legal opinions and the reasoning used to derive them.

ribat: a frontier fortress and residence for Muslim warriors and mystics.

ru'asa': see *ra'is*.

ruh: the soul, sometimes the equivalent of *qalb* (q.v.).

rustaq: an administrative district comprising a town and subordinate villages.

sabr: steadfastness, patience, endurance in fulfillment of religious obligations.

sadaqa: voluntary alms, sometimes a synonym for *zakat* (q.v.).

sajjada nishin: "one who sits on the prayer carpet"; the successor to the leadership of a *khanaqa* (q.v.) or the custodian of a Sufi shrine.

salah: Muslim ritual prayer performed five times daily; in Persian called *namaz*.

sama': Sufi musical session intended to inculcate states of ecstasy.

santri: in Indonesia, a student of Islam; a devout and correct Muslim.

sarkin: a Hausa title for headman, ruler.

sawafi: the crown estates seized by the Umayyad dynasty from former Sasanian royal and noble landowners.

sayyid: a prince, lord, chief; a descendant of Husayn, the son of 'Ali.

shahada: "witnessing"; the Muslim profession of faith.

Shah-en-shah: the king of kings; a Persian title of the emperor.

shahid: a witness, martyr.

Shari'a: the path to be followed; Muslim law, the totality of the Islamic way of life.

sharif (pl. *ashraf* or *shurafa'*): a noble; a descendant of the Prophet.

shaykh: an elder, head, chief, respected man of religion, Sufi leader, teacher.

shaykh al-Islam: a chief jurisconsult or *mufti* (q.v.); the head of the religious establishment in the Ottoman Empire.

Shi'is: the group of Muslims who regard 'Ali and his heirs as the only legitimate successors to the Prophet, divided into sects according to allegiance to different lines of 'Alid descent.

shirk: polytheism, associating other beings with God, the ultimate blasphemy.

shura: a council; specifically the council established by the Caliph 'Umar to choose his successor.

shurafa': see *sharif*.

shurta: the governor's police.

silsila: the sequence of Sufi masters reaching back to the Prophet through whom a particular Sufi acquires his knowledge.

sipahi: a cavalry soldier in the Ottoman Empire; appears in India as *sepoy*.

sira: biographical narratives of the Prophet.

Sufi: a Muslim mystic; named after the early ascetics who wore garments of coarse wool; *see also ishan, murshid, pir, shaykh*.

sultan: "power," authority; the title of a Muslim monarch.

sunna: "the trodden path," custom; the practice of the Prophet and the early community, which becomes for all Muslims an authoritative example of the correct way to live a Muslim life.

Sunnis: those who accept the *sunna* (q.v.) and the historical succession of caliphs, as opposed to the *'Alids* (q.v.); the majority of the Muslim community.

sura: a group of Quranic verses collected in a single chapter.

tafsir: commentary and interpretation, the exegesis of the Quran.

tajdid: renewal; applied to the post-eighteenth-century movement to revive the true practice of Islam based on the Quran and hadith; *see also islah*.

talakawata: a Hausa term for the peasants and working poor.

talji'a: commendation; *see also himaya*.

Tanzimat: reorganization; the name for the Ottoman reforms of the nineteenth century.

taqlid: "imitation"; the principle of following the established doctrines of the Muslim schools of law; the opposite of *ijtihad* (q.v.).

tariqa: a way, the Sufi path; the system of beliefs and training transmitted by particular schools of Sufis; a brotherhood of Sufis.

tasdiq: faith, affirmation of the truth of God's existence.

tawakkul: trust in God.

tawba: repentance, turning to God.

tawhid: unity, the oneness of God's being and the unity of the mystic with the divine being.

ta'wil: allegorical exegesis of the Quran.

ta'ziya: the lamentation for a martyr; the mourning for Husayn displayed in processions and mystery plays in the month of Muharram; also refers to models of Husayn's tomb at Karbala kept in *imamzadas* (q.v.).

tekke: the Turkish name for a Sufi residence; *see also khanaqa*.

timar: the Turkish and Ottoman term for a grant of tax revenues to support a military retainer of the sultan.

tyeddo: the name of the warrior slave elite in Senegambia.

'ulama': the collective term for the scholars, especially scholars of law, or learned men of Islam; *see also 'alim*.

uleebalang: an intermediary administrative official in the Malayan sultanates.

umma: people or community; the whole of the brotherhood of Muslims.

'ushr: the tenth of the produce levied on Muslim-owned lands.

uymaq: in Iran and Inner Asia, a chieftaincy under the authority of a headman supported by military retainers and allied lineages.

wahdat al-shuhud: unity of witness.

wahdat al-wujud: unity of being, existential monism.

wali: a protector, a benefactor, a companion, a governor; a friend of God, a saint or a Sufi whose tomb is visited for its blessing; the legal guardian of a minor, woman, or incapacitated person.

waqf (pl. *awqaf*): an endowment; an irrevocable grant of the income of property set aside in perpetuity for a religious or charitable purpose.

watan: country, motherland.

wazir: "a helper"; the chief secretary of a ruler; head of the bureaucracy; prime minister.

wilayat: a legal competence; power delegated to a governor or *wali* (q.v.); in Ottoman usage, a term for an administrative district.

wird: a litany or patterned devotion chanted by Sufis.

yasa: Mongol law.

zahir: the external, literal meaning of a text, as opposed to *batin* (q.v.), its inner significance.

zakat: a legal alms tax raised from Muslims.

zamindar: landowner; under the Mughals, a person with a right to collect revenues from the land.

zanadiqa: people who held dualistic or other heretical beliefs.

zawaya: Berber North African religious lineages.

zawiya: a building that functions as a Sufi residence, place of prayer, school, and the tomb of a saint; *see also khanaqa*.

ziyara: a visit to the tomb of a saint or holy man to pray for intercession before God.

BIBLIOGRAPHY

Surveys of Islamic History

J. Berkey, *The Formation of Islam*, Cambridge, 2003; M. G. S. Hodgson, *The Venture of Islam*, v. 1–3, Chicago, 1974.

CHAPTER 1. MIDDLE EASTERN SOCIETIES BEFORE ISLAM

A. General and Interpretive Works on Late Antiquity

G. W. Bowersock, *Hellenism in Late Antiquity*, Ann Arbor, MI, 1990; G. W. Bowersock, P. Brown, and O. Grabar, eds., *Interpreting Late Antiquity: Essays on the Postclassical World*, Cambridge, MA, 2001; G. W. Bowersock, *Mosaics as History: The Near East from Late Antiquity to Islam*, Cambridge, MA, 2006; P. Brown, *The Rise of Western Civilization*, Oxford, 2003; and the classic, P. Brown, *The World of Late Antiquity*, London, 1971; B. Dignas and E. Winter, *Rome and Persia in Late Antiquity*, Cambridge, 2007; J. Howard-Johnson, *The Two Great Powers in Late Antiquity: A Comparison, East Rome, Sasanian Persia and the End of Antiquity*, Burlington, VT, 2006, pp. 158–226; S. F. Johnson, *Greek Literature in Late Antiquity*, Ashgate, Burlington, VT, 2006; T. Sizgorich, *Violence and Belief in Late Antiquity*, Philadelphia, 2009.

B. The Roman and Byzantine Empires

A. Cameron, *Changing Cultures in Early Byzantium*, Brookfield, VT, 1996; G. Fowden, *Empire to Commonwealth*, Princeton, NJ, 1993; D. Gutas, "Language and Imperial Ideology in Late Antiquity and Early Islam," W. M. Bloomer, ed., *The Contest of Language*, Notre Dame, IN, 2005, pp. 99–110; J. F. Haldon, *Byzantium in the Seventh Century*, Cambridge, 1990; P. Sarris, *Economy and Society in the Age of Justinian*, Cambridge, 2006; M. Whitby, "The Role of the Emperor," D. M. Gwynn, ed., *A.H.M. Jones and the Later Roman Empire*, Leiden, 2008, pp. 65–96.

C. Persian Empires and Societies

P. Christensen, *The Decline of Iranshahr*, Copenhagen, 1993; V. S. Curtis and S. Stewart, eds., *The Sasanian Era: The Idea of Iran, III*, London, 2008; P. O. Harper, *In Search of a Cultural Identity: Monuments and Artifacts of the Sasanian Near East, 3rd to 7th century A.D.*, New York, 2006; M. Morony, *Encyclopedia of Islam, Sasanids*, Leiden, 1960–2006; J. Neusner, *Israel and Iran in Talmudic Times*, New York, 1986; P. Pourshariati, *Decline and Fall of the Sasanian Empire*, London, 2008; S. Shaked, *Dualism in Transformation: Varieties of Religion in Sasanian Iran*, London, 1994.

D. Women and Family

J. Z. Abrams, *The Women of the Talmud*, Northvale, NJ, 1995; M. Alexandre, "Early Christian Women," G. Duby and M. Perrot, eds., *A History of Women in the West: From Ancient Goddesses to Christian Saints*, Cambridge, 1992, pp. 409–444; M. Brosius, *Women in Ancient Persia, 559–331 BC*, Oxford, 1996; M. J. Broyde, "Jewish Law and the Abandonment of Marriage: Diverse Models of Sexuality and Reproduction in the Jewish View, and the Return to Monogamy in the Modern Era," M. Broyde, ed., *Marriage, Sex, and Family in Judaism*, Oxford, 2005, pp. 88–115; J. E. Grubbs, *Law and Family in Late Antiquity: The Emperor Constantine's Marriage Legislation*, Oxford, 1999; J. E. Grubbs, "'Pagan' and 'Christian' Marriage: The State of the Question," E. Ferguson, ed., *Recent Studies in Early Christianity*, New York, 1999, pp. 185–237; C. Leduc, "Marriage in Ancient Greece," G. Duby and M. Perrot, eds., *A History of Women in the West: From Ancient Goddesses to Christian Saints*, Cambridge, 1992, pp. 235–294; D. L. Lieber, B. Schereschewsky, and M. Drori, "Divorce," M. Berenbaum and F. Skolnik, eds., *Encyclopaedia Judaica, v. 5*, Detroit, 2007, pp. 710–721; Y. Thomas, "The Division of the Sexes in Roman Law," G. Duby and M. Perrot, eds., *A History of Women in the West, v. I*, Cambridge, 1992, pp. 83–138; H. J. Wolff, *Written and Unwritten Marriages in Hellenistic and Post-Classical Roman Law, Philological Monographs, IX*, Haverford, PA, 1939.

CHAPTER 2. HISTORIANS AND THE SOURCES

A. The Radical Skeptics

P. Crone and M. Cook, *Hagarism: The Making of the Islamic World*, Cambridge, England, 1977; G. W. Hawting, *The Idea of Idolatry and the emergence of Islam*, Cambridge, 1999; G. Luling, *A Challenge to Islam for Reformation*, Delhi, 2003; C. Luxenberg, *The Syro-Aramaic Reading of the Koran*, Berlin, 2007; J. Wansbrough, *The Sectarian Milieu*, Amherst, NY, 2006.

B. Efforts at Reconstruction

J. Bacharach, I. C. Lawrence, and P. Crone, eds., *Studies in Early Islamic History, Studies in Late Antiquity and Early Islam 4*, Princeton, NJ, 1996; F. M. Donner,

"From Believers to Muslims," *Al-Abhath*, 50–51 (2002–3), pp. 9–53; F. M. Donner, *Narratives of Islamic Origins, Studies in Late Antiquity and Early Islam*, Princeton, NJ, 1998; A. Elad, "Community of Believers of 'Holy Men' and 'Saints' or Community of Muslims? The Rise and Development of Early Muslim Historiography," *Journal of Semitic Studies*, XLVII (2002), pp. 241–308; R. G. Hoyland, "History, Fiction and Authorship in the First Centuries of Islam," J. Bray, ed., *Writing and Representation in Medieval History: Muslim Horizons*, London, 2006, pp. 16–46; R. S. Humphreys, *Islamic History: A Framework for Inquiry*, revised edition, Princeton, NJ, 1991.

CHAPTER 3. ARABIA

R. Hoyland, *Arabia and the Arabs: From the Bronze Age to the Coming of Islam*, London and New York, 2001; R. Hoyland, "Epigraphy and the Emergence of Arab Identity," P. M. Sijpesteijn et al., eds., *From al-Andalus to Khurasan*, Leiden, 2007, pp. 219–242; J. W. Jandora, "The Rise of Mecca: Geopolitical Factors," *Muslim World*, 85 (1995), pp. 333–344; M. J. Kister, *Society and Religion from Jahiliyya to Islam*, Aldershot, 1990; M. Lecker, *Jews and Arabs in Pre- and Early Islamic Arabia*, Aldershot and Brookfield, VT, 1998; M. Lecker, *Muslims, Jews, and Pagans: Studies in Early Islamic Medina*, Leiden, 1995; M. Lecker, *People, Tribes and Society in Arabia Around the Time of Muhammad*, Aldershot and Brookfield, VT, 2005; M. G. Morony, "The Late Sasanian Economic Impact on the Arabian Peninsula," *International Journal of Ancient Iranian Studies*, 1 (2001–2), pp. 25–38; F. E. Peters, ed., *The Arabs and Arabia on the Eve of Islam*, Aldershot and Brookfield, VT, 1998; I. Shahid, "Islam and Oriens Christianus: Makka 610–622 AD," E. Grypeou, M. Swanson, and D. Thomas, eds., *The Encounter of Eastern Christianity with Early Islam*, Leiden, 2006, pp. 9–33.

CHAPTER 4. MUHAMMAD: PREACHING, COMMUNITY, AND STATE FORMATION

A. The Biography of the Prophet

J. Horovitz and L. I. Conrad, ed., *The Earliest Biographies of the Prophet and Their Authors*, Princeton, NJ, 2002; R. Hoyland, "New Documentary Texts and the Early Islamic State," *Bulletin of the School of Oriental and African Studies*, 69 (2006), pp. 395–416; R. Hoyland, "Writing the Biography of the Prophet Muhammad: Problems and Solutions," *History Compass*, 5 (2007), pp. 581–602; M. Lecker, *The "Constitution of Medina": Muhammad's First Legal Document, Studies in Late Antiquity and Early Islam*, Princeton, NJ, 2004; H. Motzki, ed., *The Biography of Muhammad: The Issue of the Sources*, Leiden, 2000; F. E. Peters, *Muhammad and the Origins of Islam*, Albany, NY, 1994; U. Rubin, *The Eye of the Beholder: The Life of Muhammad as Viewed by the Early Muslims*, Princeton, NJ, 1995; U. Rubin, *The Life of Muhammad*, Brookfield, VT, 1998.

B. The Quran

The best overview is J. D. McAuliffe, *The Cambridge Companion to the Qur'an*, Cambridge, 2006. Also important are M. Bernards, "Canonization in Early Islam: Reception of the 'Uthmanic Codex in the Arabic Linguistic Tradition," W. J. Van Bekkum and P. M. Cobb, eds., *Strategies of Medieval Communal Identity: Judaism, Christianity and Islam*, Leuven, 2004, pp. 29–46; Y. Dutton, "An Early Mushaf According to the Reading of Ibn 'Amir," *Journal of Quranic Studies*, 3 (2001), pp. 71–89; Y. Dutton, "An Umayyad Fragment of the Qur'an and Its Dating, *Journal of Qur'anic Studies*, 9 (2007), pp. 57–87; J. E. Fossum, "The Apostle Concept in the Qur'an and Pre-Islamic Near Eastern Literature," M. Mir and J. Fossum, eds., *Literary Heritage of Classical Islam: Arabic and Islamic Studies in Honor of James A. Bellamy*, Princeton, NJ, 1993, pp. 149–167; C. Gilliot, "The Beginnings of Qur'anic Exegesis," A. Rippin, ed., *The Qur'an: Formative Interpretation*, Brookfield, VT, 1999, pp. 1–27; C. Gilliot, "Une reconstruction critique de Coran ou comment en finir avec les merveilles de la lampe d'Aladin," M. S. Kropp, ed., *Results of Contemporary Research on the Qur'an*, Beirut, 2007, pp. 33–137; C. Melchert, "Ibn Mujahid and the Establishment of Seven Qur'anic Readings," *Studia Islamica*, 91 (2000), pp. 5–22; A. Neuwirth, "Qur'an and History: A Disputed Relationship," *Journal of Quranic Studies*, 5 (2003), pp. 1–18; A. Neuwirth, "Structure and the Emergence of Community," A. Rippin, ed., *The Blackwell Companion to the Qur'an*, Oxford, 2006, pp. 140–158; M. E. Pregill, "The Hebrew Bible and the Quran: The Problem of the Jewish "Influence" on Islam," *Religion Compass*, 2007, pp. 643–659; G. S. Reynolds, *The Qur'an in Its Historical Context*, London, 2008; A. Rippin, ed., *The Blackwell Companion to the Qur'an*, Oxford, 2006; A. Rippin, "Literary Analysis of Qur'an, Tafsir and Sira: The Methodologies of John Wansbrough," A. Rippin, *The Qur'an and Its Interpretive Tradition*, Burlington, VT, 2001, pp. 151–163; A. Rippin, *The Qur'an: Formative Interpretation*, Brookfield, VT, 1999; W. A. Saleh, *The Formation of the Classical Tafsir Tradition: The Qur'an Commentary of al-Tha'labi (d. 427/1035)*, Leiden, 2004; I. Warraq, *The Origins of the Koran*, Amherst, NY, 1998.

CHAPTERS 5 AND 6. INTRODUCTION TO THE ARAB-MUSLIM EMPIRES; THE ARAB-MUSLIM CONQUESTS AND THE SOCIOECONOMIC BASES OF EMPIRE

A. Afsaruddin, *The First Muslims: History and Memory*, Oxford, 2008; H. Kennedy, *The Great Arab Conquests*, Philadelphia, 2007; M. G. Morony, "Social Elites in Iraq and Iran: After the Conquest," J. Haldon and L. I. Conrad, eds., *The Byzantine and Early Islamic Near East*, Princeton, NJ, 2004, pp. 275–284; P. Sijpesteijn, "The Arab Conquest of Egypt and the Beginning of Muslim Rule," R. S. Bagnall, ed., *Byzantine Egypt*, Cambridge, 2007, pp. 437–459; P. Sijpesteijn, "The Archival Mind in Early Islamic Egypt," P. M. Sijpesteijn et al., eds., *From al-Andalus to Khurasan*, Leiden,

2007, pp. 163–186; R. Stroumsa, "Peoples and Identities in Nessana," Dissertation, Duke University, 2008; C. Wickham, "The Mediterranean around 800: On the Brink of the Second Trade Cycle," *Dumbarton Oaks Papers*, 58 (2004), pp. 161–174.

CHAPTER 7. REGIONAL DEVELOPMENTS: ECONOMIC AND SOCIAL CHANGE

A. Economy
G. Frantz-Murphy, "A New Interpretation of the Economic History of Medieval Egypt: The Textile Industry," M. G. Morony, ed., *Manufacturing and Labour*, Burlington, VT, 2003, pp. 119–142; G. R. D. King and A. Cameron, eds., *The Byzantine and Early Islamic Near East: Land Use and Settlement Patterns*, Princeton, NJ, 1994; M. G. Morony, ed., *Manufacturing and Labour*, Burlington, VT, 2003; P. M. Sijpesteijn et al., eds., *From al-Andalus to Khurasan*, Leiden, 2007, pp. 201–215; A. Watson, "The Arab Agricultural Revolution and Its Diffusion, 700–1100," *Journal of Economic History*, 34 (1974), pp. 29–58.

B. Conversions
R. W. Bulliet, "Conversion Based Patronage and Onomastic Evidence in Early Islam," M. Bernards and J. Nawas, eds., *Patronate and Patronage in Early and Classical Islam*, Leiden, 2005, pp. 246–262; M. Gervers and R. J. Bikhazi, eds., *Conversion and Continuity: Indigenous Christian Communities in Islamic Lands*, Toronto, 1990, pp. 1–14; N. Levtzion, *Islam in Africa and the Middle East: Studies on Conversion and Renewal*, Burlington, VT, 2007.

C. Arabic and Other Languages
M. Bernards, "The Contribution of the Mawali to the Arabic Linguistic Tradition," M. Bernards and J. Nawas, eds., *Patronate and Patronage in Early and Classical Islam*, Leiden, 2005, pp. 426–453; J. C. Robin, "La reforme de l'écriture Arabe a l'époque du califat medinois," *Les Mélanges de l'Université Saint-Joseph*, 59 (2006), pp. 319–364.

CHAPTER 8. THE CALIPHATE TO 750

A. History and Historiography: The First Hundred Years
R. Firestone, *Jihad: The Origin of Holy War in Islam*, Oxford, 1999; C. Foss, "The Near Eastern Countryside in Late Antiquity: A Review Article," *The Roman and Byzantine Near East: Some Recent Archaeological Research*, Ann Arbor, MI, 1995, pp. 213–234; G. Fox, *A Gift for the Sultan*, Torre del Rayo, 2010; J. Johns, "Archaeology and the History of Early Islam: The First Seventy Years," *Journal of Economic and Social History of the Orient*, 46 (2003), pp. 411–436; H. Kennedy, "The Decline and Fall of the First Muslim Empire," *Der Islam*, 81 (2004), pp. 3–30; H. Kennedy, "Elite Incomes in the Long Eighth Century," J. Haldon and L. I. Conrad, eds., *The*

Byzantine and Early Islamic Near East, Princeton, NJ, 2004, pp. 13–28; Y. Masarwa, "Early Islamic Military Architecture: The Birth of Ribats on the Palestinian Coast," *Al-'Usur al-Wusta*, 19 (2007), pp. 36–42; M. G. Morony, "Economic Boundaries? Late Antiquity and Early Islam," *Journal of the Economic and Social History of the Orient*, 47 (2004), pp. 166–194; S. A. Mourad, *Early Islam between Myth and History*, Leiden, 2006; T. Sizgorich, "Narrative and Community in Late Islamic Antiquity," *Past and Present*, 185 (2004), pp. 9–42.

B. Umayyad Administration
I. Bligh-Abramski, "The Judiciary (Qadis) as a Governmental-Administrative Tool in Early Islam," *Journal of Economic and Social History of the Orient*, 35 (1992), pp. 40–71; P. Crone, "Were the Qays and the Yemen of the Umayyad Period Political Parties," *Der Islam*, 71 (1994), pp. 95–111; G. R. Hawting, *The First Dynasty of Islam: The Umayyad Caliphate*, 2nd edition, London and New York, 1986; H. Kennedy, *The Armies of the Caliphs: Military and Society in the Early Islamic State*, London and New York, 2001; H. Kennedy, *The Byzantine and Early Islamic Near East*, Burlington, VT, 2006; W. Madelung, *The Succession to Muhammad: A Study of the Early Caliphate*, Cambridge, 1997; W. al-Qadi, "Population Census and Land Surveys under the Umayyds (41–132/661–750)," *Der Islam*, 83 (2008), pp. 341–416; C. F. Robinson, *'Abd al-Malik*, Oxford, 2005; C. F. Robinson, *Empire and Elites after the Muslim Conquest: The Transformation of Northern Mesopotamia*, Cambridge, 2000.

CHAPTER 9. THE 'ABBASID EMPIRE

A. 'Abbasid Revolution
S. S. Agha, *The Revolution Which Toppled the Umayyads: Neither Arab nor 'Abbasid*, Leiden, 2003; F. Amabe, *The Emergence of the 'Abbasid Autocracy: The 'Abbasid Army, Khurasan and Adharbayjan*, Kyoto, 1995; M. L. Bates, "Khurasani Revolutionaries and al-Mahdi's Title," F. Daftary and J. W. Meri, eds., *Culture and Memory in Medieval Islam*, London, 2003, pp. 279–317; K. A. Blankinship, *The End of the Jihad State: The Reign of Hisham Ibn Abd al-Malik and the Collapse of the Umayyads*, Albany, NY, 1994; E. L. Daniel, "The 'Ahl al-Taqadum' and the Problem of the Constituency of the Abbasid Revolution in the Merv Oasis," *Journal of Islamic Studies*, 7 (1996), pp. 150–179; E. L. Daniel, *The Political and Social History of Khurasan under Abbasid Rule 747–820*, Minneapolis, 1979; A. Elad, "The Ethnic Composition of the 'Abbasid Revolution: A Reevaluation of Some Recent Research," *Jerusalem Studies in Arabic and Islam*, 24 (2000), pp. 246–326.

B. 'Abbasid-Era Society
M. Bernards and J. Nawas, *Patronate and Patronage in Early and Classical Islam*, Leiden, 2005; I. Bligh-Abramski, "Evolution versus Revolution: Umayyad Elements

in the ʿAbbasid Regime, 133/750–320/932," *Der Islam*, 26 (1988), pp. 226–243; J. K. Choksy, *Conflict and Cooperation: Zoroastrian Subalterns and Muslim Elites in Medieval Iranian Society*, New York, 1997; A. Elad, "Mawali in the Composition of al-Maʾmun's Army," M. Bernards and J. Nawas, eds., *Patronate and Patronage in Early and Classical Islam*, Leiden, 2005, pp. 278–325; H. Kennedy, *The Court of the Caliphs*, London, 2004; W. Madelung, *Religious Trends in Early Islamic Iran*, Albany, NY, 1988; U. Mitter, "Origin and Development of the Islamic Patronate," M. Bernards and J. Nawas, eds., *Patronate and Patronage in Early and Classical Islam*, Leiden, 2005, pp. 70–133; S. Sabari, *Mouvements populaires à Bagdad à l'époque ʿAbbaside IX–XI siècles*, Paris, 1981; A. Silverstein, "A Neglected Chapter in the History of Caliphal State Building," *Jerusalem Studies in Arabic and Islam*, 30 (2005), pp. 293–317; J. P. Turner, "The Abna' al-Dawla: The Definition and Legitimation of Identity in Response to the Fourth Fitna," *Journal of the American Oriental Society*, 124 (2004), pp. 1–22; M. Q. Zakari, *Sasanid Soldiers in Early Muslim Society*, Wiesbaden, 1995.

C. ʿAbbasid Politics and Government

P. M. Cobb, *White Banners: Contention in ʿAbbasid Syria, 750–880*, Albany, NY, 2001; T. El-Hibri, *Reinterpreting Islamic Historiography: Harun al-Rashid and the Narrative of the ʿAbbasid Caliphate*, Cambridge, 1999; A. al-Hasan, "The Financial Reforms of the Caliph al-Muʾtadid (892–901)," *Journal of Islamic Studies*, 18 (2007), pp. 1–13.

CHAPTER 12. THE IDEOLOGY OF IMPERIAL ISLAM

A. General Works on Political Theory

A. Al-Azmeh, *Muslim Kingship: Power and the Sacred in Muslim, Christian, and Pagan Politics*, London, 1997; A. Black, *The History of Islamic Political Thought: From the Prophet to the Present*, New York, 2001; P. Crone and M. Hinds, *God's Caliph*, Cambridge, 1986; P. Crone, *God's Rule: Government and Islam*, New York, 2004; M. Q. Zaman, *Religion and Politics Under the Early ʿAbbasids: The Emergence of the Proto-Sunni Elite*, Leiden, 1997.

B. Islamic Art: Surveys

W. Ali, *The Arab Contribution to Islamic Art*, Cairo, 1999; J. Bloom and S. Blair, *The Grove Encyclopedia of Islamic Art and Architecture*, Oxford and New York, 2009; J. Bloom, S. Blair, and R. Ettinghausen, *The Art and Architecture of Islam, 1250–1800*, New Haven, CT, 1994; J. Bloom and S. Blair, *Images of Paradise in Islamic Art*, Hanover, NH, 1991; J. Bloom and S. Blair, *Islam: A Thousand Years of Faith and Power*, New Haven, CT, and London, 2002; R. Ettinghausen, O. Grabar, and M. Jenkins-Madina, *Islamic Art and Architecture, 650–1250*, New Haven, CT, 2001.

C. *Umayyad Art and Architecture*

A. Elad, *Medieval Jerusalem and Islamic Worship*, Brill, 1999; F. B. Flood, *The Great Mosque of Damascus*, Leiden, 2001; G. Fowden, *Qusayr Amra: Art and Umayyad Elite in Late Antique Syria*, Berkeley, CA, 2004; G. Fowden and E. K. Fowden, *Studies on Hellenism, Christianity and the Umayyads*, Athens, 2004; O. Grabar, *The Dome of the Rock*, Cambridge, MA, 2006; O. Grabar, *Early Islamic Art, 650–1100*, Burlington VT, 2005; O. Grabar, *The Shape of the Holy: Early Islamic Jerusalem*, Princeton, NJ, 1996; R. Hillenbrand, "La Dolce Vita in Early Islamic Syria: The Evidence of Later Umayyad Palaces," J. M. Bloom, ed., *Early Islamic Art and Architecture*, Burlington, VT, 2002, pp. 333–372; J. Johns, *Bayt al-Maqdis: Jerusalem and Early Islam*, Oxford, 1999; J. Raby and J. Johns, *Bayt al-Maqdis: ʿAbd al-Malik's Jerusalem*, Oxford, 1992; E. Whelan, "The Origins of the Mihrab Mujawwaf: A Reinterpretation," J. M. Bloom, ed., *Early Islamic Art and Architecture*, Burlington, VT, 2002, pp. 374–391.

D. *ʿAbbasid Architecture*

C. F. Robinson, *A Medieval Islamic City Reconsidered: Samarra*, Oxford, 2001.

CHAPTER 13. THE ʿABBASIDS: CALIPHS AND EMPERORS

A. *The Concept of the Caliphate*

S. M. Ali, "Early Islam: Monotheism or Henotheism? A View from the Court," *Journal of Arabic Literature*, 39 (2008), pp. 14–37; N. Calder, "The Significance of the Term Imam in Early Islamic Jurisprudence," J. Mojaddedi and A. Rippen, eds., *Interpretation and Jurisprudence in Medieval Islam*, Burlington, VT, 2006, pp. 253–264; D. Gutas, "Language and Imperial Ideology in Late Antiquity and Early Islam," W. M. Bloomer, ed., *The Contest of Language*, Notre Dame, IN, 2005, pp. 99–110; A. Hakim, "ʿUmar b. al-Khattab and the title khalifat Allah," *Jerusalem Studies in Arabic and Islam*, 30 (2005), pp. 207–230; H. Kennedy, "The Decline and Fall of the First Muslim Empire," *Der Islam*, 81 (2004), pp. 3–30; W. al-Qadi, "The Term 'Khalifa' in Early Exegetical Literature," *Die Welt des Islams*, 28 (1988), pp. 392–411; M. Q. Zaman, "The Caliphs, the ʿUlama' and the Law: Defining the Role and Function of the Caliph in the Early ʿAbbasid Period," *Islamic Law and Society*, 4 (1997), pp. 1–36.

B. *The Inquisition*

Z. Chokr, *Zandaqa et zindiqs en Islam au second siècle de l'hégire*, Damascus, 1993; M. Cooperson, *Classical Arabic Biography: The Heirs of the Prophets in the Age of al-Maʾmun*, Cambridge, 2000; N. Hurvitz, "Mihna as Self Defense," *Studia islamica*, 92 (2001), pp. 93–111; C. Melchert, "Religious Policies of the Caliphs from al-Mutawakkil to al-Muqtadir, AH 232–295/AD 847–908," *Islamic Law and Society*,

3 (1996), pp. 316–342; J. A. Nawas, "The Mihna of 218A.H./833 A.D. Revisited: An Empirical Study," *Journal of the American Oriental Society*, 116 (1996), pp. 698–708; J. A. Nawas, "A Reexamination of Three Current Explanations of al-Ma'mun's Introduction of the Mihna," *International Journal of Middle East Studies*, 26 (1994), pp. 615–629.

C. Arabic Humanities and Court Culture
L. I. Conrad, "The Mawali and Early Arabic Historiography," M. Bernards and J. Nawas, eds., *Patronate and Patronage in Early and Classical Islam*, Leiden, 2005, pp. 370–425; L. E. Goodman, "The Sacred and the Secular," M. Mir, ed., *Literary Heritage of Classical Islam*, Princeton, NJ, 1993, pp. 289–330; A. al-Heitty, *The Role of the Poetess at the Abbasid Court (132–247 A.H./750–861 A.D.)*, Beirut, 2005; T. Khalidi, *Arabic Historical Thought in the Classical Period*, Cambridge, 1994; T. Khalidi, *Classical Arab Islam: The Culture and Heritage of the Golden Age*, Princeton, NJ, 1985; A. Noth, *The Early Arabic Historical Tradition: A Source-Critical Study*, M. Bonner, trans., Princeton, NJ, 1994; C. F. Robinson, *Islamic Historiography*, Cambridge, 2003; S. P. Stetkevych, *The Poetics of Islamic Legitimacy*, Bloomington, IN, 2002.

D. Hellenism
P. Adamson and R. C. Taylor, eds., *The Cambridge Companion to Arabic Philosophy*, Cambridge, 2005; J. W. Drijvers, "The School of Edessa: Greek Learning and Local Culture," J. W. Dijvers and A. A. MacDonald, eds., *Centres of Learning: Learning and Location in Pre-Modern Europe and the Near East*, Leiden, 1995, pp. 49–59; D. Gutas, *Greek Thought, Arabic Culture*, New York, 1998; S. Rissanen, *Theological Encounter of Oriental Christians with Islam during Early Abbasid Rule*, Abo, 1993; F. Rosenthal, *The Classical Heritage in Islam*, London, 1975; U. Vagelpohl, *Aristotle's Rhetoric in the East*, Leiden, 2008; J. W. Watt, "Eastward and Westward Transmission of Classical Rhetoric," J. W. Dijvers and A. A. MacDonald, eds., *Centres of Learning: Learning and Location in Pre-Modern Europe and the Near East*, Leiden, 1995, pp. 63–76; H. Zia, "Islamic Philosophy," T. Winter, ed., *The Cambridge Companion to Classical Islamic Theology*, Cambridge, 2008, pp. 55–76.

CHAPTER 15. SUNNI ISLAM

A. Veneration of the Prophet
H. Berg, *The Development of Exegesis in Early Islam: The Authenticity of Muslim Literature from the Formative Period*, Curzon Studies in the Qur'ān, Richmond, Surrey, 2000. M. H. Katz, *The Birth of the Prophet Muhammad: Devotional Piety in Sunni Islam*, London, 2007.

B. Surveys of Theology

R. M. Frank, *Philosophy, Theology and Mysticism in Medieval Islam*, Burlington, VT, 2005; G. F. Hourani, *Reason and Tradition in Islamic Ethics*, Cambridge, 1985; S. A. Jackson, *On the Boundaries of Theological Tolerance in Islam*, Oxford, 2002; T. Nagel, *The History of Islamic Theology: From Muhammad to the Present*, Princeton, NJ, 2000; A. K. Reinhart, *Before Revelation: The Boundaries of Muslim Moral Thought*, Albany, NY, 1995; J. Van Ess, The Flowering of Muslim Theology, Cambridge and London, 2006; T. Winter, ed., *The Cambridge Companion to Classical Islamic Theology*, Cambridge, 2008, pp. 1–16.

C. History of Theology

B. Abrahamov, *Islamic Theology: Traditionalism and Rationalism*, Edinburgh, 1998; K. Athamina, "The Early Murji'a: Some Notes," *Journal of Semitic Studies*, xxxv (1990), pp. 109–130; K. Blankinship, "The Early Creed," T. Winter, ed., *The Cambridge Companion to Classical Islamic Theology*, Cambridge, 2008, pp. 33–54; M. Ceric, *Roots of Synthetic Theology in Islam: A Study of the Theology of Abu Mansur al-Maturidi*, Kuala Lumpur, 1995; A. El Shamsy, "The Social Construction of Orthodoxy," T. Winter, ed., *The Cambridge Companion to Classical Islamic Theology*, Cambridge, 2008, pp. 97–120; S. H. Griffith, *The Beginnings of Christian Theology in Arabic*, Burlington, VT, 2002; S. Leaman and S. Rizvi, "The Developed Kalam Tradition," T. Winter, ed., *The Cambridge Companion to Classical Islamic Theology*, Cambridge, 2008, pp. 77–96; R. C. Martin and M. R. Woodward, *Defenders of Reason in Islam*, Oxford, 1997; S. Schmidtke, "Theological Rationalism in the Medieval Islamic World," *Bulletin of Middle East Medievalists Al-Usur Al-Wusta*, 20 (2008), pp. 17–30.

D. Topics in Theology

N. El-Bizri, "God: Essence and Attributes," T. Winter, ed., *The Cambridge Companion to Classical Islamic Theology*, Cambridge, 2008, pp. 121–140; M. Fakhry, *Ethical Theories in Islam*, Leiden, 1991; R. M. Frank, *Creation and the Cosmic System: Ghazali and Avicenna*, Heidelberg, 1992; D. Gimaret, *Dieu à l'image de l'homme: les anthropomorphismes de la sunna et leur interprétation par les théologiens*, Paris, 1997; M. Hermansen, "Eschatology," T. Winter, ed., *The Cambridge Companion to Classical Islamic Theology*, Cambridge, 2008, pp. 308–324; S. Stelzer, "Ethics," T. Winter, ed., *The Cambridge Companion to Classical Islamic Theology*, Cambridge, 2008, pp. 161–179.

E. Ash'arism

R. M. Frank, *Beings and Their Attributes, Albany, NY, 1978*; R. M. Frank, *Early Islamic Theology: The Mu'tazilites and al-Ash'ari*, Burlington, VT, 2007; D. Gimaret, *La doctrine d'al-Ash'ari*, Paris, 1990.

F. History of Law

J. E. Bockoff, "The Minor Compendium of Ibn ʿAbd al-Hakam (d.214/829) and Its Reception in the Early Maliki School," *Islamic Law and Society*, 12 (2005), pp. 149–181; N. Calder, *Studies in Early Muslim Jurisprudence*, Oxford, 1993; P. Crone, *Roman, Provincial and Islamic Law*, Cambridge, 1987; Y. Dutton, *The Origins of Islamic Law: The Qurʾan, the Muwattaʾ and Madinan ʿAmal*, Richmond, Surrey, 1999; W. B. Hallaq, *Authority, Continuity and Change in Islamic Law*, Cambridge, 2001; W. B. Hallaq, "From Regional to Personal Schools of Law? A Reevaluation," *Islamic Law and Society*, 8 (2001), pp. 1–26; W. B. Hallaq, *An Introduction to Islamic Law*, Cambridge and New York, 2009; W. B. Hallaq, "Logic, Formal Arguments and Formalization of Arguments in Sunni Jurisprudence," *Arabica*, 37 (1990), pp. 315–358; W. B. Hallaq, *The Origins and Evolution of Islamic Law*, Cambridge, 2005; W. B. Hallaq, "Was al-Shafiʿi the Master Architect of Islamic Jurisprudence?," *International Journal of Middle East Studies*, 25 (1993), pp 587–605; A. Hasan, *The Early Development of Islamic Jurisprudence*, Islamabad, Lahore, 1970; N. Hurvitz, *The Formation of Hanbalism*, London, 2002; B. Johansen, *Contingency in a Sacred Law*, Leiden, 1999; C. Melchert, *The Formation of the Sunni Schools of Law: 9th–10th Centuries C.E.*, Leiden and New York, 1997; C. Melchert, "How Hanafism Came to Originate in Kufa and Traditionalism in Medina," *Islamic Law and Society*, 6 (1999), pp. 318–347; C. Melchert, "Traditionist-Jurisprudents and the Framing of Islamic Law," *Islamic Law and Society*, 8 (2001), pp. 383–406; H. Motzki, *The Origins of Islamic Jurisprudence: Meccan Fiqh before the Classical Schools*, M. H. Katz, trans., Leiden and Boston, 2002; B. G. Weiss, *Studies in Islamic Legal History*, Leiden, 2002.

G. Hadith

J. A. C. Brown, *The Canonization of Al-Bukhari and Muslim*, Leiden, 2007; J. A. C. Brown, "Critical Rigor vs. Juridical Pragmatism: How Legal Theorists and Hadith Scholars Approached the Backgrowth of Isnads in the Genre of ʿIlal al-Hadith," *Islamic Law and Society*, 14 (2007), pp. 1–41; J. A. C. Brown, *Hadith: Muhammad's Legacy in the Medieval and Modern World*, Oxford, 2009; R. Gleave, "Between Hadith and Fiqh: The 'Canonical' Imami Collections of Akhbar," *Islamic Law and Society*, 8 (2001), pp. 350–382; S. C. Lucas, *Constructive Critics, Hadīth Literature, and the Articulation of Sunnī Islam: The Legacy of the Generation of Ibn Saʾd, Ibn Maʾīn, and Ibn Hanbal*, Brill, Leiden, and Boston, 2004; S. Spectorsky, "Hadith in the Responses of Ishaq b. Rahayh," *Islamic Law and Society*, 8 (2001), pp. 407–431.

H. Political and Social History of Law

M. Bernards and J. Nawas, "The Geographic Distribution of Muslim Jurists during the First Four Centuries AH," *Islamic Law and Society*, 10 (2003), pp. 168–181;

N. Hurvitz, "Schools of Law and Historical Context: Re-Examining the Formation of the Hanbali Madhhab," *Islamic Law and Society*, 7 (2000), pp. 37–64; N. Tsafrir, "The Beginnings of the Hanafi School in Isfahan," *Islamic Law and Society*, 5 (1998), pp. 1–21; N. Tsafrir, *The History of an Islamic School of Law: The Early Spread of Hanafism*, Cambridge, MA, 2004.

I. Topics in Law

R. Gauvain, "Ritual Rewards: A Consideration of Three Approaches to Sunni Purity Law," *Islamic Law and Society*, 12 (2005), pp. 333–393; L. Halevi, *Muhammad's Grave: Death Rites and the Making of Islamic Society*, New York, 2007; M. H. Katz, *Body of Text: The Emergence of the Sunni Law of Ritual Purity*, Albany, NY, 2002; D. S. Powers, "The Islamic Inheritance System: A Socio-Historical Approach," C. Mallat and J. Connors, eds., *Islamic Family Law*, London, 1990, pp. 11–30; D. S. Powers, *Studies in Qur'an and Hadith: The Formation of Islamic Inheritance Law*, Berkeley, CA, 1986; L. Salaymeh, "Alms-Giving, Poverty and Islamic Legal Reasoning," paper for ASLH, November 2008; L. Salaymeh, "Early Islamic Legal-Historical Precedents: Prisoners of War," *Law and History Review*, 26 (2008), pp. 521–544; S. Spectorsky, *Chapters on Marriage and Divorce: Responses of Ibn Hanbal and Ibn Rahwayh*, Austin, TX, 1993.

J. Sufism

A. T. Karamustafa, *God's Unruly Friends: Dervish Groups in the Islamic Later Middle Period*, Salt Lake City, 1994; A. Khysh, *Islamic Mysticism, A Short History*, Leiden, 2000; L. Lewisohn, ed., *The Heritage of Sufism, 1: Classical Persian Sufism from Its Origins to Rumi (700–1300); II: The Legacy of Persian Sufism (1150–1500)*, Oxford, 1999; L. Massignon, *Essay on the Origins of the Technical Language of Islamic Mysticism*, B. Clark, trans., Notre Dame, IN, 1997; T. Mayer, "Theology and Sufism," T. Winter, ed., *The Cambridge Companion to Classical Islamic Theology*, Cambridge, 2008, pp. 258–287. M. A. Sells, *Early Islamic Mysticism: Sufi, Qur'an, Mi'raj, Poetic and Theological Writings*, Mahwah, NJ, and New York, 1996; S. Sviri, "The Early Mystical Schools of Baghdad and Nishapur," *Jerusalem Studies in Arabic and Islam*, 30 (2005), pp. 450–482.

K. Popular Religion

M. H. Katz, *The Birth of the Prophet Muhammad: Devotional Piety in Sunni Islam*, London, 2007; B. Shoshan, *Popular Culture in Medieval Cairo*, Cambridge, 1993; C. S. Taylor, *In the Vicinity of the Righteous: Ziyara and the Veneration of Muslim Saints in Late Medieval Egypt*, Leiden, 1999.

CHAPTER 16. SHI'I ISLAM

M. M. Bar-Asher, *Scripture and Exegesis in Early Imami Shiism*, Leiden, 1999; H. Modarressi, *Crisis and Consolidation in the Formative Period of Shi'ite Islam*,

Princeton, NJ, 1993; D. Stewart, *Islamic Legal Orthodoxy: Twelver Shiite Responses to the Sunni Legal System*, Salt Lake City, 1998; H. M. Tabataba'i, *An Introduction to Shi'i Law*, London, 1984.

CHAPTER 17. MUSLIM URBAN SOCIETIES TO THE TENTH CENTURY

A. 'Abd al-Raziq, *Le femme au temps des Mamlouks en Égypte*, Textes Arabes et Etudes Islamique, 5, Caire, 1973; L. Brubaker and J. M. H. Smith, eds., *Gender in the Early Medieval World: East and West, 300–900*, Cambridge, 2004; D. Cortese and S. Calderini, *Women and the Fatimids in the World of Islam*, Edinburgh, 2006; N. M. El Cheikh, "Gender and Politics in the Harem of al-Muqtadir," L. Brubaker and J. M. H. Smith, eds., *Gender in the Early Medieval World: East and West, 300–900*, Cambridge, 2004, pp. 146–161; N. M. El Cheikh, "Revisiting the Abbasid Harems," *Journal of Middle East Women's Studies*, 1 (2005), pp. 1–19, G. R. G. Hambly, "Becoming Visible: Medieval Islamic Women in Historiography and History," G. R. G. Hambly, ed., *Women in the Medieval Islamic World: Power, Patronage, and Piety*, New York, 1998, pp. 3–27; E. J. Hanne, "Women, Power, and the Eleventh and Twelfth Century Abbasid Court," *Hawwa: Journal of Women of the Middle East and Islamic World*, 3 (2005), pp. 80–110; N. Keddie and B. Baron, eds., *Women in Middle Eastern History*, New Haven, CT, 1991; C. Melchert, "Whether to Keep Women out of the Mosque: A Survey of Medieval Islamic Law," B. Michalak-Pikulska and A. Pikulski, eds., *Authority, Privacy and Public Order in Islam*, Leuven, 2006, pp. 59–69; Y. Rapoport, *Marriage, Money and Divorce in Medieval Islamic Society*, Cambridge, 2005; R. Roded, *Women in Islamic Biographical Collections from Ibn Sa'd to Who's Who*, Boulder, CO, 1994; M. Shatzmiller, "Women and Wage Labour in the Medieval Islamic West: Legal Issues in an Economic Context," *Journal of the Economic and Social History of the Orient*, 40 (1997), pp. 174–206; D. A. Spellberg, *Politics, Gender, and the Islamic Past: The Legacy of 'A'isha bint Abi Bakr*, New York, 1994; M. Tillier, "Women before the Qāḍī under the Abbasids," *Islamic Law and Society*, 16 (2009), pp. 280–301; U. Vermeulen, K. D. Hulster, and J. van Steenbergen, eds., *Continuity and Change in the Realms of Islam: Studies in Honour of Professor Urbain Vermeulen*, Leuven, 2008.

CHAPTER 18. THE NON-MUSLIM MINORITIES

A. General Works and Collected Essays

H. Badr, ed., *Christianity: A History in the Middle East*, Beirut, 2005; Y. Friedmann, *Tolerance and Coercion in Islam*, Cambridge, 2003; M. Gervers and R. J. Bikhazi, eds., *Conversion and Continuity: Indigenous Christian Communities in Islamic Lands, Eighth to Eighteenth Century*, Toronto, 1990; E. Grypeou, M. Swanson, and D. Thomas, eds., *The Encounter of Eastern Christianity with Early Islam*, The History of Christian-Muslim Relations, v. 5, Leiden, 2006; B. H. Hary, J. L. Hayes, and F. Astren, eds., *Judaism and Islam: Boundaries, Communication, and Interaction;*

Essays in Honor of William M. Brinner, Leiden and Boston, 2000; R. Hoyland, ed., *Muslim and Others in Early Islamic Society*, Burlington, VT, 2004; R. Hoyland, *Seeing Islam as Others Saw It; A Survey and Evaluation of Christian, Jewish and Zoroastrian Writings on Early Islam*, Princeton, NJ, 1997; M. Morony, "Religious Communities in Late Sasanian and Early Muslim Iraq," *Journal of the Economic and Social History of the Orient*, 17 (1974), pp. 113–135; S. Shaked, *From Zoroastrian Iran to Islam: Studies in Religious History and Intercultural Contacts*, Aldershot and Brookfield, VT, 1995; J. J. Van Ginkel et al., eds., *Redefining Christian Identity: Cultural Interaction in the Middle East since the Rise of Islam*, Leuven, 2005.

B. Muslim-Non-Muslim Cultural Relations

C. Cahen, "Histoire économico-sociale et islamologie: le problème préjudiciel de l'adaptation entre les autochtones et l'Islam," Correspondence d'Orient (1961), pp. 197–215; S. H. Griffith, *The Beginnings of Christian Theology in Arabic: Muslim-Christian Encounters in the Early Islamic Period*, Aldershot, 2002; S. H. Griffith, "Comparative Religion in the Apologetics of the First Christian Arabic Theologians," *Proceedings of the Patristic, Medieval and Renaissance Conference, Villanova University, Pennsylvania*, 4 (Philadelphia, 1979), pp. 63–86; M. J. Kister, "'Do Not Assimilate Yourselves ...' La Tashabbahū ... ," *Jerusalem Studies in Arabic and Islam*, 12 (1989), pp. 321–353; U. Rubin, *Between Bible and Qur'an: The Children of Israel and the Islamic Self-Image*, Princeton, NJ, 1999; U. Rubin, "Muhammad the Exorcist: Aspects of Islamic-Jewish Polemics," *Jerusalem Studies in Arabic and Islam*, 30 (2005), pp. 94–112; K. Samir and J. S. Nielsen, eds., *Christian Arabic Apologetics During the Abbasid Period, 750–1258*, Leiden, 1994. S. Stroumsa, "Jewish Polemics Against Islam and Christianity in the Light of Judeo-Arabic Texts," N. Golb, ed., *Judeo-Arabic Studies: Proceedings of the Founding Conference of the Society for Judeo-Arabic Studies, Studies in Muslim-Jewish Relations, v. 3*, Amsterdam, 1997, pp. 241–250; F. Von der Velden, "Relations Between Jews, Syriac Christians and Early Muslim Believers in Seventh-Century Iraq," *Al-usur al-wusta*, 19 (2007), pp. 27–33; S. Wasserstrom, *Between Muslim and Jew: The Problem of Symbiosis under Early Islam*, Princeton, NJ, 1995.

C. Non-Muslims and Islamic Law

M. Ayoub, "Dhimmah in Qur'an and Hadith," *Arab Studies Quarterly*, 5 (1983), pp. 172–182; C. E. Bosworth, "The Concept of *Dhimma* in Early Islam," B. Braude and B. Lewis, eds., *Christians and Jews in the Ottoman Empire: The Functioning of a Plural Society, v. 1: Central Lands*, New York and London, 1982, pp. 37–54; N. Edebly, "L'autonomie législative des chrétiens en terre d'islam," *Archives d'histoire du droit oriental*, 5 (1950–1), pp. 307–351; A. Fattal, "Comment les Dhimmīs étaient jugés en terre d'Islam," *Cahiers d'histoire égyptienne*, 3 (1951), pp. 321–341; S. D. Goitein, "Minority Self-Rule and Government Control in Islam," *Studia Islamica*, 31 (1970), pp. 101–116; M. Levy-Rubin, "Shurut 'Umar and Its Alternatives: The Legal

Debate on the Status of the Dhimmis," *Jerusalem Studies in Arabic and Islam*, 30 (2005), pp. 170–206; U. I. Simonsohn, "Overlapping Jurisdictions: Confessional Boundaries and Judicial Choice among Christians and Jews under Early Muslim Rule," Dissertation, Princeton University, 2008.

D. Jewish History
Books and Collected Articles
C. Adang, "The Karaites as Portrayed in Medieval Islamic Sources," *Karaite Judaism: A Guide to Its History and Literary Sources*, Leiden and Boston, 2003, pp. 179–197; F. Astren, *Karaite Judaism and Historical Understanding*, Columbia, SC, 2004; D. Biale, ed., *Cultures of the Jews: A New History*, New York, 2002; R. Brody, *The Geonim of Babylonia and the Shaping of Medieval Jewish Culture*, New Haven, 1998; J. Cohen and D. Sorkin, eds., *The Oxford Handbook of Jewish Studies*, Oxford, 2002; M. R. Cohen, *Jewish Self-Government in Medieval Egypt: The Origins of the Office of Head of the Jews, ca. 1065–1126*, Princeton, NJ, 1980; M. R. Cohen and A. L. Udovitch, eds., *Jews Among Arabs: Contacts and Boundaries*, Princeton, NJ, 1989; M. R. Cohen, *Under Crescent and Cross: The Jews in the Middle Ages*, Princeton, NJ, 1994; W. Fischel, *Jews in the Economic and Political Life of Medieval Islam*, New York, 1969; D. Frank, ed., *The Jews of Medieval Islam: Community, Society, and Identity*, Etudes sur le judaïsme médiéval, v. 16, Leiden and New York, 1992; M. Gil, *Jews in Islamic Countries in the Middle Ages*, Leiden and Boston, 2004; S. D. Goitein, *Jews and Arabs: Their Contacts Through the Ages*, New York, 1955; S. D. Goitein et al., *A Mediterranean Society: The Jewish Communities of the Arab World as Portrayed in the Documents of the Cairo Geniza, v. 1–6*, Berkeley, CA, 1967–88; S. D. Goitein, *Religion in a Religious Age*, Cambridge, MA, 1974; B. Lewis, *The Jews of Islam*, Princeton, NJ, 1984; G. Newby, *A History of the Jews of Arabia: From Ancient Times to Their Eclipse Under Islam*, Columbia, SC, 1988; M. Polliack, ed., *Karaite Judaism: A Guide to Its History and Literary Sources*, Leiden, 2003; N. A. Stillman, *The Jews of Arab Lands: A History and Source Book*, Philadelphia, 1979.

Jews of North Africa and Iran
D. Corcos, "The Jews of Morocco under the Marinides," *Jewish Quarterly Review*, 54 (1964), pp. 271–287; E. Gottreich, *The Mellah of Marrakesh: Jewish and Muslim Space in Morocco's Red City*, Bloomington, IN, 2007; H. Z. Hirschberg, *A History of the Jews in North Africa*, Leiden, 1974; S. Shaked and A. Netzer, eds., *Irano-Judaica: Studies Relating to Jewish Contact with Persian Culture Through the Ages*, v. 1–5, Jerusalem, 1982–2003.

Jewish Culture and Jewish-Muslim Cultural Relations
W. M. Brinner et al., eds., *Judaism and Islam: Boundaries, Communications and Interaction: Essays in Honor of William M. Brinner*, Leiden and Boston, 2000; R. Firestone, *Journeys in Holy Lands: The Evolution of Abraham-Ishmael Legends in Islamic Exegesis*, Albany, NY, 1990; B. Grévin, A. Nef, and Emanuelle Tixier, eds.,

Chrétiens, Juifs et Musulmans dans la Méditerranée medieval: Études en hommage à Henri Bresc, Paris, 2008; B. Hary and H. Ben-Shammai, eds., *Esoteric and Exoteric Aspects in Judeo-Arabic Culture*, Leiden, 2006; H. Lazarus-Yafeh et al., eds., *The Majlis: Interreligious Encounters in Medieval Islam*, Wiesbaden, 1999; R. L. Nettler, ed., *Studies in Muslim-Jewish Relations*, Oxford, 1993; S. M. Wasserstrom, *Between Muslim and Jew: The Problems of Symbiosis under Early Islam*, Princeton, NJ, 1995.

E. Christian Communities and Churches
G. Frantz-Murphy, "Conversion in Early Islamic Egypt: The Economic Factor," Y. Raghib, ed., *Documents d'Islam m'diéval: nouvelles perspectives de recherché*, Cairo, 1991, pp. 11–17; S. H. Griffith, *Arabic Christianity in the Monasteries of Ninth-Century Palestine*, Variorum, Aldershot, 1992; M. N. Swanson, *The Coptic Papacy in Islamic Egypt (641–1517)*, Cairo and New York, 2010; D. Thomas, ed., *Syrian Christians Under Islam: The First Thousand Years*, Leiden, 2001; J. R. Zaborowski, "From Coptic to Arabic in Medieval Egypt," *Medieval Encounters: Jewish, Christian, and Muslim Culture in Confluence and Dialogue*, 14 (2008), pp. 15–40.

CHAPTER 20. THE POST-ʿABBASID MIDDLE EASTERN STATE SYSTEM

A. Iraq: Buwayhids and Saljuqs
J. Donohue, *The Buwayhid Dynasty in Iraq 334H./945 to 403H./1012 Shaping Institutions for the Future*, Leiden and Boston, 2003; D. Ephrat, *A Learned Society in a Period of Transition*, Albany, NY, 2000; R. P. Mottohadeh, *Loyalty and Leadership in an Early Islamic Society*, Princeton, NJ, 1980; S. Sabari, *Mouvements Populaires à Bagdad, ix–xi siècles, Studies in Islamic Culture and History, v. 5*, Paris, 1981.

B. Mongols and Timurids
T. T. Allsen, *Culture and Conquest in Mongol Eurasia*, Cambridge and New York, 2001; O. Grabar, *Toward an Aesthetic of Persian Painting, Islamic Visual Art, 1100–1800*, Burlington, VT, 2006; R. G. Hovannsian and G. Sabagh, *The Persian Presence in the Islamic World*, New York, 1998; T. W. Lentz and G. D. Lowry, *Timur and the Princely Vision: Persian Art and Culture in the Fifteenth Century*, Los Angeles County Museum of Art, Los Angeles, 1989; M. E. Subtelny, *Timurids in Transition*, Leiden, 2007.

C. Fatimids
M. Brett, *The Rise of the Fatimids*, Leiden, 2001; Y. Lev, *State and Society in Fatimid Egypt*, Leiden, 1991; P. Sanders, *Ritual, Politics, and the City in Fatimid Cairo*, Albany, NY, 1994; P. E. Walker, "Fatimid Institutions of Learning," P. E. Walker, *Fatimid History and Ismaili Doctrine*, Cairo, 1997, pp. 179–200; P. E. Walker,

"The Ismaili Da'wa in the Reign of the Fatimid Caliph al-Hakim," *Journal of the American Research Center in Egypt*, 30 (1993), pp. 161–182.

D. Syria: Crusades and Counter-Crusades

Y. Frenkel, "The Impact of the Crusades on Rural Society and Religious Endowments: The Case of Medieval Syria (Bilad Al-Sham)," Y. Lev, ed., *War and Society in the Eastern Mediterranean, 7th–15th Centuries*, Leiden and New York, 1997, pp. 237–248; D. T. Heller, "The Shaykh and the Community: Popular Hanbalite Islam in 12th–13th Century Jabal Nablus and Jabal Qasyun,"*Studia Islamica*, 79 (1994), pp. 103–120; J. Riley-Smith, "Government and the Indigenous in the Latin Kingdom of Jerusalem," D. Abulafia and N. Berend, eds., *Medieval Frontiers: Concepts and Practices*, Ashgate, 2002, pp. 121–132; D. Stewart, "The Doctorate of Islamic Law in Mamluk Egypt and Syria," J. Lowry, D. Stewart, and S. Toorawa, eds., *Law and Education in Medieval Islam Studies in Memory of Professor George Makdisi*, Cambridge, 2004, S. Tsugitaka, *State and Rural Society in Medieval Islam*, Leiden, 1997.

CHAPTER 26. ISLAMIC NORTH AFRICA TO THE THIRTEENTH CENTURY

J. Clancy-Smith, ed., *North Africa, Islam, and the Mediterranean World: From the Almoravids to the Algerian War*, Portland, OR, 2001; E. Gottreich, *Mellah of Marakesh: Jewish and Muslim Space in Morocco's Red City*, Bloomington, IN, 2007; A. Hess, *The Foreign Frontier: A History of the 16th Century Ibero-African Frontier*, Chicago, 1978; H. Z. Hirschberg, *A History of the Jews in North Africa, v. 1: From Antiquity to the Sixteenth Century*, Leiden, 1974; A. Laroui, *The History of the Maghrib: An Interpretive Essay*, Princeton, NJ, 1977; S. G. Miller, A. Petruccioli, and M. Bertagnin, "The Mallah, the Third City of Fez," S. G. Miller and M. Bertagnin, eds., *The Architecture and Memory of the Minority Quarter in the Muslim Mediterranean City*, Cambridge, MA, 2010, pp. 79–108; D. Robinson, *Muslim Societies in African History*, Cambridge, 2004; P. von Sivers, "Egypt and North Africa," N. Levtzion and R. L. Pouwels, eds., *The History of Islam in Africa*, Athens, Oxford, and Cape Town, 2000, pp. 21–36.

CHAPTER 27. SPANISH-ISLAMIC CIVILIZATION

A. Christians under Muslim Rule

T. E. Burman, *Religious Polemic and the Intellectual History of the Mozarabs, c. 1050–1200*, Leiden, 1994; A. Christys, *Christians in al-Andalus (711–1000)*, Richmond, Surrey, 2002; J. A. Coope, *The Martyrs of Cordoba; Community and Family Conflict in an Age of Mass Conversion*, Lincoln, NE, 1995; M. Gervers and R. J. Bikhazi, eds., *Conversion and Continuity: Indigenous Christian Communities in*

Islamic Lands, Eighth to Eighteenth Centuries, Toronto, 1990; T. F. Glick, *Islamic and Christian Spain in the Early Middle Ages*, Leiden, 2005; R. Hitchcock, *Mozarabs in Medieval and Early Modern Spain: Identities and Influences*, Aldershot and Burlington, VT, 2008; J. V. Tolan, ed., *Medieval Christian Perceptions of Islam*, New York, 1996; K. B. Wolf, *Christian Martyrs in Muslim Spain*, Cambridge and New York, 1988.

B. Mudejar Culture: Muslims under Christian Rule

M. Gervers and R. J. Bikhazi, eds., *Conversion and Continuity: Indigenous Christian Communities in Islamic Lands, Eighth to Eighteenth Centuries*, Toronto, 1990; L. P. Harvey, *Islamic Spain, 1250 to 1500*, Chicago and London, 1990; L. P. Harvey, *Muslims in Spain, 1500 to 1614*, Chicago and London, 2005; M. D. Meyerson, *The Muslims of Valencia: In the Age of Fernando and Isabel: Between Coexistence and Crusade*, Berkeley, CA, Los Angeles, and Oxford, 1991; K. A. Miller, *Guardians of Islam: Religious Authority and Muslim Communities of Late Medieval Spain*, New York, 2008; M. Shatzmiller, *Her Day in Court: Women's Property Rights in Fifteenth Century Granada*, Cambridge, MA, 2007.

C. Jews in Spain

E. Ashtor, *The Jews of Moslem Spain, v. 1*, Philadelphia, 1973; Y. Baer, *A History of the Jews in Christian Spain, v. 1: From the Age of Reconquest to the Fourteenth Century*, Philadelphia, 1961; Y. Baer, *A History of the Jews in Christian Spain, v. 2: From the Fourteenth Century to Expulsion*, Philadelphia, 1966; J. S. Gerber, *The Jews of Spain: A History of the Sephardic Experience*, New York, 1992; M. D. Meyerson, *A Jewish Renaissance in Fifteenth-Century Spain*, Princeton, NJ, 2004; M. D. Meyerson, *Jews in an Iberian Frontier Kingdom: Society, Economy, and Politics in Morvedre, 1248–1391*, Leiden and Boston, 2004.

D. Convivencia

R. I. Burns, *Muslims, Christians and Jews in the Crusader Kingdom of Valencia: Societies in Symbiosis*, Cambridge, 1984; N. Daniel, *The Arabs and Medieval Europe*, London, 1975; J. D. Dodds, M. R. Menocal, and A. K. Balbale, *The Arts of Intimacy: Christians, Jews, and Muslims in the Making of Castilian Culture*, New Haven, CT, and London, 2008; E. Lourie, *Crusade and Colonisation: Muslims, Christians and Jews in Medieval Aragon*, Aldershot, 1990; V. B. Mann, T. F. Glick, and J. D. Dodds, eds., *Convivencia: Jews, Muslims and Christians in Medieval Spain*, New York, 1992; M. R. Menocal, *The Ornament of the World: How Muslims, Jews and Christians Created a Culture of Tolerance in Medieval Spain*, Boston, 2002; M. D. Meyerson and E. D. English, eds., *Christians, Muslims and Jews in Medieval and Early Modern Spain: Interaction and Social Change*, Notre Dame, IN, 1999; N. Roth, *Jews, Visigoths and Muslims in Medieval Spain; Cooperation and Conflict*, Leiden, 1994.

CHAPTER 30. INTRODUCTION: EMPIRES AND SOCIETIES

A. *Theory and Early Modern Empires*

V. H. Aksan, "Locating the Ottomans among Early Modern Empires," *Journal of Early Modern History*, 3 (1999), pp. 103–134; D. Armitage and S. Subrahmanyam, eds., *The Age of Revolutions in Global Contexts, c. 1760–1840*, New York, 2010; K. Barkey and M. von Hagen, eds., *After Empire: Multiethnic Societies and Nation-Building, the Soviet Union and Russian, Ottoman, and Habsburg Empires*, Boulder, CO, 1997; C. A. Bayly and P. F. Bang, "Introduction: Comparing Pre-Modern Empires," *Medieval History Journal*, 6 (2003), pp. 169–188; T. A. Brady Jr., H. A. Oberman, and J. D. Tracy, eds., *Handbook of European History, 1400–1600: Late Middle Ages, Renaissance, and Reformation*, Leiden, 1994; S. N. Eisenstadt, *The Political System of Empires*, London, 1963; T. Ertman, *Birth of the Leviathan: Building States and Regimes in Medieval and Early Modern Europe*, Cambridge, 1997; H. Islamoglu, *Constituting Modernity: Private Property in the East and West*, London and New York, 2004; H. Islamoglu, "Modernities Compared: State Transformations and Constitutions of Property in the Qing and Ottoman Empires," *Journal of Early Modern History*, 5 (2001), pp. 353–386; H. Islamoglu and P. Perdue, eds., *Shared Histories of Modernity in China, India and the Ottoman Empire*, New Delhi, 2009; A. J. Motyl, *Imperial Ends: The Decay, Collapse, and Revival of Empires*, New York, 2001; P. O'Brien, "Historiographical Traditions and Modern Imperatives for the Restoration of Global History," *Journal of Global History*, 1 (2006), pp. 3–39; S. Subrahmanyam, "Connected Histories: Notes Towards a Reconfiguration of Early Modern Eurasia," *Modern Asia Studies*, 31, no. 3 (1997): 735–762; S. Subrahmanyam, "A Tale of Three Empires," *Common Knowledge*, 12 (2006), pp. 66–92; I. Wallerstein, *The Modern World-System I: Capitalist Agriculture and the Origins of the European World-Economy in the Sixteenth Century*, New York, 1974; I. Wallerstein, *The Modern World-System II: Mercantilism and the Consolidation of the European World-Economy, 1600–1750*, New York, 1980; I. Wallerstein, *The Modern World-System III: The Second Era of Great Expansion of the Capitalist World-Economy, 1730s–1840s*, San Diego, 1989; K. Wittfogel, *Oriental Despotism; A Comparative Study of Total Power*, New Haven, CT, 1957.

B. *Turko-Mongol Empires, Comparisons*

A. Anooshar, *The Ghazi Sultans and the Frontiers of Islam*, London, 2009; L. Balabanlilar, "Lords of the Auspicious Conjunction: Turco-Mongol Imperial Identity on the Subcontinent," *Journal of World History*, 18 (2007), pp. 1–39; H. Berktay and S. Faroqhi, eds., *New Approaches to State and Peasant in Ottoman History*, London, 1992; R. C. Canfield, ed., *Turko-Persia in Historical Perspective*, Cambridge, 1991; S. Dale, *The Muslim Empires of the Ottomans, Safavids, and Mughals*, New York, 2010; R. C. Foltz, *Mughal India and Central Asia*, Karachi, New York, 1998;

F. Robinson, "Ottomans-Safavids-Mughals: Shared Knowledge and Connective Systems," *Journal of Islamic Studies*, 8 (1997), pp. 151–184.

CHAPTER 31. THE TURKISH MIGRATIONS AND THE OTTOMAN EMPIRE

A. *Surveys and General Works*
S. N. Faroqhi, ed., *The Cambridge History of Turkey, v. 1–3*, Cambridge, 2006.

B. *Conquest and the Classical Empire*
V. H. Aksan and D. Goffman, eds., *The Early Modern Ottomans: Remapping the Empire*, Cambridge and New York, 2007; P. J. Brummett, *Ottoman Seapower and Levantine Diplomacy in the Age of Discovery*, Albany, NY, 1994; A. Bryer and H. Lowry, eds., *Continuity and Change in Late Byzantine and Early Ottoman Society*, Birmingham, 1986; J. V. A. Fine, *The Late Medieval Balkans: A Critical Survey from the Late Twelfth Century to the Ottoman Conquest*, Ann Arbor, 1987; C. Finkel, *Osman's Dream: The Story of the Ottoman Empire, 1300–1923*, London, 2005; C. Imber, *The Ottoman Empire, 1300–1650: The Structure of Power*, New York, 2002; H. Inalcik, *The Middle East and the Balkans under the Ottoman Empire*, Bloomington, IN, 1993; C. Kafadar, *Between Two Worlds: The Construction of the Ottoman State*, Berkeley, CA, 1995; C. Kafadar, "The Ottomans and Europe," T. A. Brady Jr., H. A. Oberman, and J. D. Tracy, eds., *Handbook of European History, 1400–1600: Late Middle Ages, Renaissance, and Reformation*, Leiden, 1994, pp. 589–636; H. W. Lowry, *The Nature of the Early Ottoman State*, Albany, NY, 2003.

C. *Ottomans and Europe*
V. H. Aksan and D. Goffman, eds., *The Early Modern Ottomans: Remapping the Empire*, Cambridge and New York, 2007; V. H. Aksan, "Locating the Ottomans among Early Modern Empires," *Journal of Early Modern History*, 3 (1999), pp. 103–134; F. Braudel, *The Mediterranean and the Mediterranean World in the Age of Philip II*, New York, 1972; P. J. Brummett, *Ottoman Seapower and Levantine Diplomacy in the Age of Discovery*, Albany, NY, 1994; A. Çırakman, *From the "Terror of the World" to the "Sick Man of Europe": European Images of Ottoman Empire and Society from the Sixteenth Century to the Nineteenth*, New York, 2002; S. N. Faroqhi, *The Ottoman Empire and the World Around It*, London and New York, 2004; O. Ghiselin, *The Turkish Letters of Ogier Ghiselin de Busbecq, Imperial Ambassador at Constantinople, 1554–1562*, E. S. Forster, trans., Baton Rouge, LA, 2005; D. Goffman, *The Ottoman Empire and Early Modern Europe*, Cambridge, 2002; M. Greene, *A Shared World: Christians and Muslims in the Early Modern Mediterranean*, Princeton, NJ, 2000; C. Kafadar, "The Ottomans and Europe," T. A. Brady Jr., H. A. Oberman, and J. D. Tracy, eds., *Handbook of European History, 1400–1600: Late Middle Ages, Renaissance, and Reformation*, Leiden, 1994,

pp. 589–636; H. T. Norris, *Islam in the Balkans: Religion and Society between Europe and the Arab World*, London, 1993.

D. Ottoman Economy and Society

E. Eldem, D. Goffman, and B. Masters, *The Ottoman City between East and West: Aleppo, Izmir, and Istanbul*, Cambridge, 1999; B. Ergene, *Local Court, Provincial Society and Justice in the Ottoman Empire: Legal Practice and Dispute Resolution in Çankırı and Kastamonu (1652–1744)*, Leiden, 2003; K. Fleet, *European and Islamic Trade in the Early Ottoman State: The Merchants of Genoa and Turkey*, Cambridge, 1999; H. Gerber, *Economy and Society in an Ottoman City: Bursa, 1600–1700*, Jerusalem, 1988; H. Inalcik and D. Quataert, eds., *An Economic and Social History of the Ottoman Empire 1300–1914*, Cambridge, 1994; H. Inalcik, "Islamization of Ottoman Laws on Land and Land Tax," C. Fragner, K. Schwarz, and J. Matuz, eds., *Osmanistik-Turkologie-Diplomatik*, Berlin, 1992, pp. 101–116, B. McGowan, *Economic Life in Ottoman Europe*, Cambridge and New York, 1981; A. Y. Ocak, ed., *Sufism and Sufis in Ottoman Society*, Ankara, 2005; A. Singer, *Constructing Ottoman Beneficence: An Imperial Soup Kitchen in Jerusalem*, Albany, NY, 2002.

E. Ottoman Architecture

G. Necipoğlu, *The Age of Sinan: Architectural Culture in the Ottoman Empire, 1539–1588*, Princeton, NJ, 1995; G. Necipoğlu, *Architecture, Ceremony, and Power: The Topkapi Palace in the Fifteenth and Sixteenth Centuries*, Cambridge, MA, 1991.

F. Ottoman Intelligentsia and Vision of State

C. H. Fleischer, *Bureaucrat and Intellectual in the Ottoman Empire: The Historian Mustafa Ali (1541–1600)*, Princeton, NJ, 1986; G. Piterberg, *An Ottoman Tragedy: History and Historiography at Play*, Berkeley, CA, 2003; D. Quataert, "Ottoman History Writing and Changing Attitudes Towards the Notion of 'Decline.'" *History Compass*, 1 (2003), pp. 1–9.

G. Ottoman Law

B. Ergene, *Local Court, Provincial Society and Justice in the Ottoman Empire: Legal Practice and Dispute Resolution in Çankırı and Kastamonu (1652–1744)*, Leiden, 2003; C. Imber, *Ebu's-su'ud: The Islamic Legal Tradition*, Edinburg, 1997; H. Inalcik, "Suleiman the Law-Giver and the Ottoman Law," *Archivum Ottomanicum*, 1 (1960), pp. 126–136; H. Islamoglu, *Constituting Modernity: Private Property in the East and West*, London and New York, 2004; H. Islamoglu, "Modernities Compared: State Transformations and Constitutions of Property in the Qing and Ottoman Empires," *Journal of Early Modern History*, 5 (2001), pp. 353–386; B. Johansen, *Contingency in a Sacred Law: Legal and Ethical Norms in the Muslim Fiqh*, Leiden, 1999;

B. Johansen, *The Islamic Law on Land Tax and Rent: The Peasants' Loss of Property Rights as Interpreted in the Hanafite Legal Literature of the Malmuk and Ottoman Periods*, London and New York, 1988; A. Y. Kaya, "Administering Conflicts: The Justice of Peace in the Russian and Ottoman Empires," paper delivered at "Law and Political Economy in the Russian and Ottoman Empires" workshop, June 2003, Bogazici University, Istanbul; B. Messick, *Islamic Legal Interpretation: Muftis and Their Fatwas*, Cambridge, MA, 1996; A. Saltzman, "An Ancient Regime Revisited: Privatization and Political Economy in the 18th Century Ottoman Empire," *Politics and Society*, 21 (1993), pp. 393–423; I. Tamdogan, "Sulh and the 18th Century Ottoman Courts of Uskudar and Adana," *Islamic Law and Society*, 15 (2008), pp. 55–83; B. Tezcan, *The Second Ottoman Empire: Political and Social Transformation in the Early Modern World*, New York, 2010; F. Zarinebaf, *Crime and Punishment in Istanbul*, Berkeley, CA, and Los Angeles, 2010; S. Zubaida, *Law and Power in the Islamic World*, London and New York, 2003.

H. Non-Muslims
Books and Articles on Non-Muslims

F. Armanios, *Coptic Christianity in Ottoman Egypt*, New York, 2011; H. Badr, ed., *Christianity: A History in the Middle East*, Beirut, 2005; M. Baer, U. Makdisi, and A. Shryock, "Tolerance and Conversion in the Ottoman Empire: A Conversation," *Comparative Studies in Society and History*, 51 (2009), pp. 927–940; B. Braude and B. Lewis, eds., *Christians and Jews in the Ottoman Empire: The Functioning of a Plural Society, v. 1: Central Lands*, New York and London, 1982; M. Gervers and R. J. Bikhazi, eds., *Conversion and Continuity: Indigenous Christian Communities in Islamic Lands, Eighth to Eighteenth Century*, Toronto, 1990; M. Greene, *A Shared World: Christians and Muslims in the Early Modern Mediterranean*, Princeton, NJ, 2000; A. Husain and K. E. Fleming, eds., *A Faithful Sea: The Religious Cultures of the Mediterranean, 1200–1700*, Oxford, 2007; B. Masters, *Christians and Jews in the Ottoman Arab World: The Roots of Sectarianism*, Cambridge, 2001; A. Minkov, *Conversion to Islam in the Balkans: Kisve Bahasi Petitions and Ottoman Social Life, 1670–1730*, Leiden, 2004; H. T. Norris, *Islam in the Balkans: Religion and Society between Europe and the Arab World*, London, 1993; N. al-Qattan, "Dhimmis in the Muslim Court: Legal Autonomy and Religious Discrimination," *International Journal of Middle East Studies*, 31 (1999), pp. 429–444.

Ottoman Jews

D. Frank, ed., *The Jews of Medieval Islam: Community, Society, and Identity, Etudes sur le judaïsme médiéval, v. 16*, Leiden and New York, 1992; A. Levy, ed., *The Jews of the Ottoman Empire*, Princeton, NJ, 1994; Y. Ben-Naeh, *Jews in the Realm of the Sultans; Ottoman Jewish Society in the Seventeenth Century*, Tübingen, 2008; A. Rodrigue, "The Ottoman Diaspora: The Rise and Fall of Ladino Culture," D. Biale, ed., *Cultures of the Jews; A New History*, New York, 2002, pp. 863–885;

G. Scholem, *Major Trends in Jewish Mysticism*, New York, 1954; S. J. Shaw, *The Jews of the Ottoman Empire and the Turkish Republic*, New York, 1991; A. Shmuelevitz, *The Jews of the Ottoman Empire in the Late Fifteenth and the Sixteenth Centuries: Administrative, Economic, Legal, and Social Relations as Reflected in the Responsa*, Leiden, 1984.

I. Women and Family

L. Abu-Lughod, *Remaking Women: Feminism and Modernity in the Middle East*, Princeton, NJ, 1998; G. Akyılmaz, "Women According to the Ottoman Law of Family," H. C. Güzel, C. C. Oguz, and O. Karatay, *The Turks, v. 3: The Ottomans*, Ankara, 2002, pp. 627–635; G. Art, "Women and Sexuality in the Fatwas of the Sheikhulislam in Seventeenth Century Ottoman Empire," P. Ilkkaracan, ed., *Women and Sexuality in Muslim Societies*, Istanbul, 2000, pp. 81–90; H. Bodman and N. Tohidi, *Women in Muslim Societies*, Boulder, CO, 1998; L. A. Brand, *Women, the State and Political Liberalization*, New York, 1998; L. Brubaker and J. M. H. Smith, eds., *Gender in the Early Medieval World: East and West, 300–900*, Cambridge, 2004; A. el-Azhary Sonbol, ed., *Beyond the Exotic: Women's Histories in Islamic Societies*, Syracuse, NY, 2005; A. el-Azhary Sonbol, *Women, the Family, and Divorce Laws in Islamic History*, Syracuse, NY, 1996; D. Fairchild Ruggles, ed., *Women, Patronage and Self-Representation in Islamic Societies*, Albany, NY, 2000; H. Gerber, "Social and Economic Position of Women in an Ottoman City, Bursa, 1600–1700," *International Journal of Middle East Studies*, 12 (1980), pp. 231–244; A. Giladi, *Infants, Parents and Wet Nurses*, Leiden, 1999; Y. Y. Haddad and J. Esposito, eds., *Islam, Gender and Social Change*, New York, 1998; G. R. G. Hambly, *Women in the Medieval Islamic World*, New York, 1998; P. Ilkkaracan, *Women and Sexuality in Muslim Societies*, Istanbul, 2000; E. Isin and E. Üstüdang, "Wills, Deeds, Acts: Women's Civic Gift-Giving in Ottoman Istanbul," *Gender, Place and Culture*, 15 (2008), pp. 519–532; R. Jennings, "Divorce in the Ottoman Sharia Court of Cyprus, 1580–1640," D. Panzac, ed., *Histoire économique et sociale de l'Empire ottoman et de la Turquie (1326–1960)*, Paris, 1995, pp. 359–372; N. R. Keddie and B. Baron, eds., *Women in Middle Eastern History: Shifting Boundaries in Sex and Gender*, New Haven, CT, 1991; S. Laiou, "Christian Women in an Ottoman World: Interpersonal and Family Cases Brought before the Shari'a Courts during the Seventeenth and Eighteenth Centuries (Cases Involving the Greek Community)," A. Buturović and I. C. Schick, eds., *Women in the Ottoman Balkans: Gender, Culture, and History*, London, 2007, pp. 243–272; M. L. Meriwether, *The Kin Who Count: Family and Society in Ottoman Aleppo, 1770–1840*, Austin, TX, 1999; M. L. Meriwether and J. E. Tucker, *A Social History of Women and Gender in the Modern Middle East*, Boulder, CO, 1999; B. F. Musallam, *Sex and Society in Islam*, Cambridge, 1983, repr. 1989; G. Nashat and J. E. Tucker, *Women in the Middle East and North Africa*, Bloomington, IN, 1999; M. Shatzmiller, *Her Day in Court: Women's Property Rights in Fifteenth-Century Granada*, Cambridge, MA, 2007; J. E. Tucker, *In the House of the Law: Gender and Islamic Law in Ottoman Syria and Palestine*, Berkeley, CA, Los Angeles, and London, 1998; D. Ze'evi, *Producing Desire: Changing Sexual Discourse in the Ottoman Middle East, 1500–1900*, Berkeley, CA, 2006; M. C. Zilfi, "Muslim Women in the Early Modern Era," S. N. Faroqhi, ed., *The Cambridge History of Turkey, v. 3: The Later Ottoman Empire, 1603–1839*, Cambridge, 2006; M. C. Zilfi, ed., *Women in the Ottoman Empire: Middle Eastern Women in the Early Modern Era*, Leiden, 1997.

CHAPTER 32. THE POSTCLASSICAL OTTOMAN EMPIRE: DECENTRALIZATION, COMMERCIALIZATION, AND INCORPORATION

R. A. Abou-el-Haj, *The 1703 Rebellion and the Structure of Ottoman Politics*, Istanbul, 1984; K. Barkay, *Empire of Difference: The Ottomans in Comparative Perspective*, Cambridge and New York, 2008; J. Hathaway, "Problems of Periodization in Ottoman History: The Fifteenth through the Eighteenth Centuries," *Turkish Studies Association Bulletin*, 20 (1996), pp. 25–31; K. Karpat, *The Politicization of Islam: Reconstructing Identity, State, Faith, and Community in the Late Ottoman State*, Oxford and New York, 2001; M. I. Kunt, *The Sultan's Servants: The Transformation of the Ottoman Provincial Government 1550–1650*, New York, 1983; D. Quataert, *The Ottoman Empire, 1700–1922: New Approaches to European History*, 2nd edition, Cambridge, 2005; A. Saltzman, "An Ancient Regime Revisited: Privatization and Political Economy in the 18th Century Ottoman Empire," *Politics and Society*, 21 (1993), pp. 393–423; B. Tezcan, *The Second Ottoman Empire: Political and Social Transformation in the Early Modern World*, New York, 2010.

CHAPTER 33. THE ARAB PROVINCES UNDER OTTOMAN RULE

K. K. Babir, *Ottoman Rule in Damascus, 1708–1758*, Princeton, NJ, 1980; B. Doumani, *Rediscovering Palestine: Merchants and Peasants in Jabal Nablus, 1700–1900*, Berkeley, CA, 1995.

CHAPTER 34. THE SAFAVID EMPIRE

A. Early Safavids

K. Babayan, *Mystics, Monarchs, and Messiahs: Cultural Landscapes of Early Modern Iran*, Cambridge, MA, 2002; A. J. Newman, *Safavid Iran: Rebirth of a Persian Empire*, London and New York, 2006; A. J. Newman, ed., *Society and Culture in the Early Modern Middle East*, Leiden, 2003.

B. Shah ʿAbbas

S. Babaie et al., *Slaves of the Shah: New Elites of Safavid Iran*, London and New York, 2004; R. P. Matthee, *The Politics of Trade in Safavid Iran: Silk for Silver,*

1600–1730, Cambridge, 1999; C. Melville, ed., *Safavid Persia: The History and Politics of an Islamic Society*, London, 1996; C. Werner, *An Iranian Town in Transition: A Social, and Economic History of the Elites of Tabriz, 1747–1848*, Wiesbaden, 2000.

C. Safavid State and Religion
R. J. Abisaab, *Converting Persia: Religion and State Power in the Safavid Empire*, London and New York, 2004; C. P. Mitchell, *The Practice of Politics in Safavid Iran: Power, Religion, and Rhetoric*, London and New York, 2009.

D. Art and Architecture
S. Blake, *Half the World: The Social Architecture of Safavid Isfahan, 1590–1722*, Costa Mesa, CA, 1999.

CHAPTER 35. THE INDIAN SUBCONTINENT: THE DELHI SULTANATES AND THE MUGHAL EMPIRE

A. Conquests and Delhi Sultanates
B. D. Chattopadhyaya, *The Making of Early Medieval India*, Delhi, 1996; S. F. Dale, *The Garden of the Eight Paradises: Babur and the Culture of Empire in Central Asia, Afghanistan and India (1483–1530)*, Leiden, 2004; R. M. Eaton, *Temple Desecration and Muslim States in Medieval India*, New Delhi, 2004; R. C. Foltz, *Mughal India and Central Asia*, Karachi and New York, 1998; S. Kumar, *The Emergence of the Delhi Sultanate 1192–1286*, New Delhi, 2007; S. Kumar et al., *Expanding Frontiers in South Asian and World History: Essays in Honour of John F. Richards*, Special Issue of *Modern Asian Studies*, 43, Cambridge, 2009; S. Kumar, "The Ignored Elites: Turks, Mongols and a Persian Secretarial Class in the Early Delhi Sultante," *Modern Asian Studies*, 43 (2008), pp. 1–33; S. Kumar, "Qutb and Modern Memory," S. Kaul, ed., *The Partitions of Memory: The Afterlife of the Division of India*, Delhi, 2001, pp. 140–182; S. Kumar, "Service, Status and Military Slavery in the Delhi Sultanate of the Thirteenth and Early Fourteenth Centuries," I. Chatterjee and R. Eaton, eds., *Slavery and South Asia*, Bloomington, IN, 2006; J. Laine, *Shivaji: Hindu King in Islamic India*, Oxford and New York, 2003; N. Peabody, "Hindu Kingship and Polity in Precolonial India," Dissertation, New York, 2003.

B. Indian Islam
J. R. I. Cole, "Popular Shiʻism," R. M. Eaton, ed., *India's Islamic Traditions, 711–1750*, New Delhi, 2003, pp. 311–339; S. J. Desiderio Pinto, "The Mystery of the Nizamuddin Dargah: The Accounts of Pilgrims," C. Troll, ed., *Muslim Shrines in India*, New Delhi, 1989, pp.112–124; S. Digby, "The Sufi Shaikh as a Source of Authority in Medieval India," R. M. Eaton, ed., *India's Islamic Traditions, 711–1750*, New Delhi, 2003, pp. 234–262; R. M. Eaton et. al, eds., *Expanding Frontiers in*

South Asian and World History: Essays in Honour of John F. Richards, Special Issue of *Modern Asian Studies*, 43 (2009); R. M. Eaton, ed., *India's Islamic Traditions, 711–1750*, New Delhi, 2003; R. M. Eaton, *The Rise of Islam and the Bengal Frontier, 1204–1706*, Berkeley, CA, 1993; F. Robinson, *Islam and Muslim History in South Asia*, Delhi, 2000; F. Robinson, "Ottomans-Safavids-Mughals: Shared Knowledge and Connective Systems," *Journal of Islamic Studies*, 8 (1997), pp. 151–184; C. Troll, ed., *Muslim Shrines in India*, New Delhi, 1989.

C. Mughal State

M. D. Faruqui, "The Forgotten Prince: Mirza Hakim and the Formation of the Mughal Empire in India," *Journal of the Economic and Social History of the Orient*, 48 (2005), pp. 487–523; J. Gommans, *Mughal Warfare: Indian Frontiers and Highroads to Empire, 1500–1700*, London and New York, 2002; D. N. MacLean, "Real Men and False Men at the Court of Akbar: The *Majalis* of Shaykh Mustafa Gujariti," D. Gilmartin and B. Lawrence, eds., *Beyond Turk and Hindu: Rethinking Religious Identities in Islamicate South Asia*, Gainesville, FL, 2000, pp. 199–215; S. Musavi, *People, Taxation, and Trade in Mughal India*, Oxford and New York, 2008; M. N. Pearson, "Political Participation in Mughal India," *Indian Economic Social History Review*, 9 (1972), pp. 113–131; J. F. Richards, *The Mughal Empire: The New Cambridge History of India, I (5)*, Cambridge and New York, 1993; J. F. Richards, *Power, Administration, and Finance in Mughal India*, Aldershot and Brookfield, VT, 1993.

D. Mughals, Indian Society, and Culture

M. Alam, *The Languages of Political Islam: India 1200–1800*, Chicago, 2004; M. Athar Ali, "Towards an Interpretation of the Mughal Empire," *Journal of the Royal Asiatic Society of Great Britain and Ireland*, 1 (1978), pp. 38–49; I. A. Bierman, *The Experience of Islamic Art on the Margins of Islam*, Reading, 2005; S. Blake, "The Patrimonial-Bureaucratic Empire of the Mughals," *Journal of Asian Studies*, 39 (1979), pp. 77–94; S. Blake, *Shahjahanabad: The Sovereign City in Mughal India, 1639–1739*, Northfield, MN, 1993; I. Chatterjee and R. Eaton, eds., *Slavery and South Asian History*, Bloomington, IN, 2006; I. Chatterjee ed., *Unfamiliar Relations: Family and History in South Asia*, New Brunswick, NJ, 2004; R. M. Eaton, "The Articulation of Islamic Space in the Medieval Deccan," I. A. Bierman, *The Experience of Islamic Art on the Margins of Islam*, Reading, 2005, pp. 113–131; D. Gilmartin and B. Lawrence, eds., *Beyond Turk and Hindu: Rethinking Religious Identities in Islamicate South Asia*, Gainesville, FL, 2000; I. A. Khan, "The Nobility Under Akbar and the Development of His Religious Policy, 1560–80," R. M. Eaton, ed., *India's Islamic Traditions, 711–1750*, New Delhi, 2003, pp. 120–132; R. Kinra, "Secretary-Poets in Mughal India and the Ethos of Persian: The Case of Chandar Bhan Brahman," Dissertation, University of Chicago, 2008; R. Lal, *Domesticity and Power in the Early Mughal World*, Cambridge, 2005.

E. Eighteenth-Century Muslim Reform

D. Ahmad, "The Origins and Objectives of Islamic Revivalist Thought, 1750–1850," *Journal of American Oriental Society*, 113 (1993), pp. 341–359; J. M. S. Baljon, "Shah Waliullah and the Dargah," C. Troll, ed., *Muslim Shrines in India*, New Delhi, 1989, pp. 189–197; J. R. I. Cole, *Roots of North Indian Shi'ism in Iran and Iraq: Religion and State in Awadh, 1722–1859*, Delhi, 1984; Y. Friedmann, *Shaykh Ahmad Sirhindi: An Outline of His Thought and a Study of His Image in the Eyes of Posterity*, Montreal, 1971.

F. Eighteenth-Century Decentralized Government

M. Alam, *The Crisis of Empire in Mughal North India: Awadh and the Punjab 1707–1748*, New Delhi, 1986; M. Alam, "The Zamindars and Mughal Power in the Deccan, 1685–1712," *Indian Economic and Social History Review*, 11 (1974), pp. 74–91; S. Alavi, ed., *The Eighteenth Century in India*, New Delhi, 2002; C. B. Asher, "Sub-Imperial Palaces: Power and Authority in Mughal India," *Ars Orientalis*, 23 (1993), pp. 281–302; M. Athar Ali, *The Mughal Nobility Under Aurangzeb*, revised edition, Delhi, 1997; M. Athar Ali, "The Mughal Polity: A Critique of Revisionist Approaches," *Modern Asian Studies*, 27 (1993), pp. 699–710; K. Chatterjee, *Merchants, Politics and Society in Early Modern India: Bihar 1733–1820*, Leiden, 1996; M. Fisher, *Indirect Rule in India: Residents and the Residency System, 1764–1858*, Delhi and New York, 1991; R. Hallisey, *The Rajput Rebellion against Aurangzeb: A Study of the Mughal Empire in Seventeenth-Century India*, Columbia, 1977; F. Hasan, *State and Locality in Mughal India: Power Relation in Western India, c. 1572–1730*, Cambridge and New York, 2004; P. J. Marshall, ed., *The Eighteenth Century in Indian History: Evolution or Revolution?*, New Delhi, 2003; P. Parthasarathi, *The Transition to a Colonial Economy: Weavers, Merchants, and Kings in South India*, Cambridge and New York, 2001; C. Singh "Centre and Periphery in the Mughal State: The Case of Seventeenth-Century Panjab," *Modern Asian Studies*, 22 (1988), pp. 299–318; C. Singh, *Region and Empire: Panjab in the Seventeenth Century*, Delhi and New York, 1991; S. Subrahmanyam, "The Mughal State – Structure or Process? Reflections on Recent Western Historiography," *Indian Economic Social History Review*, 29 (1992), pp. 291–322; R. Travers, "The Eighteenth Century in Indian History," *Eighteenth Century Studies*, 40 (2007), pp. 492–508.

G. Economy and Trade

M. Alam, "Trade, State Policy and Regional Change: Aspects of Mughal-Uzbek Commercial Relations, c. 1550–1750," *Journal of the Economic and Social History of the Orient*, 37 (1994), pp. 202–227; C. A. Bayly, *The Birth of the Modern World, 1780–1914*, Malden, MA, 2004; S. F. Dale, *Indian Merchants and Eurasian Trade, 1600–1750*, Cambridge, 1994; R. Datta, *Society, Economy and the Market: Commercialization in Rural Bengal, c. 1760–1800*, New Delhi, 2000.

H. The British Empire in India

C. A. Bayly, *Indian Society and the Making of the British Empire*, Cambridge and New York, 1988; S. Kaul, ed., *The Partitions of Memory: The Afterlife of the Division of India*, Delhi, 2001; O. Prakash, *European Commercial Enterprise in Pre-Colonial India: The New Cambridge History of India, II (5)*, New York and Cambridge, 1998; S. Sen, *Empire of Free Trade: The East India Company and the Making of the Colonial Market Place*, Philadelphia, 1998.

CHAPTER 37. INNER ASIA FROM THE MONGOL CONQUESTS TO THE NINETEENTH CENTURY

R. C. Caneld, ed., *Turko-Persia in Historical Perspective*, Cambridge, 1991; R. Crews, *For Prophet and Tsar: Islam and Empire in Russia and Central Asia*, Cambridge, MA, 2006; R. C. Foltz, *Mughal India and Central Asia*, Karachi and New York, 1998; A. Khalid, *The Politics of Muslim Cultural Reform: Jadidism in Central Asia*, Berkeley, CA, 1998.

CHAPTER 38. ISLAMIC SOCIETIES IN SOUTHEAST ASIA

An excellent one-volume history is M. C. *Ricklefs, A History of Modern Indonesia since c. 1300*, Stanford, CA, 1993.

A. Southeast Asia to the Eighteenth Century

B. W. Andaya and J. Hadler, "To Live as Brothers: Southeast Sumatra in the Seventeenth and Eighteenth Centuries," *Journal of Asian Studies*, 57 (1998), pp. 269; K. N. Chaudhuri, *Trade and Civilisation in the Indian Ocean: An Economic History from the Rise of Islam to 1750*, Cambridge, 1985; J. Hadler, *Muslims and Matriarchs: Cultural Resilience in Indonesia through Jihad and Colonialism*, Ithaca, NY, 2008; J. Hadler, "Places like Home: Islam, Matriliny, and the History of Family in Minangkabau," Dissertation, Cornell University, 2000; M. F. Laffan, "Finding Java: Muslim Nomenclature of Insular Southeast Asia from Srîvijaya to Snouck Hurgronje," E. Tagliacozzo, *Southeast Asia and the Middle East: Islam, Movement and the Longue Durée*, Stanford, CA, 2009, pp. 17–64; V. Lieberman, *Strange Parallels: Southeast Asia in Global Context, c. 800–1830, vol. 1: Integration on the Mainland*, Cambridge, 2003; M. Pearson, *The Indian Ocean*, London and New York, 2003; A. Reid, *Southeast Asia in the Early Modern Era: Trade, Power, and Belief*, Ithaca, NY, and London, 1993.

B. Modernization and Islamic Reform

A. B. Adam, *The Vernacular Press and the Emergence of Modern Indonesian Consciousness (1855–1913)*, Ithaca, NY, 1995; C. A. Bayly and D. H. A. Kolff, eds., *Two Colonial Empires: Comparative Essays on the History of India and Indonesia in the Nineteenth Century*, Dordrecht, Boston, and Lancaster, 1986; R. M. Feener, *Muslim Legal Thought in Modern Indonesia*, Cambridge, 2007; R. W. Hefner, ed., *Making Modern Muslims: The Politics of Islamic Education in Southeast Asia*, Honolulu, 2009; M. F. Laffan, *Islamic Nationhood and Colonial Indonesia: The Umma below the Winds*, London and New York, 2003; M. C. Ricklefs, "The Birth of the Abangan," *Bijdragen tot de Taal- Land- en Volkenkunde (BKI)*, 162 (2006), pp. 35–55; M. C. Ricklefs, *Polarizing Javanese Society: Islamic and Other Visions (c. 1830–1930)*, Honolulu, 2007.

C. International Networks

A. Azra, *The Origins of Islamic Reformism in Southeast Asia: Networks of Malay-Indonesian and Middle Eastern 'Ulama in the Seventeenth and Eighteenth Centuries*, Honolulu, 2004; H. De Jonge and N. Kaptein, eds., *Transcending Borders: Arabs, Politics, Trade and Islam in Southeast Asia*, Leiden, 2002; U. Freitag and W. Clarence-Smith, eds., *Hadhrami Traders, Scholars, and Statesmen in the Indian Ocean, 1750s–1960s*, Leiden, New York, and Köln, 1997; E. Ho, *The Graves of Tarim: Genealogy and Mobility across the Indian Ocean*, Berkeley, CA, Los Angeles, and London, 2006.

CHAPTERS 39–42. ISLAM IN AFRICA

A. General Surveys

A. Atmore and R. Oliver, *Medieval Africa, 1250–1800*, Cambridge, 2001; J. A. Azumah, *The Legacy of Arab-Islam in Africa: A Quest for Inter-Religious Dialogue*, Oxford, 2001; P. D. Curtin, *Precolonial African History*, Washington, DC, 1974; M. Hiskett, *The Course of Islam in Africa*, Edinburgh, 1994; I. Hrebk, ed., *General History of Africa III: Africa from the Seventh to the Eleventh Century*, Berkeley, CA, 1992; N. Levtzion and R. L. Pouwels, eds., *The History of Islam in Africa*, Athens, Oxford, and Cape Town, 2000: D. Robinson, *Muslim Societies in African History*, Cambridge, 2004; E. E. Rosander and D. Westerlund, *African Islam and Islam in Africa: Encounters between Sufis and Islamists*, Athens, OH, 1997; L. Sanneh, *The Crown and the Turban: Muslims and West African Populism*, Boulder, CO, 1997; J. Spaulding and L. Kapteijns, "The Periodization of Pre-Colonial African History," Working Paper, Boston University, 1987; C. N. Ubah, *Islam in African History*, Kaduna, 2001.

B. West Africa

E. A. McDougall, "The View from Awdaghust: War, Trade and Social Change in the Southwestern Sahara; Eighth through Fifteenth Centuries," *Journal of African History*, 26 (1985), pp. 35–63; H. T. Norris, "Muslim Sanhaja Scholars of Mauritania," J. R. Willis, ed., *Studies in West African Islamic History, v. 1: The Cultivators of Islam*, London, 1979, pp. 147–151.

C. East Africa

R. L. Pouwels, *Horn and Crescent: Cultural Change and Traditional Islam on the East African Coast, 800–1900*, Cambridge, 1987.

D. Surveys of the Nineteenth Century

J. F. A. Ajayi, ed., *General History of Africa VI: Africa in the Nineteenth Century until the 1800s*, Paris, Oxford, and Berkeley, CA, 1989; C. Coquery-Vidrovitch, *Africa and the Africans in the Nineteenth Century: A Turbulent History*, New York, 2009.

ANNOTATED BIBLIOGRAPHY FROM A HISTORY OF ISLAMIC SOCIETIES, *2ND EDITION*

Although this book is extensively revised, it is to a significant degree based on the second edition of *A History of Islamic Societies*. The following section reproduces the relevant portions of the bibliography from the second edition of *A History of Islamic Societies* to give the interested reader further suggestions for in-depth study, and to honor the earlier scholarship on which this book is based.

INTRODUCTION

This bibliography is intended as a guide to further reading and includes the most important translations and scholarly works. Most of the citations are to English-language works, but important materials in French, German, and other languages are suggested. Readers will find further bibliographical references in many of the cited works. J. D. Pearson, *Index Islamicus*, Cambridge, 1958–, covers the periodical literature of all Islamic regions from 1906 to the present and book literature from 1976 to the present.

The following abbreviations are used in the bibliography:

AIEO	*Annales de l'institut des études orientales*
BEO	*Bulletin d'études orientales*
BSOAS	*Bulletin of the School of Oriental and African Studies*
	CMRS *Cahiers du monde russe et soviétique*
IJAHS	*International Journal of African Historical Studies*
IJMES	*International Journal of Middle East Studies*
JAH	*Journal of African History*
JAOS	*Journal of the American Oriental Society*
JESHO	*Journal of the Economic and Social History of the Orient*
	JRAS *Journal of the Royal Asiatic Society*
REI	*Revue des études islamiques*

ROMM   *Revue de l'Occident musulman et de la Méditerranée*
RSO   *Revista degli studi orientali*
SI   *Studia Islamica*
ZDMG   *Zeitschrift der deutschen morganländischen Gesellschaft*

PART I

Introduction
On Islamic history as a whole see M. G. S. Hodgson, *The Venture of Islam*, 3 vols., Chicago, 1974. Hodgson is particularly sensitive to religious and literary issues and to the existential meaning of Islamic discourses. The *Encyclopaedia of Islam*, new edn, ed. H. A. R. Gibb et al., Leiden, 1960 is an inexhaustible reference work on all topics related to this volume. The following atlases are useful reference works: R. Roolvink, *Historical Atlas of the Muslim Peoples*, Amsterdam, 1957; F. Robinson, *Atlas of the Islamic World since 1500*, Oxford, 1982; J. L. Bacharach, *A Middle East Studies Handbook*, Seattle, 1984; C. F. Beckingham, *Atlas of the Arab World and the Middle East*, New York, 1960; D. E. Pitcher, *An Historical Geography of the Ottoman Empire*, Leiden, 1972; J. E. Schwartzberg, *A Historical Atlas of South Asia*, Chicago, 1978; G. S. P. Freeman-Grenville, *A Modern Atlas of African History*, London, 1976; and J. D. Fage, *An Atlas of African History*, New York, 1978; H. Kennedy, *An Historical Atlas of Islam*, Leiden, 2002.

On early Islamic history and civilization see J. J. Saunders, *A History of Medieval Islam*, London, 1965; H. A. R. Gibb, *Mohammedanism*, 2nd edn, London, 1969; F. Rahman, *Islam*, 2nd edn, Chicago, 1979; G. E. von Grunebaum, *Medieval Islam*, 2nd edn, Chicago, 1956. In French there is L. Gardet, *L'Islam, religion et communauté*, Paris, 1967; R. Mantran, *L'Expansion musulmane, VIIe-IXe siècles*, 2nd edn, Paris, 1979; C. Cahen, *Les Peuples musulmans dans l'histoire médiévale*, Paris, 1977. See also F. Robinson, *The Cambridge Illustrated History of the Islamic World*, Cambridge, 1996; J. Esposito, ed., *The Oxford History of Islam*, Oxford, 2000; J. Bloom and S. Blair, *Islam: A Thousand Years of Faith and Power*, New Haven, 2002.

Chapter 1
A useful introduction to pre-Islamic Arabia is I. Shahid, "Pre-Islamic Arabia," *Cambridge History of Islam*, I, ed. P. M. Holt, A. K. S. Lambton, and B. Lewis, Cambridge, 1970, pp. 3–29. The pre-Islamic kingdoms of Yemen may be studied in J. Ryckmans, *L'Institution monarchique en Arabie méridionale avant l'Islam*, Louvain, 1951. On Arabian bedouin society see H. Lammens, *Le Berceau de l'Islam*, Rome, 1914; H. Lammens, *L'Arabie occidentale avant l'hégire*, Beirut, 1928; A. Musil, *Arabia Deserta*, New York, 1927; F. Gabrieli, *L'antica società beduina*, Rome, 1959. On the bedouinization of Arabia: W. Caskel, *Die Bedeutung der Beduinen*

in der Geschichte der Araber, Cologne, 1953; W. Caskel, "The Bedouinization of Arabia," *American Anthropologist*, Memoirs, 76 (1954), pp. 36–46.

Pre-Islamic Arabian poetry is the principal literary source of our knowledge of Arabian peoples: see C. Lyall, tr. and ed., *Translations of Ancient Arabian Poetry*, London, 1885; C. Lyall, tr. and ed., *The Mufaddaïyyat*, 2 vols., Oxford, 1918–21; C. Lyall, tr. and ed., *The Poems of ʿAmr son of Qamiʿah*, Cambridge, 1919.

On pre-Islamic Arabian religion see B. Farès, *L'Honneur chez les Arabes avant l'Islam*, Paris, 1932; G. Ryckmans, *Les Religions arabes préislamiques*, 2nd edn, Louvain, 1951; J. Chelhod, *Le Sacrifice chez les Arabes*, Paris, 1955; J. Chelhod, *Introduction à la sociologie de l'Islam: De l'animisme a l'universalisme*, Paris, 1958, which gives an important evolutionary theory; J. Chelhod, *Les Structures du sacré chez les Arabes*, Paris, 1964; T. Fahd, *La Divination arabe*, Leiden, 1966; T. Fahd, *Le Panthéon de l'Arabie centrale à la veille de l'hégire*, Paris, 1968; M. M. Bravmann, *The Spiritual Background of Early Islam*, Leiden, 1972.

Arabian family and social institutions are the subject of W. R. Smith, *Kinship and Marriage in Early Arabia*, New York, 1979; G. H. Stern, *Marriage in Early Islam*, London, 1939; W. M. Watt, *Muhammad at Medina*, Oxford, 1956, pp. 261–302.

Mecca is the subject of H. Lammens, *Le Mecque à la veille de l'hégire*, Beirut, 1924, which develops the theory of the importance of Mecca as a trading center. On Meccan society and commerce: M. J. Kister, *Studies on Jahiliyya and Early Islam*, London, 1980.

Chapter 2

The most important source for the rise of Islam is the Quran itself. A vivid but not always literal translation is A. J. Arberry, tr., *The Koran Interpreted*, New York, 1955. More literal translations include J. M. Rodwell, tr., *The Koran*, London, 1939; E. H. Palmer, tr., *The Koran*, London, 1951. Introductions to the Quran include R. Bell, *Introduction to the Qur'an*, Edinburgh, 1953; A. Jeffries, *The Qur'an as Scripture*, New York, 1952; R. Blachère, *Introduction au Coran*, 2nd edn, Paris, 1959. R. Roberts, *The Social Laws of the Quran*, London, 1971 is a convenient compilation of all the texts dealing with social issues.

The earliest authoritative Muslim biography of the Prophet is made up of the traditions collected in the second century after his death by Ibn Ishaq, and edited by Ibn Hisham, *Life of Muhammad*, tr. A. Guillaume, Lahore, 1955. The most important Western biography is W. M. Watt, *Muhammad at Mecca*, Oxford, 1953; and W. M. Watt, *Muhammad at Medina*, Oxford, 1956. See also M. Rodinson, *Mohammed*, tr. A. Carter, London, 1971.

The relationship of the Quran to the Bible and of Muhammad to Jewish and Christian tradition is the subject of Tor Andrae, *Les Origines de l'Islam et le Christianisme*, tr. Jules Roche, Paris, 1955, summarized in English in Tor Andrae, *Mohammed: The Man and his Faith*, tr. T. Menzel, London, 1956; R. Bell, *The Origins of Islam in its Christian Environment*, London, 1968; H. Speyer, *Die biblischen*

Erzählungen im Qoran, Hildesheim, 1961; C. C. Torrey, *The Jewish Foundation of Islam*, New York, 1933. The most important contributions to understanding the Quran in its Arabian context are T. Izutsu, *Ethico-Religious Concepts in the Qur'an*, Montreal, 1966; and T. Izutsu, *God and Man in the Koran*, Tokyo, 1964.

Chapters 3 and 4

On the Arab conquests and settlement see al-Baladhuri, *Futah al-Buldan*, Leiden, 1866; P. K. Hitti and E. C. Murgotten, tr., *The Origins of the Islamic State*, 2 vols., New York, 1916–24; Fred M. Donner, *The Early Islamic Conquests*, Princeton, 1981; E. Shoufany, *Al-Riddah and the Muslim Conquest of Arabia*, Toronto, 1972. The classic history of the Umayyad period is J. Wellhausen, *The Arab Kingdom and its Fall*, Calcutta, 1927. A good recent general history is M. A. Shaban, *Islamic History*, I, Cambridge, 1971, with fresh but sometimes controversial interpretations. A useful collective work is G. H. A. Juynboll, ed., *Studies on the First Century of Islamic Society*, Carbondale, Ill., 1982. On the transition from ancient to Islamic times see M. Morony, *Iraq after the Muslim Conquest*, Princeton, 1983. E. L. Peterson, *'Ali and Mu'awiya in Early Arabic Tradition*, Copenhagen, 1964 is of exceptional historiographical importance.

On the Umayyad Caliphs see G. Rotter, *Die Umayyaden und der zweite Burgerkreig, 680–692*, Wiesbaden, 1982; F. Gabrieli, "Il califfato di Hisham," *Mémoires de la Société royale d'archéologie d'Alexandrie*, VII, Alexandria, 1935. Fiscal administration is the subject of D. B. Dennett, *Conversion and the Poll Tax in Early Islam*, Cambridge, Mass., 1950.

Art and architecture: K. A. C Creswell, *Early Muslim Architecture*, Oxford, 1969; J. Sauvaget, *La Mosquée omeyyade de Médine*, Paris, 1947; O. Grabar, *The Formation of Islamic Art*, New Haven, 1973; O. Grabar, *City in the Desert: Qasr al-Hayr East*, 2 vols., Cambridge, Mass., 1978. See also Grabar's dissertation, "Ceremonies and Art at the Umayyad Court," Princeton, 1954; and his collected papers, *Studies in Medieval Islamic Art*, London, 1972.

On Umayyad urbanism see Salih al-'Ali, *Al-Tanzīmāt al-ijtimā'iya wa'l-iqtisādīya fi'l-Basra*, Baghdad, 1953; and I. M. Lapidus, "Arab Settlement and Economic Development of Iraq and Iran in the Age of the Umayyad and Early 'Abbasid Caliphs," *The Islamic Middle East, 700–1900: Studies in Economic and Social History*, ed. A. L. Udovitch, Princeton, 1981, pp. 177–208, with further references.

The anti-Umayyad movements to 750: S. M. Jafri, *Origins and Early Developments of Shi'a Islam*, London, 1979; W. M. Watt, "Shiism under the Umayyads," *JRAS* (1960), pp. 158–72; W. M. Watt, "Kharijite Thought in the Umayyad Period," *Der Islam*, 36 (1961), pp. 215–31. The messianic movements of the late Umayyad era may be studied in G. Van Vloten, *Recherches sur la dominion arabe, le chiitisme et les croyances messianiques sous le khalifat des Omayades*, Amsterdam, 1894; B. Lewis, "An Apocalyptic Vision of Islamic History," *BSOAS*, 13 (1950), pp. 308–38.

The ʿAbbasid revolution is the subject of M. Shaban, *The ʿAbbasid Revolution*, Cambridge, 1970; F. Omar, *The ʿAbbasid Caliphate*, Baghdad, 1969; C. Cahen, "Points de vue sur la révolution ʿabbaside," *Revue historique*, 230 (1963), pp. 295–338.

The first century of the ʿAbbasid empire is covered by H. Kennedy, *The Early ʿAbbasid Caliphate*, London, 1981; and J. Lassner, *The Shaping of ʿAbbasid Rule*, Princeton, 1980.

ʿAbbasid urbanism is treated in I. M. Lapidus, "The Evolution of Muslim Urban Society," *Comparative Studies in Society and History*, 15 (1973), pp. 21–50; J. Lassner, *The Topography of Baghdad in the Early Middle Ages*, Detroit, 1970. For ʿAbbasid military institutions see P. Crone, *Slaves on Horses: The Evolution of the Islamic Polity*, Cambridge, 1980; D. Pipes, *Slaves, Soldiers and Islam*, New Haven, 1981. ʿAbbasid administration: the legal sources are translated by A. Ben Shemesh, *Taxation in Islam*, 3 vols., Leiden, 1958–69; D. Sourdel, *Le Vizirat ʿabbaside*, 2 vols., Damascus, 1959–60; S. D. Goitein, "The Origin of the Vizierate and its True Character," *Islamic Culture*, 16 (1942), pp. 255–392; E. Tyan, *Histoire de l'organisation judiciaire en pays d'Islam*, Leiden, 1960; and his summary, "Judicial Organization," *Law in the Middle East*, ed. M. Khadduri and H. Liebesny, Washington, D.C., 1955, pp. 236–78. For provincial tax administration see F. Hussein, *Das Steuersystem in Ägypten, 639–868*, Frankfurt am Main, 1982; A. K. S. Lambton, *Landlord and Peasant in Persia*, London, 1953; C. Cahen, "L'Evolution de l'iqtaʾdu IXᵉ au XIIIᵉ siècle," *Annales ESC*, 8 (1953), pp. 25–52.

Provincial histories: for Iran see the *Cambridge History of Iran*, iv, ed. R. N. Frye, Cambridge, 1975; W. Barthold, *Turkestan Down to the Mongol Invasion*, London, 1968; G. H. Sadiqi, *Les Mouvements religieux Iraniens au IIᵉ, et au IIIᵉ siècle de l'hégire*, Paris, 1938, C. E. Bosworth, *Sistan under the Arabs: From the Islamic Conquest to the Rise of the Saffarids*, Rome, 1968, and the relevant articles in his collected *Medieval History of Iran, Afghanistan and Central Asia*, London, 1977. For Egypt see G. Wiet, *L'Egypte arabe*, Paris, 1937; 2. M. Hassan, *Les Tulunides*, Paris, 1933.

Chapter 5

The theory of the Caliphate is reviewed by T. Arnold, *The Caliphate*, London, 1965; E. Tyan, *Institutions du droit public musulman*, I, Paris, 1954; L. Gardet, *La Cité musulmane*, Paris, 1954; H. A. R. Gibb, "Constitutional Organization," *Law in the Middle East*, ed. M. Khadduri and H. Liebesny, Washington, D.C., 1955, pp. 3–28; D. Sourdel, "Questions de cérémonial ʿabbaside," *REI*, 27 (1960), pp. 121–48.

Reviews of the development of Arabic literature include R. Blachère, *Histoire de la littérature arabe des origines à la fin du XVᵉ siècle de J.-C.*, 3 vols., Paris, 1952–66; A. F. L. Beeston et al., eds., *Arabic Literature to the End of the Umayyad Period*, Cambridge, 1983; H. A. R. Gibb, *Arabic Literature: An Introduction*, 2nd edn, Oxford, 1963; G. E. von Grunebaum, *Themes in Medieval Arabic Literature*, London, 1981; A. Hamori, *On the Art of Medieval Arabic Literature*, Princeton,

1974; M. Zwettler, *The Oral Tradition of Classical Arabic Poetry: Its Character and Implications*, Columbus, Ohio, 1978. For Arabic literary criticism see V. Cantarino, *Arabic Poetics in the Golden Age*, Leiden, 1975; K. Abu Deeb, *Al-Jurjani's Theory of Poetic Imagery*, Warminster, 1979.

On Persian literature see G. Morrison, J. Baldick, and S. Kadkani, *History of Persian Literature from the Beginning of the Islamic Period to the Present Day*, Leiden and Cologne, 1981. J. Rypka, *History of Iranian Literature*, Dordrecht, 1968 is the classic work in the field. See also G. Lazard, ed. and tr., *Les Premiers poètes persans*, Tehran, 1964.

Adab, or courtly literatures of the ʿAbbasid era, are treated in F. Rosenthal, *Knowledge Triumphant: The Concept of Knowledge in Medieval Islam*, Leiden, 1970; G. E. von Grunebaum, *Medieval Islam*, Chicago, 1946; J. C. Vadet, *L'Esprit courtois en Orient dans les cinq premiers siècles de l'hégire*, Paris, 1968; V. Monteil, *Abu-Nuwas: Le vin, le vent, la vie*, Paris, 1979.

For Ibn al-Muqaffaʾ, see D. Sourdel, "La Biographie d'Ibn al-Muqaffaʾ d'après les sources anciennes," *Arabica*, 1 (1954), pp. 307–23. Ibn Qutayba (d. 889) is the subject of G. Lecomte, *Ibn Qutayba: L'Homme, son oeuvre, ses idées*, Damascus, 1965. A partial translation of Ibn Qutayba's major work is provided by J. Horovitz, "Ibn Quteiba's ʿUyun al-Akhbar," *Islamic Culture*, 4 (1930), pp. 171–98, 331–62, 488–530, 5 (1931), pp. 1–27, 194–224. For Jahiz: C Pellat, ed. and tr., *The Life and Works of Jahiz*, Berkeley, 1969; C. Pellat, *Le Milieu Basrien et la formation de Jahiz*, Paris, 1953.

A brief overview of Islamic philosophy may be found in W. M. Watt, *Islamic Philosophy and Theology*, Edinburgh, 1962; R. Walzer, *Greek into Arabic*, Oxford, 1962. On Shiʿi philosophy see H. Corbin, *Histoire de la philosophie islamique*, Paris, 1964. The transmission of Greek thought into Arabic is discussed in D. L. E. O'Leary, *How Greek Science Passed to the Arabs*, London, 1949; F. E. Peters, *Aristotle and the Arabs*, New York, 1968.

For the major Arab philosophers: G. N. Atiyeh, *Al-Kindi: The Philosopher of the Arabs*, Rawalpindi, 1966; *Al-Kindi's Metaphysics: A Translation of "On First Philosophy*,*"* tr. A. L. Ivry, Albany, N.Y., 1974; J. Jolivet, *L'Intellect selon Kindi*, Leiden, 1971; al-Farabi, *Idées des habitants de la cité vertueuse*, tr. R. P. Jaussen, Cairo, 1949; al-Farabi, *Fusul al-Madanï: Aphorisms of the Statesman*, tr. D. M. Dunlop, Cambridge, 1961; al-Farabi, *Philosophy of Plato and Aristotle*, tr. M. Mahdi, New York, 1962.

Chapter 6

Hadith and law: al-Bukhari, *Al-Sahih: Les Traditions islamiques*, 4 vols., tr. O. Houdas, Paris, 1903–14. A convenient later collection of hadith is al-Khatib al-Tibrizi, *Mishkat al-Masahih*, 4 vols., tr. J. Robson, Lahore, 1960–65. Important studies on hadith include W. Graham, *Divine Word and Prophetic Word in Early*

Islam, The Hague, 1977; G. H. A. Juynboll, *Muslim Tradition: Studies in Chronology, Provenance and Authorship of Early Hadith*, Cambridge, 1983. The classic studies in the field are I. Goldziher, *Muslim Studies*, 2 vols., tr. C. R. Barber and S. M. Stern, London, 1968–71; I. Goldziher, *Le Dogme et la loi de l'Islam*, Paris, 1973; I. Goldziher, *Introduction to Islamic Theology and Law*, tr. A. Hamori and R. Hamori, Princeton, 1980; J. Schacht, *The Origins of Muhammadan Jurisprudence*, Oxford, 1959. Good summary reviews of these findings are found in J. Schacht, *An Introduction to Islamic Law*, Oxford, 1964; N. J. Coulson, *A History of Islamic Law*, Edinburgh, 1964. Two important texts in the development of Muslim legal theory are M. Khadduri, tr., *Islamic Jurisprudence: Shafi'i's Risala*, Baltimore, 1961; Malik b. Anas, *Al-Muwatta'* tr. A. A. Tarjumana and Y. Johnson, Norwich, 1982. Important collections of articles on Islamic law include N. J. Coulson, *Conflicts and Tensions in Islamic Jurisprudence*, Chicago, 1969. For commercial law, see A. L. Udovitch, *Partnership and Profit in Medieval Islam*, Princeton, 1970. For law of war and peace; M. Khadduri, *War and Peace in the Law of Islam*, Baltimore, 1955; al-Shaybani, *The Islamic Law of Nations*, tr. M. Khadduri, Baltimore, 1966.

On theology (*kalam*): L. Gardet and M. Anawati, *Introduction à la théologie musulmane: Essai de théologie comparée*, Paris, 1948; P. Morewedge, *Islamic Philosophical Theology*, Albany, N.Y., 1979; L. Gardet, *Dieu et la destinée de l'homme*, Paris, 1967. For the origins and first century of Muslim theology see W. M. Watt, *The Formative Period of Islamic Thought*, Edinburgh, 1973; J. van Ess, *Zwischen Hadit und Theologie*, Berlin and New York, 1975; J. van Ess, *Anfänge muslimischer Theologie*, Beirut, 1977; M. Cook, *Early Muslim Dogma: A Source-Critical Study*, Cambridge, 1981; A.J. Wensinck, *The Muslim Creed: Its Genesis and Historical Development*, London, 1965. On Mu'tazilism see J. van Ess, *Frühe Mu'tazilitische Haresiographie*, Beirut, 1971; A. Nader, *Le Systeme philosophique des Mu'tazila*, Beirut, 1956. For al-Ash'ari see M. Allard, *Le Problème des attributs divins dans la doctrine d'al-As'ari et de ses premiers grands disciples*, Beirut, 1965; al-Ash'ari, *The Theology of al-Ash'ari*, tr. R. J. McCarthy, Beirut, 1953.

Important works on special problems in Muslim theology include T. Izutsu, *The Concept of Belief in Islamic Theology*, Tokyo, 1965; L. Gardet, "Les Noms et les statuts: Le Problème de la foi et des oeuvres en Islam," *SI*, 5 (1956), pp. 61–123.

Sufism: M. G. S. Hodgson, *The Venture of Islam*, I, Chicago, 1974, pp. 359–409 gives a good general introduction. For a Muslim convert's point of view, see T. Burck-hardt, *An Introduction to Sufi Doctrine*, tr. D.M. Matheson, Lahore, 1959. On early Sufism the pathbreaking work of L. Massignon, *Essai sur les origines du lexique technique de la mystique musulmane*, 2nd edn, Paris, 1954; L. Massignon, *La Passion d'al-Husayn ibn Mansour al-Hallaj*, 2 vols., Paris, 1922, tr. H. Mason as *The Passion of al-Hallaj*, 4 vols., Princeton, 1982; and P. Nwyia, *Exégèse coranique et language mystique*, Beirut, 1970 are indispensable. For other good general histories see A. Schimmel, *The Mystical Dimensions of Islam*, Chapel Hill, N.C., 1975;

G. C. Anawati and L. Gardet, *La Mystique musulmane*, Paris, 1961. On the relation of Sufism to other mysticisms see L. Gardet, *Expériences mystiques en terres non-chrétiennes*, Paris, 1953; R. C. Zaehner, *Hindu and Muslim Mysticism*, New York, 1969; R. C. Zaehner, *Mysticism, Sacred and Profane*, Oxford, 1957.

Translations and works dealing with the principal early Sufi masters include H. Ritter, "Studien zur Geschichte der islamischen Frömmigkeit; Hasan el-Basri," *Der Islam*, 21 (1933), pp. 1–83; J. van Ess, *Die Gedankenwelt des Harit al-Muhāsibi*, Bonn, 1961; M. Smith, *An Early Mystic of Baghdad. A Study of the Life, Teaching and Writings of al-Muhasibi*, London, 1935; M. Smith, *Rabi'a the Mystic*, Cambridge, 1928; al-Kharraz, *The Book of Truthfulness [Kitāb al-sidq]*, tr. A. J. Arberry, London, 1937; A. H. Abdel-Kader, *The Life, Personality and Writings of al-Junayd*, London, 1962; al-Niffari, *Kitab al-mawaqif wa-l-mukhatabat*, ed. and tr. A. J. Arberry, London, 1935; M. I. el-Geyoushi, "Al-Tirmidhī's Theory of Saints and Sainthood," *Islamic Quarterly*, 15 (1971), pp. 17–61.

For ʿAbbasid-period Shiʿism, see H. Laoust, *Les Schismes dans l'Islam*, Paris, 1965. For Ismaʾilism see B. Lewis, *The Origins of Ismaʿilism*, Cambridge, 1940; T. Nagel, *Frühe Ismailiya und Fatimiden*, Bonn, 1972; W. Madelung, "Das Imamat in der frühen ismailitischen Lehre," *Der Islam*, 37 (1961), pp. 43–135.

Chapter 7

On the political and religious struggles of the reign of al-Maʾmun, see I. M. Lapidus, "The Separation of State and Religion," *IJMES*, 6 (1975), pp. 363–85, where references may be found to earlier literature.

Chapter 8

On the century of ʿAbbasid decline see H. Bowen, *The Life and Times of ʿAli ibn ʿIsa, the Good Vizier*, Cambridge, 1928; M. Forstner, *Das Kalifat des Abbasiden al-Mustaʾn*, Mainz, 1968; W. Hellige, *Die Regentschaft al-Muwaffaqs*, Berlin, 1936; A. Popović, *La Révolte des esclaves en Iraq*, Paris, 1976.

Chapter 9

For the history of Iran in the late ʿAbbasid, Saljuq, and Mongol eras see the *Cambridge History of Iran*, IV, *The Period from the Arab Invasion to the Saljuqs*, ed. R. N. Frye, Cambridge, 1975, and V, *The Saljuq and Mongol Periods*, ed. J. A. Boyle, Cambridge, 1968. See also R. Frye, *Islamic Iran and Central Asia (7th–12th centuries)*, London, 1979; A. K. S. Lambton, *Theory and Practice in Medieval Persian Government*, London, 1980; D. S. Richards, ed., *Islamic Civilization 950–1150*, Oxford, 1973.

For the Buwayhids see M. Kabir, *The Buwayhid Dynasty of Baghdad*, Calcutta, 1964; H. Busse, *Chalif und Grosskönig, die Buyiden im Iraq*, Beirut, 1969. R. Mottahedeh, *Loyalty and Leadership in an Early Islamic Society*, Princeton, 1980 deals with the concepts that underlay Buwayhid social and political practices.

On the Ghaznavids see C. E. Bosworth, *The Ghaznavids*, Edinburgh, 1963. A regional history of the Caspian area is V. Minorsky, *A History of Sharvan and Darband in the 10th–11th Century*, Cambridge, 1958.

On the Saljuq period see C. Cahen, "The Turkish Invasion: The Selchukids," *A History of the Crusades*, I, ed. M. W. Baldwin, Philadelphia, 1958, pp. 135–76; C. Cahen, "The Historiography of the Seljuqid Period," *Historians of the Middle East*, ed. B. Lewis and P. Holt, London, 1962, pp. 59–78; E. Tyan, *Institutions du droit public musulman: Sultanat et califat*, II, Paris, 1957; Nizam al-Mulk, *Siyasat-Nama: The Book of Government*, tr. H. Darke, London, 1960. On the Khwarazmshahs see H. Horst, *Die Staatsverwaltung der Grosselğūqen und Hōrazmsahs, 1038–1231*, Wiesbaden, 1964.

Political and cultural geography is the subject of X. de Planhol, *Le Monde islamique: Essai de géographie religieuse*, Paris, 1957; X. de Planhol, *Les Fondements géographiques de l'histoire de l'Islam*, Paris, 1968; A. Miquel, *La Géographie humaine du monde musulman jusqu'au milieu du XIe siecle*, Paris, 1967. On economy and technology see R. Bulliet, *The Camel and the Wheel*, Cambridge, Mass., 1975; A. M. Watson, *Agricultural Innovation in the Early Islamic World: The Diffusion of Crops and Farming Techniques, 700–1100*, Cambridge, 1983; M. Lombard, *Les Textiles dans le monde musulman du VIIe au XIIe siècle*, Paris, 1978.

On the economic history of the Middle East from the origins of Islam to the thirteenth century see A. L. Udovitch, ed., *The Islamic Middle East, 700–1900: Studies in Economic and Social History*, Princeton, 1981; E. Ashtor, *A Social and Economic History of the Near East*, London, 1976; D. S. Richards, *Islam and the Trade of Asia*, Oxford, 1970.

The basic history of Mediterranean trade through the late Middle Ages is W. von Heyd, *Histoire du commerce du levant au moyen âge*, 2 vols., tr. F. Reynaud, Amsterdam, 1959. The study of Mediterranean trade in the early Middle Ages was for decades dominated by H. Pirenne, *Mohammed and Charlemagne*, New York, 1958. The controversy that followed is summed up in a pamphlet by A. F. Havighurst, *The Pirenne Thesis*, 3rd edn, Lexington, Mass., 1976. Important revisions include A. R. Lewis, *Naval Power and Trade in the Mediterranean*, Princeton, 1951; E. Eickhoff, *Seekrieg und Seepolitik zwischen Islam und Abendland. Das Mittelmeer unter byzantinischer und arabischer Hegemonie (650–1040)*, Berlin, 1966. For the period of the Crusades see E. H. Byrne, *Genoese Shipping in the Twelfth and Thirteenth Centuries*, Cambridge, Mass., 1930.

Chapter 10

For the social organization of the 'ulama' see R. P. Mottahedeh, *Loyalty and Leadership in an Early Islamic Society*, Princeton, 1980; R. W. Bulliet, *The Patricians of Nishapur*, Cambridge, 1972; J. Gilbert, "Institutionalization of Muslim Scholarship and Professionalization of the 'Ulama' in Medieval Damascus," SI, 52 (1980), pp. 105–34. For the madrasa see G. Makdisi, "Muslim Institutions of Learning in

Eleventh-century Baghdad," *BSOAS*, 24 (1961), pp. 1–56. A. L. Tibawi, "Origin and Character of al Madrasah," *BSOAS*, 25 (1962), pp. 225–38 is a rebuttal of Makdisi's views. Also important are D. Sourdel, "Reflexions sur la diffusion de la madrasa en Orient du XIe au XIIIe siècle," *REI*, 44 (1976), pp. 165–84; G. Makdisi, "Ash'ari and the Ash'arites in Islamic Religious History," *SI*, 17 (1962), pp. 37–80, 18(1962), pp. 19–39.

For religion and politics in the Saljuq era see H. Laoust, "La Pensée et l'action politiques d'Al-Mawardi," *REI*, 36 (1968), pp. 11–92; H. Laoust, *La Politique de Gazali*, Paris, 1970. On Hanbalism see G. Makdisi, *Ibn 'Aqil et la résurgence de l'Islam traditionaliste au XIe siècle*, Damascus, 1963; and G. Makdisi, "Hanbalite Islam," *Studies on Islam*, ed. M. L. Swartz, New York, 1981, pp. 216–74.

On the social history of Sufism see J. S. Trimingham, *The Sufi Orders in Islam*, Oxford, 1971. On veneration of saints see I. Goldziher, "Veneration of Saints in Islam," *Muslim Studies*, II, London, 1971, pp. 253–341; J. Sourdel-Thomine, "Les Anciens lieux de pèlerinage damascains," *BEO*, 14 (1952–54), pp. 65–85.

On urbanism see I. M. Lapidus, "The Early Evolution of Muslim Urban Society," *Comparative Studies in Society and History*, 15 (1973), pp. 21–50; I. M. Lapidus, "Muslim Cities and Islamic Societies," *Middle Eastern Cities*, ed. I. M. Lapidus, Berkeley, 1969, pp. 47–79; and I. M. Lapidus, *Muslim Cities in the Later Middle Ages*, Cambridge, 1984. Collective works devoted to cities include A. Hourani and S. M. Stern, *The Islamic City*, Oxford, 1970; L. C. Brown, *From Madina to Metropolis*, Princeton, 1973; M. Haneda and T. Miura, eds., *Islamic Urban Studies*, London, 1994.

S. D. Goitein, *A Mediterranean Society: The Jewish Communities of the Arab World as Portrayed in the Documents of the Cairo Geniza*, 4 vols., Berkeley, 1967–78 portrays the Jewish communities of the Mediterranean but throws light on Muslim societies as well. On the Muslim merchant classes see S. D. Goitein, "The Rise of the Near-Eastern Bourgeoisie," *Journal of World History*, 3 (1956), pp. 583–604; M. Rodinson, "Le Marchand musulman," *Islam and the Trade of Asia*, ed. D. S. Richards, Oxford, 1970, pp. 21–36; M. Rodinson, *Islam and Capitalism*, tr. B. Pearce, Austin, Tex., 1978. For guilds and working classes see R. Brunschvig, "Métiers vils en Islam," *SI*, 16 (1962), pp. 41–60; S. D. Goitein, "Artisans en Méditerranée orientale au haut moyen âge," *Annales ESC*, 19 (1964), pp. 847–68.

Futuwwa, *'ayyarun*, and urban young men's gangs: C. Cahen, "Mouvements populaires et autonomisme urbain dans l'Asie musulmane du moyen âge," *Arabica*, 5 (1958), pp. 225–50, 6 (1959), pp. 25–56, 233–65; F. Taeschner, "Das Futuwwa-Rittertum des islamischen Mittelalters," *Beiträge zur Arabistik, Semitistik und Islamwissenschaft*, ed. R. Hartmann and H. Scheel, Leipzig, 1944, pp. 340–85.

Non-Muslim peoples under Muslim rule: A. Fattal, *Le Statut légal des non-musulmans en pays d'Islam*, Beirut, 1958; A. S. Tritton, *The Caliphs and their*

Non-Muslim Subjects, London, 1970; S. D. Goitein, *Jews and Arabs: Their Contacts through the Ages*, New York, 1964; N. A. Stillman, *The Jews of Arab Lands*, Philadelphia, 1979; A. S. Atiya, *A History of Eastern Christianity*, 2 vols., London, 1968–69; P. Rondot, *Les Chrétiens d'Orient*, Paris, 1955; M. Morony, "Religious Communities in Late Sassanian and Early Muslim Iraq," *JESHO*, 17 (1974), pp. 113–35.

Conversion to Islam has been little studied. See N. Levtzion, ed., *Conversion to Islam*, New York, 1979; R. Bulliet, *Conversion to Islam in the Medieval Period*, Cambridge, Mass., 1979; I. M. Lapidus, "The Conversion of Egypt to Islam," *In Memoriam S. M. Stern (Israel Oriental Studies)*, 2 (1972), pp. 248–62.

Chapter 11

Important overviews of the literature are E. I. J. Rosenthal, *Political Thought in Medieval Islam*, Cambridge, 1958; W. M. Watt, *Islamic Political Thought*, Edinburgh, 1968. On juristic political theory see A. K. S. Lambton, *State and Government in Medieval Islam*, Oxford, 1981, Y. Ibish, *The Political Doctrine of al-Baqillani*, Beirut, 1968; al-Mawardi, *Les Statuts gouvernementaux*, tr. E. Fagnan, Algiers, 1915; Ibn Taymiya, *Ibn Taymiyah on Public and Private Law in Islam*, Beirut, 1968; H. Laoust, *Essai sur les doctrines sociales et politiques de Taki-d-Din Ahmad b. Taimiya*, Cairo, 1939.

Translations of the works of al-Farabi on political theory include *Idées des habitants de la cité vertueuse*, tr. R. P. Jaussen, Y. Karam, and J. Chlala, Cairo, 1949; *Fusūl al-Madanī: Aphorisms of the Statesman*, ed. and tr. D. M. Dunlop, Cambridge, 1961; *Philosophy of Plato and Aristotle*, tr. M. Mahdi, New York, 1962. Averroes' principal political work is the *Commentary on Plato's Republic*, ed. and tr. E. I. J. Rosenthal, Cambridge, 1966.

Translations of Mirrors for Princes include al-Jahiz, *Le Livre de la couronne*, tr. C. Pellat, Paris, 1954; Nizam al-Mulk, *The Book of Government or Rules for Kings*, tr. H. Darke, 2nd edn, London, 1978; al-Ghazali, *Book of Counsel for Kings*, tr. F. Bagley, London, 1964; Kai Ka'us b. Iskandar, *A Mirror for Princes: The Qabus Nama*, tr. R. Levy, New York, 1951; see also G. Richter, *Studien zur Geschichte der älteran arabischen Fürstenspiegel*, Leipzig, 1932.

The *Muqaddima* or *Prolegomena* of Ibn Khaldun is translated by W. M. de Slane, *Les Prolégomènes d'Ibn Khaldoun*, 3 vols., Paris, 1934–38; F. Rosenthal, *Ibn Khaldun, The Muqaddimah*, 3 vols., New York, 1958. Among recent scholarly works on Ibn Khaldun see M. Mahdi, *Ibn Khaldun's Philosophy of History*, London, 1957; W. J. Fischel, *Ibn Khaldun in Egypt*, Berkeley, 1967; Y. Lacoste, *Ibn Khaldoun: Naissance de l'histoire passé du Tiers-Monde*, Paris, 1966; M. M. Rabi, *The Political Theory of Ibn Khaldun*, Leiden, 1967; P. von Sivers, *Khalifat, Königtum und Verfall: Die Politische Theorie Ibn Khaldüns*, Munich, 1968; A. al-Azmeh, *Ibn Khaldün in Modern Scholarship: A Study in Orientalism*, London, 1981; and A. al-Azmeh, *Ibn Khaldun: An Essay in Reinterpretation*, London, 1982.

Chapter 12

On ethics see M. Arkoun, "L'Ethique musulmane d'après Mawardī," *REI*, 31 (1963), pp. 1–31; M. Arkoun, *Contribution à l'étude de l'humanisme arabe au IVe/Xe siècle: Miskawayh (320/325–421–932/936–1030), philosophe et historien*, Paris, 1970; Ibn Miskawayh, *Traité d'éthique*, tr. M. Arkoun, Damascus, 1969; Muhammad Abul Qassem, *The Ethics of al-Ghazali*, Petaling Jaya, 1975.

The post-945 development of Sufism is represented by al-Kalabadhi, *The Doctrine of the sūfīs*, tr. A. J. Arberry, Cambridge, 1935; al-Sarraj, *The Kitab al-Luma' fi'l-Tasawwuf of Abu Nasr*, tr. R. A. Nicholson, London, 1963; al-Hujwīrī, *The Kashf al-Mahjub*, tr. R. A. Nicholson, London, 1911; S. de Laugier de Beaurecueil, *Khwadja 'Abdullah Ansārī mystique hanbalite*, Beirut, 1965.

For al-Ghazali, see M. Bouyges, *Essai de chronologie des oeuvres d'al-Ghazali*, Beirut, 1959; H. Laoust, *La Politique de Gazzali*, Paris, 1970; H. Lazarus-Yafeh, *Studies in al-Ghazali*, Jerusalem, 1975. The works of F. Jabré explore al-Ghazali's conceptual vocabulary: *La Notion de certitude selon Ghazali*, Paris, 1958; *La Notion de la ma'rifa chez Ghazali*, Beirut, 1958; *Essai sur la lexique de Ghazali*, Beirut, 1970.

Translations of al-Ghazali include W. M. Watt, *The Faith and Practice of al-Ghazali*, London, 1953; a translation of the autobiography, *Deliverance from Error: The Book of Knowledge*, tr. N. A. Faris, Lahore, 1962; *The Alchemy of Happiness*, tr. C. Field, London, 1980; *Al-Ghazali's Book of 'Fear and Hope*, tr. W. McKane, Leiden, 1965; G. H. Bousquet, *Ihya': ou Vivication des sciences de la foi, analyse et index*, Paris, 1955 – a résumé of al-Ghazali's principal work; *Tahafut al-Falasifah* [Incoherence of the Philosophers], tr. S. A. Kamali, Lahore, 1958. On Suhrawardi al-Maqtul (d. 1191) see S. H. Nasr, *Three Muslim Sages*, Cambridge, Mass., 1964; H. Corbin, *Les Motifs zoroastriens dans la philosophie de Suhrawardi*, Tehran, 1946; and H. Corbin, *Suhrawardi d'Alep*, Paris, 1939. Translations include *Opera metaphysica et mystica*, tr. H. Corbin, I, Istanbul, 1945, II, Tehran, 1952.

On Ibn al-'Arabi (d. 1240) see A. E. Affifi, "Ibn 'Arabi," *History of Muslim Philosophy*, I, ed. M. M. Sharif, Wiesbaden, 1963, pp. 398–420; A. E. Affifi, *The Mystical Philosophy of Muhyid Din Ibnul'Arabi*, Cambridge, 1939; H. Corbin, *Creative Imagination in the Sufism of Ibn 'Arabi*, tr. R. Manheim, Princeton, 1969; T. Izutsu, *A Comparative Study of the Key Philosophical Concepts in Sufism and Taoism*, Berkeley, 1984.

Translations of Ibn al'Arabi's works include *Sufis of Andalusia. The Rūh al-quds and al-Durrat al-fakhirah of Ibn 'Arabī*, tr. R. W. J. Austin, Berkeley, 1977; *La Profession de foi*, tr. R. Deladrière, Paris, 1978; *The Bezels of Wisdom*, tr. R. W. J. Austin, New York, 1980; *The Seals of Wisdom*, tr. A. al-Tarjumana, Norwich, 1980; *Journey to the Lord of Power: A Sufi Manual on Retreat*, tr. T. Harris, New York, 1981.

On the philosophy of Ibn Sina see L. Gardet, *La Pensée religieuse d'Avicenne (Ibn Sīnā)*, Paris, 1951; A. M. Goichon, *La Philosophie d'Avicenne et son influence en Europe médiévale*, 2nd edn, Paris, 1951; A. Afnan, *Avicenna: His Life and Works*, London, 1958; H. Corbin, *Avicenna and the Visionary Recital*, tr. W. Trask, New York, 1960. Translations include *Avicenna on Theology*, tr. A. J. Arberry, London, 1951; *Livre des directives et remarques*, tr. A. M. Goichon, Beirut, 1951; *Avicenna's Psychology*, tr. F. Rahman, London, 1952; *The Metaphysica of Avicenna*, tr. P. Morewedge, New York, 1973. Translations of Ibn Rushd include *Tahafut al-Tahafut* [The Incoherence of the Incoherence], 2 vols., tr. S. van den Bergh, London, 1954; *On the Harmony of Religion and Philosophy*, tr. G. Hourani, London, 1961; *Aver-roes' Three Short Commentaries on Aristotle's "Topics," "Rhetoric," and "Poetics,"* tr. C. E. Butterworth, Albany, N.Y., 1977.

For special topics in Islamic philosophy see M. Fakhry, *Islamic Occasionalism and its Critique by Averroes and Aquinas*, London, 1958; A. J. Arberry, *Revelation and Reason in Islam*, London, 1957; F. Rahman, *Prophecy in Islam*, London, 1958; S. H. Nasr, *An Introduction to Islamic Cosmological Doctrines*, Cambridge, Mass., 1964; I. R. Netton, *Muslim Neoplatonists: An Introduction to the Thought of the Brethren of Purity*, London, 1982.

The transmission of Arabic and Hebrew philosophy to Europe and the development of Christian scholasticism are the subjects of F. van Steenberghen, *Aristotle in the West: The Origins of Latin Aristotelianism*, tr. L. Johnston, Louvain, 1955; F. van Steenberghen, *The Philosophical Movement in the Thirteenth Century*, Edinburgh, 1955; E. Gilson, "Les Sources gréco-arabes de l'Augustinisme avicennisant," *Archives d'histoire doctrinale et littéraire du moyen âge*, 14 (1929), pp. 5–149; M. Steinschneider, *Die europäischen Übersetzungen aus dem Arabischen bis mitte des 17. Jahrhunderts*, Graz, 1956. For relations between Islam and the West more generally see R. W. Southern, *Western Views of Islam in the Middle Ages*, Cambridge, Mass., 1978; N. Daniel, *Islam and the West: The Making of an Image*, Edinburgh, 1960; N. Daniel, *The Arabs and Medieval Europe*, 2nd edn, London, 1979; J. Kritzech, *Peter the Venerable and Islam*, Princeton, 1964; K. I. Semaan, ed., *Islam and the Medieval West*, Albany, N.Y., 1980.

PART II

Chapter 13

For Iran under the Mongols see the relevant chapters of the *Cambridge History of Iran*, v, ed. J. A. Boyle, Cambridge, 1968; C. Cahen, "The Turks in Iran and Anatolia before the Mongol Invasions," *History of the Crusades*, ii, ed. R. L. Wolff and H. W. Hazard, Madison, Wis., 1969, pp. 661–92; C. Cahen, "The Mongols and the Near East," *ibid.*, pp. 715–34; B. Spuler, *Die Mongolen in Iran: Politik, Verwaltung und Kultur der Ilchanzeit, 1220–1350*, Berlin, 1968. On Mongol art see D. N. Wilber, *The Architecture of Islamic Iran*, Princeton, 1955; O. Grabar and S. Blair, *Epic Images and Contemporary History: The Illustrations of the Great Mongol*

Shah-nama, Chicago, 1980. See bibliography for chapter 17 for further references to Mongols and Inner Asia.

For the political system of Iran in the fifteenth century see J. E. Woods, *The Aqquyunlu: Clan, Confederation, Empire*, Minneapolis, 1976. On the rise of the Safavid dynasty see M. Mazzaoui, *The Origins of the Safawids*, Wiesbaden, 1972. A general history of the Safavid period in English is R. Savory, *Iran under the Safavids*, Cambridge, 1980. L. L. Bellan, *Chah ʿAbbas*, I, Paris, 1932 covers the principal reign of the dynasty. For Safavid and later Iranian relations with Europe see R. K. Ramazani, *The Foreign Policy of Iran: 1500–1941*, Charlottesville, Va., 1966.

Safavid state organization: A. K. S. Lambton, *Landlord and Peasant in Persia*, London, 1953. For the theory of Iranian monarchy see A. K. S. Lambton, "Quis cus-todiet custodes? Some Reflections on the Persian Theory of Government," *SI*, 5 (1956), pp. 125–48, 6 (1956), pp. 125–46. For Safavid art and architecture see S. C. Welch, *A King's Book of Kings: The Shah-nameh of Shah Tahmasp*, London, 1972; S. C. Welch, *Persian Painting: Five Royal Safavid Manuscripts of the Sixteenth Century*, New York, 1976; J. Bloom and S. Blair, *Art and Architecture of Islam, 1250–1800*, New Haven, 1994.

The relations between state and religion in Safavid Iran are the subject of J. Aubin, "Etudes safavides: I, Šāh Ismāʿīl; et les notables de l'Iraq persan," *JESHO*, 2 (1959), pp. 37–81; J. Aubin, "La Politique religieuse des Safavides," *Le Shīʿisme imamite, Colloque* de Strasbourg, Paris, 1970, pp. 235–44; S. Arjomand, "Religion, Political Action and Legitimate Domination in Shiʿite Iran: 14th to 18th Centuries," *European Journal of Sociology*, 20 (1979), pp. 59–109; S. Arjomand, "Religious Extremism (Ghuluww), Sufism and Sunnism in Safavid Iran: 1501–1722," *Journal of Asian History*, 15 (1981), pp. 1–35.

Iranian illuminationist philosophy has been examined by S. H. Nasr, "The School of Isfahan," *A History of Muslim Philosophy*, II, ed. M. M. Sharif, Wiesbaden, 1966, pp. 904–31; H. Corbin, *En Islam iranien*, 3 vols., Paris, 1974; and H. Corbin, *La Philosophie iranienne islamique aux XVIIe et XVIIe siècles*, Paris, 1981. See also F. Rahman, *The Philosophy of Mulla Sadra (Sadr al-Din al-Shirazi)*, Albany, N.Y., 1976.

The work of James Reid on *uymaq* and tribal structures has contributed to my interpretation of the dynamics of Iranian history. See his *Tribalism and Society in Islamic Iran, 1500–1629*, Malibu, Calif., 1983; "The Qajar Uymaq in the Safavid Period, 1500–1722," *Iranian Studies*, 11 (1978), pp. 117–143; and "Rebellion and Social Change in Astarabad, 1537–1744," *IJMES*, 13 (1981), pp. 35–53.

On the Iranian economy see R. Quiring-Zoche, *Isfahan im funfzehnten und sechzehnten Jahrhundert*, Freiburg, 1980; M. Keyvani, *Artisans and Guild life in the Later Safavid Period*, Berlin, 1982.

For the eighteenth-century collapse of the Safavid regime see L. Lockhart, *The Fall of the Safavi Dynasty and the Afghan Occupation of Persia*, Cambridge, 1958;

L. Lockhart, *Nadir Shah: A Critical Study*, London, 1938; and J. R. Perry, *Karim Khan Zand: A History of Iran, 1747–1779*, Chicago, 1979. Other studies of Turko-Iranian tribal societies in the eighteenth and nineteenth centuries include G. Garthwaite, "Pastoral Nomadism and Tribal Power," *Iranian Studies*, 11 (1978), pp. 173–97; R. Loeffler, "Tribal Order and the State: The Political Organization of the Boir Ahmad, *Iranian Studies*, 11 (1978), pp. 144–71.

Chapter 14

The classic history of the Ottoman empire is H. Inalcik, *The Ottoman Empire: The Classical Age, 1300–1600*, tr. N. Itzkowitz and C. Imber, London, 1973- H. A. R. Gibb and H. Bowen, *Islamic Society and the West*, 2 parts, Oxford, 1950, 1957, despite out-of-date sections, is still an indispensable introduction. See also N. Itzkowitz, *The Ottoman Empire and Islamic Tradition*, New York, 1972; S. J. Shaw, *History of the Ottoman Empire and Modern Turkey*, 2 vols., Cambridge, 1976.

On pre-Ottoman Turkey see C. Cahen, *Pre-Ottoman Turkey, 1071–1330*, tr. J. Jones-Williams, London, 1968. Important studies of the Turkish principalities include B. Flemming, *Landschaftsgeschichte von Pamphylien, Pisidien und Lykien im Spätmittelalter*, Wiesbaden, 1964; P. Lemerle, *L'Emirat d'Aydin: Byzance et l'Occident. Recherches sur "La Geste d'Umur Pacha,"* Paris, 1957; P. Wittek, *Das fürstentum Mentesche*, Amsterdam, 1967; S. Vryonis, Jr., *The Decline of Medieval Hellenism in Asia Minor*, Berkeley, 1971; and S. Vryonis, Jr., "Nomadization and Islamization in Asia Minor," *Dumbarton Oaks Papers*, 29 (1975), pp. 41–71.

On Ottoman conquests see P. Wittek, *Rise of the Ottoman Empire*, London, 1938; F. Babinger, *Mahomet II, le Conquérant, et son temps*, Paris, 1954; S. Runciman, *The Fall of Constantinople*, Cambridge, 1965. Ottoman wars with the Austro-Hungarian empire: D. Vaughan, *Europe and the Turk: A Pattern of Alliances, 1350–1700*, Liverpool, 1954; C. M. Kortepeter, *Ottoman Imperialism during the Reformation: Europe and the Caucasus*, New York, 1972; S. A. Fischer-Galati, *Ottoman Imperialism and German Protestantism*, Cambridge, Mass., 1959. For Ottoman expansion in the Crimea see H. Inalcik, "The Origin of the Ottoman-Russian Rivalry and the Don-Volga Canal (1569)," *Annales de l'Université d Ankara*, 1 (1946–47), pp. 47–106; W. E. D. Allen, *Problems of Turkish Power in the Sixteenth Century*, London, 1963.

On Ottoman expansion in the Mediterranean see F. Braudel, *The Mediterranean and the Mediterranean World*, 2 vols., tr. S. Reynolds, New York, 1972; A. Hess, *The Forgotten Frontier: A History of the Sixteenth-century Ibero-African Frontier*, Chicago, 1978. For Ottoman–Safavid wars see E. Eberhard, *Osmanische Polemik gegen die Safawiden im 16. Jahrhundert. nach arabischen Handschriften*, Freiburg, 1970. A useful collection of documents is J. C. Hurewitz, *Diplomacy in the Near and Middle East: A Documentary Record, 1535–1914*, I, New York, 1956.

For Ottoman rule in the Balkans see P. F. Sugar, *Southeastern Europe under Ottoman Rule, 1354–1804*, Seattle, 1977; N. Beldiceanu, *Le Monde ottoman des Balkans (1402–1566)*, London, 1976.

For the institutions of the Ottoman state see A. D. Alderson, *The Structure of the Ottoman Dynasty*, Oxford, 1956; I. M. Kunt, *The Sultan's Servants: The Transformation of Ottoman Provincial Government, 1550–1650*, New York, 1983; H. Inalcik, "Military and Fiscal Transformation in the Ottoman Empire, 1600–1700," *Archivum Ottomanicum*, 6 (1980), pp. 283–337. B. Miller, *The Palace School of Muhammad the Conqueror*, Cambridge, Mass., 1941 depicts the education of the janissaries.

For Islamic religious elites see H. A. R. Gibb and H. Bowen, *Islamic Society and the West*, Oxford, 1950–57, I, pp. 19–38, II, pp. 70–261; J. Birge, *The Bektashi Order of Dervishes*, London, 1937.

On the non-Muslim populations: F. W. Hasluck, *Christianity and Islam under the Sultans*, 2 vols., Oxford, 1929; T. Ware, *Eustratios Argenti: A Study of the Greek Church under Turkish Rule*, Oxford, 1964; N. J. Pantazopoulos, *Church and Law in the Balkan Peninsula during the Ottoman Rule*, Thessaloniki, 1967; S. Runciman, *The Great Church in Captivity*, London, 1968; L. Arpee, *A History of Armenian Christianity from the Beginning to our Own Time*, New York, 1946. On the Jewish communities see M. A. Epstein, *The Ottoman Jewish Communities and their Role in the Fifteenth and Sixteenth Centuries*, Freiburg, 1980; C. Roth, *The House of Nasi: The Duke of Naxos*, New York, 1948. The relations between Ottomans and Europeans are discussed in B. Homsy, *Les Capitulations et la protection des chrétiens au Proche-Orient aux XVIᵉ, XVIIᵉ et XVIIIᵉ siècles*, Paris, 1956; C. A. Frazee, *Catholics and Sultans: The Church and the Ottoman Empire, 1453–1923*, Cambridge, 1983. A major reinterpretation of the "millet" system is advanced by B. Braude, "Foundation Myths of the Millet System," *Christians and Jews in the Ottoman Empire*, i, ed. B. Braude and B. Lewis, New York, 1982, pp. 69–88.

For the development of Istanbul see B. Lewis, *Istanbul and the Civilization of the Ottoman Empire*, Norman, Okla., 1963; R. Mantran, *La Vie quotidienne à Constantinople au temps de Soliman le Magnifique et de ses successeurs*, Paris, 1965. Balkan cities are the subject of N. Todorov, ed., *La Ville balkanique sous les Ottomans, XVᵉ–XIXᵉ siècles*, London, 1977. On the small towns of Anatolia see S. Faroqhi, *Towns and Townsmen of Ottoman Anatolia*, Cambridge, 1984.

The demographic and economic development of Anatolia is treated by M. A. Cook, *Population Pressure in Rural Anatolia, 1450–1600*, London, 1972. See also H. Islamoglu and S. Faroqhi, "Crop Patterns and Agricultural Production Trends in Sixteenth-Century Anatolia," *Review* (New York), 2 (1979), pp. 401–36. Ottoman trade: H. Inalcik, "Bursa and the Commerce of the Levant," *JESHO*, 3 (1960), pp. 131–47; H. Inalcik, "Capital Formation in the Ottoman Empire," *Journal of Economic History*, 29 (1969), pp. 97–140; H. Islamoglu-Inan, *State and Peasant in the Ottoman Empire*, New York, 1994.

The struggle for control of the international spice trade is the subject of S. Y. Labib, *Handelsgeschichte Ägyptens im Spätmittelalter (1171–1517)*, Wiesbaden,

1965. For the rise of Europe and the transformation of the world economy see I. Wallerstein, *The Modern World System*, 2 vols., New York, 1974–80; P. Pachi, "The Shifting of International Trade Routes in the 15th–17th Centuries," *Acta Historica*, 14 (1968), pp. 287–321; R. Mantran, "Transformation du commerce dans l'Empire Ottoman au dix-huitième siècle," *Studies in Eighteenth-Century Islamic History*, ed. T. Naff and R. Owen, Carbondale, Ill., 1977, pp. 217–35.

The growth of European commerce in the seventeenth and eighteenth centuries is studied in P. Masson, *Histoire du commerce français dans le Levant au XVIe siècle*, Paris, 1896; P. Masson, *Histoire du commerce français dans le Levant au XVIIIe siècle*, Paris, 1911; N. G. Svoronos, *Le Commerce de Salonique au XVIIe siècle*, Paris, 1956; A. C. Wood, *A History of the Levant Company*, London, 1935. See also D. Goffman, *Izmir and the Levantine World*, Seattle, 1990; E. Eldem, D. Goffman, and B. Masters, *The Ottoman City between East and West*, Cambridge, 1999.

On Turkish art and literature see E. Atil, ed., *Turkish Art*, Washington, D.C., 1980; G. Goodwin, *A History of Ottoman Architecture*, Baltimore, 1971; O. Aslanapa, *Turkish Art and Architecture*, London, 1971; M. And, *A History of Theatre and Popular Entertainment in Turkey*, Ankara, 1963–64; M. And, *Turkish Miniature Painting*, Ankara, 1974; E. Atil, *Turkish Miniature Painting*, Tokyo, 1960.

On the seventeenth and eighteenth centuries see S. J. Shaw, *Between Old and New: The Ottoman Empire under Sultan Selim III, 1789–1807*, Cambridge, Mass., 1971; T. Naff and R. Owen, eds., *Studies in Eighteenth Century Islamic History*, London, 1977. Specialized studies on the internal condition of the Ottoman empire include W. J. Griswold, *The Great Anatolian Rebellion: 1000–1020/1591–1611*, Berlin, 1983; K. Barkey, *Bandits and Bureaucrats: The Ottoman Route to State Centralization*, Ithaca, N.Y., 1994.

Ottoman military and political relations with Europe in the eighteenth century are treated in M. S. Anderson, *The Eastern Question, 1774–1923*, London, 1966; L. Cassels, *The Struggle for the Ottoman Empire, 1717–1740*, London, 1966; A. W. Fisher, *The Russian Annexation of the Crimea, 1772–1783*, Cambridge, 1970; B. H. Sumner, *Peter the Great and the Ottoman Empire*, Oxford, 1949; G. S. Thomson, *Catherine the Great and the Expansion of Russia*, London, 1947.

Chapter 15

For Fatimid art see K. A. C. Creswell, *The Muslim Architecture of Egypt*, 2 vols., Oxford, 1952–59; O. Grabar, "Imperial and Urban Art in Islam: The Subject Matter of Fatimid Art," *Colloque international sur l'histoire du Caire*, Cairo, 1973, pp. 173–89; J. M. Bloom, "The Mosque of al-Hakim in Cairo," *Muqarnas*, 1 (1983), pp. 15–36; C. Williams, "The Cult of Alid Saints in the Fatimid Monuments of Cairo," *Muqarnas*, 1 (1983), pp. 37–52; M. Canard, "Le Cérémonie fatimite et le cérémonie byzantin," *Byzantion*, 21 (1951), pp. 355–420; and M. Canard, "La Procession du nouvel an chez les Fatimides," *AIEO*, 10 (1952), pp. 364–98.

For Syria in the early Islamic era see K. S. Salibi, *Syria under Islam: Empire on Trial, 634–1097*, Delmar, N.Y., 1976; M. Canard, *Histoire de la dynastie des Ham-danides de jazïra et de Syrie*, Paris, 1953. Histories of the Crusades include S. Runci-man, *A History of the Crusades*, 3 vols., Cambridge, 1951–54; H. E. Mayer, *The Crusades*, tr. J. Gillingham, London, 1972; J. Prawers, *Crusader Institutions*, Oxford, 1980; H. W. Hazard, *The Art and Architecture of the Crusader States*, Madison, Wis., 1977.

For the history of Muslim Syria in the crusading era the fundamental work is C. Cahen, *La Syrie du Nord à lépoque des croisades*, Paris, 1940. Good general accounts may be found in K. M. Setton, ed., *A History of the Crusades*, 2nd edn, 4 vols., Madison, Wis., 1969–77. See also N. Elisseeff, *Nür ad-Dïn: Un grand prince musulman de Syrie au temps des croisades (511–569 h/1 118–1174)*, 3 vols., Damascus, 1967; E. Sivan, *L'Islam et la croisade*, Paris, 1968.

Useful translations of Arabic sources include E. Gabrieli, ed., *Arab Historians of the Crusades*, Berkeley, 1969; F. Gabrieli, *Recueil des historiens des croisades*, Académie des inscriptions et belles-lettres, 14 vols., Paris, 1966–67; Ibn al-Qalānisī, *The Damascus Chronicle of the Crusades*, tr. H. A. R. Gibb., London, 1932; Usämah ibn Munqidh, *An Arab-Syrian Gentleman and Warrior in the Period of the Crusades*, tr. P. K. Hitti, New York, 1929.

Isma'ilism in the Crusades period is the subject of M. G. S. Hodgson, *The Order of Assassins*, The Hague, 1955; B. Lewis, *The Assassins*, London, 1967. See especially M. G. S. Hodgson, "The Isma'ili State," *Cambridge History of Iran*, v, ed. J. A. Boyle, Cambridge, 1968, pp. 422–82.

For Egypt and Syria under Saladin and the Ayyubids see A. Ehrenkreutz, *Saladin*, Albany, N.Y., 1972; R. S. Humphreys, *From Saladin to the Mongols*, Albany, N.Y., 1972. Ayyubid military organization is treated by S. Elbeheiry, *Les Institutions de l'Egypte au temps desAyyübides. L'organisation de l'armée et des institutions militaires*, Paris, 1971; R. S. Humphreys, "The Emergence of the Mamluk Army," *SI*, 45 (1977), pp. 67–100, 46 (1977), pp. 147–82. Ayyubid administration has been extensively studied by C. Cahen, *Makhzūmiyyāt: Etudes sur l'histoire économique et financière de l'Egypte médiévale*, Leiden, 1977.

For Syrian Muslim towns see E. Ashtor-Strauss, "L'Administration urbaine en Syrie médiévale, "*RSO*, 31 (1956), pp. 73–128; C. Cahen, "Mouvements populaires et autonomisme urbain dans l'Asie musulmane du moyen âge," *Arabica*, 5 (1958), pp. 225–50, 6 (1959), pp. 25–56, 233–65; and the relevant chapters of J. Sauvaget, *Alep*, Paris, 1941. On the 'ulama' and the schools of law in Syria see N. Elisseeff, *Nur ad-Dïn: Un grand prince musulman de Syrie au temps des croisades (511–569h/1118–1174)*, 3 vols., Damascus, 1967.

Ayyubid architecture is treated by E. Herzfeld, "Damascus: Studies in Architecture," *Ars Islamica*, 9 (1942), pp. 1–53, 10 (1943), pp. 13–70, 11 (1946), pp. 1–71, 13–14 (1948), pp. 118–38; J. Sauvaget, M. Ecochard, and J. Sourdel-Thomine, *Les Monuments ayyoubides de Damas*, Paris, 1938–50.

An extensive bibliography of works on the Mamluk era in Egypt and Syria is found in I. M. Lapidus, *Muslim Cities in the Later Middle Ages*, Cambridge, Mass., 1967, with supplements in the 2nd edn, Cambridge, 1984.

The history of Egypt under Ottoman rule is given by P. M. Holt, *Egypt and the Fertile Crescent, 1516–1922*, London, 1966; S. J. Shaw, *The Financial and Administrative Organization and Development of Ottoman Egypt, 1517–1798*, Princeton, 1962; S. J. Shaw, *Ottoman Egypt in the Eighteenth Century*, Cambridge, Mass., 1962. The economy of Ottoman Egypt: A. Raymond, *Artisans et commerçants au Caire*, 2 vols., Damascus, 1973–74; A. Raymond, "The Economic Crisis of Egypt in the Eighteenth Century," *The Islamic Middle East, 700–1900: Studies in Economic and Social History*, ed. A. L. Udovitch, Princeton, 1981, pp. 687–707; G. Baer, *Egyptian Guilds in Modern Times*, Jerusalem, 1964.

On Egyptian Islam see A. L. Marsot, "The Ulama of Cairo in the Eighteenth and Nineteenth Centuries," *Scholars, Saints and Sufis: Muslim Religious Institutions since 1500*, ed. N. R. Keddie, Berkeley, 1972, pp. 149–65; M. Winter, *Society and Religion in Early Ottoman Egypt*, New Brunswick, N.J., 1982.

On the Arab provinces under Ottoman rule see H. Laoust, *Les Gouverneurs de Damas sous les Mamlouks et les premiers Ottomans*, Damascus, 1952; M. A. Bakhit, *The Ottoman Province of Damascus in the Sixteenth Century*, Beirut, 1982; K. K. Barbir, *Ottoman Rule in Damascus 1708–1758*, Princeton, 1980; A. K. Rafeq, *The Province of Damascus, 1723–1783*, Beirut, 1966.

For the 'ulama' and Sufism in Syria see M. Winter, "Sheikh ʿAlī ibn Maymūn and Syrian Sufism in the Sixteenth Century," *Israel Oriental Studies*, 7 (1977), pp. 281–308; A. Hourani, "Sheikh Khalid and the Naqshbandi Order," *Islamic Philosophy and the Classical Tradition*, éd. S. M. Stern and V. Brown, Columbia, S.C., 1972, pp. 89–103; J. Voll, "Old 'Ulama' Families and Ottoman Influence in 18th-century Damascus," *The American Journal of Arabic Studies*, 3 (1975), pp. 48–59.

Palestine has been the subject of U. Heyd, *Ottoman Documents on Palestine, 1552–1615*, Oxford, 1960; A. Cohen and B. Lewis, *Population and Revenue in the Towns of Palestine in the Sixteenth Century*, Princeton, 1978; M. Mabr, ed., *Studies on Palestine during the Ottoman Period*, Jerusalem, 1975; A. Cohen, *Palestine in the Eighteenth Century*, Jerusalem, 1973. On Lebanon see K. S. Salibi, *The Modern History of Lebanon*, London, 1965; I. F. Harik, *Politics and Change in a Traditional Society: Lebanon, 1711–1845*, Princeton, 1968; B. Doumani, *Rediscovering Palestine: Merchants and Peasants infabal Nablus*, Berkeley, 1995.

On Iraq see T. Nieuwenhuis, *Politics and Society in Early Modern Iraq (1802–1831*, The Hague, 1982; S. H. Longrigg, *Four Centunes of Modern Iraq*, Oxford, 1925.

Chapter 16

General histories of North Africa include J. M. Abun-Nasr, *A History of the Maghrib*, 2nd edn, Cambridge, 1975; A. Laroui, *The History of the Maghrib*, Princeton, 1977;

L. Valensi, *On the Eve of Colonialism: North Africa before the French Conquest*, New York, 1977; C. A. Julien, *History of North Africa: Tunisia, Algeria, Morocco, from the Arab Conquest to 1830*, New York, 1970.

The Arab conquests to the thirteenth century: H. R. Idris, *La Berbèrie orientale sous les Zīrīdes*, Paris, 1962; G. Marçais, *Les Arabes en Berbèrie du XIᵉ au XIVᵉ siècle*, Paris, 1913; M. Talbi, *L'Emirat aghlabide: Histoire politique*, Paris, 1966. For the Fatimids see the previous section on Egypt and Syria. Kharijism has been studied by T. Lewicki, "La Répartition géographique des groupements ibâdites dans l'Afrique du Nord au moyen âge," *Rocznik orientalistyczny*, 21 (1957), pp. 301–43; and T. Lewicki, "The Ibadites in Arabia and Africa," *Journal of World History*, 13 (1971), pp. 51–130.

The origin of the Almoravid movement has been reinterpreted by P. F. de Moraes Farias, "The Almoravids: Some Questions Concerning the Character of the Movement during its Periods of Closest Contact with the Western Sudan," *Bulletin de l'Institut français d'Afrique Noire*, 29 (1967), pp. 794–878; H. T. Norris, "New Evidence on the Life of ʿAbdullah b. Yâsïn and the Origins of the Almoravid Movement," *JAH*, 12 (1971), pp. 255–68; V. Lagardere, "Esquisse de l'organization militaire des Murâbitün à l'époque de Yusuf b. Tâsfïn, 430 H/1039 à 500 H/1106," *ROMM*, 27 (1979), pp. 99–114; N. Levtzion, "ʿAbd Allah b. Yâsïn and the Almoravids," *Studies in West African Islamic History*, ı, ed. J. R. Willis, London, 1979, pp. 78–112.

The impact of the Hilali invasions is much debated: H. R. Idris, "L'Invasion hilälienne et ses conséquences," *Cahiers de civilisation médiévale*, 11 (1968), pp. 353–69; J. Poncet, "Prospérité et décadence ifrikiyennes," *Cahiers de Tunisie*, 9 (1961), pp. 221–43; J. Poncet, "Le Mythe de la 'catastrophe' hilälienne," *Annales ESC*, 22 (1967), pp. 1099–1120.

On Saharan, North African, and Mediterranean trade see N. Pacha, *Le Commerce au Maghreb du XIᵉ au XIVᵉ siècle*, Tunis, 1976; J. Devisse, "Routes de commerce et échanges en Afrique Occidentale en relation avec la Méditerranée," *Revue d'histoire économique et sociale*, 50 (1972), pp. 42–73, 357–97.

The basic study of Tunisian society from the thirteenth to the sixteenth centuries is R. Brunschvig, *La Berbèrie orientale sous les Hafsides*, 2 vols., Paris, 1940–47. See also L. C. Brown, "The Religious Establishment in Husainid Tunisia," *Scholars, Saints and Sufis*, ed. N. R. Keddie, Berkeley, 1972, pp. 47–91; J. Abun-Nasr, "The Beylicate in Seventeenth-Century Tunisia," *IJMES*, 6 (1975), pp. 70–93; J. Pignon, "La Milice des janissaires du Tunis au temps des Deys (1590–1650)," *Cahiers de Tunisie*, 4 (1956), pp. 301–26.

For the economic history of Tunisia in the eighteenth and early nineteenth centuries see L. Valensi, "Islam et capitalisme, production et commerce des Chéchias en Tunisie et en France aux XVIIIᵉ et XIXᵉ siècles," *Revue d'histoire moderne et contemporaine*, 16 (1969), pp. 376–400; L. Valensi, *Tunisian Peasants in the Eighteenth and Nineteenth Centuries*, Cambridge, 1985; M. H. Cherif, "Expansion européenne et difficultés tunisiennes de 1815 à 1830," *Annales ESC,* 25 (1961), pp. 714–45; L. C. Brown, *The Tunisia of Ahmad Bey, 837–1855,* Princeton, 1974.

For Algeria under the Turks see P. Boyer, *L'Evolution de l'Algérie médiane,* Paris, 1960; P. Boyer, *La Vie quotidienne à Alger,* Paris, 1964; W. Spencer, *Algiers in the Age of the Corsairs,* Norman, Okla., 1976. On piracy and trade in the Mediterranean from the sixteenth to the nineteenth centuries see G. Fisher, *Barbary Legend: War, Trade and Piracy in North Africa, 1415–1830,* Oxford, 1957; P. Masson, *Histoire des établissements et du commerce français dans l'Afrique barbaresque (1560–1793),* Paris, 1903; A. E. Sayous, *Le Commerce des Européens à Tunis,* Paris, 1929.

On Algerian society see P. Boyer, "Contribution à l'étude de la politique religieuse des Turcs dans la Régence d'Alger (XVI^c-XIX^c siècles)," *ROMM,* 1 (1966), pp. 11–49. R. Gallissot, *L'Algérie pré-coloniale: Classes sociales en système précapitaliste,* Paris, 1968; R. Gallissot, "Pre-colonial Algeria," *Economy and Society,* 4 (1975), pp. 418–45; J. C. Vatin, "L'Algérie en 1830: Essai d'interprétation des recherches historiques sous l'angle de la science politique," *Revue algerienne,* 7 (1970), pp. 977–1058; A. Nouschi, "La vita rurale in Algeria prima de 1830," *Studi Storici,* 4 (1963), pp. 449–78.

Morocco's history is covered by the work of H. Terrasse, *Histoire du Maroc,* 2 vols., Casablanca, 1950; E. Lévi-Provençal, *Les Historiens des Chorfa: Essai sur la littérature historique et biographique au Maroc du XVIe au XX^c siècle,* Paris, 1922. On the Moroccan economy before the nineteenth century see P. Berthier, *Les Anciennes Sucreries du Maroc, 2* vols., Rabat, 1966; A. Hammoudi, "Sainteté, pouvoir et société: Tamgrout aux XVII^c et XVIII^c siècles," *Annales ESC,* 35 (1980), pp. 615–41.

For Moroccan urban society, see K. Brown, *People of Salé,* Manchester, 1976; R. Le Tourneau, *Fes avant le protectorat,* Casablanca, 1949; R. Le Tourneau, *Les Villes musulmanes de VAfrique du Nord,* Algiers, 1957; R. Le Tourneau, *Fez in the Age of the Marinides,* Norman, Okla., 1961; J. S. Gerber, *Jewish Society in Fez, 1450–1700,* Leiden, 1980.

On North African Sufism see A. Bel, *La Religion musulmane en Berbèrie,* Paris, 1938; G. Drague, *Esquisse d'histoire religieuse du Maroc: confréries et zaouias,* Paris, 1951; P. J. André, *Contribution à l'tudes des confréries religieuses musulmanes,* Algiers, 1956; J. Abun-Nasr, *The Tijaniyya,* London, 1965; R. G. Jenkins, "The Evolution of Religious Brotherhoods in North and Northwest Africa 1523–1900, "*Studies in West African Islamic History,* i, ed. J. R. Willis, London, 1979, pp. 40–77; C. Geertz, *Islam Observed,* New Haven, 1968; V. J. Cornell, "The Logic of Analogy and the Role of the Sufi Shaykh," *IJMES,* 15 (1983), pp. 67–93.

Introductory accounts of Muslim Spain include A. Chejne, *Muslim Spain,* Minneapolis, 1974; J. O'Callaghan, *A History of Medieval Spain,* Ithaca, N.Y., 1975; and the classic E. Lévi-Provençal, *Histoire de l'Espagne musulmane,* 3 vols., Paris, 1950–53. Important interpretations of the economic and social bases of Spanish and Muslim civilization are T. Glick, *Irrigation and Society in Medieval Valencia,*

Cambridge, Mass., 1970; T. Glick, *Islamic and Christian Spain in the Early Middle Ages*, Princeton, 1979; P. Guichard, *Structures sociales, orientales et occidentales dans l'Espagne musulmane*, Paris, 1977. See also D. Wasserstein, *The Rise and Fall of the Party-Kings*, Princeton, 1985.

Muslim urban communities and the supervision of markets are treated in the work of P. Chalmeta Gendrón, *El "señor del zoco" en España*, Madrid, 1973; L. Torres Balbás, "Les Villes musulmanes d'Espagne et leur urbanisation," *AIEO, 6* (1942–47), pp. 5–30; L. Torres Balbás, "Extensión y demografia de las ciudades hispano musulmanas," *SI*, 3 (1955), pp. 37–59.

On Islam in Spain see H. Mones, "Le Rôle des hommes de religion dans l'histoire de l'Espagne musulmane jusqu'à la fin du Califat," *SI*, 20 (1964), pp. 47–88. For Spanish Sufism see P. Nwyia, *Ibn 'Abbād de Ronda (1332–1390)*, Beirut, 1961.

For the Reconquista and relations between Muslims and Christians see R. Burns, *Islam under the Crusaders: Colonial Survival in the Thirteenth-Century Kingdom of Valencia*, Princeton, 1973; R. Burns, *The Crusader Kingdom of Valencia: Reconstruction on a Thirteenth-Century Frontier*, 2 vols., Cambridge, Mass., 1967; J. Boswell, *The Royal Treasure: Muslim Communities under the Crown of Aragon in the Fourteenth Century*, New Haven, 1978; J. Edwards, *Christian Cordoba: The City and its Region in the Late Middle Ages*, Cambridge, 1982.

On Arabic literature see the contributions of J. Monroe, *The Shu'ubiyya in al-Andalus: The Risala of Ibn Garcia and Five Refutations*, Berkeley, 1969; J. Monroe, *Hispano-Arabic Poetry*, Berkeley, 1974; S. Stern, *Hispano-Arabic Strophic Poetry*, Oxford, 1974; L. Compton, *Andalusian Lyrical Poetry and Old Spanish Love Songs*, New York, 1976. A vivid interpretation of Spanish architecture and its cultural significance is O. Grabar, *The Alhambra*, London, 1978.

Chapter 17

For the dynamics of steppe empires see R. Grousset, *The Empire of the Steppes: A History of Central Asia*, tr. N. Walford, New Brunswick, N.J., 1970. D. Sinor, *Introduction à l'étude de l'Eurasie centrale*, Wiesbaden, 1963 contains ample bibliographies. O. Lattimore, *Inner Asian Frontiers of China*, New York, 1951 is an imaginative interpretation of the formation of nomadism in Inner Asia and its relation to sedentary empires. L. Krader discusses Inner Asian social organization: *Peoples of Central Asia*, Bloomington, 1963; and *Social Organization of the Mongol-Turkic Pastoral Nomads*, The Hague, 1963.

On the Mongol, Chaghatay, and Timurid periods in Inner Asia see P. Brent, *The Mongol Empire: Genghis Khan, his Triumph and Legacy*, London, 1976; V. V. Bar-told, *Histoire des Turcs d Asie centrale*, Paris, 1945; V. V. Bartold, *Four Studies on the History of Central Asia*, tr. V. Minorsky and T. Minorsky, 3 vols., Leiden, 1956–62; J. A. Boyle, *The Mongol World Empire, 1206–1370*, London, 1977. Two important early histories have been translated: Rashid al-Din Tabib, *The Successors of Genghis Khan*, tr. J. A. Boyle, New York, 1971; and M. Haydar (Dughlat), *A History of the Moghuls of Central Asia (Tarikh-i Rashidi)*, tr. E. D. Ross, New York, 1970.

For the Golden Horde see G. Vernadsky, *The Mongols and Russia*, New Haven, 1953. For the Russian conquest: A. S. Donnelly, *The Russian Conquest of Bashkiria, 1552–1740*, New Haven, 1968; C Lemercier-Quelquejay, "Les Missions orthodoxes en pays musulmans de Moyenne et Basse Volga, 1552–1865," *CMRS, 8* (1967), pp. 363–403; H. Carrère d'Encausse, "Les Routes commerciales de l'Asie Centrale et les tentatives de reconquête d'Astrakhan," *CMRS*, 11 (1970), pp. 391–422. For the Crimea see A. Bennigsen et al, *Le Khanat de Crimée dans les archives du Musée du Palais de Topkapi*, Paris, 1978; A. W. Fisher, *The Russian Annexation of the Crimea*, Cambridge, 1970.

On Kazakhs see R. Majerczak, "Renseignements historiques sur les Kazaks ou Kirghizes-Kazaks depuis la formation de la Horde Kazak jusqu'à la fin du XIXe siècle," *Revue du monde musulman*, 43 (1921), pp. 54–220; A. Hudson, *Kazak Social Structure*, New Haven, 1938; T. G. Winner, *The Oral Art and Literature of the Kazakhs of Russian Central Asia*, Durham, N.C., 1958; E. Bacon, *Central Asia under Russian Rule*, Ithaca, N.Y., 1966.

Bukhara and the Central Asian Khanates: M. Holdsworth, *Turkestan in the Nineteenth Century: A Brief History of the Khanates of Bukhara, Kokand and Khiva*, London, 1959; H. Carrère d'Encausse, *Réforme et révolution chez les musulmans de l'Empire russe: Bukhara, 1867–1924*, Paris, 1966. On Central Asian culture see E. Knobloch, *Beyond the Oxus: Archaeology, Art and Architecture of Central Asia*, London, 1972; N. Chadwick and V. Zhirmunsky, *Oral Epics of Central Asia*, London, 1969.

On Islam in Inner Asia see H. Algar, "The Naqshbandi Order: A Preliminary Survey of its History and Significance," *SI*, 44 (1976), pp. 123–52. Important Russian scholarship on Sufism in Turkestan and Turkmenistan includes S. M. Demidov, *Sufizm v Turkmenii: Evolutsiia i perezhitki* [Sufism in Turkmenia: Evolution and Remnants], Ashkhabad, 1978; M. B. Durdyev, "Dukhovenstvo v sisteme obshchestvennykh institutov turkmen kontsa XIX-nachala XX v." [The Clergy in the System of Social Institutions of the Turkmen at the End of the Nineteenth – beginning of the Twentieth Century], *Vestnik Moskovskogo Universiteta* [Moscow University Review] (1970), pp. 27–42; S. M. Demidov, "Magtymy" [The Magtyms], *Domusu-Vmanskie verovanie i obriady v srednei azii* [Pre-Muslim Beliefs and Rites in Central Asia], Moscow, 1975; V. N. Basilov, "Honour Groups in Traditional Turk-menian Society," *Islam in Tubai Societies: From the Atlas to the Indus*, ed. A. S. Ahmed and D. M. Hart, London, 1984, pp. 220–43.

For the Muslims of China before the Chinese occupation of eastern Turkestan see M. Rossabi, *China and Inner Asia*, New York, 1975; M. Rossabi, "The Muslims in the Early Yuan Dynasty," *China under Mongol Rule*, ed. J. Langlois, Princeton, 1981, pp. 257–95; R. Israeli, "The Muslim Minority in Traditional China," *Asian and*

African Studies, 10 (1974–75), pp. 101–26; and R. Israeli, "The Muslims under the Manchu Reign in China," *SI*, 49 (1979), pp. 159–79.

The *khwajas* of Kashgar and the nineteenth-century struggle for eastern Turkestan are the subject of T. Saguchi, "The Eastern Trade of the Khoqand Khanat," *Memoirs of the Research Department of the Toyo Bunko*, 24 (1965), pp. 47–114; H. G. Schwarz, "The Khwajas of Eastern Turkestan," *Central Asiatic Journal*, 20 (1976), pp. 266–96; T. Yuan, "Yakub Beg (1820–1877) and the Moslem Rebellion in Chinese Turkestan," *Central Asiatic Journal*, 6(1961), pp. 134–67. On other nineteenth-century Muslim rebellions see R. Israeli, "The Muslim Revival in 19th-century China," *SI*, 43 (1976), pp. 119–38; Wen-djang Chu, *The Moslem Rebellion in Northwest China*, The Hague, 1966.

Chapter 18

For an overview of the history of Muslims in India see P. Hardy, *The Muslims of British India*, New York, 1973. See also H. G. Behr, *Die Moguln: Macht und Pracht der indischen Kaiser von 1369–1857*, Vienna, 1979. For histories written in the subcontinent see S. M. Ikram, *Muslim Civilization in India*, New York, 1964; M. Mujeeb, *The Indian Muslims*, Montreal, 1967; I. H. Qureshi, *The Muslim Community of the Indo-Pakistan Sub-continent, 610–1947*, Karachi, 1977; S. M. Haq, *Islamic Thought and Movements in the Subcontinent, 711–1947*, Karachi, 1979.

On the Delhi regime see V. D. Mahajan, *The Delhi Sultanate*, Delhi, 1981. Provincial regimes: S. Dale, *Islamic Society on the South Asian Frontier: The Mappilas of Malabar 1498–1922*, Oxford, 1980; R. M. Eaton, *Sufis of Bijapur 1300–1700: Social Roles of Sufis in Medieval India*, Princeton, 1978; J. F. Richards, *Mughal Administration in Golconda*, London, 1976; A. Karim, *A Social History of the Muslims in Bengal down to ad 1538*, Dacca, 1959; R. M. Eaton, *The Rise of Islam and the Bengal Frontier*, Berkeley, 1993.

On Mughal administration see I. Habib, *The Agrarian System of Mughal India 1556–1707*, Bombay, 1963; W. H. Moreland, *The Agrarian System of Moslem India*, Delhi, 1968; M. Athar 'Ali, *The Mughal Nobility under Aurangzeb*, Bombay, 1966; J. F. Richards, *Kingship and Authority in South Asia*, Madison, Wis., 1978.

For Islamic religion and culture see Aziz Ahmad, *Studies on Islamic Culture in the Indian Environment*, Oxford, 1969; Aziz Ahmad, *An Intellectual History of 'Islam in India*, Edinburgh, 1969; A. Schimmel, *Islam in the Indian Subcontinent*, London, 1980; B. D. Metcalf, ed., *Moral Conduct and Authority: The Place of Adab in South Asian Islam*, Berkeley, 1984; A. Schimmel, *Mystical Dimensions of Islam*, Chapel Hill, N.C., 1975; J. A. Subhan, *Sufism: Its Saints and Shrines*, Lucknow, 1960; S. A. A. Rizvi, *A History of Sufism in India*, New Delhi, 1978.

On Islam under the Delhi Sultanate the principal contributor is K. A. Nizami: see *Some Aspects of Religion and Politics in India during the Thirteenth Century*, Aligarh, 1961; and *Studies in Medieval Indian History and Culture*, Allahabad, 1966.

On Sufism in the Mughal period see A. A. Rizvi, *Muslim Revivalist Movements in Northern India in the Sixteenth and Seventeenth Centuries*, Agra, 1965. Sirhindi is the subject of Y. Friedmann, *Shaykh Ahmad Sirhindi: An Outline of his Thought and a Study of his Image in the Eyes of Posterity*, Montreal, 1971. For translations and works concerning Shah Waliallah: Shah Waliullah, *Sufism and the Islamic Tradition: The Iamahat and Sata'at of Shah Waliullah*, tr. G. N. Jalbani, London, 1980; S. A. A. Rizvi, *Shah Wali-Allah and his Times: A Study of 18th Century Islam, Politics and Society in India*, Canberra, 1980.

Commerce in India and the Indian Ocean is the subject of M. N. Pearson, *Merchants and Rulers in Gujarat: The Response to the Portuguese in the Sixteenth Century*, Berkeley, 1976; A. Das Gupta, *Malabar in Asian Trade: 1740–1800*, Cambridge, 1967; A. Das Gupta, *Indian Merchants and the Decline of Surat c. 1700–1750*, Wiesbaden, 1979; O. P. Singh, *Surat and its Trade in the Second Half of the 17th Century*, Delhi, 1977.

On Muslim "sects": S. C. Misra, *Muslim Communities in Gujarat*, Bombay, 1964; A. Nanji, *The Nizari Isma'ili Tradition in the Indo-Pakistan Subcontinent*, Delmar, N.Y., 1978.

Indian architecture and art are the subjects of S. C. Welch and M. C Beach, *Gods, Thrones and Peacocks: Northern Indian Painting from Two Traditions: Fifteenth to Nineteenth Centuries*, New York, 1965; P. Brown, *Indian Architecture: Islamic Period*, Bombay, 1968; G. Hambly, *Cities of Mughal India*, New Delhi, 1977; R. Nath, *History of Sultanate Architecture*, New Delhi, 1978. On Mughal poetry see R. Russell and K. Islam, *Three Mughal Poets: Mir, Sauda, Mir Hasan*, Cambridge, 1968.

The decline of the Mughal empire and the transition to the British era are interpreted in C. A. Bayly, *Rulers, Townsmen, and Bazaars: North Indian Society in the Age of British Expansion*, Cambridge and New York, 1983; R. B. Barnett, *North India between Empires: Awdh, the Mughals, and the British, 1720–1801*, Berkeley, 1980.

Chapter 19

A survey of Southeast Asian peoples is given by H. Geertz, "Indonesian Cultures and Communities," *Indonesia*, ed. R. T. McVey, New Haven, 1963, pp. 24–96. Brief historical introductions are to be found in H. J. Benda, "The Structure of Southeast Asian History: Some Preliminary Observations," *Journal of Southeast Asian History*, 3 (1962), pp. 106–38; W. Roff, "South-East Asian Islam in the Nineteenth Century," *Cambridge History of Islam*, ed. P. M. Holt, A. K. S. Lambton, and B. Lewis, Cambridge, 1970, pp. 155–81. For a fuller history see B. H. M. Vlekke, *Nusantara: A History of Indonesia*, The Hague, 1959. On trade and society see J. C van Leur, *Indonesian Trade and Society*, tr. J. S. Holmes and A. van Marie, The Hague, 1955; B. J. O. Schrieke, *Indonesian Sociological Studies*, 2 vols., The Hague, 1955, 1957; W. F. Wertheim, *Indonesian Society in Transition*, The Hague, 1959.

Origins and diffusion of Islam in Indonesia: C. A. Majul, "Theories on the Introduction and Expansion of Islam in Malaysia," *Sulliman journal*, 11 (1964), pp. 335–98; M. C. Ricklefs, "Six Centuries of Islamization in Java," *Conversion to Islam*, ed. N. Levtzion, New York and London, 1979, pp. 100–28; C. C. Berg, "The Islamisation of Java," *SI*, 4 (1955), pp. 111–42; A. H. Johns, "From Coastal Settlement to Islamic School and City: Islamization in Sumatra, the Malay Peninsula and Java," *Hamdard Islamicus*, 4 (1981), pp. 3–28.

For Southeast Asian trade see O. W. Wolters, *The Fall of Srivijaya in Malay History*, Ithaca, N.Y., 1970. For Dutch and British commerce and colonial empires see F. S. Gaastra, J. R. Bruijn, and I. Schoffer, eds., *Dutch-Asiatic Shipping in the Seventeenth and Eighteenth Centuries*, 3 vols., The Hague, 1979; K. Glamann, *Dutch-Asiatic Trade, 1620–1740*, Copenhagen, 1958; A. Reid, *The Contest for North Sumatra: Atjeh, the Netherlands, and Britain, 1858–1898*, Kuala Lumpur and New York, 1969; J. S. Bastin, *The Changing Balance of the Early Southeast Asian Pepper Trade*, Kuala Lumpur, 1980; J. S. Bastin and R. Roolvink, eds., *Malayan and Indonesian Studies*, Oxford, 1964; J. S. Furnivall, *Colonial Policy and Practice: A Comparative Study of Burma and Netherlands India*, Cambridge, 1948; J. S. Furnivall, *Netherlands India: A Study of Plural Economy*, Cambridge, 1944.

For Java see C. Geertz, *The Religion of Java*, Glencoe, Ill., 1960; B. Anderson, "The Idea of Power in Javanese Culture," *Culture and Politics in Indonesia*, ed. C. Holt, Ithaca, N.Y., 1972, pp. 1–69; S. Moertono, *State and Statecraft in Old Java. A Study of the Later Mataram Period, 16th to 19th Century*, Ithaca, N.Y., 1968.

Minangkabau and the Padri movement have been studied by C. Dobbin, *Islamic Revivalism in a Changing Peasant Economy: Central Sumatra 1784–1847*, London, 1983; P. E. Josselin de Jong, *Minangkabau and Negri Sembilan: Socio-Political Structure in Indonesia*, Leiden, 1951. C. S. Hurgronje, *The Achenese*, 2 vols., tr. A. W. S. O'Sullivan, Leiden and London, 1906 is the classical study of this North Sumatran Muslim society.

On Sufism there are several articles by A. H. Johns: "Muslim Mystics and Historical Writing," *Historians of South-East Asia*, ed. D. G. E. Hall, London, 1961–62, pp. 37–49; "Islam in Southeast Asia: Reflections and New Directions," *Indonesia*, 19 (1975), pp. 33–55; "Friends in Grace: Ibrahim al-Kurani and 'Abd al-Ra'uf al-Singkeli," *Spectrum: Essays Presented to Sultan Takdir Alisjahbana on his Seventieth Birthday*, ed. S. Udin, Jakarta, 1978, pp. 469–85.

The history of Malaya is treated by J. Kennedy, *A History of Malaya, ad 1400–1959*, London and New York, 1962; K. G. Tregonning, *Papers on Malayan History*, Singapore, 1962; R. O. Winstedt, *The Malays: A Cultural History*, London, 1961; R. O. Winstedt, *A History of Classical Malay Literature*, Kuala Lumpur, 1969. For political institutions see J. M. Gullick, *Indigenous Political Systems of Western Malaya*, London, 1965.

Chapter 20

Two good bibliographies are P. E. Ofori, *Islam in Africa South of the Sahara: A Select Bibliographic Guide*, Nendeln, 1977; S. M. Zoghby, *Islam in Sub-Saharan Africa: A Partially Annotated Guide*, Washington, D.C., 1978. Valuable introductory histories include R. A. Oliver and J. D. Fage, *A Short History of Africa*, 3rd edn, Harmondsworth, 1970; *The Cambridge History of Africa*, 8 vols., Cambridge, 1975-; J. S. Trimingham, *The Influence of Islam upon Africa*, Beirut, 1968. Important collections of articles include I. M. Lewis, ed., *Islam in Tropical Africa*, London, 1966; and J. Kritzeck and W. H. Lewis, eds., *Islam in Africa*, New York, 1969. Studies of special topics with Africa-wide scope are J. N. D. Anderson, *Islamic Law in Africa*, London, 1954; A. G. B. Fisher and H. J. Fisher, *Slavery and Muslim Society in Africa: The Institution in Saharan and Sudanic Africa, and the Trans-Saharan Trade*, London, 1970; C. Meillassoux, ed., *L'Ésclavage en Afrique pré-coloniale*, Paris, 1975.

For histories of Islam in West Africa see J. S. Trimingham, *A History of Islam in West Africa*, London and New York, 1962; J. D. Fage, *History of West Africa*, Cambridge, 1969; D. McCall and N. Bennett, *Aspects of West African Islam*, Boston, 1971; C. Meillassoux, *The Development of Indigenous Trade and Markets in West Africa*, London, 1971; J. F. A. Ajayi and M. Crowder, eds., *History of West Africa*, 2 vols., London, 1976; J. R. Willis, ed., *Studies in West African Islamic History*, London, 1979; P. B. Clarke, *West Africa and Islam*, London, 1982. An unusual study of the integration of pagan and Muslim culture in West Africa is R. A. Bravman, *Islamic and Tribal Art in West Africa*, London, 1974. For the Almoravid movement see the bibliography for chapter 16.

On Mali, an early Muslim empire, see C. Monteil, *Les Empires du Mali*, Paris, 1930; D. T. Niane, *Sundiata: An Epic of Old Mali*, tr. G. D. Pickett, London, 1965; N. Levtzion, *Ancient Ghana and Mali*, London, 1973. For the Songhay empire see J. Boulnois and B. Hama, *L'Empire de Gao*, Paris, 1954.

Timbuktu is the subject of H. M. Miner, *The Primitive City of Timbucktoo*, Garden City, N.Y., 1965; S. M. Cissoko, *Tombouctou et l'empire Songhai*, Dakar, 1976; M. Abitbol, *Tombouctou et les arma*, Paris, 1979; E. N. Saad, *Social History of Timbuktu: The Role of Muslim Scholars and Notables, 1400–1900*, Cambridge, 1983.

For Hausaland from the fourteenth century to the jihad of ʿUthman Don Fodio see M. G. Smith, "The Beginnings of Hausa Society, AD 1000–1500," *The Historian in Tropical Africa*, ed., J. Vansina, R. Mauny, and L. V. Thomas, London, 1964, pp. 339–57; F. Fuglestad, "A Reconstruction of Hausa History before the Jihad," *JAH*, 19 (1978), pp. 319–39; J. E. G. Sutton, "Towards a Less Orthodox History of Hausaland," *JAH*, 20 (1979), pp. 179–201; M. Hiskett, "An Islamic Tradition of Reform in the Western Sudan from the Sixteenth to the Eighteenth Century," *BSOAS*, 25 (1962), pp. 577–96.

For Bornu see A. Schultze, *The Sultanate of Bornu*, tr. P. A. Benton, London, 1968; L. Brenner, *The Shehus of Kukawa: A History of the Al-Kanemi Dynasty of Bornu*, Oxford, 1973.

Mauritania: D. G. Lavroff, *Introduction à la Mauritanie*, Paris, 1979; C. C. Stewart with E. K. Stewart, *Islam and Social Order in Mauritania*, Oxford, 1973; H. T. Norris, *Shinqiti Folk Literature and Songs*, Oxford, 1968; and H. T. Norris, *The Tuaregs: Their Islamic Legacy and its Diffusion in the Sah el*, Warminster, 1975.

On Muslim merchants and scholars: P. D. Curtin, *Economic Change in Precolonial Africa*, Madison, Wis., 1974; P. E. Lovejoy, "The Role of the Wangara in the Economic Transformation of the Central Sudan in the Fifteenth and Sixteenth Centuries," *JAH*, 19 (1978), pp. 173–93; C. C. Stewart, "Southern Saharan Scholarship and the *BiladAl-Sudan*," *JAH*, 17 (1976), pp. 73–93. L. O. Sanneh stresses the clerical rather than the commercial groups: *The Jakhanke: The History of an Islamic Clerical People of the Senegambia*, London, 1979.

On Islam in Ghana the principal contribution is N. Levtzion, *Muslims and Chiefs in West Africa*, Oxford, 1968. On Muslims in the Ashanti empire of Ghana see I. Wilks, *The Northern Factor in Ashanti History*, Legon, Ghana, 1961; and I. Wilks, *Asante in the Nineteenth Century*, London, 1975.

For Sierra Leone see D. Skinner, "Islam and Education in the Colony and Hinterland of Sierra Leone (1750–1914)," *Canadian Journal of African Studies*, 10 (1976), pp. 499–520; and D. Skinner, "Mande Settlement and the Development of Islamic Institutions in Sierra Leone," *IJAHS*, 11 (1978), pp. 32–62.

Important studies of the great eighteenth- and nineteenth-century jihads include J. R. Willis, "Jihad fi Sabil Allah: Its Doctrinal Basis in Islam and Some Aspects of its Evolution in Nineteenth Century West Africa," *JAH*, 8 (1967), pp. 395–415; M. Hiskett, "The Nineteenth-Century Jihads in West Africa," *The Cambridge History of Africa, 1790–1870*, v, ed. J. E. Flint, Cambridge, 1976, pp. 125–69; M. Last, *The Sokoto Caliphate*, New York, 1967; H. A. S. Johnston, *The Fulani Empire of Sokoto*, London, 1967; M. Hiskett, *The Sword of Truth: The Life and Times of the Shehu Usuman Dan Fodio*, New York, 1973. For the Sokoto Caliphate: M. G. Smith, *Government in Zazzau, 1800–1950*, London and New York, 1960; R. A. Adeleye, *Power and Diplomacy in Northern Nigeria, 1804–1906*, London, 1971; V. N. Low, *Three Nigerian Emirates*, Evanston, 111., 1972. On the trade and economy of northern Nigeria in this period see J. P. Smaldane, *Warfare in the Sokoto Caliphate*, Cambridge, 1974; P. E. Lovejoy, "Plantations in the Economy of the Sokoto Caliphate," *JAH*, 19 (1978), pp. 341–68.

The eastern offshoots of ʿUthman's jihad are treated in S. Abubakar, *The Lamibe of Fombina: A Political History of Adamawa, 1809–1901*, Zaria (Nigeria), 1977; A. D. Babikir, *L'Empire de Rabeh*, Paris, 1950. On the western offshoots: A. H. Ba and J. Daget, *L'Empire peul du Macina*, Paris, 1962.

For the jihads in Senegambia and Mauritania see M. A. Klein, "Social and Economic Factors in the Muslim Revolution in Senegambia," *JAH*, 13 (1972), pp. 419–41; J. R. Willis, "The Torodbe Clerisy: A Social View," *JAH*, 19 (1978), pp. 195–212.

For al-Hajj ʿUmar see B. G. Martin, *Muslim Brotherhoods in Nineteenth-Century Africa*, Cambridge, 1976, pp. 68–217. For the Umarian state see B. O. Oloruntimehin, *The Segu TukulorEmpire*, London, 1972; Y. Saint-Martin, *L'Empire toucouleur, 1848–1897*, Paris, 1970; R. L. Roberts, "Production and Reproduction of Warrior States: Segu Bambara and Segu Tokolor, c 1712–1890," *IJAHS*, 13 (1980), pp. 389–419; J. R. Willis, *In the Path of Allah: The Passion of Al-Hajj Vmar*, London: 1989. For comparative purposes see D. Forde and P. M. Kaberry, eds., *West African Kingdoms in the Nineteenth Century*, London, 1967.

The principal contributions to the study of the Senegambian region in the nineteenth century are M. A. Klein, *Islam and Imperialism in Senegal*, Stanford and Edinburgh, 1968; Charlotte A. Quinn, *Mandingo Kingdoms of the Senegambia*, Evanston, 111., 1972; P. D. Curtin, *Economic Change in Precolonial Africa: Senegam-bia in the Era of the Slave Trade*, Madison, Wis., 1975; D. W. Robinson, *Chiefs and Clerics: Abdul Bokar Kan and Futa Toro, 1853–1891*, Oxford, 1975; T. Diallo, *Les Institutions politiques du Fouta Dyallon au XIXe siècle*, Dakar, 1972. See also L. G. Colvin, "Islam and the State of Kajoor: A Case of Successful Resistance to Jihad," *JAH*, 15 (1974), pp. 587–606. The conversion of the Wolof is discussed in L. Behrman, "The Islamization of the Wolof by the End of the Nineteenth Century," *Western African History*, IV, ed. D. McCall, N. Bennett, and J. Butler, New York, 1969, pp. 102–31. On French policy in Senegal at the beginning of the colonial era see G. W. Johnson, *The Emergence of Black Politics in Senegal: The Struggle for Power in the Four Communes, 1900–1920*, Stanford, 1971.

The principal study of Samory is Y. Person, *Samori: Une révolution dyula*, Dakar, 1968–75.

On Muslim brotherhoods and religious teaching in West Africa see J. M. Abun-Nasr, *The Tijaniyya: A Sufi Order in the Modern World*, London and New York, 1965; B. G. Martin, *Muslim Brotherhoods in Nineteenth-Century Africa*, Cambridge, 1976.

Chapter 21

For overviews of East African history see R. Oliver and G. Matthew, eds., *History of East Africa*, 1, Oxford, 1963; V. Harlow and E. M. Chilver, eds., *History of East Africa*, 11, Oxford, 1965; *The Cambridge History of Africa, 1050–1600*, III, ed. K. Oliver, Cambridge, 1977; *The Cambridge History of Africa, 1600–1790*, IV, ed. R. Gray, Cambridge, 1975.

On the early history of Muslim settlement see H. N. Chittick, *Kilwa: An Islamic Trading City on the East African Coast*, Nairobi, 1974; P. S. Garlake, *The Early Islamic Architecture of the East African Coast*, Nairobi and London, 1966; G. S. P. Freeman-Grenville, *The Medieval History of the Coast of Tanganyika*, London and New York, 1962. An important revision of the subject is under way. See R. L. Pouwels, "The Medieval Foundations of East African Islam," *IJAHS*, 11 (1978), pp. 201–26, 393–409; J. de V. Allen, "Swahili Culture and the Nature of East Coast Settlement," *IJAHS*, 14 (1981), pp. 306–34; J. C. Wilkinson, "Oman and East Africa: New Light on Early Kilwan History from the Omani Sources," *IJAHS*, 14 (1981), pp. 272–305.

On Zanzibar and the development of coastal trade with the interior see C. S. Nicholls, *The Swahili Coast: Politics, Diplomacy and Trade on the East African Littoral, 1798–1856*, London, 1971; L. Farrant, *Tippu Tip and the East African Slave Trade*, London, 1975; N. R. Bennett, *Mirambo of Tanzania ca. 1840–1884*, New York, 1971.

For Ethiopia see J. S. Trimingham, *Islam in Ethiopia*, London, 1965; M. Abir, *Ethiopia: The Era of the Princes*, New York, 1968; J. Cuoq, *L'Islam en Ethiopie des origines au seizième siècle*, Paris, 1981.

On Somalia see I. M. Lewis, *Peoples of the Horn of Africa, Somali, Afar and Saho*, London, 1969; D. D. Laitin, *Polity, Language and Thought: The Somali Experience*, Chicago, 1977; L. V. Cassanelli, *The Shaping of Somali Society: Reconstructing the History of a Pastoral People, 1600–1900*, Philadelphia, 1982.

For the Sudan see J. S. Trimingham, *Islam in the Sudan*, London, 1965; P. M. Holt and M. W. Daly, *The History of the Sudan from the Coming of Islam to the Present Day*, 3rd edn, London, 1979; Y. F. Hasan, *The Arabs and the Sudan: From the Seventh to the Early Sixteenth Century*, Edinburgh, 1967; R. S. O'Fahey and J. L. Spaulding, *Kingdoms of the Sudan*, London, 1974; R. S. O'Fahey, *State and Society in Dar Fur*, London, 1980.

For African society on the eve of colonialism see E. Colson, "African Society at the Time of the Scramble," *Colonialism in Africa: The History and Politics of Colonialism 1870–1914*, I, ed. L. H. Gann and P. Duignan, Cambridge, 1969, pp. 27–65 and other essays in this volume. On the rise of colonial domination see M. Crowder, "West Africa and the Europeans: Five Hundred Years of Direct Contact," *Colonial West Africa: Collected Essays*, London, 1978, pp. 1–25; P. Ehrensaft, "The Political Economy of Informal Empire in Pre-Colonial Nigeria, 1807–1884," *Canadian Journal of African Studies*, 6 (1972), pp. 451–90. The diplomatic background of the European scramble for Africa is included in R. Robinson and J. Gallagher, *Africa and the Victorians*, New York, 1961; J. D. Hargreaves, *Prelude to the Partition of West Africa*, London and New York, 1963.

INDEX

poetry, 131–132
  Arabia, 37–38
  Baghdadi, post-ʿAbbasid era, 254
  bedouins, 34
  court, Ottoman Empire,
  ghazal (lyric), 257
  Hebrew, 396
  Hispano-Arabic culture, 386
  Indian, 518–519
  Mahmud of Ghazna, 257
  masnavi (rhyming couplet), 257
  new blend of Arabic literary form and oral
    Iranian literature, 256
  qasida (panegyric), 132, 254, 256, 257
  romantic, Azarbayjan, 257
  rubaʿi (quatrain), 257
  saz shairi (itinerant minstrel poets),
    461–462
  Sufi, 257–258
  Sufi, post-ʿAbbasid era, 254
  Turkish, European influence on, 477
political institutions, Ottoman Empire, 472–475
political theory, 293–301
  Greek, philosophic political theory,
    298–301
  Persian mirror literature, 295–298
  Sunni theory, 293–295
Polo, Marco, 564
polyandrous marriage, 183
polygamous marriage, 183
pondoks, 566
popular Islam, 327–328
Porphyry, 137
Portuguese
  colonialism and defeat of Muslim
    expansion, 630
  colonialism in Africa, 586–587
  East Africa and, 624–625
  expulsion of Jews, 401–404
  Southeast Asia and, 566–569
post-ʿAbbasid Middle Eastern state system,
  225–263
  concept of state, 262–263
  Fatimid Egypt, 238–243
  iqtaʿ system and Middle Eastern feudalism,
    250–254
  Iraq and Iran, 227–230
  Mamluk Empire, 247–249
  military slavery, 249–250
  Mongols, 233–236
  royal courts and regional cultures, 254–262
  Saljuq Empire, 230–233
  Sufism in, 304–306

Syria, 243–247
Timurids, 236–238
post-imperial succession regimes (late tenth
  century), 226
priyayi, 571–572, 667
property and inheritance
  India, Mughal Empire, 524–525
  medieval Muslim jurists, 270
  Middle Eastern societies before Islam,
    21–22
  women, Ottoman Empire, 464
  women and family, 187–190
protocol, royal court
  ʿAbbasids, 130–131
  Fatimid dynasty, 239–241
  Umayyads, 332–333
provincial government
  ʿAbbasid Empire, 97–99
  ʿAbbasid Empire, decline of, 109–113
  Ottoman empire, 442–444
Pumbedita (Babylonian yeshivas), 208
purification, Sufi, 309–313
al-Qabisi, 380

qadaʾ, 303–329
Qadaris (theological school), 150, 326–329
qadi (judge), 96, 156–157, 278, 364–368, 667
al-Qadir (Caliph), 289
Qadiriyya Sufi order
  Somalia and Eritrea, 628
  Sufis, 283
  in West Africa, 600
qaʾid, 667
al-Qaʾim (Caliph), 289
Qajars, 506
Qalandariyya, 461
qalb, 307–309, 329, 667
qanat, 667
Qarakhanid Empire, 230, 258, 543–544,
  647–648
Qarakhitay, 233
Qaramanli, Ahmad, 407
Qarluq peoples, 230
Qarmatian movement, 111
qasaba, 667
qasida (panegyric), 132, 254, 256, 257, 386,
  388, 396, 667. *See also* poetry
Qasr Shirin treaty, 434
qawm (lineages), 575–576, 667. *See also*
  lineages
Qayrawan, 206, 379–380
qibla, 328–329, 667
qital, 53

CPSIA information can be obtained
at www.ICGtesting.com
Printed in the USA
LVOW10s2331050917
547623LV00014B/198/P